# BUSINESS   Process & Product

# COMMUNICATION

Fourth Canadian Edition

**Mary Ellen Guffey**
Professor of Business, Emeritus
Los Angeles Pierce College

**Kathleen Rhodes**
Durham College

**Patricia Rogin**
Durham College

THOMSON

NELSON

Australia   Canada   Mexico   Singapore   Spain   United Kingdom   United States

**THOMSON**

**NELSON**

**Business Communication: Process and Product,
Fourth Canadian Edition**

by Mary Ellen Guffey, Kathleen Rhodes,
and Patricia Rogin

**Editorial Director and Publisher:**
Evelyn Veitch

**Executive Editor:**
Chris Carson

**Marketing Manager:**
Lisa Rahn

**Senior Developmental Editor:**
Rebecca Rea

**Permissions Coordinator:**
Karen Becker

**Production Editor:**
Natalia Denesiuk

**Copy Editor:**
Erin Moore

**Proofreader:**
June Trusty

**Indexer:**
Chris Blackburn

**Production Coordinator:**
Helen Locsin

**Creative Director:**
Angela Cluer

**Interior Design:**
Liz Harasymczuk Design

**Cover Design:**
Katherine Strain

**Cover Image:**
Michael Aveto/The Stock
Illustration Source

**Compositor:**
Tammy Gay

**Printer:**
Quebecor World

**National Library of Canada
Cataloguing in Publication**

Guffey, Mary Ellen

Business communication : process
and product / Mary Ellen Guffey,
Kathleen Rhodes, Patricia Rogin.—
4th Canadian ed.

Includes bibliographical references
and index.
ISBN 0-17-622515-3

1. Business communication. 2.
Business writing. I. Rhodes,
Kathleen, 1951– II. Rogin, Patricia,
1958– III. Title.

HF5718.3.G82 2004    651.7
C2004-901252-5

# Brief Contents

# Detailed Contents

# Preface

*The Foundation for Successful Business Communication*
Previous editions of *Business Communication: Process & Product*
achieved success due to the book's unique, time-tested, interactive
teaching and learning system. Now in its fourth edition, this text
prepares students to thrive in the digital and global workplace.

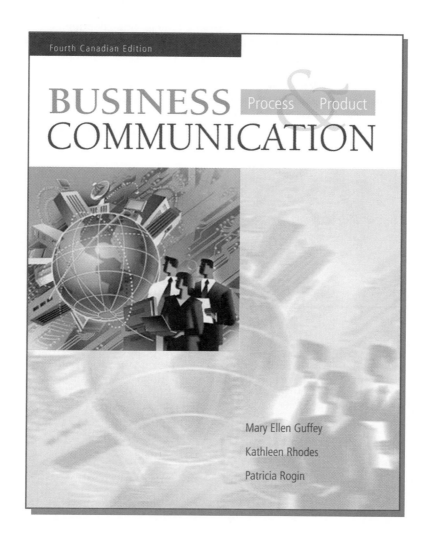

# Partnership

Mary Ellen Guffey and co-authors Kathleen Rhodes and Patricia Rogin dedicate themselves to business communication instructors and students. The student and instructor Web sites, student CD-ROM, newsletters, and plethora of teaching materials prove the authors' commitment to providing you and your students with the best business communication teaching and learning experience. Guffey is a valuable resource inside and outside the classroom.

# 3-×-3 Writing Process

The text's unique 3-×-3 process approach provides students with a practical plan for solving communication problems and creating successful communication products. This multi-stage approach of analyzing-anticipating-adapting, researching-organizing-approaching, and revising-proofreading-evaluating makes the process understandable.

Developed by Mary Ellen Guffey, this systematic approach was the first of its kind to provide a straightforward method for business communications. Learn about these nine steps in chapters 5, 6, and 7.

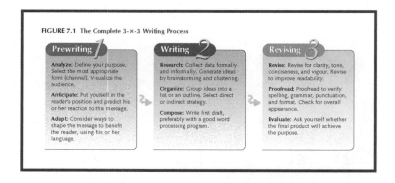

FIGURE 7.1 The Complete 3-×-3 Writing Process

**Prewriting 1**

**Analyze:** Define your purpose. Select the most appropriate form (channel). Visualize the audience.

**Anticipate:** Put yourself in the reader's position and predict his or her reaction to this message.

**Adapt:** Consider ways to shape the message to benefit the reader, using his or her language.

**Writing 2**

**Research:** Collect data formally and informally. Generate ideas by brainstorming and clustering.

**Organize:** Group ideas into a list or an outline. Select direct or indirect strategy.

**Compose:** Write first draft, preferably with a good word processing program.

**Revising 3**

**Revise:** Revise for clarity, tone, conciseness, and vigour. Revise to improve readability.

**Proofread:** Proofread to verify spelling, grammar, punctuation, and format. Check for overall appearance.

**Evaluate:** Ask yourself whether the final product will achieve the purpose.

Graphics serve as visual guides and demonstrate the process in action. Through consistent utilization and visual representations, the book provides an invaluable business communication problem-solving strategy.

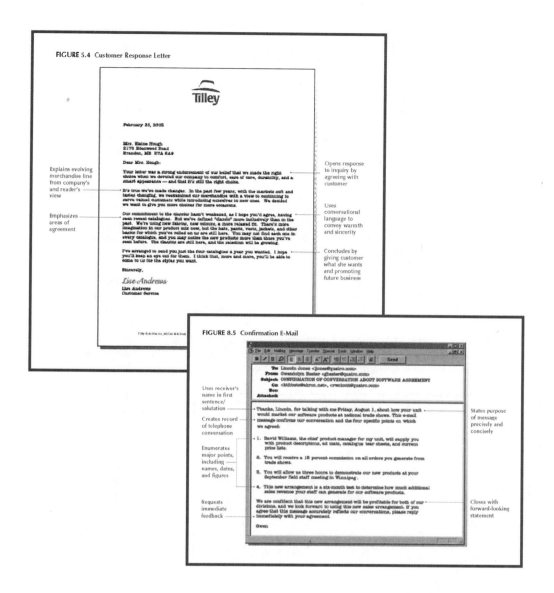

FIGURE 5.4 Customer Response Letter

FIGURE 8.5 Confirmation E-Mail

## Product

Through direct application of the 3-×-3 strategy to all forms of business communication, students obtain the tools they need to create well-crafted memos, letters, e-mails, résumés, reports, and presentations.

# New and Expanded Features

**E-mail** – Recognizing the growing importance of e-mail as a channel of communication, the text devotes Chapter 8 to writing, organizing, and formatting messages. The chapter's new content includes e-mail management, etiquette, formatting, and safety. A new three-part case study in Chapter 8 examines e-mail use within Research in Motion Limited (RIM), a Canadian company that produces innovative wireless solutions for the mobile communication market.

**Small Groups & Teams** – The text now allocates all of Chapter 2 to small-group and team communication. This chapter explores the dynamics of team communication and offers tips, techniques, and strategies that prepare readers to collaborate effectively with others. New topics include recognizing team and group roles, dealing with dysfunctional members, and managing meetings.

**Listening and Nonverbal Communication** – Successful careers depend on the ability to listen. Due to the importance of this topic, the authors increased the coverage of workplace listening and nonverbal communication strategies in Chapter 3.

**Cross-Cultural Work Force Diversity** – Chapter 4 addresses work force diversity and offers practical skills for communicating in the global environment. This chapter encourages awareness, tolerance, and the need for intercultural sensitivity.

---

*13.17 Yardstick Report: Evaluating Equipment (Obj. 5)*

**CRITICAL THINKING**

You recently complained to your boss that you were unhappy with a piece of equipment that you use (printer, computer, copier, fax, or the like). After some thought, the boss decided you were right and told you to go shopping.
**Your Task.** Compare at least three different manufacturers' models and recommend one. Since the company will be purchasing ten or more units and since several managers must approve the purchase, write a careful report documenting your findings. Establish at least five criteria for comparing the models. Submit a memo report to your boss.

*13.18 Yardstick Report: Measuring the Alternatives (Obj. 5)*

**CRITICAL THINKING**

**Your Task.** Consider a problem where you work or in an organization you know. Select a problem with several alternative solutions or courses of action (retaining the present status could be one alternative). Develop criteria that could be used to evaluate each alternative. Write a report measuring each alternative by the yardstick you have created. Recommend a course of action to your boss or to the organization head.

### Self-Contained Report Activities

**NO ADDITIONAL RESEARCH REQUIRED**

*13.19 Justification/Recommendation Report: Improving Village Market's Service\* (Obj. 5)*

**CRITICAL THINKING**

You are a recently hired manager for Village Market, a high-end fast-food restaurant, which has been in business for three years. The restaurant specializes in a wide selection of quality "deli-style" sandwiches, desserts, and coffees. The restaurant's owner, Jill Hillings, tells you that the volume of business, especially at lunch hour, has increased considerably lately.

After your first month on the job, you notice that, because of the increased volume, the method of delivering orders to customers seems to be inadequate. At present, the ordering system consists of the following: (1) the customer's order and table number are recorded by counter staff on a ticket; (2) after the customers pays, the ticket is given to the sandwich makers, who complete the order; (3) one of the counter staff then takes the order to the customer's table. Coffee and desserts are also brought to the customer's table. Additional beverages are located in a refrigerated display case, where customers help themselves. You also note that three counter staff work with one cash register and two sandwich makers are on duty.

You bring the problem to Jill's attention, and she responds by saying, "As a business increases, one must keep up with the times and continually assess ways to do business better." She asks you to help solve the problem by analyzing how similar businesses handle their service during lunch hour. You begin by selecting three fast-food restaurants similar to Village Market. You observe each restaurant during its lunch hour to determine its serving techniques. You also decide to determine the amount of time it takes for a customer to receive an order relative to Village Market. Presently, the average time it takes for a customer to receive an order at Village Market is 4.6 minutes. The following is a rough account of your observations.

**Country Custard**
- Limited menu selection
- Orders are taken using an electronic system that includes the customer's number
- Customers pay immediately
- Customers pick up their orders after number has been called and retrieve their own beverages
- Each sandwich maker is assigned a different task
- Four counter employees at four registers; three sandwich makers
- Average time customer waits to receive order: 2.7 minutes

**Jimmy Jack's**
- Limited menu selection
- Order takers call out menu item as order is taken
- Tickets are used to inform sandwich makers of extras like cheese, mayo, etc.
- Counter employees serve beverages
- Customers pay immediately
- Three sandwich makers make each sandwich in assembly-line fashion
- Customers wait at the counter to pick up their orders
- One counter employee at one register; three sandwich makers
- Average time customer waits to receive order: 2.3 minutes

**Red Hound Bagels**
- Limited menu selection
- Tickets are used to record menu selection; customers pay immediately
- Food and beverages are brought to the customer's table
- Four employees are assigned different tasks: one takes the customer's order, another makes the food, another delivers the order
- Average time customer waits to receive order: 3.5 minutes

**Your Task.** Now it is up to you to sift through the data you've collected and present your findings (conclusions) to

\*Instructors: See the Instructor's Manual for additional resources regarding these activities.

RICH CHAPTER RESOURCES ARE AVAILABLE AT THE WEB SITE

NEL

---

**Self-Contained Report Problems** – Chapters 12, 13, and 14 introduce a brand new element: *self-contained report problems*. These problems contain all the information needed to write five challenging, analytical reports. As students may not have an opportunity to conduct primary and secondary research outside the classroom, these problems put all the information they need at their fingertips. The Instructor's Manual provides recommendations and a set of conclusions for these problems, thus saving time in the development of report assignments.

# New and Updated Case Studies

Applying a concept to a real-life situation is the best way to learn and retain important information. Through three-part case studies, readers apply their problem-solving skills to reality-based situations.

At the beginning of each chapter, *Communication in Process* introduces the featured company and its business communication scenario. New critical-thinking questions link the case to the chapter and encourage student discussion. Part Two of the case study, *Process in Progress*, offers additional information and poses critical-thinking questions. *Process to Product*, at the end of the chapter, provides the opportunity to play the role of employee and resolve the communication issue.

The fourth Canadian edition provides 10 new case studies of Canadian and global companies, including Tim Hortons, Research in Motion Limited (RIM), United Way-Centraide, Statistics Canada, Hudson's Bay Company, and Esteem Team, Canada's only athlete role-model program. In addition the authors kept six of the most interesting case studies from the third Canadian edition and updated them to reflect changes in the companies since the last publication.

---

**CASE STUDY  Communication in Process**

## Tim Hortons

Tim Hortons is one of Canada's top 75 companies of all time, and for a simple reason, according to Ron Joyce, the former Hamilton cop who turned one doughnut shop into an empire. "We take a lot of pride in that it was a Canadian-born chain—made in Canada."[1] In 1963, Ronald Joyce bought a Dairy Queen outlet in Hamilton. Two years later, he invested $10 000 to become a franchisee in the first Tim Hortons. By 1967, Joyce had opened up two more stores, and he and Tim Horton became full partners in the business. In 1975, Joyce became the chain's sole owner, and 20 years later, Joyce received $480 million when Wendy's bought out the chain.[2]

The first Tim Hortons offered only two products—coffee and doughnuts. The most popular, and Tim Hortons' creations, were the Apple Fritter and the Dutchie. This franchise has grown into Canada's number one quick-service chain with a goal to have 3000 units by 2005. Presently, Tim Hortons has more than 2200 locations coast to coast and 160 in the United States. The company posted revenues of US$1.7 billion in 2002, while fast-food stores such as McDonald's struggled.[3]

The company has positioned itself not only in the coffee and doughnut business but also as a fast-food lunch alternative. In the past, Tim Hortons was seen as a breakfast solution, but now it attracts customers at breakfast, lunch, and dinner. Hortons is the largest seller of soup in Canadian food service, and it sells one of every two bagels sold at restaurants.[4] The burger business has also experienced significant losses in the past year, and Tim's has filled the void. Jim Robinson, NPD Group Canada vice president and market researcher, notes part of Hortons' success has been the ability to anticipate cultural shifts. A decade ago, one in ten quick-service meals were bought at a drive-through; that number is now one in four.[5]

Although Tim Hortons has had stores in the United States dating back to the late 1970s, aggressive expansion began in 1995 when Wendy's International purchased the chain. However, Tim Hortons is still operated by the TDL Group Ltd., based in Oakville, Ontario. Although Tim Hortons has a U.S. parent company, spokesperson Patti Jameson asserts that Tim Hortons remains quintessentially Canadian, with no intention of relocating. She continues, "I don't think that we market Canadiana. I think we market ourselves as a chain that always offers top quality and cleanliness and good value for money spent. If there's any part of the Canadiana aspect it will probably be the kind of personality people perceive our chain to have, which is friendly and caring because of all of the things we do within the community."[6]

CRITICAL THINKING
- In what ways would research (gathering information) be important to business communicators at Tim Hortons and other companies?
- Why is it important to gather all necessary information before beginning to write a business message or make a presentation?
- What techniques can business communicators at Tim Hortons and other companies use to generate ideas for new projects, such as preparing a training brochure for employees?

www.timhortons.com

---

**CASE STUDY  Process in Progress**

## Tim Hortons Revisited

"There is always something new going on at Tim Hortons" is one of the reasons for its success. The menu at Tim's is always evolving to keep up with changing consumer tastes and preferences. The 1976 introduction of Timbits was one of the biggest changes in the company's focus. New product introductions of muffins, cakes, pies, croissants, soups, chili, and "Tim's Own" sandwiches followed in the 1980s. In the 1990s, the company expanded its offerings to include bagels, flavoured cappuccino, café mocha, and iced cappuccino. In 2000, the company introduced "Tim's Own" coffeecake and hot chicken stew in an edible bread bowl. Of course the famous coffee remains, available not only by the cup, but also in cans for the customer to make and enjoy at home.

Such diversity and response to change have proven to be invaluable to Tim Hortons' success. In 2002, the company had about $2.1 billion in Canadian sales, compared to $2.2 billion for McDonald's Corporation. The company plans to overtake the burger giant in sales. South of the border, Tim's now accounts for 30 to 35 percent of Wendy's total revenue.[11]

In addition to being successful on the balance sheet, Tim Hortons also gives back to the community. Ron Joyce states, "Everybody should give back, if you can afford it. Giving is what it's all about. I think that there is an obligation to give back, especially if you've been financially successful. Government can't do it as well as the private sector, and the private sector should."[12]

When Tim Horton died on February 21, 1974, Ron Joyce announced the establishment of the Tim Horton Children's Foundation to honour Tim Horton's love of children and desire to help those less fortunate. The foundation is a non-profit charitable organization that operates camps for economically disadvantaged children from communities in which Tim Hortons operates. The first camp opened in 1975; now there are six—five in Canada and one in the United States. In 2003, over 9000 children attended the camps. Since 1974, more than 54 000 children have participated in the camp program. Funding for the camps comes from donations from store owners, the parent company (TDL Group Ltd.), suppliers, and public donations. As the company states on its Web site, "The Tim Horton Children's Foundation is committed to providing an enriched and memorable camp experience for children, giving them confidence in their abilities, pride in their accomplishments, and a more positive view of the world and their place in it."

CRITICAL THINKING
- When a business communicator responds to an inquiry, such as asking for the criteria for choosing the candidates to attend camp, is "research" necessary?
- What is the difference between formal and informal research?
- What are the advantages and disadvantages of brainstorming with groups?

www.timhortons.com

---

**CASE STUDY  Process to Product**

## Applying Your Skills at Tim Hortons

After its huge success in Canada, Tim Hortons posted its first-ever annual profit in 2002 in the United States.[19] The goal is to follow the Canadian business model and have 70 percent of U.S. units franchised.[20] However, the competition in the United States remains intense. Competitors such as Dunkin' Donuts, Krispy Kreme, and Starbucks are strong forces in the U.S. market, and Tim Hortons is relying on its diversified product mix to compete.

Ron Joyce believes the Krispy Kreme phenomenon is similar to the Tim Hortons phenomenon when it first started. "We used to have those huge lineups. When the novelty wears off, what's their staying power?" he asks.[21] According to Paul House, Tim Hortons' president and chief operating officer, "We're not just in the coffee-and-baked goods business anymore. If we were still selling only coffee and doughnuts, we wouldn't be in the position we are today."[22]

Coffee accounts for 50 percent of all sales in Canada, baked goods contribute 22.5 percent, and lunch yields 10.5 percent. Tim Hortons estimates that it has 70 percent of the coffee-and-baked goods market in Canada and 22 percent of the overall quick-service market.[23] To improve drive-through service, Tim Hortons implemented a tandem ordering system to speed up customer service. In Canada, Tim Hortons has a top drive-through time of 101.58 seconds, topping the best score held at a U.S. Wendy's at 134.67 seconds.[24]

Tim Hortons' motto of "Always Fresh" translates into concepts, ideas, and thoughts and extends beyond the food being sold. Tim Hortons is "Always Fresh," whether it is uniforms, quality of the products, chains, and so on.[25]

Your Task

To remain competitive and capture market share, Tim Hortons must be aware of the competition. Your boss has asked you to examine the major competitors to Tim Hortons and would like an analysis on the direction that the company should take to keep its number one spot in Canada and expand that success to the franchises south of the border. She also wants you to examine the U.S. market to see any trends or differences that should be acknowledged.

In small groups, brainstorm about where you can collect information for this project. Based on what you learned in this chapter, list possible sources of information for informal research. Your instructor may further ask you to brainstorm about potential problems in preparing this report. If directed, make a cluster diagram showing the results of your brainstorming.

www.timhortons.com

# Model Documents

An abundance of perfectly formatted models, complete with proper documentation, visually reinforce students' understanding of concepts. Pointers on the letters, memos, and reports lead to concise annotations that explain communication strategies and applications of theory. In addition, before-and-after messages help students visualize the writing process and revision techniques.

Complete coverage of employment communication products, including current model résumés and letters of application, plus job-search skills from interview through follow-up, provides useful tools and guidance for the job seeker.

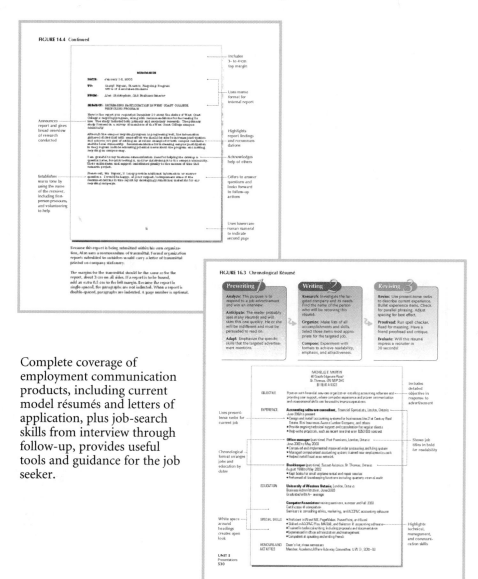

# Critical Thinking Focus

Employers place increasing importance on critical-thinking skills. The workplace needs employees who can analyze situations, make decisions, and solve problems. This text sharpens the ability to think critically through the incorporation of case studies and end-of-chapter problem-solving activities. *Business Communication: Process & Product* equips future business communicators with these skills.

# Applied Career Skills Coverage

*Career Coach*
Career Coach boxes offer practical advice and information on transferring communication skills to future careers. Topics such as "He Said, She Said: Gender Issues and Gender Tension" and "Casual Apparel in the Workplace" examine communication issues and challenges in the workplace.

---

## CAREER COACH

### Practising Courteous and Responsible Cell Phone Use

Business communicators find cell phones to be enormously convenient and real time-savers. But rude users have generated a backlash of sorts. Most of us have experienced thoughtless and offensive cell phone behaviour. Although the cell phone industry vigorously opposes restrictive legislation, many major manufacturers admonish users to be courteous. Here are specific suggestions for using cell phones safely and responsibly:

- **Be courteous to those around you.** Don't force those near you to hear your business. Think first of those in close proximity instead of those on the other end of the phone. Apologize and make amends gracefully for occasional cell phone blunders.

- **Observe wireless-free quiet areas.** Don't allow your cell phone to ring in theatres, restaurants, museums, classrooms, important meetings, and similar places. Use the cell phone's silent/vibrating ring option. A majority of travellers prefer that cell phone conversations not be held on most forms of public transportation.

- **Speak in low, conversational tones.** Microphones on cell phones are quite sensitive, thus making it unnecessary to talk loudly. Avoid "cell yell."

- **Take only urgent calls.** Make full use of your cell phone's caller ID feature to screen incoming calls. Let voice mail take those calls that are not pressing.

- **Drive now, talk later.** Pull over if you must make a call. Talking while driving increases the chance of accidents fourfold, about the same as driving while intoxicated.

#### Career Application

How do you feel when you must listen to nearby cell phone conversations? Should cell phone use in cars be prohibited? During business meetings, how should participants react if their cell phones ring?

# Tech Talk

Communicating successfully in the business world includes the ability to communicate effectively with people by computer. *Business Communication: Process & Product* helps the business communicator understand and prepare for electronic communication challenges. Tech Talk boxes provide important information on technology issues and tools.

# Ethical Communication

To stress the importance of ethics, the first chapter introduces ethical challenges and provides the business communication tools to deal with them. This approach puts ethical conduct in context, rather than isolating these issues from the reality of daily business interactions.

Additionally, Ethical Insights boxes address issues or dilemmas and provide strategies for communicating information within a complex business environment. Every chapter includes an *Ethical Issue* question that can be used for class discussion or assigned for homework.

# C.L.U.E.

## Back to the Basics

The *Competent Language Usage Essentials* appendix reviews and reinforces grammar and language principles. This business writer's handbook contains 54 of the most used and abused language elements, along with frequently misspelled and misused words. In addition, end-of-chapter C.L.U.E. exercises challenge the spelling and punctuation skills of students while simultaneously reviewing key concepts. The end of the book provides the answers to C.L.U.E. exercises.

---

# Appendix A

## Competent Language
## Usage Essentials (C.L.U.E.)

### A BUSINESS COMMUNICATOR'S GUIDE

In the business world, people are often judged by the way they speak and write. Using the language competently can mean the difference between individual success and failure. Often a speaker sounds accomplished; but when that same individual puts ideas in print, errors in language usage destroy his or her credibility. One student observed, "When I talk, I get by on my personality; but when I write, the flaws in my communication show through. That's why I'm in this class."

### What C.L.U.E. Is

This appendix provides a condensed guide to competency in language usage essentials (C.L.U.E.). Fifty-four guidelines review sentence structure, grammar, usage, punctuation, capitalization, number style, and abbreviations. These guidelines focus on the most frequently used—and abused—language elements. Presented from a business communicator's perspective, the guidelines also include realistic tips for application. And frequent checkpoint exercises enable you to try out your skills immediately. In addition to the 54 language guides in this appendix, you'll find a list of 165 frequently misspelled words plus a quick review of selected confusing words.

The concentrated materials in this guide will help novice business communicators focus on the major areas of language use. The guide is not meant to teach or review *all* the principles of English grammar and punctuation. It focuses on a limited number of language guidelines and troublesome words. Your objective should be mastery of these language principles and words, which represent a majority of the problems typically encountered by business writers.

### How to Use C.L.U.E.

Your instructor may give you a language diagnostic test to help you assess your competency. After taking this test, read and work your way through the 54 guidelines. Concentrate on areas where you are weak. Memorize the spelling list and definitions for the confusing words located at the end of this appendix.

NEL

---

### C.L.U.E. REVIEW 15

On a separate sheet edit the following sentences to correct faults in grammar, punctuation, spelling, and word use.

1. The CEOs assistant asked my colleague and I to explain why our proposed method was better then the one previously used.

2. My friend and me were definitely inexperienced in making presentations, therefore him and I decided to learn more about public speaking.

3. We learned that the introduction to a presentation should accomplish 3 goals (a) capture attention, (b) establish credibility and (c) preview main points.

4. In the body of a short presentation which is usually 20 or less minutes we should focus on 2 to 4 principle points.

5. One of the most important ways to end a presentation are focusing on what you want the audience to do think or remember.

6. Speakers must remember that listeners unlike readers' can not controll the rate of presentation, or flip back thorough pages to review main points.

7. In working with electronic presentation softwear experts suggest chosing 1 transition effect, and using it consistantly.

8. The range of effects are staggering but presenters using electronic slides must control there urge to pile on to many dazzling features.

9. Every good speaker adapt to his audience and cross cultural presentations call for special adjustments and sensitivity.

10. One study found that 2/3 of telephone calls were less important then the work it interrupted.

520

MORE CHAPTER RESOURCES ARE AVAILABLE AT THE WEB SITE

NEL

# End-of-Chapter Materials

## Applying the Concepts

Comprehensive end-of-chapter materials strengthen and apply concepts. Every chapter offers a variety of short, long, easy, and difficult exercises, activities, and problems. Selected activities, such as Team, Web, Critical Thinking, and InfoTrac, provide a variety of stimulating assignment choices.

### CHAPTER REVIEW

1. List seven reasons that explain why organizations are forming groups and teams. (Obj. 1)
2. How are virtual teams different from intact teams? (Obj. 1)
3. To be most successful, self-directed teams need to have what characteristics? (Obj. 1)
4. What are the four phases of team development? Is it best to move through the stages quickly? Why or why not? (Obj. 2)
5. Name five team roles that relate to tasks and five roles that relate to developing relationships. Which roles do you think are most important and why? (Obj. 2)
6. Name five dysfunctional team roles. (Obj. 2)
7. What is the difference between *cognitive* and *affective* conflict? (Obj. 2)
8. What is *groupthink*? (Obj. 2)
9. Why can diverse teams be more effective than homogeneous teams? (Obj. 3)
10. Why are team decisions based on consensus generally better than decisions reached by majority rule? (Obj. 3)
11. What is the best way to set team deadlines when time is short to complete a project? (Obj. 4)
12. In completing a team-written report, should all team members work together to write the report? Why or why not? (Obj. 4)
13. When groups or teams meet, what are seven ground rules with which they should begin? (Obj. 5)
14. Name five techniques for handling dysfunctional group members. (Obj. 5)
15. What is groupware? What are three important functions it serves? (Obj. 5)

### CRITICAL THINKING

1. Compare the advantages and disadvantages of using teams in today's workplace. (Objs. 1, 2, and 3)
2. What kinds of conflict could erupt during the "storming" phase of team development? Should conflict be avoided? (Obj. 2)
3. What are the advantages and disadvantages of diverse teams? (Obj. 3)
4. How would you comment on this statement made by an executive: "If you can't orchestrate a meeting, then you are of little use to an organization." (Obj. 5)
5. **Ethical Issue:** You're disturbed that Randy, one member of your team, is selling Amway products to other members of the team. He shows catalogues and takes orders at lunch, and he distributes products after work and during lunch. He also leaves an order form on the table during team meetings. What should you do? What if Randy were selling Girl Guide cookies?

### ACTIVITIES

#### 2.1 Advantages of Teams: Convincing Your Boss (Obj. 1)

Your boss or organization leader comes to you and asks you to take on a big job. Use your imagination to select a task such as developing a Web site or organizing a fund-raising campaign. You are flattered that your boss respects you and thinks you capable of completing the task, but you think that a team could do a better job than an individual.

**Your Task.** What arguments would you use to convince your boss that a team could work better than an individual?

#### 2.2 Group Decision Strategies: Which Method? (Objs. 1 and 2)

TEAM

In small groups decide which decision strategy is best for the following situations:

a. A steering committee at your office must decide on the format for an upcoming company conference.
b. The owner of your company is meeting with all managers to decide whether to purchase new ergonomic chairs and workstations.
c. Members of a condominium association must decide which members will become directors.
d. Your project team must decide among several candidates in hiring a new member.
e. The human resources department of a large company must work with employees to hammer out a new benefits package within its budget.
f. A large association of realtors must decide how to organize a member Web site. Only a few members have technical expertise.
g. Three employees must decide who gets a large vacant corner office.

#### 2.3 Analyzing Team Formation, Decision Making, and Group Roles (Objs. 1, 2, and 3)

TEAM

Members of small groups play a number of different roles as their groups are formed and decisions are made. To better

66

NEL

# Resources That Enhance Learning

## Student Resources

*Student CD-ROM* (0-17-622523-4 comes packaged with text)
The student CD-ROM provides a wealth of additional resources: chapter review quizzes, letter and memo exercises, letter and memo case studies, grammar review, an employment interview kit, and links to CBC video clips. A CD-ROM accompanies every new copy of *Business Communication: Process and Product,* Fourth Canadian Edition.

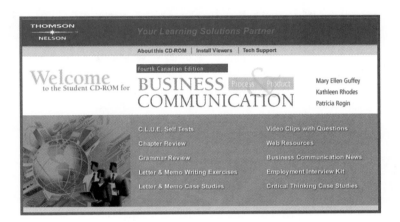

*Student Web Site* (www.businesscommunication-4th.nelson.com)
Students can test their knowledge of chapter concepts with interactive review exercises that provide immediate feedback. In addition to text-specific items, the Web site provides a guide to business etiquette, public speaking tips, report topics, and links to the best search engines and employment sites. Panteli Tritchew, Chair of Applied Communications at Kwantlen University College, is the site leader.

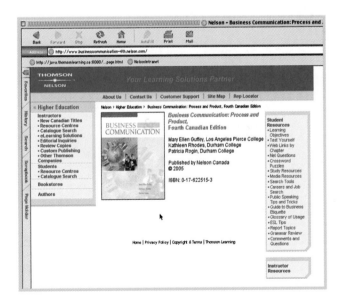

## InfoTrac® College Edition

Today's digital workplace requires employees to find and evaluate information on the Internet. Students have the opportunity to develop these research skills with activities and questions that use InfoTrac® College Edition, a comprehensive Web-based collection of over 10 million full-text articles from nearly 5 000 scholarly and popular periodicals. Students can access this database 24 hours a day, 7 days a week.

### CHAPTER REVIEW

1. How are business communicators affected by the emergence of global competition, flattened management hierarchies, and expanded team-based management? (Obj. 1)
2. How are business communicators affected by the emergence of innovative communication technologies, new work environments, and an increasingly diverse work force? (Obj. 1)
3. What are knowledge workers? Why are they hired? (Obj. 1)
4. Define *communication* and explain its most critical factor. (Obj. 2)
5. Describe the five steps in the process of communication. (Obj. 2)
6. List four barriers to interpersonal communication. Be prepared to discuss each. (Obj. 3)
7. Name five specific ways in which you can personally reduce barriers in your communication. (Obj. 3)
8. What are the three main functions of organizational communication? (Obj. 4)
9. What are the advantages of oral, face-to-face communication? (Obj. 4)
10. What are the advantages of written communication? (Obj. 4)
11. How do formal and informal channels of communication differ within organizations? (Obj. 5)
12. Describe three directions in which communication flows within organizations and what barriers can obstruct each. (Obj. 5)
13. How can barriers to the free flow of information in organizations be reduced? (Obj. 5)
14. Discuss five thinking traps that block ethical behaviour. (Obj. 6)
15. When faced with a difficult ethical decision, what questions should you ask yourself? (Obj. 6)

### INFOTRAC® COLLEGE EDITION

#### Building Knowledge and Research Skills

Today's digital workplace requires you to find and evaluate information on the Internet. As a student purchasing a new copy of *Business Communication: Process and Product*, Fourth Canadian Edition, you have an extraordinary opportunity to develop these research skills. For four months, you have special access to InfoTrac College Edition, a comprehensive Web-based collection of over 10 million full-text articles from nearly 5 000 scholarly and popular periodicals. You can access this online database 24 hours a day, 7 days a week from any computer with Internet access. Since InfoTrac

College Edition's articles are updated daily, you can access the most current information. At the time of publication, InfoTrac links were up-to-date. You will find research activities and questions in this text that will help you build knowledge and develop research skills using InfoTrac. Watch for the InfoTrac icon.

**How to Use InfoTrac College Edition**
1. Visit the InfoTrac site at <http://infotrac.thomsonlearning.com>. Click on *Register New Account*.
2. Enter the passcode on the card packaged with your textbook.
3. Create your own user name.
4. Fill out the registration form completely to activate your account. Enter your newly created user name (step 3). Create your own password. Make up a question to which only you know the answer; then provide the answer. Provide your contact information. Your account is now registered. (If you forget your password, InfoTrac uses the security question to verify access and will e-mail your password back to you.)

**Search Methods**

**Subject Search:** Select *Subject Guide* on the menu bar. Enter the subject, and click *Search*.
a. After a list of articles appears, select an article by clicking on its title. If your search words do not match the Subject Guide database, a list of similar and related subjects will appear.
b. Select the subject that most closely matches your topic. A list containing bibliographic information for each article appears.
c. To view an article, click on the citation.
d. To print the article, click *Print* on the menu bar.
e. To return to the citation list, click *Citations* on the menu bar.
f. To start a new search, click *Search* on the menu bar.

**Keyword Search:** Click *Keyword Search* on the menu bar. This search matches key words in the articles.
a. Click on the entry box, and type your search term. Click *Search*.
The search will return with a list of articles containing the keyword(s). Results are listed from most recent to oldest publication date.
b. To print an article, return to the citation list, or start a new search, refer to the above.

**Advanced Search:** Click *Advanced Search* on the menu bar. This allows you to select from the index to narrow your search.
a. Select an index. Each article is indexed by variables such as author, title, publication name, and where and when it was published.
b. Type your search criteria into the entry box. Click *Search*

35

## Instructor Resources

*Instructor's Manual* (0-17-622518-8)
This comprehensive resource includes course outlines, chapter synopses, teaching ideas, lecture enrichment material, classroom management techniques, answers for chapter review questions, suggested discussion guidelines for critical thinking questions, and solutions for the case study questions, applications, and memo-writing assignments in the textbook.

*Instructor's CD-ROM* (0-17-622522-6)
Using course resources has never been easier! The Instructor's CD-ROM puts supplement material in an easy-to-use format. The CD-ROM includes the Instructor's Manual (chapter outlines, bonus lecture material, before-and-after documents, and solutions to select chapter activities), Microsoft® PowerPoint® presentation slides, and the test bank, which provides feedback for every question.

*Instructor Web Site* (www.businesscommunication-4th.nelson.com)
The Instructor site provides textbook information, links to professional organizations, and current event items that can enrich business communication lectures. Panteli Tritchew, Chair of Applied Communication at Kwantlen University College, serves as the site leader.

*Microsoft® PowerPoint® Presentation Slides* (0-17-622521-8)
This lecture system offers summaries, explanations, and illustrations of key chapter concepts, plus lecture material not included in the text. With Microsoft® PowerPoint® software, you can easily customize any slide to support lectures.

*Printed Test Bank* (0-17-622519-6)
Each chapter of the test bank contains 60–150 questions. Every chapter opens with a correlation table that identifies questions by chapter learning objective and by content (factual, conceptual, or application). Page references to the text provide quick access.

*Computerized Test Bank* (0-17-622520-X)
All items from the printed test bank are available through this automated testing program. Create tests by selecting provided questions, modifying existing questions, and adding questions.

# Appreciation for Support

It is our pleasure to present the fourth Canadian edition of *Business Communication: Process and Product* to you. The Canadian edition continues to build on the excellent foundation created by Dr. Mary Ellen Guffey, who recognizes the trends in today's workplace and economy and responds accordingly. Through her insight and creativity, the text continues to evolve and provide information that is timely and relevant.

This Canadian edition benefits in many ways from its strong American foundation. In response to the changing needs of our students, new information has been added to the text, including enhanced team information, expanded e-mail coverage, and new and updated exercises. In addition to updates in content and structure, you will also notice ten new case studies of companies to which our students can relate. Canadian companies, such as Tim Hortons, the Hudson's Bay Company, and Research in Motion, are profiled, and critical thinking cases are built around them. The remaining case studies have all been updated.

Many changes are the result of extensive reviewer feedback and comments. The valuable and insightful reviews that we receive allow us to modify the text to meet the needs of our users. We are grateful for the feedback from Denise Blay, Fanshawe College; Laura Reave, University of Western Ontario; Jean M. Mills, Mount Saint Vincent University; Melanie A. Rubens, Seneca College; Bryan Scully, Northern Alberta Institute of Technology; Clark Cook, British Columbia Institute of Technology; David Warrick, Humber College; and Lynn Morrissey, Memorial University of Newfoundland. The support and insight offered by these professionals allow us to make the necessary changes to respond to the evolving world of work and school.

We must also acknowledge the support of our colleagues at Nelson, who continue to provide a professional approach, attention to detail, and a genuine caring and concern that bring this book to life. Special thanks go to the amazing sales representatives who promote our books—our Durham College representative, Bill More, and others across Canada. We particularly appreciate the assistance of the entire Nelson team: Rebecca Rea, Natalia Denesiuk, Natalie Barrington, Erin Moore, June Trusty, Lisa Rahn, Chris Carson, and Evelyn Veitch.

We also appreciate our friends and colleagues at Durham College who continue to offer their support through positive feedback and suggestions. Finally, thanks to our families—Bryan, Tim, and Emily Rhodes, and Howie and Alison Rogin—who are always there for us.

*Kathleen Rhodes*          *Patricia Rogin*

# Unit 1
## Communication Foundations

# Chapter 1

## Communicating at Work

## LEARNING OBJECTIVES

*1* Identify changes in the workplace and the importance of communication skills.

*2* Describe the process of communication.

*3* Discuss barriers to interpersonal communication and the means of overcoming those barriers.

*4* Analyze the functions and procedures of communication in organizations.

*5* Assess the flow of communication in organizations including barriers and methods for overcoming those barriers.

*6* List the goals of ethical business communication and describe important tools for doing the right thing.

# *Canadian Tire*

Founded in 1922, Canadian Tire is seen by many as a Canadian institution with its nostalgic advertising and even its own money. The company has the most successful customer loyalty program in Canada, with more than $100 million in Canadian Tire "money" distributed every year.[1] In the 1990s, business analysts wrote the company off, calling it the "retailer that was going to die." However, in 1993, the company imported Stephen Bachand from the United States and aggressively remodelled its stores. In 2000, Wayne Sales became president and CEO. In comparison to the fate of other domestic retailers, such as Woolco, Eaton's, and BiWay, Rob Gerlsbeck, editor of *Hardware Merchandising Magazine*, calls Canadian Tire "the last of the true great Canadian retailers."

The company is successfully competing with Wal-Mart, Home Depot, and other U.S. retailers, and has done "exceptionally well," according to Gerlsbeck.[2] Canadian Tire's survival and success is no accident—the company successfully undertook a series of corporate-wide changes that positioned the Toronto-based retailer for profitability.

Canadian Tire has been extremely resilient over the past years, and the balance sheets reflect the results. Despite a soft economy and increased competition, in 2001 Canadian Tire had record sales of $5.3 billion, up 6.9 percent from the previous year. The company also has implemented a series of strategic changes. Canadian Tire plans to open more new-format stores with more selling space and more items to appeal to women, including housewares, home office accessories, and a gift registry.

Canadian Tire has also invested significantly in its electronic commerce Web site, which can be used for both research and shopping. The site sells over 13 000 products online and is an extension of the bricks and mortar of the business. Bryan Murphy, divisional vice president and general manager of CT Direct (the Canadian Tire online retail division), states, "We haven't been afraid to try different things, but we also haven't strayed from the core of what Canadian Tire is known for."[3] With 450 stores, which service 91 percent of the Canadian population, the numbers keep adding up for the company. It is reported that more than half of Canadians shop at Canadian Tire on a monthly basis and nearly 80 percent have been in Canadian Tire stores in the past six months.

Currently, the company consists of five distinct divisions: retail, financial services, petroleum, PartSource, and Mark's Work Wearhouse.

The ultimate goal is not only to reach customers, but also to retain them. "You can't be a successful retailer if you spend your life emulating," according to former Canadian Tire president and CEO Stephen Bachand.

The Canadian Tire initiatives have brought more customers and prompted the media to recognize Canadian Tire as being "on a roll." In a *Canadian Business* article, writer Kevin Libin stated that Canadian Tire "is one of the few homegrown retailers still managing to keep investors happy."[4] According to Sales, while speaking to shareholders, "The message I want to leave with you is that Canadian Tire is truly a growth performer across the entire enterprise."[5]

## CRITICAL THINKING

- How is Canadian Tire similar to many retailers today? What kinds of changes are other companies undergoing?
- Why is communication within an organization especially important in times of change?
- How can effective communication help Canadian Tire remain successful?

**www.canadiantire.ca**

# ENSURING THAT YOU SUCCEED IN THE NEW WORKPLACE

*1*

Employees at many organizations are experiencing the kind of change felt at Canadian Tire. In fact, the entire work world you are about to enter is changing dramatically. The kind of work you'll do, the tools you'll use, the form of management, the environment where you'll work, the people with whom you'll interact—all are undergoing a profound transformation. Many of the changes in this dynamic workplace revolve around processing and communicating information. As a result, the most successful players in this new world of work will be those with highly developed communication skills.

**Succeeding in today's world of work demands that you read, listen, speak, and write effectively.**

The abilities to read, listen, speak, and write effectively, of course, are not inborn. Thriving in the dynamic and demanding work world depends on many factors, some of which you cannot control. But one factor that you do control is how well you communicate. The goals of this book and this course are to teach you basic business communication skills, such as how to write a memo or letter and how to make a presentation. You will also learn additional powerful communication skills, as summarized in Figure 1.1. Because they will equip you with the skills most needed in today's dynamic workplace, *this book and this course may well be the most important in your entire postsecondary curriculum.*

The book provides you with not only the process but also the products of effective communication. You'll be able to use it throughout your training for its many models of successful business and professional documents. When you are ready to enter the job market, you'll find it to be an invaluable source of excellent résumés

**FIGURE 1.1  Succeeding in Today's Dynamic and Demanding Workplace**

## This Business Communication Book and This Course Will Help You

- Apply a universal process that enables you to solve communication problems now and throughout your entire career

- Learn specific writing techniques and organizational strategies to compose clear, concise, and purposeful business messages

- Master effective speaking skills for getting your ideas across to small and large groups

- Learn to be a valuable team player

- Work productively with the Internet and other rapidly evolving communication technologies

- Recognize the importance of nonverbal communication cues

- Value diversity and function with sensitivity in multicultural work environments

- Develop tools for meeting ethically challenging situations

- Feel confident that you will always have excellent document models to follow now and on the job

- Land the job of your dreams by providing invaluable job-search, résumé-writing, and interviewing tips and cover letters. On the job you'll refer to it for examples of business letters, e-mail messages, reports, and other documents. That's why many students decide that this is one book they will keep.

To become an effective communicator, though, you need more than a good book. You also need practice—with meaningful feedback. You need someone such as your instructor to tell you how to modify your responses so that you can improve. We've designed this book and its supplements to provide you and your instructor with principles, processes, products, and practice—everything necessary to make you a successful business communicator in today's dynamic workplace.

**This book and your instructor provide you with the principles, processes, products, and practice that you need to succeed.**

Yes, the workplace is undergoing profound changes. As a businessperson and especially as a business communicator, you will undoubtedly be affected by many transformations. Some of the most significant changes include global competition, flattened management hierarchies, and team-based projects. Other changes reflect our constantly evolving information technology, new work environments, a diverse work force, and the emergence of a knowledge-based economy. In fact, Prime Minister Paul Martin once made the analogy of Canada's economy moving from "brick to click."[6] The following brief look at this new world of work reveals how directly your success in it will be tied to possessing excellent communication skills.

## Heightened Global Competition

Small, medium, and large companies increasingly find themselves competing in global rather than local markets. Improved systems of telecommunication, advanced forms of transportation, and saturated local markets—all of these developments have encouraged companies to move beyond familiar territories to emerging markets around the world. PepsiCo fights Coca-Cola for new customers in India. Yahoo! soars to success in Japan and Korea.[7] FedEx learns the ropes in South America. Burger King challenges McDonald's for fast-food supremacy in Europe,[8] and Starbucks opens a coffee shop in the heart of the Forbidden City in Beijing.[9]

**Communication is more complicated with people who have different religions, customs, and lifestyles.**

Doing business in far-flung countries means dealing with people who are very different from you. They have different religions, engage in different customs, live different lifestyles, and rely on different approaches in business. Now add the complications of multiple time zones, vast distances between offices, and different languages. No wonder global communicators can blunder.[10] Take, for example, FedEx's offer of a money-back guarantee in South America. The concept was so unfamiliar to the culture that people automatically thought something must be wrong with the service.[11] FedEx quickly withdrew the offer.

Successful communication in these new markets requires developing new skills and attitudes such as cultural knowledge and sensitivity, flexibility, patience, and tolerance. Because these are skills and attitudes that most of us need to polish, you will receive special communication training to help you deal with intercultural business transactions.

Facing saturated local markets, many North American companies are becoming global competitors. This Nike store in Bangalore, India, is an example.

## Flattened Management Hierarchies

In response to intense global competition and other pressures, businesses have for years been cutting costs and flattening their management hierarchies. This flattening means that fewer layers of managers separate decision makers from line workers. In traditional companies, information flows through many levels of managers. In flat organizations, however, where the lines of communication are shorter, decision makers can react more quickly to market changes. Companies such as IBM have gone from about ten levels in the corporate hierarchy to five.[12]

But today's flatter organizations also bring greater communication challenges. In the past, authoritarian and hierarchical management structures did not require that every employee be a skilled communicator. Managers simply passed along messages to the next level. Today, however, front-line employees as well as managers participate in decision making. Their input and commitment are necessary for their organizations to be successful in global markets. What's more, everyone has become a writer and a communicator.[13] According to Tim Wilson, a senior research analyst at International Data Corporation (Canada) Ltd. of Toronto, communication skills are more important than technical skills. "If you're not understanding what the client wants, and can't articulate it, all your IT skills are wasted."[14] Nearly all employees have computers and write their own messages. Administrative assistants no longer "clean up" their bosses' writing.

## Expanded Team-Based Management

Along with flatter chains of command, companies are also turning to the concept of team-based operations. Nearly 80 percent of employees in all industries have adopted some form of quality circles or self-directed teams. An Ipsos-Reid survey revealed that more than 57 percent of urban workers in Canada believe the need to work in teams as opposed to individually has increased in the last five years. Ninety-one percent of workers in the same study reported they collaborate with others in their organization on the same documents either frequently (52 percent) or sometimes (39 percent).[15] At Cigna Corporation, a huge national insurance company, three organizational layers were flattened and teams were formed to reduce backups in processing customer claims. Formation of these teams forced technology specialists to communicate constantly with business specialists. Suddenly, computer programmers had to do more than code and debug; they had to listen, interpret, and explain. All members of the team had to analyze problems and negotiate solutions.[16]

When companies form cross-functional teams, individuals must work together and share information. What's tough is that these individuals often don't share the same background, knowledge, or training. Dr. George Gekas, of Algoma University College in Sault Ste. Marie, explains, "Employees are now working more collaboratively, and gone are the days of 'that's not my department, I cannot get involved.' The knowledge worker and the knowledge environment require synergy and collaboration more than ever."[17] Some companies must hire communication coaches to help existing teams get along. They work to develop interpersonal, negotiation, and collaboration techniques. But companies would prefer to hire new workers who already possess these skills. That's why so many advertisements for new employees say "must possess good communication skills."

## Innovative Communication Technologies

Because technology is completely revolutionizing the way we communicate, recruiters are also looking for people with good computer skills. We now exchange information and stay in touch through e-mail, fax, voice mail, two-way pagers, cellular phones, powerful laptop computers, and satellite communications.[18] Through teleconferencing and videoconferencing, we can conduct meetings with associates around the world. Interactive software enables dozens or even hundreds of users to collaborate on projects.

We now make tremendous use of the Internet and the Web for collecting information, serving customers, and selling products and services. Canadian Tire has divided its Web site into three categories: automotive, leisure/recreation, and home. The site offers more than 13 000 products for sale online and over 1 000 are exclusive to the Web site.[19] Part of the reason for the success of the site is that it is an extension of the bricks and mortar brand. See Figure 1.2.

Just as companies are scrambling to use the Web most effectively, individual businesspeople are eagerly embracing the new technologies and revamping the way they communicate. With 84 percent of Internet users connecting to e-mail, e-mail is considered the most often used means of communication. According to a Statistics Canada General Social Survey, approximately two thirds of Internet users send and receive e-mail several times a week. Additionally, e-mail has extended beyond national borders, with users reporting they use e-mail to communicate extensively with people outside the country.[20] To use these new resources most effectively, you, as a skilled business communicator, must develop a tool kit of new communication skills. For example, you will want to know how to design documents for screen appeal, how to select the best medium for a message, and how to use online search tools efficiently.

## New Work Environments

As a result of global competition, restructuring, and the Internet, it's no surprise that we are also seeing dramatic changes in work environments. Thanks to advances in communication and mobile technologies, experts estimate that there are over 1.5 million teleworkers in Canada.[21] They have flexible working arrangements so that they can work at home at least part of the time. Many workers live thousands of miles from the office, and others carry their work with them as they travel.[22] IMRglobal Ltd., a Clearwater, Florida-based IT service firm with offices in Canada,

**FIGURE 1.2  Canadian Tire Web Site**

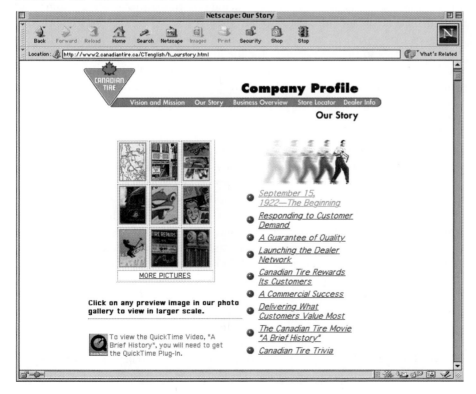

After its launch in November 2000, canadiantire.ca became one of Canada's top five visited sites. In 2001, the Retail Council of Canada named it the best e-commerce site in Canada.[23]

Global competition, restructuring, and mobile technologies
are encouraging flexible
working arrangements such as
telecommuting and hotelling.

has created a system to take advantage of the new work environment. By establishing a "virtual work day," IMRglobal assembles teams from posts throughout the world to work with teams in Canada. This "worldwide" team not only addresses time and space constraints, but also cuts down on labour costs.[24] Some Big Five accounting firms are even instituting the practices of hotelling and hot-desking.[25] Hotelling describes the practice of an open office with unassigned desks. Employees do not have personal work spaces; they reserve a desk for the days or hours they will be in the office. Hot-desking refers to a desk that's still warm from its previous occupant (similar to hot-bunking for sailors on crowded ships). Hotelling makes sense for companies with staffs that spend most of their time outside the office, such as accountants who work at clients' businesses. Why should a company rent offices for empty desks gathering dust in expensive office buildings?

Although hotelling and hot-desking will probably never become commonplace, many office workers are admittedly working in tighter quarters and under greater stress. Some are in open offices divided into small work cubicles, resulting in the need for new rules of office etiquette and civility. For example, instead of wandering into a cubicle, visitors should knock on the frame (they have no doors) to ask permission to enter.[26]

Tight quarters, intense cost-cutting measures, demands for increased produc-
tivity, and round-the-clock workdays—all are creating stress for today's workers. Combined with new responsibilities of team problem solving, business communicators can expect to need interpersonal skills that deal with heightened levels of emo-
tion. Especially important are listening to and empathizing with fellow employees. Equally significant is respecting others' periodic need for uninterrupted, focused work time.[27] And employees at home face added communication challenges since staying connected with the office often requires exchanging more messages than if they were face to face with their colleagues.[28]

## Increasingly Diverse Work Force

Changes in today's work environments include more than innovative technology, team management, and different work routines. You can also expect to see hordes of new faces. No longer, say the experts, will the workplace be overwhelmingly male- or Anglo-oriented. In the last two decades, the number of women working in Canada increased almost 50 percent to more than 7.5 million, while the number of men working rose only 18 percent to 8.5 million.[29] Statistics Canada reports that 18 percent of the population was born outside Canada[30] and immigrants now account for a 70 percent growth in the labour force.[31] Statistics Canada predicts that if current trends continue, one in five Canadians will be a visible minority in 2016.[32] Refer to Figure 1.3 for information on the diversity of Canadian cities. In addition to increasing numbers of minorities, the work force will see a big jump in older workers. In 2001, people in the 37 to 55 age group made up 47 percent of the labour force. In 2011, more than half of this group will be 55 or older.[33] As a result of these and other demographic trends, you can count on interacting with many coworkers who differ from you in race, ethnicity, gender, age, and many other ways.

Communicating with workers
who differ in race, ethnicity,
gender, and age requires new
attitudes and skills.

Communicating in this diverse work environment requires new attitudes and skills. Acquiring these new employment skills is certainly worth the effort because of the benefits diversity brings to consumers, work teams, and business organizations. A diverse staff is better able to read trends and respond to the increasingly diverse customer base in local and world markets. In the workplace, diversity also makes good business sense. Teams made up of different people with different experiences are more likely to create the different products that consumers demand. Customers also want to deal with companies that respect their values. They are more likely to say, "If you're a company whose ads don't include me, or whose work force doesn't

**FIGURE 1.3** Diversity in Canadian Cities

# Canadian Cities More Diverse

**Visible minorities in Canadian cities, shown as a percentage of the municipal population:**

**Foreign-born residents in Toronto as a percentage of the population, compared to other Canadian cities:**

| City | % growth 1996–2001 | % |
|------|------|------|
| Richmond, BC | 31.9% | 59% |
| Markham, ON | 44.7 | 55.5% |
| Vancouver, BC | 16.3 | 49% |
| Burnaby, BC | 33.7 | 48.6% |
| Toronto, ON | 19.1 | 42.8% |
| Richmond Hill, ON | 61.6 | 40.4% |
| Mississauga, ON | 33.9 | 40.3% |
| Brampton, ON | 63.0 | 40.2% |
| St-Laurent, QC | 9.4 | 38.1% |
| Surrey, BC | 45.7 | 36.7% |
| Coquitlam, BC | 37.7 | 34.3% |
| Brossard, QC | 4.0 | 27.7% |
| Pickering, ON | 42.1 | 26.4% |
| Canada | 19.6 | 13.4% |

| City | % |
|------|------|
| Toronto, ON | 43.7% |
| Vancouver, BC | 37.5% |
| Hamilton, ON | 23.6% |
| Windsor, ON | 22.3% |
| Kitchener, ON | 22.1% |
| Calgary, AB | 20.9% |
| Montreal, QC | 18.4% |
| St. Catharines-Niagara, ON | 17.8% |
| Ottawa-Hull*, ON | 17.6% |
| Oshawa, ON | 15.7% |
| Kingston, ON | 12.4% |

**Compared to some large cities outside Canada:**

| City | % |
|------|------|
| Miami, FL | 40.2% |
| Sydney, AUS | 30.9% |
| Los Angeles, CA | 30.9% |
| New York City, NY | 24.4% |

*Now known as Ottawa-Gatineau

include me, I won't buy from you."[34] Learning to cooperate and communicate successfully with diverse coworkers should be a major priority for all businesspeople.

## Thriving in the Age of Knowledge

**Knowledge workers deal with symbols, such as words, figures, and data.**

We're now witnessing the emergence of a new economy based on information and knowledge. Physical labour, raw materials, and capital are no longer the key ingredients in the creation of wealth. Economists predict that two thirds of new jobs in the Canadian economy will require more than 12 years of education and training, and half of those will require more than 17 years. Repetitive jobs are decreasing and being replaced by new jobs that require workers to constantly change and adapt. Constant change means that most jobs now require continuous learning. The fluid labour market requires people to keep learning so they may move more easily from one job to the next.[35] Knowledge workers engage in mind work. They deal with symbols: words, figures, and data.

What does all this mean for you? As a future knowledge worker, you can expect to be generating, processing, and exchanging information. Whether you work in the new economy of *dot-coms* (Internet-based businesses) or the old economy of *brick and mortar* companies, three out of four jobs will involve some form of mind work. Management and employees alike will be making decisions in such areas as product development, quality control, and customer satisfaction.

*Learning to Think Critically.* You will be asked to think critically. This means having opinions that are backed by reasons and evidence. When your boss or team leader says, "What do you think we ought to do?" you want to be able to supply good ideas. The accompanying Career Coach box provides a five-point critical thinking plan to help you solve problems and make decisions. But having a plan is not enough. You also need chances to try the plan out and get feedback from colleagues and your boss (your instructor, for the time being). At the end of each chapter, you'll find activities and problems that will help you develop and apply your critical thinking skills.

**Constantly changing technologies and work procedures mean continual training for employees.**

*Taking Charge of Your Career.* In the new world of work, you can look forward to being in constant training to acquire new skills that will help you keep up with improved technologies and procedures. You can also expect to be exercising greater control over your career. Many workers today will not find nine-to-five jobs, lifetime security, predictable promotions, and even conventional workplaces, as you have learned earlier. Don't presume that companies will provide you with a clearly defined career path or planned developmental experiences. And don't wait for someone to "empower" you. You have to empower yourself.[36] To thrive in the new work world, you must be flexible and continually willing to learn new skills that supplement the strong foundation of basic skills you acquire in college.

*Learning to Communicate.* Probably the most important foundation skill for knowledge workers in the new environment is the ability to communicate. This means being able to listen and to express your ideas effectively in writing and in speech. As you advance in your career, communication skills become even more important. The number one requirement for promotion to management is the ability to communicate. Corporate president Ben Ordover explained how he makes executive choices: "Many people climbing the corporate ladder are very good. When faced with a hard choice between candidates, I use writing ability as the deciding factor. Sometimes a candidate's writing is the only skill that separates him or her from the competition."[37]

## Sharpening Your Skills for Critical Thinking, Problem Solving, and Decision Making

Gone are the days when management expected workers to do only as told. As a knowledge worker, you'll be expected to think critically. You'll be solving problems and making decisions. Much of this book is devoted to helping you learn how to solve problems and communicate those decisions to management, coworkers, clients, the government, and the public.

Faced with a problem or an issue, most of us do a lot of worrying before separating the issues or making a decision. All that worrying can become directed thinking by channelling it into the following procedure.

1. **Identify and Clarify the Problem.** Your first task is to recognize that a problem exists. Some problems are big and unmistakable, such as failure of an air-freight delivery service to get packages to customers on time. Other problems may be continuing annoyances, such as regularly running out of toner for an office copy machine. The first step in reaching a solution is pinpointing the problem area.

2. **Gather Information.** Learn more about the problem situation. Look for possible causes and solutions. This step may mean checking files, calling suppliers, or brainstorming with fellow workers. For example, the air-freight delivery service would investigate the tracking systems of the commercial airlines carrying its packages to determine what went wrong.

3. **Evaluate the Evidence.** Where did the information come from? Does it represent various points of view? What biases could be expected from each source? How accurate is the information gathered? Is it fact or opinion? For example, it is a fact that packages are missing; it is an opinion that they are merely lost and will turn up eventually.

4. **Consider Alternatives and Implications.** Draw conclusions from the gathered evidence and pose solutions. Then weigh the advantages and disadvantages of each alternative. What are the costs, benefits, and consequences? What are the obstacles, and how can they be handled? Most important, what solution best serves your goals and those of your organization? Here's where your creativity is especially important.

5. **Choose and Implement the Best Alternative.** Select an alternative and put it into action. Then, follow through on your decision by monitoring the results of implementing your plan. The freight company decided to give its unhappy customers free delivery service to make up for the lost packages and downtime. Be sure to continue monitoring and adjusting the solution to ensure its effectiveness over time.

### Career Application

As the owner of a popular local McDonald's franchise, you recognize a problem. Customers are unhappy with the multiple lines for service. They don't seem to know where to stand to be next served. Tempers flare when aggressive customers cut in line, and other customers spend so much time protecting their places in line that they fail to study the menu. Then they don't know what to order when they approach the counter. As a franchise owner, you would like to solve this problem. How would the steps discussed here be helpful in approaching this problem? See Activity 1.15 for additional analysis.

## EXAMINING THE PROCESS OF COMMUNICATION

Since communication is a central factor in the emerging knowledge economy and a major consideration for anyone entering today's work force, we need to look more closely at the total process of communication. Just what is communication? For our purposes, communication is the *transmission of information and meaning from one individual or group to another.* The crucial element in this definition is *meaning.* Communication has as its central objective the transmission of meaning. The process of communication is successful only when the receiver understands an idea as the sender intended it. Both parties must agree not only on the information transmitted but also on the meaning of that information. This entire book is devoted to one objective: teaching you the skills of communication so that you can transmit meaning along with information. How does an idea travel from one person to another? Despite what you may have seen in futuristic science fiction movies, we can't just glance at another person and transfer meaning directly from mind to mind. We engage in a sensitive process of communication that generally involves five steps, discussed here and depicted in Figure 1.4.

## Sender Has Idea

**The communication process has five steps: idea formation, message encoding, message transmission, message decoding, and feedback.**

The process of communication begins when the person with whom the message originates—the *sender*—has an idea. The form of the idea will be influenced by complex factors surrounding the sender: mood, frame of reference, background, culture, and physical makeup, as well as the context of the situation and many other factors. The way you greet people on campus or on the job, for example, depends a lot on how you feel, whom you are addressing (a classmate, a professor, a colleague, or your boss), and what your culture has trained you to say ("Good morning," "Hey," "Hi," or "How ya doing?").

**Predicting the effect of a message and adapting the message to a receiver are key factors in successful communication.**

The form of the idea, whether a simple greeting or a complex idea, is shaped by assumptions based on the sender's experiences. A manager sending an e-mail announcement to employees assumes they will be receptive, while direct mail advertisers assume that receivers will give only a quick glance to their message. The ability to accurately predict how a message will affect its receiver and skill in adapting that message to its receiver are key factors in successful communication.

**FIGURE 1.4** The Communication Process

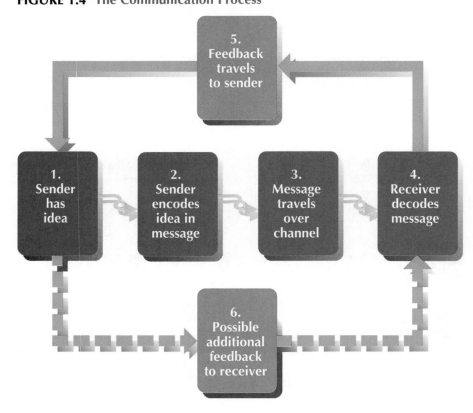

## Sender Encodes Idea in Message

The next step in the communication process involves *encoding*. This means converting the idea into words or gestures that will convey meaning. A major problem in communicating any message verbally is that words have different meanings for different people. When misunderstandings result from missed meanings, it's called *bypassing*. Recognizing how easy it is to be misunderstood, skilled communicators choose familiar words with concrete meanings on which both senders and receivers agree. In selecting proper symbols, senders must be alert to the receiver's communication skills, attitudes, background, experiences, and culture: How will the selected words affect the receiver? Consider the Roots Canada logo sported by Canadian athletes at the 2000 Olympics in Sydney. In Australia, the word "root" has a sexual connotation. Although the word "root" is not considered swearing in Australia, some receivers may be offended.[38] A Dr. Pepper cola promotion failed miserably in Great Britain because North American managers had not done their homework. They had to change their "I'm a Pepper" slogan after learning that *pepper* is British slang for *prostitute*.[39] Because the sender initiates a communication transaction, he or she has primary responsibility for its success or failure. Choosing appropriate words or symbols is the first step.

Messages can also be delivered through handheld wireless devices, a recent technology being used and accepted by many businesses.

## Message Travels Over Channel

The medium over which the message is physically transmitted is the *channel*. Messages may be delivered by computer, telephone, cell phone, letter, memorandum, report, announcement, picture, spoken word, fax, pager, Web page, or through some other channel. Because communication channels deliver both verbal and nonverbal messages, senders must choose the channel and shape the message carefully. A company may use its annual report, for example, as a channel to deliver many messages to shareholders. The verbal message lies in the report's financial and organizational news. Nonverbal messages, though, are conveyed by the report's appearance (showy versus bland), layout (ample white space versus tightly packed columns of print), and tone (conversational versus formal).

Anything that interrupts the transmission of a message in the communication process is called *noise*. Channel noise ranges from static that disrupts a telephone conversation to typographical and spelling errors in a letter or e-mail message. Such errors damage the credibility of the sender. Channel noise might even include the annoyance a receiver feels when the sender chooses an improper medium for sending a message, such as announcing a loan rejection via postcard or firing an employee by e-mail.

**Channels are the media—computer, telephone, letter, fax, and so on—that transmit messages.**

## Receiver Decodes Message

The individual for whom the message is intended is the *receiver*. Translating the message from its symbol form into meaning involves *decoding*. Only when the receiver understands the meaning intended by the sender—that is, successfully decodes the message—does communication take place. Such success, however, is difficult to achieve because no two people share the same life experiences and because many barriers can disrupt the process.

Decoding can be disrupted internally by the receiver's lack of attention to or bias against the sender. It can be disrupted externally by loud sounds or illegible words.

Decoding can also be sidetracked by semantic obstacles, such as misunderstood words or emotional reactions to certain terms. A memo that refers to all the women in an office as "girls," for example, may disturb its receivers so much that they fail to comprehend the total message.

## Feedback Travels to Sender

The verbal and nonverbal responses of the receiver create *feedback*, a vital part of the communication process. Feedback helps the sender know that the message was received and understood. If, as a receiver, you hear the message "How are you," your feedback might consist of words ("I'm fine") or body language (a smile or a wave of the hand). Although the receiver may respond with additional feedback to the sender (thus creating a new act of communication), we'll concentrate here on the initial message flowing to the receiver and the resulting feedback.

Senders can encourage feedback by asking questions such as, *Am I making myself clear?* and *Is there anything you don't understand?* Senders can further improve feedback by timing the delivery appropriately and by providing only as much information as the receiver can handle. Receivers can improve the process by paraphrasing the sender's message with comments, such as, *Let me try to explain that in my own words.* The best feedback is descriptive rather than evaluative. For example, here's a descriptive response: *I understand you want to launch a used golf ball business.* Here's an evaluative response: *Your business ideas are always weird.* An evaluative response is judgmental and doesn't tell the sender whether the receiver actually understood the message.

## OVERCOMING INTERPERSONAL COMMUNICATION BARRIERS

*3*

The communication process is successful only when the receiver understands the message as intended by the sender. It sounds quite simple. Yet, it's not. How many times have you thought that you delivered a clear message, only to learn later that your intentions were totally misunderstood? Most messages that we send reach their destination, but many are only partially understood.

## Obstacles That Create Misunderstanding

You can improve your chances of communicating successfully by learning to recognize barriers that are known to disrupt the process. The most significant barriers for individuals are bypassing, frames of reference, lack of language skill, and distractions.

*Bypassing.* One of the biggest barriers to clear communication involves words. Each of us attaches a little bundle of meanings to every word, and these meanings are not always similar. *Bypassing* happens when people miss each other with their meanings.[40] Let's say your boss asks you to "help" with a large customer mailing. When you arrive to do your share, you learn that you are expected to do the whole mailing yourself. You and your boss attached different meanings to the word *help*. Bypassing can lead to major miscommunication because people assume that meanings are contained in words. Actually, meanings are in people. For communication to be successful, the receiver and sender must attach the same symbolic meanings to their words.

*Differing Frames of Reference.* Another barrier to clear communication is your *frame of reference*. Everything you see and feel in the world is translated through your individual frame of reference. Your unique frame is formed by a combination of your experiences, education, culture, expectations, personality, and many other elements. As a result, you bring your own biases and expectations to any communication situation. Because your frame of reference is totally different from everyone else's, you will never see things exactly as others do. The merger of the Daimler-Benz and Chrysler companies to create DaimlerChrysler experienced some serious cultural differences in working habits, planning, conducting meetings, and exchanging information. To ensure the smooth integration of the companies, management had to accept the differences and allow each group to follow its experiences. The manager in charge of the international management integration of the combined companies stated, "When you say something it does not necessarily have the same meaning, depending on the person you talk to. So we established a discussion culture. We have not had a cultural gap. It is only a gap in the way people express themselves."[41] Wise business communicators strive to prevent communication failure by being alert to both their own frames of reference and those of others.

Miscommunication often results when the sender's frame of reference differs markedly from the receiver's.

*Lack of Language Skill.* No matter how extraordinary the idea, it won't be understood or fully appreciated unless the communicators involved have good language skills. Each individual needs an adequate vocabulary, a command of basic punctuation and grammar, and skill in written and oral expression. Moreover, poor listening skills can prevent us from hearing oral messages clearly and thus responding properly.

Successful communication requires good oral and written language skills.

*Distractions.* Other barriers include emotional interference and physical distractions. Shaping an intelligent message is difficult when you're feeling joy, fear, resentment, hostility, sadness, or some other strong emotion. To reduce the influence of emotions on communication, both senders and receivers should focus on the content of the message and try to remain objective. Physical distractions such as faulty acoustics, noisy surroundings, or a poor cell phone connection can disrupt oral communication. Similarly, sloppy appearance, poor printing, careless formatting, and typographical or spelling errors can disrupt written messages.

## Overcoming the Obstacles

Careful communicators can conquer barriers in a number of ways. Half the battle in communicating successfully is recognizing that the entire process is sensitive and susceptible to breakdown. Like a defensive driver anticipating problems on the road, a good communicator anticipates problems in encoding, transmitting, and decoding a message. Effective communicators also focus on the receiver's environment and frame of reference. They ask themselves questions such as, *How is that individual likely to react to my message?* or *Does the receiver know as much about the subject as I do?*

Misunderstandings are less likely if you arrange your ideas logically and use words precisely. Mark Twain was right when he said, "The difference between an almost-right word and the right word is like the difference between lightning and the lightning bug." But communicating is more than expressing yourself well. A large part of successful communication is listening. Management adviser Peter Drucker observed that "too many executives think they are wonderful with people because they talk well. They don't realize that being wonderful with people means listening well."[42]

Overcoming interpersonal barriers often involves questioning your preconceptions. Successful communicators continually examine their personal assumptions, biases, and prejudices. The more you pay attention to subtleties and know "where

To overcome obstacles, communicators must anticipate problems in encoding, transmitting, and decoding.

you're coming from" when you encode and decode messages, the better you'll communicate. A North American software company, for example, failed unnecessarily in Japan because it simply translated its glossy brochure from English into Japanese. The software company employees didn't realize that in Japan such brochures are associated with low-priced consumer products. The software producer wrongly assumed that since glossy was upscale here, it would be perceived similarly in Japan.

**Good communicators ask questions to stimulate feedback.**

Finally, effective communicators create an environment for useful feedback. In oral communication this means asking questions such as, *Do you understand?* and *What questions do you have?* as well as encouraging listeners to repeat instructions or paraphrase ideas. As a listener it means providing feedback that describes rather than evaluates. And in written communication it means asking questions and providing access: *Do you have my telephone number in case you have questions?* or *Here's my e-mail address so that you can give me your response immediately.*

## COMMUNICATING IN ORGANIZATIONS

Until now, you've probably been thinking about the communication you do personally. But business communicators must also be concerned with the bigger picture, and that involves sharing information in organizations. Creating and exchanging knowledge are critical to fostering innovation, the key challenge in today's knowledge economy. On the job you'll be exchanging information by communicating internally and externally.

### Internal and External Functions

**Internal communication often consists of e-mail, memos, and voice messages; external communication generally consists of letters.**

Internal communication includes sharing ideas and messages with superiors, coworkers, and subordinates. When those messages must be written, you'll probably choose e-mail or a printed memorandum, such as the memo shown in Figure 1.5. When you are communicating externally with customers, suppliers, government, and the public, you will generally send letters on company stationery, such as the Canadian Tire letter also shown in Figure 1.5.

Some of the functions of internal communication are to issue and clarify procedures and policies, inform management of progress, develop new products and services, persuade employees or management to make changes or improvements, coordinate activities, and evaluate and reward employees. External functions are to answer inquiries about products or services, persuade customers to buy products or services, clarify supplier specifications, issue credit, collect bills, respond to government agencies, and promote a positive image of the organization.

**Organizational communication has three basic functions: to inform, to persuade, and/or to promote goodwill.**

In all of these tasks employees and managers use a number of communication skills: reading, listening, speaking, and writing. As postsecondary students and workers, you probably realize that you need to improve these skills to the proficiency level required for success in today's knowledge society. This book and this course will provide you with practical advice on how to do just that.

Now look back over the preceding discussion of internal and external functions of communication in organizations. Although there appear to be a large number of diverse business communication functions, they can be summarized in three simple categories, as Figure 1.6 shows: (1) to inform, (2) to persuade, and/or (3) to promote goodwill.

# FIGURE 1.5  Internal and External Forms of Communication

August 14, 2005

Audrey Lovelace
2180 Yonge Street, 9th Floor
Toronto, ON  M4P 2V8

Dear Ms. Lovelace:

Great news! On September 5th, the Options® Cardmember Reward Program® will change to **Canadian Tire 'Money' On The Card**™. You'll automatically be rewarded with Canadian Tire 'Money' On the Card just for using your Options® MasterCard Card®—and you can use it for instant savings on store merchandise and auto service at Canadian Tire. It's that simple!

**Start earning Canadian Tire 'Money' On the Card electronically
everywhere you use your Options MasterCard.**

Imagine making a purchase at any of the over 15 million locations worldwide where MasterCard is accepted, and receiving Canadian Tire 'Money' On the Card—at the rate of 1% for every dollar you spend—as a "Thank You" for using your Options MasterCard.

But there's a lot more to the story . . .

- Earn More!
  You can earn 20% MORE Canadian Tire 'Money' On The Card by using your Options MasterCard than you'd earn in paper Canadian Tire 'Money'™ if you paid with cash for the same purchase in Canadian Tire stores.

- Multiply your earnings at Canadian Tire Gas Bars!
  The GasAdvantage® program will change, so you'll be able to earn Canadian Tire 'Money' On The Card when you buy gas. Canadian Tire 'Money' On The Card will begin rolling out to Canadian Tire Gas Bars in November and be completed during December. Until the program changes at your local Gas Bar, you'll continue to receive your GasAdvantage discount when you qualify.

**Get instant savings on Canadian Tire merchandise and auto service**

With so many opportunities to earn Canadian Tire 'Money' On The Card, you'll want to reach for your Options MasterCard first, wherever and whenever you make a purchase. That means you'll be able to SAVE MORE on the Canadian Tire merchandise you want to buy when you use your Canadian Tire 'Money' On The Card.

Remember, there are just a few short days until you can start earning Canadian Tire 'Money' On The Card. So please take a moment to read the enclosed Cardmember Benefits Booklet. It will help you get the most from your Options MasterCard.

Sincerely,

*Kevin Gould*

T. Kevin Gould, President
Canadian Tire Acceptance Ltd.

> Letters on company stationery communicate with outsiders. Notice how this one builds a solid relationship between Canadian Tire and a satisfied customer.

> E-mail messages and printed memorandums typically deliver messages within organizations. They use a standardized format and are direct and concise.

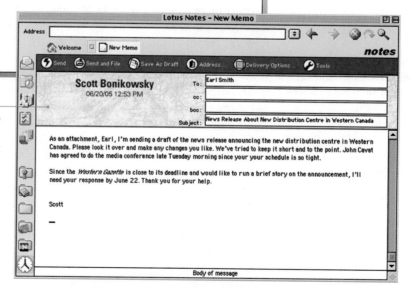

**FIGURE 1.6** Functions of Business Communication

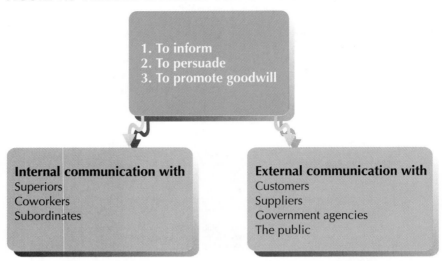

1. To inform
2. To persuade
3. To promote goodwill

**Internal communication with**
Superiors
Coworkers
Subordinates

**External communication with**
Customers
Suppliers
Government agencies
The public

## New Emphasis on Interactive and Mobile Communication

The flattening of organizations coupled with the development of sophisticated information technology has greatly changed the way we communicate internally and externally. We're seeing a major shift away from one-sided and rather slow forms of communication, such as memos and letters. More companies are seeking customer and employee input to learn ways to improve business.

To convey information to various audiences, organizations prefer more interactive, fast-results communication, such as e-mail, instant messaging, voice mail, pagers, and cell phones. Cell phones have proliferated so rapidly that their careless use has become an annoyance in many public places. See the accompanying Career Coach box for tips on using this technological privilege courteously and responsibly.

Other forms of interactive communication include intranets (company versions of the Internet), Web sites, video transmission, and videoconferencing. You'll be learning more about these forms of communication in subsequent chapters. Despite the range of interactive technologies, communicators are still working with two basic forms of communication: oral and written. Each has advantages and disadvantages.

**Oral communication minimizes miscommunication but provides no written record.**

*Oral Communication.* Nearly everyone agrees that the best way to exchange information is orally in face-to-face conversations or meetings. Oral communication has many advantages. For one thing, it minimizes misunderstandings because communicators can immediately ask questions to clarify uncertainties. For another, it enables communicators to see each other's facial expressions and hear voice inflections, further improving the process. Oral communication is also an efficient way to develop consensus when many people must be consulted. Finally, most of us enjoy face-to-face interpersonal communication because it's easy, feels warm and natural, and promotes friendships.

The main disadvantages of oral communication are that it produces no written record, sometimes wastes time, and may be inconvenient. When individuals meet face to face or speak on the telephone, someone's work has to be interrupted. And how many of us are able to limit a conversation to just business? Nevertheless, oral communication has many advantages. The forms and advantages of both oral and written communication are summarized in Figure 1.7.

# Practising Courteous and Responsible Cell Phone Use

**B**usiness communicators find cell phones to be enormously convenient and real time-savers. But rude users have generated a backlash of sorts. Most of us have experienced thoughtless and offensive cell phone behaviour. Although the cell phone industry vigorously opposes restrictive legislation, many major manufacturers admonish users to be courteous. Here are specific suggestions for using cell phones safely and responsibly:

- **Be courteous to those around you.** Don't force those near you to hear your business. Think first of those in close proximity instead of those on the other end of the phone. Apologize and make amends gracefully for occasional cell phone blunders.

- **Observe wireless-free quiet areas.** Don't allow your cell phone to ring in theatres, restaurants, museums, classrooms, important meetings, and similar places. Use the cell phone's silent/vibrating ring option. A majority of travellers prefer that cell phone conversations not be held on most forms of public transportation.

- **Speak in low, conversational tones.** Microphones on cell phones are quite sensitive, thus making it unnecessary to talk loudly. Avoid "cell yell."

- **Take only urgent calls.** Make full use of your cell phone's caller ID feature to screen incoming calls. Let voice mail take those calls that are not pressing.

- **Drive now, talk later.** Pull over if you must make a call. Talking while driving increases the chance of accidents fourfold, about the same as driving while intoxicated.

**Career Application**

How do you feel when you must listen to nearby cell phone conversations? Should cell phone use in cars be prohibited? During business meetings, how should participants react if their cell phones ring?

**FIGURE 1.7  Forms of Organizational Communication**

| Oral Communication | Written Communication |
|---|---|
| **Form**<br>Phone call<br>Conversation<br>Interview<br>Meeting<br>Conference | **Form**<br>Announcement<br>Memo, e-mail, fax<br>Letter<br>Report, proposal<br>Newsletter |
| **Advantages**<br>Immediate feedback<br>Nonverbal clues<br>Warm feeling<br>Forceful impact<br>Multiple input | **Advantages**<br>Permanent record<br>Convenience<br>Economy<br>Careful message<br>Easy distribution |

*Written Communication.* Written communication is impersonal in the sense that two communicators cannot see or hear each other and cannot provide immediate feedback. Most forms of business communication—including e-mail, announcements, memos, faxes, letters, newsletters, reports, proposals, and manuals—fall into this category.

Written communication provides a permanent record but lacks immediate feedback.

Written messages demand good
writing skills, which can be
developed through training.

Organizations rely on written communication for many reasons. It provides a permanent record, a necessity in these times of increasing litigation and extensive government regulation. Writing out an idea instead of delivering it orally enables communicators to develop an organized, well-considered message. Written documents are also convenient. They can be composed and read when the schedules of both communicators permit, and they can be reviewed if necessary.

Written messages have drawbacks, of course. They require careful preparation and sensitivity to audience and anticipated effects. Words spoken in conversation may soon be forgotten, but words committed to hard or soft copy become a public record—and sometimes an embarrassing one. A former IBM chairman, for example, must have had second thoughts about his e-mail memo blasting managers for complacency and product defects. When leaked to the press, the memo shook up the financial world and damaged IBM's image and morale.

Another drawback to written messages is that they are more difficult to prepare. They demand good writing skills, and such skills are not inborn. But writing proficiency can be learned. Because as much as 90 percent of all business transactions may involve written messages and because writing skills are so important to your business success, you will be receiving special instruction in becoming a good writer.

## Avoiding Information Overload and Productivity Meltdown

"What information consumes is rather obvious: It consumes the attention of its recipients. Hence a wealth of information creates a poverty of attention," according to Herbert Simon, economist and Nobel Prize recipient.[43] Although technology provides a myriad of communication channel choices, the sheer volume of messages is overwhelming many employees. A study by the Institute for the Future revealed each employee receives 192 messages per day in all media.[44] According to Christina Cavanaugh of the Richard Ivey School of Business, interviews with executives and managers at companies from General Motors to CIBC found 80 percent of managers receiving more than 80 e-mails daily believe it is out of control. She calculates that the typical executive may spend two hours per day handling e-mail. Additionally, meaning may also be lost since reading on a computer screen has been shown to yield just 75 percent of the comprehension of reading on paper.[45] According to a study by Emailthatpays and Ipsos-Reid, e-mail is accessed multiple times weekly by 88 percent of online Canadians, and daily by 62 percent. The average user receives 22 messages per day at work and home. Eighty-five percent of online Canadians believe that e-mail has made them more efficient in the workplace.[46] Figure 1.8 shows the results of a survey conducted by Pitney Bowes. "Messaging is at the core of virtually all business processes, and managing it now

Information overload is a serious problem. Today, individuals may be bombarded with electronic, audio, and print messages. One expert warns that the use of e-mail, cell phones, and PDAs can become more time-consuming than time-saving if allowed.

controls people's daily priorities and focus," said Meredith Fischer, vice president of corporate marketing at Pitney Bowes, which specializes in communication products and services.[47]

Information overload and resulting productivity meltdown are becoming serious problems for workers and their employers. One midlevel manager at a global company solves his overload problem by deleting all the messages in his e-mail in-box when it gets too full. "If it's important," he reasons, "people will get back to me."[48] That technique, however, flirts with disaster. While some software programs can now automatically sort messages into limited categories, one expert says that "human brainpower"—not new technology—is the key to managing e-mail overload.[49] Suggestions for controlling the e-mail monster are shown in the Tech Talk box on page 22.

Although communication tools like e-mail and voice mail were expected to make workers more productive, the truth is that many employees are feeling stressed and unable to function. Solutions? Some workers are beginning to telecommute. Working from home means fewer interruptions. Others are blocking out work time when they turn off pagers and cell phones and log off the Internet.

## IMPROVING THE FLOW OF INFORMATION IN ORGANIZATIONS

Information within organizations flows through formal and informal communication channels. A free exchange of information helps organizations respond rapidly to changing markets, increase efficiency and productivity, build employee morale, serve

5

**FIGURE 1.8  Volume and Source of Daily Messages for Average Worker**

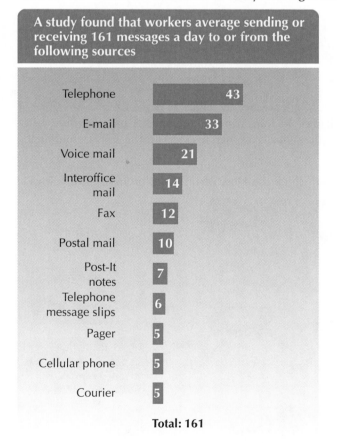

A study found that workers average sending or receiving 161 messages a day to or from the following sources

| Source | Messages |
| --- | --- |
| Telephone | 43 |
| E-mail | 33 |
| Voice mail | 21 |
| Interoffice mail | 14 |
| Fax | 12 |
| Postal mail | 10 |
| Post-It notes | 7 |
| Telephone message slips | 6 |
| Pager | 5 |
| Cellular phone | 5 |
| Courier | 5 |

**Total: 161**

## Tips for Controlling the E-Mail Monster

In an amazingly short time, e-mail has become one of the most powerful and useful communication channels in the workplace. But it has also produced information overload for many workers. The following techniques can help you control the e-mail monster:

- Send only business messages that you would have sent in a memo format. If a quick phone call or a short in-person chat could solve the problem immediately, avoid sending an e-mail.

- Check your e-mail in-box only at specific times each day, say at 9 a.m. and again at 4 p.m.

- Print important memos to read during free time away from your desk.

- Avoid using the copy function and sending unnecessary replies.

- Pick up your incoming messages online, but answer them offline. Take time to think about your responses. Compose them on your word processor and upload them to your mail program, thus saving valuable network connection time.

- Practise e-mail triage. This means focusing on the most urgent messages first. Read the subject lines; then delete unwanted messages (*spam*) and those that require no response.

- Devise a logical storage system, and religiously move incoming mail into electronic folders.

- Subscribe only to mailing lists in which you are really interested. (Some high-volume Internet mailing lists disgorge 30 or more messages a day.[50])

the public, and take full advantage of the ideas of today's knowledge workers. Barriers, however, can obstruct the flow of communication, as summarized in Figure 1.9.

### Formal Channels

**Formal communication channels follow an organization's chain of command.**

Formal channels of communication generally follow an organization's hierarchy of command, as shown in Figure 1.10. Information about policies and procedures originates with executives and flows down through managers to supervisors and finally

**FIGURE 1.9  Barriers That Block the Flow of Information in Organizations**

**FIGURE 1.10** Formal Communication Channels

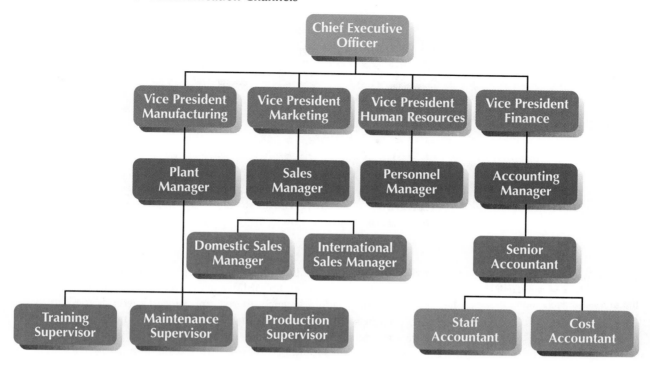

to lower-level employees. Many organizations have formulated official communication policies that encourage regular open communication, suggest means for achieving it, and spell out responsibilities. As summarized in Figure 1.11, official information among workers typically flows through formal channels in three directions: downward, upward, and horizontally.

*Downward Flow.* Information flowing downward generally moves from decision makers, including the CEO and managers, through the chain of command to workers. This information includes job plans, policies, and procedures. Managers also provide feedback about employee performance and instill a sense of mission in achieving the organization's goals.

One obstacle that can impede the downward flow of information is distortion resulting from long lines of communication. If, for example, the CEO in Figure 1.10 wanted to change an accounting procedure, she or he would probably not send a memo directly to the staff or cost accountants who would implement the change. Instead, the CEO would relay the idea through proper formal channels—from the vice president for finance, to the accounting manager, to the senior accountant, and so on—until the message reached the affected employees. Obviously, the longer the lines of communication, the greater the chance that a message will be distorted.

To improve communication and to compete more effectively, many of today's companies have "reengineered" themselves into smaller operating units and work teams. Rather than being bogged down with long communication chains, management speaks directly to team leaders, thus speeding up the entire process.[51] Management is also improving the downward flow of information through newsletters, announcements, meetings, videos, and company intranets. Instead of hoarding information at the top, today's managers recognize how essential it is to let workers know how well the company is doing and what new projects are planned.

**Job plans, policies, instructions, feedback, and procedures flow downward from managers to employees.**

**FIGURE 1.11** How Communication Flow Serves Organizations

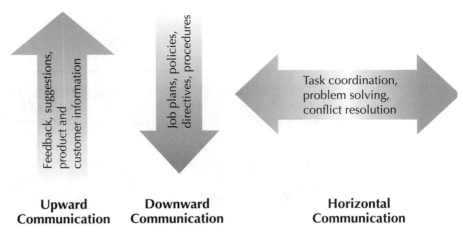

| Upward Communication | Downward Communication | Horizontal Communication |

*Upward Flow.* Information flowing upward provides feedback from nonmanagement employees to management. Subordinate employees describe progress in completing tasks, report roadblocks encountered, and suggest methods for improving efficiency. Channels for upward communication include phone messages, e-mail, memos, reports, departmental meetings, and suggestion systems. Ideally, the heaviest flow of information should be upward, with information being fed steadily to decision makers.

A number of obstacles, however, can interrupt the upward flow of communication. Employees who distrust their employers are less likely to communicate openly. Employees cease trusting managers if they feel they are being tricked, manipulated, criticized, or treated unfairly. Unfortunately, some employees today no longer have a strong trusting attitude toward employers. Downsizing, cost-cutting measures, the tremendous influx of temporary workers, discrimination and harassment suits, substantial compensation packages for chief executives, and many other factors have eroded the feelings of trust and pride that employees once felt toward their employers and their jobs. Other obstacles include fear of reprisal for honest communication, lack of adequate communication skills, and differing frames of reference. Imperfect communication results when individuals are not using words or symbols with similar meanings, when they cannot express their ideas clearly, or when they come from different backgrounds.

To improve the upward flow of communication, some companies are (1) hiring communication coaches to train employees, (2) asking employees to report customer complaints, (3) encouraging regular meetings with staff, (4) providing a trusting, nonthreatening environment in which employees can comfortably share their observations and ideas with management, and (5) offering incentive programs that encourage employees to collect and share valuable feedback. Companies are also building trust by setting up hotlines for anonymous feedback to management and by installing *ombudsman* programs. An *ombudsman* is a mediator who hears employee complaints, investigates, and seeks to resolve problems fairly.

*Horizontal Flow.* Lateral channels transmit information horizontally among workers at the same level, such as between the training supervisor and maintenance supervisor in Figure 1.10. These channels enable individuals to coordinate tasks, share information, solve problems, and resolve conflicts. Horizontal communication takes place through personal contact, telephone, e-mail, memos, voice mail, and

**Feedback from employees forms the upward flow of communication in most organizations.**

meetings. Most traditional organizations have few established regular channels for the horizontal exchange of information. Restructured companies with flattened hierarchies and team-based management, however, have discovered that when employees combine their knowledge with that of other employees, they can do their jobs better. Much of the information in these organizations is travelling horizontally among team members.[52]

**Workers coordinate tasks, share information, solve problems, and resolve conflicts through horizontal communication.**

Obstacles to the horizontal flow of communication, as well as to upward and downward flow, include poor communication skills, prejudice, ego involvement, and turf wars. Some employees avoid sharing information if doing so might endanger their status or chances for promotion within the organization. Competition within units and an uneven reward system may also prevent workers from freely sharing information.

To improve horizontal communication, companies are (1) training employees in teamwork and communication techniques, (2) establishing reward systems based on team achievement rather than individual achievement, and (3) encouraging full participation in team functions. However, employees must also realize that they are personally responsible for making themselves heard, for really understanding what other people say, and for getting the information they need. Developing those business communication skills is exactly what this book and this course will do for you.

**To improve horizontal communication, companies are training and rewarding employees.**

## Informal Channels

Not all information within an organization travels through formal channels. Often, it travels in informal channels called the *grapevine*. These channels are usually based on social relationships in which individuals talk about work when they are having lunch, meeting at the water cooler, working out, golfing, or car-pooling to work. Alert managers find the grapevine an excellent source of information about employee morale and problems. They have also used the grapevine as a "break it to them gently" device, planting "rumours," for example, of future layoffs or other changes.

**Informal organizational communication transmits unofficial news through the grapevine.**

In many organizations information exchanged informally is nearly as important as that flowing through formal channels. Wise managers take the time to stop and talk with employees to learn how employees are interpreting what's being communicated formally.

## *Canadian Tire Revisited*

One of Canadian Tire's initiatives was the launch of the "Next Generation" retail store. This initiative is the most extensive store renewal and redevelopment program in Canadian history and was established to keep Canadian Tire's competitive edge. The company's strategic repositioning in the marketplace began in 1993. Since that time, more than 300 of its 450 stores have been built, replaced, and/or renovated. By 2005, 350 new-format stores will have been opened, representing approximately three quarters of the Canadian Tire retail store network. As part of the store expansion program, Canadian Tire plans to build approximately 30 incremental locations, for a total of more than 480 stores.

In addition, the company plans to open at least 100 locations in 2003, including Canadian Tire stores, gas bars, and Mark's Work Wearhouse stores. The company also intends to convert more gas bars to the Canadian Tire name.[53] After acquiring Mark's Work Wearhouse, Canadian Tire initiated its new "Let's Get Started" positioning and began making some noise—something seen by some as being not characteristically Canadian.[54]

In the town of Okotoks, Alberta, at the foot of the mountains, Associate Dealer Rick Siddon helped to open a new "Next Generation" retail store, which has become a key anchor in the community of just over 12 000 people. The "Next Generation" store includes all of the products normally associated with Canadian Tire, but it also focuses on the "stores-within-a-store" concept, which includes a kitchen place, hardware store, paint gallery, and enhanced sporting goods and automotive departments. The store is easy to shop, with excellent signage and multiple cash lines, making the stores more shopper-friendly.

In the midst of all of the change, effective and clear communication between the head office and Canadian Tire's dealers and its employees is what has ensured the company's status as a success story. Shifts in strategy are based on honest and simple communication with the head office, as well as constant feedback from across the organization. "From the creative stage to testing to implementation—associate dealers are involved every step of the way," explains Scott Bonikowsky, senior director of Corporate Communication. "It's just how we do business." The key to effective communication, both internal and external, according to Bonikowsky, is honesty. "You've got to be open about the bad news and the challenges as well as the good stuff."

### CRITICAL THINKING

- Canadian Tire's executives recognized that informal communication would not be appropriate during the company's many new campaigns and initiatives designed to revitalize the retail chain across Canada. Why would informal channels of communication be dangerous at such a time of upheaval?
- What obstacles might hinder the downward, upward, and horizontal flow of information across the organization with as many employees and stores as Canadian Tire? Why is it important that communication experts like Scott Bonikowsky consult with dealers, employees, and customers before dramatic changes are made to stores and product lines?
- Canadian Tire launched its "Foundation for Families" with an eye to raising funds for families and communities in need. How might such an initiative enhance the competitive spirit and positive atmosphere at a company facing stiff challenges from rival retailers?

**www.canadiantire.ca**

Researchers studying communication flow within organizations know that the grapevine can be a major source of information. One study found that as much as two thirds of an employee's information comes from informal channels.[55] Is this bad? Well, yes and no. The grapevine can be a fairly accurate and speedy source of organization information. The Workplace Safety and Insurance Board (WSIB) of Ontario has created a unique way to handle informal communication. To encourage staff to share information, Ash Sooknanan, WSIB's knowledge manager, created a virtual water cooler where the agency's staff of over 5 000, spread throughout the province, could "shoot the breeze." In the first three days, the WSIB water cooler received more than 19 000 hits. Employees began sharing not only work-related information but also personal matters. This relaxed atmosphere encouraged new ideas with less formality.[56] However, grapevine information is often incomplete because it travels in headlines. When employees obtain most of their company news from the grapevine, it's a pretty sure bet that management is not releasing sufficient information through formal channels.

The truth is that most employees want to know what's going on. In fact, one study found that regardless of how much information organization members reported receiving, they wanted more.[57] Many companies today have moved away from a rigid authoritarian management structure in which only managers were privy to vital information, such as product success and profit figures. Employees who know the latest buzz feel like important members of the team.[58] Through formal lines of communication, smart companies are keeping employees informed. Thus, the grapevine is reduced to carrying gossip about who's dating whom and what restaurant is trendy for lunch.

**Employees prefer to receive vital company information through formal channels.**

## FACING INCREASING ETHICAL CHALLENGES

The work world is indeed changing. One of the most remarkable changes involves ethics in the workplace. At one time the expression "business ethics" was considered an oxymoron, a combination of contradictory words. How could a business, which is obviously governed by profits, also be ethical? Yet corporations made a remarkable turnabout in the 1990s. Following the "greed is good" era of the 1980s, business-people became increasingly concerned with ethics. Today many organizations recognize the benefits of discussing and implementing codes of conduct. Although this trend is more pronounced in the United States, the phenomenon is spreading throughout the rest of the western world.[59] According to Eugene Ellen, executive director of the Social Investment Organization in Canada, the issue of business ethics is becoming more mainstream. "It has become good hard business practice to establish corporate liability in various areas, including ethics and environment."[60]

What causes this explosion of ethical awareness? According to David King, regional manager of Robert Half Management Resources, many executives recognize the benefits of adopting a comprehensive corporate social responsibility program. "Community involvement is an effective way for companies to encourage employee participation, improve morale, and strengthen team-building skills."[61] Actually, however, many businesses simply recognized that ethical practices make good business sense. Ethical companies endure less litigation, less resentment, and less government regulation.[62] As a result, companies are adding ethics officers, hotlines, workshops, training programs, and codes of conduct. If you go to work for a large company, chances are good that you'll be asked to comply with its code of conduct.

**Ethical awareness grows as companies recognize that ethical practices make good business sense.**

## Violating Business Ethics

Despite this trend, however, the business world continues to be plagued by unethical behaviour and a poor public image. Consider Calgary-based Talisman Energy's four-year venture into Sudan—which has been in a civil war for nearly two decades—that angered international human rights activists, who accused the company of generating oil revenue that allows the Sudanese government to fund violent human rights abuses of civilians in South Sudan.[63] One study revealed that 56 percent of the

**The business world suffers from a poor public image resulting from unethical behaviour by some organizations.**

employees surveyed felt some pressure to act unethically or illegally. Another 48 percent admitted they had engaged in one or more unethical and/or illegal actions during the past year. The most common violations follow:[64]

**Employees revealed common ethical violations.**

- Cutting corners on quality
- Covering up incidents
- Abusing or lying about sick days
- Deceiving customers
- Lying to a supervisor or underling
- Taking credit for a colleague's ideas

## Achieving Ethical Behaviour

With downsized staffs and fewer resources, employees feel pressure to increase productivity—by whatever means. Knowingly or not, managers under pressure to make profit quotas may send the message to workers that it's OK to lie, cheat, or steal to achieve company goals.[65] Couple these pressures with a breakdown in the traditional attitudes of trust and loyalty toward employers, and it's easy to see why ethical lapses are causing concern in the workplace.

**Ethical behaviour means doing the *right* thing given the circumstances.**

Just what is ethical behaviour? According to Linda Crompton of Citizen's Bank of Canada, "How well you stand up in a controversy—that's also what ethics are all about. People understand the effect of business on the environment or children in other countries." The bank's ethical policy means Citizen's does not invest in or do business with companies that have a poor record of employee relations or are involved in the production of nuclear energy.[66] Ethical behaviour involves four principles: honesty, integrity, fairness, and concern for others. "These four principles are like the four legs of a stool," explains ethics authority Michael Josephson. "If even one leg is missing, the stool wobbles, and if two are missing, the stool falls. It's not enough to pride oneself on your honesty and integrity if you're not fair or caring."[67] Consider a manager who would never dream of behaving dishonestly on the job or off. Yet this same manager forces a key employee to choose between losing her job and staying home with a sick child. The manager's lack of caring and failure to consider the circumstances create a shaky ethical position that would be difficult to justify.

Founded in 1995, Canadian Business for Social Responsibility (CBSR) has more than 100 members, including VanCity, Alcan, Bell Canada, the Hudson's Bay Company, and Mountain Equipment Co-Op. CBSR's goal is to foster a positive relationship among businesses, governments, and consumers.

## Five Common Ethical Traps

Canadian companies must abide by the rules set out by the Competition Bureau, which is an independent organization responsible for administration and enforcement of the *Competition Act*, the *Consumer Packaging and Labelling Act*, the *Textile Labelling Act*, and the *Precious Metals Marking Act*. Its role is to promote and maintain fair competition so that Canadians can benefit from lower prices, product choice, and quality services. The Bureau's operating principles can be summarized in five words: *confidentiality, fairness, predictability, timeliness,* and *transparency*.[68] In making ethical decisions, business communicators commonly face five traps that can make arriving at the right decision more difficult.[69]

***The False Necessity Trap.*** People act from the belief that they're doing what they must do. They convince themselves that they have no other choice, when in fact it's generally a matter of convenience or comfort. Consider the Beech-Nut Corporation's actions when it discovered that its supplier was providing artificial apple juice. Beech-Nut cancelled its contracts but continued to advertise and sell the adulterated "apple" juice as a 100 percent natural product in its baby food line. Apparently falling into the false necessity trap, Beech-Nut felt it had no choice but to continue the deception.

Recognizing five ethical traps can help communicators avoid them.

*The Doctrine-of-Relative-Filth Trap.* Unethical actions sometimes look good when compared with the worse behaviour of others. What's a little padding on an expense account compared with the pleasure cruise the boss took and charged as a business trip? Or how about using your PC at work to send a little personal e-mail (just a few quick notes) and perhaps do some much-needed research on an SUV you are considering buying. After all, the fellows in Engineering told you that they spend hours on their PCs checking sports scores, playing games, and conducting recreational Web surfing. They even have bookmarked "Don's Boss Page" so that they can look busy while cruising the Internet.[70] Your minor infraction is insignificant compared with what's happening regularly in Engineering.

*The Rationalization Trap.* In falling into the rationalization trap, people try to explain away unethical actions by justifying them with excuses. Consider employees who "steal" time from their employers by taking long lunch and coffee breaks, claiming sick leave when not ill, and completing their own tasks on company time. It's easy to rationalize such actions: "I deserve an extra-long lunch break because I can't get all my shopping done in such a short lunch hour" or "I'll just write my class report at the office because the computer printer is much better than mine, and they aren't paying me what I'm worth anyway."

Explaining unethical actions by justifying them with excuses is a form of rationalization.

*The Self-Deception Trap.* Applicants for jobs often fall into the self-deception trap. They are all too willing to inflate grade-point averages or exaggerate past accomplishments to impress prospective employers. One applicant, for example, claimed experience as a broker's assistant at a prestigious securities firm. A background check revealed that he had interviewed for the securities job but was never offered it.[71] Another applicant claimed that in his summer job he was "responsible for cross-corporate transferal of multidimensional client receivables." In other words, he moved boxes from sales to shipping. Self-deception can lead to unethical and possibly illegal behaviour.

*The Ends-Justify-the-Means Trap.* Taking unethical actions to accomplish a desirable goal is a common trap. Consider a manager in the claims division of a large health insurance company who coerced clerical staff into working overtime without pay. The goal was the reduction of a backlog of unprocessed claims. Despite the worthy goal, the means of reaching it was unethical.

## Goals of Ethical Business Communication

Business communicators can minimize the danger of falling into ethical traps by setting specific ethical goals. Although the following goals hardly comprise a formal code of conduct, they will help business writers maintain a high ethical standard.

*Telling the Truth.* Ethical business communicators do not intentionally make statements that are untrue or deceptive. We become aware of dishonesty in business when violators break laws, notably in advertising, packaging, and marketing. The

Competition Bureau fined the Hudson's Bay Company $600 000 for advertising limited-time availability of bicycles; however, the sale continued much longer. In supporting the decision, the director of the investigation said, "Consumers can be easily misled by sales promotions that create a general sense of urgency."[72] Some companies may engage in the unethical principle of *bait and switch* promotions, in which a product may be offered at a very low price, but there are insufficient quantities to meet the demand. The customer may then be encouraged to purchase a more expensive, yet similar, product. The Competition Bureau has cracked down on electronic muscle-stimulation devices, such as Abtronic and the Abtronic Pro, which gave the impression that a person could lose weight and obtain an athletic physique without participating in any physical exercise. "Consumers are particularly vulnerable when it comes to unsubstantiated product performance claims, and more specifically when the claims relate to sensitive issues such as weight loss and physical appearance," says Raymond Pierce, deputy commissioner of the Competition Bureau.[73]

Half-truths, exaggerations, and deceptions constitute unethical communication. But conflicting loyalties in the workplace sometimes blur the line between right and wrong. Let's say you helped the marketing director, who is both your boss and your friend, conduct consumer research about a new company product. When you see the final report, you are astonished at how the findings have been distorted to show a highly favourable product approval rating. You are torn between loyalty to your boss (and friend) and loyalty to the company. Tools for helping you solve such ethical dilemmas will be discussed shortly.

*Labelling Opinions.* Sensitive communicators know the difference between facts and opinions. Facts are verifiable and often are quantifiable; opinions are beliefs held with confidence but without substantiation. It's a fact, for example, that women in the last decade started new businesses twice as fast as men.[74] It's an opinion, though, that increasing numbers of women are abandoning the corporate employment arena to start these businesses. Such a statement can't be verified. Stating opinions as if they were facts is unethical.

*Being Objective.* Ethical business communicators recognize their own biases and strive to keep them from distorting a message. Suppose you are asked to investigate laptop computers and write a report recommending a brand for your office. As you visit stores and watch computer demonstrations, you discover that an old high school friend is selling Brand X. Because you always liked this individual and have faith in his judgment, you may be inclined to tilt your recommendation in his direction. However, it's unethical to misrepresent the facts in your report or to put a spin on your arguments based on friendship. To be ethical, you could note in your report that you have known the person for ten years and that you respect his opinion. In this way, you have disclosed your relationship as well as the reasons for your decision. Honest reporting means presenting the whole picture and relating all facts fairly.

*Communicating Clearly.* Ethical business communicators feel an obligation to write clearly so that receivers understand easily and quickly. Many organizations, such as banks and insurance companies, have even created "Plain English" guidelines to ensure that policies, warranties, and contracts are in language comprehensible to average readers. Plain English means short sentences, simple words, and clear organization. Communicators who intentionally obscure the meaning with long sentences and difficult words are being unethical. A thin line, however, separates unethical communication from ethical communication. Some might argue that writers and speakers who deliver wordy, imprecise messages requiring additional correspondence or inquiry to clarify the meaning are acting unethically. However, the problem may be one of experience and skill rather than ethics. Such messages waste the time and resources of both senders and receivers. However, they are not unethical unless the intent is to deceive.

*Giving Credit.* As you probably know, using the written ideas of others without credit is called plagiarism. Ethical communicators give credit for ideas by (1) referring to originators' names within the text; (2) using quotation marks; and (3) documenting sources with endnotes, footnotes, or internal references. (You'll learn how to do this in Chapter 12 and Appendix C.) One student writer explained his reasons for plagiarizing material in his report by rationalizing, "But the encyclopedia said it so much better than I could!" This may be so, yet such an argument is no justification for appropriating the words of others. Quotation marks and footnotes could have saved the student. In school or on the job, stealing ideas or words from others is unethical.

## Tools for Doing the Right Thing

In composing messages or engaging in other activities on the job, business communicators can't help being torn by conflicting loyalties. Do we tell the truth and risk our jobs? Do we show loyalty to friends even if it means bending the rules? Should we be tactful or totally honest? Is it our duty to make a profit or to be socially responsible? Acting ethically means doing the right thing given the circumstances. Each set of circumstances requires analyzing issues, evaluating choices, and acting responsibly.

Resolving ethical issues is never easy, but the task can be made less difficult if you know how to identify key issues. The following questions may be helpful.

- **Is the action you are considering legal?** No matter who asks you to do it or how important you feel the result will be, avoid anything that is prohibited by law. Giving a kickback to a buyer for a large order is illegal, even if you suspect that others in your field do it and you know that without the kickback you will lose the sale.

- **How would you see the problem if you were on the opposite side?** Looking at all sides of an issue helps you gain perspective. Consider the issue of mandatory drug testing among employees. From management's viewpoint such testing could stop drug abuse, improve job performance, and lower health insurance premiums. From the employees' viewpoint mandatory testing reflects a lack of trust of employees and constitutes an invasion of privacy. By weighing both sides of the issue, you can arrive at a more equitable solution.

  > Business communicators can help resolve ethical issues through self-examination.

- **What are alternative solutions?** Consider all dimensions of other options. Would the alternative be more ethical? Under the circumstances, is the alternative feasible? Can an alternative solution be implemented with a minimum of disruption and with a high degree of probable success? In the situation involving your boss's distortion of consumer product research, you could go to the head of the company and tell what you know. A more tactful alternative, however, would be to approach your boss and ask whether you misunderstood the report's findings or whether an error might have been made.

- **Can you discuss the problem with someone whose advice you trust?** Suppose you feel ethically bound to report accurate information to a client even though your boss has ordered you not to do so. Talking about your dilemma with a coworker or with a colleague in your field might give you helpful insights and lead to possible alternatives.

  > Discussing an ethical problem with a coworker or colleague might lead to helpful alternatives.

- **How would you feel if your family, friends, employer, or coworkers learned of your action?** If the thought of revealing your action publicly produces cold sweats, your choice is probably not a wise one. Losing the faith of your friends or the confidence of your customers is not worth whatever short-term gains might be realized.

Perhaps the best advice in ethical matters is contained in the Golden Rule: Do unto others as you would have others do unto you. The ultimate solution to all ethics problems is treating others fairly and doing what is right to achieve what is good. Consider the advice of U.S. General Norman Schwarzkopf on dealing with ethical dilemmas: "The truth of the matter is that you always know the right thing to do. The hard part is doing it."[75] In succeeding chapters you will find additional discussions of ethical questions as they relate to relevant topics.

## STRENGTHENING YOUR COMMUNICATION SKILLS

You've just taken a brief look at the changing workplace, the process of communication, the flow of communication in organizations, and ethical challenges facing business communicators today. Each topic provided you not only with the latest information about an issue but also with tips and suggestions that will help you function successfully in the changing workplace. After all, it's not enough to know the problems; you also need to know some of the solutions. Our goal is to help you recognize the problems and also to equip you with techniques for overcoming the obstacles that others have faced. This book is crammed with model documents, practice exercises, procedures, tips, strategies, suggestions, summaries, and checklists— all meant to ensure that you develop the superior communication skills that are so vital to your success as a businessperson today.

Remember, communication skills are not inherent; they must be learned. Remember, too, to take advantage of the unique opportunity you now have. You have an expert who is willing to work with you to help improve your writing, speaking, and other communication skills. Many organizations pay thousands of dollars to communication coaches and trainers to teach employees the very skills that you are learning in this course. Your coach is your instructor. Get your money's worth! Pick his or her brains. With this book as your guide and your instructor as your coach, you will find that this course, as we mentioned earlier, could very well be the most important in your entire postsecondary curriculum.

> You can improve your communication skills by making use of the model documents, practice exercises, procedures, tips, strategies, summaries, and checklists in this book.

## SUMMARY OF LEARNING OBJECTIVES

*1* **Identify changes in the workplace and the importance of communication skills.** The workplace has undergone profound changes, such as the emergence of heightened global competition, flattened management hierarchies, expanded team-based management, innovative communication technologies, new work environments, and an increasingly diverse work force. In this dynamic workplace you can expect to be a knowledge worker; that is, you will deal with words, figures, and data. The most important foundation skill for knowledge workers is the ability to communicate. You can improve your skills by studying the principles, processes, and products of communication provided in this book and in this course.

## *Applying Your Skills at Canadian Tire*

A secret to the retail success of Canadian Tire is in the people. Canadian Tire associate dealers are involved in the planning and evaluation process and in the daily life of the community. "We have a unique advantage in Canadian retailing—our Associate Dealers. They are men and women who have a vested interest in succeeding, and they work tirelessly with us to implement initiatives within the Strategic Plan to accelerate growth and performance," according to the company's 2002 annual report.

The company realizes the great importance of communicating with its associate dealers. In the midst of the "Next Generation" changes, there has been positive feedback on the staggered height of aisles and the repositioning of the various departments to make them more shopper-friendly. Revenues and profits have also climbed considerably at the stores involved in Next Generation retail.

Canadian Tire's next retail initiative is the Concept 20/20 strategy, which will incorporate significant design changes both inside and outside the store, anchored with dining, driving, fixing, playing, and living areas, including an expanded assortment of home decor items, sports-related footwear and apparel, and storage and organization and ready-to-assemble furniture, along with the cornerstone businesses of automotive, tools, hardware, and lawn and garden products. After testing the four new Concept 20/20 stores in the fall of 2003, the company will determine how to proceed with this vision. The strategic goal is to apply the Concept 20/20 plan to new-format stores and to retrofit chosen existing stores in the 2004–2005 plan.

### Your Task

Your boss asks you to determine what will be the best way to communicate with associate dealers the principles of the Concept 20/20 strategy. Associate dealers meet every year, but the next meeting is not for nine months. In light of this, the suggestion has been made that a formal teleconference would work best. You are exploring the idea of using the Internet to conduct an informal question-and-answer session followed by a virtual, real-time meeting. What would be the advantages and disadvantages of an online session? Would a teleconferencing session allow for free flow of ideas, or simply complicate matters? How important would it be to include senior corporate managers in any communication exercise?

In a memo addressed to your boss, outline the advantages of an online meeting, and present a strong argument for holding a teleconference based on the need to avoid a breakdown in communication while overcoming any obstacles that might create misunderstandings.

**www.canadiantire.ca**

---

2 **Describe the process of communication.** The sender encodes (selects) words or symbols to express an idea. The message is sent verbally over a channel (such as a letter, e-mail message, or telephone call) or is expressed nonverbally, perhaps with gestures or body language. "Noise"—such as loud sounds, misspelled words, or other distractions—may interfere with the transmission. The receiver decodes (interprets) the message and attempts to make sense of it. The receiver responds with feedback, informing the sender of the effectiveness of the message. The objective of communication is the transmission of meaning so that a receiver understands a message as intended by the sender.

3 **Discuss barriers to interpersonal communication and the means of overcoming those barriers.** *Bypassing* causes miscommunication because people have different meanings for the words they use. One's *frame of reference* creates

a filter through which all ideas are screened, sometimes causing distortion and lack of objectivity. *Weak language skills* as well as *poor listening skills* impair communication efforts. *Emotional interference*—joy, fear, anger, and so forth—hampers the sending and receiving of messages. *Physical distractions*—noisy surroundings, faulty acoustics, and so forth—can disrupt oral communication. You can reduce or overcome many interpersonal communication barriers if you (a) realize that the communication process is imperfect, (b) adapt your message to the receiver, (c) improve your language and listening skills, (d) question your preconceptions, and (e) plan for feedback.

**4** **Analyze the functions and procedures of communication in organizations.** Internal functions of communication include issuing and clarifying procedures and policies, informing management of progress, persuading others to make changes or improvements, and interacting with employees. External functions of communication include answering inquiries about products or services, persuading customers to buy products or services, clarifying supplier specifications, and so forth. Oral, face-to-face communication is most effective, but written communication is often more expedient. The volume of messages today is overwhelming many employees, who must institute techniques to control information overload and productivity meltdown.

**5** **Assess the flow of communication in organizations including barriers and methods for overcoming those barriers.** Formal channels of communication follow an organization's hierarchy of command. Information flows downward from management to workers. Long lines of communication tend to distort information. Many organizations are improving the downward flow of communication through newsletters, announcements, meetings, videos, and company intranets. Information flows upward from employees to management, thus providing vital feedback for decision makers. Obstacles include mistrust, fear of reprisal for honest communication, lack of adequate communication skills, and differing frames of reference. To improve upward flow, companies are improving relations with staff, offering incentive programs that encourage employees to share valuable feedback, and investing in communication training programs. Horizontal communication is among workers at the same level. Obstacles include poor communication skills, prejudice, ego involvement, competition, and turf wars. Techniques for overcoming the obstacles include (a) training employees in communication and teamwork techniques, (b) establishing reward systems, and (c) encouraging full participation in team functions. Informal channels of communication, such as the grapevine, deliver unofficial news—both personal and organizational—among friends and coworkers.

**6** **List the goals of ethical business communication and describe important tools for doing the right thing.** Ethical business communicators strive to (a) tell the truth, (b) label opinions so that they are not confused with facts, (c) be objective and avoid distorting a message, (d) write clearly and avoid obscure language, and (e) give credit when using the ideas of others. When you face a difficult decision, the following questions serve as valuable tools in guiding you to do the right thing: (a) Is the action you are considering legal? (b) How would you see the problem if you were on the opposite side? (c) What are alternative solutions? (d) Can you discuss the problem with someone whose advice you trust? (e) How would you feel if your family, friends, employer, or coworkers learned of your action?

# CHAPTER REVIEW

1. How are business communicators affected by the emergence of global competition, flattened management hierarchies, and expanded team-based management? (Obj. 1)

2. How are business communicators affected by the emergence of innovative communication technologies, new work environments, and an increasingly diverse work force? (Obj. 1)

3. What are knowledge workers? Why are they hired? (Obj. 1)

4. Define *communication* and explain its most critical factor. (Obj. 2)

5. Describe the five steps in the process of communication. (Obj. 2)

6. List four barriers to interpersonal communication. Be prepared to discuss each. (Obj. 3)

7. Name five specific ways in which you can personally reduce barriers in your communication. (Obj. 3)

8. What are the three main functions of organizational communication? (Obj. 4)

9. What are the advantages of oral, face-to-face communication? (Obj. 4)

10. What are the advantages of written communication? (Obj. 4)

11. How do formal and informal channels of communication differ within organizations? (Obj. 5)

12. Describe three directions in which communication flows within organizations and what barriers can obstruct each. (Obj. 5)

13. How can barriers to the free flow of information in organizations be reduced? (Obj. 5)

14. Discuss five thinking traps that block ethical behaviour. (Obj. 6)

15. When faced with a difficult ethical decision, what questions should you ask yourself? (Obj. 6)

INFOTRAC® COLLEGE EDITION

## Building Knowledge and Research Skills

Today's digital workplace requires you to find and evaluate information on the Internet. As a student purchasing a new copy of *Business Communication: Process and Product,* Fourth Canadian Edition, you have an extraordinary opportunity to develop these research skills. For four months, you have special access to InfoTrac College Edition, a comprehensive Web-based collection of over 10 million full-text articles from nearly 5 000 scholarly and popular periodicals. You can access this online database 24 hours a day, 7 days a week from any computer with Internet access. Since InfoTrac

College Edition's articles are updated daily, you can access the most current information. At the time of publication, InfoTrac links were up-to-date. You will find research activities and questions in this text that will help you build knowledge and develop research skills using InfoTrac. Watch for the InfoTrac icon.

### How to Use InfoTrac College Edition

1. Visit the InfoTrac site at <http://infotrac.thomsonlearning.com>. Click on *Register New Account.*
2. Enter the passcode on the card packaged with your textbook.
3. Create your own user name.
4. Fill out the registration form completely to activate your account. Enter your newly created user name (step 3). Create your own password. Make up a question to which only you know the answer; then provide the answer. Provide your contact information. Your account is now registered. (If you forget your password, InfoTrac uses the security question to verify access and will e-mail your password back to you.)

### Search Methods

**Subject Search:** Select *Subject Guide* on the menu bar. Enter the subject, and click *Search.*

a. After a list of articles appears, select an article by clicking on its title. If your search words do not match the Subject Guide database, a list of similar and related subjects will appear.

b. Select the subject that most closely matches your topic. A list containing bibliographic information for each article appears.

c. To view an article, click on the citation.

d. To print the article, click *Print* on the menu bar.

e. To return to the citation list, click *Citations* on the menu bar.

f. To start a new search, click *Search* on the menu bar.

**Keyword Search:** Click *Keyword Search* on the menu bar. This search matches key words in the articles.

a. Click on the entry box, and type your search term. Click *Search.*

The search will return with a list of articles containing the keyword(s). Results are listed from most recent to oldest publication date.

b. To print an article, return to the citation list, or start a new search, refer to the above.

**Advanced Search:** Click *Advanced Search* on the menu bar. This allows you to select from the index to narrow your search.

a. Select an index. Each article is indexed by variables such as author, title, publication name, and where and when it was published.

b. Type your search criteria into the entry box. Click *Search.*

# CRITICAL THINKING

1. Why should you, as a business student and communicator, strive to improve your communication skills, and why is it difficult or impossible to do so on your own? (Obj. 1)

2. Recall a time when you experienced a problem as a result of poor communication. What were the causes of and possible remedies for the problem? (Objs. 2 and 3)

3. How would you respond to this complaint? Some companies say that the more information provided to employees, the more employees want. (Objs. 4 and 5)

4. How would you describe the communication climate in an organization to which you belonged or for which you worked? (Objs. 4 and 5)

5. How are the rules of ethical behaviour that govern businesses different from those that govern your personal behaviour? (Obj. 6)

6. **Ethical Issue:** Suppose your superior asked you to alter year-end financial data, and you knew that if you didn't you might lose your job. What would you do if it were a small amount? A large amount?

# ACTIVITIES

## 1.1 Communication Assessment: How Do You Stack Up? (Objs. 2 and 3)

You know more about yourself than anyone else. That makes you the best person to assess your present communication skills. Take an honest look at your current skills and rank them using the chart below. How well you communicate will be an important factor in your future career—particularly if you are promoted into management, as many postsecondary graduates are. For each skill, circle the number from 1 (indicating low ability) to 5 (indicating high ability) that best reflects your perception of yourself.

Now analyze your scores. Where are you strongest? Weakest? How do you think outsiders would rate you on these skills and traits? Are you satisfied with your present skills? The first step to improvement is recognition of a need. Put check marks next to the five traits you feel you should begin working on immediately.

| Writing Skills | Low | | | | High |
|---|---|---|---|---|---|
| 1. Possess basic spelling, grammar, and punctuation skills | 1 | 2 | 3 | 4 | 5 |
| 2. Am familiar with proper memo, letter, and report formats for business documents | 1 | 2 | 3 | 4 | 5 |
| 3. Can analyze a writing problem and quickly outline a plan for solving the problem | 1 | 2 | 3 | 4 | 5 |
| 4. Am able to organize data coherently and logically | 1 | 2 | 3 | 4 | 5 |
| 5. Can evaluate a document to determine its probable success | 1 | 2 | 3 | 4 | 5 |

| Reading Skills | | | | | |
|---|---|---|---|---|---|
| 1. Am familiar with specialized vocabulary in my field as well as general vocabulary | 1 | 2 | 3 | 4 | 5 |
| 2. Can concentrate despite distractions | 1 | 2 | 3 | 4 | 5 |
| 3. Am willing to look up definitions whenever necessary | 1 | 2 | 3 | 4 | 5 |
| 4. Am able to move from recreational to serious reading | 1 | 2 | 3 | 4 | 5 |
| 5. Can read and comprehend postsecondary material | 1 | 2 | 3 | 4 | 5 |

| Speaking Skills | | | | | |
|---|---|---|---|---|---|
| 1. Feel at ease in speaking with friends | 1 | 2 | 3 | 4 | 5 |
| 2. Feel at ease in speaking before a group of people | 1 | 2 | 3 | 4 | 5 |
| 3. Can adapt my presentation to the audience | 1 | 2 | 3 | 4 | 5 |
| 4. Am confident in pronouncing and using words correctly | 1 | 2 | 3 | 4 | 5 |
| 5. Sense that I have credibility when I make a presentation | 1 | 2 | 3 | 4 | 5 |

| Listening Skills | | | | | |
|---|---|---|---|---|---|
| 1. Spend at least half the time listening during conversations | 1 | 2 | 3 | 4 | 5 |
| 2. Am able to concentrate on a speaker's words despite distractions | 1 | 2 | 3 | 4 | 5 |
| 3. Can summarize a speaker's ideas and anticipate what's coming during pauses | 1 | 2 | 3 | 4 | 5 |
| 4. Provide feedback, such as nodding, paraphrasing, and asking questions | 1 | 2 | 3 | 4 | 5 |
| 5. Listen with the expectation of gaining new ideas and information | 1 | 2 | 3 | 4 | 5 |

**RICH CHAPTER RESOURCES ARE AVAILABLE AT THE WEB SITE**

## 1.2 Getting to Know You (Objs. 1 and 2)

Your instructor wants to know more about you, your motivation for taking this course, your career goals, and your writing skills.

**Your Task.** Send an e-mail or write a memo of introduction to your instructor. See Appendix B for memo formats and Chapter 8 for tips on preparing an e-mail message. In your message include the following:

a. Your reasons for taking this class
b. Your career goals (both temporary and long term)
c. A brief description of your employment, if any, and your favourite activities
d. An assessment and discussion of your current communication skills, including your strengths and weaknesses
e. A brief discussion of your familiarity with e-mail and other communication technologies

## 1.3 Collaborating on the Opening Case Study (Objs. 1–5)

Each chapter contains a three-part case study of a well-known company. To help you develop collaboration skills as well as to learn about the target company and apply the chapter concepts, your instructor may ask you to do the following.

**Your Task.** As part of a three-student team during your course, work on one of the 16 case studies in the textbook. Answer the questions posed in all parts of the case study, look for additional information in articles or Web sites, complete the application assignment, and then make a five- to ten-minute presentation to the class with your findings.

## 1.4 Information Overload: Dangerous to Employees? (Obj. 4)

Psychologist David Lewis coined the phrase "Information Fatigue Syndrome." He warns that businesses may face litigation and financial liability for failing to protect employees from the health consequences of exposure to excessive amounts of information. (Proceed to "Your Task.")

**Your Task.** To learn more about information overload, use InfoTrac to find Marsha White and Steve M. Dorman's article, "Confronting Information Overload," *Journal of School Health*, April 2000, Article No. A61995006. After reading the article, organize into teams to discuss these questions:

a. What evidence did you find in the article to support the contention that North Americans are overwhelmed with information?

b. How could employers avoid the possibility of being sued for allowing employees to suffer from information overload?

c. What strategies are suggested for living with information overload? Can you add other strategies?

## 1.5 Small-Group Presentation: Getting to Know Each Other (Objs. 1 and 2)

Many business organizations today use teams to accomplish their goals. To help you develop teamwork skills, your instructor may assign team projects. One of the first jobs in any team is selecting members.

**Your Task.** Your instructor will divide your class into small groups or teams. At your instructor's direction, either (a) interview another group member and introduce that person to the group or (b) introduce yourself to the group. Think of this as an informal interview for a team assignment or for a job. You'll want to make notes from which to speak. Your introduction should include information such as the following:

a. Where did you grow up?
b. In what work and extracurricular activities have you engaged?
c. What are your interests and talents? What are you good at doing?
d. What have you achieved?
e. How familiar are you with various computer technologies?
f. What are your professional and personal goals?
g. Where do you expect to be five years from now?

## 1.6 Want Ads: Analyzing Job Requirements (Obj. 1)

What do the electronic job advertisements in your field say about communication skills?

**Your Task.** To give you practice in using a job board, visit <www.monster.ca>. Locate job categories and locations. Study the jobs listed. Find five or more job listings in which you might be interested. If possible, print the results of your search. If you cannot print, make notes on what you find. Study the skills requested. How often do the ads mention communication, teamwork, and computer skills? What tasks do the ads mention? Your instructor may ask you to submit your findings and/or report to the class. If you are not satisfied with the job selection at this site, choose another job board.

## 1.7 Information Flow: What's the Latest Buzz? (Obj. 5)

Consider an organization to which you belong or a business where you've worked. How did members learn what was going on in the organization? What kind of information flowed through formal channels? What were those channels? What kind of information was delivered through informal channels? Was the grapevine as accurate as official channels? What barriers obstructed the flow of information? How could the flow be improved?

## 1.8 Communication Process: Analyzing the Process (Obj. 2)

Review the communication process and its barriers as described in the text. Now imagine that you are the boss in an organization where you've worked and you wish to announce a new policy aimed at improving customer service. Examine the entire communication process from sender to feedback. How will the message be encoded? What assumptions must you make about your audience? How should you announce the new policy? How can you encourage feedback? What noise may interfere with transmission? What barriers should you expect? How can you overcome them? Your instructor may ask you to write a memo describing your responses to these questions.

## 1.9 Workplace Writing: Separating Myths From Facts (Obj. 1)

Today's knowledge workers are doing more writing on the job than ever before. Flattened management hierarchies, heightened global competition, expanded team-based management, and heavy reliance on e-mail have all contributed to more written messages.
**Your Task.** In teams discuss the following statements. Are they myths or facts?

a. Because I'm in a technical field, I'll work with numbers, not words.
b. Administrative assistants will clean up my writing problems.
c. Technical writers do most of the real writing on the job.
d. Computers can fix any of my writing mistakes.
e. I can use form letters for most messages.

## 1.10 Document Analysis: Barriers to Communication (Objs. 3, 4, and 5)

The following memo was actually written in a large business organization.
**Your Task.** Comment on the memo's effectiveness, tone, and potential barriers to communication.

**TO:**   All Department Personnel

**SUBJECT:** FRIDAY P.M. CLEAN-UP

Every Friday afternoon starting at 3 p.m. there is suppose to be a departmental clean-up. This practice will commence this Friday and continue until otherwise specified.

All CC162 employees will partake in this endeavour. This means not only cleaning his own area, but contributing to the cleaning of the complete department.

Thank you for your cooperation.

## 1.11 Communicating in Organizations: Reducing Information Overload (Obj. 4)

Eric S. has been working at HotStuff Software for six months. He loved e-mail when he first joined HotStuff, but now it's overwhelming him. Every day he receives between 200 and 300 messages, some important and some junk. To keep caught up, Eric checks his e-mail every hour—sometimes more often if he's expecting a response. He joined five mailing lists because they sounded interesting and helpful. But when a topic really excites the subscribers, Eric's e-mail box is jammed with 50 or 60 postings at once. Reading all his messages prevents him from getting his real work done. If he ignores his e-mail, though, he may miss something important. What really frustrates him is what to do with messages that he must retain until he gathers the necessary information to respond.
**Your Task.** What suggestions can you make to lessen Eric's e-mail overload?

## 1.12 Communication Process: Avoiding Misunderstanding (Obj. 2)

Communication is not successful unless the receiver understands the message as the sender meant it.
**Your Task.** Analyze the following examples of communication failures. What went wrong?

a. A supervisor issued the following announcement: "Effective immediately the charge for copying services in Repro will be raised 1/2 to 2 cents each." Receivers scratched their heads.
b. The pilot of a military airplane about to land decided that the runway was too short. He shouted to his engineer, "Takeoff power!" The engineer turned off the engines; the plane crashed.
c. The following statements actually appeared in letters of application for an advertised job opening. One applicant wrote, "Enclosed is my résumé in response to Sunday's *Calgary Herald*." Another wrote, "Enclosed is my résumé in response to my search for an editorial/creative position." Still another wrote, "My experience in the production of newsletters,

magazines, directories, and on-line data bases puts me head and shoulders above the crowd of applicants you have no doubtedly been inundated with."

**d.** The following sign in English appeared in an Austrian hotel that catered to skiers: "Not to perambulate the corridors in the hours of repose in the boots of ascension."

**e.** The editor of *The Montreal Gazette* told his staff to "change the picture" of film icon James Dean, who had a cigarette dangling from his lips. The staff thought that the editor wanted the cigarette digitally removed from the picture, which was done. When published, the altered picture drew considerable criticism. The editor later explained that he had expected the staff to find a new picture.

## 1.13 Workplace Ethics: Where Do You Stand? (Obj. 6)

How do your ethics compare with those of workers across the continent?

**Your Task.** Answer yes or no to each item in the following *The Wall Street Journal Workplace Ethics Quiz*.[76] Be prepared to discuss your responses in class. At the end of this Activities section you can see how others responded to this quiz.

1. Is it wrong to use company e-mail for personal reasons?
2. Is it wrong to use office equipment to help your children or spouse do schoolwork?
3. Is it wrong to play computer games on office equipment during the workday?
4. Is it wrong to use office equipment to do Internet shopping?
5. Is it unethical to blame an error you made on a technological glitch?
6. Is it unethical to visit pornographic Web sites using office equipment?
7. Is a $50 gift TO a boss unacceptable?
8. Is a $50 gift FROM a boss unacceptable?
9. Is it OK to accept a $200 pair of football tickets from a supplier?
10. Can you accept a $75 prize won at a raffle at a supplier's conference?

## 1.14 Ethical Traps: Milking Microsoft (Obj. 6)

Microsoft recently offered a $400 rebate if customers bought a computer and subscribed to its online service. To comply with California law, Microsoft was forced to allow consumers to cancel the service at any time. Many people bought a computer, immediately cancelled the service, and pocketed $400.

**Your Task.** Since Microsoft must have anticipated that some customers would do this, was the customer behaviour unethical? Is it all right to milk Microsoft for the rebate because it's a huge company making obscene profits and it would never miss these small sums? Compared with other bigger white-collar crimes, isn't this "small potatoes"? Is the immediate cancellation acceptable if the consumer really needs the $400 to pay for schooling or some other necessity? What ethical traps might be at work here?

## 1.15 Developing Critical Thinking Skills: Serpentine Lines at McDonald's (Obj. 1)

**CRITICAL THINKING**

As a McDonald's franchise owner, you have a big problem. During rush times, customers complain about the chaotic multiple waiting lines to approach the service counter. You once saw two customers nearly get into a fistfight over cutting into a line. And customers often are so intent on looking for ways to improve their positions in line that they fail to focus on the menu. When they arrive at the counter, they are clueless about what to order. You wonder whether a single-line (serpentine) system would work better. You know that McDonald's management feels that the multiline system accommodates higher volumes of customers more quickly than a single-line system. Moreover the problem of perception is important. What happens when customers open the door to a restaurant and see a long, single line? Do they stick around to learn how fast the line is moving?

**Your Task.** Use the steps outlined in the Career Coach box on page 11 to clarify this problem.

**a.** Where could you gather information to solve this problem?

**b.** Would it be wise to see what your competitors are doing? How do banks handle customer lines? Airlines? Sports events?

**c.** Evaluate your findings and consider alternatives. What are the pros and cons of each alternative?

**d.** Choose the best alternative. Present your recommendation to your class and give your reasons for choosing it.

**Responses to *The Wall Street Journal Workplace Ethics Quiz* in Activity 1.13.**

1. 34 percent said using company e-mail for personal reasons is wrong.
2. 37 percent said using office equipment to help your children or spouse do schoolwork is wrong.
3. 49 percent said playing computer games at work is wrong.
4. 54 percent said using office equipment to do Internet shopping is wrong.

5.  61 percent said blaming your own error on faulty technology is unethical.

6.  87 percent said visiting pornographic Web sites using office equipment is unethical.

7.  35 percent said making a $50 gift to a boss is unacceptable.

8.  35 percent said accepting a $50 gift from a boss is unacceptable.

9.  70 percent said accepting a $200 pair of football tickets from a supplier is unacceptable.

10. 40 percent said accepting a $75 prize won at a raffle at a supplier's conference is unacceptable.

# C.L.U.E. REVIEW 1

Each chapter includes an exercise based on Appendix A, "Competent Language Usage Essentials (C.L.U.E.)." This appendix is a business communicator's condensed guide to language usage, covering 54 of the most used, and abused, language elements. It also includes a list of 165 frequently misspelled words and a quick review of selected confusing words. The following ten sentences are packed with errors based on concepts and spelling words from the appendix. If you are rusty on these language essentials, spend some time studying the guidelines and examples in Appendix A. Then, test your skills with the chapter C.L.U.E. exercises. You will find the corrections for these exercises at the end of the appendix. Remember, these exercises contain only usage and spelling words from Appendix A. On a separate sheet, edit the following sentences to correct faults in grammar, punctuation, numbers, spelling, and word use.

1.  In todays average buziness office employes spend approximately 60% of there time processing documents.

2.  My friend and me was serprised to learn that more information has been produced in the last thirty years then in the previous five thousand years.

3.  A typical Manager by the way reads 1 000 000 words every week. Which is equal to reading one and a half full length novels everyday.

4.  If you are defining *communication* a principle element are the transmission of information and meaning.

5.  When Ms Diaz had 3 messages to send she chose e-mail because it was definitly the most fastest comunication channel.

6.  5 factors that make up your unique frame of reference are the following, Experience, Education, Culture, Expectations and Personality.

7.  Just between you and I whom do you think will be reccomended for the award.

8.  To many workers balancing family and work demands are more important then earning big salarys.

9.  Matt felt that he done good on the exam but he wants to do even better when its given again next Fall.

10. The grapevine may be a excelent source of employe information however it should not replace formal lines of communication.

# Chapter 2
## Communicating in Small Groups and Teams

## LEARNING OBJECTIVES

1 Discuss why groups and teams are formed and how they are different.

2 Describe team development, team and group roles, dealing with conflict, and methods for reaching group decisions.

3 Identify the characteristics of successful teams.

4 List techniques for organizing team-based written and oral presentations.

5 Discuss how to plan and participate in productive meetings.

# National Public Relations

When Bell Canada was having problems with its 416 area code on a Sunday evening, a team of National Public Relations' employees and senior Bell executives worked through the night to ensure both that the problem was solved and that all of Bell's employees, customers, and partners were not only informed of the situation but also confident that it had been fixed.[1]

Canada's largest public relations firm, National Public Relations, founded in 1976, is a sprawling communications firm with a talent pool spread across six offices in Canada and another in New York City. In today's world, people are inundated with corporate messages. The job of technology specialists such as Ronald Alepian is to create a communications strategy that enables clients to cut through the noise and reach customers. Alepian states, "Our ability as communicators is to take this very complex, often nebulous, concept and articulate it into a very clear value proposition to the public and make it relevant to them."[2]

There is a natural and necessary diversification process that develops when dealing with clients that require assistance with mergers, restructuring, expansion, initial public offerings, and almost every other issue under the sun. In tackling everything from media relations to research analysis to crisis management to environmental communications, National draws on a staff of approximately 300, who trouble-shoot, promote, and problem-solve on behalf of clients ranging from high-tech companies to high-profile individuals.

"National's strength lies in the experience and resourcefulness of our people," says Francine La Haye, managing partner, based in the company's Montreal headquarters. "We have always attracted strong individuals who combine superior industry knowledge and communications expertise with an ability to work as a team and deliver results."

National's prowess stems from an ability to elicit cooperation from staff and clients alike. "It's all about building the best team," says Ronald Alepian, senior consultant with National. "Clients come to us because we can work across disciplines and with various levels of management, using a team composed of different players." In fact, a team of consultants working on a given project may total 20 members, and address such issues as a Web strategy, corporate communications, and investor relations.

"There is no way that I can counsel on all of those subjects," says Alepian. "What I can do is put the specialists around the table that will address a problem or situation from all 360 degrees."

## CRITICAL THINKING

- Why do firms such as National Public Relations benefit from working in teams?
- How can smaller operating units be helpful in responding to client concerns?
- What kinds of problems would you expect work groups or teams to experience when they form to make decisions?

www.national.ca

## PREPARING TO WORK WITH GROUPS AND TEAMS

*1*

Like employees at National Public Relations, you will probably find yourself working with small groups or in a team-oriented environment. You may already be part of one or more groups or teams. That's good, because experience on a team has become one of the top requests among recruiters looking over job candidates. To participate most effectively on a team, however, you need to learn about groups and teams. In this chapter you'll study why groups and teams are formed, how they differ, how they develop, typical roles members play, and how to deal with dysfunctional behaviour. In addition, you'll study how to collaborate in team-based written and oral presentations and how to plan and participate in productive meetings.

# Why Form Groups and Teams?

As organizations in the past decade were downsized, restructured, and reengineered, one reality became increasingly clear: Companies were expected to compete globally, meet higher standards, and increase profits—but often with fewer people and fewer resources.[3] Striving to meet these seemingly impossible goals, organizations began developing groups and teams for the following specific reasons:[4]

- **Better decisions.** Decisions are generally more accurate and effective because group and team members contribute different expertise and perspectives.

- **Faster response.** When action is necessary to respond to competition or to solve a problem, small groups and teams can act rapidly.

- **Increased productivity.** Because they are often closer to the action and to the customer, team members can see opportunities for improving efficiencies.

- **Greater "buy-in."** Decisions derived jointly are usually better received because members are committed to the solution and are more willing to support it.

- **Less resistance to change.** People who have input into making decisions are less hostile, aggressive, and resistant to change.

- **Improved employee morale.** Personal satisfaction and job morale increase when teams are successful.

- **Reduced risks.** Responsibility for a decision is diffused, thus carrying less risk for any individual.

Teams can be very effective in solving problems. Take, for example, the production of one of the world's first light, small, and high-quality cellular phones. Motorola teams blew away the Japanese competition by designing a superior phone. And the new phone had only a few hundred parts, compared with thousands of parts in rival phones.[5]

Despite the current popularity of teams, however, they are not a panacea for all workplace problems. Some critics complain that they are the latest in a succession of management fads. Others charge that they are a screen behind which management intensifies its control over labour.[6] Companies such as Ford, Levi Strauss, Honda, and GM's Saturn plant retreated from teams, finding that they slowed decision

**Organizations are forming teams for better decisions, faster response, increased productivity, greater "buy-in," less resistance to change, improved morale, and reduced risks.**

**Some companies rejected teams because they slowed decisions, shielded workers from responsibility, and reduced productivity.**

Organizations are forming teams for better decisions, faster response, increased productivity, greater "buy-in," less resistance to change, improved morale, and reduced risk.

## Techniques for Staying Connected in Virtual Teams

When Roger Richards goes to work at WishBone Software in Waterloo, Ontario, he connects with a team of customer support people in Maryland, the United Kingdom, and Japan. He has never met these people and probably never will. Richards is one of many workers and managers who belong to *virtual teams*. These are teams with members in remote locations who communicate electronically. With videoconferences, e-mail, the Internet, and sophisticated groupware, it's possible for teams to complete projects no matter where they are geographically based. You'll learn more about groupware and videoconferencing shortly.

Richards and others working on virtual teams must overcome many obstacles not faced by intact groups. Because team members may be separated by geography, time zones, and cultures, they must work especially hard to develop understanding, commitment, and trust. Virtual team managers offer the following recommendations to help members work together.

- **Select team members carefully.** Choose team members who are self-starters, good communicators, flexible, trusting, and experts in areas needed by the team.

- **Invest in beginnings.** Team processes are expedited by spending time initially in reaching consensus about goals, tasks, and procedures. If possible, meet face to face to work out procedures and to bond.

- **Redefine "we."** Team members should be present in one another's thoughts even when not in their physical presence. Encourage behaviour that

reflects unity, such as including one another in decisions and sharing information. Consider having a team photograph taken and made into something used frequently, such as a mouse pad or computer wallpaper.

- **Get the maximum benefit from technology.** Make use of speaker phones, groupware, the Internet, and videoconferencing. But be sure that members are well trained in their use.

- **Concentrate on building credibility and trust.** Team members should pay close attention to the way that others perceive them. Consistency of actions, fulfilling promises, considering other members' schedules, and responding promptly to e-mail and voice messages help to build credibility and trust.

- **Put communication on the agenda.** Members should discuss how and when it is appropriate to communicate with one another. They should establish clear expectations about response times.

- **Avoid misinterpreting messages.** Because it's so easy to misunderstand e-mail messages, one virtual manager advises team members to always doubt their first instinct about another team member if the response is negative. Always take time to question your reactions.

### Career Application

Why do you think increasing numbers of employees are joining virtual teams? What are the advantages and disadvantages for employees and for employers?

making, shielded workers from responsibility, and created morale and productivity problems.[7] Yet, in most models of future organizations, teams, not individuals, function as the primary performance unit.[8]

Some organizations are even creating *virtual teams*, which are connected by the Internet, intranets, and electronic media. To learn more about communicating in these digital groups, see the Tech Talk box above.

## Comparing Groups and Teams

Although teams and groups are similar, they are not identical. A *group* is a collection of three or more individuals who perceive themselves as a group but who may work independently to achieve organization goals. For example, members of an advertising department within a company are a group. Members of the department often complete their tasks independently, and their leader is a manager. A *team* is a group of individuals who interact over time to achieve a purpose. Members recognize a need for each other's expertise, talents, and commitment to achieve their goals. For example, a task force established to increase sales in a given territory is a team. Although the word *team* is used loosely to describe many combinations of workers, no one would dispute that the workplace trend today is definitely toward teams. Although some statistics cite the number of employees who participate in teams in the workplace as ranging from 54 to 80 percent,[9] other researchers argue that unless employees work in an "isolated, non-interactive vacuum, they are on some kind of team." Although there may not be regular meetings or a team title, as long as the members share a common goal and rely on one another to attain goals, they are a team.[10]

A group may work independently, but a team must interact.

Much of the emphasis today is on *self-directed teams*. They are different from single-leader work groups in a number of dimensions, as shown in Figure 2.1. Self-directed teams are most useful to solve problems that require people with different skills to work together. Single-leader work groups are most useful in solving problems quickly when the leader already knows how to proceed. Ideally, the most successful self-directed teams will have many of the following characteristics.

Self-directed teams are best to solve problems requiring people with different skills.

- **Clearly stated goals.** They are able to state their purpose and assess progress toward it.
- **Autonomy.** They can hire, fire, and discipline their own members. They complete jobs on their own with little or no supervision.
- **Decision-making authority.** They do not require a manager's approval for decisions.
- **Frequent communication.** They meet often or exchange messages to coordinate activities, avoid duplication, and make decisions.
- **Ongoing training.** They emphasize improving their skills to meet their goals.

## UNDERSTANDING TEAM DEVELOPMENT AND ROLES

Small groups and teams may be formed to complete single tasks or to function as permanent ongoing bodies. Regardless of their purpose, successful teams normally go through predictable phases as they develop. Team members also perform in a number of functional and dysfunctional roles.

*2*

## Four Phases of Team Development

When groups are formed, they generally evolve through four phases, as identified by psychologist B. A. Tuckman. These phases include *forming*, *storming*, *norming*, and *performing*.[11] Some groups get lucky and move quickly from forming to performing. But most struggle through disruptive, although ultimately constructive, team-building stages.

Successful teams generally go through four phases: forming, storming, norming, and performing.

*Forming.* During the first stage individuals get to know one another. They often are overly polite and feel a bit awkward. As they search for similarities and attempt to bond, they begin to develop trust in each other. Members will discuss fundamental topics such as why the team is necessary, who "owns" the team, whether membership is mandatory, how large it should be, and what talents members can contribute. A leader functions primarily as a traffic director. Groups and teams should resist the

**FIGURE 2.1** Comparing Self-Directed Teams and Single-Leader Work Groups

| DIMENSION | SELF-DIRECTED TEAM | SINGLE-LEADER WORK GROUP |
|---|---|---|
| Best business use | Most useful to solve problems that require people with various skill sets working together | Most useful to solve problems in which time is of the essence and the leader already knows how to proceed |
| Leadership | Shifts to member best suited to lead tasks at hand | Formally assigned to one person, usually the senior member |
| Goals and agenda | Set by group, based on dialogue about purpose | Set by leader, often in consultation with sponsoring executive |
| Conflict | Recognized as constructive | Avoided by members |
| Work style | Determined by members | Determined by leader |
| Success | Defined by members' aspirations | Defined by leader's aspirations |
| Speed and efficiency | Low until group learns to function as a team; afterward, as fast as a single-leader group | Higher at first because members need no time to develop commitment or to learn to work as a team |
| End products | Best produced by collective group working together | Best produced by individuals working on their own |
| Accountability | Set by team who hold one another mutually accountable | Set by leader who holds individuals accountable for their output |

efforts of some members to sprint through the first stages and vault to the performing stage. Moving slowly through the stages is necessary in building a cohesive, productive unit.

*Storming.* During the second phase, members define their roles and responsibilities, decide how to reach their goals, and iron out the rules governing how they interact. Unfortunately, this stage often produces conflict, resulting in *storming*. A good leader, however, should step in to set limits, control the chaos, and offer suggestions. The leader will be most successful if she or he acts like a coach rather than

Heightened global competition has pushed many organizations into team-based projects where collective brain power makes products faster, cheaper, and better. But before teams can function harmoniously, they often go through four developmental stages.

a cop. Teams composed of dissimilar personality types may take longer to progress through the storming phase. Tempers may flare, sleep may be lost, leaders may be deposed. But most often the storm passes, and a cohesive group emerges.

*Norming.* Once the sun returns to the sky, teams and groups enter the *norming* stage. Tension subsides, roles clarify, and information begins to flow among members. The group periodically checks its agenda to remind itself of its progress toward its goals. People are careful not to shake the hard-won camaraderie and formation of a single-minded purpose. Formal leadership is unnecessary since everyone takes on leadership functions. Important data is shared with the entire group, and mutual interdependence becomes typical. The group or team begins to move smoothly in one direction. Members make sure that procedures are in place to resolve future conflicts.

**In the norming stage, tensions subside, roles clarify, and information flows among team members.**

*Performing.* In Tuckman's team growth model, some groups never reach the final stage of *performing*. Problems that may cause them to fail are shown in Figure 2.2. For those that survive the first three phases, however, the final stage is gratifying. Group members have established a pace and a shared language. They develop loyalty and a willingness to resolve all problems. A "can-do" mentality pervades as they progress toward their goal. Fights are clean, and members continue working together without grudges. Best of all, information flows freely, deadlines are met, and production exceeds expectations.

## Typical Team and Group Roles

Team members play different roles when they work together in groups. These roles can be grouped into three categories. *Task roles* are those that help the group meet its goals. *Relationship roles* facilitate the smooth functioning of the group. *Dysfunctional roles* are those that hinder a group from moving forward to achieve its purpose.[12]

Members of effective teams play different task and relationship roles to help the group run efficiently in accomplishing its task.

*Group Task Roles.* Group members who are committed to achieving the group's purpose contribute to the group in a number of positive roles. You can be a better group member if you assume one or more of the following task roles.

**Members who assume positive task roles help a team achieve its purpose.**

- **Initiator.** Defines problems, sets rules, contributes ideas (e.g., "I think the problem is not lack of funds but rather lack of support from upper management").

- **Information seeker/information giver.** Asks for or supplies relevant information (e.g., "Didn't we have a similar situation two years ago?").

- **Opinion giver/opinion seeker.** Asks for and offers personal opinions, attitudes, and beliefs (e.g., "Matt, I think your position needs more facts to support it").

- **Direction giver.** Tells how to perform task at hand.

- **Summarizer.** Reviews significant points, synthesizing points of agreement and group's progress toward goal.

- **Diagnoser.** Analyzes task and discussion. Tells what is needed to reach goal.

**FIGURE 2.2  Why Teams Fail: Typical Problems, Symptoms, and Solutions**

| PROBLEM | SYMPTOM | SOLUTION |
|---|---|---|
| Confused goals | People don't know what they're supposed to do | Clarify team purpose and expected outcomes |
| Mismatched needs | People with private agendas working at cross-purposes | Get hidden agendas on table by asking what people personally want from team |
| Unresolved roles | Team members are uncertain what their jobs are | Inform team members what is expected of them |
| Senseless procedures | Team is at the mercy of an ineffective employee handbook | Throw away the book and develop procedures that make sense |
| Bad leadership | Leader is tentative, inconsistent, or foolish | Leader must learn to serve the team and keep its vision alive or give up role |
| Antiteam culture | Organization is not committed to the idea of teams | Team for the right reasons or don't team at all; never force people onto a team |
| Poor feedback | Performance is not being measured; team members are groping in the dark | Create system of free flow of useful information to and from all team members |

- **Energizer.** Exhorts members to stay on task, offers encouraging remarks.
- **Gatekeeper.** Controls participants, drawing in nontalkers and cutting off monopolizers (e.g., "You've described your plan, Eric, but now I'd like to hear what Karen thinks").
- **Reality tester.** Compares group's ideas with feasibility of real-world implementation.

**Members who carry out relationship roles help teams achieve harmony and strong bonds.**

*Group Relationship Roles.* In addition to contributing to task functions, effective members of groups perform relationship functions. When you assume these roles, you are helping to build harmony and strong relationships among group members.

- **Participation encourager.** Seeks to involve silent members (e.g., "Matt, what do you think about Lisa's ideas?").
- **Harmonizer/tension reliever.** Resolves differences, relaxes atmosphere, reduces tension—sometimes with the use of humour or informality.
- **Evaluator of emotional climate.** Reflects the feelings of the group (e.g., "I sense that we're becoming destructive instead of constructive. Does anyone else feel that way?").
- **Praise giver.** Encourages warm, supportive climate by praising and agreeing with others (e.g., "I really like Lisa's idea; let's build on it").
- **Empathic listener.** Shows interest by listening actively without interrupting or evaluating.

*Dysfunctional Group Roles.* When group members perform the following roles, they disrupt the group and slow progress toward its goal. As you study the following list, think about groups you know and individuals who may have played these self-serving roles.

- **Blocker.** Constantly puts down the ideas and suggestions of others.

- **Attacker.** Insults, criticizes, and aggresses against others (e.g., "Why should we listen to your ideas when you've been wrong so many times in the past?").
- **Recognition-seeker.** Wastes group's time with unnecessary and irrelevant recounting of personal achievements and successes.
- **Joker.** Distracts group with excessive joke-telling, inappropriate comments, and disruptive antics.
- **Withdrawer.** Participates very little or not at all. Refuses to be drawn out or to offer opinions.

## Dealing With Conflict and Groupthink

As teams develop, they should expect conflict to arise—not only in the storming phase but also at other times. How a team manages that conflict often determines whether a team survives; it also affects the quality of its performance and its decisions. Teams may experience two kinds of conflict. *Cognitive conflict* centres on issues[13] and is considered healthy and functional. Cognitive conflict arouses discussion and stimulates creative thinking. It makes team members get involved as they examine, compare, and reconcile their differences. Cognitive conflict also promotes acceptance of a team decision. Team members "buy into" the decision and are more willing to implement it when they have been able to speak their minds.

*Affective conflict* aims not at issues but at feelings and personalities. It is disruptive and dysfunctional. Affective conflict tends to be emotional and focuses on people, not on substantive matters. Such conflict may erupt into name-calling and criticism, which destroys team unity. Research shows that the best decisions are made by teams that experience healthy differences of opinion but are able to keep their conflict aimed at issues. As one member of a successful team remarked, "We scream a lot, then laugh, and then resolve the issues."[14]

Without conflict and free discussions, teams may fall victim to *groupthink*. This is a term coined by theorist Irving Janis to describe faulty decision-making processes by team members who are overly eager to agree with one another. Several conditions can lead to groupthink: team members with similar backgrounds, a lack of methodical procedures, a demand for a quick decision, and a strong leader who favours a specific decision. Symptoms of groupthink include pressures placed on a member who argues against the group's shared beliefs, self-censorship of thoughts that deviate from the group consensus, collective efforts to rationalize, and an unquestioned belief in the group's inherent morality. Teams suffering from groupthink fail to examine alternatives, are biased in collecting and evaluating information, and ignore the risks of the preferred choice. They may also forget to work out a contingency plan in case the preferred choice fails.[15]

Effective teams avoid groupthink by striving for team diversity—in age, gender, backgrounds, experience, and training. They encourage open discussion, search for relevant information, evaluate many alternatives, consider how a decision will be implemented, and plan for contingencies in case the decision doesn't work out.

## Reaching Group Decisions

The manner in which teams reach decisions greatly affects the morale and commitment of a team, as well as the implementation of any team decision. In North American culture the majority usually rules, but other methods, five of which are discussed here, may be more effective. As you study these methods, think about which methods would be best for routine decisions and which methods would be best for dealing with emergencies.

**Members who play dysfunctional roles disrupt the group's progress toward its goal.**

**Cognitive conflict centres on issues and is considered healthy and functional.**

**Affective conflict centres on feelings and personalities and is considered disruptive.**

**Groupthink means that team members agree without examining alternatives or considering contingency plans.**

- **Majority.** Group members vote and a majority wins. This method results in a quick decision but may leave an alienated minority uncommitted to implementation.

- **Consensus.** Discussion continues until all team members air their opinions and, ultimately, agree. This method is time-consuming, but it produces creative, high-quality discussion and generally elicits commitment by all members to implement the decision.

- **Minority.** Typically, a subcommittee investigates and makes a recommendation for action. This method is useful when the full group cannot get together to make a decision or when time is short.

- **Averaging.** Members haggle, bargain, cajole, and negotiate to reach a middle position, which often requires compromise. With this method, the opinions of the least knowledgeable members may cancel the opinions of the most knowledgeable.

- **Authority rule with discussion.** The leader, boss, or manager listens to team members' ideas, but the final decision is his or hers. This method encourages lively discussion and results in participatory decision making. However, team members must have good communication skills. This method also requires a leader who is willing to make decisions.

**Although time-consuming, consensus decisions generally produce the most team commitment.**

## CHARACTERISTICS OF SUCCESSFUL TEAMS

*3*

The use of teams has been called the "solution" to many ills in the current workplace.[16] Someone even observed that as an acronym, TEAM means "Together, Everyone Achieves More."[17] Yet, many teams do not work well together. In fact, some teams can actually increase frustration, lower productivity, and create employee dissatisfaction. Experts who have studied team workings and decisions have discovered that effective teams share some or all of the following characteristics.

**Small, diverse teams often produce more creative solutions with broader applications than homogeneous teams.**

*Small Size, Diverse Makeup.* For most functions the best teams range from 2 to 25 members, although 4 or 5 is optimum for many projects. The Conference Board of Canada describes a "team" as consisting of 3 to 20 persons, whose functions on the team are interdependent.[18] Larger groups have trouble interacting constructively, much less agreeing on actions.[19] For the most creative decisions, teams generally have male and female members who differ in age, social background, training, and experience. Members should bring complementary skills to a team. Paul Fireman, founder of sports shoe manufacturer Reebok, wisely remarked, "If you put five centres on the basketball court, you're going to lose the game. You need, we all need, people of different strengths and talents—and that means, among other things, people of different backgrounds."[20] Diverse teams can produce innovative solutions with broader applications than homogeneous teams can.

*Agreement on Purpose.* An effective team begins with a purpose. Xerox scientists who invented personal computing developed their team purpose after the chairman of Xerox called for an "architecture of information." A team at Sealed Air Corporation developed its purpose when management instructed it to cut waste and reduce downtime.[21] Working from a general purpose to specific goals typically requires a huge investment of time and effort. Meaningful discussions, however, motivate team members to "buy into" the project.

*Agreement on Procedures.* The best teams develop procedures to guide them. They set up intermediate goals with deadlines. They assign roles and tasks, requiring all members to contribute equivalent amounts of real work. They decide how they will reach decisions using one of the strategies discussed earlier. Procedures are continually evaluated to ensure movement toward attainment of the team's goals.

*Ability to Confront Conflict.* Poorly functioning teams avoid conflict, preferring sulking, gossip, or backstabbing. A better plan is to acknowledge conflict and address the root of the problem openly. Although it may feel emotionally risky, direct confrontation saves time and enhances team commitment in the long run. To be constructive, however, confrontation must be task-oriented, not person-oriented. An open airing of differences, in which all team members have a chance to speak their minds, should focus on strengths and weaknesses of the different positions and ideas—not on personalities. After hearing all sides, team members must negotiate a fair settlement, no matter how long it takes. Good decisions are based on consensus: all members agree.

*Use of Good Communication Techniques.* The best teams exchange information and contribute ideas freely in an informal environment. Team members speak clearly and concisely, avoiding generalities. They encourage feedback. Listeners become actively involved, read body language, and ask clarifying questions before responding. Tactful, constructive disagreement is encouraged. Although a team's task is taken seriously, successful teams are able to inject humour into their interactions.

**Good teams exchange information freely and collaborate rather than compete.**

*Ability to Collaborate Rather Than Compete.* Effective team members are genuinely interested in achieving team goals instead of receiving individual recognition. They contribute ideas and feedback unselfishly. They monitor team progress, including what's going right, what's going wrong, and what to do about it. They celebrate individual and team accomplishments.

*Acceptance of Ethical Responsibilities.* Teams as a whole have ethical responsibilities to their members, to their larger organizations, and to society. Members have a number of specific responsibilities to each other, as described in the Ethical Insights box on page 52. As a whole, groups have a responsibility to represent the organization's view and respect its privileged information. They should not discuss with outsiders any sensitive issues without permission. In addition, groups have a broader obligation to avoid advocating actions that would endanger members of society at large.

**Ethical teams should represent the organization's view and respect its privileged information.**

*Shared Leadership.* Effective teams often have no formal leader. Instead, leadership rotates to those with the appropriate expertise as the team evolves and moves from one phase to another. Many teams operate under a democratic approach. This approach can achieve buy-in to team decisions, boost morale, and create fewer hurt feelings and less resentment. But in times of crisis, a strong team member may need to step up as leader.

## CHECKLIST FOR DEVELOPING TEAM EFFECTIVENESS

 **Establish small teams.** Teams with fewer members are thought to function more efficiently and more effectively than larger teams.

## Ethical Responsibilities of Group Members and Leaders

When people form a group or a team to achieve a purpose, they agree to give up some of their individual sovereignty for the good of the group. They become interdependent and assume responsibilities to one another and to the group. Here are important ethical responsibilities for members to follow:

- **Determine to do your best.** When you commit to the group process, you are obligated to offer your skills freely. Don't hold back, perhaps fearing that you will be repeatedly targeted because you have skills to offer. If the group project is worth doing, it's worth the best effort you can offer.

- **Decide to behave with the group's good in mind.** You may find it necessary to set aside your personal goals in favour of the group goals. Decide to keep an open mind and to listen to evidence and arguments objectively. Strive to evaluate information carefully, even though it may contradict your own views or thwart your personal agendas.

- **Make a commitment to fair play.** Group problem solving is a cooperative, not a competitive, event. Decide that you cannot grind your private axe at the expense of the group project.

- **Expect to give and receive a fair hearing.** When you speak, others should give you a fair hearing.

You have a right to expect them to listen carefully, provide you with candid feedback, strive to understand what you say, and treat your ideas seriously. Listeners do not have to agree with you, of course. However, all speakers have a right to a fair hearing.

- **Be willing to take on a participant/analyst role.** As a group member, it is your responsibility to pay attention, evaluate what is happening, analyze what you learn, and help make decisions.

- **As a leader, be ready to model appropriate team behaviour.** It is a leader's responsibility to coach team members in skills and teamwork, to acknowledge achievement and effort, to share knowledge, and to periodically remind members of the team's missions and goals.

### Career Application

Assume you're a member of a campus committee to organize a celebrity auction to raise funds for a local homeless shelter. Your friend Eric is committee chair, but he is carrying a heavy course load and is also working part time. As a result, he has taken no action. You call him, but he is evasive when you try to pin him down about committee plans. What should you do?

✓ **Encourage diversity.** Innovative teams typically include members who differ in age, gender, and background. Team members should possess technical expertise, problem-solving skills, and interpersonal skills.

✓ **Determine purpose, procedures, and roles.** Members must understand the task at hand and what is expected of them. Teams function best when operating procedures are ironed out early on and each member has a specific role.

✓ **Acknowledge and manage conflict.** Conflict is productive when it motivates a team to search for new ideas, increase participation, delay premature decisions, or discuss disagreements. Keep conflict centred on issues rather than on people.

✓ **Cultivate good communication skills.** Effective team members are willing and able to articulate ideas clearly and concisely, recognize nonverbal cues, and listen actively.

✓ **Advance an environment of open communication.** Teams are most productive when members trust each other and feel free to discuss all viewpoints openly in an informal atmosphere.

✓ **Encourage collaboration and discourage competition.** Sharing information in a cooperative effort to achieve the team purpose must be more important than competing with other members for individual achievement.

✓ **Share leadership.** Members with the most expertise should lead at various times during the project's evolution.

✓ **Create a sense of fairness in making decisions.** Effective teams resolve issues without forcing members into a win–lose situation.

✓ **Lighten up.** The most successful teams take their task seriously, but they are also able to laugh at themselves and interject humour to enliven team proceedings.

✓ **Continually assess performance.** Teams should establish checkpoints along the way to determine whether they are meeting their objectives and adjust procedures if progress is unsatisfactory.

## ORGANIZING TEAM-BASED WRITTEN AND ORAL PRESENTATIONS

Companies form teams for many reasons. The goal of some teams is an oral presentation to pitch a new product or to win a high-stakes contract. Before Bill Gates and his Microsoft team roll out their latest software product, you can bet that team members spend months preparing the presentation so that everything flows smoothly. The goal of other teams is to investigate a problem and submit recommendations to decision makers in a report. At Kodak, for example, the "Zebra Team" advised management regarding the development and marketing of all black-and-white film products. The end product of any team is often a written report or an oral presentation.

*4*

## Guidelines for Team Writing and Oral Presentations

Whether your team's project produces written reports or oral presentations, you generally have considerable control over how the project is organized and completed. If you've been part of any team efforts before, you also know that such projects can be very frustrating—particularly when some team members don't carry their weight or when members cannot resolve conflict. On the other hand, team projects can be harmonious and productive when members establish ground rules and follow guidelines related to preparing, planning, collecting information for, organizing, rehearsing, and evaluating team projects.

**Team projects proceed more smoothly when members agree on ground rules.**

***Preparing to Work Together.*** Before you begin talking about a specific project, it's best to discuss some of the following issues in regard to how your group will function.

- Name a meeting leader to plan and conduct meetings, a recorder to keep a record of group decisions, and an evaluator to determine whether the group is on target and meeting its goals.

- Decide whether your team will be governed by consensus (everyone must agree), by majority rule, or by some other method.

**Teams must decide whether they will be governed by consensus, by majority rule, or by some other method.**

Eugene Melnyk, the owner of the NHL's Ottawa Senators and CEO and chairperson of Biovail Corporation, realizes the importance of having an effective team both on and off the ice. Melnyk's rules to hire the very best and ensure company leaders keep everyone informed of what they are doing are definite keys to success.

**In planning a team document or presentation, develop a work plan, assign jobs, and set deadlines.**

**Unless facts are accurate, reports and presentations will fail.**

- Compare schedules of team members in order to set up the best meeting times. Plan to meet often. Make team meetings a top priority. Avoid other responsibilities that might cause disruption during these meetings.

- Discuss the value of conflict. By bringing conflict into the open and encouraging confrontation, your team can prevent personal resentment and group dysfunction. Confrontation can actually create better final products by promoting new ideas and avoiding groupthink. Conflict is most beneficial when team members are allowed to air their views fully.

- Discuss how you will deal with team members who are not pulling their share of the load.

*Planning the Document or Presentation.* Once you've established ground rules, you're ready to discuss the final document or presentation. Be sure to keep a record of the following decisions your team makes.

- Establish the specific purpose for the document or presentation. Identify the main issues involved.

- Decide on the final format. For a report determine what parts it will include, such as an executive summary, figures, and an appendix. For a presentation, decide on its parts, length, and graphics.

- Discuss the audience(s) for the product and what questions it would want answered in your report or oral presentation. If your report is persuasive, consider what appeals might achieve its purpose.

- Develop a work plan (see Chapter 12). Assign jobs. Set deadlines. If time is short, work backward from the due date. For oral presentations build in time for content and creative development as well as for a series of rehearsals.

- For oral presentations give each team member a written assignment that details his or her responsibilities for researching content, producing visuals, developing handout materials, building transitions between segments, and showing up for rehearsals.

- For written reports decide how the final document will be composed: individuals working separately on assigned portions, one person writing the first draft, the entire group writing the complete document together, or some other method.

*Collecting Information.* The following suggestions help teams generate and gather accurate information. Unless facts are accurate, the most beautiful report or the best high-powered presentation will fail.

- Brainstorm for ideas; consider cluster diagramming (see Figure 6.2 in Chapter 6).

- Assign topics. Decide who will be responsible for gathering what information.

- Establish deadlines for collecting information.

- Discuss ways to ensure the accuracy of the information collected.

*Organizing, Writing, and Revising.* As the project progresses, your team may wish to modify some of its earlier decisions.

- Review the proposed organization of your final document or presentation and adjust it if necessary.

- Compose the first draft of a written report or presentation. If separate team members are writing segments, they should use the same word processing and/or presentation graphics program to facilitate combining files.

- Meet to discuss and revise the draft(s) or rehearse the presentation.

- If individuals are working on separate parts of a written report, appoint one person (probably the best writer) to coordinate all the parts, striving for consistent style and format. Work for a uniform look and feel to the final product.

- For oral presentations be sure each member builds a bridge to the next presenter's topic and launches it smoothly. Strive for logical connections between segments.

**For team reports assign one person to coordinate all the parts and make the style consistent.**

*Editing, Rehearsing, and Evaluating.* Before the presentation is made or the final document is submitted, complete the following steps.

- For a written report give one person responsibility for finding and correcting grammatical and mechanical errors.

- For a written report meet as a group to evaluate the final document. Does it fulfill its purpose and meet the needs of the audience? Successful group documents emerge from thoughtful preparation, clear definition of contributors' roles, commitment to a group-approved plan, and willingness to take responsibility for the final product.

- For oral presentations assign one person the task of merging the various files, running a spell checker, and examining the entire presentation for consistency of design, format, and vocabulary.

- Schedule at least five rehearsals, say the experts.[22] Consider videotaping one of the rehearsals so that each presenter can critique his or her own performance.

- Schedule a dress rehearsal with an audience at least two days before the actual presentation. Practise fielding questions.

**Schedule at least five rehearsals for a team presentation.**

More information about writing business reports and making individual presentations appears in subsequent chapters of this book.

## PLANNING AND PARTICIPATING IN PRODUCTIVE MEETINGS

As businesses become more team-oriented and management becomes more participatory, people are attending more meetings than ever. It is estimated that senior managers spend three quarters of their workdays in meetings,[23] and other workers estimate that they spend 5.2 hours per week in meetings. Employees in larger organizations spend more time in meetings than those in small and medium-sized organizations.[24] Yet, meetings are almost universally disliked. Typical comments include "We have too many of them," "They don't accomplish anything," and "What a waste of time!" In spite of employee reluctance and despite terrific advances in communication and team technology, face-to-face meetings are not going to disappear. In discussing the future of meetings, Akio Morita, former chairman of the Sony Corporation, said that he expects "face-to-face meetings will still be the number one form of communication in the twenty-first century."[25] So, get used to them. Meetings are here to stay. Our task, then, as business communicators, is to learn how to make them efficient, satisfying, and productive.

Meetings, by the way, consist of three or more individuals who gather to pool information, solicit feedback, clarify policy, seek consensus, and solve problems. But

5

# National Public Relations Revisited

A leading brewer sues its biggest competitor for appropriating its trademark and misleading consumers, then launches an aggressive assault in the media and a comprehensive communications program to tell its story to customers, trade partners, employees, and investors. National Public Relations is the storyteller of choice.

Eventually a consultant will speak with analysts, members of the media, customers, and potential customers to gauge how the client is perceived from the outside, but the first thing National does is open the lines of communication. This happens as soon as contact is made with a client, says consultant Ronald Alepian, who explains that an initial meeting may be held over the phone or in person. Either way, he poses plenty of questions in an attempt to understand the client's business.

"I spend extraordinary amounts of time talking to people and asking questions in an effort to get the pulse of an organization," says Alepian. "This means talking with everyone from the president of the company right down to the guy in the mailroom in an effort to see how the company views itself, what the corporate culture and internal attitudes are like, and what is needed to go forward. The first step toward meaningful communication is gaining knowledge."

Getting information from intelligent and informed individuals is one thing; getting them to agree is quite another. Effective communication in teams is "all about reaching a consensus," says Alepian, adding that the exchange of ideas "cannot be a free-for-all." There must be a leader who stimulates conversation in a non-threatening and collaborative manner, refines goals, and commands the respect of team members while bringing a plan to fruition. But above all else, "there has to be a loyalty to the team," Alepian says.

## CRITICAL THINKING

- Through what stages of development could teams formed by National expect to pass?
- Why are decisions by consensus harder to achieve than those from a majority vote or an authoritative leader? Why might consensus be a better route than the latter two ways of deciding an issue?

www.national.ca

---

**Because you can expect to attend many meetings, learn to make them efficient, satisfying, and productive.**

meetings have another important purpose for you. They represent opportunities. Because they are a prime tool for developing staff, they are career-critical. "If you can't orchestrate a meeting, you're of little use to the corporation," says Morris Schechtman, head of a leadership training firm.[26] At meetings judgments are formed and careers are made. Therefore, instead of treating them as thieves of your valuable time, try to see them as golden opportunities to demonstrate your leadership, communication, and problem-solving skills. So that you can make the most of these opportunities, here are techniques for planning and conducting successful meetings.

## Deciding Whether a Meeting Is Necessary

**Call meetings only when necessary, and invite only key people.**

No meeting should be called unless the topic is important, can't wait, and requires an exchange of ideas. If the flow of information is strictly one way and no immediate feedback will result, then don't schedule a meeting. For example, if people are merely being advised or informed, send an e-mail, memo, or letter. Leave a telephone or voice mail message, but don't call a costly meeting. Remember, the real expense of a meeting is the lost productivity of all the people attending. To decide whether the purpose of the meeting is valid, it's a good idea to consult the key people who will be attending. Ask them what outcomes are desired and how to achieve those goals. This consultation also sets a collaborative tone and encourages full participation.

## Selecting Participants

The number of meeting participants is determined by the purpose of the meeting, as shown in Figure 2.3. If the meeting purpose is motivational, such as an awards ceremony for sales reps of Mary Kay Cosmetics, then the number of participants is unlimited. But to make decisions, according to studies at 3M Corporation, the best number is five or fewer participants.[27] Ideally, those attending should be people who will make the decision and people with information necessary to make the decision. Also attending should be people who will be responsible for implementing the decision and representatives of groups who will benefit from the decision.

**Problem-solving meetings should involve five or fewer people.**

## Distributing Advance Information

At least two days in advance of a meeting, distribute an agenda of topics to be discussed. Also include any reports or materials that participants should read in advance. For continuing groups, you might also include a copy of the minutes of the previous meeting. To keep meetings productive, limit the number of agenda items. Remember, the narrower the focus, the greater the chances for success. A good agenda, as illustrated in Figure 2.4, covers the following information:

**Pass out a meeting agenda showing topics to be discussed and other information.**

- Date and place of meeting
- Start time and end time
- Brief description of each topic, in order of priority, including the names of individuals who are responsible for performing some action

**FIGURE 2.3  Meeting Purpose and Number of Participants**

| Purpose | Ideal Size |
|---------|-----------|
| Intensive problem solving | 5 or fewer |
| Problem identification | 10 or fewer |
| Information reviews and presentations | 30 or fewer |
| Motivational | Unlimited |

- Proposed allotment of time for each topic
- Any premeeting preparation expected of participants

## Getting the Meeting Started

**Start meetings on time and open with a brief introduction.**

To avoid wasting time and irritating attendees, always start meetings on time—even if some participants are missing. Waiting for latecomers causes resentment and sets a bad precedent. For the same reasons, don't give a quick recap to anyone who arrives late. At the appointed time, open the meeting with a three- to five-minute introduction that includes the following:

- Goal and length of the meeting
- Background of topics or problems

**FIGURE 2.4  Typical Meeting Agenda**

Heading identifies all important details including time allocation.

Items, responsibilities, and time lines provide clarity and ensure the meeting proceeds smoothly.

### AGENDA

Quantum Travel International
Staff Meeting September 4, 2005
10 to 11 a.m.
Conference Room

I. Call to order; roll call

II. Approval of agenda

III. Approval of minutes from previous meeting

|  | Person | Proposed Time |
|---|---|---|
| IV. Committee reports |  |  |
| A. Web site update | Kevin | 5 minutes |
| B. Tour packages | Lisa | 10 minutes |
| V. Old business |  |  |
| A. Equipment maintenance | John | 5 minutes |
| B. Client escrow accounts | Alicia | 5 minutes |
| C. Internal newsletter | Adrienne | 5 minutes |
| VI. New business |  |  |
| A. New accounts | Sarah | 5 minutes |
| B. Pricing policy for trips | Marcus | 15 minutes |

VII. Announcements

VIII. Chair's summary, adjournment

- Possible solutions and constraints
- Tentative agenda
- Ground rules to be followed

A typical set of ground rules might include arriving on time, communicating openly, being supportive, listening carefully, participating fully, confronting conflict frankly, and following the agenda. More formal groups follow parliamentary procedures based on *Robert's Rules of Order*. After establishing basic ground rules, the leader should ask if participants agree thus far. The next step is to assign one attendee to take minutes and one to act as a recorder. The recorder stands at a flipchart or whiteboard and lists the main ideas being discussed and agreements reached.

## Moving the Meeting Along

After the preliminaries, the leader should say as little as possible. Like a talk show host, an effective leader makes "sure that each panel member gets some air time while no one member steals the show."[28] Remember that the purpose of a meeting is to exchange views, not to hear one person, even the leader, do all the talking. If the group has one member who monopolizes, the leader might say, "Thanks, Kurt, for that perspective, but please hold your next point while we hear how Ann would respond to that." This technique also encourages quieter participants to speak up.

To avoid allowing digressions to sidetrack the group, try generating a "Parking Lot" list. This is a list of important but divergent issues that should be discussed at a later time. Another way to handle digressions is to say, "Folks, we are getting off track here. Forgive me for pressing on, but I need to bring us back to the central issue of . . . ."[29] It's important to adhere to the agenda and the time schedule. Equally important, when the group seems to have reached a consensus, is to summarize the group's position and check to see whether everyone agrees.

**Keep the meeting moving by avoiding issues that sidetrack the group.**

## Recording Information

Ensure minutes of the meeting are transcribed for consistency of information and distribution to all stakeholders. Minutes must be objective and action-oriented. Verbatim minutes are long and tedious, and may include personal and irrelevant "chatter." To capture discussion, a point-by-point summary is effective. Action-oriented minutes permit one to chair the meeting and take notes at the same time.[30]

## Dealing With Conflict

Before reaching decisions, most groups go through a "storming" or conflict stage. Conflict is natural and even desirable, but it can cause awkwardness and uneasiness. In meetings, conflict typically develops when people feel unheard or misunderstood. If two people are in conflict, the best approach is to encourage each to make a complete case while group members give their full attention. Let each one question the other. Then, the leader should summarize what was said, and the group should offer comments. The group may modify a recommendation or suggest alternatives before reaching consensus on a direction to follow.

**When a conflict develops between two members, allow each to make a complete case before the group.**

## Handling Dysfunctional Group Members

When individuals are performing in any of the dysfunctional roles described earlier (such as blocker, attacker, joker, and withdrawer), they should be handled with care and tact. The following specific techniques can help a leader or gatekeeper control some group members and draw others out.[31]

- **Lay down the rules in an opening statement.** Give a specific overall summary of topics, time allotment, and expected behaviour. Warn that speakers who digress will be interrupted.

- **Seat potentially dysfunctional members strategically.** Experts suggest seating a difficult group member immediately next to the leader. It's easier to bypass a person in this position. Make sure the person with dysfunctional behaviour is not seated in a power point, such as at the end of the table or across from the leader.

- **Avoid direct eye contact.** In North American society, direct eye contact is a nonverbal signal that encourages talking. Thus, when asking a question of the group, look only at those whom you wish to answer.

- **Assign dysfunctional members specific tasks.** Ask a potentially disruptive person, for example, to be the group recorder.

- **Ask members to speak in a specific order.** Ordering comments creates an artificial, rigid climate and should be done only when absolutely necessary. But such a regimen ensures that everyone gets a chance to participate.

- **Interrupt monopolizers.** If a difficult member dominates a discussion, wait for a pause and then break in. Summarize briefly the previous comments or ask someone else for an opinion.

- **Encourage nontalkers.** Give only positive feedback to the comments of reticent members. Ask them direct questions about which you know they have information or opinions.

- **Give praise and encouragement** to those who seem to need it, including the distracters, the blockers, and the withdrawn.

## Ending With a Plan

End the meeting at the agreed time. The leader should summarize what has been decided, who is going to do what, and by what time. It may be necessary to ask people to volunteer to take responsibility for completing action items agreed to in the meeting. No one should leave the meeting without a full understanding of what was accomplished. One effective technique that encourages full participation is "once around the table." Everyone is asked to summarize briefly his or her interpretation of what was decided and what happens next. Of course, this closure technique works best with smaller groups. The leader should conclude by asking the group to set a time for the next meeting. He or she should also assure the group that a report will follow and thank participants for attending.

## Following Up Actively

Minutes should be distributed within a couple of days after the meeting. It is up to the leader to see that what was decided at the meeting is accomplished. The leader may need to call people to remind them of their assignments and also to volunteer to help them if necessary.

Meetings are a necessary evil for today's team-oriented workplace. The following checklist can help you use them effectively and perhaps accelerate your career.

## Before the Meeting

✓ **Consider alternatives.** Unless a topic is important and pressing, avoid calling a meeting. Perhaps an e-mail message, telephone call, or announcement would serve the purpose as well.

✓ **Invite the right people.** To make decisions, invite those people who have information and authority to make the decision and implement it.

✓ **Distribute an agenda.** Prepare and distribute an agenda that includes the date and place of meeting, the starting and ending times, a brief description of each topic, the names of people responsible for any action, and a proposed time allotment for each topic.

## During the Meeting

✓ **Start on time and introduce the agenda.** Discuss the goal and length of the meeting, provide background of topics for discussion, suggest possible solutions and constraints, propose a tentative agenda, and clarify the ground rules for the meeting.

✓ **Appoint a secretary and a recorder.** Ask one attendee to make a record of the proceedings, and ask another person to record discussion topics on a flipchart or whiteboard.

✓ **Encourage balanced participation.** Strive to be sure that all participants' views are heard and that no one monopolizes the discussion. Avoid digressions by steering the group back to the topics on the agenda.

✓ **Confront conflict frankly.** Encourage people who disagree to explain their positions completely. Then, restate each position and ask for group comments. The group may modify a recommendation or suggest alternatives before agreeing on a plan of action.

✓ **Summarize along the way.** When the group seems to reach a consensus, summarize and see whether everyone agrees.

## Ending the Meeting and Following Up

✓ **Review meeting decisions.** At the end of the meeting, summarize what has been decided, discuss action items, and establish a schedule for completion.

✓ **Distribute minutes of meeting.** A few days after the meeting, arrange to have the recorder or scribe distribute the minutes.

✓ **Remind people of action items.** Follow up by calling people to see if they are completing the actions recommended at the meeting.

# USING GROUPWARE TO MANAGE PROJECTS, FACILITATE MEETINGS, AND MAKE DECISIONS

*Groupware* **(also known as** *teamware***) is software that facilitates group activities.**

*Groupware* (sometimes called *teamware*) is a generic term for software designed to facilitate group activities. The term relates to a number of constantly evolving technologies that help groups exchange information, collaborate in project management, and reach consensus. For example, groupware is helpful in planning and managing focus groups, executive retreats, strategic planning sessions, product development meetings, team-building seminars, and other meetings and training programs. Groupware is also effective when members of organizations must work together to solve problems, write mission statements, and develop proposals. It's equally useful whether team members are just down the hall, across the country, or around the world.

**Second-generation groupware systems use the Web to help teams collaborate on projects.**

First-generation groupware systems involved full-featured proprietary software systems such as Lotus Notes. These text-based systems were expensive and often required local area networks with well-trained technical staffs to keep everything functioning. Second-generation groupware systems use the Web, which enables any user to gain access to applications with any computer as long as it has a Web browser. Claudine Simard, Lotus Canada's national technology manager, explains the spontaneous exchange of information between users. SameTime informs users if any members of their group are online, so that discussions may begin. To facilitate this process, "meeting centres" are created to allow for sharing of ideas that can then be saved and referred to at a later time.[32] Such groupware can help teams collaborate on projects regardless of their office locations, time zones, travel schedules, or "flex hours."

Groupware is most often used to help teams with three important functions: project management, meeting facilitation, and decision support.

**Project management software helps distant team members, suppliers, partners, and others clarify project goals, set deadlines, and anticipate obstacles.**

*Project Management.* Completing a project successfully generally requires unrestricted sharing of information. Project management software can allow remote team members, suppliers, partners, and others with an interest in the project's successful completion to view the project and modify their own tasks via the Web. For example, users can input time sheet information, submit status reports, and delegate tasks. Some programs provide guides that help managers identify project phases, clarify goals, establish deadlines, and anticipate obstacles. Executives can even create a portfolio view to determine the status of all projects under way as well as search more deeply for detailed descriptions of key events.

**Videoconferencing enables remote groups to meet electronically.**

*Meeting Facilitation.* For the past decade *videoconferencing* has been an important means of enabling groups to meet electronically. Videoconferencing combines audio, video, and communications networking technologies for real-time interaction. Generally, participants meet in special conference rooms equipped with cameras and television screens for transmitting images and documents. Because participants did not have to journey to far-flung meetings, organizations could reduce travel expenses, travel time, and employee fatigue. But videoconferencing equipment was expensive, and only large organizations could afford it.

**Desktop videoconferencing uses the Web to reduce the cost of electronic meetings.**

Recently, *desktop videoconferencing* has reduced the cost of electronic meetings. Desktop videoconferencing combines personal computing with audio, video, and communications technologies to provide real-time interaction from personal computers. The latest technologies use the Web to facilitate team meetings. Instead of investing in expensive videoconference rooms and equipment, teams need only a

Web cam and a headset or microphone to conduct real-time virtual meetings. With increasing power in personal computing and the spread of broadband delivery, videoconferencing is becoming more flexible and more accessible.

*Decision Support.* Large groups that must solve problems quickly may turn to group decision support software (GDSS). For example, Harley-Davidson wanted to lure "higher class" riders without tarnishing a brand made famous by big-screen bad boys like Marlon Brando, James Dean, and Dennis Hopper. One way to generate ideas is with a GDSS brainstorming session bringing together engineers, managers, production crews, suppliers, and customers to present ideas and evaluate reactions.

A typical GDSS session involves participants seated at networked computers with a large screen at the front of a room. This screen functions as an electronic flipchart displaying participant ideas and responses. With a facilitator guiding the group, the software may be used to poll participants, capture large amounts of verbatim feedback, analyze voting results, and create detailed reports including meeting minutes.

Group decision support software offers a number of advantages over traditional face-to-face meetings. It promises equality of participation; group members are less able to monopolize available meeting time. Because communication is anonymous, group members are more willing to make critical comments, question solutions, and ask clarifying questions. Anonymity also helps to equalize influence; thus the comments of powerful members do not carry more weight. Research has shown that GDSS elicits higher quality input from attendees and helps keep group decisions on track. However, this software is so complex that a facilitator is required to instruct participants and organize sessions.

**Group decision support software helps large groups solve problems quickly.**

# STRENGTHENING YOUR TEAMWORK SKILLS NOW

At one time or another in your current or future job and certainly in your postsecondary career, you will be working on a team. It may be a temporary team created to complete one specific task, such as developing a new product or completing a project. It could be a permanent team with a continuing function, such as overseeing a complete line of products. In your personal life you could be a committee member or part of the governing body for a volunteer organization, a social group, or a housing group. Most assuredly, however, in your professional life you will be part of a team effort. You may be thinking, "Yeah, down the road a bit I might need some of these skills, but why worry about them now?"

The truth is that you need to start developing teamwork skills now. You can't just turn them on when you want them. They need to be studied, modelled, nurtured, and practised. You've just taken a look at the inner workings of teams, including the four phases of team development, the role of conflict, the characteristics of successful teams, functional and dysfunctional team roles, and participating in productive meetings. In this book, in this course, and throughout your academic career, you will have opportunities to work with teams. Begin to analyze their dynamics. Who has the power and why? Who are the most successful team members and why? What would make a team function more effectively? How can you improve your teamwork skills?

Remember, job recruiters consider team skills among the most important requirements for many of today's jobs. You can become the number one candidate for your dream job by developing team skills and acquiring experience now.

**Developing effective teamwork skills requires study, modelling, nurturing, and practice.**

## *Applying Your Skills at National Public Relations*

The staff at National dialogue freely and in confidence with clients ranging from heads of corporations to former heads of state. So how is success gauged?

"At National, people are evaluated on the ability to build teams," says Ronald Alepian. "It's not necessarily how many clients you bring through the door or the revenue you generate, but 'Can you build great teams?' That's how you create wealth: by bringing good people together and empowering them to be successful."

Only when ideas are shared freely can a program be received, approved, and moved ahead. Says Alepian: "When things are stalled, that's when you know there has been a breakdown in communication."

### Your Task

As an assistant to a senior consultant at National Public Relations, you have been asked to prepare a summary of suggestions for developing effective meetings. Discuss how to prepare for meetings, how to conduct meetings that allow for the effective flow of ideas, and how to follow up after meetings. Your suggestions will eventually become part of a Web site page called "Think National, Act Global." Suggest ways to illustrate your ideas on the Internet or submit your ideas in a memo with descriptive side headings.

**www.national.ca**

## SUMMARY OF LEARNING OBJECTIVES

*1* **Discuss why groups and teams are formed and how they are different.** Many organizations have found that groups and teams are more effective than individuals because groups make better decisions, respond faster, increase productivity, achieve greater buy-in, reduce resistance to change, improve employee morale, and result in reduced risk for individuals. A *group* is a collection of three or more individuals who perceive themselves as a group but who may complete their tasks independently. A *team* is a group that interacts over time to achieve a purpose. Businesses are increasingly turning to *self-directed teams*, which are characterized by clearly stated goals, autonomy, decision-making authority, frequent communication, and ongoing training.

*2* **Describe team development, team and group roles, dealing with conflict, and methods for reaching group decisions.** Teams typically go through four stages of development. In the *forming* stage, they get to know each other and discuss general topics. In the second stage, *storming*, they define their roles, goals, and governing procedures. Tempers may flare as conflict erupts. Once team members work through this stage, they enter the *norming* stage in which tension subsides, roles clarify, and information begins to flow. Finally, in the *performing* stage, teams develop loyalty and progress toward their goals. Team members perform in a number of different positive task and group roles. But some team members play dysfunctional roles, such as blocking, attacking, seeking recognition, joking, and withdrawing. Conflict that centres on issues can generate new ideas and help the group progress toward consensus. Open discussion of conflict prevents *groupthink*, a condition that leads to faulty decisions. Methods for reaching group decisions include majority, consensus, minority, averaging, and authority rule with discussion.

3 **Identify the characteristics of successful teams.** The most effective teams are usually small and diverse; that is, they are made up of people representing different ages, genders, and backgrounds. Successful teams agree on their purpose and procedures. They are able to channel conflict into constructive discussion and reach consensus. They accept their ethical responsibilities, encourage open communication, listen actively, provide feedback, and have fun. Members are able to collaborate rather than compete, and leadership is often a shared responsibility depending on the situation and expertise required.

4 **List techniques for organizing team-based written and oral presentations.** In preparing to work together, teams should limit their size, name a meeting leader, and decide whether they wish to make decisions by consensus, majority rule, or some other method. They should work out their schedules, discuss the value of conflict, and decide how to deal with team members who do not do their share. They should decide on the purpose, form, and procedures for preparing the final document or presentation. They must brainstorm for ideas, assign topics, establish deadlines, and discuss how to ensure information accuracy. In composing the first draft of a report or presentation, they should use the same software and meet to discuss drafts and rehearsals. For written reports one person should probably compose the final draft, and the group should evaluate it. For group presentations they need to work for consistency of design, format, and vocabulary. At least five rehearsals, one of which should be videotaped, will enhance the final presentation.

5 **Discuss how to plan and participate in productive meetings.** Call a meeting only when urgent two-way communication is necessary. Limit participants to those directly involved. Distribute an agenda in advance, start the meeting on time, and keep the discussion on track. Confront conflict openly by letting each person present her or his views fully before having the group decide which direction to take. Summarize what was said and end the meeting on time. Follow up by distributing minutes of the meeting and verifying that action items are being accomplished. *Groupware* is software that helps groups exchange information, collaborate in project management, facilitate meetings, and support decision making. Group decision support software automates traditional meeting functions, such as brainstorming, capturing feedback, analyzing voting results, and creating reports including meeting minutes.

# CHAPTER REVIEW

1. List seven reasons that explain why organizations are forming groups and teams. (Obj. 1)

2. How are virtual teams different from intact teams? (Obj. 1)

3. To be most successful, self-directed teams need to have what characteristics? (Obj. 1)

4. What are the four phases of team development? Is it best to move through the stages quickly? Why or why not? (Obj. 2)

5. Name five team roles that relate to tasks and five roles that relate to developing relationships. Which roles do you think are most important and why? (Obj. 2)

6. Name five dysfunctional team roles. (Obj. 2)

7. What is the difference between *cognitive* and *affective* conflict? (Obj. 2)

8. What is *groupthink*? (Obj. 2)

9. Why can diverse teams be more effective than homogeneous teams? (Obj. 3)

10. Why are team decisions based on consensus generally better than decisions reached by majority rule? (Obj. 3)

11. What is the best way to set team deadlines when time is short to complete a project? (Obj. 4)

12. In completing a team-written report, should all team members work together to write the report? Why or why not? (Obj. 4)

13. When groups or teams meet, what are seven ground rules with which they should begin? (Obj. 5)

14. Name five techniques for handling dysfunctional group members. (Obj. 5)

15. What is groupware? What are three important functions it serves? (Obj. 5)

# CRITICAL THINKING

1. Compare the advantages and disadvantages of using teams in today's workplace. (Objs. 1, 2, and 3)

2. What kinds of conflict could erupt during the "storming" phase of team development? Should conflict be avoided? (Obj. 2)

3. What are the advantages and disadvantages of diverse teams? (Obj. 3)

4. How would you comment on this statement made by an executive? "If you can't orchestrate a meeting, then you are of little use to an organization." (Obj. 5)

5. **Ethical Issue:** You're disturbed that Randy, one member of your team, is selling Amway products to other members of the team. He shows catalogues and takes orders at lunch, and he distributes products after work and during lunch. He also leaves an order form on the table during team meetings. What should you do? What if Randy were selling Girl Guide cookies?

# ACTIVITIES

## 2.1 Advantages of Teams: Convincing Your Boss (Obj. 1)

Your boss or organization leader comes to you and asks you to take on a big job. Use your imagination to select a task such as developing a Web site or organizing a fund-raising campaign. You are flattered that your boss respects you and thinks you capable of completing the task, but you think that a team could do a better job than an individual.

**Your Task.** What arguments would you use to convince your boss that a team could work better than an individual?

## 2.2 Group Decision Strategies: Which Method? (Objs. 1 and 2)

**TEAM**

In small groups decide which decision strategy is best for the following situations:

a. A steering committee at your office must decide on the format for an upcoming company conference.

b. The owner of your company is meeting with all managers to decide whether to purchase new ergonomic chairs and workstations.

c. Members of a condominium association must decide which members will become directors.

d. Your project team must decide among several candidates in hiring a new member.

e. The human resources department of a large company must work with employees to hammer out a new benefits package within its budget.

f. A large association of realtors must decide how to organize a member Web site. Only a few members have technical expertise.

g. Three employees must decide who gets a large vacant corner office.

## 2.3 Analyzing Team Formation, Decision Making, and Group Roles (Objs. 1, 2, and 3)

**TEAM**

Members of small groups play a number of different roles as their groups are formed and decisions are made. To better understand the dynamics of group formation, decision making, and group roles, you will form small groups to discuss one of the topics below.

**Your Task.** Decide on a team leader and a recorder. Discuss a topic for ten minutes (or as long as your instructor directs). As the discussion progresses, analyze the comments made and the group roles they represent. Then as a group, draft an outline of the major points discussed, your team decision, and the specific roles played in the discussion. Your instructor may ask you to report to the class or prepare a group memo summarizing your discussion.

a. Should an employee be allowed to sell products such as Amway items or Girl Guide cookies at work? (See Critical Thinking Question 5 for more details.)

b. Should an employee be allowed to send personal e-mail messages during breaks or lunch hours? How about using company computers after hours to prepare a college report? What if your supervisor gives her permission but asks you to keep quiet about it?

c. Should companies have the right to monitor e-mail messages sent by employees? If so, is it necessary for an organization to inform the employees of its policy?

## 2.4 Group Roles: Observing a Group in Action (Objs. 1, 2, 3, and 5)

Watching a school board, city council, campus organization, or other public meeting in which problems and solutions are discussed can be useful in understanding group actions and roles.

**Your Task.** Attend the meeting of an organized group. Analyze the roles played by participants. What roles related to completing the task at hand? What roles related to developing group relationships? Did any participants play dysfunctional roles? How was conflict resolved?

## 2.5 Characteristics of Successful Teams: Being a Team Consultant (Objs. 1, 2, and 3)

**TEAM**

Your consulting company has been hired to make a presentation before a conference of entrepreneurs. They want to learn more about effective teams.

**Your Task.** In small groups, outline an appropriate presentation. Why do some teams succeed and others fail? Make a list of significant elements and be prepared to support each with evidence, examples, or description.

## 2.6 Group Roles: Revealing Comments (Obj. 2)

In teams or in class discussion, analyze the following statements in relation to the group roles presented in this chapter.

What group role does each statement represent? Is it a positive or negative contribution to the team?

a. "I don't think the two of you are as far apart as you think. Kevin, are you saying . . . . And Jeff, you seem to be saying . . . . Is that what you mean?"

b. "Does anyone else have an opinion on this issue?"

c. "Hey, did you all hear the one about the . . . ."

d. "Don't we all need a break about now? I'm tired and confused. How about the rest of you?"

e. "What a great idea! Stacy, you're really on to something. We need more input like this."

f. "I know it's a little off the subject, but you're going to love this. Wait till I tell you about what happened to me today."

g. "I think we should . . . . When I was in charge of . . . , I was able to . . . . Don't you think I'm right?" (Don't you think I'm wonderful?)

h. "Rachel, you've been awfully quiet. What do you think about this?"

i. "Well, let's see what we have here. Thus far, we seem to be agreed on these points: . . . . Does everyone think this is a fair synopsis?"

j. "That's about the dumbest thing I've ever heard. Why don't you come out from under your rock and see what's happening in the real world?"

k. "Before we go down that road, does anyone know how this method has worked with other groups?"

l. "It sounds as if you think we're all against you, Kevin."

m. "Based on what you have all said, I think our next step is to . . . ."

## 2.7 Teamwork: Moving From "Me" Thinking to "We" Thinking (Obj. 3)

**INFOTRAC**

James E. Perella, former CEO of industrial engineering giant Ingersoll-Rand, gave an inspiring speech about teamwork to a leadership group at Purdue University.

**Your Task.** To read that speech, use InfoTrac and keyword search for "work teams." Scroll down the listings until you find "The Importance of Working Together: Individuals Add; Team Players Multiply," *Vital Speeches*, 1 May 1999; Article No. A54772989. (For a faster search, use PowerTrac with the author's name, a few words from the title, or the article number.) After reading the article, answer these questions.

a. What specific benefits did Ingersoll-Rand experience as a result of implementing work teams?

b. What is the "maturity continuum," and how does it relate to "we" thinking?

c. What is meant by "individuals add, team players multiply"?

d. Who are "glue people"?

**e.** Based on what you learned in this chapter, what are some of the group roles that could be filled by "glue people"?

**f.** What do you think is the best advice given by Perella?

## 2.8 Group Roles: Analyzing the Roles You Play (Obj. 2)

Think about work groups or social groups in which you have interacted. Based on the discussion in this chapter, what group role do you usually play? Do you play more than one role? What roles could you adopt to improve the functioning of your group?

## 2.9 Groupthink: Reaching a Unanimous Decision (Obj. 2)

You are a member of the Community Service Committee, which is part of the Business Newcomers Club in your town. Your committee must decide what local cause to support with funds earned at the Newcomers' annual celebrity auction. Matt, the committee chair, suggested that the group support a local literacy program. His aunt is literacy coordinator at the Davis Outreach Centre, and he knows that the group would be delighted with any contribution. Heather said that she favoured any cause that was educational. Eric announced that he had to leave for an appointment in five minutes. Mona described an article she read in the newspaper about surprisingly large numbers of people who were functionally illiterate. Kevin said that he thought they ought to consider other causes such as the homeless centre, but Matt dismissed the idea saying, "The homeless already receive lots of funding. Besides, our contribution could make a real difference with the literacy program." The other members of the committee persuaded Kevin to agree with them. The committee voted unanimously to support the literacy program.

**Your Task.**

**a.** What aspects of groupthink were at work in this committee?

**b.** What conditions contribute to groupthink?

**c.** What can groups do to avoid groupthink?

## 2.10 Teams: Converting Low Performance Into High Performance (Obj. 3)

**WEB**

The Legacee consulting firm lists rules for converting low-performing teams into high-performing teams.
**Your Task.** Go to <www.legacee.com> and, in the Legacee site Search box, insert the words "rules for team building." How do the Legacee rules for team building differ from the characteristics of successful teams discussed in this chapter?

## 2.11 Meetings: Planning a Gathering (Obj. 5)

Assume that the next meeting of your associated students organization will discuss preparations for a careers day in the spring. The group will hear reports from committees working on speakers, business recruiters, publicity, reservation of campus space, setup of booths, and any other matters you can think of.
**Your Task.** As president of your ASO, prepare an agenda for the meeting. Compose your introductory remarks to open the meeting. Your instructor may ask you to submit these two documents or use them in staging an actual meeting in class.

## 2.12 Evaluating Meetings: Effective or Ineffective? (Obj. 5)

Attend a structured meeting of an academic, social, business, or other organization. Compare the manner in which the meeting is conducted with the suggestions presented in this chapter. Why did the meeting succeed or fail? Prepare a memo for your instructor or be ready to discuss your findings in class.

## 2.13 Videoconferencing: Using the Web for Research (Obj. 5)

**WEB**

Your boss wants to learn more about workplace videoconferencing, but she is busy and a Web novice. She asks you to find three or four sites that will help her learn more about terminology, resources, and services.

**Your Task.** Use a search engine such as <**www.google.ca**> to locate helpful sites. Consider sites with videoconferencing glossaries, FAQs (frequently asked questions), and guides. Submit a list of the three best sites that you find. Provide a short description of each site and why you think it will be helpful.

## 2.14 Making Meetings Count: Do's and Don'ts (Obj. 5)

> **INFOTRAC**

Most businesspeople feel that meetings are the bane of their existence, leading the list of top time wasters. An excellent article by Catherine L. Carlozzi provides advice for ensuring that meetings are efficient and effective.

**Your Task.** Use InfoTrac to locate "Make Your Meetings Count," *Journal of Accountancy*, February 1999, Article No. A53878198. After reading the article, answer these questions:

a. What two well-known companies have made good use of virtual meetings? How have they done this?

b. What are three suggestions regarding meeting preparation or participation that were not contained in this chapter?

c. If you are a group leader, how should you react when discussion becomes bogged down or sidetracked?

# C.L.U.E. REVIEW 2

On a separate sheet edit the following sentences to correct faults in grammar, punctuation, spelling, numbers, proofreading, and word use.

1. Companys are forming teams for at least 3 good reasons; better decisions, more faster response times and increase productivity.

2. Although they do not hold face to face meetings virtual teams exchange information and make desisions electronically.

3. Successful self directed teams are autonomous, that is they can hire fire and discipline there own member.

4. We all ready have a number of teams, however our CEO and several Vice Presidents are advicing us to add more.

5. At last months Staff meeting the Manager and him encouraged a warm supportive climate with praise and helpful comments.

6. When conflict erupted at our teams febuary meeting we made a conscience effort to confront the underlying issues.

7. The best method for reaching group decisions involve consensus but this method is very time-consuming.

8. The Team Leader and myself think however that all speakers have a right to a fair hearing.

9. 75 people are expected to attend the Training Session on May 15th consequently her and I must find a more larger room.

10. Lawyers in our legal services department distributed a agenda for participants attending there January 3rd meeting.

**69**

# Chapter 3

## Workplace Listening and Nonverbal Communication

## LEARNING OBJECTIVES

*1* Explain the importance of listening in the workplace and describe three types of workplace listening.

*2* Discuss the listening process and its barriers.

*3* Enumerate ten techniques for improving workplace listening.

*4* Define nonverbal communication and explain its functions.

*5* Describe the forms of nonverbal communication and how they can be used positively in your career.

*6* List specific techniques for improving nonverbal communication skills in the workplace.

# Minacs Worldwide Inc.

It's the entrepreneurial dream—to grow a small business into a worldwide corporation. It took Elaine Minacs 20 years to accomplish this dream. Starting as a four-person temporary staffing agency established in 1981 in Pickering, Ontario, Minacs Worldwide Inc. now employs over 4 500 people in 20 locations in Canada, the United States, and Europe and is traded publicly on the Toronto Stock Exchange.[1] Along the way, Elaine Minacs has been ranked among the top five of the top 100 Women Business Owners by *Profit* magazine and is a recipient of the Canadian Professional Sales Association Hall of Fame Canadian Woman Entrepreneur of the Year and the Toronto YWCA's Woman of Distinction awards. The company was listed on the Profit 100 (the fastest growing companies in Canada) in 2001, 2002, and 2003 and named a General Motors Supplier of the Year in 2002. Bo Andersson, vice president, GM Worldwide Purchasing Production Control & Logistics, said, "Minacs is representative of the companies GM expects to grow with us as we seek to increase market share. They serve as a role model for other suppliers."[2]

Minacs Worldwide Inc. is a leader in customer relationship management (CRM) services and lists clients in the automotive, financial services, and technology fields. CRM is a "customer-focused strategy that boosts customer loyalty and profitability."[3] It involves a number of elements that help companies better understand their customers' needs. This knowledge allows companies to improve product and service offerings to optimize the customer experience and build lasting relationships.

To customers that include General Motors, OnStar, the Ford Motor Company, and the American Honda Motor Company, Minacs offers inbound services such as customer care, technical support, complaint tracking, and equipment sales; outbound services such as customer acquisition, loyalty programs, welcome calling, and customer surveys; and e-channel/self-service such as Web site design, development, and hosting, interactive voice response, e-mail and Web communications, and e-business support. In addition, the company offers data mining, in which experts analyze client databases and collect intelligence about customers and prospects from service records, warranty reports, and sales data.

Employees at Minacs understand that today's customers demand when and how they communicate with service and product providers. CRM provides customers with what they want, when they want it, and how they want it: by phone, fax, e-mail, or Web chat. Minacs offers its clients a flexible platform to support their CRM initiatives while minimizing the capital costs associated with creating their own infrastructure. This enables clients to concentrate on their core business and customer-facing strategies, while Minacs delivers on its promise of improved customer value, satisfaction, profitability, and retention.[4]

## CRITICAL THINKING

- What do you think really influences long-term customer retention and loyalty? Products? Promotions? Prices? Staff? Convenience? Reward programs?
- How could feedback from call centre representatives be helpful to organizations?
- In what ways is listening to customers similar to listening to friends and colleagues?

www.minacs.com

---

"Companies that listen are very successful. They listen to their clients, employees, and vendors to monitor and take corrective action when necessary to maintain alignment with their business environment."[5] Today's employers are becoming increasingly aware that listening is a critical employee and management skill. In addition, listening to customers takes on increasing importance as our economy becomes ever more service-oriented.

But, you may be thinking, everyone knows how to listen. Most of us believe that listening is an automatic response to noise. We do it without thinking. Perhaps that explains why so many of us are poor listeners. You can develop good listening habits by learning more about the process and by studying specific techniques. In this chapter we'll explore the importance of listening, the kinds of listening required in the workplace, the listening process, listening barriers, and how to become a better listener. Although many of the tips will be effective in your personal life, our discussion centres primarily on workplace and employment needs.

## LISTENING IN THE WORKPLACE

*1*

As you learned earlier, workers are doing more communicating than ever before, largely because of the Internet, team environments, global competition, and an increasing emphasis on customer service. A vital ingredient in every successful workplace is high-quality communication. And three quarters of high-quality communication involves listening.[6]

Listening skills are important for career success, organization effectiveness, and worker satisfaction. Numerous studies report that good listeners make good managers and that good listeners advance more rapidly in their organizations.[7] In its *Employability Skills 2000+*, The Conference Board of Canada lists communication skills (reading and understanding information, writing and speaking so others understand, listening and asking questions, sharing information, and using relevant knowledge and skills to explain ideas) among those fundamental skills required as a base for further development.[8] Other studies show that listening skills are an important part of the new emphasis on customer service. The enduring success of many companies is largely a result of listening to customers. Such attention to customers is becoming increasingly feasible and a major cause of marketing effectiveness.[9] Listening is equally significant within organizations. Workers are most satisfied when they feel that management listens to their concerns.

Listening is especially important in the workplace because we spend so much time doing it. Most workers spend 30 to 45 percent of their communication time listening,[10] while executives spend 60 to 70 percent of their communication time listening.[11]

**Listening skills are critical for career success, organization effectiveness, and worker satisfaction.**

### Poor Listening Habits

**Most of us listen at only 25 percent efficiency.**

Although executives and workers devote the bulk of their communication time to listening, research suggests that they're not very good at it. In fact, most of us are poor listeners. Some estimates indicate that only half of the oral messages heard in a day are completely understood.[12] Experts say that we listen at only 25 percent efficiency. In other words, we ignore, forget, distort, or misunderstand 75 percent of everything we hear.

**We are inefficient listeners due to lack of training, competing sounds, slowness of speech, and daydreaming.**

Poor listening habits may result from several factors. Lack of training is one significant reason. Few schools give as much emphasis to listening as they do to the development of reading, speaking, and writing skills. In addition, our listening skills may be less than perfect because of the large number of competing sounds and stimuli in our lives that interfere with concentration. Finally, we are inefficient listeners because we are able to process speech much faster than others can speak. While most speakers talk at about 125 to 250 words per minute, listeners can think at 1 000 to 3 000 words per minute.[13] The resulting lag time fosters daydreaming, which clearly reduces listening efficiency.

### Types of Workplace Listening

In an employment environment, you can expect to be involved in many types of listening. These include listening to superiors, listening to employees, and listening to customers. As an entry-level employee, you will be most concerned with listening to superiors. But as you advance in your career and enter the ranks of management, you will need skills for listening to employees. Finally, the entire organization must listen to customers to compete in today's service-oriented economy.

*Listening to Superiors.* On the job one of your most important tasks will be listening to instructions, assignments, and explanations about how to do your work. You will be listening to learn and to comprehend. To focus totally on the speaker, be sure you are not distracted by noisy surroundings or other tasks. Don't take phone calls, and don't try to complete another job while listening with one ear. Show your interest by learning forward and striving for good eye contact.

> Above all, take notes. Don't rely on your memory. Details are easy to forget. Taking selective notes also conveys to the speaker your seriousness about hearing accurately and completely. Don't interrupt. When the speaker finishes, paraphrase the instructions in your own words. Ask pertinent questions in a nonthreatening manner. And don't be afraid to ask "dumb" questions, if it means you won't have to do a job twice. Avoid criticizing or arguing when you are listening to a superior. Your goals should be to hear accurately and to convey an image of competence.

**Listening to superiors involves hearing instructions, assignments, and explanations of work procedures.**

**Listen carefully, take selective notes, and don't interrupt.**

*Listening to Employees.* In the best organizations, listening works in both directions. Employees listen to their superiors, but management also listens to employees. Organizations that listen to employees reap many benefits, including higher productivity and morale. When employees feel that they are being listened to, they are more committed to the success of the entire enterprise. Over the past 40 years management books have observed that senior managers can lead their organizations only if they know what is going on inside them. Employees often know more about daily workplace realities than the boss. They may know about brewing problems—with a new hire, a new process, a slow-paying customer—long before management finds out.[14] Listening organizations take advantage of the ideas, creativity, and commitment of employees, which one expert called the "most underutilized and underdeveloped resource in North American business."[15]

**Organizations that listen to employees take advantage of ideas, encourage creativity, and build commitment.**

> But many organizations are not committed to listening to employees. In a poll of 9 144 employees, only about a third felt that their companies actively sought their opinions and suggestions, as shown in Figure 3.1.[16] Moreover, many managers are not good listeners. Sometimes they are judgmental; other times they listen at lower levels of intensity and think they are saving time. This kind of marginal listening is counterproductive and stressful for employees. As listeners, managers must confirm the message being sent and also affirm the relationship between the speaker and the listener. You'll learn more techniques for improving listening skills shortly.

**Marginal listening is counterproductive for managers.**

*Listening to Customers.* As the North American economy becomes increasingly service-oriented, the new management mantra has become "customers rule." Yet, despite 50 years of talk about customer service, the concept of "customer-centric" business is still in its infancy.[17] Many organizations are just learning that listening to customers results in increased sales and profitability as well as improved customer acquisition and retention. As one salesperson says, "Price is almost always the number one factor for the buyer. But once you develop a relationship, even if your price is a little high, the customers will want to find a reason to stay with you."[18] The simple truth is that consumers just feel better about companies that value their opinions. Listening is an acknowledgment of caring and is a potent retention tool. Customers want to be cared about, thus fulfilling a powerful human need.

**Organizations that listen to customers improve sales and profitability.**

> How can organizations improve their customer listening techniques? Since employees are the eyes and ears of the organization, smart companies begin by hiring

**FIGURE 3.1  Are Companies Really Listening to Their Employees?**

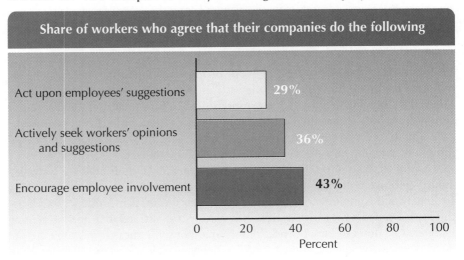

**Share of workers who agree that their companies do the following**

Act upon employees' suggestions — 29%

Actively seek workers' opinions and suggestions — 36%

Encourage employee involvement — **43%**

(Percent: 0, 20, 40, 60, 80, 100)

employees who genuinely care about customers. Listening organizations also train their employees to listen actively and to ask gentle, probing questions to ensure clear understanding. As you can see in Figure 3.2, employees trained in listening techniques are far more likely to elicit customer feedback and promote goodwill than untrained employees.

Many organizations today stay in touch with customers through *call centres* that process hundreds of thousands of telephone calls daily. For example, if you call a major hotel or airline to make a reservation, you will doubtless speak to a call centre representative. Similarly, if you need help with your new computer or your satellite cable service, the help desk you reach is probably a call centre. As service expands to the Web, call centres and voice communications are rapidly evolving into key, integrated components of new customer relation management programs.

**Call centres are an important customer access channel and a major source of customer-related information.**

The better a call centre agent listens to a customer, the better she or he will be at resolving disputes, reducing uncertainty, and matching expectations and perceptions. Any employee listening to a customer should learn to defer judgment, pay attention to content rather than surface issues, and avoid replying to sidetracking issues.

**FIGURE 3.2** Listening to Customers: Comparing Trained and Untrained Listeners

| Untrained Listeners | Trained Listeners |
| --- | --- |
| You tune out some of what the customer is saying because you know what the answer is. | You defer judgment. You listen for the customer's feelings and assess the situation. |
| You are quick to mentally criticize grammar, voice tone, speaking style. You focus on style. | You pay most attention to content, not to appearances, form, or other surface issues. |
| You tend to listen mainly for facts and specific bits of information. | You listen completely, trying to really understand every nuance. This enthralls speakers. |
| You attempt to take in everything the customer is saying, including exaggerations and errors (referred to as "fogging") so that you can refute each comment. | You listen primarily for the main idea and avoid replying to everything, especially sidetracking issues. |
| You divide your attention among multiple tasks because listening is automatic. | You do one thing at a time, realizing that listening is a full-time job. |
| You tend to become distracted by emotional words and have difficulty controlling your angry responses. | You control your anger, refusing to allow your emotions to govern. |
| You interrupt the customer. | You are silent for a few seconds after a customer finishes to be sure the thought is complete. |
| You give few, if any, verbal responses. | You give affirming statements and invite additional comments. |

Call centres have become an important customer access channel as well as a significant source of customer-related information. In call centres and in all contacts with customers, effective listening is an essential business skill.

## THE LISTENING PROCESS AND ITS BARRIERS

Skillful listening to superiors, employees, and customers can mean the difference between workplace success and failure. To help you build effective listening skills, we'll begin by examining the process of listening, as well as its barriers.

Listening takes place in four stages, including perception, interpretation, evaluation, and action, as illustrated in Figure 3.3. Barriers, however, can obstruct the listening process. These barriers may be mental or physical.

*Perception.* The listening process begins when you hear sounds and concentrate on them. Stop reading for a moment and become conscious of the sounds around you. Do you notice the hum of your computer or printer, background sounds from a TV

The four stages of listening are perception, interpretation, evaluation, and action.

## FIGURE 3.3 The Listening Process and Its Barriers

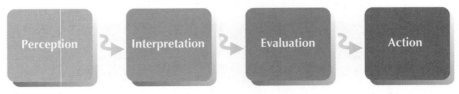

Perception ↝ Interpretation ↝ Evaluation ↝ Action

**COMMON LISTENING BARRIERS**

| Mental Barriers | Physical and Other Barriers |
| --- | --- |
| Inattention | Hearing impairment |
| Prejudgment | Noisy surroundings |
| Frame of reference | Speaker's appearance |
| Closed-mindedness | Speaker's mannerisms |
| Pseudolistening | Lag time |

program, muffled traffic noise, or the murmur of distant voices? Until you "tuned in" to them, these sounds went unnoticed. The conscious act of listening begins when you focus on the sounds around you and select those you choose to hear. You tune in when you (1) sense that the message is important, (2) are interested in the topic, or (3) are in the mood to listen. Perception is reduced by impaired hearing, noisy surroundings, inattention, and pseudolistening. *Pseudolistening* occurs when listeners "fake" it. They look as if they are listening, but their minds are wandering far off.

*Interpretation.* Once you have focused your attention on a sound or message, you begin to interpret, or decode, it. As described in Chapter 1, interpretation of a message is coloured by your cultural, educational, and social frames of reference. The meanings you attach to the speaker's words are filtered through your expectations and total life experiences. Thus, your interpretation of the speaker's meaning may be quite different from what the speaker intended because your frame of reference is different.

**Evaluation involves separating fact from opinion and judging messages objectively.**

*Evaluation.* After interpreting the meaning of a message, you analyze its merit and draw conclusions. To do this, you attempt to separate fact from opinion. Good listeners try to be objective, and they avoid prejudging the message. In a study of college students, one researcher determined that closed-mindedness and opinionated attitudes functioned as major barriers to listening. Certain students were not good listeners because their prejudices prevented them from opening up to a speaker's ideas.[19] The appearance and mannerisms of the speaker can also affect a listener's evaluation of a message. A juror, for example, might jump to the conclusion that an accused man is guilty because of his fierce expression or his substandard English. Thus, to evaluate a message accurately and objectively, you should (1) consider all the information, (2) be aware of your own biases, and (3) avoid jumping to hasty conclusions.

**Action involves storing a message in memory, reacting, or supplying feedback.**

*Action.* Responding to a message may involve storing the message in memory for future use, reacting with a physical response (a frown, a smile, a laugh), or supplying feedback to the speaker. Listener feedback is essential because it helps clarify the message so that it can be decoded accurately. Feedback also helps the speaker to find out whether the message is getting through clearly. In one-to-one conversation, of course, no clear distinction exists between the roles of listener and speaker—you give or receive feedback as your role alternates.

***Improving Retention.*** Unfortunately, most of us will be able to recall only 50 percent of information we heard a day earlier and only 20 percent after two days, as shown in Figure 3.4.[20] How can we improve our retention?

Memory training specialists say that effective remembering involves three factors: (1) deciding to remember, (2) structuring the incoming information to form relationships, and (3) reviewing. In the first step you determine what information is worth remembering. Once you have established a positive mindset, you look for a means of organizing the incoming information to form relationships. Chain links can help you associate the unfamiliar with something familiar. For instance, make an acronym of the first letters of the item to be remembered. To recall the names of the Great Lakes—Huron, Ontario, Michigan, Erie, and Superior—remember the word "HOMES." To remember the listening process—perception, interpretation, evaluation, action—think "PIE-A." Rhyming is another helpful chain-link tool. To remember how to spell words with "EI" combinations, think "I before E except after C."

> Retention can be improved by deciding to remember, structuring incoming information to form relationships, and reviewing.

The world memory champion uses a device called *loci*. To remember the sequence of a pack of 52 playing cards, for example, he associates each card with a character. The queen of diamonds he might imagine covered head to foot in diamonds. Then he places each character in a location (hence, *loci*), say around the local golf course, which has 52 stages.[21]

One of the most reliable ways to improve retention is to take notes of the important ideas to be remembered. Rewriting within ten minutes of completing listening improves your notes and takes advantage of peak recall time, which immediately follows listening.

> To further improve retention, take notes and rewrite them immediately after listening.

The final step in improving retention is reviewing your notes, repeating your acronym, or saying your rhyme to move the targeted information into long-term memory. Frequent reviews help strengthen your memory connections.

## IMPROVING WORKPLACE LISTENING

Listening on the job is more difficult than listening in university or college classes where experienced professors present well-organized lectures and repeat important points. Workplace listening is more challenging because information is often exchanged casually. It may be disorganized, unclear, and cluttered with extraneous

**FIGURE 3.4** The Forgetting Curve

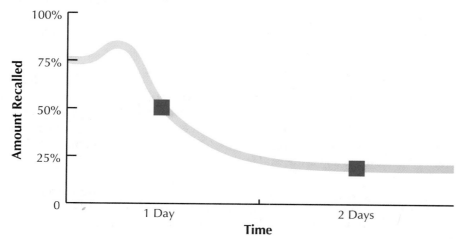

facts. Moreover, your coworkers are usually friends. Because they are familiar with one another, they may not be as polite and respectful as they are with strangers. Friends tend to interrupt, jump to conclusions, and take each other for granted.

Listening in groups or listening to nonnative speakers further complicates the listening process. In groups, more than one person talks at once, and topics change rapidly. Group members are monitoring both verbal and nonverbal messages to learn what relates to their group roles. Listening to nonnative speakers often creates special challenges. The accompanying Career Coach box offers suggestions for improving communication between native and nonnative speakers. You'll find more suggestions for communicating across cultures in Chapter 4.

Despite the complexities and challenges of workplace listening, good listeners on the job must remember that their goal is to listen carefully and to *understand* what is being said so that they can do their work well. The following recommendations can help you improve your workplace listening effectiveness.

*Control External and Internal Distractions.* Move to an area where you can hear without conflicting noises or conversations. Block out surrounding physical distractions. Internally, try to focus totally on the speaker. If other projects are on your mind, put them on the back burner temporarily. When you are emotionally upset, whether angry or extremely happy, it's a good idea to postpone any serious listening.

*Become Actively Involved.* Show that you are listening closely by leaning forward and maintaining eye contact with the speaker. Don't fidget or try to complete another task at the same time you are listening. Listen to more than the spoken words. How are they said? What implied meaning, reasoning, and feelings do you hear behind the spoken words? Does the speaker's body language (eye contact, posture, movements) support or contradict the main message?

*Separate Facts From Opinions.* Facts are truths known to exist; for example, *The Bay, Zellers, and Home Outfitters are all part of Hbc.* Opinions are statements of personal judgments or preferences; for example, *The Bay has a better selection of linens than Zellers.* Some opinions are easy to recognize because speakers preface them with statements such as *I think, It seems to me,* and *As far as I'm concerned.*[22] Often, however, listeners must evaluate assertions to decide their validity. Good listeners consider whether speakers are credible and speaking within their areas of competence. They don't automatically accept assertions as facts.

*Identify Important Facts.* Speakers on the job often intersperse critical information with casual conversation. Unrelated topics pop up—ball scores, a customer's weird request, a computer glitch, the boss's extravagant new sports utility van. Your task is to select what's important and register it mentally. What step is next in your project? Who does what? What is your role?

*Don't Interrupt.* While someone else has the floor, don't interrupt with a quick reply or opinion. And don't show nonverbal disagreement such as negative head shaking, rolling eyes, sarcastic snorting, or audible sighs. Good listeners let speakers have their say. Interruptions are not only impolite, but they also prevent you from hearing the speaker's complete thought. Listeners who interrupt with their opinions sidetrack discussions and cause hard feelings.

*Ask Clarifying Questions.* Good listeners wait for the proper moment and then ask questions that do not attack the speaker. Instead of saying, "But I don't understand how you can say that," a good listener seeks clarification with questions such as,

Workplace listening is challenging because information may be disorganized, unclear, and cluttered with extraneous facts.

You listen better when you control distractions, become actively involved, separate facts from opinions, and identify important facts.

You listen better when you don't interrupt, ask clarifying questions, paraphrase, capitalize on lag time, take notes, and observe gender differences.

## Listening to Nonnative Speakers in the Workplace

Many workplaces today involve interaction between native and nonnative English speakers. As immigration increases and as local businesses expand into global markets, the chances are that you will at times be listening to speakers for whom English is a second language. Although many speakers have studied English and comprehend it, they may have difficulty speaking it. Why? Vowels and consonants are pronounced differently. Learning the inflection and sentence patterns of English is difficult when they conflict with the speaker's native tongue. And most "errors" in pronunciation occur in meaningful patterns traced to their home languages.

Moreover, nonnative speakers are intimidated by the fluency of native speakers; therefore, they don't try to become fluent. They worry about using incorrect verb forms and tenses. They may be trying to translate thoughts from their own language word for word into the foreign language. Often, they spend so long thinking about how to express a thought that the conversation moves on. And many worry about being judged negatively and losing face. What can native speakers do to become better listeners when nonnatives speak?

- **Avoid negative judgment of accented speech.** Many nonnative speakers of English speak an articulate, insightful, and complex variety of English. Their speech may retain remnants of their native language. But don't assume that a nonnative speaker struggling with pronunciation is unintelligent. Instead, imagine how difficult it would be for you to learn that person's language.

- **Be patient.** North Americans are notoriously poor listeners. Strive to overcome the need to hurry a

conversation along. Give nonnative speakers time to express their thoughts.

- **Don't finish sentences.** Allow nonnative speakers to choose their words and complete their sentences without volunteering your help. You may find that they are saying something quite different from what you expected.

- **Don't correct grammar and pronunciation.** Although you are trying to "help" a nonnative speaker, it's better to focus on what's being expressed and forget about teaching English. As one company caller said, "If I could speak better English, I'd already be doing it."

- **Don't pretend to understand.** It's perfectly all right to tell a speaker that you're having a little difficulty understanding him or her.

- **Practise listening to many varieties of English.** Improving your skill at comprehending many accents as well as native dialects (for example, East Coast, Ottawa Valley, and mid-Western) can be a valuable skill in today's diverse and intercultural workplace.

### Career Application

In a class forum, discuss these questions. How do you think nonnative speakers feel when they must converse with native speakers in a work environment? For nonnative speakers, what is most frustrating in conversation? For native speakers, what is awkward or frustrating in talking with nonnative speakers? What embarrassing moments have you experienced as a result of mispronunciations or misunderstandings? What suggestions can native and nonnative speakers make for improving communication?

"Please help me understand by explaining more about . . . ." Because questions can put you in the driver's seat, think about them in advance. Use open questions (those without set answers) to draw out feelings, motivations, ideas, and suggestions. Use closed fact-finding questions to identify key factors in a discussion.[23] And, by the way, don't ask a question unless you are ready to be quiet and listen to the answer.

***Paraphrase to Increase Understanding.*** To make sure you understand a speaker, rephrase and summarize a message in your own words. Be objective and non-judgmental. Remember, your goal is to understand what the speaker has said—not to show how mindless the speaker's words sound when parroted. Remember, too, that other workplace listeners will also benefit from a clear summary of what was said.

Leaning forward and maintaining good eye contact tells the receiver you are listening actively.

**Capitalize on Lag Time.** While you are waiting for a speaker's next idea, use the time to review what the speaker is saying. Separate the central idea, key points, and details. Sometimes you may have to supply the organization. You can also use lag time to silently rephrase and summarize the speaker's message in your own words. Most important, keep your mind focused on the speaker and her or his ideas—not on all the other work waiting for you.

**Take Notes to Ensure Retention.** Don't trust your memory. A wise person once said that he'd rather have a short pencil than a long memory. If you have a hallway conversation with a colleague and don't have a pencil handy, make a mental note of the important items. Then write them down as soon as possible. Even with seemingly easily remembered facts or instructions, jot them down to ease your mind and also to be sure you understand them correctly. Two weeks later you'll be glad that you did. Be sure you have a good place to store notes of various projects, such as file folders, notebooks, or computer files.

**Be Aware of Gender Differences.** Men tend to listen for facts, whereas women tend to perceive listening as an opportunity to connect with the other person on a personal level.[24] Men tend to use interrupting behaviour to control conversations, while women generally interrupt to communicate assent, to elaborate on an idea of another group member, or to participate in the topic of conversation.[25] Women listeners tend to be attentive, provide steady eye contact, remain stationary, and nod their heads.[26] Male listeners are less attentive, provide sporadic eye contact, and move around. Being aware of these tendencies will make you a more sensitive and knowledgeable listener. To learn more about gender differences in communication, see the Career Coach box in Chapter 4.

## CHECKLIST FOR IMPROVING LISTENING

✓ **Stop talking.** Accept the role of listener by concentrating on the speaker's words, not on what your response will be.

✓ **Work hard at listening.** Become actively involved; expect to learn something.

✓ **Block out competing thoughts.** Concentrate on the message. Don't allow yourself to daydream during lag time.

✓ **Control the listening environment.** Move to a quiet area where you won't be interrupted by telephone calls or visitors. Check to be certain that listeners can hear speakers.

✓ **Maintain an open mind.** Know your biases and try to correct for them. Be tolerant of less-abled and different-looking speakers. Provide verbal and nonverbal feedback. Encourage the speaker with comments such as "Yes," "I see," "OK," and "Uh huh," and ask polite questions. Look alert by leaning forward.

✓ **Paraphrase the speaker's ideas.** Silently repeat the message in your own words, sort out the main points, and identify supporting details. In conversation sum up the main points to confirm what was said.

✓ **Listen between the lines.** Observe nonverbal cues and interpret the feelings of the speaker: What is really being said?

✓ **Distinguish between facts and opinions.** Know the difference between factual statements and opinions stated as assertions.

✓ **Capitalize on lag time.** Use spare moments to organize, review, anticipate, challenge, and weigh the evidence.

✓ **Use memory devices.** If the information is important, develop acronyms, links, or rhymes to help you remember.

✓ **Take selective notes.** If you are hearing instructions or important data, record the major points; then, revise your notes immediately or verify them with the speaker.

## COMMUNICATING THROUGH NONVERBAL MESSAGES

Understanding messages often involves more than merely listening to spoken words. Nonverbal clues also carry powerful meanings. Nonverbal communication includes all unwritten and unspoken messages, both intentional and unintentional. Eye contact, facial expression, body movements, space, time, distance, appearance—all of these nonverbal clues influence the way a message is interpreted, or decoded, by the receiver. Many of the nonverbal messages that we send are used intentionally to accompany spoken words. When Stacy pounds her desk and shouts "This computer just crashed again!" we interpret the loudness of her voice and the act of slamming her fist as intentional emphasis of her words. But people can also communicate nonverbally even when they don't intend to. And not all messages accompany words. When Jeff hangs on to the podium and barely looks at the audience, he sends a nonverbal message of fear and lack of confidence.

> Nonverbal communication includes all unwritten and unspoken messages, both intentional and unintentional.

Because nonverbal communication can be an important tool for you to use and control in the workplace, you need to learn more about its functions and forms.

## Functions of Nonverbal Communication

Nonverbal communication functions in at least five ways to help convey meaning. As you become more aware of the following functions of nonverbal communication, you will be better able to use these silent codes to your advantage in the workplace.

> Nonverbal cues function in five ways: to complement and illustrate, to reinforce and accentuate, to replace and substitute, to control and regulate, and to contradict.

- **To complement and illustrate.** Nonverbal messages can amplify, modify, or provide details for a verbal message. For example, in describing the size of a cell phone, a speaker holds his fingers apart 12 cm. In pumping up sales reps, the manager jams his fist into the opposite hand to indicate the strong effort required.

- **To reinforce and accentuate.** Skilled speakers raise their voices to convey important ideas, but they whisper to suggest secrecy. A grimace forecasts painful news, while a big smile intensifies good news. A neat, well-equipped office reinforces a message of professionalism.

# *Minacs Worldwide Inc. Revisited*

Minacs employs over 500 people at its state-of-the-art customer contact centre in Oshawa, Ontario. This particular centre is responsible for responding to enrolment requests from dealers and customers from the United States. In the near future, OnStar plans to expand full service delivery through Minacs to its Canadian subscribers, who will benefit from the proximity, localized geographic knowledge, and bilingual (English and French) language skills of the Minacs agents.

Training is a critical component for all employees, and 5 percent of gross revenue is devoted to training. Customer service representatives (CSRs), for example, can expect five weeks of full-time, paid training before they begin their new jobs.

This extensive training prepares CSRs to respond effectively and thoroughly to a wide variety of customer issues, using a computerized information system. CSRs may be taking orders, explaining available services, providing information, or dealing with concerns. Many responses are scripted to ensure consistency with all customers, and often calls will be forwarded to in-company or client third parties for handling. CSRs may also be required to follow up with clients through outbound calling to deliver scripted sales dialogue and to engage in problem solving.

CSRs are also trained to evaluate the need for call escalation and are authorized to forward problem-type calls to a specialist or team leader for resolution or more detailed information. They may also contact internal specialists to obtain clarification or further detail before responding to some questions. Finally, they must be prepared to read and research relevant material and resources to stay current in programs.[27]

## CRITICAL THINKING

- What listening skills are important in establishing rapport with customers?
- Why are CSRs given scripts to follow?
- How might you respond to a customer who is frustrated and angry? What listening skills are appropriate?

**www.minacs.com**

---

- **To replace and substitute.** Many gestures substitute for words: nodding your head for "yes," giving a "V" for victory, making a thumbs-up sign for approval, and shrugging your shoulders for "I don't know" or "I don't care." In fact, a complex set of gestures totally replaces spoken words in sign language.

- **To control and regulate.** Nonverbal messages are important regulators in conversation. Shifts in eye contact, slight head movements, changes in posture, raising of eyebrows, nodding of the head, and voice inflection—all of these cues tell speakers when to continue, to repeat, to elaborate, to hurry up, or to finish.

- **To contradict.** To be sarcastic, a speaker might hold his nose while stating that your new perfume is wonderful. In the workplace, individuals may send contradictory messages with words or actions. The boss, for example, says he wants to promote Kevin, but he fails to submit the necessary recommendation. Or, when your boss asks you at the last minute to work overtime, you may say yes, but then sigh heavily, run your fingers through your hair, and begin massaging your temples as if you have a headache.

In the workplace people may not be aware that they are sending contradictory messages. Researchers have found that when verbal and nonverbal messages contradict each other, listeners tend to believe and act on the nonverbal message. How would you interpret the following?

- Allison assures her boss that she has enough time to complete her assigned research, but she misses two deadlines.

- Stewart protests that he's not really angry but slams the door when he leaves a group meeting.

- Kyoko claims she's not nervous about a team presentation, but her brow is furrowed and she perspires profusely.

The nonverbal messages in these situations speak louder than the words uttered. In one experiment speakers delivered a positive message but averted their eyes as they spoke. Listeners perceived the overall message to be negative. Moreover, listeners thought that gaze aversion suggested nonaffection, superficiality, lack of trust, and nonreceptivity.[28] The lesson to be learned here is that effective communicators must make sure that all their nonverbal messages reinforce their spoken words and their professional goals. As one expert advises, "Either say what you mean, or act out what you mean. But don't make the messages contradictory."[29] To make sure that you're on the right track to nonverbal communication competency, let's look more carefully at the specific forms of nonverbal communication.

## Forms of Nonverbal Communication

Instead of conveying meaning with words, nonverbal messages carry their meaning in a number of different forms ranging from facial expressions to body language and even clothes. Each of us sends and receives thousands of nonverbal messages daily in our business and personal lives. Although the following discussion covers all forms of nonverbal communication, we will be especially concerned with workplace applications. As you learn about the messages sent by eye contact, facial expressions, posture, and gestures, as well as the use of time, space, territory, and appearance—think about how you can use these nonverbal cues positively in your career.

During his election campaign, Mexican President Vicente Fox flashed a "V" for victory, a nonverbal gesture symbolizing triumph and winning. But gestures have different meanings in different cultures.

*Eye Contact.* The eyes have been called the "windows to the soul." Even if communicators can't look directly into the soul, they consider the eyes to be the most accurate predictor of a speaker's true feelings and attitudes. Most of us cannot look another person straight in the eyes and lie. As a result, we tend to believe people who look directly at us. We have less confidence in and actually distrust those who cannot maintain eye contact. Sustained eye contact suggests trust and admiration; brief eye contact signifies fear or stress. Prolonged eye contact, however, can be intrusive and intimidating. One successful CEO says that he can tell from people's eyes whether they are focused, receptive, or distant. He also notes the frequency of eye blinks when judging a person's honesty.[30]

Good eye contact enables the message sender to determine whether a receiver is paying attention, showing respect, responding favourably, or feeling distress. From the receiver's perspective, good eye contact reveals the speaker's sincerity, confidence, and truthfulness. Since eye contact is a learned skill, however, you must be respectful of people who do not maintain it. You must also remember that nonverbal cues, including eye contact, have different meanings in various cultures. You'll learn more about the cultural influence of nonverbal cues in Chapter 4.

5

**FIGURE 3.5** Olympic Games staff working with international visitors were trained in what to say and how to gesture. This illustration shows several examples.

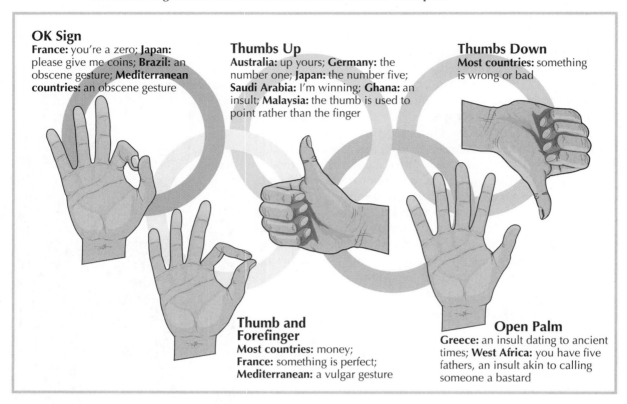

**OK Sign**
**France:** you're a zero; **Japan:** please give me coins; **Brazil:** an obscene gesture; **Mediterranean countries:** an obscene gesture

**Thumbs Up**
**Australia:** up yours; **Germany:** the number one; **Japan:** the number five; **Saudi Arabia:** I'm winning; **Ghana:** an insult; **Malaysia:** the thumb is used to point rather than the finger

**Thumbs Down**
**Most countries:** something is wrong or bad

**Thumb and Forefinger**
**Most countries:** money; **France:** something is perfect; **Mediterranean:** a vulgar gesture

**Open Palm**
**Greece:** an insult dating to ancient times; **West Africa:** you have five fathers, an insult akin to calling someone a bastard

*Facial Expression.* The expression on a communicator's face can be almost as revealing of emotion as the eyes. Researchers estimate that the human face can display over 250 000 different expressions.[31] Although a few people can control these expressions and maintain a "poker face" when they want to hide their feelings, most of us display our emotions openly. Raising or lowering the eyebrows, squinting the eyes, swallowing nervously, clenching the jaw, smiling broadly—these voluntary and involuntary facial expressions supplement or entirely replace verbal messages. In the workplace, maintaining a pleasant expression with frequent smiles promotes harmony.

*Posture and Gestures.* An individual's general posture can convey anything from high status and self-confidence to shyness and submissiveness. Leaning toward a speaker suggests attraction and interest; pulling away or shrinking back denotes fear, distrust, anxiety, or disgust. Similarly, gestures can communicate entire thoughts via simple movements. But remember that these nonverbal cues may have vastly different meanings in different cultures. An individual who signals success by forming the thumb and forefinger into a circle would be in deep trouble in Germany or parts of South America. The harmless OK sign is actually an obscene gesture in those areas.[32] See Figure 3.5 for information provided to Olympic Games staff.

In the workplace a simple way to leave a good impression is to make sure your upper body is aligned with the person to whom you're talking. Former U.S. President Nixon was famous for talking to someone while his body was facing another direction, thus giving the impression that his heart wasn't in the conversation. Erect posture sends a message of confidence, competence, diligence, and

> Erect posture sends a message of confidence, competence, diligence, and strength.

strength. Gestures are also important, if used effectively. Using an upward palm gesture can help you immediately establish rapport, either across a meeting room or one on one. This trust-generating gesture shows that you are friendly without being too aggressive. Women are advised to avoid tilting their heads to the side when making an important point. This gesture diminishes the main thrust of the message.[33]

*Time.* How we structure and use time tells observers about our personality and attitudes. For example, when Maritza Samuelson, a banking executive, gives a visitor a prolonged interview, she signals her respect for, interest in, and approval of the visitor or the topic to be discussed. By sharing her valuable time, she sends a clear nonverbal message. Likewise, when David Ing twice arrives late for a meeting, it could mean that the meeting has low priority to David, that he is a self-centred person, or that he has little self-discipline. These are assumptions that typical North Americans might make. In other cultures and regions, though, punctuality is viewed differently.

**Being on time sends a positive nonverbal message in North American workplaces.**

In the workplace you can send positive nonverbal messages by being on time for meetings and appointments, staying on task during meetings, and giving ample time to appropriate projects and individuals.

*Space.* How we arrange things in the space around us tells something about ourselves and our objectives. Whether the space is a dorm room, an office, or a department, people reveal themselves in the design and grouping of furniture within that space. Generally, the more formal the arrangement, the more formal and closed the communication environment. An executive who seats visitors in a row of chairs across from his desk sends a message of aloofness and desire for separation. A team leader who arranges chairs informally in a circle rather than in straight rows or a rectangular pattern conveys her desire for a more open, egalitarian exchange of ideas. A manager who creates an open office space with few partitions separating workers' desks seeks to encourage an unrestricted flow of communication and work among areas.

**The way an office is arranged can send nonverbal messages about the openness of its occupant.**

*Territory.* Each of us has certain areas that we feel are our own territory, whether it's a specific spot or just the space around us. Your father may have a favourite chair in which he is most comfortable, a cook might not tolerate intruders in his or her kitchen, and veteran employees may feel that certain work areas and tools belong to them. We all maintain zones of privacy in which we feel comfortable. Figure 3.6 categorizes the

**FIGURE 3.6 Four Space Zones for Social Interaction**

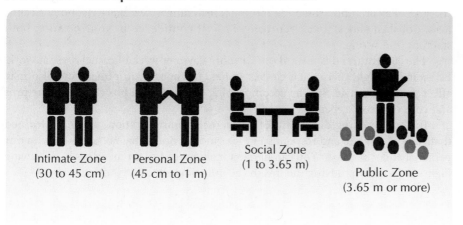

Intimate Zone (30 to 45 cm)

Personal Zone (45 cm to 1 m)

Social Zone (1 to 3.65 m)

Public Zone (3.65 m or more)

four zones of social interaction among North Americans, as formulated by anthropologist Edward T. Hall. Notice that North Americans are a bit standoffish; only intimate friends and family may stand closer than about 0.5 m. If someone violates that territory, we feel uncomfortable and defensive and may step back to reestablish our space. The distance between two people can convey different messages: a desire for intimacy, a lack of interest, or an attempt to increase or decrease domination. Police interrogators, for instance, have been taught that this violation of personal space can nonverbally intimidate a suspect and give the officer a psychological advantage.[34] In the workplace be aware of the territorial needs of others and don't invade their space.

**Your appearance and the appearance of your documents convey nonverbal messages.**

*Appearance of Business Documents.* The way a letter, memo, or report looks can have either a positive or a negative effect on the receiver. Envelopes through their postage, stationery, and printing can suggest routine, important, or junk mail. Letters and reports can look neat, professional, well organized, and attractive—or just the opposite. Sloppy, hurriedly written documents convey negative nonverbal messages regarding both the content and the sender. Among the worse offenders are e-mail messages.

Although they seem like conversation, e-mails are business documents that create a permanent record and often a bad impression. Sending an e-mail message full of errors conveys a damaging nonverbal message. It says that the writer doesn't care enough about this message to take the time to make it read well or look good. The sender immediately doubts the creditability of the sender. How much faith can you put in someone who can't spell, capitalize, or punctuate and won't make the effort to communicate clearly?

In succeeding chapters you'll learn how to create documents that send positive nonverbal messages through their appearance, format, organization, readability, and correctness.

*Appearance of People.* The way you look—your clothing, grooming, and posture—telegraphs an instant nonverbal message about you. Based on what they see, viewers make quick judgments about your status, credibility, personality, and potential. Business communicators who look the part are more likely to be successful in working with superiors, colleagues, and customers. Because appearance is such a powerful force in business, some aspiring professionals are turning for help to image consultants (who charge up to $500 an hour!).

What do image consultants say? They suggest investing in appropriate, professional-looking clothing and accessories; quality is more important than quantity. Avoid flashy garments, clunky jewellery, garish makeup, and overpowering colognes. Pay attention to good grooming, including a neat hairstyle, body cleanliness, polished shoes, and clean nails. Project confidence in your posture, both standing and sitting.

The current trend is toward one or more days per week of casual dress at work. Be aware, though, that casual clothes change the image you project and also may affect your work style. See the accompanying Career Coach box regarding the pros and cons of casual apparel.

In the preceding discussion of nonverbal communication, you have learned that each of us gives and responds to thousands of nonverbal messages daily in our personal and work lives. You can harness the power of silent messages by reviewing Figure 3.7 and by studying the tips in the following checklist (both on page 88).

# Casual Apparel in the Workplace

As you read in Chapter 1, the workplace is changing: heightened global competition, flattened management hierarchies, expanded team-based management, and innovative communication technologies have all affected today's workplace. But these are not the only areas of evolution.

Standards of dress are also shifting. The mid- to late-1990s saw many workers adopt a much more casual appearance. This more relaxed approach was due in part to the proliferation of high-tech and Internet companies that seemed to throw out many traditional business practices. In addition, many organizations not directly connected to the technology industry adopted casual dress policies in an attempt to improve employee morale and thus increase productivity.

There is strong evidence that some workers took casual dressing a step too far. Anne Sowden, president of a professional image-consulting firm, Here's Looking at You, asserts, "People have forgotten how important the way you dress is. People need to remember they are going to work. The way you dress really reflects the way people respond to you and your professionalism."[35]

So how should you dress for work? D-Code, a Toronto-based company specializing in gathering information on the behaviours, beliefs, and aspirations of the Information Age Generation (18- to 34-year-olds), states that there is a swing toward "dressing to incorporate more of the 'business' in business casual" and that "people who are conscious of their potential for advancement want to be perceived as the people in an office who are the most in control and together."[36] Although the trend may be to more business than casual, D-Code believes that it's still possible to incorporate comfort and personal expression into your business wardrobe.

Queen's University advises job-seekers that there are three general categories of workplace dress: business, business casual, and casual. Business dress is the traditional matched suit with white or plain-coloured shirt or blouse. Business casual is a much broader category—corporate business casual might be a jacket with dress pants or skirt while a more casual level might be a shirt or sweater with dress pants or skirt. Casual workplace dress includes casual pants and skirts with shirts (with or without a collar).[37]

## Advice from the Experts

The following suggestions, gleaned from surveys and articles about casual dress trends in the workplace, can help future and current employees avoid casual dress blunders.

- For job interviews, dress conservatively or call ahead to ask the interviewer or the receptionist what is appropriate.

- Find out what your company allows. Ask whether a dress-down policy is available. Observe what others are wearing on casual dress days.

- If your company has no casual dress policy, volunteer to work with management to develop relevant guidelines, including illustrations of suitable casual attire.

- One expert advises that you "show respect for yourself and management" by avoiding jeans, shorts, cut-offs, sleeveless or tank-top shirts or dresses, halter tops, spandex, sheer clothes, exposed bra straps, and bare midriffs.[38]

- When meeting customers, dress as well as or better than they do. Again, this is a sign of professional respect.

- Dress for the job you want rather than the job you have.

- Above all, make sure that your clothes fit well, are well maintained, and suit you in colour and style.

## Career Application

Assume that you have been asked to draft a casual dress policy for your workplace. Working individually or as part of a team, consult at least three current sources of information, provide a rationale for this new policy, and prepare a list of casual dress guidelines. Look for information beyond that presented here.

**FIGURE 3.7** Sending Positive Nonverbal Signals in the Workplace

| | |
|---|---|
| Eye contact | Maintain direct but not prolonged eye contact. |
| Facial expression | Express warmth with frequent smiles. |
| Posture | Convey self-confidence with erect stance. |
| Gestures | Suggest accessibility with open-palm gestures. |
| Time | Be on time, use time judiciously. |
| Space | Maintain neat, functional work area. |
| Territory | Use closeness to show warmth and to reduce status differences. |
| Business documents | Produce careful, neat, professional, well-organized messages. |
| Appearance | Be well groomed, neat, and appropriately dressed |

## CHECKLIST OF TECHNIQUES FOR IMPROVING NONVERBAL COMMUNICATION SKILLS IN THE WORKPLACE

✓ **Establish and maintain eye contact.** Remember that in North America appropriate eye contact signals interest, attentiveness, strength, and credibility.

✓ **Use posture to show interest.** Encourage communication interaction by leaning forward, sitting or standing erect, and looking alert.

✓ **Reduce or eliminate physical barriers.** Move out from behind a desk or lectern; shorten lines of communication; arrange meeting chairs in a circle.

✓ **Improve your decoding skills.** Watch facial expressions and body language to understand the complete verbal and nonverbal message being communicated.

✓ **Probe for more information.** When you perceive nonverbal cues that contradict verbal meanings, politely seek additional clues (*I'm not sure I understand, Please tell me more about . . .*, or *Do you mean that . . .*).

✓ **Avoid assigning nonverbal meanings out of context.** Make nonverbal assessments only when you understand a situation or a culture.

✓ **Associate with people from diverse cultures.** Learn about other cultures to widen your knowledge and tolerance of intercultural nonverbal messages.

✓ **Appreciate the power of appearance.** Keep in mind that the appearance of your business documents, your business space, and yourself send immediate positive or negative messages to receivers.

✓ **Observe yourself on videotape.** Ensure that your verbal and nonverbal messages are in sync by taping and evaluating yourself making a presentation.

## Applying Your Skills at Minacs Worldwide Inc.

One of the areas in which Minacs specializes is the automotive industry. "With over 20 years of providing services to the automotive sector, Minacs has a deep understanding of the unique customer relationship needs of this highly competitive industry. As a result, we have the ability to deploy timely, innovative business solutions that produce significant returns on customer loyalty and retention," says Elaine Minacs.[39]

In February 2003, Minacs announced that it had been selected by American Honda Motor Company Inc. to manage its Service Reminder Program. Minacs provides all marketing support services including program management, information systems, creative, and inbound and outbound contact centres, as well as printing and fulfillment services.

This program provides Honda customers with regular service reminders using a variety of media, including e-mail, fax, and phone. In addition, the Minacs Dealer Services Group is responsible for maintaining a dealer support centre to manage inquiries and work with dealers to customize their program to meet their customers' needs. Over 900 dealers throughout North America are currently enrolled in the Service Reminder Program. Staff at the Minacs facilities in Milwaukee, Wisconsin; Farmington Hills, Michigan; and Costa Mesa, California, will handle approximately 1 million mailings on a monthly basis.

### Your Task

Based on what you learned in this and previous chapters, how can the pointers on listening and nonverbal communication be converted to training for e-mail or Web contacts? Prepare a memo (or e-mail message) describing five or more suggestions for providing effective online customer service. Remember that you will be writing, rather than speaking, to customers.

**www.minacs.com**

---

 **Enlist friends and family.** Ask them to monitor your conscious and unconscious body movements and gestures to help you become a more effective communicator.

## SUMMARY OF LEARNING OBJECTIVES

*1* **Explain the importance of listening in the workplace and describe three types of workplace listening.** A large part of the communication process involves listening. Good listeners advance more rapidly in their careers, and listening skills are increasingly important in our economy's emphasis on customer service. Workers spend 30 to 45 percent of their communication time listening, while executives spend 60 to 70 percent. However, most of us listen at only 25 percent efficiency. Workplace listening involves listening to superiors, to employees, and to customers. When listening to superiors, take selective notes, don't interrupt, ask pertinent questions, and paraphrase what you hear. When listening to employees, managers should avoid being judgmental, confirm the message being sent, and affirm the relationship. When listening to customers, employees should defer judgment, pay attention to content rather than form, listen completely, control emotions, give affirming statements, and invite additional comments.

**2** **Discuss the listening process and its barriers.** The listening process involves (a) perception of sounds, (b) interpretation of those sounds, (c) evaluation of meaning, and (d) action, which might involve a physical response or storage of the message in memory for future use. Mental barriers to listening include inattention, prejudgments, differing frames of reference, closed-mindedness, and pseudolistening. Physical and other barriers include hearing impairment, noisy surroundings, speaker's appearance, speaker's mannerisms, and lag time. Retention can be improved by developing a positive mindset, structuring the incoming information to form relationships, and reviewing.

**3** **Enumerate ten techniques for improving workplace listening.** Listeners can improve their skills by controlling external and internal distractions, becoming actively involved, separating facts from opinions, identifying important facts, refraining from interrupting, asking clarifying questions, paraphrasing, taking advantage of lag time, taking notes to ensure retention, and being aware of gender differences.

**4** **Define nonverbal communication and explain its functions.** Nonverbal communication includes all unwritten and unspoken messages, both intentional and unintentional. Its primary functions are to complement and illustrate, to reinforce and accentuate, to replace and substitute, to control and regulate, and to contradict. When verbal and nonverbal messages contradict each other, listeners tend to believe the nonverbal message.

**5** **Describe the forms of nonverbal communication and how they can be used positively in your career.** Nonverbal communication takes many forms including eye contact, facial expressions, posture and gestures, as well as the use of time, space, and territory. Appearance of business documents and of people also sends silent messages. Eye contact should be direct but not prolonged; facial expression should express warmth with frequent smiles. Posture should convey self-confidence, and gestures should suggest accessibility. Being on time and maintaining neat, functional work areas send positive nonverbal messages. Use closeness to show warmth and to reduce status differences. Strive for neat, professional, well-organized business messages, and be well groomed, neat, and appropriately dressed.

**6** **List specific techniques for improving nonverbal communication skills in the workplace.** To improve your nonverbal skills, establish and maintain eye contact, use posture to show interest, reduce or eliminate physical barriers, improve your decoding skills, probe for more information, avoid assigning nonverbal meanings out of context, associate with people from diverse cultures, appreciate the power of appearance, observe yourself on videotape, and enlist friends and family to monitor your conscious and unconscious body movements and gestures.

# CHAPTER REVIEW

1. What percent of workers' communication time is spent listening? What percent of executives' time is spent listening? Why do you think the figures are so different? (Obj. 1)

2. How can workers improve their listening when superiors are giving instructions, assignments, and explanations? (Obj. 1)

3. How can companies and managers do a better job of listening to employees? (Obj. 1)

4. How can employees do a better job of listening to customers? (Obj. 1)

5. Describe the four elements in the listening process. (Obj. 2).

6. How can listeners improve retention? (Obj. 2)

7. What are ten techniques for improving workplace listening? Be prepared to explain each. (Obj. 3)

8. Define *nonverbal communication*. (Obj. 4)

9. List five functions of nonverbal communication. Give an original example of each. (Obj. 4)

10. When verbal and nonverbal messages disagree, which message does the receiver consider more truthful? Give an example. (Obj. 4)

11. North Americans are said to be a little "standoffish." What does this mean? (Obj. 5)

12. How does good eye contact help a speaker/sender? How does it benefit a listener/receiver? (Obj. 5)

13. How can the use of space send nonverbal messages? (Obj. 5)

14. What nonverbal messages are sent by organizations with casual dress codes? (Obj. 5)

15. List ten techniques for improving nonverbal communication skills in the workplace. (Obj. 6)

# CRITICAL THINKING

1. How are listening skills important to employees, supervisors, and executives? Who should have the best listening skills? (Obj. 1)

2. North Americans are said to have the world's worst listening skills.[40] Why do you think this reputation has been earned? (Objs. 1–3)

3. Why is it acceptable behaviour for two 127-kg professional football players to slap each other on the rear end during a game but inappropriate during a business meeting? What principle of nonverbal communication can you extract from this example? (Obj. 4)

4. What arguments could you give for or against the idea that body language is a science with principles that can be interpreted accurately by specialists? (Obj. 4)

5. **Ethical Issue:** Tim, a member of your workplace team, talks too much, hogs the limelight, and frequently strays from the target topic. In an important meeting he announces, "Hey, I want you all to listen up. I've got this cool new idea, and you're gonna love it!" Is it unethical for you to tune Tim out based on your past experience with his digressions? You want to sigh deeply and shout "Not again!" You're inclined to slump in your chair, slam your pencil down on the table, and stop taking notes. What is your ethical responsibility? What nonverbal message should you send?

# ACTIVITIES

## 3.1 Bad Listening Habits (Objs. 1–3)

Focusing on your own listening can reveal a number of bad habits.
**Your Task.** Concentrate for three days on your listening habits in class and on the job. What bad habits do you detect? Be prepared to discuss five bad habits and specific ways you could improve your listening skills. Your instructor may ask you to report your analysis in a memo.

## 3.2 Listening and Retention (Objs. 2 and 3)

After studying the suggestions in this chapter for improving listening, you should be able to conduct a before-and-after study.
**Your Task.** Record and listen to a 30-minute segment of TV news using your normal listening habits. When you finish, make a list of the major items you remember, recording names, places, and figures. A day later watch the same 30-minute segment but put to use the good-listening tips in this chapter, including taking selective notes and possibly using memory devices. When the segment is completed, make a list of the major items you remember. Which experience provided more information? What made a major difference for you?

## 3.3 Listening Check (Objs. 1–3)

You can sharpen your listening habits with practice.
**Your Task.** Your instructor will read a short passage (say, 200 words) about a relevant topic from a business magazine, newspaper, or journal. When finished, your instructor will ask two short questions: (a) What is the thesis of the passage? and (b) What is one piece of evidence that supports the thesis?

## 3.4 How Good Are Your Listening Skills? Self-Checked Rating Quiz (Objs. 1–3)

WEB

You can learn whether you are a poor, fair, good, or excellent listener by completing a 16-point quiz.

**Your Task.** Take the listening quiz at the Los Angeles Pierce College Web site. At this book's Student Resources Web site <**www.businesscommunication-4th.nelson.com**>, click on "Web Links by Chapter," and go to "Chapter 3" and "Listening Quiz." What two listening behaviours do you think you need to work on the most?

## 3.5 Listening to Customers (Objs. 1–3)

Play the part of a training consultant hired to help improve customer service at a high-volume travel agency. During a get-acquainted training session, you hear the following comments from current customer service representatives.

**Your Task.** Based on what you learned in this chapter (and especially Figure 3.2), would you characterize the speaker as a trained or untrained listener, and what advice would you give to improve listening skills?

a. "It's pretty hard to take seriously a customer whose accent and grammar are so bad that you know he could never afford the trip to Tahiti that he's asking about."

b. "You know what I really hate are those people who want to complain about a trip but can't stick to the facts. They want to tell you each little detail."

c. "My biggest gripe is those people who distort and exaggerate what happened. I nail them on every point that I know can't be true."

d. "When I have a customer who wants to tell a long story, I cut her off and get the conversation under control with my questions."

e. "I think the best way to handle unhappy customers is silence. I try not to encourage them."

f. "When I have an upset customer, I try to listen carefully and occasionally give affirming comments."

g. "You know all the forms we have to fill out? The best time to do that is while you're working with customers. I save a lot of time that way."

h. "When someone gets snippy with me, I come right back with more of the same. Works every time."

i. "I don't waste my time with verbose customers. After the first few words, I can always tell what they want."

## 3.6 Listening to Nonnative Speakers (Objs. 1–3)

In our increasingly multicultural workplace and global economy, you will probably have occasion to listen to nonnative speakers. To improve your skills and widen your perspective, your instructor will present a video, audio tape, or person speaking a nonnative variety of English (preferably on a topic with "real" content). You should have a copy of the pronunciation guide from a postsecondary-level dictionary showing how vowels and consonants are pronounced in standard English.

**Your Task.** As you listen to the presentation, focus on any differences in the pronunciation of vowels and consonants. Study your chart. Then list the differences and similarities between the pronunciation you heard and that on your dictionary chart. Do you hear any patterns, such as the substitution of *b*'s for *p*'s, *v*'s for *w*'s, and *r*'s for *l*'s? If you recognize a pattern, how can that help you improve your listening comprehension? Also summarize the content of the presentation. Did any misunderstandings result from mispronunciation? Submit your written observations to your instructor or discuss them in class.

## 3.7 Bias-free Listening and Reporting (Objs. 1–3)

One of the most important listening techniques you can learn is bias-free reporting. This involves paraphrasing accurately and without bias what a speaker has said. This skill is especially important during disagreements or discussion of controversial topics.

**Your Task.** Throughout this course you will be asked to discuss controversial issues related to ethics, cross-culture, technology, and other topics. You will probably also be listening to the presentations of fellow students. Your instructor may ask you to develop your bias-free listening skills by summarizing and restating key points without critiquing what was said. Your task will be to offer a bias-free, fair report of what was said in terms that the speaker accepts.

## 3.8 Finding Relevant Listening Advice (Objs. 1–3)

INFOTRAC

Your manager, Bryan Evans, has been asked to be part of a panel discussion at a management conference. The topic is "Workplace Communication Challenges," and his area of expertise is listening. He asks you to help him prepare for the discussion by doing some research.

**Your Task.** Using an InfoTrac subject search, locate at least three articles with suggestions for improving listening skills. The articles should contain information that would be helpful in the workplace. Use full-text articles, not abstracts. In a memo to Bryan Evans, present a two- to three-sentence summary explaining why each article is helpful. Include the author's name, publication, date of publication, and page number.

## 3.9 Eavesdropping on Customers (Objs. 1–3)

**E-MAIL**

Some consultants recommend that CEOs and even board members regularly visit online chat rooms to listen to customers who might be praising or badmouthing their products.

**Your Task.** Write an e-mail message to your instructor that summarizes four ways in which businesses benefit from listening to their customers.

## 3.10 Silent Messages (Objs. 4–6)

We all send nonverbal messages, and many are unconscious.

**Your Task.** Analyze the kinds of silent messages you send your instructor, your classmates, and your employer. How do you send these messages? What do they mean? What functions do they serve? What forms do they take? Be prepared to discuss them in small groups or in a memo to your instructor.

## 3.11 Document Appearance (Objs. 5 and 6)

How does the appearance of a document send a nonverbal message?

**Your Task.** Select a business letter and envelope that you have received at home or work. Analyze the appearance and nonverbal message the letter and envelope send. Consider the amount of postage, method of delivery, correctness of address, kind of stationery, typeface(s), format, and neatness. What assumptions did you make when you saw the envelope? How about the letter itself?

## 3.12 Surveying Gender Differences (Objs. 5 and 6)

Some researchers in the field of nonverbal communication report that women are better than men at accurately interpreting nonverbal signals.[41]

**Your Task.** Conduct a class survey. On a scale of 1 (low) to 5 (high), how would you rank men in general on their ability to interpret the meaning of eye, voice, face, and body signals? Then rank women in general. Tabulate the class votes. Why do you think gender differences exist in the decoding of nonverbal signals?

## 3.13 Body Language (Objs. 5 and 6)

What attitudes do the following body movements suggest to you? Do these movements always mean the same thing? What part does context play in your interpretations?

a. Whistling, wringing hands
b. Bowed posture, twiddling thumbs
c. Steepled hands, sprawling position
d. Rubbing hand through hair
e. Open hands, unbuttoned coat
f. Wringing hands, tugging ears

## 3.14 Nonverbal Communication: Universal Sign for "I Goofed" (Objs. 4–6)

**CRITICAL THINKING       TEAM**

In an effort to promote tranquillity on the highways and reduce road rage, motorists submitted the following suggestions. They were sent to a newspaper columnist who asked for a universal nonverbal signal admitting that a driver "goofed."[42]

**Your Task.** In small groups consider the pros and cons for each of the following gestures intended as an apology when a driver makes a mistake. Why would some fail?

a. Lower your head slightly and bonk yourself on the forehead with the side of your closed fist. The message is clear: "I'm stupid. I shouldn't have done that."
b. Make a temple with your hands, as if you were praying.
c. Move the index finger of your right hand back and forth across your neck—as if you are cutting your throat.
d. Flash the well-known peace sign. Hold up the index and middle fingers of one hand, making a V, as in Victory.
e. Place the flat of your hands against your cheeks, as children do when they've made a mistake.
f. Clasp your hand over your mouth, raise your brows, and shrug your shoulders.
g. Use your knuckles to knock on the side of your head. Translation: "Oops! Engage brain."
h. Place your right hand high on your chest and pat a few times, like a basketball player who drops a pass or a football player who makes a bad throw. This says, "I'll take the blame."
i. Place your right fist over the middle of your chest and move it in a circular motion. This is universal sign language for "I'm sorry."
j. Open your window and tap the top of your car roof with your hand.
k. Smile and raise both arms, palms outward, which is a universal gesture for surrender or forgiveness.
l. Use the military salute, which is simple and shows respect.
m. Flash your biggest smile, point at yourself with your right thumb and move your head from left to right, as if to say, "I can't believe I did that."

## 3.15 Verbal vs. Nonverbal Signals (Objs. 4–6)

To show the power of nonverbal cues, the president of a large East Coast consulting company uses the following demonstration with new employees. Raising his right hand, he touches his pointer finger to his thumb to form a circle. Then he asks new employees in the session to do likewise. When everyone has a finger-thumb circle formed, the president tells them to touch that circle to their *chin*. But as he says this, he touches is own finger-thumb circle to his *cheek*. What happens? You guessed it! About 80 percent of the group follow what they see the president do rather than following what they hear.[43]

**Your Task.** Try this same demonstration with several of your friends, family members, or work colleagues. Which is more effective—verbal or nonverbal signals? What conclusion could you draw from this demonstration? Do you think that nonverbal signals are always more meaningful than verbal ones? What other factors in the communication process might determine whether verbal or nonverbal signals were more important?

## 3.16 Nonverbal Signals Sent by Business Casual Dress (Objs. 5 and 6)

**TEAM**

Although many employers are beginning to allow casual dress, not all employers and customers are happy with the results. To learn more about the implementation, acceptance, and effects of casual dress programs, select one of the following activities.

**Your Task.**

a. In teams, gather information from human resources directors to determine which companies allow business casual dress, how often, and under what specific

conditions. The information may be collected by personal interviews, by e-mail, or by telephone. You can learn how to conduct interviews by visiting this book's Student Resources Web site. Click "Web Links by Chapter," "Chapter 3," and "Conducting Successful Interviews." Pay special attention to the checklist for conducting interviews.

b. In teams, conduct inquiring-reporter interviews. Ask individuals in the community how they react to casual dress in the workplace. Develop a set of standard interview questions.

c. In teams, visit local businesses on both business casual days and on traditional business dress days. Compare and contrast the effects of different business dress standards on such factors as the projected image of the company, the nature of the interactions with customers and with fellow employees, the morale of employees, and the productivity of employees. What generalizations can be drawn from your findings?

## 3.17 Role-Playing Business Casual Dress-Related Guidance (Objs. 5 and 6)

Supervisors in the workplace must occasionally deliver dress-related guidance to workers who may have dressed inappropriately for work. The following situations, written by Dr. James Calvert Scott, provide excellent opportunities for you to develop skills in applying diplomatic, positive, and nondiscriminatory feedback in realistic workplace contexts.[44]

**Your Task.** Volunteer (or be assigned) the role of supervisor. Assume your organization has an existing business casual dress policy. Your job is to encourage an employee to comply with the dress code in the following situations:

a. A 35-year-old male systems analyst is working in his glass-walled private office wearing a T-shirt that has an obscene slogan printed on the back.

b. A 21-year-old clerk working in an open-office area is wearing a tight-fitting cropped top and hip-hugger pants that expose her pierced navel.

c. A 17-year-old high school marketing intern is wearing low-riding baggy pants that expose the top three inches of his underwear as he works in the public area assigned to the marketing division.

d. A 43-year-old custodian is wearing loose-fitting sandals as he tries to move a 250-L drum of carpet-cleaning solution from the loading dock to his supply room.

e. A 54-year-old obese female customer service representative who always wears tight-fitting pantsuits and frequently works with offsite clients in their offices shakes uncontrollably every time she moves, causing those around her to smirk and chuckle behind her back—and occasionally to her face.

## 3.18 Backlash Against Business Casual Dress (Objs. 5 and 6)

**INFOTRAC**

Not all businesses are jumping on the casual dress bandwagon. In fact, one study reports a 10 percent drop in the number of companies allowing casual dress.

**Your Task.** Using InfoTrac, conduct a keyword search for "business casual dress." Find Eva Kaplan-Leiserson's article "Back-to-Business Attire," *Training & Development*, November 2000, Article No. A67590797.

**a.** According to the author, what is causing the decline in casual dress in the workplace?

**b.** Do you agree with the statement that "people think you're smarter when you're well dressed, and they think you come from a high socioeconomic class"? Why or why not?

**c.** What is "Dress Up Thursday"?

## 3.19 Defining "Business Casual" (Objs. 5 and 6)

**WEB** **TEAM**

Although many business organizations are adopting business casual dress, most people cannot define the term. Your boss asks your internship team to use the Web to find out exactly what "business casual" means.

**Your Task.** Using a good search engine, such as <**www.google.ca**>, search the Web for "business casual dress code." A few Web sites actually try to define the term and give examples of appropriate clothing. Visit several sites and decide whether they are reliable enough to use as sources of accurate information. Print several relevant pages. Get together with your team and compare notes. Then write a memo to your boss explaining what men and women should and shouldn't wear on business casual days.

## C.L.U.E. REVIEW 3

On a separate sheet edit the following sentences to correct faults in grammar, punctuation, numbers, spelling, proofreading, and word use.

1. Although listening is a principle activity of employees experts say that many listen at only twenty-five percent effecency.

2. When listening too instructions be sure to take notes and review them immedeately.

3. In a poll of over nine thousand employees only 1/3 felt that their companys' sought their opinions and suggestion.

4. Well trained customer service representatives ask gentle probing questions to insure clear understanding.

5. The appearance and mannerisms of a speaker effects a listeners evaluation of a message.

6. Remembering important points involve 3 factors, (1) Deciding to remember, (2) Forming relationships, and (c) Reviewing.

7. A list of suggestions for paraphrasing a speakers ideas are found in an article titled Best Listening Habits which appeared in Fortune.

8. Skilled speakers raise there voices to convey important ideas, however they whisper to infer secrecy.

9. One successful Manager says that he can tell from peoples eyes whether they are focused receptive or distant.

10. On March 5th the President of the Company announced a casual dress policy consequently I must buy a hole new wardrobe.

# Chapter 4

## Communicating Across Cultures

## LEARNING OBJECTIVES

*1* Discuss three significant trends related to the increasing importance of intercultural communication.

*2* Define culture. Describe five significant characteristics of culture, and compare and contrast five key dimensions of culture.

*3* Explain the effects of ethnocentrism, tolerance, and patience in achieving intercultural sensitivity.

*4* Illustrate how to improve nonverbal and oral communication in multicultural environments.

*5* Illustrate how to improve written messages in multicultural environments.

*6* Discuss intercultural ethics, including ethics abroad, bribery, prevailing customs, and methods for coping.

*7* Explain the challenge of capitalizing on work force diversity, including its dividends and its divisiveness. List tips for improving harmony and communication among diverse workplace audiences.

# G.A.P Adventures

If your idea of a dream vacation involves groomed beaches, five-star hotels, and all-you-can-eat North American-style buffets, don't call G.A.P Adventures. Built on a philosophy of offering individuals the freedom of independent travel with the security of a group, Great Adventure People (G.A.P) offers adventure travel as a grassroots, low-impact activity that encourages participants to travel responsibly and use locally owned accommodation.

G.A.P Adventures offers trips to over 100 destinations through its 21 offices worldwide and annually serves over 10 000 travellers. President and CEO Bruce Poon Tip began his eco-tourism company in 1991 based on the belief that people should behave ethically at work and play. G.A.P Adventures has developed its own Operator Standards and holds itself responsible for ensuring that its actions are not environmentally or culturally harmful to the destinations it visits.

This commitment has paid off. In 1999, Poon Tip was named one of Canada's top 40 business leaders under the age of 40 and in 2002 was honoured with the regional Entrepreneur of the Year Award in Canada in the category of consumer services. The company itself has received the Ethics in Action Millennium Award in recognition of its high standards, has twice been a finalist as one of Canada's 50 best-managed companies, and has been on the *Profit* 100 list for a record five consecutive years. Today, 70 percent of the company's business is derived from exporting outside North America.

In October 2002, G.A.P purchased Vancouver-based Global Connections, making the adventure travel firm not only Canada's largest, but also the most significant, supplier of free independent traveller product to Latin America and a major airfare wholesaler. G.A.P is also launching two new affiliate companies: Real Traveller, which will become the exclusive provider for all foreign adventure travel operators previously handled by G.A.P, allowing G.A.P to remain focused on its niche market in Latin America; and Great Ocean Technologies, which customizes and markets FileMaker, the electronic reservation system that G.A.P has developed.

The typical Great Adventure Person doesn't have to be exceptionally athletic, but does need to have a spirit of adventure and the desire to experience a completely different world. G.A.P travellers are also culturally and environmentally sensitive and realize it's a privilege and not a right to visit any country. Perhaps most important is a lot of patience for the unexpected—delayed buses and broken-down vans might just be part of the package! Groups of no more than 12 travel together, giving the group the advantage of security and intimacy while still allowing flexibility and spontaneity.

Once you've arrived at your destination, you can expect to travel as the locals do—on a vintage bus, a train, a native canoe, a rickshaw, or even on elephant back. Accommodations include clean, simple hotels or perhaps a farm, a converted monastery, or a quaint bed and breakfast. Meals are provided if camping or in remote areas, but expect to savour the local cuisine if you are in towns or cities.

According to Bruce Poon Tip, "Most people say eco-tourism means 'leave only footprints.' I disagree with that. I think that we've got to get those 10 000 people off the cruise ships and into 200 small groups. I think that tourists can leave behind a huge impact."[1] This impact includes respecting local people and cultures, providing economic benefit to local communities, and protecting the environment.[2]

## CRITICAL THINKING
- What are some of the mistakes travellers make when they visit other countries?
- What consequences can occur if business travellers fail to observe local customs?
- What types of training could ensure success for business travellers?

www.gapadventures.ca

*1*

John Ralston Saul, vice-regal consort to Canada's Governor General Adrienne Clarkson, asserts that modern Canada is a success because it was founded on three pillars—aboriginal, anglophone, and francophone. The compromises that allowed the three communities to coexist and flourish seeped into the national psyche and explain why Canada, unlike many other nations, has largely avoided internal strife.[3] But the face of our nation has broadened far beyond these three pillars. The 2001 Canadian census data reports that over 130 different languages are spoken in Canada today, with about 40 of those being aboriginal tongues.[4] This diversity in our population is reflected in the workplace, mostly in large urban centres in Ontario, Quebec, British Columbia, and Alberta.

Not only can you expect to work in a multicultural work force in many parts of Canada, but with increases in globalization, you may also have the opportunity to represent your organization in other countries. Or you may simply want to take advantage of travel adventures like those offered by G.A.P Adventures.

The demographic differences of our population combined with the geographic differences of the land itself make it impossible to define a "Canadian culture." Instead, this chapter will help you understand the powerful effect that culture has on behaviour and will offer you some strategies for overcoming intercultural obstacles. Three significant trends—globalization of markets, technological advancements, and a multicultural work force—will be examined.

## Globalization of Markets

Doing business beyond our borders is now commonplace. Procter & Gamble is selling disposable diapers in Asia, Rubbermaid would like to see its plastic products in all European kitchens, and Unilever promotes its detergents around the world. Not only are market borders blurring, but acquisitions, mergers, and alliances are obscuring the nationality of many companies. Firestone is owned by Japan's Bridgestone, Sylvania is controlled by German lighting giant OSARM, and Chrysler has merged with Daimler-Benz, makers of Mercedes luxury cars. Two thirds of Colgate-Palmolive's employees work outside North America, and half of Sony's employees are not Japanese.

To be successful in this interdependent global village, North American companies are increasingly finding it necessary to adapt to other cultures. In China and Korea, Procter & Gamble learned to promote unisex white diapers. Although Americans preferred pink for girls and blue for boys, Korean and Chinese housewives balked at pink diapers. In a society where intense sexism favours boys, shoppers preferred white diapers that did not signal their child's gender.[5] In Europe, Rubbermaid met resistance when it offered products in neutral blues and almond, favourite North American colours. Southern Europeans prefer red, while customers in Holland want white.[6] To sell its laundry products in Europe, Unilever learned that Germans demand a product that's gentle on lakes and rivers. Spaniards wanted cheaper products that get shirts white and soft, and Greeks preferred small packages that were cheap and easy to carry home.[7] To sell ketchup in Japan, H. J. Heinz had to overcome a cultural resistance to sweet flavours. Thus, it offered Japanese homemakers cooking lessons instructing them how to use the sugary red sauce on omelettes, sausages, and pasta.[8] Domino's Pizza also catered to the Japanese by adding squid to its pizza toppings.[9]

What has caused this rush toward globalization of markets and blurring of national identities? One significant factor is the passage of favourable trade agreements. The General Agreement on Tariffs and Trade (GATT) promotes open trade globally, while the North American Free Trade Agreement (NAFTA) expands free trade among Canada, the United States, and Mexico. NAFTA created the largest and richest free-trade region on earth.[10] The opening of Eastern Europe and the shift away from communism in Russia have also fuelled the progress toward expanding world markets.

Another important factor in the new global market is the explosive growth of the middle class. Parts of the world formerly considered underdeveloped now boast robust middle classes. And these consumers crave everything from cola to cellular phones. But probably the most important factor in the rise of the global market is the development of new transportation and information technologies.

## Technological Advancements

Amazing new transportation and information technologies are major contributors to the development of our global interconnectivity. Supersonic planes now carry goods and passengers to other continents overnight. As a result, produce shoppers in Japan can choose from the finest apples, artichokes, avocados, and pears only hours after they were picked in California. North Americans enjoy bouquets of tulips, roses, and exotic lilies soon after harvesting in Holland and Colombia. Continent-hopping planes are so fast and reliable that most of the world is rapidly becoming an open market.

Doing business in the interdependent global village often means adapting to other cultures and observing local business practices. Distribution channels for Coca Cola in Prague, Czechoslovakia, are quite different from those in Canada.

Equally significant in creating the global village are incredible advancements in communication technologies. The Internet now permits instantaneous oral and written communication across time zones and continents. Managers in Moncton or Moose Jaw can use high-speed data systems to swap marketing plans instantly with their counterparts in Milan or Munich. Some software firms depend on programmers in India to solve intricate computer problems and return the solutions overnight via digital transmission. Fashion designers at Liz Claiborne can snap a digital photo of a garment and immediately transmit the image to manufacturers in Hong Kong and Djakarta, Indonesia.[11] They can even include a video clip to show a tricky alteration.

Moreover, the Web is emerging as a vital business tool. Companies depend on the Web to sell products, provide technical support, offer customer service, investigate the competition, and link directly to suppliers. Many multinational companies are now establishing country-specific Web sites, as discussed in the Tech Talk box on page 101 and illustrated by the Sony Music Germany site shown in Figure 4.1.

Internal web networks called *intranets* streamline business processes and improve access to critical company information. Through intranets employees have access to information that formerly had to be printed, such as a company phone book, training manuals, job postings, employee newsletters, sales figures, price lists, and even confidential reports, which can be password-protected. The Internet and the Web are changing the way we do business and the way we communicate. These advancements in communication and transportation have made markets more accessible and the world of business more efficient and more globally interdependent.

## Multicultural Work Force

As world commerce mingles more and more, another trend gives intercultural communication increasing importance: people are on the move. Lured by the prospects of

## FIGURE 4.1

Sony Music Germany is one of the increasing number of Web sites directed at specific countries. Many Web developers continue to offer content and interactions only in English. But 80 percent of European corporate sites are multilingual, with English as the preferred second language.

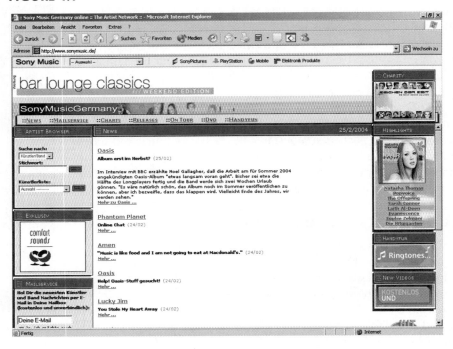

**Canadian society is often referred to as a cultural mosaic.**

peace, prosperity, education, or a fresh start, persons from many cultures are moving to countries promising to fulfill their dreams. For generations the two most popular destinations have been Canada and the United States.

Because of increases in immigration, foreign-born persons are an ever-growing portion of the total Canadian population. The Canadian Council of Social Development's John Anderson states, "Immigrants are a crucial part of Canada, economically and socially, since Canada needs immigrants to deal with its aging population." According to census statistics, 5.4 million people (18.4 percent of the population) report being foreign born.[12]

This influx of immigrants has reshaped Canadian society. While Americans have traditionally supported the "melting pot" approach to ethnic groups, Canada has often been compared to a cultural mosaic. In 1971, Canada became the first country in the world to adopt a multiculturalism policy. In 1988, it passed the Canadian Multiculturalism Act, which provides "specific direction to the federal government to work toward achieving equality in the economic, social, cultural, and political life of the country."[13] Individuals are invited to join the nation and still retain their cultural identifies, complete with traditions, languages, and customs. Although Canada's two official languages are English and French, unofficially it is a land of many languages. In Toronto, street signs are frequently printed both in English and in the predominant language of the neighbourhood, such as Greek, Italian, or Chinese. In British Columbia, drivers' licence tests are available in English, French, Chinese, and Punjabi, and Nunavut's primary language of government is Inuktitut, with secondary services available in English as required. Instead of being the exception, cultural diversity is increasingly the norm. As we seek to accommodate multiethnic neighbourhoods, multinational companies, and a multicultural work force, we can expect some changes to happen smoothly. Other changes may involve conflict and resentment, especially for people losing their positions of power and privilege. Learning how to manage multicultural conflict is an important part of the education of any business communicator.

## Being Interculturally Correct on the Web

Early Web sites were almost always in English and meant for North Americans. But as online access grows around the world, multinational companies are taking a second look at their sites. Sony Music Entertainment, Inc., for example, now boasts 13 country-specific Web sites. French fans can see which Sony artists are "en tournée" in Nice, and German fans, as shown in Figure 4.1, can see which Sony records topped the local album charts "diese woche." United Parcel Service, Inc., allows customers in 13 European countries to track packages in their native languages. And Reebok considers its multilingual Web presence a necessity in expanding its global sales and marketing. What should companies do when they decide to go global on the Web?

- **Learn the local lingo.** Other countries have developed their own Web jargon and iconography. *Home page* is "page d'accueil" (welcome page) in French and "pagina inicial" (initial page) in Spanish. Experts warn against simply translating English words page by page. Hiring a proficient translator is a better idea.[14]

- **Check icons.** North American Web surfers easily recognize the mailbox, but in Europe a more universal icon would be an envelope. Test images with local residents.

- **Relax restrictions on consistency.** Allow flexibility to meet local tastes. For example, McDonald's main site greets visitors with the golden arches and a Ronald McDonald-red background. The

Japanese site, though, complements the McDonald's red and gold with pinks and browns, which are more pleasing in their culture.

- **Keep the message simple.** Whether in English or the local language, use simple, easily translated words. Avoid slang, jargon, acronyms, or ambiguous expressions.

- **Customize Web content.** Avoid conflict with local customs and attitudes. For example, the Web page of a car manufacturer showed a hiker standing next to a car. But in Mexico, hikers are poor people who can't afford cars, so it wasn't acceptable to show someone who wanted to be a hiker.[15] Tailor Web marketing content to local holidays and events.

- **Develop the site together.** The best foreign Web sites for multinational companies are developed when domestic and foreign webmasters work together. Start early and build rapport, recommends Judy Newby, McDonald's webmaster.[16]

### Career Application

Compare the foreign and domestic sites of several multinational companies such as Sony Music Entertainment <**www.sonymusic.com**>, IBM <**www.ibm.com**>, United Parcel Service <**www.ups.com**>, Reebok <**www.reebok.com**>, and McDonald's <**www.mcdonalds.com**>. Are design, content, and navigation similar for the domestic and foreign sites? Is any English used on the foreign site?

## UNDERSTANDING CULTURE

Every country or region within a country has a unique common heritage, joint experience, or shared learning. This shared background produces the culture of a region, country, or society. For our purposes, *culture* may be defined as the complex system of values, traits, morals, and customs shared by a society. Culture teaches people how to behave, and it conditions their reactions.

Anthropologists Edward T. Hall and Mildred Reed Hall suggested that culture is "a system for creating, sending, storing, and processing information." Society programs men and women to act differently. Gender, race, age, religion, and many other factors affect our behaviour and cause us to behave in certain patterns.

2

Wayne Gretzky's first advertisement for Ford Motor Company was featured on *Hockey Night in Canada* during a game between the Toronto Maple Leafs and the Detroit Red Wings. Canadians think of Gretzky as a team player with strong family values, high standards of excellence, and a will to succeed. The use of Gretzky as a spokesperson builds on the strong Canadian hockey culture.

People from one culture may have difficulty getting through to those from another culture because individuals do not always behave as expected. People are further differentiated by their environments. For example, work cultures differ remarkably from one organization to another. When people conditioned to work in casual surroundings are placed in work cultures that are more formal and regimented, they may experience culture shock.

The important thing to remember is that culture is a powerful operating force that conditions the way we think and behave. As thinking individuals, we are extraordinarily flexible and are capable of phenomenal change. The purpose of this chapter is to broaden your view of culture and open your mind to flexible attitudes so that you can avoid frustration when cultural adjustment is necessary.

## Characteristics of Culture

**Understanding basic characteristics of culture helps us make adjustments and accommodations.**

Culture is shaped by attitudes learned in childhood and later internalized in adulthood. As we enter this current period of globalization and multiculturalism, we should expect to make adjustments and adopt new attitudes. Adjustment and accommodation will be easier if we understand some basic characteristics of culture.

*Culture Is Learned.* Rules, values, and attitudes of a culture are not inherent. They are learned and passed down from generation to generation. For example, in many Middle Eastern and some Asian cultures, same-sex people may walk hand in hand in the street, but opposite-sex people may not do so. In Arab cultures conversations are often held in close proximity, sometimes nose to nose. But in Western cultures if a person stands too close, one may react as if violated: "He was all over me like a rash." Cultural rules of behaviour learned from your family and society are conditioned from early childhood.

*Cultures Are Inherently Logical.* The rules in any culture originated to reinforce that culture's values and beliefs. They act as normative forces. For example, in Japan the original Barbie doll was a failure for many reasons, one of which was her toothy smile.[17] This is a country where women cover their mouths with their hands when they laugh so as not to expose their teeth. Exposing one's teeth is not only immodest but also aggressive. Although current cultural behaviour may sometimes seem silly and illogical, nearly all serious rules and values originate in deep-seated beliefs. Rules about exposing teeth or how close to stand are linked to values about sexuality, aggression, modesty, and respect. Acknowledging the inherent logic of a culture is extremely important when learning to accept behaviour that differs from one's own cultural behaviour.

*Culture Is the Basis of Self-Identity and Community.* Culture is the basis for how we tell the world who we are and what we believe. People build their identities through cultural overlays to their primary culture. North Americans, for example, make choices in education, career, place of employment, and life partner. Each of these choices brings with it a set of rules, manners, ceremonies, beliefs, language, and values. They add to one's total cultural outlook, and they represent major expressions of a person's self-identity.

Culture determines our sense of who we are and our sense of community.

*Culture Combines the Visible and Invisible.* To outsiders, the way we act— those things that we do in daily life and work—are the most visible parts of our culture. In Japan, for instance, harmony with the environment is important. Thus, when attending a flower show, a woman might dress in pastels rather than primary colours to avoid detracting from the beauty of the flowers. And in India people may avoid stepping on ants or insects because they believe in reincarnation and are careful about all forms of life.[18] These practices are outward symbols of deeper values that are invisible but that pervade everything we think and do.

*Culture Is Dynamic.* Over time, cultures will change. Changes are caused by advancements in technology and communication, as discussed earlier. Change is also caused by events such as migration, natural disasters, and wars. Canada's tradition of tolerance is highlighted by the decision made in 1849 by the government of Lower Canada not to use troops to subdue riots against British rule. At the same time in Europe and in the United States, armies were frequently turned against their own people to suppress antigovernment demonstrations.[19] Attitudes, behaviours, and beliefs change in open societies more quickly than in closed societies.

Attitudes, behaviours, and beliefs in a culture change as a result of migration, disasters, and wars.

## About Stereotypes, Prototypes, Prejudices, and Generalizations

Most experts recognize that it is impossible to talk about cultures without using mental categories, representations, and generalizations to describe groups. These categories are sometimes considered *stereotypes*. Because the term *stereotype* has a negative meaning, intercultural authors Varner and Beamer suggest that we distinguish between *stereotype* and *prototype*.

A *stereotype* is an oversimplified behavioural pattern applied uncritically to groups. The term was used originally by printers to describe identical type set in two frames, hence *stereo type*. Stereotypes are fixed and rigid. Although they may be exaggerated and overgeneralized beliefs when applied to groups of people, stereotypes are not always entirely false.[20] Often they contain a grain of truth. When a stereotype develops into a rigid attitude and when it's based on erroneous beliefs or preconceptions, then it should be called a *prejudice*.

Varner and Beamer recommend the use of the term *prototype* to describe "mental representations based on general characteristics that are not fixed and rigid, but rather are open to new definitions."[21] Prototypes, then, are dynamic and change with fresh experience. Prototypes based on objective observations usually have a considerable amount of truth in them. That's why they can be helpful in studying

*Stereotypes* are oversimplified behavioural patterns applied uncritically to groups; *prototypes* describe general characteristics that are dynamic and may change.

culture. For example, Latin businesspeople often talk about their families before getting down to business. This prototype is generally accurate, but it may not universally apply and it may change over time.

Some people object to making any generalizations about cultures whatsoever. Yet, it is wise to remember that whenever we are confronted with something new and unfamiliar, we naturally strive to categorize the data in order to make sense out of it. In categorizing these new data, we are making generalizations. Significant intellectual discourse is impossible without generalizations. In fact, science itself would be impossible without generalizations, for what are scientific laws but valid generalizations? Much of what we teach in university or college courses could be called generalizations. Being able to draw generalizations from masses of data is a sign of intelligence and learning. Unfounded generalizations about people and cultures, of course, can lead to bias and prejudice. But for our purposes, when we discuss cultures, it's important to be able to make generalizations and describe cultural prototypes.

## Dimensions of Culture

The more you know about culture in general and your own culture in particular, the better able you will be to adapt to a multicultural perspective. The diverse Canadian society is really a group of cultures. Canada also has several regional subcultures. Those living on the west coast of Canada may have a different way of thinking and a different spirit from those on the east coast; Canadians living on the Prairies are distinct from those in Ontario, as are Québécois and Newfoundlanders.[22] A typical Canadian has habits and beliefs similar to those of other members of Western, technologically advanced societies. In our limited space in this book, it's impossible to cover fully the infinite facets of culture. But we can outline some key dimensions of culture and look at them from different views.

So that you will better understand your culture and how it contrasts with other cultures, we will describe five key dimensions of culture: context, individualism, formality, communication style, and time orientation.

*Context.* Context is probably the most important cultural dimension and also the most difficult to define. It's a concept developed by cultural anthropologist Edward T. Hall. In his model, context refers to the stimuli, environment, or ambience surrounding an event. Communicators in low-context cultures (such as those in North America, Scandinavia, and Germany) depend little on the context of a situation to convey their meaning. They assume that listeners know very little and must be told practically everything. In high-context cultures (such as those in Japan, China, and Arab countries), the listener is already "contexted" and does not need to be given much background information.[23] To identify low- and high-context countries, Hall arranged them on a continuum, as shown in Figure 4.2.

Low-context cultures tend to be logical, analytical, and action-oriented. Business communicators stress clearly articulated messages that they consider to be objective, professional, and efficient. High-context cultures are more likely to be intuitive and contemplative. Communicators in high-context cultures pay attention to more than the words spoken. They emphasize interpersonal relationships, nonverbal expression, physical setting, and social setting. They are more aware of the communicator's history, status, and position. Communication cues are transmitted by posture, voice inflection, gestures, and facial expression. Establishing relationships is an important part of communicating and interacting.

In terms of thinking patterns, low-context communicators tend to use *linear logic*. They proceed from Point A to Point B to Point C and finally arrive at a conclusion. High-context communicators, however, may use *spiral logic*, circling around

Low-context cultures (North America, Western Europe) depend less on the environment of a situation to convey meaning than do high-context cultures (Japan, China, and Arab countries).

People in low-context cultures tend to be logical, analytical, and action-oriented.

## FIGURE 4.2 Comparing Low- and High-Context Cultures

| Low Context | High Context |
|---|---|
| Tends to prefer direct verbal interaction | Tends to prefer indirect verbal interaction |
| Tends to understand meaning at one level only | Tends to understand meanings embedded at many sociocultural levels |
| Is generally less proficient in reading nonverbal cues | Is generally more proficient in reading nonverbal cues |
| Values individualism | Values group membership |
| Relies more on logic | Relies more on context and feeling |
| Employs linear logic | Employs spiral logic |
| Says *no* directly | Talks around point; avoids saying *no* |
| Communicates in highly structured (contexted) messages, provides details, stresses literal meanings, gives authority to written information | Communicates in simple, ambiguous, noncontexted messages; understands visual messages readily |

German    North    French   Spanish   Greek   Chinese
          American

**Low-Context Cultures** ⟵————————————————⟶ **High-Context Cultures**

German-   Scandinavian   English   Italian   Mexican   Arab   Japanese
Swiss

a topic indirectly and looking at it from many tangential or divergent viewpoints. A conclusion may be implied but not argued directly. For a concise summary of important differences between low- and high-context cultures, see Figure 4.2.

*Individualism.* An attitude of independence and freedom from control characterizes individualism. Members of low-context cultures, particularly North Americans, tend to value individualism. They believe that initiative and self-assertion result in personal achievement. They believe in individual action and personal responsibility, and they desire a large degree of freedom in their personal lives.

Members of high-context cultures are more collectivist. They emphasize membership in organizations, groups, and teams; they encourage acceptance of group values, duties, and decisions. They typically resist independence because it fosters competition and confrontation instead of consensus. In group-oriented cultures like many Asian societies, for example, self-assertion and individual decision making are discouraged. "The nail that sticks up gets pounded down" is a common Japanese saying.[24] Business decisions are often made by all who have competence in the matter under discussion. Similarly, in China managers also focus on the group rather than on the individual, preferring a "consultative" management style over an autocratic style.[25]

Many cultures, of course, are quite complex and cannot be characterized as totally individualistic or group-oriented. For example, Canadians of European descent are generally quite individualistic, while those with Asian backgrounds may be closer to the group-centred dimension.[26]

**Members of many low-context cultures value independence and freedom from control.**

**Tradition, ceremony, and social rules are more important in some cultures.**

Isadore Sharp, chairperson and founder of the Four Seasons luxury hotel chain, has extended operations worldwide. Especially aware of multicultural sensitivity, Four Seasons looks for overseas managers with strong listening skills, alertness to body language, and open minds. In working abroad, Four Seasons managers must be able to suspend judgment because right and wrong may not be the same as they would be at home.

*Formality.* People in some cultures place less emphasis on tradition, ceremony, and social rules than do members of other cultures. While Canadians tend to be generally reserved and formal in their business dealings,[27] levels of formality vary across the country. In Quebec, where etiquette and politeness are considered very important, first names and informal greetings are generally not used, and modes of dress are more conservative than in the rest of Canada.[28] In other parts of Canada, business dress may be more casual, and business acquaintances are soon on a first-name basis. While French Canadians may be more formal in business settings, they may also have a tendency to be less reserved—gesturing more expansively, requiring less personal space, and engaging in more touching—than English Canadians.[29] Directness and a tendency to come right to the point often characterize a lack of formality in business. In many cases, lack of directness is thought to be a waste of time—another valuable commodity in Western culture.

This informality and directness may be confusing abroad. In Mexico, for instance, a typical business meeting begins with handshakes, coffee, and an expansive conversation about the weather, sports, and other light topics. An invitation to "get down to business" might offend a Mexican executive.[30] In Japan signing documents and exchanging business cards are important rituals. In Europe first names are never used without invitation. In Arab, South American, and Asian cultures, a feeling of friendship and kinship must be established before business can be transacted.

In Western cultures people are more relaxed about social status and appearance of power.[31] Deference is not generally paid to individuals merely because of their wealth, position, seniority, or age. In many Asian cultures, however, these characteristics are important and must be respected. Marriott Hotel managers, for example, have learned never to place a lower-level Japanese employee on a floor above a higher-level executive from the same company.

**Words are used differently by people in low- and high-context cultures.**

*Communication Style.* People in low- and high-context cultures tend to communicate differently with words. To North Americans and Germans, words are very important, especially in contracts and negotiations. People in high-context cultures, on the other hand, place more emphasis on the surrounding context than on the words describing a negotiation. A Greek may see a contract as a formal statement announcing the intention to build a business for the future. The Japanese may treat contracts as statements of intention, and they assume changes will be made as a project develops. Mexicans may treat contracts as artistic exercises of what might be accomplished in an ideal world. They do not necessarily expect contracts to apply consistently in the real world. An Arab may be insulted by merely mentioning a contract; a person's word is more binding.[32]

**Westerners value a direct, straightforward communication style.**

Westerners tend to take words literally, while Hispanics enjoy plays on words. Arabs and South Americans sometimes speak with extravagant or poetic figures of speech that may be misinterpreted if taken literally. Nigerians prefer a quiet, clear form of expression; and Germans tend to be direct but understated.[33]

In communication style Canadians value straightforwardness, are suspicious of evasiveness, and distrust people who might have a "hidden agenda" or who "play their cards too close to the chest."[34] Canadians and Americans also tend to be uncomfortable with silence and impatient with delays. Some Asian businesspeople have learned that the longer they drag out negotiations, the more concessions impatient North Americans are likely to make.

Western cultures have developed languages that use letters describing the *sounds* of words. But Asian languages are based on pictographical characters representing the *meanings* of words. Asian language characters are much more complex than the Western alphabet; therefore, Asians are said to have a higher competence in the discrimination of visual patterns.

*Time Orientation.* North Americans consider time a precious commodity to be conserved. They correlate time with productivity, efficiency, and money. Keeping people waiting for business appointments wastes time and is also rude.

In other cultures time may be perceived as an unlimited and never-ending resource to be enjoyed. A Canadian businessperson, for example, was kept waiting two hours past a scheduled appointment time in South America. She wasn't offended, though, because she was familiar with Hispanics' more relaxed concept of time.

Although Asians are punctual, their need for deliberation and contemplation sometimes clashes with our desire for speedy decisions. They do not like to be rushed. A Japanese businessperson considering the purchase of Western appliances, for example, asked for five minutes to consider the seller's proposal. The potential buyer crossed his arms, sat back, and closed his eyes in concentration. A scant 18 seconds later, the seller resumed his sales pitch to the obvious bewilderment of the Japanese buyer.[35]

## ACHIEVING INTERCULTURAL SENSITIVITY

Being aware of your own culture and how it contrasts with others is an important first step in achieving multicultural sensitivity. Another step involves recognizing barriers to intercultural accommodation and striving to overcome them. Some of these barriers occur quite naturally and require conscious effort to surmount. You might be thinking, why bother? Probably the most important reasons for becoming interculturally competent are that your personal life will be more satisfying and your work life will be more productive, gratifying, and effective. According to international banker Wing Morse, "many business talks go sour because of poor understanding of non-verbal communication cues."[36]

*3*

## Avoiding Ethnocentrism

The belief in the superiority of one's own race is known as *ethnocentrism*, a natural attitude inherent in all cultures. If you were raised in North America, many of the dimensions of culture described previously probably seem "right" to you. For example, it's only logical to think that time is money and you should not waste it. Everyone knows that, right? That's why a Canadian businessperson in an Arab or Asian country might feel irritated at time spent over coffee or other social rituals before any "real" business is transacted. In these cultures, however, time is viewed differently. And personal relationships must be established and nurtured before credible negotiations may proceed.

Ethnocentrism causes us to judge others by our own values. As Professor Usha George points out, "We all try to interpret the world through our own cultural lens."[37] We expect others to react as we would, and they expect us to behave as they would. Misunderstandings naturally result. A North American who wants to set a deadline for completion of negotiations is considered pushy by an Arab. That same Arab, who prefers a handshake to a written contract, is seen as naïve and possibly untrustworthy by a North American. These ethnocentric reactions can be reduced through knowledge of other cultures and development of increased multicultural sensitivity.

*Ethnocentrism*, the belief in the superiority of one's own race, tends to cause us to judge others by our own values.

## Bridging the Gap

Developing cultural competence often involves changing attitudes. Remember that culture is learned. Through exposure to other cultures and through training, such as you are receiving in this course, you can learn new attitudes and behaviours that help bridge gaps between cultures.

*Tolerance.* One desirable attitude in achieving multicultural sensitivity is that of *tolerance*. Closed-minded people cannot look beyond their own ethnocentrism. But as global markets expand and as our own society becomes increasingly multiethnic, tolerance becomes especially significant. Some job descriptions now include statements such as "Must be able to interact with ethnically diverse personnel."

To improve tolerance, you'll want to practise *empathy*. This means trying to see the world through another's eyes. It means being less judgmental and more eager to seek common ground. For example, one of the most ambitious cross-cultural business projects ever attempted joined Siemens AG, the giant German technology firm, with Toshiba Corporation of Japan and IBM. Scientists from each country worked at the IBM facility on the Hudson River in New York State to develop a revolutionary computer memory chip. All sides devoted extra effort to overcome communication and other problems. The Siemens employees had been briefed on America's "hamburger style of management." When American managers must criticize subordinates, they generally start with small talk, such as "How's the family?" That, according to the Germans, is the bun on the top of the hamburger. Then they slip in the meat, which is the criticism. They end with encouraging words, which is the bun on the bottom. "With Germans," said a Siemens cross-cultural trainer, "all you get is the meat. And with the Japanese, it's all the soft stuff—you have to *smell* the meat."[38] Along the continuum of high-context, low-context cultures, you can see that the Germans are more direct, the Americans are less direct, and the Japanese are very subtle.

Recognizing these cultural differences enabled the scientists to work together with greater tolerance. They also sought common ground when trying to solve disagreements, such as one involving workspace. The Toshiba researchers were accustomed to working in big crowded areas like classrooms where constant supervision and interaction took place. But IBMers worked in small isolated offices. The solution was to knock out some walls for cooperative work areas while also retaining smaller offices for those who wanted them. Instead of passing judgment and telling the Japanese that solitary workspaces are the best way for serious thinkers to concentrate, the Americans acknowledged the difference in work cultures and sought common ground. Accepting cultural differences and adapting to them with tolerance and empathy often results in a harmonious compromise.

*Saving Face.* In business transactions North Americans often assume that economic factors are the primary motivators of people. It's wise to remember, though, that strong cultural influences are also at work. *Saving face*, for example, is important in many parts of the world. *Face* refers to the image a person holds in his or her social network. Positive comments raise a person's social standing, but negative comments lower it. People in low-context cultures are less concerned with face. Germans and North Americans, for instance, value honesty and directness; they generally come right to the point and "tell it like it is." Mexicans, Asians, and members of other high-context cultures, on the other hand, are more concerned with preserving social harmony and saving face. They are indirect and go to great lengths to avoid giving offence by saying *no*. The Japanese, in fact, have 16 different ways to avoid an outright *no*. The empathic listener recognizes the language of refusal and pushes no further.

*Patience.* Being tolerant also involves patience. If a foreigner is struggling to express an idea in English, North Americans must avoid the temptation to finish the sentence and provide the word that they presume is wanted. When we put words into their mouths, our foreign friends often smile and agree out of politeness, but our words may in fact not express their thoughts. Remaining silent is another means of exhibiting tolerance. Instead of filling every lapse in conversation, North Americans, for example, should recognize that in Asian cultures people deliberately use periods of silence for reflection and contemplation.

Tolerance sometimes involves being patient and silent.

## IMPROVING COMMUNICATION WITH MULTICULTURAL AUDIENCES

Thus far we've discussed the increasing importance of multicultural sensitivity as a result of globalization of markets, increasing migration, and technological advancements. We've described characteristics and dimensions of cultures, and we've talked about avoiding ethnocentrism. Our goal was to motivate you to unlock the opportunities offered by multiculturalism. Remember, the key to future business success may very well lie in finding ways to work harmoniously with people from different cultures.

Business success may depend on working harmoniously with people from different cultures.

### Adapting Messages to Multicultural Audiences

As business communicators, we need to pay special attention to specific areas of communication to enhance the effectiveness of intercultural messages. To minimize the chance of misunderstanding, we'll look more closely at nonverbal communication, oral messages, and written messages.

*Nonverbal Communication.* Verbal skills in another culture can generally be mastered if one studies hard enough. But nonverbal skills are much more difficult to learn. Nonverbal behaviour includes the areas described in Chapter 3, such as eye contact, facial expression, posture, gestures, and the use of time, space, and territory. The messages sent by body language and the way we arrange time and space have always been open to interpretation. Does a raised eyebrow mean that your boss doubts your statement or just that she is seriously considering it? Does that closed door to an office mean that your coworker is angry or just that he is working on a project that requires concentration? Deciphering nonverbal communication is difficult for people who are culturally similar, and it is even more troublesome when cultures differ.

Understanding nonverbal messages is particularly difficult when cultures differ.

In Western cultures, for example, people perceive silence as a negative trait. It suggests rejection, unhappiness, depression, regret, embarrassment, or ignorance. However, the Japanese admire silence and consider it a key to success. A Japanese proverb says, "Those who know do not speak; those who speak do not know." Over 60 percent of Japanese businesswomen said that they would prefer to marry silent men.[39] Silence is equated with wisdom.

Although nonverbal behaviour is ambiguous within cultures and even more problematic between cultures, it nevertheless conveys meaning. If you've ever had to talk with someone who does not share your language, you probably learned quickly to use gestures to convey basic messages. Since gestures can create very different reactions in different cultures, one must be careful in using and interpreting them. In some societies it is extremely bad form to point one's finger, as in giving directions. Other hand gestures can also cause trouble. The "thumbs up" symbol may be

Gestures can create different reactions in multicultural environments.

## G.A.P Adventures Revisited

The hugely successful reality television series *Survivor* pits teams and individuals against one other and the elements. Contestants must compete in immunity challenges and are voted off the show by their own teammates. So popular is the program that "voting someone off the island" has become part of the lexicon.

When the show was taping its Australian series, G.A.P's local office managed the ground operations and was responsible for all of the company's transportation. In exchange, G.A.P secured the use of the property for spin-off tours so *Survivor* "wannabes" can pretend they are doing the real thing: eating overcooked rice and conducting their own immunity challenges.

In 2000, the show's producers called Bruce Poon Tip again to ask his advice about future destinations. "*Survivor* is really interested in perceived risk as opposed to actual risk. They want something that's fairly challenging, but don't want to put their Survivors in life-threatening situations."[40] Poon Tip suggested Kenya because of its dry climate and more highly developed tourism industry. He believed they would have more facilities to house the crew and that the plains of Africa would be a great backdrop.

Recently, former *Survivor* contestants have taken part in G.A.P tours and some have become tour guides.

### CRITICAL THINKING

- What cultural considerations would Bruce Poon Tip and the producers of *Survivor* need to think about when contemplating a new site?
- What responsibilities would the show's producers have for "leaving nothing but footprints"?[41]

**www.gapadventures.ca**

---

used to indicate approval in North America, but in Iran and Ghana it is a vulgar gesture.[42]

As businesspeople increasingly interact with their counterparts from other cultures, they will become more aware of these differences. Some behaviours are easy to warn against, such as touching people from the Middle East with the left hand (because it is considered unclean and is used for personal hygiene). We're also warned not to touch anyone's head (even children) in Thailand, as the head is considered sacred. Numerous lists of cultural do's and don'ts have been compiled. However, learning all the nuances of nonverbal behaviour in other cultures is impossible, and such lists are merely the tip of the cultural iceberg.

**Becoming more aware of your own use of nonverbal cues can make you more sensitive to variations in other cultures.**

Although we can't ever hope to understand fully the nuances of meaning transmitted by nonverbal behaviour in various cultures, we can grow more tolerant, more flexible, and eventually, more competent. An important part of achieving nonverbal competence is becoming more aware of our own nonverbal behaviours and their meanings. Much of our nonverbal behaviour is learned in early childhood from our families and from society, and it is largely unconscious. Once we become more aware of the meaning of our own gestures, posture, eye gaze, and so on, we will become more alert and more sensitive to variations in other cultures. Striving to associate with people from different cultures can further broaden our intercultural competence.

In achieving competence, one multicultural expert, M. R. Hammer, suggests that three processes or attitudes are effective. *Descriptiveness* refers to the use of concrete and specific feedback. As you learned in Chapter 1 in regard to the process of communication, descriptive feedback is more effective than judgmental feedback. For example, using objective terms to describe the modest attire of Moslem women is more effective than describing it as unfeminine or motivated by oppressive and unequal treatment of females. A second attitude is what Hammer calls *nonjudgmentalism*. This attitude goes a long way in preventing defensive reactions from communicators. Most important in achieving effective communication is *supportiveness*. This attitude requires us to support others positively with head nods, eye contact, facial expression, and physical proximity.[43]

Descriptiveness, nonjudgmentalism, and supportiveness all help you broaden your intercultural competence.

From a practical standpoint, when interacting with businesspeople in other cultures, it's always wise to follow their lead. If they avoid intense eye contact, don't stare. If no one is putting his or her elbows on a table, don't be the first to do so. Until you are knowledgeable about the meaning of gestures, it's probably a good idea to keep yours to a minimum. Learning the words for *please*, *yes*, and *thank you*, some of which are shown in Figure 4.3, is even better than relying on gestures.[44] Multicultural competence in regard to nonverbal behaviour may never be totally attained, but sensitivity, nonjudgmentalism, and tolerance go a long way toward improving interactions.

*Oral Messages.* Although it's best to speak a foreign language fluently, many of us lack that skill. Fortunately, global business transactions are often conducted in English, although the level of proficiency may be limited among those for whom it is a second language. Travellers abroad make a big mistake in thinking that people who speak English always understand what is being said. Comprehension can be fairly superficial. The following suggestions are helpful for situations in which one or both communicators may be using English as a second language.

- **Learn foreign phrases.** In conversations, even when English is used, foreign nationals appreciate it when you learn greetings and a few phrases in their language. See Figure 4.3 for a list of basic expressions in some of the world's major languages. Practise the phrases phonetically so that you will be understood.

- **Use simple English.** Speak in short sentences (under 15 words), and try to stick to the 3 000 to 4 000 most common English words. For example, use *old* rather than *obsolete* and *rich* rather than *luxurious* or *sumptuous*. Eliminate puns, sports and military references, slang, and jargon (special business terms). Be especially alert to idiomatic expressions that can't be translated, such as *burn the midnight oil* and *under the weather*.

Use simple English and avoid puns, sports references, slang, and jargon when communicating with people for whom English is a second language.

- **Speak slowly and enunciate clearly.** Avoid fast speech, but don't raise your voice. Overpunctuate with pauses and full stops. Always write numbers for all to see.

- **Observe eye messages.** Be alert to a glazed expression or wandering eyes—these tell you the listener is lost.

- **Encourage accurate feedback.** Ask probing questions, and encourage the listener to paraphrase what you say. Don't assume that a *yes*, a nod, or a smile indicates comprehension.

- **Check frequently for comprehension.** Avoid waiting until you finish a long explanation to request feedback. Instead, make one point at a time, pausing to check for comprehension. Don't proceed to B until A has been grasped.

- **Accept blame.** If a misunderstanding results, graciously accept the blame for not making your meaning clear.

- **Listen without interrupting.** Curb your desire to finish sentences or to fill out ideas for the speaker. Keep in mind that North Americans abroad are often accused of listening too little and talking too much.

- **Remember to smile!** Roger Axtell, international behaviour expert, calls the smile the single most understood and most useful form of communication in either personal or business transactions.[45]

**FIGURE 4.3** Basic Expressions in Other Languages

| COUNTRY | GOOD MORNING | PLEASE | THANK YOU | YES | NO | GOODBYE |
|---|---|---|---|---|---|---|
| Arabic | saBAH al-khayr | minFUDlak | shookRAAN | NAA-am | LAA | MAA-a salAAMuh |
| French | Bonjour [bohnzhoor] | S'il vous plaît [see voo pleh] | Merci (beaucoup) [mare-see (bo-coo)] | Oui [weeh] | Non [nonh] | Au revoir [oh vwar] |
| German | Guten morgen [Goo-ten more-gen] | Bitte [Bitt-eh] | Danke [Dahnk-eh] | Ja [Yah] | Nein [Nine] | Auf Wiedersehen [auwf vee-dur-zain] |
| Italian | Buon giorno | Per favore/per piacere | Grazie (tante) | Si | No | Arrivederla (Arrivederci, informal) |
| Japanese | Ohayoo [Ohio (go-ZAI-mahss) or simply Ohio] | oh-NEH-ga-ee she-mahss (when requesting) | Arigato [Ah-ree-GAH-tow (go-ZAI-mahss)] | High, so-dess | Ee-yeh | Sayonara |
| Norwegian | God morgen | Vaer sa snill [var so snill] | Takk [tahk] | Ja [yah] | Nei [nay] | Adjo [adieu] |
| Russian | Do'braye oo-tra | Pa-JAH-loos-tah | Spa-SEE-bah | Dah | N'yet | DasviDANya |
| Spanish | Buenos días [BWEH-nos DEE-ahs] | Con permiso [Con pair-ME-soh], Por favor [Pohr fah-VOHR] | Gracias [GRAH-seeahs] | Sí [SEEH] | No [NOH] | Adiós |

- **Follow up in writing.** After conversations or oral negotiations, confirm the results and agreements with follow-up letters. For proposals and contracts, engage a translator to prepare copies in the local language.

5

*Written Messages.* In sending letters and other documents to businesspeople in other cultures, try to adapt your writing style and tone appropriately. For example, in cultures where formality and tradition are important, be scrupulously polite. Don't even think of sharing the latest joke. Humour translates very poorly and can cause misunderstanding and negative reactions. Familiarize yourself with accepted channels of communication. Are letters, e-mail, and faxes common? Would a direct or indirect organizational pattern be more effective? The following suggestions, coupled with the earlier guidelines, can help you prepare successful written messages for multicultural audiences.

To improve written messages, adopt local formats, use short sentences and short paragraphs, avoid ambiguous expressions, strive for clarity, use correct grammar, cite numbers carefully, and accommodate readers in organization, tone, and style.

- **Adopt local formats.** Learn how documents are formatted and addressed in the intended reader's country. Use local formats and styles.

- **Use short sentences and short paragraphs.** Sentences with fewer than 15 words and paragraphs with fewer than 7 lines are most readable.

- **Avoid ambiguous expressions.** Include relative pronouns (*that, which, who*) for clarity in introducing clauses. Stay away from contractions (especially ones like *Here's the problem*). Avoid idioms (*once in a blue moon*), slang (*my presentation really bombed*), acronyms (*ASAP* for *as soon as possible*), abbreviations (*DBA* for *doing business as*), jargon (*input, bottom line*), and sports references (*play ball, slam dunk, ballpark figure*). Use action-specific verbs (*purchase a printer* rather than *get a printer*).

- **Strive for clarity.** Avoid words that have many meanings (the word *light* has 18 different meanings!). If necessary, clarify words that may be confusing.

Replace two-word verbs with clear single words (*return* instead of *bring back*; *delay* instead of *put off*; *maintain* instead of *keep up*).

- **Use correct grammar.** Be careful of misplaced modifiers, dangling participles, and sentence fragments. Use conventional punctuation.

- **Cite numbers carefully.** For international trade it's a good idea to learn and use the metric system. In citing numbers use figures (*15*) instead of spelling them out (*fifteen*). Always convert dollar figures into local currency. Avoid using figures to express the month of the year. See Figure 4.4 on page 114 for additional guidelines on data formats.

- **Accommodate the reader in organization, tone, and style.** Organize your message to appeal to the reader. If flowery tone, formal salutations, indirectness, references to family and the seasons, or unconditional apologies are expected, strive to accommodate.

Making the effort to communicate with sensitivity across cultures pays big dividends. "Much of the world wants to like us," says businessman and international consultant Kevin Chambers. "When we take the time to learn about others, many will bend over backward to do business with us."[46] The following checklist summarizes suggestions for improving communication with multicultural audiences.

## CHECKLIST FOR IMPROVING INTERCULTURAL SENSITIVITY AND COMMUNICATION

✓ **Study your own culture.** Learn about your customs, biases, and views and how they differ from those in other societies. This knowledge can help you better understand, appreciate, and accept the values and behaviour of other cultures.

✓ **Learn about other cultures.** Education can help you alter cultural misconceptions, reduce fears, and minimize misunderstandings. Knowledge of other cultures opens your eyes and teaches you to expect differences. Such knowledge also enriches your life.

✓ **Curb ethnocentrism.** Avoid judging others by your personal views. Get over the view that the other cultures are incorrect, defective, or primitive. Try to develop an open mindset.

✓ **Avoid judgmentalism.** Strive to accept other behaviour as different, rather than as right or wrong. Try not to be defensive in justifying your culture. Strive for objectivity.

✓ **Seek common ground.** When cultures clash, look for solutions that respect both cultures. Be flexible in developing compromises.

✓ **Observe nonverbal cues in your culture.** Become more alert to the meanings of eye contact, facial expression, posture, gestures, and the use of time, space, and territory. How do they differ in other cultures?

✓ **Use plain English.** Speak and write in short sentences using simple words and standard English. Eliminate puns, slang, jargon, acronyms, abbreviations, and any words that cannot be easily translated.

**FIGURE 4.4** Typical Data Formats

|  | CANADA | UNITED KINGDOM | FRANCE | GERMANY | PORTUGAL |
|---|---|---|---|---|---|
| **Dates** | May 15, 2005<br>5/15/05 | 15th May 2005<br>15/5/05 | 15 mai 2005<br>15.05.05 | 15. Mai 2005<br>15.5.05 | 05.05.15 |
| **Time** | 10:32 p.m. | 10:32 pm | 22.32<br>22 h 32 | 22:32 Uhr<br>22.32 | 22H32m |
| **Currency** | $123.45<br>CDN$123.45 | £123.45<br>GB£123.45 | 123F45<br>123,45F<br>123.45 euros | DM 123,45<br>123,45 DM<br>123.45 euros | 123$45<br>ESC 123.45<br>123.45 euros |
| **Large numbers** | 1 234 567.89 | 1,234,567.89 | 1.234.567,89<br>1 234 567 | 1.234.567,89 | 1.234.567,89 |
| **Phone numbers** | (205) 555-1234 | (081) 987 1234<br>0255 876543 | (15) 61-87-34-02<br>(15) 61.87.34.02 | (089) 2 61 39 12 | 056-244 33<br>056 45 45 45 |

✓ **Encourage accurate feedback.** In conversations ask probing questions and listen attentively without interrupting. Don't assume that a yes or a smile indicates assent or comprehension.

✓ **Adapt to local preferences.** Shape your writing to reflect the reader's document styles, if appropriate. Express currency in local figures. Write out months of the year for clarity.

## COPING WITH INTERCULTURAL ETHICS

A perplexing problem faces conscientious organizations and individuals who do business around the world. Whose values, culture, and, ultimately, laws do you follow? Do you heed the customs of your country or those of the country where you are engaged in business? Some observers claim that when Western businesspeople venture abroad, they're wandering into an "ethical no-man's land, where each encounter holds forth a fresh demand for a 'gratuity,' or baksheesh."[47]

### Business Practices Abroad

**When Westerners conduct business abroad, their ethics are put to the test.**

As companies do more and more business around the globe, their assumptions about ethics are put to the test. Businesspeople may face simple questions regarding the appropriate amount of money to spend on a business gift or the legitimacy of payments to agents and distributors to "expedite" business. Or they may encounter out-and-out bribery, child-labour abuse, environment mistreatment, and unscrupulous business practices.

**The least corrupt countries are Finland, Iceland, Denmark, New Zealand, Singapore, and Sweden.**

All countries, of course, are not corrupt. Transparency International, a Berlin-based watchdog group, compiles an annual ranking of corruption in many countries. Based on polls and surveys of businesspeople and journalists, the index shown in Figure 4.5 presents a look at the perceptions of corruption. Gauging corruption precisely, of course, is impossible, but this graph reflects the feelings of individuals doing business in the countries shown. Of the countries selected for this graph, the least corrupt countries are Finland, Iceland, Denmark, New Zealand, Singapore, and Sweden. The most corrupt were Bangladesh, Cameroon, and Indonesia.

## FIGURE 4.5 Transparency International Corruption Perceptions Index 2003

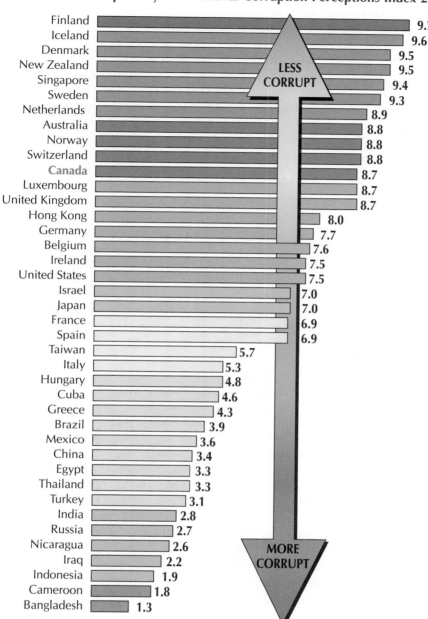

| | |
|---|---|
| Finland | 9.7 |
| Iceland | 9.6 |
| Denmark | 9.5 |
| New Zealand | 9.5 |
| Singapore | 9.4 |
| Sweden | 9.3 |
| Netherlands | 8.9 |
| Australia | 8.8 |
| Norway | 8.8 |
| Switzerland | 8.8 |
| Canada | 8.7 |
| Luxembourg | 8.7 |
| United Kingdom | 8.7 |
| Hong Kong | 8.0 |
| Germany | 7.7 |
| Belgium | 7.6 |
| Ireland | 7.5 |
| United States | 7.5 |
| Israel | 7.0 |
| Japan | 7.0 |
| France | 6.9 |
| Spain | 6.9 |
| Taiwan | 5.7 |
| Italy | 5.3 |
| Hungary | 4.8 |
| Cuba | 4.6 |
| Greece | 4.3 |
| Brazil | 3.9 |
| Mexico | 3.6 |
| China | 3.4 |
| Egypt | 3.3 |
| Thailand | 3.3 |
| Turkey | 3.1 |
| India | 2.8 |
| Russia | 2.7 |
| Nicaragua | 2.6 |
| Iraq | 2.2 |
| Indonesia | 1.9 |
| Cameroon | 1.8 |
| Bangladesh | 1.3 |

**LESS CORRUPT**

**MORE CORRUPT**

This international corruption index is a compilation of polls and surveys put together by Transparency International, a Berlin-based watchdog organization whose purpose is curbing the increasingly rampant corruption stunting the development of poor countries. The index relates to perceptions of the degree of corruption as seen by businesspeople, risk analysts, and the general public. It ranges between 10 (highly clean) and 0 (highly corrupt).

## Laws Forbidding Bribery

Canada performs consistently well on the index of least corruptible countries and has taken a global lead in fighting corruption. In 1999, the Canadian government passed legislation governing the corruption of foreign public officials in international transactions. Legislation prohibiting bribery and corruption exists both in Canada (Corruption of Foreign Public Officials Act) and in the United States (Foreign Corrupt Practices Act). Dr. Wesley Craig, chairperson of Transparency International Canada, believes that such legislation is a "vitally important step in raising the standard of conduct in global business transactions ... which will help to create a more level playing field in pursuing global contracts." Craig asserts, "Bribery is an impediment to economic development. We want Canada to take a leading role in removing that impediment."[48]

Most other industrialized countries looked the other way when their corporations used bribes. They considered the "greasing of palms" just a cost of doing business in certain cultures. In fact, German corporations were even allowed to deduct bribes as a business expense when they calculated taxes. But in Canada, bribery is a criminal offence, and corporate officials found guilty are fined and sent to jail.

After years of U.S. negotiating, however, the tide is turning. Many of the world's industrialized countries formally agreed in 1997 to a new global treaty promoted by the Organization for Economic Cooperation and Development (OECD). This treaty bans the practice of bribery of foreign government officials. Although 29 countries signed the treaty, only 21 have passed implementing legislation.[49] Canada has been a member of the OECD since 1961 and is perceived to be an international leader in fighting corruption.

## Whose Ethics Should Prevail?

**Although world leaders agree that bribery of officials is wrong, they do not agree on other ethical behaviour.**

Although world leaders seem to agree that bribery of officials is wrong, many other shady areas persist. Drawing the lines of ethical behaviour here at home is hard enough. When faced with a cultural filter, the picture becomes even murkier. Most people agree that mistreating children is wrong. But in some countries, child labour is not only condoned, it is considered necessary for a family to subsist. While most countries want to respect the environment, they might also sanction the use of DDT because crops would be consumed by insects without it.

In some cultures "grease" payments to customs officials may be part of their earnings—not blackmail. In parts of Africa, a "family" celebration at the conclusion of a business deal includes a party for which you are asked to pay. This payment is a sign of friendship and lasting business relationship, not a personal payoff. In some Third World countries, requests for assistance in developing technologies or reducing hunger may become part of a business package.[50]

**Gifts may be a sign of gratitude and hospitality, but they also suggest future obligation.**

The exchanging of gifts is another tricky subject. In many non-Western cultures, the gift exchange tradition has become a business ritual. Gifts are not only a sign of gratitude and hospitality, but they also generate a future obligation and trust. North Americans, of course, become uneasy when gift-giving seems to move beyond normal courtesy and friendliness. If it even remotely suggests influence-peddling, they back off.

Whose ethics should prevail across borders? Unfortunately, no clear-cut answers can be found. North Americans are sometimes criticized for being ethical "fanatics," wishing to impose their "moralistic" views on the world. Also criticized are ethical "relativists" who contend that no absolute values exist.[51]

## Making Ethical Decisions Across Borders

**Finding practical solutions to ethical problems is most important.**

Instead of trying to distinguish "good ethics" and "bad ethics," perhaps the best plan is to look for practical solutions to the cultural challenges of global business interaction. Following are suggestions that acknowledge different values but also respect the need for moral initiative.[52]

- **Broaden your view.** Become more sensitive to the values and customs of other cultures. Look especially at what they consider moral, traditional, practical, and effective.

- **Avoid reflex judgments.** Don't automatically judge the business customs of others as immoral, corrupt, or unworkable. Assume they are legitimate and workable until proved otherwise.

- **Find alternatives.** Instead of caving in to government payoffs, perhaps offer nonmonetary public service benefits, technical expertise, or additional customer service.

- **Refuse business if options violate your basic values.** If an action seriously breaches your own code of ethics or that of your firm, give up the transaction.

- **Work in the fresh air.** Conduct all relations and negotiations as openly as possible.

- **Don't rationalize shady decisions.** Avoid agreeing to actions that cause you to say, "This isn't *really* illegal or immoral," "This is in the company's best interest," or "No one will find out."

- **Resist legalistic strategies.** Don't use tactics that are legally safe but ethically questionable. For example, don't call "agents" (who are accountable to employers) "distributors" (who are not). When faced with an intercultural ethical dilemma, you can apply the same five-question test you learned in Chapter 1. Even in another culture, these questions can guide you to the best decision.

  1. Is the action you are considering legal?
  2. How would you see the problem if you were on the opposite side?
  3. What are alternative solutions?
  4. Can you discuss the problem with someone whose advice you trust?
  5. How would you feel if your family, friends, employer, or coworker learned of your action?

Businesspeople abroad can choose many alternatives that acknowledge different values but also respect the need for moral initiative.

## CAPITALIZING ON WORK FORCE DIVERSITY

At the same time that North American businesspeople are interacting with people from around the world, the domestic work force is becoming more diverse. This diversity has many dimensions—race, ethnicity, age, religion, gender, national origin, physical ability, and countless other qualities. No longer, say the experts, will the workplace be predominantly Anglo-oriented or male. According to Statistics Canada, women and minorities will significantly outnumber white males entering the work force in this decade, and by 2005, more than 15 percent of the work force will be 55 years or older.[53] And because of technological advances, more physically challenged people are joining the work force.

## Dividends of Diversity

As society and the work force become more diverse, successful interaction and communication among the various identity groups brings distinct challenges and dividends in three areas.

***Consumers.*** A diverse staff is better able to read trends and respond to the increasingly diverse customer base in local and world markets. Diverse consumers now want specialized goods and services tailored to their needs. Teams made up of different people with different experiences are better able to create the different products that these markets require. Consumers also want to deal with companies that respect their values.

A diverse work force benefits consumers, work teams, and business organizations.

***Work Teams.*** As you learned in Chapter 2, employees today work in teams. Team members with different backgrounds may come up with more creative and effective

Developing a diverse staff that can work together cooperatively is one of the biggest challenges facing business organizations today. Ultimately, customers need to look into your company and see people like themselves.

problem-solving techniques than homogeneous teams. Chains of command, narrow job descriptions, and hierarchies are gradually becoming things of the past. Today's teams are composed of knowledgeable, diverse individuals who are concerned with sustainability, competence, and ownership within the project, team, and organization.[54]

**Diversity can improve employee relationships and increase productivity.**

***Business Organizations.*** Companies that set aside time and resources to cultivate and capitalize on diversity will suffer fewer discrimination lawsuits, fewer union clashes, and less government regulatory action. Most important, though, is the growing realization among organizations that diversity is a critical bottom-line business strategy to improve employee relationships and to increase productivity. Developing a diverse staff that can work together cooperatively is one of the biggest challenges facing business organizations today.

## Divisiveness of Diversity

**Diversity can cause divisiveness, discontent, and clashes.**

Diversity can be a positive force within organizations. But all too often it can also cause divisiveness, discontent, and clashes. Many of the identity groups, the so-called work force "disenfranchised," have legitimate gripes.

**The *glass ceiling* is an invisible barrier of attitudes, prejudices, and "old boy networks" that block women from reaching important positions.**

Women complain of the *glass ceiling*, that invisible barrier of attitudes, prejudices, and "old boy networks" blocking them from reaching important corporate positions. Some women feel that they are the victims of sexual harassment, unequal wages, sexism, and even their style of communication. See the accompanying Career Coach box to learn more about gender talk and gender tension. On the other hand, men, too, have gender issues. One manager described gender discrimination in his office: "My boss was a woman and was very verbal about the opportunities for women to advance in my company. I have often felt she gave much more attention to the women in the office than the men."[55]

Older employees feel that the deck is stacked in favour of younger employees. Minorities complain that they are discriminated against in hiring, retention, wages, and promotions. Physically challenged individuals feel that their limitations should not hold them back, and they fear that their potential is often prejudged. Individuals with different religions may feel uncomfortable working beside each other.

## He Said, She Said: Gender Talk and Gender Tension

Has the infiltration of gender rhetoric done great damage to the workplace? Are men and women throwing rotten tomatoes at each other as a result of misunderstandings caused by stereotypes of "masculine" and "feminine" attitudes? Deborah Tannen's book *You Just Don't Understand: Women and Men in Conversation*, as well as John Grey's *Men Are From Mars, Women Are From Venus*, caused an avalanche of discussion (and some hostility) by comparing the communication styles of men and women. Here are some of their observations (greatly simplified):[56]

|  | WOMEN | MEN |
|---|---|---|
| **Object of talk** | Establish rapport, make connections, negotiate inclusive relationships | Preserve independence, maintain status, exhibit skill and knowledge |
| **Listening behaviour** | Attentive, steady eye contact; remain stationary; nod head | Less attentive, sporadic eye contact; move around |
| **Pauses** | Frequent pauses, giving chance for others to take turns | Infrequent pauses; interrupt each other to take turns |
| **Small talk** | Personal disclosure | Impersonal topics |
| **Focus** | Details first, pulled together at end | Big picture |
| **Gestures** | Small, confined | Expansive |
| **Method** | Questions; apologies; "we" statements; hesitant, indirect, soft speech | Assertions; "I" statements; clear, loud, take-charge speech |

Gender theorists suggest that one reason women can't climb above the glass ceiling is that their communication style is less authoritative than that of men.

### Career Application

In small group or class discussion, consider these questions: Do men and women have different communication styles? Which style is more appropriate for today's team-based management? Do we need a kind of communicative affirmative action to give more recognition to women's ways of talking? Should training be given to men and women encouraging the interchangeable use of these styles depending on the situation?

## Tips for Improving Communication Among Diverse Workplace Audiences

Integrating all this diversity into one seamless work force is a formidable task and a vital one. Harnessed effectively, diversity can enhance productivity and propel a company to success well into the twenty-first century. Mismanaged, it can become a tremendous drain on a company's time and resources. How companies deal with diversity will make all the difference in how they compete in an increasingly global environment. And that means that organizations must do more than just pay lip service to these issues. Harmony and acceptance do not happen automatically when people who are dissimilar work together. The following suggestions can help you and your organization find ways to improve communication and interaction.

**A diverse work force may reduce productivity unless trained to value differences.**

- **Seek training.** Especially if an organization is experiencing problems in managing diversity, awareness-raising sessions may be helpful. Spend time reading and learning about work force diversity and how it can benefit organizations. Look on diversity as an opportunity, not a threat. Intercultural communication, team building, and conflict resolution are skills that can be learned in diversity training programs.

- **Understand the value of differences.** Diversity makes an organization innovative and creative. Sameness fosters an absence of critical thinking called "groupthink," which you learned about in Chapter 2. Diversity in problem-solving groups encourages independent and creative thinking.

- **Don't expect conformity.** Gone are the days when businesses could say, "This is our culture. Conform or leave."[57] Paul Fireman, CEO of Reebok, stresses seeking people who have new and different stories to tell. "And then you have to make real room for them, you have to learn to listen, to listen closely, to their stories. It accomplishes next to nothing to employ those who are different from us if the condition of their employment is that they become the same as us. For it is their differences that enrich us, expand us, provide us the competitive edge."[58]

- **Learn about your cultural self.** Begin to think of yourself as a product of your culture, and understand that your culture is just one among many. Try to stand outside and look at yourself. Do you see any reflex reactions and automatic thought patterns that are a result of your upbringing? These may be invisible to you until challenged by difference. Remember, your culture was designed to help you succeed and survive in a certain environment. Be sure to keep what works and yet be ready to adapt as environments change.

- **Make fewer assumptions.** Be careful of seemingly insignificant, innocent workplace assumptions. For example, don't assume that everyone wants to observe the holidays with a Christmas party and a decorated tree. Celebrating only Christian holidays in December and January excludes those who honour Hanukkah, Kwanza, and the Chinese New Year. Moreover, in workplace discussions don't assume that everyone is married or wants to be or is even heterosexual, for that matter. For invitations, avoid phrases such as *managers and their wives*. *Spouses* or *partners* is more inclusive. Valuing diversity means making fewer assumptions that everyone is like you or wants to be like you.

- **Build on similarities.** Look for areas where you and others not like you can agree or at least share opinions. Be prepared to consider issues from many perspectives, all of which may be valid. Accept that there is room for different points of view to coexist peacefully. Although you can always find differences, it's much harder to find similarities. Look for common ground in shared experiences, mutual goals, and similar values. Concentrate on your objective even when you may disagree on how to reach it.[59]

## SUMMARY OF LEARNING OBJECTIVES

*1* **Discuss three significant trends related to the increasing importance of intercultural communication.** Three trends are working together to crystallize the growing need for developing multicultural sensitivities and improved communication techniques. First, the globalization of markets means that you can expect to be doing business with people from around the world. Second, technological advancements in transportation and information are making the world smaller and more intertwined. Third, more and more immigrants from other cultures are settling in North America, thus changing the complexion of the work force. Successful interaction requires awareness, tolerance, and accommodation.

## Applying Your Skills at G.A.P Adventures

Let's assume that you're working at G.A.P's head office in Toronto as part of the sales and promotions team. You have been asked to work on the promotional campaign for Real Traveller, G.A.P's newest affiliate company. This new company is designed for less eco-minded tourists, offering essentially the same products without such a large emphasis on sustainability. As Bruce Poon Tip points out, the new company is designed to appeal to customers who don't want to travel with a "bunch of tree huggers."[60]

Although eco-tourism traditionally referred to environmentally friendly nature-based tourism, it has more recently, in large part thanks to the efforts of G.A.P, come to refer to the use of tourism as a tool for sustainable development, conservation, and biological diversity.[61]

### Your Task

As a member of the sales and promotions team, you've been asked to come up with some ideas for promoting Real Traveller. Bruce Poon Tip believes that companies should celebrate employees' failures as learning opportunities,[62] so feel comfortable in being as creative as you can with your ideas. Consider what type of person a Real Traveller might be (age, gender, interests, background, income, etc.), and prepare a summary of the key points for your promotional ideas as well as the various communication channels you would use.

**www.gapadventures.ca**

---

**2** Define *culture.* **Describe five significant characteristics of culture, and compare and contrast five key dimensions of culture.** *Culture* is the complex system of values, traits, morals, and customs shared by a society. Each of us is shaped by the elements of our culture. Some of the significant characteristics of culture include the following: (1) culture is learned, (2) cultures are inherently logical, (3) culture is the basis of self-identity and community, (4) culture combines the visible and invisible, and (5) culture is dynamic. Members of low-context cultures (such as those in North America, Scandinavia, and Germany) depend on words to express meaning, while people in high-context cultures (such as those in Japan, China, and Arab countries) rely more on context (social setting, a person's history, status, and position) to communicate meaning. Other key dimensions of culture include individualism, degree of formality, communication style, and time orientation.

**3** **Explain the effects of ethnocentrism, tolerance, and patience in achieving intercultural sensitivity.** *Ethnocentrism* refers to an individual's feeling that the culture you belong to is superior to all others and holds all truths. To function effectively in a global economy, we must acquire knowledge of other cultures and be willing to change attitudes. Developing tolerance often involves practising *empathy*, which means trying to see the world through another's eyes. Saving face and promoting social harmony are important in many parts of the world. Moving beyond narrow ethnocentric views often requires tolerance and patience.

*4* **Illustrate how to improve nonverbal and oral communication in multicultural environments.** We can minimize nonverbal miscommunication by recognizing that meanings conveyed by eye contact, posture, and gestures are largely culture dependent. Nonverbal messages are also sent by the use of time, space, and territory. Becoming aware of your own nonverbal behaviour and what it conveys is the first step in broadening your intercultural competence. In improving oral messages, you can learn foreign phrases, use simple English, speak slowly and enunciate clearly, observe eye messages, encourage accurate feedback, check for comprehension, accept blame, listen without interrupting, smile, and follow up important conversations in writing.

*5* **Illustrate how to improve written messages in multicultural environments.** To improve written messages, adopt local formats, use short sentences and short paragraphs, avoid ambiguous expression, strive for clarity, use correct grammar, and cite numbers carefully. Also try to accommodate the reader in organization, tone, and style.

*6* **Discuss intercultural ethics, including ethics abroad, bribery, prevailing customs, and methods for coping.** In doing business abroad, businesspeople should expect to find differing views about ethical practices. Although deciding whose ethics should prevail is tricky, the following techniques are helpful. Broaden your understanding of values and customs in other cultures, and avoid reflex judgments regarding the morality or corruptness of actions. Look for alternative solutions, refuse business if the options violate your basic values, and conduct all relations as openly as possible. Don't rationalize shady decisions, resist legalistic strategies, and apply a five-question ethics test when faced with a perplexing ethical dilemma.

*7* **Explain the challenge of capitalizing on work force diversity, including its dividends and its divisiveness. List tips for improving harmony and communication among diverse workplace audiences.** Having a diverse work force can benefit consumers, work teams, and business organizations. However, diversity can also cause divisiveness among various identity groups. To promote harmony and communication, many organizations develop diversity training programs. As an individual, you must understand and accept the value of differences. Don't expect conformity, and create zero tolerance for bias and prejudice. Learn about your cultural self, make fewer assumptions, and seek common ground when disagreements arise.

# CHAPTER REVIEW

1. Why is it increasingly important for businesspeople to develop multicultural communication skills? (Obj. 1)

2. What is culture and how is culture learned? (Obj. 2)

3. Describe five major dimensions of culture. (Obj. 2)

4. Briefly, contrast high- and low-context cultures. (Obj. 2)

5. What is *ethnocentrism*? (Obj. 3)

6. How is a *stereotype* different from a *prototype*? (Obj. 3)

7. Why is nonverbal communication more difficult to study and learn than verbal communication? (Obj. 4)

8. Name three processes that are effective in achieving competence in dealing with nonverbal messages in other cultures. (Obj. 4)

9. Describe five specific ways in which you can improve oral communication with a foreigner. (Obj. 4)

10. Describe five specific ways in which you can improve written communication with a foreigner. (Obj. 5)

11. What is the Corruption of Foreign Public Officials Act? (Obj. 6)

12. List seven techniques for making ethical decisions across borders. (Obj. 6)

13. Name three groups that benefit from work force diversity and explain why. (Obj. 7)

14. Describe six tips for improving communication among diverse workplace audiences. (Obj. 7)

# CRITICAL THINKING

1. Since English is becoming the world's business language, why should Canadians bother to learn about other cultures? (Objs. 1, 2, and 7)

2. If the rules, values, and attitudes of a culture are learned, can they be unlearned? Explain. (Obj. 2)

3. Some economists argue that the statement that "diversity is an economic asset" is an unproved and perhaps unprovable assertion. Should social responsibility or market forces determine whether an organization strives to create a diverse work force? Why? (Obj. 7)

4. **Ethical Issue:** In many countries government officials are not well paid, and "tips" (called "bribes" in North America) are a way of compensating them. If such payments are not considered wrong in those countries, should you pay them as a means of accomplishing your business? (Objs. 2 and 6)

# ACTIVITIES

## 4.1 Learning From Cultural Mishaps (Objs. 1–3)

As North American companies become increasingly global in their structure and marketing, employees face communication problems resulting from cultural misunderstandings. The following situations really happened.

**Your Task.** Based on what you have learned in this chapter, describe several broad principles that could be applied in helping the individuals involved understand what went wrong in the following events. What suggestions could you make for remedying the problems involved?

a. The employees of a large pharmaceutical firm became angry over the e-mail messages they received from the firm's employees in Spain. The messages weren't offensive. Generally, these routine messages just explained ongoing projects. What riled the employees was that every Spanish message was copied to the hierarchy within its division. The Canadians could not understand why e-mail messages had to be sent to people who had little or nothing to do with the issues being discussed. But this was accepted practice in Spain.[63]

b. A North American businessperson guided a group of Japanese to a local hospital on a business trip. The hospital director threw a handful of his business cards on a table for the Japanese to pick up. Why might the Japanese be offended?[64]

c. A T-shirt maker in Toronto printed shirts for the Spanish market that promoted the Pope's visit. Instead of the desired "I Saw the Pope" in Spanish, the shirts proclaimed "I Saw the Potato."

## 4.2 From Waterloo, Wisconsin, Trek Bicycles Goes Global (Objs. 1, 3, and 7)

The small town of Waterloo, Wisconsin (population 2 888), is about the last place you would expect to find the world's largest specialty bicycle maker. But Trek Bicycles started its global business in a red barn smack in the middle of Wisconsin farm country. Nearly 40 percent of the sales of the high-tech, Y-frame bicycles come from international markets. And future sales abroad look promising. Europeans buy 15 million bikes a year, while Americans and Canadians together purchase only 10 million. In Asia bicycles are a major means of transportation. To accommodate domestic and international consumers, Trek maintains a busy Web site at <**www.trekbikes.com**>.

Like many companies, Trek encountered problems in conducting multicultural transactions. For example, in Mexico, cargo was often pilfered while awaiting customs clearance.

Distributors in Germany were offended by catalogues featuring pictures of Betty Boop, a cartoon character that decorated Allied bombers during World War II. In Singapore a buyer balked at a green bike helmet, explaining that when a man wears green on his head it means his wife is unfaithful. In Germany, Trek had to redesign its packaging to reduce waste and meet environmental requirements. Actually, the changes required in Germany helped to bolster the company's overall image of environmental sensitivity.

**Your Task.** Based on principles you studied in this chapter, name several lessons that other entrepreneurs can learn from Trek's international experiences.[65]

## 4.3 Interpreting Intercultural Proverbs (Objs. 2 and 3)

Proverbs, which tell truths with metaphors and simplicity, often reveal fundamental values held by a culture.

**Your Task.** Discuss the following proverbs and explain how they relate to some of the cultural values you studied in this chapter. What additional proverbs can you cite and what do they mean?

*Japanese proverbs*
> The pheasant would have lived but for its cry.
> The nail that sticks up gets pounded down.
> To say nothing is a flower.

*North American proverbs*
> The squeaking wheel gets the grease.
> A stitch in time saves nine.
> A bird in hand is worth two in the bush.
> A man's home is his castle.

*German proverbs*
> No one is either rich or poor who has not helped himself to be so.
> He who is afraid of doing too much always does too little.

## 4.4 Negotiating Traps (Objs. 2, 3, 4, and 5)

It's often difficult for businesspeople to reach agreement on the terms of contracts, proposals, and anything that involves bargaining. It's even more difficult when the negotiators are from different cultures.

**Your Task.** Discuss the causes and implications of the following common mistakes made by North Americans in their negotiations with foreigners.

a.  Assuming that a final agreement is set in stone
b.  Lacking patience and insisting that matters progress more quickly than the pace preferred by the locals
c.  Thinking that an interpreter is always completely accurate
d.  Believing that individuals who speak English understand every nuance of your meaning
e.  Ignoring or misunderstanding the significance of rank

## 4.5 Global Economy (Obj. 1)

Fred Smith, founder of Federal Express, said, "It is an inescapable fact that the North American economy is becoming much more like the European and Asian economies, entirely tied to global trade."

**Your Task.** Read your local newspapers for a week and peruse national news magazines (*The Globe and Mail, Maclean's, Canadian Business,* and so forth) for articles that support this assertion. Your instructor may ask you to (a) report on many articles or (b) select one article to summarize. Report your findings orally or in a memo to your instructor. This topic could be expanded into a long report for Chapter 13 or 14.

## 4.6 Learning About Other Cultures: Multicultural Panel (Objs. 1–7)

**TEAM**

Probably the best way to learn about people from other countries and cultures is to travel extensively. A second-best way, though, is learning from visitors to your country.

**Your Task.** Locate two or three students from other countries (possibly members of your class or international students on campus) who could report on differences between their cultures and Western culture. In addition to context, individualism, formality, communication style, and time, consider such topics as the importance of family and gender roles. Study attitudes toward education, clothing, leisure time, and work. You may want to try some questions such as these:

a.  What behaviour or practices shocked you when you first arrived?
b.  What are some things visitors should or shouldn't do in your country?
c.  What is your educational system like?
d.  What do you consider a proper greeting for a friend? For a teacher? For your boss?
e.  What could we say or do to increase your comfort in social or business settings?

Conduct a panel discussion. At the chalkboard or on an overhead transparency, you might want to develop a chart contrasting Western values with those of the interviewees. See Activity 14.3 in Chapter 14 for additional questions and a research report focused on this topic.

## 4.7 Designing a Cell Phone Manual for Low- and High-Context Cultures (Obj. 2)

**CRITICAL THINKING**

Sometime in the early twenty-first century, many are predicting that China will emerge as the world's largest consumer of electronics products.[66] Well aware of this prediction, Siemens AG, a German cellular telephone manufacturer, is preparing to sell its popular German model to the Chinese. To develop the cell phone user manual, the firm conducted focus groups with Chinese and German consumers. The traditional German manual was translated into Chinese, and both German and Chinese focus groups were given nine tasks to perform using the same manual.

The focus groups produced contrasting results. When Chinese users first approach a manual, they want to see basic operations illustrated in colour on single pages with pictures. They reported having "no patience" to learn functions they might not use. They also noted that they learned to use the phone by asking friends, but if they had a problem they would never admit it to a friend. The Germans, on the other hand, wanted a manual that would present a clear but detailed overview of all the phone functions, not just basic operations. They thought that it would be useful in the long run to know all the different functions. The Germans read the words in the manual carefully, sometimes complaining when sentences were illogical or contradictory.

The Chinese preferred the "help" key to the printed manual. One said, "It gives you a very foolish feeling to use the phone at the same time you use the manual. It is ridiculous." The Chinese requested a videotape to show operations, and they also recommended that the size of the characters in the manual correlate with the importance of the information. **Your Task.** Based on your knowledge of high- and low-context cultures, how do the reactions of these focus groups reflect cultural expectations? If you were the researcher in this study, would you suggest to Siemens that a totally different user manual be developed for the Chinese market? What design recommendations would you make regarding the Chinese manual?

## 4.8 Helping Workers From High-Context Cultures Fit In (Obj. 2)

Cultural differences can undermine the effectiveness of day-to-day communications between workers from abroad and their North American colleagues. In an article in *HR Focus*, Cornelius Grove describes problems and offers solutions when individuals from high- and low-context cultures must work together. **Your Task.** Use InfoTrac to locate "Easing Overseas Workers into the U.S. Business Environment," *HR Focus*, October 1999, Article No. A55822581. After reading the article, answer these questions.

a. According to Grove, what are some of the office communication expectations of workers from high- and low-context cultures?

b. Cross-cultural training for both sides should focus on what topics?

c. What are four specific techniques that would help a high-context newcomer fit into a low-context office?

If this article is unavailable, use the search term "cross-cultural communication" to find another article that you can summarize.

## 4.9 Analyzing a Problem International Letter (Obj. 5)

North American writers sometimes forget that people in other countries, even if they understand English, are not aware of the meanings of certain words and phrases. **Your Task.** Study the following letter[67] to be sent by a North American firm to a potential supplier in another country. Identify specific weaknesses that may cause troubles for intercultural readers.

Dear Madeleine:

Because of the on-again/off-again haggling with one of our subcontractors, we have been putting off writing to you. We were royally turned off by their shoddy merchandise, the excuses they made up, and the way they put down some of our customers. Since we have our good name to keep up, we have decided to take the bull by the horns and see if you would be interested in bidding on the contract for spare parts.

By playing ball with us, your products are sure to score big. So please give it your best shot and fire off your price list ASAP. We'll need it by 3/8 if you are to be in the running.

Yours,

**125**

## 4.10 Talking Turkey: Avoiding Ambiguous Expressions (Obj. 5)

When a German firm received a message from a North American firm saying that it was "time to talk turkey," it was puzzled but decided to reply in Turkish, as requested. **Your Task.** Assume you are a businessperson engaged in exporting and importing. As such, you are in constant communication with suppliers and customers around the world. In messages sent abroad, what kinds of ambiguous expressions should you avoid? In teams or individually, list three to five original examples of idioms, slang, acronyms, sports references, abbreviations, jargon, and two-word verbs.

## 4.11 Making Grease Payments Abroad (Obj. 6)

**CRITICAL THINKING**

The Corruption of Foreign Public Officials Act prohibits giving anything of value to a foreign official in an effort to win or retain business. However, the Act does allow payments that may be necessary to expedite or secure "routine governmental action." For instance, a company could make "facilitation" payments to obtain permits and licences or to process visas or work orders. Also allowed are payments to provide telephone service, power and water supply, and loading and unloading of cargo.

**Your Task.** In light of what you have learned in this chapter, how should you act in the following situations? Are the actions legal or illegal?[68]

a. Your company is moving toward final agreement on a contract in Pakistan to sell farm equipment. As the contract is prepared, officials ask that a large amount be included to enable the government to update its agriculture research. The extra amount is to be paid in cash to the three officials you have worked with. Should your company pay?

b. You have been negotiating with a government official in Niger regarding an airplane maintenance contract. The official asks to use your Visa card to charge $2 028 in airplane tickets as a honeymoon present. Should you do it to win the contract?

c. You are trying to collect an overdue payment of $163 000 on a shipment of milk powder to the Dominican Republic. A senior government official asks for $20 000 as a collection service fee. Should you pay?

d. Your company is in the business of arranging hunting trips to East Africa. You are encouraged to give guns and travel to officials in a wildlife agency that has authority to issue licences to hunt big game. The officials have agreed to keep the gifts quiet. Should you make the gifts?

e. Your firm has just moved you to Malaysia, and your furniture is sitting on the dock. Cargo handlers won't unload it until you or your company pays off each local dock worker. Should you pay?

f. In Mexico your firm has been working hard to earn lucrative contracts with the national oil company, Pemex. One government official has hinted elaborately that his son would like to do marketing studies for your company. Should you hire the son?

## 4.12 Diversity Role-Playing: Hey, We're All Clones! (Obj. 7)

Reebok International, the athletic footwear and apparel company, swelled from a $12-million-a-year company to a $3-billion footwear powerhouse in less than a decade. "When we were growing very, very fast, all we did was bring another friend into work the next day," recalls Sharon Cohen, Reebok vice president. "Everybody hired nine of their friends. Well, it happened that nine white people hired nine of their friends, so guess what? They were white, all about the same age. And then we looked up and said, 'Wait a minute. We don't like the way it looks here.'"[69] Assume you are a manager for a successful, fast-growing company like Reebok. One day you look around and notice that everyone looks alike. **Your Task.** Pair off with a classmate to role-play a discussion in which you strive to convince another manager that your organization would be better if it were more diverse. The other manager (your classmate), however, is satisfied with the status quo. Suggest advantages for diversifying the staff. The opposing manager argues for homogeneity.

## 4.13 Locating Diversity Training Consultants (Obj. 7)

**WEB** **E-MAIL**

Management thought it was doing the right thing in diversifying its staff. But now signs of friction are appearing. Staff meetings are longer, and conflicts have arisen in solving problems. Some of the new people say they aren't taken seriously and that they are expected to blend in and become just like everybody else. A discrimination suit was filed in one department.

**Your Task.** CEO William Somers asks you, a human resources officer, to present suggestions for overcoming this staff problem. Make a list of several suggestions, based on what you have learned in this chapter. In addition, go to the Web and locate three individuals, teams, or firms who you think might be possibilities for developing a diversity training program for your company. Prepare a memo or an e-mail to Mr. Somers outlining your suggestions and listing your rec-

ommendations for possible diversity training consultants. Describe the areas of expertise of each potential consultant.

## 4.14 Searching International Publications for Business News

**WEB**

Your company seeks to expand its markets overseas. Your boss asks you to check three newspapers (your choice) every week to keep track of business-related events. She's interested in a variety of subjects and is always intrigued by whatever you uncover.

**Your Task.** Go to <**www.businessindepth.com**>, where you'll find English editions of international newspapers from many countries. Select three to five articles to summarize in a memo to your boss, Susan Plutsky. Include a short description of each newspaper.

## 4.15 Learning About Workers From India

**INFOTRAC**

North American companies are heavily recruiting skilled workers from India. And many companies have relocated technical jobs to India. An interesting article in *Global Workforce* provides insights into Indian culture and customs. The aim of the article is to prevent miscommunication in organizations with Indian workers.

**Your Task.** Use InfoTrac to locate Valerie Frazee's article, "Working With Indians," *Global Workforce*, July 1998, Article No. A20978819. After reading the article, answer the following questions.

**a.** How is diversity in India different from diversity in North America?

**b.** What two core social values are paramount to Indians, and how do these values affect their work efforts?

**c.** How do Indians differ from Westerners on the issue of control?

## C.L.U.E. REVIEW 4

On a separate sheet edit the following sentences to correct faults in grammar, punctuation, spelling, and word use.

**1.** Gifts for the children of an arab are welcome however gifts for an arabs wife are not advisible.

**2.** In latin america knifes are not proper gifts, they signify cutting off a relationship.

**3.** statistics canada reports that 1/3 of the foreign born population of canada are from: asia, the caribbean, and the middle east.

**4.** Although international business was all ready common among big companys we now find many smaller companys seeking global markets.

**5.** On April 15th an article entitled Practicle Cross-Cultural persuasion strategies appeared in The Journal of International Business.

**6.** 3 executives agreed that there companys overseas project with france was taking twice as long as expected.

**7.** They reccommend therefor that a committee study the cultural and language issues for a 3 week period, and submit a report of it's findings.

**8.** The three hundred represenatives were told that the simple act of presenting a bussiness card is something to which canadians give little thought but it is a serious formality in japan.

**9.** Each of the seventy-five delegates were charged a fee of forty dollars to attend the cultural training session although formally the charge had been only thirty dollars.

**10.** Both the President and Senior Vice President agrees that all staff members suggestions should be sent to: Human Relations.

# Unit 2
## The Writing Process

**CHAPTER 5**

*Preparing to Write Business Messages*

**CHAPTER 6**

*Organizing and Writing Business Messages*

**CHAPTER 7**

*Revising Business Messages*

# Chapter 5

## Preparing to Write Business Messages

## LEARNING OBJECTIVES

**1** Describe three basic elements that distinguish business writing and summarize the three phases of the 3-×-3 writing process.

**2** Explain how the writing process may be altered and how it is affected by team projects and technology.

**3** Clarify what is involved in analyzing a writing task and selecting a communication channel.

**4** Describe anticipating and profiling the audience for a message.

**5** Specify six writing techniques that help communicators adapt messages to the task and audience.

**6** Explain why four areas of communication hold legal responsibilities for writers.

## *Tilley Endurables*

Alex Tilley, an avid sailor, was tired of his hats blowing into the water and sinking into oblivion and decided to do something about it. After consulting with a variety of specialists, Tilley created a hat that floats, doesn't blow off, has pockets, sports a brim that stiffens in the rain, and blocks harmful UV rays.

Tilley was born in Mount Albert, Ontario, and grew up all over Ontario. At an early age, his entrepreneurial spirit emerged as he re-sold pumpkins bought from a Kitchener farmer. He spent his high school years in Sudbury, and his spotty academic career is part of the folklore.[1] After working at various ventures, he began dealing art. This pursuit allowed him the leisure time to sail—a passion that brought forth the famous Tilley hat.

Tilley began selling hats in 1980, hoping to make a small profit. Because the hats were priced higher than his competitors', early sales were disappointing. Tilley's big break came when he donated his hats to the Canadian entry in the 1983 America's Cup sailing race. The word-of-mouth advertising paid off, and the family business grew into a mail-order company that led to a retail operation when customers began showing up at the door.

The classic Tilley hat is a Canadian design icon that has expanded into a global business. Customers' stories include one about a Bowmanville (Ontario) Zoo elephant that ate the hat right off his trainer's head three times. Each time, the persistent trainer washed, dried, and returned that hat to his head. This legendary elephant story is part of the appeal that makes the Tilley name unique and memorable. Tilley hats are famous and are endorsed by Sir Edmund Hillary (the only person who receives payment for his endorsement—30 hats and 30 windbreakers for his Sherpa friends),[2] U.S. General Norman Schwarzkopf, and the Canadian Armed Forces, which purchased 6 000 hats for its troops during the Gulf War.

Tilley hats are sold in 17 countries, with sales in excess of "tens of millions of dollars,"[3] and the family owns four stores: two in Toronto, one in Montreal, and another in Vancouver. Tilley Endurables was one of the first companies in the world to showcase its catalogue on the Web in the mid-1990s. In addition to the making of hats, Tilley Endurables has evolved into a company with over 9 000 stockkeeping units (SKUs). The company sells apparel, shoes, totes, belts, and other items. The most popular travel products are hats, bush shirts, and a 16-pocket vest called VOMP (vest of many pockets).

Tilley Endurables recognizes the importance of its customers. Alex Tilley knows it's not enough to have an excellent product; customer satisfaction leads to positive word-of-mouth marketing for the company and its clothes.

### CRITICAL THINKING
- Why might a company like Tilley change its image?
- In messages it sends to customers, how would Tilley present a new image?
- What communication skills are important to Tilley's marketing representatives?

**www.tilley.com**

## APPROACHING THE WRITING PROCESS SYSTEMATICALLY

As Tilley Endurables continues to succeed, its representatives must finely tune their communication skills to project a new image and capture new clients. Preparing and writing any business message—whether a letter, e-mail, memo, or sales presentation—is easier when the writer or presenter has a systematic plan to follow.

*1*

# The Basics of Business Writing

**Business writing is purposeful, economical, and reader-oriented.**

Business writing differs from other writing you may have done. Secondary or post-secondary compositions and term papers may have required you to describe your feelings, display your knowledge, and meet a minimum word count. Business writing, however, has different goals. In preparing business messages and oral presentations, you'll find that your writing needs to be:

- **Purposeful.** You will be writing to solve problems and convey information. You will have a definite purpose to fulfill in each message.

- **Economical.** You will try to present ideas clearly but concisely. Length is not rewarded.

- **Reader-oriented.** You will concentrate on looking at a problem from the reader's perspective instead of seeing it from your own.

**Business writers seek to *express* rather than *impress*.**

These distinctions actually ease the writer's task. In writing most business documents, you won't be searching your imagination for creative topic ideas. You won't be stretching your ideas to make them appear longer. One writing consultant complained that "most college graduates entering industry have at least a subliminal perception that in technical and business writing, quantity enhances quality."[4] Wrong! Get over the notion that longer is better. Conciseness is what counts in business. Furthermore, you won't be trying to dazzle readers with your extensive knowledge, powerful vocabulary, or graceful phrasing. The goal in business writing is to *express* rather than *impress*. You will be striving to get your ideas across naturally, simply, and clearly.

In many ways business writing is easier than academic writing, yet it still requires hard work, especially from beginners. But following a process, studying models, and practising the craft can make nearly anyone a successful business writer and speaker. This book provides all three components: process, products (models), and practice. First, you'll focus on the process of writing business messages.

## The 3-×-3 Writing Process for Business Messages and Oral Presentations

**The phases of the 3-×-3 writing process are prewriting, writing, and revising.**

This book divides the writing process into three distinct phases: prewriting, writing, and revising. As shown in Figure 5.1, each phase is further divided into three major activities. The 3-×-3 process provides you with a systematic plan for developing all your business communications, from simple memos and informational reports to corporate proposals and oral presentations.

The time spent on each phase varies with the deadline, purpose, and audience for the message. Let's consider how the 3-×-3 writing process might work in a typical business situation. Suppose you must write a letter to a department store buyer about an order that you, as a manufacturer of jeans, cannot fill. The first phase (prewriting) prepares you to write and involves analyzing, anticipating, and adapting. In analyzing the situation, you decide to focus your letter on retaining the order. That can best be done by persuading the buyer to accept a different jeans model. You anticipate that the buyer will be disappointed that the original model is unavailable. What's more, she will probably be reluctant to switch to a different model. Thus, you must find ways to adapt your message to reduce her reluctance and convince her to switch.

The second phase (writing) involves researching, organizing, and then composing the message. To collect facts for this letter, you would probably investigate the buyer's past purchases. You would check to see what jeans you have in stock that she might accept as a substitute. You might do some brainstorming or consult your colleagues for their suggestions about how to retain this order. Then, you would

**FIGURE 5.1** The 3-×-3 Writing Process

| Prewriting *1* | Writing *2* | Revising *3* |
| --- | --- | --- |
| Analyze | Research | Revise |
| Anticipate | Organize | Proofread |
| Adapt | Compose | Evaluate |

organize your information into a loose outline and decide on a strategy or plan for revealing your information most effectively. Equipped with a plan, you're ready to compose the first draft of the letter.

**Collecting data, organizing it, and composing a first draft make up the second phase of the writing process.**

The third phase of the process (revising) involves revising, proofreading, and evaluating your letter. After writing the first draft, you'll revise the message for clarity, conciseness, tone, and readability. You'll proofread carefully to ensure correct spelling, grammar, punctuation, and format. Finally, you'll evaluate the message to see whether it accomplishes your goal.

Although our diagram of the writing process shows the three phases equally, the time you spend on each varies. One expert gives these rough estimates for scheduling a project: 25 percent worrying and planning (Phase 1), 25 percent writing (Phase 2), 45 percent revising, and 5 percent proofreading (Phase 3). These are rough guides, yet you can see that good writers spend most of their time revising. Much depends, of course, on your project, its importance, and your familiarity with it. What's critical to remember, though, is that revising is a major component of the writing process.

**In the writing process revising takes the most time.**

This process may seem a bit complicated for the daily messages and oral presentations that many businesspeople prepare. Does this same process apply to memos and short letters? And how do collaborators and modern computer technologies affect the process?

## Adapting and Altering the Process

Although good writers proceed through each phase of the writing process, some steps may be compressed for short, routine messages. Brief, everyday documents enlist the 3-×-3 process, but many of the steps are performed quickly, without prolonged deliberation. For example, prewriting may take the form of a few moments of reflection. The writing phase may consist of looking in the files quickly, jotting a few notes in the margin of the original document, and composing at your computer. Revising might consist of reading a printout, double-checking the spelling and grammar, and making a few changes. Longer, more involved documents—such as persuasive memos, sales letters, management reports, proposals, and résumés—require more attention to all parts of the process.

One other point about the 3-×-3 writing process needs clarification. It may appear that you perform one step and progress to the next, always following the same order. Most business writing, however, is not that rigid. Although writers perform the tasks described, the steps may be rearranged, abbreviated, or repeated. Some writers revise every sentence and paragraph as they go. Many find that new ideas occur after they've begun to write, causing them to back up, alter the organization, and rethink their plan. You should expect to follow the 3-×-3 process closely as you begin developing your business communication skills. With experience, though, you'll become like other good writers and presenters who alter, compress, and rearrange the steps as needed.

**Steps in the writing process may be rearranged, shortened, or repeated.**

*Working With Teams.* As you learned in Chapter 2, many of today's workers will spend some time working with teams to complete projects. Experts say that 40 to 50 percent of the work force will soon be working in some kind of team environment.[5] And a study of business professionals showed that nine out of ten sometimes write as part of a team.[6]

When is writing collaboration necessary? It is especially important for (1) big tasks, (2) items with short deadlines, and (3) team projects that require the expertise or consensus of many people. Businesspeople sometimes collaborate on short documents, such as memos, letters, information briefs, procedures, and policies. But more often, teams work together on big documents and presentations. For example, let's say that a product development team at Mattel comes up with a new line of educational computer toys for infants. The team will probably have to prepare a proposal that persuades management to manufacture and market the new toys. This proposal would be developed and written by many members of a team.

<aside>Team-written documents and presentations produce better products.</aside>

Team-written documents and presentations are standard in most organizations because collaboration has many advantages. Most important, collaboration produces a better product. Many heads are better than one. In addition, team members and organizations benefit from team processes. Working together helps socialize members. They learn more about the organization's values and procedures. They are able to break down functional barriers, and they improve both formal and informal chains of communication. Additionally, they "buy into" a project when they are part of its development. Members of effective teams are eager to implement their recommendations.

In preparing big projects, teams may not actually function together for each phase of the writing process. Typically, team members gather at the beginning to brainstorm. They iron out answers to questions about the purpose, audience, content, organization, and design of their document or presentation. They develop procedures for team functioning, as you learned in Chapter 2. Then, they often assign segments of the project to individual members. Thus, teams work together closely in Phase 1 (prewriting) of the writing process. However, members generally work separately in Phase 2 (writing), when they conduct research, organize their findings, and compose a first draft. During Phase 3 (revising) teams may work together to synthesize their drafts and offer suggestions for revision. They might assign one person the task of preparing the final document and another the job of proofreading. The revision and evaluation phase might be repeated several times before the final product is ready for presentation.

<aside>Computer technology helps you generate ideas, conduct research, and organize facts.</aside>

*Working With Technology.* The composition process—whether you are writing a business document, preparing an oral presentation, or creating a Web page—is further affected by today's amazing computer tools. Software exists to help you generate ideas, conduct research electronically, and organize facts into outlines. In fact, many phases of the writing process—such as keyboarding, revision, and collaboration—are simplified and supported by word processing programs, discussed more fully in the accompanying Tech Talk box.

Wonderful as these powerful technological tools are, however, they do not automatically produce effective letters, persuasive oral presentations, or cool Web sites. They can neither organize data into concise and logical presentations nor shape ideas into persuasive arguments. Only a well-trained author can do that. Nevertheless, today's technology enhances every aspect of writing. Therefore, skill in using software is essential for anyone whose job requires composition.

## Seven Ways Computer Software Can Help You Create Better Written Messages, Oral Presentations, and Web Pages

Although computers and software programs cannot actually do the writing for you, they provide powerful tools that make the composition process easier and the results more professional. Here are seven ways your computer can help you improve your written documents, oral presentations, and even Web pages.

1. **Fighting writer's block.** Because word processors enable ideas to flow almost effortlessly from your brain to a screen, you can expect fewer delays resulting from writer's block. You can compose rapidly, and you can experiment with structure and phrasing, later retaining and polishing your most promising thoughts. Many authors "sprint write," recording unedited ideas quickly, to start the composition process and also to brainstorm for ideas on a project. Then, they tag important ideas and use computer outlining programs to organize those ideas into logical sequences.

2. **Collecting information electronically.** As a knowledge worker in an information economy, you will need to find information quickly. Much of the world's information is now accessible by computer. You can locate the titles of books, as well as many full-text articles from magazines, newspapers, and government publications. Massive amounts of information are available from the Internet, CD-ROMs, and online services. Through specialized information-retrieval services (such as ABI-INFORM, InfoTrac, or Dow Jones News/Retrieval Service), you can have at your fingertips up-to-the-minute legal, scientific, scholarly, and business information. The most amazing source of electronic information is the Web, with its links to sites around the world, some incredibly helpful and others worthless. You'll learn more about these exciting electronic resources in Unit 4.

3. **Outlining and organizing ideas.** Most high-end word processors include some form of "outliner," a feature that enables you to divide a topic into a hierarchical order with main points and subpoints. Your computer keeps track of the levels of ideas automatically so that you can easily add, cut, or rearrange points in the outline. This feature is particularly handy when you're preparing a report or organizing a presentation. Some programs even enable you to transfer your outline directly to slide frames to be used as visual aids in a talk.

4. **Improving correctness and precision.** Nearly all word processing programs today provide features that catch and correct spelling and typographical errors. Poor spellers and weak typists universally bless their spell checkers for repeatedly saving them from humiliation. Most high-end word processing programs today also provide grammar checkers that are markedly improved over earlier versions. They now detect many errors in capitalization, word use (such as *it's*, *its*), double negatives, verb use, subject-verb agreement, sentence structure, number agreement, number style, and other writing faults. However, most grammar programs don't actually correct the errors they detect. You must know how to do that. Still, grammar checkers can be very helpful. In addition to spelling and grammar programs, thesaurus programs help you choose precise words that say exactly what you intend.

5. **Adding graphics for emphasis.** Your letters, memos, and reports may be improved by the addition of graphs and artwork to clarify and illustrate data. You can import charts, diagrams, and illustrations created in database, spreadsheet, graphics, or draw-and-paint programs. Moreover, ready-made pictures, called clip art, can be used to symbolize or illustrate ideas.

6. **Designing and producing professional-looking documents, presentations, and Web pages.** Most high-end word processing programs today include a large selection of scalable fonts (for different character sizes and styles), italics, boldface, symbols, and styling techniques to aid you in producing consistent formatting and professional-looking results. Moreover, today's presentation software enables you to incorporate

*(continued)*

showy slide effects, colour, sound, pictures, and even movies into your talks for management or customers. Web document builders also help you design and construct Web pages.

7. **Using collaborative software for team writing.** Assume you are part of a group preparing a lengthy proposal to secure a government contract. You expect to write one segment of the proposal yourself and help revise parts written by others. Special word processing programs with commenting and strikeout features allow you to revise easily and to identify each team member's editing. Some collaborative programs, called groupware, as you learned in Chapter 2, also include decision-support tools to help groups generate, organize, and analyze ideas more efficiently than in traditional meetings.

**Career Application**

Individually or in teams, identify specific software programs that perform the tasks described here. Prepare a table naming each program, its major functions, and its advantages and disadvantages for business writers in your field.

## ANALYZING THE TASK

*3*

Whether you're writing with a team, composing by yourself, or preparing an oral presentation, the product of your efforts can be improved by following the steps described in the 3-×-3 writing process. Not only are you more likely to get your message across, but you'll feel less anxious and your writing will progress more quickly. The remainder of this chapter concentrates on the prewriting phase of composition: analyzing, anticipating, and adapting.

In analyzing the composition task, you'll first need to identify the purpose of the message and select the best channel or form in which to deliver it.

### Identifying Your Purpose

As you begin to compose a message, ask yourself two important questions: (1) Why am I sending this message? and (2) What do I hope to achieve? Your responses will determine how you organize and present your information.

Your message may have primary and secondary purposes. For academic work your primary purpose may be merely to complete the assignment; secondary purposes might be to make yourself look good and to get a good grade. The primary purposes for sending business messages are typically to inform and to persuade. A secondary purpose is to promote goodwill: you and your organization want to look good in the eyes of your audience.

**Most business communication has both primary purposes (to inform or persuade) and secondary purposes (to promote goodwill).**

Most business messages do nothing more than *inform*. They explain procedures, announce meetings, answer questions, and transmit findings. Some business messages, however, are meant to *persuade*. These messages sell products, convince managers, motivate employees, and win over customers. Informative messages are developed differently than persuasive messages.

### Selecting the Best Channel

After identifying the purpose of your message, you need to select the most appropriate communication channel. As you learned in Chapter 1, some information is most efficiently and effectively delivered orally. Other messages should be written, and still others are best delivered electronically. Whether to set up a meeting, send a message by e-mail, or write a report depends on some of the following factors:

- Importance of the message
- Amount and speed of feedback required
- Necessity of a permanent record
- Cost of the channel
- Degree of formality desired

The foregoing factors could help you decide which of the channels shown in Figure 5.2 is most appropriate for delivering a message. Tilley store managers, for example, would probably choose face-to-face conversations or group meetings as the most effective communication channel in delivering any new product message.

**FIGURE 5.2  Choosing Communication Channels**

| Channel | Best Use |
|---|---|
| Face-to-face conversation | When you want to be persuasive, deliver bad news, or share a personal message. |
| Telephone call | When you need to deliver or gather information quickly, when nonverbal cues are unimportant, and when you cannot meet in person. |
| Voice mail message | When you wish to leave important or routine information that the receiver can respond to when convenient. |
| Fax | When your message must cross time zones or international boundaries, when a written record is significant, or when speed is important. |
| E-mail | When you need feedback but not immediately. Insecurity makes it problematic for personal, emotional, or private messages. Effective for communicating with a large, dispersed audience. |
| Face-to-face group meeting | When group decisions and consensus are important. Inefficient for merely distributing information. |
| Video or teleconference | When group consensus and interaction are important, but members are geographically dispersed. |
| Memo | When you want a written record to clearly explain policies, discuss procedures, or collect information within an organization. |
| Letter | When you need a written record of correspondence with customers, the government, suppliers, or others outside an organization. |
| Report or proposal | When you are delivering complex data internally or externally. |

Choosing the best channel to deliver a message depends on the importance of the message, the feedback required, the need for a permanent record, the cost, and the degree of formality needed.

Some messages miss the mark. Consider this letter that responds to a nine-year-old boy who requested a toy rocket launcher from a breakfast cereal company: "Due to the overwhelming response this promotion has generated, we have unfortunately depleted our stock temporarily. We are, therefore, holding your request pending stock replenishment." The breakfast cereal company's representative had no sense of audience; as a result, the language was totally inappropriate.

A good writer anticipates the audience for a message: What is the reader like? How will that reader react to the message? Although you can't always know exactly who the reader is, you can imagine some characteristics of the reader. The breakfast cereal company writer could have pictured a typical young boy and imagined the vocabulary and expectations he might have. Even writers of direct-mail sales letters have a general idea of the audience they wish to target. Picturing a typical reader is important in guiding what you write. One catalogue copywriter pictures his sister-in-law whenever he writes product descriptions for the catalogue. By profiling your audience and shaping a message to respond to that profile, you are more likely to achieve your communication goals.

## Profiling the Audience

**By profiling your audience before you write, you can identify the appropriate tone, language, and channel.**

Visualizing your audience is a pivotal step in the writing process. The questions in Figure 5.3 will help you profile your audience. How much time you devote to answering these questions depends greatly on your message and its context. An analytical report that you compose for management or an oral presentation before a big group would, of course, demand considerable audience anticipation. On the other hand, a memo to a coworker or a letter to a familiar supplier might require only a few moments of planning. No matter how short your message, though, spend some time thinking about the audience so that you can tailor your words to your readers or listeners. "The most often unasked question in business and professional communication," claims a writing expert, "is as simple as it is important: *Have I thought enough about my audience?*"[7]

## Responding to the Profile

Valuable advice on how to improve your messages includes profiling your audience and responding to that profile.

Anticipating your audience helps you make decisions about shaping the message. You'll discover what kind of language is appropriate, whether you're free to use specialized technical terms, whether you should explain everything, and so on. You'll decide whether your tone should be formal or informal, and you'll select the most desirable channel. Imagining whether the receiver is likely to be neutral, positive, or negative will help you determine how to organize your message.

Another result of profiling your audience will be knowing whether a secondary audience is possible. If so, you'll provide more background information and be more specific in identifying items than would be necessary for the primary audience only. Analyzing the task and anticipating the audience assists you in adapting your message so that it will accomplish what you intend.

**FIGURE 5.3** Asking the Right Questions to Profile Your Audience

| Primary Audience | Secondary Audience |
|---|---|
| Who is my primary reader or listener? | Who might see or hear this message in addition to the primary audience? |
| What is my personal and professional relationship with that person? | How do these people differ from the primary audience? |
| What position does the individual hold in the organization? | |
| How much does that person know about the subject? | |
| What do I know about that person's education, beliefs, culture, and attitudes? | |
| Should I expect a neutral, positive, or negative response to my message? | |

## ADAPTING TO THE TASK AND AUDIENCE

After analyzing your purpose and anticipating your audience, you must convey your purpose to that audience. Adaptation is the process of creating a message that suits your audience.

5

One important aspect of adaptation is *tone*. Conveyed largely by the words in a message, tone reflects how a receiver feels upon reading or hearing a message. For example, think how you would react to these statements:

You must return the form by 5 p.m.

Would you please return the form by 5 p.m.

The wording of the first message establishes an aggressive or negative tone—no one likes being told what to do. The second message is reworded in a friendlier, more positive manner. Poorly chosen words may sound demeaning, condescending, discourteous, pretentious, or demanding. Notice in the Tilley Endurable's letter in Figure 5.4 (page 141) that the writer achieves a courteous and warm tone. The letter responds to a customer's concern about the changing merchandise mix available in Tilley's catalogues. The customer also wanted to receive fewer catalogues. The writer explains the company's expanded merchandise line and reassures the customer that Tilley has not abandoned its emphasis on classic styles.

Skilled communicators create a positive tone in their messages by using a number of adaptive techniques, some of which are unconscious. These include spotlighting receiver benefits; cultivating a "you" attitude; and avoiding gender, racial, age, and disability bias. Additional adaptive techniques include being courteous, using familiar words, and choosing precise words.

**Ways to adapt to the audience include choosing the right words and tone, spotlighting reader benefits, cultivating a "you" attitude, and using sensitive, courteous language.**

# Spotlighting Receiver Benefits

**Empathic communicators envision the receiver and focus on benefits to that person.**

Focusing on the audience sounds like a modern idea, but in describing effective writing over 200 years ago, Ben Franklin observed, "To be good, it ought to have a tendency to benefit the reader."[8] These wise words have become a fundamental guideline for today's business communicators. A contemporary communication consultant gives this solid advice to his business clients: "Always stress the benefit to the readers of whatever it is you're trying to get them to do. If you can show them how you're going to save *them* frustration or help them meet their goals, you have the makings of a powerful message."[9]

**Empathy means trying to understand another's situation, feelings, and motives.**

Adapting your message to the receiver's needs means putting yourself in that person's shoes. It's called *empathy*. Empathic senders think about how a receiver will decode a message. They try to give something to the receiver, solve the receiver's problems, save the receiver's money, or just understand the feelings and position of that person. Which of the following messages are more appealing to the receiver?

| **Sender-Focused** | **Receiver-Focused** |
|---|---|
| To enable us to update our share-holder records, we ask that the enclosed card be returned. | So that you may promptly receive dividend cheques and information related to your shares, please return the enclosed card. |
| Our warranty becomes effective only when we receive an owner's registration. | Your warranty begins working for you as soon as you return your owner's registration. |
| We offer an audiocassette language course in which we have complete faith. | The sooner you order the audio-cassette language program, the sooner the rewards will be yours. |
| The Human Resources Department requires that the enclosed question-naire be completed immediately so that we can allocate our training resource funds. | You can be one of the first employees to sign up for the new career development program. Fill out the attached questionnaire and return it immediately. |

# Cultivating the "You" View

**Effective communicators develop the "you" view in a sincere, not manipulative or critical, tone.**

Notice how many of the previous receiver-focused messages included the word *you*. In concentrating on receiver benefits, skilled communicators naturally develop the "you" view. They emphasize second-person pronouns (*you, your*) instead of first-person pronouns (*I/we, us, our*). Whether your goal is to inform, persuade, or promote goodwill, the catchiest words you can use are *you* and *your*. Compare the following examples.

| **"I/We" View** | **"You" View** |
|---|---|
| I have scheduled your vacation to begin May 1. | You may begin your vacation May 1. |
| **"I/We" View** | **"You" View** |
| We have shipped your order by FedEx, and we are sure it will arrive in time for the sales promotion January 15. | Your order will be delivered by FedEx in time for your sales promotion January 15. |

## FIGURE 5.4 Customer Response Letter

Explains evolving merchandise line from company's and reader's view

Emphasizes areas of agreement

**Opens response to inquiry by agreeing with customer**

**Uses conversational language to convey warmth and sincerity**

**Concludes by giving customer what she wants and promoting future business**

Tilley

February 23, 2005

Mrs. Elaine Hough
2175 Edenwood Road
Brandon, MB  R7A 6A9

Dear Mrs. Hough:

Your letter was a strong endorsement of our belief that we made the right choice when we devoted our company to comfort, ease of care, durability, and a smart appearance — and that it's still the right choice.

It's true we've made changes. In the past few years, with the markets soft and tastes changing, we reexamined our merchandise with a view to continuing to serve valued customers while introducing ourselves to new ones. We decided we want to give you more choices for more occasions.

Our commitment to the classics hasn't weakened, as I hope you'd agree, having seen recent catalogues. But we've defined "classic" more inclusively than in the past. We're using new fabrics, new colours, a more relaxed fit. There's more imagination in our product mix now, but the hats, pants, vests, jackets, and other basics for which you've relied on us are still here. You may not find each one in every catalogue, and you may notice the new products more than those you've seen before. The classics are still here, and the selection will be growing.

I've arranged to send you just the four catalogues a year you wanted. I hope you'll keep an eye out for them. I think that, more and more, you'll be able to come to us for the styles you want.

Sincerely,

*Lise Andrews*

Lise Andrews
Customer Service

Tilley Endurables Inc., 900 Don Mills Road, Don Mills, Ontario M3C 1V6 • Telephone (416) 441-6141 • Fax (416) 444-3860

---

| | |
|---|---|
| I'm asking all of our employees to respond to the attached survey regarding working conditions. | Because your ideas count, please complete the attached survey regarding working conditions. |

To see if you're really concentrating on the reader, try using the "empathy index." In one of your messages, count all the second-person references. Then, count all the first-person references. Your empathy index is low if *I* and *we* outnumber *you* and *your*.

But the use of *you* is more than merely a numbers game. Second-person pronouns can be overused and misused. Readers appreciate genuine interest; on the other hand, they resent obvious attempts at manipulation. Some sales messages, for example, are guilty of overkill when they include *you* dozens of times in a direct-mail promotion. Furthermore, the word can sometimes create the wrong impression.

Consider this statement: *You cannot return merchandise until you receive written approval. You* appears twice, but the reader feels singled out for criticism. In the following version the message is less personal and more positive: *Customers may return merchandise with written approval.* In short, avoid using *you* for general statements that suggest blame and could cause ill will.

In recognizing the value of the "you" attitude, however, writers do not have to sterilize their writing and totally avoid any first-person pronouns or words that show their feelings. Skilled communicators are able to convey sincerity, warmth, and enthusiasm by the words they choose. Don't be afraid to use phrases such as *I'm happy* or *We're delighted*, if you truly are.

When speaking face to face, communicators show sincerity and warmth with nonverbal cues such as a smile and pleasant voice tone. In letters, memos, and e-mail messages, however, only expressive words and phrases can show these feelings. These phrases suggest hidden messages that say to readers and customers "You are important, I hear you, and I'm honestly trying to please you." Mary Kay Ash, one of the most successful cosmetics entrepreneurs of all times, gave her salespeople wise advice. She had them imagine that any person they were addressing had a sign around her neck saying "Make me feel important."

## Using Bias-Free Language

In adapting a message to its audience, be sure your language is sensitive and bias-free. Few writers set out to be offensive. Sometimes, though, we all say things that we never thought might be hurtful. The real problem is that we don't think about the words that stereotype groups of people, such as *the boys in the mailroom* or *the girls in the front office*. Be cautious about expressions that might be biased in terms of gender, race, ethnicity, age, and disability.[10]

*Avoiding Gender Bias.* You can defuse gender time bombs by replacing words that exclude or stereotype women (sometimes called *sexist language*) with neutral, inclusive expressions. The following examples show how sexist terms and phrases can be replaced with neutral ones.

| Gender-Biased | Improved |
|---|---|
| female doctor, woman lawyer, cleaning woman | doctor, lawyer, cleaner |
| waiter/waitress, authoress, stewardess | server, author, cabin attendant |
| mankind, man-hour, man-made | humanity, working hours, artificial |
| office girls | office workers |
| the doctor . . . he | doctors . . . they |
| the teacher . . . she | teachers . . . they |
| executives and their wives | executives and their spouses |
| foreman, flagman, workman | lead worker, flagger, worker |
| businessman, salesman | businessperson, sales representative |
| Each worker had his picture taken. | Each worker had a picture taken. |
|  | All workers had their pictures taken. |
|  | Each worker had his or her picture taken. |

Generally, you can avoid gender-biased language by leaving out the words *man* or *woman*, by using plural nouns and pronouns, or by changing to a gender-free word (*person* or *representative*). Avoid the "his or her" option whenever possible. It's wordy and conspicuous. With a little effort, you can usually find a construction that is graceful, grammatical, and generic.

# Tilley Endurables Revisited

After over two decades as an adventure-apparel catalogue/retail Internet company that takes in over $20 million a year,[11] Tilley Endurables decided to revamp its catalogue. Founder Alex Tilley's daughter, Alison Tilley, led the redesign, using thicker paper, a new logo, and a much cleaner look. Other elements that had previously been eliminated, such as customer testimonials and photographs plus the Tilleys' own testimonials, were reintroduced. According to Alison, "We have very loyal customers—400 000 of them—and they missed that in the old catalogue."[12]

Tilley's target market is consumers 50 and up, and the catalogue reflects this group by portraying older models and "real" customers. Although the advertising for the products focuses on mountains and deserts, Tilley's customers live predominately in the "urban jungle" but may aspire to more exciting possibilities in the future.

The clothing is considered classically conservative, and the prices are somewhat higher than some of their competitors'. Quality sometimes comes with a price tag; however, Tilley products come with a lifetime guarantee. This excellent quality also has other benefits. The outstanding reputation and endurance of Tilley products often help their suppliers. According to David Freedman, owner of Freedman Harness Limited in Toronto, Tilley's major competitors, such as Mountain Equipment Co-op, Eddie Bauer, and Lands' End, often want merchandise from his company since Freedman has passed the Tilley test.

## CRITICAL THINKING

- In planning a catalogue for a potential customer, why is analyzing the task and anticipating the audience such an important part of the preparation?
- If the company were considering opening another retail location and needed financing, what kinds of questions should be asked to profile the audience?
- How important is it to consider reader benefits before communicating a message, particularly the kinds of messages that the Tilley catalogue sends?

**www.tilley.com**

*Avoiding Racial or Ethnic Bias.* You need indicate racial or ethnic identification only if the context demands it.

| Racially or Ethnically Biased | Improved |
| --- | --- |
| An Indian accountant was hired. | An accountant was hired. |
| James Lee, a Native Canadian, applied. | James Lee applied. |

*Avoiding Age Bias.* Again, specify age only if it is relevant, and avoid expressions that are demeaning or subjective.

| Age-Biased | Improved |
| --- | --- |
| The law applied to old people. | The law applied to people over 65. |
| Sally Kay, 55, was transferred. | Sally Kay was transferred. |
| a spry old gentleman | a man |
| a little old lady | a woman |

*Avoiding Disability Bias.* Unless relevant, do not refer to an individual's disability. When necessary, use terms that do not stigmatize disabled individuals.

| Disability-Biased | Improved |
|---|---|
| afflicted with, suffering from, crippled by | has |
| defect, disease | condition |
| confined to a wheelchair | uses a wheelchair |

The preceding examples give you a quick look at a few problem expressions. The real key to bias-free communication, though, lies in your awareness and commitment. Always be on the lookout to be sure that your messages do not exclude, stereotype, or offend people.

## Expressing Yourself Positively

Certain negative words create ill will because they appear to blame or accuse readers. For example, opening a letter to a customer with *You claim that* suggests that you don't believe the customer. Other loaded words that can get you in trouble are *complaint, criticism, defective, failed, mistake,* and *neglected.* Often the writer is unconscious of the effect of these words. To avoid angry reactions, restrict negative words and try to find positive ways to express ideas. You provide more options to the reader when you tell what can be done instead of what can't be done.

| Negative | Positive |
|---|---|
| You failed to include your credit card number, so we can't mail your order. | We'll mail your order as soon as we receive your credit card number. |
| Your letter of May 2 claims that you returned a defective headset. | Your May 2 letter describes a headset you returned. |
| You cannot park in Lot H until April 1. | You may park in Lot H starting April 1. |
| You won't be sorry that . . . . | You will be happy that . . . . |
| The problem cannot be solved without the aid of top management. | With the aid of top management, the problem can be solved. |

## Being Courteous

Maintaining a courteous tone involves not just guarding against rudeness but also avoiding words that sound demanding or preachy. Expressions like *you should, you must,* and *you have to* cause people to instinctively react with "Oh, yeah?" One remedy is to turn these demands into rhetorical questions that begin with *Will you please* . . . . Giving reasons for a request also softens the tone.

| Less Courteous | More Courteous |
|---|---|
| You must complete this report before Friday. | Will you please complete the report by Friday. |
| You should organize a car pool in this department. | Organizing a car pool will reduce your transportation costs and help preserve the environment. |

Many receivers of business messages today are frazzled and suffering from information overload. Capturing their attention requires a message that is "you"-oriented and emphasizes reader benefits. Show how your message can help solve their problems.

**Positive language creates goodwill and gives more options to readers.**

Customer service representatives hear many complaints, often from frustrated and unhappy customers, but they are trained to respond courteously. In business correspondence, you are more likely to achieve your goals if you keep your cool and display courtesy.

Even when you feel justified in displaying anger, remember that losing your temper or being sarcastic will seldom accomplish your goals as a business communicator to inform, to persuade, and to create goodwill. When you are irritated, frustrated, or infuriated, keep cool and try to defuse the situation. Concentrate on the real problem. What must be done to solve it?

| You May Be Thinking This | Better to Say This |
|---|---|
| This is the second time I've written. Can't you get anything right? | Please credit my account for $843. My latest statement shows that the error noted in my letter of June 2 has not been corrected. |
| Am I the only one who can read the operating manual? | Let's review the operating manual together so that you can get your documents to print correctly next time. |
| Hey, don't blame me! I'm not the promoter who took off with the funds. | Please accept our sincere apologies and two complimentary tickets to our next event. Let me try to explain why we had to substitute performers. |

**Negative expressions can often be rephrased to sound positive.**

## Simplifying Your Language

In adapting your message to your audience, whenever possible use short, familiar words that you think readers will recognize. Don't, however, avoid a big word that conveys your idea efficiently and is appropriate for the audience. Your goal is to shun pompous and pretentious language. Instead, use "GO" words. If you mean *begin*, don't say *commence* or *initiate*. If you mean *give*, don't write *render*.[13] By substituting everyday, familiar words for unfamiliar ones, as shown in the following list, you help your audience comprehend your ideas quickly.

| Unfamiliar | Familiar |
|---|---|
| commensurate | equal |
| conceptualization | idea |
| interrogate | question |
| materialize | appear |
| remunerate | pay |
| terminate | end |

At the same time, be selective in your use of jargon. *Jargon* describes technical or specialized terms within a field. These terms enable insiders to communicate complex ideas briefly, but to outsiders they mean nothing. Human resources professionals, for example, know precisely what's meant by *cafeteria plan* (a benefits option program), but most of us would be thinking about lunch. Geologists refer to *plate tectonics*, and physicians discuss *metastatic carcinomas*, but these terms mean little to most of us. Use specialized language only when the audience will understand it. And don't forget to consider secondary audiences: Will those potential readers understand any technical terms used?

## Using Precise, Vigorous Words

**Using familiar but precise language helps receivers understand.**

Strong verbs and concrete nouns give readers more information and keep them interested. Don't overlook the thesaurus (or the thesaurus program on your computer) for expanding your word choices and vocabulary. Whenever possible, use specific words as shown here.

| Imprecise, Dull | More Precise |
|---|---|
| a gain in profits | |
| a jump in profits | a 23 percent hike in profits |
| it takes memory | it requires 32 megabytes of RAM |
| to think about | to identify, diagnose, analyze to probe, examine, inspect |

By reviewing the tips in the following checklist, you can master the steps of writing preparation. As you review these tips, remember the three basics of prewriting: analyzing, anticipating, and adapting.

## CHECKLIST FOR ADAPTING A MESSAGE TO ITS AUDIENCE

✓ **Identify the message purpose.** Ask yourself why you are communicating and what you hope to achieve. Look for primary and secondary purposes.

✓ **Select the most appropriate form.** Determine whether you need a permanent record or whether the message is too sensitive to put in writing.

✓ **Profile the audience.** Identify your relationship with the reader and your knowledge about that individual or group. Assess how much the receiver knows about the subject.

✓ **Focus on reader benefits.** Phrase your statements from the reader's viewpoint, not the writer's. Concentrate on the "you" view (*Your order will arrive, You can enjoy, Your ideas count*).

✓ **Avoid gender and racial bias.** Use bias-free words (*businessperson* instead of *businessman; working hours* instead of *man-hours*). Omit ethnic identification unless the context demands it.

✓ **Avoid age and disability bias.** Include age only if relevant. Avoid potentially demeaning expressions (*spry old gentleman*), and use terms that do not stigmatize disabled people (*he is disabled* instead of *he is a cripple* or *he has a handicap*).

✓ **Express ideas positively rather than negatively.** Instead of *Your order can't be shipped before June 1*, say *Your order can be shipped June 1*.

✓ **Use short, familiar words.** Use technical terms and big words only if they are appropriate for the audience (*end* not *terminate, required* not *mandatory*).

✓ **Search for precise, vigorous words.** Use a thesaurus if necessary to find strong verbs and concrete nouns (*announces* instead of *says, brokerage* instead of *business*).

## ADAPTING TO LEGAL RESPONSIBILITIES

One of your primary responsibilities in writing for an organization or for yourself is to avoid language that may land you in court. In our current business environment, lawsuits abound, many of which centre on the use and abuse of language. You can protect yourself and avoid litigation by knowing what's legal and by adapting your language accordingly. Be especially careful when communicating in the following four areas: investments, safety, marketing, and human resources. Because these information areas generate the most lawsuits, we will examine them more closely.[14]

## Investment Information

Writers describing the sale of stocks or financial services must follow specific laws written to protect investors. Any messages—including letters, newsletters, and pamphlets—must be free from misleading information, exaggerations, and half-truths. One U.S. company inadvertently violated the law by declaring that it was "recession-proof." After going bankrupt, the company was sued by angry stockholders claiming that they had been deceived. Another company, Lotus Development Corporation, caused a flurry of lawsuits by withholding information that revealed problems in a new version of its 1-2-3 program. Stockholders sued, charging that managers had deliberately concealed the bad news, thus keeping stock prices artificially high. Experienced financial writers know that careless language and even poor timing may provoke litigation.

**Careful communicators should familiarize themselves with information in four information areas: investments, safety, marketing, and human resources.**

## Safety Information

Writers describing potentially dangerous products worry not only about protecting people from physical harm but also about being sued. Although there are far fewer product liability cases filed in Canada than in the United States,[15] litigation arising

**Warnings on dangerous products must be written especially clearly.**

from these cases is an active area of tort law (tort law involves compensating those who have been injured by the wrongdoing of others).[16] Under the law of product liability, a manufacturer is responsible to those injured by a product with a defect caused by either the manufacturing process or the product's design.[17] Manufacturers are obligated to warn consumers of any risks in their products. These warnings must do more than suggest danger; they must also clearly tell people how to use the product safely. In writing warnings, concentrate on major points. Omit anything that is not critical. In the work area describe a potential problem and tell how to solve it. For example, *Lead dust is harmful and gets on your clothes. Change your clothes before leaving work.*

Clearly written safety messages use easy-to-understand words, such as *doctor* instead of *physician*, *clean* instead of *sanitary*, and *burn* instead of *incinerate*. Technical terms are defined. For example, *Asbestos is a carcinogen (something that causes cancer).*[18] Effective safety messages also include highlighting techniques, such as using headings and bullets. In coming chapters you'll learn more about these techniques for improving readability.

## Marketing Information

**Sales and marketing messages must not make claims that can't be verified.**

Sales and marketing messages are illegal if they falsely advertise prices, performance capability, quality, or other product characteristics. Marketing messages must not deceive the buyer in any way. According to Canada's Competition Bureau, "misleading advertising occurs when representation is made to the public that is materially misleading."[19] If the consumer purchases the product or service based on the advertising, it is material. To determine whether an advertisement is misleading, the courts consider the "general impression" it conveys as well as the literal meaning.[20] Sellers of services must also be cautious about the language they use to describe what they will do. Letters, reports, and proposals that describe services to be performed are interpreted as contracts in court. Therefore, the language must not promise more than intended. Here are some dangerous words (and recommended alternatives) that have created misunderstandings leading to lawsuits.[21]

| Dangerous Word | Court Interpretation | Recommended Alternative |
|---|---|---|
| inspect | to examine critically, to investigate and test officially, to scrutinize | to review, to study, to tour the facility |
| determine | to come to a decision, to decide, to resolve | to evaluate, to assess, to analyze |
| assure | to render safe, to make secure, to give confidence, to cause to feel certain | to facilitate, to provide further confidence, to enhance the reliability of |

## Human Resources Information

**The safest employment recommendations contain positive, job-related information.**

The vast number of lawsuits relating to employment makes this a treacherous area for business communicators. In evaluating employees in the workplace, avoid making unsubstantiated negative comments. It's also unwise to assess traits (*she is unreliable*) because they require subjective judgment. Concentrate instead on specific incidents (*in the last month she missed four work days and was late three times*). Defamation lawsuits have become so common that some companies no longer

# Applying Your Skills at Tilley Endurables

Tilley's headquarters in Don Mills reflects the novel approach of the company. Witty slogans such as "Practise Safe Sun" and "Prepare—for Adventure" set the tone for the company. A huge, rusty moose greets customers who head into the store. Customers are then greeted by a totem pole, replicas of French cave paintings, and corkboards with endorsements from satisfied Tilley customers. After passing the free cookies and coffee, customers are greeted with a burst of colour. The store has silks, denim, and Linda Lundström's elegant Tilley line, in addition to the vests, pants, shirts, and shorts that are made from the famous polycotton blend.[22]

The product line changes constantly, and Alex Tilley remains true to listening to the customer. When he received a letter from a man in New Hampshire who complained that he loved his Tilley winter hat, but the ear flaps were too short to keep his ears warm, Tilley redesigned the hat to make the flaps longer and sent the customer a new, free hat.

Although hats are still the company's top-selling item, the firm sells a wide range of products. Alex Tilley is always looking for new opportunities for growth. Future plans include a new line of clothing—"the different drummer," dedicated to "the uncommon man and woman."[23] The new strategy is to increase the demographic appeal of the product.

There is a question of how to get younger people interested in the Tilley merchandise. As Alex Tilley states, "We're beloved by the older crowd; most of our clients are 40 and up, but we don't have any young people coming in. We're hoping to come up with things that will make us more attractive to them, and have established a Design 2000 Group that is working on that."[24]

## Your Task

You have been hired as a communication trainer to provide a training program for the retail staff at the stores. Sales associates do not always adapt their approach to the audience. You are required to provide the sales associates with specific techniques for dealing with a wide range of customers. Before developing your training program, you are asked to submit a list of points that you feel are important.

Individually or in small groups, review the suggestions in this chapter for adapting a message to its audience. Prepare a list of at least ten points. For each point, try to supply an example of the type of customer and the approach that could be taken to ensure appropriate analysis and interaction.

www.tilley.com

---

provide letters of recommendation for former employees. To be safe, give recommendations only when the former employee authorizes the recommendation and when you can say something positive. Stick to job-related information.

Statements in employee handbooks also require careful wording, because a court might rule that such statements are "implied contracts." Consider the following handbook remark: "We at Data Corporation show our appreciation for hard work and team spirit by rewarding everyone who performs well." This seemingly harmless statement could make it difficult to fire an employee because of the implied employment promise.[25] Companies are warned to avoid promissory phrases in writing job advertisements, application forms, and offer letters. Phrases that suggest permanent employment and guaranteed job security can be interpreted as contracts.[26]

In adapting messages to meet today's litigious business environment, be sensitive to the rights of others and to your own rights. The key elements in this adaptation process are awareness of laws, sensitivity to interpretations, and careful use of language.

*1* **Describe three basic elements that distinguish business writing and summarize the three phases of the 3-×-3 writing process.** Business writing differs from academic writing in that it strives to solve business problems, it is economical, and it is reader-oriented. Phase 1 of the writing process (prewriting) involves analyzing the message, anticipating the audience, and considering ways to adapt the message to the audience. Phase 2 (writing) involves researching the topic, organizing the material, and composing the message. Phase 3 (revising) includes proofreading and evaluating the message.

*2* **Explain how the writing process may be altered and how it is affected by team projects and technology.** The writing process may be compressed for short messages; steps in the process may be rearranged. Team writing, which is necessary for large projects or when wide expertise is necessary, alters the writing process. Teams often work together in brainstorming and working out their procedures and assignments. Then individual members write their portions of the report or presentation during Phase 2. During Phase 3 (revising) teams may work together to combine their drafts. Technology assists writers with word processing, revision, and collaboration tools.

*3* **Clarify what is involved in analyzing a writing task and selecting a communication channel.** Communicators must decide why they are delivering a message and what they hope to achieve. Although many messages only inform, some must also persuade. After identifying the purpose of a message, communicators must choose the most appropriate channel. That choice depends on the importance of the message, the amount and speed of feedback required, the need for a permanent record, the cost of the channel, and the degree of formality desired.

*4* **Describe anticipating and profiling the audience for a message.** A good communicator tries to envision the audience for a message. What does the receiver know about the topic? How well does the receiver know the sender? What is known about the receiver's education, beliefs, culture, and attitudes? Will the response to the message be positive, neutral, or negative? Is the secondary audience different from the primary audience?

*5* **Specify six writing techniques that help communicators adapt messages to the task and audience.** Skilled communicators strive to (a) spotlight reader benefits; (b) look at a message from the receiver's perspective (the "you" view); (c) use sensitive language that avoids gender, racial, ethnic, and disability biases; (d) state ideas positively; (e) show courtesy; and (f) use short, familiar, and precise words.

*6* **Explain why four areas of communication hold legal responsibilities for writers.** Actions and language in four information areas generate the most lawsuits: investments, safety, marketing, and human resources. In writing about investments, communicators must avoid misleading information, exaggerations, and half-truths. Safety information, including warnings, must tell people clearly how to use a product safely and motivate them to do so. In addition to being honest, marketing information must not promise more than intended. And communicators in the area of human resources must use careful wording (particularly in employment recommendations and employee handbooks) to avoid potential lawsuits.

# CHAPTER REVIEW

1. Name three ways in which business writing differs from other writing. (Obj. 1)

2. Describe the components in each stage of the 3-×-3 writing process. (Obj. 1)

3. List five factors to consider when selecting a communication channel. (Obj. 3)

4. Why should you "profile" your audience before composing a message? (Obj. 4)

5. What is *empathy*, and how does it apply to business writing? (Obj. 5)

6. Discuss the effects of first- and second-person pronouns. (Obj. 5)

7. What is gender-biased language? Give examples. (Obj. 5)

8. Name replacements for the following gender-biased terms: *waitress, stewardess, foreman* (Obj. 5)

9. When should a writer include racial or ethnic identification, such as *Ellen Lee, an Asian, . . .*? (Obj. 5)

10. Revise the following expression: *He is crippled by muscular dystrophy.* (Obj. 5)

11. Revise the following expression to show more courtesy: *You must submit your budget before noon.* (Obj. 5)

12. What is *jargon*, and when is it appropriate for business writing? (Obj. 5)

13. What's wrong with using words such as *commence, mandate,* and *interrogate*? (Obj. 5)

14. What four information areas generate the most lawsuits? (Obj. 6)

15. How can business communicators protect themselves against litigation? (Obj. 6)

# CRITICAL THINKING

1. Business communicators are encouraged to profile or "visualize" the audience for their messages. How is this possible if you don't really know the people who will receive a sales letter or who will hear your business presentation? (Obj. 4)

2. How can the 3-×-3 writing process help the writer of a business report as well as the writer of an oral presentation? (Obj. 1)

3. If adapting your tone to the receiving audience and developing reader benefits are so important, why do we see so much writing that does not reflect these suggestions? (Objs. 3–5)

4. Discuss the following statement: "The English language is a landmine—it is filled with terms that are easily misinterpreted as derogatory and others that are blatantly insulting. . . . Being fair and objective is not enough; employers must also appear to be so."[27] (Obj. 5)

5. **Ethical Issue:** As a supervisor, you have been asked to recommend a former employee. He was fired after he had an accident while driving a company car. You believe that he was driving under the influence. He had a history of drinking problems. How much are you ethically obliged to reveal to the potential new employer?

# ACTIVITIES

## 5.1 Document for Analysis (Obj. 5)

**Your Task.** Discuss the following memo, which is based on an actual document sent to employees. How can you apply what you learned in this chapter to improving this memo? Revise the memo to make it more courteous, positive, and precise. Focus on developing the "you" view and using familiar language. Remove any gender-biased references.

**TO:**   All Employees Using HP 5000 Computers

It has recently come to my attention that a computer security problem exists within our organization. I understand that the problem is twofold in nature:

a. You have been sharing computer passwords.
b. You are using automatic log-on procedures.

Henceforth, you are prohibited from sharing passwords for security reasons that should be axiomatic. We also must forbid you to use automatic log-on files because they empower anyone to have access to our entire computer system and all company data.

151

Enclosed please find a form that you must sign and return to the aforementioned individual, indicating your acknowledgment of and acquiescence to the procedures described here. Any computer user whose signed form is not returned will have his personal password invalidated.

## 5.2 Selecting Communication Channels (Obj. 3)

**Your Task.** Using Figure 5.2, suggest the best communication channels for the following messages. Assume that all channels shown are available. Be prepared to explain your choices.

a. As department manager, you wish to inform four department members of a training session scheduled for three weeks from now.

b. As assistant to the vice president, you are to investigate the possibility of developing internship programs with several nearby colleges and universities.

c. You wish to send price quotes for a number of your products in response to a request from a potential customer in Taiwan.

d. You must respond to a notice from Canada Customs and Revenue Agency insisting that you did not pay the correct amount for last quarter's employer's taxes.

e. As a manager, you must inform an employee that continued tardiness is jeopardizing her job.

f. Members of your task force must meet to discuss ways to improve communication among 5000 employees at 32 branches of your large company. Task force members are from Laval, Ottawa, Winnipeg, Regina, and Victoria.

g. You need to know whether Paula in Printing can produce a special pamphlet for you within two days.

## 5.3 Analyzing Audiences (Obj. 4)

**Your Task.** Using the questions in Figure 5.3, write a brief analysis of the audience for each of the following communication tasks.

a. Your letter of application for a job advertised in your local newspaper. Your qualifications match the job description.

b. An e-mail memo to your boss persuading her to allow you to attend a computer class that will require you to leave work early two days a week for ten weeks.

c. An unsolicited sales letter promoting life insurance to a targeted group of executives.

d. A letter from the municipal water department explaining that the tap water may taste and smell bad, but it poses no threats to health.

e. A letter from a credit card organization refusing credit to an applicant.

## 5.4 Reader Benefits and the "You" View (Obj. 5)

**Your Task.** Revise the following sentences to emphasize the reader's perspective and the "you" view.

a. To prevent us from possibly losing large sums of money, our bank now requires verification of any large cheque presented for immediate payment.

b. We take pride in announcing a new schedule of low-cost flights to Halifax.

c. So that we may bring our customer records up to date and eliminate the expense of duplicate mailings, we are asking you to complete the enclosed card.

d. For just $300 per person, we have arranged a three-day trip to Las Vegas that includes deluxe accommodations, the "City Lights" show, and selected meals.

e. I give my permission for you to attend the two-day workshop.

f. We're requesting all employees to complete the enclosed questionnaire so that we may develop a master schedule for summer vacations.

g. I think my background and my education match the description of the manager trainee position you advertised.

h. We are offering an in-house training program for employees who want to improve their writing skills.

i. We are pleased to announce an arrangement with Dell that allows us to offer discounted computers in the student bookstore.

j. Our safety policy forbids us from renting power equipment to anyone who cannot demonstrate proficiency in its use.

## 5.5 Language Bias (Obj. 5)

**Your Task.** Revise the following sentences to eliminate gender, racial, age, and disability stereotypes.

a. Any applicant for the position of fireman must submit a medical report signed by his physician.

b. We hired Todd Shimoyama, a Japanese Canadian, for the position of communications coordinator.

c. Because she is confined to a wheelchair, we look for restaurants without stairs.

d. Every employee is entitled to see his personnel file.

e. Some restaurants have a special menu for old people.

f. How many man-hours will the project require?

g. James is afflicted with arthritis, but his crippling rarely interferes with his work.

h. Debbie Sanchez, 24, was hired; Tony Morris, 57, was promoted.

i. All conference participants and their wives are invited to the banquet.

j. Our company encourages the employment of handicapped people.

152

## 5.6 Positive Expression (Obj. 5)

**Your Task.** Revise the following statements to make them more positive.

- **a.** If you fail to pass the examination, you will not qualify.
- **b.** In the message you left at our Web site, you claim that you returned a defective headset.
- **c.** Although you apparently failed to read the operator's manual, we are sending you a replacement blade for your food processor. Next time read page 18 carefully so that you will know how to attach this blade.
- **d.** We can't process your application because you neglected to insert your social insurance number.
- **e.** Construction cannot begin until the building plans are approved.
- **f.** Because of a mistake in its address, your letter did not arrive until January 3.
- **g.** In response to your e-mail complaint, we are investigating our agent's poor behaviour.
- **h.** It is impossible to move forward without community support.
- **i.** Customers are ineligible for the 10 percent discount unless they show their membership cards.
- **j.** You won't be disappointed with the many electronic services we now offer.

## 5.7 Courteous Expression (Obj. 5)

**Your Task.** Revise the following messages to show greater courtesy.

- **a.** You must sign and return this form immediately.
- **b.** This is the last time I'm writing to try to get you to record my January 6 payment of $500 to my account. Anyone who can read can see from the attached documents that I've tried to explain this to you before.
- **c.** As manager of your department, you will have to get your employees to use the correct forms.
- **d.** To the Staff: Can't anyone around here read instructions? Page 12 of the operating manual for our copy machine very clearly describes how to remove jammed paper. But I'm the only one who ever does it, and I've had it! No more copies will be made until you learn how to remove jammed paper.
- **e.** If you had listened to our agent more carefully, you would know that your policy does not cover accidents outside Canada.

## 5.8 Familiar Words (Obj. 5)

**Your Task.** Revise the following sentences to avoid unfamiliar words.

- **a.** Pursuant to your invitation, we will interrogate our manager.

- **b.** To expedite ratification of this agreement, we urge you to vote in the affirmative.
- **c.** In a dialogue with the manager, I learned that you plan to terminate our agreement.
- **d.** Did the steering problem materialize subsequent to our recall effort?
- **e.** Once we ascertain how much it costs, we can initiate the project.

## 5.9 Precise Words (Obj. 5)

**Your Task.** From the choices in parentheses, select the most precise, vigorous words.

- **a.** If you find yourself (*having, engaged in, juggling*) many tasks, find ways to remind yourself of them.
- **b.** He is (*connected to, associated with, employed by*) the Dana Corporation.
- **c.** We plan to (*acknowledge, publicize, applaud*) the work of exemplary employees.
- **d.** The splendid report has (*a lot of, many, a warehouse of*) facts.
- **e.** All the managers thought the new software was (*good, nice, helpful*).

For the following sentences provide more precise alternatives for the italicized words.

- **f.** If necessary, we will (a) *drop* overtime hours in order to (b) *fix* the budget.
- **g.** The CEO (a) *said* that only (b) *the right kind* of applicants should apply.
- **h.** After (a) *reading* the report, I decided it was (b) *bad*.
- **i.** Jenny said the movie was (a) *different*, but her remarks weren't very (b) *clear* to us.
- **j.** I'm (a) *going* to Hamilton tomorrow, and I plan to (b) *find out* the real problem.

## 5.10 Legal Language (Obj. 6)

**Your Task.** To avoid possible litigation, revise the italicized words in the following sentences taken from proposals.

- **a.** We will *inspect* the building plans before construction begins.
- **b.** Our goal is to *assure* completion of the project on schedule.
- **c.** We will *determine* the amount of stress for each supporting column.

## 5.11 Is Instant Messaging a Valid Business Channel Choice? (Obj. 3)

**INFOTRAC**

Should instant messaging become one of the accepted communication channels for business? Once "dismissed as a toy for teenagers and lonely hearts," instant messaging is making its way into the office.

**Your Task.** Using InfoTrac, conduct a keyword search for "instant messaging." Find David LaGesse's article "Instant Message Phenom Is, Like, Way Beyond E-mail," *U.S. News & World Report*, 5 March 2001, Article No. A70910699.

a. How many users are estimated to be sending instant messages by 2004?

b. What are the advantages to instant messages for businesspeople?

c. What are the disadvantages?

## 5.12 Looking at the Upside and the Downside of Computers (Obj. 2)

**TEAM** **CRITICAL THINKING**

As a member of your local Better Business Bureau, you have been asked to participate in a forum on the use of computers by businesspeople. You are expected to explain the "good, the bad, and the ugly" in a balanced presentation.

**Your Task.** In teams of three to five, develop a list of ways that computer software can help businesspeople create better written messages, oral presentations, and Web pages. Then make a list of disadvantages to using software. What can go wrong? What is the downside? After making your lists, draw conclusions. Is software all that it's cracked up to be? Your instructor may ask you to submit your team lists and conclusions in a memo or make a presentation of your findings before the class.

## 5.13 Learning More About Gender-Biased Language (Obj. 5)

**WEB**

As part of an in-service training program at your place of work, you've been asked to make a presentation about gender-biased language.

**Your Task.** Using one or more search engines (such as <**www.google.ca**>), search the Web for "gender-biased language." Remember to enclose your search term in quotation marks. Why does gender-biased language matter? How can gender-biased language be avoided? Find at least four suggestions that are not discussed in this chapter. Submit an outline of your presentation in a memo or e-mail to your instructor.

# C.L.U.E. REVIEW 5

On a separate sheet edit the following sentences to correct faults in grammar, punctuation, spelling, and word use.

1. If I was you I would memorize the following three parts of the writing process; prewriting writing and revising.

2. A writers time is usualy spent as follows; twenty-five percent worrying, twenty-five percent writing, forty-five percent revising and five percent proofreading.

3. At least 4 or 5 members of our team will probaly attend the meeting scheduled with our company Vice President at three p.m. on Tuesday March 4th.

4. Were not asking the team to altar it's proposal we are asking team members to check the proposals figures.

5. A writer may use computer software to fight writers block as well as to help him collect information electronically.

6. Will you please fax me a list of all independant pubishers names and addresses?

7. A writer has many communication channels from which to chose, therefore he should choose carefully.

8. Over two hundred fifty years ago one of Canada's founding fathers recognized a fundamental writing principal.

9. If you are trying to persuade someone be sure that your proposal and request is benificial to him.

10. By substituting every day familiar words for unfamilar ones you can make you audience comprehend your ideas more quicker.

# Chapter 6
## Organizing and Writing Business Messages

## LEARNING OBJECTIVES

*1* Contrast formal and informal methods for researching data and generating ideas.

*2* Specify how to organize data into lists and alphanumeric or decimal outlines.

*3* Compare direct and indirect patterns for organizing ideas.

*4* Discuss composing the first draft of a message, focusing on techniques for creating effective sentences.

*5* Define a paragraph and describe three classic paragraph plans and techniques for composing meaningful paragraphs.

# Tim Hortons

Tim Hortons is one of Canada's top 75 companies of all time, and for a simple reason, according to Ron Joyce, the former Hamilton cop who turned one doughnut shop into an empire. "We take a lot of pride in that it was a Canadian-born chain—made in Canada."[1] In 1963, Ronald Joyce bought a Dairy Queen outlet in Hamilton. Two years later, he invested $10 000 to become a franchisee in the first Tim Hortons. By 1967, Joyce had opened up two more stores, and he and Tim Horton became full partners in the business. In 1975, Joyce became the chain's sole owner, and 20 years later, Joyce received $480 million when Wendy's bought out the chain.[2]

The first Tim Hortons offered only two products—coffee and doughnuts. The most popular, and Tim Hortons' creations, were the Apple Fritter and the Dutchie. This franchise has grown into Canada's number one quick-service chain with a goal to have 3000 units by 2005. Presently, Tim Hortons has more than 2200 locations coast to coast and 160 in the United States. The company posted revenues of US$1.7 billion in 2002, while fast-food stores such as McDonald's struggled.[3]

The company has positioned itself not only in the coffee and doughnut business but also as a fast-food lunch alternative. In the past, Tim Hortons was seen as a breakfast solution, but now it attracts customers at breakfast, lunch, and dinner. Hortons is the largest seller of soup in Canadian food service, and it sells one of every two bagels sold at restaurants.[4] The burger business has also experienced significant losses in the past year, and Tim's has filled the void. Jim Robinson, NPD Group Canada vice president and market researcher, notes part of Hortons' success has been the ability to anticipate cultural shifts. A decade ago, one in ten quick-service meals were bought at a drive-through; that number is now one in four.[5]

Although Tim Hortons has had stores in the United States dating back to the late 1970s, aggressive expansion began in 1995 when Wendy's International purchased the chain. However, Tim Hortons is still operated by the TDL Group Ltd., based in Oakville, Ontario. Although Tim Hortons has a U.S. parent company, spokesperson Patti Jameson asserts that Tim Hortons remains quintessentially Canadian, with no intention of relocating. She continues, "I don't think that we market Canadiana. I think we market ourselves as a chain that always offers top quality and cleanliness and good value for money spent. If there's any part of the Canadiana aspect it will probably be the kind of personality people perceive our chain to have, which is friendly and caring because of all of the things we do within the community."[6]

## CRITICAL THINKING

- In what ways would research (gathering information) be important to business communicators at Tim Hortons and other companies?
- Why is it important to gather all necessary information before beginning to write a business message or make a presentation?
- What techniques can business communicators at Tim Hortons and other companies use to generate ideas for new projects, such as preparing a training brochure for employees?

**www.timhortons.com**

## RESEARCHING DATA AND GENERATING IDEAS

*1*

Communicators at Tim Hortons face daily challenges that require data collection, idea generation, and concept organization. These activities are part of the second phase of the writing process, which includes researching, organizing, and composing.

No smart businessperson would begin writing a message before collecting all the needed information. We call this collection process *research*, a rather formal-sounding term. For simple documents, though, the procedure can be quite informal. Research is necessary before beginning to write because the information you collect helps shape the message. Discovering significant data after a message is half-completed often means starting over and reorganizing. To avoid frustration and inaccurate messages, collect information that answers a primary question:

- *What does the receiver need to know about this topic?*

When the message involves action, search for answers to secondary questions:

- *What is the receiver to do?*
- *How is the receiver to do it?*
- *When must the receiver do it?*
- *What will happen if the receiver doesn't do it?*

Whenever your communication problem requires more information than you have in your head or at your fingertips, you must conduct research. This research may be formal or informal.

## Formal Research Methods

Long reports and complex business problems generally require some use of formal research methods. Let's say you are a market specialist for Coca-Cola, and your boss asks you to evaluate the impact on Coke sales of private-label or generic soft drinks (the bargain-basement-brand knockoffs sold at Zellers and other outlets). Or, let's assume you must write a term paper for one of your classes. Both tasks require more data than you have in your head or at your fingertips. To conduct formal research, you could:

- **Search manually.** You'll find helpful background and supplementary information through manual searching of resources in public and institutional libraries. These traditional sources include periodical indexes for lists of newspaper, magazine, and journal articles, along with the card catalogue for books. Other manual sources are book indexes, encyclopedias, reference books, handbooks, dictionaries, directories, and almanacs.

- **Access electronically.** Like other facets of life, the research process has been changed considerably by the computer. Much of the printed material just described is now available from the Internet, databases, or compact discs that can be accessed by computer. Institutional and public libraries subscribe to retrieval services that permit you to access thousands of bibliographic or full-text databases. You'll learn more about using the Internet and other electronic information resources in Unit 4.

- **Investigate primary sources.** To develop firsthand, primary information for a project, go directly to the source. For the Coca-Cola report, for example, you could find out what consumers really think by conducting interviews or surveys, by putting together questionnaires, or by organizing focus groups. Formal research includes scientific sampling methods that enable investigators to make accurate judgments and valid predictions.

- **Experiment scientifically.** Another source of primary data is experimentation. Instead of merely asking for the target audience's opinion, scientific researchers present choices with controlled variables. Assume, for example, that Coca-Cola wants to determine at what price and under what circumstances consumers would switch from Coca-Cola to a generic brand. The results of such experimentation would provide valuable data for managerial decision making.

Because formal research techniques are particularly necessary for reports, you'll study resources and techniques more extensively in Unit 4.

**Before writing, conduct formal or informal research to collect or generate necessary data.**

**Formal research may involve searching libraries and electronic databases or investigating primary sources (interviews, surveys, and experimentation).**

## Informal Research

Informal research may involve looking in the files, talking with your boss, interviewing the audience, and conducting an informal survey.

Most routine tasks—such as composing e-mail messages, memos, letters, informational reports, and oral presentations—require data that you can collect informally. For some projects, though, you rely more on your own ideas instead of—or in addition to—researching existing facts. Here are some techniques for collecting informal data and for generating ideas:

- **Look in the files.** Before asking others for help, see what you can find yourself. For many routine messages you can often find previous documents to help you with content and format.

- **Talk with your boss.** Get information from the individual making the assignment. What does that person know about the topic? What slant should be taken? What other sources would she or he suggest?

- **Interview the target audience.** Consider talking with individuals at whom the message is aimed. They can provide clarifying information that tells you what they want to know and how you should shape your remarks.

- **Conduct an informal survey.** Gather unscientific but helpful information via questionnaires or telephone surveys. In preparing a memo report predicting the success of a proposed fitness centre, for example, circulate a questionnaire asking for employee reactions.

## Generating Ideas by Brainstorming

The most productive group brainstorming sessions begin with defining the problem and creating an agenda.

One popular method for generating ideas is brainstorming. We should point out, however, that some critics argue that brainstorming groups "produce fewer and poorer quality ideas than the same number of individuals working alone."[7] Proponents say that if "you've had bad luck with brainstorming, you're just not doing it right."[8] Here are suggestions for productive group brainstorming:

- Define the problem and create an agenda that outlines the topics to be covered.
- Establish time limits, remembering that short sessions are best.
- Set a quota, such as a minimum of 100 ideas. The goal is quantity, not quality.
- Require every participant to contribute ideas, accept the ideas of others, or improve on ideas.
- Encourage wild, "out of the box" thinking. Allow no one to criticize or evaluate ideas.
- Write ideas on flipcharts or on sheets of paper hung around the room.
- Organize and classify the ideas, retaining the best. Consider using cluster diagrams, discussed shortly.

## Collecting Information and Generating Ideas on the Job

Let's follow Susanne Tully to see how she collected data and generated ideas for two projects at Liz Claiborne, the women's clothing manufacturer. One of Susanne's tasks is simple, and one is complex.

*Writing an Informational E-Mail Memo.* Susanne's first task is to write an informational memo, shown in Figure 6.1. It describes a photo contest sponsored by Liz Claiborne. For this memo Susanne began by brainstorming with her staff, other employees, and her boss to decide on a photo contest theme. After naming a theme,

## FIGURE 6.1 Informational E-Mail Memo at Liz Claiborne

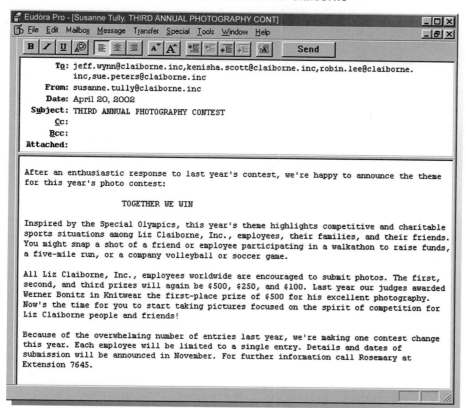

```
Eudora Pro - [Susanne Tully, THIRD ANNUAL PHOTOGRAPHY CONT]
File  Edit  Mailbox  Message  Transfer  Special  Tools  Window  Help

B  /  U  ⟳  ☰ ☰ ☰  A▾ A̋  ⁺☰ ⁺☰ ⁺☰ ⁺☰  🄰̲        Send

     To:  jeff.wynn@claiborne.inc,kenisha.scott@claiborne.inc,robin.lee@claiborne.
          inc,sue.peters@claiborne.inc
   From:  susanne.tully@claiborne.inc
   Date:  April 20, 2002
Subject:  THIRD ANNUAL PHOTOGRAPHY CONTEST
     Cc:
    Bcc:
Attached:
```

After an enthusiastic response to last year's contest, we're happy to announce the theme for this year's photo contest:

                         TOGETHER WE WIN

Inspired by the Special Olympics, this year's theme highlights competitive and charitable sports situations among Liz Claiborne, Inc., employees, their families, and their friends. You might snap a shot of a friend or employee participating in a walkathon to raise funds, a five-mile run, or a company volleyball or soccer game.

All Liz Claiborne, Inc., employees worldwide are encouraged to submit photos. The first, second, and third prizes will again be $500, $250, and $100. Last year our judges awarded Werner Bonitz in Knitwear the first-place prize of $500 for his excellent photography. Now's the time for you to start taking pictures focused on the spirit of competition for Liz Claiborne people and friends!

Because of the overwhelming number of entries last year, we're making one contest change this year. Each employee will be limited to a single entry. Details and dates of submission will be announced in November. For further information call Rosemary at Extension 7645.

"Together We Win," inspired by the Special Olympics, she consulted the files to see who had won prizes in last year's contest. She also double-checked with management to ensure that the prize money of $500, $250, and $100 remained the same. Then she made the following quick scratch list outlining the points she wanted to cover in her memo.

*To develop ideas for a memo announcing a contest, the writer brainstormed with employees and also checked the files.*

### Photo Contest E-Mail Memo

1. Announce theme; give examples

2. Encourage all employees to participate

3. Review prizes; name last year's first-place winner

4. Limit: one entry each

5. Details in November; call Rosemary for more info

Many business messages, like Susanne's finished memo, require only simple data-collection and idea-generation techniques.

***Preparing a Recruitment Brochure.*** Susanne's second project, though, demanded both formal and informal research, along with considerable creativity. She needed to produce a recruitment brochure that explained career opportunities for postsecondary graduates at Liz Claiborne. She had definite objectives for the brochure: It should be colourful, exciting, concise, lightweight (because she had to carry stacks of them to campuses!), and easily updated. Moreover, she wanted the brochure to promote Liz Claiborne, describing its progressive benefits, community involvement, career potential, and corporate values program (called "Priorities").

Some of her thoughts about this big project are shown in the cluster diagram in Figure 6.2. Cluster diagramming sparks our creativity; it encourages ideas to spill forth because the process is unrestricted. From the jumble of ideas in the initial cluster diagram, main categories—usually three to five—are extracted. At this point some people are ready to make an outline; others need further visualization, such as a set of subclusters, shown in Figure 6.3. Notice that four major categories (Purposes, Content, Development, and Form) were extracted from the initial diagram. These categories then became the hub of related ideas. This set of subclusters forms the basis for an outline, to be discussed shortly.

To collect data for this project, Susanne employed both formal and informal research methods. She studied recruiting brochures from other companies. She talked with students to ask what information they sought in a brochure. She conducted more formal research among the numerous division presidents and executives within her company to learn what really went on in all the departments, such

**FIGURE 6.2** Using a Cluster Diagram to Generate Ideas for Liz Claiborne College Recruiting Brochure

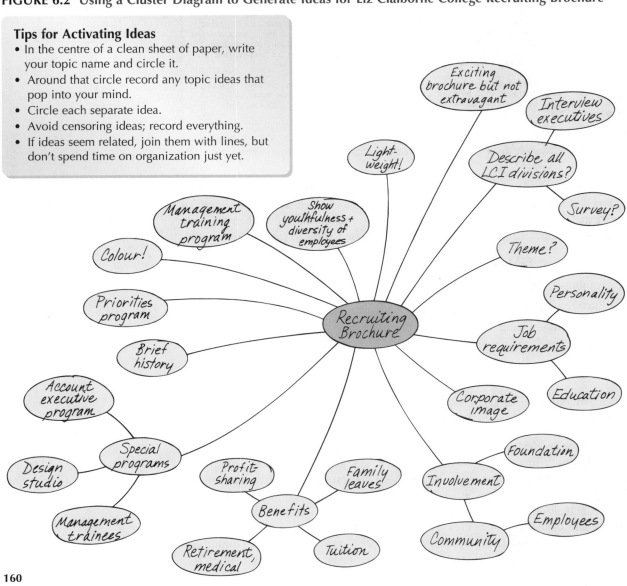

**Tips for Activating Ideas**
- In the centre of a clean sheet of paper, write your topic name and circle it.
- Around that circle record any topic ideas that pop into your mind.
- Circle each separate idea.
- Avoid censoring ideas; record everything.
- If ideas seem related, join them with lines, but don't spend time on organization just yet.

## FIGURE 6.3 Organizing Ideas From a Cluster Diagram Into Subclusters

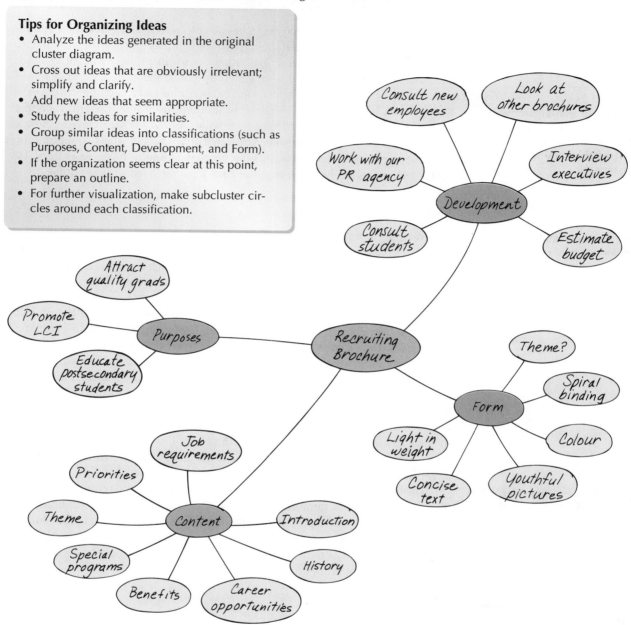

**Tips for Organizing Ideas**
- Analyze the ideas generated in the original cluster diagram.
- Cross out ideas that are obviously irrelevant; simplify and clarify.
- Add new ideas that seem appropriate.
- Study the ideas for similarities.
- Group similar ideas into classifications (such as Purposes, Content, Development, and Form).
- If the organization seems clear at this point, prepare an outline.
- For further visualization, make subcluster circles around each classification.

as Information Systems, Operations Management, Production, and Design. She also had to learn the specific educational and personality requirements for careers in those areas. Working with an outside consultant, she prepared a questionnaire, which was used in personal interviews with company executives. The interviews included some open-ended questions, such as "How did you start with the company?" It also contained more specific questions about the number of employees in their departments, intended career paths, degree requirements, personality traits desired, and so forth. Organizing the mass of data collected was the next task.

**More complex projects may require both formal and informal research.**

2

The process of organization may begin before you collect data, as it did for Susanne, or occur simultaneously with data collection. For complex projects, organization may be ongoing. Regardless of when organization occurs, its primary goals are grouping and patterning. Well-organized messages group similar items together; ideas follow a sequence that helps the reader understand relationships and accept the writer's views. Unorganized messages proceed freeform, jumping from one thought to another. Such messages fail to emphasize important points. Puzzled readers can't see how the pieces fit together, and they become frustrated and irritated. Many communication experts regard poor organization as the greatest failing of business writers. Two simple techniques can help you organize data: the scratch list and the outline.

## Listing and Outlining

In developing simple messages, some writers make a quick scratch list of the topics they wish to cover, as Susanne did for her memo in Figure 6.1. Writers often jot this scratch list in the margin of the letter or memo to which they are responding—and the majority of business messages are written in response to other documents. These writers then compose a message at their computers directly from the scratch list.

Most writers, though, need to organize their ideas—especially if the project is complex—into a hierarchy, such as an outline. The beauty of preparing an outline is that it gives you a chance to organize your thinking before you get bogged down in word choice and sentence structure.[9] Figure 6.4 shows two outline formats: alphanumeric and decimal. The familiar alphanumeric format uses Roman numerals, letters, and numbers to show major and minor ideas. The decimal format, which takes a little getting used to, has the advantage of showing how every item at every level relates to the whole. Both outlining formats force you to focus on the topic, identify major ideas, and support those ideas with details, illustrations, or evidence. Many computer outlining programs now on the market make the mechanics of the process a real breeze.

The hardest part of outlining is grouping ideas into components or categories—ideally three to five in number. By the way, these major categories will become the major headings in your report. If you have more than five components, look for ways to combine smaller segments into broader topics. The following example shows how a portion of the Liz Claiborne brochure subcluster (Figure 6.3) can be organized into an alphanumeric outline.

I. Introduction
   A. Brief history of Liz Claiborne
      1. Founding, Fortune 500 status
      2. Product lines
   B. Corporate environment
      1. System of values: "Priorities"
      2. Team spirit; corporate image
II. Career opportunities
   A. Operations management
      1. Traffic
      2. International trade and corporate customs
      3. Distribution
   B. Accounting and finance
      1. General accounting

**FIGURE 6.4** Two Outlining Formats

## Tips for Making Outlines

- Define the main topic (purpose of message) in the title.
- Divide the main topic into major components or classifications (preferably three to five). If necessary, combine small components into one larger category.
- Break the components into subpoints.

- Don't put a single item under a major component; if you have only one subpoint, integrate it with the main item above it or reorganize.
- Strive to make each component exclusive (no overlapping).
- Use details, illustrations, and evidence to support subpoints.

### Format for Alphanumeric Outline

Title: Major Idea, Purpose

I. First major component
  A. First subpoint
    1. Detail, illustration, evidence
    2. Detail, illustration, evidence
  B. Second subpoint
    1.
    2.
II. Second major component
  A. First subpoint
    1.
    2.
  B. Second subpoint
    1.
    2.
III. Third major component
  A.
    1.
    2.
  B.
    1.
    2.

*(This method is simple and familiar.)*

### Format for Decimal Outline

Title: Major Idea, Purpose

1.0. First major component
  1.1. First subpoint
    1.1.1. Detail, illustration, evidence
    1.1.2. Detail, illustration, evidence
  1.2. Second subpoint
    1.2.1.
    1.2.2.
2.0. Second major component
  2.1. First subpoint
    2.1.1.
    2.1.2.
  2.2. Second subpoint
    2.2.1.
    2.2.2.
3.0. Third major component
  3.1.
    3.1.1.
    3.1.2.
  3.2.
    3.2.1.
    3.2.2.

*(This method relates every item to the overall outline.)*

    2. Internal audit
    3. Treasury and risk management
  C. Special opportunities
    1. Management training program
    2. Account executive sales training program
    3. Design studio

Notice that each major category is divided into at least two subcategories. These categories are then fleshed out with examples, details, statistics, case histories, and other data. In moving from major point to subpoint, you are progressing from large abstract concepts to small concrete ideas. And each subpoint could be further subdivided with more specific illustrations if you desired. You can determine the appropriate amount of detail by considering what your audience (primary and secondary) already knows about the topic and how much persuading you must do.

**Every major category in an outline should have at least two subcategories.**

How you group ideas into components depends on your topic and your channel of communication. The finished Liz Claiborne recruitment brochure, shown on this page, required careful editing so that each component fit into the page layout. Business documents, on the other hand, do not have rigid page constraints. They usually contain typical components arranged in traditional patterns, as shown in Figure 6.5.

Thus far, you've seen how to collect information, generate ideas, and prepare an outline. How you order the information in your outline, though, depends on what pattern or strategy you choose.

**FIGURE 6.5  Typical Major Components in Business Outlines**

**Letter or Memo**
I. Opening
II. Body
III. Close

**Procedure**
I. Step 1
II. Step 2
III. Step 3
IV. Step 4

**Informational Report**
I. Introduction
II. Facts
III. Summary

**Analytical Report**
I. Introduction
II. Facts/findings
III. Conclusions
IV. Recommend-ations (if requested)

**Proposal**
I. Introduction
II. Proposed solution
III. Staffing
IV. Schedule, cost
V. Authoritization

In organizing this Liz Claiborne recruitment brochure, Susanne Tully and her staff achieved coherence and readability by converting each topic from the outline into a consistent, reader-centred heading. Notice the emphasis on "you," an important lesson for every business communicator to learn.

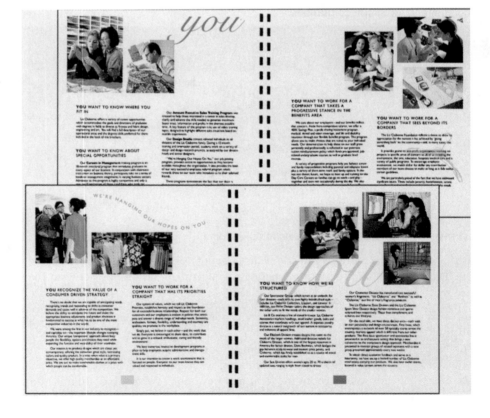

## ORGANIZING IDEAS INTO PATTERNS

Two organizational patterns provide plans of action for typical business messages: the direct pattern and the indirect pattern. The primary difference between the two patterns is where the main idea is placed. In the direct pattern the main idea comes first, followed by details, explanation, or evidence. In the indirect pattern the main idea follows the details, explanation, and evidence. The pattern you select is determined by how you expect the audience to react to the message, as shown in Figure 6.6.

### The Direct Pattern for Receptive Audiences

In preparing to write any message, you need to anticipate the audience's reaction to your ideas and frame your message accordingly. When you expect the reader to be pleased, mildly interested, or, at worst, neutral—use the direct pattern. That is, put your main point—the purpose of your message—in the first or second sentence. Dianna Booher, renowned writing consultant, points out that typical readers begin any message by saying, "So what am I supposed to do with this information?" In business writing you have to say, "Reader, here is my point!"[10] As quickly as possible, tell why you are writing. Compare the direct and indirect patterns in the following memo openings. Notice how long it takes to get to the main idea in the indirect opening.

Business messages typically follow either the (1) direct pattern, with the main idea first, or (2) the indirect pattern, with the main idea following explanation and evidence.

**Indirect Opening**
Our company has been concerned with attracting better-qualified prospective job candidates. For this reason, the Management Council has been gathering information about an internship program for postsecondary students. After considerable investigation, we have voted to begin a pilot program starting next fall.

**Direct Opening**
The Management Council has voted to begin a postsecondary internship pilot program next fall.

Explanations and details should follow the direct opening. What's important is getting to the main idea quickly. This direct method, also called *frontloading*, has at least three advantages:

- **Saves the reader's time.** Many of today's businesspeople can devote only a few moments to each message. Messages that take too long to get to the point may lose their readers along the way.

- **Sets a proper frame of mind.** Learning the purpose up front helps the reader put the subsequent details and explanations in perspective. Without a clear opening, the reader may be thinking, "Why am I being told this?"

- **Prevents frustration.** Readers forced to struggle through excessive verbiage before reaching the main idea become frustrated. They resent the writer. Poorly organized messages create a negative impression of the writer.

Frontloading saves the reader's time, establishes the proper frame of mind, and prevents frustration.

This frontloading technique works best with audiences that are likely to be receptive to or at least not disagree with what you have to say. Typical business messages that follow the direct pattern include routine requests and responses, orders and acknowledgments, nonsensitive memos, e-mail messages, informational reports, and informational oral presentations. All these tasks have one element in common: none has a sensitive subject that will upset the reader.

**FIGURE 6.6** Audience Response Determines Pattern of Organization

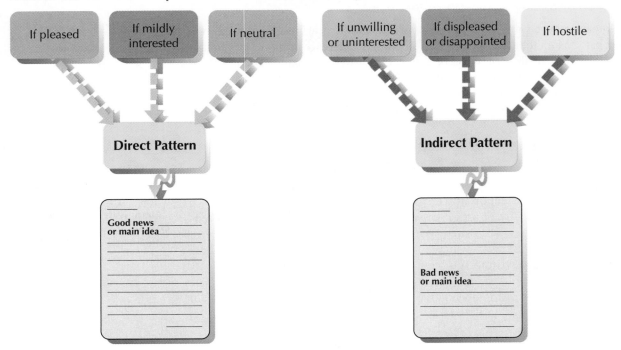

## The Indirect Pattern for Unreceptive Audiences

**The indirect pattern respects the feelings of the audience, facilitates a fair hearing, and minimizes a negative reaction.**

When you expect the audience to be uninterested, unwilling, displeased, or perhaps even hostile, the indirect pattern is more appropriate. In this pattern you don't reveal the main idea until after you have offered explanation and evidence. This approach works well with three kinds of messages: (1) bad news, (2) ideas that require persuasion, and (3) sensitive news, especially when being transmitted to superiors. The indirect pattern has these benefits:

- **Respects the feelings of the audience.** Bad news is always painful, but the trauma can be lessened when the receiver is prepared for it.

- **Encourages a fair hearing.** Messages that may upset the reader are more likely to be read when the main idea is delayed. Beginning immediately with a piece of bad news or a persuasive request, for example, may cause the receiver to stop reading or listening.

- **Minimizes a negative reaction.** A reader's overall reaction to a negative message is generally improved if the news is delivered gently.

Typical business messages that could be developed indirectly include letters and memos that refuse requests, deny claims, and disapprove credit. Persuasive requests, sales letters, sensitive messages, and some reports and oral presentations also benefit from the indirect strategy. You'll learn more about how to use the indirect pattern in Chapters 10 and 11.

In summary, business messages may be organized directly, with the main idea first, or indirectly, with the main idea delayed. Although these two patterns cover many communication problems, they should be considered neither universal nor inviolate. Every business transaction is distinct. Some messages are mixed: part good news, part bad; part goodwill, part persuasion. In upcoming chapters you'll practise

## *Tim Hortons Revisited*

"There is always something new going on at Tim Hortons" is one of the reasons for its success. The menu at Tim's is always evolving to keep up with changing consumer tastes and preferences. The 1976 introduction of Timbits was one of the biggest changes in the company's focus. New product introductions of muffins, cakes, pies, croissants, soups, chili, and "Tim's Own" sandwiches followed in the 1980s. In the 1990s, the company expanded its offerings to include bagels, flavoured cappuccino, café mocha, and iced cappuccino. In 2000, the company introduced "Tim's Own" coffeecake and hot chicken stew in an edible bread bowl. Of course the famous coffee remains, available not only by the cup, but also in cans for the customer to make and enjoy at home.

Such diversity and response to change have proven to be invaluable to Tim Hortons' success. In 2002, the company had about $2.1 billion in Canadian sales, compared to $2.2 billion for McDonald's Corporation. The company plans to overtake the burger giant in sales. South of the border, Tim's now accounts for 30 to 35 percent of Wendy's total revenue.[11]

In addition to being successful on the balance sheet, Tim Hortons also gives back to the community. Ron Joyce states, "Everybody should give back, if you can afford it. Giving is what it's all about. I think that there is an obligation to give back, especially if you've been financially successful. Government can't do it as well as the private sector, and the private sector should."[12]

When Tim Horton died on February 21, 1974, Ron Joyce announced the establishment of the Tim Horton Children's Foundation to honour Tim Horton's love of children and desire to help those less fortunate. The foundation is a non-profit charitable organization that operates camps for economically disadvantaged children from communities in which Tim Hortons operates. The first camp opened in 1975; now there are six—five in Canada and one in the United States. In 2003, over 9000 children attended the camps. Since 1974, more than 54 000 children have participated in the camp program. Funding for the camps comes from donations from store owners, the parent company (TDL Group Ltd.), suppliers, and public donations. As the company states on its Web site, "The Tim Horton Children's Foundation is committed to providing an enriched and memorable camp experience for children, giving them confidence in their abilities, pride in their accomplishments, and a more positive view of the world and their place in it."

### CRITICAL THINKING

- When a business communicator responds to an inquiry, such as asking for the criteria for choosing the candidates to attend camp, is "research" necessary?
- What is the difference between formal and informal research?
- What are the advantages and disadvantages of brainstorming with groups?

**www.timhortons.com**

---

applying the direct and indirect patterns in typical situations. Then, you'll have the skills and confidence to evaluate communication problems and vary these patterns depending on the goals you wish to achieve.

## COMPOSING THE FIRST DRAFT

Once you've researched your topic, organized the data, and selected a pattern of organization, you're ready to begin composing. Communicators who haven't completed the preparatory work often suffer from "writer's block" and sit staring at a piece of paper or at the computer screen. It's difficult to get started without organized ideas and a plan. Composition is also easier if you have a quiet environment in which to concentrate. Businesspeople with messages to compose set aside a given time and allow no calls, visitors, or other interruptions. This is a good technique for students as well.

As you begin composing, keep in mind that you are writing the first draft, not the final copy. Experts suggest that you write quickly (*sprint writing*). Get your thoughts down now and refine them in later versions.[13] As you take up each idea, imagine that you are talking to the reader. Don't let yourself get bogged down. If you can't think of the right word, insert a substitute or type "find perfect word later."[14] Sprint writing works especially well for those composing on a computer because it's simple to make changes at any point of the composition process. If you are handwriting the first draft, double-space so that you have room for changes.

## Creating Effective Sentences

**Sentences must have subjects and verbs and must make sense.**

As you create your first draft, you'll be working at the sentence level of composition. Although you've used sentences all your life, you may be unaware of how they can be shaped and arranged to express your ideas most effectively. First, let's review some basic sentence elements.

Complete sentences have subjects and verbs and make sense.

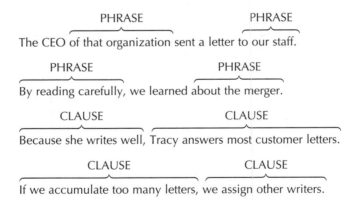

SUBJECT VERB      SUBJECT VERB

This report is clear and concise. Our employees write many reports.

**Clauses have subjects and verbs, but phrases do not.**

Clauses and phrases, the key building blocks of sentences, are related groups of words. Clauses have subjects and verbs; phrases do not.

PHRASE      PHRASE

The CEO of that organization sent a letter to our staff.

PHRASE      PHRASE

By reading carefully, we learned about the merger.

CLAUSE      CLAUSE

Because she writes well, Tracy answers most customer letters.

CLAUSE      CLAUSE

If we accumulate too many letters, we assign other writers.

**Independent clauses may stand alone; dependent clauses may not.**

Clauses may be divided into two groups: independent and dependent. Independent clauses are grammatically complete. Dependent clauses depend for their meaning on independent clauses. In the two preceding examples, the clauses beginning with *If* and *Because* are dependent. Dependent clauses are often introduced by words such as *if, when, because,* and *as.*

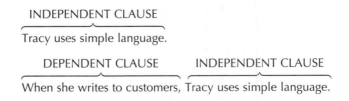

INDEPENDENT CLAUSE

Tracy uses simple language.

DEPENDENT CLAUSE      INDEPENDENT CLAUSE

When she writes to customers, Tracy uses simple language.

By learning to distinguish phrases, independent clauses, and dependent clauses, you'll be able to punctuate sentences correctly and avoid three basic sentence faults: the fragment, the run-on sentence, and the comma splice. In Guide 1, Appendix A, we examine these writing problems in greater detail. For now, however, let's look at some ways to make your sentences more readable.

*Using Short Sentences.* Because your goal is to communicate clearly, you're better off limiting your sentences to about 20 or fewer words. In prose, the average sentence length for a general reader has gone from about 23–24 words per sentence in the 1950s to 17–18 in the 1990s. Harlequin romances use about 7–8 words per sentence, and popular thrillers fall into the 10–12 words per sentence range. This shortening of sentences is to accommodate the shortened attention span of readers.[15] The American Press Institute reports that reader comprehension drops off markedly as sentences become longer.[16] Thus, in crafting your sentences, think about the relationship between sentence length and comprehension:

**Effective sentences are short and stress important ideas.**

| Sentence Length | Comprehension Rate |
|---|---|
| 8 words | 100% |
| 15 words | 90% |
| 19 words | 80% |
| 28 words | 50% |

**Sentences of 20 or fewer words have the most impact.**

Instead of stringing together clauses with *and, but,* and *however,* break some of those complex sentences into separate segments. Business readers want to grasp ideas immediately. They can do that best when thoughts are separated into short sentences. On the other hand, too many monotonous short sentences will sound "grammar schoolish" and may bore or even annoy the reader. Strive for a balance between longer sentences and shorter ones. Your computer probably can point out long sentences and give you an average sentence length.

Ensure instructions are readable by shortening sentences, emphasizing important ideas with graphic highlighting, and using active-voice verbs.

*Emphasizing Important Ideas.* You can stress prominent ideas mechanically by underscoring, italicizing, or boldfacing. You'll learn more about these graphic highlighting devices shortly. You can also emphasize important ideas with five stylistic devices.

- **Use vivid words.** Vivid words are emphatic because the reader can picture ideas clearly.

| **General** | **Vivid** |
|---|---|
| One business uses personal selling techniques. | Avon uses face-to-face selling techniques. |

- **Label the main idea.** If an idea is significant, tell the reader.

| **Unlabelled** | **Labelled** |
|---|---|
| Explore the possibility of leasing a site, but also hire a consultant. | Explore the possibility of leasing a site; but, *most important,* hire a consultant. |

**Emphasize an important idea by using vivid words, labelling the main idea, placing the idea first or last in a sentence, and making the idea the sentence subject.**

- **Place the important idea first or last in the sentence.** Ideas have less competition from surrounding words when they appear first or last in a sentence. Observe from the following how the date of the meeting can be emphasized.

| **Unemphatic** | **Emphatic** |
|---|---|
| All production and administrative personnel will meet on May 23, at which time we will announce a new plan of salary incentives. | On May 23 all personnel will meet to learn about salary incentives. |

- **Place the important idea in a simple sentence or in an independent clause.** Don't dilute the effect of the idea by making it share the spotlight with other words and clauses.

| **Unemphatic** | **Emphatic** |
|---|---|
| Although you are the first trainee that we have hired for this program, we have interviewed many candidates and expect to expand the program in the future. (Main idea lost in introductory dependent clause.) | You are the first trainee that we have hired for this program. (Simple sentence contains main idea.) |

- **Make sure the important idea is the sentence subject.** You'll learn more about active and passive voice shortly, but at this point just focus on making the important idea the subject.

| **Unemphatic** | **Emphatic** |
|---|---|
| The environmental report was written by Michelle. (Deemphasizes *Michelle*; emphasizes the report.) | Michelle wrote the environmental report. (Emphasizes *Michelle*.) |

*In active-voice sentences the subject is the doer; in passive-voice sentences, the subject is acted upon.*

*Using Active and Passive Voice.* In sentences with active-voice verbs, the subject is the doer of the action. In passive-voice sentences, the subject is acted upon.

| **Passive verb** | **Active verb** |
|---|---|
| The tax return *was completed* before the April 30 deadline. (The subject, *tax return*, is acted upon.) | Brandon *completed* his tax return before the April 30 deadline. (The subject, *Brandon*, is the doer of the action.) |

In the first sentence, the active-voice verb emphasizes Brandon. In the second sentence, the passive-voice verb emphasizes the tax return. Active-voice sentences are more direct because they reveal the performer immediately. They're easier to understand and shorter. Most business writing should be in the active voice.

Yet, passive verbs are useful in certain instances. In sentences with passive-voice verbs, the doer of the action may be revealed or left unknown. In business writing, as well as in personal interactions, some situations demand tact and sensitivity. Instead of using a direct approach with active verbs, we may prefer the indirectness that passive verbs allow. Rather than making a blunt announcement with an active verb (*Tyler made a major error in the estimate*), we can soften the sentence with a passive construction (*A major error was made in the estimate*).

*Passive-voice sentences are useful for tact and to direct attention to actions instead of people.*

Here's a summary of the best uses of active- and passive-voice verbs:

- **Use the active voice for most business writing.** *Our company gives drug tests to all applicants.*

- **Use the passive voice to emphasize an action or the recipient of the action.** *Drug tests are given to all applicants.*

- **Use the passive voice to deemphasize negative news.** *Your monitor cannot be repaired.*
- **Use the passive voice to conceal the doer of an action.** *A major error was made in the estimate.*

How can you tell whether a verb is active or passive? Identify the subject of the sentence and decide whether the subject is doing the acting or whether it is being acted upon. For example, in the sentence *An appointment was made for January 1*, the subject is *appointment*. The subject is being acted upon; therefore, the verb (*was made*) is passive. Another clue in identifying passive-voice verbs is that they generally include a *to be* helping verb, such as *is, are, was, were, being,* or *been*.

### Avoiding Dangling and Misplaced Modifiers.
For clarity, modifiers must be close to the words they describe or limit. A dangling modifier describes or limits a word or words that are missing from the sentence. A misplaced modifier occurs when the word or phrase it describes is not close enough to be clear. In both instances, the solution is to position the modifier closer to the word(s) it describes or limits. Introductory verbal phrases are particularly dangerous; be sure to follow them immediately with the words they can logically describe or modify.

**Modifiers must be close to the words they describe or limit.**

| Dangling Modifier | Improved |
|---|---|
| To win the lottery, a ticket must be purchased. (*The introductory verbal phrase must be followed by a logical subject.*) | To win the lottery, you must purchase a ticket. |
| Driving on the Cabot Trail, the ocean suddenly came into view. (*Is the ocean driving on the Cabot Trail?*) | As we drove on the Cabot Trail, the ocean suddenly came into view. |
| Speaking before the large audience, my knees began to knock. (*Are your knees making a speech?*) | Speaking before the large audience, I felt my knees begin to knock. |

Try this trick for detecting and remedying these dangling modifiers. Ask the question *who?* or *what?* after any introductory phrase. The words immediately following should tell the reader *who* or *what* is performing the action. Try the "who?" test on the previous danglers and on the following misplaced modifiers.

| Misplaced Modifier | Improved |
|---|---|
| Seeing his error too late, the envelope was immediately resealed by Mark. (*Did the envelope see the error?*) | Seeing his error too late, Mark immediately resealed the envelope. |
| A wart appeared on my left hand that I want removed. (*Is the left hand to be removed?*) | A wart that I want removed appeared on my left hand. |
| The busy personnel director interviewed only candidates who had excellent computer skills in the morning. (*Were the candidates skilled only in the morning?*) | In the morning the busy personnel director interviewed only candidates who had excellent computer skills. |

**A modifier is misplaced when the word or phrase it describes is not close enough to be clear.**

# 5 Drafting Meaningful Paragraphs

From composing sentences, we progress to paragraphs. A paragraph is one or more sentences designated as a separate thought group. To avoid muddled paragraphs, writers must recognize basic paragraph elements, conventional sentence patterns, and ways to organize sentences into one of three classic paragraph patterns. They must also be able to polish their paragraphs by linking sentences and using transitional expressions.

*Discussing One Topic.* Well-constructed paragraphs discuss only one topic. They reveal the primary idea in a main sentence that usually, but not always, appears first. Other ideas, connected logically with transitional expressions (verbal road signs), support or illustrate that idea.

*Organizing Sentences Into Paragraphs.* Paragraphs are generally composed of three kinds of sentences:[17]

**Main sentence:** Expresses the primary idea of the paragraph.

**Supporting sentence:** Illustrates, explains, or strengthens the primary idea.

**Limiting sentence:** Opposes the primary idea by suggesting a negative or contrasting thought; may precede or follow the main sentence.

These sentences may be arranged in three classic paragraph plans: direct, pivoting, and indirect.

*Using the Direct Paragraph Plan.* Paragraphs arranged in the direct plan begin with the main sentence, followed by supporting sentences. Most business messages use this paragraph plan because it clarifies the subject immediately. This plan is useful whenever you must define (a new product or procedure), classify (parts of a whole), illustrate (an idea), or describe (a process). Simply start with the main sentence; then strengthen and amplify that idea with supporting ideas, as shown here:

| | |
|---|---|
| Main Sentence | A social audit is a report on the social performance of a company. |
| Supporting Sentences | Such an audit may be conducted by the company itself or by outsiders who evaluate the company's efforts to produce safe products, engage in socially responsible activities, and protect the environment. Many companies publish the results of their social audits in their annual reports. Commitment to the environment and social responsibility have been core values for Vancouver City Savings Credit Union (Vancity) since 1993. The company conducts social audits to combine measures of financial return, social responsibility, and environmental performance.[18] |

You can alter the direct plan by adding a limiting sentence if necessary. Be sure, though, that you follow with sentences that return to the main idea and support it, as shown here:

| | |
|---|---|
| Main Sentence | Flexible work scheduling could immediately increase productivity and enhance employee satisfaction in our entire organization. |

The direct paragraph pattern is appropriate when defining, classifying, illustrating, or describing.

| Limiting Sentence | Such scheduling, however, is impossible for all employees. |
| Supporting Sentences | Managers would be required to maintain their regular hours. For many other employees, though, flexible scheduling permits extra time to manage family responsibilities. Feeling less stress, employees are able to focus their attention better at work; hence they become more relaxed and more productive. |

*Using the Pivoting Paragraph Plan.* Paragraphs arranged in the pivoting plan start with a limiting sentence that offers a contrasting or negative idea before delivering the main sentence. Notice in the following example how two limiting sentences about drawbacks to military careers open the paragraph; only then do the main and supporting sentences describing rewards in military service appear. The pivoting plan is especially useful for comparing and contrasting ideas. In using the pivoting plan, be sure you emphasize the turn in direction with an obvious *but* or *however*.

The pivoting paragraph pattern is appropriate when comparing and contrasting.

| Limiting Sentences | Military careers are certainly not for everyone. Many are in remote countries where harsh climates, health hazards, security risks, and other discomforts exist. |
| Main Sentence | However, careers in the military offer special rewards for the special people who qualify. |
| Supporting Sentences | Military employees enjoy the pride and satisfaction of representing their country abroad. They enjoy frequent travel, enriching cultural and social experiences in living abroad, and action-oriented work. |

*Using the Indirect Paragraph Plan.* Paragraphs arranged in the indirect plan start with the supporting sentences and conclude with the main sentence. This useful plan enables you to build a rationale, a foundation of reasons, before hitting the audience with a big idea—possibly one that is bad news. It enables you to explain your reasons and then in the final sentence draw a conclusion from them. In the following example the vice president of a large accounting firm begins by describing the trend toward casual dress and concludes with a recommendation that his firm change its dress code. This indirect plan works well for describing causes followed by an effect.

The indirect paragraph pattern is appropriate when delivering bad news.

| Supporting Sentences | According to a recent poll, more than half of all white-collar workers are now dressing casually at work. Many high-tech engineers and professional specialists have given up suits and ties, favouring khakis and sweaters instead. In our own business our consultants say they stand out like "sore thumbs" because they are attired in traditional buttoned-down styles, while the businesspeople they visit are usually wearing comfortable, casual clothing. |
| Main Sentence | Therefore, I recommend that we establish an optional "business casual" policy allowing consultants to dress casually, if they wish, as they perform their duties both in and out of the office. |

You'll learn more techniques for implementing direct and indirect writing strategies when you prepare letters, memos, e-mail messages, reports, and oral presentations in subsequent chapters.

**Linking Ideas to Build Coherence.** Paragraphs are coherent when ideas are linked, that is, when one idea leads logically to the next. Well-written paragraphs take the reader through a number of steps. When the author skips from Step 1 to Step 3 and forgets Step 2, the reader is lost. You can use several techniques to keep the reader in step with your ideas.

> **Sustaining the Key Idea.** This involves simply repeating a key expression or using a similar one. For example:

Coherent paragraphs link ideas by sustaining the main idea, using pronouns, dovetailing sentences, and using transitional expressions.

> Our philosophy holds that every customer is really a guest. All new employees to our theme parks are trained to treat *guests* as *VIPs*. These *VIPs* are never told what they can or cannot do.

Notice how the repetition of *guest* and *VIP* connects ideas.

> **Using Pronouns.** Familiar pronouns, such as *we, they, he, she,* and *it,* help build continuity, as do demonstrative pronouns, such as *this, that, these,* and *those.* These words confirm that something under discussion is still being discussed. For example:

Using pronouns strategically helps build coherence and continuity.

> All new park employees receive a two-week orientation. They learn that every staffer has a vital role in preparing for the show. This training includes how to maintain enthusiasm.

Be careful with *this, that, these,* and *those,* however. These words usually need a noun with them to make their meaning absolutely clear. In the last example notice how confusing *this* becomes if the word *training* is omitted.

> **Dovetailing Sentences.** Sentences are "dovetailed" when an idea at the end of one connects with an idea at the beginning of the next. For example:

Dovetailing sentences means connecting ending and beginning ideas.

> New hosts and hostesses learn about the theme park and its *facilities*. These facilities include telephones, food services, bathrooms, and attractions, as well as the location of *offices*. Knowledge of administrative offices and internal workings of the company, such as who's who in administration, ensures that staffers will be able to *serve guests* fully. *Serving guests,* of course, is our number one priority.

Dovetailing of sentences is especially helpful with dense, difficult topics. This technique, however, should not be overused.

**Using Transitional Expressions to Build Coherence.** Transitional expressions are another excellent device for achieving paragraph coherence. These words, some of which are shown in Figure 6.7, act as verbal road signs to readers and listeners. Transitional expressions enable the receiver to anticipate what's coming, to reduce uncertainty, and to speed up comprehension. They signal that a train of thought is moving forward, being developed, possibly detouring, or ending. Transitions are especially helpful in persuasive writing.

Transitional expressions help readers anticipate what's coming, reduce uncertainty, and speed comprehension.

As Figure 6.7 shows, transitions can add or strengthen a thought, show time or order, clarify ideas, show cause and effect, contradict thoughts, and contrast ideas. Thus, you must be careful to select the best transition for your purpose. Look back at the examples of direct, pivoted, and indirect paragraphs to see how transitional expressions and other devices build paragraph coherence. Remember that coherence in communication rarely happens spontaneously; it requires effort and skill.

**FIGURE 6.7** Transitional Expressions to Build Coherence

| TO ADD OR STRENGTHEN | TO SHOW TIME OR ORDER | TO CLARIFY | TO SHOW CAUSE AND EFFECT | TO CONTRADICT | TO CONTRAST |
|---|---|---|---|---|---|
| additionally | after | for example | accordingly | actually | as opposed to |
| again | before | for instance | as a result | but | at the same time |
| also | earlier | I mean | consequently | however | by contrast |
| besides | finally | in other words | for this reason | in fact | conversely |
| likewise | first | that is | so | instead | on the contrary |
| moreover | meanwhile | this means | therefore | rather | on the other hand |
| further | next | thus | thus | still | |
| furthermore | now | to put it another way | under the circumstances | though | |
| | previously | | | yet | |

*Composing Short Paragraphs.* Although no rule regulates the length of paragraphs, business writers recognize the value of short paragraphs. Paragraphs with eight or fewer lines look inviting and readable, whereas long, solid chunks of print appear formidable. If a topic can't be covered in eight or fewer printed lines (not sentences), consider breaking it up into smaller segments.

**Paragraphs with eight or fewer lines are inviting and readable.**

The following checklist summarizes the key points of writing a first draft.

## CHECKLIST FOR COMPOSING SENTENCES AND PARAGRAPHS

### For Effective Sentences

✓ **Use short sentences.** Keep in mind that sentences with 20 or fewer words are easier to read. Use longer sentences occasionally, but rely primarily on short sentences.

✓ **Emphasize important ideas.** Place main ideas at the beginning of short sentences for emphasis.

✓ **Apply active and passive verbs carefully.** Use active verbs (*She sent the e-mail* instead of *The e-mail was sent by her*) most frequently; they immediately identify the doer. Use passive verbs to be tactful, to emphasize an action, or to conceal the performer.

✓ **Eliminate misplaced modifiers.** Be sure that introductory verbal phrases are followed by the words that can logically be modified. To check the placement of modifiers, ask *who?* or *what?* after such phrases.

### For Meaningful Paragraphs

✓ **Develop one idea.** Use main, supporting, and limiting sentences to develop a single idea within each paragraph.

# Applying Your Skills at Tim Hortons

After its huge success in Canada, Tim Hortons posted its first-ever annual profit in 2002 in the United States.[19] The goal is to follow the Canadian business model and have 70 percent of U.S. units franchised.[20] However, the competition in the United States remains intense. Competitors such as Dunkin' Donuts, Krispy Kreme, and Starbucks are strong forces in the U.S. market, and Tim Hortons is relying on its diversified product mix to compete.

Ron Joyce believes the Krispy Kreme phenomenon is similar to the Tim Hortons phenomenon when it first started. "We used to have those huge lineups. When the novelty wears off, what's their staying power?" he asks.[21] According to Paul House, Tim Hortons' president and chief operating officer, "We're not just in the coffee-and-baked goods chain anymore. If we were still selling only coffee and doughnuts, we wouldn't be in the position we are today."[22]

Coffee accounts for 50 percent of all sales in Canada, baked goods contribute 22.5 percent, and lunch yields 10.5 percent. Tim Hortons estimates that it has 70 percent of the coffee-and-baked goods market in Canada and 22 percent of the overall quick-service market.[23] To improve drive-through service, Tim Hortons implemented a tandem ordering system to speed up customer service. In Canada, Tim Hortons has a top drive-through time of 101.58 seconds, topping the best score held at a U.S. Wendy's at 134.67 seconds.[24]

Tim Hortons' motto of "Always Fresh" translates into concepts, ideas, and thoughts and extends beyond the food being sold. Tim Hortons is "Always Fresh," whether it is uniforms, quality of the products, chains, and so on.[25]

## Your Task

To remain competitive and capture market share, Tim Hortons must be aware of the competition. Your boss has asked you to examine the major competitors to Tim Hortons and would like an analysis on the direction that the company should take to keep its number one spot in Canada and expand that success to the franchises south of the border. She also wants you to examine the U.S. market to see any trends or differences that should be acknowledged.

In small groups, brainstorm about where you can collect information for this project. Based on what you learned in this chapter, list possible sources of information for informal research. Your instructor may further ask you to brainstorm about potential problems in preparing this report. If directed, make a cluster diagram showing the results of your brainstorming.

**www.timhortons.com**

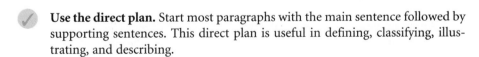

**Use the direct plan.** Start most paragraphs with the main sentence followed by supporting sentences. This direct plan is useful in defining, classifying, illustrating, and describing.

**Use the pivoting plan.** To compare and contrast ideas, start with a limiting sentence; then, present the main sentence followed by supporting sentences.

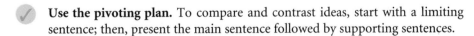

**Use the indirect plan.** To explain reasons or causes first, start with supporting sentences. Build to the conclusion with the main sentence at the end of the paragraph.

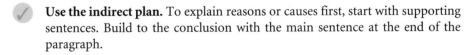

**Build coherence by linking sentences.** Hold ideas together by repeating key words, using pronouns, and dovetailing sentences (beginning one sentence with an idea from the end of the previous sentence).

- ✓ **Provide road signs with transitional expressions.** Use verbal signals to help the audience know where the idea is going. Words like *moreover, accordingly, as a result,* and *thus* function as idea pointers.

- ✓ **Limit paragraph length.** Remember that paragraphs with eight or fewer printed lines look inviting. Consider breaking up longer paragraphs if necessary.

## SUMMARY OF LEARNING OBJECTIVES

*1* **Contrast formal and informal methods for researching data and generating ideas.** Formal research for long reports and complex problems may involve searching library data manually or electronically, as well as conducting interviews, surveys, focus groups, and experiments. Informal research for routine tasks may include looking in company files, talking with your boss, interviewing the target audience, conducting informal surveys, brainstorming for ideas, and cluster diagramming.

*2* **Specify how to organize data into lists and alphanumeric or decimal outlines.** One method for organizing data in simple messages is to list the main topics to be discussed. Organizing more complex messages usually requires an outline. To prepare an outline, divide the main topic into three to five major components. Break the components into subpoints consisting of details, illustrations, and evidence. For an alphanumeric outline arrange items using Roman numerals (I, II), capital letters (A, B), and numbers (1, 2). For a decimal outline show the ordering of ideas with decimals (1.0., 1.1., 1.1.1.).

*3* **Compare direct and indirect patterns for organizing ideas.** The direct pattern places the main idea first. This pattern is useful when audiences will be pleased, mildly interested, or neutral. It saves the reader's time, sets the proper frame of mind, and prevents reader frustration. The indirect pattern places the main idea after explanations. This pattern is useful for audiences that will be unwilling, displeased, or hostile. It respects the feelings of the audience, encourages a fair hearing, and minimizes negative reactions.

*4* **Discuss composing the first draft of a message, focusing on techniques for creating effective sentences.** Compose the first draft of a message in a quiet environment where you won't be interrupted. Compose quickly, preferably at a computer. Plan to revise. As you compose, remember that sentences are most effective when they are short (under 20 words). A main idea may be emphasized by making it the sentence subject, placing it first, and removing competing ideas. Effective sentences use active verbs, although passive verbs may be necessary for tact or deemphasis. Effective sentences avoid dangling and misplaced modifiers.

*5* **Define a paragraph and describe three classic paragraph plans and techniques for composing meaningful paragraphs.** A paragraph consists of one or more sentences designated as a separate thought group. Typical paragraphs follow one of three plans. Direct paragraphs (main sentence followed by supporting sentences) are useful to define, classify, illustrate, and describe. Pivoting paragraphs (limiting sentence followed by main sentence and supporting sentences) are useful to compare and contrast. Indirect paragraphs (supporting sentences followed by main sentence) build a rationale and foundation of ideas before presenting the main idea. Paragraphs may be improved through the use of coherence techniques and transitional expressions.

## CHAPTER REVIEW

1. Name seven specific techniques for a productive group "brainstorming" session. (Obj. 1)

2. What is a cluster diagram, and when might it be useful? (Obj. 1)

3. Describe an alphanumeric outline. (Obj. 2)

4. What is the relationship between the major categories in an outline and those in a report written from the outline? (Obj. 2)

5. Distinguish between the direct and indirect patterns of organization for typical business messages. (Obj. 3)

6. Why should most messages be "frontloaded"? (Obj. 3)

7. List some business messages that should be frontloaded and some that should not be frontloaded. (Obj. 3)

8. Why should writers plan for revision? How can they do it? (Obj. 4)

9. Distinguish an independent clause from a dependent clause. Give examples. (Obj. 4)

10. Name three ways to emphasize important ideas in sentences. (Obj. 4)

11. Distinguish between active-voice sentences and passive-voice sentences. Give examples. (Obj. 4)

12. Give an original example of a dangling or misplaced modifier. Why are introductory verbal phrases dangerous? (Obj. 4)

13. Describe three kinds of sentences used to develop ideas in paragraphs. (Obj. 5)

14. Describe three paragraph plans. Identify the uses for each. (Obj. 5)

15. What is coherence, and how is it achieved? (Obj. 5)

## CRITICAL THINKING

1. Why is cluster diagramming considered an intuitive process while outlining is considered an analytical process? (Obj. 1)

2. Why is audience analysis so important in choosing the direct or indirect pattern of organization for a business message? (Obj. 3)

3. In what ways do you imagine that writing on the job differs from the writing you do in your academic studies? Consider process as well as product. (Obj. 1)

4. Why are short sentences and short paragraphs appropriate for business communication? (Objs. 4 and 5)

5. **Ethical Issue:** Discuss the ethics of the indirect pattern of organization. Is it manipulative to delay presentation of the main idea in a message?

## ACTIVITIES

### 6.1 Document for Analysis (Objs. 3, 4, and 5)

The following interoffice memo is hard to read. It suffers from numerous writing faults discussed in this chapter. **Your Task.** First, read the memo to see whether you can understand what the writer requests from all Western Division employees. Then, discuss why this memo is so hard to read. How long are the sentences? How many passive-voice constructions can you locate? How effective is the paragraphing? Can you spot four dangling or misplaced modifiers? In the next activity you'll improve the organization of this message. (Superscript numbers in the following sentences are provided to help you identify problem sentences.)

**TO:** All Western Division Employees

[1]Personal computers and all the software to support these computers are appearing on many desks of Western Division employees. [2]After giving the matter considerable attention, it has been determined by the Systems Development Department (SDD) that more control should be exerted in coordinating the purchase of hardware and software to improve compatibility throughout the division so that a library of resources may be developed. [3]Therefore, a plan has been developed by SDD that should be followed in making all future equipment selections and purchases. [4]To make the best possible choice, SDD should be contacted as you begin your search because questions about personal computers, word processing programs, hardware, and software can be answered by our knowledgeable staff, who can also provide you with invaluable assistance in making the best choice for your needs at the best possible cost.

178

[5]After your computer and its software arrive, all your future software purchases should be channelled through SDD. [6]To actually make your initial purchase, a written proposal and a purchase request form must be presented to SDD for approval. [7]A need for the purchase must be established; benefits that you expect to derive resulting from its purchase must be analyzed and presented, and an itemized statement of all costs must be submitted. [8]By following these new procedures, coordinated purchasing benefits will be realized by all employees. [9]I may be reached at X466 if you have any questions.

## 6.2 Organizing Data (Obj. 2)

The interoffice memo in Activity 6.1 is hard to read and hard to follow. One of its biggest problems is organization.
**Your Task.** Use either a cluster diagram or an outline to organize the garbled message in Activity 6.1. Beyond the opening and closing of the message, what are the three main points the writer is trying to make? Should this message use the direct pattern or the indirect pattern? Your instructor may ask you to discuss how this entire message could be revised or to actually rewrite it.

## 6.3 Collaborative Brainstorming (Obj. 1)

**TEAM**

Brainstorming can be a productive method for generating problem-solving ideas. You can improve your brainstorming skills through practice.
**Your Task.** In teams of four or five, analyze a problem on your campus such as the following: unavailable classes, unrealistic degree requirements, lack of student intern programs, poor parking facilities, inadequate registration process, lack of diversity among students on campus, and so forth. Use brainstorming techniques to generate ideas that clarify the problem and explore its solutions. Each team member should prepare a cluster diagram to record the ideas generated. Either individually or as a team, organize the ideas into an outline with three to five main points and numerous subpoints. Assume that your ideas will become part of a letter to be sent to an appropriate campus official or to your campus newspaper discussing the problem and your solution. Remember, however, your role as a student. Be polite, positive, and constructive—not negative, hostile, or aggressive.

## 6.4 Individual Brainstorming (Objs. 1 and 2)

**E-MAIL**

Brainstorming techniques can work for individuals as well as groups. Assume that your boss or department chair wants you to submit a short report analyzing a problem.

**Your Task.** Analyze a problem that exists where you work or go to school, such as long lines at the copy or fax machines, overuse of express mail services, understaffing during peak customer service hours, poor scheduling of employees, inferior or inflexible benefit package, outdated office or other equipment, or one of the campus problems discussed in Activity 6.3. Select a problem about which you have some knowledge. Prepare a cluster diagram to develop ideas. Then, organize the ideas into an outline with three to five main points and numerous subpoints. Be polite, positive, and constructive. Send the outline to your boss (your instructor). Include an introduction (such as *Here is the outline you requested in regard to. . . .*). Include a closing that offers to share your cluster diagram if your boss would like to see it.

## 6.5 Researching and Outlining "How-to" Techniques for Productive Brainstorming (Objs. 1 and 2)

**INFOTRAC**

Casandra M., your supervisor, has been asked to lead a brainstorming group in an effort to generate new ideas for the company's product line. Although Casandra knows a great deal about the company and its products, she doesn't know much about brainstorming. She asks you to research the topic quickly and give her a concise guide on how to brainstorm. One other thing—Casandra doesn't want to read an entire article. She wants you to outline it.
**Your Task.** Conduct an InfoTrac keyword search for "brainstorming." Locate an article with specific instructions for running a productive brainstorming session. Prepare an outline that tells how to (a) prepare for a brainstorming session, (b) conduct the session, and (c) follow up after the meeting. Submit your outline in a memo or an e-mail message to your supervisor (your instructor).

## 6.6 Using the Web to Compare Brainstorming Resources (Obj. 1)

You are part of an internship program at a large company. Ron W., the manager in charge of interns, wants your group to use the Web to research two topics: (a) group brainstorming and (b) brainstorming software. Ron wants to know the two best Web sites that provide free advice about brainstorming, but he also wants your group to recommend two software products that teach people how to brainstorm.
**Your Task.** Using one or more search engines (such as Google), locate a few good Web sites that provide free advice on how to conduct brainstorming sessions. Then locate sites that sell software teaching individuals how to brainstorm. As a team, discuss which sites seemed most useful and trustworthy. How can you judge a Web software product if you have not seen it? In an e-mail or a memo to Ron, tell him what two sites you thought were best for free advice and what two software products you would recommend. Explain and defend your choices.

## 6.7 Outlining (Obj. 2)

You were hired as a consultant to a group of investors who requested information about starting a new radio station in Frederiction, New Brunswick. You collected information for a report to the investors, but you realize that your information would be easier to read if it were outlined.
**Your Task.** Arrange the following topics into a coherent alphanumeric outline. Clue: The items are already in the right order.

Problem: Determining program format for new radio station CFSD-FM

Background: Current radio formats available to listeners in Frederiction

Background: Demographics of target area (population, age, gender, income)

Survey results: Music preferences

Survey finds that top two favourites are easy listening and soft rock

Next two favourites are country and rock

Other kinds of music mentioned in survey: classical, jazz

Survey results: Newscast preferences

News emphasis: Respondents prefer primarily national news but with some local items

Respondents say yes to news but only short, hourly newscasts

Analysis of findings: Discussion of all findings in greater detail

Recommendations: Hybrid format combining easy listening and soft rock

Recommendations: News in three- to five-minute newscasts hourly; cover national news but include local flavour

We recommend starting a new station immediately.

## 6.8 Collaborative Letter (Objs. 3–5)

One of the best ways to learn about the skills required in your field is to interview individuals working in that field.
**Your Task.** Divide into teams of three to five people who have similar majors. Work together to compose an inquiry letter requesting career information from someone in your field. Include questions about technical and general courses to take, possible starting salaries, good companies to apply to, technical skills required, necessary interpersonal skills, computer tools currently used, and tips for getting started in the field. Although this is a small project, your team can work more harmoniously if you apply some of the suggestions from Chapter 2. For example, appoint a meeting leader, recorder, and evaluator.

## 6.9 Sentence Elements (Obj. 4)

**Your Task.** In the following sentences underscore and identify dependent clauses (DC), independent clauses (IC), and phrases (P). Circle subjects and verbs in clauses.

a. We had a company problem, and we tried brainstorming.
b. Because we wanted creativity, we gave everyone a pad of sticky notes.
c. Our team leader installed flipcharts around the room.
d. With different-coloured markers, each team member wrote ideas on the appropriate flipchart.

## 6.10 Sentence Length (Obj. 4)

**Your Task.** Break the following sentences into shorter sentences. Use appropriate transitional expressions.

a. If firms have a substantial investment in original research or development of new products, they should consider protecting those products with patents, although all patents eventually expire and what were once trade secrets can become common knowledge in the industry.
b. As soon as consumers recognize a name associated with a product or service, that name is entitled to legal protection as a trademark; in fact, consumers may even create a trademark where none existed or create a second trademark by using a nickname as a source indicator, such as the name "Coke," which was

legally protected even before it had ever been used by the company.

c. Although no magic formula exists for picking a good trademark name, firms should avoid picking the first name that pops into someone's head; moreover, they should be aware that unique and arbitrary marks are best, while descriptive terms such as "car" or "TV repair" are useless, and surnames and geographic names are weak because they lack distinction and exclusivity.

## 6.11 Active and Passive Voice (Obj. 4)

**Your Task.** In the following sentences convert passive-voice verbs to active-voice verbs. Add subjects if necessary. Be prepared to discuss which sentence version is more effective.

a. A decision to focus on customer service was made by the board.

b. First, the product line was examined to determine whether it met customers' needs.

c. In the past, products had been built to the company's internal expectations of market needs.

d. When it was realized that changes were in order, a new product line was designed.

e. After just-in-time inventory procedures were introduced, our inventories were cut in half.

f. Our company was recently named "Vendor of the Year" by Texas Instruments.

Now convert active-voice verbs to passive-voice verbs, and be prepared to discuss which sentence version is more effective.

g. We cannot authorize repair of your VCR since you have allowed the warranty period to expire.

h. I cannot give you a cash refund for merchandise that you purchased 60 or more days ago.

i. Valley Golf Course does not accept players who are not members.

j. You must submit all reports by Friday at 5 p.m.

k. Joan added the two columns instead of subtracting them, thus producing the incorrect total.

## 6.12 Dangling and Misplaced Modifiers (Obj. 4)

**Your Task.** Remedy any dangling or misplaced modifiers in the following sentences. Add subjects as needed, but retain the introductory phrases. Mark "C" if correct.

a. To stay in touch with customers, telephone contacts were encouraged among all sales reps.

b. By making sales reps a part of product design, a great deal of money was saved.

c. Acting as president, the contract was immediately signed by Rachel.

d. To receive a bachelor's degree, complete 120 units of study. (*Tricky!*)

e. Noxious fumes made the office workers sick coming from the storage tanks of a nearby paint manufacturer.

f. Using available evidence, it becomes apparent that the court has been deceived by the witness.

g. Having found the misplaced report, the search was ended.

h. The parliamentary candidate announced his intentions to run as a national candidate in his hometown of Blue Bell, Saskatchewan.

i. Although T-Mart is a self-service department store, every effort is made to give customers personalized, patient service. (*Tricky!*)

## 6.13 Transitional Expressions (Obj. 5)

**Your Task.** Add transitional expressions to the following sentences to improve the flow of ideas (coherence).

a. Computer style checkers rank somewhere between artificial intelligence and artificial ignorance. They are like clever children: smart but not wise. Business writers should be fully aware of the limitations and the usefulness of style checkers.

b. Our computerized file includes all customer data. It provides space for name, address, and other vital information. It has an area for comments, a feature that comes in handy and helps us keep our records up to date.

c. No one likes to turn out poor products. We began highlighting recurring problems. Employees make a special effort to be more careful in doing their work right the first time. It doesn't have to be returned to them for corrections.

d. In-depth employment interviews may be structured or unstructured. Structured interviews have little flexibility. All candidates are asked the same questions in the same order. Unstructured interviews allow a free-flowing conversation. Topics are prepared for discussion by the interviewer.

e. Fringe benefits consist of life, health, and dental insurance. Some fringe benefits might include paid vacations and sick pay. Other fringe benefits include holidays, funeral leave, and emergency leave. Paid lunch, rest periods, tuition reimbursement, and child care are also sometimes provided.

## 6.14 Paragraph Organization (Obj. 5)

**Your Task.** The following poorly written paragraphs follow the indirect plan. Locate the main sentence in each paragraph. Then revise each paragraph so that it is organized directly. Improve coherence by using the techniques described in this chapter.

**a.** Many of our customers limp through their business despite problems with their disk drives, printers, and peripherals. We cannot service their disk drives, printers, and peripherals. These customers are unable to go without this equipment long enough for the repair. We've learned that there are two times when we can get to that equipment. We can do our repairs in the middle of the night or on Sunday. All of our staff of technicians now works every Sunday. Please authorize additional budget for my department to hire technicians for night and weekend service hours.

**b.** Air express is one of the ways SturdyBilt power mowers and chain saws may be delivered. Air express promises two-day delivery but at a considerable cost. The cheapest method is for retailers to pick up shipments themselves at our nearest distribution centre. We have distribution centres in Regina, Winnipeg, and Thunder Bay. Another option involves having our trucks deliver the shipment from our distribution centre to the retailer's door for an additional fee. These are the options SturdyBilt provides for the retailers purchasing our products.

## C.L.U.E. REVIEW 6

Edit the following sentences to correct faults in grammar, punctuation, spelling, and word use.

**1.** Whether you are writting a short memo or a thirty page report you should expect to conduct formal, or informal research.

**2.** Our company Vice President came to the President and I asking for help with 2 complex but seperate desktop publishing problems.

**3.** Because neither of us are particularly creative we decided to organize a brainstorming session.

**4.** To develop a better sense of design we collected desireable samples from: books, magazines, brochures and newsletters.

**5.** We noticed that, poorly-designed projects often was filled with cluttered layouts, incompatible typefaces, and to many typefaces.

**6.** Our brain storming session included the following individuals; Troy, Rhonda, Amanda and Matt.

**7.** We encouraged participants to think visually but most was reluctant to draw pictures.

**8.** One of our principle goals were to create one hundred ideas in thirty minutes however we were prepared to meet up to 1 hour.

**9.** Because we know that ideas continue to incubate we encouraged every one to continue too submit ideas, after the session ended.

**10.** Robyn Clarkes article titled A Better way to brainstorm which appeared in the magazine Black Enterprise proved to be very helpful.

# Chapter 7
## Revising Business Messages

## LEARNING OBJECTIVES

*1* Identify revision techniques that make a document clear, conversational, and concise.

*2* Describe revision tactics that make a document vigorous and direct.

*3* Discuss revision strategies that improve readability.

*4* List problem areas that good proofreaders examine carefully.

*5* Compare the proofreading of routine and complex documents.

*6* Evaluate a message to judge its success.

# *Stiff Sentences Inc.*

How critical to your personal and professional success is your ability to write well? To the writers of Stiff Sentences Inc., it's very critical. In fact, they contend that in today's wired workplace, no single skill is more critical to the success of an overall enterprise than writing intelligence.

Believing that English is now the predominant language of international affairs and that mastery of English is a precondition for success in most ventures, the writers at Stiff Sentences offer their clients a methodical approach to writing that achieves impressive and consistent results—no matter the medium. It is this methodical approach that has earned them the distinction of being the first company of writers to receive ISO 9000 certification. Their approach involves mastery of what the writers refer to as the machinery of language—diction (word choice), grammar, punctuation, syntax (word order), logic, and rhetoric.

At Stiff Sentences, the sole purpose of writing is to reveal the intelligence of the writer. It is not the writing itself that informs or persuades, rather it is the writer. Writing intelligence involves, among other things, an ability to choose exactly the right words for your intended audience and purpose, and requires a substantial vocabulary. The writers at Stiff Sentences must undertake a demanding professional development program, no matter how proficient they may already be. All writing is reviewed and assessed by at least two other writers. The ability to accept constructive criticism is essential. In addition, writers are expected to be adept at client service, project management, and marketing.

Located just outside Ottawa, Ontario, Stiff Sentences serves clients across Canada and in Bermuda, the United Kingdom, Europe, and the United States. Its diverse client base requires an understanding of the differing standards of language from one country to another. Failing to respect the language standards of the intended audience can cause the writer to appear uneducated. It is this premise that makes the editing phase of any writing project so critical.

Over 15 years of working with clients in business, government, and non-profit sectors, the writers have identified the causes of weak writing—and have developed an executive writing system called BackDRAFT™ that helps average writers become excellent. This interactive writing curriculum is delivered in five self-paced semesters and involves approximately 30 hours of one-on-one interactive coaching. By setting realistic, visible, and achievable benchmarks for the machinery of language, BackDRAFT offers mastery of professional writing skills in just three months.[1]

## CRITICAL THINKING

- Why is the editing phase of a writing project so critical?
- How would you go about improving your own writing intelligence? What activities could you do on your own? What courses might you take?
- Is it important to revise your personal writing style to meet the needs of your intended audience? Why or why not?

**www.stiffsentences.com**

## REVISING MESSAGES

*1*

The final phase of the 3-×-3 writing process focuses on revising, proofreading, and evaluating. Revising means improving the content and sentence structure of your message. Proofreading involves correcting its grammar, spelling, punctuation, format, and mechanics. Evaluating is the process of analyzing whether your message achieved its purpose. Many businesspeople realize that their ideas are worth little unless they can be communicated effectively to coworkers and to management. In the communication process the techniques of revision can often mean the difference between the acceptance or rejection of ideas.

While the composition process differs for individuals and situations, this final phase should occupy a significant share of the total time you spend on a message. As you learned earlier, some experts recommend devoting about half of the total composition time to revising and proofreading.[2]

Rarely is the first or even second version of a message satisfactory. One authority says, "Only the amateur expects writing perfection on the first try."[3] The revision stage is your chance to make sure your message says what you mean. Many professional writers compose the first draft quickly without worrying about language, precision, or correctness. Then they revise and polish extensively. Other writers, however, prefer to revise as they go—particularly for shorter business documents. At Stiff Sentences, for example, writing is subject to a review system wherein it is read by at least two other writers in the firm. Members of the writing team have already closely scrutinized the first draft the client sees.

Because few writers can produce a satisfactory copy on the first attempt, revision is an important step in the writing process.

Important messages—such as those you send to management or to customers or turn in to instructors for grades—deserve careful revision and proofreading. When you finish a first draft, plan for a cooling-off period. Put the document aside and return to it after a break, preferably after 24 hours or longer.[4]

Whether you revise immediately or after a break, you'll want to examine your message critically. You should be especially concerned with ways to improve its clarity, conciseness, vigour, and readability.

## Keeping It Clear

One of the first revision tasks is assessing the clarity of your message. A clear message is one that is immediately understood. To achieve clarity, resist the urge to show off or be fancy. Remember that your goal is not to impress an instructor. Instead, the goal of business writing is to *express*, not *impress*. This involves two simple rules: (1) keep it simple and (2) keep it conversational.

The goal of business writing is to express rather than impress.

Why do some communicators fail to craft simple, direct messages? For several reasons:

- Untrained executives and professionals worry that plain messages don't sound important.

- Subordinates fear that plain talk won't impress the boss.

- Unskilled writers create foggy messages because they have not learned how to communicate clearly.

- Unethical writers intentionally obscure a message to hide the truth.

Whatever the cause, you can eliminate the fog by applying the familiar KISS formula: Keep It Short and Simple! One way to achieve clear writing is to use active-voice sentences that avoid foggy, indirect, and pompous language.

To achieve clarity, remember to KISS: Keep It Short and Simple!

| **Foggy** | **Clear** |
|---|---|
| Employees have not been made sufficiently aware of the potentially adverse consequences involved regarding these chemicals. | Warn your employees about these chemicals. |
| To be sure of obtaining optimal results, it is essential that you give your employees the implements that are necessary for completion of the job. | To get the best results, give employees the tools they need to do the job. |

# Keeping It Conversational

To achieve a conversational tone, sound professional but not stilted.

Clarity is further enhanced by language that sounds like conversation. This doesn't mean that your letters and memos should be chatty or familiar. Rather, you should strive to sound professional, yet not artificial or formal. This means avoiding legal terminology, technical words, and third-person constructions (*the undersigned, the writer*). Business messages should sound warm, friendly, and conversational—not stuffy and formal.[5] To sound friendly, include occasional contractions (*can't, doesn't*) and first-person pronouns (*I/we*). This warmth is appropriate in all but the most formal business reports. You can determine whether your writing is conversational by trying the kitchen test. If it wouldn't sound natural in your kitchen, it probably needs revision. Note how the following formal sentences were revised to pass the kitchen test.

| **Formal** | **Conversational** |
|---|---|
| As per your verbal instruction, steps will be undertaken immediately to investigate your billing problem. | At your suggestion I'm investigating your billing immediately. |
| Our organization would like to inform you that your account is being credited in the aforementioned sum. | We're crediting your account for $78. |

# Keeping It Concise

Main points are easier to understand in concise messages.

In revising, make certain that a message makes its point in the fewest possible words. In explaining a five-page letter to a friend, former British Prime Minister Winston Churchill once said, "I would have written a short letter, but I didn't have the time."[6]

Messages without flabby phrases and redundancies are easier to comprehend and more emphatic because main points stand out. Efficient messages also save the reader valuable time.

Many busy executives today won't read wordy reports. Chairman Martin Kallen, of Monsanto Europe, "flipped" because too much paper was clogging the company. He complained that reports were too long, too frequent, and too unread. He then decreed that all writing be more concise, and he refused to read any report that was not summarized in two or fewer pages.[7] Similarly, the late chairman of General Motors, Alfred P. Sloan, had a rule that any memo submitted for his signature be no longer than one page. When he received any memo, regardless of its length, he signed the bottom of the first page and threw the rest of the memo into the wastebasket.[8] And Microsoft chairman Bill Gates is said to stop reading e-mail messages after three screens.

Short messages require more effort than long, flabby ones.

But concise writing is not easy. As one expert copyeditor observed, "Trim sentences, like trim bodies, usually require far more effort than flabby ones."[9] To turn out slim sentences and lean messages, you do not have to be brusque, rude, or simpleminded. Instead, you must take time in the revision stage to "trim the fat." And before you can do that, you must learn to recognize it. Locating and excising wordiness involves (1) removing opening fillers, (2) eliminating redundancies, (3) reducing compound prepositions, and (4) purging empty words.

***Removing Opening Fillers.*** Openers like *there is* and *it is* fill in sentences but generally add no meaning. These fillers reveal writers spinning their wheels until deciding where the sentence is going. Train yourself to question these constructions.

About 75 percent of sentence-opening fillers can be eliminated, almost always resulting in more emphatic and more efficient sentences.

| Wordy | Concise |
|---|---|
| There are three things I want you to do. | I want you to do three things. |
| It is important to start meetings on time. | Starting meetings on time is important. |

*Eliminating Redundancies.* Expressions that repeat meaning or include unnecessary words are redundant. To say *unexpected surprise* is like saying "surprise surprise" because *unexpected* carries the same meaning as *surprise.* Excessive adjectives, adverbs, and phrases often create redundancies and wordiness. The following list represents a tiny segment of the large number of redundancies appearing in business writing today.

**Redundancies convey the same meaning more than once.**

**Redundancies to Avoid**

| | | |
|---|---|---|
| advance warning | exactly identical | perfectly clear |
| alter or change | few in number | personal opinion |
| assemble together | free and clear | potential opportunity |
| basic fundamentals | grateful thanks | positively certain |
| collect together | great majority | proposed plan |
| consensus of opinion | integral part | serious interest |
| contributing factor | last and final | refer back |
| dollar amount | midway between | true facts |
| each and every | new changes | visible to the eye |
| end result | past history | unexpected surprise |

**What word in each expression creates the redundancy?**

Although stockbrokers understand the meaning of their finger gestures in buying and selling stocks, investors were often confused by the language appearing in investment literature. Plain language guidelines offer suggestions to avoid redundancies, long sentences, wordy phrases, passive voice, and abstract words. These techniques are helpful to all business communicators.

Wordy prepositional phrases
can be shortened to single
words.

*Reducing Compound Prepositions.* Single words can often replace wordy prepositional phrases. In the following examples notice how the shorter forms say the same thing but more efficiently.

| Wordy Compound Preposition | Shorter Form |
| --- | --- |
| as to whether | whether |
| at a later date | later |
| at this point in time | now |
| at such time, at which time | when |
| by means of, in accordance with | by |
| despite the fact that | although |
| due to the fact that, inasmuch as,<br>    in view of the fact that | because |
| for the amount of | for |
| in advance of, prior to | before |
| subsequent to | after |
| the manner in which | how |
| until such time as | until |

*Purging Empty Words.* Familiar phrases roll off the tongue easily, but many contain expendable parts. Be alert to these empty words and phrases: *case, degree, the fact that, factor, instance, nature,* and *quality.* Notice how much better the following sentences sound when we remove all the empty words:

~~In the case of~~ the *Halifax Gazette* ~~the newspaper~~ improved its readability.

Because of ~~the degree of~~ active participation by our sales reps, profits soared.

We are aware ~~of the fact~~ that many managers need assistance.

Except for ~~the instance of~~ Mazda, Japanese imports sagged.

She chose a career in a field that was analytical ~~in nature~~. (Or, *She chose a career in an analytical field.*)

Student writing in that class is excellent ~~in quality~~.

Also avoid saying the obvious. In the following examples notice how many unnecessary words we can omit through revision:

~~When it arrived,~~ I cashed your cheque immediately. (*Announcing the cheque's arrival is unnecessary. That fact is assumed in its cashing.*)

~~We need printer cartridges; therefore,~~ please send me two dozen laser cartridges. (*The first clause is obvious.*)

~~This is to inform you that~~ the meeting will start at 2 p.m. (*Avoid unnecessary lead-in.*)

Finally, look carefully at clauses beginning with *that, which,* and *who.* They can often be shortened without loss of clarity. Search for phrases, such as *it appears that.* Such phrases can be reduced to a single adjective or adverb, such as *apparently.*

successful

Changing the name of a company ~~that is successful~~ is always risky.

All employees ~~who are among those~~ completing the course will be reimbursed.

final
Our proposal, ~~which was~~ slightly altered ~~in its final form~~, won approval.
^

weekly
We plan to schedule meetings ~~on a weekly basis~~.
^

## REVISING FOR VIGOUR AND DIRECTNESS

Much business writing has been criticized as lifeless, cautious, and "really, really boring."[10] This boredom results not so much from content as from wordiness and dull, trite expressions. An Edmonton lawyer, David C. Elliott, has capitalized on the legalese of the judicial system by proposing a "Gobbledygook Fee Scale" in his "Model Plain Language Act." For example, using *above-referenced* involves a $100 fee; *herein*, $125; *pursuant to*, $100; and *witnesseth*, $200. If a phrase is used more than ten times in a document, the fines are tripled.[11] You've already studied ways to improve clarity and conciseness. You can also reduce wordiness and improve vigour by (1) kicking the noun habit and (2) dumping trite business phrases.

### Kicking the Noun Habit

Some writers become addicted to nouns, needlessly transforming verbs into nouns (*we make a recommendation of* instead of *we recommend*). This bad habit increases sentence length, drains verb strength, slows the reader, and muddies the thought. Notice how efficient, clean, and forceful the verbs below sound compared with their noun phrase counterparts.

| Wordy Noun Phrase | Verb |
|---|---|
| conduct a discussion of | discuss |
| create a reduction in | reduce |
| engage in the preparation of | prepare |
| give consideration to | consider |
| make an assumption of | assume |
| make a discovery of | discover |
| perform an analysis of | analyze |
| reach a conclusion about | conclude |
| take action on | act |

**Much business writing is plagued by wordiness and triteness.**

### Dumping Trite Business Phrases

To sound "businesslike," many writers repeat the same stale expressions that other writers have used over the years. Your writing will sound fresher and more vigorous if you eliminate these phrases or find more original ways to convey the idea.

| Trite Phrase | Improved Version |
|---|---|
| as per your request | as you request |
| pursuant to your request | at your request |
| enclosed please find | enclosed is |
| every effort will be made | we'll try |
| in accordance with your wishes | as you wish |
| in receipt of | have received |
| please do not hesitate to | please |
| thank you in advance | thank you |
| under separate cover | separately |
| with reference to | about |

**Avoid trite expressions that are overused in business writing.**

*3*

To help receivers anticipate and comprehend ideas quickly, two special writing techniques are helpful: (1) parallelism, which involves balanced writing, and (2) highlighting, which makes important points more visible. And to ensure that your document is readable, consider using the readability statistics feature in your word processing software.

## Developing Parallelism

**Parallelism means matching nouns with nouns, verbs with verbs, phrases with phrases, and so on.**

As you revise, be certain that you express similar ideas in balanced or parallel construction. For example, the phrase *clearly, concisely,* and *correctly* is parallel because all the words end in *-ly*. To express the list as *clearly, concisely, and with correctness* is jarring because the last item is not what the receiver expects. Instead of an adverb, the series ends with a noun. To achieve parallelism, match nouns with nouns, verbs with verbs, phrases with phrases, and clauses with clauses. Avoid mixing active-voice verbs with passive-voice verbs.

| **Not Parallel** | **Improved** |
|---|---|
| The policy affected all vendors, suppliers, and those involved with consulting. | The policy affected all vendors, suppliers, and consultants. *(Series matches nouns.)* |
| Good managers analyze a problem, collect data, and alternatives are evaluated. | Good managers analyze a problem, collect data, and evaluate alternatives. *(Series matches verb forms.)* |

Be alert to a list or series of items; the use of *and* or *or* should signal you to check for balanced construction. When elements cannot be balanced fluently, consider revising to subordinate or separate the items.

| **Not Parallel** | **Improved** |
|---|---|
| Foreign service employees must be able to communicate rapidly, concisely, and be flexible in handling diverse responsibilities. | Foreign service employees must be able to communicate rapidly and concisely; they must also be flexible in handling diverse responsibilities. |

## Applying Graphic Highlighting

**Graphic devices such as lists, bullets, headings, and white space spotlight important ideas.**

One of the best ways to improve comprehension is through graphic highlighting techniques. Spotlight important items by setting them off with

- Letters, such as (a), (b), and (c), within the text
- Numerals, such as 1, 2, and 3, listed vertically
- Bullets—black squares, raised periods, or other symbols
- Headings
- Capital letters, underscores, boldface, and italics

Ideas formerly buried within sentences or paragraphs stand out when targeted with one of these techniques. Readers not only understand your message more rapidly and easily but also consider you efficient and well organized. In the following sentence notice how highlighting with letters makes the three items more visible and emphatic.

**Without Highlighting**
Chez Hélène attracts upscale customers by featuring quality fashions, personalized service, and a generous return policy.

**Highlighted With Letters**
Chez Hélène attracts upscale customers by featuring (a) quality fashions, (b) personalized service, and (c) a generous return policy.

If you have the space and wish to create even greater visual impact, you can list items vertically. Capitalize the word at the beginning of each line. Don't add end punctuation unless the statements are complete sentences. And be sure to use parallel construction whenever you itemize ideas. In the following examples, each item in the bulleted list follows an adjective/noun sequence. In the bulleted list, each item begins with a verb. Notice, too, that we use bullets when items have no particular order or importance. Numbers, however, are better to show a sequence or to identify items for reference.

Lists offset from the text and introduced with bullets or numbers have a strong visual impact.

**Highlighted With Bullets**
Chez Hélène attracts upscale customers by featuring the following:
- Quality fashions
- Personalized service
- Generous return policy

**Highlighted With Numbers**
Chez Hélène advises recruiters to follow these steps in hiring applicants:
1. Examine application
2. Interview applicant
3. Check references

Headings are another choice for highlighting information. They force the writer to organize carefully so that similar data are grouped together. And they help the reader separate major ideas from details. Moreover, headings enable a busy reader to skim familiar or less important information. They also provide a quick preview or review. Although headings appear more often in reports, they are equally helpful in complex letters and memos. Here, they informally summarize items within a message:

Headings help writers to organize information and enable readers to absorb important ideas.

**Highlighted With Headings**
Chez Hélène focuses on the following areas in the employment process:
- **Attracting applicants.** We advertise for qualified applicants, and we also encourage current employees to recommend good people.
- **Interviewing applicants.** Our specialized interviews include simulated customer encounters as well as scrutiny by supervisors.
- **Checking references.** We investigate every applicant thoroughly, including conversations with former employers and all listed references.

To highlight individual words, use CAPITAL letters, underlining, **bold** type, or *italics*. Be careful with these techniques, though, because they SHOUT at the reader. Consider how the reader will react.

The following chapters supply additional ideas for grouping and spotlighting data. Although highlighting techniques can improve comprehension, they can also clutter a message if overdone. Many of these techniques also require more space, so use them judiciously.

## Measuring Readability

Experts have developed methods for measuring how easy, or difficult, a message is to read. Probably the best known is Robert Gunning's Fog Index, which measures long words and sentence length to determine readability. The foggier a message, the more difficult it is to read and thus understand. For more information about the Fog Index, visit <http://lfa.atu.edu/Brucker/Fog.html>.

# *Stiff Sentences Inc. Revisited*

The writing team at Stiff Sentences has been asked to create a guide for preparing internal and external corporate correspondence. One of its major clients, an accounting firm, has a new president who believes memos should be no longer than a single page. In fact, he has been heard to say that he refuses to read beyond the first page of any internal correspondence he receives.

The company has been in business for more than 20 years, and many of the employees have been there since the beginning. They are accustomed to using a certain style for memos and are not eager to change. The president, however, has other ideas.

## CRITICAL THINKING

- Based on what you learned in this chapter, what specific advice can you give about keeping a message clear? Should a business message be conversational? If so, how is a conversational tone achieved?
- Why is conciseness important and what techniques can be used to achieve it?
- What advice can you give for improving the directness and readability of a business message?
- What arguments can you provide to convince all employees to adopt a consistent format?

**www.stiffsentences.com**

---

The National Literacy Secretariat (NLS) promotes the use of plain language to make written material from the government easily understood and accessible to as many Canadians as possible. To support this, the NLS has published *Plain Language: Clear and Simple*, a guide to show how to use straightforward language.[12] In 2001, the Department of Finance Canada released four model plain-language loan disclosure documents designed to make it easier for consumers to understand these types of agreements. The four documents cover credit card applications, credit card agreements, personal lines of credit, and vehicle loan agreements. "Canadians have told us that they want to be provided with clear, easy-to-understand information to help them make important financial decisions," said former Secretary of State Jim Peterson.[13] In addition, Canada Customs and Revenue Agency conducts a literacy sensitivity training workshop for staff, monitors 1 000 publications and 800 forms for plain language, and uses a large font for letters to taxpayers.[14]

Remember that your goal as a business communicator is to make your message understood. By following the tips outlined in this chapter and occasionally using your word processor to calculate the readability of your writing, you can ensure that you stay within the appropriate range for your audience. Long words—those over two syllables—and long sentences can make your writing foggy.

**Readability formulas based on word and sentence length do not always measure meaningfulness.**

Readability formulas, however, don't always tell the full story. Although they provide a rough estimate, those based solely on word and sentence counts fail to measure meaningfulness. Even short words (such as *skew, onus*, and *wane*) can cause trouble if readers don't recognize them. More important than length are a word's familiarity and meaningfulness to the reader. In Chapter 5 you learned to adapt your writing to the audience by selecting familiar words. Other techniques that can improve readability include well-organized paragraphs, transitions to connect ideas, headings, and lists.

The task of revision, summarized in the following checklist, is hard work. It demands objectivity and a willingness to cut, cut, cut. Although painful, the process is gratifying. It's a great feeling when you realize your finished message is clear, concise, and readable.

## CHECKLIST FOR REVISING MESSAGES

✓ **Keep the message simple.** Express ideas directly. Don't show off or use fancy language.

✓ **Be conversational.** Include occasional contractions (*hasn't, don't*) and first-person pronouns (*I/we*). Use natural-sounding language.

✓ **Avoid opening fillers.** Omit sentence fillers such as *there is* and *it is* to produce more direct expression.

✓ **Shun redundancies.** Eliminate words that repeat meanings, such as *mutual cooperation*. Watch for repetitious adjectives, adverbs, and phrases.

✓ **Tighten your writing.** Check phrases that include *case, degree, the fact that, factor,* and other words and phrases that unnecessarily increase wordiness. Avoid saying the obvious.

✓ **Don't convert verbs to nouns.** Keep your writing vigorous by avoiding the noun habit (*analyze,* not *make an analysis of*).

✓ **Avoid trite phrases.** Keep your writing fresh, direct, and contemporary by skipping such expressions as *enclosed please find* and *pursuant to your request.*

✓ **Strive for parallelism.** Help receivers anticipate and comprehend your message by using balanced writing (*planning, drafting, and constructing,* not *planning, drafting, and construction*).

✓ **Highlight important ideas.** Use graphic techniques such as letters, numerals, bullets, headings, capital letters, underlining, boldface, and italics to spotlight ideas and organization.

✓ **Test readability.** Check your writing occasionally to identify its reading level. Remember that short, familiar words and short sentences help readers comprehend.

## PROOFREADING FOR THE FINISHING TOUCH

Once you have the message in its final form, it's time to proofread it. Don't proofread earlier because you may waste time checking items that eventually are changed or omitted.

### What to Watch for in Proofreading

Careful proofreaders check for problems in these areas:

- **Spelling.** Now's the time to consult the dictionary. Is *recommend* spelled with one *c* or two? Do you mean *affect* or *effect*? Use your computer spell checker, but don't rely on it totally. See the Tech Talk box on the next page to learn more about the benefits and hazards of computer spell checkers.

- **Grammar.** Locate sentence subjects. Do their verbs agree with them? Do pronouns agree with their antecedents? Review the C.L.U.E. principles in Appendix A if necessary. Use your computer's grammar checker, but be suspicious. See the Tech Talk box on page 197.

**Proofreading before a document is completed is generally a waste of time.**

## Spell Checkers Are Wonderful, But . . .

Nearly all high-end word processing programs now include sophisticated spell checkers. Also called *dictionaries*, these programs compare your typed words with those in the computer's memory. Microsoft uses a wavy red line to underline misspelled words caught "on the fly."

Although some writers dismiss spell checkers as an annoyance,[15] most of us are only too happy to have our typos and misspelled words detected. The real problem is that spell checkers (and grammar checkers, which are discussed in a subsequent box) don't find all spelling and word usage errors. In the following poem, for example, only two problems were detected (*your* and *it's*):

I have a spell checker
That came with my PC.
It plainly marks four my review
Mistakes I cannot sea.

I've run this poem threw it,
I'm sure your pleased too no.
Its letter perfect in it's weigh
My checker tolled me sew.[16]

The lesson to be learned here is that you can't rely totally on any spell checker. Misused words may not be highlighted because the spell checker doesn't know what meaning you have in mind. That's why you're wise to print out every message and proofread it word by word.

**Career Application**

Use the latest version of Word as you write an assignment for this class. Note any words that it underlined with wavy red lines. Then, have a friend or classmate proofread it to see what the computer missed.

---

- **Punctuation.** Make sure that introductory clauses are followed by commas. In compound sentences put commas before coordinating conjunctions (*and, or, but, nor*). Double-check your use of semicolons and colons.

- **Names and numbers.** Compare all names and numbers with their sources because inaccuracies are not immediately visible. Especially verify the spelling of the names of individuals receiving the message. Most of us immediately dislike someone who misspells our name.

- **Format.** Be sure that your document looks balanced on the page. Compare its parts and format with those of standard documents shown in Appendix B. If you indent paragraphs, be certain that all are indented.

### How to Proofread Routine Documents

5 Most routine documents require a light proofreading. You may be working with a handwritten or a printed copy or on your computer screen. If you wish to print a copy, make it a rough draft (don't print it on letterhead stationery). In time, you may be able to produce a "first-time-final" message, but beginning writers seldom do.

For handwritten or printed messages, read the entire document. Watch for all of the items just described. Use standard proofreading marks, shown on the inside front cover of this book, to indicate changes.

For computer messages you can read the document on the screen, preferably in WYSIWYG mode (what you see is what you get). Use the down arrow to reveal one line at a time, thus focusing your attention at the bottom of the screen. A safer proofreading method, however, is reading from a printed copy. You're more likely to find errors and to observe the tone. "Things really look different on paper,"

For both routine and complex documents, it's best to proofread from a printed copy, not on a computer screen.

UNIT 2
The Writing Process
**194**

In many ways business communicators can learn to improve readability of their messages by emulating newspaper and magazine articles. These writers enhance comprehension by writing concisely, using short sentences, controlling paragraph length, including headings, and developing parallelism (expressing similar ideas in similar grammatical constructions).

observes veteran writer Louise Lague at *People* magazine. "Don't just pull a letter out of the printer and stick it in an envelope. Read every sentence again. You'll catch bad line endings, strange page breaks, and weird spacing. You can also get a totally different feeling about what you've said when you see it in print. Sometimes you can say something with a smile on your face; but if you put the same thing in print, it won't work."[17]

## How to Proofread Complex Documents

Long, complex, or important documents demand more careful proofreading using the following techniques:

- Print a copy, preferably double-spaced, and set it aside for at least a day. You'll be more alert after a breather.

- Allow adequate time to proofread carefully. A common excuse for sloppy proofreading is lack of time.

- Be prepared to find errors. One student confessed, "I can find other people's errors, but I can't seem to locate my own." Psychologically, we don't expect to find errors, and we don't want to find them. You can overcome this obstacle by anticipating errors and congratulating, not criticizing, yourself each time you find one.

- Read the message at least twice—once for word meanings and once for grammar/mechanics. For very long documents (book chapters and long articles or reports), read a third time to verify consistency in formatting.

- Reduce your reading speed. Concentrate on individual words rather than ideas.

- For documents that must be perfect, have someone read the message aloud. Spell names and difficult words, note capitalization, and read punctuation.

- Use standard proofreading marks, shown on the inside front cover of this book, to indicate changes.

Your computer word processing program may include a style or grammar checker. These programs generally analyze aspects of your writing style, including readability level and use of passive voice, trite expressions, split infinitives, and

## The Canadian Spelling Dilemma

An order-in-council, dated June 1890, stated that "in all official documents, in the *Canada Gazette*, and in the Dominion Statutes, the English practice of *-our* endings shall be followed." However, times have changed and much uncertainty exists about what form of spelling to use.

The federal government has produced a helpful manual, *The Canadian Style*,[18] which provides guidance in matters of usage and style. According to *The Canadian Style*, spelling is a major problem in English, not only because of the various rules but also because of differences between the United Kingdom and the United Sates. Canadian spelling fluctuates between the two, and as Mark Orkin states, "To this day, there is no clearly established Canadian standard.[19]

*Editing Canadian English*, by the Editors' Association of Canada (Douglas & McIntyre, 2000), also recognizes the spelling dilemma. Ruth Chernia, the association's professional development chair, describes the association's typically Canadian non-committal stance: "Sometimes it's British and sometimes it's American and sometimes it's our own version of the way things work.[20]

*The Nelson Canadian Dictionary of the English Language* (1997) acknowledges the distinct nature of Canadian spelling as an "erratic blend of U.S. and British usages." To the British and Europeans, we often sound like Americans, and to the Americans, we spell like the British. The use of the *-our* in *honour* and *colour*, the *-re* in *centre* and *metre*, and the doubling of the *l* in words such as *cancelled* and *traveller* reflect British influence. But we are very inconsistent: we cash a *cheque* and order from a *catalogue*, we fly in an *airplane* (not the British *aeroplane*) and we repair a flat *tire* (as opposed to the British *tyre*). Adding to this confusion, to make words such as *beau* and *bureau* plural, many Canadians use the French form of adding *-x* (*beaux* and *bureaux*) rather than adding *-s*.

### Career Application

The spelling issue remains unresolved. What form of spelling do you think is preferable? What spelling should you use when you are writing to represent your organization? Review Canadian newspapers and magazines to determine their spelling choices.

---

**Computer programs can help analyze writing, calculate readability, and locate some grammar and punctuation errors.**

wordy expressions. The latest grammar checkers use sophisticated technology (and a lot of computer memory) to identify significant errors. In addition to finding spelling and typographical errors, they find subject-verb lack of agreement, word misuse, spacing irregularities, punctuation problems, and many other faults. But these programs won't find everything, as you see in the Tech Talk box about grammar checkers on the next page.

## EVALUATING THE PRODUCT

*6*

As part of applying finishing touches, take a moment to evaluate your writing. How successful will this message be? Does it say what you want it to? Will it achieve your purpose? How will you know if it succeeds?

As you learned in Chapter 1, the best way to judge the success of your communication is through feedback. Thus, you should encourage the receiver to respond to your message. This feedback will tell you how to modify future efforts to improve your communication technique.

**A good way to evaluate messages is through feedback.**

Your instructor will also be evaluating some of your writing. Although any criticism is painful, try not to be defensive. Look on these comments as valuable advice tailored to your specific writing weaknesses—and strengths. Many businesses today spend thousands of dollars bringing in communication consulting companies like Stiff Sentences to improve employee writing skills. You're getting the same training

## Grammar Checkers: Not the Final Answer

When first introduced, grammar and style checkers were not too helpful. They were limited in scope, awkward to use, and identified many questionable "errors." But today's built-in grammar checkers detect an amazing number of legitimate writing lapses. Microsoft's Word marks faults in word use (such as *there, their*), capitalization, punctuation, subject-verb agreement, sentence structure, singular and plural endings, repeated words, wordy expression, gender-specific expressions, and many other problems.

How does a grammar checker work? Let's say you typed the sentence, *The office and its equipment is for sale.* You would see a wavy green line appear under *is.* When you point your cursor at "Tools" in the tool bar and click on "Spelling and Grammar," a box opens up. It identifies the subject-verb agreement error and suggests the verb *are* as a correction. When you click on "Change," the error is corrected.

The capabilities of these grammar checkers are truly astounding, given the complexity of the English language. However, before you decide that all your writing problems are solved, think again. Even Word's sophisticated program misses plenty of errors, and it also mismarks some correct expressions. For example, in one document the checker suggested that *company's goals* be changed to *companies goals*, which is clearly wrong. It also thought that the word *italics* should be capitalized.

Despite their limitations, grammar checkers definitely enhance the proofreading process. They find many errors—especially for inexperienced writers. But keep in mind that they are far from perfect. Be prepared to question their suggestions. If in doubt, consult your instructor, a good reference manual, your school writing lab, or one of the online writing labs.

### Career Application

Use a word processing program with a built-in grammar checker in preparing letters and memos for this class. Analyze the suggestions made by the checker. Revise your documents using your judgment about what changes improve message effectiveness.

---

in this course. Take advantage of this chance—one of the few you may have—to improve your skills. The best way to improve your skills, of course, is through instruction, practice, and evaluation.

In this class you have all three elements: instruction in the writing process (summarized in Figure 7.1), practice materials, and someone willing to guide and evaluate your efforts. Those three elements are the reasons that this book and this course may be the most valuable in your entire curriculum. Because it's almost impossible to improve your communication skills alone, grab this chance!

**FIGURE 7.1** The Complete 3-×-3 Writing Process

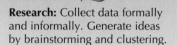

**Prewriting** *1*

**Analyze:** Define your purpose. Select the most appropriate form (channel). Visualize the audience.

**Anticipate:** Put yourself in the reader's position and predict his or her reaction to this message.

**Adapt:** Consider ways to shape the message to benefit the reader, using his or her language.

**Writing** *2*

**Research:** Collect data formally and informally. Generate ideas by brainstorming and clustering.

**Organize:** Group ideas into a list or an outline. Select direct or indirect strategy.

**Compose:** Write first draft, preferably with a good word processing program.

**Revising** *3*

**Revise:** Revise for clarity, tone, conciseness, and vigour. Revise to improve readability.

**Proofread:** Proofread to verify spelling, grammar, punctuation, and format. Check for overall appearance.

**Evaluate:** Ask yourself whether the final product will achieve the purpose.

197

# *Applying Your Skills at Stiff Sentences Inc.*

As a student intern, you are invited to attend the weekly professional development sessions held in your office. This week's session will review the steps for writing clear internal communication.

The team leader talks about the importance of using the direct approach, being concise, and using graphic highlighting to make your memos more readable. The group is also reminded to think of the reader as an "internal customer."

As an example, the group is provided with the first draft of a memo written by the culinary product manager of a Mexican fast-food restaurant (Figure 7.2). The product manager is eager to incorporate some of the rich, complex flavours of Mexican cuisine in ways that will appeal to Canadians. She has exceptional talent in the field of cuisine, but her writing skills are not as well developed as her cooking skills. Suggestions for revising the first two paragraphs of the memo have been included.

## Your Task

To see how much you've learned during your time as a student intern, the team leader asks you to finish revising the memo. He says, "The writer's ideas are right on target, but the main points are totally lost in wordy sentences and solid paragraphs. Revise this and concentrate on conciseness, parallelism, and readability." Revise the remaining four paragraphs of the memo using the techniques presented in this chapter. Type a copy of the complete memo to submit to the team leader.

**www.stiffsentences.com**

## SUMMARY OF LEARNING OBJECTIVES

*1* **Identify revision techniques that make a document clear, conversational, and concise.** Clear documents use active-voice sentences and simple words and avoid negative expressions. Clarity is further enhanced by language that sounds like conversation, including occasional contractions and first-person pronouns (*I/we*). Conciseness can be achieved by excluding opening fillers (*There are*), redundancies (*basic essentials*), and compound prepositions (*by means of*).

*2* **Describe revision tactics that make a document vigorous and direct.** Writers can achieve vigour in messages by revising wordy phrases that needlessly convert verbs into nouns. For example, instead of *we conducted a discussion of*, write *we discussed*. To make writing more direct, good writers replace trite business phrases, such as *please do not hesitate to*, with similar expressions, such as *please*.

*3* **Discuss revision strategies that improve readability.** One revision technique that improves readability is the use of balanced constructions (*parallelism*). For example, *collecting, analyzing, and illustrating data* is balanced and easy to read. *Collecting, analysis of, and illustration of data* is more difficult to read because it is unbalanced. Parallelism involves matching nouns with nouns, verbs with verbs, phrases with phrases, and clauses with clauses. Another technique that improves readability is graphic highlighting. It incorporates devices such as lettered items, numerals, bullets, headings, capital letters, underlining, italics, and bold print to highlight and order ideas. A readability scale is helpful in measuring how easy or difficult a document is to read.

**FIGURE 7.2  Partially Revised First Draft**

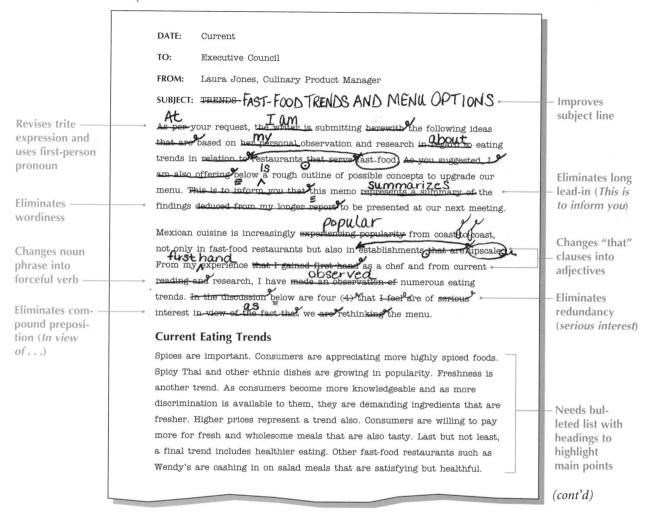

Revises trite expression and uses first-person pronoun

Eliminates wordiness

Changes noun phrase into forceful verb

Eliminates compound preposition (*In view of . . .*)

Improves subject line

Eliminates long lead-in (*This is to inform you*)

Changes "that" clauses into adjectives

Eliminates redundancy (*serious interest*)

Needs bulleted list with headings to highlight main points

*(cont'd)*

---

**4** **List problem areas that good proofreaders examine carefully.** Proofreaders must be especially alert to these problem areas: spelling, grammar, punctuation, names, numbers, and document format.

**5** **Compare the proofreading of routine and complex documents.** Routine documents may be proofread immediately after completion. They may be read line by line on the computer screen or, better yet, from a printed draft copy. More complex documents, however, should be proofread after a breather. To do a good job, you must read from a printed copy, allow adequate time, reduce your reading speed, and read the document at least three times—for word meanings, for grammar/mechanics, and for formatting.

**6** **Evaluate a message to judge its success.** Encourage feedback from the receiver so that you can determine whether your communication achieved its goal. Welcome any advice from your instructor on how to improve your writing skills. Both techniques contribute to helping you evaluate the success of a message.

## FIGURE 7.2 Continued

Given the increasing degree of acceptance of Mexican cuisine and the rich array of flavours and textures in Mexican cuisine, we find that we have many possibilities for the expansion of our menu. Despite the fact that my full report contains a number of additional trends and menu ideas, I will concentrate below on four significant concepts.

*Needs to reduce wordy phrases*

### New Menu Concepts

First, I am of the opinion that we should add **More Grilled Items**. Offer spicy chicken marinated in lime juice or chipotle-rubbed ahi tuna served with cranberry mango salsa. A second idea involves **Salad Meals.** Consider a variety of chicken- or steak-based salads using baby spinach or mixed greens. Third, concentrate on Higher Quality, More Expensive Dishes. Consider churrascos, made with prime beef tenderloin basted with a South American pesto sauce. Lastly, we should consider a Self-Serve Salsa Bar. In relation to this, we could offer exotic fresh salsas with bold flavours and textures.

*Needs bulleted list with headings to improve readability*

I would be more than happy to have a discussion of these ideas with you in greater detail and to have a demonstration of them in the kitchen. Thanks for this opportunity to work with you in the expansion of our menu in a move to ensure that Pepi's Grill remains tops in Mexican cuisine.

*Needs to eliminate empty words*

*Must convert noun phrases to verbs*

# CHAPTER REVIEW

1. Approximately how much of the total composition time should be spent revising, proofreading, and evaluating? (Obj. 1)

2. What is the KISS method? In what three ways can it apply to business writing? (Obj. 1)

3. What is a redundancy? Give an example. Why should writers avoid redundancies? (Obj. 1)

4. Why should communicators avoid openings such as *there is*? (Obj. 1)

5. What shorter forms could be substituted for the expressions *by means of, despite the fact that,* and *at this point in time*? (Obj. 1)

6. Why should a writer avoid the opening *This memo is to inform you that our next committee meeting is Friday*? (Obj. 1)

7. Why should a writer avoid an expression such as *We hope you will give consideration to our proposal*? (Obj. 2)

8. What's wrong with businesslike expressions such as *enclosed please find* and *as per your request*? (Obj. 2)

9. Discuss five ways to highlight important ideas. (Obj. 3)

10. What two characteristics increase the Fog Index of written matter? (Obj. 3)

11. What is parallelism, and how can you achieve it? (Obj. 3)

12. Name five specific items to check in proofreading. Be ready to discuss methods you find useful in spotting these errors. (Obj. 4)

13. In proofreading, what major psychological problem do you face in finding errors? How can you overcome this barrier? (Obj. 4)

14. List four or more techniques for proofreading complex documents. (Obj. 5)

15. How can you overcome defensiveness when your writing is criticized constructively? (Obj. 6)

# CRITICAL THINKING

1. Why is it difficult to recommend a specific process that all writers can follow in composition? (Obj. 1)

2. Would you agree or disagree with the following statement by writing expert William Zinsser? "Plain talk will not be easily achieved in corporate America. Too much vanity is on the line." (Objs. 1 and 2)

3. To be conversational, should business writing be exactly as we talk? Support your opinion. (Obj. 1)

4. Why should the proofreading process for routine documents differ from that for complex documents? (Objs. 4 and 5)

5. **Ethical Issue:** What advice would you give in this ethical dilemma? Lisa is serving as interim editor of the company newsletter. She receives an article written by the company president describing, in abstract and pompous language, the company's goals for the coming year. Lisa thinks the article will need considerable revising to make it readable. Attached to the president's article are complimentary comments by two of the company vice presidents. What action should Lisa take?

# ACTIVITIES

## 7.1 Document for Analysis (Objs. 1 and 3)

The following interoffice memo is hard to read because it is poorly written.
**Your Task.** After reading the memo, discuss its faults. How many wordy constructions can you spot? Revise the memo to improve its clarity, conciseness, vigour, and readability.

| | |
|---|---|
| **DATE:** | Current |
| **TO:** | All Management |
| **FROM:** | S. A. Jones, Vice President |
| **SUBJECT:** | SUITABLE BUSINESS ATTIRE |

This memo is addressed to all members of management to advise you that once a year we like to remind management of our policy in relation to the matter of business attire. In this policy there is a recommendation that all employees should wear clothing that promotes a businesslike atmosphere and meets requirements of safety.

Employees who work in offices and who, as part of their jobs, meet the public and other outsiders should dress in a professional manner, including coat, tie, suit, dress, and so forth. In areas of industrial applications, supervisors may prohibit loose clothing (shirttails, ties, cuffs) that could become entangled in machinery that moves.

Where it is necessary, footwear should provide protection against heavy objects or sharp edges at the level of the floor. In the manufacturing and warehousing areas, prohibited footwear includes the following: shoes that are open toe, sandals, shoes made of canvas or nylon, tennis shoes, spiked heels, and heels higher than approximately 4 cm.

Each and every manager has the responsibility for the determination of suitable business attire, and employees should be informed of what is required.

## 7.2 Document for Analysis (Objs. 4 and 5)

The following letter suffers from many writing and proofreading faults.

**Your Task.** Use standard proofreading marks to show corrections. Check spelling, typos, grammar, punctuation, names and numbers, and format.

Current date

Ms. Amanda M. Willis
53 Pendell Road
Windsor, ON  N8N 4W3

Dear Ms. Willis,

We appreciate you interest in employe leasing through Dominion Staff Network. Our programs and our service has proved to be powerful management tools for business owners, like you.

Our seventeen year history, Ms. Williams, provide the local service and national strength neccesary to offer the best employee leasing programs available, we save business owners time, and money, employee hassles and employer liability.

Your employees' will receive health care benifits, retirement plan choices and a national credit union. As a small business owner you can eliminate personel administration. Which involves alot of goverment paperwork today.

Whether you have one or 1,000 employees and offer no benefits to a full-benefits package employee leasing will get you back to the basics of running your business more profitably. I will call you to arrange a time to meet, and talk about your specific needs.

Cordially,

## 7.3 Revising for Readability (Obj. 3)

The following letter is poorly written and suffers from a number of faults.

**Your Task.** As an in-class project or for homework, do the following:

a. Revise the following letter using proofreading marks. Reduce its length and improve its readability by eliminating redundancies, wordiness, and trite expressions. Use simple, clear words. Shorten sentences.

b. Prepare a clean copy of the revised letter.

Current date

Mr. Brian T. Sato
1364 Wakefield Circle
Vancouver, BC V6R 3G7

Dear Mr. Sato:

Pursuant to your request, the undersigned is transmitting to you herewith the attached materials and documents with regard to the improvement of security in your business. To ensure the improvement of your after-hours security, you should initially make a decision with regard to exactly what you contemplate must have protection. You are, in all probability, apprehensive not only about your electronic equipment and paraphernalia but also about your company records, information, and data.

Inasmuch as we feel you will want to obtain protection for both your equipment and data, we will make suggestions for taking a number of judicious steps to inhibit crime. First and foremost, we recommend that you install defensive lighting. A consultant for lighting, currently on our staff, can design both outside and inside lighting, which brings me to my second point. Exhibit security signs, due to the fact that nonprofessional thieves are often as not deterred by posted signs on windows and doors. As my last and final recommendation, you should install space alarms, which are sensors that look down over the areas that are to receive protection, and activate bells or additional lights, thus scaring off intruders.

After reading the enclosed materials, please call me to further discuss the protection of your business.

Sincerely,

## 7.4 Interview (Objs. 1–6)

How much writing is required by people working in your career area? The best way to learn about on-the-job writing is to talk with someone who has a job similar to one you hope to have some day.

**Your Task.** Interview someone in your field of study. Ask questions such as these: • *What kind of writing do you do?* • *What kind of planning do you do before writing?* • *Where do you get information? Do you brainstorm? Make lists?* • *Do you compose with pen and paper, a computer, or a dictating machine?* • *How long does it take you to compose a routine one- or two-page memo or letter? Do you revise? How often?* • *Do you have a preferred method for proofreading? When you have questions about grammar and mechanics, what or whom do you consult? Does anyone read your drafts and make suggestions?* • *Can you describe your entire composition process?* • *Do you ever work with others to produce a document? How does this process work?* • *What makes writing easier or harder for you? Have your writing methods and skills changed since you left school?* Your instructor may ask you to present your findings orally or in a written report.

## 7.5 Making You a Better Writer (Objs. 1–6)

Accountants and other technical experts often think of themselves as accumulators of data rather than as communicators of information. Instead of merely presenting information, you can make yourself more valuable to your organization by becoming a better communicator.

**Your Task.** Use InfoTrac to locate David R. Koeppen's article entitled "Writing for Success: Some Tips for the Accountant," *The National Public Accountant*, February 2000, Article No. A59833208. After reading the article, answer these questions:

a.   How are Koeppen's three writing steps different from your textbook's writing process?

b.   According to Koeppen, how is your audience for writing assignments in school different from the audience in the workplace?

c.   What does the author think is the most difficult part of any communication task? Do you agree?

d.   What are three of the best writing techniques described in this article?

## 7.6 Searching for Deadwood (Obj. 1)

Many writers and speakers are unaware of "deadwood" phrases they use. Some of these are redundancies, compound prepositions, and trite business phrases.

**Your Task.** Using your favourite Web browser, locate two or three sites devoted to deadwood phrases. Your instructor may ask you to (a) submit a list of ten deadwood phrases (and their preferred substitutes) not mentioned in this textbook, or (b) work in teams to prepare a comprehensive "Dictionary of Deadwood Phrases," including as many as you can find. Be sure to include a preferred substitute.

## 7.7 How Plain Is the English in Your Apartment Lease? (Objs. 1–3)

Have you read your apartment lease carefully? Did you understand it? Many students (and their friends and family members) are intimidated, frustrated, or just plain lost when they try to comprehend an apartment lease.

**Your Task.** Locate an apartment lease (yours, a friend's, or a family member's). In teams, analyze its format and readability. What size is the paper? How large are the margins? Is the type large or small? How much white space appears on the page? Are paragraphs and sentences long or short? Does the lease contain legalese or obscure language? What makes it difficult to understand? In an e-mail message to your instructor, summarize your team's reaction to the lease. Your instructor may ask you to revise sections or the entire lease to make it more readable. In class, discuss how ethical it is for an apartment owner to expect a renter to read and comprehend a lease while sitting in the rental office.

## 7.8 Clarity (Obj. 1)

**Your Task.** Revise the following sentences to make them direct, simple, and conversational.

a.   As per your written instruction, we will undertake the task of studying your investment program.

b.   A request that we are making to managers is that they not spend all their time in their departments and instead visit other departments one hour a month.

c.   We in management are of the opinion that employees have not been made sufficiently aware of the problem of computer security.

d.   Our organization is honoured to have the pleasure of extending a welcome to you as a new customer.

e.   Please be advised that it is our intention to make every effort to deliver your order by the date of your request, December 1.

f.   Enclosed herewith please find the proposal which we have the honour to submit to your esteemed organization in regard to the acquisition and purchase of laptop computers.

g.   It has been established that the incontestable key to the future success of QuadCam is a deep and firm commitment to quality.

h.   It is our suggestion that you do not attempt to move forward until you seek and obtain approval of the plan from the team leader prior to beginning this project.

## 7.9 Conciseness (Obj. 1)

**Your Task.** Suggest shorter forms for the following expressions.

a.   at this point in time

b.   in reference to

c.   in regard to

d.   without further delay

e.   on an annual basis

f.   in the event that

g.   a report for which you have no use

h.   a project manager who took great care

i.   arranged according to numbers

j.   a program that is intended to save time

## 7.10 Conciseness (Obj. 1)

**Your Task.** Revise and shorten the following sentences.

a. There are three people who volunteered for the new team.

b. As per your suggestion, we will not attempt to make alterations or changes in the proposal at this point in time.

c. Because of the fact that his visit was an unexpected surprise, we were totally unprepared to make a presentation of profit and loss figures.

d. It is perfectly clear that meetings held on a weekly basis are most effective.

e. Despite our supposition that the bill appeared erroneous, we sent a cheque in the amount of $250.

f. We have received your letter, and we are sending the brochures you request.

g. A great majority of companies are unaware of the fact that college or university interns cannot displace regular employees.

h. There are numerous benefits that can result from a good program that focuses on customer service.

i. Because of the degree of active employee participation, we are of the opinion that our team management program will be successful.

j. At this point in time in the program, I wish to extend my grateful thanks to all the support staff who helped make this occasion possible.

## 7.11 Vigour (Obj. 2)

**Your Task.** Revise the following sentences to reduce noun conversions, trite expressions, and other wordiness.

a. We must make the assumption that you wish to be transferred.

b. Please give consideration to our latest proposal, despite the fact that it comes into conflict with the original plan.

c. The committee reached the conclusion that a great majority of students had a preference for mail-in registration.

d. Please conduct an investigation of employee turnover in that department for the period of June through August.

e. After we engage in the preparation of a report, our recommendations will be presented in their final form before the Executive Committee.

f. There are three members of our staff who are making every effort to locate your lost order.

g. Whether or not we make a continuation of the sales campaign is dependent upon its success in the city of Calgary.

## 7.12 Parallelism (Obj. 2)

**Your Task.** Revise the following sentences to improve parallelism. If elements cannot be balanced fluently, use appropriate subordination.

a. Your goal should be to write business messages that are concise, clear, and written with courteousness.

b. Ensuring equal opportunities, the removal of barriers, and elimination of age discrimination are our objectives.

c. Ms. Thomas tries to read all e-mail messages daily, but responses may not be made until the following day.

d. Last year Mr. Alvarro wrote letters and was giving presentations to promote investment in his business.

e. Because of its air conditioning and since it is light and attractive, I prefer this office.

f. For this position we assess oral and written communication skills, how well individuals solve problems, whether they can work with teams, and we're also interested in interpersonal skills, such as cultural awareness and sensitivity.

## 7.13 Highlighting (Obj. 3)

**Your Task.** Revise the following statements using the suggested highlighting techniques. Improve parallel construction and reduce wordiness if necessary.

a. Revise using letters, such as (a) and (b), within the sentence.

The benefits for employees that our organization offers include annual vacations of two weeks, insurance for group life, provision for insurance coverage of medical expenses for the family, and a private retirement fund.

b. Revise using a vertical list with bullets.

The Canadian Automobile Association makes a provision of the following tips for safe driving. You should start your drive well rested. You should wear sunglasses in bright sunshine. To provide exercise breaks, plan to stop every two hours. Be sure not to drink alcohol or take cold and allergy medications before you drive.

204

**c.** Revise using a vertical list with numbers.

Our lawyer made a recommendation that we take several steps to avoid litigation in regard to sexual harassment. The first step we should take involves establishing an unequivocal written statement prohibiting sexual harassment within our organization. The second thing we should do is make sure training sessions are held for supervisors regarding a proper work environment. Finally, some kind of procedure for employees to lodge complaints is necessary. This procedure should include investigation of complaints.

## 7.14 Proofreading (Objs. 4 and 5)

Use proofreading marks to mark spelling, grammar, punctuation, capitalization, and other errors in the following sentences.

**a.** To be elligible for this job, you must: (1) Be a Canadian citizen, (2) Be able to pass a through back ground investigation, and (3) Be available for world wide assignment.

**b.** Some businesses view "quality" as a focus of the organization rather then as a atribute of goods or services.

**c.** Its easy to get caught up in internal problems, and to overlook customers needs.

**d.** Incidently we expect both the ceo and the president to give there speechs before noon.

**e.** This is to inform you that wordiness destroys clarity therefore learn to cut the fat from your writing.

**f.** A clothing outlet opened at lakeland plaza in june, however business is slow.

# C.L.U.E. REVIEW 7

Edit the following sentences to correct faults in grammar, punctuation, spelling, and word use.

1. Business documents must be written clear to insure that readers comprehend the message quick.

2. The prominant Chairman of Monsanto in europe complained that his managers reports were to long, to frequent and too unread.

3. The report contained so many redundancys that it's main principals requesting Provincial and Federal funding was lost.

4. The information was sited in an recent article entitled "Whats new in grammer-checking softwear, however I can't locate the article now.

5. All 3 of our companys recruiters: Jim Lucus, Doreen Delgado, and Brad Kirby—critisized there poorly-written procedures.

6. To help recievers anticipate and comprehend ideas quick 2 special writing techniques is helpful, parallalism which involves balanced writing and highlighting which makes important points more visible.

7. When you must proof read a important document all ways work from a printed copy.

8. Have you all ready ordered the following? a dictionary a reference manual and a style book.

9. As we completed the final step in the writing process we wondered how feasable it would be to evaluate our message?

10. Its almost impossible to improve your communication skills alone, therefore you should take advantage of this oppertunity.

# Unit 3
## Business Correspondence

# Chapter 8

## Routine E-Mail Messages and Memos

## LEARNING OBJECTIVES

*1* Discuss the characteristics of and the writing process for successful routine e-mail messages and memos.

*2* Analyze the organization of e-mail messages and memos.

*3* Describe smart e-mail practices, including getting started; content, tone, and correctness; netiquette; replying to e-mail; and formatting.

*4* Write procedure and information e-mail messages and memos.

*5* Write request and reply e-mail messages and memos.

*6* Write confirmation e-mail messages and memos.

# Research in Motion Limited

Research in Motion Limited (RIM) is a leading designer, manufacturer, and marketer of innovative wireless solutions for the worldwide mobile communications market. Through the development of integrated hardware, software, and services that support multiple network standards, RIM provides platforms and solutions for seamless access to time-sensitive information including e-mail, phone, SMS messaging, Internet, and intranet-based applications. RIM technology also enables a broad array of third-party developers and manufacturers to enhance their products and services with wireless connectivity to data.

RIM's award-winning products, services, and embedded technologies are used by thousands of organizations around the world and include the BlackBerry™ wireless platform, the RIM Wireless Handhelds™ product line, software development tools, radio modems, and software/hardware licensing agreements. Awards received in early 2003 alone include the Reader's Choice Award for Best Mobility Solution, the Government Computer News' Best New Technology Award, Andy Seybold's Outlook 4Mobility Innovation Award as the first complete wireless e-mail solution, and first place in the Innovation category on KPMG/Ipsos-Reid's list of Canada's most-respected corporations. Founded in 1984 and based in Waterloo, Ontario, RIM operates offices in North America, Europe, and Asia Pacific.

RIM's first-quarter revenue for the three months ending May 31, 2003, was US$104.5 million, up from US$87.5 million in the previous quarter. Of this, 50 per-cent was for handhelds. The total number of BlackBerry subscribers increased by approximately 81 000 from the prior quarter to 615 000 subscribers. "RIM continues to grow its business and strengthen its market position through close-knit alliances with leading product and service providers," said Jim Balsillie, chairperson and co-CEO at RIM. "Together with our partners, we are expanding the global reach of the BlackBerry platform through new product, distribution, and licensing initiatives." RIM's partners include Rogers AT&T Wireless, T-Mobile, and Onset Technologies.

According to Mark Guibert, vice president, Brand Management, at RIM, "BlackBerry has become the leading wireless platform for the enterprise because it provides secure, push-based connectivity to corporate e-mail and data." David Bean, president of eAccess Solutions in Palatine, Illinois, adds, "Data access is the hot button now; everyone is looking for a fast way to connect BlackBerry handhelds to data sources."[1]

## CRITICAL THINKING

- In what ways have e-mail and instant messaging changed our behaviour, our way of interacting with people, and our institutions?
- How long will it take to learn to adapt to this new wireless form of communication? What adaptation(s) or preparation might be necessary?
- Why do some people find it easier than others do to adapt to new technologies?

**www.rim.com**

---

# GETTING RESULTS THROUGH WELL-WRITTEN E-MAIL MESSAGES AND MEMOS

In most organizations today, an amazing change has taken place in internal communication. In the past, written messages from insiders took the form of hard-copy memorandums. But recently e-mail has become the communication channel of choice. In a survey conducted by Emailthatpays and Ipsos-Reid, results indicate that e-mail has fundamentally changed the way we communicate with people and has become an essential tool for office communications. A full 85 percent of online Canadians believe that e-mail has made them much more efficient, and nearly two thirds (62 percent) prefer to communicate via e-mail than through other methods.[2]

**E-mail has become the primary communication channel for internal communication.**

CHAPTER 8
Routine E-Mail Messages
and Memos
**209**

Technology allows increasing numbers of employees to work at home and telecommute to the office. As a result, more and more messages—especially memos—need to be written to keep the lines of communication open between remote employees and the office.

A primary function of e-mail is exchanging messages within organizations. Such internal communication has taken on increasing importance today. Organizations are downsizing, flattening chains of command, forming work teams, and empowering rank-and-file employees. Given more power in making decisions, employees find that they need more information. They must collect, exchange, and evaluate information about the products and services they offer. Management also needs input from employees to respond rapidly to local and global market changes. This growing demand for information means an increasing use of e-mail, although hard-copy memos are still written.

Developing skill in writing e-mail messages and memos brings you two important benefits. First, well-written documents are likely to achieve their goals. They create goodwill by being cautious, caring, and clear. They do not intentionally or unintentionally foment ill feelings. Second, well-written internal messages enhance your image within the organization. Individuals identified as competent, professional writers are noticed and rewarded; most often, they are the ones promoted into management positions.

This chapter concentrates on routine e-mail messages and memos. These straightforward messages open with the main idea because their topics are not sensitive and require little persuasion. You'll study the characteristics, writing process, and organization for e-mail messages and memos. Because e-mail is such a new and powerful channel of communication, we'll devote special attention to using it safely and effectively. Finally, you'll learn to write procedure, information, request, reply, and confirmation memos.

## Characteristics of Successful E-Mail Messages and Memos

Because e-mail messages and memos are standard forms of communication within most organizations, they will probably become your most common business communication medium. These indispensable messages inform employees, request data, supply responses, confirm decisions, and give directions. Good e-mail messages and memos generally share certain characteristics.

**Effective e-mail messages and memos contain guide-word headings, focus on a single topic, are concise and conversational, and use graphic highlighting.**

*To, From, Date, Subject Headings.* E-mails and memos contain guide-word headings as shown in Figure 8.1. These headings help readers immediately identify the date, origin, destination, and purpose of a message. Please note that outgoing e-mail messages will not show a dateline because it is inserted automatically by your computer. The position of the dateline in incoming e-mail messages varies depending on your program. The position of the dateline in hard-copy memos also is flexible.

*Single Topic.* Good e-mail messages and memos generally discuss only one topic. Notice that Figure 8.1 considers only one topic. Limiting the topic helps the receiver act on the subject and file it appropriately. A memo writer who, for example, describes a computer printer problem and also requests permission to attend a conference runs a 50 percent failure risk. The reader may respond to the printer problem but forget about the conference request.

*Conversational Tone.* The tone of e-mail messages and memos is expected to be conversational because the communicators are usually familiar with one another.

**FIGURE 8.1  Guide-Word Headings for Memos**

System inserts date, which is only seen on incoming messages

Uses salutation for friendly tone

Closes with date and action request

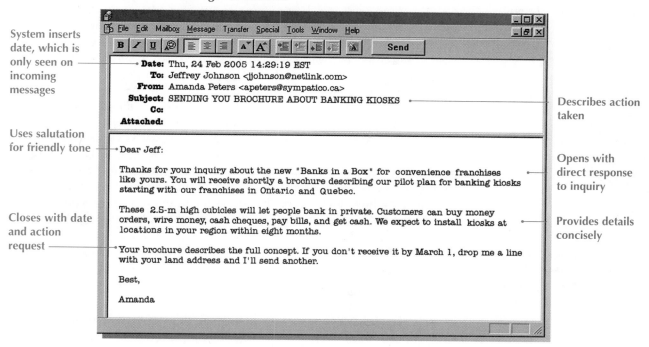

Describes action taken

Opens with direct response to inquiry

Provides details concisely

---

This means using occasional contractions (*I'm, you'll*), ordinary words, and first-person pronouns (*I/we*). Yet, the tone should also be professional. E-mail is so fast and so easy to use that some writers have been seduced into an "astonishing lack of professionalism."[3] Although warm and friendly, e-mail messages should not be emotional. They should never include remarks that would not be said to the face of an individual.

*Conciseness.* As functional forms of communication, e-mails and memos contain only what's necessary to convey meaning and be courteous. Often, they require less background explanation and less attention to goodwill efforts than do letters to outsiders. Be particularly alert to eliminating wordiness. Avoid opening fillers (*there is, it is*), long lead-ins (*I am writing this memo to inform you that*), and wordy phrases (*because of the fact that*).

*Graphic Highlighting.* To make important ideas stand out and to improve readability, e-mail and memo writers make liberal use of graphic highlighting techniques. The content of many printed memos is enhanced by numbered or bulleted items, headings, tables, and other techniques you studied in Chapter 6. Some e-mail programs may not transmit italics, bolding, or double sets of columns. However, you can improve readability with good paragraphing, bullet or asterisk points, and side headings, especially for longer messages. Readers hate to scroll through screen after screen of solid writing. Although corporate North America has fallen in love with e-mail, users are less and less tolerant of writers who fail to follow writing conventions. They won't tolerate unattractive, unintelligible, and "impenetrable data dumps."[4]

Graphic highlighting includes numbered and bulleted lists and headings.

## The Writing Process

"One of the most amazing features of the information revolution," says a technology vice president, is that the "momentum has turned back to the written word."[5]

Businesspeople are writing more messages than ever before, and many of them are e-mails and memos. To be effective, good internal messages require careful preparation. Although they often seem routine, e-mails and memos may travel farther than you expect. Consider the market researcher in Vancouver, new to her job and eager to please her boss, who was asked to report on the progress of her project. Off the top of her head, she dashed off a quick summary of her work in an e-mail to her boss. Later that week a vice president asked her boss how the project was progressing, and her boss forwarded the market researcher's hurried memo. The resulting poor impression was difficult for the new employee to overcome.

Careful writing takes time—especially at first. By following a systematic plan and practising your skill, however, you can speed up your efforts and greatly improve the product. Bear in mind, moreover, that the effort you make to improve your communication skills can pay big dividends. Frequently, your speaking and writing abilities determine how much influence you'll have in your organization. As with other writing tasks, e-mail and memo writing follows the familiar three-phase writing process.

*Analysis, Anticipation, and Adaptation.* In Phase 1 (prewriting) you'll need to spend some time analyzing your task. It's amazing how many of us are ready to put our pens or computers into gear before engaging our minds. Ask yourself three important questions:

- **Do I really need to write this e-mail or memo?** A phone call or a quick visit to a nearby coworker might solve the problem—and save the time and expense of a written message. On the other hand, some written messages are needed to provide a permanent record. Another decision is whether to write a hard-copy memo or send an electronic one. Many offices are moving toward a *paperless workplace,* as discussed in the accompanying Tech Talk box.

- **Why am I writing?** Know why you are writing and what you hope to achieve. This will help you recognize what the important points are and where to place them.

- **How will the reader react?** Visualize the reader and the effect your message will have. Consider ways to shape the message to benefit the reader.

*Research, Organization, and Composition.* In Phase 2 (writing) you'll first want to check the files, gather documentation, and prepare your message. Make an outline of the points you wish to cover. For short messages you can jot down notes on the document you are answering. Be sure to prepare for revision, because excellence is rarely achieved on the first effort.

*Revision, Proofreading, and Evaluation.* Careful and caring writers revise their messages, proofread the final copy, and make an effort to evaluate the success of their communication.

- **Revise for clarity.** Viewed from the receiver's perspective, are the ideas clear? Do they need more explanation? If the memo is passed on to others, will they need further explanation? Consider having a colleague critique your message if it is an important one.

- **Proofread for correctness.** Are the sentences complete and punctuated properly? Did you overlook any typos or misspelled words? Remember to use your spell checker and grammar checker to proofread your message before sending it.

- **Plan for feedback.** How will you know whether this message is successful? You can improve feedback by asking questions (such as *Do you agree with these suggestions?*) and by making it easy for the receiver to respond.

## The Paperless Workplace: Probable or Improbable?

Promises, promises. We've been hearing for years that the paperless office was just around the corner, but it never seems to happen. People thought that paper use would shrink with the rise of the computer. But just the opposite is happening. According to Michael Barr, a senior business consultant for the Ivey Business Consulting Group, "The digital revolution has not led to a paperless office." In fact, the average user at a large corporation prints almost 50 pages per day, while those at small or medium-sized enterprises print out more than 35 pages per day. And astonishingly, 40 percent of corporate employees print at least 60 percent of the information they receive electronically. As the Forest Products Association of Canada reports, demand for paper has doubled in the past 20 years.[6]

Why are people so attached to paper? Part of the reason is psychological. "There are a lot of paper hoarders, people who want the security net of the paper copy," says a paper industry spokesman.[7] But businesspeople have numerous, more pragmatic reasons for printing:

- Paper offers more portability.
- On paper, print is easier to read.
- Studies indicate that people retain 30 percent more when reading from paper than when reading from computer screens.
- Paper documents are easier to annotate and compare.

Some organizations have been partially successful in convincing people to give up paper. Many organizations now make internal reports electronically accessible. Others create manuals and other texts only on computers. Moreover, companies are increasingly using *intranets*, which are internal Web sites, to publish and store company files and data.

### Career Application

Do you print e-mail messages? Why? Are you currently using more paper than you were a year ago? What can businesses do to reduce paper consumption?

## Organization of E-Mail Messages and Memos

Whether electronic or hard-copy, routine memos generally contain four parts: (1) a subject line that summarizes the message, (2) an opening that reveals the main idea immediately, (3) a body that explains and justifies the main idea, and (4) an action closing. Remember that routine messages deliver good news or standard information.

*Subject Line.* In e-mails and memos a subject line is mandatory. It summarizes the central idea, thus providing quick identification for reading and for filing. A subject line is usually written in an abbreviated style, often without articles (*a, an, the*). It need not be a complete sentence, and it does not end with a period. E-mail subject lines are particularly important. Meaningless ones (such as *Hello* or *Important*) may cause readers to delete the message without ever opening it. Good subject lines often contain a verb form or an action request:

**SUBJECT:** Need You to Showcase Two Items at Our Next Trade Show (rather than *Trade Show*)

**SUBJECT:** Beefing Up Our Messaging Capabilities (rather than *New Software*)

**SUBJECT:** Staff Meeting to Discuss Summer Vacation Schedules (rather than *Meeting*)

***Opening.*** Most memos and e-mails cover nonsensitive information that can be handled in a straightforward manner. "The memos that grab me tell right away what the writer has in mind," says corporate executive Doris Margonine.[8] Begin by frontloading; that is, reveal the main idea immediately. Even though the purpose of the memo or e-mail is summarized in the subject line, that purpose should be restated—and amplified—in the first sentence. Some readers skip the subject line and plunge right into the first sentence. Notice how the following indirect openers can be improved by frontloading.

| **Indirect Opening** | **Direct Opening** |
|---|---|
| For the past six months, the Human Resources Development Department has been considering changes in our employees' benefit plan. | Please review the following proposal regarding employees' benefits, and let me know by May 20 if you approve these changes. |
| As you may know, employees in Document Production have been complaining about eye fatigue as a result of the overhead fluorescent lighting in their centre. | If you agree, I'll order six high-intensity task desk lamps at $189 each for use in the Document Production Centre. |

**The body explains data and should use graphic devices to improve readability.**

***Body.*** The body provides more information about the reason for writing. It explains and discusses the subject logically. Design your data for easy comprehension by using numbered lists, headings, tables, and other graphic highlighting techniques. Compare the following versions of the same message. Observe how the graphic devices of columns, headings, and white space make the main points easy to comprehend.

**Hard-to-Read Paragraph Version**
Effective immediately are the following air travel guidelines. Between now and December 31, only account executives may take company-approved trips. These individuals will be allowed to take a maximum of two trips, and they are to travel economy or budget class only.

**Improved Version With Graphic Highlighting**
Effective immediately are the following air travel guidelines:

- Who may travel:   Account executives only
- How many trips:   A maximum of two trips
- By when:   Between now and December 31
- Air class:   Economy or budget class only

**Memos should close with (1) action information including dates and deadlines, (2) a summary, or (3) a closing thought.**

***Closing.*** Generally end with (1) action information, dates, or deadlines; (2) a summary of the message; or (3) a closing thought. Here again the value of thinking through the message before actually writing it becomes apparent. The closing is where readers look for deadlines and action language. An effective memo or e-mail closing might be, *Please submit your report by June 15 so that we can have your data before our July planning session.*

In more complex messages a summary of main points may be an appropriate closing. If no action request is made and a closing summary is unnecessary, you might end with a simple concluding thought (*I'm glad to answer your questions* or *This sounds like a useful project*). Although you needn't close messages to coworkers with goodwill statements such as those found in letters to customers or clients, some closing thought is often necessary to prevent a feeling of abruptness. Closings can show gratitude or encourage feedback with remarks such as *I sincerely appreciate your cooperation* or *What are your ideas on this proposal?* Other closings look forward to what's next, such as *How would you like to proceed?* Avoid closing with *Please let me know if I may be of further assistance.* This overused ending sounds mechanical and insincere.

***Putting It All Together.*** Now let's compose a complete e-mail message. The following is the first draft of an e-mail message Matt Barnes, marketing manager, wrote to his supervisor, Debbie Pickett. Although it contains solid information, the message is so wordy and poorly organized that the reader will have trouble grasping its significance.*

✗ *Poorly Written First Draft*

**E-MAIL TO:** Debbie Pickett

This is in response to your recent inquiry about our customer database. Your message of May 9 said that you wanted to know how to deal with the database problems.

— **Fails to reveal purpose quickly and concisely**

I can tell you that the biggest problem is that it contains a lot of outdated information, including customers who haven't purchased anything in five or more years. Another problem is that the old database is not compatible with the new Access software that is being used by our mailing service, and this makes it difficult to merge files.

— **Does not help reader see the two problems or the three recommendations**

I think I can solve both problems, however, by starting a new database. This would be the place where we put the names of all new customers. And we would have it keyed using Access software. The problem with outdated information could be solved by finding out if the customers in our old database wish to continue receiving our newsletter and product announcements. Finally, we would rekey the names of all active customers in the new database.

— **Forgets to conclude with next action and end date**

Matt's revised version of this e-mail appears in Figure 8.2. Notice that it opens directly. Both the subject line and the first sentence explain the purpose for writing. Notice how much easier the revised version is to read. Bullets and headings emphasize the actions necessary to solve the database problems. Notice, too, that the revised version ends with a deadline and refers to the next action to be taken.

## USING E-MAIL SAFELY AND EFFECTIVELY

Early e-mail users were encouraged to "ignore stylistic and grammatical considerations." They thought that "words on the fly," as e-mail messages were considered, required little editing or proofing. Correspondents used emoticons (such as sideways happy faces) to express their emotions. And some e-mail today is still quick and dirty. But as this communication channel matures, messages are becoming more proper and more professional. Today, the average e-mail message may remain in the company's computer system for up to five years. And in some instances the only impression a person has of the e-mail writer is from a transmitted message.

Wise e-mail business communicators are aware of its dangers. They know that thoughtless messages can cause irreparable harm. They know that their messages can

*3*

**E-mail messages are becoming more proper and more professional.**

---

*Some unformatted e-mail messages, memos, and letters such as that shown here will appear in this textbook. They illustrate content rather than form. Documents that illustrate form are shown in figures, such as Figure 8.2.

## FIGURE 8.2 Information E-Mail Message

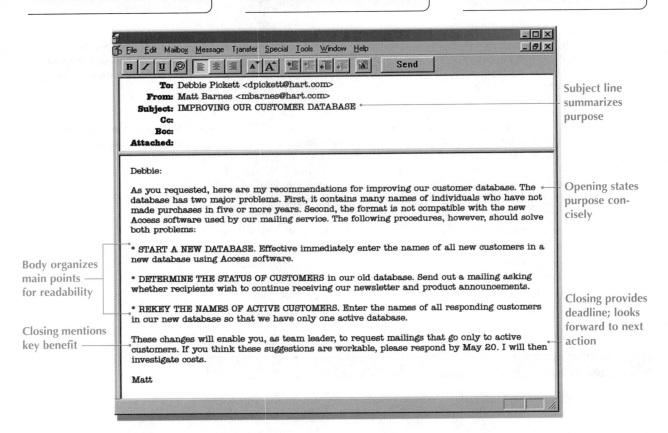

**Prewriting** 1

**Analyze:** The purpose of this memo is to describe database problems and recommend solutions.

**Anticipate:** The audience is the writer's boss, who is familiar with the topic and who appreciates brevity.

**Adapt:** Because the reader requested this message, the direct pattern is most appropriate.

**Writing** 2

**Research:** Gather data documenting the customer database and how to use Access software.

**Organize:** Announce recommendations and summarize problems. In the body, list the three actions for solving the problem. In the closing, describe reader benefits, provide a deadline, and specify the next action.

**Compose:** Prepare the first draft.

**Revising** 3

**Revise:** Highlight the two main problems and the three recommendations. Use asterisks, caps, and headings to improve readability. Make the bulleted ideas parallel.

**Proofread:** Double-check to see whether *database* is one word or two. Use spell checker.

**Evaluate:** Does this e-mail supply concise information the boss wants in an easy-to-read form?

**To:** Debbie Pickett <dpickett@hart.com>
**From:** Matt Barnes <mbarnes@hart.com>
**Subject:** IMPROVING OUR CUSTOMER DATABASE ——— Subject line summarizes purpose
**Cc:**
**Bcc:**
**Attached:**

Debbie:

As you requested, here are my recommendations for improving our customer database. The ——— Opening states purpose concisely
database has two major problems. First, it contains many names of individuals who have not
made purchases in five or more years. Second, the format is not compatible with the new
Access software used by our mailing service. The following procedures, however, should solve
both problems:

Body organizes main points for readability ——— * START A NEW DATABASE. Effective immediately enter the names of all new customers in a
new database using Access software.

* DETERMINE THE STATUS OF CUSTOMERS in our old database. Send out a mailing asking
whether recipients wish to continue receiving our newsletter and product announcements.

* REKEY THE NAMES OF ACTIVE CUSTOMERS. Enter the names of all responding customers ——— Closing provides deadline; looks forward to next action
in our new database so that we have only one active database.

Closing mentions key benefit ——— These changes will enable you, as team leader, to request mailings that go only to active
customers. If you think these suggestions are workable, please respond by May 20. I will then
investigate costs.

Matt

**E-mail messages may be dangerous because they travel long distances and are difficult to erase.**

travel (intentionally or unintentionally) long distances. A quickly drafted note may end up in the boss's mailbox or be forwarded to an adversary's box. Making matters worse, computers—like elephants and spurned lovers—never forget.[9] Even erased messages can remain on disk drives. "It's as if people put their brains on hold when they write e-mail," said one expert. They think that e-mail "is a substitute for a phone call, and that's the danger."[10] E-mail represents a number of dangers, both to employees and to employers, as discussed in the accompanying Career Coach box.

## Your Internet Use Could Get You Fired

Employee Internet abuse costs employers millions of dollars in litigation and lost productivity. Many companies have fired or disciplined employees for online shopping, gambling, gossiping, and pursuing various nonbusiness activities. These intentional activities, as well as unintentional but careless miscues, can gobble up precious network resources and waste valuable work time. Small wonder that companies are increasingly monitoring and restricting employee Internet use. Here are some of the Internet problems facing employers:

- **Sexual harassment.** Companies must maintain a workplace free of harassment. If employees download pornography, transmit sexually explicit jokes, or use inappropriate screen savers, the work environment can become "poisoned" and employers are liable.

- **Personal use on company time.** Because some employees do not have Internet access at home, they rely on their employers for access. These employees may spend hours surfing, chatting, shopping, or exchanging e-mails that have little to do with their jobs.

- **Copyright infringement.** Employees may copy or distribute graphics, pictures, logos, cartoons, and so forth without permission. For example, a report writer may cut and paste a picture into a report, thus violating copyright laws.

- **Viruses.** Employees frequently forget to scan incoming attachments or files for viruses. Attachments with executable files or video files are especially vulnerable. Many of these files are personal, making the sting of viruses even worse.

- **Confidential information.** Sensitive organizational information may find its way into the wrong hands when transmitted electronically.

- **Defamation.** Employees can defame other individuals or organizations in e-mail messages, bulletin boards, or in chat rooms.

### Career Application

Based on what you learned in this chapter, what can employees do to avoid jeopardizing their jobs because of Internet misuse? Do employees deserve limited access to the Internet if they are responsible? Should employers block access to Web sites in these categories: adult content, gambling, illegal activities, racism, abortion or anti-abortion advocacy, activist groups, cultural institutions (including galleries and museums), educational institutions, gay and lesbian issues, health information, hobbies, job search, news, personals, political groups, religion, restaurants, search engines, sex education, shopping, sports, and travel?

## Smart E-Mail Practices

Despite its dangers and limitations, however, e-mail is increasingly the channel of choice for sending many business messages. Because e-mail has become a mainstream channel of communication, it's important to take the time to organize your thoughts, compose carefully, and be concerned with correct grammar and punctuation.

> **Because e-mail is now a mainstream communication channel, messages should be well organized, carefully composed, and grammatically correct.**

*Getting Started.* The following pointers will help you get off to a good start in using e-mail safely and effectively.

- **Compose offline.** Instead of dashing off hasty messages, consider using your word processing program to write offline. Then upload your message to the e-mail network. This avoids "self destructing" (losing all your writing through some glitch or pressing the wrong key) when working online.

- **Get the address right.** E-mail addresses are sometimes complex, often illogical, and always unforgiving. Omit one character or misread the letter *l* for the number *1*, and your message bounces. Solution: Use your electronic address book for people you write frequently. And double-check every address that you key in manually. Also be sure that you don't reply to a group of receivers when you intend to answer only one.

- **Avoid misleading subject lines.** With an abundance of spam (junk mail) clogging most inboxes, make sure your subject line is relevant and helpful. Generic tags such as *Hi!* and *Great Deal* may cause your message to be deleted before it is opened.

*Content, Tone, and Correctness.* Although e-mail seems as casual as a telephone call, it's not. Because it produces a permanent record, think carefully about what you say and how you say it.

- **Be concise.** Don't burden readers with unnecessary information. Remember that monitors are small and typefaces are often difficult to read. Organize your ideas tightly.

- **Don't send anything you wouldn't want published.** Because e-mail seems like a telephone call or a person-to-person conversation, writers sometimes send sensitive, confidential, inflammatory, or potentially embarrassing messages. Beware! E-mail creates a permanent record that often does not go away even when deleted. And every message is a corporate communication that can be used against you or your employer. Don't write anything that you wouldn't want your boss, your family, or a judge to read.

- **Don't use e-mail to avoid contact.** E-mail is inappropriate for breaking bad news or for resolving arguments. For example, it's improper to fire a person by e-mail. It's also not a good channel for dealing with conflict with supervisors, subordinates, or others. If there's any possibility of hurt feelings, pick up the telephone or pay the person a visit.

- **Never respond when you're angry.** Always allow some time to cool off before shooting off a response to an upsetting message. You often come up with different and better alternatives after thinking about what was said. If possible, iron out differences in person.

- **Care about correctness.** People are still judged by their writing, whether electronic or paper-based. Sloppy e-mail messages (with missing apostrophes, haphazard spelling, and stream-of-consciousness writing) make readers work too hard. They resent not only the information but also the writer.

- **Resist humour and tongue-in-cheek comments.** Without the nonverbal cues conveyed by your face and your voice, humour can easily be misunderstood.

*Netiquette.* Although e-mail is a new communication channel, a number of rules of polite online interaction are emerging.

- **Limit any tendency to send blanket copies.** Send copies only to people who really need to see a message. It is unnecessary to document every business decision and action with an electronic paper trail.

- **Never send "spam."** Forty-three percent of Internet users say that their number one pet peeve of e-mail usage is spam (unsolicited e-mail messages).[11]

- **Consider using identifying labels.** When appropriate, add one of the following labels to the subject line: ACTION (action required, please respond); FYI (for

People are becoming increasingly dependent on access to their e-mail and their ability to stay in contact with work, family, and friends when away from home. In response to such demand, Sherpa Tsering Gyalzen plans the world's highest cyber-café to be built 5000 m above the sea-level base camp of Mount Everest, the world's highest peak. The café will be open during the spring and fall and available to the thousands of trekkers who visit the Everest region each year.

your information, no response needed); RE (this is a reply to another message); URGENT (please respond immediately). Some e-mail programs allow you to flag urgent messages.

- **Use capital letters only for emphasis or for titles.** Avoid writing entire messages in all caps, which is like SHOUTING.
- **Announce attachments.** If you're sending a lengthy attachment, tell your receiver. You might also ask what format is preferred.
- **Don't forward without permission.** Obtain approval before forwarding a message.

*Replying to E-Mail.* The following tips can save you time and frustration when answering messages.

- **Scan all messages in your inbox before replying to each individually.** Because subsequent messages often affect the way you respond, read them all first (especially all of those from the same individual).
- **Don't automatically return the sender's message.** When replying, cut and paste the relevant parts. Avoid irritating your recipients by returning the entire "thread" (sequence of messages) on a topic. More advanced users can set their program options so that only the response is sent.
- **Revise the subject line if the topic changes.** When replying or continuing an e-mail exchange, revise the subject line as the topic changes.

*Personal Use.* Remember that office computers are intended for work-related communication.

- **Don't use company computers for personal matters.** Unless your company specifically allows it, never use your employer's computers for personal messages, personal shopping, or entertainment.
- **Assume that all e-mail is monitored.** Employers legally have the right to monitor e-mail, and many do.

*Other Smart E-Mail Practices.* Depending on your messages and audience, the following tips promote effective electronic communication.

- **Use design to improve the readability of longer messages.** When a message requires several screens, help the reader with headings, bulleted listings, side headings, and perhaps an introductory summary that describes what will follow. Although these techniques lengthen a message, they shorten reading time.

- **Consider cultural differences.** When using this borderless tool, be especially clear and precise in your language. Remember that figurative clichés (*pull up stakes, playing second fiddle*), sports references (*hit a home run, play by the rules*), and slang (*cool, stoked*) cause confusion abroad.

- **Double-check before hitting the *Send* button.** Have you included everything? Avoid the necessity of sending a second message, which makes you look careless. Use spell check and reread for fluency before sending.

## Formatting E-Mail Messages

Because e-mail is a developing communication channel, its formatting and usage conventions are still fluid. Users and authorities, for instance, do not always agree on what's appropriate for salutations and closings. The following suggestions, however, can guide you in formatting most e-mail messages, but always check with your organization to observe its practices.

**The position of *To, From, Date, and Subject* vary, depending on your e-mail program.**

*Guide Words.* Following the guide word *To*, some writers insert just the recipient's electronic address, such as *ptuckman@accountpro.com.* Other writers prefer to include the receiver's full name plus the electronic address, as shown in Figure 8.3. By including full names in the *To* and *From* slots, both receivers and senders are better able to identify the message. By the way, the order of *Date, To, From, Subject,* and other guide words varies, depending on your e-mail program and whether you are sending or receiving the message.

Most e-mail programs automatically add the current date after *Date.* On the *Cc* line (which stands for *carbon* or *courtesy copy*) you can type the address of anyone who is to receive a copy of the message. Remember, though, to send copies only to those people directly involved with the message. Most e-mail programs also include a line for *Bcc* (*blind carbon copy*). This sends a copy without the addressee's knowledge. Many wise writers today use *Bcc* for the names and addresses of a list of receivers, a technique that avoids revealing the addresses to the entire group. On the subject line, identify the subject of the memo. Be sure to include enough information to be clear and compelling.

**Salutations for e-mail messages are optional, and practice is as yet unsettled.**

*Salutation.* What to do about a salutation is sticky. Many writers omit a salutation because they consider the message a memo. In the past, hard-copy memos were sent only to company insiders, and salutations were omitted. However, when e-mail messages travel to outsiders, omitting a salutation seems curt and unfriendly. Because the message is more like a letter, a salutation is appropriate (such as *Dear Jake; Hi, Jake; Greetings;* or just *Jake*). Including a salutation is also a visual cue to where the message begins. Many messages are transmitted or forwarded with such long headers that finding the beginning of the message can be difficult. A salutation helps, as shown in Figure 8.3. Other writers do not use a salutation; instead, they use the name of the recipient in the first sentence.

**FIGURE 8.3  E-Mail Request**

### Tips for E-Mail Formatting

- After *To*, type the receiver's electronic address. If you include the receiver's name, enclose the address in angle brackets.
- After *From*, type your name and electronic address, if your program does not insert it automatically.
- After *Subject*, provide a clear description of your message.
- Insert the addresses of anyone receiving carbon or blind copies.
- Include a salutation (such as *Dear Marilyn; Hi; Marilyn; Greetings*) or weave the receiver's name into the first line (see Figure 8.5 on page 228). Some writers omit a salutation.
- Set your line length for no more than 80 characters. If you expect your message to be forwarded, set it for 60 characters.
- Use word-wrap rather than pressing *Enter* at line ends.
- Double-space (press *Enter*) between paragraphs.
- Do not type in all caps or in all lowercase letters.
- Include a complimentary close, your name, and your address if you wish.

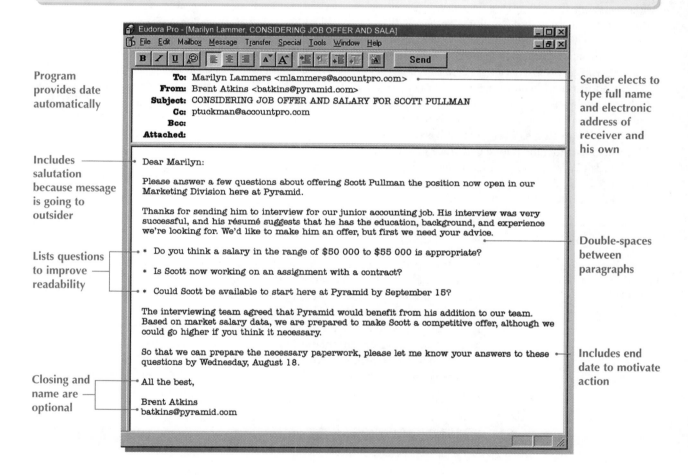

Program provides date automatically

Includes salutation because message is going to outsider

Lists questions to improve readability

Closing and name are optional

Sender elects to type full name and electronic address of receiver and his own

Double-spaces between paragraphs

Includes end date to motivate action

*Eudora Pro - [Marilyn Lammer, CONSIDERING JOB OFFER AND SALA]*
File  Edit  Mailbox  Message  Transfer  Special  Tools  Window  Help

**To:** Marilyn Lammers <mlammers@accountpro.com>
**From:** Brent Atkins <batkins@pyramid.com>
**Subject:** CONSIDERING JOB OFFER AND SALARY FOR SCOTT PULLMAN
**Cc:** ptuckman@accountpro.com
**Bcc:**
**Attached:**

Dear Marilyn:

Please answer a few questions about offering Scott Pullman the position now open in our Marketing Division here at Pyramid.

Thanks for sending him to interview for our junior accounting job. His interview was very successful, and his résumé suggests that he has the education, background, and experience we're looking for. We'd like to make him an offer, but first we need your advice.

* Do you think a salary in the range of $50 000 to $55 000 is appropriate?

* Is Scott now working on an assignment with a contract?

* Could Scott be available to start here at Pyramid by September 15?

The interviewing team agreed that Pyramid would benefit from his addition to our team. Based on market salary data, we are prepared to make Scott a competitive offer, although we could go higher if you think it necessary.

So that we can prepare the necessary paperwork, please let me know your answers to these questions by Wednesday, August 18.

All the best,

Brent Atkins
batkins@pyramid.com

**Body.** The body of an e-mail message should be typed with upper- and lowercase characters—never in all uppercase or all lowercase characters. Cover just one topic, and try to keep the total message under three screens in length. To assist you, many e-mail programs have basic text-editing features, such as cut, copy, paste, and word-wrap. However, avoid boldface and italics because they may create a string of control characters that may cause chaos on the recipient's computer.

# RIM Revisited

With the introduction of wireless devices such as RIM's BlackBerry, businesspeople can be in constant contact with their e-mail. In fact, RIM views the BlackBerry as "a device that can significantly improve the quality of life of its users. Among the benefits RIM highlights are stress relief for those who hate to miss e-mail messages when they are travelling; increased freedom for workers, who no longer feel obliged to be tied to their desks past normal working hours; and enhanced flexibility for working parents who must juggle family and business responsibilities."[12] According to RIM president and CEO Mike Lazaridis (pictured on the first page of this chapter), "The true innovation of BlackBerry is that it's always connected."[13]

In addition to keeping up with e-mail, wireless technology allows users to surf the Net, keep contacts and appointments, and even send quick messages during slow meetings. More recent versions of the BlackBerry also include phone and voice mail capabilities. Randall Wilson, an information technology executive, says, "I can't imagine living without my BlackBerry. I can't even fathom the idea."[14]

Lawyer Mark Plotkin takes his devotion to his BlackBerry a step further. "It sounds kind of sick to say you can't live without wireless e-mail, but it has made a huge difference in my quality of life. I have [a BlackBerry] wired to my hand."[15] Although constant access may seem like a benefit to many, there are those who wonder if their lives may have become consumed. "The BlackBerry has definitely made me more productive. But it's kind of a double-edged sword. I'm always accessible. I have no downtime, and everyone knows it."[16]

## CRITICAL THINKING

- While many users seem to agree that 24/7 access is a benefit, there may also be a downside. In teams of three to four, discuss the pros and cons of "having a BlackBerry wired to your hand." Prepare a one-page summary of your discussion.

**www.rim.com**

---

**Closing lines may include the writer's name, title, and organization.**

***Closing Lines.*** Writers of e-mail messages sent within organizations may omit closings and even skip their names at the end of messages. They can omit these items because receivers recognize them from identification in the opening lines. But for outside messages, a writer might include a closing such as *Cheers* or *All the best* followed by the writer's name and e-mail address (because some systems do not transmit your address automatically). If the recipient is unlikely to know you, it's wise to include your title and organization. Some veteran e-mail users include a *signature file* with identifying information embellished with keyboard art. Use restraint, however, because signature files take up precious bandwidth (Internet capacity).

## KINDS OF INTERNAL MESSAGES

Business communicators write many different kinds of internal messages to conduct the operations of organizations. They may be e-mails or hard-copy memos. This chapter focuses on routine messages that can be grouped into three categories: (1) procedure and information messages, (2) request and reply messages, and (3) confirmation messages.

### Procedure and Information E-Mail Messages and Memos

Most internal messages describe procedures and distribute information. These messages typically flow downward from management to employees and relate to the daily operation of an organization. When the topics are nonsensitive, follow the overall memo plan: clear subject line, direct opening, concise explanation, and action closing. They have one primary function: conveying your idea so clearly that no further explanation (return message, telephone call, or personal visit) is necessary.

In writing information and procedure memos, be careful of tone. Today's managers and team leaders seek employee participation and cooperation, but they can't achieve that rapport if they sound like dictators or autocrats. Avoid making accusations and fixing blame. Rather, explain changes, give reasons, and suggest benefits to the reader. Assume that employees want to contribute to the success of the organization and to their own achievement. Remember, too, that saying something negatively (*Don't park in Lot A*) is generally less helpful than saying it positively (*Park in Lot B until Lot A is repaired*).

The following procedure memo about large printing bills is disappointing both in content and tone.

**✗ Ineffective Memo**

**MEMO TO:** Staff Members

Lately, very large expenditures for printing jobs have been submitted, particularly bills being paid to PrintMasters. These bills are suspiciously large and can no longer be honoured without careful scrutiny.

*Fails to reveal the purpose of the memo (new procedures). Uses accusatory language.*

Henceforth, all employees may not send out printing jobs without prior written notice. Using PrintMasters as our sole source must stop. Therefore, authorization is now required for all printing. Two copies of any printing order must be submitted to Kelly before any job is commenced. Please see Kelly if you have any questions.

*Concentrates on what should* not *be done instead of what should be done. Word choice (must stop, is now required) conveys authoritarian tone.*

Thank you for your cooperation.

*Sounds insincere.*

The following improved version of this memo delivers essentially the same message. It reflects, however, a more cooperative tone and illustrates clear thinking and expression.

**✓ Improved Memo**

**MEMO TO:** Staff

To improve budget planning and to control costs, please follow the new procedures listed below in submitting future requests for outside printing jobs.

*Opening reveals purpose immediately and offers brief explanation.*

In our business, of course, printing is a necessary expenditure. However, our bills seem very high lately, particularly those from PrintMasters. The following procedures should help protect us from being overcharged:

*Body uses conversational language in justifying reasons for change in procedures.*

1. Determine your exact printing specifications for a particular job.

2. Secure two estimates for the job.

3. Submit the written estimates to Kelly.

4. Place the order after receiving approval.

*Listing of steps in chronological order tells readers exactly how to implement the new procedure. Beginning each numbered item with a verb improves readability and comprehension.*

Following these new procedures will result in more competitive pricing and perhaps may even provide you with new creative printing options.

The preceding procedure memo applies a direct strategy in telling how to complete a task. Information memos also use that straightforward approach in supplying details about organization activities, services, and actions. The following memo describes four child-care options. Notice how the information was designed for maximum visual impact and readability. Imagine how it would have looked if it had been presented in one or two big paragraphs.

✓ *Effective Memo*

**MEMO TO:** Staff

Straightforward opening immediately sets forth the purpose
from the reader's viewpoint.
→ Members of your employee council have met with representatives from management in considering the following four options to provide child care.

- *On-site day-care centres.* This option accommodates employees' children on the premises. Weekly rates would be competitive with local day-care facilities. This option is most costly but is worth pursuing, particularly if local facilities are deficient.

Since these items reflect no
particular order, they are
bulleted to present a slightly
cleaner appearance than a
numbered list.
→ - *Off-site centres in conjunction with other local employers.* We are looking into the possibility of developing central facilities to be shared with nearby firms.

- *Neighbourhood child-care centres.* We would contract with local centres to buy open slots for employees' children, perhaps at a discount.

- *Sick-child services.* This plan would provide employees with alternatives to missing work when children are ill. We are investigating sick-child programs at local hospitals and services that send workers to employees' homes to look after sick children.

Ends with forward-looking statement. No action is required.
→ As soon as we gather more information about these options, we will pass that data along to you.

## Request and Reply E-Mail Messages and Memos

*5*

Request and reply messages
follow the direct pattern
in seeking or providing
information.

In requesting routine information or action within an organization, the direct approach works best. Generally, this means asking for information or making the request without first providing elaborate explanations and justifications. Remember that readers are usually thinking, "Why me? Why am I receiving this?" Readers can understand the explanation better once they know what you are requesting.

If you are seeking answers to questions, you have two options for opening the message: (1) ask the most important question first, followed by an explanation and then the other questions, or (2) use a polite command, such as *Please answer the following questions regarding . . . .*

In the body of the memo, you can explain and justify your request or reply. When many questions must be asked, list them, being careful to phrase them similarly. Be courteous and friendly. In the closing include an end date (with a reason, if possible) to promote a quick response. For simple requests some writers encourage their readers to jot responses directly on the request memo. In answering e-mail messages, writers may request a quick reply.

The following request seeks information from managers about the use of temporary office workers. It begins with a polite command followed by numbered questions. Notice that the writer develops reader benefits by describing how the data collected will be used to help the reader. Notice, too, the effort to promote the feeling that the writer is part of a team working with employees to achieve their common goals.

**MEMO TO:** Department Managers

Please answer the questions listed below about the use of temporary help in your department. •——— **Opens with polite command**

With your ideas we plan to develop a policy that will help us improve the process of budgeting, selecting, and hiring temporaries. •——— **Explains the purpose concisely**

1. What is the average number of temporary office workers you employ each month?

2. What is the average length of a temporary worker's assignment in your department?

3. What specific job skills are you generally seeking in your temporaries?

4. What temporary agencies are you now using?

**Enumerates parallel questions for easy reading, comprehension, and reference**

By replying before January 20, you will have direct input into the new policy, •——— which we will be developing at the end of the month. This improved policy will help you fill your temporary employment needs more quickly and more efficiently. **Includes end date, along with reason and reader benefit**

Writers sometimes fall into bad habits in answering memos. Here are some trite and long-winded openers that are best avoided:

**Overused and long-winded openers bore readers and waste their time.**

In response to your message of the 15th . . . (*States the obvious.*)

Thank you for your memo of the 15th in which you . . . (*Suggests the writer can think of nothing more original.*)

I have before me your memo of the 15th in which you . . . (*Unnecessarily identifies the location of the previous message.*)

Pursuant to your request of the 15th . . . (*Sounds old-fashioned.*)

This is to inform you that . . . (*Delays getting to the point.*)

Please refer to your memo of . . . (*Asks reader to search for the original document. Always supply a copy if necessary or summarize its points.*)

Instead of falling into the trap of using one of the preceding shopworn openings, start directly by responding to the writer's request. If you agree to the request, show your cheerful compliance immediately. Consider these good-news openers:

**Direct opening statements can also be cheerful and empathic.**

Yes, we will be glad to . . . (*Sends message of approval by opening with "Yes."*)

Here are answers to the questions you asked about . . . (*Sounds straightforward, businesslike, and professional.*)

You're right in seeking advice about . . . (*Opens with two words that every reader enjoys seeing and hearing.*)

We are happy to assist you in . . . (*Shows writer's helpful nature and goodwill.*)

The information you requested is shown on the attached . . . (*Gets right to the point.*)

When businesspeople make significant oral decisions and commitments, it's always a good idea to write a confirmation memo that creates a permanent record of the facts.

After a direct and empathic opener, provide the information requested in a logical and coherent order. If you're answering a number of questions, arrange your answers in the order of the questions. In the favourable reply shown in Figure 8.4, information describing dates, speakers, and topics is listed in columns with headings. Although it requires more space than the paragraph format, this arrangement vastly improves readability and comprehension.

In providing additional data, use familiar words, short sentences, short paragraphs, and active-voice verbs. When alternatives exist, make them clear. Consider using graphic highlighting techniques, as shown in Figure 8.4, for both the speakers' schedules and the two program choices offered farther along in the letter. Imagine how much more effort would be required to read and understand the letter without the speaker list or the numbered choices.

If further action is required, be specific in spelling it out. What may be crystal clear to you (because you have been thinking about the problem) is not always immediately apparent to a reader with limited time and interest. Figure 8.4 not only illustrates a readable, well-organized reply, it also specifies formatting tips for hard-copy memos.

## Confirmation E-Mail Messages and Memos

*6*

**Confirmation messages provide a permanent record of oral discussions, decisions, and directives.**

Confirmation messages—also called *to-file reports* or *incident reports*—record oral decisions, directives, and discussions. They create a concise, permanent record that could be important in the future. Because individuals may forget, alter, or retract oral commitments, it's wise to establish a written record of significant happenings. Such records are unnecessary, of course, for minor events. The confirmation e-mail message shown in Figure 8.5 on page 228 reviews the significant points of a sales agreement discussed in a telephone conversation. When you write to confirm an oral agreement, remember these tips:

• Include the names and titles of involved individuals.

• Itemize major issues or points concisely.

• Request feedback regarding unclear or inaccurate points.

Another type of confirmation message simply verifies the receipt of materials or a change of schedule. It is brief and often kept on file to explain your role in a project. For example, suppose you are coordinating an interdepartmental budget report. Marie Nadeau from Human Resources calls to let you know that her portion of the report will be a week late. To confirm, you would send Marie the following one-sentence message: *This message verifies our telephone conversation of November 5 in which you said that your portion of the budget report will be submitted November 14 instead of November 7.* Be sure to print a copy if you are using e-mail. Notice that the tone is objective, not accusatory. However, if you are later asked about why your project is running late (and you probably will be), you'll have a record of the explanation. In fact, you should probably send a copy to your superior so that he or she can intervene if necessary.

**FIGURE 8.4  Reply Memo**

**Tips for Formatting Hard-Copy Memos**
- Set one tab to align entries evenly after *Subject.*
- Leave two blank lines after the subject line.
- Single-space all but the shortest memos. Double-space between paragraphs.
- For full-page memos on plain paper, leave a 5-cm top margin.
- For half-page memos, leave a 2.5-cm top margin.
- Use 3-cm side margins.
- For a two-page memo, use a second-page heading with the addressee's name, page number, and date.
- Handwrite your initials after your typed name.

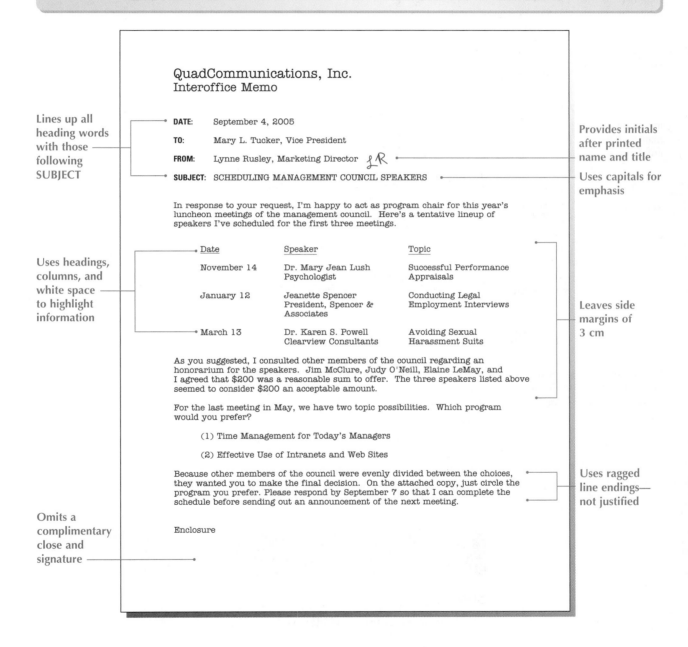

Lines up all heading words with those following SUBJECT

Uses headings, columns, and white space to highlight information

Omits a complimentary close and signature

Provides initials after printed name and title

Uses capitals for emphasis

Leaves side margins of 3 cm

Uses ragged line endings—not justified

---

QuadCommunications, Inc.
Interoffice Memo

**DATE:**     September 4, 2005

**TO:**       Mary L. Tucker, Vice President

**FROM:**     Lynne Rusley, Marketing Director

**SUBJECT:**  SCHEDULING MANAGEMENT COUNCIL SPEAKERS

In response to your request, I'm happy to act as program chair for this year's luncheon meetings of the management council.  Here's a tentative lineup of speakers I've scheduled for the first three meetings.

| Date | Speaker | Topic |
|------|---------|-------|
| November 14 | Dr. Mary Jean Lush Psychologist | Successful Performance Appraisals |
| January 12 | Jeanette Spencer President, Spencer & Associates | Conducting Legal Employment Interviews |
| March 13 | Dr. Karen S. Powell Clearview Consultants | Avoiding Sexual Harassment Suits |

As you suggested, I consulted other members of the council regarding an honorarium for the speakers.  Jim McClure, Judy O'Neill, Elaine LeMay, and I agreed that $200 was a reasonable sum to offer.  The three speakers listed above seemed to consider $200 an acceptable amount.

For the last meeting in May, we have two topic possibilities.  Which program would you prefer?

(1) Time Management for Today's Managers

(2) Effective Use of Intranets and Web Sites

Because other members of the council were evenly divided between the choices, they wanted you to make the final decision.  On the attached copy, just circle the program you prefer.  Please respond by September 7 so that I can complete the schedule before sending out an announcement of the next meeting.

Enclosure

**FIGURE 8.5** Confirmation E-Mail

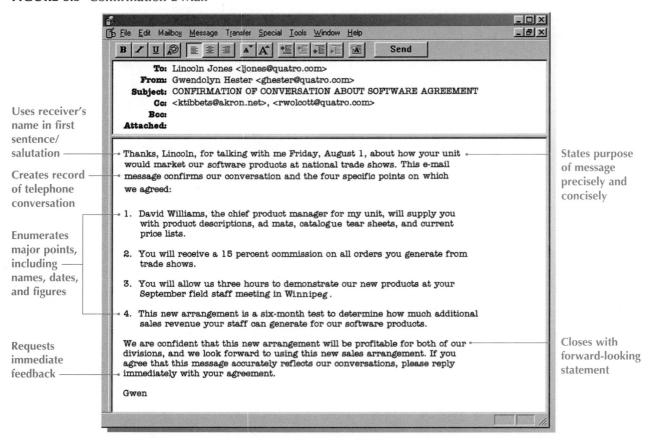

Uses receiver's name in first sentence/salutation

Creates record of telephone conversation

Enumerates major points, including names, dates, and figures

Requests immediate feedback

States purpose of message precisely and concisely

Closes with forward-looking statement

---

**Confirmation messages can save employees from being misunderstood or blamed unfairly.**

Some critics complain that too many "cover-your-tail" messages are written, thus creating excessive and unnecessary paperwork.[17] However, legitimate messages that confirm and clarify events have saved many thoughtful workers from being misunderstood or blamed unfairly.

Sometimes taken lightly, office memos and e-mail messages, like other business documents, should be written carefully. Once they leave the author's hands, they are essentially published. They can't be retrieved, corrected, or revised. Review the following checklist for tips in writing memos that accomplish what you intend.

## CHECKLIST FOR WRITING ROUTINE E-MAIL MESSAGES AND MEMOS

### Subject Line

✓ **Summarize the central idea.** Make the subject line read like a newspaper headline—brief but clear.

✓ **Use an abbreviated style.** Omit articles (*a, an, the*), and do not try to make the subject line a complete sentence. Omit an ending period.

## *Applying Your Skills at RIM*

RIM president and CEO Mike Lazaridis believes in homegrown talent and maintains close ties with the academic community. "We have everything we need in Canada," he says.[18] In fact, one of the reasons that RIM is located in the Waterloo region is its proximity to the University of Waterloo. Believing in the need for "young, aggressive talent," RIM employs more than 120 co-op students each year from Canadian universities and community colleges and regularly recruits promising second- and third-year students from U of W, Sir Wilfrid Laurier University, and Conestoga College.

As is often the case, young people are quick to adopt new technologies, and many have embraced short message system (SMS) and instant messaging since their early teens. Along with the technology, a new "language" has developed. "SMS-speak uses a combination of symbols, abbreviations, and phonetics for speed and brevity, and capitals for emphasis. The number 8, for example, substitutes for the 'ate' sound, used in words such as gr8, h8, or st8. Capital letters are pronounced as written so that 'accurate and balanced article' becomes 'aQr8 & balNsd RTcL.'"[19]

In addition, abbreviations such as BRB (be right back), LOL (I'm laughing out loud), and G2G (I've got to go) and emoticons (smilies) provide meaning. Developing proficiency in instant messaging is almost like learning another language.

The problem arises when SMS-speak is carried over into e-mails intended for business use. While no one would likely send an entire business message consisting of symbols and abbreviations, occasional references do creep in.

### Your Task

You are working in one of the research areas at RIM where a number of "techie" co-op students are employed. Proficient in SMS-speak, they often have difficulty preparing business messages that are not peppered with symbols and abbreviations. At the request of your supervisor, prepare a one-page guide for writing concise, yet understandable, e-mail messages.

**www.rim.com**

## Opening

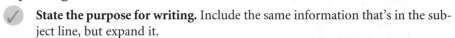

**State the purpose for writing.** Include the same information that's in the subject line, but expand it.

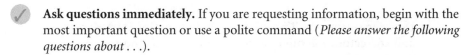

**Ask questions immediately.** If you are requesting information, begin with the most important question or use a polite command (*Please answer the following questions about . . .*).

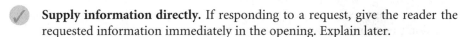

**Supply information directly.** If responding to a request, give the reader the requested information immediately in the opening. Explain later.

## Body

**Explain details.** Arrange information logically. For complex topics use separate paragraphs developed coherently.

**Enhance readability.** Use short sentences, short paragraphs, and parallel construction for similar ideas.

**Supply graphic highlighting.** Provide bulleted and/or numbered lists, tables, or other graphic devices to improve readability and comprehension.

CHAPTER 8
Routine E-Mail Messages
and Memos
**229**

**Be cautious.** Remember that memos and e-mail messages often travel far beyond their intended audiences.

## Closing

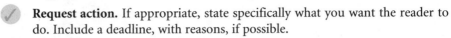 **Request action.** If appropriate, state specifically what you want the reader to do. Include a deadline, with reasons, if possible.

**Summarize the memo or provide a closing thought.** For long memos provide a summary of the important points. If neither an action request nor a summary is necessary, end with a closing thought.

**Avoid cliché endings.** Use fresh remarks rather than overused expressions such as *If you have additional questions, please do not hesitate to call* or *Thank you for your cooperation.*

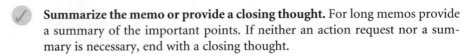
## SUMMARY OF LEARNING OBJECTIVES

*1* **Discuss the characteristics of and the writing process for successful routine e-mail messages and memos.** Successful e-mails and memos begin with TO, FROM, SUBJECT, and DATE, and they generally cover just one topic. They are written conversationally and concisely. Their content often can be highlighted with numbered or bulleted lists, headings, and tables. Before writing, determine whether you really must write. If you must, analyze your purpose and audience. Collect information, prepare an outline, and compose the first draft using a word processing program. Revise for clarity and correctness. Encourage feedback from the reader.

*2* **Analyze the organization of e-mail messages and memos.** The subject line summarizes the central idea, while the opening repeats that idea and amplifies it. The body explains and provides more information. The closing includes (a) action information, dates, and deadlines; (b) a summary of the memo; and/or (c) a closing thought.

*3* **Describe smart e-mail practices, including getting started; content, tone, and correctness; netiquette; replying to e-mail; and formatting.** Careful e-mail users compose offline, get the address right, avoid misleading subject lines, and are concise. They don't send anything they wouldn't want published, and they don't use e-mail to avoid contact. They don't respond when angry, and they care about correctness. They resist humour, and they limit any tendency to send blanket copies. They never send "spam," they use identifying labels, and they reserve capital letters for emphasis or titles. They announce attachments and don't forward without permission. In replying, they scan all messages before replying to each individually, and they don't automatically return the sender's message. They revise the subject line if a topic changes. Smart e-mail users do not use company computers for personal matters, and they assume that all e-mail is monitored. In formatting, they single-space, with double-spacing between paragraphs. Salutations and closings are optional.

**4** **Write procedure and information e-mail messages and memos.** Messages delivering information or outlining procedures follow the direct memo plan, with the main idea stated immediately. Ideas must be explained so clearly that no further explanation is necessary. The tone of the memo should encourage cooperation.

**5** **Write request and reply e-mail messages and memos.** Messages requesting action or information open with a specific request, followed by details. Messages that reply to requests open with information the reader most wants to learn. The body contains details, and the closing may summarize the important points or look forward to a subsequent event or action.

**6** **Write confirmation e-mail messages and memos.** Sometimes called "to-file reports" or "incident reports," confirmation messages create a permanent record of oral decisions, directives, and discussions. They should include the names and titles of involved individuals, the major issues discussed, and a request for approval by the receiver.

## CHAPTER REVIEW

1. Name five characteristics of successful e-mail messages and memos. (Obj. 1)

2. What is graphic highlighting, and why is it particularly useful in e-mail messages and memos? (Obj. 1)

3. Briefly describe the writing process for e-mail messages and memos. (Obj. 1)

4. What three questions should you ask yourself before writing an e-mail message or memo? (Obj. 1)

5. Name three ways to close a memo or an e-mail message. (Obj. 2)

6. What are some of the dangers for users of e-mail? (Obj. 3)

7. Suggest at least ten pointers that you could give to a first-time e-mail user. (Obj. 3)

8. Name at least five rules of e-mail etiquette that show respect for others. (Obj. 3)

9. What are three possibilities in handling the salutation for an e-mail message? (Obj. 3)

10. What tone should managers avoid in writing procedure or information e-mail messages and memos? (Obj. 4)

11. Why should writers of information e-mail messages and memos strive to express ideas positively instead of negatively? (Obj. 4)

12. Should a request e-mail message or memo open immediately with the request or with an explanation? Why? (Obj. 5)

13. What's wrong with a message opener such as *This is to inform you that . . .*? (Obj. 5)

14. What is a confirmation e-mail message or memo? What other names could it be given? (Obj. 6)

15. What three elements should most confirmation e-mail messages and memos include? (Obj. 6)

## CRITICAL THINKING

1. How can the writer of a business e-mail message or memo develop a conversational tone and still be professional? Why do e-mail writers sometimes forget to be professional? (Objs. 1–3)

2. What factors would help you decide whether to write a memo, send an e-mail, make a telephone call, leave a

voice mail message, or deliver a message in person? (Objs. 1 and 2)

3. Why are lawyers and technology experts warning companies to store, organize, and manage computer data, including e-mail, with sharper diligence? (Obj. 3)

4. Discuss the ramifications of the following statement: Once a memo or any other document leaves your hands, you have essentially published it. (Objs. 2–6)

5. **Ethical Issue:** Should managers have the right to monitor the e-mail messages of employees? Why or why not? What if employees are warned that e-mail could be monitored? If a company sets up an e-mail policy, should only in-house transmissions be monitored? Only outside transmissions?

# ACTIVITIES

## 8.1 Openers for E-Mail Messages and Memos (Objs. 1–3)

**Your Task.** Revise the following e-mail and memo openers so that they are more direct.

a. I enjoyed talking with you at our last committee meeting. You mentioned a number of new ergonomic products that might solve some of the repetitive stress injuries among our office employees. You said that you had written a report on it, and you said you would be willing to share it with me. I would be very pleased if you would send me a copy of your report.

b. I appreciate your asking me for my ideas on processing data electronically. In the nearly 15 years since EDI (electronic data interchange) was first introduced, large companies have always wanted their smaller suppliers to use it. But now with Internet-based systems, it's much more usable and less expensive. I've worked out six suggestions for how your company can switch to Internet-based EDI. They are discussed below.

c. I have before me your memo of the 16th in which you request permission to attend the Web Site Design Seminar sponsored by Presentation Planners. As I understand it, this is a two-day seminar scheduled for February 25 and 26. Your reasons for attending were well stated and convincing. You have my permission to attend.

d. As you are aware, the document specialists in our department have been unhappy about their chairs and their inability to adjust the back height. The chairs are uncomfortable and cause back fatigue. As a result, I looked into the possibility of purchasing new adjustable chairs that I think will be just right for these employees. New chairs have been ordered for all these employees. The new chairs should be arriving in about three weeks.

## 8.2 Subject Lines (Objs. 1–3)

**Your Task.** Write effective subject lines for the messages represented by the openings in Activity 8.1.

## 8.3 Graphic Highlighting Techniques (Objs. 1 and 3)

**Your Task.** Revise the following hard-to-read paragraphs. Include an introductory statement or a title before presenting the data in bulleted or numbered lists.

a. A recent survey of car buyers uncovered some very interesting information about what electronic options they really wanted in new cars. Some technology visionaries have been saying that car buyers wanted a lot of fancy electronic gadgets, but the survey showed that only 5.1 percent, for example, wanted a trip computer. Most car buyers mentioned cruise control (79.1 percent). A total of 61.1 percent said that they wanted antilock brakes. A smaller percentage (50.5 percent) wanted keyless entry. Farther down the list we found that buyers wanted CD players (34.1 percent).

b. Our employee leasing program has proven to be an efficient management tool for business owners because we take care of everything. Our program will handle your payroll preparation. Moreover, benefits for employees are covered. We also know what a chore calculating workers' compensation premiums can be, so we do that for you. And we make all the necessary provincial and federal reports that are required today.

c. We are concerned about your safety in using our automated teller machines (ATMs) at night, so we think you should consider the following tips. Users of ATMs are encouraged to look around—especially at night—before using the service. If you notice anything suspicious, the use of another ATM is recommended. Or you could come back later. Another suggestion that we give our customers involves counting your cash. Be sure that the cash you receive is put away quickly. Don't count it as soon as you get it. It's better to check it in the safety of your car or at home. Also, why not take a friend with you if you must use an ATM at night? We also suggest that you park in a well-lighted area as close to the actual location of the ATM as possible.

## 8.4 Document for Analysis: Information E-Mail (Obj. 4)

**Your Task.** Analyze the following e-mail message. It suffers from wordiness and lack of graphic highlighting techniques to improve readability. List its weaknesses. If your instructor directs, revise it.

**To:** Todd Shimoyama
<todd.shimoyama@chemco.com>

**From:** Avianca Harper
<avianca.harper@chemco.com>

**Subject:** REPORT

**Cc:**

Todd:

I went to the OfficePro conference on May 2. The topic was how to prevent workplace violence, and I found it very fascinating. Although we have been fortunate to avoid serious incidents at our company, it's better to be safe than sorry. Since I was the representative from our company, I thought you would like me to report about some suggestions for preventing workplace violence. Robert Mather was the presenter, and he made suggestions in three categories, which I will summarize here.

Mr. Mather cautioned organizations to prescreen job applicants. As a matter of fact, wise companies do not offer employment until after a candidate's background has been checked. Just the mention of a background check is enough to make some candidates withdraw. These candidates, of course, are the ones with something to hide.

A second suggestion was that companies should prepare a good employee handbook that outlines what employees should do when they suspect potential workplace violence. This handbook should include a way for informers to be anonymous.

A third recommendation had to do with recognizing red-flag behaviour. This involves having companies train managers to recognize signs of potential workplace violence. What are some of the red flags? One sign is an increasing number of arguments (most of them petty) with coworkers. Another sign is extreme changes in behaviour or statements indicating depression over family or financial problems. Another sign is bullying or harassing behaviour. Bringing a firearm to work or displaying an extreme fascination with firearms is another sign.

By the way, the next OfficePro conference is in September, and the topic is the new WSIB standards.

I think that the best recommendation is prescreening job candidates. This is because it is most feasible. If you want me to do more research on prescreening techniques, do not hesitate to let me know. Let me know by May 7 if you want me to make a report at our management meeting, which is scheduled for June.

Avianca

## 8.5 Document for Analysis: Request Memo (Obj. 5)

**Your Task.** Analyze the following memo. List its weaknesses. If your instructor directs, revise it.

**DATE:** Current

**TO:** All Employees

**FROM:** Elizabeth Mendoza, Human Resources

**SUBJECT:** NEW HOLIDAY PLAN

In the past we've offered all employees 11 holidays (starting with New Year's Day in January and proceeding through Christmas Day the following December). Other companies offer similar holiday schedules.

In addition, we've given all employees one floating holiday. As you know, we've determined that day by a companywide vote. As a result, all employees had the same day off. Now, however, management is considering a new plan that we feel would be better. This new plan involves a floating holiday that each individual employee may decide for herself or himself. We've given it considerable thought and decided that such a plan could definitely work. We would allow each employee to choose a day that he or she wants. Of course, we would have to issue certain restrictions. Selections would have to be subject to our staffing needs within individual departments. For example, if everyone wanted the same day, we could not allow everyone to take it. In that case, we would allow the employee with the most seniority to have the day off.

Before we institute the new plan, though, we wanted to see what employees thought about this. Is it better to continue our current companywide uniform floating holiday? Or should we try an individual floating holiday? Please let us know what you think as soon as possible.

## 8.6 Document for Analysis: Confirmation E-Mail (Obj. 6)

**Your Task.** Analyze the following e-mail message. List its weaknesses. If your instructor directs, revise it.

**To:** William.Morrison@commercial.com
**From:** TracyAnnPhillips@aol.com
**Subject:** COMMERCIALS
**Cc:**

Bill:

It was good to talk to you on the telephone yesterday after exchanging letters with you and after reading so much about

Bermuda. I was very interested in learning about the commercials you want me to write. As I understand it, Mr. Morrison, you want a total of 240 one-minute radio commercials. These commercials are intended to rejuvenate the slumping tourist industry in Bermuda. You said that these commercials would be broadcast from March 30 through June 30. You said these commercials would be played on three radio stations. These stations are in the major cities on the East Coast. The commercials would be aimed at morning and evening drive time, for drivers who are listening to their radios, and the campaign would be called "Radio Bermuda."

I am sure I can do as you suggested in reminding listeners that Bermuda is less than three hours away. You expect me to bring to these commercials the colour and character of the island. You want me to highlight the attractions and the civility of Bermuda, at least as much as can be done in one-minute radio commercials. In my notes I wrote that you also mentioned that I should include references to tree frogs and royal palm trees. Another item you suggested that I include in some of the commercials was special Bermuda food, such as delicacies like shark on toast, conch fritters, and mussel stew.

I wanted to be sure to write these points down so that we both agreed on what we said in our telephone conversation. I am eager to begin working on these commercials immediately, but I would feel better if you looked over these points to see if I have it right. I look forward to working with you.

Tracy

## 8.7 Information Memo: What I Do on the Job (Obj. 4)

Some employees have remarked to the boss that they are working more than other employees. Your boss has decided to study the matter by collecting memos from everyone. **Your Task.** He asks you to write a memo describing your current duties and the skills required for your position. If some jobs are found to be overly demanding, your boss may redistribute job tasks or hire additional employees. Based on your own work or personal experience, write a well-organized memo describing your duties, the time you spend on each task, and the skills needed for what you do. Provide enough details to make a clear record of your job. Use actual names and describe actual tasks. Report to the head of the organization. The organization could be a campus club or committee on which you serve. Don't make your memo a list of complaints. Just describe what you do in an objective tone. And by the way, your boss appreciates brevity. Keep your memo under one page.

## 8.8 Information Memo: Party Time (Obj. 4)

Staff members in your office were disappointed that no holiday party was given last year. They don't care what kind of party it is, but they do want some kind of celebration this year. **Your Task.** You have been asked to draft a memo to the office staff about the upcoming December holiday party. Decide what kind of party you would like. Include information about where the party will be held, when it is, what the cost will be, what kind of food will be served, whether guests are allowed, and with whom to make reservations.

## 8.9 Reply Memo or E-Mail: One Sick Day Too Many (Obj. 5)

`TEAM`  `CRITICAL THINKING`

As director of Human Resources at a midsize insurance company, you received an inquiry from Suzette Chase, who is supervisor of Legal Support. It seems that one of Suzette's veteran employees recently implemented a four-day workweek for herself. On the fifth morning, the employee calls in with some crisis or sickness that makes it impossible for her to get to work. Suzette asks for your advice in how to handle this situation.

In the past you've told supervisors to keep a written record (a log) of each absence. This record should include the financial and productive impact of the absence. It should include a space where the employee can include her comments and signature. You've found that a written document always increases the significance of the event. You've also told supervisors that they must be objective and professional. It's difficult, but they should not personalize the situation.

Occasionally, of course, an absence is legitimate. Supervisors must know what is unavoidable and what is a lame excuse. In other words, they must know how to separate reasons from excuses. Another thing to consider is how the employee reacts when approached. Is her attitude sincere, or does she automatically become defensive?

You also tell supervisors that "if they talk the talk, they must walk the walk." In other words, they must follow the same policies that are enforced. The best plan, of course, is to clearly define what is and is not acceptable attendance policy and make sure every new hire is informed. **Your Task.** In teams discuss what advice to give to Suzette Chase regarding her habitually absent worker. Why is a log important? What other suggestions can you make? How should you conclude this message? Individually or in teams, write a well-organized reply memo or e-mail message to Suzette Chase, supervisor of Legal Support. Remember that bulleted items improve readability.

## 8.10 Information Memo: Retirement Questions (Obj. 4)

`TEAM`

Your company hired a writing consultant to help employees improve their communication skills.

**Your Task.** The following memo was assigned as an exercise to train your team in recognizing good and bad writing. In small groups discuss its weaknesses and then compose, either individually or as a team, an improved version.

**DATE:** Current

**TO:** All Employees

**FROM:** Mark Grist, Employee Benefits Division

**SUBJECT:** RETIREMENT

We are aware that many employees do not have sufficient information that relates to the prospect of their retirement. Many employees who are approaching retirement age have come to this office with specific questions about their retirement. It would be much easier for us to answer all these questions at once, and that is what we will try to do.

We would like to answer your questions at a series of retirement planning sessions in the company conference room. The first meeting is September 6. We will start at 4 p.m., which means that the company is giving you one hour of released time to attend this important session. We will meet from 4 to 6 p.m. when we will stop for dinner. We will begin again at 7 p.m. and finish at 8 p.m.

We have arranged for three speakers. They are: our company benefits supervisor, a financial planner, and a psychologist who treats retirees who have mental problems. The three sessions are planned for: September 6, October 4, and November 1.

## 8.11 Information Memo or E-Mail*: Wilderness Retreat (Obj. 4)

**E-MAIL**

Assume you are Mark Peters, president of a small printing operation employing 25 workers. On Friday, June 7, your print shop employees will join you at an expense-paid, one-day retreat that you hope will improve teamwork among the workers. The retreat will be led by Wilderness Retreats, which offers companies outdoor team training designed to build employee trust, teamwork, and loyalty. Employees will meet at work at 8 a.m., and a Wilderness Retreats van will pick them up and take them to a nearby provincial park. Employees will spend the day on team-building activities, including a map-reading exercise that will require employee teams to find their way through a wooded area to a "home base." The retreat will provide a catered picnic lunch and time for socializing. The group will return to work by 4 p.m. Since the print shop will be closed during the retreat, you consider the retreat a workday and expect all employees to attend. Employees should dress casually. They'll be outside most of the day.

**Your Task.** Write a memo to employees announcing the retreat.

*All e-mail activities may be used as memos if e-mail is unavailable.

## 8.12 Information Memo or E-Mail: Sick and Tired of Spam (Obj. 4)

**INFOTRAC**

Your boss wants to do something about all the spam (unwanted e-mail messages) being delivered to her computer and other computers in your company. She's sick and tired of wading through mortgage offers, work-at-home schemes, get-rich offers, and pyramid letters. She asks you to use the Internet to learn about techniques for avoiding unsolicited e-mail.

**Your Task.** Using an InfoTrac subject or power search, read several articles on fighting spam. A good article is Helen Bradley's "Fight Back Against Spam!" in *Home Office Computing*, April 2001, Article No. A72790790. After looking at several articles, prepare an information memo or e-mail message to send to your boss, Cheryl Lupton. In your own words describe ten techniques for reducing the amount of incoming spam in your office. Be sure to include an appropriate opening and closing, along with listing techniques for your tips. Do you think items should be bulleted or numbered?

## 8.13 Information Memo or E-Mail: Sweet Rewards (Obj. 4)

**E-MAIL**

The summer Candy Show is a "must-attend" trade show for all manufacturers of sweets, including cereals and even fruit drinks. One year's event, held in Chicago, produced a number of trends including novelty items, tie-ins with books and movies, and high-tech products. "Nobody sells just candy anymore," observed one visitor. "You need a gimmick, such as a connection with a cartoon character, a book or movie, a sports team, or something high-tech." Among the novelty items were Crispy Chocolate Candies (chocolate-covered rice) by M&M/Mars. A novelty item by Amurol featured Chocolate Chip Cookie Doh, a candy that looks like raw cookie dough. Concord brought out edible candy stampers, an interesting concept. Some novelties combined candy with toys. For example, Cap Toy introduced White Ranger, a spin-top candy, and Candy Popper, a battery-operated spin toy.

After novelty products, the most popular new items incorporated tie-in products. For example, a Willy Wonka candy line featured an animated character and a Web site said to have a "substantial" advertising budget. Another tie-in product was a Dilbert Desktop Dispenser for M&Ms, as well as numerous candies connected with current films. Sports licences were also hot, such as a Team NFL gum bank. Some of the most interesting new products involved high-tech items, such as the Web site for Willy Wonka candy. Amural Confections featured a refillable "gumputer," available in three different flavours.

**Your Task.** As Peter Kim <pkim@candy.com>, assistant marketing director at a large Montreal-area candy manufacturer, you have been sent to this year's Candy Show to observe what's hot. You are exhausted after visiting nearly all the exhibits in two days. But you must respond to your boss's request that you use your laptop computer to send her an e-mail message summarizing what you saw. She asked you to pick out three trends that could affect your company's product development. Describe each trend briefly and give examples. You'll provide a full report when you return to the office. Address an e-mail message to Tanya Smith <tsmith@candy.com>.[20]

## 8.14 Procedure Memo: Ticket-Free Parking (Obj. 4)

Assume that you are Tran Crozier, director of the Human Resources Division of IBM in Markham, Ontario. Both day- and swing-shift employees need to be reminded of the parking guidelines. Day-shift employees must park in Lots A and B in their assigned spaces. If they have not registered their cars and received their white stickers, the cars will be ticketed.

Day-shift employees are forbidden to park at the curb. Swing-shift employees may park at the curb before 3:30 p.m. Moreover, after 3:30 p.m., swing-shift employees may park in any empty space—except those marked Tandem, Handicapped, Van Pool, Car Pool, or Management. Day-shift employees may loan their spaces to other employees if they know they will not be using the space.

One serious problem is lack of registration (as evidenced by white stickers). Registration is done by Employee Relations. Any car without a sticker will be ticketed. To encourage registration, Employee Relations will be in the cafeteria May 12 and 13 from 11:30 a.m. to 1:30 p.m. and from 3 p.m. to 5 p.m. to take applications and issue white parking stickers.
**Your Task.** Write a procedure memo to employees that reviews the parking guidelines and encourages them to get their cars registered. Use itemization techniques and strive for a tone that fosters a sense of cooperation rather than resentment.

## 8.15 Procedure E-Mail or Memo: Countdown to Performance Appraisal Deadline (Obj. 4)

It's time to remind all supervisory personnel that they must complete employee performance appraisals by April 15. Your boss, James Robinson, director, Human Resources, asks you to draft a procedure memo announcing the deadline. In talking with Jim, you learn that he wants you to summarize some of the main steps in writing these appraisals. Jim says that the appraisals are really important this year because of changes in work and jobs. Many offices are installing new technologies, and some offices are undergoing reorganization. It's been a hectic year.

Jim also mentions that some supervisors will want to attend a training workshop on February 20 where they can update their skills. Supervisors who want to reserve a space at the training workshop should contact Lynn Jeffers <ljeffers@rainco.com>. When you ask Jim what procedures

you should include in the memo, he tells you to consult the employee handbook and pick out the most important steps.

In the handbook you find suggestions that say each employee should have a performance plan with three or four main objectives. In the appraisal the supervisor should mention three strengths the employee has, as well as three areas for improvement. One interesting comment in the handbook indicated that improvements should focus on skills, such as time management, rather than on things like being late frequently. Supervisors are supposed to use a scale of 1 to 5 to assess employees: 1 = consistently exceeds requirements; 5 = does not meet requirements at all. You think to yourself that this scale is screwy; it's certainly not like grades in school. But you can't change the scale. Finally, supervisors should meet with employees to discuss the appraisal. The completed appraisal should be sent to your office.
**Your Task.** Draft a memo from James Robinson, director, Human Resources, to all department heads, managers, and supervisors. Announce the April 15 deadline for performance appraisals. List five or six steps to be taken by supervisors in completing performance appraisals. If you need more information about writing performance appraisals, search that term on the Web. You'll find many sites with helpful advice.

## 8.16 Procedure Memo: Hot Calls in August (Obj. 4)

Play the part of Sally Chernoff, division sales manager of DataCom Electronics. The company's long-distance and cell phone bills have been skyrocketing. Sales reps use the telephone to make "hot" calls to close deals or to persuade hard-sells. However, Paul Wilson, vice president, Sales, is not sure that the cost of these calls is worth the return. He suggested sharply reducing or even eliminating *all* long-distance calls made by sales reps, but you want to collect information first. You propose a plan.

For the month of August, all sales reps are to place their long-distance calls through the company operator (rather than dialing direct). They are to keep a log of all calls, including the date, time, city, and reason for the call. In September you'd like them to give you that telephone log. Then you can analyze the data and perhaps solve this telephone budget crisis. Privately, you hope that the cumbersome procedure will, by itself, decrease the number of calls.
**Your Task.** Write a memo to all sales reps describing this procedure. Attach a telephone log. Include reader benefits and itemization techniques.

## 8.17 Procedure Memo: Managing Your Time More Wisely (Obj. 4)

**INFOTRAC**

You work with a group of engineers who are constantly putting in 60- and 70-hour workweeks. The vice president worries

**RICH CHAPTER RESOURCES ARE AVAILABLE AT THE WEB SITE**

that major burnout will occur. Personally, he believes that some of the engineers simply manage their time poorly. He asks you to look into the topic of time management and put together a list of procedures that might help these professionals use their time more wisely. Your suggestions may become the basis for an in-service training program.

**Your Task.** Using InfoTrac, conduct a keyword search for articles about time management. Read several articles. Summarize five or six procedures that might be helpful to employees. Write a memo to Thomas Sawicky, vice president, with your suggestions.

## 8.18 Request Memo: Protecting the CEO From Prying Eyes (Obj. 5)

E-MAIL    CRITICAL THINKING

As an experienced executive assistant, you really never had any problems with the confidentiality aspect of your job. Your boss, however, was recently promoted to CEO of your company. Now it seems that both your office and his have become Grand Central Station. Company officers float in and out because the CEO has an open-door policy. They have a barrage of questions about projects, budgets, and problems. When the CEO is out of town, they inquire about his travel schedule and what he's doing. Some of them even enter his office and go through papers on his desk.

Because your boss and you are increasingly processing a huge amount of sophisticated, confidential information, you are afraid that the wrong person is going to lay hands on company information. And if something confidential ever leaks, you worry that you will be held responsible.[21]

**Your Task.** You decide to write to your boss to gain some understanding about managing sensitive information. You wonder about his open-door policy. You don't know whether to stop company officers when he is on the telephone and they walk right in. When he's away, the open-door policy becomes even more problematic. You would like to clarify what documents are strictly confidential—for your eyes and your boss's eyes only. When packages or mail arrive with items marked "Personal" or "Confidential," you don't know whether to open them. What should you do, for example, when his paycheque arrives in an envelope? You're concerned about who should have access to what information and under what circumstances. You worry about sharing materials related to current projects. When a department head asks for documents related to her department and the CEO is gone, what should you do? Should anyone be allowed to use the boss's computer? Who? Under what circumstances should you be allowed to talk to the media? Think of other matters of confidentiality. Spell them out in a request memo to Sebastian Watts. You prefer to have his response in writing so that you can use it to back up enforcement. Because he's leaving on another trip next week, you want his written

response before he leaves. You know how busy he is. How could you make it easy for him to respond?

## 8.19 Request Memo or E-Mail: Smokers vs. Nonsmokers (Obj. 5)

E-MAIL    CRITICAL THINKING

The city of Thunder Bay has mandated that employers "shall adopt, implement, and maintain a written smoking policy which shall contain a prohibition against smoking in restrooms and infirmaries." Employers must also "maintain a nonsmoking area of not less than two thirds of the seating capacity in cafeterias, lunchrooms, and employee lounges, and make efforts to work out disputes between smokers and nonsmokers."

**Your Task.** As Lindsay English, director of Human Resources, write a memo to all department managers of General Wheat, a large foods company. Announce the new restriction, and tell the managers that you want them to set up departmental committees to mediate any smoking conflicts before the complaints surface. Explain why this is a good policy.

## 8.20 Reply Memo or E-Mail: Enforcing Smoking Ban (Obj. 5)

E-MAIL

As Bruni Comenic, manager of accounting services for General Wheat, you want to respond to Ms. English's memo in the preceding activity. You could have called Ms. English, but you prefer to have a permanent record of this message. You are having difficulty enforcing the smoking ban in restrooms. Only one men's room serves your floor, and 9 of your 27 male employees are smokers. You have already received complaints, and you see no way to enforce the ban in the restrooms. You have also noticed that smokers are taking longer breaks than other employees. Smokers complain that they need more time because they must walk to an outside area. Smokers are especially unhappy when the weather is cold, rainy, or snowy. Moreover, smokers huddle near the building entrances, thus creating a negative impression for customers and visitors. Your committee members can find no solutions; in fact, they have become polarized in their meetings to date. You need help from a higher authority.

**Your Task.** Write an e-mail or memo to Ms. English appealing for solutions. Perhaps she should visit your department.

## 8.21 Reply to Request: Chocolates on the Web (Obj. 5)

E-MAIL    WEB

Again act as Peter Kim, assistant marketing director at a large Montreal-area candy manufacturer. Your boss asks you to

237

check out a competitor's World Wide Web site: <**www.godiva.com**>. Godiva chocolates, according to your boss, has a much-acclaimed Web site. You are to access the site, examine what it offers, and report your findings. Godiva is an upscale chocolatier offering its delights in the best department stores, as well as through its own stores and catalogue. Your boss wonders if a Web site might be a good investment for your company. In an e-mail message, report to your boss (your instructor, in this instance) how Godiva uses the site and what it features.

## 8.22 Reply Memo: Rescheduling Interviews (Obj. 5)

Your boss, Fred Knox, had scheduled three appointments to interview applicants for an accounting position. All of these appointments were for Friday, October 7. However, he now must travel to Halifax on that weekend. He asks you to reschedule all the appointments for one week later. He also wants a brief summary of the background of each candidate.

You call each person and arrange these times. Paul Scheffel, who has been an accountant for 15 years with Bechtel Corporation, agreed to come at 10:30 a.m. Mark Cunningham, who is a CPA and a consultant to many companies, will come at 11:30. Geraldine Simpson, who has a B.A. degree and eight years of experience in payroll accounting, will come at 9:30 a.m. You're wondering if Mr. Knox forgot to include Don Stastry, operations personnel officer, in these interviews. Mr. Stastry usually is part of the selection process. **Your Task.** Write a memo to Mr. Knox including all the vital information he needs.

## 8.23 Request Memo or E-Mail: Dress-Down Day for Us? (Obj. 5)

**E-MAIL**

According to a poll funded by Levi Strauss & Co., more than half of all white-collar workers now can dress casually at work. The dress-down trend reflects larger changes in work patterns. Top-down management is less prevalent, and more people work at home or have flexible hours. Even John Molloy, the guru of the 1980s "dress for success" movement, now works with "befuddled executives," teaching them what to wear in a casual world.

As Thomas Marshall, CEO of Marshall & Associates, a sedate accountancy firm, you have had some inquiries from your accountants and other employees about the possibility of dressing casually—not all the time, but occasionally. You decide to ask a few key people what they think about establishing a casual-dress day. It sounds like a good idea, especially if it makes people feel more at ease in the office. But you worry that it might look unprofessional and encourage sloppy work and horsing around. Moreover, you are concerned about what people might wear, such as shorts, tank

tops, T-shirts with slogans, baseball caps, and dirty athletic clothes. Would a dress-down policy make the office atmosphere less professional? Perhaps a written dress code will be necessary if a casual-dress policy is allowed.

**Your Task.** To solicit feedback, you write the same memo to two partners and your office manager. Ask for their opinions, but do so with specific questions. Be sure to include an end date so that you can decide on a course of action before the next management council meeting. Address the same memo or e-mail to Mary E. Leslie <mel@marsh.com>, Sam W. Miller <sam@marsh.com>, and Jonathon Galston <jon@marsh.com>.[22]

## 8.24 Reply E-Mail: Dress-Down Discussion and Decision (Obj. 5)

**E-MAIL**     **TEAM**     **CRITICAL THINKING**

Casual dress in professional offices seems to be increasingly common. Should the accountancy firm in Activity 8.23 allow employees one dress-down day a week? Why or why not? If you decide to recommend a dress-down day, consider whether a dress code is appropriate. Give reasons. Then decide whether a dress-down day would affect the professional environment of the office. You can tell from the CEO's words that he favours a limited dress-down program, but your team should make up its own mind.

**Your Task.** Get together in groups to discuss a suitable response to the request made in Activity 8.23. Once you reach consensus, respond to the boss either in individual memos or a team-written memo. Be sure to answer the questions and issues raised in Activity 8.23. Your reply memo should go to CEO Thomas Marshall <tmarshall@marsh.com>.

## 8.25 Reply Memo: Someone's Going to Get Dumped On (Obj. 5)

**WEB**     **TEAM**

The IS (Information Systems) network manager at a large organization in Burnaby, British Columbia, worried that his company would have to upgrade its Internet connection because operations were noticeably slower than in the past. On checking, however, he discovered that extensive recreational Web surfing among employees was the real reason for the slowdown. Since the company needed a good policy on using e-mail and the Internet, he assigned your team the task of investigating existing policies. Your team leader, Rick Rodriquez, who has quite a sense of humour, said, "Adopting an Internet policy is a lot like hosting a convention of pigeons. Both will result in a lot of squawking, ruffled feathers, and someone getting dumped on." Right! No one is going to like having e-mail and Internet use restricted. It is, indeed, a dirty job, but someone has to do it.

**Your Task.** Working individually, locate examples or models of company e-mail and Internet policies. For best results use several search engines and try variations of the search term "company e-mail policy." Print out any helpful material. Then meet as a group and select six to eight major topics that you think should be covered in a company policy. Your investigation will act as a starting point in the long process of developing a policy that provides safeguards but is not overly restrictive. You are not expected to write the policy at this time, but you could attach copies of anything interesting. Your boss would especially like to know where he could see or purchase model company policies. Send a reply memo or an e-mail message to Rick Rodriquez, your team leader.[23]

## 8.26 Confirmation Memo or E-Mail: Looking Over the Employee's Shoulder (Obj. 6)

**E-MAIL**

At lunch one day you had a stimulating discussion with Barbara Wilson, your company attorney, about e-mail privacy. You brought up the topic because you will be attending a conference shortly on Internet uses and abuses, and you will be serving on a panel discussing e-mail privacy. As you recall, Ms. Wilson emphasized the fact that the employer owns the workplace. She said, "It owns the desks, machines, stationery, computers, and everything else. Employees have no legal right to use the employer's property for personal business."

Equally important, however, is the recognition of a right to privacy, even in the workplace. "If an employee can demonstrate that the employer violated his or her reasonable *expectation* of privacy," said Ms. Wilson, "then he or she can hold the employer liable for that violation." You also remember a rather startling comment: Ms. Wilson said that an employer may listen to or read only as much of a communication as is necessary for the employer to determine whether it is personal or business.[24] You wonder if you remembered this conversation accurately.

**Your Task.** Because one of the topics your panel will discuss is whether employers may monitor e-mail, you decide to write to Ms. Wilson to confirm what she said.

## 8.27 Confirmation Memo: Dream Vacation (Obj. 6)

Play the role of Jack Mendoza. You had a vacation planned for September 2 through 16. But yesterday your wife suggested delaying the vacation for several weeks so that you could travel through Quebec's Eastern Townships when the fall colours are most beautiful. She said it would be the vacation of her dreams, and you agree. Perhaps you could change your vacation dates. Unfortunately, you remember that you're scheduled to attend the Winnipeg marketing exhibit September 29–30. But maybe Melanie Grasso would fill in for you and make the presentation of the company's newest product, JuiceMate. You see your boss, Mas Watanabe, in the

hall and decide to ask if you can change your vacation to September 28 through October 12. To your surprise, he agrees to the new dates. He also assures you that he will ask Melanie to make the presentation and encourage her to give a special demonstration to the Dana Corporation, which you believe should be targeted.

**Your Task.** Back in your office, you begin to worry. What if Mas forgets about your conversation? You can't afford to take that chance. Write a confirmation memo that summarizes the necessary facts and also conveys your gratitude.

## 8.28 Confirmation Memo: Verifying a Job Severance Package (Obj. 6)

You're congratulating yourself on landing a fantastic job. Terrific title. Terrific salary. Terrific boss. You were even smart enough to talk about an exit package during your interviewing. You had read an article in the *National Post* suggesting that the best time to win a generous departure deal is before you accept a position.

Because you knew your skills were in high demand for this position and because you would be giving up a good position, you wanted to know what the typical severance package involved. What would you receive if this job disappeared through a merger or downturn in the economy or similar unforeseen event? The hiring manager told you that the standard severance package includes one week's salary for every year of service, out-placement counseling for up to six months, accrued but unused vacation pay, and extended medical coverage. After a little bargaining, you were able to increase the severance pay to two weeks' salary for each year of service and medical insurance for you and your family up to one year or until you found another position.

Then you begin to worry. You didn't get any of this in writing.

**Your Task.** You decide to write a confirmation memo outlining the severance package discussed in your interview. The *National Post* says that your memo becomes an enforceable contract. Write a memo to Jefferson Walker, operations manager, describing your understanding of what you were promised.[25] If Mr. Walker doesn't agree with any of the details, ask him to respond immediately. Show your enthusiasm for the job and keep the tone of your message upbeat. Add any necessary details.

# C.L.U.E. REVIEW 8

Edit the following sentences to correct all language faults, including grammar, punctuation, spelling, and word use.

1. Todays organizations however are encouraging rank and file employees to share information, and make decisions.

2. Because managers, and employees, are writing more messages then ever before its definitely important that they develop good communication skills.

3. Memos generally contain 4 nesessary parts; subject line, opening, body and action closing.

4. The federal trade commission are holding hearings to illicit information about IBMs request to expand marketing in twenty-one city's.

5. Consumer buying and spending for the past 5 years, is being studied by a Federal team of analysts.

6. When you respond too a e-mail message you should not automaticly return the senders message.

7. Wasnt it Dr Ben Cohen not Mr Temple who allways wrote their e-mails in all capitol letters.

8. A list of the names' and addresses' of e-mail recipients were sent using the "bcc" function.

9. Our human resources department which was formerally in room 35 has moved it's offices to room 5.

10. The Post Dispatch our local newspaper featured as its principle article a story entitled, Smarter E-Mail is here.

# Chapter 9

## Routine Letters and Goodwill Messages

## LEARNING OBJECTIVES

*1* List three characteristics of good letters and describe the direct pattern for organizing letters.

*2* Write letters requesting information and action.

*3* Write letters placing orders.

*4* Write letters making claims.

*5* Write letters complying with requests.

*6* Write letters of recommendation.

*7* Write letters granting claims and making adjustments.

*8* Write goodwill messages.

*9* Modify international letters to accommodate other cultures.

# Rocky Mountaineer Railtours

When the Canadian government decided to drastically cut the heavily subsidized VIA Rail (Canada's national passenger train company) operation and privatize the daylight service, Great Canadian Railtour Company was awarded the rights to the service. Led by president Peter Armstrong, former railroad executives and leading tourism experts were brought in to impart 120 years of combined railroad experience to the newly established company.

In 1990, the first year that Rocky Mountaineer Railtours pulled out of the station, 11 000 passengers took the "trip of a lifetime." In 2001, Rocky Mountaineer welcomed over 73 000 guests and celebrated its 500 000th guest in 2002. The mix of passengers from the United States, the United Kingdom, Australia, Germany, Mexico, and many other countries attests to the organization's international reach.

The two-day, all-daylight rail journey follows the historical train route constructed over 100 years ago through Canada's West and the Canadian Rockies. The entire trip takes place in daylight hours to ensure that travellers enjoy all the scenery. Guests stay overnight midway in historic Kamloops, British Columbia. Built around the two-day train trip are more than 40 package tours that explore the breathtaking scenery of British Columbia and Alberta by land, sea, and rail.

Rocky Mountaineer offers two choices of service: Redleaf Service provides guests with assigned, spacious, comfortable reclining seats, large picture windows, and at-your-seat meal service, in a nonsmoking, air-conditioned, traditional rail coach environment. Goldleaf Service offers guests reserved seating in bi-level domed coaches featuring panoramic views on the upper level and an elegant dining room on the main level where à la carte breakfasts and lunches are served.

Over 350 people make the Rocky Mountaineer the success it is. The principles of guest service have been the driving force behind the company's high level of guest satisfaction. An executive team that offers a combined 48 years of experience with the organization leads the talented staff and crew.[1]

The growing popularity of the Rocky Mountaineer has the potential to generate a great deal of correspondence. Satisfied customers might write to express how much they had enjoyed their trip; the occasional unhappy customer might write to complain about unsatisfactory service or accommodation—or even about the weather. Prospective customers might write to inquire about routes, accommodation, and prices. Responding to customer letters is a critical element in maintaining customer goodwill and market position for organizations like Rocky Mountaineer Railtours.

## CRITICAL THINKING
- Have you ever written a letter or sent an e-mail to a company? What might motivate you to do so? Would you expect a response?
- If a company such as Rocky Mountaineer receives a letter complimenting its service, is it necessary to respond?
- Why is it important for companies to answer claim (complaint) letters immediately?

**www.rockymountaineer.com**

## STRATEGIES FOR ROUTINE LETTERS

*1*

Letters sent to customers are a primary channel of communication for delivering messages *outside* an organization. Although e-mail is incredibly successful for both internal and external communication, many important messages still require written letters. Business letters are important when a permanent record is required, when formality is necessary, and when a message is sensitive and requires an organized, well-considered presentation. In this book we'll divide letters into three groups: (1) routine letters communicating straightforward requests, replies, and goodwill messages; (2) persuasive messages including sales pitches; and (3) negative messages delivering refusals and bad news.

This chapter concentrates on routine, straightforward letters through which we conduct everyday business and convey goodwill to outsiders. Such letters go to suppliers, government agencies, other businesses, and, most important, customers. The letters to customers receive a high priority because these messages encourage product feedback, project a favourable image of the company, and promote future business.

Publisher Malcolm Forbes understood the power of business letters when he said, "A good business letter can get you a job interview, get you off the hook, or get you money. It's totally asinine to blow your chances of getting *whatever* you want—with a business letter that turns people off instead of turning them on."[2] This chapter teaches you what turns readers on. You'll study the characteristics of good letters, techniques for organizing direct requests and responses, and ways to apply the 3-×-3 writing process. You'll learn how to write six specific kinds of direct letters, along with special goodwill messages. Finally, you'll study how to modify letters to accommodate other cultures.

## Characteristics of Good Letters

Although routine letters deliver straightforward facts, they don't have to sound and look dull or mechanical. At least three characteristics distinguish good business letters: clear content, a tone of goodwill, and correct form.

*Clear Content.* A clearly written letter separates ideas into paragraphs, uses short sentences and paragraphs, and guides the reader through the ideas with transitional expressions. Moreover, a clear letter uses familiar words and active-voice verbs. In other words, it incorporates the writing techniques you studied in Chapters 5, 6, and 7.

Clear letters feature short sentences and paragraphs, transitional expressions, familiar words, and active-voice verbs.

But many business letters are not written well. As many as one third of business letters do nothing more than seek clarification of earlier correspondence. Clear letters avoid this problem by answering all the reader's questions or concerns so that no further correspondence is necessary. Clear letters also speak the language of the receiver. One expert says, "The only sure-fire way to avoid miscommunication is to determine your audience's characteristics" and write in her or his language.[3] This doesn't mean "dumbing down" your remarks. It means taking into consideration what your reader knows about the subject and using appropriate words.

*A Tone of Goodwill.* Good letters, however, have to do more than deliver clear messages; they also must build goodwill. Goodwill is a positive feeling the reader has toward an individual or an organization. By analyzing your audience and adapting your message to the reader, your letters can establish an overall tone of goodwill.

Letters achieve a tone of goodwill by emphasizing a "you" view and reader benefits.

To achieve goodwill, look for ways to present the message from the reader's perspective. In other words, emphasize the "you" view and point out benefits to the reader. In addition, be sensitive to words that might suggest gender, racial, age, or disability bias. Finally, frame your ideas positively because they will sound more pleasing and will give more information than negative constructions. For example, which sounds better and gives more information? *We cannot send your order until April 1* or *We can send your order April 1.*

*Correct Form.* A business letter conveys silent messages beyond that of its printed words. The letter's appearance and format reflect the writer's carefulness and experience. A short letter bunched at the top of a sheet of paper, for example, looks as if it was prepared in a hurry or by an amateur.

Appropriate letter formats send silent but positive messages.

For your letters to make a good impression, you need to select an appropriate format. The block style shown in Figure 9.1 is a popular format. Other letter formats are illustrated later in this chapter and shown in Appendix C. In the block style, the parts of your letter—dateline, inside address, body, and so on—are set flush left on the page. Also, the letter is formatted so that it is centred on the page and framed by white space. Most letters will have margins of 2.5 to 4 cm.

Finally, be sure to use ragged-right margins; that is, don't allow your computer to justify the right margin and make all lines end evenly. Unjustified margins improve readability, say experts, by providing visual stops and by making it easier to tell where the next line begins. Although book publishers use justified right margins, as you see on this page, your letters should be ragged right. Study Figure 9.1 for more tips on making your letters look professional.

**FIGURE 9.1  Business Letter Formatting**

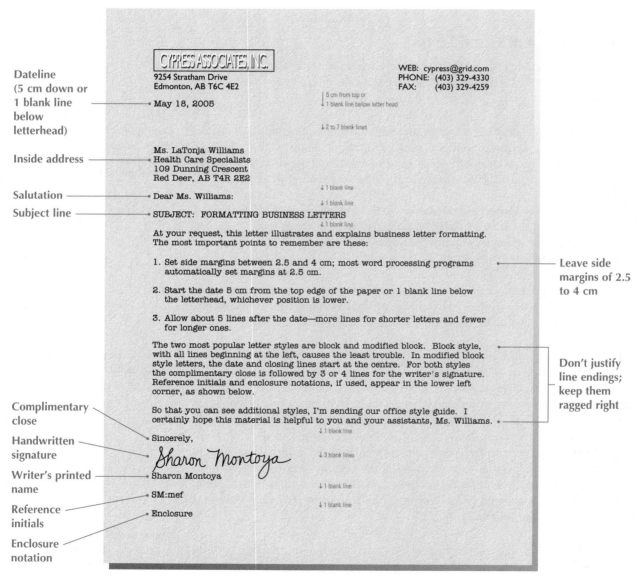

UNIT 3
Business Correspondence
**244**

# Using the Direct Pattern for Routine Letters

The everyday transactions of a business consist mainly of routine requests and responses. Because you expect the reader's response to be positive or neutral, you won't need special techniques to be convincing, to soften bad news, or to be tactful. Thus, in composing routine letters, you can organize your message, as shown in Figure 9.2, into three parts:

Most business messages are routine requests or routine responses.

- **Opening:** A statement that announces the purpose immediately
- **Body:** Details that explain the purpose
- **Closing:** A request for action or a courteous conclusion

*Frontloading in the Opening.* You should begin everyday messages in a straightforward manner by frontloading the main idea. State immediately why you are writing so that the reader can anticipate and comprehend what follows. Remember, every time a reader begins a message, he or she is thinking, "Why was this sent to me?" "What am I to do?"

Everyday business messages "frontload" by presenting the main idea or purpose immediately.

Some writers make the mistake of organizing a message as if they were telling a story or solving a problem.[4] They start at the beginning and follow the same sequence in which they thought through the problem. This means reviewing the background, discussing the reasons for action, and then requesting an action. Most business letters, though, are better written "backwards." Start with the action desired or the main idea. Don't get bogged down in introductory material, history, justifica-

**FIGURE 9.2  Three-Part Direct Pattern for Routine Requests and Responses**

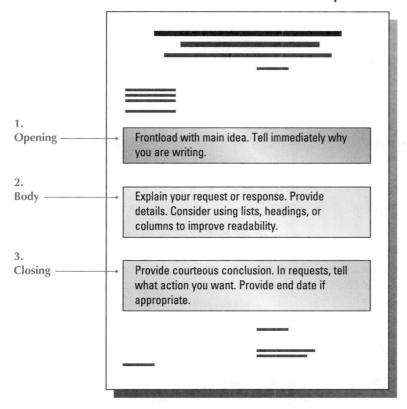

1. Opening — Frontload with main idea. Tell immediately why you are writing.

2. Body — Explain your request or response. Provide details. Consider using lists, headings, or columns to improve readability.

3. Closing — Provide courteous conclusion. In requests, tell what action you want. Provide end date if appropriate.

tions, or old-fashioned "business" language.[5] Instead, reveal your purpose immediately. Compare the following indirect and direct openers to see the differences:

**Indirect Opening**
Our company is experiencing difficulty in retaining employees. We also need help in screening job applicants. Our current testing program is unsatisfactory. I understand that you offer employee testing materials, and I have a number of questions to ask.

**Direct Opening**
Please answer the following questions about your personnel testing materials.

Most simple requests should open immediately with a statement of purpose (*Please answer these questions about...*). Occasionally, however, complex requests may require a sentence or two of explanation or background before the purpose is revealed. What you want to avoid, though, is delaying the purpose of the letter beyond the first paragraph.

*Explaining in the Body.* After a direct opening that tells the reader why you are writing, present details that explain your request or response. This is where your planning pays off, allowing you to structure the information for maximum clarity and readability. Here you should consider using some graphic devices to highlight the details: a numbered or bulleted list, headings, columns, or boldface or italic type.

If you have considerable information, you'll want to develop each idea in a separate paragraph with effective transitions to connect them. The important thing to remember is to keep similar ideas together. The biggest problem in business writing is poor organization, and the body of a letter is where that failure becomes apparent.

*Being Specific and Courteous in the Closing.* In the last paragraph of direct letters, readers look for action information: schedules, deadlines, activities to be completed. Thus, at this point, you should specify what you want the reader to do. If appropriate, include an end date—a date for completion of the action. If possible, give reasons for establishing the deadline. Research shows that people want to know why they should do something—even if the reasons seem obvious. Moreover, people want to be treated courteously (*Please answer these questions before April 1, when we must make a final decision*), not bossed around (*Send this information immediately*).

## Applying the 3-×-3 Writing Process to Routine Letters

Although routine letters may be short and straightforward, they benefit from attention to the composition process. "At the heart of effective writing is the ability to organize a series of thoughts," says writing expert and executive Max Messmer. Taking the time to think through what you want to achieve and how the audience will react makes writing much easier.[6] Here's a quick review of the 3-×-3 writing process to help you think through its application to routine letters.

*Analysis, Anticipation, and Adaptation.* Before writing, spend a few moments analyzing your task and audience. Your key goals here are (1) determining your purpose, (2) anticipating the reaction of your audience, and (3) visualizing the audience. Too often, letter writers start a message without enough preparation. According to British poet and critic Matthew Arnold, you must "have something to say and say it as clearly as you can."[7]

*Sidenotes (left margin):*

The body explains the purpose for writing, perhaps using graphic devices to highlight important ideas.

The closing courteously specifies what the receiver is to do.

Before writing routine letters, analyze your purpose and anticipate the audience's response.

***Research, Organization, and Composition.*** Collect information and make a list of the points you wish to cover. For short messages such as an answer to a customer's inquiry, jot your notes down on the document you are answering. For longer documents that require formal research, use a cluster diagram or the outlining techniques discussed in Chapter 6. When business letters carry information that won't upset the receiver, you can organize them in the direct manner described earlier. And be sure to plan for revision. A writer can seldom turn out an excellent message on the first attempt.

***Revision, Proofreading, and Evaluation.*** When you finish the first draft, revise for clarity. The receiver should not have to read the message twice to grasp its meaning. Proofread for correctness. Check for punctuation irregularities, typos, misspelled words, or other mechanical problems. *Always* take time to examine the words highlighted by your spell checker. Finally, evaluate your product. Before any letter leaves your desk, always reread it and put yourself in the shoes of the reader, asking yourself, "How would I feel if I were receiving it?"

After completing the first draft, revise for clarity, proofread for correctness, and evaluate for effectiveness.

## DIRECT REQUEST LETTERS

Many of your routine business letters will fall into one of three categories: (1) asking for information or action, (2) placing orders for products, or (3) making a claim requiring an adjustment when something has gone wrong. In this section you'll learn how to write good letters for each of these circumstances. Before you write any letter, though, consider its costs in terms of your time and workload. Whenever possible, don't write! Instead of asking for information, could you find it yourself? Would a telephone call, an e-mail message, or a brief visit to a coworker solve the problem quickly? If not, use the direct pattern to present your request efficiently.

### Requesting Information and Action

The majority of your business letters will request information or action. Suppose you have questions about a payroll accounting service your company is considering or you need to ask a customer to supply missing data from an order. For these routine messages put the main idea first. If your request involves several questions, you could open with a polite request, such as *Will you please answer the following questions about your payroll service.* Note that although this request sounds like a question, it's actually a disguised command. Since you expect an action rather than a reply, punctuate this polite command with a period instead of a question mark.

*A direct letter may open with a question or a polite request.*

***Clarifying Requests.*** In the letter body explain your purpose and provide details. If you have questions, express them in parallel form so that you balance them grammatically. To elicit the most information, pose open-ended questions (*What computer lock-down device can you recommend?*) instead of yes-or-no questions (*Do you carry computer lock-down devices?*). If you are asking someone to do something, be sure your tone is polite and undemanding. Remember that your written words cannot be softened by a smile. When possible, focus on benefits to the reader (*To ensure that you receive the exact sweater you want, send us your colour choice*). In the closing tell the reader courteously what is to be done. If a date is important, set an end date to take action and explain why. Some careless writers end request letters simply with *Thank you,* forcing the reader to review the contents to determine what is expected and when. You can save the reader time by spelling out the action to be

*Questions in a direct letter should be parallel (balanced grammatically).*

taken. Avoid other overused endings such as *Thank you for your cooperation* (trite), *Thank you in advance for . . .* (trite and presumptuous), and *If you have any questions, do not hesitate to call me* (suggests that you didn't make yourself clear).

**Direct request letters maintain a courteous tone, spell out what needs to be done, and focus on reader benefits.**

***Showing Appreciation.*** It's always appropriate to show appreciation, but try to do so in a fresh and efficient manner. For example, you could hook your thanks to the end date (*Thanks for returning the questionnaire before May 5, when we will begin tabulation*). You might connect your appreciation to a statement developing reader benefits (*We are grateful for the information you will provide because it will help us serve you better*). Or you could describe briefly how the information will help you (*I appreciate this information that will enable me to . . .*). When possible, make it easy for the reader to comply with your request (*Note your answers on this sheet and return it in the postage-paid envelope* or *Here's my e-mail address so that you can reach me quickly*).

Let's now analyze the first draft of a direct request letter written by office manager Melanie Marshall. She wants information about computer security devices, but the first version of her letter is confusing and inefficient. Melanie makes a common mistake: starting the message with a description of the problem instead of starting with the main idea. Here is Melanie's first version.*

✗ *Poorly Written First Draft*

Dear Ms. Ivorson:

**Starts with background infor- ——→** Our insurance rates will be increased soon if we don't install security devices on our computer equipment. We have considered some local suppliers, but none had exactly what we wanted.
**mation and explanation instead of request.**

**Fails to organize information ——→** We need a device that can be used to secure separate computer components at a workstation including a computer, keyboard, and monitor. We currently own 18 computers, keyboards, and monitors, along with six printers.
**into logical order.**

**Confuses reader by jumping ——→** We wonder if professionals are needed to install your security devices. We're also interested in whether the devices can be easily removed when we need to move equipment around. We are, of course, very interested in prices and quantity discounts, if you offer them.
**around among many topics. Fails to ask specific questions.**

**Ends with cliché. Does not ——→** Thank you for your attention to this matter.
**reveal what to do and when to do it.**

Sincerely,

Melanie Marshall

Melanie's second version, shown in Figure 9.3, begins more directly. The opening sentence introduces the purpose immediately so that the reader quickly knows why the letter was sent. Melanie then provides background information. Most important, she organizes all her requests into specific questions, which are sure to bring a better result than her previous diffuse request. Study the 3-×-3 writing process outlined in Figure 9.3 to see the plan Melanie followed in improving her letter.

## 3 Placing Orders

You may occasionally need to write a letter that orders supplies, merchandise, or services. Generally, such purchases are made by telephone, catalogue order form, fax,

*Some unformatted letters and memos such as that shown here will appear in this textbook. They illustrate content rather than form. Documents that illustrate form are shown in figures, such as Figure 9.3.

**FIGURE 9.3  Direct Request Letter**

## The Three Phases of the Writing Process

**Prewriting  1**

**Analyze:** The purpose of this letter is to gain specific data about devices to lock down computer equipment.

**Anticipate:** The audience is expected to be a busy but receptive customer service representative.

**Adapt:** Because the reader will probably react positively to this inquiry, the direct pattern is best.

**Writing  2**

**Research:** Determine how much equipment must be locked down and what questions must be answered. Learn the name of the receiver.

**Organize:** Open with a general inquiry about security devices. In the body give details; arrange any questions logically. Close by courteously providing a specific deadline.

**Compose:** Draft the first copy on a computer.

**Revising  3**

**Revise:** Improve the clarity by grouping similar ideas together. Improve readability by listing and numbering questions. Eliminate wordiness.

**Proofread:** Look for typos and spelling errors. Check punctuation and placement. Indent the second line of all listed items for a clean look.

**Evaluate:** Is this message attractive and easily comprehended?

---

inner **Circle** graphics

32 Hershey Road, Dartmouth, NS B2Y 2H5

(902) 488-3310 phone (902) 488-3319 fax

February 3, 2005

Ms. Sue Ivorson, Customer Service
Micro Supplies and Software
P.O. Box 800
Montreal, QC G5B 2G6

**Addresses receiver by name** → Dear Ms. Ivorson:

Please provide information and recommendations regarding security equipment to prevent the theft of office computers, keyboards, monitors, and printers. ← **Introduces purpose immediately**

**Explains need for information** → Our office now has 18 computer workstations and 6 printers that we must secure to desks or counters. Answers to the following questions will help us select the best devices for our purpose.

1. What device would you recommend that can secure a workstation consisting of a computer, monitor, and keyboard?

2. What expertise and equipment are required to install and remove the security device?

3. How much is each device? Do you offer quantity discounts, and if so, how much?

← **Groups open-ended questions into list for quick comprehension and best feedback**

**Courteously provides end date and reason** → Your response before February 15 will help us meet an April 1 deadline from our insurance company for locking down this equipment.

Sincerely,

*Melanie Marshall*

Melanie Marshall
Office Manager

**CHAPTER 9**
Routine Letters and
Goodwill Messages
**249**

**Letters placing orders specify items or services, quantities, dates, prices, and payment method.**

or Web page. Sometimes, however, you may not have a telephone number, order form, or Web address—only a street address. To order items by letter, supply the same information that an order blank would require. In the opening let the reader know immediately that this is a purchase authorization and not merely an information inquiry. Instead of *I saw a number of interesting items in your catalogue*, begin directly with order language such as *Please send me by FedEx the following items from your fall merchandise catalogue.*

If you're ordering many items, list them vertically in the body of your letter. Include as much specific data as possible: quantity, order number, complete description, unit price, and total price. Show the total amount, and figure the tax and shipping costs if possible. The more information you provide, the less likely that a mistake will be made.

In the closing tell how you plan to pay for the merchandise. Enclose a cheque, provide a credit card number, or ask to be billed. Many business organizations have credit agreements with their regular suppliers that enable suppliers to send goods without prior payment. In addition to payment information, tell when the merchandise should be sent and express appreciation. The following letter from the human resources department of a business illustrates the pattern of an order letter.

**Opens directly with authorization for purchase, method of delivery, and catalogue source.** ⟶ Please send by express mail the following items from your summer catalogue.

**Uses columns to make quantity, catalogue number, description, and price stand out.**

| | | | |
|---|---|---|---|
| 250 | No. OG-18 | Payroll greeting cards | $102.50 |
| 250 | No. OG-22 | Payroll card envelopes | 21.95 |
| 100 | No. OM-01 | Performance greeting cards | 80.00 |
| | Subtotal | | $204.45 |
| | GST at 7% | | 14.31 |
| | PST at 8% (ON) | | 16.36 |
| | Shipping | | 24.00 |
| | Total | | $259.12 |

**Calculates totals to prevent possible mistakes.**

**Expresses appreciation and tells when items are expected. Identifies method of payment.** ⟶ My company would appreciate receiving these cards immediately since we are starting an employee recognition program February 12. Enclosed is our cheque for $259.12. If additional charges are necessary, please bill my company.

## Making Straightforward Claims

In business many things can go wrong—promised shipments are late, warrantied goods fail, or service is disappointing. When you as a customer must write to identify or correct a wrong, the letter is called a *claim*. Straightforward claims are those to which you expect the receiver to agree readily. But even these claims often require a letter. While your first action may be a telephone call or a visit to submit your claim, you may not be satisfied with the result. Written claims are often taken more seriously, and they also establish a record of what happened. Straightforward claims use a direct approach. Claims that require persuasion are presented in Chapter 10.

Most businesses today honestly want to please their customers. To compete globally and to pump up local markets, North American industry is particularly sold on the idea of improving the quality of its service. Since winning a new customer is three times as expensive as retaining a current one, businesses especially want to hear what customers have to say—even when it's a complaint. One industry expert observed, "You're most likely to hear from customers when they have a complaint, and that's a good thing. They're not only giving you a chance to help them, but they're initiating a dialogue, which is exactly what you want to have with your best customers."[8]

*Opening Directly.* When you, as a customer, have a legitimate claim, you can expect a positive response from a company. Smart businesses want to hear from their customers. That's why you should open a claim letter with a clear statement of the problem or with the action you want the receiver to take. You might expect a replacement, a refund, a new order, credit to your account, correction of a billing error, free repairs, free inspection, or cancellation of an order. When the remedy is obvious, state it immediately (*Please send us 24 Royal hot-air popcorn poppers to replace the 24 hot-oil poppers sent in error with our order shipped January 4*). When the remedy is less obvious, you might ask for a change in policy or procedure or simply for an explanation (*Because three of our employees with confirmed reservations were refused rooms September 16 in your hotel, would you please clarify your policy regarding reservations and late arrivals*).

*Explaining.* In the body of a claim letter, explain the problem and justify your request. Provide the necessary details so that the difficulty can be corrected without further correspondence. Avoid becoming angry or trying to fix blame. Bear in mind that the person reading your letter is seldom responsible for the problem. Instead, state the facts logically, objectively, and unemotionally; let the reader decide on the causes. Include copies of all pertinent documents such as invoices, sales slips, catalogue descriptions, and repair records. (By the way, be sure to send copies and NOT your originals, which could be lost.) When service is involved, cite names of individuals spoken to and dates of calls. Assume that a company honestly wants to satisfy its customers—because most do. When an alternative remedy exists, spell it out (*If you are unable to send 24 Royal hot-air popcorn poppers immediately, please credit our account now and notify us when they become available*).

*Concluding.* Conclude a claim letter with a courteous statement that promotes goodwill and expresses a desire for continued relations. If appropriate, include an end date (*We realize that mistakes in ordering and shipping sometimes occur. Because we've enjoyed your prompt service in the past, we hope that you will be able to send us the hot-air poppers by January 15*). Finally, in making claims, act promptly. Delaying claims makes them appear less important. Delayed claims are also more difficult to verify. By taking the time to put your claim in writing, you indicate your seriousness. A written claim starts a record of the problem, should later action be necessary. Be sure to keep a copy of your letter.

Figure 9.4 shows a first draft and revision of a hostile claim that vents the writer's anger but accomplishes little else. Its original tone is belligerent, and it assumes that the company intentionally mischarged the customer. Furthermore, it fails to tell the reader how to remedy the problem. The revision tempers the tone, describes the problem objectively, and provides facts and figures. Most important, it specifies exactly what the customer wants done.

To sum up, use the direct pattern with the main idea first when you expect little resistance to letters making requests. The checklist that follows Figure 9.4 reviews the direct strategy for information and action requests, orders, and adjustments.

**Claim letters open with a clear problem statement, support the claim with specifics, and close with a statement of goodwill.**

**Providing details without getting angry improves the effectiveness of a claim letter.**

**Written claims submitted promptly are taken more seriously than delayed ones.**

**FIGURE 9.4** Direct Claim Letter

**First Draft**

Dear Premier Quality Systems, Inc.:

You call yourselves Premier Quality, but all I'm getting from your service is garbage! I'm furious that you have your salespeople slip in unwanted service warranties to boost your sales.

*Sounds angry; jumps to conclusions*

When I bought my Panatronic DVD from PQS, Inc., in August, I specifically told the salesperson that I did NOT want a three-year service warranty. But there it is on my VISA statement this month! You people have obviously billed me for a service I did not authorize. I refuse to pay this charge.

*Forgets that mistakes happen*

How can you hope to stay in business with such fraudulent practices? I was expecting to return this month and look at CD players, but you can be sure I'll find an honest dealer this time.

*Fails to suggest solution*

Sincerely,

**Revision**

2352 Hall Avenue
Windsor, ON N8X 3L9

*Personal business letter style*

September 3, 2005

Mr. Sam Lee, Customer Service
Premier Quality Systems, Inc.
41 Bricker Avenue
Waterloo, ON N2L 3B6

Dear Mr. Lee:

Please credit my VISA account, No. 0000-0046-2198-9421, to correct an erroneous charge of $99.

*States simply and clearly what to do*

*Explains objectively what went wrong*

On August 8 I purchased a Panatronic DVD from PQS, Inc. Although the salesperson discussed a three-year extended warranty with me, I decided against purchasing that service for $99. However, when my credit card statement arrived this month, I noticed an extra $99 charge from PQS, Inc. I suspect that this charge represents the warranty I declined.

*Doesn't blame or accuse*

*Documents facts*

Enclosed is a copy of my sales invoice along with my VISA statement on which I circled the charge. Please authorize a credit immediately and send a copy of the transaction to me at the above address.

*Suggests continued business once problem is resolved*

I'm enjoying all the features of my Panatronic DVD and would like to be shopping at PQS for a CD player shortly.

*Uses friendly tone*

Sincerely,

Keith Cortez

Keith Cortez

Enclosure

252

### Information or Action Request Letters

✓ **Open by stating the main idea.** To elicit information, ask a question or issue a polite command (*Will you please answer the following questions . . .*).

✓ **Explain and justify the request.** In seeking information, use open-ended questions structured in parallel, balanced form.

✓ **Request action in the closing.** Express appreciation, and set an end date if appropriate. Avoid clichés (*Thank you for your cooperation*).

### Order Letters

✓ **Open by authorizing the purchase.** Use order language (*Please send me . . .*), designate the delivery method, and state your information source (such as a catalogue, advertisement, or magazine article).

✓ **List items in the body.** Include quantity, order number, description, unit price, extension, tax, shipping, and total costs.

✓ **Close with the payment data.** Tell how you are paying and when you expect delivery. Express appreciation.

### Claim Letters

✓ **Begin with the purpose.** Present a clear statement of the problem or the action requested—such as a refund, replacement, credit, explanation, or correction of an error.

✓ **Explain objectively.** In the body tell the specifics of the claim. Provide copies of necessary documents.

✓ **End by requesting action.** Include an end date if important. Add a pleasant, forward-looking statement. Keep a copy of the letter.

## DIRECT REPLY LETTERS

Occasionally, you will receive requests for information or action. In these cases your first task is deciding whether to comply. If the decision is favourable, your letter should let the reader know immediately by using the direct pattern and frontloading the good news.

**When you can respond favourably to requests, use the direct pattern.**

This section focuses on routine reply letters in three situations: (1) complying with requests for information or action, (2) writing letters of recommendation, and (3) granting claims and making adjustments.

## Complying With Requests

Often, your messages will respond favourably to requests for information or action. A customer wants information about a product. A supplier asks to arrange a meeting. Another business inquires about one of your procedures or about a

5

A logically arranged request usually ensures effective and prompt feedback.

**Letters responding to requests may open with a subject line to identify the topic immediately.**

**Responding to customer inquiries provides a good opportunity to promote your business.**

former employee. In complying with such requests, you'll want to apply the same direct pattern you used in making requests.

The opening of a direct reply letter might contain a subject line, as shown in Figure 9.5. A subject line helps the reader recognize the topic immediately. Usually appearing two lines below the salutation, the subject line refers in abbreviated form to previous correspondence and/or summarizes a message (*Subject: Your July 12 Inquiry About WorkZone Software*). It often omits articles (*a, an, the*), is not a complete sentence, and does not end with a period. Knowledgeable business communicators use a subject line to refer to earlier correspondence so that in the first sentence, the most emphatic spot in a letter, they are free to emphasize the main idea.

*Opening Directly.* In the first sentence of a direct reply letter, deliver the information the reader wants. Avoid wordy, drawn-out openings such as *I have before me your letter of August 5, in which you request information about . . . .* More forceful and more efficient is an opener that answers the inquiry (*Here is the information you wanted about . . .*). When agreeing to a request for action, announce the good news promptly (*Yes, I will be happy to speak to your business communication class on the topic of . . .*).

In the body of your reply, supply explanations and additional information. Because a letter written on company stationery is considered a legally binding contract, be sure to check facts and figures carefully. If a policy or procedure needs authorization, seek approval from a supervisor or executive before writing the letter.

*Arranging Information Logically.* When answering a group of questions or providing considerable data, arrange the information logically and make it readable by using lists, tables, headings, boldface, italics, or other graphic devices. When customers or prospective customers inquire about products or services, your response should do more than merely supply answers. You'll also want to promote your organization and products. Often, companies have particular products and services they want to spotlight. Thus, when a customer writes about one product, provide helpful information that satisfies the inquiry, but consider using the opportunity to introduce another product as well. Be sure to present the promotional material with attention to the "you" view and to reader benefits (*You can use our standardized tests to free you from time-consuming employment screening*). You'll learn more about special techniques for developing sales and persuasive messages in Chapter 10.

In concluding, make sure you are cordial and personal. Refer to the information provided or to its use (*The enclosed list summarizes our recommendations. We wish you all the best in redesigning your Web site*). If further action is required, describe the procedure and help the reader with specifics (*The federal government's Canada Business Service Centres Web site provides helpful information about doing business on the Internet. Its Web address is <http://bsa.cbsc.org>*).

*Illustrating Reply Letters.* In replying to a customer's request for information, the writer in Figure 9.5 uses the first sentence to present the most important information. Then she itemizes her list of responses to the customer's questions. If she had written these responses in paragraph form, they would have been less emphatic and more difficult to read. She goes on to describe and promote the product, being careful to show how it would benefit the customer. And she concludes by referring specifically to pages in an enclosed pamphlet and providing a number for the customer's response.

**FIGURE 9.5 Customer Reply Letter**

## The Three Phases of the Writing Process

### Prewriting

**Analyze:** The purpose of this letter is to provide helpful information and to promote company products.

**Anticipate:** The reader is the intelligent owner of a small business who needs help with personnel administration.

**Adapt:** Because the reader requested this data, she will be receptive to the letter. Use the direct pattern.

### Writing

**Research:** Gather facts to answer the business owner's questions. Consult brochures and pamphlets.

**Organize:** Prepare a scratch outline. Plan for a fast, direct opening. Use numbered answers to the business owner's three questions.

**Compose:** Write the first draft on a computer. Strive for short sentences and paragraphs.

### Revising

**Revise:** Eliminate jargon and wordiness. Look for ways to explain how the product fits the reader's needs. Revise for "you" view.

**Proofread:** Double-check the form of numbers (*July 12, page 6, 8 to 5 PST*).

**Evaluate:** Does this letter answer the customer's questions and encourage an order?

---

## KELOWNA SOFTWARE, INC.

**777 Raymer Road**
**Kelowna, BC V1W 1H7**
**www.kelownasoft.ca**

July 15, 2005

Mr. Jeffrey M. White
White-Rather Enterprises
220 Telford Court
Leduc, AB T9E 5M6

Dear Mr. White:

SUBJECT: YOUR JULY 12 INQUIRY ABOUT WORKZONE SOFTWARE  ⟵ *Identifies previous correspondence and subject*

*Puts most important information first* ⟶ Yes, we do offer personnel record-keeping software specially designed for small businesses like yours. Here are answers to your three questions about this software:

*Lists answers to sender's questions in order asked* ⟶

1. Our WorkZone software provides standard employee forms so that you are always in compliance with current government regulations.

2. You receive an interviewer's guide for structured employee interviews, as well as a scripted format for checking references by telephone.   ⟵ *Emphasizes "you" view*

3. Yes, you can update your employees' records easily without the need for additional software, hardware, or training.

Our WorkZone software was specially designed to provide you with expert forms for interviewing, verifying references, recording attendance, evaluating performance, and tracking the status of your employees. We even provide you with step-by-step instructions and suggested procedures. You can treat your employees as if you had a professional human resources specialist on your staff.   ⟵ *Links sales promotion to reader benefits*

*Helps reader find information by citing page number* ⟶ On page 6 of the enclosed pamphlet you can read about our WorkZone software. To receive a preview copy or to ask questions about its use, just call 1-800-354-5500. Our specialists are eager to help you weekdays from 8 to 5 PST. If you prefer, visit our Web site to receive more information or to place an order.   ⟵ *Makes it easy to respond*

Sincerely,

*Linda DeLorme*

Linda DeLorme
Senior Marketing Representative

Enclosure

The direct reply letter, as shown in Figure 9.6, responds to a request from a teacher and a Toronto Raptors fan. The opening announces the letter's purpose immediately and also establishes rapport with the reader by thanking him for his support in the previous season. The body of the letter includes a bulleted list and an explanation of the information being sent. Notice how the writer invites future business by offering an "exclusive advanced booking opportunity." The cordial, personalized closing that concludes the direct reply letter is sure to build goodwill and promote future business while delivering the information sought.

In mixed-news messages the good news should precede the bad.

*Treating Mixed Messages.* The direct pattern is also appropriate for messages that are mostly good news but may have some negative elements. For example, a return policy has time limits; an airfare may contain holiday restrictions; a speaker can come but not at the time requested; an appliance can be repaired but not replaced. When the message is mixed, emphasize the good news by presenting it first (*Yes, I would be delighted to address your marketing class on the topic of . . .*). Then, explain why a problem exists (*My schedule for the week of October 10 takes me to Calgary and Edmonton, where I am . . .*). Present the bad news in the middle (*Although I cannot meet with your class at that time, perhaps we can schedule a date during the week of . . .*). End the message cordially by returning to the good news (*Thanks for the invitation. I'm looking forward to arranging a date in October when I can talk with your students about careers in marketing*).

Your goal is to present the negative news clearly without letting it become the focus of the message. Thus, you want to spend more time talking about the good news. And by placing the bad news in the middle of the letter, you deemphasize it. You'll learn other techniques for presenting bad news in Chapter 11.

## Writing Letters of Recommendation

6

Letters of recommendation present honest, objective evaluations of individuals and help match candidates to jobs.

Letters of recommendation may be written to nominate people for awards and for membership in organizations. More frequently, though, they are written to evaluate present or former employees. The central concern in these messages is honesty. Thus, you should avoid exaggerating or distorting a candidate's qualifications to cover up weaknesses or to destroy the person's chances. Ethically and legally, you have a duty to the candidate as well as to other employers to describe that person truthfully and objectively. You don't, however, have to endorse everyone who asks. Since recommendations are generally voluntary, you can—and should—resist writing letters for individuals you can't truthfully support. Ask these people to find other recommenders who know them better.

Some businesspeople today refuse to write recommendations for former employees because they fear lawsuits. See the Ethical Insights box on page 258 for tips on using caution in these letters. Other businesspeople argue that recommendations are useless because they're always positive. Despite the general avoidance of negatives, well-written recommendations do help match candidates with jobs. Hiring companies learn more about a candidate's skills and potential. As a result, they are able to place a candidate properly. Therefore, you should learn to write such letters because you will surely be expected to do so in your future career.

*Opening.* Begin an employment recommendation by identifying the candidate and the position sought, if it is known. State that your remarks are confidential, and suggest that you are writing at the request of the applicant. Describe your relationship with the candidate, as shown here:

## FIGURE 9.6 Direct Reply from Toronto Raptors

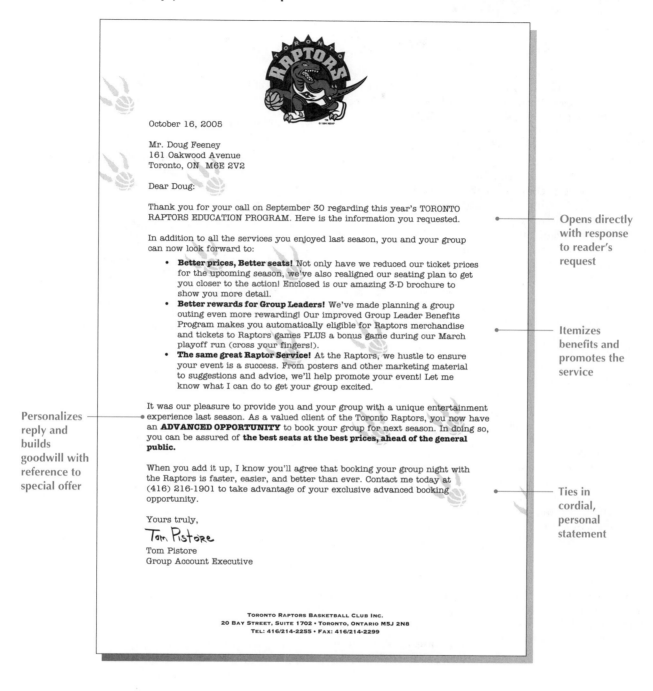

October 16, 2005

Mr. Doug Feeney
161 Oakwood Avenue
Toronto, ON  M6E 2V2

Dear Doug:

Thank you for your call on September 30 regarding this year's TORONTO RAPTORS EDUCATION PROGRAM. Here is the information you requested. — **Opens directly with response to reader's request**

In addition to all the services you enjoyed last season, you and your group can now look forward to:

- **Better prices, Better seats!** Not only have we reduced our ticket prices for the upcoming season, we've also realigned our seating plan to get you closer to the action! Enclosed is our amazing 3-D brochure to show you more detail.
- **Better rewards for Group Leaders!** We've made planning a group outing even more rewarding! Our improved Group Leader Benefits Program makes you automatically eligible for Raptors merchandise and tickets to Raptors games PLUS a bonus game during our March playoff run (cross your fingers!). — **Itemizes benefits and promotes the service**
- **The same great Raptor Service!** At the Raptors, we hustle to ensure your event is a success. From posters and other marketing material to suggestions and advice, we'll help promote your event! Let me know what I can do to get your group excited.

**Personalizes reply and builds goodwill with reference to special offer** — It was our pleasure to provide you and your group with a unique entertainment experience last season. As a valued client of the Toronto Raptors, you now have an **ADVANCED OPPORTUNITY** to book your group for next season. In doing so, you can be assured of **the best seats at the best prices, ahead of the general public.**

When you add it up, I know you'll agree that booking your group night with the Raptors is faster, easier, and better than ever. Contact me today at (416) 216-1901 to take advantage of your exclusive advanced booking opportunity. — **Ties in cordial, personal statement**

Yours truly,

Tom Pistore

Tom Pistore
Group Account Executive

**TORONTO RAPTORS BASKETBALL CLUB INC.**
**20 BAY STREET, SUITE 1702 • TORONTO, ONTARIO M5J 2N8**
**TEL: 416/214-2255 • FAX: 416/214-2299**

Ms. Cindy Robertson, whom your organization is considering for the position of media trainer, requested that I submit confidential information on her behalf. Ms. Robertson worked under my supervision for the past two years in our Video Training Centre. — The opening establishes the reason for writing and the relationship of the writer.

Letters that recommend individuals for awards may open with more supportive statements, such as *I'm very pleased to nominate Robert Walsh for the Employee-of-the-Month award. For the past sixteen months, Mr. Walsh served as staff accountant in my division. During that time he distinguished himself by . . . .*

## Using Caution in Writing Letters of Recommendation

Fearing lawsuits, many companies prohibit their managers from recommending ex-employees. Instead, they provide only the essentials, such as date of employment and position held. Is it ethical for employers to refuse such requests? In truth, employers have little reason to fear providing honest references. Lawyer Malcolm MacKillop asserts, "As long as a reference is accurate, it will defeat any question of malice."[9] Truth is an absolute defence against defamation.

An even more worrisome ethical problem involves companies that fail to provide references revealing problems with employees. A growing trend in lawsuits involves judgments against employers who conceal knowledge of demonstrated violent or dangerous behaviour of former employees. Take, for example, a past employer who does not reveal information about a child molester who applies for work with a school. One executive admitted that he felt ethically bound to reveal serious deficiencies in former employees, even if his company prohibited the writing of recommendations. "When it comes to . . . anything that can cause really serious problems, I'll find a way to send up a red flag." Like many employers, this executive believes that the consequences of withholding critical data "can just be too great—for the new employer, for its customers and other employees—and for us."[10]

Regardless of the problems involved, most ethical and conscientious businesspeople recognize that references serve a valuable purpose in conveying personnel data. Yet, they are cautious in writing them.

Here are six guidelines that a careful writer can follow in writing recommendations:

- **Respond only to written requests.** Moreover, don't volunteer information, particularly if it's negative.

- **State that your remarks are confidential.** While such a statement does not prevent legal review, it does suggest the intentions of the writer.

- **Provide only job-related information.** Avoid commenting on behaviour or activities away from the job.

- **Avoid vague or ambiguous statements.** Keep in mind that imprecise, poorly explained remarks (*she left the job suddenly*) may be made innocently but could be interpreted quite differently.

- **Supply specific evidence for any negatives.** Support any damaging information with verifiable facts.

- **Stick to the truth.** Avoid making any doubtful statements. Truth is always a valid defence against libel or slander.

### Career Application

You are the manager of productions at a mid-sized graphics company. A well-regarded former employee asks for your recommendation, which you want to write. However, your boss has recently prohibited the writing of any letters of recommendation. You feel strongly that you should write this recommendation. What should you do?

---

**The body of a letter of recommendation should describe the candidate's job performance and potential in specific terms.**

**A good recommendation describes general qualities ("organizational and interpersonal skills") backed up by specific evidence that ———→ illustrates those qualities.**

**Body.** The body of an employment recommendation should describe the applicant's job performance and potential. Employers are particularly interested in such traits as communication skills, organizational skills, people skills, ability to work with a team, ability to work independently, honesty, dependability, ambition, loyalty, and initiative. In describing these traits, be sure to back them up with evidence. One of the biggest weaknesses in letters of recommendation is that writers tend to make global, nonspecific statements (*He was careful and accurate* versus *He completed eight financial statements monthly with about 99 percent accuracy*). Employers prefer definite, task-related descriptions:

As a training development specialist, Ms. Robertson demonstrated superior organizational and interpersonal skills. She started as a Specialist I, writing scripts for interactive video modules. After six months she was promoted to team leader. In that role she supervised five employees who wrote, produced, evaluated, revised, and installed 14 computer/videodisc training courses over a period of 18 months.

Be especially careful to support any negative comments with verification (not *He was slower than other customer service reps* but *He answered 25 calls per hour, while most service reps average 40 calls per hour*). In reporting deficiencies, be sure to describe behaviour (*Her last two reports were late and had to be rewritten by her supervisor*) rather than evaluate it (*She is unreliable and her reports are careless*).

***Conclusion.*** In the final paragraph of a recommendation, you should offer an overall evaluation. Indicate how you would rank this person in relation to others in similar positions. Many managers add a statement indicating whether they would rehire the applicant, given the chance. If you are strongly supportive, summarize the candidate's best qualities. In the closing you might also offer to answer questions by telephone. Such a statement, though, could suggest that the candidate has weak skills and that you will make damaging statements orally but not in print. Here's how our sample letter might close:

> Ms. Robertson is one of the most productive employees I have supervised. I would rank her in the top 10 percent of all the media specialists with whom I have worked. Were she to return to Regina, we would be pleased to rehire her. If you need additional information, call me at (306) 440-3019.

The closing of a recommendation presents an overall ranking and may provide an offer to supply more information by telephone.

General letters of recommendation, written when the candidate has no specific position in mind, often begin with the salutation TO PROSPECTIVE EMPLOYERS. More specific recommendations, to support applications to known positions, address an individual. When the addressee's name is unknown, consider using the simplified letter format, shown in Figure 9.7, which avoids a salutation.

The letter shown in Figure 9.7 illustrates a complete employment letter of recommendation and shows a summary of writing tips. After naming the applicant and the position sought, the letter describes the applicant's present duties. Instead of merely naming positive qualities (*he is personable, possesses superior people skills, works well with a team, is creative, and shows initiative*), these attributes are demonstrated with specific examples and details.

## Granting Claims and Making Adjustments

Even the best-run and best-loved businesses occasionally receive claims or complaints from consumers. Most businesses grant claims and make adjustments promptly—they replace merchandise, refund money, extend discounts, send coupons, and repair goods. Businesses make favourable adjustments to legitimate claims for two reasons. First, consumers are protected by law for recovery of damages. Consumer protection is a joint effort of both federal and provincial legislation.[11] Second, and more obviously, most organizations genuinely want to satisfy their customers and retain their business.

Customer goodwill and retention have an important effect on profits. One study showed that losing a customer reduces profits by $118. Keeping that customer satisfied, however, costs only $20.[12] Marketing author Vic Hunter reports that a 5 percent increase in overall customer retention equates to a 25 to 55 percent increase in the profitability of a business unit.[13] When customers are unhappy, they don't return. A staggering 91 percent of disgruntled customers swear they will never do business again with a company that does not resolve their complaints.[14] What's worse, today's unhappy customers are wired; they have the Web to broadcast their protests to the world. In fact, Web pages launched by angry customers or former employees have taken aim at a wide range of companies, including BMW, Apple Computer, and Burger King.[15] Small wonder that businesses are increasingly concerned with improving customer service and listening to what customers are saying.

Businesses generally respond favourably to claims because of legal constraints and the desire to maintain customer goodwill.

## FIGURE 9.7  Employment Recommendation Letter

**Tips for Writing Letters of Recommendation**
- Identify the purpose and confidentiality of the message.
- Establish your relationship with the applicant.
- Describe the length of employment and job duties, if relevant.
- Provide specific examples of the applicant's professional and personal skills.
- Compare the applicant with others in his or her field.
- Offer an overall rating of the applicant.
- Summarize the significant attributes of the applicant.
- Draw a conclusion regarding the recommendation.

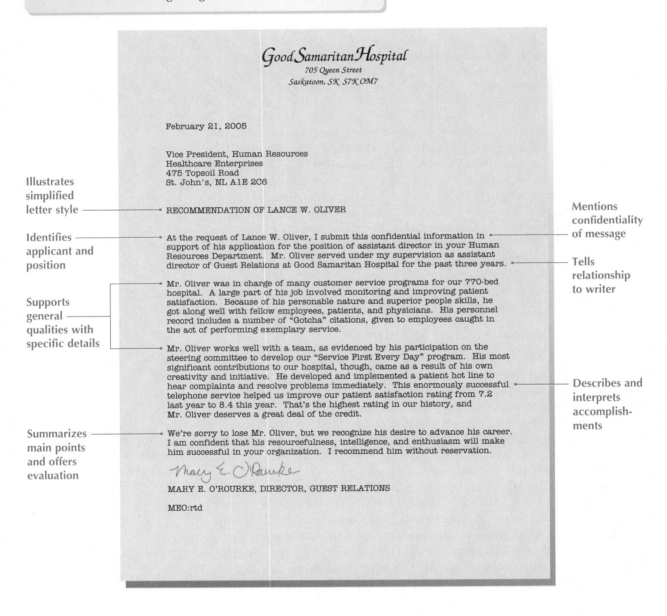

Illustrates simplified letter style

Identifies applicant and position

Supports general qualities with specific details

Summarizes main points and offers evaluation

*Good Samaritan Hospital*
705 Qyeen Street
Saskatoon, SK S7K OM7

February 21, 2005

Vice President, Human Resources
Healthcare Enterprises
475 Topsoil Road
St. John's, NL A1E 2C6

RECOMMENDATION OF LANCE W. OLIVER

At the request of Lance W. Oliver, I submit this confidential information in support of his application for the position of assistant director in your Human Resources Department. Mr. Oliver served under my supervision as assistant director of Guest Relations at Good Samaritan Hospital for the past three years.

Mr. Oliver was in charge of many customer service programs for our 770-bed hospital. A large part of his job involved monitoring and improving patient satisfaction. Because of his personable nature and superior people skills, he got along well with fellow employees, patients, and physicians. His personnel record includes a number of "Gotcha" citations, given to employees caught in the act of performing exemplary service.

Mr. Oliver works well with a team, as evidenced by his participation on the steering committee to develop our "Service First Every Day" program. His most significant contributions to our hospital, though, came as a result of his own creativity and initiative. He developed and implemented a patient hot line to hear complaints and resolve problems immediately. This enormously successful telephone service helped us improve our patient satisfaction rating from 7.2 last year to 8.4 this year. That's the highest rating in our history, and Mr. Oliver deserves a great deal of the credit.

We're sorry to lose Mr. Oliver, but we recognize his desire to advance his career. I am confident that his resourcefulness, intelligence, and enthusiasm will make him successful in your organization. I recommend him without reservation.

*Mary E. O'Rourke*

MARY E. O'ROURKE, DIRECTOR, GUEST RELATIONS

MEO:rtd

Mentions confidentiality of message

Tells relationship to writer

Describes and interprets accomplishments

Wise organizations value complaints not only as a chance to retain customers but also as a significant source of feedback. Comments from complainers often provide more useful information than expensive customer surveys and focus groups.

In responding to customer claims, you must first decide whether to grant the claim. Unless the claim is obviously fraudulent or represents an excessive sum, you'll probably grant it. When you say yes, your adjustment letter will be good news to the reader, so you'll want to use the direct pattern. When your response is no, the indirect pattern might be more appropriate. Chapter 11 discusses the indirect pattern for conveying negative news.

You'll have three goals in adjustment letters:

- Rectifying the wrong, if one exists

- Regaining the confidence of the customer

- Promoting further business

**Adjustment letters seek to right wrongs, regain customer confidence, and promote further business.**

*Opening With the Good News.* The opening of a positive adjustment letter should approve the customer's claim immediately. Notice how quickly the following openers announce the good news:

**Opening sentences tell the good news quickly.**

> You're right! We agree that the warranty on your American Standard Model UC600 dishwasher should be extended for six months.

> The enclosed $250 refund cheque demonstrates our desire to satisfy our customers and earn their confidence.

> You will be receiving shortly a new slim Nokia 8860 cell phone to replace the one that shattered when dropped recently.

> Please take your Sanyo cassette tape deck to A-1 Appliance Service, 220 Orange Street, Saskatoon, where it will be repaired at no cost to you.

Occasionally, customers merely want to lodge a complaint and know that something is being done about it. Here's the opening from a bank responding to such a complaint:

> We agree with you completely. Some of our customers have recently spent too much time "on hold" while waiting to speak to a customer service representative. These delays are unacceptable, and we are taking strong measures to eliminate them.

In making an adjustment, avoid sounding resentful or grudging. Once you decide to grant a claim, do so willingly. Remember that a primary goal in adjustments is retaining customer loyalty. Statements that sound reluctant (*Although we generally refuse to extend warranties, we're willing to make an exception in this case*) may cause greater dissatisfaction than no response at all.

*Explaining the Reasons.* In the body of an adjustment letter, your goal is to win back the confidence of the customer. You can do this by explaining what caused the problem (if you know) or by describing the measures you are taking to avoid recurrences of the problem, such as in the following:

**Explain what caused the problem and the measures taken to avoid future recurrence.**

> In preparing our products, we take special care to see that they are wholesome and free of foreign matter. Approved spraying procedures in the field control insects when necessary during the growing season. Our processing plants use screens, air curtains, ultraviolet lights, and other devices to exclude insects. Moreover, we inspect and clean every product to ensure that insects are not present.

Notice that this explanation does not admit error. Many companies sidestep the issue of responsibility because they feel that such an admission damages their credibility or might even encourage legal action. Others admit errors indirectly (*Oversights may sometimes occur*) or even directly (*Once in a while a product that is less than perfect goes out*). The major focus of attention, however, should be on explaining how you are working to prevent recurrence of the problem, as illustrated in the following:

> Waiting "on hold" is as unacceptable to us as it is to you. This delay was brought about when we installed a new automated system. Unfortunately, it took longer than we expected to implement the system and to train our people in their new roles. We are now taking strong measures to eliminate the problem. We have made a significant investment in new technology that will free our customer representatives from routine calls so that they can help you with those banking needs that require personal attention. We are also rerouting calls and modifying the way they are handled.

**Explain what went wrong without admitting liability or making excuses.**

When an explanation poses no threat of admitting liability, provide details. But don't make your explanation sound like an excuse. Customers resent it when organizations don't take responsibility or try to put the blame elsewhere. When Intel Corp. was swamped with a flood of unfavourable responses regarding a flawed Pentium chip, President Andy Grove posted a letter to the Internet. His letter said, "I'd like to comment a bit on the conversations that have been taking place here. First of all, I'm truly sorry for the anxiety created among you by our floating-point issue." He went on to explain how Intel had tested the chip and appointed a group of mathematicians and scientists to study the problem. Eventually, Intel decided to replace all flawed chips. His letter concluded, "Please don't be concerned that the passing of time will deprive you of the opportunity to get your problem resolved. We will stand behind these chips for the life of your computer."[16] The tone of a response is extremely important, and Grove sounded sincere in his explanation.

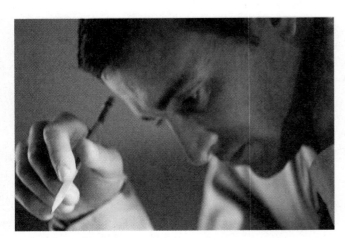

When unhappy customers launch a complaint, 7 of 10 will do business with the company again as long as their concern is handled properly. A staggering 19 of 20 will do business with the company again if the grievance is dealt with swiftly.

***Should You Apologize?*** Another sticky issue is whether to apologize. Notice that Andy Grove of Intel apologized in his Internet letter. Studies of adjustment letters received by consumers show that a majority do contain apologies, either in the opening or in the closing.[17] Many business writing experts, however, advise against apologies, contending that they are counterproductive and merely remind the customer of unpleasantness related to the claim. However, if it seems natural to you to apologize, do so. People like to hear apologies. It raises their self-esteem and shows the humility of the writer.[18] Don't, however, fall back on the familiar phrase, "I'm sorry for any inconvenience we may have caused." It sounds mechanical and totally insincere. Instead try something like this: *We understand the frustration our delay has caused you. We're sorry you didn't receive better service,* or *You're right to be disappointed.* If you feel that an apology is appropriate, do it early and briefly, as Andy Grove did in his Internet response. Remember that the primary focus of your letter is on (1) how you are complying with the request, (2) how the problem occurred, and (3) how you are working to prevent its recurrence.

The language of adjustment letters must be particularly sensitive, since customers are already upset. Here are some don'ts:

Focus on complying with the request, explaining reasons, and preventing recurrence.

- Don't use negative words (*trouble, regret, misunderstanding, fault, error, inconvenience, you claim*).

- Don't blame customers—even when they may be at fault.

- Don't blame individuals or departments within your organization; it's unprofessional.

- Don't make unrealistic promises; you can't guarantee that the situation will never recur.

To regain the confidence of your reader, consider including resale information. Describe a product's features and any special applications that might appeal to the reader. Promote a new product if it seems appropriate.

***Closing an Adjustment Letter.*** To close an adjustment letter, assume that the problem has been resolved and that future business will continue. You might express appreciation that the reader wrote, extend thanks for past business, refer to your desire to be of service, or mention a new product. Here are some effective adjustment letter closings for various purposes:

Close an adjustment letter with appreciation, thanks for past business, desire to be of service, or promotion of new product.

> You were most helpful in informing us of this situation and permitting us to correct it. We appreciate your thoughtfulness in writing to us.

> Thanks for writing. Your satisfaction is important to us. We hope that this refund cheque convinces you that service to our customers is our number one priority. Our goals are to earn your confidence and continue to justify that confidence with quality products and excellent service.

> Your Nokia 8860 cell phone will come in handy when you're playing and working outside this summer. For additional summer enjoyment take a look at the portable MP3 player on page 37 of the enclosed catalogue. We value your business and look forward to your future orders.

The adjustment letter in Figure 9.8 offers to replace dead rose bushes. It's very possible that grower error caused the plants to die, yet the letter doesn't blame the customer. Notice, too, how resale information and sales promotion material are introduced without seeming pushy. Most important, the tone of the letter suggests that the company is in the customer's corner and wants to do what is right.

Although the direct pattern works for many requests and replies, it obviously won't work for every situation. With more practice and experience, you'll be able to alter the pattern and apply the writing process to other communication problems. The following checklist summarizes the process of writing direct replies.

## CHECKLIST FOR WRITING DIRECT REPLIES

## Complying With Requests

✓ **Use a subject line.** Identify previous correspondence and the topic of this letter.

✓ **Open directly.** In the first sentence deliver the information the reader wants (*Yes, I can meet with your class* or *Here is the information you requested*). If the message is mixed, present the best news first.

**FIGURE 9.8** Adjustment Letter

**Rose World**
Beamsville, ON L0R 1B1
1-800-543-2000

June 3, 2005

Mr. James Bronski
68 Wingate Crescent
Richmond Hill, ON L4B 2Y9

Dear Mr. Bronski:

You may choose six rose bushes as replacements, or you may have a full cash refund for the roses you purchased last year.

The quality of our plants and the careful handling they receive assure you of healthy, viable roses for your garden. Even so, plants sometimes fail without apparent cause. That's why every plant carries a guarantee to grow and to establish itself in your garden.

Along with this letter is a copy of our current catalogue for you to select six new roses or reorder the favourites you chose last year. Two of your previous selections—Red Velvet and Rose Princess—were last season's best-selling roses. For fragrance and old-rose charm, you might like to try the new David Austin English Roses. These enormously popular hybrids resulted from crossing full-petalled old garden roses with modern repeat-flowering shrub roses.

To help you enjoy your roses to the fullest, you'll also receive a copy of our authoritative *Home Gardener's Guide to Roses*. This comprehensive booklet provides easy-to-follow planting tips as well as sound advice about sun, soil, and drainage requirements for roses.

To receive your free replacement order, just fill out the order form inside the catalogue and attach the enclosed certificate. Or return the certificate, and you will receive a full refund of the purchase price.

The quality of Rose World plants reflects the expertise of over a century of hybridizing, growing, harvesting, and shipping top-quality garden stock. Your complete satisfaction is our primary goal. If you're not happy, Mr. Bronski, we're not happy. To ensure your satisfaction and your respect, we maintain our 100 percent guarantee policy.

Sincerely,

*Michael Vanderer*

Michael Vanderer
General Manager

mv:meg

Enclosures

*Annotations (left):*
- Tactfully skirts the issue of what caused plant failure
- Offers resale information to assure customer of wise choice
- Projects personal, conversational tone
- Shows pride in the company's products and concern for its customers

*Annotations (right):*
- Approves customer's claim immediately
- Avoids blaming customer
- Includes some sales promotion without overkill
- Tells reader clearly what to do next
- Strives to regain customer's confidence in both products and service

---

✓ **In the body provide explanations and additional information.** Arrange this information logically, perhaps using a list, headings, or columns. For prospective customers build your company image and promote your products.

✓ **End with a cordial, personalized statement.** If further action is required, tell the reader how to proceed and give helpful details.

## Writing Letters of Recommendation

✓ **Open with identifying information.** Name the candidate, identify the position, and explain your relationship. State that you are writing at the request of the candidate and that the letter is confidential.

## *Rocky Mountaineer Railtours Revisited*

Rocky Mountaineer's president, Peter Armstrong, strongly believes in serving customers well. His principles of guest services have been the driving force behind the company's high level of guest satisfaction. Armstrong realizes that his passengers are not looking for cheap, efficient transportation, but rather "a rail experience where the scenery, service, and history are the attractions—more of an enjoyable excursion than a means of transportation."[19]

One aspect of customer satisfaction is the ability of a company to respond quickly and appropriately to customer requests for information, positive feedback, and concerns. While companies enjoy hearing from customers who have enjoyed their services and products, they also understand the importance of responding, in particular, to unhappy customers and, wherever possible, making things right.

Current and prospective guests of Rocky Mountaineer can contact the company directly through its Web site or through more traditional means such as land mail, fax, or phone.

### CRITICAL THINKING

- When customers write to Rocky Mountaineer for information and the response must contain both positive and negative news, what strategy should the respondent follow?
- If a customer writes to complain about something for which Rocky Mountaineer is not responsible (such as the weather), should the response letter contain an apology? Why or why not?
- Why is letter writing an important function for a company like Rocky Mountaineer?

**www.rockymountaineer.com**

---

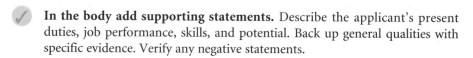

**In the body add supporting statements.** Describe the applicant's present duties, job performance, skills, and potential. Back up general qualities with specific evidence. Verify any negative statements.

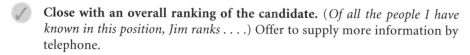

**Close with an overall ranking of the candidate.** (*Of all the people I have known in this position, Jim ranks . . . .*) Offer to supply more information by telephone.

## Granting Claims and Making Adjustments

**Open with approval.** Comply with the customer's claim immediately. Avoid sounding grudging or reluctant.

**In the body win back the customer's confidence.** Explain the cause of the problem or describe your ongoing efforts to avoid such difficulties. Focus on your efforts to satisfy customers. If you apologize, do so early and briefly. Avoid negative words, accusations, and unrealistic promises. Consider including resale and sales promotion information.

**Close positively.** Express appreciation to the customer for writing, extend thanks for past business, anticipate continued patronage, refer to your desire to be of service, and/or mention a new product if it seems appropriate.

Goodwill messages, which include thanks, recognition, and sympathy, seem to intimidate many communicators. Finding the right words to express feelings is sometimes more difficult than writing ordinary business documents. Writers tend to procrastinate when it comes to goodwill messages, or else they send a ready-made card or pick up the telephone. Remember, though, that the personal sentiments of the sender are always more expressive and more meaningful to readers than are printed cards or oral messages. Taking the time to write gives more importance to our well-wishing. Personal notes also provide a record that can be reread, savoured, and treasured.

In expressing thanks, recognition, or sympathy, you should always do so promptly. These messages are easier to write when the situation is fresh in your mind. They also mean more to the recipient. And don't forget that a prompt thank-you note carries the hidden message that you care and that you consider the event to be important. The best goodwill messages—whether thanks, congratulations, praise, or sympathy—concentrate on the five *S*s. These goodwill messages are

- **Selfless.** Be sure to focus the message solely on the receiver not the sender. Don't talk about yourself; avoid such comments as *I remember when I . . . .*

- **Specific.** Personalize the message by mentioning specific incidents or characteristics of the receiver. Telling a colleague *Great speech* is much less effective than *Great story about McDonald's marketing in Moscow.* Take care to verify names and other facts.

- **Sincere.** Let your words show genuine feelings. Rehearse in your mind how you would express the message to the receiver orally. Then transform that conversational language to your written message. Avoid pretentious, formal, or flowery language (*It gives me great pleasure to extend felicitations on the occasion of your firm's 20th anniversary*).

- **Spontaneous.** Keep the message fresh and enthusiastic. Avoid canned phrases (*Congratulations on your promotion, Good luck in the future*). Strive for directness and naturalness, not creative brilliance.

- **Short.** Although goodwill messages can be as long as needed, try to accomplish your purpose in only a few sentences. What is most important is remembering an individual. Such caring does not require documentation or wordiness. Individuals and business organizations often use special note cards or stationery for brief messages.

## Thanks

When someone has done you a favour or when an action merits praise, you need to extend thanks or show appreciation. Letters of appreciation may be written to customers for their orders, to hosts and hostesses for their hospitality, to individuals for kindnesses performed, and especially to customers who complain. After all, complainers are actually providing you with "free consulting reports from the field." Complainers who feel that they were listened to often become the greatest promoters of an organization.[20]

Because the receiver will be pleased to hear from you, you can open directly with the purpose of your message. The letter in Figure 9.9 thanks a speaker who addressed a group of marketing professionals. Although such thank-you notes can be quite short, this one is a little longer because the writer wants to lend importance to the receiver's efforts. Notice that every sentence relates to the receiver and offers enthusiastic praise.

## FIGURE 9.9 Thank-You Letter for a Favour

**Prewriting** *1*

**Analyze:** The purpose of this letter is to express appreciation to a business executive for presenting a talk before professionals.

**Anticipate:** The reader will be more interested in personalized comments than in general statements showing gratitude.

**Adapt:** Because the reader will be pleased, use the direct pattern.

**Writing** *2*

**Research:** Consult notes taken during the talk.

**Organize:** Open directly by giving the reason for writing. Express enthusiastic and sincere thanks. In the body provide specifics. Refer to facts and highlights in the talk. Supply sufficient detail to support your sincere compliments. Conclude with appreciation. Be warm and friendly.

**Compose:** Write the first draft.

**Revising** *3*

**Revise:** Revise for tone and warmth. Use the reader's name. Include concrete detail but do it concisely. Avoid sounding gushy or phony.

**Proofread:** Check the spelling of the receiver's name; verify facts. Check the spelling of *gratitude, patience, advice, persistence,* and *grateful.*

**Evaluate:** Does this letter convey sincere thanks?

---

*Hamilton–Wentworth Chapter*
**North American Marketing Association**
P.O. Box 3598
Hamilton, ON L8V 4X2

March 20, 2005

Mr. Bryant Huffman
Marketing Manager, Western Division
Toys "R" Us, Inc.
2777 Langstaff Avenue
Thornhill, ON L3T 3M8

Dear Bryant:

You have our sincere gratitude for providing the Hamilton-Wentworth chapter of the NAMA with one of the best presentations our group has ever heard. — *Tells purpose and delivers praise*

*Personalizes the message by using specifics rather than generalities* — Your description of the battle Toys "R" Us waged to begin marketing products in Japan was a genuine eye-opener for many of us. Nine years of preparation establishing connections and securing permissions seems an eternity, but obviously such persistence and patience pays off. We now understand better the need to learn local customs and nurture relationships when dealing in Japan.

In addition to your good advice, we particularly enjoyed your sense of humour and jokes—as you must have recognized from the uproarious laughter. What a great routine you do on faulty translations! — *Spotlights the reader's talents*

*Concludes with compliments and thanks* — We're grateful, Bryant, for the entertaining and instructive evening you provided our marketing professionals. Thanks!

Cordially,

*Joyce Barnes*

Joyce Barnes
Program Chair, NAMA

JRB:grw

And, by using the receiver's name along with contractions and positive words, the writer makes the letter sound warm and conversational.

Written notes that show appreciation and express thanks are significant to their receivers. In expressing thanks, you generally write a short note on special notepaper or heavy card stock. The following messages provide models for expressing thanks for a gift, for a favour, and for hospitality.

### To Express Thanks for a Gift

Thanks, Laura, to you and the other members of the department for honouring me with the elegant Waterford crystal vase at the party celebrating my twentieth anniversary with the company.

The height and shape of the vase are perfect to hold roses and other bouquets from my garden. Each time I fill it, I'll remember your thoughtfulness in choosing this lovely gift for me.

**Identify the gift, tell why you appreciate it, and explain how you will use it.**

### To Send Thanks for a Favour

I sincerely appreciate your filling in for me last week when I was too ill to attend the planning committee meeting for the spring exhibition.

Without your participation much of my preparatory work would have been lost. It's comforting to know that competent and generous individuals like you are part of our team, Mark. Moreover, it's my very good fortune to be able to count you as a friend. I'm grateful to you.

**Tell what the favour means using sincere, simple statements.**

### To Extend Thanks for Hospitality

Jeffrey and I want you to know how much we enjoyed the dinner party for our department that you hosted Saturday evening. Your charming home and warm hospitality, along with the lovely dinner and sinfully delicious chocolate dessert, combined to create a truly memorable evening.

Most of all, though, we appreciate your kindness in cultivating togetherness in our department. Thanks, Jennifer, for being such a special person.

**Compliment the fine food, charming surroundings, warm hospitality, excellent host and hostess, and/or good company.**

## Response

Should you respond when you receive a congratulatory note or a written pat on the back? By all means! These messages are attempts to connect personally; they are efforts to reach out, to form professional and/or personal bonds. Failing to respond to notes of congratulations and most other goodwill messages is like failing to say "You're welcome" when someone says "Thank you." Responding to such messages is simply the right thing to do. Do avoid, though, minimizing your achievements with comments that suggest you don't really deserve the praise or that the sender is exaggerating your good qualities.

**Take the time to respond to any goodwill message you may receive.**

### To Answer a Congratulatory Note

Thanks for your kind words regarding my award, and thanks, too, for sending me the newspaper clipping. I truly appreciate your thoughtfulness and warm wishes.

### To Respond to a Pat on the Back

Your note about my work made me feel good. I'm grateful for your thoughtfulness.

## Sympathy

Most of us can bear misfortune and grief more easily when we know that others care. Notes expressing sympathy, though, are probably more difficult to write than any other kind of message. Commercial "In sympathy" cards make the task easier—but they are far less meaningful. Grieving friends want to know what you think—not what Hallmark's card writers think. To help you get started, you can always glance through cards expressing sympathy. They will supply ideas about the kinds of thoughts you might wish to convey in your own words. In writing a sympathy note, (1) refer to the death or misfortune sensitively, using words that show you understand what a crushing blow it is; (2) in the case of a death, praise the deceased in a personal way; (3) offer assistance without going into excessive detail; and (4) end on a reassuring, forward-looking note. Sympathy messages may be typed, although handwriting seems more personal. In either case, use notepaper or personal stationery.

**Sympathy notes should refer to the misfortune sensitively and offer assistance.**

### To Express Condolences

We are deeply saddened, Gayle, to learn of the death of your husband. Warren's kind nature and friendly spirit endeared him to all who knew him. He will be missed.

— Mentions the loss tactfully and recognizes good qualities of the deceased.

Although words seem empty in expressing our grief, we want you to know that your friends at QuadCom extend their profound sympathy to you. If we may help you or lighten your load in any way, you have but to call.

— Assures receiver of your concern. Offers assistance.

We know that the treasured memories of your many happy years together, along with the support of your family and many friends, will provide strength and comfort in the months ahead.

— Concludes on positive, reassuring note.

## CHECKLIST FOR WRITING GOODWILL MESSAGES

## General Guidelines: The Five Ss

✓ **Be selfless.** Discuss the receiver, not the sender.

✓ **Be specific.** Instead of generic statements (*You did a good job*), include special details (*Your marketing strategy to target key customers proved to be outstanding*).

✓ **Be sincere.** Show your honest feelings with conversational, unpretentious language (*We're all very proud of your award*).

✓ **Be spontaneous.** Strive to make the message natural, fresh, and direct. Avoid canned phrases (*If I may be of service, please do not hesitate . . .*).

✓ **Keep the message short.** Remember that, although they may be as long as needed, most goodwill messages are fairly short.

## Giving Thanks

✓ **Cover three points in gift thank-yous.** (1) Identify the gift, (2) tell why you appreciate it, and (3) explain how you will use it.

✓ **Be sincere in sending thanks for a favour.** Tell what the favour means to you. Avoid superlatives and gushiness. Maintain credibility with sincere, simple statements.

✓ **Offer praise in expressing thanks for hospitality.** Compliment, as appropriate, the (1) fine food, (2) charming surroundings, (3) warm hospitality, (4) excellent host and hostess, and (5) good company.

## Answering Congratulatory Messages

✓ **Respond to congratulations.** Send a brief note expressing your appreciation. Tell how good the message made you feel.

✓ **Accept praise gracefully.** Don't make belittling comments (*I'm not really all that good!*) to reduce awkwardness or embarrassment.

## Extending Sympathy

✓ **Refer to the loss or tragedy directly but sensitively.** In the first sentence mention the loss and your personal reaction.

✓ **For deaths, praise the deceased.** Describe positive personal characteristics (*Howard was a forceful but caring leader*).

✓ **Offer assistance.** Suggest your availability, especially if you can do something specific.

✓ **End on a reassuring, positive note.** Perhaps refer to the strength the receiver finds in friends, family, colleagues, or religion.

## WRITING INTERNATIONAL MESSAGES

*9*

International letters should conform to the organizational, format, and cultural conventions of the receiver's country.

The letter-writing suggestions you've just studied work well for correspondence in this country. You may wish, however, to modify the organization, format, and tone of letters going abroad.

Western businesspeople appreciate efficiency, straightforwardness, and conciseness in letters. Moreover, North American business letters tend to be informal and conversational. Correspondents in other countries, however, may look upon such directness and informality as inappropriate, insensitive, and abrasive. Letters in Japan, for example, may begin with deference, humility, and references to nature:

> The season for cherry blossoms is here with us and everybody is beginning to feel refreshed. We sincerely congratulate you on becoming more prosperous in your business.[21]

Chinese letters strive to build relationships. A sales letter might begin with the salutation *Honoured Company*, indicating a high level of respect. While North American business writers use direct requests, Chinese writers are more tentative. For example, a Chinese sales letter might say *I hope you'll take a moment to complete and mail the enclosed application.* The verb *hope* reduces the imposition of a direct request. Avoiding pressure tactics results from the cultural need to show respect and preserve harmony. A typical closing in Chinese letters is *wishing good health*, which emphasizes the importance of showing respect and developing reciprocal relationships.[22]

Letters in Germany commonly start with a long, formal lead-in, such as *Referring to your kind inquiry from the 31st of the month, we take the liberty to remind you with this letter . . . .*[23] Italian business letters may refer to the receiver's family and children. And French correspondents would consider it rude to begin a letter with a request before it is explained. French letters typically include an ending with this phrase (or a variation of it): *I wish to assure you* [insert reader's most formal title] *of my most respectful wishes* [followed by the writer's title and signature].[24] Foreign let-

## *Applying Your Skills at Rocky Mountaineer Railtours*

As a new member of the Guest Services division at Rocky Mountaineer, you have been asked to review and suggest responses to some of the letters received from customers. One customer acknowledges that the service, food, and accommodation were excellent, but her trip was marred by poor weather. Constant rain made it difficult for her to enjoy the scenery to its fullest, and her pictures are not at all satisfactory. In closing, she asks about the possibility of travelling through the Rockies in the winter.

Your supervisor explains that the company cannot guarantee the weather, and it will not be possible to offer this customer any form of compensation (with the possible exception of a free roll of film on her next Rocky Mountaineer trip). She also informs you of a new "winter wonderland" service being offered in December and January.

### Your Task

Respond to all three of the comments in the letter of Diane Gruber, 1968 West Griswold Road, Phoenix, AZ 85051, USA. Although her complaint about the weather is not something the company can control, it can still be addressed. In your response, strive to maintain her goodwill and favourable opinion of Rocky Mountaineer while promoting a second trip.

**www.rockymountaineer.com**

---

ters are also more likely to include passive-voice constructions (*your letter has been received*), exaggerated courtesy (*great pleasure, esteemed favour*), and obvious flattery (*your eminent firm*).[25]

Foreign letters may use different formatting techniques. Whereas North American business letters are typewritten and single-spaced, in other countries they may be handwritten and single- or double-spaced. Address arrangements vary as well, as shown in the following:

**German**
Herr [title, Mr., on first line]
Deiter Woerner [name]
Fritz-Kalle-Strasse 4 [street, house number]
6200 Wiesbaden [postal district, city]
Germany [country]

**Japanese**
Ms. Atsuko Takagi [title, name]
5-12 Koyo-cho 4 chome [street, house number]
Higashinada-ku [city]
Tokyo 194 [prefecture, postal district]
Japan [country]

Dates and numbers can be particularly confusing, as shown here:

**Canadian**
June 3, 2005
6/3/05
CDN$5 320.00

**Some European Countries**
3rd of June 2005
3.6.05
CDN$5.320,00

To be safe, spell out the names of months instead of using figures. Verify sums of money and identify the currency unit.

Because the placement and arrangement of letter addresses and closing lines vary greatly, you should always research local preferences before writing. For important letters going abroad, it's also wise to have someone familiar with local customs read and revise the message. One graduate student learned this lesson when she wrote a letter, in French, to a Paris museum asking for permission to do research. She received no response. Before writing a second time, she took the letter to her French tutor. "No, no, mademoiselle! It will never do! It must be more respectful. You must be very careful of individuals' titles. Let me show you!" The second letter won the desired permission.

## SUMMARY OF LEARNING OBJECTIVES

*1* **List three characteristics of good letters and describe the direct pattern for organizing letters.** Good letters are characterized by clear content, a tone of goodwill, and correct form. Letters carrying positive or neutral messages should be organized directly. That means introducing the main idea (the purpose for writing) immediately in the opening. The body of the letter explains and gives details. Letters that make requests close by telling what action is desired and establishing a deadline (end date) for that action.

*2* **Write letters requesting information and action.** The opening immediately states the purpose of the letter, perhaps asking a question. The body explains and justifies the request. The closing tells the reader courteously what to do and shows appreciation.

*3* **Write letters placing orders.** The opening introduces the order and authorizes a purchase (*Please send me the following items . . .*). The body lists the desired items including quantity, order number, description, unit price, and total price. The closing describes the method of payment, tells when the merchandise should be sent, and expresses appreciation.

*4* **Write letters making claims.** The opening describes the problem clearly or tells what action is to be taken. The body explains and justifies the request without anger or emotion. The closing, which might include an end date, describes the desired action.

*5* **Write letters complying with requests.** A subject line identifies previous correspondence, while the opening immediately delivers the good news. The body explains and provides additional information. The closing is cordial and personalized.

*6* **Write letters of recommendation.** The opening identifies the candidate, the position, your relationship, and the confidentiality of the letter. The body describes the candidate's job duties, performance, skills, and potential. The closing provides an overall ranking of the candidate and offers to give additional information by telephone.

**7** **Write letters granting claims and making adjustments.** The opening immediately grants the claim without sounding grudging. To regain the confidence of the customer, the body may explain what went wrong and how the problem will be rectified. However, it may avoid accepting responsibility for any problems. The closing expresses appreciation, extends thanks for past business, refers to a desire to be of service, and/or mentions a new product. An apology is optional.

**8** **Write goodwill messages.** Goodwill messages deliver thanks, praise, or sympathy. They should be selfless, specific, sincere, spontaneous, and short. Gift thank-yous should identify the gift, tell why you appreciate it, and explain how you will use it. Thank-yous for favours should tell, without gushing, what they mean to you. Expressions of sympathy should mention the loss tactfully; recognize good qualities in the deceased (in the case of a death); offer assistance; and conclude on a positive, reassuring note.

**9** **Modify international letters to accommodate other cultures.** Letters going to individuals in some areas, such as Japan and Europe, should probably use a less direct organizational pattern and be more formal in tone. They should also be adapted to appropriate regional letter formats.

# CHAPTER REVIEW

1. What is goodwill? Briefly describe five ways to develop goodwill in a letter. (Obj. 1)

2. Why is it best to write most business letters "backwards"? (Obj. 1)

3. What kind of questions elicit the most information? Give an example. (Obj. 2)

4. Why is the direct letter strategy appropriate for most business messages? (Obj. 2)

5. For order letters what information goes in the opening? In the body? In the closing? (Obj. 3)

6. What is a claim? (Obj. 4)

7. Why are most companies today particularly interested in listening to customers? (Obj. 4)

8. In complying with requests, why is it especially important that all facts are correct in letters written on company stationery? (Obj. 5)

9. When answering many questions for a customer, how can the information be grouped to improve readability? (Obj. 5)

10. What information should the opening of a letter of recommendation contain? (Obj. 6)

11. What is an appropriate salutation for a letter of recommendation when the candidate has no specific position in mind? (Obj. 6)

12. What are a writer's three goals for adjustment letters? (Obj. 7)

13. Name four things to avoid in adjustment letters. (Obj. 7)

14. Name five characteristics of goodwill messages. (Obj. 8)

15. Name three elements of business letters going abroad that might be modified to accommodate readers from other cultures. (Obj. 9)

# CRITICAL THINKING

1. What's wrong with using the indirect pattern for writing routine requests and replies? If in the end the reader understands the message, why make a big fuss over the organization? (Obj. 1)

273

2. Is it insensitive to include resale or sales promotion information in an adjustment letter? Why or why not? (Obj. 7)

3. Why is it important to regain the confidence of a customer in an adjustment letter? How can it be done? (Obj. 7)

4. How are North American business letters different from those written in other countries? Why do you suppose this is so? (Obj. 9)

5. **Ethical Issue:** Let's say you've drafted a letter to a customer in which you apologize for the way the customer's account was fouled up by the accounting department. You show the letter to your boss, and she instructs you to remove the apology. It admits responsibility, she says, and the company cannot allow itself to be held liable. You're not a lawyer, but you can't see the harm in a simple apology. What should you do? Refer to the section "Tools for Doing the Right Thing" on page 31 in Chapter 1 to review the five questions you might ask yourself in trying to do the right thing.

# ACTIVITIES

## 9.1 Direct Openings (Objs. 1–8)

**Your Task.** Revise the following openings so that they are more direct. Add information if necessary.

a. Please allow me to introduce myself. I am Christie Montgomery, and I am assistant to the director of Human Resources at MicroSynergy. Our company has an intranet, which we would like to use more efficiently to elicit feedback on employee issues and concerns. I understand that you have a software product called "Opinionware" that might do this, and I need to ask you some questions about it.

b. Because I've lost your order blank, I have to write this letter. I hope that it's all right to place an order this way. I am interested in ordering a number of things from your summer catalogue, which I still have although the order blank is missing.

c. Pursuant to your letter of January 15, I am writing in regard to your inquiry about whether or not we offer our European-style patio umbrella in colours. This unique umbrella receives a number of inquiries. Its 3-m canopy protects you when the sun is directly overhead, but it also swivels and tilts to virtually any angle for continuous sun protection all day long. It comes in two colours: off-white and forest green.

d. Your letter of March 21, which was originally sent to *Mountain Bike Action*, has been referred to my desk for response. In your letter you inquire about the mountain bike featured on the cover of the magazine in April. That particular bike is a Series 70 Paramount and is manufactured by Schwinn.

e. I am pleased to receive your inquiry regarding the possibility of my acting as a speaker at the final semester meeting of your business management club on April 30. The topic of online résumés interests me and is one on which I think I could impart helpful information to your members. Therefore, I am responding in the affirmative to your kind invitation.

f. Thank you for your recent order of November 2. We are sure you will enjoy the low-profile, brushed-cotton ball caps that you ordered from our spring catalogue. Your order is currently being processed and should leave our production facility in Montreal early next week. We use UPS for all deliveries in Ontario. Because you ordered caps with your logo embroidered in a two-tone combination, your order cannot be shipped until November 12. You should not expect it until November 15.

g. We have just received your letter of March 12 regarding the unfortunate troubles you are having with your Magnum videocassette recorder. In your letter you ask if you may send the flawed VCR to us for inspection. Although we normally handle all service requests through our local dealers, in your circumstance we are willing to take a look at your unit here at our St. Catharines plant. Therefore, please send it to us so that we may determine what's wrong.

## 9.2 Subject Lines (Objs. 1–8)

**Your Task.** Write efficient subject lines for each of the messages in Activity 9.1. Add dates and other information if necessary.

## 9.3 Letter Formatting (Obj. 1)

**Your Task.** On a sheet of paper draw two rectangles about 10 cm by 15 cm. Within these rectangles show where the major parts of letters go: letterhead, dateline, inside address, salutation, body, complimentary close, signature, and author's name. Use lines to show how much space each part would occupy. Illustrate two different letter styles, such as block and personal business style. Be prepared to discuss your drawings. Consult Appendix B for format guidelines.

## 9.4 Document for Analysis: Information Request (Obj. 2)

**Your Task.** Analyze the following letter. List its weaknesses. If your instructor directs, revise the letter.

Dear Sir:

I am a new member of the Corporate Travel Department of my company, QuadCom, and I have been assigned the task of writing to you to inquire about our next sales meeting. We would like to find a resort with conference facilities, which is why I am writing.

We are interested in banquet facilities where we can all be together, but we will also need at least four smaller meeting rooms. Each of these rooms should accommodate about 75. We hope to arrange our conference August 4 through August 9, and we expect about 250 sales associates. Most of our associates will be flying in so I'm interested in what airport is closest and transportation to and from the airport.

Does your hotel have public address systems in the meeting rooms? How about audio-visual equipment and computer facilities for presentations? Thank you for any information you can provide.

Sincerely,

## 9.5 Document for Analysis: Claim Request (Obj. 4)

**Your Task.** Analyze the following letter. List its weaknesses. If your instructor directs, revise the letter.

*X Poorly Written Letter*

Dear Customer Service Manager Kent Fowler:

This is to inform you that you can't have it both ways. Either you provide customers with cars with full gas tanks or you don't. And if you don't, you shouldn't charge them when they return with empty tanks!

In view of the fact that I picked up a car in Fredericton August 22 with an empty tank, I had to fill it immediately. Then I drove it until August 25. When I returned to Wolfville, I naturally let the tank go nearly empty, since that is the way I received the car in Fredericton.

But your attendant in Wolfville charged me to fill the tank—$26.50 (premium gasoline at premium prices)! Although I explained to him that I had received it with an empty tank, he kept telling me that company policy required that he charge for a fill-up. My total bill came to $266.50, which, you must agree, is a lot of money for a rental period of only three days. I have the signed rental agreement and a receipt showing that I paid the full amount and that it included $26.50 for a gas fill-up when I returned the car.

Inasmuch as my company is a new customer and inasmuch as we had hoped to use your agency for our future car rentals because of your competitive rates, I trust that you will give this matter your prompt attention.

Disappointedly yours,

## 9.6 Document for Analysis: Favourable Adjustment (Obj. 7)

**Your Task.** Analyze the following letter. List its weaknesses. If your instructor directs, revise the letter.

*X Poorly Written Letter*

Dear Mr. Yoder:

I have before me your letter in which you complain about a missing shipment. May I suggest that it is very difficult for us to deliver merchandise when we have been given an erroneous address.

Our investigators made an investigation of your problem shipment and arrived at the determination that it was sent immediately after we received the order. According to the shipper's records, it was delivered to the warehouse address given on your stationery: 3590 University Avenue, Toronto, ON M5X 7S7. Unfortunately, no one at that address would accept delivery, so the shipment was returned to us. I see from your current stationery that your company has a new address: 2293 Bay Street, Toronto, ON M5V 7J3. With the proper address, we probably could have delivered this shipment.

When an order cannot be delivered, we usually try to verify the shipping address by telephoning the customer. Apparently, we could not find you.

Although we feel that it is entirely appropriate and right to charge you shipping and restocking fees, as is our standard practice on returned goods, in this instance we will waive those fees. We hope this second shipment finally catches up with you.

Sincerely,

## 9.7 Information Request: Touring Europe on a Shoestring (Obj. 2)

You just saw a great TV program about cheap travel in Europe, and you think you'd like to try it next summer. The program described how some people want to get away from it all; others want to see a little of the world. Some want to learn a different language; some want to soak up a bit of culture. The "get-away" group, the program advised, should book a package trip to a Contiki resort where they relax and soak up the sun. But "culture vultures" and FITs (frequent independent travellers) should select the countries they want to

275

visit and plan their own trips. You decide to visit France, Spain, and Portugal (or any other countries you select).

Begin planning your trip by gathering information from the country's tourist office. Many details need to be worked out. What about visas? How about inoculations? Since your budget will be limited, you need to stay in youth hostels whenever possible. Where are they? Are they private? Some hostels accept only people who belong to their organization. You really need to get your hands on a list of hostels for every country before departure. You are also interested in any special transport passes for students, such as a Eurail Pass. And while you are at it, find out whether they have any special guides for student travellers.

**Your Task.** Most of this specific information is not available at the country's tourist Web site. Thus, you must write a letter requesting information. Address your inquiry to Maison de la France, 1981 av. McGill College, Suite 490, Montreal, QC H3A 2W9, e-mail <mfrance@attcanada.net>, or access <**www.franceguide.com**>. If you prefer another country, find its tourist office address. Because this is a personal business letter, include your return address above the date. See Appendix B.

## 9.8 Information Request: Reducing Junk Mail (Obj. 2)

As editor of your company newsletter, you have a bright idea. On the radio you heard the tail end of an announcement about reducing the amount of direct-mail advertising (junk mail) that people receive. You think you heard that people can write to the Canadian Direct Marketing Association and request that their names be removed from direct-mail lists. This would make a good article for your newsletter. Nearly everyone hates junk mail. Because you believe that a written request will receive a better response, you decide to write a letter to the Canadian Direct Marketing Association. You have many questions. You are curious about who sponsors this program. You wonder why the association would support a program to reduce direct-mail advertising. How could this program possibly serve its members? You need to know what to tell your readers about how the program works. It occurs to you that your employees might also be interested in how to reduce calls from telephone marketers.

**Your Task.** Write to the Mail Preference Service, Canadian Direct Marketing Association, Suite 800, 840 6th Avenue SW, Calgary, AB T2P 3E5. Use your imagination to develop a good list of questions so that you can write an interesting and helpful article for *The Inside Scoop*, your company newsletter. You'd like a reply within three weeks to meet your next newsletter deadline. How should the CDMA respond to your letter? Call you? Send an e-mail? Write a letter? Since you don't have the name of an individual to address, you can either use "Greetings" or "Dear Canadian Direct Marketing Association" as your salutation.

## 9.9 Information Request: Las Vegas Meeting at the Fabulous Mandalay Bay (Obj. 2)

Your company, Software.com, has just had an enormously successful two-year sales period. CEO Ryan Wayburn has asked you, as marketing manager, to arrange a fabulous conference/retreat. "This will be a giant thank-you gift for all 75 of our engineers, product managers, and salespeople," he says. Warming up to the idea, he says, "I want the company to host a four-day combination sales conference/vacation/retreat at some spectacular location. Let's begin by inquiring at the new Mandalay Bay Resort and Casino in Las Vegas. I heard that it's awesome!" You check its Web site and find some general information. However, you decide to write a letter so that you can have a permanent, formal record of all the resorts you investigate. You estimate that your company will require about 75 rooms. You'll also need about three conference rooms for one and a half days. You want to know room rates, conference facilities, and entertainment possibilities for families. The CEO gave you two possible times: July 18–22 or August 4–8. You know that these are off-peak times, and you wonder whether you can get a good room rate. What entertainment will be showing at the Mandalay Bay during these times? One evening the CEO will want to host a banquet for about 140 people. Oh yes, he wants a report from you by April 1.

**Your Task.** Write a well-organized information request to Ms. Carol Mintus, Manager, Convention Services, Mandalay Bay Resort and Casino, 240 Mandalay Bay Drive, Las Vegas, NV 87550. Spell out your needs and conclude with a logical end date.

## 9.10 Information Request: Computer Code of Conduct (Obj. 2)

**WEB**

As an assistant in the campus computer laboratory, you have been asked by your boss to help write a code of conduct for use of the laboratory facilities. This code will spell out what behaviour and activities are allowed in your lab. The first thing you are to do is conduct a search of the Internet to see what other college or university computing labs have written as conduct codes.

**Your Task.** Using at least two search engines, search the Web employing variations of the keywords "computer code of conduct." Print two or three codes that seem appropriate. Write a letter (or an e-mail message, if your instructor agrees) to the director of an educational computer laboratory asking for further information about its code and its effectiveness. Include at least five significant questions. Attach your printouts to your letter.

## 9.11 Information Request: Backpacking Cuisine (Obj. 2)

Assume that you are Benjamin Spring, manager of a health spa and also an ardent backpacker. You are organizing a group of hikers for a wilderness trip to northern Manitoba. One item that must be provided is freeze-dried food for the three-week trip. You are unhappy with the taste and quality of backpacking food products currently available. You expect to have a group of hikers who are older, affluent, and natural-food enthusiasts. Some are concerned about products containing preservatives, sugar, and additives. Others are on diets restricting cholesterol, fat, and salt.

You heard that Outfitters, Inc., offers a new line of freeze-dried products. You want to know what they offer and whether they have sufficient variety to serve all the needs of your group. You need to know where their products can be purchased and what the cost range is. You'd also like to try a few of their items before placing a large order. You are interested in how they produce the food products and what kinds of ingredients they use. If you have any items left over, you wonder how long they can be kept and still be usable.

**Your Task.** Write an information request letter to Tia Osborne, Outfitters, Inc., 2380 Westside Drive, Vancouver, BC V6P 1W8.

## 9.12 Information Request: Online Microbrewery (Obj. 2)

Play the part of brewmaster Carol Fischer, owner of Crystal Ale Microbrewery, 147 Ruby Lane, St. John's, NL A1G 1P9. Your Crystal Ale beers have won local taste awards. However, sales are dismal, perhaps because your beer is pricier than mass-produced beers and because you have a meagre advertising and sales budget.

Then you hear about MicroBeer Online, a service that sells microbrewed beer via the World Wide Web. When you visit the Web site, you find descriptions of beer from many microbreweries, along with ratings for each beer. An order page enables customers to order beer directly from the Web site.

You wonder if you might sell your beer via MicroBeer Online, but you're not exactly sure how the service works. For example, who writes the product descriptions, and who rates the beer? Furthermore, because you offer some seasonal varieties of Crystal Ale, you are concerned about being able to change the selection of beer offered on the service. Of course, you also need to know the specifics of working with MicroBeer Online. For example, how much does it cost to sell online? In addition, since Crystal Ale badly needs customers, you would like to know how many customers Crystal Ale might gain through MicroBeer Online. You have many questions! You could e-mail Mr. Fahlk, but you prefer a paper copy as a permanent record of the correspondence.

**Your Task.** Write a letter to Peter Fahlk, Webmaster, MicroBeer Online, 22050 Ontario Street, Lennoxville, QC J1M 1Z7. Provide an end date and a logical reason for it.

## 9.13 Order Letter: Camera Jumble (Obj. 3)

**Your Task.** Study the following ineffective request for merchandise. Revise the letter and place your return address above the date. Send the letter to Cameratone, Inc., 200 Main Street, Mississauga, ON L5B 3X3. Add any necessary information.

✗ *Poorly Written Letter*

Dear Sir:

I saw a number of items in your summer/fall catalogue that would fit my Lentax ME camera. I am particularly interested in your Super Zoom 55-200-mm lens. Its number is SF39971, and it costs $139.95. To go with this lens I will need a polarizing filter. Its number is SF29032 and costs $22.95 and should fit a 52-mm lens. Also include a 05CC magenta filter for a 52-mm lens. That number is SF29036 and it costs $9.95. Please send also a Hikemaster camera case for $24.95. Its number is SF29355.

I am interested in having these items charged to my credit card. I'd sure like to get them quickly because my vacation starts soon.

Sincerely,

## 9.14 Order Letter: Office Supplies to Go (Obj. 3)

You are Hector Rivera, manager, Lasertronics, Inc., 627 Nordstrum Road, Lethbridge, AB T1R 3L5. You want to order some items from an office supply catalogue, but your catalogue is a year old and you have lost the order form. Because you're in a hurry, you decide to place a fax order. Rather than write for a new catalogue, you decide to take a chance and order items from the old catalogue, realizing that prices may be somewhat different. You want three Panasonic electric pencil sharpeners, Item 22-A, at $19.95 each. You want one steel desktop organizer, 1.5 m long, Item No. 23-K. Its price is $117.50. Order two Roll-a-Flex files for 5- by 10-cm cards at $14.50 each. This is Item 23-G. The next item is No. 29-H, file folders, box of 100, letter size, at $5.29. You need ten boxes. You would like to be invoiced for this purchase, and you prefer UPS delivery. Even though the prices may be somewhat higher, you decide to list the prices shown in your catalogue so that you have an idea of what the total order will cost.

**Your Task.** Write a letter to Monarch Discount Office Furniture, 2890 Monarch Road, Lethbridge, Alberta T1K 1L6. Between the date and the inside address, type TRANSMITTED BY FAX.

## 9.15 Direct Claim: Free Samples Are Surprisingly Costly (Obj. 4)

As marketing manager of Advantage, you are ticked off at Quantum Enterprises. Quantum is a catalogue company that provides imprinted promotional products for companies. Your travel company was looking for something special to offer in promoting its cruise ship travel packages. Quantum offered free samples of its promotional merchandise, under its "No Surprise" policy.

You figured, what could you lose? So on January 11 you placed a telephone order for a number of samples. These included three kinds of jumbo tote bags, a square-ended barrel bag with fanny pack, as well as a deluxe canvas attaché case and two colours of garment-dyed sweatshirts. All items were supposed to be free. You did think it odd that you were asked for your company's MasterCard number, but Quantum promised to bill you only if you kept the samples.

When the items arrived, you were not pleased, and you returned them all on January 21 (you have a postal receipt showing the return). But your February credit card statement showed a charge of $239.58 for the sample items. You called Quantum in February and spoke to Diane, who assured you that a credit would appear on your next statement. However, your March statement showed no credit. You called again and received a similar promise. It's now April and no credit has been received. You decide to write and demand action. **Your Task.** Write a claim letter that documents the problem and states the action that you want taken. Add any information you feel is necessary. Address your letter to Ms. Cheryl Butler, Customer Services, Quantum Enterprises, 7024 Glover Road, Langley, BC V2Y 2R1.

## 9.16 Direct Claim: Deep Desk Disappointment (Obj. 4)

Assume that you are Monica Keil, president, Keil Consulting Services, 9802 Founders Drive, Antigonish, NS B2G 1C0. Since your consulting firm was doing very well, you decided to splurge and purchase a fine executive desk for your own office. You ordered an expensive desk described as "North American white oak embellished with hand-inlaid walnut cross-banding." Although you would not ordinarily purchase large, expensive items by mail, you were impressed by the description of this desk and by the money-back guarantee promised in the catalogue.

When the desk arrived, you knew that you had made a mistake. The wood finish was rough, the grain looked splotchy, and many of the drawers would not pull out easily. The advertisement had promised "full suspension, silent ball-bearing drawer slides."
**Your Task.** Because you are disappointed with the desk, you decide to send it back, taking advantage of the money-back

guarantee. Write a letter to Rodney Harding, Marketing Manager, Harbourview Wood Products, 49 Harbourview Drive, Sydney, NS B1S 2A8, asking for your money back. You're not sure whether the freight charges can be refunded, but it's worth a try. Supply any details needed.

## 9.17 Direct Claim: Earth First Runs Dry (Obj. 4)

Assume that you are Megan Phillips, public relations assistant for a grassroots environmental organization, Earth First, 1971 Bowler Drive, Pickering, ON L1V 3K3. You are responsible for printing 250 flyers for an upcoming Earth First rally, but the ink cartridges for your two Stellar printers aren't working properly. Although the cartridges are clearly full, no ink is dispensed. When you tried to return the faulty cartridges to your local office supply store, The Office Centre, the store refused to take them because you had purchased the cartridges more than 30 days ago.

On the advice of the store manager, you purchase two new cartridges that enable you to print your flyers on time. However, you are frustrated about spending Earth First's meagre funds on faulty equipment. The store manager said that many customers recently had returned Stellar ink cartridges. You hope Stellar isn't losing its commitment to quality. After all, you are particularly fond of Stellar ink cartridges, since they are the only cartridges on the market that use environmentally safe soy-based ink. Decide what will resolve your complaint: a cash refund of $126.50, replacement cartridges, or some other action.
**Your Task.** Send a claim letter, the cartridges, and a copy of your receipt to Stellar Printers, 1110 Birchmount Road, Toronto, ON M1K 5G4.

## 9.18 Direct Claim: Undersized French Doors (Obj. 4)

As Julie Chen, owner of Smart Interiors, you recently completed a kitchen remodel that required double-glazed, made-to-order oak French doors. You ordered them, by telephone, on July 2 from Custom Wood, Inc. When they arrived on July 25, your carpenter gave you the bad news: The doors were cut too small. Instead of measuring a total of 3.5 m, the doors measured 3.4 m. In your carpenter's words, "No way can I stretch those doors to fit these openings!" You waited three weeks for these doors, and your clients wanted them installed immediately. Your carpenter said, "I can rebuild this opening for you, but I'm going to have to charge you for my time." His extra charge came to $455.50.

You feel that the people at Custom Wood should reimburse you for this amount since it was their error. In fact, you actually saved them a bundle of money by not returning the doors. You decide to write to Custom Wood and enclose a copy of your carpenter's bill. You wonder whether you should also include a copy of Custom Wood's invoice, even though it does not show the exact door measurements. You are a good customer of Custom Wood, having used their quality doors and windows on many other jobs. You're confident that it will grant this claim.

**Your Task.** Write a claim letter to Jay Brandt, Marketing Manager, Custom Wood, Inc., 17 Portsmouth Close, St. John's, NL A1N 3Y1.

## 9.19 Direct Claim: The Real Thing (Obj. 4)

Let's face it. Like most consumers, you've probably occasionally been unhappy with service or with a product you have used.

**Your Task.** Select a product or service that has disappointed you. Write a claim letter requesting a refund, replacement, explanation, or whatever seems reasonable. Generally, such letters are addressed to customer service departments. For claims about food products, be sure to include bar-code identification from the package, if possible. Your instructor may ask you to actually mail this letter. Remember that smart companies want to know what their customers think, especially if a product could be improved. Give your ideas for improvement. When you receive a response, share it with your class.

## 9.20 Direct Reply: River Rafting on the Web (Obj. 5)

WEB

As the program chair for the campus Ski Club, you have been asked by the president to investigate river rafting. The Ski Club is an active organization, and its members want to schedule a summer activity. A majority favoured rafting. Search the Web for relevant information. Select five of the most promising Web sites offering rafting. If possible, print copies of your findings.

**Your Task.** Summarize your findings in a memo to Brian Krauss, Ski Club president. The next meeting of the Ski Club is May 8, but you think it would be a good idea if you could discuss your findings with Brian before the meeting.

## 9.21 Direct Reply: McDonald's Goes Green (Obj. 5)

TEAM

Diane LaSala, director of Customer Service for McDonald's Corporation, has received a letter from Sandi Escalante, an environmentalist. Ms. Escalante wants to know what McDonald's is doing to reduce the huge amounts of waste products that its restaurants generate. She argues that these wastes not only deplete world resources but also clog our already overburdened landfills. Diane LaSala thinks that this is a good opportunity for her student interns to sharpen their reasoning and writing skills on the job. She asks you and the other interns to draft a response to the inquiry telling how McDonald's is cleaning up its act. Here are some of the facts that Diane supplies your group.

Actually, McDonald's has been quite active in its environmental efforts. Working with the Environmental Defense Fund, McDonald's has initiated a series of 42 resolutions that are cutting by more than 80 percent the huge waste stream from its 12 000 restaurants. McDonald's efforts meant making changes in packaging, increasing its recycling campaign, trying more composting, and retraining employees.

McDonald's was one of the food industry leaders in abandoning the polystyrene "clamshell" box for hamburgers and sandwiches. Formerly using an average of 9 kg of polystyrene a day per restaurant, McDonald's now uses only 10 percent of that figure. McDonald's suppliers have been asked to use corrugated boxes that contain at least 35 percent recycled content. Moreover, suppliers will be asked to make regular reports to McDonald's that measure their progress in reaching new waste-reduction goals. Other environmental efforts include testing a starch-based material in consumer cutlery to replace plastic forks, knives, and spoons. Many restaurants have also begun trial composting of eggshells, coffee grounds, and food scraps. McDonald's is also starting a nationwide program for recycling corrugated boxes. In addition, the company is testing reusable salad lids and shipping pallets, pump-style bulk dispensers for condiments, and refillable coffee mugs.

McDonald's has retrained its restaurant crews to give waste reduction equal weight with other priorities, such as quickness, cleanliness, and quality service. The company is trying to reduce the waste both behind the counter (which accounts for 80 percent of the total waste) and over the counter.[26]

**Your Task.** Prepare a letter that can be used for similar inquiries. To promote goodwill, you might wish to throw in a few coupons for free sandwiches. Send this letter to Sandi Escalante, 1762 Evergreen Road, Waterloo, ON M2A 3G6.

## 9.22 Direct Reply: Scannable Résumés (Obj. 5)

WEB    TEAM    CRITICAL THINKING

You've worked at MegaTech for a couple of years. It's a great place to work, and it receives many letters from job applicants. Some of them inquire about the company's résumé-scanning techniques. You generally send out the following letter, which has been in the files for some time.

Dear Sir or Madam:

Your letter of April 11 has been referred to me for a response. We are pleased to learn that you are considering employment here at MegaTech, and we look forward to receiving your résumé, should you decide to send same to us.

You ask if we scan incoming résumés. Yes, we certainly do. Actually, we use SmartTrack, an automated résumé-tracking system. SmartTrack is terrific! We sometimes receive as many as 300 résumés a day, and SmartTrack helps us sort, screen, filter, and separate the résumés. It also processes them, helps us organize them, and keeps a record of all of these résumés. Some of the résumés, however, cannot be scanned, so we have to return those—if we have time.

The reasons that résumés won't scan may surprise you. Some applicants send photocopies or faxed copies, and these can cause misreading, so don't do it. The best plan is to send an original copy. Some people use coloured paper. Big mistake! White paper (Letter-sized) printed on one side is the best bet. Another big problem is unusual type fonts, such as script or fancy gothic or antique fonts. They don't seem to realize that scanners do best with plain, readable fonts such as Helvetica or Universe in a 10- to 14-point size.

Other problems occur when applicants use graphics, shading, italics, underlining, horizontal and vertical lines, parentheses, and brackets. Scanners like plain "vanilla" résumés! Oh yes, staples can cause misreading. And folding of a résumé can also cause the scanners to foul up. To be safe, don't staple or fold, and be sure to use wide margins and a quality printer.

When a hiring manager within MegaTech decides to look for an appropriate candidate, he is told to submit keywords to describe the candidate he has in mind for his opening. We tell him (or sometimes her) to zero in on nouns and phrases that best describe what they want. Thus, my advice to you is to try to include those words that highlight your technical and professional areas of expertise.

If you do decide to submit your résumé to MegaTech, be sure you don't make any of the mistakes described herein that would cause the scanner to misread it.

Sincerely,

**Your Task.** Your boss saw this letter one day and thought it was miserable. She asks you and your team to produce an informative and effective letter that can be sent to anyone who inquires. Discuss how this letter could be improved. Decide what information is necessary to send to potential job applicants. Use the Web to search for additional information that might be helpful. Individually or as a team, develop a better letter. Address your first letter to Mr. Michael Madzar, 1101 Copeland Street, Winnipeg, MB R2C 3H8.

## 9.23 Direct Reply: Tell Me About Your Major (Obj. 5)

A friend in a distant city is considering moving to your area for more education and training in your field. This individual wants to know about your program of study.

**Your Task.** Write a letter describing a program in your field (or any field you wish to describe). What courses must be taken? Toward what degree-diploma, certificate, or employment position does this program lead? Why did you choose it? Would you recommend this program to your friend? How long does it take? Add any information you feel would be helpful.

## 9.24 Direct Reply: Backpacking Cuisine (Obj. 5)

As Tia Osborne, owner of Outfitters, Inc., producer of freeze-dried backpacking foods, answer the inquiry of Benjamin Spring (described in Activity 9.11). You are eager to have Mr. Spring sample your new all-natural line of products containing no preservatives, sugar, or additives. You want him to know that you started this company two years ago after you found yourself making custom meals for discerning backpackers who rejected typical camping fare. Some of your menu items are excellent for individuals on restricted diets. Some dinners are cholesterol-, fat-, and salt-free, but he'll have to look at your list to see for himself.

You will send him your complete list of dinner items and the suggested retail prices. You will also send him a sample "Saturday Night on the Trail," a four-course meal that comes with fruit candies and elegant appetizers. All your food products are made from choice ingredients in sanitary kitchens that you personally supervise. They are flash-frozen in a new vacuum process that you patented. Although your dried foods are meant to last for years, you don't recommend that they be kept beyond 18 months because they may deteriorate. This could happen if a package were punctured or if the products became overheated.

**Your Task.** Your products are currently available at Glen Elm Sports Centre, 14003 12th Avenue S, Regina, SK S4N 0M6. Large orders may be placed directly with you. You offer a 5-percent discount on direct orders. Write a response to Benjamin Spring, 2631 28th Avenue, Regina, SK S4S 6X3.

## 9.25 Direct Reply: MicroBeer Online (Obj. 5)

As Peter Fahlk, webmaster for MicroBeer Online, respond to a letter from a potential customer, microbrewer Carol Fischer (see Activity 9.12). In addition to answering Ms. Fischer's questions, you hope to gain her company, Crystal Ale Microbrewery, as a new customer by highlighting the benefits of MicroBeer Online. Of course, you want to clarify for Ms. Fischer that MicroBeer Online doesn't brew beer; it simply advertises and collects orders on its Web site. Orders are then forwarded to microbrewers, who fill the orders, ship the product to the consumer, and fork over 4 percent of online sales receipts to MicroBeer. (The fee of 4 percent of sales is well under the amount allocated for advertising in most company budgets.)

Although you can't predict how many customers each brewer will gain through MicroBeer Online, you do know that the service reaches thousands of consumers a day, 365 days a year, 24 hours a day. Small brewers appreciate MicroBeer Online because it brings in orders while brewers concentrate on brewing their specialty beers. Furthermore, by cutting out intermediaries and reducing distribution costs, MicroBeer Online enables brewers to maintain reasonable beer prices. Consumers particularly appreciate MicroBeer's product write-ups and beer ratings by Ted Groebles, a well-known brew-master. However, since Groebles is able to review only a reasonable number of beers at a time, MicroBeer limits its service to 50 breweries and about 250 beers. Brewers may sell up to five beers on the service, and the beers may change seasonally.

It is very inexpensive for MicroBeer to run its Web site; the cost of setting up the Web site was less than the cost of four half-page ads in a major newspaper. Gaining new customers, however, hasn't been easy, so MicroBeer now offers short-term contracts to brewers new to the service. Brewers may call you personally at (517) 756-1456 for more information.

**Your Task.** Write to Carol Fischer, Crystal Ale Microbrewery, 147 Ruby Lane, St. John's, NL A1G 1P9. Answer the questions in her inquiry (Activity 9.12). Along with your reply, send her your brochure "MicroBeer Online."

## 9.26 Direct Reply: Avoiding Employee Gifts That Become Doorstops (Obj. 5)

### INFOTRAC

A friend of yours, Megan Stowe, is an executive with a large insurance company. One day you see her at a software conference, and afterward you decide to have cappuccino together at a nearby cafe. After the usual small talk, she says, "You know, I'm beginning to hate the holidays. Every year it gets harder and harder to choose presents for our staff. Once we gave fruitcakes, which I thought were excellent, but it turns out that some people used them for doorstops." As an executive training coach, you say, "Well, what is your gift goal? Do you want to encourage your employees? Are you just saying thanks? Or do you want your gifts to act as a retention tool to keep good people on your team?" Megan responds, "I never thought of it that way. Our company doesn't really have a strategy for the gifts. It's just something we do every year. Do you have any ideas?"

As it turns out, you have many ideas. You've developed a gift list based on the reasons talented people stay with organi-zations. Megan asks you to send her a letter explaining some of the gift ideas. She thinks that she will be able to retain your services for this advice.

**Your Task.** Using InfoTrac, find the article by Beverly L. Kaye and Sharon Jordan-Evans entitled "The ABCs of Management Gift-Giving," *Training & Development*, December 2000, Article No. A68217191. As a consultant, prepare a letter with a sampling of gift-giving ideas addressed to Megan Stowe, Vice President, Alliance Insurance Company, 1586 Albert Avenue, Regina, SK S4V 6W3. Because you don't want to give away all of your best advice in this letter, limit your suggestions to ten or twelve. How would you like to present additional ideas?

## 9.27 Letter of Recommendation: Recommending Yourself (Obj. 6)

You are about to leave your present job. When you ask your boss for a letter of recommendation, to your surprise he tells you to write it yourself and then have him sign it. [Actually, this is not an unusual practice today. Many businesspeople find that employees are very perceptive and accurate when they evaluate themselves.]

**Your Task.** Use specifics from a current or previous job. Describe your duties and skills. Be sure to support general characteristics with specific examples.

## 9.28 Order Response: Office Supplies to Go (Obj. 7)

As a member of the Order Department at Monarch Discount Office Furniture (2890 Monarch Road, Lethbridge, AB T1K 1L6), respond to the order placed by Hector Rivera at Lasertronics (described in Activity 9.14). Yes, all of the prices listed in your old catalogue have increased. That's the bad news. The good news is that you have in stock nearly everything he ordered. The only item not immediately available is the desktop organizer, Item No. 23-K. That has to be shipped from the manufacturer in Calgary. You've been having trouble with that supplier lately, perhaps because of heavy demand. However, you think that the organizer will be shipped no later than three weeks from the current date. You're pleased to have Lasertronics' order. They might be interested in your new line of office supply products at discount prices. Send Mr. Rivera a new catalogue and call his attention to the low, low price on continuous-form computer paper. It's just $39.95 for a box containing 2 700 sheets of 9½- by 11-inch, 20-pound printout paper. All the items he ordered, except the organizer, are on their way by UPS and should arrive in three days.

**Your Task.** Respond to Hector Rivera, manager, Lasertronics, Inc., 627 Nordstrum Road, Lethbridge, AB T1R 3L5. Tell him the good and bad news about his order.

## 9.29 Claim Response: Undersized French Doors (Obj. 7)

**CRITICAL THINKING**

As Jay Brandt, manager of Custom Wood, Inc., you have a problem. Your firm manufactures quality precut and custom-built doors and frames. You have received a letter dated August 3 from Julie Chen (described in Activity 9.18). Ms. Chen is an interior designer, and she complains that the oak French doors she recently ordered for a client were made to the wrong dimensions.

Although they were the wrong size, she kept the doors and had them installed because her clients were without outside doors. However, her carpenter charged an extra $455.50 to install them. She claims that you should reimburse her for this amount, since your company was responsible for the error. You check her July 2 order and find that the order was filled correctly. In a telephone order, Ms. Chen requested doors that measured 3.4 m, and that's what you sent. Now she says that the doors should have been 3.5 m. Your policy forbids refunds or returns on custom orders. Yet, you remember that around July 2 you had two new people working the phones taking orders. It's possible that they did not hear or record the measurements correctly. You don't know whether to grant this claim or refuse it. But you do know that you must look into the training of telephone order takers and be sure that they verify all custom-order measurements. It might also be a good idea to have your craftsmen call a second time to confirm custom measurements.

Ms. Chen is a successful interior designer and has provided Custom Wood with a number of orders. You value her business but aren't sure how to respond.

**Your Task.** Decide how to treat this claim and then write to Julie Chen, Smart Interiors, 8 Prince of Wales Street, St. John's, NL A1C 4N7. In your letter remind her that Custom Wood has earned a reputation as the manufacturer of the finest wood doors and frames on the market. Your doors feature prime woods, and the craftsmanship is meticulous. The designs of your doors have won awards, and the engineering is ingenious. You have a new line of greenhouse windows that are available in three sizes. Include a brochure describing these windows.

## 9.30 Claim Response: Deep Desk Disappointment (Obj. 7)

As Rodney Harding, marketing manager, Harbourview Wood Products, it is your job to reply to customer claims, and today you must respond to Monica Keil (described in Activity 9.16). You are disappointed that she is returning the executive desk (Invoice No. 3499), but your policy is to comply with customer wishes. If she doesn't want to keep the desk, you will certainly return the purchase price plus shipping charges. On occasion,

desks are damaged in shipping, and this may explain the marred finish and the sticking drawers.

You want Ms. Keil to give Harbourview Wood Products another chance. After all, your office furniture and other wood products are made from the finest hand-selected woods by master artisans. Since she is apparently furnishing her office, send her another catalogue and invite her to look at the traditional conference desk on page 10-E. This is available with a matching credenza, file cabinets, and accessories.

**Your Task.** Write a letter granting the claim of Monica Keil, President, Keil Consulting Services, 9802 Founders Drive, Antigonish, NS B2G 1C0. She might be interested in your furniture-leasing plan, which can produce substantial savings. Be sure to promise that you will personally examine any furniture she may order in the future.

## 9.31 Claim Response: Earth First Runs Dry (Obj. 7)

As Antonio Garcia, customer service manager for Stellar Printers (1110 Birchmount Road, Toronto, ON M1K 5G4), respond to a claim letter from Megan Phillips, public relations assistant, Earth First (see Activity 9.17). Explain to Ms. Phillips that Stellar Printers will refund to Earth First $126.50 for the two faulty cartridges it purchased. The cartridges were apparently among the 10 percent of cartridges shipped to retailers in December and January that were made with a new type of protective tape. The tape worked well in manufacturing, and it was much cheaper for Stellar to use. Unfortunately, when printer owners removed the protective tape as instructed, residue from the tape clogged the cartridges' ink holes, causing the cartridges to malfunction even though they were still full of ink.

You would like Earth First to know that Stellar is committed to improving the quality of its soy-based ink cartridges, but not at the expense of customer satisfaction. Clearly the protective tape wasn't a successful product improvement, and customer feedback from companies such as Earth First has helped Stellar to improve product quality. In February, Stellar stopped using the defective tape. Instead, it returned to its original protective tape to seal cartridges. This tape never failed. Cartridges with the new tape were removed from store shelves.

**Your Task.** Grant the claim of Megan Phillips, Public Relations, Earth First, 1971 Bowler Drive, Pickering, ON L1V 3K3.

## 9.32 Thanks for a Favour: Got the Job! (Obj. 8)

Congratulations! You completed your degree or diploma and got a terrific job in your field. One of your instructors was especially helpful to you when you were a student. This instructor also wrote an effective letter of recommendation that was instrumental in helping you obtain your job.

**Your Task.** Write a letter thanking your instructor.

### 9.33 Thanks for a Favour: The Century's Biggest Change in Job Finding (Obj. 8)

**TEAM**

Your business communication class was fortunate to have author Joyce Lain Kennedy speak to you. She has written many books including *Electronic Job Search Revolution; Hook Up, Get Hired!;* and *Electronic Résumé Revolution.* Ms. Kennedy talked about writing a scannable résumé, using keywords to help employers hire you, keeping yourself visible in databases on the Internet, and finding online classified ads. The class especially liked hearing the many examples of real people who had found jobs on the Internet. Ms. Kennedy shared many suggestions from human resources people, and she described how large and small employers are using computers to read résumés and track employees. You know that she did not come to plug her books, but when she left, most class members wanted to head straight for a bookstore to get some of them. Her talk was a big hit.

**Your Task.** Individually or in groups, draft a thank-you letter to Joyce Lain Kennedy, P.O. Box 3502, Madeira Park, BC V0N 2H0.

### 9.34 Thanks for the Hospitality: Holiday Entertaining (Obj. 8)

You and other members of your staff or organization were entertained at an elegant dinner during the winter holiday season.

**Your Task.** Write a thank-you letter to your boss (supervisor, manager, vice president, president, or chief executive officer) or to the head of an organization to which you belong. Include specific details that will make your letter personal and sincere.

### 9.35 Sending Good Wishes: Personalizing Group Greeting Cards (Obj. 8)

**WEB**     **TEAM**

When a work colleague has a birthday, gets promoted, or retires, someone generally circulates a group greeting card. In the past it wasn't a big deal. Office colleagues just signed their names and passed the store-bought card along to others. But the current trend is toward personalization with witty, oh-so-clever quips. And that presents a problem. What should you say—or not say? You know that people value special handwritten quips, but you realize that you're not particularly original and you don't have a store of "bon mots" (clever sayings, witticisms). You're tired of the old standbys, such as "This place won't be the same without you" and "You're only as old as you feel."

**Your Task.** To be prepared for the next greeting card that lands on your desk at work, you decide to work with some friends to make a list of remarks appropriate for business occasions. Use the Web to research witty sayings appropriate for promotions, birthdays, births, weddings, illnesses, or personal losses. Use a search term such as "birthday sayings," "retirement quotes," or "cool sayings." You may decide to assign each category (birthday, retirement, promotion, and so forth) to a separate team. Submit the best sayings in a memo to your instructor.

### 9.36 Responding to Good Wishes: Saying Thank You (Obj. 8)

**Your Task.** Write a short note thanking a friend who sent you good wishes when you recently completed your degree or diploma.

### 9.37 Extending Sympathy: To a Spouse (Obj. 8)

**Your Task.** Imagine that a coworker was killed in an automobile accident. Write a letter of sympathy to her or his spouse.

## C.L.U.E. REVIEW 9

Edit the following sentences to correct faults in grammar, punctuation, spelling, and word use.

1. Although we've saw a extrordinary increase in the use of e-mail some business letters must still be wrote.

2. She acts as if she was the only person who ever received a complement about their business writting.

3. Good business letters are distinguished by three characteristics. Clear content, a goodwill tone and correct form.

4. Cynthia Jones whom I think is our newly-appointed Vice President writes many business letters for our Company.

5. After the Office Manager and him returned from their meeting we were able to sort the customer's letters more quick.

6. Even the best run and best loved businesses ocassionaly recieve claims, or complaints from consumers'.

7. On Wenesday we received 2 claims, on Thursday we received 4 more.

8. We enclosed a refund cheque for two hundred dollars, however we worried that it was not enough to regain the confidence of the customer.

9. If you could of saw the customers letter you would have been as upset as Rona and me.

10. To express thanks and show apreciation most people write a short note. On special notepaper or heavy card stock.

# Chapter 10

## Persuasive and Sales Messages

## LEARNING OBJECTIVES

*1* Apply the 3-×-3 writing process to persuasive messages.

*2* Explain the components of a persuasive message.

*3* Request favours and action effectively.

*4* Write convincing persuasive messages within organizations.

*5* Request adjustments and make claims successfully.

*6* Compose successful sales messages.

*7* Describe the basic elements included in effective news releases.

# United Way-Centraide

Each year, volunteers across Canada call on their colleagues to give generously to the United Way campaign. Nationwide, 125 United Way-Centraide organizations provide direct financial support to more than 7 000 funded agencies and provide funding to an additional 10 000 organizations through donor-directed giving. In 2002, that financial support totalled more than $354 million, a 6.2 percent increase over the 2001 campaign. Forty organizations and their affiliated labour partners each contributed $1 million or more and were recipients of the "Thanks a Million" award.

United Way of Canada-Centraide Canada, a national organization created in 1939, acts as a voice for members within the Canadian voluntary sector and provides leadership, programs, and services to its members. In the early part of the twentieth century, Catholic, Protestant, and Jewish charities began to raise funds to strengthen their communities. Over the years, United Way-Centraide was known as Red Feather, Community Chest, and United Appeal. In the 1970s, these organizations adopted the name of United Way and Centraide. Each United Way-Centraide is an autonomous organization operated by a voluntary board of directors chosen from the community it serves.

The familiar United Way-Centraide symbol can be seen at health agencies, daycare facilities, and neighbourhood centres, and on all United Way-Centraide posters and publications. The symbol consists of three distinct parts: a rainbow to represent the hope of a better life possible through United Way-Centraide, the universal symbol of humankind symbolizing that all people are supported and uplifted by United Way-Centraide efforts, and a helping hand representing the services and programs supported by United Way-Centraide that in turn support the people in our communities.

The United Way-Centraide organizations are dependent on volunteers for their success. The benefits of volunteering include giving something back to the community; making a difference in someone's life; sharing your skills, talents, and time with others; enjoying a feeling of satisfaction; and making important business contacts.[1]

## CRITICAL THINKING

- How can United Way-Centraide organizations be persuasive in their local communities?
- What are the potential benefits to students and recent graduates of becoming volunteers? How would you go about persuading a peer to volunteer with a charitable agency?
- How often do you use persuasion in your daily life? For what purposes?

**www.unitedway.ca**

# PERSUASIVE REQUESTS

The ability to persuade is one of life's important skills. *Persuading* means using argument or discussion to change an individual's beliefs or actions. Persuasion, of course, is a very important part of any business that sells goods or services. And selling online is even more challenging than other forms of persuasion because of the technology barrier that must be overcome. However, many of the techniques used online are similar to those you will use in persuasion at home, at school, and on the job.

Doubtless you've had to be persuasive to convert others to your views or to motivate them to do what you want. The outcome of such efforts depends largely on the reasonableness of your request, your credibility, and the ability to make your request attractive to the receiver. In this chapter you will learn many techniques and strategies to help you be successful in any persuasive effort.

When you think that your listener or reader is inclined to agree with your request, you can start directly with the main idea. But when the receiver is likely to resist, don't reveal the purpose too quickly. Ideas that require persuasion benefit from a slow approach that includes ample preparation.

**Successful persuasion results from a reasonable request and a well-presented argument.**

Let's say you want to replace your outdated office PC with a new, powerful computer that is fast as lightning and enables you to access the Internet instantly. In a memo to your boss, Laura, who is likely to resist this request because of budget constraints, you wisely decide not to open with a direct request. Instead, you gain her attention and move to logical reasons supporting your request. This indirect pattern is effective when you must persuade people to grant you favours, accept your recommendations, make adjustments in your favour, or grant your claims.

The same is true for sales messages. Instead of making a sales pitch immediately, smart communicators prepare a foundation by developing credibility and hooking their requests to benefits for the receiver. In persuasive messages other than sales, you must know precisely what you want the receiver to think or do. You must also anticipate what appeals to make or "buttons to push" to motivate action. Achieving these goals in both written and oral messages requires special attention to the initial steps in the process.

## Applying the 3-×-3 Writing Process to Persuasive Messages

Persuasion means changing people's views, and that's a difficult task. Pulling it off demands planning and perception. The 3-×-3 writing process provides you with a helpful structure for laying a foundation for persuasion. Of particular importance here are (1) analyzing the purpose, (2) adapting to the audience, (3) collecting information, and (4) organizing the message.

*Analyzing the Purpose.* The purpose of a persuasive message is to convert the receiver to your ideas or to motivate action. A message without a clear purpose is doomed. Not only must you know what your purpose is and what response you want, but you must know these things when you start writing a letter or planning a presentation. Too often, ineffective communicators reach the end of a message before discovering exactly what they want the receiver to do. Then they must start over, giving the request a different "spin" or emphasis. Because your purpose establishes the strategy of the message, determine it first.

Let's return to your memo requesting a new computer. What exactly do you want your boss to do? Which of these actions do you expect Laura to take? (1) Meet with you so that you can show her how much computer time is lost with slow software and poor Internet connections? (2) Purchase a Brand X computer for you now? (3) Include your computer request in the department's five-year equipment forecast? By identifying your purpose up front, you can shape the message to point toward it. This planning effort saves considerable rewriting time and produces the most successful persuasive messages.

*Adapting to the Audience.* While you're considering the purpose of a persuasive message, you also need to concentrate on the receiver. How can you adapt your request to that individual so that your message is heard? Zorba the Greek wisely observed, "You can knock forever on a deaf man's door." A persuasive message is equally futile unless it meets the needs of its audience. In a broad sense, you'll be seeking to show how your request helps the receiver achieve some of life's major goals or fulfills key needs: money, power, comfort, confidence, importance, friends, peace of mind, and recognition, to name a few.

On a more practical level, you want to show how your request solves a problem, achieves a personal or work objective, or just makes life easier for your audience. In your request for a new computer, for example, you could appeal to your boss's expressed concern for increasing productivity. If you were asking for a four-day work schedule, you could cite the need for improved efficiency and better employee morale.

**Effective sales messages reflect thorough product knowledge, writer credibility, and specific reader benefits.**

*1*

**The key components of a persuasive request are gaining attention, showing the worth of the proposal, overcoming resistance, and motivating action.**

**Persuasive messages require careful analysis of the purpose for writing.**

**Effective persuasive messages focus on audience needs or goals.**

To adapt your request to the receiver, consider these questions that receivers will very likely be asking themselves:

- Why should I?
- What's in it for me?
- What's in it for you?
- Who cares?

Adapting to your audience means being ready to answer these questions. It means learning about audience members and analyzing why they might resist your proposal. It means searching for ways to connect your purpose with their needs. If completed before you begin writing, such analysis goes a long way toward overcoming resistance and achieving your goal. The accompanying Career Coach box presents additional strategies that can make you a successful persuader.

## CAREER COACH

### Seven Rules Every Persuader Should Know

Successful businesspeople create persuasive memos, letters, reports, and presentations that get the results they want. Yet, their approaches are all different. Some persuaders are gentle, leading readers by the hand to the targeted recommendation. Others are brisk and authoritative. Some are objective, examining both sides of an issue like a judge deciding a difficult case. Some move slowly and carefully toward a proposal, while others erupt like a volcano in their eagerness to announce a recommendation.

Because of the immense number of variables involved, no single all-purpose strategy works for every persuasive situation. You wouldn't, for example, use the same techniques in asking for a raise from a stern supervisor as you would use in persuading a close friend to see a movie of your choice. Different situations and different goals require different techniques. The following seven rules suggest various strategies—depending on your individual need.

1. **Consider whether your views will create problems for your audience.** A student engineer submitted a report recommending a simple change at a waste-treatment facility. His recommendation would save $200 000 per year, but the report met with a cool reception. Why? His supervisors would have to explain to management why they had allowed a waste of $200 000 per year! If your views make trouble for the audience, think of ways to include the receivers in your recommendation if possible. Whatever your strategy, be tactful and empathic.

2. **Don't offer new ideas, directives, or recommendations for change until your audience is prepared for them.** Receivers are threatened by anything that upsets their values or interests. The greater the change you suggest, the more slowly you should proceed. For example, if your boss is enthusiastic about a new marketing scheme (that would cost $50 000 to develop), naturally you will go slowly in shooting it down. If, on the other hand, your boss has little personal investment in the scheme, you could be more direct in your attack.

3. **Select a strategy that supports your credibility.** If you have great credibility with your audience, you can proceed directly. If not, you might want to establish that credibility first. *Given* credibility results from position or reputation, such as that of the boss of an organization or a highly regarded scientist. *Acquired* credibility is earned. To acquire credibility, successful persuaders often identify themselves, early in the message, with the goals and interests of the audience (*As a small business owner myself . . .*). Another way to acquire credibility is to mention evidence or ideas that support the audience's existing views (*We agree that small business owners need more government assistance*). Finally, you can acquire credibility by citing authorities who rate highly with your audience (*Richard Love, recently named Small Businessperson of the Year, supports this proposal*).

*(continued)*

4. **If your audience disagrees with your ideas or is uncertain about them, present both sides of the argument.** You might think that you would be most successful by revealing only one side of an issue—your side, of course. But persuasion doesn't work that way. You'll be more successful—particularly if the audience is unfriendly or uncertain—by disclosing *all* sides of an argument. This approach suggests that you are objective. It also helps the receiver remember your view by showing the pros and cons in relation to one another. Thus, if you want to convince the owners of a realty firm that an expensive new lockbox system is a wise investment, be truthful about any shortcomings, weaknesses, and limitations.

5. **Win respect by making your opinion or recommendation clear.** Although you should be truthful in presenting both sides of an argument, don't be shy in supporting your conclusions or final proposals. You will, naturally, have definite views and should persuade your audience to accept them. The two-sided strategy is a means to an end, but it does not mean compromising your argument. One executive criticized reports from his managers because they presented much data and concluded, in effect, with "Here is what I found out and maybe we should do this or maybe we should do that." Be decisive and make specific recommendations.

6. **Place your strongest points strategically.** Some experts argue that if your audience is deeply concerned with your subject, you can afford to begin with your weakest points. Because of its commitment, the audience will stay with you until you reach the strongest points at the end. For an unmotivated audience, begin with your strongest points to get them interested. Other experts feel that a supportive audience should receive the main ideas or recommendations immediately, to avoid wasting time. Whichever position you choose, don't bury your recommendation, strongest facts, or main idea in the middle of your argument.

7. **Don't count on changing attitudes by offering information alone.** "If customers knew the truth about our costs, they would not object to our prices," some companies reason. Well, don't bet on it. Companies have pumped huge sums into advertising and public relations campaigns that provided facts alone. Such efforts often fail because learning something new (that is, increasing the knowledge of the audience) is rarely an effective way to change attitudes. Researchers have found that presentations of facts alone may strengthen opinions—but primarily for people who already agree with the persuader. The added information reassures them and provides ammunition for defending themselves in discussions with others.

### Career Application

Consider a career-oriented problem in a current or past job: customer service must be improved, workers need better training, inventory procedures are inefficient, equipment is outdated, worker scheduling is arbitrary, and so forth. Devise a plan to solve the problem. How could the preceding rules help you persuade a decision maker to adopt your plan? In a memo to your instructor or in class discussion, outline the problem and your plan for solving it. Describe your persuasive strategy.

*Researching and Organizing Data.* Once you've analyzed the audience and considered how to adapt your message to its needs, you're ready to collect data and organize it. You might brainstorm and prepare cluster diagrams to provide a rough outline of ideas. For your computer request, if your strategy was to show that a new computer would increase your productivity, you would gather data to show how much time and effort could be saved with the new machine. To overcome resistance to cost, you would need information about prices. To ensure getting exactly what you want, you would study many computer configurations.

The next step is organizing your data. Suppose you have already decided that your request will meet with resistance. Thus, you decide not to open directly with your request. Instead, you follow the components of a persuasive message, listed below and shown graphically in Figure 10.1:

## FIGURE 10.1 Components of a Persuasive Message

| GAINING ATTENTION | BUILDING INTEREST | REDUCING RESISTANCE | MOTIVATING ACTION |
|---|---|---|---|
| Summary of problem | Facts, figures | Anticipate objections | Describe specific request |
| Unexpected statement | Expert opinion | Offer counterarguments | Sound confident |
| Reader benefit | Examples | Play *What if?* scenarios | Make action easy to take |
| Compliment | Specific details | Establish credibility | Offer incentive |
| Related fact | Direct benefits | Demonstrate competence | Don't provide excuses |
| Stimulating question | Indirect benefits | Show value of proposal | Repeat main benefit |

- Gain attention
- Build interest
- Reduce resistance
- Motivate action

## Blending the Components of a Persuasive Message

Although the indirect pattern appears to contain separate steps, successful persuasive messages actually blend these steps into a seamless whole. However, the sequence of the components may change depending on the situation and the emphasis. Regardless of where they are placed, the key elements in persuasive requests are (1) gaining the audience's attention, (2) convincing them that your proposal is worthy, (3) overcoming resistance, and (4) motivating action.

*Gaining Attention.* To grab attention, the opening statement in a persuasive request should be brief, relevant, and engaging. When only mild persuasion is necessary, the opener can be low-key and factual. If, however, your request is substantial and you anticipate strong resistance, provide a thoughtful, provocative opening. The following examples suggest possibilities.

- **Problem description.** In a recommendation to hire temporary employees: *Last month Legal Division staff members were forced to work 120 overtime hours, costing us $6 000 and causing considerable employee unhappiness.* With this opener you've presented a capsule of the problem your proposal will help solve.

- **Unexpected statement.** In a memo to encourage employees to attend an optional sensitivity seminar: *Men and women draw the line at decidedly different places in identifying what behaviour constitutes sexual harassment.* Note how this opener gets readers thinking immediately.

- **Reader benefit.** In a proposal offering writing workshops to an organization: *For every letter or memo your employees can avoid writing, your organization saves $78.50.* Companies are always looking for ways to cut costs, and this opener promises significant savings.

- **Compliment.** In a letter inviting a business executive to speak: *Because our members admire your success and value your managerial expertise, they want you to be our speaker.* In offering praise or compliments, however, be careful to avoid obvious flattery.

Successful openers to persuasive requests should be brief, targeted, and interesting.

- **Related fact.** In a memo encouraging employees to start car-pooling: *A car pool is defined as two or more persons who travel to work in one car at least once a week.* An interesting, relevant, and perhaps unknown fact sets the scene for the interest-building section that follows.

- **Stimulating question.** In a plea for funds to support environmental causes: *What do Avril Lavigne, the maple leaf, and hockey have in common?* Readers will be curious to find the answer to this intriguing question.

*Building Interest.* After capturing attention, a persuasive request must retain that attention and convince the audience that the request is reasonable. To justify your request, be prepared to invest in a few paragraphs of explanation. Persuasive requests are likely to be longer than direct requests because the audience must be convinced rather than simply instructed. You can build interest and conviction through the use of the following:

- Facts, statistics
- Expert opinion
- Direct benefits
- Examples
- Specific details
- Indirect benefits

Showing how your request can benefit the audience directly or indirectly is a key factor in persuasion. If you were asking colleagues to contribute money to the United Way, for example, you might promote *direct benefits* such as using the contribution as a tax write-off. An *indirect benefit* comes from feeling good about helping the community and knowing that others will benefit from the gift. Nearly all charities rely in large part on indirect benefits—the selflessness of givers—to promote their causes.

*Reducing Resistance.* One of the biggest mistakes in persuasive requests is the failure to anticipate and offset audience resistance. How will the receiver object to your request? In brainstorming for clues, try *What if?* scenarios. Let's say you are trying to convince management that the employees' cafeteria should switch from paper and plastic plates and cups to ceramic. What if they say the change is too expensive? What if they argue that they are careful recyclers of paper and plastic? What if they contend that ceramic dishes would increase cafeteria labour and energy costs tremendously? What if they protest that ceramic is less hygienic? For each of these *What if?* scenarios, you need a counterargument.

Unless you anticipate resistance, you give the receiver an easy opportunity to dismiss your request. Countering this resistance is important, but you must do it with finesse (*Although ceramic dishes cost more at first, they actually save money over time*). You can minimize objections by presenting your counterarguments in sentences that emphasize benefits: *Ceramic dishes may require a little more effort in cleaning, but they bring warmth and graciousness to meals. Most important, they help save the environment by requiring fewer resources and eliminating waste.* However, don't spend too much time on counterarguments, thus making them overly important. Finally, avoid bringing up objections that may never have occurred to the receiver in the first place.

Another factor that reduces resistance is credibility. Receivers are less resistant if your request is reasonable and if you are believable. When the receiver does not know you, you may have to establish your expertise, refer to your credentials, or demonstrate your competence. Even when you are known, you may have to establish your knowledge in a given area. In making your request for a new computer, you might have to establish your credibility by showing your boss articles you have read about the latest computers and how much more efficient you could be with better Internet connections. Some charities establish their credibility by displaying on their stationery the names of famous people who serve on their boards. The credibility of speakers making presentations is usually outlined by someone who introduces them.

*Motivating Action.* After gaining attention, building interest, and reducing resistance, you'll want to inspire the receiver to act. This is where your planning pays dividends. Knowing exactly what action you favour before you start to write enables you to point your arguments toward this important final paragraph. Here you will make your recommendation as specifically and confidently as possible—without seeming pushy. A proposal from one manager to another might conclude with, *So that we can begin using the employment assessment tests by May 1, please send a return e-mail immediately.* In making a request, don't sound apologetic (*I'm sorry to have to ask you this, but . . .*), and don't supply excuses (*If you can spare the time, . . .*). Compare the following closings for a persuasive memo recommending training seminars in communication skills.

**Persuasive requests motivate action by specifying exactly what should be done.**

### Too General
We are certain we can develop a series of training sessions that will improve the communication skills of your employees.

### Too Timid
If you agree that our training proposal has merit, perhaps we could begin the series in June.

### Too Pushy
Because we're convinced that you will want to begin improving the skills of your employees immediately, we've scheduled your series to begin in June.

### Effective
You will see decided improvement in the communication skills of your employees. Please call me at (613) 439-2201 by May 1 to give your approval so that training sessions may start in June, as we discussed.

Note how the last opening suggests a specific and easy-to-follow action. Figure 10.2 summarizes techniques for overcoming resistance and crafting successful persuasive messages.

## FIGURE 10.2 Four-Part Indirect Pattern for Sales or Persuasion

| GAINING ATTENTION | BUILDING INTEREST | REDUCING RESISTANCE | MOTIVATING ACTION |
|---|---|---|---|
| Free offer | Rational appeals | Testimonials | Gift |
| Promise | Emotional appeals | Satisfied users | Incentive |
| Question | Dual appeals | Guarantee | Limited offer |
| Quotation | Product description | Free trial | Deadline |
| Product feature | Reader benefits | Sample | Guarantee |
| Testimonial | Cold facts mixed with | Performance | Repetition of |
| Action setting | warm feelings | tests | selling feature |
| | | Polls, awards | |

## What's Fair in Persuasion? Avoiding Common Logical Fallacies

While being persuasive, we must be careful to remain ethical. In our eagerness to win others over to our views, we may inadvertently overstep the bounds of fair play. Philosophers through the years have pinpointed a number of logical fallacies. Here are three you'll want to avoid in your persuasive messages. For an online discussion of many logical fallacies, try using a Web search engine to find "Stephen's Guide to the Logical Fallacies."

- **Circular reasoning.** When the support given for a contention merely restates the contention, the reasoning is circular. For example, *Investing in the stock market is dangerous for short-term investors because it is unsafe.* The evidence (*because it is unsafe*) offers no proof. It merely circles back to the original contention. Revision: *Investing in the stock market is dangerous for short-term investors because stock prices fluctuate widely.*

- **Begging the question.** A statement such as *That dishonest CEO should be replaced* begs the question. Merely asserting that the CEO is dis-

honest is not enough. Be sure to supply solid evidence for such assertions. Revision: *That CEO is dishonest because he awards contracts only to his friends. A good manager would require open bidding.*

- **Post hoc (after, thus, because).** Although two events may have happened in immediate sequence, the first did not necessarily cause the second. For example, *The company switched to team-based management, and its stock price rose immediately afterward.* Switching to teams probably had no effect on the stock price. Revision: *At about the same time the company switched to team-based management, its stock price began to rise, although the two events are probably unrelated.*

### Career Application

In teams or in class discussion, cite examples of how these fallacies could be used in persuasive messages or sales letters. Provide a logical, ethical revision for each.

## Being Persuasive but Ethical

**Ethical business communicators maintain credibility and respect by being honest, fair, and objective.**

Business communicators may be tempted to make their persuasion even more forceful by fudging on the facts, exaggerating a point, omitting something crucial, or providing deceptive emphasis. Consider the case of a manager who sought to persuade employees to accept a change in insurance benefits. His memo emphasized a small perk (easier handling of claims) but deemphasized a major reduction in total coverage. Some readers missed the main point—as the manager intended. Others recognized the deception, however, and before long the manager's credibility was lost. A persuader is effective only when he or she is believable. If receivers suspect that they are being manipulated or misled, or if they find any part of the argument untruthful, the total argument fails. Persuaders can also fall into traps of logic without even being aware of it. Take a look at the accompanying Ethical Insights box to learn about common logical fallacies that you will want to avoid.

Persuasion becomes unethical when facts are distorted, overlooked, or manipulated with an intent to deceive. Of course, persuaders naturally want to put forth their strongest case. But that argument must be based on truth, objectivity, and fairness.

In prompting ethical and truthful persuasion, two factors act as powerful motivators. The first is the desire to preserve your reputation and credibility. Once lost, a good name is difficult to regain. An equally important force prompting ethical behaviour, though, is your opinion of yourself. One stockbroker admits that she's in the business to make money, but she still has to be able to look at herself in the mirror each morning. "We've gone through the '80s, when it was tough for morality.

Now we're in the process of doing a complete turnaround; people are saying that honesty is what's really important. If you're unethical, you may make all the money in the world. But you won't retain family, friends, or lasting business relationships."[2]

## WRITING SUCCESSFUL PERSUASIVE REQUESTS

*3*

Convincing someone to change a belief or to perform an action when that individual is reluctant requires planning and skill—and sometimes a little luck. If the request is in writing, rather than face to face, the task is even more difficult. The indirect pattern, though, can help you shape effective persuasive appeals that (1) request favours and action, (2) persuade within organizations, and (3) request adjustments and make claims.

## Requesting Favours and Actions

Persuading someone to do something that largely benefits you is not easy. Fortunately, many individuals and companies are willing to grant requests for time, money, information, special privileges, and cooperation. They grant these favours for a variety of reasons. They may just happen to be interested in your project, or they may see goodwill potential for themselves. Often, though, they comply because they see that others will benefit from the request. Professionals sometimes feel obligated to contribute their time or expertise to "pay their dues."

**The indirect pattern is appropriate when requesting favours and action, persuading within organizations, and requesting adjustments or making claims.**

You may find that you have few direct benefits to offer in your persuasion. Instead, you'll focus on indirect benefits, as the writer does in Figure 10.3 (on page 295). In asking a manager to speak before a marketing meeting, the writer has little to offer as a direct benefit other than a $300 honorarium. But indirectly, the writer offers enticements such as an enthusiastic audience and a chance to help other companies solve overseas marketing problems. This persuasive request appeals primarily to the reader's desire to serve his profession—although a receptive audience and an opportunity to talk about one's successes have a certain ego appeal as well. Together, these appeals—professional, egoistic, monetary—make a persuasive argument rich and effective.

As another example, consider the following persuasive message, which asks a company to participate in a survey requesting salary data. This is usually a touchy subject. Few organizations are willing to reveal how much they pay their employees. Yet, this request may succeed because of the explanation provided and the benefit offered (free salary survey data).

✓ *Effective Letter*

Dear Ms. Masi:

Has your company ever lost a valued employee to another organization that offered 20 percent more in salary for the same position? Have you ever added a unique job title but had no idea what compensation the position demanded?

— Gains attention with two short questions that suggest problems the reader knows.

To remain competitive in hiring and to retain qualified workers, companies rely on survey data showing current salaries. My organization collects such data, and we need your help. Would you be willing to complete the enclosed questionnaire so that we can supply companies like yours with accurate salary data?

— Discusses a benefit that leads directly to the frank request for help. Notice that the request is coupled with a reader benefit.

Your information, of course, will be treated confidentially. The questionnaire takes but a few moments to complete, and it can provide substantial dividends for professional organizations that need comparative salary data.

— Anticipates and counters resistance to confidentiality and time/effort objections.

*(continued)*

# *United Way-Centraide Revisited*

Durham College, serving the Durham Region in Ontario, is one of the thousands of organizations across Canada that encourages employee contribution campaigns. In 2003, Canada's newest university, the University of Ontario Institute of Technology (UOIT), welcomed its first students and the many employees who would serve them. Durham College and UOIT are located on the same campus in Oshawa. While the two institutions are separate entities, they share many facilities and resources. One of these is the United Way employee contribution campaign.

The campaign committee consists of faculty, administrative and support staff, and students and is co-chaired by a representative from each of the two institutions. Although the campaign itself is formally kicked off in the fall, planning begins in the early spring. The 2003–04 campaign will be the first in which the two institutions worked together. The committee's first task was to establish campaign goals. These included increasing the participation rate (in 2002, approximately 12 percent of employees had participated in the campaign), increasing the total amount raised, and increasing the involvement of students both in planning and in participating in the campaign.

The committee knows from experience that the bulk of its donations will come from pledge forms that allow donors to make a one-time contribution or authorize regular payroll deductions. It will also plan a series of events that don't necessarily raise a great deal of money (particularly given the amount of time and effort required to organize them), but go a long way toward providing social activities and team activities that contribute to employee morale.

## CRITICAL THINKING

- What factors will the campaign organizers need to consider as they encourage staff and students from two completely different organizations to participate in the United Way campaign?
- Why is it difficult to change attitudes (such as a reluctance to complete the pledge forms) by offering information only?
- How is the four-part plan for persuasion effective for messages such as Durham College/UOIT might send to employees and students?

**www.unitedway.ca**

---

Offers free salary data as a direct benefit. Describes the benefit in detail to strengthen its appeal.

To show our gratitude for your participation, we'll send you comprehensive salary surveys for your industry and your metropolitan area. Not only will you find basic salaries, but you'll also learn about bonus and incentive plans, special pay differentials, expense reimbursements, perquisites such as a company car and credit card, and special payments such as beeper pay.

Appeals to professionalism. Motivates action with a deadline and a final benefit that relates to the opening questions.

Comparative salary data are impossible to provide without the support of professionals like you. Please complete the questionnaire and return it in the prepaid envelope before November 1, our fall deadline. You'll no longer be in the dark about how much your employees earn compared with others in your industry.

Sincerely yours,

Notice that the last paragraph gives details about how to comply with the request. It also takes advantage of an "emphasis spot" (the end of a letter) to provide a final benefit reminder echoing the opening questions.

## FIGURE 10.3 Persuasive Favour Request

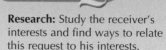

**Prewriting** *1*

**Analyze:** The purpose of this letter is to persuade the reader to speak at a dinner meeting.

**Anticipate:** Although the reader is busy, he may respond to appeals to his ego (describing his successes before an appreciative audience) and to his professionalism.

**Adapt:** Because the reader will be uninterested at first and require persuasion, use the indirect pattern.

**Writing** *2*

**Research:** Study the receiver's interests and find ways to relate this request to his interests.

**Organize:** Gain attention by opening with praise or a stimulating remark. Build interest with explanations and facts. Show how compliance benefits the reader and others. Reduce resistance by providing ideas for the dinner talk.

**Compose:** Prepare a first draft on a computer.

**Revising** *3*

**Revise:** Revise to show direct and indirect benefits more clearly.

**Proofread:** Use quotes around "R" to reflect company usage. In the fourth paragraph, use a semicolon in the compound sentence. Start all lines at the left for block-style letter.

**Evaluate:** Will this letter convince the reader to accept the invitation?

---

### *North American Marketing Association*

Hamilton–Wentworth Chapter
1624 Fennell Street
Hamilton, ON
L8V 4X2

(905) 469-8274

January 28, 2005

Mr. Bryant Hoffman
Marketing Manager
Toys "R" Us, Inc.
2777 Langstaff Avenue,
Thornhill, ON L3J 3M8

Dear Mr. Hoffman:

*Piques reader's curiosity* —

One company is legendary for marketing North American products successfully in Japan.

— *Gains attention*

That company, of course, is Toys "R" Us. The triumph of your thriving toy store in Amimachi, Japan, has given other North American marketers hope. But this success story has also raised numerous questions. Specifically, how did Toys "R" Us circumvent local trade restrictions? How did you solve the complex distribution system? And how did you negotiate with all the levels of Japanese bureaucracy?

— *Builds interest*

*Notes indirect benefit* —

*Notes direct benefit* —

The members of the Hamilton-Wentworth chapter of the North American Marketing Association asked me to invite you to speak at our March 19 dinner meeting on the topic of "How Toys 'R' Us Unlocked the Door to Japanese Trade." By describing your winning effort, Mr. Hoffman, you can help launch other North American companies who face the same quagmire of Japanese restrictions and red tape that your organization overcame. Although we can offer you only a small honorarium of $300, we can assure you of a big audience of enthusiastic marketing professionals eager to hear your dramatic story.

*Offsets reluctance by making the talk informal and easy to organize* —

Our relaxed group doesn't expect a formal address; our members are most interested in what steps Toys "R" Us took to open its Japanese toy outlet. To make your talk easy to organize, I've enclosed a list of questions our members submitted. Most talks are about 45 minutes long.

— *Reduces resistance*

*Makes acceptance as simple as a telephone call* —

Can we count on you to join us for dinner at 7 p.m. on March 19 at the Fisherman's Inn in Hamilton? Just call me at (905) 860-4320 by February 15 to make arrangements.

— *Motivates action*

Sincerely,

*Joyce Barnes*

Joyce Barnes
Program Chair, NAMA

JCB:grw
Enclosure

An offer to work as an intern, at no cost to a company, would seem to require little persuasion. Actually, though, companies hesitate to participate in internship programs because student interns require supervision, desk space, and equipment. They also pose an insurance liability threat.

In Figure 10.4 college student Melanie Harris seeks to persuade Software Enterprises to accept her as an intern. In the analysis process before writing, Melanie thought long and hard about what benefits she could offer the reader and how she could present them strategically. She decided that the offer of a trained college student's free labour was her strongest benefit. Thus, she opens with it, as well as mentioning the same benefit in the letter body and in the closing. After opening with the main audience benefit, she introduces the actual request ("Could you use the part-time services of a college senior . . . ?").

In the interest section, Melanie tells why she is making the request and describes its value in terms of direct and indirect benefits. Notice how she transforms obstacles (lack of equipment or desk space) into helpful suggestions about how her serv-

## FIGURE 10.4  Persuasive Action Request

1777 North Dinosaur Trail
Drumheller, AB T0J 0Y1

January 12, 2005

Ms. Nancy Ashley, Director
Human Resources Department
Software Enterprises, Inc.
268 Redmond Avenue
Calgary, AB T3B 6W7

Dear Ms. Ashley:

How often do college-trained specialists offer to work for nothing?

Very infrequently, I imagine. But that's the offer I'm making to Software Enterprises. During the next 14 weeks, could you use the part-time services of a college senior with communication and computer skills?

To gain work experience and to earn three units of credit, I would like to become an intern at Software Enterprises. My skills in Word and Excel, as well as training in letter and report writing, could be put to use in your Customer Service, Human Resources, Legal, Documentation, or other departments.

By granting this internship, your company not only secures the skills of an enthusiastic and well-trained college student, but it also performs a valuable service to your local community college. Your cooperation provides an opportunity for students to acquire the kind of job training that college classrooms simply cannot give.

If equipment and desk space at Software Enterprises are limited, you may want me to fill in for employees who can then be freed up for other projects, training, or release time. In regard to supervision you'll find that I require little direction once I start a project. Moreover, you don't need to worry about insurance, as our college provides liability coverage for all students at internship sites.

Although I'm taking classes in the mornings, I'm available to work afternoons for 15 hours per week. Please examine the attached résumé to confirm my education and qualifications.

Do you have any questions about my proposal to become an intern? To talk with me about it, please call 893-2155. I could begin working for you as early as February 1. You gain a free employee, and you also provide an appreciative local college student with much-needed job training.

Sincerely,

*Melanie E. Harris*

Melanie E. Harris

Enclosure

*Marginal annotations:*

- Starts with date and address in personal business style
- Uses strongest benefit for stimulating opener
- Notes direct benefit
- Notes indirect benefit
- Anticipates three obstacles and answers each
- Refers to enclosure only after presenting main points
- Introduces request after presenting main benefit
- Introduces a negative in a positive way
- Couples action request with reference to direct and indirect benefits

ices would free up other staff members to perform more important tasks. She delays mentioning a negative (being able to work only 15 hours per week and only in the afternoon) until she builds interest and reduces resistance. And she closes confidently and motivates action with reference to both direct and indirect benefits.

## Persuading Within Organizations

Instructions or directives moving downward from superiors to subordinates usually require little persuasion. Employees expect to be directed in how to perform their jobs. These messages (such as information about procedures, equipment, or customer service) follow the direct pattern, with the purpose immediately stated. However, employees are sometimes asked to perform in a capacity outside their work roles or to accept changes that are not in their best interests (such as pay cuts, job transfers, or reduced benefits). In these instances, a persuasive memo using the indirect pattern may be most effective.

The goal is not to manipulate employees or to seduce them with trickery. Rather, the goal is to present a strong but honest argument, emphasizing points that are important to the receiver. In business, honesty is not just the best policy—it's the *only* policy. Especially within your own organization, people see right through puffery and misrepresentation. For this reason, the indirect pattern is effective only when supported by accurate, honest evidence.

Another form of persuasion within organizations centres on suggestions made by subordinates. Convincing management to adopt a procedure or invest in a product or new equipment generally requires skillful communication. Managers are just as resistant to change as others. Providing evidence is critical when subordinates submit recommendations to their bosses. "The key to making a request of a superior," advises communication consultant Patricia Buhler, "is to know your needs and have documentation [facts, figures, evidence]." Another important factor is moderation. "Going in and asking for the world [right] off the cuff is most likely going to elicit a negative response," she adds.[3] Equally important is focusing on the receiver's needs. What about your suggestion is appealing to the receiver?

The following draft of a request for a second copy machine fails to present convincing evidence of the need. Although the request is reasonable, the argument lacks credibility because of its high-pressure tactics and lack of proof.

*4*

**Internal persuasive memos present honest arguments detailing specific reader benefits.**

*✗ Ineffective Memo*

TO:     Peggy Brunyansky, Vice President
FROM:  Mike Montgomery, Marketing
DATE:   April 12, 2005
SUBJECT: COPIERS

Although you've opposed the purchase of additional copiers in the past, I think I've found a great deal on a copier that's just too good to pass up but we must act before May 1!

**Begins poorly by reminding reader of negative past feelings.**

Copy City has reconditioned copiers that are practically being given away. If we move fast, they will provide many free incentives—like a free copier stand, free starter supplies, free delivery, and free installation.

**Sounds high-pressured and poorly conceived.**

We must find a way to reduce copier costs in my department. Our current copier can't keep up with our demand. Thus, we're sending secretaries or sales reps to Copy Quick for an average of 10 000 copies a month. These copies cost 5 cents a page and waste a lot of time. We're making at least eight trips a week, adding up to a considerable expense in travel time and copy costs.

**Presents persuasive arguments illogically. Fails to tell exactly how much money could be saved.**

*(continued)*

⟶ Please give this matter your immediate attention and get back to me as soon as possible. We don't want to miss this great deal!

The preceding memo will probably fail to achieve its purpose. Although the revised version in Figure 10.5 is longer, it's far more effective. Remember that a persuasive message will typically take more space than a direct message because proving a case requires evidence. Notice that the subject line in Figure 10.5 tells the purpose of the memo without disclosing the actual request. By delaying the request until he's had a chance to describe the problem and discuss a solution, the writer prevents the reader's premature rejection.

The strength of this revision, though, is in the clear presentation of comparison figures showing how much money can be saved by purchasing a remanufactured copier. Although the organization pattern is not obvious, the revised memo begins with an attention-getter (frank description of problem), builds interest (with easy-to-read facts and figures), provides benefits, and reduces resistance. Notice that the conclusion tells what action is to be taken, makes it easy to respond, and repeats the main benefit to motivate action.

## Complaint Letters: Requesting Adjustments and Making Claims

*5*

**Effective complaint/adjustment letters make reasonable claims backed by solid evidence.**

Persuasive adjustment letters make claims about damaged products, mistaken billing, inaccurate shipments, warranty problems, return policies, insurance mix-ups, faulty merchandise, and so on. Generally, the direct pattern is best for requesting straightforward adjustments (see Chapter 9). When you feel your request is justified and will be granted, the direct strategy is most efficient. But if a past request has been refused or ignored or if you anticipate reluctance, then the indirect pattern is appropriate.

In a sense, an adjustment letter is a complaint letter. Someone is complaining about something that went wrong. Some complaint letters just vent anger; the writers are mad, and they want to tell someone about it. But if the goal is to change something (and why bother to write except to motivate change?), then persuasion is necessary. Effective adjustment letters make a reasonable claim, present a logical case with clear facts, and adopt a moderate tone. Anger and emotion are not effective persuaders.

### Logical Development

Strive for logical development in an adjustment letter. You'll want to open with sincere praise, an objective statement of the problem, a point of agreement, or a quick review of what you have done to resolve the problem. Then you can explain precisely what happened or why your claim is legitimate. Don't provide a blow-by-blow chronology of details; just hit the highlights. Be sure to enclose copies of relevant invoices, shipping orders, warranties, and payments. And close with a clear statement of what you want done: refund, replacement, credit to your account, or other action. Be sure to think through the possibilities and make your request reasonable.

### Moderate Tone

The tone of the letter is important. You should never suggest that the receiver intentionally deceived you or intentionally created the problem. Rather, appeal to the

**FIGURE 10.5** Persuasive Memo

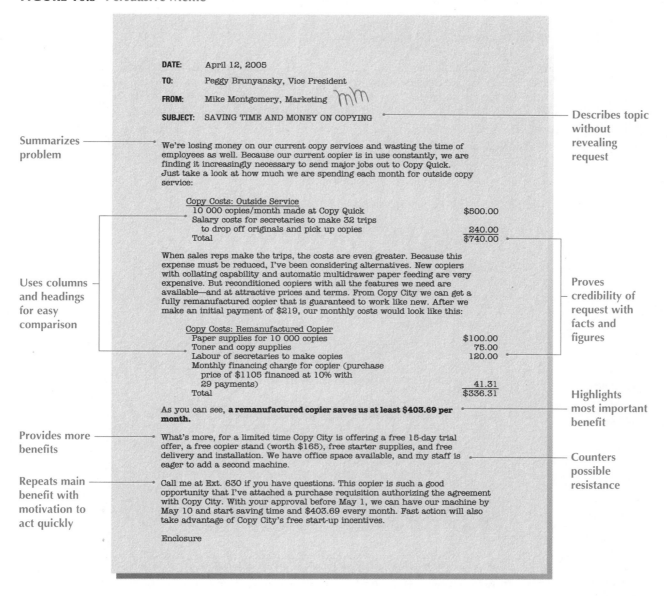

Summarizes problem

Uses columns and headings for easy comparison

Provides more benefits

Repeats main benefit with motivation to act quickly

Describes topic without revealing request

Proves credibility of request with facts and figures

Highlights most important benefit

Counters possible resistance

DATE:     April 12, 2005

TO:       Peggy Brunyansky, Vice President

FROM:     Mike Montgomery, Marketing

SUBJECT:  SAVING TIME AND MONEY ON COPYING

We're losing money on our current copy services and wasting the time of employees as well. Because our current copier is in use constantly, we are finding it increasingly necessary to send major jobs out to Copy Quick. Just take a look at how much we are spending each month for outside copy service:

Copy Costs: Outside Service
10 000 copies/month made at Copy Quick                    $500.00
Salary costs for secretaries to make 32 trips
     to drop off originals and pick up copies               240.00
Total                                                     $740.00

When sales reps make the trips, the costs are even greater. Because this expense must be reduced, I've been considering alternatives. New copiers with collating capability and automatic multidrawer paper feeding are very expensive. But reconditioned copiers with all the features we need are available—and at attractive prices and terms. From Copy City we can get a fully remanufactured copier that is guaranteed to work like new. After we make an initial payment of $219, our monthly costs would look like this:

Copy Costs: Remanufactured Copier
Paper supplies for 10 000 copies                          $100.00
Toner and copy supplies                                     75.00
Labour of secretaries to make copies                       120.00
Monthly financing charge for copier (purchase
     price of $1105 financed at 10% with
     29 payments)                                           41.31
Total                                                     $336.31

As you can see, **a remanufactured copier saves us at least $403.69 per month.**

What's more, for a limited time Copy City is offering a free 15-day trial offer, a free copier stand (worth $165), free starter supplies, and free delivery and installation. We have office space available, and my staff is eager to add a second machine.

Call me at Ext. 630 if you have questions. This copier is such a good opportunity that I've attached a purchase requisition authorizing the agreement with Copy City. With your approval before May 1, we can have our machine by May 10 and start saving time and $403.69 every month. Fast action will also take advantage of Copy City's free start-up incentives.

Enclosure

---

receiver's sense of responsibility and pride in its good name. Calmly express your disappointment in view of your high expectations of the product and of the company. Communicating your feelings, without rancour, is often your strongest appeal.

Janet Walker's letter, shown in Figure 10.6, follows the persuasive pattern as she seeks to return three answering machines. Notice that she uses simplified letter style (skipping the salutation and complimentary close) because she doesn't have a person's name to use in addressing the letter. Note also her positive opening; her calm, well-documented claims; and her request for specific action.

The checklist on page 301 reviews pointers for helping you make persuasive requests of all kinds.

**Adjustment requests should adopt a moderate tone, appeal to the receiver's sense of responsibility, and specify needed actions.**

**FIGURE 10.6 Request for Adjustment (Complaint Letter)**

## Tips for Requesting Adjustments and Making Complaints

- Begin with a compliment, point of agreement, statement of the problem, or brief review of action you have taken to resolve the problem.
- Provide identifying data.
- Prove that your claim is valid; explain why the receiver is responsible.

- Enclose document copies supporting your claim.
- Appeal to the receiver's fairness, ethical and legal responsibilities, and desire for customer satisfaction.
- Describe your feelings and your disappointment.
- Avoid sounding angry, emotional, or irrational.
- Close by telling exactly what you want done.

# CHAMPLAIN AUTOMOTIVES
141 Rue Champlain, Gatineau, QC J8T 3H9 (819) 690-3500

November 21, 2005

Customer Service
Raytronic Electronics
57 Émile Simard Avenue
Edmunston, NB E3V 3N9

SUBJECT: CODE-A-PHONE MODEL 100S ●————— *Uses simplified letter style when name of receiver is unknown*

*Begins with compliment* ————— Your Code-A-Phone Model 100S answering unit came well recommended. We liked our neighbour's unit so well that we purchased three for different departments in our business.

*Describes problem calmly* ————— After the three units were unpacked and installed, we discovered a problem. Apparently our office fluorescent lighting interferes with the electronics in these units. When the lights are on, heavy static interrupts every telephone call. When the lights are off, the static disappears.

We can't replace the fluorescent lights, so we tried to return the Code-A-Phones to the place of purchase (Office Mart, 479 Pleasant Street, Truro, NS B2N 3J9). A salesperson inspected the units and said they could not be returned since they were not defective and they had been used.

*Suggests responsibility* ————— Because the descriptive literature and instructions for the Code-A-Phones say nothing about avoiding use in rooms with fluorescent lighting, we expected no trouble. We were quite disappointed that this well-engineered unit—with its time/date stamp, room monitor, and auto-dial features—failed to perform as we hoped it would.

*Stresses disappointment* —————

*Appeals to company's desire to preserve good reputation* ————— If you have a model with similar features that would work in our offices, give me a call. Otherwise, please authorize the return of these units and refund the purchase price of $519.45 (see enclosed invoice). We're confident that a manufacturer with your reputation for excellent products and service will want to resolve this matter quickly. —————— *Tells what action to take*

*Janet Walker*

JANET WALKER, PRESIDENT

JPW:ett
Enclosure

## CHECKLIST FOR MAKING PERSUASIVE REQUESTS

✓ **Gain attention.** In requesting favours, begin with a compliment, statement of agreement, unexpected fact, stimulating question, reader benefit, summary of the problem, or candid plea for help. For claims and complaints, also consider opening with a review of action you have taken to resolve the problem.

✓ **Build interest.** Prove the accuracy and merit of your request with solid evidence, including facts, figures, expert opinion, examples, and details. Suggest direct and indirect benefits for the receiver. Avoid sounding high-pressured, angry, or emotional.

✓ **Reduce resistance.** Identify what factors will be obstacles to the receiver; offer counterarguments. Demonstrate your credibility by being knowledgeable. In requesting favours or making recommendations, show how the receiver or others will benefit. In making claims, appeal to the receiver's sense of fairness and desire for goodwill. Express your disappointment.

✓ **Motivate action.** Confidently ask for specific action. For favours include an end date (if appropriate) and try to repeat a key benefit.

## PLANNING AND COMPOSING SALES MESSAGES

Traditional direct-mail marketing involves the sale of goods and services through letters, catalogues, brochures, and other messages delivered by land mail. Electronic marketing, on the other hand, involves sales messages delivered by e-mail, Web sites, and, less frequently, by fax. To some marketers, e-mail sounds like "the promised land," guaranteeing instant delivery and at only pennies per message. However, unsolicited e-mail, called "spam," has generated an incredible backlash from recipients, who want their e-mail addresses to remain private and unviolated. One of the leading direct-mail marketers correctly sensed the pulse of the times when he remarked, "Nothing is more powerful than goodwill—except ill will."[4] Unsolicited e-mail seems to create enormous ill will today. Although marketing by e-mail may one day eclipse traditional direct mail, for today's markets, traditional sales messages are still key. Sellers feel that "even with all the new media we have available today, a letter remains one of the most powerful ways to make sales, generate leads, boost retail traffic, and solicit donations."[5]

Professionals who specialize in traditional direct-mail services have made a science of analyzing a market, developing an effective mailing list, studying the product, preparing a sophisticated campaign aimed at a target audience, and motivating the reader to act. You've probably received many direct-mail packages, often called "junk" mail. These packages typically contain a sales letter, a brochure, a price list, illustrations of the product, testimonials, and other persuasive appeals.

We're most concerned here with the sales letter: its strategy, organization, and evidence. Because sales letters are generally written by specialists, you may never write one on the job. Why, then, learn how to write a sales letter? In many ways, every letter we create is a form of sales letter. We sell our ideas, our organizations, and ourselves. Learning the techniques of sales writing will help you be more successful in any communication that requires persuasion and promotion. Furthermore, you'll recognize sales strategies, thus enabling you to become a more perceptive consumer of ideas, products, and services.

# Applying the 3-×-3 Writing Process to Sales Messages

Successful sales messages require research on the product or service offered and analysis of the purpose for writing.

Marketing professionals analyze every aspect of a sales message because consumers reject most direct-mail offers. Like the experts, you'll want to pay close attention to the preparatory steps of analysis and adaptation before writing the actual message.

*Analyzing the Product and Purpose.* Before writing a sales letter, you should study the product carefully. What can you learn about its design, construction, raw materials, and manufacturing process? About its ease of use, efficiency, durability, and applications? Be sure to consider warranties, service, price, and special appeals. At the same time, evaluate the competition so that you can compare your product's strengths against the competitor's weaknesses.

Now you're ready to identify your central selling points. At Amazon.com the central selling points are reliability, selection, and convenience. The company has won scores of loyal customers by delivering packages on time, often exceeding customers' expectations.[6] The central selling point for Pitney Bowes was service. It used the following testimonial: "When we went looking for copiers, service was our number one concern . . . and Pitney Bowes was our number one choice." Analyzing your product and studying the competition help you determine what to emphasize in your sales letter.

Another important decision in the preparatory stage involves the specific purpose of your letter. Do you want the reader to call for a free video and brochure? Fill out an order form? See a demonstration? Send a credit card authorization? Before you write the first word of your message, know what features of the product you will emphasize and what response you want.

*Adapting to the Audience.* Blanket mailings sent "cold" to occupants generally produce low responses—typically only 2 percent. That means that 98 percent of us usually toss direct-mail sales letters directly into the garbage. But the response rate can be increased dramatically by targeting the audience through selected mailing lists. These lists can be purchased or compiled. By directing your message to a selected group, you can make certain assumptions about the receivers. You would expect similar interests, needs, and demographics (age, income, and other characteristics). With this knowledge you can adapt the sales letter to a specific audience.

## Crafting a Winning Sales Message

Your primary goal in writing a sales message is to get someone to devote a few moments of attention to it.[7] You may be promoting a product, a service, an idea, or yourself. In each case the most effective messages will (1) gain attention, (2) build interest, (3) reduce resistance, and (4) motivate action. This is the same recipe we studied earlier, but the ingredients are different.

Openers for sales messages should be brief, honest, relevant, and provocative.

*Gaining Attention.* One of the most critical elements of a sales letter is its opening paragraph. This opener should be short (one to five lines), honest, relevant, and stimulating. Marketing pros have found that eye-catching typographical arrangements or provocative messages, such as the following, can hook a reader's attention:

- **Offer:** *A free trip to Hawaii is just the beginning!*
- **Promise:** *Now you can raise your sales income by 50 percent or even more with the proven techniques found in . . . .*
- **Question:** *Do you yearn for an honest, fulfilling relationship?*
- **Quotation or proverb:** *Necessity is the mother of invention.*

Many people wrote off Mac computers a long time ago and switched to Windows platforms. But Steve Jobs returned to Macintosh and gave its sales a shot in the arm. Colourful, cool designs attract attention, while promises of frustration-free operation reduce resistance. Knowing your product and audience enable you to find ways to gain attention and reduce resistance in any sales presentation.

- **Fact:** *The Greenland Eskimos ate more fat than anyone in the world. And yet . . . they had virtually no heart disease.*

- **Product feature:** *Volvo's snazzy new convertible ensures your safety with a roll bar that pops out when the car tips 40 degrees to the side.*

- **Testimonial:** *"It is wonderful to see such a well-written and informative piece of work." (Thomas J. Bata, chairman, Bata Ltd., about* Secrets of Power Presentations*)*

- **Startling statement:** *Let the poor and hungry feed themselves! For just $100 they can.*

- **Personalized action setting:** *It's 4:30 p.m. and you've got to make a decision. You need everybody's opinion, no matter where they are. Before you pick up your phone to call them one at a time, pick up this card: Bell Canada Teleconference Services.*

Other openings calculated to capture attention might include a solution to a problem, an anecdote, a personalized statement using the receiver's name, or a relevant current event.

***Building Interest.*** In this phase of your sales message, you should describe clearly the product or service. In simple language emphasize the central selling points that you identified during your prewriting analysis. Those selling points can be developed using rational or emotional appeals.

Rational appeals are associated with reason and intellect. They translate selling points into references to making or saving money, increasing efficiency, or making the best use of resources. In general, rational appeals are appropriate when a product is expensive, long-lasting, or important to health, security, and financial success. Emotional appeals relate to status, ego, and sensual feelings. Appealing to the emotions is sometimes effective when a product is inexpensive, short-lived, or non-essential. Many clever sales messages, however, combine emotional and rational strategies for a dual appeal. Consider the following examples.

### Rational Appeal

You can buy the things you need and want, pay household bills, pay off higher-cost loans and credit cards—as soon as you're approved and your Credit-Line account is opened.

### Emotional Appeal

Leave the urban bustle behind and escape to sun-soaked Bermuda! To recharge your batteries with an injection of sun and surf, all you need is your bathing suit, a little suntan lotion, and your Credit-Line card.

### Dual Appeal

New Credit-Line cardholders are immediately eligible for a $100 travel certificate and additional discounts at fun-filled resorts. Save up to 40 percent while lying on a beach in picturesque, sun-soaked Bermuda, the year-round resort island.

A physical description of your product is not enough, however. Zig Ziglar, thought by some to be the United States' greatest salesperson, points out that no matter how well you know your product, no one is persuaded by cold, hard facts alone. In the end, he contends, "People buy because of the product benefits."[8] Your job is to translate those cold facts into warm feelings and reader benefits. Let's say a sales letter promotes a hand cream made with aloe and cocoa butter extracts, along with Vitamin A. Those facts become, "Nature's hand helpers—including soothing aloe and cocoa extracts, along with firming Vitamin A—form invisible gloves that protect your sensitive skin against the hardships of work, harsh detergents, and constant environmental assaults."

Techniques for reducing resistance include testimonials, guarantees, warranties, samples, and performance polls.

*Reducing Resistance.* Marketing pros use a number of techniques to overcome resistance and build desire. When price is an obstacle, consider these suggestions:

- Delay mentioning price until after you've created a desire for the product.
- Show the price in small units, such as the price per issue of a magazine.
- Demonstrate how the reader saves money by, for instance, subscribing for two or three years.
- Compare your prices with those of a competitor.

In addition, you need to anticipate other objections and questions the receiver may have. When possible, translate these objections into selling points (*If you've never ordered software by mail, let us send you our demonstration disks at no charge*). Other techniques to overcome resistance and prove the credibility of the product include the following:

- **Testimonials:** *"I learned so much in your language courses that I began to dream in French." —Holly Franker, Woodstock, Ontario*
- **Names of satisfied users** (with permission, of course): *Enclosed is a partial list of private pilots who enthusiastically subscribe to our service.*
- **Money-back guarantee or warranty:** *We offer the longest warranties in the business—all parts and service on-site for two years!*
- **Free trial or sample:** *We're so confident that you'll like our new accounting program that we want you to try it absolutely free.*
- **Performance tests, polls, or awards:** *Our TP-3000 was named Best Web Phone, and Etown.com voted it Cell Phone of the Year.*

*Motivating Action.* All the effort put into a sales message is wasted if the reader fails to act. To make it easy for readers to act, you can provide a reply card, a stamped and preaddressed envelope, a toll-free telephone number, an easy Web site, or a promise of a follow-up call. Because readers often need an extra push, consider including additional motivators, such as the following:

- **Offer a gift:** *You'll receive a free cell phone with the purchase of any new car.*

- **Promise an incentive:** *With every new, paid subscription, we'll plant a tree in one of Canada's national parks.*

- **Limit the offer:** *Only the first 100 customers receive free cheques.*

- **Set a deadline:** *You must act before June 1 to get these low prices.*

- **Guarantee satisfaction:** *We'll return your full payment if you're not entirely satisfied—no questions asked.*

The final paragraph of the sales letter carries the punch line. This is where you tell readers what you want done and give them reasons for doing it. Most sales letters also include postscripts because they make irresistible reading. Even readers who might skim over or bypass paragraphs are drawn to a P.S. Therefore, use a postscript to reveal your strongest motivator, to add a special inducement for a quick response, or to reemphasize a central selling point.

*Putting It All Together.* Sales letters are a preferred marketing medium because they can be personalized, directed to target audiences, and filled with a more complete message than other advertising media. But direct mail is expensive. That's why the total sales message is crafted so painstakingly.

Let's examine a sales letter, shown in Figure 10.7, addressed to a target group of small-business owners. To sell the new magazine *Small Business Monthly*, the letter incorporates all four components of an effective persuasive message. Notice that the personalized action-setting opener places the reader in a familiar situation (getting into an elevator) and draws an analogy between failing to reach the top floor and failing to achieve a business goal. The writer develops a rational central selling point (a magazine that provides valuable information for a growing small business) and repeats this selling point in all the components of the letter. Notice, too, how a testimonial from a small-business executive lends support to the sales message, and how the closing pushes for action. Since the price of the magazine is not a selling feature, it's mentioned only on the reply card. This sales letter saves its strongest motivator—a free booklet—for the high-impact P.S. line.

## Writing Online Sales Letters

As consumers become more comfortable with online shopping, they will be receiving more e-mail sales letters. If your organization requires an online sales letter, you can make it more acceptable by following these techniques:

- **Be selective.** Send messages only to targeted, preselected customers. E-mail users detest "spam" (unsolicited sales and other messages). However, receivers are surprisingly receptive to offers specifically for them. Remember that today's customer is *somebody*—not *anybody*.

- **Keep the message short, conversational, and focused.** Because on-screen text is taxing to read, be brief. Focus on one or two central selling points only.

- **Provide a means for being removed from the mailing list.** It's polite and good business tactics to include a statement that tells receivers how to be removed from the sender's mailing database.

> Techniques for motivating action include offering a gift or incentive, limiting an offer, and guaranteeing satisfaction.

> Because direct mail is an expensive way to advertise, messages should present complete information in a personalized tone for specific audiences.

> Send only targeted, not "blanket," mailings with something special for select group.

**FIGURE 10.7  Sales Letter**

## Prewriting

**Analyze:** The purpose of this letter is to persuade the reader to return the reply card and subscribe to *Small Business Monthly*.

**Anticipate:** The targeted audience consists of small-business owners. The central selling point is providing practical data to help their businesses grow.

**Adapt:** Because readers will be reluctant, use the indirect pattern.

## Writing

**Research:** Gather facts to promote your product, including testimonials.

**Organize:** Gain attention by opening with a personalized action picture. Build interest with an analogy and a description of magazine features. Use a testimonial to reduce resistance. Motivate action with a free booklet and an easy-reply card.

**Compose:** Prepare a first draft for a pilot study.

## Revising

**Revise:** Use short paragraphs and short sentences. Replace words like *malfunction* with words like *glitch*.

**Proofread:** Indent long quotations on the left and right sides. Italicize or underscore titles of publications. Hyphenate *first-of-its-kind* and *hard-headed*.

**Evaluate:** Monitor the response rate to this letter to assess its effectiveness.

---

**small business monthly**
160 Duncan Mills Road • Toronto ON M3B 1Z5

April 15, 2005

Mr. James Wehrley
1608 Davidson Avenue North
Listowel, ON N4W 3A2

Dear Mr. Wehrley:

*(Puts reader into action setting)* — You walk into the elevator and push the button for the top floor.  The elevator glides upward.  You step back and relax. — *(Gains attention)*

But the elevator never reaches the top.  A glitch in its electronics prevents it from processing the information it needs to take you to your destination.

*(Suggests analogy)* — Do you see a similarity between your growing company and this elevator?  You're aiming for the top, but a lack of information halts your progress.  Now you can put your company into gear and propel it toward success with a new publication—*Small Business Monthly*.

*(Emphasizes central selling point)* — This first-of-its-kind magazine brings you marketing tips, hard-headed business pointers, opportunities, and inspiration.  This is the kind of current information you need today to be where you want to be tomorrow.  One executive wrote: — *(Builds interest)*

*(Uses testimonial for credibility)* —
> As president of a small manufacturing company, I read several top business publications, but I get my "bread and butter" from *Small Business Monthly*.  I'm not interested in a lot of "pie in the sky" and theory.  I find practical problems and how to solve them in *SBM*.
> —Mitchell M. Perry, Oshawa, Ontario

*(Reduces resistance)*

Mr. Perry's words are the best recommendation I can offer you to try *SBM*.  In less time than you might spend on an average business lunch, you learn the latest in management, operations, finance, taxes, business law, compensation, and advertising.

*(Repeats central sales pitch in last sentence)* — To evaluate *Small Business Monthly* without cost or obligation, let me send you a free issue.  Just initial and return the enclosed card to start receiving a wealth of practical information that could keep your company travelling upward to its goal. — *(Motivates action)*

Cordially,

*Cheryl Owings*

Cheryl Owings
Vice President, Circulation

*(Spotlights free offer in P.S. to prompt immediate reply)* — P.S.  Act before May 15 and I'll send you our valuable booklet *Managing for Success*, revealing more than 100 secrets for helping small businesses grow.

- **Project sincerity.** Sending a simple, low-key message and encouraging feedback help establish a tone of sincerity.

Whether you actually write sales letters on the job or merely receive them, you'll better understand their organization and appeals by reviewing this chapter and the tips in the following checklist.

## CHECKLIST FOR WRITING SALES LETTERS

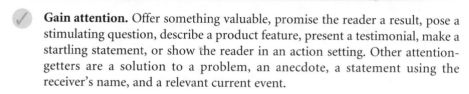 **Gain attention.** Offer something valuable, promise the reader a result, pose a stimulating question, describe a product feature, present a testimonial, make a startling statement, or show the reader in an action setting. Other attention-getters are a solution to a problem, an anecdote, a statement using the receiver's name, and a relevant current event.

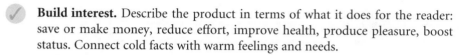 **Build interest.** Describe the product in terms of what it does for the reader: save or make money, reduce effort, improve health, produce pleasure, boost status. Connect cold facts with warm feelings and needs.

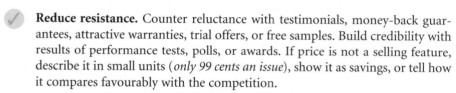 **Reduce resistance.** Counter reluctance with testimonials, money-back guarantees, attractive warranties, trial offers, or free samples. Build credibility with results of performance tests, polls, or awards. If price is not a selling feature, describe it in small units (*only 99 cents an issue*), show it as savings, or tell how it compares favourably with the competition.

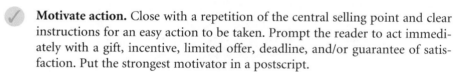 **Motivate action.** Close with a repetition of the central selling point and clear instructions for an easy action to be taken. Prompt the reader to act immediately with a gift, incentive, limited offer, deadline, and/or guarantee of satisfaction. Put the strongest motivator in a postscript.

## DEVELOPING PERSUASIVE NEWS RELEASES

News (press) releases announce information about your company to the media: new products, new managers, new facilities, participation in community projects, awards given or received, joint ventures, donations, or seminars and demonstrations. Naturally, you hope that this news will be published and provide good publicity for your company. But this kind of largely self-serving information is not always appealing to magazine and newspaper editors or to TV producers. To get them to read beyond the first sentence, try these suggestions:

- Open with an attention-getting lead or a summary of the important facts.

- Include answers to the five Ws and one H (who, what, when, where, why, and how) in the article—but not all in the first sentence!

- Appeal to the audience of the target media. Emphasize reader benefits written in the style of the focus publication or newscast.

- Present the most important information early, followed by supporting information. Don't put your best ideas last because they may be chopped off or ignored.

- Make the release visually appealing. Limit the text to one or two double-spaced pages with attractive formatting.

Effective news releases feature an attention-getting opener, place key information up front, appeal to the target audience, and maintain visual interest.

## FIGURE 10.8 News Release

Provides optional headline ————

Opens with dateline and attention-getting lead

Uses visually appealing formatting

Uses -30- symbols to signal end of release

Supplies names and telephone numbers of persons who can answer questions

Answers five Ws: *who, what, when, where,* and *why*

Places key information up front

**United Way of Greater Toronto**

For Immediate Release

# Vince Carter Launches Team Toronto for United Way

TORONTO, ON – July 10, 2003 – Toronto Raptor **Vince Carter,** Olympic cyclist **Curt Harnett** and Olympic hockey player **Lori Dupuis** held a basketball clinic for dozens of kids today at the downtown YMCA to kick off Team Toronto, a unique program created by Bell Canada and United Way of Greater Toronto designed to increase giving to the charity's 2003 fall fundraising campaign.

Team Toronto features a team of sports celebrities including Carter – the team captain, the Toronto Maple Leafs' **Pat Quinn** and **Owen Nolan,** members of Canada's gold-medal winning Olympic hockey team **Cassie Campbell, Lori Dupuis,** and **Vicky Sunohara,** and Olympic cyclist **Curt Harnett.** Members of Team Toronto will attend selected United Way events to encourage increased giving and participation during this year's United Way fundraising campaign.

Team Toronto will also feature special personal experience incentive packages available to workplaces that run United Way fundraising campaigns. These incentives aim to increase:

- the level of employee giving and participation
- the total number of workplaces that donate to United Way
- and the number of people who donate at the leadership level of $1000 or more.

As well, Bell and United Way are excited to include Team Toronto in student campaigns this fall.

"One of my goals as this year's campaign chair was to create a unique program that would encourage corporations and their employees to more actively support the campaign," said John Sheridan, 2003 United Way campaign chair and group president of Bell Canada. "The Team Toronto initiative is a fantastic partnership with local sports heroes who understand that great things can happen when everyone works as a team."

"We're very excited that Team Toronto and Bell Canada have come together to score big for United Way," said United Way of Greater Toronto president and CEO **Frances Lankin.** "Team Toronto will help increase awareness of United Way's role in the community and how we help hundreds of thousands of people each year through 200 social and health service agencies in neighbourhoods across the city."

...../2

**United Way of Greater Toronto**
26 Wellington St E 11th Floor
Toronto ON M5E 1W9
Tel: (416) 777-2001 Fax: (416) 777-0962
www.unitedwaytoronto.com

-2-

United Way of Greater Toronto runs the largest annual fundraising campaign in Canada, and raised $81 million last year. Thanks to the community's generosity, United Way is able to help hundreds of thousands of Torontonians, giving young children a healthier start in life, helping seniors live more independently, providing opportunities for youth and assisting newcomers to settle. It will announce the 2004 fundraising goal on September 4.

Bell Canada, Canada's national leader in communications, provides connectivity to residential and business customers through wired and wireless voice and data communications, local and long distance phone services, high speed and wireless Internet access, IP-broadband services, e-business solutions and satellite television services. Bell Canada is wholly owned by BCE Inc. For more information please visit www.bell.ca.

-30-

**Media contacts:**
United Way of Greater Toronto – Lynn Beauchamp, James Ip or Kim Barnhardt (416) 777-2001.
Don Blair, Bell Canada Media Relations, 416-581-3311

## Applying Your Skills at United Way-Centraide

Historically, Durham College has worked directly with the United Way of Oshawa, Whitby, Clarington, Brock, and Scugog. Many of its employees, however, don't live within the area served by this particular United Way agency. The number of new employees hired for the University of Ontario Institute of Technology further compounds this situation. Although most of these employees are willing to support the United Way, they would prefer to see the money go back into their own communities.

To address this concern, the Durham College/UOIT campaign organizers invited a representative from the United Way of Ajax, Pickering to participate in the planning for their next campaign. This way, the entire Durham Region was represented on the planning team. A second step was to customize the donor pledge form to make it easier for donors to direct their pledges. The existing United Way pledge forms provided donors with the opportunity to direct their donation to the United Way agency of their choice or to any other registered charity. However, the "give where you live" philosophy still remained a stumbling block. Thirdly, the organizers decided to highlight the tax benefits to donors.

The campaign organizers hoped that by involving a second agency, making the forms more user-friendly, and focusing on donor benefits, they could accomplish their campaign goal of increasing their employee participation rate as well as their total campaign contribution.

### Your Task

Prepare a memo to all Durham College/UOIT employees encouraging them to contribute to this year's United Way campaign. Include at least three direct or indirect benefits to being a United Way donor. Be sure to include information that will convince potential donors that their money will be directed as they wish.

**www.unitedway.ca**

---

- Look and sound credible—no typos, no imaginative spelling or punctuation, no factual errors.

The most important ingredient of a press release, of course, is *news*. Articles that merely plug products end up in the circular file. Bell Canada, recipient of one of the United Way's "Thanks a Million" awards, sent out the press release in Figure 10.8 announcing that Toronto Raptor Vince Carter and other celebrity athletes had held a basketball clinic to kick off Bell's 2003 United Way campaign. Naturally, it provides information about both the United Way and Bell Canada, but it also provides a great deal of news about the clinic and the campaign.

## SUMMARY OF LEARNING OBJECTIVES

*1* **Apply the 3-×-3 writing process to persuasive messages.** The first step in the writing process for a persuasive message is analysis of the audience and purpose. Writers must know exactly what they want the receiver to do or think. The second step involves thinking of ways to adapt the message to the audience. Particularly important is expressing the request so that it may benefit the reader. Next, the writer must collect data and organize it into an appropriate strategy. An indirect strategy is probably best if the audience will resist the request.

**2** **Explain the components of a persuasive message.** The most effective persuasive messages gain attention by opening with a problem, unexpected statement, reader benefit, compliment, related fact, stimulating question, or similar device. They build interest with facts, expert opinions, examples, details, and additional reader benefits. They reduce resistance by anticipating objections and presenting counterarguments. They conclude by motivating a specific action and making it easy for the reader to respond. Skilled communicators avoid distortion, exaggeration, and deception when making persuasive arguments.

**3** **Request favours and action effectively.** When writing to ask for a favour, the indirect pattern is appropriate. This means delaying the request until after logical reasons have been presented. Such memos should emphasize, if possible, benefits to the reader. Appeals to professionalism are often a useful technique. Writers can counter any anticipated resistance with explanations and motivate action in the closing.

**4** **Write convincing persuasive messages within organizations.** In writing internal messages that require persuasion, the indirect pattern is appropriate. These messages might begin with a frank discussion of a problem. They build interest by emphasizing points that are important to the readers. They support the request with accurate, honest evidence.

**5** **Request adjustments and make claims successfully.** When writing about damaged products, mistaken billing, or other claims, the indirect pattern is appropriate. These messages might begin with a sincere compliment or an objective statement of the problem. They explain concisely why a claim is legitimate. Copies of relevant documents should be enclosed. The message should conclude with a clear statement of the action to be taken.

**6** **Compose successful sales messages.** Before writing a sales message, it's necessary to analyze the product and purpose carefully. The letter begins with an attention-getting statement that is short, honest, relevant, and stimulating. It builds interest by describing the product or service clearly in simple language, incorporating appropriate appeals. Testimonials, a money-back guarantee, a free trial, or some other device can reduce resistance. A gift, incentive, deadline, or other device can motivate action.

**7** **Describe the basic elements included in effective news releases.** Effective news releases usually open with an attention-getting lead or summary of the important facts. They attempt to answer the questions who, what, when, where, why, and how. They are written carefully to appeal to the audience of the target media. The best news releases present the most important information early, make the release visually appealing, and look and sound credible.

# CHAPTER REVIEW

1. List the four steps in the indirect pattern for persuasive messages. (Objs. 1 and 2)

2. List six or more techniques for opening a persuasive request for a favour. (Obj. 3)

3. List techniques for building interest in a persuasive request for a favour. (Obj. 3)

4. Describe ways to reduce resistance in persuasive requests. (Obj. 3)

5. How should a persuasive request end? (Objs. 2 and 3)

6. When does persuasion become unethical? (Obj. 2)

7. What are the differences between direct and indirect reader benefits? Give an original example of each (other than those described). (Obj. 3)

8. When would persuasion be necessary in messages moving downward in organizations? (Obj. 4)

9. Why are persuasive messages usually longer than direct messages? (Objs. 1–7)

10. When is it necessary to use the indirect pattern in requesting adjustments or making claims? (Obj. 5)

11. What is an appropriate tone for a letter requesting an adjustment? (Obj. 5)

12. Name eight or more ways to attract attention in opening a sales message. (Obj. 6)

13. How do rational appeals differ from emotional appeals? Give an original example of each. (Obj. 6)

14. Name five or more ways to motivate action in closing a sales message. (Obj. 6)

15. List five or more topics that an organization might feature in a press release. (Obj. 7)

# CRITICAL THINKING

1. How are requests for action and sales letters similar and how are they different? (Objs. 3 and 6)

2. What are some of the underlying motivations that prompt individuals to agree to requests that do not directly benefit themselves or their organizations? (Objs. 2–7)

3. In view of the burden that "junk" mail places on society (depleted landfills, declining timber supplies, overburdened postal system), how can "junk" mail be justified? (Obj. 6)

4. Why is it important to know your needs and have documentation when you make requests of superiors? (Obj. 4)

5. **Ethical Issue:** Identify and discuss direct-mail sales messages that you consider unethical.

# ACTIVITIES

## 10.1 Document for Analysis: Weak Persuasive Invitation (Obj. 3)

**Your Task.** Analyze the following document. List its weaknesses. If your instructor directs, revise it.

### ✗ *Ineffective Letter*

Dear Dr. Thomas:

Because you're a local Guelph author, we thought it might not be too much trouble for you to speak at our U of G banquet May 5.

Some of us business students here at Guelph University admired your book *Beyond Race and Gender*, which appeared last spring and became such a hit across the nation. One of our professors said you were now the nation's diversity management guru. What exactly did you mean when you said that Canada is no longer a blend of two cultures—that it's now a "smorgasbord of multicultural expectations"?

Because we have no funds for honoraria, we have to rely on local speakers. The Reverend James R. Jones and Vice Mayor Rebecca A. Timmons were speakers in the past. Our banquets usually begin at 6:30 with a social hour, followed by dinner at 7:30 and the speaker from 8:30 until 9:00 or 9:15. We can arrange transportation for you and your wife if you need it.

We realize that you must be very busy, but we hope you'll agree. Please let our advisor, Professor Alexa North, have the favour of an early response.

Cordially,

## 10.2 Document for Analysis: Weak Persuasive Memo (Obj. 4)

**Your Task.** Analyze the following document. List its weaknesses. If your instructor directs, revise it.

### ✗ *Poorly Written Memo*

**TO:** Jennifer Ritter, VP, Media Relations
**FROM:** Phillip Pitino, Product Manager
**SUBJECT:** OUR TRADE BOOTH

We have all enjoyed attending the many trade shows where we exhibit our products. I particularly look forward to the Toronto Comdex show, which, as you know, is the biggest software and hardware trade show in the country.

My fellow product managers and I try to get visitors to come to our booth, but it's not easy. In the past we've tried promotions with T-shirts, coffee mugs, and pens all sporting our company logo. We also tried "freemiums," but we lost a bundle on these $50 coupons. You will recall that they were supposed to be used toward future software purchases, but we learned too late that they could be easily photocopied and multiple copies printed out. What a bummer!

But here's a promotion idea that is not going to lose us a lot of money. Digital Equipment Corporation, at its exhibit at Networld a couple of months ago in Toronto, had a way of making personalized Web pages for visitors. They used a template, took a picture of the visitor with a digital camera, and made a Web page for each visitor. They then gave a disk to the visitor with the page in HTML format, ready to upload to their personal Web sites. It was a huge hit! The great part about this is that visitors have to leave their names, addresses, and contact information to insert into their Web pages. We get all this great information—they get a free disk. Doesn't this sound like a winner? About all we have to do in the way of preparation is have our Web design team make a Web page template. This shouldn't be too difficult.

Let me know what you think. Our next big trade show is June 10 in Vancouver.

## 10.3 Document for Analysis: Weak Adjustment Request (Obj. 5)

**Your Task.** Analyze the following document. List its weaknesses. If your instructor directs, revise it.

X *Poorly Written Letter*

Dear Sir:

Three months ago we purchased four of your CopyMaster Model S-5 photocopiers, and we've had nothing but trouble ever since.

Your salesperson, Kevin Woo, assured us that the S-5 could easily handle our volume of 3000 copies a day. This seemed strange since the sales brochure said that the S-5 was meant for 500 copies a day. But we believed Mr. Woo. Big mistake! Our four S-5 copiers are down constantly; we can't go on like this. Because they're still under warranty, they eventually get repaired. But we're losing considerable business in downtime.

Your Mr. Woo has been less than helpful, so I telephoned the district manager, Keith Sumner. I suggested that we trade in our S-5 copiers (which we got for $2 500 each) on two S-55 models (at $13 500 each). However, Mr. Sumner said he would have to charge 50 percent depreciation on our S-5 copiers. What a ripoff! I think that 20 percent depreciation is more reasonable since we've had the machines only three months. Mr. Sumner said he would get back to me, and I haven't heard from him since.

I'm writing to your headquarters because I have no faith in either Mr. Woo or Mr. Sumner, and I need action on these machines. If you understood anything about business, you would see what a sweet deal I'm offering you. I'm willing to

stick with your company and purchase your most expensive model—but I can't take such a loss on the S-5 copiers. The S-5 copiers are relatively new; you should be able to sell them with no trouble. And think of all the money you'll save by not having your repair technicians making constant trips to service our S-5 copiers! Please let me hear from you immediately.

Sincerely yours,

## 10.4 Sales Letter Analysis (Obj. 6)

**Your Task.** Select a one- or two-page sales letter received by you or a friend. Study the letter and then answer these questions:

a. What techniques capture the reader's attention?
b. Is the opening effective? Explain.
c. What are the central selling points?
d. Does the letter use rational, emotional, or a combination of appeals? Explain.
e. What reader benefits are suggested?
f. How does the letter build interest in the product or service?
g. How is price handled?
h. How does the letter anticipate reader resistance and offer counterarguments?
i. What action is the reader to take? How is the action made easy?
j. What motivators spur the reader to act quickly?

## 10.5 Persuasive Favour/Action Request: Paying Your Tuition (Obj. 3)

**TEAM**    **CRITICAL THINKING**

After high school you started taking postsecondary courses but found that you needed to get a job. Your academic courses had to be put on hold. After working for a few years, you want to go back to school. You know that your education can benefit your employer, but you can't really afford the fees for tuition and books. You've heard that many companies (General Motors, Marriott Hotels, Procter & Gamble Canada, and others) offer reimbursement for fees and books when employees complete approved courses with a C or higher.
**Your Task.** In teams discuss the best way to approach an employer whom you wish to persuade to start a tuition/books reimbursement program. How could such a program help the employer? Remember that the most successful requests help receivers see what's in it for them. What objections might your employer raise? How can you counter them? After discussing strategies in teams, write a team memo or individual memos to your boss (for a company where you now work or one with which you are familiar). Persuade her or him to act on your action request.

## 10.6 Persuasive Favour/Action Request: Celebrity Auction (Obj. 3)

**TEAM** **CRITICAL THINKING**

Your student organization must find ways to raise money. The president of your group appoints a team and asks it to brainstorm for ways to meet your group's pledge to aid your school's scholarship and bursary fund. The fund provides monetary rewards to academic high achievers and much needed support to students who might otherwise be unable to afford a postsecondary education. After considering and rejecting a number of creative, but impractical, ideas, your team decides on a celebrity auction. At a spring function, items or services from local and other celebrities would be auctioned. Your organization approves your idea and asks your team to persuade an important person in your community (or your institution's president) to donate an object to be auctioned. If you have higher aspirations, write to a movie star or athlete of your choice (perhaps one who attended your school).

**Your Task.** As a team, discuss the situation and decide what action to take. Then write a persuasive letter to secure an item for the auction. For example, you might wish to ask a movie star to donate a prop from her or his recent movie.

## 10.7 Persuasive Favour/Action Request: Cultivating an Internship (Obj. 3)

Your school has no internship program in your field. You realize that work experience is invaluable both to acquaint you with the field and to help you find employment. You decide to write to Ranch Enterprises, Inc., asking this company to hire you as an intern.

Although you're taking a full load of courses, you feel you could work 12 to 15 hours per week for one semester. You would have to arrange the internship hours around your existing class schedule. Describe your desire to function in a specific capacity, but express your willingness to serve wherever the company can accommodate you. Of course, you expect no remuneration, but you will be receiving up to three units of credit if Ranch can take you for one semester.

**Your Task.** Write a persuasive letter to Phyllis Laranjo, Manager, Human Resources, Ranch Enterprises, 1901 St. Clair Avenue, Toronto, ON M5W 6R1.

## 10.8 Persuasive Favour/Action Request: Dining Gratuity Guidelines (Obj. 3)

As a server in the Tejas Grill, you have occasionally been "stiffed" by customers who left no tip. You know your service is excellent, but some customers just don't get it. They seem to think that tips are optional, a sign of appreciation. For servers, however, tips are 80 percent of their income. In a recent newspaper article, you learned that some restaurants—like the new Coach House in Victoria—automatically add a 15 percent tip to the bill. In Montreal the Porte Rouge restaurant prints "gratuity guidelines" on cheques, showing customers what a 15 or 20 percent tip would be. You also know that American Express recently developed a gratuity calculation feature on its terminals. This means that diners don't even have to do the math!

**Your Task.** Your fellow servers have asked you, as a business communication student, to write a serious letter to Doug Young, general manager of Tejas (3150 Signal Hill Drive SW, Calgary, AB T3H 3T2), persuading him to adopt mandatory tipping guidelines. Talk with fellow servers (classmates) to develop logical persuasive arguments. Follow the four-part plan developed in this chapter.

## 10.9 Persuasive Action Request: Asking Your Member of Parliament to Listen and Act (Obj. 3)

**WEB** **CRITICAL THINKING**

Assume you are upset about an issue, and you want your member of Parliament to know your position. Choose a national issue about which you feel strongly: student loans, social insurance depletion, human rights in other countries, federal safety regulations for employees, environmental protection, employment equity, gun control, Aboriginal issues, the federal deficit, or some other area regulated by government.

**Your Task.** Obtain your MP's address and appropriate title by visiting the Government of Canada Web site at <www.parl.gc.ca>. You'll find e-mail and land addresses, along with fax and telephone numbers. Remember that although e-mail and fax messages are fast, they don't carry as much influence as personal letters. And MPs are having trouble responding to the overload of e-mail messages they receive. Decide whether it's better to send an e-mail message or a letter to your representative outlining your feelings. For best results, consider these tips. (1) Use the proper form of address (*The Honourable John Smith, Dear Mr. Smith* or *The Honourable Joan Doe, Dear Ms. Doe*). (2) Identify yourself as a member of his or her province or territory. (3) Immediately state your position (*I urge you to support/oppose . . . because*). (4) Present facts and illustrations and how they affect you personally. If legislation were enacted, how would you or your organization be better off or worse off? Avoid generalities. (5) Offer to provide further information. (6) Keep the message polite, constructive, and brief (one page maximum).

## 10.10 Persuasive Favour/Action Request: How to Spend $5 Million (Obj. 3)

As you're having your second cup of coffee and reading the morning newspaper, you see an article that gets you thinking. One of your school's alumni has made a fortune in the software business. Before the dot-com bust, he sold his company for over $70 million. The article says that like many successful people, he wants to give back something to the school that gave him his education and his start. As a result, he has donated $5 million to your school! As you try to imagine how much $5 million would buy, you begin to wonder how your school will use this windfall.

**Your Task.** Write a persuasive letter to your school's chief operating officer outlining some of the ways you think the money could be spent at your school. From your perspective, how could programs, services, or equipment be improved? How about tutoring in some of your classes? Use specific examples of areas that could be improved.

## 10.11 Persuasive Action Request: Solving the Problem of Chaotic Service Lines at McDonald's (Obj. 3)

**TEAM** **CRITICAL THINKING**

As Parker Williams, the franchise owner of a popular local McDonald's restaurant, you are unhappy about one thing. At rush times customers complain about the chaotic multiple waiting lines to approach the service counter. You once saw two customers nearly get into a fistfight over cutting into a line. Customers often are so intent on looking for ways to improve their positions in line that they fail to examine the menu and are clueless when their turn arrives. At moderately busy times, no lines form at all and shy customers are served last.

You get together with a small group of other franchise owners to discuss the problem. Your goal is to work out a solution to the problem and then write a letter to other owners to convince them of your decision. A district meeting of McDonald's owners is scheduled in one month, and you would like to see action taken. All restaurant owners in a district must agree on a plan, if a change is made.

In teams, discuss the pros and cons of multiple lines versus a single-line (serpentine) system. It seems like a simple thing, but for many businesses it is a major decision. In fact, some academics devote their careers to studying the psychology of lines. Within your group, discuss the advantages of each system (or any other system). What do banks do? How about the competition, such as Wendy's, Burger King, and other fast-food restaurants? Is this totally an issue of speed? Some McDonald's executives contend that the multiline system accommodates higher volumes of customers more quickly. But the problem of perception is equally important. What happens when you open the door to a restaurant and see a long, long single line? Do you stick around to learn how quickly the line is moving?

**Your Task.** Within your group decide on a course of action based on your own experience in fast-food restaurants and other service organizations. Perhaps a trial program at a group of restaurants would be possible. Consult the Career Coach box on page 11 and Activity 1.15 in Chapter 1 for fur-

ther analysis of this problem. Write a letter to other franchise owners in your region persuading them to agree with your position at the next district meeting. Although a similar letter will go to many franchise owners, address the first one to Matthew and Cynthia Ames, co-owners of a McDonald's at 12 Queen's Road, St. John's, NL A1C 2B1. Your letter should gain attention, build interest, reduce resistance, and motivate action.[9]

## 10.12 Persuasive Internal Memo or E-Mail: We Need a Change (Obj. 4)

**CRITICAL THINKING**

In your own work or organization experience, identify a problem for which you have a solution. Should a procedure be altered to improve performance? Would a new or different piece of equipment help you perform your work better? Could some tasks be scheduled more efficiently? Are employees being used most effectively? Could customers be better served by changing something? Do you want to work other hours or perform other tasks? Do you deserve a promotion? Do you have a suggestion to improve profitability?

**Your Task.** Once you have identified a situation requiring persuasion, write a memo or an e-mail to your boss or organization head. Use actual names and facts. Employ the concepts and techniques in this chapter to help you convince your boss that your idea should prevail. Include concrete examples, anticipate objections, emphasize reader benefits, and end with a specific action to be taken.

## 10.13 Persuasive Internal Request: Overusing Overnight Shipments (Obj. 4)

As office manager of Cupertino Software, write a memo persuading technicians, engineers, programmers, and other employees to reduce the number of overnight or second-day mail shipments. Your Federal Express and other shipping bills have been sky high, and you feel that staff members are overusing these services.

You think employees should send messages by fax. Sending a fax costs only about 35 cents a page to most long-distance areas and nothing to local areas. There's a whopping difference between 35 cents and $12 to $18 for FedEx service! Whenever possible, staff members should obtain the FedEx account number of the recipient and use it for charging the shipment. If staff members plan ahead and allow enough time, they can use Canada Post ground service, which takes three to five days. You wonder whether staff members consider whether the recipient is *really* going to use the message as soon as it arrives. Does it justify an overnight shipment? You'd like to reduce overnight delivery services voluntarily by 50 percent over the next two months. Unless a sizable reduction occurs, the CEO threatens severe restrictions in the future.

**Your Task.** Address your memo to all employees. Include any other ways in which employees could reduce shipping costs.

## 10.14 Persuasive Internal Request: Supporting Project H.E.L.P. (Obj. 4)

E-MAIL

As employee relations manager of the Prudential Insurance Company, one of your tasks is to promote Project H.E.L.P. (Higher Education Learning Program), an on-the-job learning opportunity. Project H.E.L.P. is a combined effort of major corporations and the Bruce County District School Board. You must recruit 12 employees who will volunteer as instructors for 50 or more students. The students will spend four hours per week at the Prudential Bruce County facility, earning an average of five units of credit a semester.

This semester the students will be serving in the Claims, Word Processing, Corporate Media Services, Marketing, Communications, Library, and Administrative Support departments. Your task is to convince employees in these departments to volunteer. They will be expected to supervise and instruct the students. In return, employees will receive two hours of release time per week to work with the students. The program has been very successful so far. School officials, students, and employees alike express satisfaction with the experience and the outcomes.

**Your Task.** Write a persuasive memo or e-mail message with convincing appeals that will bring you 12 volunteers to work with Project H.E.L.P.

## 10.15 Persuasive Internal Request: Scheduling Meetings More Strategically (Obj. 4)

The following memo (with names changed) was actually sent. **Your Task.** Based on what you have learned in this chapter, improve the memo. Expect the staff to be somewhat resistant because they've never before had meeting restrictions.

*✗ Poorly Written Memo*

TO:         All Managers and Employees

FROM:     Lynn Wasson, CEO

SUBJECT: SCHEDULING MEETINGS

Please be reminded that travel in the greater Toronto area is time-consuming. In the future we're asking that you set up meetings that

1. Are of critical importance
2. Consider travel time for the participants
3. Consider phone conferences (or video or e-mail) in lieu of face-to-face meetings
4. Meetings should be at the location where most of the participants work and at the most opportune travel times

5. Travelling together is another way to save time and resources.

We all have our traffic stories. A recent one is that a certain manager was asked to attend a one-hour meeting in Guelph. This required one hour of travel in advance of the meeting, one hour for the meeting, and two and a half hours of travel through Toronto afterward. This meeting was scheduled for 4 p.m. Total time consumed by the manager for the one-hour meeting was four and a half hours.

Thank you for your consideration.

## 10.16 Persuasive Internal Request: Rapid Reviews Land Top Recruits (Obj. 4)

As Cassandra Carpenter, associate director of Human Resources at Techtronics computer consulting, you must improve company recruitment and retention rates soon. Employee turnover at the company is higher than 20 percent, and filling vacancies can take up to a year. Recruiting trends in the high-tech industry are clear. Record low unemployment rates, a burgeoning computer industry, and too few computer systems graduates have made the hiring game extremely competitive. To stay ahead, most firms have pumped up recruiting tactics, using hiring bonuses, unusually high salaries, extra vacation, and early reviews and raises to win the best employees. "I asked for a six-month review from ComputerTech," said one especially promising candidate, "and they agreed to it. They'll even offer a raise after three months if my performance is up to it."

You're certain that your boss will never agree to giving new employees salary raises after only three months on the job. However, offering reviews and pay raises at six months would enable you to snare the best hires without paying top dollar up front. Company pay scales simply don't allow for outlandish starting salaries, and reviews typically are given after 12 months. By offering early reviews for the best candidates, you could honour the internal pay scales while offering applicants the opportunity for early raises.

At a recent recruiting seminar, you learned that many companies are resorting to early reviews because they must. Nearly 30 percent of all high-tech companies offer them. Raises based on those reviews range from 2 percent to 8 percent, and a few star employees manage to gain even more. Companies using the tactic report great results. One company apparently reduced its usual 10 percent turnover to 1 percent for those who received raises. Those expecting early reviews performed well right away because they wanted the early pay raise. When they got it, they stayed on.

**Your Task.** You are determined to make early reviews part of your hiring arsenal, and you plan to pitch the plan to your boss, Director of Public Relations Jonathon Richards, in a persuasive memo. You have checked with his assistant, and he is available for a meeting on Wednesday, November 15, at

315

10:30. You would like to meet with him then to discuss the issue, but your memo should precede the visit. Write a convincing memo that wins the appointment.

## 10.17 Persuasive Internal Request: Training Telecommuters (Obj. 4)

INFOTRAC      TEAM      CRITICAL THINKING

You see the handwriting on the wall. More and more employees are asking to telecommute. They want to work at home, where they feel they can be more productive and avoid the hassle of driving to work. Some need to telecommute only temporarily, while they take care of family obligations, births, illnesses, or personal problems. Others are highly skilled individuals who can do their work at home as easily as in the office. As human resources director at a large corporation, you know that at least 157 of your current employees have permission to telecommute.

But the results have not been totally satisfactory. Teleworkers don't always have the best work habits, and lack of communication is a major problem. Unless the telecommuter is expert at coordinating projects and giving instructions, productivity can fizzle. Another problem for managers is measuring productivity. Then there's the issue of resentment among other workers in the office.

All the trends seem to indicate that telecommuting will increase in the future. You come to the conclusion that if your company is to continue to grant permission for employees to work at remote locations, then workers and their managers must receive training on how to do it effectively. You would like to hire a consultant to train your prospective telecommuters and their managers. Another possibility is developing an in-house training program.

**Your Task.** As human resources director, you must convince Robert Richardson, vice president, that your company needs a training program for all individuals who are currently telecommuting or who plan to do so. Their managers should also receive training. You decide to ask your staff of four to help you gather information. Using InfoTrac, you and your team read several articles on what such training should include. Now you must decide what action you want the vice president to take. Meet with you to discuss a training program? Commit to a budget item for future training? Hire a consultant or agency to come in and conduct training programs?

Individually or as a team, write a convincing memo that describes the problem, suggests what the training should include, and asks for action by a specific date. Add any reasonable details necessary to build your case.[10]

## 10.18 Claim Request: Excessive Legal Fees (Obj. 5)

You are the business manager for McConnell's, a producer of gourmet ice cream. McConnell's has 12 ice cream parlours in the Winnipeg area and a reputation for excellent ice cream. Your firm was approached by an independent ice cream vendor who wanted to use McConnell's name and recipes for ice cream to be distributed through grocery stores and drugstores. As business manager you worked with a law firm, Lancomb, Pereigni, and Associates, to draw up contracts regarding the use of McConnell's name and quality standards for the product. When you received the bill from Louis Lancomb, you couldn't believe it. The bill itemized 38 hours of lawyer preparation, at $300 per hour, and 55 hours of paralegal assistance, at $75 per hour. The bill also showed $415 for telephone calls, which might be accurate because Mr. Lancomb had to converse with McConnell's owners, who were living in Ireland at the time. However, you doubt that an experienced lawyer would require 38 hours to draw up the contracts in question.

Perhaps some error was made in calculating the total hours. Moreover, you have checked with other businesses and found that excellent legal advice can be obtained for $150 per hour. McConnell's would like to continue using the services of Lancomb, Pereigni, and Associates for future legal business. Such future business is unlikely if an adjustment is not made on this bill.

**Your Task.** Write a persuasive request to Louis Lancomb, L.L.B., Lancomb, Pereigni, and Associates, 1675 Croydon Avenue, Winnipeg, MB R3N 0J8.

## 10.19 Claim Request: Kodak Ruins His Round-the-World Trip (Obj. 5)

Pictures of himself in front of the Great Pyramids of Giza, shots of the famous Blue Mosque in Istanbul, and photographs of himself dancing with children around a fire in a Thailand village—all lost because of a faulty shutter mechanism on his camera. Twenty-seven year-old Brian P. Coyle made a once-in-a-lifetime trip around the world last fall. To record the sights and adventures, he invested in a Kodak Advantix camera.

Coyle selected the Advantix because of the extensive marketing of its easy-load feature, which worked well. But when he returned, he discovered that 12 of the 15 rolls of film he shot were ruined. He learned later that the camera shutter had malfunctioned. Needless to say, Coyle is very unhappy. After all, half of the fun of a trip lies in the memories summoned forth by photographs that can be enjoyed years after one returns. The emotional value of his pictures is far greater than the film on which they are recorded. He decides that he won't settle for 12 rolls of new film and perhaps replacement of the camera. He wants Kodak to send him around the world to repeat his trip. He figures that it is the only way he can recapture and record his lost adventure. He figures it would cost him about $20 000 to repeat his 27-day trip.

Coyle asks you, as a business communication student, to help him write a convincing letter to Kodak. You respond that it's highly unlikely that Kodak will grant this claim, and Coyle says, "Hey, what have I got to lose? Kodak ruined my trip, and I think a lot of travellers would be interested in hearing about my troubles with Kodak's Advantix camera."[11] **Your Task.** Write a persuasive claim to Mr. Charles Smith, Customer Relations, Eastman Kodak Company, 258 West Main Street, Rochester, NY 14605. Return the defective camera, copies of the purchase papers, and 12 rolls of ruined film. Should you send your package by Certified Mail with a return receipt requested? Determine the best way to send the message.

## 10.20 Claim Request: Outrageous Charge for Pancake Breakfast (Obj. 5)

As regional manager for an electronics parts manufacturer, you and two other employees attended a conference in Montreal. You stayed at the Excelsior Hotel because your company recommends that employees use it. Generally, your employees have liked their accommodations, and the rates have been within your company's budget. The hotel's service has been excellent.

Now, however, you're unhappy with the charges you see on your company's credit statement from the Excelsior. When your department's administrative assistant made the reservations, she was assured that you would receive the weekend rates and that a hot breakfast—in the hotel restaurant, the Atrium—would be included in the rate. You hate those cold sweet rolls and instant coffee "continental" breakfasts, especially when you have to leave early and won't get another meal until afternoon. So you and the other two employees went to the restaurant and ordered a hot meal from the menu.

When you received the credit card statement, though, you see a charge for $79 for three champagne buffet breakfasts in the Atrium. You hit the ceiling! For one thing, you didn't have a buffet breakfast and certainly no champagne. The three of you got there so early that no buffet had been set up. You ordered pancakes and sausage, and for this you were billed $25 each. You're outraged! What's worse, your company may charge you personally for exceeding the expected rates.

In looking back at this event, you remembered that other guests on your floor were having a "continental" breakfast in a lounge on your floor. Perhaps that's where the hotel expected all guests on the weekend rate to eat. However, your administrative assistant had specifically asked about this matter when she made the reservations, and she was told that you could order breakfast from the menu at the hotel's restaurant.

**Your Task.** You want to straighten out this matter, and you can't do it by telephone because you suspect that you will need a written record of this entire mess. Write a claim request to Customer Service, Montreal Excelsior Hotel, 1221 22nd Street, Montreal, QC J1M 1R7. Decide whether you should include a copy of the credit card statement showing the charge.

## 10.21 Sales Letter: Becoming a Bridal Consultant (Obj. 6)

As a communication consultant, you receive all kinds of requests. Your most recent job is writing a sales letter promoting the Professional Bridal Consultant program. Now, you are the first to admit that you don't know a lot about bridal consulting and weddings, but you do know what it takes to write a good direct-mail letter. You didn't hesitate for a minute in accepting the job assignment from Harcourt Learning Direct, an educational institution. It wants you to prepare a letter that sells its online bridal consulting course.

Unfortunately, Harcourt did not provide you with much to go on. You visit its Web site and quickly see that the Web site focuses primarily on instructional information, such as books, learning aids, and access to Web services. But it doesn't provide many details about how important a professional consultant is in achieving a perfect wedding day. To sell this online training program, you feel that you need to make both rational and emotional appeals. You decide to look at other wedding consultant Web sites for more information. Many of them have information about what a consultant does, including establishing a realistic budget; recommending venues, caterers, florists, musicians, and photographers; scheduling appointments; and coordinating everybody on the wedding day. Harcourt's Professional Bridal Consultant program provides training in all of these aspects of wedding planning.

**Your Task.** Visit the Harcourt site by using a Web search engine (such as <**www.google.ca**>). Search for "Harcourt Professional Bridal Consultant Program." Look at other bridal consultant Web sites also. Then write a letter promoting the Harcourt program. It will be sent to a targeted database of people who sell wedding dresses or gifts, maintain wedding registries, subscribe to selected bridal magazines, or work as caterers. Harcourt figures that within this group some people will be interested in becoming professional bridal consultants. Students can earn a career diploma in as little as nine months. Because your letter will be reviewed thoroughly by Harcourt, you feel free to "pull out all the stops" in your first draft. Your goal is to have receivers return an enclosed postal card requesting more information (free, of course) about the program. If they act by a certain date, they will receive *Basics of a Bridal Business*, a fact-filled book with valuable tips on successful bridal consulting.

## 10.22 Sales Letter: Fitness at Crowne Pizza (Obj. 6)

The Canadian Council on Integrated Healthcare reports that employee absences cost Canadian employers an estimated $8.6 billion a year. Many of these absences are related to employee fitness (or lack of it). Dofasco in Hamilton, Ontario, found in an employee audit that obese nonsmokers lost an average of 72 hours per year and obese smokers lost an average of 106 hours per year. Many companies are responding to these concerns by offering wellness programs such as weight loss (Dofasco's Big Steel Men and Women; the Kitchener, Ontario Home & Park Motorhomes' Fat Cat Club) and smoking cessation (Home & Park's Kick Ash Club), and on-site fitness facilities.[12]

As a sales representative for Fitness Associates, you think your fitness equipment and programs could be instrumental in helping people lose weight. With regular exercise at an on-site fitness centre, employees lose weight and improve their overall health. As employee health improves, absenteeism is reduced and overall productivity increases. And employees love working out before or after work. They make the routine part of their workday, and they often have work buddies who share their fitness regimen.

Although many companies resist spending money to save money, fitness centres need not be large or expensive to be effective. Studies show that moderately sized centres coupled with motivational and training programs yield the greatest success. For just $30 000, Fitness Associates (FA) will provide exercise equipment including stationary bikes, weight machines, and treadmills. Their fitness experts will design a fitness room, set up the fitness equipment, and design appropriate programs. Best of all, the one-time cost is usually offset by cost savings within one year of centre installation. For additional fees FA can also provide fitness consultants for employee fitness assessments. FA specialists will also train employees on proper use of equipment and clean and manage the facility—for an extra charge, of course.

**Your Task.** Write a sales letter to Ms. Kathleen Stewart, Human Resources Vice President, Crowne Pizza, 3939 West Highland Blvd., Fredericton, NB E3A 8T4. Assume you are writing on company letterhead paper. Ask for an appointment to meet with her. Send her a brochure detailing the products and services that Fitness Associates provides. As an incentive offer a free fitness assessment for all employees if Crowne Pizza installs a fitness facility by December 1.

## 10.23 Sales Letter: Promoting Your Product or Service (Obj. 6)

Identify a situation in your current job or a previous one in which a sales letter is (was) needed. Using suggestions from this chapter, write an appropriate sales letter that promotes a product or service. Use actual names, information, and examples. If you have no work experience, imagine a business you'd like to start: word processing, student typing, pet grooming, car detailing, tutoring, specialty knitting, balloon decorating, delivery service, child care, gardening, lawn care, or something else. Write a letter selling your product or service to be distributed to your prospective customers. Be sure to tell them how to respond.

## 10.24 News Release: Vintage Nikes Wanted in Japan (Obj. 7)

TEAM

Ever hear of the Nike "Dunk," a brightly coloured basketball shoe sold in the 1980s? Although it bombed in North America, a pair of Dunks might now sell for $2 000 in Japan, where vintage (translation: old) athletic footwear is all the rage. Why would anyone pay exorbitant prices for smelly, old athletic shoes? Here's how Robert Smith, of Farley Enterprises, explains the craze. Japanese young people are forced to wear look-alike outfits six days a week. But out of school, they desperately want to break out of the school uniform mould to look different. And they're not interested in standard Nike, Reebok, and Adidas items that anyone can pick up at an outlet. Instead, they clamour for unique, hard-to-find older sneakers, such as the Nike Dunk in bright purple or neon yellow.

Vancouver-based Farley Enterprises has been scouring North America seeking vintage articles for the Japanese market. Although the company continues to offer old Levi's jeans (small sizes preferred) and aged Hawaiian shirts, its main interest right now is in older but well-known Nikes. As Smith says, "Nike has spent a lot more money on advertising, and everyone knows who Michael Jordan is." For anyone willing to part with an old pair of Nike Dunks, Farley would offer as much as $500 (maybe more for a really clean pair). But Farley is also interested in other vintage athletic shoes. In fact, the company has gone so far as to search through running magazines for the names of athletes who might have kept their old shoes around. One Toronto-based wholesaler of used clothing made $2.3 million in 1996 exporting vintage items to Japan.

**Your Task.** As an intern for Farley Enterprises, you have been asked to work with two other interns in writing an effective news release for local newspapers and radio and TV stations around the country. Discuss what should be included in the news release and the best way to develop the information. Be sure to describe Farley's search efforts. Encourage people to call 1-800-VINTAGE if they have distinctive, old athletic shoes or old Levi's. As a contact person, you can be reached at 1-604-867-4673. Individually or as a team, write a persuasive news release.[13]

## 10.25 News Release: EarthShell Wants You (Obj. 7)

You have been interviewed for a terrific job in corporate communications at EarthShell, which produces biodegradable packaging materials for traditional food service items. Its clamshell sandwich containers are made from potato starch and have been approved for 300 McDonald's stores. The best part of the job offer is that you could work in Victoria, one of BC's most beautiful cities. However, EarthShell wants you to submit a news release as a writing sample. EarthShell features a number of news releases at its Web site, and many articles about its products have appeared in periodicals. The EarthShell recruiter wants you to submit a news release that would appeal to the publisher of your local newspaper.
**Your Task.** Using InfoTrac, search for EarthShell information. Read several articles. Also go to its Web site (use a search engine to find it) and look at its current news releases. Select one event or product that you think would be of interest to your local newspaper. Although you can use the information from current EarthShell news releases, don't copy the exact wording because it will be obvious to EarthShell. As a contact person to be named in your new release, use a name from a current EarthShell news release.

## 10.26 News Release: It's New! (Obj. 7)

**Your Task.** In a company where you now work or for an organization you belong to, identify a product or service that could be publicized. Consider writing a press release announcing a new course at your school, a new president, new equipment, or a campaign to raise funds. Write the press release for your local newspaper.

# C.L.U.E. REVIEW 10

Edit the following sentences to correct faults in grammar, punctuation, spelling, and word use.

1. Sucessful persuasion results from 2 important elements; a reasonable request, and a well presented argument.

2. If we wanted to persuade a bank to lend you and I ten thousand dollars we would probibly use rational appeals.

3. Our Senior Marketing Director and the sales manager wants to send a sales letter to our current customers therefore they analyzed the product, purpose and audience.

4. 4 important parts of a persuasive message are: (1) Gaining the audiences attention (2) Convincing them that your purpose is worthy (3) Overcoming resistance and (4) Motivating action.

5. One of the most biggest mistakes in persuasive request's are the failure to anticipate, and off set audience resistance.

6. If the CEO and him had behaved more professional the chances of a practicle settlement would be considerably greater.

7. A adjustment letter is a form of complaint consequently its wise to use the indirect strategy.

8. Anger and emotion is not effective in persuasion but many writers cannot controll there tempers.

9. When we open our office in Montreal we will need at least 3 people whom are fluent in french and english.

10. A good news release looks and sound credible that is it has no typos no imaginative spelling and no factual errors.

# Chapter 11
## Negative Messages

## LEARNING OBJECTIVES

*1* Describe the goals and strategies of business communicators in delivering bad news.

*2* Explain techniques for delivering bad news sensitively.

*3* Identify routine requests and describe a strategy for refusing such requests.

*4* Explain techniques for managing bad news to customers.

*5* Explain techniques for managing bad news within organizations.

*6* Compare strategies for revealing bad news in different cultures.

## Hyundai Auto Canada

Hyundai aims to be among the world's best in technology and quality. Through steady progress in technology, its quality and expectations continue to rise.

Just over 30 years old, Hyundai has already become a major global player, with plants and dealerships that span six continents. The Hyundai Group is among the world's largest and most diversified business organizations, with 45 affiliated domestic companies and 254 overseas companies in nearly 200 countries. In addition to automotive production, Hyundai is active in such varied industries as shipbuilding, steel, petrochemicals, heavy machinery, aerospace, electronics, and financial services.

Hyundai now operates eight research centres in Korea, along with four international centres, including Hyundai America Technical Centre, Inc., in Ann Arbor, Michigan, and Hyundai California Design Centre in Fountain Valley, California. The company is currently pursuing the development of electric, solar, hybrid-fuelled cars, and compressed natural gas–fuelled cars, as well as intelligent vehicle systems.

Hyundai entered the Canadian market in 1983 at a time when most automobile manufacturers had abandoned the entry-level market in favour of high-end, high-priced vehicles. First-time car buyers such as college and university students and young families were unable to find adequate, value-equipped cars that met their needs and their budgets. The Hyundai Pony filled this void and, as a result, was the most successful launch of an import car in Canada. Hyundai continues to expand its product line with the launch of its SUV, the Santa Fe, and its newest luxury car, the XG350.

Hyundai Auto Canada is an active supporter of local and national organizations such as the United Way, the Canadian Cancer Society, the Children's Wish Foundation, and the Markham Stouffville Hospital Foundation.

The road to success, however, has not been without its potholes. In September 2002, Hyundai Auto Canada discovered that horsepower ratings on some of its vehicles had been mistakenly reported. Because president and CEO Steve Kelleher values his company's relationship with its customers, a letter of apology was quickly sent to all affected customers.[1] You'll learn more about this case later in this chapter.

### CRITICAL THINKING

- If you had to reveal bad news to your parents or to your spouse (such as denting the fender of that person's car), would you break the bad news quickly or build up to it? Why?
- What are some techniques you could use to soften the blow of bad news?
- When an organization has to reveal disappointing news to customers, employees, or others, what goals should it try to achieve?

**www.hyundaicanada.com**

# STRATEGIES FOR DELIVERING BAD NEWS

Breaking bad news is a fact of business life for nearly every business communicator. In all businesses, things occasionally go wrong. Goods are not delivered, a product fails to perform as expected, service is poor, billing gets fouled up, or customers are misunderstood. Because bad news disappoints, irritates, and sometimes angers the receiver, such messages must be written carefully. The bad feelings associated with disappointing news can generally be reduced if (1) the reader knows the reasons for the rejection and (2) the bad news is revealed with sensitivity. You've probably heard people say, "It wasn't so much the bad news that I resented. It was the way I was told!"

The direct strategy, which you learned to apply in earlier chapters, frontloads the main idea, even when it's bad news. This direct strategy appeals to efficiency-oriented writers who don't want to waste time with efforts to soften the effects of bad news.[2] Many business writers, however, prefer to use the indirect pattern in delivering negative messages. The indirect strategy is especially appealing to relationship-oriented writers. They care about how a message will affect its receiver.

*1*

**The sting of bad news can be reduced by giving reasons and communicating sensitively.**

**CHAPTER 11**
Negative Messages
**321**

In this chapter you'll learn when to use the direct or indirect pattern to deliver bad news. You'll study the goals of business communicators in working with bad news, and you'll examine three causes for legal concerns. The major focus of this chapter, however, is on developing the indirect strategy and applying it to situations in which you must refuse routine requests, decline invitations, and deliver negative news to employees and customers. You'll also learn how bad news is handled in other cultures.

## Goals in Communicating Bad News

In communicating bad news, key goals include getting the receiver to accept it, maintaining goodwill, and avoiding legal liability.

Delivering bad news is not the happiest writing task you may have, but it can be gratifying if you do it effectively. As a business communicator working with bad news, you will have many goals, the most important of which are these:

- **Acceptance.** Make sure the reader understands and *accepts* the bad news. The indirect pattern helps in achieving this objective.

- **Positive image.** Promote and maintain a good image of yourself and your organization. Realizing this goal assumes that you will act ethically.

- **Message clarity.** Make the message so clear that additional correspondence is unnecessary.

- **Protection.** Avoid creating legal liability or responsibility for you or your organization.

These are ambitious goals, and we're not always successful in achieving them all. The patterns you're about to learn, however, provide the beginning communicator with strategies and tactics that many writers have found successful in conveying disappointing news sensitively and safely. With experience, you'll be able to vary these patterns and adapt them to your organization's specific writing tasks.

## Using the Indirect Pattern to Prepare the Reader

The indirect pattern softens the impact of bad news by giving reasons and explanations first.

Whereas good news can be revealed quickly, bad news is generally easier to accept when broken gradually. Revealing bad news slowly and indirectly shows sensitivity to your reader. By preparing the reader, you tend to soften the impact. A blunt announcement of disappointing news might cause the receiver to stop reading and toss the message aside. The indirect strategy enables you to keep the reader's attention until you have been able to explain the reasons for the bad news. In fact, the most important part of a bad-news letter is the explanation, which you'll learn about shortly. The indirect plan consists of four parts, as shown in Figure 11.1:

- **Buffer.** Offer a neutral but meaningful statement that does not mention the bad news.

- **Reasons.** Give an explanation of the causes for the bad news before disclosing it.

- **Bad news.** Provide a clear but understated announcement of the bad news that may include an alternative or compromise.

- **Close.** Include a personalized, forward-looking, pleasant statement.

## When to Use the Direct Pattern

Many bad-news letters are best organized indirectly, beginning with a buffer and reasons. The direct pattern, with the bad news first, may be more effective, though, in situations such as the following.

**FIGURE 11.1** **Four-Part Indirect Pattern for Bad News**

**Buffer**
Open with a neutral but meaningful statement that does not mention the bad news.

➤

**Reasons**
Explain the causes of the bad news before disclosing it.

➤

**Bad News**
Reveal the bad news without emphasizing it. Provide an alternative or compromise, if possible.

➤

**Closing**
End with a personalized, forward-looking, pleasant statement. Avoid referring to the bad news.

- **When the receiver may overlook the bad news.** With the crush of mail today, many readers skim messages, looking only at the opening. If they don't find substantive material, they may discard the message. Rate increases, changes in service, new policy requirements—these critical messages may require boldness to ensure attention.

- **When organization policy suggests directness.** Some companies expect all internal messages and announcements—even bad news—to be straightforward and presented without frills.

- **When the receiver prefers directness.** Busy managers may prefer directness. Such shorter messages enable the reader to get in the proper frame of mind immediately. If you suspect that the reader prefers that the facts be presented straightaway, use the direct pattern.

- **When firmness is necessary.** Messages that must demonstrate determination and strength should not use delaying techniques. For example, the last in a series of collection letters that seek payment of overdue accounts may require a direct opener.

- **When the bad news is not damaging.** If the bad news is insignificant (such as a small increase in cost) and doesn't personally affect the receiver, then the direct strategy certainly makes sense.

> The direct pattern is appropriate when the receiver might overlook the bad news, when directness is preferred, when firmness is necessary, or when the bad news is not damaging.

Rate increases represent bad news to customers. However, small increases, such as that announced in the Harmony letter shown in Figure 11.2, can be announced directly. Notice that Harmony includes many letter components discussed earlier. The letter presents the rate increase but immediately points out that other service rates remain the same or are decreasing. In fact, the entire balance of the letter promotes reader benefits, including committed delivery, 24-hour access to shipment information, money-back guarantees, an enhanced Web site, and Sunday delivery. The letter emphasizes the "you" view throughout and closes with a forward-looking thought. Clever organizations like Harmony can turn bad news into an opportunity to sell their services.

> Small rate increases may be announced directly.

Harmony placed its rate increase right up front. Generally, however, North American writers prefer to use an indirect strategy, especially for more serious bad news. On the other hand, some researchers report that *where* the writer places the bad news is not nearly as important as the *tone* of the message.[3] Many of the techniques you've just learned will help you achieve a sensitive, personal tone in messages delivering negative news.

## Applying the 3-×-3 Writing Process

Thinking through the entire process is especially important in bad-news letters. Not only do you want the receiver to understand and accept the message, but you want to be careful that your words say only what you intend. Thus, you'll want to apply the familiar 3-×-3 writing process to bad-news letters.

**FIGURE 11.2** Harmony Shipping Uses Direct Strategy for Rate Increase

# HARMONYShipping

Uses direct strategy because bad news (small rate increase) is not damaging

Promotes reader benefits (economical, committed delivery, 24-hour shipment information, etc.)

Emphasizes "you" view

Uses bullets to highlight customer benefits

Closes with appreciation and forward-looking thought

Dear Valued Harmony Customer:

Effective February 15, your rates for Harmony Shipping domestic services will change to those in the enclosed rate agreement. These new rates reflect an average increase of between 3% and 4%. However, rates for Harmony Regular Overnight® are decreasing for heavier weights, and Harmony Quick Saver® rates are staying the same for heavier weights.

Harmony Quick Saver® gives you Harmony value for your less-urgent shipments. It provides delivery in three business days at some of our most affordable rates ever, yet with such Harmony extras as committed delivery, 24-hour access to shipment status information, and our Money-Back Guarantees.*

In addition, recognizing the growing number of businesses whose work extends right through the weekend, Harmony announces a welcome innovation: Sunday delivery. Starting March 15, shipments dropped off or picked up on Friday or Saturday* can be delivered to 40 metro areas on Sunday via Harmony Express Overnight® service for a $20 special handling fee.

Enhancements to our Web site (www.harmonyshipping.ca) make using Harmony as easy and fast as ever. Here's just some of what you can do:

• Use Harmony E-Ship® to prepare shipping documentation, store recipient addresses, and send a Harmony Ship Alert—an e-mail to the recipient that a package is on its way.
• Go to our Drop-Off Locator to find a map of your nearest Harmony location.
• Track your shipment status 24 hours a day.

Harmony gives you many ways to satisfy your customers' expectations, from reliable, on-time delivery to consistent, dependable handling. We appreciate your choosing Harmony, and strive always to meet your express shipping needs. If you have any questions, please call 1•800•HAR•MONY® (800-427-6669).

Sincerely,

Harmony Shipping Corporation

*See the Harmony Service Guide for details and limitations.

Offsets bad news with some good news (lower rates and stay-even rates)

Starts each line with a verb for parallelism and readability

Shows empathy by looking at its services through the eyes of the receiver

---

**The 3-×-3 writing process is especially important in crafting bad-news messages because of the potential consequences of poorly written messages.**

*Analysis, Anticipation, and Adaptation.* In Phase 1 (prewriting) you need to analyze the bad news so that you can anticipate its effect on the receiver. If the disappointment will be mild, announce it directly. If the bad news is serious or personal, consider techniques to reduce the pain. Adapt your words to protect the receiver's ego. Instead of *You neglected to change the oil, causing severe damage to the engine,* switch to the passive voice: *The oil wasn't changed, causing severe damage to the engine.* Choose words that show you respect the reader as a responsible, valuable person.

*Research, Organization, and Composition.* In Phase 2 (writing) you can gather information and brainstorm for ideas. Jot down all the reasons you have that explain the bad news. If four or five reasons prompted your negative decision, concentrate on the strongest and safest ones. Avoid presenting any weak reasons; readers may seize on them to reject the entire message. After selecting your best reasons, outline the four parts of the bad-news pattern: buffer, reasons, bad news, closing. Flesh out each section as you compose your first draft.

***Revision, Proofreading, and Evaluation.*** In Phase 3 (revising) you're ready to switch positions and put yourself into the receiver's shoes. Have you looked at the problem from the receiver's perspective? Is your message too blunt? Too subtle? Does the message make the refusal, denial, or bad-news announcement clear? Prepare the final version, and proofread for format, punctuation, and correctness.

## Avoiding Three Causes of Legal Problems

Before we examine the components of a bad-news message, let's look more closely at how you can avoid exposing yourself and your employer to legal liability in writing negative messages. Although we can't always anticipate the consequences of our words, we should be alert to three causes of legal difficulties: (1) abusive language, (2) careless language, and (3) the "good-guy syndrome."

***Abusive Language.*** Calling people names (such as *deadbeat, crook,* or *quack*) can get you into trouble. *Defamation* is the legal term for any false statement that harms an individual's reputation. When the abusive language is written, it's called *libel*; when spoken, it's *slander.*

To be actionable (likely to result in a lawsuit), abusive language must be (1) false, (2) damaging to one's good name, and (3) "published"—that is, spoken within the presence of others or written. Thus, if you were alone with Jane Doe and accused her of accepting bribes and selling company secrets to competitors, she couldn't sue because the defamation wasn't published. Her reputation was not damaged. But if anyone heard the words or if they were written, you might be legally liable.

In a new wrinkle, you may now be prosecuted if you transmit a harassing or libelous message by e-mail on a computer bulletin board. Such electronic transmission is considered to be "published." Moreover, a company may incur liability for messages sent through its computer system by employees. That's why many companies do not allow employees to post Internet messages using the company's return address. Employees must add a "not speaking for the company" disclaimer to private messages transmitted over networks.[4]

Obviously, competent communicators avoid making unproven charges and letting their emotions prompt abusive language—in print or electronically.

***Careless Language.*** As the marketplace becomes increasingly litigious, we must be certain that our words communicate only what we intend. Take the case of a factory worker injured on the job. His lawyer subpoenaed company documents and discovered a seemingly harmless letter sent to a group regarding a plant tour. These words appeared in the letter: "Although we are honoured at your interest in our company, we cannot give your group a tour of the plant operations as it would be too noisy and dangerous." The court found in favour of the worker, inferring from the letter that working conditions were indeed hazardous.[5] Although a legal case would not result in Canada in such an instance due to provincial workers' compensation plans, companies here must still be on guard against such careless wording. The letter writer did not intend to convey the impression of dangerous working conditions, but the court accepted that interpretation.

This case points up two important cautions. First, be careful in making statements that are potentially damaging or that could be misinterpreted. Be wary of explanations that convey more information than you intend. Second, be careful

**Abusive language becomes legally actionable when it is false, harmful to the person's good name, and "published."**

**Careless language includes statements that could be damaging or misinterpreted.**

about what documents you save. Lawyers may demand, in pursuing a lawsuit, all company files pertaining to a case. Even documents marked "Confidential" or "Personal" may be used.

Remember, too, that e-mail messages are especially risky. You may think that a mere tap of the *Delete* key makes a file disappear; however, messages continue to exist on backup storage devices in the files of the sender and the recipient. "Everyone needs to understand that anything typed onto the system remains out there forever," says lawyer Ronald J. James. "There is no such thing as a delete key."[6]

**Avoid statements that make you feel good but may be misleading or inaccurate.**

*The Good-Guy Syndrome.* Most of us hate to have to reveal bad news—that is, to be the bad guy. To make ourselves look better, to make the receiver feel better, and to maintain good relations, we are tempted to make statements that are legally dangerous. Consider the case of a law firm interviewing job candidates. One of the firm's partners was asked to inform a candidate that she was not selected. The partner's letter said, "Although you were by far the most qualified candidate we interviewed, unfortunately, we have decided we do not have a position for a person of your talents at this time." To show that he personally had no reservations about this candidate and to bolster the candidate, the partner offered his own opinion. But he differed from the majority of the recruiting committee. When the rejected interviewee learned later that the law firm had hired two male lawyers, she sued, charging sexual discrimination. The court found in favour of the rejected candidate, agreeing that a reasonable inference could be made from the partner's letter that she was the "most qualified candidate."[7] Because the Canadian Human Rights Act prohibits discrimination in employment, such a case might have ended with a similar ruling in this country.

**Use organizational stationery for official business only, and beware of making promises that can't be fulfilled.**

Two important lessons emerge. First, business communicators act as agents of their organizations. Their words, decisions, and opinions are assumed to represent those of the organization. If you want to communicate your personal feelings or opinions, use your home computer or write on plain paper (rather than company letterhead) and sign your name without title or affiliation. Second, volunteering extra information can lead to trouble. Thus, avoid supplying data that could be misused, and avoid making promises that can't be fulfilled. Don't admit or imply responsibility for conditions that caused damage or injury. Even apologies (*We're sorry that a faulty bottle cap caused damage to your carpet*) may suggest liability.

In Chapter 5 we discussed four information areas that generate the most lawsuits: investments, safety, marketing, and human resources. In this chapter we'll make specific suggestions for avoiding legal liability in writing responses to claim letters, credit letters, and personnel documents. You may find that in the most critical areas (such as collection letters or hiring/firing messages) your organization provides language guidelines and form letters approved by legal counsel. As the business environment becomes more perilous, we must not only be sensitive to receivers but also keenly aware of risks to ourselves and to the organizations we represent.

## 2 TECHNIQUES FOR DELIVERING BAD NEWS SENSITIVELY

Legal matters aside, let's now study specific techniques for using the indirect pattern in sending bad-news messages. In this pattern the bad news is delayed until after explanations have been given. The four components of the indirect pattern, shown in Figure 11.3, include buffer, reasons, bad news, and closing.

## FIGURE 11.3 Delivering Bad News Sensitively

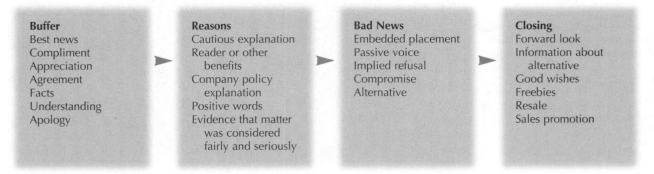

**Buffer**
Best news
Compliment
Appreciation
Agreement
Facts
Understanding
Apology

**Reasons**
Cautious explanation
Reader or other
   benefits
Company policy
   explanation
Positive words
Evidence that matter
   was considered
   fairly and seriously

**Bad News**
Embedded placement
Passive voice
Implied refusal
Compromise
Alternative

**Closing**
Forward look
Information about
   alternative
Good wishes
Freebies
Resale
Sales promotion

## Buffering the Opening

A buffer is a device to reduce shock or pain. To buffer the pain of bad news, begin with a neutral but meaningful statement that makes the reader continue reading. The buffer should be relevant and concise and provide a natural transition to the explanation that follows. The individual situation, of course, will help determine what you should put in the buffer. Avoid trite buffers such as *Thank you for your letter.* Here are some possibilities for opening bad-news messages.

*To reduce negative feelings, use a buffer opening for sensitive bad-news messages.*

**Best News.** Start with the part of the message that represents the best news. For example, in a memo that announces a new service along with a cutback in mailroom hours, you might write, *To ensure that your correspondence goes out with the last pickup, we're starting a new messenger pickup service at 2:30 p.m. daily beginning June 1.*

**Compliment.** Praise the receiver's accomplishments, organization, or efforts. But do so with honesty and sincerity. For instance, in a letter declining an invitation to speak, you could write, *The Thalians have my sincere admiration for their fund-raising projects on behalf of hungry children. I am honoured that you asked me to speak Friday, November 5.*

*Openers can buffer the bad news with compliments, appreciation, agreement, relevant facts, and understanding.*

**Appreciation.** Convey thanks to the reader for doing business, for sending something, for conveying confidence in your organization, for expressing feelings, or simply for providing feedback. Suppose you had to draft a letter that refuses employment. You could say, *I appreciated learning about the hospitality management program at George Brown College and about your qualifications in our interview last Friday.* Avoid thanking the reader, however, for something you are about to refuse.

**Agreement.** Make a relevant statement with which both reader and receiver can agree. A letter that rejects a loan application might read, *We both realize how much the export business has been affected by the relative strength of the dollar in the past two years.*

**Facts.** Provide objective information that introduces the bad news. For example, in a memo announcing cutbacks in the hours of the employees' cafeteria, you might say, *During the past five years the number of employees eating breakfast in our cafeteria has dropped from 32 percent to 12 percent.*

**Understanding.** Show that you care about the reader. Notice how in this letter to customers announcing a product defect, the writer expresses concern: *We know that you expect superior performance from all the products you purchase from OfficeCity. That's why we're writing personally about the Exell printer cartridges you recently ordered.*

Although popular outdoor retailer REI (Recreational Equipment Inc.) contributes more than $7.5 million to local outdoor recreation clubs and conservation groups, it must refuse many requests for funds and donations. The indirect pattern with its reasons-before-refusal works well for messages that deliver bad news.

*Apology.* As you learned in Chapter 9, an apology may be appropriate. A study of actual letters responding to customer complaints revealed that 67 percent carried an apology of some sort.[8] If you do apologize, do it early, briefly, and sincerely. For example, a manufacturer of premium ice cream might respond to a customer's complaint with, *We're genuinely sorry that you were disappointed in the price of the ice cream you recently purchased at one of our scoop shops. Your opinion is important to us, and we appreciate your giving us the opportunity to look into the problem you describe.* In responding to a complaint about poor service, a company might write, *I appreciate the frustration our delay has caused you. I'm sorry you didn't receive better service.* Or, *You're right to be concerned.*

Good buffers avoid revealing the bad news immediately. Moreover, they do not convey a false impression that good news follows. Additionally, they provide a natural transition to the next bad-news letter component—the reasons.

## Presenting the Reasons

**Bad-news messages should explain reasons before stating the negative news.**

The most important part of a bad-news letter is the section that explains why a negative decision is necessary. Without sound reasons for denying a request or refusing a claim, a letter will fail, no matter how cleverly it is organized or written. As part of your planning before writing, you analyzed the problem and decided to refuse a request for specific reasons. Before disclosing the bad news, try to explain those reasons. Providing an explanation reduces feelings of ill will and improves the chances that the reader will accept the bad news.

*Being Cautious in Explaining.* If the reasons are not confidential and if they will not create legal liability, you can be specific: *Growers supplied us with a limited number of patio roses, and our demand this year was twice that of last year.* In refusing a speaking engagement, tell why the date is impossible: *On January 17 we have a board of directors meeting that I must attend.* Don't, however, make unrealistic or dangerous statements in an effort to be the "good guy."

*Citing Reader or Other Benefits if Plausible.* Readers are more open to bad news if in some way, even indirectly, it may help them. In refusing a customer's request for free hemming of skirts and slacks, one clothing company wrote: "We tested our ability to hem skirts a few months ago. This process proved to be very time-consuming. We have decided not to offer this service because the additional cost would have increased the selling price of our skirts substantially, and we did not want to impose that cost on all our customers."[9] Readers also accept bad news better if they recognize that someone or something else benefits, such as other workers or the environment: *Although we would like to consider your application, we prefer to fill managerial positions from within.* Avoid trying to show reader benefits, though, if they appear insincere: *To improve our service to you, we're increasing our brokerage fees.*

**Readers accept bad news more readily if they see that someone benefits.**

*Explaining Company Policy.* Readers resent blanket policy statements prohibiting something: *Company policy prevents us from making cash refunds* or *Contract bids may be accepted from local companies only* or *Company policy requires us to promote from within.* Instead of hiding behind company policy, gently explain why the policy makes sense: *We prefer to promote from within because it rewards the loyalty of our employees. In addition, we've found that people familiar with our organization make the quickest contribution to our team effort.* By offering explanations, you demonstrate that you care about readers and are treating them as important individuals.

*Choosing Positive Words.* Because the words you use can affect a reader's response, choose carefully. Remember that the objective of the indirect pattern is holding the reader's attention until you've had a chance to explain the reasons justifying the bad news. To keep the reader in a receptive mood, avoid expressions with punitive, demoralizing, or otherwise negative connotations. Stay away from such words as as *cannot, claim, denied, error, failure, fault, impossible, mistaken, misunderstand, never, regret, rejected, unable, unwilling, unfortunately,* and *violate.*

**Don't use expressions with punitive, demoralizing, or other negative meanings.**

*Showing That the Matter Was Treated Seriously and Fairly.* In explaining reasons, demonstrate to the reader that you take the matter seriously, have investigated carefully, and are making an unbiased decision. Consumers are more accepting of disappointing news when they feel that their requests have been heard and that they have been treated fairly. Avoid passing the buck or blaming others within your organization. Such unprofessional behaviour makes the reader lose faith in you and your company.

## Cushioning the Bad News

Although you can't prevent the disappointment that bad news brings, you can reduce the pain somewhat by breaking the news sensitively. Be especially considerate when the reader will suffer personally from the bad news. A number of thoughtful techniques can cushion the blow.

*Positioning the Bad News Strategically.* Instead of spotlighting it, sandwich the bad news between other sentences, perhaps among your reasons. Don't let the refusal begin or end a paragraph—the reader's eye will linger on these high-visibility spots. Another technique that reduces shock is putting a painful idea in a subordinate clause: *Although another candidate was hired, we appreciate your interest in our organization and wish you every success in your job search.* Subordinate clauses often begin with words like *although, as, because, if,* and *since.*

**Techniques for cushioning bad news include positioning it strategically, and using the passive voice.**

*Using the Passive Voice.* Passive-voice verbs enable you to depersonalize an action. Whereas the active voice focuses attention on a person (*We don't give cash refunds*), the passive voice highlights the action (*Cash refunds are not generally given because . . .*). Use the passive voice for the bad news. In some instances you can combine passive-voice verbs and a subordinate clause: *Although franchise scoop shop owners cannot be required to lower their ice cream prices, we are happy to pass along your comments for their consideration.*

*Accentuating the Positive.* As you learned earlier, messages are far more effective when you describe what you can do instead of what you can't do. Rather than *We will no longer allow credit card purchases*, try a more positive appeal: *We are now selling gasoline at discount cash prices.*

**Implying the refusal and offering alternatives or compromises help to soften bad news.**

*Implying the Refusal.* It's sometimes possible to avoid a direct statement of refusal. Often, your reasons and explanations leave no doubt that a request has been denied. Explicit refusals may be unnecessary and at times cruel. In this refusal to contribute to a charity, for example, the writer never actually says no: *Because we will soon be moving into new offices in Glendale, all our funds are earmarked for moving and furnishings. We hope that next year we'll be able to support your worthwhile charity.* The danger of an implied refusal, of course, is that it is so subtle that the reader misses it. Be certain that you make the bad news clear, thus preventing the need for further correspondence.

*Suggesting a Compromise or an Alternative.* A refusal is not so depressing— for the sender or the receiver—if a suitable compromise, substitute, or alternative is available. In denying permission to a group of students to visit a historical private residence, for instance, this writer softens the bad news by proposing an alternative: *Although private tours of the grounds are not given, we do open the house and its gardens for one charitable event in the fall.* You can further reduce the impact of the bad news by refusing to dwell on it. Present it briefly (or imply it), and move on to your closing.

## Closing Pleasantly

**Closings to bad-news messages might include a forward look, an alternative, good wishes, freebies, and resale or sales promotion information.**

After explaining the bad news sensitively, close the message with a pleasant statement that promotes goodwill. The closing should be personalized and may include a forward look, an alternative, good wishes, freebies, resale information, or an off-the-subject remark.

*Forward Look.* Anticipate future relations or business. A letter that refuses a contract proposal might read: *Thanks for your bid. We look forward to working with your talented staff when future projects demand your special expertise.*

*Alternative.* If an alternative exists, end your letter with follow-through advice. For example, in a letter rejecting a customer's demand for replacement of landscaping plants, you might say: *I will be happy to give you a free inspection and consultation. Please call (905) 746-8112 to arrange a date for my visit.*

*Good Wishes.* A letter rejecting a job candidate might read: *We appreciate your interest in our company, and we extend to you our best wishes in your search to find the perfect match between your skills and job requirements.*

*Freebies.* When customers complain—primarily about food products or small consumer items—companies often send coupons, samples, or gifts to restore confidence and to promote future business. In response to a customer's complaint about a frozen dinner, you could write, *Your loyalty and your concern about our frozen entrées is genuinely appreciated. Because we want you to continue enjoying our healthful and convenient dinners, we're enclosing a coupon that you can take to your local market to select your next Green Valley entrée.*

*Resale or Sales Promotion.* When the bad news is not devastating or personal, references to resale information or promotion may be appropriate: *The computer workstations you ordered are unusually popular because of their stain-, heat-, and scratch-resistant finishes. To help you locate hard-to-find accessories for these workstations, we invite you to visit our Web site where our online catalogue provides a huge selection of surge suppressors, multiple-outlet strips, security devices, and PC tool kits.*

Avoid endings that sound canned, insincere, inappropriate, or self-serving. Don't invite further correspondence (*If you have any questions, do not hesitate . . .*), and don't refer to the bad news. To review these suggestions for delivering bad news sensitively, take another look at Figure 11.3.

## REFUSING ROUTINE REQUESTS

Every business communicator will occasionally have to say no to a request. Depending on how you think the receiver will react to your refusal, you can use the direct or the indirect pattern. If you have any doubt, use the indirect pattern.

*3*

### Rejecting Requests for Favours, Money, Information, and Action

Most of us prefer to be let down gently when we're being refused something we want. That's why the reasons-before-refusal pattern works well when you must turn down requests for favours, money, information, action, and so forth.

Requests for contributions to charity are common. Many large and small companies receive requests for contributions of money, time, equipment, and support. Although the causes may be worthy, resources are usually limited. If you were required to write frequent refusals, you might prepare a form letter, changing a few variables as needed. See the Tech Talk box on the next page to learn how you can personalize form letters by using word processing equipment.

As you read the following letter, think about how it could be adapted, using word processing equipment, to serve other charity requests.

**The reasons-before-refusal pattern works well when turning down requests for favours, money, information, or action.**

Dear Ms. Brown:

We appreciate your letter describing the good work your Tri-Valley County chapter of the National Reye's Syndrome Foundation is doing in preventing and treating this serious affliction. Your organization is to be commended for its significant achievements resulting from the efforts of dedicated members.

Supporting the good work of your organization and others, although unrelated to our business, is a luxury we have enjoyed in past years. Because of sales declines and organizational downsizing, we're forced to take a much harder look at funding requests that we receive this year. We feel that we must focus our charitable contributions on areas that relate directly to our business.

*Opens with acknowledgment of inquiry and praise for the writer. Doesn't say yes or no.*

*Repeats the key idea of good work. Explains that a decline in sales requires a cutback in gifts. Reveals refusal gently without actually stating it.*

*(continued)*

# Using Technology to Personalize Form Letters

If you had to send the same information to 200 or more customers, would you write a personal letter to each? Probably not! Responding to identical requests can be tedious, expensive, and time-consuming. That's why many businesses turn to form letters for messages like these: announcing upcoming sales, responding to requests for product information, and updating customers' accounts.

But your letters don't have to sound or look as if a computer wrote them. Word processing equipment can help you personalize those messages so that receivers feel they are being treated as individuals. Here's how the process works.

First, create a form letter (main document) with the basic text that is the same in every document. Insert codes or "merge fields" at each point where information will vary, for example, for the customer's name and address, item ordered, balance due, or due date. A database contains the recipient list. The main document is then merged with the recipient list to create a personalized letter for each individual. It's usually wise to minimize the variable information within the body of your message to keep the merging operation as simple as possible.

## Form Letter (Main Document)

Current Date
<<Title>> <<First_Name>> <<Last_Name>>
<<Address 1>>
<<City>>, <<Province>> <<Postal_Code>>

Dear <<Title>> <<Last_Name>>:

Thanks for your recent order from our fall catalogue.

One item that you requested, <<Item>>, has proved to be very popular this season. Occasionally, we are able to appeal to our manufacturers to make more of a popular item. In this instance, though, our pleas went unanswered.

More than anything, we hate to disappoint customers like you, <<Title>> <<Last_Name>>. We pledge to do better with your future orders.

Sincerely,

Cindy Scott

## List of Variable Information in Data Source

<<Title>> Mr.
<<First_Name>> Drew
<<Last_Name>> Jamison
<<Address 1>> 7700 Glover Road
<<City>>Langley
<<Province>>BC
<<Postal_Code>>V3A 4P9
<<Item>> No. 8765 ivory pullover.

## Completed Form Letter

Current Date

Mr. Drew Jamison
7700 Glover Road
Langley, BC V3A 4P9

Dear Mr. Jamison:

Thanks for your recent order from our fall catalogue.

One item that you requested, No. 8765 ivory pullover, has proved to be very popular this season. Occasionally, we are able to appeal to our manufacturers to make more of a popular item. In this instance, though, our pleas went unanswered.

More than anything, we hate to disappoint customers like you, Mr. Jamison. We pledge to do better with your future orders.

Sincerely,

Cindy Scott

## Career Application

Bring in a business letter that could be adapted as a form letter. Using it as a guide, prepare a rough draft of the same message indicating the exact locations of all necessary variables. Then ask someone from your class or your campus computer centre to demonstrate how this letter would be set up and merged using word processing software.

We're hopeful that the worst days are behind us and that we'll be able to renew •——— Closes graciously by looking
our support for worthwhile projects like yours next year.                                                                forward to next year.

Sincerely,

Just as managers must refuse requests from outsiders, they must also occasionally refuse requests from employees. In Figure 11.4 you see the first draft and revision of a message responding to a request from a key manager, Mark Stevenson. He
wants permission to attend a conference. However, he can't attend the conference
because the timing is bad; he must be present at budget planning meetings scheduled
for the same two weeks. Normally, this matter would be discussed in person. But
Mark has been travelling among branch offices, and he just hasn't been in the office
recently.

The vice president's first inclination was to send a quick memo, as shown in
Figure 11.4, and "tell it like it is." In revising, the vice president realized that this message was going to hurt and that it had possible danger areas. Moreover, the memo
misses a chance to give Mark positive feedback. An improved version of the memo
starts with a buffer that delivers honest praise (*pleased with your leadership* and *your
genuine professional commitment*). By the way, don't be stingy with compliments;
they cost you nothing. As a philosopher once observed, *We don't live by bread alone.
We need buttering up once in a while.* The buffer also includes the date of the meeting,
used strategically to connect the reasons that follow. You will recall from Chapter 6
that repetition of a key idea is an effective transitional device to provide smooth flow
between components of a message.

The middle paragraph provides reasons for the refusal. Notice that they focus on
positive elements: Mark is the specialist; the company relies on his expertise; and
everyone will benefit if he passes up the conference. In this section it becomes
obvious that the request will be refused. The writer is not forced to say, *No, you may
not attend.* Although the refusal is implied, the reader gets the message.

The closing suggests a qualified alternative (*if our workloads permit, we'll try to
send you then*). It also ends positively with gratitude for Mark's contributions to the
organization and with another compliment (*you're a valuable player*). Notice that the
improved version focuses on explanations and praise rather than on refusals and
apologies.

The success of this message depends on attention to the entire writing process,
not just on using a buffer or scattering a few compliments throughout.

## Declining Invitations

When we must decline an invitation to speak or attend a program, we generally try
to provide a response that says more than *I can't* or *I don't want to.* Unless the reasons are confidential or business secrets, try to explain them. Because responses to
invitations are often taken personally, make a special effort to soften the refusal. In
the letter on page 335, an accountant must say no to the invitation from a friend's
son to speak before the young man's college business club. The refusal is embedded
in a long paragraph and deemphasized in a subordinate clause (*Although I must
decline your invitation*). The reader naturally concentrates on the main clause that
follows. In this case that main clause contains an alternative that draws attention
away from the refusal.

Notice that the tone of a refusal is warm, upbeat, and positive. This refusal starts
with conviviality and compliments.

## FIGURE 11.4 Refusing a Request

First Draft

**DATE:** July 2, 2005

**TO:** Mark Stevenson
Manager, Telecommunications

**FROM:** Ann Wells-Freed  *AWF*
VP, Management Information Systems

**SUBJECT:** CONFERENCE REQUEST

We can't allow you to attend the conference in September, Mark. Perhaps you didn't know that budget planning meetings are scheduled for that month. — Announces the bad news too quickly and painfully

Your expertise is needed here to help keep our telecommunications network on schedule. Without you, the entire system—which is shaky at best—might fall apart. I'm sorry to have to refuse your request to attend the conference. I know this is small thanks for the fine work you have done for us. Please accept our humble apologies. — Gives reasons, but includes a dangerous statement

In the spring I'm sure your work schedule will be lighter, and we can release you to attend a conference at that time. — Makes a promise that might be difficult to keep

Revision

**DATE:** July 2, 2005

**TO:** Mark Stevenson
Manager, Telecommunications

**FROM:** Ann Wells-Freed  *AWF*
VP, Management Information Systems

**SUBJECT:** REQUEST TO ATTEND SEPTEMBER CONFERENCE

Transition: Uses date to move smoothly from buffer to reasons

The Management Council and I are extremely pleased with the leadership you have provided in setting up live video transmission to our regional offices. Because of your genuine professional commitment, Mark, I can understand your desire to attend the conference of the Telecommunication Specialists of North America September 23 to 28 in Kelowna. — Buffer: Includes sincere praise

Bad news: Implies refusal

The last two weeks in September have been set aside for budget planning. As you and I know, we've only scratched the surface of our teleconferencing projects for the next five years. Since you are the specialist and we rely heavily on your expertise, we need you here for those planning sessions. — Reasons: Tells why refusal is necessary

Closing: Contains realistic alternative, praise, and appreciation

If you're able to attend a similar conference in the spring and if our workloads permit, we'll try to send you then. You're a valuable player, Mark, and I'm grateful you're on our MIS team.

Dear William:

News of your leadership position in your campus student association fills me with delight and pride. Your father must be proud also of your educational and extracurricular achievements.

You honour me by asking me to speak to your group in the spring about codes of ethics in the accounting field. Because our firm has not yet adopted such a code, we have been investigating the codes developed by other accounting firms. I am decidedly not an expert in this area, but I have met others who are. Although your invitation must be declined, I would like to recommend Dr. Carolyn S. Marshall, who is a member of the ethics subcommittee of the Institute of Internal Auditors. Dr. Marshall is a professor who often addresses groups on the subject of ethics in accounting. I spoke with her about your club, and she indicated that she would be happy to consider your invitation.

It's good to learn that you are guiding your organization toward such constructive and timely program topics. Please call Dr. Marshall at (416) 389-2210 if you would like to arrange for her to address your club.

Sincerely,

*Opens cordially with buffer statement praising reader's accomplishments.*

*Explains the writer's ignorance on the topic of ethics. Lessens the impact of the refusal by placing it in a subordinate clause (Although your invitation must be declined) using the passive voice. Concentrates attention on the alternative.*

*Ends positively with compliments and assistance for arranging the substitute speaker.*

Although the direct refusal in this letter is softened by a subordinate clause, perhaps the refusal could have been avoided altogether. Notice how the following statement implies the refusal: *I'm certainly not an expert in this area, but I have met others who are. May I recommend Dr. Marshall . . . .* If no alternative is available, focus on something positive about the situation: *Although I'm not an expert, I commend your organization for selecting this topic.*

The following checklist reviews the steps in composing a letter refusing a routine request.

## CHECKLIST FOR REFUSING ROUTINE REQUESTS

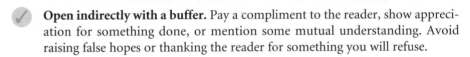 **Open indirectly with a buffer.** Pay a compliment to the reader, show appreciation for something done, or mention some mutual understanding. Avoid raising false hopes or thanking the reader for something you will refuse.

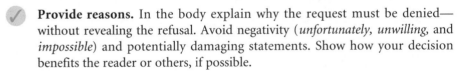 **Provide reasons.** In the body explain why the request must be denied—without revealing the refusal. Avoid negativity (*unfortunately, unwilling,* and *impossible*) and potentially damaging statements. Show how your decision benefits the reader or others, if possible.

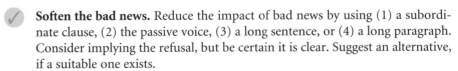 **Soften the bad news.** Reduce the impact of bad news by using (1) a subordinate clause, (2) the passive voice, (3) a long sentence, or (4) a long paragraph. Consider implying the refusal, but be certain it is clear. Suggest an alternative, if a suitable one exists.

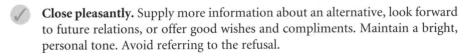 **Close pleasantly.** Supply more information about an alternative, look forward to future relations, or offer good wishes and compliments. Maintain a bright, personal tone. Avoid referring to the refusal.

Businesses must occasionally respond to disappointed customers. In Chapter 9 you learned to use the direct strategy in granting claims and making adjustments because these were essentially good-news messages. But in some situations you have little good news to share. Sometimes your company is at fault, in which case an apology is generally in order. Other times the problem is with product orders you can't fill, claims you must refuse, or credit that you must deny. Messages with bad news for customers generally follow the same pattern as other negative messages. Customer letters, though, differ in one major way: they usually include resale or sales promotion emphasis.

## Damage Control: Dealing With Disappointed Customers

**When a customer problem arises and the company is at fault, many businesspeople call and apologize, explain what happened, and follow up with a goodwill letter.**

All companies occasionally disappoint their customers. Merchandise is not delivered on time, a product fails to perform as expected, service is deficient, charges are erroneous, or customers are misunderstood. All businesses offering products or services must sometimes deal with troublesome situations that cause unhappiness to customers. Whenever possible, these problems should be dealt with immediately and personally. One study found that a majority of business professionals strive to control the damage and resolve such problems in the following manner:[10]

- Call the individual involved.

- Describe the problem and apologize.

- Explain why the problem occurred, what you are doing to resolve it, and how you will prevent it from happening again.

- Follow up with a letter that documents the phone call and promotes goodwill.

Dealing with problems immediately is very important in resolving conflict and retaining goodwill. Written correspondence is generally too slow for problems that demand immediate attention. But written messages are important (1) when personal contact is impossible, (2) to establish a record of the incident, (3) to formally confirm follow-up procedures, and (4) to promote good relations.

A bad-news follow-up letter is shown in Figure 11.5. Consultant Maris Richfield found herself in the embarrassing position of explaining why she had given out the name of her client to a salesperson. The client, Data.com, Inc., had hired her firm, Richfield Consulting Services, to help find an appropriate service for outsourcing its payroll functions. Without realizing it, Maris had mentioned to a potential vendor (Payroll Services, Inc.) that her client was considering hiring an outside service to handle its payroll. An overeager salesperson from Payroll Services immediately called on Data.com, thus angering the client. The client had hired the consultant to avoid this very kind of intrusion. Data.com did not want to be hounded by vendors selling their payroll services.

When she learned of the problem, the first thing consultant Maris Richfield did was call her client to explain and apologize. But she also followed up with the letter shown in Figure 11.5. The letter not only confirms the telephone conversation but also adds the right touch of formality. It sends the nonverbal message that the matter is being taken seriously and that it is important enough to warrant a written letter.

When situations involve many unhappy customers, companies may need to write personalized form letters. United Airlines found itself in this situation when it had to delay or cancel many flights because of a pilot slowdown and other factors. To

**FIGURE 11.5** Bad-News Follow-Up Message

## Tips for Resolving Problems and Following Up
- Whenever possible, call or see the individual involved.
- Describe the problem and apologize.
- Explain why the problem occurred.
- Describe what you are doing to resolve it.
- Explain how it will not happen again.
- Follow up with a letter that documents the personal message.
- Look forward to positive future relations.

## Richfield Consulting Services

1642 Sherbrooke St. West
Montreal, QC H3G 1H6

Voice: 514.499.8224
Web: www.richfieldconsulting.ca

October 23, 2005

Ms. Angela Ranier
Vice President, Human Resources
Data.com, Inc.
21067 Lacombe Avenue
Montreal, QC H5B 2G6

Dear Angela:

*Opens with agreement and apology* — You have every right to expect complete confidentiality in your transactions with an independent consultant. As I explained in yesterday's telephone call, I am very distressed that you were called by a salesperson from Payroll Services, Inc. This should not have happened, and I apologize to you again for inadvertently mentioning your company's name in a conversation with a potential vender, Payroll Services, Inc.

*Explains what caused problem and how it was resolved* — All clients of Richfield Consulting are assured that their dealings with our firm are held in the strictest confidence. Because your company's payroll needs are so individual and because you have so many contract workers, I was forced to explain how your employees differed from those of other companies. The name of your company, however, should never have been mentioned. I can assure you that it will not happen again. *Promises to prevent recurrence* — I have informed Payroll Services that it had no authorization to call you directly and its actions have forced me to reconsider using its services for my future clients.

*Closes with forward look* — A number of other payroll services offer excellent programs. I'm sure we can find the perfect partner to enable you to outsource your payroll responsibilities, thus allowing your company to focus its financial and human resources on its core business. I look forward to our next appointment when you may choose from a number of excellent payroll outsourcing firms.

Sincerely yours,

*Maris Richfield*

Maris Richfield

**Personalized form letters may be necessary when delivering bad news to large groups of customers.**

respond to bad publicity and growing customer annoyance, United's CEO wrote a "damage control" letter to its frequent flyers. The letter contains many elements in the indirect strategy, beginning with an apology:

> Dear Mr. Victor:
>
> I want to tell you how sorry I am about all of the flight delays and cancellations we at United have subjected you to during the past few weeks.

The letter continued with a no-excuses explanation of the cause of its delays and cancellations and a frank admission that United's service was worse than that of its competitors:

> While all airlines have been affected by weather, air traffic control problems, and unprecedented load factors, our performance has been noticeably worse than that of our competitors. Let me explain why and, more important, tell you what we are doing about it.

The letter went on to explain that United had finally reached an agreement with its pilots, which was a "first step in returning our service to the high standards you deserve." The next sentence began by assuming responsibility but quickly shifted the focus to what United is doing for its customers:

When something goes wrong in customer transactions and damage control is necessary, the first thing most businesspeople do is call the individual involved, explain what happened, and apologize. Written messages follow up.

> We accept the responsibility for our current situation, and we are working on every front—from the negotiating table to the airports—to improve your experience.

The next portion of the letter used bullet points to list the steps that United was taking to solve its problems, including tripling the number of extra aircraft ready for use at the airports, reducing its flight schedule, and adding time to its schedule to reflect operational realities. The letter also waived service fees for changing flights and offered bonus mileage points. Concluding the United letter, the CEO used warm words and personal entreaties to win back its lost customers:

> These actions are only a beginning. We recognize that we need to get our operation back on track to truly regain your loyalty. If you have stayed with us during our recent difficulties, I want to personally thank you for showing more patience than any company has a right to expect. If you have taken your business elsewhere, I assure you that we will do everything possible to win back your confidence.[11]

As exemplified in United Airlines' letter, the following specific strategies are effective in dealing with unhappy customers.

- Apologize if your organization is to blame.
- Identify the problem and take responsibility.

- Explain the steps being taken to prevent recurrence.
- Offer gifts, benefits, or bonuses to offset disappointment and to reestablish relationship.
- Thank customers for their past business and patience.
- Look forward to future warm relations.

## Handling Problems With Orders

Not all customer orders can be filled as received. Suppliers may be able to send only part of an order or none at all. Substitutions may be necessary, or the delivery date may be delayed. Suppliers may suspect that all or part of the order is a mistake; the customer may actually want something else. In writing to customers about problem orders, it's generally wise to use the direct pattern if the message has some good-news elements. But when the message is disappointing, the indirect pattern is more appropriate.

> **In handling problems with orders, the indirect pattern is appropriate unless the message has some good-news elements.**

Let's say you represent Live and Learn Toys, a large West Coast toy manufacturer, and you're scrambling for business in a slow year. A big customer, Child Land, calls in August and asks you to hold a block of your best-selling toy, the Space Station. Like most vendors, you require a deposit on large orders. September rolls around, and you still haven't received any money from Child Land. You must now write a tactful letter asking for the deposit—or else you will release the toy to other buyers. The problem, of course, is delivering the bad news without losing the customer's order and goodwill. Another challenge is making sure the reader understands the bad news. The following letter sandwiches the bad news (*without a deposit, we must release this block to other retailers*) between resale information and sales promotion information.

✓ *Effective Letter*

Dear Mr. Ronzelli:

You were smart to reserve a block of 500 Space Stations, which we have been holding for you since August. As the holidays approach, the demand for all our learning toys, including Space Station, is rapidly increasing.

> Opening compliments the receiver while establishing the facts.

Toy stores from St. John's to Victoria are asking us to ship these Space Stations. One reason the Space Station is moving out of our warehouses so quickly is its assortment of gizmos that children love, including a land rover vehicle, a shuttle craft, a hovercraft, astronauts, and even a robotic arm. As soon as we receive your deposit of $4 000, we'll have this popular item on its way to your stores. Without a deposit by September 20, though, we must release this block to other retailers. Use the enclosed envelope to send us your cheque immediately. You can begin showing this fascinating Live and Learn toy in your stores by November 1.

> Reasons justify the coming bad news. Instead of focusing on the writer's needs (*we have a full warehouse* and *we need your deposit*), the reasons concentrate on motivating the reader. After the reasons, the bad news is clearly spelled out.

Please visit our Web site, which replaces our paper catalogue, for pictures, descriptions, and prices of other popular Live and Learn toys. We were voted one of the best online toy stores—with higher ratings than even FAO Schwarz and Etoys. We look forward to your cheque as well as to continuing to serve all your toy needs.

> Closing promotes the company's Web site and looks ahead to future business.

Sincerely,

## Denying Claims

In denying claims, the reasons-before-refusal pattern sets an empathic tone and buffers the bad news.

Customers occasionally want something they're not entitled to or that you can't grant. They may misunderstand warranties or make unreasonable demands. Because these customers are often unhappy with a product or service, they are emotionally involved. Letters that say no to emotionally involved receivers will probably be your most challenging communication task. As publisher Malcolm Forbes observed, "To be agreeable while disagreeing—that's an art."[12]

Fortunately, the reasons-before-refusal plan helps you be empathic and artful in breaking bad news. Obviously, in denial letters you'll need to adopt the proper tone. Don't blame customers, even if they are at fault. Avoid *you* statements that sound preachy (*You would have known that cash refunds are impossible if you had read your contract*). Use neutral, objective language to explain why the claim must be refused. Consider offering resale information to rebuild the customer's confidence in your products or organization. In Figure 11.6 the writer denies a customer's claim for the difference between the price the customer paid for speakers and the price he saw advertised locally (which would have resulted in a cash refund of $151). While the catalogue service does match any advertised lower price, the price-matching policy applies only to exact models. This claim must be rejected because the advertisement the customer submitted showed a different, older speaker model.

The letter to Matthew Tyson opens with a buffer that agrees with a statement in the customer's letter. It repeats the key idea of product confidence as a transition to the second paragraph. Next comes an explanation of the price-matching policy. The writer does not assume that the customer is trying to pull a fast one. Nor does he suggest that the customer is a dummy who didn't read or understand the price-matching policy. The safest path is a neutral explanation of the policy along with precise distinctions between the customer's speakers and the older ones. The writer also gets a chance to resell the customer's speakers and demonstrate what a quality product they are. By the end of the third paragraph, it's evident to the reader that his claim is unjustified.

## Refusing Credit

Goals when refusing credit include maintaining customer goodwill and avoiding actionable language.

As much as companies want business, they can extend credit only when payment is likely to follow. Credit applications, from individuals or from businesses, are generally approved or disapproved on the basis of the applicant's credit history. This record is supplied by a credit-reporting agency, such as Equifax. After reviewing the applicant's record, a credit manager applies the organization's guidelines and approves or disapproves the application.

If you must deny credit to prospective customers, you have four goals in conveying the refusal:

- Avoiding language that causes hard feelings
- Retaining customers on a cash basis
- Preparing for possible future credit without raising false expectations
- Avoiding disclosures that could cause a lawsuit

Because credit applicants are likely to continue to do business with an organization even if they are denied credit, you'll want to do everything possible to encourage that patronage. Thus, keep the refusal respectful, sensitive, and upbeat. To avoid possible litigation, some organizations give no explanation of the reasons for the refusal. Instead, they provide the name of the credit-reporting agency and suggest that inquiries be directed to it. Here's a credit refusal letter that uses a buffer but does

## FIGURE 11.6 Denying a Claim

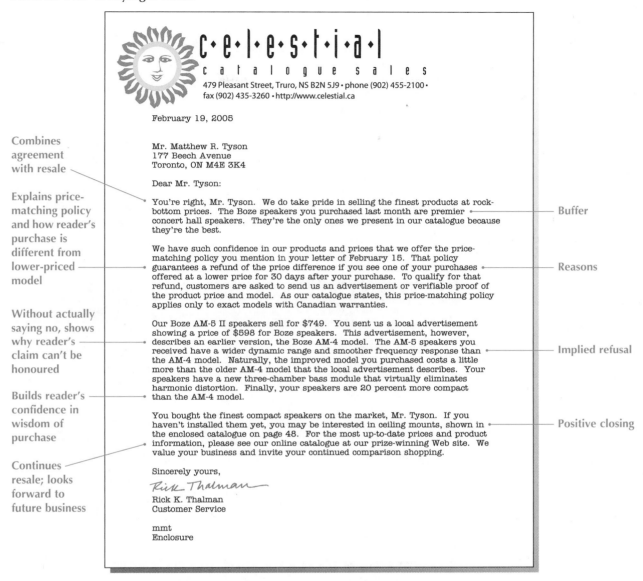

**Combines agreement with resale**

**Explains price-matching policy and how reader's purchase is different from lower-priced model**

**Without actually saying no, shows why reader's claim can't be honoured**

**Builds reader's confidence in wisdom of purchase**

**Continues resale; looks forward to future business**

c·e·l·e·s·t·i·a·l
c a t a l o g u e   s a l e s

479 Pleasant Street, Truro, NS B2N 5J9 · phone (902) 455-2100 ·
fax (902) 435-3260 · http://www.celestial.ca

February 19, 2005

Mr. Matthew R. Tyson
177 Beech Avenue
Toronto, ON M4E 3K4

Dear Mr. Tyson:

You're right, Mr. Tyson. We do take pride in selling the finest products at rock-bottom prices. The Boze speakers you purchased last month are premier concert hall speakers. They're the only ones we present in our catalogue because they're the best. — **Buffer**

We have such confidence in our products and prices that we offer the price-matching policy you mention in your letter of February 15. That policy guarantees a refund of the price difference if you see one of your purchases offered at a lower price for 30 days after your purchase. To qualify for that refund, customers are asked to send us an advertisement or verifiable proof of the product price and model. As our catalogue states, this price-matching policy applies only to exact models with Canadian warranties. — **Reasons**

Our Boze AM-5 II speakers sell for $749. You sent us a local advertisement showing a price of $598 for Boze speakers. This advertisement, however, describes an earlier version, the Boze AM-4 model. The AM-5 speakers you received have a wider dynamic range and smoother frequency response than the AM-4 model. Naturally, the improved model you purchased costs a little more than the older AM-4 model that the local advertisement describes. Your speakers have a new three-chamber bass module that virtually eliminates harmonic distortion. Finally, your speakers are 20 percent more compact than the AM-4 model. — **Implied refusal**

You bought the finest compact speakers on the market, Mr. Tyson. If you haven't installed them yet, you may be interested in ceiling mounts, shown in the enclosed catalogue on page 48. For the most up-to-date prices and product information, please see our online catalogue at our prize-winning Web site. We value your business and invite your continued comparison shopping. — **Positive closing**

Sincerely yours,

*Rick Thalman*

Rick K. Thalman
Customer Service

mmt
Enclosure

---

not explain the reasons for the denial. Notice how the warm tone reassures the reader that she is respected and that her patronage is valued. The letter implies that her current credit condition is temporary, but it does not raise false hopes by promising future credit.

✓ *Effective Letter*

Dear Ms. Love:

We genuinely appreciate your application of January 12 for a Fashion Express credit account. — **Buffer identifies application and shows appreciation for it.**

After receiving a report of your current credit record from Equifax, it is apparent that credit cannot be extended at this time. To learn more about your record, you may call an Equifax credit counsellor at (800) 356-0922. We've

*(continued)*

Long sentence and passive
voice deemphasize bad news.
To prevent possible litigation,
offers no reason for denial.

Closes cordially and looks forward to continued patronage.

arranged for you to take advantage of this service for 60 days from the date of this letter at no charge to you.

Thanks, Ms. Love, for the confidence you've shown in Fashion Express. We invite you to continue shopping at our stores, and we look forward to your reapplication in the future.

Some businesses do provide reasons explaining credit denials (*Credit cannot be granted because your firm's current and long-term credit obligations are nearly twice as great as your firm's total assets*). They may also provide alternatives, such as deferred billing or cash discounts. When the letter denies a credit application that accompanies an order, the message may contain resale information. The writer tries to convert the order from credit to cash.

Whatever form the bad-news letter takes, it's a good idea to have the message reviewed by legal counsel because of the litigation landmines awaiting unwary communicators in this area. The following checklist provides tips on how to craft effective bad-news letters.

## CHECKLIST FOR DELIVERING BAD NEWS TO CUSTOMERS

✓ **Begin indirectly.** Express appreciation (but don't thank the reader for requesting something you're about to refuse), show agreement on some point, review facts, or show understanding. Consider apologizing if your organization was responsible for disappointing its customers.

✓ **Provide reasons.** Except in credit denials, justify the bad news with objective reasons. Use resale, if appropriate, to restore the customer's confidence. Avoid blaming the customer or hiding behind company policy. Look for reader benefits.

✓ **Present the bad news.** State the bad news objectively or imply it. Although resale or sales promotion is appropriate in order letters, it may offend in claim or credit refusals.

✓ **Offer gifts, benefits, or tokens of appreciation.** When appropriate, look for ways to offset your customers' disappointment.

✓ **Close pleasantly.** Look forward to future business, suggest action on an alternative, offer best wishes, refer to gifts, or use resale sensitively. Don't mention the bad news.

## DELIVERING BAD NEWS WITHIN ORGANIZATIONS

5

A tactful tone and a reasons-first approach help preserve friendly relations with customers. These same techniques are useful when delivering bad news to employees and when rejecting job applicants.

## Announcing Bad News to Employees

Bad news within organizations might involve declining profits, lost contracts, harmful lawsuits, public relations controversies, and changes in policy. Whether you use a direct or an indirect pattern in delivering that news depends primarily on the anticipated reaction of the receiver. When bad news affects employees personally—such as cutbacks in pay, reduction of benefits, or relocation plans—you can generally lessen its impact and promote better relations by explaining reasons before revealing the bad news.

The first version of the following memo, which announces a substantial increase in the cost of employee health care benefits, suffers from many problems.

Internal bad-news memos should use the indirect pattern to convey news that adversely affects employees.

✗ *Ineffective Memo*

TO:        Employees

FROM:    David P. Martinez, President

SUBJECT: INCREASE IN YOUR PAYMENTS

Beginning January 1 your monthly payment for supplementary health care benefits will be increased to $109 (up from $42 last year).

*Hits readers with bad news without any preparation.*

Every year supplementary health care costs go up. Although we considered dropping other benefits, Midland decided that the best plan was to keep the present comprehensive package. Unfortunately, we can't do that unless we pass along some of the extra cost to you. Last year the company was forced to absorb the total increase in health care premiums. However, such a plan this year is inadvisable.

*Offers no explanation of why health care costs are rising. Action sounds arbitrary. Fails to take credit for absorbing previous increases.*

We did everything possible to avoid the sharp increase in costs to you this year. A rate schedule describing the increases in payments for your family and dependants is enclosed.

*Sounds defensive; fails to provide reasons.*

The improved version of this bad-news memo, shown in Figure 11.7, uses the indirect pattern. Notice that it opens with a relevant, upbeat buffer regarding health care—but says nothing about increasing costs. For a smooth transition, the second paragraph begins with a key idea from the opening (*comprehensive package*). The reasons section discusses rising costs with explanations and figures. The bad news (*you will be paying $109 a month*) is clearly presented but embedded within the paragraph. Throughout, the writer strives to show the fairness of the company's position. The ending, which does not refer to the bad news, emphasizes how much the company is paying and what a wise investment it is. Notice that the entire memo demonstrates a kinder, gentler approach than that shown in the first draft. Of prime importance in breaking bad news to employees is providing clear, convincing reasons that explain the decision.

Many organizations involved in a crisis (serious performance problems, major relocation, massive layoffs, management shakeup, or public controversy) prefer to communicate the news openly to employees, customers, and shareholders. Instead of letting rumours distort the truth, they explain the organization's side of the story honestly and early. Morale can be destroyed when employees learn of major events affecting their jobs through the grapevine or from news accounts—rather than from management.

Organizations can sustain employee morale by communicating bad news openly and honestly.

## Saying No to Job Applicants

Being refused a job is one of life's major rejections. The blow is intensified by tactless letters (*Unfortunately, you were not among the candidates selected for . . .*).

**FIGURE 11.7** Announcing Bad News to Employees

**Prewriting**

**Analyze:** The purpose of this memo is to tell employees that they must share the increasing costs of health care.

**Anticipate:** The audience will be employees who are unaware of health care costs and, most likely, reluctant to pay more.

**Adapt:** Because the readers will probably be unhappy and resentful, use the indirect pattern.

**Writing**

**Research:** Collect facts and statistics that document health care costs.

**Organize:** Begin with a buffer describing the company's commitment to health benefits. Provide an explanation of health care costs. Announce the bad news. In the closing, focus on the company's major share of the cost.

**Compose:** Draft the first version on a computer.

**Revising**

**Revise:** Remove negativity (*unfortunately, we can't, we were forced, inadvisable, we don't think*). Explain the increase with specifics.

**Proofread:** Use a semicolon before however. Use quotes around *defensive* to show its special sense. Spell out *percent* after *300*.

**Evaluate:** Is there any other way to help readers accept this bad news?

---

DATE:     November 6, 2005

TO:       Fellow Employees

FROM:     David P. Martinez, President  DPM

SUBJECT:  MAINTAINING QUALITY HEALTH CARE

Supplementary health care programs have always been an important part of our commitment to employees at Midland, Inc. We're proud that our total benefits package continues to rank among the best in the country.

Such a comprehensive package does not come cheaply. In the last decade health care costs alone have risen over 300 percent. We're told that several factors fuel the cost spiral: inflation, technology improvements, increased cost of outpatient services, and "defensive" medicine practised by doctors to prevent lawsuits.

Just two years ago our monthly health care cost for each employee was $415. It rose to $469 last year. We were able to absorb that jump without increasing your contribution, but this year's hike to $539 forces us to ask you to share the increase. To maintain your current health care benefits, you will be paying $109 a month. The enclosed rate schedule describes the costs for families and dependants.

Midland continues to pay the major portion of your supplementary health care program ($430 each month). We think it's a wise investment.

Enclosure

*Begins with positive buffer*

*Offers reasons explaining why costs are rising*

*Reveals bad news clearly but embeds it in paragraph*

*Ends positively by stressing the company's major share of the costs*

---

You can reduce the receiver's disappointment somewhat by using the indirect pattern—with one important variation. In the reasons section it's wise to be vague in explaining why the candidate was not selected. First, giving concrete reasons may be painful to the receiver (*Your grade point average of 2.7 was low compared with GPAs*

# *Hyundai Auto Canada Revisited*

When Steve Kelleher, president and CEO of Hyundai Auto Canada, learned of an error in marketing information given to customers, he offered his personal apology: "I am very sorry for these errors and for any concerns it raises among Hyundai customers. We are announcing these errors because we want our relationship with our customers, our dealers, and all our business partners to be open and honest."

The error in this case was the misreporting of information regarding horsepower ratings on a number of vehicle lines over a period of several years. Although a Hyundai press release explained that these errors originated with Hyundai Motor America, Kelleher chose not to point fingers in his letter to affected customers. Instead, he assured readers that the error did not impact the safety or reliability of their automobiles, indicated that he had taken steps to ensure the error didn't happen again, and directed readers to a specific Web site for more details.

To back up his apology, Kelleher offered affected customers a choice of three warranty-enhancement options for year 2000 models onward, or, for 1999 and earlier models, three-year unlimited-kilometre roadside assistance coverage. The letter included a self-addressed, postage-paid envelope and a personalized Customer Reply Form. Respondents had only to check off their choice and sign and return the completed form. Hyundai followed up with a letter confirming the customer's choice and reiterating the company's desire to maintain open and honest communication.[13]

## CRITICAL THINKING

- How closely does Steve Kelleher's letter (as described above) follow the four-part plan suggested in this chapter?
- Why might Kelleher have chosen not to reveal the source of the problem in his letter to affected customers?
- When would form letters make sense for a company such as Hyundai Auto Canada?

www.hyundaicanada.com

---

of other candidates). Second, and more important, providing extra information may prove fatal in a lawsuit. Hiring and firing decisions generate considerable litigation today. To avoid charges of discrimination or wrongful actions, legal advisors warn organizations to keep employment rejection letters general, simple, and short.

The following job refusal letter is tactful but intentionally vague. It implies that the applicant's qualifications don't match those needed for the position, but the letter doesn't reveal anything specific.

**Letters that deny applications for employment should be courteous and tactful but free of specifics that could trigger lawsuits.**

✓ *Effective Letter*

Dear Mr. Fisher:

Thanks for letting us review your résumé submitted for our advertised management trainee opening.

*Shows appreciation. Doesn't indicate good or bad news.*

We received a number of impressive résumés for this opening. Although another candidate was selected, your interest in our organization is appreciated. So that you may continue your search for a position at another organization, we are writing to you immediately.

*To prevent possible lawsuits, gives no explanation. Places bad news in a dependent clause.*

We wish you every success in finding a position that exactly fits your qualifications.

*Ends with best wishes.*

Sincerely,

The following checklist gives tips on how to communicate bad news within an organization.

## CHECKLIST FOR DELIVERING NEGATIVE NEWS WITHIN ORGANIZATIONS

✓ **Start with a relevant, upbeat buffer.** Open with a small bit of good news, praise, appreciation, agreement, understanding, or a discussion of facts leading to the reasons section.

✓ **Discuss reasons.** Except in job refusal letters, explain what caused the decision necessitating the bad news. Use objective, nonjudgmental, and nondiscriminatory language. Show empathy and fairness.

✓ **Reveal the bad news.** Make the bad news clear but don't accentuate it. Avoid negative language.

✓ **Close harmoniously.** End on a positive, friendly note. For job refusals, extend good wishes.

## PRESENTING BAD NEWS IN OTHER CULTURES

*6*

**Communicating bad news in other cultures may require different strategies.**

To minimize disappointment, Westerners generally prefer to present negative messages indirectly. Other cultures may treat bad news differently.

In Germany, for example, business communicators occasionally use buffers but tend to present bad news directly. British writers also tend to be straightforward with bad news, seeing no reason to soften its announcement. In Latin countries the question is not how to organize negative messages but whether to present them at all. It's considered disrespectful and impolite to report bad news to superiors. Thus, reluctant employees may fail to report accurately any negative messages to their bosses.

In Asian cultures, harmony and peace are sought in all relationships. Disrupting the harmony with bad news is avoided. To prevent discord, Japanese communicators use a number of techniques to indicate *no*—without being forced to say it. In conversation they may respond with silence or with a counter question, such as "Why do you ask?" They may change the subject or tell a white lie to save face for themselves and for the questioner. Sometimes the answer sounds like a qualified *yes*: "I will do my best, but if I cannot, I hope you will understand," "Yes, but . . . ," or "yes" followed by an apology. All of these responses should be recognized as *no*.

In China, Westerners often have difficulty understanding the "hints" given by communicators.

"I agree" might mean "I agree with 15 percent of what you say."

"We might be able to" could mean "Not a chance."

"We will consider" could mean "WE will, but the real decision maker will not."

"That is a little too much" might equate to "That is outrageous."[14]

In Thailand the negativism represented by a refusal is completely alien; the word *no* does not exist. In many cultures negative news is offered with such subtleness or

## Applying Your Skills at Hyundai Auto Canada

Large organizations such as Hyundai Auto Canada receive many inquiries requesting donations to charities, sponsorships of charitable projects, and contributions of free merchandise. As a good corporate citizen, Hyundai Auto Canada sponsors many national and local organizations as well as a number of multicultural charities such as the Danak Festival and the Korean Canadian Cultural Association.

Unfortunately, Hyundai Auto Canada can't possibly say yes to all requests and so must sometimes respond with disappointing news. Assume that you are working in the Communications division at Hyundai Auto Canada, and you have been asked to prepare a set of guidelines to be used when turning down requests. Knowing that bad news is more palatable if it's accompanied by an explanation, your supervisor suggests that you first research how other companies handle this situation.

### Your Task

Using the Internet to check the corporate donation policies of at least three different companies, draft a one-page outline for a set of guidelines for Hyundai Auto Canada. If your instructor directs, prepare a form letter that could be used as an example.

**www.hyundaicanada.com**

in such a positive light that it may be overlooked or misunderstood by literal-minded low-context cultures. To understand the meaning of what's really being communicated, we must look beyond an individual's actual words, considering the communication style, the culture, and especially the context.

You've now studied the indirect method for revealing bad news and analyzed many examples of messages applying this method. As you observed, business writers generally try to soften the blow; however, they do eventually reveal the bad news. No effort is made to sweep it under the carpet or ignore it totally.

## SUMMARY OF LEARNING OBJECTIVES

*1* **Describe the goals and strategies of business communicators in delivering bad news.** All businesses will occasionally deal with problems. Good communicators have several goals in delivering bad news: (a) making the reader understand and accept the bad news, (b) promoting and maintaining a good image of themselves and their organizations, (c) making the message so clear that additional correspondence is unnecessary, and (d) avoiding creating legal liability or responsibility. The indirect pattern involves delaying the bad news until reasons have been presented. The direct pattern reveals the main idea immediately. The direct pattern is preferable when (a) the receiver may overlook the bad news, (b) organization policy suggests directness, (c) the receiver prefers directness, (d) firmness is necessary, and (e) the bad news is not damaging. Careful communicators will avoid careless and abusive language, which is actionable when it is false, damages a person's reputation, and is "published" (spoken within the presence of others or written). Messages written on company stationery represent that company and can be legally binding.

**2** **Explain techniques for delivering bad news sensitively.** Begin with a buffer, such as a compliment, appreciation, a point of agreement, objective information, understanding, or some part of the message that represents good news. Then explain the reasons that necessitate the bad news, trying to cite benefits to the reader or others. Choose positive words, and clarify company policy if necessary. Announce the bad news strategically, mentioning a compromise or alternative if possible. Close pleasantly with a forward-looking goodwill statement.

**3** **Identify routine requests and describe a strategy for refusing such requests.** Routine requests ask for favours, money, information, action, and other items. When the answer will be disappointing, use the reasons-before-refusal pattern. Open with a buffer; provide reasons; announce the refusal sensitively; suggest possible alternatives; and end with a positive, forward-looking comment.

**4** **Explain techniques for managing bad news to customers.** When a company disappoints its customers, most organizations (a) call the individual involved, (b) describe the problem and apologize (when it is to blame), (c) explain why the problem occurred and what is being done to prevent its recurrence, and (d) follow up with a letter that documents the phone call and promotes goodwill. Some organizations also offer gifts or benefits to offset customers' disappointment and to reestablish the business relationship. In denying claims or refusing credit, begin indirectly, provide reasons for the refusal, and close pleasantly, looking forward to future business. When appropriate, resell a product or service.

**5** **Explain techniques for managing bad news within organizations.** When breaking bad news to employees, use the indirect pattern but be sure to provide clear, convincing reasons that explain the decision. In refusing job applicants, however, keep letters short, general, and tactful.

**6** **Compare strategies for revealing bad news in different cultures.** North American communicators often prefer to break bad news slowly and indirectly. In other low-context cultures, such as Germany and Britain, however, bad news is revealed directly. In high-context cultures, straightforwardness is avoided. In Latin cultures bad news may be totally suppressed. In Asian cultures negativism is avoided and hints may suggest bad news. Subtle meanings must be interpreted carefully.

# CHAPTER REVIEW

1. Discuss four goals of a business communicator who must deliver bad news. (Obj. 1)

2. How can business documents in an organization's files become part of a lawsuit? (Obj. 1)

3. Describe the four parts of the indirect message pattern. (Obj. 1)

4. Name five situations in which the direct pattern should be used for bad news. (Obj. 1)

5. Name five or more techniques to buffer the opening of a bad-news message. (Obj. 2)

6. Name four or more techniques to deemphasize bad news when it is presented. (Obj. 2)

7. Name four kinds of routine requests that businesses must frequently refuse. (Obj. 3)

8. Why should you be especially careful in cushioning the refusal to an invitation? (Obj. 3)

9. What is the major difference between bad-news messages for customers and those for other people? (Obj. 4)

10. Identify a process used by many business professionals in resolving problems with disappointed customers. (Obj. 4)

11. List four goals a writer seeks to achieve in writing messages that deny credit to prospective customers. (Obj. 4)

12. Why should a writer be somewhat vague in the reasons section of a letter rejecting a job applicant? (Obj. 4)

13. When organizations must reveal a crisis (such as Firestone/Ford's deadly pattern of tire failures), how should they communicate the news to employees, customers, shareholders, and the public? (Objs. 4 and 5)

14. Why is the reasons-before-refusal strategy appropriate for customers who are unhappy with a product or service? (Obj. 4)

15. In Latin countries why may employees sometimes fail to report accurately any negative messages to management? (Obj. 6)

# CRITICAL THINKING

1. Does bad news travel faster and farther than good news? Why? What implications would this have for companies responding to unhappy customers? (Objs. 1–5)

2. Some people feel that all employee news, good or bad, should be announced directly. Do you agree or disagree? Why? (Objs. 1–5)

3. Consider times when you have been aware that others have used the indirect pattern in writing or speaking to you. How did you react? (Objs. 1–5)

4. In considering negative organization news, should companies immediately reveal grave illnesses of key executives? Or should executives be entitled to keep their health a private matter? Does it matter if the company is public or private? (Objs. 4 and 5)

5. **Ethical Issue:** You work for a large corporation with headquarters in a small town. Recently you received shoddy repair work and a huge bill from a local garage. Your car's transmission has the same problems that it did before you took it in for repair. You know that a complaint letter written on your corporation's stationery would be much more authoritative than one written on plain stationery. Should you use corporation stationery? (Obj. 1)

# ACTIVITIES

## 11.1 Organizational Patterns (Objs. 1–5)

**Your Task.** Identify which organizational pattern you would use for the following messages: direct or indirect.

a. A letter refusing a request by a charitable organization asking your restaurant chain to provide refreshments for a large reception.

b. A memo from the manager denying an employee's request for computer access to the Web. Although the employee works closely with the manager on many projects, the employee's work does not require Internet access.

c. An announcement to employees that a financial specialist has cancelled a scheduled lunchtime talk and cannot reschedule.

d. A letter from a bank refusing to fund a company's overseas expansion plan.

e. A form letter from an insurance company announcing new policy requirements that many policyholders may resent. If policyholders do not indicate the plan they prefer, they may lose their insurance coverage.

f. A letter from an amusement park refusing the request of a customer who was unhappy with a substitute concert performer.

g. The last in a series of letters from a collection agency demanding payment of a long-overdue account. The next step will be hiring a lawyer.

h. A letter from a computer company refusing to authorize repair of a customer's computer on which the warranty expired six months ago.

i. A memo from an executive refusing a manager's plan to economize by purchasing reconditioned computers.

The executive and the manager both appreciate efficient, straightforward messages.

j. A letter informing a customer that the majority of the customer's recent order will not be available for six weeks.

## 11.2 Passive-Voice Verbs (Obj. 2)

**Your Task.** Revise the following sentences to present the bad news with passive-voice verbs.

a. We do not serve meals on any flights other than those during meal times.

b. No one is allowed to park in the yellow zone.

c. Because of our Web site, we are no longer offering a printed catalogue.

d. We are unable to grant your request for a loan.

## 11.3 Subordinating Bad News (Obj. 2)

**Your Task.** Revise the following sentences to position the bad news in a subordinate clause. (*Hint:* Consider beginning the clause with *Although.*) Use passive-voice verbs for the bad news.

a. We cannot refund your purchase price, but we are sending you two coupons toward your next purchase.

b. We appreciate your interest in our organization. Unfortunately, we are unable to extend an employment offer to you at this time.

c. It is impossible for us to ship your complete order at this time. However, we are able to send the four oak desks now; you should receive them within five days.

d. You are able to increase the number of physician visits you make, but we find it necessary to increase the cost of your monthly health benefit contribution.

## 11.4 Implying Bad News (Obj. 2)

**Your Task.** Revise the following statements to *imply* the bad news. Use passive-voice verbs and subordinate clauses to further deemphasize the bad news.

a. I already have an engagement in my appointment calendar for the date you mention. Therefore, I am unable to speak to your group. However, I would like to recommend another speaker who might be able to address your organization.

b. Because of the holiday period, all our billboard space was used this month. Therefore, we are sorry to say that we could not give your charitable group free display space. However, next month, after the holidays, we hope to display your message as we promised.

c. We cannot send you a price list nor can we sell our equipment directly to customers. Our policy is to sell only through dealers, and your dealer is Stereo City, located on Yonge Street in Toronto.

## 11.5 Evaluating Bad-News Statements (Obj. 2)

**Your Task.** Discuss the strengths or weaknesses of the following bad-news statements.

a. It's impossible for us to ship your order before May 1.

b. Frankly, we like your résumé, but we were hoping to hire someone a little younger who might be able to stay with us longer.

c. I'm thoroughly disgusted with this entire case, and I will never do business with shyster lawyers like you again.

d. We can assure you that on any return visit to our hotels, you will not be treated so poorly.

e. We must deny your credit application because your record shows a history of late payments, nonpayment, and irregular employment.

f. *(In a confidential company memo:)* I cannot recommend that we promote this young lady into any position where she will meet the public. Her colourful facial decoration, as part of her religion, may offend our customers.

## 11.6 Negative News in Other Cultures (Obj. 6)

**Your Task.** Interview fellow students or work colleagues who are from other cultures. How is negative news handled in their cultures? How would typical individuals refuse a request for a favour, for example? How would a business refuse credit to customers? How would an individual be turned down for a job? Is directness practised? Report your findings to the class.

## 11.7 Document for Analysis: Request Refusal (Objs. 1–4)

**Your Task.** Analyze the following letter. List its weaknesses. If your instructor directs, revise it.

X *Ineffective Letter*

Dear Mr. Waters:

Unfortunately, we cannot permit you to apply the lease payments you've been making for the past ten months toward the purchase of your Sako 600 copier.

Company policy does not allow such conversion. Have you ever wondered why we can offer such low leasing and purchase prices? Obviously, we couldn't stay in business long if we agreed to proposals such as yours.

You've had the Sako 600 copier for ten months now, Mr. Waters, and you say you like its versatility and reliability. Perhaps we could interest you in another Sako model—one that's more within your price range. Do give us a call.

## 11.8 Document for Analysis: Bad News for Customers (Objs. 1–4)

**Your Task.** Analyze the following letter. List its weaknesses. If your instructor directs, revise it.

✗ *Ineffective Letter*

Dear Charge Customers:

This letter is being sent to you to announce the termination of in-house charge accounts at Golden West Print and Frame Shop. We are truly sorry that we can no longer offer this service.

Because some customers abused the privilege, we must eliminate local charge accounts. We regret that we must take this action, but we found that carrying our own credit had become quite costly. To continue the service would have meant raising our prices. As a small but growing business, we decided it was more logical to drop the in-house charges. As a result, we are forced to begin accepting bank credit cards, including VISA and MasterCard.

Please accept our apologies and deepest regrets in reducing our services. We hope to see you soon when we can show you our new collection of museum-quality gilded wood frames.

## 11.9 Document for Analysis: Saying No to a Job Applicant (Objs. 1, 2, and 5)

**Your Task.** Analyze the following letter. List its weaknesses. If your instructor directs, revise it.

✗ *Ineffective Letter*

Dear Mr. Franklin:

Ms. Sievers and I wish to thank you for the pleasure of allowing us to interview you last Thursday. We were delighted to learn about your superb academic record, and we also appreciated your attentiveness in listening to our description of the operations of the Maxwell Corporation.

However, we had many well-qualified applicants who were interested in the advertised position of human resources assistant. As you may have guessed, we were particularly eager to find a minority individual who could help us fill out our employment equity goals. Although you did not fit one of our goal areas, we enjoyed talking with you. We hired a female graduate of Ryerson Polytechnic University who had most of the qualities we sought.

Although we realize that the job market is difficult at this time, you have our heartfelt wishes for good luck in finding precisely what you are looking for.

## 11.10 Request Refusal: Too Much to Ask (Obj. 3)

Dustin O'Hair, a magazine editor, asks your organization, Panatronics International, for confidential information regarding the salaries and commissions of your top sales representatives. The magazine, *Marketing Monthly*, plans to spotlight young sales professionals "whose stars are ascending." You've got some great young superstars, as well as many excellent mature sales representatives. Frankly, the publicity would be excellent.

You would agree in a minute except that (1) you don't want to be forced to pick favourites among your sales reps and (2) you can't reveal private salary data. Every sales rep operates under an individual salary contract. During salary negotiations several years ago, an agreement was reached in which both sales staff members and management agreed to keep the terms of these individual contracts confidential. Perhaps the editor would be satisfied with a list that ranks your top sales reps for the past five years. You could also send a fact sheet describing your top reps. You notice that three of the current top sales reps are under the age of thirty-five. **Your Task.** Write a refusal that explains your position but retains the goodwill of Dustin O'Hair, *Marketing Monthly*, 1326 Henderson Avenue, Calgary, AB T3Z 1X5.

## 11.11 Request Refusal: Saying No to Under-21 Crowd on Carnival Cruises (Obj. 3)

**WEB**

The world's largest cruise line finds itself in a difficult position. Carnival climbed to the number one spot by promoting fun at sea and pitching its appeal to younger customers who were drawn to on-board discos, swim-up bars, and hassle-free partying. But apparently the partying of high school and college students went too far. Roving bands of teens had virtually taken over some cruises in recent years. Travel agents complained of "drunken, loud behaviour," as reported by Mike Driscall, editor of *Cruise Week*.

To crack down, Carnival raised the drinking age from 18 to 21 and required more chaperoning of school groups. But young individual travellers were still unruly and disruptive. Thus, Carnival instituted a new policy, effective immediately. No one under 21 may travel unless accompanied by an adult over 25. Says Vicki Freed, Carnival's vice president for marketing, "We will turn them back at the docks, and they will not get refunds." As Eric Rivera, a Carnival marketing manager, you must respond to the inquiry of April Corcoran of Counsellor Travel, a travel agency that features special spring- and summer-break packages for college and high school students.

Counsellor Travel has been one of Carnival's best customers. However, Carnival no longer wants to encourage unaccompanied young people. You must refuse the request of Ms. Corcoran to help set up student tour packages. Carnival discourages even chaperoned tours. Its real market is now family packages. You must write to Counsellor and break the bad news. Try to promote fun-filled, carefree cruises destined for sunny, exotic ports of call that remove guests from the stresses of everyday life. By the way, Carnival attracts more passengers than any other cruise line—over a million people a year from all over the world. And over 98 percent of Carnival's guests say that they were well satisfied. For more information about Carnival, visit its Web site: <www.carnival.com>. There's no need to register; simply click "About Carnival."

**Your Task.** Write your letter to April Corcoran, Counsellor Travel Agency, 103 Juniper Crescent, Eastern Passage, NS B3G 1M1. Send her a schedule for spring and summer Caribbean cruises. Tell her you will call during the week of January 5 to help her plan special family tour packages.[15]

## 11.12 Request Refusal: Mountain Bike Race Regrets (Obj. 3)

As president of CycleWorld you must refuse a request from the North American Biking Association. This group wants your company to become a major sponsor of the first annual Durango World Mountain Bike Championship—for $30 000! You applaud NABA for its proactive stance in encouraging families to participate in the sport of mountain biking. NABA was also instrumental in opening up ski resorts to mountain bikers during the summer months. Actually, you'd like to support the Durango World Mountain Bike Championship. There's no doubt that such races increase interest in mountain biking and ridership. You have sponsored some bike races in the past, but for small amounts—usually under $500—which paid for trophies. But the NABA wants to offer large cash prizes and pay the expenses of big-name champions to enter.

You are a small Kamloops, BC, company, and all your current profits are being ploughed into research to compete with the Japanese imports. You're very proud of your newly introduced brake pads and trigger-action shift levers. But these kinds of engineering breakthroughs are costly. You don't have the big bucks NABA wants. You wouldn't mind taking an ad in its program or contributing $500 toward trophies. But that's the limit.

**Your Task.** Write a refusal to Christopher Van Wijk, North American Biking Association, 1720 Waterloo Street, Vancouver, BC V6R 3G2.

## 11.13 Request Refusal: Getting Rid of Noisy Tenant (Obj. 4)

CRITICAL THINKING    INFOTRAC

As Arman Aryai, you must respond to the request of Robert Brockway, one of the tenants in your three-story office building. Mr. Brockway, a CPA, demands that you immediately evict a neighbouring tenant who plays loud music

throughout the day, interfering with Mr. Brockway's conversations with clients and with his concentration. The noisy tenant, Ryan McInnis, seems to operate an entertainment booking agency and spends long hours in his office. You know you can't evict Mr. McInnis immediately because of his lease. Moreover, you hesitate to do anything drastic because tenants are hard to find. However, Mr. McInnis has not been terribly reliable in his rent payments. Occasionally, he's been late.

**Your Task.** Before responding to Mr. Brockway, you decide to find out more about eviction on the Internet. Use InfoTrac to search the keywords "commercial eviction." Then develop a course of action. In writing to Mr. Brockway, deny his request but retain his goodwill. Tell him how you plan to resolve the problem. Write to Robert Brockway, CPA, Suite 203, 120 Wentworth Road, Hamilton, ON L9B 2F5.

## 11.14 Request Refusal: Rock Band Banned for Violating Sound Limits (Obj. 3)

Residents living near The Centre, an outdoor amphitheatre, were more than relieved when the rock band Greed was banned from future concerts. At the recent Greed concert, the head-banging band exceeded Centre sound limits for its entire show. Despite persistent warnings from Centre personnel, Greed played at levels of over 110 decibels. The Centre limit is 102. After the performance, Greed was fined $3 000 and banned from future appearances.

Ian Martin, a teenager who had attended the Greed concert, thinks the ban is excessive punishment. In a letter, Martin implores the general manager of The Centre to invite Greed back for its summer tour. He argues that a previous concert surpassed decibel limits, but that the band was fined only a few hundred dollars. He also points to a statement from a Centre spokesman that nearly every performer breaks decibel limits at The Centre, although admittedly not as badly as Greed did. Moreover, sound limits were established in the 1970s, Martin argues, before bands like Greed learned to rely on volume to deliver their unique sound. "Sound limits just aren't valid anymore," writes Martin, "and they interfere with the artists' creative freedom."

Although Martin's arguments may have some validity, it is Sam Scranton's job to enforce current sound limits, not change them. As general manager of The Centre, he's responsible for informing visiting bands of the sound limits. His crew monitors sound levels and warns bands when they play too loudly. Those that don't comply are fined, says Scranton, but most bands do stay within the limits or exceed them only once or twice during a show. Greed seemed to ignore them completely, although the band was aware of the limits and before the show agreed to comply. The noise was so loud that police reported nearly twice the average number of noise complaints from area residents during the concert.

**Your Task.** As Scranton's assistant, it is your job to reply to Ian Martin. You need to tell Martin about Centre sound limits and explain that Greed will not be invited back for its summer tour. You think that concert sites away from residential areas would be more inviting for a band like Greed. Incidentally, The Centre does have a great summer lineup, including Our Lady Peace, Sum 41, and the Tragically Hip. For Sam Scranton's signature, write a convincing letter to Ian Martin, 2390 Silver Creek Drive, Windsor, ON N8N 4W2.

## 11.15 Request Refusal: Cancelling Free Trip to Europe (Obj. 3)

"As I'm sure you've noticed, Cadillac has been on a bit of a roll lately with the worldwide launch of the all-new Seville and the introduction of the innovative Escalade," began the GM invitation letter. This letter was sent to many of the top automotive journalists in the country, inviting them to join GM's executives on a five-day all-expenses paid press trip to Paris. Such junkets were not unusual. Big Three automakers routinely sponsored the trips of reporters to ensure favourable local coverage from the big auto shows in Paris, Frankfurt, Geneva, and Tokyo. GM particularly wanted reporters at the Paris show. This is the show where it hoped to position Cadillac as a global luxury car manufacturer. The invitation letter, mailed in July, promised a "sneak peek at Cadillac's first major concept vehicle in nearly ten years." But GM had only 20 spots available for the trip, and journalists had to request one of the spots. Suddenly, in late July, GM found itself in the midst of an expensive strike. "All at once, what had seemed like a good idea started to look fiscally irresponsible," said J. Christopher Preuss, Cadillac spokesman. Although exact figures were not available, some estimates held that the Paris trip could easily cost $12 000 per reporter. That's a large bill for a company facing a prolonged, damaging strike.

**Your Task.** As part of a group of interns working in the communications division of GM, you and your team have been asked to draft a letter to the journalists who signed up for the trip. Announce that GM must back out. About the best thing they can expect now is an invitation to the gala unveiling and champagne reception GM will sponsor in January at the Vancouver auto show. At that time GM will brief reporters about Cadillac's "new vision" and unveil the eye-popping Escalade. Mr. Preuss is embarrassed about cancelling the Paris trip, but he feels GM must do what is financially prudent. Prepare a draft of the letter for the signature of J. Christopher Preuss. Address the first letter to Rodney M. Puckett, 31 rue Prévost, Hull, QC J8A 1P1.[16]

## 11.16 Request Refusal: Declining Returned Books (Obj. 3)

As the customer service manager of Kent Publishers, you must refuse most of a shipment of books returned from the MacKenzie College Bookstore. Your policy is to provide a 100 percent return on books if the books are returned prepaid in *new*, *unmarked*, and *resalable* condition.

The return must be within 12 months of the original invoice date. Old editions of books must be returned within 90 days of your announcement that you will no longer be printing that edition. These conditions are published and sent with every order of books shipped. The return shipment from MacKenzie looks as if someone was housecleaning and decided to return all unsold books to you. Fourteen books are not your titles; return them. You could have accepted the 22 copies of Donner's *Introduction to Marketing*—if they were not imprinted with "MacKenzie College," the price, and return instructions on the inside cover. The 31 copies of Heigel's *College Writing Handbook* are second editions. Since you've been selling the third edition for 14 months, you can't accept them. Five copies of Quigley's *Business Law* appear to be water-damaged; they're unsalable. From the whole mess it looks as if you'll be able to give them credit for 25 copies of Miller's *The Promotable Woman* (wholesale price $31). However, since MacKenzie sent no invoice information, you'll have to tack on a 15 percent service charge to cover the effort involved in locating the order in your records.

**Your Task.** Write a letter to Christopher Lorenze, Manager, MacKenzie College Bookstore, Peterborough, ON K9H 5Z4, that denies his request but retains his business. MacKenzie has been a valued customer in the past. This bookstore placed orders on time and paid on time. Tell Mr. Lorenze what is being returned and how much credit you are allowing. From the credit total, deduct $32.50 for return shipping costs.

## 11.17 Damage Control for Disappointed Customers: J. Crew Goofs on Cashmere Turtleneck. (Obj. 4)

Who wouldn't want a cashmere zip turtleneck sweater for $18? At the J. Crew Web site, <www.jcrew.com>, many delighted shoppers scrambled to order the bargain cashmere. Unfortunately, the price should have been $218! Before J. Crew officials could correct the mistake, several hundred e-shoppers had bagged the bargain sweater for their digital shopping carts.

When the mistake was discovered, J. Crew immediately sent an e-mail message to the soon-to-be disappointed shoppers. The subject line shouted "Big Mistake!" Emily Woods, chairwoman of J. Crew, began her message with this statement: "I wish we could sell such an amazing sweater for only $18. Our price mistake on your new cashmere zip turtleneck probably went right by you, but rather than charge you such a large difference, I'm writing to alert you that this item has been removed from your recent order."

As an assistant in the communication department at J. Crew, you saw the e-mail message that was sent to customers and you tactfully suggested that the bad news might have been broken differently. Your boss says, "Okay, hot stuff. Give it your best shot."

**Your Task.** Although you have only a portion of the message, analyze the customer bad news message sent by J. Crew.

Using the principles suggested in this chapter, write an improved e-mail message. In the end, J. Crew decided to allow customers who ordered the sweater at $18 to reorder it for $118.80 to $130.80, depending on the size. Customers were given a special Web site to reorder (make up an address). Remember that J. Crew customers are youthful and hip. Keep your message upbeat.[17]

## 11.18 Damage Control for Disappointed Customers: No Credit in Paris (Obj. 4)

Travel writer Becky Grant was mystified when the sales clerk at the Paris department store refused her credit card. "Sorry," the clerk said, "your credit card is not being accepted. I don't know why." Grant found out soon enough. Her bank had frozen her account because of an "unusual" spending pattern. The problem? "We've never had a charge from you in France before," a bank official told her. The bank didn't seem to remember that Grant had repeatedly used that card in cities ranging from Boston to Tokyo to Cape Town over the past six years, each time without incident.

Grant was a victim of neural-network technology, a tool that is intended to protect credit cardholders from thieves who steal cards and immediately run up huge purchases. This technology tracks spending patterns. If it detects anything unusual—such as a sudden splurge on easy-to-fence items like jewellery—it sets off an alarm. Robert Boxberger, senior

vice president of fraud management at Fleet Credit Card Services, says that the system is "geared toward not declining any travel and entertainment expenses, like hotels, restaurants, or car rentals." But somehow it goofed and did not recognize that Becky Grant was travelling, although she had used her card earlier to rent a car in Paris, a sure sign that she was travelling.

Grant was what the credit card industry calls a false positive—a legitimate cardholder inconvenienced by the hunt for fraudsters. What particularly riled her was finding out that 75 percent of the transactions caught in the neural network turn out to be legitimate. Yet the technology has been immensely successful for credit card companies. Since VISA started using the program, its fraud rate dropped from 15 cents to 6 cents per $100. To avoid inconveniencing cardholders, the company doesn't automatically suspend a card when it suspects fraud. Instead, it telephones the cardholder to verify purchases. Of course, if the cardholder is travelling, it's impossible to reach her.

Angry at the inconvenience and embarrassment she experienced, Grant sent a letter to VISA demanding an explanation in writing.

**Your Task.** As an assistant to the vice president in charge of fraud detection at VISA, you have been asked to draft a letter that can be used to respond to Becky Grant as well as to other unhappy customers whose cards were wrongly refused by your software. You know that the program has been an overwhelming success, but it can inconvenience people, especially when they are travelling. You've heard your boss tell travellers that it's a good idea to touch base with their bank before leaving and take along the card's customer service number (1-800-553-0321). Write a letter that explains what happened, retains the goodwill of the customer, and suggests reader benefits. Address your letter to Ms. Becky Grant, 68 Riverside Drive, Apt. 35, Ottawa, ON K1A 1A2.

## 11.19 Damage Control for Disappointed Customers: Million-Dollar Upgrade Falls Short (Obj. 4)

As an Internet service provider, your company, WeConnect, is growing rapidly. To keep up with increased customer demand, you decided to install a million-dollar network upgrade. From Robotech you bought what you thought were the finest modems on the market. They passed your rigorous lab tests with flying colours, but apparently some bugs in the operating system slipped through the cracks. The modems clearly were not "field ready" when they were installed. Now you are hearing from customers complaining of slower speeds in connecting to the Internet and even disconnections.

Derek Jones, manager, Information Systems, Big Dog Catalogue Company, your most profitable local customer, is very upset. Jones says, "You promised a million-dollar upgrade, and now service is worse than ever!" You replied, "Look, we're very sorry. These bugs didn't show up in our lab tests. But Robotech is providing excellent support for their hardware and we've cleared up most of the initial problems. Although we've fixed all the major technical problems, some other little things remain, and we're fully committed to a complete resolution." You ask for Big Dog's patience. Things will get better, you promise!

**Your Task.** Write a follow-up letter to Mr. Derek Jones, Manager, Information Systems, Big Dog Catalogue Company, 1326 Henderson Avenue, Calgary, AB T3Z 1X5. You have set up a special Web site where customers can report any connection problems: http://home.weconnect.net/disconnect .html. However, you also want to assure customers that they can contact you personally with questions or comments. You promise that all their issues will be resolved as soon as possible. You might wish to write this letter so that you can use it to respond to other inquiries.

## 11.20 Damage Control for Disappointed Customers: Virus Infects Rocket Launcher (Obj. 4)

TEAM      CRITICAL THINKING

"How could you sell me a program with a virus! I hold your company personally responsible for contaminating my hard drive," wrote Jennifer M. Sage in a letter to software game manufacturer Quixell. Ms. Sage has ample reason to be angry with Quixell. Its Rocket Launcher program carried a computer virus, unknown to Quixell at the time of distribution.

Computer viruses are programs written to perform malicious tasks. They attach themselves secretly to data files and are then copied either by disk or by a computer network. Some viruses are carried as attachments to e-mail. The particular virus contaminating Quixell's program is called "Stoned IV." First reported in Europe, it represents a class of "stealth" viruses. They mask their location and are extremely difficult to detect. Both manufacturers and consumers get stung by viruses. Quixell already had an extensive virus-detection program, but this new virus slipped by. Actually, Quixell has just licensed special digital-signature software that will make it difficult for future viruses to spread undetected. But this new technology won't do much for current angry customers like Ms. Sage.

In the past, courts have generally found that if a company has been reasonably prudent in its production process, that company is not liable for damage caused by a third person (the individual who planted the virus). Nevertheless, Quixell feels an obligation to do whatever is possible—within reason—to rectify the situation. Some customers would like to have software companies like Quixell give them new computers, or at the very least, install new hard drives. Ms. Sage is making what she thinks is a reasonable request. Since she is no computer techie, she wants Quixell to pay for a computer specialist to clean up her hard drive and restore it to its previous uncontaminated state. Such a solution, say most of the Quixell man-

agers, is out of the question. It's much too expensive. Moreover, Quixell can't be sure that her computer doesn't have problems that have nothing to do with the Rocket Launcher virus. When faced with viruses, other software manufacturers have simply offered a clean disk and advice.

Because of its vigilance and concern for product quality, Quixell has never had a virus contaminate any of its 350 products—until Stoned IV. When the virus was discovered, Quixell immediately stopped production and recalled all unsold disks. Like other companies facing virus attacks, Quixell has assigned a specialist to answer specific questions from affected customers. He is Jason John at (416) 344-9901. Quixell has also located an antivirus program, AntiVirus Max by Integrity Software. This program has special routines that detect, remove, and prevent more than 400 viruses, including Stoned IV. AntiVirus Max costs $59.95 and can be purchased by calling Integrity's toll-free number (1-800-690-3220). This program removes the virus and restores the hard drive. Quixell fears that as many as 300 of its customers were affected by the virus. As a small company with a very slim profit margin, Quixell cannot afford to provide the antivirus program to that many customers.

**Your Task.** You are part of the customer service team at Quixell that must decide how to handle this request and others. Remember that Quixell cannot afford to have technicians make personal visits. Discuss possible options, make a group decision, and then individually or as a group write a letter to Ms. Jennifer M. Sage, 2360 Red Rock Road, Willowdale, ON L9C 2F6.[18]

## 11.21 Damage Control for Disappointed Customers: A Mess With King Fisher and Pick Pocket (Obj. 4)

Assume you are Deborah Pool Dixon, manager, Promotions and Advertising, Seven Flags Lake Point Park. You are upset by the letter you received from Melissa Sledgeman, who complained that she was "taken" by Seven Flags when the park had to substitute performers for King Fisher and the Pick Pocket band concert. Explain to her that the concert was planned by an independent promoter. Your only obligation was to provide the theatre facility and advertising. Three days before the event, the promoter left town, taking with him all advance payments from financial backers. As it turned out, many of the artists he had promised to deliver were not even planning to attend.

Left with a pretty messy situation, you decided on Thursday to go ahead with a modified version of the event since you had been advertising it and many would come expecting some kind of talent. At that time you changed your radio advertising to say that for reasons beyond your control, King Fisher and the Pick Pocket band would not be appearing. You described the new talent and posted signs at the entrance and in the parking lot announcing the change.

355

Contrary to Ms. Sledgeman's claim, no newspaper advertising featuring Fisher and Pick Pocket appeared on the day of the concert (at least you did not pay for any to appear that day). Somehow she must have missed your corrective radio advertising and signs at the entrance. You feel you made a genuine effort to communicate the changed program. In your opinion most people who attended the concert thought that Seven Flags had done everything possible to salvage a rather unfortunate situation.

Ms. Sledgeman wants a cash refund of $70 (two tickets at $35 each). Seven Flags has a no-money-back policy on concerts after the event takes place. If Ms. Sledgeman had come to the box office before the event started, you could have returned her money. But she stayed to see the concert. She claims that she didn't know anything about the talent change until after the event was well under way. This sounds unlikely, but you don't quarrel with customers. Nevertheless, you can't give her cash back. You already took a loss on this event. But you can give her two complimentary passes to Seven Flags Lake Point Park.

**Your Task.** Write a refusal letter to Ms. Sledgeman, P.O. Box 4300, Dartmouth, NS B2Z 5B2. Invite her and a friend to return as guests under happier circumstances.

## 11.22 Problem With Customer Order: The StairClimber or the LifeStep? (Obj. 4)

You are delighted to receive a large order from Kendra Coleman at Gold's Gym. This order includes two Lifecycle Trainers (at $1295 each), four Pro Abdominal Boards (at $295 each), three Tunturi Muscle Trainers (at $749 each), and three Dual-Action StairClimbers (at $1545 each).

You could ship immediately except for one problem. The Dual-Action StairClimber is intended for home use, not for gym or club use. Customers like it because they say it's more like scaling a mountain than climbing a flight of stairs. With each step, users exercise their arms to pull or push themselves up. And its special cylinders absorb shock so that no harmful running impact results. However, this model is not what you would recommend for gym use. You feel Ms. Coleman should order your premier stairclimber, the LifeStep (at $2395 each). This unit has sturdier construction and is meant for heavy use. Its sophisticated electronics provide a selection of customer-pleasing programs that challenge muscles progressively with a choice of workouts. It also quickly multiplies workout gains with computer-controlled interval training. Electronic monitors inform users of step height, calories burned, elapsed time, upcoming levels, and adherence to fitness goals. For gym use the LifeStep is clearly better than the StairClimber. The bad news is that the LifeStep is considerably more expensive.

You get no response when you try to telephone Ms. Coleman to discuss the problem. Should you ship what you can, or hold the entire order until you learn whether she wants the StairClimber or the LifeStep? Or perhaps you should substitute the LifeStep and send only two of them.

**Your Task.** Decide what to do and write a letter to Kendra Coleman, Gold's Gym, 2439 Green Street, Toronto, ON M4E 1H3.

## 11.23 Claim Denial: Kodak Refuses Customer's Request to Repeat World Trip (Obj. 4)

Kodak Customer Service manager Charlie Smith can't believe what he reads in a letter from Brian P. Coyle (see Activity 10.19 in Chapter 10). This 27-year-old actually wants Kodak to foot the bill for a repeat round-the-world trip because his Advantix camera malfunctioned and he lost 12 rolls of film! As soon as Smith saw the letter and the returned camera, he knew what was wrong. Of the 2 million Advantix cameras made in the previous year, 20 000 malfunctioned. A supplier squirted too much oil in the shutter mechanism, and the whole lot was recalled. In fact, Kodak spent almost $1 million to remove these cameras from store shelves. Kodak also contacted all customers who could be reached. In addition to the giant recall, the company quickly redesigned the cameras so that they would work even if they had excess oil. But somehow Coyle was not notified of the recall. When Smith checked the warranty files, he learned that this customer had not returned his warranty. Had the customer done so, he would have been notified in August, well before his trip.

Although Customer Service manager Smith is sorry for the mishap, he thinks that a request for $20 000 to replace "lost memories" is preposterous. Kodak has never assumed any responsibility beyond replacing a camera or film. This customer, however, seems to have suffered more than a routine loss of snapshots. Therefore, Smith decides to sweeten the deal by offering to throw in a digital camera valued at $225, more than double the cost of the Advantix. One of the advantages of a digital camera is that it contains an LCD panel that enables the photographer to view stored images immediately. No chance of losing memories with this digital camera!

**Your Task.** As the assistant to Customer Service manager Charles Smith, you must write a letter that refuses the demand for $20 000 but retains the customer's goodwill. Tell this customer what you will do, and be sure to explain how Kodak reacted immediately when it discovered the Advantix defect. Write a sensitive refusal to Brian P. Coyle, 22050 Ontario Street, Lennoxville, QC J1M 1Z7.[19]

## 11.24 Claim Denial: Please Replace My MP3 Player (Obj. 4)

As part of the customer service team at Rio, Inc., you must respond to Jason Jordan, who wants a replacement for his portable CD player, your best-selling RioVolt. His letter said that he hears "popping" and "skipping" in some MP3 tracks. They are always in the same place, and he thinks his player is defective. He also complains that when he leaves the player in a "stop" or "pause" state, it turns itself off. Although he has heard that this is the best portable CD MP3 player, he thinks that he has a lemon and wants it replaced. The dealer from whom he bought it referred him to the manufacturer.

You know that the "popping" sounds and "skipping" on some MP3 tracks could be the result of a file that had a sound defect that was transferred when the CD was created. When other customers mentioned this problem, you generally told them to reencode the same audio track and therefore verify that the troublesome file was created correctly originally. In regard to the player turning itself off, this is intentional. When the player is left unattended, even if set for "stop" or "pause," it will shut itself off. This preserves battery life.

**Your Task.** Refuse the request of Jason Jordan. Although you think it's unreasonable for a customer to expect a replacement for the reasons given, you try to be polite in your response. You wonder why Jason didn't go to your Web site, www.riovolt.com, and look at the Frequently Asked Questions. He could have found answers to his questions in the "Troubleshooting" section. You decide to mention this resource for any future problems.

## 11.25 Claim Denial: Depressed Mattress (Obj. 4)

```
TEAM
```

The following letter was sent in response to a customer's complaint about depressions in your company's BeautyTest mattress. Your company receives enough of these kinds of letters to warrant preparation of a standard response.

✗ *Ineffective Letter*

Dear Mrs. Kearney:

We have received your letter of May 23 demanding repair or replacement of your newly purchased BeautyTest mattress. You say that you enjoy sleeping on it; but in the morning when you and your husband get up, you claim that the mattress has body impressions that remain all day.

Unfortunately, Mrs. Kearney, we can neither repair nor replace your mattress because those impressions are perfectly normal. If you will read your warranty carefully, you will find this statement: "Slight body impressions will appear with use and are not indicative of structural failure. The body-conforming coils and comfort cushioning materials are beginning to work for you and impressions are caused by the natural settling of these materials."

When you purchased your mattress, I'm sure your salesperson told you that the BeautyTest mattress has a unique, scientifically designed system of individually pocketed coils that provide separate support for each person occupying the bed. This unusual construction, with those hundreds of independently operating coils, reacts to every body contour, providing luxurious comfort. At the same time, this system provides firm support. It is this unique design that's causing the body impressions that you see when you get up in the morning.

Although we never repair or replace a mattress when it merely shows slight impressions, we will send our representative out to inspect your mattress, if it would make you feel better. Please call for an appointment at (800) 322-9800. Remember, on a BeautyTest mattress you get the best night's rest possible.

Cordially,

**Your Task.** To evaluate your writing skills, your boss asks you and some other interns to come up with a better response. If your letter is better, he may begin using it as a pattern for similar responses. The problem seems to be that customers don't understand how the unique coil system works. And they have not read the mattress warranty. Get together with your intern team and discuss the faults in this letter before generating a new, more effective letter. Write to the same customer.

## 11.26 Claim Denial: Long, Hot Summer (Obj. 4)

As Kissandra Powell, owner of Town & Country Landscaping, you must refuse the following request. Mr. and Mrs. Paul Alexander have asked that you replace the landscaping of the home they recently purchased in Regina. You had landscaped that home nearly a year ago for the former owner, Mrs. Hunter, installing a sod lawn and many shrubs, trees, and flowers. It looked beautiful when you finished, but six months later, Mrs. Hunter sold the property and moved to Summerville. Four months elapsed before the new owners moved in. After four months of neglect and a hot, dry summer, the newly installed landscaping suffered.

You guarantee all your work and normally would replace any plants that do not survive. Under these circumstances, however, you do not feel justified in making any refund because your guarantee necessarily presumes proper maintenance on the part of the property owner. Moreover, your guarantee is made only to the individual who contracted with you—not to subsequent owners. You would like to retain the goodwill of the new owners, since this is an affluent neighbourhood and you hope to attract additional work here. On the other hand, you can't afford to replace the materials invested in this job. You believe that the lawn could probably be rejuvenated with deep watering and fertilizer.

**Your Task.** Write to Mr. and Mrs. Paul Alexander, 3318 Clearview Drive, Regina, SK S4R 7W4 refusing their claim. You would be happy to inspect the property and offer suggestions to the Alexanders. In reality, you wonder if the Alexanders might not have a claim against the former owner or the escrow agency for failing to maintain the property. Clearly, however, the claim is not against you.

## 11.27 Credit Refusal: The Sports Connection (Obj. 4)

As manager of The Sports Connection, you must refuse the application of Wendy Takahashi for an extended membership in your athletic club. This is strictly a business decision. You liked Wendy very much when she applied, and she seems genuinely interested in fitness and a healthful lifestyle. However, your "extended membership" plan qualifies the member for all your testing, exercise, aerobics, and recreation programs. This multiservice program is necessarily expensive and requires a solid credit rating. To your disappointment, however, you learned that Wendy's credit rating is decidedly negative. Her credit report indicates that she is delinquent in payments to four businesses, including Holiday Health Spa, your principal competitor.

You do have other programs, including your "Drop In and Work Out" plan that offers use of available facilities on a cash basis. This plan enables a member to reserve space on the racquetball and handball courts; the member can also sign up for exercise and aerobics classes, space permitting. Since Wendy is far in debt, you would feel guilty allowing her to plunge in any more deeply.

**Your Task.** Refuse Wendy Takahashi's credit application, but encourage her cash business. Suggest that she make an inquiry to the credit reporting company Equifax to learn about her credit report. She is eligible to receive a free credit report if she mentions this application. Write to Wendy Takahashi, Mountain View Apartments, Apartment 16E, Brandon, MB R3J 7F3.

## 11.28 Credit Refusal: GodMother Wants to Cater (Obj. 4)

**Your Task.** Revise the following ineffective letter that refuses credit to Mrs. Andria Moreno, GodMother Enterprises, 225 Stafford Road South, Lethbridge, AB T1J 4R5.

✗ *Ineffective Letter*

Dear Ms. Moreno:

This is to inform you that we have received your recent order. However, we are unable to fill this order because of the bad credit record you have on file at Equifax.

We understand that at this point in time you are opening a new gourmet catering business called "The GodMother." Our sales rep left us one of your sample menus, and I must say that we were all impressed with your imaginative international selections, including duck lasagna and chicken fettuccine verde. Although we are sure your catering business will be a success, we cannot extend credit because of your current poor credit rating.

Did you know that you can find out what's in your credit file? If you would like to see what prevented you from obtaining credit from us, you should call 1-800-EQUIFAX.

We are truly sorry that we cannot fill your initial order totaling $1 430. We pride ourselves on serving most of Lethbridge's finest restaurants and catering services. We would be proud to add The GodMother to our list of discerning customers. Perhaps the best way for you to join that select list is with a smaller order to begin with. We would be happy to serve you on a cash basis. If this plan meets with your approval, do let me know.

Sincerely,

## 11.29 Credit Refusal: No Credit for Cordless Phones (Obj. 4)

As Julie Abrams, sales manager, CyberSound, you are delighted to land a sizable order for your new 25-channel cordless telephone. This great phone has speed dialing, auto scan to ensure clear conversations, caller ID, and call waiting.

The purchase order comes from High Point Electronics, a retail distributor in Regina, SK. You send the order on to Shane Simmons, your credit manager, for approval of the credit application attached. To your disappointment, Shane tells you that High Point doesn't qualify for credit. Equifax reports that credit would be risky for High Point.

You decide to write to High Point with the bad news and an alternative. Suggest that High Point order a smaller number of the cordless phones. If it pays cash, it can receive a 2 percent discount. After High Point has sold these fast-

358

moving units, it can place another cash order through your toll-free order number. With your fast delivery system, its inventory will never be depleted. High Point can get the phones it wants now and can replace its inventory almost overnight. Credit manager Simmons tells you that your company generally reveals to credit applicants the name of the credit reporting service and encourages them to investigate their credit record.

**Your Task.** Write a credit refusal to Ryan Bardens, High Point Electronics, 1586 Albert Avenue, Regina, SK S4V 6W3.

### 11.30 Employee Bad News: Strikeout for Expanded Office Teams (Obj. 5)

Assume you are Hank James, vice president of Human Resources at Tissue Mills Paper Co. in Kingston, Ontario. Recently several of your employees requested that their spouses or friends be allowed to participate in Tissue Mills' intramural sports teams. Although the teams play only once a week during the season, these employees claim that they can't afford more time away from friends and family. Over 100 employees currently participate in the eight coed volleyball, softball, and tennis teams, which are open to company employees only. The teams were designed to improve employee friendships and to give employees a regular occasion to have fun together.

If nonemployees were to participate, you're afraid that employee interaction would be limited. And while some team members might have fun if spouses or friends were included, you're not so sure all employees would enjoy it. You're not interested in turning intramural sports into "date night." Furthermore, the company would have to create additional teams if many nonemployees joined, and you don't want the administrative or equipment costs of more teams. Adding teams also would require changes to team rosters and game schedules, which could be a problem for some employees. You do understand the need for social time with friends and families, but guests are welcome as spectators at all intramural games. Besides, the company already sponsors a family holiday party and an annual company picnic.

**Your Task.** Write an e-mail or hard-copy memo to the staff denying the request of several employees to include nonemployees on Tissue Mills' intramural sports teams.

### 11.31 Employee Bad News: Refusing Christmas (Obj. 5)

In the past your office has always sponsored a Christmas party at a nice restaurant. Because your company, RedLine Software, has undergone considerable downsizing and budget cuts during the past year, you know that no money is available for holiday entertaining. Moreover, as the staff becomes

more diverse, you decide that it might be better to celebrate a "holiday" party instead of a Christmas event.

**Your Task.** As executive vice president, respond to the e-mail request of Dina Gillian, office manager. Dina asks permission to make restaurant reservations for this year's Christmas party. Prepare a memo that refuses the request but offer some alternatives. How about a potluck dinner?

## C.L.U.E. REVIEW 11

Edit the following sentences to correct all language faults, including grammar, punctuation, spelling, and word confusions.

1. When delivering bad news you can reduce the disapointment by: (1) telling the reasons for the rejection, and (2) reveal the news with sensitivity.

2. Its important that you make sure the reciever understands the bad news, and excepts it.

3. The indirect pattern consists of 4 parts, buffer, reasons, bad news, and close.

4. Undoubtlessly the indirect pattern can not be used in every situation, however, it is often better than a blunt announcement of bad news.

5. When the bad news is not devastating references to re-sale, or promotion may be apropriate.

6. If the Vice President of our Company must announce a big increase in each employees contributions to health benefits should he use the indirect strategy.

7. Most of us prefer to be let down gently when were being refused something, thats why the reasons before refusal pattern is effective.

8. Publisher Malcolm Forbes said "To be agreeable while disagreeing—thats an art.

9. When a well known Tire company recalled 100s of thousands of tires it's President issued an apology to all injured customers'.

10. If I was you I would be more concerned with long term not short term returns on the invested capitol.

# Unit 4
## Reports and Proposals

# Chapter 12

## Preparing to Write Business Reports

Statistics Canada

Statistique Canada

**Welcome to Statistics Canada**

**Bienvenue à Statistique Canada**

English

Français

Important notices

Avis importants

Canada

## LEARNING OBJECTIVES

*1* Describe business report basics, including functions, patterns, formats, and writing style.

*2* Apply the 3-×-3 writing process to business reports.

*3* Understand where to find and how to use print and electronic sources of secondary data.

*4* Understand where to find and how to use sources of primary data.

*5* Illustrate reports with graphics that create meaning and interest.

*6* Recognize the purposes and techniques of documentation in business reports.

# Statistics Canada

In the 1666 census collected by Jean Talon, Statistics Canada has the first statistics collected by Europeans in the New World. In addition to compiling the results and performing his other tasks, Talon had to knock on most of the doors himself. In the early 1900s, Canada began collecting regular records of agriculture and manufacturing. On the prairies, teachers collected information by having students report their families' crop estimates and herd sizes.[1] Times have certainly changed since the first census over 300 years ago, and the man now in charge of gathering the information is Dr. Ivan Fellegi, the chief statistician of Statistics Canada. Although Fellegi does not knock on the doors, he is keenly aware of what is going on in the country. Statistics Canada does not operate in a vacuum. Fellegi consults with different groups such as teachers, nurses, and parents to find out what they want to know. Then he instructs his staff to get the information.[2]

Unknown to many Canadians, Statistics Canada is considered the world's best statistics agency due to the quantity, quality, and credibility of its work, which is free of political interference. According to Fellegi, StatsCan offers "neither policy criticism nor advocacy, only insights that can inform decision making."[3]

Survey respondents are the most valuable asset of Statistics Canada; as a result, two commitments are made to them. StatsCan promises to protect the confidentiality of information and to continually search for innovative ways to save respondents time in completing surveys.

"Fun might not be the word that comes to mind when talking about statistics," according to Fellegi. However, the impact of the information collected by Statistics Canada affects everyone on a daily basis. For example, it helps people with their finances by reporting on the inflation rate, enables people to make better heath care decisions by analyzing medical treatments, and offers data on the best environment for children. "We try to shed light on issues, rather than just issue numbers," according to Fellegi.[4]

So the next time you are listening to a newscast or reading a newspaper that says, "According to Statistics Canada," you can be certain that the information is accurate, trustworthy, and reliable. Behind the seemingly simple numbers cited in the media lies "state-of-the-art computing technology and expertise in survey methodology and statistical methods."[5]

## CRITICAL THINKING

- In your present work or organization experience, with what kinds of reports are you familiar? What is their purpose and how are they presented?
- Should researchers be familiar with the services offered by Statistics Canada? What would you recommend about the types of information generated by this organization?
- Before funding a project, what types of information would most companies require?

www.statcan.ca

# UNDERSTANDING REPORT BASICS

Reports are a fact of life in North American business. In a low-context culture such as North America, our values and attitudes seem to prompt us to write reports. We analyze the pros and cons of problems, studying alternatives and assessing facts, figures, and details. We pride ourselves on being practical and logical. We solve problems by applying scientific procedures. When we must persuade management to support a project, we generally write a report laying out the case.

Management decisions in many organizations are based on information submitted in the form of reports. This chapter examines the functions, patterns, formats, and writing styles of typical reports. It also introduces the report-writing process and discusses methods of collecting, illustrating, and documenting data.

*1*

Effective business reports solve problems and answer questions systematically.

Because of their abundance and diversity, business reports are difficult to define. They may range from informal half-page trip reports to formal 200-page financial forecasts. Reports may be presented orally in front of a group or electronically on a computer screen. Some reports appear as words on paper in the form of memos and letters. Others are primarily numerical data, such as tax reports or profit-and-loss statements. Some seek to provide information only; others aim to analyze and make recommendations. Although reports vary greatly in length, content, form, and formality level, they all have one common purpose: *Business reports are systematic attempts to answer questions and solve problems.*

## Functions

In terms of what they do, most reports can be placed in two broad categories: informational reports and analytical reports.

Informational reports simply present data without analysis or recommendations.

*Informational Reports.* Reports that present data without analysis or recommendations are primarily informational. Although writers collect and organize facts, they are not expected to analyze the facts for readers. A trip report describing an employee's visit to a trade show, for example, simply presents information. Other reports that present information without analysis involve routine operations, compliance with regulations, and company policies and procedures.

Analytical reports provide data, analyses, conclusions, and, if requested, recommendations.

*Analytical Reports.* Reports that provide data, analyses, and conclusions are analytical. If requested, writers also supply recommendations. Analytical reports may intend to persuade readers to act or to change their beliefs. Assume you're writing a feasibility report that compares several potential locations for a workout/fitness club. After analyzing and discussing alternatives, you might recommend one site, thus attempting to persuade readers to accept this choice.

## Organizational Patterns

Like letters and memos, reports may be organized directly or indirectly. The reader's expectations and the content of a report determine its pattern of development, as illustrated in Figure 12.1. In long reports, such as corporate annual reports, some parts may be developed directly while other parts are arranged indirectly.

The direct pattern places conclusions and recommendations near the beginning of a report.

*Direct Pattern.* When the purpose for writing is presented close to the beginning, the organizational pattern is direct. Informational reports, such as the letter report shown in Figure 12.2 (on page 366), are usually arranged directly. They open with an introduction, followed by the facts and a summary. In Figure 12.2 the writer explains a legal services plan. The letter report begins with an introduction. Then it presents the facts, which are divided into three subtopics identified by descriptive headings. The letter ends with a summary and a complimentary close.

Analytical reports may also be organized directly, especially when readers are supportive or are familiar with the topic. Many busy executives prefer this pattern because it gives them the results of the report immediately. They don't have to spend time wading through the facts, findings, discussion, and analyses to get to the two items they are most interested in—conclusions and recommendations. Figure 12.3 on page 368 illustrates such an arrangement. This analytical memo report describes environmental hazards of a property that a realtor has just listed. The realtor is familiar with the investigation and eager to find out the recommendations. Therefore, the memo is organized directly. You should be aware, though, that unless

**FIGURE 12.1** Audience Analysis and Report Organization

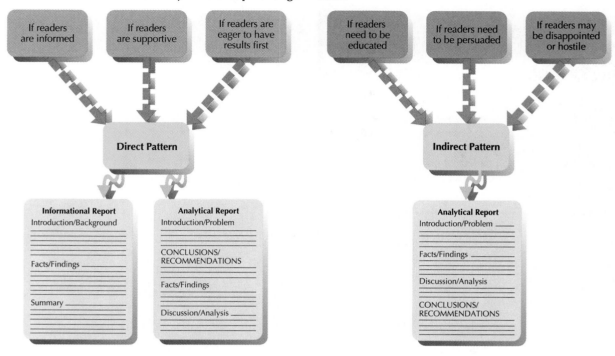

readers are familiar with the topic, they may find the direct pattern confusing. Many readers prefer the indirect pattern because it seems logical and mirrors the way we solve problems.

*Indirect Pattern.* When the conclusions and recommendations, if requested, appear at the end of the report, the organizational pattern is indirect. Such reports usually begin with an introduction or description of the problem, followed by facts and interpretation from the writer. They end with conclusions and recommendations. This pattern is helpful when readers are unfamiliar with the problem. It's also useful when readers must be persuaded or when they may be disappointed in or hostile toward the report's findings. The writer is more likely to retain the reader's interest by first explaining, justifying, and analyzing the facts and then making recommendations. This pattern also seems most rational to readers because it follows the normal thought process: problem, alternatives (facts), solution.

**The indirect pattern is appropriate for analytical reports that seek to persuade or that convey bad news.**

## Formats

The format of a report is governed by its length, topic, audience, and purpose. After considering these elements, you'll probably choose from among the following four formats:

**A report's format depends on its length, topic, audience, and purpose.**

*Letter Format.* Use letter format for short (say, ten or fewer pages) informal reports addressed outside an organization. Prepared on office stationery, a letter report contains a date, inside address, salutation, and complimentary close, as shown in Figure 12.2. Although they may carry information similar to that found in correspondence, letter reports usually are longer and show more careful organization than most letters. They also include headings.

## FIGURE 12.2 Informational Report—Letter Format

 *Centre for Consumers of Legal Services*
P.O. Box 260
Kitchener, ON N2K 2V5

— Uses letterhead stationery for an informal report addressed to an outsider

September 7, 2005

Ms. Lisa Burgess, Secretary
Westwood Homeowners
3902 Westwood Drive
Guelph, ON N1H 6Y7

Dear Ms. Burgess:

As executive director of the Centre for Consumers of Legal Services, I'm pleased to send you this information describing how your homeowners' association can sponsor a legal services plan for its members. After an introduction with background data, this report will discuss three steps necessary for your group to start its plan.

**Introduction**

A legal services plan promotes preventive law by letting members talk to lawyers whenever problems arise. Prompt legal advice often avoids or prevents expensive litigation. Because groups can supply a flow of business to the plan's lawyers, groups can negotiate free consultation, follow-up, and discounts.

Two kinds of plans are commonly available. The first, a free plan, offers free legal consultation along with discounts for services when the participating groups are sufficiently large to generate business for the plan's lawyers. These plans actually act as a substitute for advertising for the lawyers. The second common type is the prepaid plan. Prepaid plans provide more benefits, but members must pay annual fees, usually of $200 or more per year.

Since you inquired about a free plan for your homeowners' association, the following information describes how to set up such a program.

*Presents introduction and facts without analysis or recommendations*

**Determine the Benefits Your Group Needs**

The first step in establishing a free legal services plan is to meet with the members of your group to decide what benefits they want. Typical benefits include the following:

*Arranges facts of report into sections with descriptive headings*

**Free consultation.** Members may consult a participating lawyer—by phone or in the lawyer's office—to discuss any matter. The number of consultations is unlimited, provided each is about a separate matter. Consultations are generally limited to 30 minutes, but they include substantive analysis and advice.

*Emphasizes benefits in paragraph headings with boldface type*

**Free document review.** Important papers—such as leases, insurance policies, and instalment sales contracts—may be reviewed with legal counsel. Members may ask questions and receive an explanation of terms.

**FIGURE 12.2  Continued**

Ms. Lisa Burgess                    Page 2                    September 7, 2005 •————— Identifies second
and succeeding
pages with
headings

**Discount on additional services.** For more complex matters, participating
lawyers will charge members 75 percent of the lawyer's normal fee. However,
some organizations choose to charge a flat fee for commonly needed services.

**Select the Lawyers for Your Plan** •

Groups with geographically concentrated memberships have an advantage in
forming legal plans. These groups can limit the number of participating lawyers
and yet provide adequate service. Generally, smaller panels of lawyers are
advantageous.

Assemble a list of candidates, inviting them to apply. The best way to compare
prices is to have candidates submit their fee schedules. Your group can then
compare fee schedules and select the lowest bidder, if price is important. Arrange
to interview lawyers in their offices.                                    Uses parallel
————— side headings
After selecting a lawyer or a panel, sign a contract. The contract should       for consistency
include the reason for the plan, what the lawyer agrees to do, what the group    and readability
agrees to do, how each side can end the contract, and the signatures of both parties.
You may also wish to include references to malpractice insurance, assurance that
the group will not interfere with the lawyer-client relationship, an evaluation
form, a grievance procedure, and responsibility for government filings.

**Publicize the Plan to Your Members** •

Members won't use a plan if they don't know about it, and a plan will not be
successful if it is unused. Publicity must be vocal and ongoing. Announce it in
newsletters, meetings, bulletin boards, and flyers.

Persistence is the key. All too frequently, leaders of an organization assume
that a single announcement is all that's needed. They expect members to see the
value of the plan and remember that it's available. Most organization members,
though, are not as involved as the leadership. Therefore, it takes more publicity
than the leadership usually expects in order to reach and maintain the desired
level of awareness.

**Summary**

A successful free legal services plan involves designing a program, choosing
the lawyers, and publicizing the plan. To learn more about these steps or to
order a $25 how-to manual, call me at (519) 884-9901.

Sincerely,

*Richard M. Ramos*                                            •————— Includes
                                                                complimentary
Richard M. Ramos                                                close and
Executive Director                                              signature

pas

*Memo Format.* For short informal reports that stay within organizations, memo
format is appropriate. Memo reports begin with DATE, TO, FROM, and SUBJECT,
as shown in Figure 12.3. Like letter reports, memo reports differ from regular memos
in length, use of headings, and deliberate organization.

*Manuscript Format.* For longer, more formal reports, use manuscript format.
These reports are usually printed on plain paper instead of letterhead stationery or
memo forms. They begin with a title followed by systematically displayed headings
and subheadings. You will see examples of proposals and formal reports using manuscript formats in Chapter 14.

# FIGURE 12.3 Analytical Report—Memo Format

## Tips for Memo Reports
- Use memo format for most short (ten or fewer pages) informal reports within an organization.
- Leave side margins of 2.5 to 3 cm.
- Sign your initials on the FROM line.
- Use an informal, conversational style.
- For direct analytical reports, put recommendations first.
- For indirect analytical reports, put recommendations last.

*Applies memo format for short, informal internal report*

### Atlantic Environmental, Inc.

*Interoffice Memo*

**DATE:**     March 7, 2005

**TO:**       Kermit Fox, President

**FROM:**     Cynthia M. Rashid, Environmental Engineer  *CMR*

**SUBJECT:** INVESTIGATION OF MOUNTAIN PARK COMMERCIAL SITE

For Laurentian Realty, Inc., I've completed a preliminary investigation of its Mountain Park property listing. The following recommendations are based on my physical inspection of the site, official records, and interviews with officials and persons knowledgeable about the site.

*Uses first paragraph as introduction*

#### Recommendations

*Presents recommendations first (direct pattern) because reader is supportive and familiar with topic*

To reduce its potential environmental liability, Laurentian Realty should take the following steps in regard to its Mountain Park listing:

- Conduct an immediate asbestos survey at the site, including inspection of ceiling insulation material, floor tiles, and insulation around a gas-fired heater vent pipe at 2539 Mountain View Drive.

- Prepare an environmental audit of the generators of hazardous waste currently operating at the site, including Mountain Technology.

- Obtain lids for the dumpsters situated in the parking areas and ensure that the lids are kept closed.

#### Findings and Analyses

*Combines findings and analyses in short report*

My preliminary assessment of the site and its immediate vicinity revealed rooms with damaged floor tiles on the first and second floors of 2539 Mountain View Drive. Apparently, in recent remodelling efforts, these tiles had been cracked and broken. Examination of the ceiling and attic revealed further possible contamination from asbestos. The insulation for the hot-water tank was in poor condition.

Located on the property is Mountain Technology, a possible hazardous waste generator. Although I could not examine its interior, this company has the potential for producing hazardous material contamination.

In the parking area large dumpsters collect trash and debris from several businesses. These dumpsters were uncovered, thus posing a risk to the general public.

In view of the construction date of the structures on this property, asbestos-containing building materials might be present. Moreover, this property is located in an industrial part of the city, further prompting my recommendation for a thorough investigation. Laurentian Realty can act immediately to eliminate one environmental concern: covering the dumpsters in the parking area.

***Printed Forms.*** Prepared forms are often used for repetitive data, such as monthly sales reports, performance appraisals, merchandise inventories, and personnel and financial reports. Standardized headings on these forms save time for the writer. Preprinted forms also make similar information easy to locate and ensure that all necessary information is provided.

## Writing Style

Like other business messages, reports can range from informal to formal, depending on their purpose, audience, and setting. Research reports from consultants to their clients tend to be rather formal. Such reports must project an impression of objectivity, authority, and impartiality. But a report to your boss describing a trip to a conference would probably be informal.

**Reports can be formal or informal depending on the purpose, audience, and setting.**

An office worker once called a grammar hot-line service with this problem: "We've just sent a report to our headquarters, and it was returned with this comment, 'Put it in the third person.' What do they mean?" The hot-line experts explained that management apparently wanted a more formal writing style, using third-person constructions (*the company* or *the researcher* instead of *we* and *I*). Figure 12.4, which compares characteristics of formal and informal report-writing styles, can help you decide the writing style that's appropriate for your reports.

**FIGURE 12.4  Report-Writing Styles**

| | FORMAL WRITING STYLE | INFORMAL WRITING STYLE |
|---|---|---|
| Use | Theses | Short, routine reports |
| | Research studies | Reports for familiar audiences |
| | Controversial or complex reports (especially to outsiders) | Noncontroversial reports Most reports for company insiders |
| Effect | Impression of objectivity, accuracy, professionalism, fairness | Feeling of warmth, personal involvement, closeness |
| | Distance created between writer and reader | |
| Characteristics | Absence of first-person pronouns; use of third-person (*the researcher, the writer*) | Use of first-person pronouns (*I, we, me, my, us, our*) |
| | Absence of contractions (*can't, don't*) | Use of contractions |
| | Use of passive-voice verbs (*the study was conducted*) | Emphasis on active-voice verbs (*I conducted the study*) |
| | Complex sentences; long words | Shorter sentences; familiar words |
| | Absence of humour and figures of speech | Occasional use of humour, metaphors |
| | Reduced use of colourful adjectives and adverbs | Occasional use of colourful speech |
| | Elimination of "editorializing" (author's opinions, perceptions) | Acceptance of author's opinions and ideas |

## APPLYING THE 3-×-3 WRITING PROCESS TO REPORTS

Because business reports are systematic attempts to answer questions and solve problems, the best reports are developed methodically. The same 3-×-3 writing process that guided memo and letter writing can be applied to reports. Let's channel the process into seven specific steps:

**The best reports grow out of a seven-step process beginning with analysis and ending with proofreading and evaluation.**

- **Step 1:** Analyze the problem and purpose.
- **Step 2:** Anticipate the audience and issues.
- **Step 3:** Prepare a work plan.
- **Step 4:** Research the data.
- **Step 5:** Organize, analyze, interpret, and illustrate the data.
- **Step 6:** Compose the first draft.
- **Step 7:** Revise, proofread, and evaluate.

How much time you spend on each step depends on your report task. A short informational report on a familiar topic might require a brief work plan, little research, and no analysis of the data. A complex analytical report, on the other hand, might demand a comprehensive work plan, extensive research, and careful analysis of the data. In this section we will consider the first three steps in the process—analyzing the problem and purpose, anticipating the audience and issues, and preparing a work plan.

To illustrate the planning stages of a report, we'll watch Diane Camas develop a report she's preparing for her boss, Mike Rivers, at Mycon Pharmaceutical Laboratories. Mike asked Diane to investigate the problem of transportation for sales representatives. Currently, some Mycon reps visit customers (mostly doctors and hospitals) using company-leased cars. A few reps drive their own cars, receiving reimbursements for use. In three months Mycon's leasing agreement for 14 cars expires, and Mike is considering a major change. Diane's task is to investigate the choices and report her findings to Mike.

### Analyzing the Problem and Purpose

**Before beginning a report, identify the problem to be solved in a clear statement.**

The first step in writing a report is understanding the problem or assignment clearly. For complex reports it's wise to prepare a written problem statement. In analyzing her report task, Diane had many questions. Is the problem that Mycon is spending too much money on leased cars? Does Mycon wish to invest in owning a fleet of cars? Is Mike unhappy with the paperwork involved in reimbursing sales reps when they use their own cars? Does he suspect that reps are submitting inflated kilometre figures? Before starting research for the report, Diane talked with Mike to define the problem. She learned several dimensions of the situation and wrote the following statement to clarify the problem—both for herself and for Mike.

> **Problem Statement:** The leases on all company cars will be expiring in three months. Mycon must decide whether to renew them or develop a new policy regarding transportation for sales reps. Expenses and paperwork for employee-owned cars seem excessive.

Diane further defined the problem by writing a specific question that she would try to answer in her report:

**Problem Question:** What plan should Mycon follow in providing transportation for its sales reps?

Now Diane was ready to concentrate on the purpose of the report. Again, she had questions. Exactly what did Mike expect? Did he want a comparison of costs for buying cars and leasing cars? Should she conduct research to pinpoint exact reimbursement costs when employees drive their own cars? Did he want her to do all the legwork, present her findings in a report, and let him make a decision? Or did he want her to evaluate the choices and recommend a course of action? After talking with Mike, Diane was ready to write a simple purpose statement for this assignment.

**Simple Statement of Purpose:** To recommend a plan that provides sales reps with cars to be used in their calls.

A simple purpose statement defines the focus of a report.

Preparing a written purpose statement is a good idea because it defines the focus of a report and provides a standard that keeps the project on target. In writing useful purpose statements, choose active verbs telling what you intend to do: *analyze, choose, investigate, compare, justify, evaluate, explain, establish, determine,* and so on. Notice that Diane's statement begins with the active verb *recommend.*

Some reports require only a simple statement of purpose: *to investigate expanded teller hours, to select a manager from among four candidates, to describe the position of accounts supervisor.* Many assignments, though, demand additional focus to guide the project. An expanded statement of purpose considers three additional factors:

- **Scope.** What issues or elements will be investigated? To determine the scope, Diane brainstormed with Mike and others to pin down her task. She learned that Mycon currently had enough capital to consider purchasing a fleet of cars outright. Mike also told her that employee satisfaction was almost as important as cost-effectiveness. Moreover, he disclosed his suspicion that employee-owned cars were costing Mycon more than leased cars. Diane had many issues to sort out in setting the boundaries of her report.

Setting boundaries on a project helps determine its scope.

- **Significance.** Why is the topic worth investigating at this time? Some topics, after initial examination, turn out to be less important than originally thought. Others involve problems that cannot be solved, making a study useless. For Diane and Mike the problem had significance because Mycon's leasing agreement would expire shortly and decisions had to be made about a new policy for transportation of sales reps.

- **Limitations.** What conditions affect the generalizations and utility of a report's findings? In Diane's case her conclusions and recommendations might apply only to reps in her Edmonton sales district. Her findings would probably not be reliable for reps in Rimouski, Windsor, or Brandon. Another limitation for Diane is time. She must complete the report in four weeks, thus restricting the thoroughness of her research.

Diane decided to expand her statement of purpose to define the scope, significance, and limitations of the report.

**Expanded Statement of Purpose:** The purpose of this report is to recommend a plan that provides sales reps with cars to be used in their calls. The report will compare costs for three plans: outright ownership, leasing, and compensation for employee-owned cars. It will also measure employee reaction to each plan. The report is significant because Mycon's current leasing agreement expires

An expanded purpose statement considers scope, significance, and limitations.

April 1 and an improved plan could reduce costs and paperwork. The study is limited to costs for sales reps in the Edmonton district.

After preparing a statement of purpose, Diane checked it with Mike Rivers to be sure she was on target.

## Anticipating the Audience and Issues

Once the purpose of a report is defined, a writer must think carefully about who will read the report. A major mistake is concentrating solely on a primary reader. Although one individual may have solicited the report, others within the organization may eventually read it, including upper management and people in other departments. A report to an outside client may first be read by someone who is familiar with the problem and then be distributed to others less familiar with the topic. Moreover, candid statements to one audience may be offensive to another audience. Diane could make a major blunder, for instance, if she mentioned Mike's suspicion that sales reps were padding their kilometre statements. If the report were made public—as it probably would be to explain a new policy—the sales reps could feel insulted that their integrity was questioned.

As Diane considered her primary and secondary readers, she asked herself these questions:

- *What do my readers need to know about this topic?*
- *What do they already know?*
- *How will they react to this information?*
- *How can I make this information understandable and readable?*

Answers to these questions help writers determine how much background material to include, how much detail to add, whether to include jargon, what method of organization and presentation to follow, and what tone to use.

In the planning stages a report writer must also break the major investigative problem into subproblems. This process, sometimes called factoring, identifies issues to be investigated or possible solutions to the main problem. In this case Mycon must figure out the best way to transport sales reps. Each possible "solution" or issue that Diane considers becomes a factor or subproblem to be investigated. Diane came up with three tentative solutions to provide transportation to sales reps: (1) purchase cars outright, (2) lease cars, or (3) compensate employees for using their own cars. These three factors form the outline of Diane's study.

Diane continued to factor these main points into the following subproblems for investigation:

**What plan should Mycon use to transport its sales reps?**
I. Should Mycon purchase cars outright?
   A. How much capital would be required?
   B. How much would it cost to insure, operate, and maintain company-owned cars?
   C. Do employees prefer using company-owned cars?
II. Should Mycon lease cars?
   A. What is the best lease price available?
   B. How much would it cost to insure, operate, and maintain leased cars?
   C. Do employees prefer using leased cars?
III. Should Mycon compensate employees for using their own cars?
   A. How much has it cost in the past to operate employee-owned cars?

B.  How much paperwork is involved in reporting expenses?

C.  Do employees prefer being compensated for using their own cars?

Each subproblem would probably be further factored into additional subproblems. These issues may be phrased as questions, as Diane did, or as statements. In factoring a complex problem, prepare an outline showing the initial problem and its breakdown into subproblems. Make sure your divisions are consistent (don't mix issues), exclusive (don't overlap categories), and complete (don't skip significant issues).

## Preparing a Work Plan

After analyzing the problem, anticipating the audience, and factoring the problem, you're ready to prepare a work plan. Preparing a plan forces you to evaluate your resources, set priorities, outline a course of action, and establish a time schedule. Such a plan keeps you on schedule and also gives management a means of measuring your progress. A good work plan includes the following:

- Statement of the problem
- Statement of the purpose including scope, significance, and limitations
- Description of the sources and methods of collecting data
- Tentative outline
- Work schedule

A work plan gives a complete picture of a project. Because the usefulness and quality of any report rest primarily on its data, you'll want to allocate plenty of time to locate sources of information. For firsthand information you might interview people, prepare a survey, or even conduct a scientific experiment. For secondary information you'll probably search printed materials such as books and magazines as well as electronic materials on the Internet and Web. Your work plan describes how you expect to generate or collect data. Since data collection is a major part of report writing, the next section of this chapter treats the topic more fully.

Figure 12.5 shows a complete work plan for a report that studies safety seals for a food company's products. This work plan is particularly useful because it outlines the issues to be investigated. Notice that considerable thought and discussion—and even some preliminary research—are necessary to be able to develop a useful work plan.

Although this tentative outline guides investigation, it does not determine the content or order of the final report. You may, for example, study five possible solutions to a problem. If two prove to be useless, your report may discuss only the three winners. Moreover, you will organize the report to accomplish your goal and satisfy the audience. Remember that a busy executive who is familiar with a topic may prefer to read the conclusions and recommendations before a discussion of the findings. If the report is authorized by someone, be sure to review the work plan with that individual (your manager, client, or professor, for example) before proceeding with the project.

A good work plan provides an overview of a project: resources, priorities, course of action, and schedule.

## GATHERING INFORMATION FROM SECONDARY SOURCES

*3*

One of the most important steps in the process of writing a report is that of gathering information (research). Because a report is only as good as its data, the remainder of this chapter describes finding, documenting, and illustrating data. As you analyze a report's purpose and audience, you'll assess the kinds of data needed to support

# FIGURE 12.5 Work Plan for a Formal Report

## Tips for Preparing a Work Plan
- Start early; allow plenty of time for brainstorming and preliminary research.
- Describe the problem motivating the report.
- Write a purpose statement that includes its scope, significance, and limitations.
- Describe data collection sources and methods.
- Divide the major problem into subproblems stated as questions to be answered.
- Develop a realistic work schedule citing dates for completion of major tasks.
- Review the work plan with whoever authorized the report.

**Statement of Problem**

Consumers worry that food and drug products are dangerous as a result of tampering. Our company may face loss of market share and potential liability if we don't protect our products. Many food and drug companies now offer tamper-resistant packaging, but such packaging is costly.

**Statement of Purpose**

*Defines purpose, scope, limits, and significance of report*

The purpose of this study is to determine whether tamper-resistant packaging is necessary and/or feasible for our jams, jellies, and preserves. The study will examine published accounts of package tampering and evaluate how other companies have solved the problem. It will also measure consumers' interest in safety-seal packaging, as well as consumers' willingness to pay a slightly higher price for safety lids. We will conduct a market survey limited to a sample of 400 local consumers. Finally, the study will investigate a method for sealing our products and determine the cost for each unit we produce. This study is significant because safety seals could enhance the sales of our products and protect us from possible liability.

**Sources and Methods of Data Collection**

*Describes primary and secondary data sources*

Magazine and newspaper accounts of product tampering will be examined for the past 15 years. Articles describing tamper-resistant lids and other safe packaging devices for food and drug manufacturers will be studied. Moreover, our marketing staff will conduct a random telephone survey of local consumers, measuring their interest in safety seals. Finally, our production department will test various devices and determine the most cost-effective method to seal our product safely.

**Tentative Outline**

*Factors problem into manageable chunks*

I. Are consumers and producers concerned about product tampering?
   A. What incidents of tampering have been reported in the past 15 years?
   B. How did consumers react to tampered products causing harm?
   C. How did food and drug producers protect their products?
II. How do consumers react to safety seals on products today?
   A. Do consumers prefer food and drug products with safety seals?
   B. Would consumers be more likely to purchase our products if safety-sealed?
   C. Would consumers be willing to pay a few cents extra for safety seals?
III. What kind of safety seal is best for our products?
   A. What devices are other producers using—plastic "blister" packs, foil seals over bottle openings, or bands around lids?
   B. What device would work for our products?

**Work Schedule**

*Estimates time needed to complete report tasks*

| | |
|---|---|
| Investigate newspaper and magazine articles | Oct. 1-10 |
| Examine safety-seal devices on the market | Oct. 8-18 |
| Interview 400 local consumers | Oct. 8-24 |
| Develop and test devices for our products | Oct. 15-Nov.14 |
| Interpret and evaluate findings | Nov. 15-17 |
| Compose first draft of report | Nov. 18-20 |
| Revise draft | Nov. 21-23 |
| Submit final report | Nov. 24 |

# *Statistics Canada Revisited*

The mandate of StatsCan is to collect, analyze, and publish statistics on the Canadian population, society, and economy. StatsCan conducts about 350 active surveys on all aspects of Canadian life on a regular basis,[6] but the most comprehensive of all of StatsCan's work is the census, which is conducted every five years. This information provides a chronicle of the country and a unique historical record.

However, Statistics Canada and historians disagreed on the use of such information. Canada's chief statistician, Dr. Ivan Fellegi, believed that the information from the 1906 and 1911 censuses should remain private, citing the Statistics Act of 1918, which introduced secrecy provisions during World War I. However, historians disagreed. They argued that the purpose of the confidentiality was to protect people who are still living. However, more than 96 years later, they argued, it would seem unlikely that an individual would suffer. Critics and genealogists argued that the 1906 and 1911 censuses provide crucial information to Western Canada during a time of increased immigration.[7]

After a three-year fight, Statistics Canada finally gave in, and in early 2003 StatsCan posted the 1906 census on the Internet. In making this decision, Statistics Canada sought legal opinion, conducted two public opinion polls, and questioned an expert panel and 22 focus groups for feedback.[8] The release of this information makes Canada consistent with other countries. The United Kingdom provides a 100-year delay between collection and release, and the United States makes its records available after 72 years. On the 2006 census, Canadians will be required to indicate if they agree to have their information released after 92 years.

## CRITICAL THINKING

- To discuss the confidentiality and privacy agreements with superiors, should StatsCan staff write an informational or an analytical report? Why?
- Should such a report be developed directly or indirectly? Why? Should it be written formally or informally?
- Describe the major components of a logical work plan for your team to follow in preparing to write a report outlining confidentiality and privacy issues.

www.statcan.ca

---

your argument or explain your topic. Do you need statistics, background data, expert opinions, group opinions, or organizational data? Figure 12.6 lists five forms of data and provides questions to guide you in making your research accurate and productive.

**A report is only as good as its data.**

Data fall into two broad categories, primary and secondary. Primary data result from firsthand experience and observation. Secondary data come from reading what others have experienced and observed. Coca-Cola and Pepsi-Cola, for example, produce primary data when they stage taste tests and record the reactions of consumers. These same sets of data become secondary after they have been published and, let's say, a newspaper reporter uses them in an article about soft drinks. Secondary data are easier and cheaper to develop than primary data, which might involve interviewing large groups or sending out questionnaires.

**Primary data come from firsthand experience and observation; secondary data, from reading.**

We're going to discuss secondary data first because that's where nearly every research project should begin. Often, something has already been written about your topic. Reviewing secondary sources can save time and effort and prevent you from "reinventing the wheel." Most secondary material is available either in print or electronically.

**FIGURE 12.6 Selecting Report Data**

| FORM OF DATA | QUESTIONS TO ASK |
|---|---|
| Statistical | What is the source? |
| | How were these figures derived? |
| | In what form do I need the statistics? |
| | Must they be converted? |
| | How recent are they? |
| Background or historical | Has this topic been explored before? |
| | What have others said about it? |
| | What sources did they use? |
| Expert opinion | Who are the experts? |
| | Are their opinions in print? |
| | Can they be interviewed? |
| | Do we have in-house experts? |
| Individual or group opinion | Do I need to interview or survey people (such as consumers, employees, or managers)? |
| | Do good questionnaires already exist? |
| | Can parts of existing test instruments be used or combined? |
| Organizational | What are the proper channels for obtaining in-house data? |
| | Are permissions required? |
| | How can I find data about public and private companies? |

## Print Resources

**Print sources are still the most visible part of libraries.**

Although we're seeing a steady movement away from print to electronic data, print sources are still the most visible part of nearly all libraries. Much information is available only in print, and you may want to use some of the following print resources.

By the way, if you are an infrequent library user, begin your research by talking with a reference librarian about your project. These librarians won't do your research for you, but they will steer you in the right direction. Wendy Newman, president of the Canadian Library Association, states, "This is the age of 'also.' We have not eliminated our traditional service, but we have added a great deal of technologically assisted service. Far from being the death of the libraries, the Internet has actually been a new draw."[9] And librarians are very accommodating. Carla Hayden, of the American Library Association, reports, "We're [libraries] one of the most respected and even venerated places in communities. People know that they're going to get pretty objective information and they're not going to be subjected to commercialism. You'd trust a librarian, but we want you to like them, too, and feel they are somebody you can relate to."[10] Many libraries help you understand their computer, cataloguing, and retrieval systems by providing advice, brochures, handouts, and workshops.

***Books.*** Although quickly outdated, books provide excellent historical, in-depth data on subjects. Books can be located through print or computer listings.

**Books provide historical, in-depth data.**

- **Card catalogue.** Some libraries still maintain card catalogues with all books indexed on 3- by 5-inch cards alphabetized by author, title, or subject.

- **Online catalogue.** Most libraries today have computerized their card catalogues. Some systems are fully automated, thus allowing users to learn not only whether a book is located in the library but also whether it is currently available.

***Periodicals.*** Magazines, pamphlets, and journals are called *periodicals* because of their recurrent or periodic publication. Journals, by the way, are compilations of scholarly articles. Articles in journals and other periodicals will be extremely useful to you because they are concise, limited in scope, current, and can supplement information in books.

**Exploration of secondary data includes searching periodicals both in print and electronic forms.**

- **Print indexes.** The *Readers' Guide to Periodical Literature* is a valuable index of general-interest magazine article titles. It includes such magazines as *Time, Newsweek, Maclean's,* and *The Canadian Forum.* More useful to business writers, though, will be the titles of articles appearing in business and industrial magazines (such as *Canadian Business, Canadian Banker,* and *Business Quarterly*). For an index of these publications, consult the *Business Periodicals Index.* The *Canadian Business Index* can be very useful too, listing articles from more than 200 Canadian business periodicals. Many of these indexes are also available in computerized form.

- **CD-ROM and Web-based bibliographic indexes.** Automated indexes similar to the print indexes just described are stored in CD-ROM and online databases. Many libraries now provide such bibliographic databases for computer-aided location of references and abstracts from magazines, journals, and newspapers, such as *The Globe and Mail.* When using CD-ROM and Web-based online indexes, follow the on-screen instructions or ask for assistance from a librarian. It's a good idea to begin with a subject search because it generally turns up more relevant citations than keyword searches (especially when searching for names

Investors in sports teams, equipment, broadcasting, sponsorship, and marketing require a steady stream of information, much of which comes from electronic databases. For example, the Sports Business Research Network offers a fee-based electronic database with information gathered from various sports governing bodies, magazines, newsletters, and the government. Sports investors and product developers use this electronic database to study leagues and teams, operating results, legal issues, and trends in major market segments, such as youth sports, women's sports, and extreme sports.

**CHAPTER 12**
Preparing to Write Business Reports
**377**

of people or companies). Once you locate usable references, print a copy of your findings and then check the shelf listings to see if the publications are available.

## Electronic Databases

**Many researchers today begin by looking in electronic databases.**

As a writer of business reports today, you will probably begin your secondary research with electronic resources. Most writers turn to them first because they are fast, cheap, and easy to use. Some are even accessible from remote locations. This means that you can conduct detailed searches without ever leaving your office, home, or dorm room. Although some databases are still presented on CD-ROMs, information is increasingly available in online databases. They have become the staple of secondary research.

A database is a collection of information stored electronically so that it is accessible by computer and is digitally searchable. Databases provide both bibliographic (titles of documents and brief abstracts) and full-text documents. Most researchers today, however, prefer full-text documents. Various databases contain a rich array of magazine, newspaper, and journal articles, as well as newsletters, business reports, company profiles, government data, reviews, and directories. Provided with this textbook is access to InfoTrac, a Web-centred database offering nearly 1 million magazine and journal articles. Web-based documents are enriched with charts, graphs, bold and italic fonts, colour, and pictures. Other well-known databases are Dialog, ABI, and Lexis-Nexis.

Although well stocked and well organized, specialized commercial databases are indeed expensive to use. Many also involve steep learning curves. While learning how to select *keywords* (or *descriptors*) and how to explore the database, you can run up quite a bill.

## The Internet

**The World Wide Web is a collection of hypertext pages that offer information and links.**

After e-mail, the most-used function of the Internet is the World Wide Web.[11] According to the federal government, Canadians surf the Internet more than any other people in the world.[12] Growing at a dizzying pace, the Web includes an enormous collection of specially formatted documents called *Web pages* located at Web sites around the world. Web offerings include online databases, magazines, newspapers, library resources, job and résumé banks, sound and video files, and many other information resources. Creators of Web pages use a special system of codes (*HTML*, i.e., Hypertext Markup Language) to format their offerings. The crucial feature of these hypertext pages is their use of links to other Web pages. Links are identified by underlined words and phrases or, occasionally, images. When clicked, links connect you to related Web pages. These pages immediately download to your computer screen, thus creating a vast web of resources at your fingertips.

**Web research is often time-consuming and frustrating because the Web is disorganized and constantly changing.**

*Web Opportunities and Frustrations.* To a business researcher, the Web offers a wide range of organizational and commercial information. You can expect to find such items as product and service facts, public relations material, mission statements, staff directories, press releases, current company news, government information, selected article reprints, collaborative scientific project reports, and employment information. The Web is unquestionably one of the greatest sources of information now available to anyone needing facts quickly and inexpensively. But finding that information can be frustrating and time-consuming. The constantly changing contents of the Web and its lack of organization make it more problematic for research than searching commercial databases. Moreover, Web content is uneven and often the quality is questionable. You'll learn more about evaluating Web sources shortly.

*Web Browsers and URLs.* Searching the Web requires a Web *browser*, such as Netscape Navigator or Microsoft Internet Explorer. Browsers are software programs that enable you to view the graphics and text, as well as access links of Web pages. To locate the Web page of a specific organization, you need its *URL* (*Uniform Resource Locator*). URLs are case- and space-sensitive, so be sure to type the address exactly as it is printed. For most companies, the URL is *http://www.xyzcompany.com.* (Tip: You can save some keystrokes by omitting "http://"; this portion of the URL is usually unnecessary.) Your goal is to locate the top-level Web page of an organization's site. On this page you'll generally find an overview of the site contents or a link to a site map. If you can't guess a company's URL, you can usually find it quickly at Hoover's Web site: <**www.hoovers.com**>.

**Web browsers are software programs that access Web pages and their links.**

*Search Tools.* Finding what you are looking for on the Web is like searching for a library book without using the card catalogue. Fortunately, you can use a number of specialized search tools, such as Google and Yahoo!, shown in Figure 12.7. These search tools can be divided into two types: search engines and directories. Search engines use automated software "spiders" that crawl through the Web to collect and index the full text of pages they find. Directories, on the other hand, rely on human

**Search tools such as Google and Yahoo! help you locate specific Web sites and information.**

### FIGURE 12.7 Favourite Search Tools

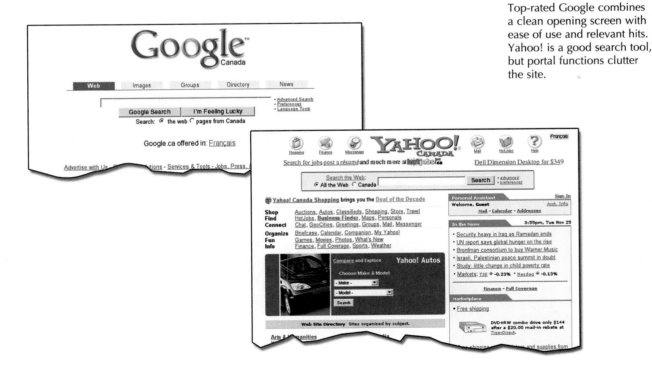

Top-rated Google combines a clean opening screen with ease of use and relevant hits. Yahoo! is a good search tool, but portal functions clutter the site.

editors to sift through pages, eliminating inappropriate ones and categorizing sites by subject. Hybrid search tools combine both spiders and directories. Many search-tool sites have tried to be "portals." They strive to provide all your Internet needs in one location, such as weather updates, stock quotes, e-mail, chat forums, shopping, and newsfeeds. Portals, though, have lost favour; researchers prefer uncluttered search tools, such as Google. According to Ellenor Innes of the Vancouver Public Library, you may also want to search the "invisible Web," which extracts information that traditional search engines don't include. Untapped information can be found at <www.completeplanet.com>, <www.metor.com>, <www.profusion.com>, and <www.incywincy.com>.[13]

Despite the many ingenious tools sprouting up (over 8 000 at this writing), Web search engines and directories cannot come close to indexing all of the pages on the Internet.[14] Even though search tools don't survey everything that's out there on the Web, they usually turn up more information than you want. Like everything else about the Web, search tools are constantly evolving as developers change their features to attract more users. Figure 12.8 shows some of the best search engines and directories as tested and ranked by *PC Magazine*. More search engines are listed at <www.businesscommunication-4th.nelson.com> (click on *Search Tools*).

You must know how to use search engines to make them most effective.

### Internet Search Tips and Techniques.

"Search engines are dumber than a box of rocks," claims one Web veteran. For example, he says, "If you ask one to look up *bathing suits*, it will find sites on *bathing* and on *suits*."[15] But enclosing the phrase in quotation marks tells most search engines to look for the words together. Knowing how to use search engines can transform that dumb box of rocks into a jewel case bulging with gems of useful information. Here's a summary of tips for wise Internet researchers.[16]

- **Use two or three search tools.** Different Internet search engines turn up different results. One expert wisely remarked: "Every search engine will give you good results some of the time. Every search engine will give you surprisingly bad results some of the time. No search engine will give you good results all of the time."[17]

- **Understand case-sensitivity.** Generally use lowercase for your searches, unless you are searching for a term that is usually written in upper and lowercase, such as a person's name.

- **Understand the AND/OR default and quotation marks.** When searching for a phrase, such as *cost-benefit analysis*, most search tools will retrieve documents having all or some of the terms. This AND/OR strategy is the default of most search tools. To locate occurrences of the complete phrase, enclose it in quotation marks.

Effective Web searches use two or more tools and precise, uncommon keywords.

- **Prefer uncommon words.** Commonly used words make poor search keywords. For example, instead of *keeping employees*, use *employee retention*.

- **Omit articles and prepositions.** These are known as "stop words," and they do not add value to a search. Instead of *request for proposal*, use *proposal request*.

- **Use wild cards.** Most search engines support wild cards, such as asterisks. For example, the search term *cent** will retrieve *cents*, while *cent*** will retrieve both *centre* and *center*.

- **Know your search tool.** When connecting to a search service for the first time, always read the description of its service, including its FAQs (Frequently Asked Questions), Help, and How to Search sections.

- **Learn basic Boolean search strategies.** You can save yourself a lot of time and frustration by narrowing your search with Boolean operators, as described in the Tech Talk box on page 382.

UNIT 4
Reports and Proposals
**380**

**FIGURE 12.8  Search Engines and Directories: Quest for the Best**

| SEARCH SITE | FEATURES | EASE OF USE | COMMENTS |
|---|---|---|---|
| **Google**<br>www.google.com<br>www.google.ca | Engine/directory. Sophisticated technology returns results based on number of other sites that link to specific information at a site. Now includes Deja's Usenet discussion service with access to many browse groups. | Excellent | Returns highly relevant results; very easy to use; few advanced features, but you may not need them to find what you're looking for. Most popular search site. Clean, uncluttered home page. |
| **Yahoo!**<br>www.yahoo.com<br>ca.yahoo.com | Portal. Catalogues over 500 000 sites; returns results from both directory and engine; searches audio, video, and newsgroups. | Good | Still the best portal and easier to use than most; flagship directory has fewer site descriptions than competing search tools. |
| **Northern Light**<br>www.northernlight.com | Engine. Sorts results into folders by topic; searches fee-based databases; many advanced features, including Boolean queries. | Good | Powerful and unique, but the topic folders don't always sort results effectively; better for business searches than for fun stuff; no directory. |
| **HotBot**<br>www.hotbot.com | Engine/directory. Advanced features include Boolean queries and much more. | Good | Good choice for serious searchers who like lots of options; basic queries may not return super-relevant results; few broken links. |
| **LookSmart**<br>www.looksmart.com | Engine/directory. Catalogues and describes over a million sites; LookSmart Live provides advice and info from real people. | Good | Solid directory with better descriptions than Yahoo!, but it seemed slower than most in tests, with more broken links. |
| **AltaVista**<br>www.altavista.com<br>ca.altavista.com | Portal. Searches news, newsgroups, audio, video, images; advanced features include Boolean queries and sorting. | Fair | Powerful engine returns high-quality results; advanced features take time to learn. Lots of clutter, but you can use its streamlined Raging.com instead. |
| **Excite**<br>www.excite.com | Portal. Searches news, images, audio, and more; advanced features include logical queries and sorting. | Fair | Busy home page makes search engine seem like an afterthought; help section is vague; doesn't specify how many links it found. |
| **Lycos**<br>www.lycos.com<br>www.lycos.ca | Portal. Searches news, audio, weather reports, and more; can restrict searches to family-friendly sites. | Fair | Lots of features, but relevance of results was erratic in tests; more broken links and duplicates than most; few advanced search options. |

- **Bookmark the best.** To keep better track of your favourite Internet sites, save them on your browser as bookmarks.

- **Keep trying.** If a search produces no results, check your spelling. If you are using Boolean operators, check the syntax of your queries. Try synonyms and

## Understanding Natural Language, Keyword, and Boolean Searching

*Natural language* searches involve posing a search question as you would normally state it. For example, "Is there a correlation between employee morale and productivity?" Using AltaVista for this search question produced nearly 5 million documents. Although the total is overwhelming, the most relevant "hits" were listed first. And the first ten items were all relevant. An increasing number of Web search engines and databases support natural language searching. It's particularly handy for vague or broad questions.

*Keyword* searches involve using the principal words in which you are interested. From the above question, you might choose to search using the phrase "employee morale" or "employee productivity." Omit useless words such as articles, conjunctions, and prepositions. Some search tools allow you to enclose keyword sequences (such as *employee morale*) in quotation marks to ensure that the specified words appear together and not separately.

*Boolean* searches involve joining keywords with "operators" (connectors) that include or exclude specific topics. For example, "employee AND morale." Using Boolean operators enables you to narrow your search and thus improve its precision. The following

Boolean operators are most commonly used:

| | |
|---|---|
| AND | Identifies only documents containing all of the specified words: **employee AND productivity AND morale** |
| OR | Identifies documents containing at least one of the specified words: **employee OR productivity OR morale** |
| NOT | Excludes documents containing the specified word: **employee productivity NOT morale** |
| NEAR | Finds documents containing target words or phrases within a specified distance, for instance, within ten words: **employee NEAR productivity** |

### Career Application

Using a search engine that supports natural language, keyword, and Boolean searching (such as AltaVista), try an experiment. Explore the same topic using (1) a natural language question, (2) key words, and (3) Boolean operators. Which method produced the most relevant hits?

variations on words. Try to be less specific in your search term. If your search produces too many hits, try to be more specific. Think of words that uniquely identify what you're looking for. And use as many relevant keywords as possible.

- **Repeat your search a week later.** For the best results, return to your search a couple of days or a week later. The same keywords will probably produce additional results. That's because hundreds of thousands of new pages are being added to the Web every day.

Remember, search tools are "dumb as rocks." Only through clever cybersearching can you uncover the jewels hidden on the Internet.

**Evaluate the currency, authority, content, and accuracy of Web sites carefully.**

*Evaluating Web Sources.* Most of us using the Web have a tendency to assume that any information turned up via a search engine has somehow been evaluated as part of a valid selection process.[18] Wrong! The truth is that the Internet is rampant with unreliable sites that reside side by side with reputable sites. Anyone with a computer and an Internet connection can publish anything on the Web. Unlike library-based research, information at many sites has not undergone the editing or scrutiny of scholarly publication procedures. The information we read in journals and most reputable magazines is reviewed, authenticated, and evaluated. That's why we have learned to trust these sources as valid and authoritative. But information on the Web is much less reliable. Some sites exist to distribute propaganda; others want to sell you something. To use the Web meaningfully, you must scrutinize what you find. For comprehensive, updated information and links to guide you in evaluating Web sources, check this book's Web site at <**www.businesscommunication-4th.nelson.com**> (click on *Search Tools*). Here are specific questions to ask as you examine a site.

- **Currency.** What is the date of the Web page? When was it last updated? Is some of the information obviously out of date? If the information is time-sensitive and the site has not been updated recently, the site is probably not reliable.

- **Authority.** Who publishes or sponsors this Web page? What makes the presenter an authority? Is a contact address available for the presenter? Learn to be skeptical about data and assertions from individuals whose credentials are not verifiable.

- **Content.** Is the purpose of the page to entertain, inform, convince, or sell? Who is the intended audience, based on content, tone, and style? Can you judge the overall value of the content compared with the other resources on this topic? Web presenters with a slanted point of view cannot be counted on for objective data.

- **Accuracy.** Do the facts that are presented seem reliable to you? Do you find errors in spelling, grammar, or usage? Do you see any evidence of bias? Are footnotes provided? If you find numerous errors and if facts are not referenced, you should be alerted that the data may be questionable.

## GATHERING INFORMATION FROM PRIMARY SOURCES

Up to this point, we've been talking about secondary data. You should begin nearly every business report assignment by probing for secondary data. However, you'll probably need primary data to give a complete picture. Business reports that solve specific current problems typically rely on primary, firsthand data. If, for example, management wants to discover the cause of increased employee turnover in its Saskatoon office, it must investigate conditions in Saskatoon by collecting recent information. Providing answers to business problems often means generating primary data through surveys, interviews, observation, or experimentation.

*4*

*Primary data comes from first-hand experience.*

### Surveys

Surveys collect data from groups of people. When companies develop new products, for example, they often survey consumers to learn their needs. The advantages of surveys are that they gather data economically and efficiently. Mailed surveys reach big groups nearby or at great distances. Moreover, people responding to mailed surveys have time to consider their answers, thus improving the accuracy of the data.

Mailed questionnaires, of course, have disadvantages. Most of us rank them with junk mail, so response rates may be no higher than 10 percent. Furthermore, those who do respond may not represent an accurate sample of the overall population, thus invalidating generalizations from the group. Let's say, for example, that an insurance company sends out a questionnaire asking about provisions in a new policy. If only older people respond, the questionnaire data cannot be used to generalize what people in other age groups might think. A final problem with surveys has to do with truthfulness. Some respondents exaggerate their incomes or distort other facts, thus causing the results to be unreliable. Nevertheless, surveys may be the

*Surveys yield efficient and economical primary data for reports.*

*Although mailed surveys may suffer low response rates, they are still useful in generating primary data.*

best way to generate data for business and student reports. In preparing print or electronic surveys, consider these pointers:

- **Explain why the survey is necessary.** In a cover letter or an opening paragraph, describe the need for the survey. Suggest how someone or something other than you will benefit. If appropriate, offer to send recipients a copy of the findings.

- **Consider incentives.** If the survey is long, persuasive techniques may be necessary. Response rates can be increased by offering money (such as a loonie), coupons, gift certificates, free books, or other gifts.

- **Limit the number of questions.** Resist the temptation to ask for too much. Request only information you will use. Don't, for example, include demographic questions (income, gender, age, and so forth) unless the information is necessary to evaluate responses.

**Effective surveys target appropriate samples and ask a limited number of specific questions with quantifiable answers.**

- **Use questions that produce quantifiable answers.** Check-off, multiple-choice, yes-no, and scale (or rank-order) questions (illustrated in Figure 12.9) provide quantifiable data that are easily tabulated. Responses to open-ended questions (*What should the bookstore do about plastic bags?*) reveal interesting, but difficult-to-quantify, perceptions.[19] To obtain workable data, give interviewees a list of possible responses (as shown in items 5–8 of Figure 12.9). For scale and multiple-choice questions, try to present all the possible answer choices. To be safe, add an "Other" or "Don't know" category in case the choices seem insufficient to the respondent. Many surveys use scale questions because they capture degrees of feelings. Typical scale headings are "agree strongly," "agree somewhat," "neutral," "disagree somewhat," and "disagree strongly."

Internet interviewing is becoming a dominant force in gathering survey data from large groups of people. It's cheaper, faster, and more consistent than mall intercepts, face-to-face interviews, and focus groups. Internet sessions reduce interviewer error, can be self-administered, and are less intrusive than other methods.

**The way a question is stated influences its response.**

- **Avoid leading or ambiguous questions.** The wording of a question can dramatically affect responses to it, as shown in a *New York Times*/CBS national poll.[20] When respondents were asked "Are we spending too much, too little, or about the right amount on *assistance to the poor* [emphasis added]?" 13 percent responded "too much." When the same respondents were asked "Are we spending too much, too little, or about the right amount on *welfare* [emphasis added]?" 44 percent responded "too much." Because words have different meanings for different people, you must strive to use objective language and pilot test your questions with typical respondents. Stay away from questions that suggest an answer (*Don't you agree that the salaries of CEOs are obscenely high?*). Instead, ask neutral questions (*Do CEOs earn too much, too little, or about the right amount?*). Also avoid queries that really ask two or more things (*Should the salaries of CEOs be reduced or regulated by government legislation?*). Instead, break them into separate questions (*Should the salaries of CEOs be regulated by government legislation? Should the salaries of CEOs be reduced by government legislation?*).

**The larger the sample, the more accurate the resulting data is likely to be.**

- **Select the survey population carefully.** Many surveys question a small group of people (a sample) and project the findings to a larger population. Let's say that a survey of your class reveals that the majority prefer deep-dish pizza. Can you then say with confidence that all students on your campus (or in the nation) prefer deep-dish pizza? To be able to generalize from a survey, you need to make the sample as large as possible. In addition, you need to determine whether the sample is like the larger population. For important surveys you will want to consult books on or experts in sampling techniques.

**FIGURE 12.9  Preparing a Survey**

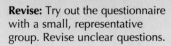

### Prewriting 1

**Analyze:** The purpose is to help the bookstore decide whether it should replace plastic bags with cloth bags for customer purchases.

**Anticipate:** The audience will be busy students who will be initially uninterested.

**Adapt:** Because students will be unwilling to participate, the survey must be short and simple. Its purpose must be significant and clear.

### Writing 2

**Research:** Ask students how they would react to cloth bags. Use their answers to form response choices.

**Organize:** Open by explaining the survey's purpose and importance. In the body ask clear questions that produce quantifiable answers. Conclude with appreciation and instructions.

**Compose:** Write the first draft of the questionnaire.

### Revising 3

**Revise:** Try out the questionnaire with a small, representative group. Revise unclear questions.

**Proofread:** Read for correctness. Be sure that answer choices do not overlap and that they are complete. Provide "other" category if appropriate (as in No. 9).

**Evaluate:** Is the survey clear, attractive, and easy to complete?

---

#### *North Shore College Bookstore*
#### STUDENT SURVEY

The North Shore College Bookstore wants to do its part in protecting the environment. Each year we give away 45 000 plastic bags for students to carry off their purchases. We are considering changing from plastic to cloth bags or some other alternative, but we need your views. ● — **Explains need for survey (use cover letter for longer surveys)**

Please place checks below to indicate your responses.

**Uses groupings that do not overlap (not 9 to 15 and 15 or more)** — ● 1. How many units are you presently carrying?
    \_\_\_ 15 or more units             \_\_\_ Male
    \_\_\_ 9 to 14 units               \_\_\_ Female
    \_\_\_ 8 or fewer units

2. How many times have you visited the bookstore this semester?
    \_\_\_ 0 times   \_\_\_ 1 time   \_\_\_ 2 times   \_\_\_ 3 times   \_\_\_ 4 or more times

3. Indicate your concern for the environment.
    \_\_\_ Very concerned   \_\_\_ Concerned   \_\_\_ Unconcerned

4. To protect the environment, would you be willing to change to another type of bag when buying books?
    \_\_\_ Yes
    \_\_\_ No

Indicate your feeling about the following alternatives.

|  | Agree | Undecided | Disagree |
|---|---|---|---|

For major purchases the bookstore should

| | Agree | Undecided | Disagree |
|---|---|---|---|
| 5. Continue to provide plastic bags. | \_\_\_ | \_\_\_ | \_\_\_ |
| 6. Provide no bags; encourage students to bring their own bags. | \_\_\_ | \_\_\_ | \_\_\_ |
| 7. Provide no bags; offer cloth bags at reduced price (about $3). | \_\_\_ | \_\_\_ | \_\_\_ |
| 8. Give a cloth bag with each major purchase, the cost to be included in registration fees. | \_\_\_ | \_\_\_ | \_\_\_ |

**Uses scale questions to channel responses into quantifiable alternatives, as opposed to open-ended questions**

**Allows respondent to add an answer in case choices provided seem insufficient** — ● 9. Consider another alternative, such as

_____

Please return the completed survey form to your instructor or to the survey box at the North Shore College Bookstore exit. Your opinion counts. ● — **Tells how to return survey form**

*Thanks for your help!*

- **Conduct a pilot study.** Try the questionnaire with a small group so that you can remedy any problems. For example, in the survey shown in Figure 12.9, a pilot study revealed that female students generally favoured cloth book bags and were willing to pay for them. Male students opposed purchasing cloth bags. By adding a gender category, researchers could verify this finding. The pilot study also revealed the need to ensure an appropriate representation of male and female students in the survey.

## Interviews

Interviews with experts yield useful report data, especially when little has been written about a topic.

Some of the best report information, particularly on topics about which little has been written, comes from individuals. These individuals are usually experts or veterans in their fields. Consider both in-house and outside experts for business reports. Tapping these sources will call for in-person, telephone, or online interviews. To elicit the most useful data, try these techniques:

- **Locate an expert.** Ask managers and individuals working in an area whom they consider to be most knowledgeable. Check membership lists of professional organizations, and consult articles about the topic or related topics. Most people enjoy being experts or at least recommending them. You could also post an inquiry to an Internet *newsgroup*. An easy way to search newsgroups in a topic area is through the browse groups now indexed by the popular search tool Google.

- **Prepare for the interview.** Learn about the individual you're interviewing as well as the background and terminology of the topic. Let's say you're interviewing a corporate communication expert about producing an in-house newsletter. You ought to be familiar with terms like *font* and software like QuarkXpress, Adobe Pagemaker, and Ventura Publisher. In addition, be prepared by making a list of questions that pinpoint your focus on the topic. Ask the interviewee if you may record the talk.

- **Make your questions objective and friendly.** Don't get into a debating match with the interviewee. And remember that you're there to listen, not to talk! Use open-ended, rather than yes-or-no, questions to draw experts out.

- **Watch the time.** Tell interviewees in advance how much time you expect to need for the interview. Don't overstay your appointment.

- **End graciously.** Conclude the interview with a general question, such as "Is there anything you'd like to add?" Express your appreciation, and ask permission to telephone later if you need to verify points.

## Observation and Experimentation

Some of the best report data come from firsthand observation and investigation.

Some kinds of primary data can be obtained only through firsthand observation and investigation. How long does a typical caller wait before a customer service rep answers the call? How is a new piece of equipment operated? Are complaints of sexual harassment being taken seriously? Observation produces rich data, but that information is especially prone to charges of subjectivity. One can interpret an observation in many ways. Thus, to make observations more objective, try to quantify them. For example, record customer telephone wait-time for 60-minute periods at different times throughout a week. Or compare the number of sexual harassment complaints made with the number of investigations undertaken and the resulting action.

Experimentation produces data suggesting causes and effects. Informal experimentation might be as simple as a pretest and posttest in a college course. Did students expand their knowledge as a result of the course? More formal experimentation is undertaken by scientists and professional researchers who control variables to test their effects. Assume, for example, that Cadbury Chocolate Canada Inc. wants to test the hypothesis (which is a tentative assumption) that chocolate lifts people out of the doldrums. An experiment testing the hypothesis would separate depressed individuals into two groups: those who ate chocolate (the experimental group) and those who did not (the control group). What effect did chocolate have? Such experiments are not done haphazardly, however. Valid experiments require sophisticated research designs and careful attention to matching the experimental and control groups.

## ILLUSTRATING DATA

After collecting information and interpreting it, you need to consider how best to present it to your audience. Whether you are delivering your report orally or in writing to company insiders or to outsiders, it will be easier to understand and remember if you include suitable graphics. Appropriate graphics make numerical data meaningful, simplify complex ideas, and provide visual interest. In contrast, readers tend to be bored and confused by text paragraphs packed with complex data and numbers. The same information summarized in a table or chart becomes clear. Tables, charts, graphs, pictures, and other graphics perform three important functions:

*5*

**Effective graphics clarify numerical data and simplify complex ideas.**

* They clarify data.
* They condense and simplify data.
* They emphasize data.

Because the same data can be shown in many different forms (for example, in a chart, table, or graph), you need to recognize how to match the appropriate graphic with your objective. In addition, you need to know how to incorporate graphics into your reports.

## Matching Graphics and Objectives

In developing the best graphics, you must first decide what data you want to highlight. Chances are you will have many points you would like to show in a table or chart. But which graphics are most appropriate for your objectives? Tables? Bar charts? Pie charts? Line charts? Surface charts? Flow charts? Organization charts? Pictures? Figure 12.10 summarizes appropriate uses for each type of graphic. The following text discusses each visual in more detail.

*Tables.* Probably the most frequently used graphic in reports is the table. Because a table presents quantitative or verbal information in systematic columns and rows, it can clarify large quantities of data in small spaces. You may have made rough tables to help you organize the raw data collected from literature, questionnaires, or interviews. In preparing tables for your readers or listeners, though, you'll need to pay more attention to clarity and emphasis. Here are tips for making good tables, one of which is illustrated in Figure 12.11:

**Tables permit the systematic presentation of large amounts of data, while charts enhance visual comparisons.**

* Provide clear heads for the rows and columns.
* Identify the units in which figures are given (percentages, dollars, units per worker hour, and so forth) in the table title, in the column or row head, with the first item in a column, or in a note at the bottom.

## FIGURE 12.10  Matching Graphics to Objectives

Selecting an appropriate graphic form depends on the purpose that it serves.

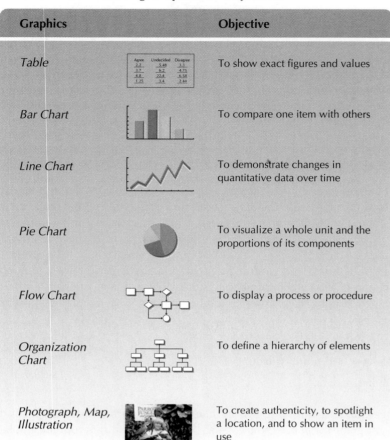

| Graphics | Objective |
|---|---|
| Table | To show exact figures and values |
| Bar Chart | To compare one item with others |
| Line Chart | To demonstrate changes in quantitative data over time |
| Pie Chart | To visualize a whole unit and the proportions of its components |
| Flow Chart | To display a process or procedure |
| Organization Chart | To define a hierarchy of elements |
| Photograph, Map, Illustration | To create authenticity, to spotlight a location, and to show an item in use |

- Place titles and labels at the top of the table.

- Arrange items in a logical order (alphabetical, chronological, geographical, highest to lowest) depending on what you need to emphasize.

- Use *N/A* (not available) for missing data.

## FIGURE 12.11  Table Summarizing Precise Data

### Figure 1
### MPM ENTERTAINMENT COMPANY
### Income by Division (in millions of dollars)

| | THEME PARKS | MOTION PICTURES | VIDEO | TOTAL |
|---|---|---|---|---|
| 2000 | $15.8 | $39.3 | $11.2 | $66.3 |
| 2001 | 18.1 | 17.5 | 15.3 | 50.9 |
| 2002 | 23.8 | 21.1 | 22.7 | 67.6 |
| 2003 | 32.2 | 22.0 | 24.3 | 78.5 |
| 2004 (projected) | 35.1 | 21.0 | 26.1 | 82.2 |

**Source:** *AET Predictors Research* (Toronto: CompDat, 2003), 225.

- Make long tables easier to read by shading alternate lines or by leaving a blank line after groups of five.

- Place tables as close as possible to the place where they are mentioned in the text.

Figure 12.10 shows how various graphics are effective in serving different purposes. Tables, as illustrated in Figure 12.11, are especially suitable in illustrating exact figures in systematic rows and columns. Figures 12.12 through 12.15 illustrate vertical, horizontal, grouped, and segmented bar charts, all of which can achieve different effects.

***Bar Charts.*** Although they lack the precision of tables, bar charts enable you to make emphatic visual comparisons. Bar charts can be used to compare related items, illustrate changes in data over time, and show segments as part of a whole. Figures 12.12 through 12.15 show vertical, horizontal, grouped, and segmented bar charts that highlight some of the data shown in the MPM Entertainment Company table (Figure 12.11). Note how the varied bar charts present information in differing ways.

## FIGURE 12.12  Vertical Bar Chart

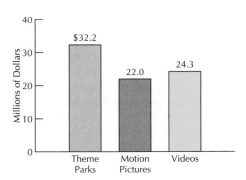

**Figure 1**

**2003 MPM INCOME BY DIVISION**

**Source:** *AET Predictors Research* (Toronto: CompDat, 2003), 225.

## FIGURE 12.13  Horizontal Bar Chart

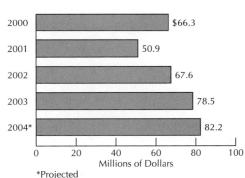

**Figure 2**

**TOTAL MPM INCOME, 2000 TO 2004**

*Projected
**Source:** *AET Predictors Research* (Toronto: CompDat, 2003), 225.

## FIGURE 12.14  Grouped Bar Chart

**Figure 3**

**MPM INCOME BY DIVISION
2000, 2002, AND 2004**

**Source:** *AET Predictors Research* (Toronto: CompDat, 2003), 225.

## FIGURE 12.15  Segmented 100% Bar Chart

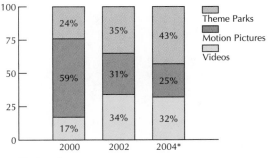

**Figure 4**

**PERCENTAGE OF TOTAL INCOME BY DIVISION
2000, 2002, 2004**

*Projected
**Source:** *AET Predictors Research* (Toronto: CompDat, 2003), 225.

Many techniques for constructing tables also hold true for bar charts. Here are a few additional tips:

- Keep the length of each bar and segment proportional.
- Include a total figure in the middle of a bar or at its end if the figure helps the reader and does not clutter the chart.
- Start dollar or percentage amounts at zero.
- Avoid showing too much information, thus producing clutter and confusion.
- Place each bar chart as close as possible to the place where it is mentioned in the text.

**Line charts illustrate trends and changes in data over time.**

***Line Charts.*** The major advantage of line charts is that they show changes over time, thus indicating trends. Simple line charts (Figure 12.16) show just one variable. Multiple-line charts combine several variables (Figure 12.17). Segmented line charts (Figure 12.18), also called surface charts, illustrate how the components of a whole change over time.

Here are tips for preparing a line chart:

- Begin with a grid divided into squares.
- Arrange the time component (usually years) horizontally across the bottom; arrange values for the other variable vertically.
- Draw small dots at the intersections to indicate each value at a given year.
- Connect the dots and add colour if desired.
- To prepare a segmented (surface) chart, plot the first value (say, video income) across the bottom; add the next item (say, motion picture income) to the first figures for every increment; for the third item (say, theme park income) add its value to the total of the first two items. The top line indicates the total of the three values.

**Pie charts are most useful in showing the proportion of parts to a whole.**

***Pie Charts.*** Pie, or circle, charts enable readers to see a whole and the proportion of its components, or wedges. Although less flexible than bar or line charts, pie charts are useful in showing percentages, as Figure 12.19 illustrates. Notice that a wedge can be "exploded" or popped out for special emphasis, as seen in Figure 12.19.

**FIGURE 12.16  Simple Line Chart**

**FIGURE 12.17  Multiple-Line Chart**

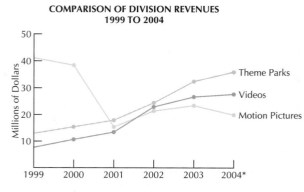

Figure 5
MOTION PICTURE REVENUES
1999 TO 2004

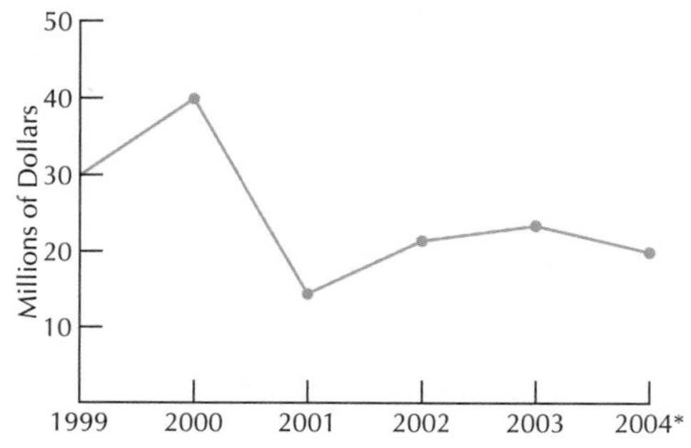

*Projected
**Source:** *AET Predictors Research* (Toronto: CompDat, 2003), 225.

Figure 6
COMPARISON OF DIVISION REVENUES
1999 TO 2004

*Projected
**Source:** *AET Predictors Research* (Toronto: CompDat, 2003), 225.

**FIGURE 12.18 Segmented Line (Surface) Chart**

Figure 7

COMPARISON OF DIVISION REVENUES
1999 TO 2004

100
80
60
40
20
Millions of Dollars
Theme Parks
Motion Pictures
Videos
1999
2000
2001
2002
2003
2004*
Year

*Projected

**Source:** *AET Predictors Research* (Toronto: CompDat, 2003), 225.

**FIGURE 12.19 Pie Chart**

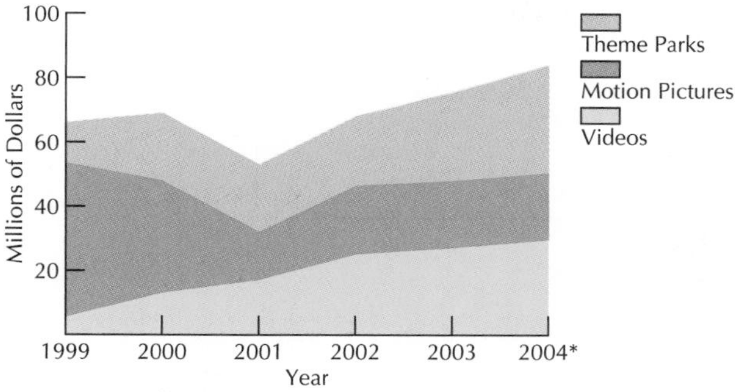

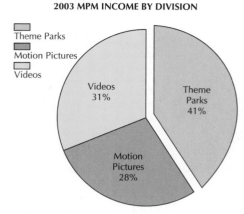

Figure 8

2003 MPM INCOME BY DIVISION

Theme Parks
Motion Pictures
Videos
Videos 31%
Theme Parks 41%
Motion Pictures 28%

**Source:** *AET Predictors Research* (Toronto: CompDat, 2003), 225.

For the most effective pie charts, follow these suggestions:

- Begin at the 12 o'clock position, drawing the largest wedge first. (Computer software programs don't always observe this advice, but if you're drawing your own charts, you can.)
- Include, if possible, the actual percentage or absolute value for each wedge.
- Use four to eight segments for best results; if necessary, group small portions into one wedge called "Other."
- Distinguish wedges with colour, shading, or crosshatching.
- Keep all the labels horizontal.

Many software programs help you prepare professional-looking charts with a minimum of effort. See the Tech Talk box on page 393 for more information.

***Flow Charts.*** Procedures are simplified and clarified by diagramming them in a flow chart, as shown in Figure 12.20. Whether you need to describe the procedure for handling a customer's purchase order or outline steps in solving a problem, flow charts help the reader visualize the process. Traditional flow charts use the following symbols:

- Ovals to designate the beginning and end of a process
- Diamonds to denote decision points
- Rectangles to represent major activities or steps

**Organization charts show the line of command and thus the flow of official communication from management to employees.**

***Organization Charts.*** Many large organizations are so complex that they need charts to show the chain of command, from the boss down to line managers and employees. Organization charts like the one in Figure 1.10 in Chapter 1 provide such information as who reports to whom, how many subordinates work for each manager (the span of control), and what channels of official communication exist. They may also illustrate a company's structure (by function, customer, or product, for example), the work being performed in each job, and the hierarchy of decision making.

**FIGURE 12.20  Flow Chart**

**FLOW OF CUSTOMER ORDER THROUGH
XYZ COMPANY**

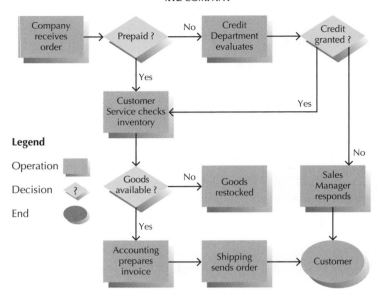

**Legend**

Operation

Decision  ?

End

**Photographs, Maps, and Illustrations.** Some business reports include photographs, maps, and illustrations to serve specific purposes. Photos, for example, add authenticity and provide a visual record. An environmental engineer may use photos to document hazardous waste sites. Maps enable report writers to depict activities or concentrations geographically, such as dots indicating sales reps in provinces across the country. Illustrations and diagrams are useful in indicating how an object looks or operates. A drawing showing the parts of a DVD player with labels describing their functions, for example, is more instructive than a photograph or verbal description. With today's computer technology, photographs, maps, and illustrations can be scanned directly into business reports.

**Computer technology permits photographs, maps, and illustrations to be scanned directly into a report.**

Many businesspeople recognize the value of ongoing research and reporting. It is crucial to collect data not only about the performance of your own company but also about that of the competition.

# Using Your Computer to Produce Charts

Designing effective bar charts, pie charts, figures, and other images has never been easier than it is now with the use of computer graphics programs.

Spreadsheet programs—such as Excel, Lotus 1-2-3, and Corel QuattroPro—and presentation graphics programs—such as Microsoft PowerPoint—allow even nontechnical people to design quality graphics. These graphics can be printed directly on paper for written reports or used for transparency masters and slides for oral presentations. The benefits of preparing graphics on a computer are near-professional quality, shorter preparation time, and substantial savings in preparation costs.

To prepare a computer graphic, begin by assembling your data, usually in table form. Let's say you work for Dynamo Products, and you prepared Table 1 below showing the number of Dynamo computers sold in each region for each quarter of the fiscal year.

Next, you must decide what type of chart you want: pie chart, grouped bar chart, vertical bar chart, horizontal bar chart, organization chart, or some other graphic. To make a pie chart showing total computers sold by division for the year, key in the data or select the data from an existing file. Add a title for the chart, as well as any necessary labels. For a bar or line chart, indicate the horizontal and vertical axes (reference lines or beginning points). Most programs will automatically generate legends for figures. If you wish, however, you can easily customize titles and legends.

The finished chart can be printed on paper or inserted into your word processing document to be printed with your finished report. The pie chart and bar chart shown here were created in a spreadsheet program and inserted into a word processing program.

Another useful feature of most word processing programs involves inserting and linking worksheets. Our table showing the total number of computers sold could be created by inserting an Excel worksheet into a Word document. The result is a nicely arranged, easy-to-read table. The table can also be "linked" to the spreadsheet program so that the latest changes made in the worksheet will be automatically reflected in the table as it appears in the word processing document.

## Career Application

Visit your local software dealer and ask for a demonstration of how to create a pie or bar chart using a computer graphics program. Ask the salesperson to print out a copy of the visual (on a colour printer, if available) for you to bring to class for discussion.

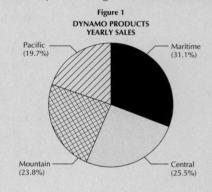

**Figure 1**
**DYNAMO PRODUCTS YEARLY SALES**

Pacific (19.7%), Maritime (31.1%), Mountain (23.8%), Central (25.5%)

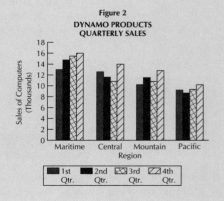

**Figure 2**
**DYNAMO PRODUCTS QUARTERLY SALES**

**Table 1**
**DYNAMO PRODUCTS**
**NUMBER OF COMPUTERS SOLD**

| Region | 1st Qtr. | 2nd Qtr. | 3rd Qtr. | 4th Qtr. | Yearly Totals |
|---|---|---|---|---|---|
| Maritime | 13 302 | 15 003 | 15 550 | 16 210 | 60 065 |
| Central | 12 678 | 11 836 | 10 689 | 14 136 | 49 339 |
| Mountain | 10 345 | 11 934 | 10 899 | 12 763 | 45 941 |
| Pacific | 9 345 | 8 921 | 9 565 | 10 256 | 38 087 |
| Total | 45 670 | 47 694 | 46 703 | 53 365 | 193 432 |

## Incorporating Graphics into Reports

Used appropriately, graphics make reports more interesting and easier to understand. In putting graphics into your reports, follow these suggestions for best effects.

**Effective graphics are accurate and ethical, avoid overuse of colour or decorations, and include titles.**

- **Evaluate the audience.** Evaluate the reader, the content, your schedule, and your budget (graphics take time and money to prepare) in deciding how many graphics to use. Six charts in an internal report to an executive may seem like overkill; but in a long technical report to outsiders, six may be too few.

- **Use restraint.** Don't overuse colour or decorations. Although colour can effectively distinguish bars or segments in charts, too much colour can be distracting and confusing. Remember, too, that colours themselves sometimes convey meaning: reds suggest deficits or negative values, blues suggest coolness, and oranges may mean warmth.

- **Be accurate and ethical.** Double-check all graphics for accuracy of figures and calculations. Be certain that your visuals aren't misleading—either accidentally or intentionally. Manipulation of a chart scale can make trends look steeper and more dramatic than they really are. Also, be sure to cite sources when you use someone else's facts. The accompanying Ethical Insights box discusses in more detail how to make ethical charts and graphics.

**Textual graphics should be introduced by statements that help readers interpret them.**

- **Introduce a graphic meaningfully.** Refer to every graphic in the text, and place the graphic close to the point where it is mentioned. Most important, though, help the reader understand the significance of a graphic. You can do this by telling the reader what to look for or by summarizing the main point of a graphic. Don't assume the reader will automatically draw the same conclusions you reached from a set of data. Instead of *The findings are shown in Figure 3*, tell the reader what to look for: *Two thirds of the responding employees, as shown in Figure 3, favour a flextime schedule.* The best introductions for graphics interpret them for readers.

- **Choose an appropriate caption or title style.** Like reports, graphics may use "talking" titles or generic, descriptive titles. "Talking" titles are more persuasive; they tell the reader what to think. Descriptive titles describe the facts more objectively.

**Talking Title**
Average Annual Health Care Costs per Worker Rise Steeply as Workers Grow Older

**Descriptive Title**
Average Annual Health Care Costs per Worker as Shown by Age Groups

Judge the style you should use by your audience and your company's preferences. Regardless of the style, make the titles consistent and specific.

## DOCUMENTING DATA

In writing business and other reports, you will often build on the ideas and words of others. In Western culture whenever you "borrow" the ideas of others, you must give credit to your information sources. This is called *documentation.*

## Purposes of Documentation

As a careful writer, you should take pains to properly document report data for the following reasons:

## Making Ethical Charts and Graphics

**B**usiness communicators must present graphical data in the same ethical, honest manner required for all other messages. Remember that the information shown in your charts and graphics will be used to inform others or help them make decisions. If this information is not represented accurately, the reader will be incorrectly informed; any decisions based on the data are likely to be faulty. And mistakes in interpreting such information may have serious and long-lasting consequences.

Chart data can be distorted in many ways. Figure 1 shows advertising expenses displayed on an appropriate scale. Figure 2 shows the same information, but the horizontal scale, from 1999 to 2004, has been lengthened. Notice that the data have not changed, but the increases and decreases are smoothed out, so changes in expenses appear to be slight. In Figure 3 the vertical scale is taller and the horizontal scale is shortened, resulting in what appear to be sharp increases and decreases in expenses.

To avoid misrepresenting data, keep the following pointers in mind when designing your graphics:

- Use an appropriate type of chart or graphic for the message you wish to convey.

- Design the chart so that it focuses on the appropriate information.

- Include all relevant or important data; don't arbitrarily leave out necessary information.

- Don't hide critical information by including too much data in one graphic.

- Use appropriate scales with equal intervals for the data you present.

**Career Application**

Locate one or two graphics in a newspaper, magazine article, or annual report. Analyze the strengths and weaknesses of each graphic. Is the information presented accurately? Select a bar or line chart. Sketch the same chart but change the vertical or horizontal scales on the graphic. How does the message of the chart change?

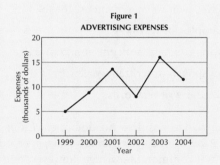

Figure 1
ADVERTISING EXPENSES

Figure 2
ADVERTISING EXPENSES

Figure 3
ADVERTISING EXPENSES

- **To strengthen your argument.** Including good data from reputable sources will convince readers of your credibility and the logic of your reasoning.

- **To protect you from charges of plagiarism.** Acknowledging your sources keeps you honest. Plagiarism, which is illegal and unethical, is the act of using others' ideas without proper documentation.

- **To instruct the reader.** Citing references enables readers to pursue a topic further and make use of the information themselves.

**Documenting data lends credibility, protects the writer from plagiarism, and aids the reader.**

## Academic Documentation vs. Business Documentation

In the academic world documentation is critical. Especially in the humanities and sciences, students are taught to cite sources by using quotation marks, parenthetical citations, footnotes, and bibliographies. Academic term papers require full documentation to demonstrate that a student has become familiar with respected sources and can cite them properly in developing an argument. Giving credit to the author is extremely important. Students who plagiarize risk a failing grade in a class and even expulsion from school.

**Business writers may not follow the same strict documentation standards as academic writers.**

In the business world, however, documentation is often viewed differently. Business communicators on the job may find that much of what is written does not follow the standards they learned in school.[21] In many instances, individual authorship is unimportant. For example, employees may write for the signature of their bosses. The writer receives no credit. Similarly, team projects turn out documents written by many people, none of whom receives individual credit. Internal business reports, which often include chunks of information from previous reports, also fail to acknowledge sources or give credit. Even information from outside sources may lack proper documentation. Yet, if facts are questioned, business writers must be able to produce their source materials.

Although both internal and external business reports are not as heavily documented as school assignments or term papers, business communication students are well-advised to learn proper documentation methods. Being accused of plagiarism is a serious charge and can lead to loss of a job if ideas or words are used without giving credit. You can avoid charges of plagiarism as well as add clarity to your work by knowing what to document and developing good research habits.

## Learning What to Document

When you write reports, especially in college or university, you are continually dealing with other people's ideas. You are expected to conduct research, synthesize ideas, and build on the work of others. But you are also expected to give proper credit for borrowed material. To avoid plagiarism, you must give credit whenever you use the following:[22]

**Give credit when you use another's ideas, when you borrow facts that are not common knowledge, and when you quote or paraphrase another's words.**

- Another person's ideas, opinions, examples, or theory
- Any facts, statistics, graphs, and drawings that are not common knowledge
- Quotations of another person's actual spoken or written words
- Paraphrases of another person's spoken or written words

Information that is common knowledge requires no documentation. For example, the statement *The Globe and Mail is a popular business newspaper* would require no citation. Statements that are not common knowledge, however, must be documented. For example, *The Globe and Mail is the largest daily newspaper in Canada* would require a citation because most people do not know this fact. Cite sources for proprietary information such as statistics organized and reported by a newspaper or magazine. Also use citations to document direct quotations and ideas that you summarize in your own words.

## Developing Good Manual and Electronic Research Habits

Report writers who are gathering information have two methods available for recording the information they find. The time-honoured manual method of notetaking works well because information is recorded on separate cards, which can then be arranged in the order needed to develop a thesis or argument. Today, though, writers rely heavily on electronic researching. Traditional notetaking methods may seem antiquated and laborious in comparison. Let's explore both methods.

*Manual Notetaking.* To make sure you know whose ideas you are using, train yourself to take excellent notes. If possible, know what you intend to find before you begin your research so that you won't waste time on unnecessary notes. Here are some pointers on taking good notes.

* Record all major ideas from various sources on separate note cards.

* Include all publication data along with precise quotations.

* Consider using one card colour for direct quotes and a different colour for your paraphrases and summaries.

* Put the original source material aside when you are summarizing or paraphrasing.

*Electronic Notetaking.* Instead of recording facts on note cards, smart researchers today take advantage of electronic tools. Beware, though, not to cut-and-paste your way into plagiarism. A recent study at a Canadian university revealed that the number of plagiarism cases between 1992 and 2002 had increased nearly 180 percent. Furthermore, almost all of the plagiarism cases involved material taken from the Web, compared with only half of the cases five years previously.[23]

* Begin your research by setting up a folder on your hard drive or on a floppy. Create subfolders for major topics, such as introduction, body, and closing.

* When you find facts on the Web or in electronic databases, highlight the material you want to record, copy it, and paste it into a document in an appropriate folder.

* Be sure to include all publication data.

* Consider archiving on a zip disk those Web pages or articles used in your research in case the data must be verified.

## Developing the Fine Art of Paraphrasing

In writing reports and using the ideas of others, you will probably rely heavily on *paraphrasing*, which means restating an original passage in your own words and in your own style. To do a good job of paraphrasing, follow these steps:

* Read the original material intently to comprehend its full meaning.

* Write your own version without looking at the original.

* Do not repeat the grammatical structure of the original, and do not merely replace words with synonyms.

* Reread the original to be sure you covered the main points but did not borrow specific language.

    To better understand the difference between plagiarizing and paraphrasing, study the following passages. Notice that the writer of the plagiarized version uses the same grammatical construction as the source and often merely replaces words with synonyms. Even the acceptable version, however, requires a reference to the source author.

**Source**
The collapse in the cost of computing has made cellular communication economically viable. Worldwide, one in two new phone subscriptions is cellular. The digital revolution in telephony is most advanced in poorer countries because they have been able to skip an outdated technological step relying on land lines.

**Handwritten note cards help writers identify sources and organize ideas.**

**Set up a folder for electronic notes, but be careful not to cut-and-paste excessively in writing reports.**

**Paraphrasing involves putting an original passage into your own words.**

**Plagiarized version**
The drop in computing costs now makes cellular communication affordable around the world. In fact, one out of every two new phones is cellular. The digital revolution in cellular telephones is developing faster in poorer countries because they could skip an outdated technological process using land lines.

**Acceptable paraphrase**
Cellular phone use around the world is increasing rapidly as a result of decreasing computing costs. Half of all new phones are now wireless. Poorer countries are experiencing the most rapid development because they can move straight to cellular without focusing on outdated technology using land lines (Henderson 44).

*The plagiarized version uses the same sentence structure as the original and makes few changes other than replacing some words.*

*The acceptable paraphrase presents ideas from a different perspective and uses a different sentence structure than the original.*

## Knowing When and How to Quote

On occasion you will want to use the exact words of a source. But beware of overusing quotations. Documents that contain pages of spliced-together quotations suggest that writers have few ideas of their own. Wise writers and speakers use direct quotations for three purposes only:

- To provide objective background data and establish the severity of a problem as seen by experts
- To repeat identical phrasing because of its precision, clarity, or aptness
- To duplicate exact wording before criticizing

*Use quotations only to provide background data, to cite experts, to repeat precise phrasing, or to duplicate exact wording before criticizing.*

When you must use a long quotation, try to summarize and introduce it in your own words. Readers want to know the gist of a quotation before they tackle it. For example, to introduce a quotation discussing the shrinking staffs of large companies, you could precede it with your words: *In predicting employment trends, Charles Waller believes the corporation of the future will depend on a small core of full-time employees.* To introduce quotations or paraphrases, use wording such as the following:

- According to Waller, . . . .
- Waller argues that . . . .
- In his recent study, Waller reported . . . .

Use quotation marks to enclose exact quotations, as shown in the following: "*The current image*," says Charles Waller, "*of a big glass-and-steel corporate headquarters on landscaped grounds directing a worldwide army of tens of thousands of employees may soon be a thing of the past.*"

## Using Citation Formats

*Guidelines for MLA and APA citation formats can be found in Appendix C; guidelines for electronic citations are at this book's Web site.*

You can direct readers to your sources with parenthetical notes inserted into the text and with bibliographies. The most common citation formats are those presented by the Modern Language Association (MLA) and the American Psychological Association (APA). Learn more about how to use these formats in Appendix C. For the most up-to-date citation formats for electronic references, check the Web site for this book at <**www.businesscommunication-4th.nelson.com**> (click "Study Resources" and go to "Documentation/Citation Style Guides"). You will find model citation formats for online magazine, newspaper, and journal articles, as well as for Web references.

# *Applying Your Skills at Statistics Canada*

*The Economist* magazine recognized Canada as the best statistics-keeping country of the industrialized world at the beginning of the 1990s. It looked at factors such as objectivity, reliability, methodology, and relevance. Statistics Canada continues to build on that trend and is acknowledged as a world leader in the gathering of information, providing models and methods to other organizations and countries.

Canadian information is also cited as being predictable and reliable. Statistics Canada releases its information at 8:30 a.m. in its bulletin, *The Daily*, unlike our American neighbours, where information is released at various times—some at 8:30 a.m., some at 9 a.m., and some at 10 a.m. StatsCan may be criticized about getting its information out more slowly than other countries; however, whereas other countries release and then revise, Canada waits until precise figures are available.[24]

The future of accessing and gathering information is electronic. "StatsCan Online," which was introduced in 1995, allows people to access databases. Most of the agency's thousands of charts, tables, and analyses are available online, making the information easily accessible for Canadians.[25]

Statistics Canada acknowledges that the transition to online data collection is the next logical step. Electronic reporting has the benefits of saving time, being convenient and available, and enhancing privacy. The prediction is that many Canadians, especially youth and businesses, may choose to complete surveys electronically. However, StatsCan wants to ensure that the cornerstones of confidentiality and privacy are not compromised, so pilot projects are being completed to ensure that these goals are met.[26]

## Your Task

You and several of your colleagues have been asked to help plan a report that analyzes some of the challenges of using electronic surveys in preparation for the 2006 census. There has been considerable study of Canadians' feelings toward new technology, and the Internet in particular, that shows that the population accepts change. Prepare a statement of purpose, sources and methods of data collection, tentative outline, and work schedule. The work schedule should cover approximately three weeks. Submit your recommendations in a memo or e-mail message to your instructor.

**www.statcan.ca**

# SUMMARY OF LEARNING OBJECTIVES

*1* **Describe business report basics, including functions, patterns, formats, and writing style.** Business reports generally function either as informational reports (without analysis or recommendations) or as analytical reports (with analysis, conclusions, and possibly recommendations). Reports organized directly present the purpose immediately. This pattern is appropriate when receivers are supportive and are familiar with the topic. Reports organized indirectly provide the conclusions and recommendations last. This pattern is helpful when receivers are unfamiliar with the problem or when they may be disappointed or hostile. Reports may be formatted as letters, memos, manuscripts, or prepared forms. Reports written in a formal style use third-person constructions, avoid contractions, and include many passive-voice verbs, complex sentences, and long words. Reports written informally use first-person constructions, contractions, shorter sentences, familiar words, and active-voice verbs.

**2** **Apply the 3-×-3 writing process to business reports.** Report writers begin by analyzing a problem and writing a problem statement, which may include the scope, significance, and limitations of the project. Writers then analyze the audience and define major issues. They prepare a work plan, including a tentative outline and work schedule. They collect, organize, interpret, and illustrate their data. Then they compose the first draft. Finally, they revise (perhaps many times), proofread, and evaluate.

**3** **Understand where to find and how to use print and electronic sources of secondary data.** Secondary data may be located by searching for books, periodicals, and newspapers through print or electronic indexes. Much report information today is located in electronic databases that are generally offered through professional information services such as Dialog and Lexis-Nexis. Much information is also available on the Internet, but searching for it requires knowledge of search tools and techniques. Popular search tools are Google, Yahoo!, and Alta-Vista. Information obtained on the Internet should be scrutinized for currency, authority, content, and accuracy.

**4** **Understand where to find and how to use sources of primary data.** Researchers generate firsthand, primary data through surveys (in-person, print, and online), interviews, observation, and experimentation. Surveys are most economical and efficient for gathering information from large groups of people. Interviews are useful when working with experts in a field. Firsthand observation can produce rich data, but it must be objective. Experimentation produces data suggesting causes and effects. Valid experiments require sophisticated research designs and careful attention to matching the experimental and control groups.

**5** **Illustrate reports with graphics that create meaning and interest.** Good graphics improve reports by clarifying, simplifying, and emphasizing data. Tables organize precise data into rows and columns. Bar and line charts enable data to be compared visually. Line charts are especially helpful in showing changes over time. Pie charts show a whole and the proportion of its components. Organization charts, pictures, maps, and illustrations serve specific purposes. In choosing or crafting graphics, smart communicators evaluate their audience, purpose, topic, and budget to determine the number and kind of graphics. They are consistent in writing "talking" titles (telling readers what to think about the graphic) or "descriptive" titles (summarizing the topic objectively).

**6** **Describe the purposes and techniques of documentation in business reports.** Documentation means giving credit to information sources. Careful writers document data to strengthen an argument, protect against charges of plagiarism, and instruct readers. Although documentation in business reports is less stringent than in academic reports, business writers should learn proper techniques to be able to verify their sources and to avoid charges of plagiarism. Report writers should document others' ideas, facts that are not common knowledge, quotations, and paraphrases. Good notetaking, either manual or electronic, enables writers to give accurate credit to sources. Paraphrasing involves putting another's ideas into your own words. Quotations may be used to provide objective background data, to repeat identical phrasing, and to duplicate exact wording before criticizing.

# CHAPTER REVIEW

1. What purpose do most reports serve? (Obj. 1)
2. How do informational and analytical reports differ? (Obj. 1)
3. How do the direct and indirect patterns of development differ? (Obj. 1)
4. Identify four common report formats. (Obj. 1)
5. List the seven steps in the report-writing process. (Obj. 2)
6. What is factoring? (Obj. 2)
7. How do primary data differ from secondary data? Give an original example of each. (Obj. 3)
8. Should data collection for most business reports begin with primary or secondary research? Why? (Obj. 3)
9. Discuss five techniques that you think are most useful in enhancing a Web search. (Obj. 3)
10. What are four major sources of primary information? (Obj. 4)
11. Why is a pilot study necessary before conducting a survey? (Obj. 4)
12. Briefly compare the advantages and disadvantages of illustrating data with charts (bar and line) versus tables. (Obj. 5)
13. What is the major advantage of using a pie chart to illustrate data? (Obj. 5)
14. What is documentation, and why is it necessary in reports? (Obj. 6)
15. Compare the advantages and disadvantages of manual notetaking and electronic notetaking. (Obj. 6)

# CRITICAL THINKING

1. Discuss this statement, made by three well-known professional business writers: "Nothing you write will be completely new."[27] (Objs. 1–4)
2. For long reports, why is a written work plan a wise idea? (Obj. 2)
3. Is information obtained on the Web as reliable as information obtained from journals, newspapers, and magazines? (Obj. 3)
4. Some people say that business reports never contain footnotes. If you were writing your first report for a business and you did considerable research, what would you do about documenting your sources? (Obj. 6)
5. **Ethical Issue:** Discuss this statement: "Let the facts speak for themselves." Are facts always truthful?

# ACTIVITIES

## 12.1 Report Functions, Writing Styles, and Formats (Obj. 1)

**Your Task.** For the following reports, (1) name the report's primary function (informational or analytical), (2) recommend a direct or indirect pattern of development, and (3) select a report format (memo, letter, or manuscript).

a. A persuasive proposal from a construction firm to the Ontario College of Art and Design describing the contractor's bid to construct the Sharp Pavilion, a controversial 15-storey table-top structure.
b. A report submitted by a sales rep to her manager describing her attendance at a sports products trade show, including the reactions of visitors to a new non-carbonated sports drink.
c. A recommendation report from a technical specialist to the vice president, Product Development, analyzing ways to prevent piracy of the software company's latest game program. The vice president values straight talk and is familiar with the project.
d. A progress report from a location manager to a Hollywood production company describing safety, fire, and environmental precautions taken for the shooting of a stunt involving blowing up a boat off the Toronto Islands.
e. A report prepared by an outside consultant examining whether a company should invest in a health and fitness centre for its employees.
f. A report from a national moving company telling provincial authorities how it has improved its safety program so that its trucks now comply with provincial regulations. The report describes but doesn't interpret the program.

## 12.2 Collaborative Project: Report Portfolio (Obj. 1)

**TEAM**

**Your Task.** In teams of three or four, collect four or more sample business reports illustrating various types of business reports. Don't forget corporate annual reports. For each report identify and discuss the following characteristics:

a. Function (informational or analytical)
b. Pattern (primarily direct or indirect)
c. Writing style (formal or informal)
d. Format (memo, letter, manuscript, preprinted form)
e. Effectiveness (clarity, accuracy, expression)

In an informational memo report to your instructor, describe your findings.

## 12.3 Data Forms and Questions (Obj. 3)

**Your Task.** In conducting research for the following reports, name at least one form of data you will need and the questions you should ask to determine whether that set of data is appropriate (see Figure 12.6).

a. A report evaluating the relocation of a Montreal company to Toronto. You find figures in a *Toronto Life* article showing the average cost of housing for 60 cities, including Montreal and Toronto.

b. A market research report to assess fan support for a name ("Raptors") and logo (a dinosaur holding a basketball) selected for a professional basketball team in Toronto.

c. A report examining the effectiveness of ethics codes in Canadian businesses.

## 12.4 Problem and Purpose Statements (Obj. 2)

**Your Task.** The following situations require reports. For each situation write (1) a concise problem question and (2) a simple statement of purpose.

a. The Confederation Bank is losing money on its Webster branch. A number of branches are being targeted for closure. Management authorizes a report that must recommend a course of action for the Webster branch.

b. New federal regulations have changed the definitions of common terms such as *fresh, fat free, low in cholesterol,* and *light.* The Big Deal Bakery worries that it must rewrite all its package labels. Big Deal doesn't know whether to hire a laboratory or a consultant for this project.

c. Customers placing telephone orders for clothing with James River Enterprises typically order only one or two items. JRE wonders whether it can train telephone service reps to motivate customers to increase the number of items ordered per call.

## 12.5 Problem and Purpose Statements (Obj. 2)

**Your Task.** Identify a problem in your current job or a previous job (such as inadequate equipment, inefficient procedures, poor customer service, poor product quality, or personnel problems). Assume your boss agrees with your criticism and asks you to prepare a report. Write (a) a two- or three-sentence statement describing the problem, (b) a problem question, and (c) a simple statement of purpose for your report.

## 12.6 Factoring and Outlining a Problem (Obj. 2)

**CRITICAL THINKING**

Japan Airlines has asked your company, Connections International, to prepare a proposal for a training school for tour operators. JAL wants to know whether Victoria would be a good spot for its school. Victoria interests JAL but only if nearby entertainment facilities can be used for tour training. JAL also needs an advisory committee consisting, if possible, of representatives of the travel community and perhaps executives of other major airlines. The real problem is how to motivate these people to cooperate with JAL.

You've heard that CBC Studios in Victoria offers training seminars, guest speakers, and other resources for tour operators. You wonder whether Magic Mountain in Vancouver would also be willing to cooperate with the proposed school. And you remember that Griffith Park is nearby and might make a good tour training spot. Before JAL will settle on Victoria as its choice, it wants to know whether access to air travel is adequate. It's also concerned about available school building space. Moreover, JAL wants to know whether city officials in Victoria would be receptive to this tour training school proposal.

**Your Task.** To guide your thinking and research, factor this problem into an outline with several areas to investigate. Further divide the problem into subproblems, phrasing each entry as a question. For example, *Should the JAL tour training program be located in Victoria?* (See the work plan model in Figure 12.5.)

## 12.7 Developing a Work Plan (Obj. 2)

**Your Task.** Select a report topic from those listed at this book's Student Resources Web site. Click on "Web Links by Chapter," "Chapter 12," and "Report Topics." For that report prepare a work plan that includes the following:

a. Statement of the problem

b. Expanded statement of purpose (including scope, limitations, and significance)

c. Sources and methods

d. Tentative outline

e. Work schedule (with projected completion dates)

## 12.8 Using Secondary Sources (Obj. 3)

**Your Task.** Conduct research in a library. Prepare a bibliography of the most important magazines and professional journals in your major field of study. Your instructor may ask you to list the periodicals and briefly describe their content, purpose, and audience. In a cover memo to your instructor, describe your bibliography and your research sources (manual or computerized indexes, databases, CD-ROM, and so on).

## 12.9 Developing Primary Data: Collaborative Survey (Obj. 4)

**TEAM**

Parking on campus has always been a problem. Students complain bitterly about the lack of spaces for them, the distance of parking lots from classrooms, and the poor condition of the lots. Some solutions have been proposed: limiting parking to full-time students, using auxiliary parking lots farther away and offering a shuttle bus to campus, encouraging bicycle and moped use, and reducing the number of spaces for visitors.

**Your Task.** In teams of three to five, design a survey for your associated student body council. The survey seeks student feedback in addressing the parking problem on campus. Discuss these solutions and add at least three other possibilities. Then prepare a questionnaire to be distributed on campus. If possible, pilot-test the questionnaire before submitting it to your instructor. Be sure to consider how the results will be tabulated and interpreted.

## 12.10 Surfing the Web for Payroll Data (Obj. 3)

**WEB**

Alisa Robertson, compensation and payroll manager for Gulf Paper Corporation, has been complaining for some time about its complex and outdated payroll processes. "We have over 2000 employees in nine different locations, and no set deadline for payroll submissions," she says. As a result of her urging, she has been named project manager for the company's "Human Resources/Payroll Business Information Systems Project."

**Your Task.** As Alisa Robertson's assistant, you are to help her learn more about payroll software programs that centralize processes, improve security, and reduce human error. You decide to begin the research process by using the Web to see what you can turn up. Employ two or more search engines, choose keywords, and search for appropriate sites. Be sure to evaluate each site for currency, authority, content, and accuracy. Select five relevant sites and print a couple of pages of information from each site. Prepare a short memo report to Robertson naming the sites and giving her a brief summary of each.[28]

## 12.11 Researching Data: Zellers Wants to Know What's Happening South of the Border (Objs. 3 and 4)

**INFOTRAC     TEAM**

With U.S. retailers, such as Wal-Mart, capturing much of the Canadian market, stores such as Zellers need to be proactive. The casualties of retailers such as Bi-Way and Eaton's have had a major impact on the retail landscape.

Looking to the south, some of the U.S. competition may provide some insightful information. Target, the U.S. discount retailer, piles it high and sells it cheap. Lauren Bacall and Robert Redford have promoted it. Oprah Winfrey thinks it is so chic that she pronounces its name in mock French ("Tar-Jay"). Despite its celebrity shoppers, Target still lags behind Wal-Mart, which stands out as the gold standard of retailing. The two companies are similar in net margins and cost structures, but Wal-Mart is way ahead in sales per square metre.

Target has indicated that it wants to narrow the gap through the sincerest form of flattery: imitation. Gerald Storch, Target's vice chairman, says his company is "the world's premier student of Wal-Mart." If it works well for Wal-Mart it might work for Target.[29]

**Your Task.** As one of several interns working in the office of Zellers' vice chairman, you have been given the task of learning about Wal-Mart and Target activities and reporting on trends, techniques, procedures, or new marketing plans that might be interesting to Zellers. For example, Wal-Mart has been experimenting with the idea of adding gas stations to more of its stores. Perhaps Zellers should consider this. You're not expected to conduct extensive research or write a long report. Your boss just wants you to think about what is happening south of the border and whether any policies or practices might be worth imitating at Zellers. Using InfoTrac, read a number of articles about Wal-Mart and/or Target. Your team should develop three to ten ideas to present to Gerry Stanton, your supervisor. Write individual informative memos or one collaborative memo.

## 12.12 Selecting Graphics (Obj. 5)

**Your Task.** Identify the best kind of graphic to illustrate the following data.

a. Instructions for workers telling them how to distinguish between worker accidents that must be reported to provincial and federal agencies and those that need not be reported

b. Figures showing what proportion of every provincial tax dollar is spent on education, social services, transportation, debt, and other expenses

c. Data showing the academic, administrative, and operation divisions of a college, from the president to department chairs and division managers

d. Figures comparing the sales of PDAs (personal data assistants), cell phones, and laptop computers over the past five years

e. Figures showing the operating profit of a company for the past five years

f. Data showing areas in Canada most likely to have earthquakes

g. Percentages showing the causes of forest fires (lightning, 73 percent; arson, 5 percent; campfires, 9 percent; and so on) in the Rocky Mountains

**h.** Figures comparing the cost of basic TV cable service in ten areas of Canada for the past ten years (the boss wants to see exact figures)

## 12.13 Evaluating Graphics (Obj. 5)

**Your Task.** Select four graphics from newspapers or magazines. Look in *The Globe and Mail, The Economist, Canadian Business, Financial Post,* or other business news publications. In a memo to your instructor, critique each graphic based on what you have learned in this chapter. What is correctly shown? What is incorrectly shown? How could the graphic be improved?

## 12.14 Drawing a Bar Chart (Obj. 5)

**Your Task.** Prepare a bar chart comparing the tax rates of eight industrial countries in the world: Canada, 34 percent; France, 42 percent; Germany, 39 percent; Japan, 26 percent; Netherlands, 48 percent; Sweden, 49 percent; United Kingdom, 37 percent; United States, 28 percent. These figures represent a percentage of the gross domestic product for each country. The sources of the figures are the International Monetary Fund and the Japanese Ministry of Finance. Arrange the entries logically. Write two titles: a talking title and a descriptive title. What should be emphasized in the graph and title?

## 12.15 Drawing a Line Chart (Obj. 5)

**Your Task.** Prepare a line chart showing the sales of Sidekick Athletic Shoes, Inc., for these years: 2004, $6.7 million; 2003, $5.4 million; 2002, $3.2 million; 2001, $2.1 million; 2000, $2.6 million; 1999, $3.6 million. In the chart title, highlight the trend you see in the data.

## 12.16 Studying Graphics in Annual Reports (Obj. 5)

**Your Task.** In a memo to your instructor, evaluate the effectiveness of graphics in three to five corporation annual reports. Critique their readability, clarity, and effectiveness in visualizing data. How were they introduced in the text? What suggestions would you make to improve them?

# C.L.U.E. REVIEW 12

On a separate sheet edit the following sentences to correct faults in grammar, punctuation, spelling, numbers, proofreading, and word use.

1. In a low context culture, such as north America our values and attitudes prompts us to write many reports.

2. A readers expectations and the content of a report determines it's pattern of development.

3. The format of a report is governed by it's length, topic, audience and purpose.

4. If a report has 10 or less pages, it's generally considered an short informal report.

5. Research reports from consultants to there clients tend to be formal, however a conference report to your boss would be informal.

6. My colleague and me followed step by step instructions in preparing a workplan for our report.

7. If your report is authorized by someone be sure to review it's workplan with them before proceding.

8. Eric was offered one thousand dollars to finish Roberts report but he said it was "to little and to late."

9. To search the internet you need a browser such as netscape navigator, or microsoft internet explorer.

10. To illustrate report data you may chose from among following visual aids, tables, charts, graphs and pictures.

# Chapter 13

## Organizing and Writing Typical Business Reports

### LEARNING OBJECTIVES

**1** Use tabulating and statistical techniques to sort and interpret report data.

**2** Draw meaningful conclusions and make practical report recommendations.

**3** Organize report data logically and provide cues to aid comprehension.

**4** Prepare typical informational reports.

**5** Prepare typical analytical reports.

# The Hudson's Bay Company

When most of the Hudson's Bay Company's suppliers did not meet the retailers' code of conduct in 2001, the company got proactive. In 2003, after applying strict standards to evaluate the suppliers, it terminated 15 percent of its suppliers. In a speech to Global Compact, a United Nations organization, The Bay's CEO George Heller insisted that the industry needs to work together to bring about change; however, he noted that change cannot happen in isolation.[1]

The Hudson's Bay Company (Hbc), established in 1670, is Canada's oldest corporation and largest department store retailer. With operations in every province, the company has more than 500 stores, led by the Bay and Zellers chains, and is Canada's fifth-largest employer, with 70 000 employees. For the past few years, Hbc, which owns The Bay, Zellers, and Home Outfitters, has worked to audit and certify every factory that provides private labels to the companies. Such vigilance, however, did not prove to be enough, as Hbc was nominated as a "Sweatshop Retailer of the Year" in the "People's Choice Award" created by the Maquila Solidarity Network, a labour rights organization. Although the 2002 award went to Wal-Mart, Canadian voters placed Disney and the Hudson's Bay Company in a tie for second, which shows how tarnished the reputation of Canada's oldest retailer has become. In 2001, Hbc was caught having clothes made for its Zellers stores in three sweatshops in Lesotho, Africa. When the company was informed of the violations to labour rights, the company abandoned the factories, leaving the workers financially stranded.[2]

In a very competitive retail environment, reputation is crucial. "Reputation management" has become a key element in determining the sustainability of organizations. Research reports that respected companies tend to suffer less in an economic downturn, and a good reputation helps a company recover from a crisis more quickly.[3]

The company responded. In 2002, Hbc issued its first Corporate Social Responsibility Report with the following goal:

*The goal of this document is to report on the manner in which Hbc acts as an agent of positive social change. In key areas of Product Sourcing, the Environment, Community Investment, and our Associates, we demonstrate our commitment to Canadians and to helping improve the way we all live.*[4]

President and CEO George Heller reinforces the aim of the report as follows:

*We hope that this, our first Corporate Social Responsibility Report, helps bring our values into focus and demonstrates that the enduring commitment to being an active and integrated force for positive change is thriving in the Hudson's Bay Company of the 21st century.*[5]

It seems as if the strategy is paying off: Maquila has since praised the efforts of Hbc for moving in the right direction.[6]

## CRITICAL THINKING
- What kind of information should a company like Hbc gather to help maintain its market-leading position?
- How can collected information be transmitted to Hbc decision makers?
- How can the organization and presentation of information in reports influence the way decision makers react?

www.hbc.com

## 1  INTERPRETING DATA

The Hudson's Bay Company and all other organizations need information to stay abreast of what's happening inside and outside of their firms. Much of that information will be presented to decision makers in the form of reports. This chapter will focus on interpreting and organizing data, drawing conclusions, providing reader cues, and writing typical business reports.

Let's assume you have collected a mass of information for a report. You may feel overwhelmed as you look at a jumble of printouts, note cards, copies of articles, interview notes, questionnaire results, and statistics. It's a little like being a contractor who allowed suppliers to dump all the building materials for a new house in a monstrous pile. Like the contractor you must sort the jumble of raw material into meaningful, usable groups. Unprocessed data become meaningful information through sorting, analysis, combination, and recombination. You'll be examining each item to see what it means by itself and what it means when connected with other data. You're looking for meanings, relationships, and answers to the research questions posed in your work plan.

## Tabulating and Analyzing Responses

If you've collected considerable numerical and other information, you must tabulate and analyze it. Fortunately, several tabulating and statistical techniques can help you create order from the chaos. These techniques simplify, summarize, and classify large amounts of data into meaningful terms. From the condensed data you're more likely to be able to draw valid conclusions and make reasoned recommendations. The most helpful summarizing techniques include tables, statistical concepts (mean, median, and mode), correlations, and grids.

*Tables.* Numerical data from questionnaires or interviews are usually summarized and simplified in tables. Using systematic columns and rows, tables make quantitative information easier to comprehend. After assembling your data, you'll want to prepare preliminary tables to enable you to see what the information means. Here is a table summarizing the response to one question from a campus survey about student parking.

Question: Should student fees be increased to build parking lots?

| | NUMBER | PERCENT | |
|---|---|---|---|
| Strongly agree | 76 | 11.5 | To simplify the table, combine these items. |
| Agree | 255 | 38.5 | |
| No opinion | 22 | 3.3 | |
| Disagree | 107 | 16.1 | To simplify the table, combine these items. |
| Strongly disagree | 203 | 30.6 | |
| **Total** | **663** | **100.0** | |

Notice that this preliminary table includes both a total number of responses and a percentage for each response. (To calculate a percentage, divide the figure for each response by the total number of responses.) To simplify the data and provide a broad overview, you can join categories. For example, combining "strongly agree" (11.5 percent) and "agree" (38.5 percent) reveals that 50 percent of the respondents supported the proposal to finance new parking lots with increased student fees.

Sometimes data become more meaningful when cross-tabulated. This process allows analysis of two or more variables together. By breaking down our student survey data into male/female responses, shown in the following table, we make an interesting discovery.

Interpreting data means sorting, analyzing, combining, and recombining to yield meaningful information.

Numerical data must be tabulated and analyzed statistically to bring order out of chaos.

Question: Should student fees be increased to build parking lots?

| | TOTAL | | MALE | | FEMALE | |
|---|---|---|---|---|---|---|
| | NUMBER | PERCENT | NUMBER | PERCENT | NUMBER | PERCENT |
| Strongly agree | 76 | 11.5 | 8 | 2.2 | 68 | 22.0 |
| Agree | 255 | 38.5 | 54 | 15.3 | 201 | 65.0 |
| No opinion | 22 | 3.3 | 12 | 3.4 | 10 | 3.2 |
| Disagree | 107 | 16.1 | 89 | 25.1 | 18 | 5.8 |
| Strongly disagree | 203 | 30.6 | 191 | 54.0 | 12 | 4.0 |
| **Total** | **663** | **100.0** | **354** | **100.0** | **309** | **100.0** |

Although 50 percent of all student respondents supported the proposal, among females the approval rating was much stronger. Notice that 87 percent of female respondents (combining 22 percent "strongly agree" and 65 percent "agree") endorsed the proposal to increase fees for new parking lots. But among male students, only 17 percent agreed with the proposal. You naturally wonder why such a disparity exists. Are female students more unhappy than males with the current parking situation? If so, why? Is safety a reason? Are male students more concerned with increased fees than females?

By cross-tabulating the findings, you sometimes uncover data that may help answer your problem question or that may prompt you to explore other possibilities. Don't, however, undertake cross-tabulation unless it serves more than mere curiosity. Tables also help you compare multiple data collected from questionnaires and surveys. Figure 13.1 shows, in raw form, responses to several survey items. To convert these data into a more usable form, you need to calculate percentages for each item. Then you can arrange the responses in some rational sequence, such as largest percentage to smallest.

Once the data are displayed in a table, you can more easily draw conclusions. As Figure 13.1 shows, Midland College students apparently are not interested in public transportation or shuttle buses from satellite lots. They want to park on campus, with restricted visitor parking; only half are willing to pay for new parking lots.

**Three statistical concepts— mean, median, and mode— help you describe data.**

*The Three Ms: Mean, Median, Mode.* Tables help you organize data, and the three Ms help you describe it. These statistical terms—mean, median, and mode— are all occasionally used loosely to mean "average." To be safe, though, you should learn to apply these statistical terms precisely. When people say *average*, they usually intend to indicate the *mean*, or arithmetic average. Let's say that you're studying the estimated starting salaries of graduates from different disciplines, ranging from education to medicine:

| | | |
|---|---|---|
| Education | $24 000 | |
| Sociology | 25 000 | |
| Humanities | 27 000 | |
| Biology | 30 000 | |
| Health sciences | 31 000 | *Median (middle point in continuum)* |
| Engineering | 33 000 | *Mode (figure occurring most frequently)* |
| Business | 33 000 | |
| Law | 35 000 | *Mean (arithmetic average)* |
| Medicine | 77 000 | |

To find the mean, you simply add up all the salaries and divide by the total number of items ($315 000 ÷ 9 = $35 000). Thus, the mean salary is $35 000. Means are very

**FIGURE 13.1  Converting Survey Data into Finished Tables**

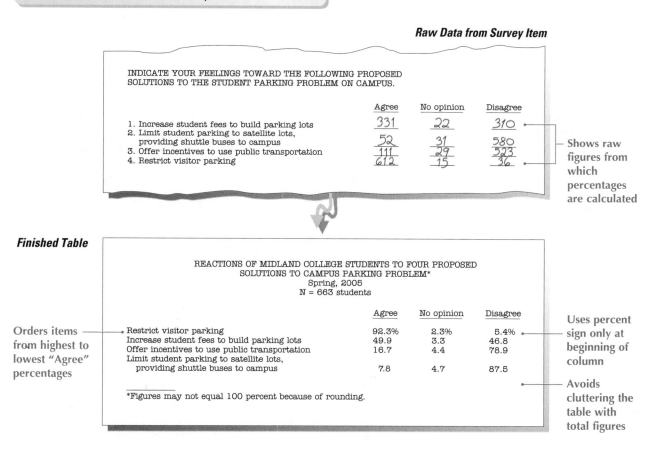

**Tips for Converting Raw Data**
- Tabulate the responses on a copy of the survey form.
- Calculate percentages (divide the score for an item by the total for all responses to that item; for example, for item 1, divide 331 by 663).
- Round off figures to one decimal point or to whole numbers.
- Arrange items in a logical order, such as largest to smallest percentage.
- Prepare a table with a title that tells such things as who, what, when, where, and why.
- Include the total number of respondents.

*Raw Data from Survey Item*

INDICATE YOUR FEELINGS TOWARD THE FOLLOWING PROPOSED
SOLUTIONS TO THE STUDENT PARKING PROBLEM ON CAMPUS.

| | Agree | No opinion | Disagree |
|---|---|---|---|
| 1. Increase student fees to build parking lots | 331 | 22 | 310 |
| 2. Limit student parking to satellite lots, providing shuttle buses to campus | 52 | 31 | 580 |
| 3. Offer incentives to use public transportation | 111 | 29 | 523 |
| 4. Restrict visitor parking | 612 | 15 | 36 |

— Shows raw figures from which percentages are calculated

*Finished Table*

REACTIONS OF MIDLAND COLLEGE STUDENTS TO FOUR PROPOSED
SOLUTIONS TO CAMPUS PARKING PROBLEM*
Spring, 2005
N = 663 students

| | Agree | No opinion | Disagree |
|---|---|---|---|
| Restrict visitor parking | 92.3% | 2.3% | 5.4% |
| Increase student fees to build parking lots | 49.9 | 3.3 | 46.8 |
| Offer incentives to use public transportation | 16.7 | 4.4 | 78.9 |
| Limit student parking to satellite lots, providing shuttle buses to campus | 7.8 | 4.7 | 87.5 |

*Figures may not equal 100 percent because of rounding.

Orders items from highest to lowest "Agree" percentages

Uses percent sign only at beginning of column

Avoids cluttering the table with total figures

useful to indicate central tendencies of figures, but they have one major flaw: extremes at either end cause distortion. Notice that the $77 000 figure makes the mean salary of $35 000 deceptively high. It does not represent a valid average for the group. Because means can be misleading, you should use them only when extreme figures do not distort the result.

The *median* represents the midpoint in a group of figures arranged from lowest to highest (or vice versa). In our list of salaries, the median is $31 000 (health sciences). In other words, half the salaries are above this point and half are below it. The median is useful when extreme figures may warp the mean. Whereas salaries for medicine distort the mean, the median, at $31 000, is still a representative figure.

The *mode* is simply the value that occurs most frequently. In our list $33 000 (for engineering and business) represents the mode since it occurs twice. The mode has the advantage of being easily determined—just a quick glance at a list of arranged values reveals it. Although mode is infrequently used by researchers, knowing the mode is useful in some situations. Let's say 7-Eleven sampled its customers to determine what drink size they preferred: 355 mL, 710 mL, or Big-Gulp 2 L. Finding the mode—the most frequently named figure—makes more sense than calculating the median, which might yield a size that 7-Eleven doesn't even offer. (To remember the meaning of *mode*, think about fashion; the most frequent response, the mode, is the most fashionable.)

Mean, median, and mode figures are especially helpful when the range of values is also known. Range represents the span between the highest and lowest values. To calculate the range, you simply subtract the lowest figure from the highest. In starting salaries for graduates, the range is $53 000 ($77 000 − $24 000). Knowing the range enables readers to put mean and median figures into perspective. This knowledge also prompts researchers to wonder why such a range exists, thus stimulating hunches and further investigation to solve problems.

*Correlations.* In tabulating and analyzing data, you may see relationships among two or more variables that help explain the findings. If your data for graduates' starting salaries also included years of schooling, you would doubtless notice that graduates with more years of education received higher salaries. For example, beginning teachers, with four years of schooling, earn less than beginning physicians, who have completed nine or more years of education. Thus, a correlation may exist between years of education and starting salary.

Intuition suggests correlations that may or may not prove to be accurate. Is there a relationship between studying and good grades? Between new office computers and increased productivity? Between the rise and fall of hemlines and the rise and fall of the stock market (as some newspaper writers have suggested)? If a correlation seems to exist, can we say that one event caused the other? Does studying cause good grades? Does more schooling guarantee increased salary? Although one event may not be said to cause another, the business researcher who sees a correlation begins to ask why and how the two variables are related. In this way, apparent correlations stimulate investigation and present possible problem solutions to be explored.

In reporting correlations, you should avoid suggesting that a cause-and-effect relationship exists when none can be proved. Only sophisticated research methods can statistically prove correlations. Instead, present a correlation as a possible relationship (*The data suggest that beginning salaries are related to years of education*). Cautious statements followed by explanations gain you credibility and allow readers to make their own decisions.

*Grids.* Another technique for analyzing raw data—especially verbal data—is the grid. Let's say you've been asked by the CEO to collect opinions from all vice presidents about the CEO's four-point plan to build cash reserves. The grid shown in Figure 13.2 enables you to summarize the vice presidents' reactions to each point. Notice how this complex verbal information is transformed into concise, manageable data; readers can see immediately which points are supported and opposed. Imagine how long you could have struggled to comprehend the meaning of this verbal information before plotting it on a grid.

**FIGURE 13.2** Grid to Analyze Complex Verbal Data About Building Cash Reserves

| | Point 1 | Point 2 | Point 3 | Point 4 | Overall Reaction |
|---|---|---|---|---|---|
| Vice President 1 | Disapproves. "Too little, too late." | Strong support. "Best of all points." | Mixed opinion. "Must wait and see market." | Indifferent. | Optimistic, but "hates to delay expansion for six months." |
| Vice President 2 | Disapproves. "Creates credit trap." | Approves. | Strong disapproval. | Approves. "Must improve receivable collections." | Mixed support. "Good self-defence plan." |
| Vice President 3 | Strong disapproval. | Approves. "Key to entire plan." | Indifferent. | Approves, but with "caveats." | "Will work only with sale of unproductive fixed assets." |
| Vice President 4 | Disapproves. "Too risky now." | Strong support. "Start immediately." | Approves, "but may damage image." | Approves. "Benefits far outweigh costs." | Supports plan. Suggests focus on Pacific Rim markets. |

Arranging data in a grid also works for projects such as feasibility studies that compare many variables. Assume you must recommend a new printer to your manager. To see how four models compare, you could lay out a grid with the names of printer models across the top. Down the left side, you would list such significant variables as price, warranty, service, capacity, compatibility, and specifications. As you fill in the variables for each model, you can see quickly which model has the lowest price, longest warranty, and so forth. *Consumer Reports* often uses grids to show information.

In addition, grids help classify employment data. For example, suppose your boss asks you to recommend one individual from among many job candidates. You could arrange a grid with names across the top and distinguishing characteristics—experience, skills, education, and other employment interests—down the left side. When you summarize each candidate's points, you'd have a helpful tool for drawing conclusions and writing a report.

## DRAWING CONCLUSIONS AND MAKING RECOMMENDATIONS

The most widely read portions of a report are the sections devoted to conclusions and recommendations. Knowledgeable readers go straight to the conclusions to see what the report writer thinks the data mean. Because conclusions summarize and explain the findings, they represent the heart of a report. Your value in an organization rises considerably if you can draw conclusions that analyze information logically and show how the data answer questions and solve problems.

### Analyzing Data to Arrive at Conclusions

Any set of data can produce a variety of conclusions. Always bear in mind, though, that the audience for a report wants to know how these data relate to the problem

Conclusions summarize and explain the findings in a report.

being studied. What do the findings mean in terms of solving the original report problem?

For example, the Marriott Corporation recognized a serious problem among its employees. Conflicting home and work requirements seemed to be causing excessive employee turnover and decreased productivity. To learn the extent of the problem and to consider solutions, Marriott surveyed its staff.[7] It learned, among other things, that nearly 35 percent of its employees had children under age twelve, and 15 percent had children under age five. Other findings, shown in Figure 13.3, indicated that one third of its staff with young children took time off because of child-care difficulties. Moreover, many current employees left previous jobs because of work and family conflicts. The survey also showed that managers did not consider child-care or family problems to be appropriate topics for discussion at work.

A sample of possible conclusions that could be drawn from these findings is shown in Figure 13.3. Notice that each conclusion relates to the initial report problem. Although only a few possible findings and conclusions are shown here, you can see that the conclusions try to explain the causes for the home/work conflict among employees. Many report writers would expand the conclusion section by explaining each item and citing supporting evidence. Even for simplified conclusions, such as those shown in Figure 13.3, you will want to number each item separately and use parallel construction (balanced sentence structure).

Effective report conclusions are objective and bias-free.

Although your goal is to remain objective, drawing conclusions naturally involves a degree of subjectivity. Your goals, background, and frame of reference all colour the inferences you make. When Federal Express, for example, tried to expand its next-day delivery service to Europe, it racked up a staggering loss of $1.2 billion in four years of operation.[8] The facts could not be disputed. But what conclusions could be drawn? The CEO might conclude that the competition is greater than anticipated but that FedEx is making inroads; patience is all that is needed. The board of directors and shareholders, however, might conclude that the competition is too well entrenched and that it's time to pull the plug on an ill-fated operation. Findings will be interpreted from the writer's perspective, but they should not be manipulated to achieve a preconceived purpose.

You can make your report conclusions more objective if you use consistent evaluation criteria. Let's say you are comparing computers for an office equipment purchase. If you evaluate each by the same criteria (such as price, specifications, service, and warranty), your conclusions are more likely to be bias-free.

You also need to avoid the temptation to sensationalize or exaggerate your findings or conclusions. Be careful of words like *many, most,* and *all.* Instead of *many of the respondents felt...,* you might more accurately write *some of the respondents....* Examine your motives before drawing conclusions. Don't let preconceptions or wishful thinking colour your reasoning.

## Preparing Report Recommendations

Conclusions explain a problem; recommendations offer specific suggestions for solving the problem.

Recommendations, unlike conclusions, make specific suggestions for actions that can solve the report problem. Consider the following examples:

**Conclusion**
Our investments are losing value because the stock market has declined. The bond market shows strength.

**Recommendation**
Withdraw at least half of our investment in stocks, and invest it in bonds.

## FIGURE 13.3 Report Conclusions and Recommendations

**Tips for Writing Conclusions**
- Interpret and summarize the findings; tell what they mean.
- Relate the conclusions to the report problem.
- Limit the conclusions to the data presented; do not introduce new material.
- Number the conclusions and present them in parallel form.
- Be objective; avoid exaggerating or manipulating the data.
- Use consistent criteria in evaluating options.

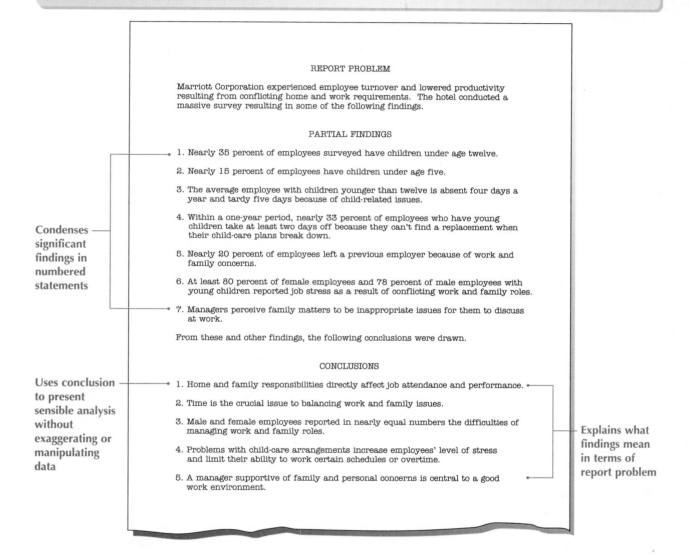

REPORT PROBLEM

Marriott Corporation experienced employee turnover and lowered productivity resulting from conflicting home and work requirements. The hotel conducted a massive survey resulting in some of the following findings.

PARTIAL FINDINGS

*Condenses significant findings in numbered statements*

1. Nearly 35 percent of employees surveyed have children under age twelve.

2. Nearly 15 percent of employees have children under age five.

3. The average employee with children younger than twelve is absent four days a year and tardy five days because of child-related issues.

4. Within a one-year period, nearly 33 percent of employees who have young children take at least two days off because they can't find a replacement when their child-care plans break down.

5. Nearly 20 percent of employees left a previous employer because of work and family concerns.

6. At least 80 percent of female employees and 78 percent of male employees with young children reported job stress as a result of conflicting work and family roles.

7. Managers perceive family matters to be inappropriate issues for them to discuss at work.

From these and other findings, the following conclusions were drawn.

CONCLUSIONS

*Uses conclusion to present sensible analysis without exaggerating or manipulating data*

1. Home and family responsibilities directly affect job attendance and performance.

2. Time is the crucial issue to balancing work and family issues.

3. Male and female employees reported in nearly equal numbers the difficulties of managing work and family roles.

4. Problems with child-care arrangements increase employees' level of stress and limit their ability to work certain schedules or overtime.

5. A manager supportive of family and personal concerns is central to a good work environment.

*Explains what findings mean in terms of report problem*

### Conclusion
The cost of constructing multilevel parking structures for student on-campus parking is prohibitive.

### Recommendation
Explore the possibility of satellite parking lots with frequent shuttle buses to campus.

Notice that the conclusions explain what the problem is, while the recommendations tell how to solve it. Typically, readers prefer specific recommendations. They

## FIGURE 13.3 Continued

**Tips for Writing Recommendations**
- Make specific suggestions for actions to solve the report problem.
- Prepare practical recommendations that will be agreeable to the audience.
- Avoid conditional words such as *maybe* and *perhaps*.
- Present each suggestion separately as a command beginning with a verb.

- Number the recommendations for improved readability.
- If requested, describe how the recommendations may be implemented.
- When possible, arrange the recommendations in an announced order, such as most important to least important.

RECOMMENDATIONS

1. Provide managers with training in working with personal and family matters.
2. Institute a flextime policy that allows employees to adapt their work schedules to home responsibilities.
3. Investigate opening a pilot child development centre for preschool children of employees at company headquarters.
4. Develop a child-care resource program to provide parents with professional help in locating affordable child care.
5. Offer a child-care discount program to help parents pay for services.
6. Authorize weekly payroll deductions, using tax-free dollars, to pay for child care.
7. Publish a quarterly employee newsletter devoted to family and child-care issues.

Arranges actions to solve problems from most important to least important

want to know exactly how to implement the suggestions. In addition to recommending satellite parking lots for campus parking, for example, the writer could have discussed sites for possible satellite lots and the cost of running shuttle buses.

The specificity of your recommendations depends on your authorization. What are you commissioned to do, and what does the reader expect? In the planning stages of your report project, you anticipate what the reader wants in the report. Your intuition and your knowledge of the audience indicate how far your recommendations should be developed.

In the recommendations section of the Marriott employee survey, shown in the continuation of Figure 13.3, many of the suggestions are summarized. In the actual report each recommendation could have been backed up with specifics and ideas for implementing them. For example, the child-care resource recommendation would be explained: it provides parents with names of agencies and professionals who specialize in locating child care across the country.

**The best recommendations offer practical suggestions that are feasible and agreeable to the audience.**

A good report provides practical recommendations that are agreeable to the audience. In the Marriott survey, for example, report researchers knew that the company wanted to help employees cope with conflicts between family and work obligations. Thus, the report's conclusions and recommendations focused on ways to resolve the conflict. If Marriott's goal had been merely to reduce employee absenteeism and save money, the recommendations would have been quite different.

If possible, make each recommendation a command. Note in Figure 13.3 that each recommendation begins with a verb. This structure sounds forceful and confident and helps the reader comprehend the information quickly. Avoid words such as *maybe* and *perhaps*; they suggest conditional statements that reduce the strength of recommendations.

Experienced writers may combine recommendations and conclusions. And in short reports, writers may omit conclusions and move straight to recommendations. The important thing about recommendations, though, is that they include practical suggestions for solving the report problem.

## ORGANIZING DATA

After collecting sets of data, interpreting them, drawing conclusions, and thinking about the recommendations you will make, you're ready to organize the parts of the report into a logical framework. Poorly organized reports lead to frustration. Readers will not understand, remember, or be persuaded. Wise writers know that reports rarely "just organize themselves." Instead, organization must be imposed on the data.

Informational reports, as you learned in Chapter 12, generally present data without interpretation. As shown in Figure 13.4, informational reports are typically organized in three parts: (1) introduction/background, (2) facts/findings, and (3) summary/conclusion. Analytical reports, which generally analyze data and draw conclusions, typically contain four parts: (1) introduction/problem, (2) facts/findings, (3) discussion/analysis, and (4) conclusions/recommendations. However, the parts in analytical reports do not always follow the same sequence. For readers who know about the project, are supportive, or are eager to learn the results quickly, the direct method is appropriate. Conclusions and recommendations, if requested, appear up front. For readers who must be educated or persuaded, the indirect method works better. Conclusions/recommendations appear last, after the findings have been presented and analyzed.

Although every report is different, the overall organizational patterns described here typically hold true. The real challenge, though, lies in (1) organizing the facts/findings and discussion/analysis sections and (2) providing reader cues.

**The direct pattern is appropriate for informed or receptive readers; the indirect pattern is appropriate when educating or persuading.**

### Ordering Information Logically

Whether you're writing informational or analytical reports, the data you've collected must be structured coherently. Five common organizational methods are by time, component, importance, criteria, or convention. Regardless of the method you choose, be sure that it helps the reader understand the data. Reader comprehension, not writer convenience, should govern organization.

**Organization by time, component, importance, criteria, or convention helps readers comprehend data.**

**FIGURE 13.4** Organizing Informational and Analytical Reports

| Informational Reports | Analytical Reports | |
| --- | --- | --- |
| | Direct Pattern | Indirect Pattern |
| I. Introduction/background | I. Introduction/problem | I. Introduction/problem |
| II. Facts/findings | II. Conclusions/recommendations | II. Facts/findings |
| III. Summary/conclusion | III. Facts/findings | III. Discussion/analysis |
| | IV. Discussion/analysis | IV. Conclusions/recommendations |

*Time.* Ordering data by time means establishing a chronology of events. Agendas, minutes of meetings, progress reports, and procedures are usually organized by time. For example, a report describing an eight-week training program would most likely be organized by weeks. A plan for step-by-step improvement of customer service would be organized by each step. A monthly trip report submitted by a sales rep might describe customers visited Week 1, Week 2, and so on. Beware of overusing time chronologies, however. Although this method is easy and often mirrors the way data are collected, chronologies—like the sales rep's trip report—tend to be boring, repetitious, and lacking in emphasis. Readers can't always pick out what's important.

*Component.* Especially for informational reports, data may be organized by components such as location, geography, division, product, or part. For instance, a report detailing company expansion might divide the plan into West Coast, East Coast, and Central expansion. The report could also be organized by divisions: personal products, consumer electronics, and household goods. A report comparing profits among makers of athletic shoes might group the data by company: Reebok, Nike, Adidas, and so forth. Organization by components works best when the classifications already exist.

**Organizing by level of importance saves the time of busy readers and increases the odds that key information will be retained.**

*Importance.* Organization by importance involves beginning with the most important item and proceeding to the least important—or vice versa. For example, a report discussing the reasons for declining product sales would present the most important reason first followed by less important ones. The Marriott report describing work/family conflicts might begin by discussing child care, if the writer considered it the most important issue. Using importance to structure findings involves a value judgment. The writer must decide what is most important, always keeping in mind the readers' priorities and expectations. Busy readers appreciate seeing important points first; they may skim or skip other points. On the other hand, building to a climax by moving from least important to most important enables the writer to focus attention at the end. Thus, the reader is more likely to remember the most important item. Of course, the writer also risks losing the attention of the reader along the way.

*Criteria.* Establishing criteria by which to judge helps writers to treat topics consistently. Let's say your report compares health plans A, B, and C. For each plan you examine the same standards: Criterion 1, cost per employee; Criterion 2, amount of deductible; and Criterion 3, patient benefits. The resulting data could then be organized either by plans or by criteria:

**To evaluate choices or plans fairly, apply the same criteria to each.**

| By Plan | By Criteria |
|---|---|
| Plan A | Criterion 1 |
|    Criterion 1 |    Plan A |
|    Criterion 2 |    Plan B |
|    Criterion 3 |    Plan C |
| Plan B | Criterion 2 |
|    Criterion 1 |    Plan A |
|    Criterion 2 |    Plan B |
|    Criterion 3 |    Plan C |
| Plan C | Criterion 3 |
|    Criterion 1 |    Plan A |
|    Criterion 2 |    Plan B |
|    Criterion 3 |    Plan C |

Although you might favour organizing the data by plans (because that's the way you collected the data), the better way is by criteria. When you discuss patient benefits, for example, you would examine all three plans' benefits together. Organizing a report around criteria helps readers make comparisons, instead of forcing them to search through the report for similar data.

*Convention.* Many operational and recurring reports are structured according to convention. That is, they follow a prescribed plan that everyone understands. For example, an automotive parts manufacturer might ask all sales reps to prepare a weekly report with these headings: *Competitive observations* (competitors' price changes, discounts, new products, product problems, distributor changes, product promotions), *Product problems* (quality, performance, needs), and *Customer service problems* (delivery, mailings, correspondence). Management gets exactly the information it needs in an easy-to-read form.

**Organizing by convention simplifies the organizational task and yields easy-to-follow information.**

Like operating reports, proposals are often organized conventionally. They might use such groupings as background, problem, proposed solution, staffing, schedule, costs, and authorization. As you might expect, reports following these conventional, prescribed structures greatly simplify the task of organization. (Proposals will be presented in Chapter 14.)

## Providing Reader Cues

When you finish organizing a report, you probably see a neat outline in your mind: major points, supported by subpoints and details. However, readers don't know the material as well as you; they cannot see your outline. To guide them through the data, you need to provide the equivalent of a map and road signs. For both formal and informal reports, devices such as introductions, transitions, and headings prevent readers from getting lost.

*Introduction.* The best way to point a reader in the right direction is to provide an introduction that does three things:

- Tells the purpose of the report
- Describes the significance of the topic
- Previews the main points and the order in which they will be developed

**Good openers tell readers what topics will be covered in what order and why.**

The following paragraph includes all three elements in introducing a report on computer security:

> The purpose of this report is to examine the security of our current computer operations and present suggestions for improving security. Lax computer security could mean loss of information, loss of business, and damage to our equipment and systems. Because many former employees, released during recent downsizing efforts, know our systems, major changes must be made. To improve security, I will present three recommendations: (1) begin using smart cards that limit access to our computer system, (2) alter sign-on and log-off procedures, (3) move central computer operations to a more secure area.

This opener tells the purpose (examining computer security), describes its significance (loss of information and business, damage to equipment and systems), and outlines how the report is organized (three recommendations). Good openers in effect set up a contract with the reader. The writer promises to cover certain topics in a specified order. Readers expect the writer to fulfill the contract. They want the

Like backpackers who need a map to reach their destination, report readers need the equivalent of a map and road signs to find their way through a report. Introductions, transitions, and headings provide cues so that readers know where they've been and where they are headed.

topics to be developed as promised—using the same wording and presented in the order mentioned. For example, if in your introduction you state that you will discuss the use of *smart cards*, don't change the heading for that section to *access cards*. Remember that the introduction provides a map to a report; switching the names on the map will ensure that readers get lost. To maintain consistency, delay writing the introduction until after you have completed the report. Long, complex reports may require introductions for each section.

**Transitional expressions inform readers where ideas are headed and how they relate.**

*Transitions.* Expressions such as *on the contrary, at the same time,* and *however* show relationships and help reveal the logical flow of ideas in a report. These transitional expressions enable writers to tell readers where ideas are headed and how they relate. Notice how abrupt the following two sentences sound without a transition: *North American car manufacturers admired Toyota's just-in-time inventory practices. Adopting a JIT system [however] means total restructuring of assembly plants.*

The following expressions (see Chapter 6, Figure 6.7 for a complete list) enable you to show readers how you are developing your ideas.

**To Present Additional Thoughts:** additionally, again, also, moreover, furthermore

**To Suggest Cause and Effect:** accordingly, as a result, consequently, therefore

**To Contrast Ideas:** at the same time, but, however, on the contrary, though, yet

**To Show Time and Order:** after, before, first, finally, now, previously, then, to conclude

**To Clarify Points:** for example, for instance, in other words, that is, thus

In using these expressions, recognize that they don't have to sit at the head of a sentence. Listen to the rhythm of the sentence, and place the expression where a natural pause occurs. Used appropriately, transitional expressions serve readers as guides;

misused or overused, they can be as distracting and frustrating as too many road signs on a highway.

*Headings.* Good headings are another structural cue that assist readers in comprehending the organization of a report. They highlight major ideas, allowing busy readers to see the big picture in a glance. Moreover, headings provide resting points for the mind and for the eye, breaking up large chunks of text into manageable and inviting segments.

Good headings provide organizational cues and spotlight key ideas.

Report writers may use functional or talking heads. Functional heads (for example, *Background, Findings, Personnel,* and *Production Costs*) describe functions or general topics. They show the outline of a report but provide little insight for readers. Functional headings are useful for routine reports. They're also appropriate for sensitive topics that might provoke emotional reactions. By keeping the headings general, experienced writers hope to minimize reader opposition or response to controversial subjects. Talking heads (for example, *Two Sides to Campus Parking Problem* or *Survey Shows Support for Parking Fees*) provide more information and interest. Unless carefully written, however, talking heads can fail to reveal the organization of a report. With some planning, though, headings can be both functional and talking, such as *Parking Recommendations: Shuttle and New Structures.* To create the most effective headings, follow a few basic guidelines:

- **Use appropriate heading levels.** The position and format of a heading indicate its level of importance and relationship to other points. Figure 13.5 both illustrates and discusses a commonly used heading format for business reports.

- **Capitalize and underline carefully.** Most writers use all capital letters (without underlines) for main titles, such as the report, chapter, and unit titles. For first- and second-level headings, they capitalize only the first letter of main words. For additional emphasis, they use a bold font, as shown in Figure 13.5.

- **Balance headings within levels.** All headings at a given level should be grammatically similar. For example, *Developing Product Teams* and *Presenting Plan to Management* are balanced, but *Development of Product Teams* and *Presenting Plan to Management* are not.

Headings should be brief, parallel, and ordered in a logical hierarchy.

- **For short reports use first- or second-level headings.** Many business reports contain only one or two levels of headings. For such reports use first-level headings (centred, bolded) and/or second-level headings (flush left, bolded). See Figure 13.5.

- **Include at least one heading per report page.** Headings increase the readability and attractiveness of report pages. Use at least one per page to break up blocks of text.

- **Keep headings short but clear.** One-word headings are emphatic but not always clear. For example, the heading *Budget* does not adequately describe figures for a summer project involving student interns for an oil company in Alberta. Try to keep your headings brief (no more than eight words), but make sure they are understandable. Experiment with headings that concisely tell who, what, when, where, and why.

**FIGURE 13.5  Levels of Headings in Reports**

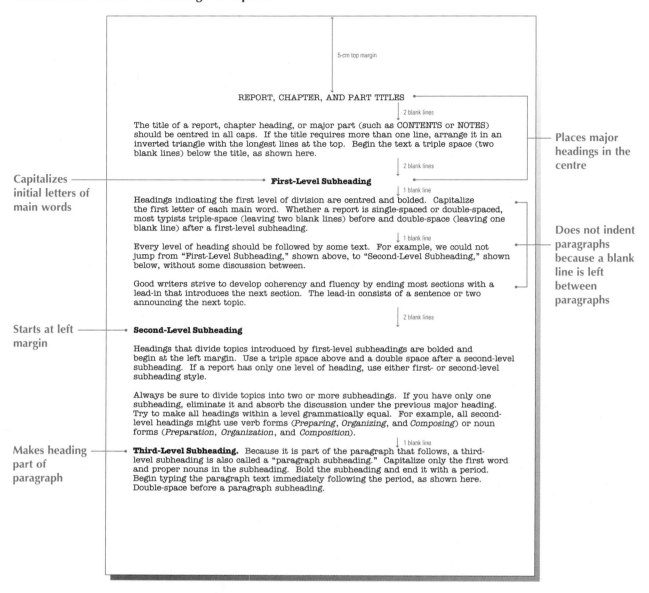

5-cm top margin

REPORT, CHAPTER, AND PART TITLES

↓ 2 blank lines

The title of a report, chapter heading, or major part (such as CONTENTS or NOTES) should be centred in all caps. If the title requires more than one line, arrange it in an inverted triangle with the longest lines at the top. Begin the text a triple space (two blank lines) below the title, as shown here.

**Places major headings in the centre**

↓ 2 blank lines

**First-Level Subheading**

↓ 1 blank line

**Capitalizes initial letters of main words**

Headings indicating the first level of division are centred and bolded. Capitalize the first letter of each main word. Whether a report is single-spaced or double-spaced, most typists triple-space (leaving two blank lines) before and double-space (leaving one blank line) after a first-level subheading.

↓ 1 blank line

Every level of heading should be followed by some text. For example, we could not jump from "First-Level Subheading," shown above, to "Second-Level Subheading," shown below, without some discussion between.

Good writers strive to develop coherency and fluency by ending most sections with a lead-in that introduces the next section. The lead-in consists of a sentence or two announcing the next topic.

**Does not indent paragraphs because a blank line is left between paragraphs**

↓ 2 blank lines

**Starts at left margin**

**Second-Level Subheading**

Headings that divide topics introduced by first-level subheadings are bolded and begin at the left margin. Use a triple space above and a double space after a second-level subheading. If a report has only one level of heading, use either first- or second-level subheading style.

Always be sure to divide topics into two or more subheadings. If you have only one subheading, eliminate it and absorb the discussion under the previous major heading. Try to make all headings within a level grammatically equal. For example, all second-level headings might use verb forms (*Preparing, Organizing,* and *Composing*) or noun forms (*Preparation, Organization,* and *Composition*).

↓ 1 blank line

**Makes heading part of paragraph**

**Third-Level Subheading.** Because it is part of the paragraph that follows, a third-level subheading is also called a "paragraph subheading." Capitalize only the first word and proper nouns in the subheading. Bold the subheading and end it with a period. Begin typing the paragraph text immediately following the period, as shown here. Double-space before a paragraph subheading.

## WRITING INFORMATIONAL REPORTS

*4*

Now that we've covered the basics of gathering, interpreting, and organizing data, we are ready to put it all together into typical informational or analytical reports. Informational reports often describe periodic, recurring activities (such as monthly sales or weekly customer calls) as well as situational, nonrecurring events (such as trips, conferences, and progress on special projects). What they have in common is delivering information to readers who do not have to be persuaded. Informational report readers usually are neutral or receptive.

You can expect to write many informational reports as an entry-level or middle-management employee. Because these reports generally deliver nonsensitive data and thus will not upset the reader, they are organized directly. Often they need little background material or introductory comments since readers are familiar with the

**Informational reports provide data on periodic and situational activities for readers who do not need to be persuaded.**

topics. Although they're generally conversational and informal, informational reports should not be so casual that the reader struggles to find the important points. Main points must be immediately visible. Headings, lists, bulleted items, and other graphic highlighting, as well as clear organization, enable readers to grasp major ideas immediately. The Career Coach box on page 422 provides additional pointers on design features and techniques that can improve your reports.

## Periodic Reports

Most businesses—especially larger ones—require periodic reports to keep management informed of operations. These recurring reports are written at regular intervals—weekly, monthly, yearly—so that management can monitor and, if necessary, remedy business strategies. Some periodic reports simply contain figures, such as sales volume, number and kind of customer service calls, shipments delivered, accounts payable, and personnel data. More challenging periodic reports require description and discussion of activities. In preparing a narrative description of their activities, employees writing periodic reports usually do the following:

- Summarize regular activities and events performed during the reporting period
- Describe irregular events deserving the attention of management
- Highlight special needs and problems

Managers naturally want to know that routine activities are progressing normally. They're often more interested, though, in what the competition is doing and in how operations may be affected by unusual events or problems. In companies with open lines of communication, managers expect to be informed of the bad news along with the good news. Jim Chrisman, sales rep for a West Coast sprinkler manufacturer, worked with a group of other sales reps and managers to produce the format for the periodic report shown in Figure 13.6 on page 423. In Jim's words, "We used to write three- and four-page weekly activity reports that, I hate to admit, rambled all over the place. When our managers complained that they weren't getting the information they wanted, we sat down together and developed a report form with four categories: (1) activity summary, (2) competition update, (3) product problems and comments, and (4) needs. Then one manager wrote several sample reports that we studied. Now, my reports are shorter and more focused. I try to hit the highlights in covering my daily activities, but I really concentrate on product problems and items that I must have to do a better job. Managers tell us that they need this kind of detailed feedback so that they can respond to the competition and also develop new products that our customers want."

## Trip, Convention, and Conference Reports

Employees sent on business trips or to conventions and conferences typically must submit reports when they return. Organizations want to know that their money was well spent in funding the travel. These reports inform management about new procedures, equipment, and laws and supply information affecting products, operations, and service.

The hardest parts of writing these reports are selecting the most relevant material and organizing it coherently. Generally, it's best not to use chronological sequencing (*in the morning we did X, at lunch we heard Y, and in the afternoon we did Z*). Instead, you should focus on three to five topics in which your reader will be interested. These items become the body of the report. Then simply add an introduction and closing, and your report is organized. A general outline for trip, conference, and convention reports appears at the top of page 424.

**Periodic reports keep management informed of operations and activities.**

**Trip and conference reports identify the event, summarize three to five main points, itemize expenses separately, and express appreciation or suggest action to be taken.**

# Ten Tips for Designing Better Documents

Desktop publishing packages, high-level word processing programs, and advanced printers now make it possible for you to turn out professional-looking documents. The temptation, though, is to overdo it by incorporating too many features in one document. Here are ten tips for applying good sense and good design principles in "publishing" your documents.

1. **Analyze your audience.** Sales brochures and promotional letters can be flashy—with colour print, oversized type, and fancy borders—to attract attention. But such effects are out of place for most conservative business documents. Also consider whether your readers will be reading painstakingly or merely browsing. Lists and headings help those readers who are in a hurry.

2. **Choose an appropriate type size.** For most business memos, letters, and reports, the body text should be 10 to 12 points tall (a point is 1/72 of an inch). Larger type looks amateurish, and smaller type is hard to read.

3. **Use a consistent type font.** Although your software may provide a variety of fonts, stay with a single family of type within one document—at least until you become more expert. The most popular fonts are Times Roman and Helvetica. For emphasis and contrast, you can vary the font size and weight with **bold**, *italic*, ***bold italic***, and other selections.

4. **Generally, don't justify right margins.** Textbooks, novels, newspapers, magazines, and other long works are usually set with justified (even) right margins. However, for shorter works ragged-right margins are recommended because such margins add white space and help readers locate the beginnings of new lines. Slower readers find ragged-right copy more legible.

5. **Separate paragraphs and sentences appropriately.** The first line of a paragraph should be indented or preceded by a blank line. To separate sentences, typists have traditionally left two spaces. This spacing is still acceptable for most business documents. If you are preparing a newsletter or brochure, however, you may wish to adopt printer's standards, leaving one space after end punctuation.

6. **Design readable headlines.** Presenting headlines and headings in all caps is generally discouraged because solid blocks of capital letters interfere with recognition of word patterns. To further improve readability, select a sans serif typeface (one without cross strokes or embellishment), such as Helvetica.

7. **Strive for an attractive page layout.** In designing title pages or graphics, provide for a balance between print and white space. Also consider placing the focal point (something that draws the reader's eye) at the optical centre of a page—about three lines above the actual centre. Moreover, remember that the average reader scans a page from left to right and top to bottom in a Z pattern. Plan your graphics accordingly.

8. **Use graphics and clip art with restraint.** Images created with spreadsheet or graphics programs can be inserted into documents. Original drawings, photographs, and clip art can also be scanned into documents. Use such images, however, only when they are well drawn, relevant, purposeful, and appropriately sized.

9. **Avoid amateurish results.** Many beginning writers, eager to display every graphic device a program offers, produce busy, cluttered documents. Too many typefaces, ruled lines, oversized headlines, and images will overwhelm readers. Strive for simple, clean, and forceful effects.

10. **Develop expertise.** Learn to use the desktop publishing features of your current word processing software, or investigate one of the special programs, such as Ventura, PageMaker, PowerPoint, or CorelDraw. Although the learning curve for many of these programs is steep, such effort is well spent if you will be producing newsletters, brochures, announcements, visual aids, and promotional literature.

## Career Application

Buy or borrow a book or two on designing documents, and select ten tips that you could share with the class. In teams of three or four, analyze the design and layout of three or four annual reports. Evaluate the appropriateness of typeface and type size, white space, headings, and graphics.

## FIGURE 13.6 Periodic Report

**Prewriting** *1*

**Analyze:** The purpose of this report is to inform management of the week's activities, customer reactions, and the rep's needs.

**Anticipate:** The audience is a manager who wants to be able to pick out the report highlights quickly. His reaction will probably be neutral or positive.

**Adapt:** Introduce the report data in a direct, straightforward manner.

**Writing** *2*

**Research:** Verify data for the landscape judging test. Collect facts about competitors. Double-check problems and needs.

**Organize:** Make lists of items for each of the four report categories. Be sure to distinguish between problems and needs. Emphasize needs.

**Compose:** Write and print first draft on a computer.

**Revising** *3*

**Revise:** Look for ways to eliminate wordiness. For greater emphasis use a bulleted list for *Competition Update* and for *Needs*. Make all items parallel.

**Proofread:** Run spell checker. Adjust white space around headings.

**Evaluate:** Does this report provide significant data in an easy-to-read format?

---

**DATE:**   March 15, 2005

**TO:**   Steve Schumacher

**FROM:**   Jim Chrisman   *JC*

**SUBJECT:**   Weekly Activity Report

> Presents internal informational report in memo format

### Activity Summary

Highlights of my activities for the week ending March 14 follow:

**Sherbrooke.** On Thursday and Friday I demonstrated our new Rain Stream drip systems at a vendor fair at Benbrook Farm Supply, where more than 500 people walked through.

**Frontenac.** Over the weekend I was a judge for the Quebec Landscape Technician test given at the college. This certification program ensures potential employers that a landscaper is properly trained. Applicants are tested in such areas as irrigation theory, repair, trouble-shooting, installation, and controller programming. The event proved to be very productive, I was able to talk to my distributors and to several important contractors whose crews were taking the tests.

> Condenses weekly activity report into topics requested by management

### Competition Update

- Toronado can't seem to fill its open sales position in the Eastern Townships.
- RainCo tried to steal the Trinity Country Club golf course contract from us by waiting until the job was spec'd our way and then submitting a lower bid. Fortunately, the Trinity people saw through this ploy and awarded us the contract nevertheless.
- Atlas has a real warranty problem with its 500 series in this area. One distributor had over 200 controllers returned in a seven-week period.

### Product Problems, Comments

A contractor in Drummondville told me that our Rain Stream No. 250 valves do not hold the adjustment screw in the throttled-down position. Are they designed to do so?

Our Remote Streamer S-100 is generating considerable excitement. Every time I mention it, people are very interested and request demos. I gave four demos last week and have three more scheduled this week. I'm not sure, though, how quickly these demos will translate into sales because contractors are waiting for our six-month special prices.

### Needs

- More information on xerigation training.
- French training videos showing our products.
- Spray nozzle to service small planter areas, say 2 to 4 m.

> Summarizes needs in abbreviated, easy-to-read form

423

- Begin by identifying the event (exact date, name, and location) and previewing the topics to be discussed.

- Summarize in the body three to five main points that might benefit the reader.

- Itemize your expenses, if requested, on a separate sheet.

- Close by expressing appreciation, suggesting action to be taken, or synthesizing the value of the trip or event.

Jeff Marchant was recently named employment coordinator in the Human Resources Department of an electronics appliance manufacturer headquartered in Windsor, Ontario. Recognizing his lack of experience in interviewing job applicants, he asked permission to attend a one-day conference on the topic. His boss, Angela Taylor, encouraged Jeff to attend, saying, "We all need to brush up on our interviewing techniques. Come back and tell us what you learned." When he returned, Jeff wrote the conference report shown in Figure 13.7. Here's how he describes its preparation: "I know my boss values brevity, so I worked hard to make my report no more than a page and a quarter. The conference saturated me with great ideas, far too many to cover in one brief report. So, I decided to discuss three topics that would be most useful to our staff. Although I had to be brief, I nonetheless wanted to provide as many details—especially about common interviewing mistakes—as possible. By the third draft, I had compressed my ideas into a manageable size without sacrificing any of the meaning."

## Progress and Interim Reports

Continuing projects often require progress or interim reports to describe their status. These reports may be external (advising customers regarding the headway of their projects) or internal (informing management of the status of activities). Progress reports typically follow this pattern of development:

- Specify in the opening the purpose and nature of the project.
- Provide background information if the audience requires filling in.
- Describe the work completed.
- Explain the work currently in progress, including personnel, activities, methods, and locations.
- Anticipate problems and possible remedies.
- Discuss future activities and provide the expected completion date.

As a location manager in the film industry, Sheila Ryan frequently writes progress reports, such as the one shown in Figure 13.8 (page 426). Producers want to be informed of what she's doing, and a phone call doesn't provide a permanent record. Here's how she describes the reasoning behind her progress report: "I usually include background information in my reports because a director doesn't always know or remember exactly what specifications I was given for a location search. Then I try to hit the high points of what I've completed and what I plan to do next, without getting bogged down in tiny details. Although it would be easier to skip them, I've learned to be up front with any problems that I anticipate. I don't tell how to solve the problems, but I feel duty-bound to at least mention them."

## Investigative Reports

Investigative or informational reports deliver data for a specific situation—without offering interpretation or recommendations. These nonrecurring reports are

**FIGURE 13.7  Conference Report**

DATE: April 22, 2005
TO: Angela Taylor
FROM: Jeff Marchant *JM*
SUBJECT: TRAINING CONFERENCE ON EMPLOYMENT INTERVIEWING

I enjoyed attending the "Interviewing People" training conference sponsored by the National Business Foundation. This one-day meeting, held in Toronto on April 19, provided excellent advice that will help us strengthen our interviewing techniques. Although the conference covered many topics, this report concentrates on three areas: structuring the interview, avoiding common mistakes, and responding to new legislation.

*Identifies topic and previews how the report is organized*

### Structuring the Interview

Job interviews usually have three parts. The opening establishes a friendly rapport with introductions, a few polite questions, and an explanation of the purpose for the interview. The body of the interview consists of questions controlled by the interviewer. The interviewer has three goals: (a) educating the applicant about the job, (b) eliciting information about the applicant's suitability for the job, and (c) promoting goodwill about the organization. In closing, the interviewer should encourage the applicant to ask questions, summarize main points, and indicate what actions will follow.

*Sets off major topics with centred headings*

### Avoiding Common Mistakes

Probably the most interesting and practical part of the conference centred on common mistakes made by interviewers, some of which I summarize here:

1. Not taking notes at each interview. Recording important facts enables you to remember the first candidate as easily as you remember the last—and all those in between.

2. Losing control of the interview. Keep control of the interview by digging into the candidate's answers to questions. Probe for responses of greater depth. Don't move on until a question has been satisfactorily answered.

3. Not testing the candidate's communication skills. To be able to evaluate a candidate's ability to express ideas, ask the individual to explain some technical jargon from his or her current position.

4. Having departing employees conduct the interviews for their replacements. Departing employees may be unreliable as interviewers because they tend to hire candidates not quite as strong as they are.

5. Failing to check references. As many as 15 percent of all résumés may contain falsified data. The best way to check references is to network: ask the person whose name has been given to suggest the name of another person.

*Covers facts that will most interest and help reader*

Angela Taylor                    Page 2                    April 22, 2005

### Responding to New Legislation

Recently enacted provisions of the Human Rights Code prohibit interviewers from asking candidates—or even their references—about candidates' disabilities. A question we frequently asked ("Do you have any physical limitations that would prevent you from performing the job for which you are applying?") would now break the law. Interviewers must also avoid asking about medical history; prescription-drug use; prior workers' compensation claims; work absenteeism due to illness; and past treatment for alcoholism, drug use, or mental illness.

### Conclusion

This conference provided me with valuable training that I would like to share with other department members at a future staff meeting. Let me know when it can be scheduled.

## FIGURE 13.8  Progress Report

### Tips for Writing Progress Reports
- Identify the purpose and the nature of the project immediately.
- Supply background information only if the reader must be educated.
- Describe the work completed.
- Discuss the work in progress, including personnel, activities, methods, and locations.
- Identify problems and possible remedies.
- Consider future activities.
- Close by telling the expected date of completion.

### QuaStar Productions

*Interoffice Memo*

**DATE:** January 7, 2005

**TO:** Rick Willens, Executive Producer

**FROM:** Sheila Ryan, Location Manager

**SUBJECT:** Sites for "Bodega Bay" Telefilm

*Identifies project and previews report*

This memo describes the progress of my search for an appropriate rustic home, villa, or ranch to be used for the wine country sequences in the telefilm "Bodega Bay." Three sites will be available for you to inspect on January 21, as you requested.

**Background:** In preparation for this assignment, I consulted Director Dave Durslag, who gave me his preferences for the site. He suggested a picturesque ranch home situated near vineyards, preferably with a scenic background. I also consulted Producer Teresa Silva, who told me that the site must accommodate 55 to 70 production crew members for approximately three weeks of filming. Ben Waters, telefilm accountant, requested that the cost of the site not exceed $24 000 for a three-week lease.

*Saves space by integrating headings into paragraphs*

**Work Completed:** For the past eight days I have searched the Niagara Escarpment area in Southern Ontario's wine country. Possible sites include turn-of-the-century estates, Victorian mansions, and rustic farmhouses in the Welland/St. Catharines area. One exceptional site is the Country Meadow Inn, a 97-year-old farmhouse nestled among vineyards with a breathtaking view of valleys and distant hills.

**Work To Be Completed:** In the next five days, I'll search the Niagara countryside. Many wineries contain charming structures that may present exactly the degree of atmosphere and mystery we need. These wineries have the added advantage of easy access. I will also inspect possible structures in and around Niagara-on-the-Lake. Finally, I've made an appointment with the director of provincial parks to discuss our project, use of provincial lands, restrictions, and costs.

*Tells the bad news as well as the good*

**Anticipated Problems:** You should be aware of two complications for filming in this area:
1. Property owners seem unfamiliar with the making of films and are suspicious of short-term leases.
2. Many trees won't have leaves again until May. You may wish to change the filming schedule somewhat.

*Concludes by giving completion date and describing what follows*

By January 14 you'll have my final report describing the three most promising locations. Arrangements will be made for you to visit these sites January 21.

generally arranged in a direct pattern with three segments: introduction, body, and summary. The body—which includes the facts, findings, or discussion—may be organized by time, component, importance, criteria, or convention. What's important is dividing the topic into logical segments, say, three to five areas that are roughly equal and don't overlap.

The subject matter of the report usually suggests the best way to divide or organize it. Beth Givens, an information specialist for a Maritime health-care consulting firm, was given the task of researching and writing an investigative report for St. John's Hospital. Her assignment: study the award-winning patient-service program at Good Samaritan Hospital, and report how it improved its patient satisfaction rating from 6.2 to 7.8 in just one year. Beth collected data and then organized her findings into four parts: management training, employee training, patient services, and follow-up program. Although we don't show Beth's complete report here, you can see a similar one in Chapter 12, Figure 12.2.

Whether you are writing a periodic, trip, conference, progress, or investigative report, you'll want to review the suggestions found in the following checklist.

> **Investigative reports provide information without interpretation or recommendations.**

## CHECKLIST FOR WRITING INFORMATIONAL REPORTS

### Introduction

✓ **Begin directly.** Identify the report and its purpose.

✓ **Provide a preview.** If the report is over a page long, give the reader a brief overview of its organization.

✓ **Supply background data selectively.** When readers are unfamiliar with the topic, briefly fill in the necessary details.

✓ **Divide the topic.** Strive to group the facts or findings into three to five roughly equal segments that do not overlap.

### Body

✓ **Arrange the subtopics logically.** Consider organizing by time, component, importance, criteria, or convention.

✓ **Use clear headings.** Supply functional or talking heads (at least one per page) that describe each important section.

✓ **Determine degree of formality.** Use an informal, conversational writing style unless the audience expects a more formal tone.

✓ **Enhance readability with graphic highlighting.** Make liberal use of bullets, numbered and lettered lists, headings, underlined items, and white space.

### Summary/Conclusion

✓ **When necessary, summarize the report.** Briefly review the main points and discuss what action will follow.

✓ **Offer a concluding thought.** If relevant, express appreciation or describe your willingness to provide further information.

# Hbc Revisited

Almost half of the Fortune 500 companies issue annual reports that provide details of their environmental and social behaviour.[9] When allegations of unfair overseas labour practices surfaced, and Hbc was accused of "cutting and running" rather than working with the suppliers to improve conditions, the company worked hard to repair its image.

Despite taking pains to improve its image, Hbc must remain vigilant. Companies are realizing the power of the Internet and have sought ways to ensure that criticism on the Web is kept to a minimum. Web sites critical of corporations, which are operated by consumers, former employees, and activists, are becoming increasingly common. The Hudson's Bay Company has responded to the concern by registering the "thebaysucks.com" domain name to prevent it from falling into less sympathetic hands.[10]

In the areas of corporate responsibility, the Hudson's Bay Company has a tradition of supporting local communities. Hbc contributes to community, heritage, health, and educational initiatives through corporate donations, sponsorships, foundations, fundraising activities, and in-kind contributions. For example, in 2002, Zellers stores raised over $2.5 million for cystic fibrosis research by conducting over 70 nationwide walks, golf tournaments, and in-store sales of cutouts.[11]

Beyond polishing its image, Hbc still has other pressing concerns. "The long-term success of any retailer rests with its ability to create and deliver value to customer segments that define value in different ways," according to George Heller, president and CEO of the Hudson's Bay Company. Therefore, Hbc is aggressively moving into other markets. "Whether Canadians are shopping for their homes or their closets, we want to ensure that they are always finding unique and exciting brands in the Hbc family of stores," said Heller.[12]

While Hbc is constantly looking ahead to catch emerging trends, it is also looking over its shoulder at what the competition is doing.

## CRITICAL THINKING

- How important to Hbc are the collection, organization, and distribution of up-to-date information regarding fashion trends, competition, and product development?
- Should Hbc monitor the information from, and concerns raised by, organizations such as the Maquila Solidarity Network and potential rogue Web sites that are critical of the company? If so, what kinds of reports might be made to management by individuals assigned to the task?
- What kinds of reports would be required from Leah Simpson, an Hbc employee assigned to organize a nationwide walk for a cystic fibrosis fundraiser? What organizational plan would the reports follow?

**www.hbc.com**

# WRITING ANALYTICAL REPORTS

5

Analytical reports present information but emphasize reasoning, conclusions, and recommendations.

Analytical reports differ significantly from informational reports. Although both seek to collect and present data clearly, analytical reports also analyze the data and typically try to persuade the reader to accept the conclusions and act on the recommendations. Informational reports emphasize facts; analytical reports emphasize reasoning and conclusions.

For some readers analytical reports may be organized directly with the conclusions and recommendations near the beginning. Directness is appropriate when the reader has confidence in the writer, based on either experience or credentials. Frontloading the recommendations also works when the topic is routine or familiar and the reader is supportive.

Directness can backfire, though. If you announce the recommendations too quickly, the reader may immediately object to a single idea, one that you had no suspicion would trigger a negative reaction. Once the reader is opposed, changing an unfavourable mind-set may be difficult or impossible. A reader may also think you have oversimplified or overlooked something significant if you lay out all the recommendations before explaining how you arrived at them. When the reader must be led through the process of discovering the solution or recommendation, use the indirect method: present conclusions and recommendations last.

Most analytical reports answer questions about specific problems. How can we use a Web site most effectively? Should we close the Bradford plant? Should we buy or lease company cars? How can we improve customer service? Three typical analytical reports answer business questions: justification/recommendation reports, feasibility reports, and yardstick reports. Because these reports all solve problems, the categories are not mutually exclusive. What distinguishes them is their goals and organization.

## Justification/Recommendation Reports

Both managers and employees must occasionally write reports that justify or recommend something, such as buying equipment, changing a procedure, hiring an employee, consolidating departments, or investing funds. Large organizations sometimes prescribe how these reports should be organized; they use forms with conventional headings. When you are free to select an organizational plan yourself, however, let your audience and topic determine your choice of direct or indirect structure.

**Justification/recommendation reports follow the direct or indirect pattern depending on the audience and the topic.**

*Direct Pattern.* For nonsensitive topics and recommendations that will be agreeable to readers, you can organize directly according to the following sequence:

**The direct pattern is appropriate for justification/recommendation reports on nonsensitive topics and for receptive audiences.**

- Identify the problem or need briefly.

- Announce the recommendation, solution, or action concisely and with action verbs.

- Explain more fully the benefits of the recommendation or steps to be taken to solve the problem.

- Include a discussion of pros, cons, and costs.

- Conclude with a summary specifying the recommendation and action to be taken.

This greenhouse at the famous Keukenhof Gardens in Holland became a key point in the justification report of a tour organizer. In supporting his inclusion of the Keukenhof in a proposed itinerary for a North American travel company, the writer argued that tourists can never be rained out. In addition to the 28 ha of outdoor gardens, thousands of flowers bloom under glass. Persuasive justification reports explain fully all the benefits of a recommendation and also anticipate possible reader objections.

**CHAPTER 13**
Organizing and Writing
Typical Business Reports
**429**

Here's how Justin Brown applied the process in justifying a purchase. Justin is operations manager in charge of a fleet of trucks for a large parcel delivery company in Quebec. When he heard about a new Goodyear smart tire with an electronic chip, Justin thought his company should give the new tire a try. Because new tires would represent an irregular purchase and because they would require a pilot test, he wrote the justification/recommendation report, shown in Figure 13.9, to his boss. Justin describes his report in this way: "As more and more parcel delivery companies crop up, we have to find ways to cut costs so that we can remain competitive. Although more expensive initially, smart tires may solve a lot of our problems and save us money in the long run. I knew Bill Montgomery, operations vice president, would be interested in them, especially in view of the huge Firestone tire fiasco.[13] Because Bill would be most interested in what they could do for us, I concentrated on benefits. In my first draft the benefits were lost in a couple of long paragraphs. Only after I read what I had written did I see that I was really talking about four separate benefits. Then I looked for words to summarize each one as a heading. So that Bill would know exactly what he should do, I concluded with specifics. All he had to do was say 'Go.'"

*Indirect Pattern.* When a reader may oppose a recommendation or when circumstances suggest caution, don't be in a hurry to reveal your recommendation. Consider using the following sequence for an indirect approach to your recommendations:

- Make a general reference to the problem, not to your recommendation, in the subject line.

- Describe the problem or need your recommendation addresses. Use specific examples, supporting statistics, and authoritative quotes to lend credibility to the seriousness of the problem.

- Discuss alternative solutions, beginning with the least likely to succeed.

- Present the most promising alternative (your recommendation) last.

- Show how the advantages of your recommendation outweigh its disadvantages.

- Summarize your recommendation. If appropriate, specify the action it requires.

- Ask for authorization to proceed if necessary.

Diane Andreas, an executive assistant at a large petroleum and mining company in Calgary, Alberta, received a challenging research assignment. Her boss, the director of Human Resources, asked her to investigate ways to persuade employees to quit smoking. Here's how she describes her task: "We banned smoking many years ago inside our buildings, but we never tried very hard to get smokers to actually kick their habits. My job was to gather information about the problem and how other companies have helped workers stop smoking. The report would go to my boss, but I knew he would pass it along to the management council for approval. If the report were just for my boss, I would put my recommendation right up front, because I'm sure he would support it. But the management council is another story. They need persuasion because of the costs involved—and because some of them are smokers. Therefore, I put the alternative I favoured last. To gain credibility, I footnoted my sources. I had enough material for a ten-page report, but I kept it to two pages in keeping with our company report policy."

Diane single-spaced her report, shown in Figure 13.10 on page 432, because that's her company's preference. Some companies prefer the readability of double spacing. Be sure to check with your organization for its preference before printing your reports.

The indirect pattern is appropriate for justification/recommendation reports on sensitive topics and for potentially unreceptive audiences.

Footnoting sources lends added credibility to justification/recommendation reports.

## FIGURE 13.9  Justification/Recommendation Report: Direct Pattern

### Prewriting 1

**Analyze:** The purpose of this report is to persuade the manager to authorize the purchase and pilot testing of smart tires.

**Anticipate:** The audience is a manager who is familiar with operations but not with this product. He will probably be receptive to the recommendation.

**Adapt:** Present the report data in a direct, straightforward manner.

### Writing 2

**Research:** Collect data on how smart tires could benefit operations.

**Organize:** Discuss the problem briefly. Introduce and justify the recommendation by noting its cost-effectiveness and paperwork benefits. Explain the benefits of smart tires. Describe the action to be taken.

**Compose:** Write and print first draft.

### Revising 3

**Revise:** Revise to break up long paragraphs about benefits. Isolate each benefit in an enumerated list with headings.

**Proofread:** Double-check all figures. Be sure all headings are parallel.

**Evaluate:** Does this report make its request concisely but emphatically? Will the reader see immediately what action is required?

---

**DATE:**  July 19, 2005
**TO:**  Bill Montgomery, Vice President
**FROM:**  Justin Brown, Operations Manager  *JB*
**SUBJECT:**  Pilot Testing Smart Tires

Next to fuel, truck tires are our biggest operating cost. Last year we spent $211 000 replacing and retreading tires for 495 trucks. This year the costs will be greater because prices have jumped at least 12 percent and because we've increased our fleet to 550 trucks. Truck tires are an additional burden since they require labour-intensive paperwork to track their warranties, wear, and retread histories. To reduce our long-term costs and to improve our tire tracking system, I recommend that we do the following:  ● *Introduces problem briefly*

- Purchase 24 Goodyear smart tires.  *← Presents recommendations immediately*
- Begin a one-year pilot test on six trucks.

**How Smart Tires Work**

Smart tires have an embedded computer chip that monitors wear, performance, and durability. The chip also creates an electronic fingerprint for positive identification of a tire. By passing a hand-held sensor next to the tire, we can learn where and when a tire was made (for warranty and other identification), how much tread it had originally, and its serial number.  *← Justifies recommendation by explaining product and benefits*

**How Smart Tires Could Benefit Us**

Although smart tires are initially more expensive than other tires, they could help us improve our operations and save us money in four ways:

1. **Retreads.**  Goodyear believes that the wear data is so accurate that we should be able to retread every tire three times, instead of our current two times. If that's true, in one year we could save at least $27 000 in new tire costs.
2. **Safety.**  Accurate and accessible wear data should reduce the danger of blowouts and flat tires. Last year, drivers reported six blowouts.
3. **Record keeping and maintenance.**  Smart tires could reduce our maintenance costs considerably. Currently, we use an electric branding iron to mark serial numbers on new tires. Our biggest headache is manually reading those serial numbers, decoding them, and maintaining records to meet safety regulations. Reading such data electronically could save us thousands of dollars in labour.
4. **Theft protection.**  The chip can be used to monitor each tire as it leaves or enters the warehouse or yard, thus discouraging theft.

*Enumerates items for maximum impact and readability →*

**Summary and Action**

Specifically, I recommend that you do the following:  *← Explains recommendation in more detail*
- Authorize the special purchase of 24 Goodyear smart tires at $450 each, plus one electronic sensor at $1 200.
- Approve a one-year pilot test in our Quebec territory that equips six trucks with smart tires and tracks their performance.  *Specifies action to be taken →*

**FIGURE 13.10** Justification/Recommendation Report: Indirect Pattern

1

| DATE: | October 11, 2005 |
| TO: | Damon Moore, Director, Human Resources |
| FROM: | Diane Andreas, Executive Assistant  *DA* |
| SUBJECT: | MEASURES TO HELP EMPLOYEES STOP SMOKING |

At your request, I have examined measures that encourage employees to quit smoking. As company records show, approximately 23 percent of our employees still smoke, despite the antismoking and clean-air policies we adopted in 1995. To collect data for this report, I studied professional and government publications; I also inquired at companies and clinics about stop-smoking programs.

This report presents data describing the significance of the problem, three alternative solutions, and a recommendation based on my investigation.

**Significance of Problem: Health Care and Productivity Losses**

Employees who smoke are costly to any organization. The following statistics show the effects of smoking for workers and for organizations:

• Absenteeism is 40 to 50 percent greater among smoking employees.
• Accidents are two to three times greater among smokers.
• Bronchitis, lung and heart disease, cancer, and early death are more frequent among smokers (Johns, 2003, p. 14).

Although our clean-air policy prohibits smoking in the building, shop, and office, we have done little to encourage employees to stop smoking. Many workers still go outside to smoke at lunch and breaks. Other companies have been far more proactive in their attempts to stop employee smoking. Many companies have found that persuading employees to stop smoking was a decisive factor in reducing their supplementary health insurance premiums. Below is a discussion of three common stop-smoking measures tried by other companies, along with a projected cost factor for each.

**Alternative 1: Literature and Events**

The least expensive and easiest stop-smoking measure involves the distribution of literature, such as "The Ten-Step Plan" from Smokefree Enterprises and government pamphlets citing smoking dangers. Some companies have also sponsored events such as Weedless Wednesday, a one-day occasion intended to develop group spirit in spurring smokers to quit. "Studies show, however," says one expert, "that literature and company-sponsored events have little permanent effect in helping smokers quit" (Woo, 2003, p. 107).

Cost: Negligible

*Annotations (left margin):*
- Avoids revealing recommendation immediately
- Uses headings that combine function and description
- Discusses least effective alternative first

*Annotations (right margin):*
- Introduces purpose of report, tells method of data collection, and previews organization
- Documents data sources for credibility; uses APA style citing author, date, and page number in the text

# Feasibility Reports

**Feasibility reports analyze whether a proposal or plan will work.**

Feasibility reports examine the practicality and advisability of following a course of action. They answer this question: Will this plan or proposal work? Feasibility reports typically are internal reports written to advise on matters such as consolidating departments, offering a wellness program to employees, or hiring an outside firm to handle a company's accounting or computing operations. These reports may also be written by consultants called in to investigate a problem. The focus in these reports is on the decision to stop or proceed with the proposal. Since your role is not to persuade the reader to accept the decision, you'll want to present the decision immediately. In writing feasibility reports, consider these suggestions:

• Announce your decision immediately.

• Provide a description of the background and problem necessitating the proposal.

**FIGURE 13.10 Continued**

2

### Alternative 2: Stop-Smoking Programs Outside the Workplace

Local clinics provide treatment programs in classes at their centres. Here in Calgary we have Smokers' Treatment Centre, ACC Motivation Centre, and the New-Choice Program for Stopping Smoking. These behaviour-modification stop-smoking programs are acknowledged to be more effective than literature distribution or incentive programs. However, studies of companies using off-workplace programs show that many employees fail to attend regularly and do not complete the programs.

> Cost:  $750 per employee, three-month individual program
> (New-Choice Program)
> $500 per employee, three-month group sessions

— Highlights costs for easy comparison

### Alternative 3: Stop-Smoking Programs at the Workplace

Many clinics offer workplace programs with counsellors meeting employees in company conference rooms. These programs have the advantage of keeping a firm's employees together so that they develop a group spirit and exert pressure on each other to succeed. The most successful programs are on company premises and also on company time. Employees participating in such programs had a 72 percent greater success record than employees attending the same stop-smoking program at an outside clinic (Manley, 2002, p. 35). A disadvantage of this arrangement, of course, is lost work time— amounting to about two hours per week for three months.

— Arranges alternatives so that most effective is last

> Cost:  $500 per employee, three-month program two hours
> per week release time for three months

### Conclusions and Recommendation

— Summarizes findings and ends with specific recommendation

Smokers seem to require discipline, counselling, and professional assistance in kicking the nicotine habit. Workplace stop-smoking programs, on company time, are more effective than literature, incentives, and off-workplace programs. If our goal is to reduce supplementary health care costs and lead our employees to healthful lives, we should invest in a workplace stop-smoking program with release time for smokers. Although the program temporarily reduces productivity, we can expect to recapture that loss in lower health care premiums and healthier employees.

— Reveals recommendation only after discussing all alternatives

Therefore, I recommend that we begin a stop-smoking treatment program on company premises with two hours per week of release time for participants for three months.

3

### References

Lists all references in APA style

Magazine ——— Johns, K. (2003, May). No smoking in your workplace. *Business Times,* 14–16.

Journal ——— Manley, D. (2002). Up in smoke: A case study of one company's proactive stance against smoking. *Management Review, 14,* 33–37.

Book ——— Woo, N. A. (2003). *The last gasp.* New York: Field Publishers.

- Discuss the benefits of the proposal.
- Describe the problems that may result.
- Calculate the costs associated with the proposal, if appropriate.
- Show the time frame necessary for implementation of the proposal.

A typical feasibility report presents the decision, background information, benefits, problems, costs, and a schedule.

Elizabeth Webb, customer service manager for a large insurance company in Surrey, British Columbia, wrote the feasibility report shown in Figure 13.11. She describes the report thus: "We had been losing customer service reps (CSRs) after they were trained and were most valuable to us. When I talked with our vice president about the problem, she didn't want me to take time away from my job to investigate what other companies were doing to retain their CSRs. Instead, we hired a consultant who suggested that we use a CSR career progression schedule. The vice president then wanted to know whether the consultant's plan was feasible. Although my report is only one page long, it provides all necessary information: background, benefits, problems, costs, and time frame."

## FIGURE 13.11 Feasibility Report

Outlines organization of the report

Evaluates positive and negative aspects of proposal objectively

Reveals decision immediately

Describes problem and background

Presents costs and schedule; omits unnecessary summary

**DATE:** November 11, 2005

**TO:** Shauna Clay-Taylor, Vice President

**FROM:** Elizabeth W. Webb, Customer Service Manager   E.W.W.

**SUBJECT:** FEASIBILITY OF PROGRESSION SCHEDULE FOR CSRs

The plan calling for a progression schedule for our customer service representatives is workable, and I think it could be fully implemented by April 1. This report discusses the background, benefits, problems, costs, and time frame involved in executing the plan.

**Background: Training and Advancement Problems for CSR Reps.** Because of the many insurance policies and agents we service, new customer service representatives require eight weeks of intensive training. Even after this thorough introduction, CSRs are overwhelmed. They take about eight more months before feeling competent on the job. Once they reach their potential, they often look for other positions in the company because they see few advancement possibilities in customer service. These problems were submitted to an outside consultant, who suggested a CSR progression schedule.

**Benefits of Plan: Career Progression and Incremental Training.** The proposed plan sets up a schedule of career progression, including these levels: (1) CSR trainee, (2) CSR Level I, (3) CSR Level II, (4) CSR Level III, (5) Senior CSR, and (6) CSR supervisor. This program, which includes salary increments with each step, provides a career ladder and incentives for increased levels of expertise and achievement. The plan also facilitates training. Instead of overloading a new trainee with an initial eight-week training program, we would train CSRs slowly with a combination of classroom and on-the-job experiences. Each level requires additional training and expertise.

**Problems of Plan: Difficulty in Writing Job Descriptions and Initial Confusion.** One of the biggest problems will be distinguishing the job duties at each level. However, I believe that, with the help of our consultant, we can sort out the tasks and expertise required at each level. Another problem will be determining appropriate salary differentials. Attached is a tentative schedule showing proposed wages at each level. We expect to encounter confusion and frustration in implementing this program at first, particularly in placing our current CSRs within the structure.

**Costs.** Implementing the progression schedule involves two direct costs. The first is the salary of a trainer, at about $40 000 a year. The second cost derives from increased salaries of upper-level CSRs, shown on the attached schedule. I believe, however, that the costs involved are within the estimates planned for this project.

**Time Frame.** Developing job descriptions should take us about three weeks. Preparing a training program will require another three weeks. Once the program is started, I expect a breaking-in period of at least three months. By April 1 the progression schedule will be fully implemented and showing positive results in improved CSR training, service, and retention.

Attachment

# Yardstick Reports

"Yardstick" reports examine problems with two or more solutions. To evaluate the best solution, the writer establishes criteria by which to compare the alternatives. The criteria then act as a yardstick against which all the alternatives are measured. This yardstick approach is effective when companies establish specifications for equipment purchases, and then compare each manufacturer's product with the established specs. The yardstick approach is also effective when exact specifications cannot be established.

Yardstick reports consider alternative solutions to a problem by establishing criteria against which to weigh options.

For example, when the giant aircraft firm McDonnell Douglas considered relocating its global headquarters, it evaluated many cities such as Montreal, Toronto, Vancouver, Halifax, and Edmonton. For each of these sites, McDonnell Douglas compared labour costs, land availability and costs, housing costs, and tax breaks. It did not set up exact specifications for each category; it merely compared each city in these various categories. The real advantage to yardstick reports is that alternatives can be measured consistently using the same criteria. Reports using a yardstick approach typically are organized this way:

- Begin by describing the problem or need.

- Explain possible solutions and alternatives.

- Establish criteria for comparing the alternatives; tell how the criteria were selected or developed.

- Discuss and evaluate each alternative in terms of the criteria.

- Draw conclusions and make recommendations.

Kelly Linden, benefits administrator for computer manufacturer CompuTech, was called on to write a report comparing outplacement agencies. These agencies counsel discharged employees and help them find new positions; fees are paid by the former employer. Kelly knew that times were bad for CompuTech and that extensive downsizing would take place in the next two years. Her task was to compare outplacement agencies and recommend one to CompuTech.

After collecting information, Kelly found that her biggest problem was organizing the data and developing a system for making comparisons. All the outplacement agencies she investigated seemed to offer the same basic package of services. Here's how she described her report, shown in Figure 13.12 on the next page.

"With the information I gathered about three outplacement agencies, I made a big grid listing the names of the agencies across the top. Down the side I listed general categories—such as services, costs, and reputation. Then I filled in the information for each agency. This grid, which began to look like a table, helped me organize all the bits and pieces of information. After studying the grid, I saw that all the information could be grouped into four categories: counselling services, secretarial and research assistance, reputation, and costs. I made these the criteria I would use to compare agencies. Next, I divided my grid into two parts, which became Table 1 and Table 2. In writing the report, I could have made each agency a separate heading, followed by a discussion of how it measured up to the criteria. Immediately, though, I saw how repetitious that would become. So I used the criteria as headings and discussed how each agency met each criterion—or failed to meet it. Making a recommendation was easy once I had the tables made and could see how the agencies compared."

Grids are a useful way to organize and compare data for a yardstick report.

## FIGURE 13.12 Yardstick Report

**DATE:** April 28, 2005

**TO:** George O. Dawes, Vice President

**FROM:** Kelly Linden, Benefits Administrator

**SUBJECT:** CHOICE OF OUTPLACEMENT SERVICES

Here is the report you requested April 1 investigating the possibility of CompuTech's use of outplacement services. It discusses the problem of counselling services for discharged staff and establishes criteria for selecting an outplacement agency. It then evaluates three prospective agencies and presents a recommendation based on that evaluation.

*Introduces purpose and gives overview of report organization*

### Problem: Counselling Discharged Staff

*Discusses background briefly because reader already knows the problem*

In an effort to reduce costs and increase competitiveness, CompuTech will begin a program of staff reduction that will involve releasing up to 20 percent of our work force over the next 12 to 24 months. Many of these employees have been with us for ten or more years, and they are not being released for performance faults. These employees deserve a severance package that includes counselling and assistance in finding new careers.

### Solution and Alternatives: Outplacement Agencies

*Uses dual headings, giving function and description*

Numerous outplacement agencies offer discharged employees counselling and assistance in locating new careers. This assistance minimizes not only the negative feelings related to job loss but also the very real possibility of litigation. Potentially expensive lawsuits have been lodged against some companies by unhappy employees who felt they were unfairly released.

In seeking an outplacement agency, we should find one that offers advice to the sponsoring company as well as to dischargees. Frankly, many of our managers need help in conducting termination sessions. A suitable outplacement agency should be selected soon so that we can learn about legal termination procedures and also have an agency immediately available when employees are discharged. Here in the metropolitan area, I have located three potential outplacement agencies appropriate to serve our needs: Gray & Associates, Right Access, and Careers Plus.

*Announces solution and the alternatives it presents*

### Establishing Criteria for Selecting Agency

*Tells how criteria were selected*

In order to choose among the three agencies, I established criteria based on professional articles, discussions with officials at other companies using outplacement agencies, and interviews with agencies. Here are the four groups of criteria I used in evaluating the three agencies:

1. <u>Counselling services</u>—including job-search advice, résumé help, crisis management, corporate counselling, and availability of full-time counsellors

2. <u>Secretarial and research assistance</u>—including availability of secretarial staff, librarian, and personal computers

3. <u>Reputation</u>—based on a telephone survey of former clients and listing with a professional association

4. <u>Costs</u>—for both group programs and executive services

*Creates four criteria to use as yardsticks in evaluating alternatives*

---

## CHECKLIST FOR WRITING ANALYTICAL REPORTS

### Introduction

 Identify the purpose of the report. Explain why the report is being written.

 Preview the organization of the report. Especially for long reports, explain to the reader how the report will be organized.

 Summarize the conclusions and recommendations for receptive audiences. Use the direct pattern only if you have the confidence of the reader.

FIGURE 13.12  **Continued**

Vice President Dawes                Page 2                April 28, 2005

**Discussion: Evaluating Agencies by Criteria**

Each agency was evaluated using the four criteria just described.  Data comparing the first three criteria are summarized in Table 1.

Table 1

A COMPARISON OF SERVICES AND REPUTATIONS
FOR THREE LOCAL OUTPLACEMENT AGENCIES

— Places table close to spot where it is first mentioned

| | Gray & Associates | Right Access | Careers Plus |
|---|---|---|---|
| Counselling services | | | |
| Résumé advice | Yes | Yes | Yes |
| Crisis management | Yes | No | Yes |
| Corporate counselling | Yes | No | No |
| Full-time counsellors | Yes | No | Yes |
| Secretarial, research assistance | | | |
| Secretarial staff | Yes | Yes | Yes |
| Librarian, research library | Yes | No | Yes |
| Personal computers | Yes | No | Yes |
| Listed by National Association of Career Consultants | Yes | No | Yes |
| Reputation (telephone survey of former clients) | Excellent | Good | Excellent |

Summarizes complex data in table for easy reading and reference

**Counselling Services**

All three agencies offered similar basic counselling services with job-search and résumé advice.  They differed, however, in three significant areas.

Right Access does not offer crisis management, a service that puts the discharged employee in contact with a counsellor the same day the employee is released.  Experts in the field consider this service especially important to help the dischargee begin "bonding" with the counsellor immediately.  Immediate counselling also helps the dischargee through the most traumatic moments of one of life's great disappointments and helps him or her learn how to break the news to family members.  Crisis management can be instrumental in reducing lawsuits because dischargees immediately begin to focus on career planning instead of concentrating on their pain and need for revenge.  Moreover, Right Access does not employ full-time counsellors; it hires part-timers according to demand.  Industry authorities advise against using agencies whose staff members are inexperienced and employed on an "as-needed" basis.

Highlights the similarities and differences among the alternatives

In addition, neither Right Access nor Careers Plus offers regular corporate counselling, which I feel is critical in training our managers to conduct exit interviews.  Careers Plus, however, suggested that it could schedule special workshops if desired.

Does not repeat obvious data from table

**Secretarial and Research Assistance**

Both Gray & Associates and Careers Plus offer complete secretarial services and personal computers.  Dischargees have access to staff and equipment to assist them in their job searches.  These agencies also provide research libraries, librarians, and databases of company information to help in securing interviews.

# Findings

 Discuss pros and cons. In recommendation/justification reports, evaluate the advantages and disadvantages of each alternative. For unreceptive audiences consider placing the recommended alternative last.

 Establish criteria to evaluate alternatives. In "yardstick" studies, create criteria to use in measuring each alternative consistently.

 Support the findings with evidence. Supply facts, statistics, expert opinion, survey data, and other proof from which you can draw logical conclusions.

**FIGURE 13.12 Continued**

**Reputation**

*Discusses objectively how each agency meets criteria*

To assess the reputation of each agency, I checked its listing with the National Association of Career Consultants. This is a voluntary organization of outplacement agencies that monitors and polices its members. Gray & Associates and Careers Plus are listed; Right Access is not.

For further evidence I conducted a telephone survey of former agency clients. The three agencies supplied me with names and telephone numbers of companies and individuals they had served. I called four former clients for each agency. Most of the individuals were pleased with the outplacement services they had received. I asked each client the same questions so that I could compare responses.

**Costs**

All three agencies have two separate fee schedules, summarized in Table 2. The first schedule is for group programs intended for lower-level employees. These include off-site or on-site single-day workshop sessions, and the prices range from $1 000 per session (at Right Access) to $1 500 per session (at Gray & Associates). An additional fee of $40 to $50 is charged for each participant.

*Selects most important data from table to discuss*

The second fee schedule covers executive services. This counselling is individual and costs from 10 percent to 18 percent of the dischargee's previous year's salary. Since CompuTech will be forced to release numerous managerial staff members, the executive fee schedule is critical. Table 2 shows fees for a hypothetical case involving a manager who earns $60 000 per year.

Table 2

A COMPARISON OF COSTS FOR THREE AGENCIES

|  | Gray & Associates | Right Access | Careers Plus |
|---|---|---|---|
| Group programs | $1 500/session, $45/participant | $1 000/session, $40/participant | $1 400/session, $50/participant |
| Executive services | 15% of previous year's salary | 10% of previous year's salary | 18% of previous year's salary plus $1 000 fee |
| Manager at $60 000/year | $9 000 | $6 000 | $11 800 |

**Conclusions and Recommendations**

*Gives reasons for making recommendation*

Although Right Access has the lowest fees, it lacks crisis management, corporate counselling, full-time counsellors, library facilities, and personal computers. Moreover, it is not listed by the National Association of Career Consultants. Therefore, the choice is between Gray & Associates and Careers Plus. Since they have similar services, the deciding factor is cost. Careers Plus would charge nearly $3 000 more for counselling a manager than would Gray & Associates. Although Gray & Associates has fewer computers available, all other elements of its services seem good. Therefore, I recommend that CompuTech hire Gray & Associates as an outplacement agency to counsel discharged employees.

*Narrows choice to final alternative*

 Organize the findings for logic and readability. Arrange the findings around the alternatives or the reasons leading to the conclusion. Use headings, enumerations, lists, tables, and graphics to focus emphasis.

## Conclusions/Recommendations

 Draw reasonable conclusions from the findings. Develop conclusions that answer the research question. Justify the conclusions with highlights from the findings.

 Make recommendations, if asked. For multiple recommendations prepare a list. Use action verbs. Explain needed action.

## *Applying Your Skills at Hbc*

The Hudson's Bay Company is continually seeking ways to remain competitive. The Hbc Rewards program continues to expand its partnerships to over 8.5 million members in Canada.[14]

To compete with Winners, the leading Canadian discount designer retailer, the Hudson's Bay Company has also entered the "off-price" segment of the market. Hbc quietly introduced this market in the fall of 2002 with the goal of making it account for 10 percent of total sales. Off-price merchandise costs less because it is purchased later in the season or may come from liquidators who are selling inventories of bankrupt retailers. Since The Bay and Winners share the same suppliers, and Winners is the fifth largest apparel retailer in Canada, with The Bay ranked fourth, the competition will be interesting.[15]

Not only does Winners compete in the fashion department, but it also creates competition in the housewares department with its Home Sense chain. The new Winners More banner carries not only brand-name clothing but also home fashions with its usual 20 to 60 percent discount,[16] which is direct competition for the Hudson's Bay Company's Home Outfitters chain.

Home Outfitters, launched in 1999, is the fastest-growing specialty chain in Canada. "For over 330 years, Hbc has changed and adapted to meet the needs of Canadians. As our customers spend more on their homes, Hbc is responding with Home Outfitters," said Marc Chouinard, president and COO of The Bay. The market for "home" and "home decorating" merchandise continues to increase. According to Statistics Canada's Large Retailer Commodity Survey, sales in the total home decorating category increased by 6.7 percent in 2002. Canadians spend more of their disposable incomes on home and home-related products (according to Statistics Canada's Annual Retail Survey). "Our goal is to continue to expand this chain over the next few years," said Bill Morrison, general manager, Home Outfitters.[17]

### Your Task

As assistant to Bill Morrison, make a list of at least six criteria to use in evaluating sites for new Home Outfitters stores. What sources of primary and secondary information would be useful in making a site choice? What kind of report would be best for arriving at a decision and reporting the search team's choice? How should that report be organized?

**www.hbc.com**

## SUMMARY OF LEARNING OBJECTIVES

*1* **Use tabulating and statistical techniques to sort and interpret report data.** Report data are more meaningful when sorted into tables or when analyzed by mean (the arithmetic average), median (the midpoint in a group of figures), and mode (the most frequent response). Range represents a span between the highest and lowest figures. Grids help organize complex data into rows and columns.

*2* **Draw meaningful conclusions and make practical report recommendations.** Conclusions tell what the survey data mean—especially in relation to the original report problem. They summarize key findings and may attempt to explain what caused the report problem. They are usually enumerated. In reports that call for recommendations, writers make specific suggestions for actions that can solve the report problem. Recommendations should be feasible and potentially agreeable to the audience. They should all relate to the initial problem. Recommendations may be combined with conclusions.

**3** Organize report data logically and provide cues to aid comprehension. Reports may be organized in many ways, including by (1) time (establishing a chronology or history of events), (2) component (discussing a problem by geography, division, or product), (3) importance (arranging data from most important to least important, or vice versa), (4) criteria (comparing items by standards), or (5) convention (using an already established grouping).

**4** Prepare typical informational reports. Periodic, trip, convention, progress, and investigative reports are examples of typical informational reports. Such reports include an introduction that may preview the report purpose and supply background data if necessary. The body of the report is generally divided into three to five segments that may be organized by time, component, importance, criteria, or convention. The body should include clear headings and may use an informal, conversational style unless the audience expects a more formal tone. The summary or conclusion reviews the main points and discusses what action will follow. The conclusion may offer a final thought, express appreciation, or express willingness to provide further information.

**5** Prepare typical analytical reports. Typical analytical reports include justification/recommendation reports, feasibility reports, and yardstick reports. Justification/recommendation reports organized directly identify a problem, immediately announce a recommendation or solution, explain and discuss its merits, and summarize the action to be taken. Justification/recommendation reports organized indirectly describe a problem, discuss alternative solutions, prove the superiority of one solution, and ask for authorization to proceed with that solution. Feasibility reports study the advisability of following a course of action. They generally announce the author's proposal immediately. Then they describe the background, advantages and disadvantages, costs, and time frame for implementing the proposal. Yardstick reports compare two or more solutions to a problem by measuring each against a set of established criteria. They usually describe a problem, explain possible solutions, establish criteria for comparing alternatives, evaluate each alternative in terms of the criteria, draw conclusions, and make recommendations. The advantage to yardstick reports is consistency in comparing various alternatives.

# CHAPTER REVIEW

1. Forms that use systematic columns and rows to enable you to summarize and simplify numerical data from questionnaires and interviews are called what? (Obj. 1)

2. What is cross-tabulation? Give an example. (Obj. 1)

3. Calculate the mean, median, and mode for these figures: 3, 4, 4, 4, 10. (Obj. 1)

4. How can a grid help classify material? (Obj. 1)

5. What are the two most widely read sections of a report? (Obj. 2)

6. How do conclusions differ from recommendations? (Obj. 2)

7. When reports have multiple recommendations, how should they be presented? (Obj. 2)

8. Name five methods for organizing report data. Be prepared to discuss each. (Obj. 3)

9. What three devices can report writers use to prevent readers from getting lost in the text? (Obj. 3)

10. Informational reports typically are organized into what three parts? (Obj. 4)

11. Describe periodic reports and what they generally contain. (Obj. 4)

**12.** What should a progress report include? (Obj. 4)

**13.** What sequence should a direct recommendation/justification report follow? (Obj. 5)

**14.** What is a feasibility report? Are they generally intended for internal or external audiences? (Obj. 5)

**15.** What is a yardstick report? (Obj. 5)

# CRITICAL THINKING

**1.** Why is audience analysis particularly important in making report recommendations? (Obj. 2)

**2.** Should all reports be organized so that they follow the sequence of investigation—that is, describing for the reader the initial problem, analysis of issues, data collection, data analysis, and conclusions? Why or why not? (Obj. 3)

**3.** Do most reports flow upward or downward? Why? (Objs. 3–5)

**4.** What are the major differences between informational and analytical reports? (Objs. 4 and 5)

**5.** **Ethical Issue:** Discuss the ethics of using persuasive tactics to convince a report's readers to accept its conclusions. Should you be persuasive only when you believe in the soundness and truth of your conclusions?

# ACTIVITIES

## 13.1 Tabulation and Interpretation of Survey Results (Obj. 1)

**TEAM**　　**CRITICAL THINKING**

Your business communication class at North Shore College was asked by the college bookstore manager, Larry Krause, to conduct a survey (see Chapter 12, Figure 12.9). Concerned about the environment, Krause wants to learn students' reactions to eliminating plastic bags, of which 45 000 are given away annually by the bookstore. Students were questioned about a number of proposals, resulting in the following raw data.

**For major purchases the bookstore should:**

|  | Agree | Undecided | Disagree |
|---|---|---|---|
| 5. Continue to provide plastic bags | 132 | 17 | 411 |
| 6. Provide no bags; encourage students to bring their own bags | 414 | 25 | 121 |
| 7. Provide no bags; offer cloth bags at reduced price (about $3) | 357 | 19 | 184 |
| 8. Give a cloth bag with each major purchase, the cost to be included in registration fees | 63 | 15 | 482 |

**Your Task.** In groups of four or five, do the following:

**a.** Convert the data into a table (see Figure 13.1) with a descriptive title. Arrange the items in a logical sequence.

**b.** How could these survey data be cross-tabulated? Would cross-tabulation serve any purpose?

**c.** Given the conditions of this survey, name at least three conclusions that could be drawn from the data.

**d.** Prepare three to five recommendations to be submitted to Mr. Krause. How could they be implemented?

## 13.2 Evaluating Conclusions (Obj. 2)

**E-MAIL**

**Your Task.** Read an in-depth article (800 or more words) in *Business Week, Fortune, Forbes, Canadian Business* or *Financial Post Magazine*. What conclusions does the author draw? Are the conclusions valid, based on the evidence presented? In an e-mail message to your instructor, summarize the main points in the article and analyze the conclusions. What conclusions would you have drawn from the data?

## 13.3 Distinguishing Between Conclusions and Recommendations (Obj. 2)

**Your Task.** For each of the following statements, indicate whether it could be classified as a conclusion or a recommendation.

**a.** In times of recession, individuals spend less money on meals away from home.

**b.** Our restaurant should offer a menu featuring a variety of low-priced items in addition to the regular menu.

**c.** Absenteeism among employees with families decreases when they have adequate child care.

**d.** Nearly 80 percent of our business comes from only 20 percent of our customers.

**e.** Datatech Company should concentrate its major sales effort on its largest accounts.

**f.** The length of vacations for employees across the country is directly correlated with their length of employment.

**g.** The employee vacation schedule of Datatech Company compares favourably with the averages of other similar Canadian companies.

**h.** Offering outplacement service (assistance in finding jobs) tends to defuse the anger that goes with involuntary separation (being released from a job).

## 13.4 Organizing Data (Obj. 3)

**Your Task.** How could the findings in the following reports be best organized? Consider these methods: time, component, importance, criteria, and convention.

**a.** A report comparing three sites for a company's new production plant. The report presents figures on property costs, construction costs, proximity to raw materials, provincial taxes, labour availability, and shipping distances.

**b.** A report describing the history of the development of dwarf and spur apple trees, starting with the first genetic dwarfs discovered about 100 years ago and progressing to today's grafted varieties on dwarfing rootstocks.

**c.** An informational brochure for job candidates that describes your company's areas of employment: accounting, finance, information systems, operations management, marketing, production, and computer-aided design.

**d.** A monthly sales report submitted to the sales manager.

**e.** A recommendation report to be submitted to management presenting four building plans to improve access to your building, in compliance with federal regulations. The plans range considerably in feasibility and cost.

**f.** A progress report submitted six months into the process of planning the program for your organization's convention.

**g.** An informational report describing a company's expansion plans in South America, Europe, Australia, and Southeast Asia.

**h.** An employee performance appraisal submitted annually.

## 13.5 Evaluating Headings and Titles (Obj. 3)

**Your Task.** Identify the following report headings and titles as "talking" or "functional/descriptive." Discuss the usefulness and effectiveness of each.

**a.** Problem
**b.** Need for Tightening Computer ID System
**c.** Annual Budget
**d.** How to Implement Self-Directed Teams That Work
**e.** Case History: Liberty Regency Hotel Focuses on Improving Service to Customers
**f.** Solving Our Records Management Problems
**g.** Comparing Copier Volume, Ease of Use, and Speed
**h.** Alternatives

## 13.6 Periodic Report: Filling in the Boss (Obj. 4)

**E-MAIL**

You work hard at your job, but you rarely see your boss and it's hard to keep him informed of your activities and accomplishments.

**Your Task.** For a job that you currently hold or a previous one, describe your regular activities, discuss irregular events that management should be aware of, and highlight any special needs or problems. Use a memo format in writing a periodic report to your boss.

## 13.7 Progress Report: Checking In (Obj. 4)

**E-MAIL**

For students writing a long report described in Chapter 14, you must keep your instructor informed of your progress.

**Your Task.** Write a progress report informing your instructor of your work. Briefly describe the project (its purpose, scope, limitations, and methodology), work you have completed, work yet to be completed, problems encountered, future activities, and expected completion date. Address the e-mail memo report to your instructor.

## 13.8 Investigative Report: Good or Bad Place to Work? (Obj. 4)

**WEB**

You are intent on working for a great company, and you want to learn as much as possible about the company.

**Your Task.** Select a company listed in *The 100 Best Companies to Work for in Canada* (a periodical that can be accessed at most libraries), and collect information about the company on the Web. Visit <**www.hoovers.com**> for a thumbnail sketch of the company. Then take a look at the company's Web site; check its background, news releases, and annual report. Learn about its major product, service, or emphasis. Find its ranking, its current stock price (if listed), and its high and low range for the year. Look up its profit-to-earnings ratio. Track down its latest marketing plan, promotion, or product. Identify its home office, major officers, and number of employees. In a memo report to your instructor, summarize your research findings. Explain why this company would be a good or bad employment choice.

## 13.9 Investigative Report: Marketing Abroad (Obj. 4)

**WEB**

You have been asked to prepare a training program for Canadian companies doing business outside Canada.

**Your Task.** Select a country to investigate (other than the United States and preferably one for which your library has *Culturgram* materials). Collect data from Culturgram files and from the country's embassy in Ottawa. Interview on-campus international students. Use the Web to discover data about the country. Collect information about formats for written communication, observance of holidays, customary greetings, business ethics, and other topics of interest to businesspeople. For more information about this assignment, see Chapter 4, Activity 4.6. Remember that your report should promote business, not tourism. Prepare a memo report addressed to Kelly Jazork, editor for the training program materials.

## 13.10 Progress Report: Heading Toward That Degree (Obj. 4)

You have made an agreement with your parents (or spouse, relative, or significant friend) that you would submit a progress report at this time.

**Your Task.** Prepare a progress report in letter format. Describe your headway toward your educational goal (such as employment, degree, diploma, or certificate). List your specific achievements, and outline what you have left to complete.

## 13.11 Conference or Trip Report: In Your Dreams (Obj. 4)

You have been sent to a meeting, conference, or seminar in an exotic spot at company expense.

**Your Task.** From a business periodical select an article describing a conference or meeting connected with your major area of study. The article must be at least 500 words long. Assume you attended the meeting. Prepare a memo report to your supervisor.

## 13.12 Justification/Recommendation Report: We Need It (Obj. 5)

Your office needs a piece of equipment, such as a photocopier, fax, VCR, computer, printer, digital camera, or the like.

**Your Task.** Select a piece of equipment and do the research necessary to write a convincing report to your boss. Although your boss did not request this report, you feel that he or she will be receptive to your request. Assume that you can be direct and straightforward in your report.

## 13.13 Justification/Recommendation Report: Time for a Change (Obj. 5)

`CRITICAL THINKING`

**Your Task.** Identify a problem or a procedure that must be changed at your job, such as poor scheduling of employees,

outdated equipment, slow order processing, failure to encourage employees to participate fully, restrictive rules, inadequate training, or disappointed customers. Using an indirect pattern, write a recommendation report suggesting one or more ways to solve the problem. Address the memo report to your boss.

## 13.14 Justification/Recommendation Report: Solving a Campus Problem (Obj. 5)

`TEAM`

**Your Task.** In groups of three to five, investigate a problem on your campus, such as inadequate parking, slow registration, poor class schedules, inefficient bookstore, weak job-placement program, unrealistic degree or diploma requirements, or lack of internship programs. Within your group develop a solution to the problem. If possible, consult the officials involved to ask for their input in arriving at a feasible solution. After reviewing persuasive techniques discussed in Chapter 10, write a group or individual justification/recommendation report(s). Address it to the proper campus official or to your instructor.

## 13.15 Feasibility Report: International Organization (Obj. 5)

`CRITICAL THINKING`

To fulfill a senior project in your department, you have been asked to submit a letter report to the dean evaluating the feasibility of starting an organization of international students on campus.

**Your Task.** Find out how many international students are on your campus, what nations they represent, how one goes about starting an organization, and whether a faculty sponsor is needed. Assume that you conducted an informal survey of international students. Of the 39 who filled out the survey, 31 said they would be interested in joining.

## 13.16 Feasibility Report: Improving Employee Fitness (Obj. 5)

`CRITICAL THINKING`

Your company is considering ways to promote employee fitness and morale.

**Your Task.** Select a possible fitness program that seems reasonable for your company. Consider a softball league, bowling teams, basketball league, lunchtime walks, lunchtime fitness speakers and demos, company-sponsored health club membership, workout room, fitness centre, fitness director, and so on. Assume that your boss has tentatively agreed to one of the programs and has asked you to write a memo report investigating its feasibility.

## 13.17 Yardstick Report: Evaluating Equipment (Obj. 5)

**CRITICAL THINKING**

You recently complained to your boss that you were unhappy with a piece of equipment that you use (printer, computer, copier, fax, or the like). After some thought, the boss decided you were right and told you to go shopping.

**Your Task.** Compare at least three different manufacturers' models and recommend one. Since the company will be purchasing ten or more units and since several managers must approve the purchase, write a careful report documenting your findings. Establish at least five criteria for comparing the models. Submit a memo report to your boss.

## 13.18 Yardstick Report: Measuring the Alternatives (Obj. 5)

**CRITICAL THINKING**

**Your Task.** Consider a problem where you work or in an organization you know. Select a problem with several alternative solutions or courses of action (retaining the present status could be one alternative). Develop criteria that could be used to evaluate each alternative. Write a report measuring each alternative by the yardstick you have created. Recommend a course of action to your boss or to the organization head.

## Self-Contained Report Activities

**NO ADDITIONAL RESEARCH REQUIRED**

## 13.19 Justification/Recommendation Report: Improving Village Market's Service* (Obj. 5)

**CRITICAL THINKING**

You are a recently hired manager for Village Market, a high-end fast-food restaurant, which has been in business for three years. The restaurant specializes in a wide selection of quality "deli-style" sandwiches, desserts, and coffees. The restaurant's owner, Jill Hillings, tells you that the volume of business, especially at lunch hour, has increased considerably lately.

After your first month on the job, you notice that, because of the increased volume, the method of delivering orders to customers seems to be inadequate. At present, the ordering system consists of the following: (1) the customer's order and table number are recorded by counter staff on a ticket; (2) after the customers pays, the ticket is given to the sandwich makers, who complete the order; (3) one of the counter staff then takes

the order to the customer's table. Coffee and desserts are also brought to the customer's table. Additional beverages are located in a refrigerated display case, where customers help themselves. You also note that three counter staff work with one cash register and two sandwich makers are on duty.

You bring the problem to Jill's attention, and she responds by saying, "As a business increases, one must keep up with the times and continually assess ways to do business better." She asks you to help solve the problem by analyzing how similar businesses handle their service during lunch hour. You begin by selecting three fast-food restaurants similar to Village Market. You observe each restaurant during its lunch hour to determine its serving techniques. You also decide to determine the amount of time it takes for a customer to receive an order relative to Village Market. Presently, the average time it takes for a customer to receive an order at Village Market is 4.6 minutes. The following is a rough account of your observations.

**Country Custard**
- Limited menu selection
- Orders are taken using an electronic system that includes the customer's number
- Customers pay immediately
- Customers pick up their orders after number has been called and retrieve their own beverages
- Each sandwich maker is assigned a different task
- Four counter employees at four registers; three sandwich makers
- Average time customer waits to receive order: 2.7 minutes

**Jimmy Jack's**
- Limited menu selection
- Order takers call out menu item as order is taken
- Tickets are used to inform sandwich makers of extras like cheese, mayo, etc.
- Counter employees serve beverages
- Customers pay immediately
- Three sandwich makers make each sandwich in assembly-line fashion
- Customers wait at the counter to pick up their orders
- One counter employee at one register; three sandwich makers
- Average time customer waits to receive order: 2.3 minutes

**Red Hound Bagels**
- Limited menu selection
- Tickets are used to record menu selection; customers pay immediately
- Food and beverages are brought to the customer's table
- Four employees are assigned different tasks: one takes the customer's order, another makes the food, another delivers the order
- Average time customer waits to receive order: 3.5 minutes

**Your Task.** Now it is up to you to sift through the data you've collected and present your findings (conclusions) to

*Instructors: See the Instructor's Manual for additional resources regarding these activities.

Jill in a short memo report. You may want to present the data using visual aids, but you also realize you must emphasize the important findings by presenting them in an easy-to-read list. If time allows, include recommendations.

## 13.20 Justification/Recommendation Report That Requires No Additional Research: Improving Register Efficiency at National TV & Appliance* (Obj. 5)

**CRITICAL THINKING**

National TV & Appliance is a high-volume market-leading retailer of consumer electronics and appliances. It has established a reputation for outstanding customer service, selection, and prices. As a supervisor at one of the store's busiest locations, you must ensure that the checkout and customer service lanes operate efficiently. To make your job easier and to ensure consistency in every store, National TV has established an action plan to prevent long waiting times at registers.

The plan includes assigning backup cashiers from other departments for each shift. Additionally, remote registers are also located in several departments to reduce customer flow at the registers nearest the exit. National's goal is to achieve at least a 35 percent "excellent" response rating from customers. Even the best plans can go awry, however, and this usually happens during holidays such as Thanksgiving, Christmas, Victoria Day, and Labour Day. With the Labour Day weekend only two months away, you want to avoid the occasional gridlock you encountered last Victoria Day.

### Customer Survey Data
To gather information from customers, you decide to tabulate responses to questions from comment cards submitted during the last month. You are particularly interested in the time customers spent in the checkout lines. The table below shows the results of 320 customer comment cards.

### Staff Survey
To gather additional information, you conduct a survey of 20 staff members, including cashiers, customer service representatives, and salespeople. Here are the results of your survey:

*Which of the following has caused a delay at a register?*

| | | |
|---|---|---|
| 1. Soft tag or CD case removal | 64% | |
| 2. Approval or override | 86 | |
| 3. Register malfunction | 3 | |
| 4. Incomplete paperwork | 7 | |
| 5. Product registration | 13 | (e.g., Internet service providers) |
| 6. Employee error | 16 | |

Figures do not total 100 percent because of multiple answers.

### Personal Observations
Finally, you selected ten registers at random (five near the front entrance, three in customer service, and one in both the TV and Digital Imaging departments) and observed them for 5 minutes, taking notes. You chose Saturday for these observations because of the typically higher volume of business. On the next page is a summary of your observations.

| | Responses/Score | | | | |
|---|---|---|---|---|---|
| | **Excellent** | **Very Good** | **Good** | **Fair** | **Poor** |
| **Questions on Comment Cards** | **5** | **4** | **3** | **2** | **1** |
| 1. Based on your shopping experience, how would you rate this National TV store? | 112 | 102 | 63 | 29 | 14 |
| 2. Based on your shopping experience, how would you rate the likelihood you will return to this National TV store? | 166 | 96 | 43 | 8 | 2 |
| 3. How would you rate the likelihood that you would recommend this National TV store to a friend? | 118 | 88 | 76 | 23 | 15 |
| 4. How would you rate your overall satisfaction with register checkout times? | 51 | 80 | 144 | 32 | 13 |
| 5. Please rate your satisfaction with the time spent in line at the customer service counter. | 19 | 38 | 128 | 96 | 39 |
| 6. How would you rate the service staff's handling of problems? | 26 | 96 | 54 | 129 | 15 |

*Instructors: See the Instructor's Manual for additional resources regarding these activities.

- During all five of your visits to registers near the front entrance, you noticed that, although a manager was often needed for a cheque approval or override, which caused delays, employee confusion about procedures and the registers themselves seemed to account for the majority of delays. You also observed five instances in which an employee needed to go to another cash register to remove security devices. Finally, you noticed several customers in line with satellite TV and wireless equipment.
- In both of your visits to the service desk, one employee was operating one of three available registers. For this reason several customers were left waiting in line for service. During one visit, you observed that when a product needed to be certified by a technician before it could be exchanged, the employee had to walk to the technical department to locate a technician, causing further delay.
- During your visits to the TV and Digital Imaging departments, you saw that floor personnel were overwhelmed with customers asking questions about products. In other words, no one seemed to be available to handle transactions at the open registers. Cheating a bit, you walked over to the kitchen appliance department, where you saw few customers but several employees in the area.

**Your Task.** After carefully comparing customer and employee perceptions, present your findings in a memo report to Tracy McGlocklin, general manager, National TV & Appliance. In your report, include as much information from the tables as possible, but present it in an easy-to-understand way. What conclusions can you draw from your findings? What recommendations will you make to Ms. McGlocklin to ensure a successful Labour Day weekend?

## 13.21 Yardstick Report That Requires No Additional Research: Comparing Clothing Retailers' Web Sites* (Obj. 5)

**CRITICAL THINKING**

You work for the Marketing Department of Rainbow Apparel, an up-and-coming specialty retailer offering clothing, accessories, and personal care products for men and women. Although Rainbow has a Web presence, it wants to update its site based on what online competitors are doing and what customers think is important about Web sites in general. Currently, Rainbow's Web site contains little more than online advertisements about its products and a store locator. You decide to analyze and evaluate Lacuna.com and Ambience.com, two companies with Web sites in direct competition with Rainbow. Your analysis is based on the following criteria: (1) speed, (2) convenience, (3) privacy/security, (4) customer service, (5) Web site design, and (6) sales promotions. You also conduct a survey of

150 shoppers to discover their online shopping habits and preferences. Below are the results of your research.

### Lacuna.com

**Speed.** The home page's average loading time, using a 56K modem, is 10 seconds.

**Convenience.** The site is convenient for finding the right size, fit, and care instructions. Virtually any size is available. Additionally, if customers aren't satisfied with an item, they may return it free of charge by mail or to any Lacuna store in Canada. One drawback is that Lacuna.com customers may find a product only by looking at images or lists; in other words, the site has no search function for locating a product by item or number.

**Privacy/Security.** The site is secure, using Secure Sockets Layer (SSL) technology. Purchases up to $50 are covered.

**Customer Service.** Overall, the service is very good to excellent. Customers may contact customer service via e-mail or use a toll-free service line any time of the day. In an experiment, two calls were made and one e-mail was sent to evaluate customer service. In general, service reps were friendly and helpful, responding politely and quickly to questions about locating products. Additional services include gift wrapping, delivery, and shopping by phone.

**Design.** The site is very well designed and is user-friendly. The home page is uncluttered and without distractions. Customers simply click either the "Men" or "Women" links to access subsequent pages. When a category is chosen, customers are linked to a well-organized collection of merchandise. The "view as a list" feature is also available for those who have slower connections.

**Promotions.** Lacuna.com's "All-Year-Long Sale" section is available to anyone. Although returns cost nothing, free shipping is offered only periodically. For customers who sign up, e-mailed specials are offered twice a month.

### Ambience.com

**Speed.** Loading time for the home page, using a 56K modem, averages 16 seconds. The ordering process is slow. Because the site is set up in an illogical fashion with both men's and women's clothing displayed on the same pages, finding an item is time-consuming. In addition, images sometimes take a long time to load.

**Convenience.** Ambience.com has a search-by-item number feature. It also offers care instructions as well as a wide-ranging size chart. If customers are unhappy with an item, they must return it by mail; Ambience stores will not accept returns of Web items.

**Privacy/Security.** The site is secure, using Secure Sockets Layer (SSL) technology. It also promotes itself as a "VeriSign" secure site. Purchases up to $50 are covered.

*Instructors: See the Instructor's Manual for additional resources regarding these activities.

**Customer Service.** Service is fair. Customers may contact customer service via e-mail or use a toll-free service line any time of the day for questions. In an experiment, however, three calls were made and one e-mail was sent to evaluate customer service. Two of the calls required an average of 45 seconds for a rep to reach the phone. Additional services include gift wrapping, delivery, and shopping by phone.

**Design.** For a first-time customer, the home page is somewhat confusing. It has too many options from which to choose. Beyond the home page, the design improves, with clearly defined categories. However, customers may view the items only as an image; no "view as a list" option is available.

**Promotions.** Ambience.com offers a new promotion every week. Repeat customers also receive an e-mailed promotion twice a month, which can include free shipping and a percentage off the total purchase.

### Consumer Survey

1.  Have you ever purchased anything online?

    Yes: 39      No: 111

2.  If you answered yes to the above question, which of the following have you ordered? Please check all that apply.

    Cosmetics: 32
    Clothing and accessories: 41
    CDs, recorded music: 90
    Flowers: 30

3.  How many purchases have you made on the Internet in the past year?

    3–4: 35      5–9: 49      10–24: 42      25 or more: 24

4.  What elements of online shopping are most important to you? Please check all that apply.

    Speed: 135          Convenience: 105
    Privacy: 105         Customer service: 83
    Design: 60           Promotions: 120

5.  What kinds of services do you expect when you shop online? Please check all that apply.

    Free shipping: 140    Free Return: 90
    Sales: 120            Promotions: 65

**Your Task.** Analyze the data you have available. What data could be presented in graphs or charts? What graphic forms should be used to best illustrate the most important data? In a memo report to your supervisor, Jim Kendrigan, director of marketing, include objective conclusions based on your analysis. Also submit recommendations regarding the steps Rainbow should take when upgrading its Web site. If your instructor directs, prepare visual aids to accompany your yardstick report.

## 13.22 Justification/Recommendation Report That Requires No Additional Research: Increasing The Axis Customer Base

You have recently accepted a position as a marketing intern at The Axis, one of four midsized live music venues in Adams, a city of 200 000. The city's image is closely tied to its university, which supplies the bulk of its business revenue. The manager of The Axis, Peter Quip, tells you that The Axis has traditionally targeted a more mature audience than the other venues in Adams. However, attendance has been flat lately—especially during the summer months—and you learn that Peter has created the internship specifically to extend The Axis customer base. In other words, he wants you to determine how The Axis can attract more college-aged students like you.

It seems to you that, initially, two things are critical: (1) how The Axis advertises relative to the other venues, and (2) how the potential target audience responds to The Axis relative to the other venues. Initially, you talk to Peter about how The Axis advertises. You learn that newspaper and radio are the primary sources of advertising. Print ads are placed in the city's only daily newspaper, and radio spots appear exclusively on the city's "classic rock" station. In examining the newspaper ads, you notice that they are somewhat lacking in visual appeal and rarely have pictures of the bands scheduled to perform.

The Axis also has a Web site, which includes concert information and ticket prices, but not much more. Average ticket prices are $10 to $25 for seminational and national acts and $6 to $8 for local acts. After you gather this initial information, you then proceed to find out as much as you can about advertising undertaken by other music venues, including The Rage, The Planet West, and The Club. You develop a survey to be distributed to university students—your target audience. Following are the results of your research.

### Advertising

**The Rage.** This venue advertises in many areas. In print, for example, The Rage advertises primarily in the city's "alternative" newspapers, *The Metro* and *The Express*. The Rage's ads always include pictures of the performers and sometimes use colour. The Rage has also occasionally run ads in *Rolling Stone, Alternative Press,* and *Music Biz* magazines. Moreover, it has an extensive, well-developed Web site that is updated daily. The Rage works closely with the city's rock/hard rock stations, which often sponsor on-site promotions and contests. For all performances, flyers are posted in local record stores and the university's student union. Ticket prices are based on a percentage of the cost of each performance, but they average about $12.

**The Planet West.** Most of the advertising is done in print—almost exclusively in the alternative weekly newspapers. While their ads do not include pictures of the performers, most ads show the performer's logo or a band's logo. Flyers are also distributed to local record stores. Ticket prices vary, but often are as low as $8 with discounts.

**The Club.** Most of The Club's ads are in the alternative weeklies, listed in the "calendar of upcoming events" section; few formal ads are placed in newspapers. However, The Club does have a contract with the national magazine *Maxim Inc.*, which provides a list of its concert dates. The Club places radio ads on the university-sponsored radio station and also distributes flyers to local coffee houses, restaurants, and record shops. Tickets for regional and national acts range from $6 to $10; local acts average about $7.

## Survey Results

A total of 220 students responded to the following survey.

1. Of the concert venues shown below, which is your favourite to see a performance?

   | The Axis | The Rage | The Planet West | The Club |
   |----------|----------|-----------------|----------|
   | 7 | 123 | 15 | 75 |

2. Of the venues shown below, how do you feel about their ticket prices?

   | | Reasonable | Undecided | Expensive |
   |---|------------|-----------|-----------|
   | The Axis | 54 | 137 | 29 |
   | The Rage | 101 | 28 | 91 |
   | The Planet West | 152 | 46 | 22 |
   | The Club | 172 | 41 | 9 |

3. Do you look for discounts on tickets to a performance you are planning to attend?

   Yes: 207     No: 13

4. Selecting *one* of the following, what is your primary source for concert information?

   | Newspaper: 44 | Magazine: 4 | Radio: 42 |
   |---|---|---|
   | Flyers: 18 | Internet: 33 | Word of mouth: 79 |

**Your Task.** Your goal is to write a concise memo report to Peter Quip. Knowing that Peter isn't going to want to linger over too many details, you must first decide how you might present the information using visual aids. Which data should be emphasized? What might be the best way to present these data? Next, what conclusions have you reached from a careful analysis of the information? Finally, what are your recommendations to Peter?

## 13.23 Feasibility Report That Requires No Additional Research: Exploring Alternative Ordering Methods for Franco's Pizza

Buyer Analysis, a leading consumer and research firm, has been asked to conduct a feasibility study on alternative ordering methods for Franco's Pizza, a 30-unit delivery and take-out chain. Fast-food franchises across the nation have become increasingly interested in using the Internet to supplement traditional take-out and delivery options. In fact, several prominent U.S. pizza chains have already adopted, or are testing, online ordering. Examples include Papa John's, Pizza Hut, and Domino's. Another more recently explored option is interactive television (i-TV). Franco Barbara, CEO of Franco's Pizza, wants to know whether the chain should continue using its conventional phone-ordering/delivery method or adopt one of the two alternatives. The following represents your preliminary research.

### The Online Consumer
- Approximately 25 percent of U.S. adults have shopped online (Scarborough Research).
- Thirteen percent of online shoppers have made food or drink purchases (Ernst & Young).
- By 2005, 85 percent of U.S. homes will be online. Approximately 75 percent will use a computer for access (Strategy Analysis).
- The composition of online shoppers is 56 percent male, 39 percent of whom are between the ages of 18 and 34 (Scarborough Research).

### Online Ordering
The most common method involves using an intermediary that accepts orders for the restaurant. For example, Food.com licenses its ROSY (Restaurant Ordering System) to Papa John's. The intermediary's Web site contains the interactive menus of its client restaurants. For example, after consumers join Food.com, they are able to access participating restaurants' menus and place orders; then, Food.com sends the completed order by fax to the restaurant. A percentage of each sale, roughly 3 percent, is billed monthly to the restaurant.

### Advantages of Online Ordering
- The intermediary handles most technological aspects of the process.
- The restaurant does not spend as much for computer technology and training.
- Most restaurants already use fax machines to conduct business with suppliers and main offices.
- Capital expenditures are minimal.
- Many pizza take-out and delivery restaurants and chains have created a Web presence.

### Disadvantages of Online Ordering
- Because of current technology, ordering by phone takes less time.
- Consumers are still concerned about online security issues.
- One Pizza Hut operator reported receiving 5 Internet orders per day compared with a typical 140 telephone orders.
- The Pizza Time delivery and restaurant chain reported sales expectations of 10 to 12 percent of total sales in a recent online ordering test.

In a recent test, Pizza Time delivery and restaurant chain expected online ordering to account for only 10 to 12 percent

448

of its total sales. This is not significant enough to justify the costs. In addition, the online grocer Web Van went bankrupt.

## The i-TV Consumer

- Satellite subscribers as of the end of last year totalled 9.39 million (OpenTV.com).
- Within three years, 117 million homes worldwide will be receiving digital TV from cable operators and 145 million households will be receiving it from satellite services (OpenTV.com).
- Approximately 85 percent of U.S. homes have cable access (Strategy Analysis).
- Roughly 6 percent of U.S. homes have i-TV (Strategy Analysis).

## Ordering i-TV

i-TV can be delivered in a number of ways. TV sets with integrated interactive receivers are on the market. However, trends suggest that more consumers will initially use i-TV through set-top boxes in the next five years. Set-top boxes, such as those provided by WebTV or DirectTV, are available at local retail stores and have a street price of about $200. The most prominent player in the i-TV market is OpenTV. Recently, Pizza Hut and Time Warner concluded test marketing in Hawaii using digital cable boxes; Pizza Hut is expected to launch nationwide next year. Domino's teamed with RespondTV, an San Francisco-based software firm, to offer pizza delivery through WebTV. Finally, i-TV is already very popular in Europe, and ordering pizza is one of its most popular uses.

## Advantages of i-TV

- A significant number of consumers already have cable TV.
- Eliminates the need for the consumer to input name and address repeatedly.
- Creates a secure channel for passing charge account information.
- Intuitive, user-friendly interface.

## Disadvantages of i-TV

- Conversion to digital cable and satellite TV has been slow.
- Arguments over technical standards have delayed a mass-market rollout in North America.
- The viability of marketing provisions like food and clothing is unproven.
- Costs are relatively expensive for businesses.

## Consumer Survey

Following are the results of a telephone survey obtained from a random sample of consumers from across the U.S.

| Questions | Yes | No |
|---|---|---|
| 1. Have you ordered pizza for delivery within the last month? | 799 | 226 |
| 2. Would you consider ordering pizza online as opposed to calling? | 133 | 892 |
| 3. Would you consider ordering pizza using your television set as opposed to calling? | 665 | 360 |

**Your Task.** As a consultant for Buyer Analysis, study the preceding information. What items are most important to show visually? Create a visual aid for your report. Then prepare a feasibility report addressed to Mr. Franco Barbara, CEO of Franco's Pizza. Your report should offer conclusions based on a careful analysis of the information. It should also make practical recommendations that can be implemented.

# C.L.U.E. REVIEW 13

On a separate sheet edit the following sentences to correct faults in grammar, punctuation, spelling, numbers, proofreading, and word use.

1. If you are conducting research for a report you will probibly face a jumble of data including: printouts, note cards, copies of articles, inter view notes, questionaire results and statistics.

2. Numerical information from surveys are usally summarized, and simplified in tables.

3. Researchers use 3 statistical terms to describe data; mean, median and mode.

4. When my boss and me use the word *average* we are refering to the mean which is the arithmetic average.

5. Readers' of reports often turn right to the conclusions and reccommendations, therefore these section must be written vary carefully.

6. Report Conclusions explain what the problem is, Recommendations tell how to solve it.

7. In writing reports you will probably organize you're data using 1 of the following 5 methods, time, component, importance, criteria or convention.

8. The Introduction to a report should tell it's purpose and significance, it should also preview the main points.

9. You should however delay writing the introduction, until after you complete the report.

10. To turn out professional looking documents be sure to design attractive pages, and avoid using to many typefaces and graphics.

# Chapter 14

## Proposals and Formal Reports

## LEARNING OBJECTIVES

*1* *Discuss the components of informal proposals.*

*2* *Discuss the special components in formal proposals.*

*3* *Identify formal report components that precede its introduction.*

*4* *Outline topics that might be covered in the introduction of a formal report.*

*5* *Describe the components of a formal report that follow the introduction.*

*6* *Specify tips that aid writers of formal reports.*

# AKA New Media, Inc.

To avoid scaring off clients with a lot of tech talk, Matthew Myers, partner and account director of AKA New Media, Inc. (pictured on the chapter-opening page), often provides them with a simple reflection document, based on discovery meetings, before he submits a formal proposal. "I like to build my customers' comfort zone," he explains, "by giving them an accessible introductory text that says, 'Here's what we see are your technological goals.'"

Matthew, along with his partner, Assadour Kirijian, runs AKA's Toronto-based New Media studio. This high-tech nerve centre builds brands, develops Web sites, designs interactive business-to-business tools, creates information architecture, and implements e-commerce integration. To ensure brand consistency, AKA also offers customers such creative and marketing support as the design of their print brochures, magazine ads, and even their trade-show display booths.

When it comes to winning new business, there is nothing flashy about this award-winning communications firm with its growing list of blue-chip clients. In the often slick world of digital entrepreneurship, AKA New Media uses old-fashioned research and thoroughness to separate its business bids from those of the competition.

"There will always be companies who are just looking at bottom-line costs," says Myers, whose company designs Web sites and other promotional material for clients such as Ericsson and Polaroid Canada. "But most companies today are looking to build relationships; they're looking to build trust. That's why it is essential that we do our homework."

Before a pen is put to a proposal—a written offer to sell its services—AKA makes sure it knows the potential client and its needs inside and out. The AKA team does a hands-on business analysis of every company it pitches, scouring marketing reports and financial statements, reviewing sales goals, and reading press releases and media coverage.

Still, there's nothing like a face-to-face encounter to get an exact understanding of corporate culture. AKA invites key company personnel to a "discovery" meeting. "We don't walk into a client selling solutions—we walk in asking questions," says Myers. "Plus, we're ready to listen. Proper listening cannot be underestimated."

The discovery meeting works for both sides. AKA gets a more intimate look inside the company, and the potential client gets a clearer understanding of what it's getting into, the expected impact on its business, and, perhaps more importantly, how it can sell AKA's services internally.

With many of the potential problems already vetted in the discovery process, AKA is ready to move forward, although it's not at the proposal stage quite yet. It first gets the client to sign off on a "reflection" document, a synopsis of everything AKA has learned in the research and discovery stages. "Once we have the signature," says Myers, "we know we're on the same page as the client, so we're free to start thinking strategically."

## CRITICAL THINKING

- How can companies use proposals to compare "apples to apples"?
- How does the preliminary planning and research affect the outcome of a report or proposal?
- How can the proposal protect the client?

www.akanewmedia.com

# PREPARING FORMAL AND INFORMAL PROPOSALS

Proposals are written offers to solve problems, provide services, or sell equipment. Although some proposals are internal, often taking the form of justification and recommendation reports, most proposals are external. External proposals are an important means of generating income for many organizations.

Because proposals are vital to their success, some businesses hire consultants or maintain specialists who do nothing but write proposals. Such proposals typically tell how a problem can be solved, what procedure will be followed, who will do it, how long it will take, and how much it will cost.

**Proposals are persuasive offers to solve problems, provide services, or sell equipment.**

CHAPTER 14
Proposals and Formal Reports
**451**

Proposals may be divided into two categories: solicited or unsolicited. When firms know exactly what they want, they prepare a request for proposal (RFP) specifying their requirements. Government agencies and large companies are likely to use RFPs to solicit competitive bids on their projects. Companies today want to be able to compare "apples with apples," and they also want the protection offered by proposals, which are legal contracts. Unsolicited proposals are written when an individual or firm sees a problem to be solved and offers a proposal to do so. Clean-Up Technology, a North American waste disposal firm, submitted several proposals, for example, to government agencies and firms in Mexico. Explaining his bid for Mexican business, the waste disposal company president said, "There's obviously a lot of clean-up work to be done in Mexico, and there's not a lot of expertise in our business."[1] Unsolicited proposals, like those of Clean-Up Technology, seize opportunities and capitalize on potential.

The most important point to remember about proposals—whether solicited or unsolicited—is that they are sales presentations. They must be persuasive, not merely mechanical descriptions of what you can do. Among other things, you may recall, effective persuasive sales messages (1) emphasize benefits for the reader, (2) "toot your horn" by detailing your expertise and accomplishments, and (3) make it easy for the reader to understand and respond.

Proposals may be informal or formal; they differ primarily in length and format. Notice in Figure 14.1 that formal proposals, described shortly, have many more components than informal proposals.

**FIGURE 14.1** Components of Formal and Informal Proposals

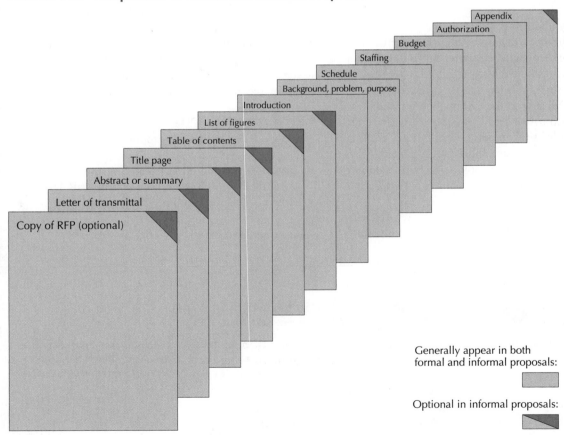

Appendix
Authorization
Budget
Staffing
Schedule
Background, problem, purpose
Introduction
List of figures
Table of contents
Title page
Abstract or summary
Letter of transmittal
Copy of RFP (optional)

Generally appear in both formal and informal proposals:

Optional in informal proposals:

452

# Components of Informal Proposals

Informal proposals may be presented in short (two- to four-page) letters. Sometimes called *letter proposals*, they may contain six principal components: introduction, background, proposal, staffing, budget, and authorization request. As you can see in Figure 14.1, both informal and formal proposals contain these six basic parts. Figure 14.2, an informal letter proposal to a London, Ontario, dentist to improve patient satisfaction, illustrates the six parts of letter proposals.

*Introduction.* Most proposals begin by briefly explaining the reasons for the proposal and by highlighting the writer's qualifications. To make your introduction more persuasive, you need to provide a "hook" to capture the reader's interest. One proposal expert suggests these possibilities:[2]

- Hint at extraordinary results with details to be revealed shortly.

- Promise low costs or speedy results.

- Mention a remarkable resource (well-known authority, new computer program, well-trained staff) available exclusively to you.

- Identify a serious problem (worry item) and promise a solution, to be explained later.

- Specify a key issue or benefit that you feel is the heart of the proposal.

For example, Jeffrey Byers, in the introduction for his proposal shown in Figure 14.2, focused on a key benefit. In his proposal to conduct a patient satisfaction survey, Jeffrey thought that Dr. Calloway would be most interested in specific recommendations for improving service to his patients. But Jeffrey didn't hit on this hook until he had written a first draft and had come back to it later. Indeed, it's often a good idea to put off writing the proposal introduction until after you have completed other parts. For longer proposals the introduction also describes the scope and limitations of the project, as well as outlining the organization of the material to come.

*Background, Problem, Purpose.* The background section identifies the problem and discusses the goals or purposes of the project. In an unsolicited proposal your goal is to convince the reader that a problem exists. Thus, you must present the problem in detail, discussing such factors as monetary losses, failure to comply with government regulations, or loss of customers. In a solicited proposal your aim is to persuade the reader that you understand the problem completely. Thus, if you are responding to an RFP, this means repeating its language. For example, if the RFP asks for the *design of a maintenance program for wireless communication equipment*, you would use the same language in explaining the purpose of your proposal. This section might include segments entitled *Basic Requirements*, *Most Critical Tasks*, and *Most Important Secondary Problems*.

*Proposal, Plan, Schedule.* In the proposal section itself, you should discuss your plan for solving the problem. In some proposals this is tricky because you want to disclose enough of your plan to secure the contract without giving away so much information that your services aren't needed. Without specifics, though, your proposal has little chance, so you must decide how much to reveal. Tell what you propose to do and how it will benefit the reader. Remember, too, that a proposal is a sales presentation. Sell your methods, product, and "deliverables"—items that will be left with the client. In this section some writers specify how the project will be managed and how its progress will be audited. Most writers also include a schedule of activities or timetable showing when events will take place.

Informal proposals may contain an introduction, background information, the proposal, staffing requirements, a budget, and an authorization request.

The actual proposal section must give enough information to secure the contract but not so much detail that the services are no longer needed.

## FIGURE 14.2 Informal Proposal

### Prewriting 1

**Analyze:** The purpose is to persuade the reader to accept this proposal.

**Anticipate:** The reader must be convinced that this survey project is worth its hefty price.

**Adapt:** Because the reader will be resistant at first, use a persuasive approach that emphasizes benefits.

### Writing 2

**Research:** Collect data about the reader's practice and other surveys of patient satisfaction.

**Organize:** Identify four specific purposes (benefits) of this proposal. Specify the survey plan. Promote the staff, itemize the budget, and ask for approval.

**Compose:** Prepare for revision by composing on a computer.

### Revising 3

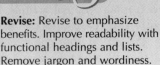

**Revise:** Revise to emphasize benefits. Improve readability with functional headings and lists. Remove jargon and wordiness.

**Proofread:** Check spelling of client's name. Verify dates and calculation of budget figures. Recheck all punctuation.

**Evaluate:** Is this proposal convincing enough to sell the client?

---

## BYERS RESEARCH CONSULTANTS

One Riverview Plaza
London, ON N6H 2V7
(519) 356-4300

May 16, 2005

Dr. Matthew M. Calloway
286 Old Bridge Road
London, ON N6H 4K4

Dear Dr. Calloway:

*Grabs attention with "hook" that focuses on key benefit* →

Helping you improve your practice is of the highest priority at Byers Research Consultants. That's why we are pleased to submit the following proposal outlining our plan to help you more effectively meet your patients' needs by analyzing their views about your practice.

← *Uses opening paragraph in place of introduction*

### Background and Purposes

We understand that you have been incorporating a total quality management system in your practice. Although you have every reason to believe your patients are pleased with the service you provide, you would like to give them an opportunity to discuss what they like and possibly don't like about your service. Specifically, your purposes are to survey your patients to (a) determine the level of their satisfaction with you and your staff, (b) elicit their suggestions for improvement, (c) learn more about how they discovered you, and (d) compare your "preferred" and "standard" patients.

← *Identifies four purposes of survey*

*Announces heart of proposal* →

### Proposed Plan

On the basis of our experience in conducting many local and national customer satisfaction surveys, Byers Research proposes the following plan to you.

*Divides total plan into logical segments for easy reading* →

**Survey.** We will develop a short but thorough questionnaire probing the data you desire. Although the survey instrument will include both open-ended and closed questions, it will concentrate on the latter. Closed questions enable respondents to answer easily; they also facilitate systematic data analysis. The questionnaire will measure patient reactions to such elements as courtesy, professionalism, accuracy of billing, friendliness, and waiting time. After you approve it, the questionnaire will be sent to a carefully selected sample of 300 patients whom you have separated into groupings of "preferred" and "standard."

**Analysis.** Data from the survey will be analyzed by demographic segments, such as patient type, age, and gender. Our experienced team of experts, using state-of-the-art computer systems and advanced statistical measures, will study the (a) degree of patient satisfaction, (b) reasons for satisfaction or dissatisfaction, and (c) relationship between responses of your "preferred" and "standard" patients. Moreover, our team will report to you specific suggestions for making patient visits more pleasant.

← *Describes procedure for solving problem or achieving goals*

**Report.** You will receive a final report with the key findings clearly spelled out, Dr. Calloway. Our expert staff will also draw conclusions based on these findings. The report will include tables summarizing all responses, broken down into groups of preferred and standard clients.

454

**FIGURE 14.2  Continued**

Dr. Matthew Calloway                Page 2                May 16, 2005

**Schedule.**  With your approval, the following schedule has been arranged for your patient satisfaction survey:

| | |
|---|---|
| Questionnaire development and mailing | June 1-6 |
| Deadline for returning questionnaire | June 24 |
| Data tabulation and processing | June 24-26 |
| Completion of final report | July 4 |

*Uses past-tense verbs to show that work has already started on the project*

*This section may be short if only one person is involved*

**Staffing**

Byers Research Consultants is a nationally recognized, experienced research consulting firm specializing in survey investigation.  I have assigned your customer satisfaction survey to Dr. Kelly Miller, our director of research.  Dr. Miller was trained at the University of Western Ontario and has successfully supervised our research program for the past nine years.  Before joining BRC, she was a marketing analyst with Procter & Gamble Company.  Assisting Dr. Miller will be a team headed by James Wilson, our vice president for operations.  Mr. Wilson earned a bachelor's degree in computer science and a master's degree in marketing from Simon Fraser University. Within our organization he supervises our computer-aided telephone interviewing (CATI) system and manages our 30-person professional interviewing staff.

*Builds credibility by describing outstanding staff and facilities*

*Itemizes costs carefully because a proposal is a contract offer*

**Budget**

| | Estimated Hours | Rate | Total |
|---|---|---|---|
| Professional and administrative time | | | |
| Questionnaire development | 3 | $150/hr. | $  450 |
| Questionnaire mailing | 4 | 40/hr. | 160 |
| Data processing and tabulation | 12 | 40/hr. | 480 |
| Analysis of findings | 15 | 150/hr. | 2 250 |
| Preparation of final report | 5 | 150/hr. | 750 |
| Mailing costs | | | |
| 300 copies of questionnaire | | | 120 |
| Postage and envelopes | | | 270 |
| Total costs | | | $4 480 |

**Authorization**

We are convinced, Dr. Calloway, that our professionally designed and administered client satisfaction survey will enhance your practice.  Byers Research Consultants can have specific results for you by July 4 if you sign the enclosed duplicate copy of this letter and return it to us with a retainer of $2 300.  The prices in this offer are in effect only until September 1.

*Closes by repeating key qualifications and main benefits*

*Makes response easy*

*Provides deadline*

Sincerely,

*Jeffrey W. Byers*

Jeffrey W. Byers
President

JWB:pem
Enclosure

**Staffing.** The staffing section of a proposal describes the credentials and expertise of the project leaders. It may also identify the size and qualifications of the support staff, along with other resources such as computer facilities and special programs for analyzing statistics. The staffing section is a good place to endorse and promote your staff. Some firms, like Hewlett-Packard, follow industry standards and include staff qualifications in an appendix. HP also uses generic résumés rather than the actual résumés of key people. This ensures privacy for individuals and also protects the company in case the staff changes after a proposal has been submitted to a customer.

**The staffing section promotes the credentials and expertise of the project leaders and support staff.**

**Budget.** A central item in most proposals is the budget, a list of proposed project costs. You need to prepare this section carefully because it represents a contract; you

**Because a proposal is a legal contract, the budget must be carefully researched.**

can't raise the price later—even if your costs increase. You can—and should—protect yourself with a deadline for acceptance. In the budget section some writers itemize hours and costs; others present a total sum only. A proposal to install a complex computer system might, for example, contain a detailed line-by-line budget. Similarly, Jeffrey Byers felt that he needed to justify the budget for his firm's patient satisfaction survey, so he itemized the costs, as shown in Figure 14.2. But the budget included for a proposal to conduct a one-day seminar to improve employee communication skills might be a lump sum only. Your analysis of the project will help you decide what kind of budget to prepare.

*Authorization Request.* Informal proposals often close with a request for approval or authorization. In addition, the closing should remind the reader of key benefits and motivate action. It might also include a deadline date beyond which the offer is invalid. At Hewlett-Packard, authorization to proceed is not part of the proposal. Instead, it is usually discussed after the customer has received the proposal. In this way the customer and the sales account manager are able to negotiate terms before a formal agreement is drawn.

## Special Components of Formal Proposals

Formal proposals differ from informal proposals not in style but in size and format. Formal proposals respond to big projects and may range from 5 to 200 or more pages. To facilitate comprehension and reference, they are organized into many parts, as shown in Figure 14.1. In addition to the six basic components just described, formal proposals may contain some or all of the following front and end parts.

**Formal proposals might also contain a copy of the RFP, a letter of transmittal, an abstract, a title page, a table of contents, a list of figures, and an appendix.**

*Copy of RFP.* A copy of the RFP may be included in the opening parts of a formal proposal. Large organizations may have more than one RFP circulating, and identification is necessary.

*Letter of Transmittal.* A letter of transmittal, usually bound inside formal proposals, addresses the person who is designated to receive the proposal or who will make the final decision. The letter describes how you learned about the problem or confirms that the proposal responds to the enclosed RFP. This persuasive letter briefly presents the major features and benefits of your proposal. Here, you should assure the reader that you are authorized to make the bid and mention the time limit for which the bid stands. You may also offer to provide additional information and ask for action, if appropriate.

**An abstract summarizes a proposal's highlights for specialists; an executive summary does so for managers.**

*Abstract or Executive Summary.* An abstract is a brief summary (typically one page) of a proposal's highlights intended for specialists or for technical readers. An executive summary also reviews the proposal's highlights, but it is written for managers and so should be less technically oriented. Formal proposals may contain one or both summaries. For more information about writing executive summaries, see pages 461–62.

*Title Page.* The title page includes the following items, generally in this order: title of proposal, name of client organization, RFP number or other announcement, date of submission, author's name, and/or her or his organization.

*Table of Contents.* Because most proposals don't contain an index, the table of contents becomes quite important. Tables of contents should include all headings and their beginning page numbers. Items that appear before the table of contents (copy of RFP, letter of transmittal, abstract, and title page) typically are not listed in the contents. However, any appendixes should be listed.

*List of Figures.* Proposals with many tables and figures often contain a list of figures. This list includes each figure or table title and its page number. If you have just a few figures or tables, however, you may omit this list.

*Appendix.* Ancillary material of interest to some readers goes in appendixes. Appendix A might include résumés of the principal investigators or testimonial letters. Appendix B might include examples or a listing of previous projects. Other appendixes could include audit procedures, technical graphics, or professional papers cited in the body of the proposal.

Proposals in the past were always paper-based and delivered by mail or special messenger. Today, however, companies increasingly prefer *online proposals.* Receiving companies may transmit the electronic proposal to all levels of management without ever printing a page, thus appealing to many environmentally conscious organizations.

Well-written proposals win contracts and business for companies and individuals. Many companies depend entirely on proposals to generate their income, so proposal writing becomes critical. For more information about industry standards and resources, visit the Web site of the Association of Proposal Management Professionals at <**www.apmp.org**>.

Another form of proposal is a business plan. Entrepreneurs who want to start a business or expand an existing business often must ask for funding. To secure financial backing, these budding businesspeople write business plans to submit to potential backers. To learn more about preparing a business plan, see the Career Coach box on the next page.

## CHECKLIST FOR WRITING PROPOSALS

### Introduction

✓ **Indicate the purpose.** Specify why the proposal is being made.

✓ **Develop a persuasive "hook."** Suggest excellent results, low costs, or exclusive resources. Identify a serious problem or name a key issue or benefit.

### Background, Problem

✓ **Provide necessary background.** Discuss the significance of the proposal and its goals or purposes.

✓ **Introduce the problem.** For unsolicited proposals convince the reader that a problem exists. For solicited proposals show that you fully understand the problem and its ramifications.

### Proposal, Plan

✓ **Explain the proposal.** Present your plan for solving the problem or meeting the need.

✓ **Discuss plan management and evaluation.** If appropriate, tell how the plan will be implemented and evaluated.

## Preparing an Effective Business Plan

Let's say you want to start your own business. Unless you can count on the Bank of Mom and Dad, you will need financial backing (called *venture capital*). A business plan is critical for securing venture capital support. Such a plan also ensures that you have done your homework and know what you are doing in launching your business. It provides you with a detailed road map to chart a course to success. Here are suggestions for preparing an effective business plan:

- **Letter of transmittal and/or executive summary.** Explain your reason for writing. Provide your name, address, and telephone number, along with contact information for all principals. Describe your business concisely, summarize the reasons it will succeed, introduce the parts of the following plan, and ask for support.

- **Table of contents.** List the page numbers and topics included in your plan.

- **Company description.** Identify the form of your business (proprietorship, partnership, or corporation) and its business type (merchandising, manufacturing, or service). For existing companies, describe the company's founding, growth, sales, and profit. For start-ups, explain why the business will be profitable.

- **Product/service description.** In jargon-free language, explain what you are providing, how it will benefit customers, and why it is better than existing products or services.

- **Market analysis.** Discuss market characteristics, trends, projected growth, customer behaviour,

complementary products and services, and barriers to entry. Identify your customers and how you will attract, hold, and increase your market share. Discuss the strengths and weaknesses of your direct and indirect competitors.

- **Operations and management.** Explain specifically how you will run your business, including location, equipment, personnel, and management. Highlight experienced and well-trained members of the management team and your advisors.

- **Financial analysis.** Outline a realistic start-up budget that includes fees for legal/professional services, occupancy, licences/permits, equipment, insurance, supplies, advertising/promotions, salaries/wages, accounting, income, and utilities. Also present an operating budget that projects costs for personnel, insurance, rent, depreciation, loan payments, salaries, taxes, repairs, and so on. Explain how much money you have, how much you will need to start up, and how much you will need to stay in business.

- **Appendixes.** Provide necessary extras such as managers' résumés, promotional materials, and product photos.

### Career Application

Have you started a business or do you know of someone who has? How are most start-up businesses funded? Why is a business plan important? What is the best place on the Web to learn more about business plans?

✓ **Outline a timetable.** Furnish a schedule showing what will be done and when.

## Staffing

✓ **Promote the qualifications of your staff.** Explain the specific credentials and expertise of the key personnel for the project.

✓ **Mention special resources or equipment.** Show how your support staff and resources are superior to those of the competition.

## *AKA New Media Revisited*

The key to a successful proposal, according to Matthew Myers, partner and account director at AKA New Media, is to tailor the document to the specific needs of the client. In tonier words, offer the client customized solutions. With all the hard work AKA does before even writing a proposal, it's not surprising the actual writing goes relatively smoothly. "Because we do our homework, the writing is the easiest part of the process," says Myers.

However, there are key factors to consider while writing a proposal. Because AKA works in a medium that's still a bit intimidating for some clients, it's important to personalize the pitch document as much as possible. Sometimes this requires educating the client. Illustrating how a technical action will affect a specific company problem allows a client to quickly overcome the fear factor and replace it with a sense of empowerment and excitement. AKA writers also endeavour to keep the language of the document as simple as possible, regardless of how technical the material is.

"We marry technology to a much larger picture," Myers reminds us. "The language of a document should reflect that hierarchy." To make the proposal even more accessible, AKA also compartmentalizes various sections of the document, targeting specific audiences within the company.

Since the relationship is meant to be long term, Myers advocates the inclusion of measurable goals or some other form of quantifying the recommendations in the proposal. "Knowing that there is a way of measuring the success of a program provides managers with some peace of mind," says Myers. "It also helps in the internal selling of the program."

### CRITICAL THINKING

- What factors does Myers identify as being important for successful proposal writing?
- Many of the contacts at AKA's client companies are not "tech-savvy." Bearing this in mind, how can a writer make the technical section of a document more accessible?

**www.akanewmedia.com**

## Budget

 **Show project costs.** For most projects itemize costs. Remember, however, that proposals are contracts.

 **Include a deadline.** Here or in the conclusion present a date beyond which the bid figures are no longer valid.

## Authorization

 **Ask for approval.** Make it easy for the reader to authorize the project (for example, *Sign and return the duplicate copy*).

## WRITING FORMAL REPORTS

Formal reports are similar to formal proposals in length, organization, and serious tone. Instead of making an offer, however, formal reports represent the end product of thorough investigation and analysis. They present ordered information to decision makers in business, industry, government, and education. In many ways formal reports are extended versions of the analytical business reports presented in Chapter 13. Figure 14.3 shows the components of typical formal reports, their normal sequence, and parts that might be omitted in informal reports.

*3*

**CHAPTER 14**
Proposals and Formal Reports
**459**

## Components of Formal Reports

**Formal reports discuss the results of a process of thorough investigation and analysis.**

A number of front and end items lengthen formal reports but enhance their professional tone and serve their multiple audiences. Formal reports may be read by many levels of managers, along with technical specialists and financial consultants. Therefore, breaking a long, formal report into small segments makes its information more accessible and easier to understand for all readers. These segments are discussed here and also illustrated in the model report shown on page 467 (Figure 14.4). This analytical report studies the recycling program at West Coast College and makes recommendations for improving its operation.

**Like proposals, formal reports are divided into many segments to make information comprehensible and accessible.**

*Cover.* Formal reports are usually enclosed in vinyl or heavy paper binders to protect the pages and to give a professional, finished appearance. Some companies have binders imprinted with their name and logo. The title of the report may appear through a cut-out window or may be applied with an adhesive label. Good stationery and office supply stores usually stock an assortment of report binders and labels.

*Title Page.* A report title page, as illustrated in the Figure 14.4 model report, begins with the name of the report typed in uppercase letters (no underscore and no

**FIGURE 14.3  Components of Formal and Informal Reports**

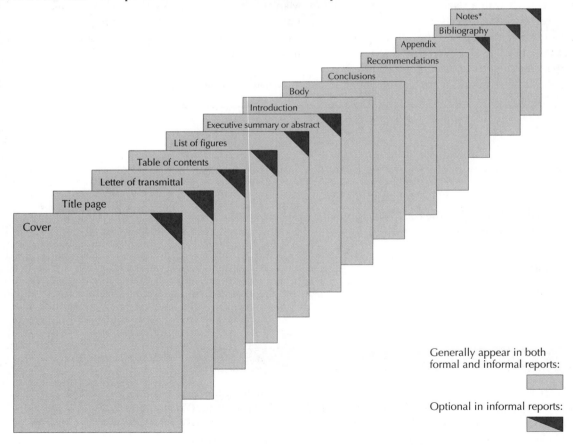

Generally appear in both formal and informal reports:

Optional in informal reports:

*Not required if parenthetic citation is used.

quotation marks). Next comes *Presented to* (or *Submitted to*) and the name, title, and organization of the individual receiving the report. Lower on the page is *Prepared by* (or *Submitted by*) and the author's name plus any necessary identification. The last item on the title page is the date of submission. All items after the title are typed in a combination of upper- and lowercase letters.

*Letter or Memo of Transmittal.* Generally written on organization stationery, a letter or memorandum of transmittal introduces a formal report. You will recall that letters are sent to outsiders and memos to insiders. A transmittal letter or memo follows the direct pattern and is usually less formal than the report itself (for example, the letter or memo may use contractions and the first-person pronouns *I* and *we*). The transmittal letter or memo typically (1) announces the topic of the report and tells how it was authorized; (2) briefly describes the project; (3) highlights the report's findings, conclusions, and recommendations, if the reader is expected to be supportive; and (4) closes with appreciation for the assignment, instruction for the reader's follow-up actions, acknowledgment of help from others, or offers of assistance in answering questions. If a report is going to different readers, a special transmittal letter or memo should be prepared for each, anticipating what each reader needs to know in using the report.

A letter or memo of transmittal gives a personalized overview of a formal report.

*Table of Contents.* The table of contents shows the headings in a report and their page numbers. It gives an overview of the report topics and helps readers locate them. You should wait to prepare the table of contents until after you've completed the report. For short reports you should include all headings. For longer reports you might want to list only first- and second-level headings. Leaders (spaced or unspaced dots) help guide the eye from the heading to the page number. Items may be indented in outline form or typed flush with the left margin.

*List of Figures.* For reports with several figures or illustrations, you may wish to include a list of figures to help readers locate them. This list may appear on the same page as the table of contents, space permitting. For each figure or illustration, include a title and page number. Some writers distinguish between tables and all other illustrations, which are called figures. If you make this distinction, you should also prepare separate lists of tables and figures. Because the model report in Figure 14.4 has few illustrations, the writer labelled them all "figures," a method that simplifies numbering (see page 469).

*Executive Summary.* The purpose of an executive summary is to present an overview of a longer report to people who may not have time to read the entire document. Generally, an executive summary is prepared by the author who is writing about his or her own report. But occasionally you may be asked to write an executive summary of a published report or article written by someone else. In either case you will probably perform the following activities:

An executive summary supplies an overview of a longer report.

- **Summarize key points.** Your goal is to summarize the important points including the purpose of the report; the problem addressed; and the findings, conclusions, and recommendations. You might also summarize the research methods, if they can be stated concisely.

- **Look for strategic words and sentences.** Read the completed report carefully. Pay special attention to first and last sentences of paragraphs, which often contain summary statements. Look for words that enumerate (*first, next, finally*) and words that express causation (*therefore, as a result*). Also look for words that signal essentials (*basically, central, leading, principal, major*) and words that contrast ideas (*however, consequently*).

- **Prepare an outline with headings.** At a minimum include headings for the purpose, findings, and conclusions/recommendations. What kernels of information would your reader want to know about these topics?

- **Fill in your outline.** Some writers use their computers to cut and paste important parts of the text. Then they condense with careful editing. Others find it most efficient to create new sentences as they prepare the executive summary.

- **Begin with the purpose.** The easiest way to begin an executive summary is with the words "The purpose of this report is to . . . ." Experienced writers may be more creative.

- **Follow the report order.** Present all your information in the order in which it is found in the report.

- **Eliminate nonessential details.** Include only main points. Don't include anything not in the original report. Use minimal technical language.

- **Control the length.** An executive summary is usually no longer than 10 percent of the original document. Thus, a 100-page report might require a 10-page summary. A 10-page report might need only a 1-page summary—or no summary at all. The executive summary for a long report may also include graphics to adequately highlight main points.

To see a representative executive summary, look at Figure 14.4 on page 470. Although it is only one page long, this executive summary includes headings to help the reader see the main divisions immediately. Let your organization's practices guide you in determining the length and form of an executive summary.

 ***Introduction.*** Formal reports begin with an introduction that sets the scene and announces the subject. Because they contain many parts serving different purposes, formal reports have a degree of redundancy. The same information may be included in the letter of transmittal, summary, and introduction. To avoid sounding repetitious, try to present the data slightly differently. But don't skip the introduction because you've included some of its information elsewhere. You can't be sure that your reader saw the information earlier. A good report introduction typically covers the following elements, although not necessarily in this order:

- **Background.** Describe events leading up to the problem or need.

- **Problem or purpose.** Explain the report topic and specify the problem or need that motivated the report.

- **Significance.** Tell why the topic is important. You may wish to quote experts or cite newspapers, journals, books, and other secondary sources to establish the importance of the topic.

- **Scope.** Clarify the boundaries of the report, defining what will be included or excluded.

- **Organization.** Launch readers by giving them a road map that previews the structure of the report.

Beyond these minimal introductory elements, consider adding any of the following information that is relevant for your readers:

- **Authorization.** Identify who commissioned the report. If no letter of transmittal is included, also tell why, when, by whom, and to whom the report was written.

- **Literature review.** Summarize what other authors and researchers have published on this topic, especially for academic and scientific reports.

- **Sources and methods.** Describe your secondary sources (periodicals, books, databases). Also explain how you collected primary data, including survey size, sample design, and statistical programs used.

- **Definitions of key terms.** Define words that may be unfamiliar to the audience. Also define terms with special meanings, such as *small business* when it specifically means businesses with fewer than 30 employees.

*Body.* The principal section in a formal report is the body. It discusses, analyzes, interprets, and evaluates the research findings or solution to the initial problem. This is where you show the evidence that justifies your conclusions. Organize the body into main categories following your original outline or using one of the patterns described earlier (such as time, component, importance, criteria, or convention).

5

Although we refer to this section as the body, it doesn't carry that heading. Instead, it contains clear headings that explain each major section. Headings may be functional or talking. Functional heads (such as *Results of the Survey, Analysis of Findings,* or *Discussion*) help readers identify the purpose of the section but don't reveal what's in it. Such headings are useful for routine reports or for sensitive topics that may upset readers. Talking heads (for example, *Recycling Habits of Campus Community*) are more informative and interesting, but they don't help readers see the organization of the report. The model report in Figure 14.4 uses functional heads for organizational sections requiring identification (*Introduction, Conclusions,* and *Recommendations*) and talking heads to divide the body.

Keep in mind the following important piece of business advice: Start with a statement of purpose. If you can't explain your idea in 25 words or less, it's probably not a good idea.

*Conclusions.* This important section tells what the findings mean, particularly in terms of solving the original problem. Some writers prefer to intermix their conclusions with the analysis of the findings—instead of presenting the conclusions separately. Other writers place the conclusions before the body so that busy readers can examine the significant information immediately. Still others combine the conclusions and recommendations. Most writers, though, present the conclusions after the body because readers expect this structure. In long reports this section may include a summary of the findings. To improve comprehension, you may present the conclusions in a numbered or bulleted list. See Chapter 13 for more suggestions on drawing conclusions.

**Recommendations.** When requested, you should submit recommendations that make precise suggestions for actions to solve the report problem. Recommendations are most helpful when they are practical and reasonable. Naturally, they should evolve from the findings and conclusions. Don't introduce new information in the conclusions or recommendations. As with conclusions, the position of recommendations is somewhat flexible. They may be combined with conclusions, or they may be presented before the body, especially when the audience is eager and supportive. Generally, though, in formal reports they come last.

Recommendations require an appropriate introductory sentence, such as *The findings and conclusions in this study support the following recommendations.* When making many recommendations, number them and phrase each as a command, such as *Begin an employee fitness program with a workout room available five days a week.* If appropriate, add information describing how to implement each recommendation. Some reports include a timetable describing the who, what, when, where, and how for putting each recommendation into operation. Chapter 13 provides more information about writing recommendations.

**Appendix.** Incidental or supporting materials belong in appendixes at the end of a formal report. These materials are relevant to some readers but not to all. Appendixes may include survey forms, copies of other reports, tables of data, computer printouts, and related correspondence. If additional appendixes are necessary, they would be named *Appendix A, Appendix B,* and so forth.

**Works Cited, References, or Bibliography.** Readers look in the bibliography section to locate the sources of ideas mentioned in a report. Your method of report documentation determines how this section is developed. If you use the MLA referencing format, all citations would be listed alphabetically in the "Works Cited." If you use the APA format, your list would be called "References." Regardless of the format, you must include the author, title, publication, date of publication, page number, and other significant data for all ideas or quotations used in your report. For electronic references include the preceding information plus a description of the electronic address or path leading to the citation. Also include the date on which you located the electronic reference. To see electronic and other citations, examine the list of references at the end of Figure 14.4. Appendix C of the text contains additional documentation information.

## Final Writing Tips

Formal reports are not undertaken lightly. They involve considerable effort in all three phases of writing, beginning with analysis of the problem and anticipation of the audience (as discussed in Chapter 5). Researching the data, organizing it into a logical presentation, and composing the first draft (Chapter 6) make up the second phase of writing. Revising, proofreading, and evaluating (Chapter 7) are the third phase. Although everyone approaches the writing process somewhat differently, the following tips offer advice in problem areas faced by most formal report writers.

- **Allow sufficient time.** The main reason given by writers who are disappointed with their reports is "I just ran out of time." Develop a realistic timetable and stick to it.

- **Finish data collection.** Don't begin writing until you've collected all the data and drawn the primary conclusions. Starting too early often means backtracking. For reports based on survey data, compile the tables and figures first.

- **Work from a good outline.** A big project such as a formal report needs the order and direction provided by a clear outline, even if the outline has to be revised as the project unfolds.

- **Provide a proper writing environment.** You'll need a quiet spot where you can spread out your materials and work without interruption. Formal reports demand blocks of concentration time.

- **Use a computer.** Preparing a report on a computer enables you to keyboard quickly; revise easily; and check spelling, grammar, and synonyms readily. A word of warning, though: save your document often and print occasionally so that you have a hard copy. Take these precautions to guard against the grief caused by lost files, power outages, and computer malfunctions.

- **Write rapidly; revise later.** Some experts advise writers to record their ideas quickly and save revision until after the first draft is completed. They say that quick writing avoids wasted effort spent in polishing sentences or even sections that may be cut later. Moreover, rapid writing encourages fluency and creativity. However, a quick-and-dirty first draft doesn't work for everyone. Many business writers prefer a more deliberate writing style, so consider this advice selectively.

- **Save difficult sections.** If some sections are harder to write than others, save them until you've developed confidence and rhythm working on easier topics.

- **Be consistent in verb tense.** Use past-tense verbs to describe completed actions (for example, *the respondents said* or *the survey showed*). Use present-tense verbs, however, to explain current actions (*the purpose of the report is, this report examines, the table shows,* and so forth). When citing references, use past-tense verbs (*Jones reported that*). Don't switch back and forth between present- and past-tense verbs in describing related data.

- **Generally avoid *I* and *we*.** To make formal reports seem as objective and credible as possible, most writers omit first-person pronouns. This formal style sometimes results in the overuse of passive-voice verbs (for example, *periodicals were consulted* and *the study was conducted*). Look for alternative constructions (*periodicals indicated* and *the study revealed*). It's also possible that your organization may allow first-person pronouns, so check before starting your report.

- **Let the first draft sit.** After completing the first version, put it aside for a day or two. Return to it with the expectation of revising and improving it. Don't be afraid to make major changes.

- **Revise for clarity, coherence, and conciseness.** Read a printed copy out loud. Do the sentences make sense? Do the ideas flow together naturally? Can wordiness and flabbiness be cut out? Make sure that your writing is so clear that a busy manager does not have to reread any part. See Chapter 7 for specific revision suggestions.

- **Proofread the final copy three times.** First, read a printed copy slowly for word meanings and content. Then read the copy again for spelling, punctuation, grammar, and other mechanical errors. Finally, scan the entire report to check its formatting and consistency (page numbering, indenting, spacing, headings, and so forth).

Smart report writers allow themselves plenty of time, research thoroughly, draw up a useful outline, and work on a computer.

Effective formal reports maintain parallelism in verb tenses, avoid first-person pronouns, and use the active voice.

## Putting It All Together

Formal reports in business generally aim to study problems and recommend solutions. Alan Christopher, business senator to the Office of Associated Students (OAS) at West Coast College, was given a campus problem to study, resulting in the formal report shown in Figure 14.4, which begins on page 467.

The campus recycling program, under the direction of Cheryl Bryant and supported by the OAS, was not attracting the anticipated level of participation. As the campus recycling program began its second year of operation, Cheryl and the OAS wondered whether campus community members were sufficiently aware of the program. They also wondered how participation could be increased. Alan volunteered to investigate the problem because of his strong support for environmental causes. He also needed to conduct a research project for one of his business courses, and he had definite ideas for improving the campus OAS recycling program.

Alan's report illustrates many of the points discussed in this chapter. Although it's a good example of typical report format and style, it should not be viewed as the only way to present a report. Wide variation exists in reports.

The following checklist summarizes the report process and report components in one handy list.

## CHECKLIST FOR PREPARING FORMAL REPORTS

### Report Process

✓ **Analyze the report problem and purpose.** Develop a problem question (*Is sexual harassment affecting employees at DataTech?*) and a purpose statement (*The purpose of this report is to investigate sexual harassment at DataTech and recommend remedies*).

✓ **Anticipate the audience and issues.** Consider primary and secondary audiences. What do they already know? What do they need to know? Divide the major problem into subproblems for investigation.

✓ **Prepare a work plan.** Include problem and purpose statements, as well as a description of the sources and methods of collecting data. Prepare a tentative project outline and a work schedule with anticipated dates of completion for all segments of the project.

✓ **Collect data.** Begin by searching secondary sources (electronic databases, books, magazines, journals, newspapers) for information on your topic. Then, if necessary, gather primary data by surveying, interviewing, observing, and experimenting.

✓ **Document data sources.** Prepare note cards or separate sheets of paper citing all references (author, date, source, page, and quotation). Select a documentation format (Chapter 12) and use it consistently.

✓ **Interpret and organize the data.** Arrange the collected information in tables, grids, or outlines to help you visualize relationships and interpret meanings. Organize the data into an outline (Chapter 6).

✓ **Prepare graphics.** Make tables, charts, graphs, and illustrations—but *only* if they serve a function. Use graphics to help clarify, condense, simplify, or emphasize your data.

✓ **Compose the first draft.** At a computer write the first draft from your outline. Use appropriate headings as well as transitional expressions (such as *however, on the contrary,* and *in addition*) to guide the reader through the report.

**FIGURE 14.4** Model Formal Report With MLA Citation Style

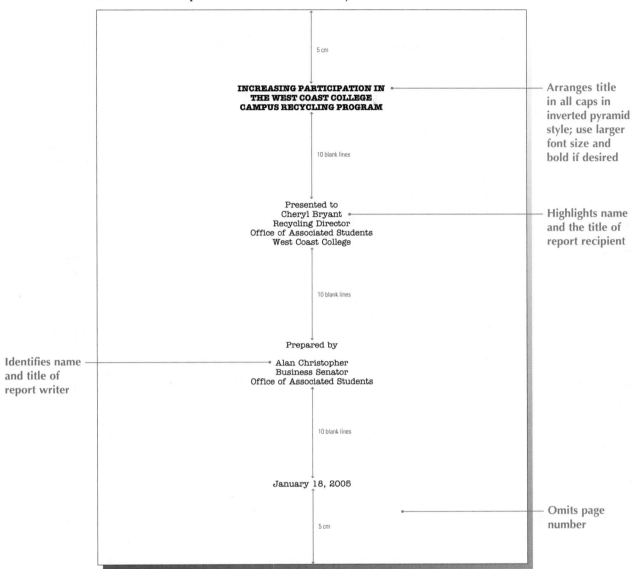

**INCREASING PARTICIPATION IN THE WEST COAST COLLEGE CAMPUS RECYCLING PROGRAM** — Arranges title in all caps in inverted pyramid style; use larger font size and bold if desired

5 cm

10 blank lines

Presented to
Cheryl Bryant
Recycling Director
Office of Associated Students
West Coast College

— Highlights name and the title of report recipient

10 blank lines

Prepared by
Alan Christopher
Business Senator
Office of Associated Students

Identifies name and title of report writer

10 blank lines

January 18, 2005

5 cm

Omits page number

Alan arranges the title page so that the amount of space above the title is equal to the space below the date. If a report is to be bound on the left, move the left margin and centre point approximately 0.5 cm to the right. Notice that no page number appears on the title page, although it is counted as page i.

If you use scalable fonts, word processing capabilities, or a laser printer to enhance your report and title page, be careful to avoid anything unprofessional (such as too many type fonts, oversized print, and inappropriate graphics).

**FIGURE 14.4** Continued

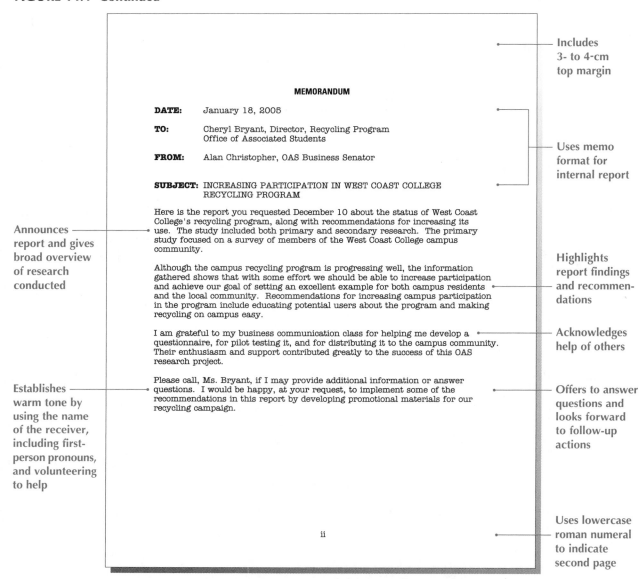

Includes
3- to 4-cm
top margin

**MEMORANDUM**

**DATE:**    January 18, 2005

**TO:**    Cheryl Bryant, Director, Recycling Program
Office of Associated Students

**FROM:**    Alan Christopher, OAS Business Senator

**SUBJECT:** INCREASING PARTICIPATION IN WEST COAST COLLEGE
RECYCLING PROGRAM

Uses memo
format for
internal report

Here is the report you requested December 10 about the status of West Coast
College's recycling program, along with recommendations for increasing its
use. The study included both primary and secondary research. The primary
study focused on a survey of members of the West Coast College campus
community.

Although the campus recycling program is progressing well, the information
gathered shows that with some effort we should be able to increase participation
and achieve our goal of setting an excellent example for both campus residents
and the local community. Recommendations for increasing campus participation
in the program include educating potential users about the program and making
recycling on campus easy.

I am grateful to my business communication class for helping me develop a
questionnaire, for pilot testing it, and for distributing it to the campus community.
Their enthusiasm and support contributed greatly to the success of this OAS
research project.

Please call, Ms. Bryant, if I may provide additional information or answer
questions. I would be happy, at your request, to implement some of the
recommendations in this report by developing promotional materials for our
recycling campaign.

ii

Announces
report and gives
broad overview
of research
conducted

Highlights
report findings
and recommen-
dations

Acknowledges
help of others

Establishes
warm tone by
using the name
of the receiver,
including first-
person pronouns,
and volunteering
to help

Offers to answer
questions and
looks forward
to follow-up
actions

Uses lowercase
roman numeral
to indicate
second page

Because this report is being submitted within his own organization, Alan uses a memorandum of transmittal. Formal organization
reports submitted to outsiders would carry a letter of transmittal
printed on company stationery.

The margins for the transmittal should be the same as for the
report, about 3 cm on all sides. If a report is to be bound,
add an extra 0.5 cm to the left margin. Because the report is
single-spaced, the paragraphs are not indented. When a report is
double-spaced, paragraphs are indented. A page number is optional.

**FIGURE 14.4** Continued

Allows top margin of 4 to 5 cm

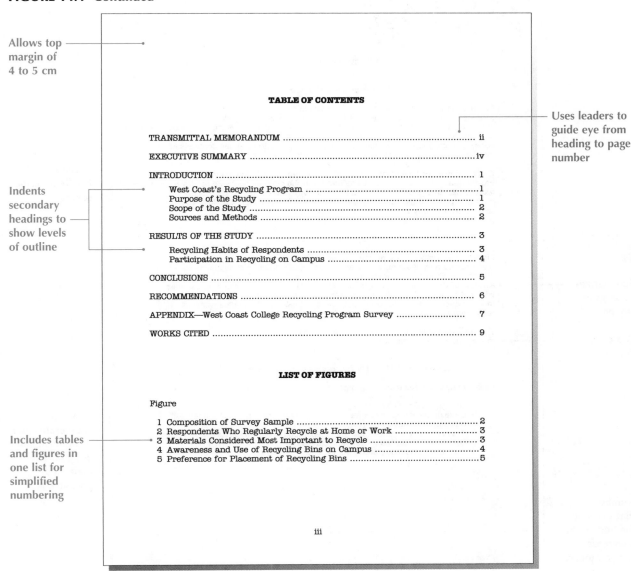

Uses leaders to guide eye from heading to page number

Indents secondary headings to show levels of outline

Includes tables and figures in one list for simplified numbering

**TABLE OF CONTENTS**

**LIST OF FIGURES**

Figure

iii

Because Alan's table of contents and list of figures are small, he combines them on one page. Notice that he uses all caps for the titles of major report parts and a combination of upper- and lowercase letters for first-level headings. This duplicates the style within the report.

Advanced word processing capabilities enable you to generate a contents page automatically, including leaders and accurate page numbering—no matter how many times you revise!

**FIGURE 14.4 Continued**

**EXECUTIVE SUMMARY**

**Purposes of the Report**

The purposes of this report are to (1) determine the West Coast College campus community's awareness of the campus recycling program and (2) recommend ways to increase participation. West Coast's recycling program was intended to respond to the increasing problem of waste disposal, to fulfill its social responsibility as an educational institution, and to meet the demands of legislation requiring individuals and organizations to recycle.

A questionnaire survey was conducted to learn about the campus community's recycling habits and to assess participation in the current recycling program. A total of 220 individuals responded to the survey. Since West Coast College's recycling program includes only aluminum, glass, paper, and plastic at this time, these were the only materials considered in this study.

Tells purpose of report and briefly describes survey

**Recycling at West Coast**

Most survey respondents recognized the importance of recycling and stated that they do recycle aluminum, glass, paper, and plastic on a regular basis either at home or at work. However, most respondents displayed a low level of awareness and use of the on-campus program. Many of the respondents were unfamiliar with the location of the bins around campus and, therefore, had not participated in the recycling program. Other responses indicated that the bins were not conveniently located.

Summarizes findings of survey

The results of this study show that more effort is needed to increase participation in the campus recycling program.

Draws primary conclusion

**Recommendations for Increasing Recycling Participation**

Recommendations for increasing participation in the program include the following:

1. Relocate the recycling bins for greater visibility
2. Develop incentive programs to gain the participation of individuals and on-campus student groups
3. Train student volunteers to give on-campus presentations explaining the benefits of using the recycling program
4. Increase advertising about the program

Concisely enumerates four recommendations using parallel (balanced) phrasing

iv

Numbers pages that precede the body with lowercase roman numerals

For readers who want a quick picture of the report, the executive summary presents its most important elements. Alan has divided the summary into three sections for increased readability.

Executive summaries generally contain little jargon or complex statistics; they condense what management needs to know about a problem and its study. Report abstracts, sometimes written in place of summaries, tend to be more technical and are aimed at specialists rather than management.

**FIGURE 14.4** Continued

Leaves 5-cm top margin on first page

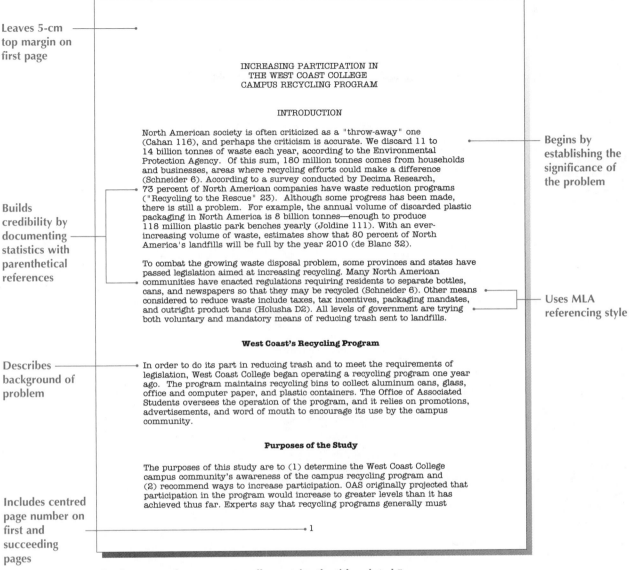

INCREASING PARTICIPATION IN
THE WEST COAST COLLEGE
CAMPUS RECYCLING PROGRAM

INTRODUCTION

North American society is often criticized as a "throw-away" one (Cahan 116), and perhaps the criticism is accurate. We discard 11 to 14 billion tonnes of waste each year, according to the Environmental Protection Agency. Of this sum, 180 million tonnes comes from households and businesses, areas where recycling efforts could make a difference (Schneider 6). According to a survey conducted by Decima Research, 73 percent of North American companies have waste reduction programs ("Recycling to the Rescue" 23). Although some progress has been made, there is still a problem. For example, the annual volume of discarded plastic packaging in North America is 8 billion tonnes—enough to produce 118 million plastic park benches yearly (Joldine 111). With an ever-increasing volume of waste, estimates show that 80 percent of North America's landfills will be full by the year 2010 (de Blanc 32).

To combat the growing waste disposal problem, some provinces and states have passed legislation aimed at increasing recycling. Many North American communities have enacted regulations requiring residents to separate bottles, cans, and newspapers so that they may be recycled (Schneider 6). Other means considered to reduce waste include taxes, tax incentives, packaging mandates, and outright product bans (Holusha D2). All levels of government are trying both voluntary and mandatory means of reducing trash sent to landfills.

**West Coast's Recycling Program**

In order to do its part in reducing trash and to meet the requirements of legislation, West Coast College began operating a recycling program one year ago. The program maintains recycling bins to collect aluminum cans, glass, office and computer paper, and plastic containers. The Office of Associated Students oversees the operation of the program, and it relies on promotions, advertisements, and word of mouth to encourage its use by the campus community.

**Purposes of the Study**

The purposes of this study are to (1) determine the West Coast College campus community's awareness of the campus recycling program and (2) recommend ways to increase participation. OAS originally projected that participation in the program would increase to greater levels than it has achieved thus far. Experts say that recycling programs generally must

1

Begins by establishing the significance of the problem

Builds credibility by documenting statistics with parenthetical references

Uses MLA referencing style

Describes background of problem

Includes centred page number on first and succeeding pages

The first page of a report generally contains the title printed 5 cm from the top edge. Titles for major parts of a report (such as *Introduction, Results, Conclusion,* and so forth) are centred in all caps. First-level headings are bold and printed with upper- and lowercase letters. Second-level headings begin at the side. For illustration of heading formats, see Figure 13.5.

Notice that Alan's report is single-spaced. Many businesses prefer this space-saving format. However, some organizations prefer double-spacing, especially for preliminary drafts. Page numbers may be centred 2.5 cm from the bottom of the page or placed 2.5 cm from the upper right corner at the margin.

**FIGURE 14.4** Continued

Describes
what the study
includes and
excludes

operate at least a year before results become apparent (de Blanc 33). The OAS program has been in operation one year, yet gains are disappointing. Therefore, OAS authorized this study to determine the campus community's awareness and use of the program. Recommendations for increasing participation in the campus recycling program will be made to the OAS based on the results of this study.

**Scope of the Study**

This study investigates potential participants' attitudes toward recycling in general, their awareness of the campus recycling program, their willingness to recycle on campus, and the perceived convenience of the recycling bins. Only aluminum, glass, paper, and plastic are considered in this study, as they are the only materials being recycled on campus at this time. The costs involved in the program were not considered in this study, since a recycling program generally does not begin to pay for itself during the first year. After the first year, the financial benefit is usually realized in reduced disposal costs (Steelman, Desmond, and Johnson 145).

**Sources and Methods**

Current business periodicals and newspapers were consulted for background information and to learn how other organizations are encouraging use of in-house recycling programs. In addition, a questionnaire survey (shown in the appendix) of administrators, faculty, staff, and students at West Coast College campus was conducted to learn about this group's recycling habits. In all, a convenience sample of 220 individuals responded to the self-administered survey. The composition of the sample closely resembles the makeup of the campus population. Figure 1 shows the percentage of students, faculty, staff, and administrators who participated in the survey.

Discusses how
the study was
conducted

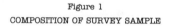

Figure 1
COMPOSITION OF SURVEY SAMPLE

Uses
computer-
generated pie
chart to
illustrate
makeup of
survey

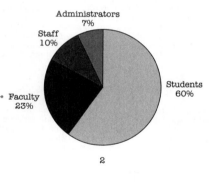

Administrators 7%

Staff 10%

Faculty 23%

Students 60%

2

Because Alan wants this report to be formal in tone, he avoids *I* and *we.* Notice, too, that he uses present-tense verbs to describe his current writing (*this study investigates*), but past-tense verbs to indicate research completed in the past (*newspapers were consulted*).

If you use figures or tables, be sure to introduce them in the text. Although it's not always possible, try to place them close to the spot where they are first mentioned. If necessary to save space, you can print the title of a figure beside it.

# FIGURE 14.4 Continued

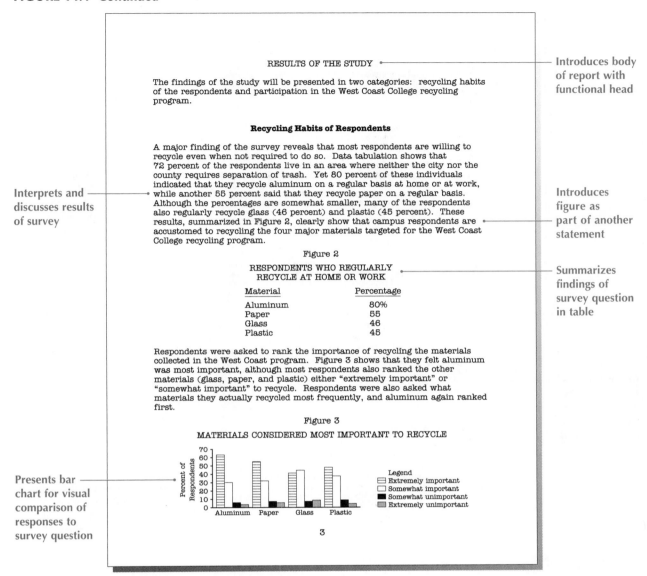

Introduces body of report with functional head

## RESULTS OF THE STUDY

The findings of the study will be presented in two categories: recycling habits of the respondents and participation in the West Coast College recycling program.

### Recycling Habits of Respondents

Interprets and discusses results of survey

A major finding of the survey reveals that most respondents are willing to recycle even when not required to do so. Data tabulation shows that 72 percent of the respondents live in an area where neither the city nor the county requires separation of trash. Yet 80 percent of these individuals indicated that they recycle aluminum on a regular basis at home or at work, while another 55 percent said that they recycle paper on a regular basis. Although the percentages are somewhat smaller, many of the respondents also regularly recycle glass (46 percent) and plastic (45 percent). These results, summarized in Figure 2, clearly show that campus respondents are accustomed to recycling the four major materials targeted for the West Coast College recycling program.

Introduces figure as part of another statement

Figure 2

RESPONDENTS WHO REGULARLY
RECYCLE AT HOME OR WORK

Summarizes findings of survey question in table

| Material | Percentage |
| --- | --- |
| Aluminum | 80% |
| Paper | 55 |
| Glass | 46 |
| Plastic | 45 |

Respondents were asked to rank the importance of recycling the materials collected in the West Coast program. Figure 3 shows that they felt aluminum was most important, although most respondents also ranked the other materials (glass, paper, and plastic) either "extremely important" or "somewhat important" to recycle. Respondents were also asked what materials they actually recycled most frequently, and aluminum again ranked first.

Figure 3

MATERIALS CONSIDERED MOST IMPORTANT TO RECYCLE

Presents bar chart for visual comparison of responses to survey question

Legend
- Extremely important
- Somewhat important
- Somewhat unimportant
- Extremely unimportant

3

Alan selects the most important survey findings to interpret and discuss for readers. Notice that he continues to use present-tense verbs (*the survey reveals* and *these results clearly show*) to discuss the current report.

Because he has few tables and charts, he labels them all as "Figures." Notice that he numbers them consecutively and places the label above each figure. Report writers with a great many tables, charts, and illustrations may prefer to label and number them separately. Tables are labelled as such; everything else is generally called a figure. When tables and figures are labelled separately, tables may be labelled above the table and figures below the figure.

**FIGURE 14.4  Continued**

Adds personal interpretation

When asked how likely they would be to go out of their way to deposit an item in a recycling bin, 29 percent of the respondents said "very likely," and 55 percent said "somewhat likely." Thus, respondents showed a willingness—at least on paper—to recycle even if it means making a special effort to locate a recycling bin.

### Participation in Recycling on Campus

For any recycling program to be successful, participants must be aware of the location of recycling centres and must be trained to use them (de Blanc 33). Another important ingredient in thriving programs is convenience to users. If recycling centres are difficult for users to reach, these centres will be unsuccessful. To collect data on these topics, the survey included questions assessing awareness and use of the current bins. The survey also investigated reasons for not participating and the perceived convenience of current bin locations.

Introduces more findings and relates them to the report's purpose

### Student Awareness and Use of Bins

Two of the most significant questions in the survey asked whether respondents were aware of the OAS recycling bins on campus and whether they had used the bins. Responses to both questions were disappointing, as Figure 4 illustrates.

Figure 4
AWARENESS AND USE OF RECYCLING BINS ON CAMPUS

| Location | Awareness of bins at this location | Use of bins at this location |
|---|---|---|
| Social sciences building | 38% | 21% |
| Bookstore | 29 | 12 |
| Administration building | 28 | 12 |
| Computer labs | 16 | 11 |
| Library | 15 | 7 |
| Student union | 9 | 5 |
| Department offices | 6 | 3 |
| Campus dormitories | 5 | 3 |
| Unaware of any bins; have not used any bins | 20 | 7 |

Arranges responses from highest to lowest with "unaware" category placed last

Only 38 percent of the respondents, as shown in Figure 4, were aware of the bins located outside the social sciences building. Even fewer were aware of the bins outside the bookstore (29 percent) and outside the administration building (28 percent). Equally dissatisfying, only 21 percent of the respondents had used the most visible recycling bins outside the social sciences

Clarifies and emphasizes meaning of findings

4

In discussing the results of the survey, Alan highlights those that have significance for the purpose of the report.

As you type a report, avoid widows and orphans (ending a page with the first line of a paragraph or carrying a single line of a paragraph to a new page). Strive to start and end pages with at least two lines of a paragraph, even if a slightly larger bottom margin results.

**FIGURE 14.4 Continued**

building. Other recycling bin locations were even less familiar to the survey respondents and, of course, were little used. These responses plainly show that the majority of the respondents in the West Coast campus community have a low awareness of the recycling program and an even lower record of participation.

**Reasons for Not Participating**

Respondents offered several reasons for not participating in the campus recycling program. Forty-five percent said that the bins are not convenient to use. Thirty percent said that they did not know where the bins were located. Another 25 percent said that they are not in the habit of recycling. Although many reasons for not participating were listed, the primary one appears to centre on convenience of bin locations.

**Location of Recycling Bins**

When asked specifically how they would rate the location of the bins currently in use, only 13 percent of the respondents felt that the bins were extremely convenient. Another 35 percent rated the locations as somewhat convenient. Over half of the respondents felt that the locations of the bins were either somewhat inconvenient or extremely inconvenient. Recycling bins are currently located outside nearly all of the major campus buildings, but respondents clearly considered these locations inconvenient or inadequate.

In indicating where they would like recycling bins placed (see Figure 5), 42 percent of the respondents felt that the most convenient locations would be outside each building on campus. Placing recycling bins near the food service facilities on campus seemed most convenient to another 33 percent of those questioned, while 15 percent stated that they would like to see the bins placed near the vending machines. Ten percent of the individuals responding to the survey did not seem to think that the locations of the bins would matter to them.

Figure 5

PREFERENCE FOR PLACEMENT OF RECYCLING BINS

| | |
|---|---|
| Outside each building on campus | 42% |
| Near food service facilities | 33 |
| Near vending machines | 15 |
| Does not matter | 10 |

CONCLUSIONS

Based on the findings of the recycling survey of members of the West Coast College campus community, the following conclusions are drawn:

1. Most members of the campus community are already recycling at home or at work without being required to do so.

5

*Discusses results of other survey questions not represented in tables or charts*

*Clarifies results of another survey question with textual discussion accompanied by table*

After completing a discussion of the survey results, Alan lists what he considers the five most important conclusions to be drawn from this survey. Some writers combine the conclusions and recommendations, particularly when they are interrelated. Alan separated them in his study because the survey findings were quite distinct from the recommendations he would make based on them.

Notice that it is unnecessary to start a new page for the conclusions.

**FIGURE 14.4  Continued**

Draws conclusions based on survey findings; summarizes previous discussion

2. Over half of the respondents recycle aluminum and paper on a regular basis; most recycle glass and plastic to some degree.

3. Most of the surveyed individuals expressed a willingness to participate in a recycling program. Many, however, seem unwilling to travel very far to participate; 42 percent would like recycling bins to be located outside every campus building.

4. Awareness and use of the current campus recycling program are low. Only a little over one third of the respondents knew of any recycling bin locations on campus, and only one fifth had actually used them.

5. Respondents considered the locations of the campus bins inconvenient. This perceived inconvenience was given as the principal reason for not participating in the campus recycling program.

## RECOMMENDATIONS

Supported by the findings and conclusions of this study, the following recommendations are offered in an effort to improve the operations and success of the West Coast recycling program:

Lists specific actions to help solve report problem; suggests practical ways to implement recommendations

1. Increase on-campus awareness and visibility by designing an eye-catching logo that represents the campus recycling program for use in promotions.

2. Enhance comprehension of recycling procedures by training users how to recycle. Use posters to explain the recycling program and to inform users of recycling bin locations. Label each bin clearly as to what materials may be deposited.

3. Add bins in several new locations, particularly in the food service and vending machine areas.

4. Recruit student leaders to promote participation in the recycling program by giving educational talks to classes and other campus groups, informing them of the importance of recycling.

5. Develop an incentive program for student organizations. Offer incentives for meeting recycling goals as determined by OAS. On-campus groups could compete in recycling drives designed to raise money for the group, the college, or a charity. Money from the proceeds of the recycling program could be used to fund the incentive program.

6

The most important parts of a report are its conclusions and recommendations. To make them especially clear, Alan enumerated each conclusion and recommendation. Notice that each recommendation starts with a verb and is stated in command language for emphasis and readability.

Report recommendations are most helpful to readers when they not only make suggestions to solve the original research problem but also describe specific actions to be taken. Notice that Alan goes beyond merely listing ideas; instead, he provides practical suggestions for ways to implement the recommendations.

**FIGURE 14.4** Continued

Includes copy of survey questionnaire so that report readers can see actual questions

Provides range of answers that will be easy to tabulate

Explains why survey is necessary, emphasizing "you" view

APPENDIX

**WEST COAST COLLEGE RECYCLING PROGRAM SURVEY**

West Coast College recently implemented a recycling program on campus. Please take a few minutes to answer the following questions so that we can make this program as convenient and helpful as possible for you to use.

1. Please indicate which items you recycle on a regular basis at home or at work.
   (Check *all* that apply.)
   ☐ Aluminum
   ☐ Glass
   ☐ Paper
   ☐ Plastic

2. Do you live in an area where the city/municipality requires separation of trash?
   ☐ Yes  ☐ No

3. How important is it to you to recycle each of the following:

|  | Extremely Important | Somewhat Important | Somewhat Unimportant | Extremely Unimportant |
|---|---|---|---|---|
| Aluminum |  |  |  |  |
| Glass |  |  |  |  |
| Paper |  |  |  |  |
| Plastic |  |  |  |  |

4. How likely would it be for you to go out of your way to put something in a recycling bin?

| Very Likely | Somewhat Likely | Somewhat Unlikely | Very Unlikely |
|---|---|---|---|
|  |  |  |  |

5. Which of the following items do you recycle *most* often? (Choose *one* item only.)
   ☐ Aluminum
   ☐ Glass
   ☐ Paper
   ☐ Plastic
   ☐ Other

6. The following are locations of the recycling bins on campus.
   (Check *all* those of which you are aware.)
   ☐ Administration building        ☐ Library
   ☐ Bookstore                      ☐ Social sciences building
   ☐ Campus dorms                   ☐ Student union
   ☐ Computer labs                  ☐ I'm unaware of any of these recycling bins.
   ☐ Engineering building

7

Alan had space to add the word "Appendix" to the top of the survey questionnaire. If space were not available, he could have typed a separate page with that title on it. If more than one item were included, he would have named them Appendix A, Appendix B, and so on.

Notice that the appendix continues the report pagination.

**FIGURE 14.4**  Continued

7. Which of the following recycling bins have you actually used?  (Check *all* that you have used.)

☐ Administration building      ☐ Library
☐ Bookstore      ☐ Social sciences building
☐ Campus dorms      ☐ Student union
☐ Computer labs      ☐ I've not used any of these recycling bins.
☐ Engineering building

8. If you don't recycle on campus, why don't you participate?

☐ I'm not in the habit of recycling.
☐ I don't know where the bins are.
☐ The bins aren't convenient for me.
☐ Other _____

9. How do you rate the convenience of the bins' locations?

☐ Extremely convenient
☐ Somewhat convenient
☐ Somewhat inconvenient
☐ Extremely inconvenient

10. Which of the following possible recycling bin locations would be most convenient for you to use? (Check *one* only.)

☐ Outside each building
☐ Near the food service facilities
☐ Near the vending machines
☐ Does not matter
☐ Other _____

11. Please indicate:

☐ Student
☐ Faculty
☐ Administrator
☐ Staff

COMMENTS:

Thank you for your responses!  Please return the questionnaire in the enclosed, stamped envelope to West Coast College, School of Business, Rm. 321.  If you have any questions, please call (555) 450-2391.

8

*Anticipates responses but also supplies "Other" category*

*Uses scale questions to capture degrees of feeling*

*Requests little demographic data to keep survey short*

*Offers comment section for explanations and remarks*

*Concludes with appreciation and instructions*

✓ **Revise and proofread.** Revise to eliminate wordiness, ambiguity, and redundancy. Look for ways to improve readability, such as bulleted or numbered lists. Proofread three times for (1) word and content meaning, (2) grammar and mechanical errors, and (3) formatting.

✓ **Evaluate the product.** Examine the final report. Will it achieve its purpose? Encourage feedback so that you can learn how to improve future reports.

## Report Components

✓ **Title page.** Balance the following lines on the title page: (1) name of the report (in all caps); (2) name, title, and organization of the individual receiving the report; (3) author's name, title, and organization; and (4) date submitted.

**FIGURE 14.4  Continued**

Works Cited

Cahan, Vicky. "Waste Not, Want Not? Not Necessarily." <u>Business Week</u>            —— Magazine
    17 July 2002: 116.

de Blanc, Susan. "Paper Recycling: How to Make It Effective." <u>The Office</u>
    Dec. 2001: 32.

Foster, David. "Recycling: A Green Idea Turns to Gold." <u>Los Angeles Times</u>            —— Online Newspaper
    5 Mar. 2003. Retrieved 7 Mar. 2003 <http://www.latimes.com/library/cyber/
    week/y05dat.html>.

Freeman, Monique M. Personal interview. 2 Nov. 2003.            —— Interview

Holusha, John. "Mixed Benefits from Recycling." <u>New York Times on the Web</u>            —— Online Newspaper
    26 July 2001. Retrieved 26 Oct 2002 <http://www.nytimes.com/2001/07/26/
    science/recycling.html>.

Joldine, Lee. <u>Spirit of the Wolf: The Environment and Canada's Future</u>.            —— Book—author with
    Ed. Jo Davis. Waterloo: Turnaround Decade Ecological Communications, 1995.            an editor

Landsburg, Steven E. "Who Shall Inherit the Earth?" <u>Slate</u> 1 May 2000. Retrieved            —— Online Magazine
    2 May 2003 <http://www.slate.com/Economics/99-05-01/Economics.asp>.

Schneider, Keith. "As Recycling Becomes a Growth Industry, Its Paradoxes Also
    Multiply." <u>The New York Times</u> 20 Jan. 2002, sec. 4: 6.            —— Newspaper

Steelman, James W., Shirley Desmond, and LeGrand Johnson. <u>Facing Global</u>            —— Book
    <u>Limitations</u>. New York: Rockford Press, 2000.

Steuteville, Robert. "The State of Garbage in America." Part 1. <u>BioCycle</u> Apr.            —— Online Magazine
    2002. Retrieved 30 Nov. 2002 <http://www.biocycle/recycle/guid.html>.

"Tips to Reduce, Reuse, and Recycle." <u>Environmental Recycling Hotline</u> May            —— World Wide Web
    2003. Retrieved 8 July 2003 <http://www.primenet.com/cgi-bin/erh.pl>.

Weddle, Bruce, and Edward Klein. "A Strategy to Control the Garbage Glut."            —— Journal
    <u>EPA Journal</u> 12.2 (2001): 28–34.

9

On this page Alan lists all the references cited in the text as well as others that he examined during his research. (Some authors list only those works cited in the report.) Alan formats his citations following the MLA referencing style. Notice that all entries are arranged alphabetically. He underlines book and periodical titles, but italics could be used. When referring to online items, he shows the full name of the citation and then identifies the path leading to that reference as well as the date on which he accessed the electronic reference. "Retrieved" or "Accessed" should be added to distinguish the retrieval date from the document date, although the MLA style does not include this.

Most word processing software today automatically updates citation references within the text and prints a complete list for you. For more information about documentation styles, see Chapter 12 and Appendix C.

# Applying Your Skills at AKA New Media

Business is booming for AKA New Media. As a result, Matthew Myers has hired you as an intern and has asked you to profile several potential clients in preparation for an AKA proposal. He reminds you to be thorough, urging you to review company products and services, strategies, and goals. He urges you to take a look at its corporate culture and its financial picture. No information is trivial when getting to know a potential client.

**Your Task**

Using the Web and any other resources available, profile the company of your choice from *Report on Business Magazine*'s "Top 1000." Submit a report, and prepare a list of questions you would ask during a "discovery" meeting. Then with a classmate simulate a discovery meeting and write a "reflection" document based on your profile and what you have learned during your one-on-one meeting.

www.akanewmedia.com

✓ **Letter of transmittal.** Announce the report topic and explain who authorized it. Briefly describe the project and preview the conclusions, if the reader is supportive. Close by expressing appreciation for the assignment, suggesting follow-up actions, acknowledging the help of others, or offering to answer questions.

✓ **Table of contents.** Show the beginning page number where each report heading appears in the report. Connect the page numbers and headings with leaders (spaced dots).

✓ **List of illustrations.** Include a list of tables, illustrations, or figures showing the title of the item and its page number. If space permits, put these lists on the same page with the table of contents.

✓ **Executive summary.** Summarize the report purpose, findings, conclusions, and recommendations. Gauge the length of the summary by the length of the report and by your organization's practices.

✓ **Introduction.** Explain the problem motivating the report; describe its background and significance. Clarify the scope and limitations of the report. Optional items include a review of relevant literature and a description of data sources, methods, and key terms. Close by previewing the report's organization.

✓ **Body.** Discuss, analyze, and interpret the research findings or the proposed solution to the problem. Arrange the findings in logical segments following your outline. Use clear, descriptive headings.

✓ **Conclusions and recommendations.** Explain what the findings mean in relation to the original problem. If requested, make enumerated recommendations that suggest actions for solving the problem.

UNIT 4
Reports and Proposals
**480**

✓ **Appendix.** Include items of interest to some, but not all, readers, such as a data questionnaire or computer printouts.

**References and bibliography.** If footnotes are not provided in the text, list all references in a bibliographical section called "Works Cited," or "References."

## SUMMARY OF LEARNING OBJECTIVES

*1* **Discuss the components of informal proposals.** Most informal proposals contain (1) a persuasive introduction that explains the purpose of the proposal and qualifies the writer; (2) background material identifying the problem and project goals; (3) a proposal, plan, or schedule outlining the project; (4) a section describing staff qualifications; (5) a budget showing expected costs; and (6) a request for approval or authorization.

*2* **Discuss the special components in formal proposals.** Beyond the six components generally contained in informal proposals, formal proposals may include these additional parts: (1) copy of the RFP (request for proposal), (2) letter of transmittal, (3) executive summary or abstract, (4) title page, (5) table of contents, (6) list of illustrations, and (7) appendix.

*3* **Identify formal report components that precede its introduction.** Formal reports may include these beginning components: (1) vinyl or heavy paper cover, (2) title page, (3) letter of transmittal, (4) table of contents, (5) list of illustrations, and (6) executive summary.

*4* **Outline topics that might be covered in the introduction of a formal report.** The introduction to a formal report sets the scene by discussing some or all of the following topics: background material, problem or purpose, significance of the topic, scope and organization of the report, authorization, review of relevant literature, sources and methods, and definitions of key terms.

*5* **Describe the components of a formal report that follow the introduction.** The body of a report discusses, analyzes, interprets, and evaluates the research findings or solution to a problem. The conclusion tells what the findings mean and how they relate to the report's purpose. The recommendations tell how to solve the report problem. The last portions of a formal report are the appendix, references, and bibliography.

*6* **Specify tips that aid writers of formal reports.** Before writing, develop a realistic timetable and collect all necessary data. During the writing process, work from a good outline, work in a quiet place, and use a computer. Also, try to write rapidly, revising later. While writing, use verb tenses consistently, and avoid *I* and *we*. A few days after completing the first draft, revise to improve clarity, coherence, and conciseness. Proofread the final copy three times.

# CHAPTER REVIEW

1. Proposals are written offers to do what? (Obj. 1)

2. What is an RFP? (Objs. 1 and 2)

3. What are the six principal parts of a letter proposal? (Obj. 1)

4. What is a "worry item" in a proposal? (Obj. 1)

5. Why should a proposal budget be prepared very carefully? (Obj. 1)

6. What is generally contained in a letter of transmittal accompanying a formal report? (Obj. 3)

7. What label can a report writer use to describe all illustrations and tables? (Obj. 3)

8. What is the purpose of an executive summary? (Objs. 2 and 3)

9. What does *scope* mean in relation to a formal report? (Obj. 4)

10. Should the body of a report include the heading *Body*? (Obj. 5)

11. What are the advantages of functional headings? Of talking headings? (Obj. 5)

12. In a formal report where do most writers place the conclusions? (Obj. 5)

13. What materials go in an appendix? (Obj. 5)

14. What environment enhances writing? (Obj. 6)

15. How should a formal report be proofread? (Obj. 6)

# CRITICAL THINKING

1. Why are proposals important to many businesses? (Obj. 1)

2. How do formal reports differ from informal reports? (Objs. 1 and 2)

3. Discuss the three phases of the writing process in relation to formal reports. What activities take place in each phase? (Objs. 3–5)

4. Compare and contrast proposals and business plans. (Objs. 1 and 2)

5. **Ethical Issue:** Is it ethical to have someone else proofread a report that you will be turning in for a grade?

# ACTIVITIES*

## 14.1 Proposal: Looking for Clients for Your Business

**TEAM     CRITICAL THINKING**

A new medical clinic, ProMed Institute, is opening its doors in your hometown, and a mutual friend has recommended your small business to the administrator of the clinic. You have received a letter asking you to provide information about your service. The new medical clinic specializes in sports medicine, physical therapy, and cardiac rehabilitation services. It is interested in retaining your company, rather than hiring its own employees to perform the service your company offers.

**Your Task.** Working in teams, first decide what service you will offer. It could be landscaping, uniform supply, laundry of uniforms, general cleaning, computerized no-paper filing systems, online medical supplies, patient transportation, supplemental hospice care, temporary office support, or food service. As a team, develop a letter proposal outlining your plan, staffing, and budget. Use persuasion to show why contracting your services is better than hiring in-house employees. In the proposal letter, request a meeting with the administrative board. In addition to a written proposal, you may be expected to make an oral presentation that includes visual aids and/or handouts. Send your proposal to Mr. Jack Dawson, Director, ProMed Institute. Supply a local address.

## 14.2 Business Plan Proposal: Starting Your Own Business (Objs. 1 and 2)

**TEAM     CRITICAL THINKING**

You and your buddies have a terrific idea for a new business in your town. For example, you might want to propose to Starbucks the concept of converting some of its coffee shops into Internet cafes. Or you might propose to the city or another organization a better Web site, which you and your team would design and maintain. You might want to start a word processing business that offers production, editing, and printing services. Often businesses, medical centres, lawyers, and other professionals have overload transcribing or word processing to contract out to a service.

**Your Task.** Working in teams, explore entrepreneurial ventures based on your experience and expertise. Write a business plan proposal to secure approval and funding. Your report should include a transmittal letter, as well as a description of your proposed company, its product or service, market analysis, operations and management plan, and financial plan.

*Instructors will find teaching suggestions and additional report topics in the Instructor's Manual.

**RICH CHAPTER RESOURCES ARE AVAILABLE AT THE WEB SITE**

## 14.3 Formal Report: Intercultural Communication (Objs. 3–6)

North American businesses are expanding into foreign markets with manufacturing plants, sales offices, and branch offices abroad. Unfortunately, most North Americans have little knowledge of or experience with people from other cultures. To prepare for participation in the global marketplace, you are to collect information for a report focused on a Pacific Rim, Latin American, or European country where English is not regularly spoken. Before selecting the country, though, consult your campus international student program for volunteers who are willing to be interviewed. Your instructor may make advance arrangements seeking international student volunteers.

**Your Task.** In teams of three to five, collect information about your target country from the library and other sources. Then invite an international student representing your target country to be interviewed by your group. As you conduct primary and secondary research, investigate the topics listed in Figure 14.5 on page 484. Confirm what you learn in your secondary research by talking with your interviewee. When you complete your research, write a report for the CEO of your company (make up a name and company). Assume that your company plans to expand its operations abroad. Your report should advise the company's executives of social customs, family life, attitudes, religions, education, and values in the target country. Remember that your company's interests are business-oriented; don't dwell on tourist information. Write your report individually or in teams.

## 14.4 Proposal and Grant Writing: Learning From the Nonprofits (Objs. 1 and 2)

You'd like to learn more about writing business proposals and especially about writing grants. The latter involves funding supplied by an institution, foundation, or the government. You might one day even decide to become a professional grant/proposal writer. But first you need experience.

**Your Task.** Volunteer your services for a local nonprofit organization, such as a United Way <**www.unitedway.ca**> member agency, an educational institution, or your local church. To learn more about writing grants, complete an InfoTrac subject guide search for "proposal." Click on articles under the categories of "business proposal writing" and "grant proposal writing." Your instructor may ask you to submit a preliminary memo report outlining ten or more pointers you learned about writing proposals and grants for nonprofit organizations.

## 14.5 Executive Summary: Keeping the Boss Informed (Objs. 5 and 6)

Many managers and executives are too rushed to read long journal articles, but they are eager to keep up with developments in their fields. Assume your boss has asked you to help him stay abreast of research in his field. He asks you to submit to him one executive summary every month on an article of interest.

**Your Task.** In your field of study, select a professional journal, such as the *Journal of Management*. Using an InfoTrac Power search, look for articles in your targeted journal. Select an article that is at least five pages long and is interesting to you. Write an executive summary in a memo format. Include an introduction that might begin with *As you requested, I am submitting this executive summary of . . . .* Identify the author, article name, journal, and date of publication. Explain what the author intended to do in the study or article. Summarize three or four of the most important findings of the study or article. Use descriptive rather than functional headings. Summarize any recommendations made. Your boss would also like a concluding statement indicating your reaction to the article. Address your memo to Matthew R. Ferranto.

## 14.6 Proposal, Business Plan, and Report Topics (Objs. 1–6)

A list with over 70 report topics is available on this book's Student Resources Web site. Click "Web Links by Chapter" and go to Chapter 12. The topics are divided into the following categories: accounting, finance, personnel/human resources, marketing, information systems, management, and general business/education/campus issues. You can collect information for many of these reports by using InfoTrac and the Web. Your instructor may assign them as individual or team projects. All involve critical thinking in organizing information, drawing conclusions, and making recommendations. The topics include assignments appropriate for proposals, business plans, and formal reports. A number of self-contained report activities that require no additional research are provided at the end of Chapter 13.

**FIGURE 14.5  Intercultural Interview Topics and Questions**

## Social Customs

1. How do people react to strangers? Friendly? Hostile? Reserved?
2. How do people greet each other?
3. What are the appropriate manners when you enter a room? Bow? Nod? Shake hands with everyone?
4. How are names used for introductions? Is it appropriate to inquire about one's occupation or family?
5. What are the attitudes toward touching?
6. How does one express appreciation for an invitation to another's home? Bring a gift? Send flowers? Write a thank-you note? Are any gifts taboo?
7. Are there any customs related to how or where one sits?
8. Are any facial expressions or gestures considered rude?
9. How close do people stand when talking?
10. What is the attitude toward punctuality in social situations? In business situations?
11. What are acceptable eye-contact patterns?
12. What gestures indicate agreement? Disagreement?

## Family Life

1. What is the basic unit of social organization? Basic family? Extended family?
2. Do women work outside of the home? In what occupations?

## Housing, Clothing, and Food

1. Are there differences in the kind of housing used by different social groups? Differences in location? Differences in furnishings?
2. What occasions require special clothing?
3. Are some types of clothing considered taboo?
4. What is appropriate business attire for men? For women?
5. How many times a day do people eat?
6. What types of places, food, and drink are appropriate for business entertainment? Where is the seat of honour at a table?

## Class Structure

1. Into what classes is society organized?
2. Do racial, religious, or economic factors determine social status?
3. Are there any minority groups? What is their social standing?

## Political Patterns

1. Are there any immediate threats to the political survival of the country?
2. How is political power manifested?
3. What channels are used for expression of popular opinion?
4. What information media are important?
5. Is it appropriate to talk politics in social situations?

## Religion

1. To which religious groups do people belong? Is one predominant?
2. Do religious beliefs influence daily activities?
3. Which places have sacred value? Which objects? Which events?
4. How do religious holidays affect business activities?

## Economic Institutions

1. What are the country's principal products?
2. Are workers organized in unions?
3. How are businesses owned? By family units? By large public corporations? By the government?
4. What is the standard work schedule?
5. Is it appropriate to do business by telephone?
6. How has technology affected business procedures?
7. Is participatory management used?
8. Are there any customs related to exchanging business cards?
9. How is status shown in an organization? Private office? Secretary? Furniture?
10. Are businesspeople expected to socialize before conducting business?

## Value Systems

1. Is competitiveness or cooperation more prized?
2. Is thrift or enjoyment of the moment more valued?
3. Is politeness more important than factual honesty?
4. What are the attitudes toward education?
5. Do women own or manage businesses? If so, how are they treated?
6. What are your people's perceptions of Canadians? Do Canadians offend you? What has been hardest for you to adjust to in Canada? How could Canadians make this adjustment easier for you?

# C.L.U.E. REVIEW 14

On a separate sheet edit the following sentences to correct faults in grammar, punctuation, spelling, numbers, proofreading, and word use.

1. Proposals are writen offers to do the following, solve problems, provide services or sell equippment.

2. Our company President and Vice President worked together in developing 2 RFP's to solicit competitive bids.

3. To make a introduction to a proposal interesting, a "hook" should be provided by the writer to capture a readers attention.

4. A central item in most Proposals, is the budget which is a list of proposed project costs.

5. Any proposal delivered to the Manager or I should definitly explain the specific credentials and expertise of key personal for the project.

6. Lisa and him wanted to start there own business, therefore they wrote a business plan, that included a detailed market analysis.

7. Nicolas Scott who is a member of our research and development department presented a formal report based on through investigation and analysis.

8. The principle sections of the report is the body, it discusses the research findings.

9. If a report is one hundred pages long it may require a ten page Executive Summary.

10. Only 1 of the executives were present at the June 10th meeting, when the report was presented.

# Unit 5
## Presentations

# Chapter 15
## Speaking Skills

## LEARNING OBJECTIVES

*1* Discuss two important first steps in preparing effective oral presentations.

*2* Explain the major elements in organizing the content of a presentation, including the introduction, body, and conclusion.

*3* Identify techniques for gaining audience rapport, including using effective imagery, providing verbal signposts, and sending appropriate nonverbal messages.

*4* Discuss designing and using effective visual aids, handouts, and electronic presentation materials.

*5* Specify delivery techniques for use before, during, and after a presentation.

*6* Explain effective techniques for adapting oral presentations to cross-cultural audiences.

*7* List techniques for improving telephone and voice mail effectiveness.

## Esteem Team

After a successful eight-year development in British Columbia, Esteem Team has spread across the country, and in March 2002 Esteem Team became Canada's first and only nationwide athlete role model program. The national program has developed partnerships with government, corporations, national sport centres, provincial sport federations, education groups, health groups, and the RCMP, according to Curt Harnett, business development director for Sport Alliance Ontario. The mission of the Esteem Team Association (ETA) is to be a world leader in youth development.

Through presentations made by Olympic, Paralympic, and other world-class athletes, the Esteem Team inspires and encourages young people to recognize their full potential by instilling in them positive characteristics and confidence. More than 80 athletes representing this nonprofit organization, funded by the Government of Canada and Webber Naturals, deliver messages to today's youth through face-to-face interactive presentations in both urban and rural communities throughout the country, sharing personal stories of failure, triumph, and determination.

Sending messages to youth about goal-setting, accepting triumph and failure, positive attitude, persistence, and overcoming obstacles, the elite athletes relate to their audiences with personal stories and experiences. The Esteem Team athletes are real people who can relate to many contemporary challenges. Topics such as motivation, making positive choices, teamwork, and peer pressure are discussed. Most of the presentations are between 45 and 60 minutes in length and are connected to the school curriculum. Pre- and post-presentation activity sheets are provided, and resource material to support the concepts discussed in the presentations is available for educators on the Web site.

Presentations not only inspire youths to reach for their potential, but they may also focus on the value of an active lifestyle and the importance of not smoking. In 2002, Esteem Team athletes partnered with the Medical Society of Nova Scotia to encourage youth to be physically active and not to smoke. Scott Logan, Sport Nova Scotia CEO, believes that "Students really look up to these athletes. These athletes are the best in their sports because of positive attitudes and healthy lifestyles. It is important for youths to see people achieving their goals by being dedicated, responsible, and drug-free."

Capturing the interest of young people through interactive and informative presentations is the challenge faced by the Esteem Team presenters, and all feedback says that it is working. "From my standpoint, I think it's a privilege to have a chance to make a difference in young people's lives," says Esteem Team founder and former Olympic wrestler Chris Wilson.[1]

### CRITICAL THINKING

- What kind of oral presentations might you have to make in your chosen career field?
- Why are most people fearful of making presentations?
- How do you think people become effective speakers?

**www.esteemteam.com**

## PREPARING EFFECTIVE ORAL PRESENTATIONS

According to Canadian speaker and author Peter Urs Bender, the greatest fear of most people is not death, but public speaking.[2] While this may seem extreme, most of us feel great stress when faced with making a speech. The physiological responses that you experience are much like those triggered by a car accident or a narrow escape from a dangerous situation.[3] Regardless, *at some point, everyone in business has to sell an idea, and such persuasion is often done in person.* A human resources director asserts that "people live and die on presentations. It's as important as being able to turn on your computer."[4] In fact, "showing you can make a good presentation is essential these days to climbing the corporate ladder and getting the attention of senior management."[5]

*1*

**Many businesspeople must make presentations as part of their careers.**

CHAPTER 15
Speaking Skills
**489**

Many future businesspeople, however, fail to take advantage of opportunities in university or college to develop speaking skills. Yet, such skills often play an important role in a successful career. You might, for example, need to describe your company's expansion plans to your banker, or you might need to persuade management to support your proposed marketing strategy. You might have to make a sales pitch before customers or speak to a professional gathering. This chapter prepares you to use speaking skills in making oral presentations and in using the telephone and voice mail to advantage.

For any presentation, you can reduce your fears and lay the foundation for a professional performance by focusing on five areas: preparation, organization, audience rapport, visual aids, and delivery.

## Knowing Your Purpose

The most important part of your preparation is deciding what you want to accomplish. Do you want to sell a health-care program to a prospective client? Do you want to persuade management to increase the marketing budget? Do you want to inform customer service reps of three important ways to prevent miscommunication? Whether your goal is to persuade or to inform, you must have a clear idea of where you are going. At the end of your presentation, what do you want your listeners to remember or do?

Eric Evans, a loan officer at Dominion Trust, faced such questions as he planned a talk for a class in small business management. Eric's former business professor had asked him to return to campus and give the class advice about borrowing money from banks in order to start new businesses. Because Eric knew so much about this topic, he found it difficult to extract a specific purpose statement for his presentation. After much thought he narrowed his purpose to this: *To inform potential entrepreneurs about three important factors that loan officers consider before granting start-up loans to launch small businesses.* His entire presentation focused on ensuring that the class members understood and remembered three principal ideas.

## Knowing Your Audience

A second key element in preparation is analyzing your audience, anticipating its reactions, and making appropriate adaptations. Audiences may fall into four categories, as summarized in Figure 15.1. By anticipating your audience, you have a better idea of how to organize your presentation. A friendly audience, for example, will respond to humour and personal experiences. A neutral audience requires an even, controlled delivery style. The talk would probably be filled with facts, statistics, and expert opinions. An uninterested audience that is forced to attend requires a brief presentation. Such an audience might respond best to humour, cartoons, colourful visuals, and startling statistics. A hostile audience demands a calm, controlled delivery style with objective data and expert opinion.

Other elements, such as age, gender, education, experience, and size of audience will affect your style and message content. Analyze the following questions to help you determine your organizational pattern, delivery style, and supporting material.

- *How will this topic appeal to this audience?*
- *How can I relate this information to their needs?*
- *How can I earn respect so that they accept my message?*
- *What would be most effective in making my point? Facts? Statistics? Personal experiences? Expert opinion? Humour? Cartoons? Graphic illustrations? Demonstrations? Case histories? Analogies?*
- *What measures must I take to ensure that this audience remembers my main points?*

Audience analysis issues include size, age, gender, experience, attitude, and expectations.

**FIGURE 15.1  Dealing With Four Audience Types**

| AUDIENCE | ORGANIZATIONAL PATTERN | DELIVERY STYLE | SUPPORTING MATERIAL |
|---|---|---|---|
| **Friendly**<br>Likes you and your topic | Any pattern; try something new; involve audience | Warm, pleasant, open; lots of eye contact, smiles | Humour, examples, personal experiences |
| **Neutral**<br>Calm, rational; have minds made up but think they are objective | Present both sides of issue; pro–con or problem–solution patterns; save time for audience questions | Controlled, even, nothing showy; confident, small gestures | Facts, statistics, expert opinion, comparison and contrast; avoid humour, personal stories, and flashy visuals |
| **Uninterested**<br>Short attention span; attending against their will | Brief, no more than three points; avoid topical and pro–con patterns that seem lengthy to audience | Dynamic and entertaining; move around, large gestures | Humour, cartoons, colorful visuals, powerful quotations, startling statistics |
| | **Avoid** darkening the room, standing motionless, passing out handouts, using boring visuals, or expecting audience to participate | | |
| **Hostile**<br>Wants to take charge or to ridicule speaker; defensive, emotional | Noncontroversial such as topical, chronological, or geographical | Calm, controlled; speak evenly and slowly | Objective data and expert opinion; avoid anecdotes and humour |
| | **Avoid** question-and-answer period, if possible; otherwise, use a moderator or accept only written questions. | | |

## ORGANIZING THE CONTENT

Once you have determined your purpose and analyzed the audience, you're ready to collect information and organize it logically. Good organization and conscious repetition are the two most powerful keys to audience comprehension and retention. In fact, many speech experts recommend the following admittedly repetitious, but effective, plan:

- **Step 1:** Tell them what you're going to say.
- **Step 2:** Say it.
- **Step 3:** Tell them what you've just said.

In other words, repeat your main points in the introduction, body, and conclusion of your presentation. Although it sounds deadly, this strategy works surprisingly well. Let's examine how to construct the three parts of an effective presentation.

# Introduction

Attention-grabbing openers include questions, startling facts, jokes, anecdotes, and quotations.

How many times have you heard a speaker begin with, *It's a pleasure to be here.* Or, *I'm honoured to be asked to speak.* Boring openings such as these get speakers off to a dull start. Avoid such banalities by striving to accomplish three goals in the introduction to your presentation:

- Capture listeners' attention and get them involved.
- Identify yourself and establish your credibility.
- Preview your main points.

If you're able to appeal to listeners and involve them in your presentation right from the start, you're more likely to hold their attention until the finish. Consider some of the same techniques that you used to open sales letters: a question, a startling fact, a joke, a story, or a quotation. Some speakers achieve involvement by opening with a question or command that requires audience members to raise their hands or stand up. Additional techniques to gain and keep audience attention are presented in the accompanying Career Coach box.

To establish your credibility, you need to describe your position, knowledge, or experience—whatever qualifies you to speak. Try also to connect with your audience. Listeners are particularly drawn to speakers who reveal something of themselves and identify with them. A consultant addressing office workers might reminisce about how she started as a clerk-typist; a CEO might tell a funny story in which the joke is on himself.

After capturing attention and establishing yourself, you'll want to preview the main points of your topic, perhaps with a visual aid. You may wish to put off actually writing your introduction, however, until after you have organized the rest of the presentation and crystallized your principal ideas.

Take a look at Eric Evans' introduction, shown in Figure 15.2 on page 494, to see how he integrated all the elements necessary for a good opening.

# Body

The best oral presentations focus on a few key ideas.

The biggest problem with most oral presentations is a failure to focus on a few principal ideas. Thus, the body of your short presentation (20 or fewer minutes) should include a limited number of main points, say, two to four. Develop each main point with adequate, but not excessive, explanation and details. Too many details can obscure the main message, so keep your presentation simple and logical. Remember, listeners have no pages to leaf back through should they become confused.

When Eric Evans began planning his presentation, he realized immediately that he could talk for hours on his topic. He also knew that listeners are not good at separating major and minor points. So, instead of submerging his listeners in a sea of information, he sorted out a few principal ideas. In the mortgage business, loan officers generally ask the following three questions of each applicant for a small business loan: (1) Are you ready to "hit the ground running" in starting your business? (2) Have you done your homework? and (3) Have you made realistic projections of potential sales, cash flow, and equity investment? These questions would become his main points, but Eric wanted to streamline them further so that his audience would be sure to remember them. He summarized the questions in three words: *experience, preparation,* and *projection.* As you can see in Figure 15.2, Eric prepared a sentence outline showing these three main ideas. Each is supported by examples and explanations.

# Nine Techniques for Gaining and Keeping Audience Attention

Experienced speakers know how to capture the attention of an audience and how to maintain that attention during a presentation. Here are nine proven techniques.

1. **A promise.** Begin with a promise that keeps the audience expectant (for example, "By the end of this presentation I will have shown you how you can increase your sales by 50 percent").

2. **Drama.** Open by telling an emotionally moving story or by describing a serious problem that involves the audience. Throughout your talk include other dramatic elements, such as a long pause after a key statement. Change your vocal tone or pitch. Professionals use high-intensity emotions such as anger, joy, sadness, and excitement.

3. **Eye contact.** As you begin, command attention by surveying the entire audience to take in all listeners. Take two to five seconds to make eye contact with as many people as possible.

4. **Movement.** Leave the lectern area whenever possible. Walk around the conference table or between the aisles of your audience. Try to move toward your audience, especially at the beginning and end of your talk.

5. **Questions.** Keep listeners active and involved with rhetorical questions. Ask for a show of hands to get each listener thinking. The response will also give you a quick gauge of audience attention.

6. **Demonstrations.** Include a member of the audience in a demonstration (for example, "I'm going to show you exactly how to implement our four-step customer courtesy process, but I need a volunteer from the audience to help me").

7. **Samples/gimmicks.** If you're promoting a product, consider using items to toss out to the audience or to award as prizes to volunteer participants. You can also pass around product samples or promotional literature. Be careful, though, to maintain control of the audience.

8. **Visuals.** Give your audience something to look at besides yourself. Use a variety of visual aids in a single session. Also consider writing the concerns expressed by your listeners on a flipchart or white board as you go along.

9. **Self-interest.** Review your entire presentation to ensure that it meets the critical "What's-in-it-for-me?" audience test. Remember that people are most interested in things that benefit them.

### Career Application

Watch a lecture series speaker on campus, a department store sales presentation, a TV "infomercial," or some other type of speaker. Note and analyze specific techniques used to engage and maintain the listener's attention. Which techniques would be most effective in a classroom presentation? Before your boss or work group?

---

How to organize and sequence main ideas may not be immediately obvious when you begin working on a presentation. Let's review and amplify some of the organizational methods employed for written reports in Chapter 12, because those methods are equally appropriate for oral presentations. You could structure your ideas according to any of the following elements:

**Main ideas can be organized according to time, component, importance, criteria, conventional groupings, problem–solution, or pro–con alternatives.**

- **Time.** Example: A presentation describing the history of a problem, organized chronologically from the first sign of trouble to the present.

- **Component.** Example: A sales report organized geographically by regions or topically by products.

- **Importance.** Example: A report describing operating problems arranged from the most important to the least.

- **Criteria.** Example: A presentation evaluating equipment by comparing each model against a set of specifications.

## FIGURE 15.2  Oral Presentation Outline

### Prewriting 1

**Analyze:** The purpose of this report is to inform listeners of three critical elements in securing business loans.

**Anticipate:** The audience members are aspiring business-people who are probably unfamiliar with loan operations.

**Adapt:** Because the audience will be receptive but uninformed, explain terms and provide examples. Repeat the main ideas to ensure comprehension.

### Writing 2

**Research:** Analyze previous loan applications; interview other loan officers. Gather critical data.

**Organize:** Group the data into three major categories. Support with statistics, details, and examples. Plan visual aids.

**Compose:** Prepare a sentence outline. Consider using presentation software to outline your talk.

### Revising 3

**Revise:** Develop transitions between topics. Prepare note cards or speaker's notes.

**Practise:** Rehearse the entire talk and time it. Practise enunciating words and projecting your voice. Practise using your visual aids. Develop natural hand motions.

**Evaluate:** Tape-record or video-tape a practice session to evaluate your movements, voice tone, enunciation, and timing.

---

### What Makes a Loan Officer Say "Yes"?

**I. INTRODUCTION**

*Captures attention* —
A. How many of you expect one day to start your own businesses? How many of you have all the cash available to capitalize that business when you start?

*Involves audience* —
B. Like you, nearly every entrepreneur needs cash to open a business, and I promise you that by the end of this talk you will have inside information on how to make a loan application that will be successful.

*Identifies speaker* —
C. As a loan officer at Dominion Trust, which specializes in small-business loans, I make decisions on requests from entrepreneurs like you applying for start-up money.
*Transition:* Your professor invited me here today to tell you how you can improve your chances of getting a loan from us or from any other lender. I have suggestions in three areas: — *Previews three main points* experience, preparation, and projection.

**II. BODY**

*Establishes main points* —
A. First, let's consider experience. You must show that you can hit the ground running.
1. Demonstrate what experience you have in your proposed business.
2. Include your résumé when you submit your business plan.
3. If you have little experience, tell us whom you would hire to supply the skills that you lack.
*Transition:* In addition to experience, loan officers will want to see that you have researched • your venture thoroughly.

B. My second suggestion, then, involves preparation. Have you done your homework?
1. Talk to local businesspeople, especially those in related fields.
2. Conduct traffic counts or other studies to estimate potential sales.
3. Analyze the strengths and weaknesses of the competition.
*Transition:* Now that we've discussed preparation, we're ready for my final suggestion. • — *Develops coherence with planned transitions*

C. My last tip is the most important one. It involves making a realistic projection of your potential sales, cash flow, and equity.
1. Present detailed monthly cash-flow projections for the first year.
2. Describe "what-if" scenarios indicating both good and bad possibilities.
3. Indicate that you intend to supply at least 25 percent of the initial capital yourself.
*Transition:* The three major points I've just outlined cover critical points in obtaining start-up • loans. Let me review them for you.

**III. CONCLUSION**

*Summarizes main points* —
A. Loan officers are most likely to say "yes" to your loan application if you do three things: (1) prove that you can hit the ground running when your business opens; (2) demonstrate that you've researched your proposed business seriously; and (3) project a realistic picture of your sales, cash flow, and equity.

B. Experience, preparation, and projection, then, are the three keys to launching your business • — *Provides final focus* with the necessary start-up capital so that you can concentrate on where your customers, not your funds, are coming from.

- **Conventional groupings.** Example: A report comparing asset size, fees charged, and yields of mutual funds arranged by these existing categories.
- **Problem–solution.** Example: A presentation describing excessive company travel expenses and three possible solutions.
- **Pro–con alternatives.** Example: A presentation outlining the advantages and disadvantages regarding whether an organization should invest only in the stocks of environmentally friendly companies.

In the presentation shown in Figure 15.2, Eric arranged the main points by importance, placing the most important point last where it had maximum effect. When organizing any presentation, prepare a little more material than you think you will actually need. Skilled speakers always have something useful in reserve (such as an extra handout, transparency, or idea)—just in case they finish early.

## Conclusion

Nervous speakers often rush to wrap up their presentations because they can't wait to flee the stage. But listeners will remember the conclusion more than any part of a speech. That's why you should spend some time to make it most effective. Strive to achieve two goals:

- Summarize the main themes of the presentation.
- Include a statement that allows you to leave the podium gracefully.

Some speakers end limply with comments such as "I guess that's about all I have to say." This leaves bewildered audience members wondering whether they should continue listening. Skilled speakers alert the audience that they are finishing. They use phrases such as, *In conclusion, As I end this presentation,* or *It's time for me to stop.* Then they proceed immediately to the conclusion. Audiences become justly irritated with a speaker who announces the conclusion but then digresses with one more story or talks on for ten more minutes.

A straightforward summary should review major points and focus on what you want the listeners to do, think, or remember. You might say, "In bringing my presentation to a close, I will restate my major purpose . . ." or, "In summary, my major purpose has been to . . . . In support of my purpose, I have presented three major points. They are (a) . . . , (b) . . . , and (c) . . . ." Notice how Eric Evans, in the conclusion shown in Figure 15.2, summarized his three main points and provided a final focus to listeners.

If you are promoting a recommendation, you might end as follows: "In conclusion, I recommend that we retain Matrixx Marketing to conduct a telemarketing campaign beginning September 1 at a cost of X dollars. To complete this recommendation, I suggest that we (a) finance this campaign from our operations budget, (b) develop a persuasive message describing our new product, and (c) name Lisa Beck to oversee the project."

In your conclusion you might want to use an anecdote, an inspiring quotation, or a statement that ties in the opener and offers a new insight. Whatever you choose, be sure to include a closing thought that indicates you are finished. For example, "This concludes my presentation. After investigating many marketing firms, we are convinced that Matrixx is the best for our purposes. Your authorization of my recommendations will mark the beginning of a very successful campaign for our new product. Thank you."

**Effective conclusions summarize main points and allow the speaker to exit gracefully.**

*3*

A number of different verbal and nonverbal techniques can help you connect with your audience. Rapport with an audience can be built by employing techniques that make you and your subject interesting and accessible. Helpful techniques include providing effective imagery, supplying verbal signposts, and using body language strategically.

## Effective Imagery

**Use analogies, metaphors, similes, personal anecdotes, personalized statistics, and worst- and best-case scenarios instead of dry facts.**

You'll lose your audience quickly if your talk is filled with abstractions, generalities, and dry facts. To enliven your presentation and enhance comprehension, try using some of these techniques:

- **Analogies.** A comparison of similar traits between dissimilar things can be effective in explaining and drawing connections. For example, *Product development is similar to the process of conceiving, carrying, and delivering a baby.* Or, *Downsizing and restructuring is similar to an overweight person undergoing a regimen of diet, habit change, and exercise.*

- **Metaphors.** A comparison between otherwise dissimilar things without using the words *like* or *as* results in a metaphor. For example, *Our competitor's CEO is a snake when it comes to negotiating* or *My desk is a garbage dump.*

- **Similes.** A comparison that includes the words *like* or *as* is a simile. For example, *Our critics used our background report like a drunk uses a lamppost—for support rather than for illumination.* Or, *She's as happy as someone who just won the lottery.*

- **Personal anecdotes.** Nothing connects you faster or better with your audience than a good personal story. In a talk about e-mail techniques, you could reveal your own blunders that became painful learning experiences. In a talk to potential investors, the founder of a new ethnic magazine might tell a story about growing up without positive ethnic role models.

- **Personalized statistics.** Although often misused, statistics stay with people—particularly when they relate directly to the audience. A speaker discussing job searching might say, *Look around the room. Only three out of five graduates will find a job immediately after graduation.* If possible, simplify and personalize facts. For example, *The sales of soft drinks totalled 2 billion cases last year. That means that six full cases were consumed by every man, woman, and child in Canada.*

- **Worst- and best-case scenarios.** Hearing the worst that could happen can be effective in driving home a point. For example, *If we do nothing about our computer backup system now, it's just a matter of time before the entire system crashes and we lose all of our customer contact information. Can you imagine starting from scratch in building all of your customer files again? However, if we fix the system now, we can expand our customer files and actually increase sales at the same time.*

**Knowledgeable speakers provide verbal signposts to spotlight organization and key ideas.**

## Verbal Signposts

Speakers must remember that listeners, unlike readers of a report, cannot control the rate of presentation or flip back through pages to review main points. As a result, listeners get lost easily. Knowledgeable speakers help the audience recognize the organization and main points in an oral message with verbal signposts. They keep listeners on track by including helpful previews, summaries, and transitions, such as these:

- **Previewing**
  *The next segment of my talk presents three reasons for . . . .*
  *Let's now consider the causes of . . . .*

- **Summarizing**
  *Let me review with you the major problems I've just discussed . . . .*
  *You see, then, that the most significant factors are . . . .*

- **Switching directions**
  *Thus far we've talked solely about . . . ; now let's move to . . . .*
  *I've argued that . . . and . . . , but an alternative view holds that . . . .*

You can further improve any oral presentation by including appropriate transitional expressions such as *first, second, next, then, therefore, moreover, on the other hand, on the contrary,* and *in conclusion.* These expressions lend emphasis and tell listeners where you are headed. Notice in Eric Evans' outline, in Figure 15.2, the specific transitional elements designed to help listeners recognize each new principal point.

## Nonverbal Messages

Although what you say is most important, the nonverbal messages you send can also have a powerful effect on how well your message is received. How you look, how you move, and how you speak can make or break your presentation. The following suggestions focus on nonverbal tips to ensure that your verbal message is well received.

**The way you look, how you move, and how you speak affect the success of your presentation.**

- **Look terrific.** Like it or not, you will be judged by your appearance. For everything but small in-house presentations, be sure you dress professionally. The rule of thumb is that you should dress at least as well as the best-dressed person in the audience.

- **Animate your body.** Be enthusiastic and let your body show it. Emphasize ideas to enhance points about size, number, and direction. Use a variety of gestures, but don't consciously plan them in advance.

- **Punctuate your words.** You can keep your audience interested by varying your tone, volume, pitch, and pace. Use pauses before and after important points. Allow the audience to take in your ideas.

- **Get out from behind the podium.** Avoid being planted to the podium. Movement makes you look natural and comfortable. You might pick a few places in the room to walk to. Even if you must stay close to your visual aids, make a point of leaving them occasionally so that the audience can see your whole body.

- **Vary your facial expression.** Begin with a smile, but change your expressions to correspond with the thoughts you are voicing. You can shake your head to show disagreement, roll your eyes to show disdain, look heavenward for guidance, or wrinkle your brow to show concern or dismay. To see how speakers convey meaning without words, mute the sound on your TV and watch the facial expressions of a talk show personality.

## PLANNING VISUAL AIDS, HANDOUTS, AND ELECTRONIC PRESENTATIONS

Before you make a business presentation, consider this wise Chinese proverb: "Tell me, I forget. Show me, I remember. Involve me, I understand." Your goals as a speaker are to make listeners understand, remember, and act on your ideas. To get them interested and involved, include effective visual aids. Some experts say that we acquire 85 percent of all our knowledge visually. Therefore, an oral presentation that incorporates visual aids is far more likely to be understood and retained than one lacking visual enhancement.

**Visual aids clarify points, improve comprehension, and aid retention.**

Good visual aids have many purposes. They emphasize and clarify main points, thus improving comprehension and retention. They increase audience interest, and they make the presenter appear more professional, better prepared, and more persuasive. Furthermore, research shows that the use of visual aids actually shortens meetings.[6] Visual aids are particularly helpful for inexperienced speakers because the audience concentrates on the aid rather than on the speaker. Good visuals also serve to jog the memory of a speaker, thus improving self-confidence, poise, and delivery.

## Types of Visual Aids

Fortunately for today's speakers, many forms of visual media are available to enhance a presentation. Figure 15.3 describes a number of visual aids and compares their cost, degree of formality, and other considerations. Three of the most popular visuals are overhead transparencies, handouts, and computer visuals.

**To maintain control, distribute handouts after you finish speaking.**

*Overhead Transparencies.* Student and professional speakers alike rely on the overhead projector for many reasons. Most meeting areas are equipped with projectors and screens. Moreover, acetate transparencies for the overhead are cheap, easily prepared on a computer or copier, and simple to use. And, because rooms need not be darkened, a speaker using transparencies can maintain eye contact with the audience. A word of caution, though: stand to the side of the projector so that you don't obstruct the audience's view.

*Handouts.* You can enhance and complement your presentations by distributing pictures, outlines, brochures, articles, charts, summaries, or other supplements. Speakers who use computer presentation programs often prepare a set of their slides along with notes to hand out to viewers. Timing the distribution of any handout, though, is tricky. If given out during a presentation, your handouts tend to distract the audience, causing you to lose control. Thus, it's probably best to discuss most handouts during the presentation but delay distributing them until after you finish.

*Computer Visuals.* With today's excellent software programs—such as PowerPoint, Freelance Graphics, and Corel Presentations—you can create dynamic, colourful presentations with your PC. The output from these programs is generally shown on a PC monitor, a TV monitor, an LCD (liquid crystal display) panel, or a screen. With a little expertise and advanced equipment, you can create a multimedia presentation that includes stereo sound, videos, and hyperlinks, as described in the following discussion of electronic presentations.

**FIGURE 15.3  Presentation Enhancers**

| MEDIUM | COST | AUDIENCE SIZE | FORMALITY LEVEL | ADVANTAGES AND DISADVANTAGES |
|---|---|---|---|---|
| Computer slides | Low | 2–200 | Formal or informal | Presentation software programs are easy to use and cheap and produce professional results. They should not, however, replace or distract from the speaker's message. Darkened room can put audience to sleep. |
| Overhead projector | Low | 2–200 | Formal or informal | Transparencies produce neat, legible visuals that are cheap and easy to make. Speaker keeps contact with audience. Transparencies may, however, look low tech. |
| Flipchart | Low | 2–200 | Informal | Easels and charts are readily available and portable. Useful for working discussions and informational presentations. Speaker can prepare display in advance or on the spot. |
| Write-and-wipe board | Medium | 2–200 | Informal | Porcelain-on-steel surface replaces messy chalkboard. Speaker can wipe clean with cloth. Useful for working discussions. |
| Video monitor | Medium | 2–100 | Formal or informal | A VCR display features motion and sound. Videos, however, require skill, time, and equipment to prepare. |
| Props | Varies | 2–200 | Formal or informal | Product samples, prototypes, symbols, or gimmicks can produce vivid images that audiences remember. |
| Handouts | Varies | Unlimited | Formal or informal | Audience appreciates take-home items such as outlines, tables, charts, reports, brochures, or summaries. Handouts, however, can divert attention from speaker. |

## DESIGNING AN ELECTRONIC PRESENTATION

The content of most presentations today hasn't changed, but the medium certainly has. At meetings and conferences smart speakers now use computer programs, such as PowerPoint, to present, defend, and sell their ideas most effectively. Business speakers have switched to computer presentations because they are economical, flexible, and easy to prepare. Changes can be made right up to the last minute. Most important, though, such presentations make even amateurs look like real pros.

Yet, PowerPoint has its critics. They charge that the program dictates the way in which information is structured and presented. PowerPoint stifles "the storyteller,

**Computer-aided presentations are economical, flexible, professional, and easy to prepare.**

the poet, the person whose thoughts cannot be arranged in the shape of an AutoContent slide."[7] PowerPoint, say its detractors, when utilized poorly can isolate and diminish the speaker in the eyes of the audience. Some speakers choose to minimize their fear by hiding behind the slides. In such a case, PowerPoint is a misused technology. Communication skills trainer James Gray cites PowerPoint as being "the most misused technological innovation since the handgun."[8] Successful business speakers, on the other hand, use PowerPoint because it increases audience enjoyment, comprehension, and retention. PowerPoint speakers, however, are effective only when they are skillful. To be effective, you must learn about using templates, working with colour, building bullet points, and adding multimedia effects.

## Using Templates

To begin your training in using an electronic presentation program, you'll want to examine its templates. These professionally designed formats combine harmonious colours, borders, and fonts for pleasing visual effects. Templates also provide guidance in laying out each slide, as shown in Figure 15.4. You can select a layout for a title page, a bulleted list, a bar chart, a double-column list, an organization chart, and so on. To present a unified and distinctive image, some companies develop a customized template with their logo and a predefined colour scheme. As one expert says, "This prevents salespeople from creating horrid colour combinations on their own."[9]

## Working With Colour

You don't need training in colour theory to create presentation images that impress your audience rather than confuse them. You can use the colour schemes from the design templates that come with your presentation program, as shown in Figure 15.5, or you can alter them. Generally, you're smart to use a colour palette of five or fewer colours for an entire presentation. Use warm colours—reds, oranges, and

**FIGURE 15.4** Selecting a Slide Layout

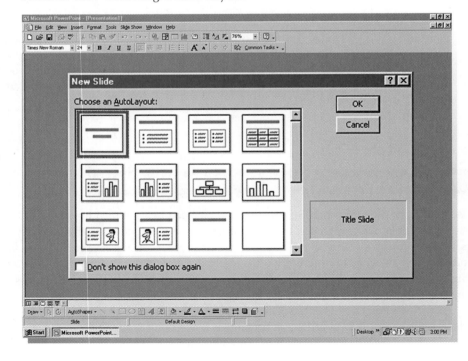

**FIGURE 15.5**  Choosing a Colour Scheme

## Tips for Choosing the Best Colours in Visuals
- Develop a colour palette of five or fewer colours.
- Use the same colour for similar elements.
- Use dark text on a light background for presentations in bright rooms.
- Use light text on a dark background for presentations in darkened rooms.
- Use dark text on a light background for transparencies.
- Beware of light text on light backgrounds and dark text on dark backgrounds.

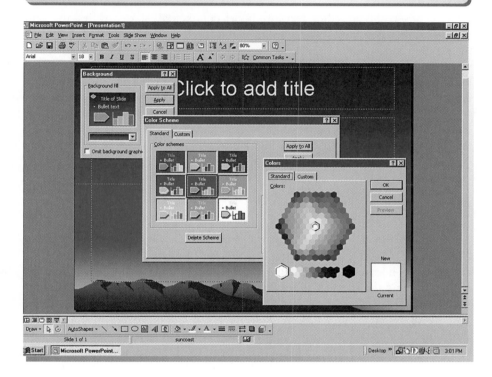

yellows—to highlight important elements. Use the same colour for like elements. For example, all slide titles should be the same colour. The colour for backgrounds and text depends on where the presentation will be given. Use light text on a dark background for presentations in darkened rooms. Use dark text on a light background for computer presentations in lighted rooms and for projecting transparencies.

## Building Bullet Points

When you prepare your slides, translate the major headings in your presentation outline into titles for slides. Then build bullet points using short phrases. In Chapter 5 you learned to improve readability by using listing techniques, including bullets, numbers, and headings. In preparing a PowerPoint presentation, you will use those same techniques.

**Bullet points should be short phrases that are parallel.**

Let's say, for example, that Matt wants to persuade management to install a voice mail system. Management is resisting because it says that voice mail will cost too much. Matt wants to emphasize benefits that result in increased productivity. Here is a portion of the text he wrote.

### Text of Presentation

*Because voice mail allows callers to deliver detailed information to office personnel with just one telephone call, telephone tag can be eliminated. In addition, some research has found that up to 75 percent of all business calls do not reach the desired party. Whatever the actual number, people do tend to make far fewer callbacks when they have a voice mailbox in which their callers can leave messages. Although voice mail can't match the timeliness of a live telephone call, it's the next best thing for getting the word out when time is of the essence. Finally, voice mail frees callers from the prospect of being placed on hold indefinitely when the person they want is temporarily unavailable. Callers can immediately leave a voice message, bypassing the "hold" interval altogether.*

**Text can be converted into bullet points by experimenting with key phrases that are concise and balanced grammatically.**

To convert the preceding text into bullet points, Matt started with a title and then listed the main ideas that related to that title. He worked with the list until all the items were parallel. That meant considerable experimenting with different wording. Matt went through many revisions before creating the following bulleted list. Notice that the heading promotes reader benefits. Notice also that the bullet points are concise and parallel. They should be key phrases, not complete sentences.

### Text Converted to Bullet Points

*Voice Mail Can Make Your Calls More Efficient*
- *Eliminates telephone tag*
- *Reduces callbacks*
- *Improves timely communication*
- *Shortens "hold" times*

In another example, Alan Christopher prepared a PowerPoint presentation based on his research report featured in Figure 14.4 in Chapter 14. Part of his presentation slides are shown in Figure 15.6. Notice that the major topics from his outline became the titles of slides. Then he developed bulleted items for major subpoints.

**Incremental bullet points enable a speaker to animate the presentation and control the flow of ideas.**

One of the best features about electronic presentation programs is the "build" capability. You can focus the viewer's attention on each specific item as you add bullet points line by line. The bulleted items may "fly" in from the left, right, top, or bottom. They can also build or dissolve from the centre. As each new bullet point is added, leave the previous ones on the slide but show them in lightened text. In building bulleted points or in moving from one slide to the next, you can use *slide transition* elements, such as "wipe-outs," glitter, ripple, liquid, and vortex effects. But don't overdo it. Experts suggest choosing one transition effect and applying it consistently.[10]

For the most readable slides, apply the *Rule of Seven*. Each slide should include no more than seven words in a line, no more than seven total lines, and no more than $7 \times 7$ or 49 total words. And remember that presentation slides summarize; they don't tell the whole story. That's the job of the presenter.

## Adding Multimedia and Other Effects

**Multimedia elements include sound, animation, and video features.**

Many presentation programs also provide libraries of *multimedia* features to enhance your content. These include sound, animation, and video elements. For example, you could use sound effects to "reward" correct answers from your audience. But using the sound of screeching tires in a Transport Canada presentation is probably unwise. Similarly, video clips—when used judiciously—can add excitement and depth to a presentation. You might use video to capture attention in a

## FIGURE 15.6  Preparing a PowerPoint Presentation

**Tips for Preparing and Using Slides**
- Keep all visuals simple; spotlight major points only.
- Use the same font size and style for similar headings.
- Apply the Rule of Seven: No more than seven words on a line, seven total lines, and 7 × 7 or 49 total words.
- Be sure that everyone in the audience can see the slides.
- Show a slide, allow the audience to read it, then paraphrase it. Do NOT read from a slide.
- Rehearse by practising talking to the audience, not to the slides.
- Bring backup transparencies in case of equipment failure.

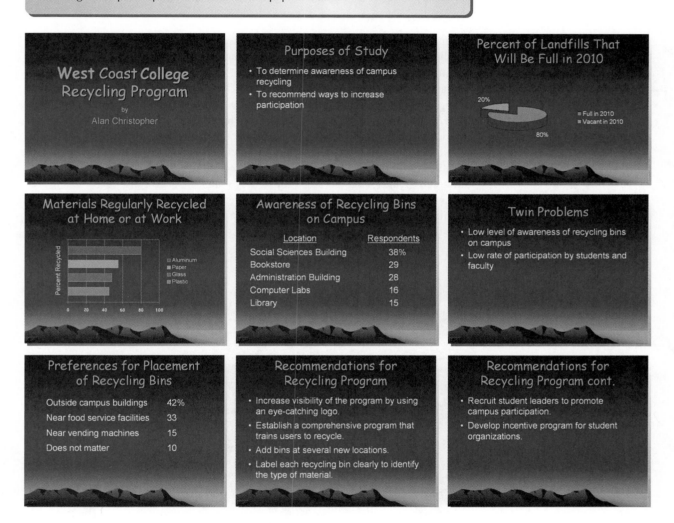

stimulating introduction, to show the benefits of a product in use, or to bring the personality of a distant expert or satisfied customer right into the meeting room.

Another way to enliven a presentation is with real-life photographic images, which are now easy to obtain thanks to the prevalence of low-cost scanners and digital cameras. Some programs are also capable of generating hyperlinks ("hot" spots on the screen) that allow you to jump instantly to relevant data or multimedia content.

## Producing Speaker's Notes and Handouts

Most electronic presentation programs offer a variety of presentation options. In addition to printouts of your slides, you can make speaker's notes, as shown in Figure 15.7. These are wonderful aids for practising your talk; they remind you of the supporting comments for the abbreviated material in your slides. Many programs allow you to print miniature versions of your slides with numerous slides to a page, if you wish. These miniatures are handy if you want to preview your talk to a sponsoring organization or if you wish to supply the audience with a summary of your presentation.

## Developing Web-Based Presentations and Electronic Handouts

**Web presentations are less expensive than videoconferencing.**

Because of many technological improvements, you can now give a talk without even travelling off-site. In other words, you can put your slides "on the road." Web presentations with slides, narration, and speaker control are emerging as a less expensive alternative to *videoconferencing*, which was discussed in Chapter 2. For example, you could initiate a meeting via a conference call, narrate using a telephone, and have participants see your slides from the browsers on their computers. If you prefer, you could skip the narration and provide a prerecorded presentation. Web-based presentations have many applications, including providing access to updated training or sales data whenever needed.[11] Larry Magid, computer expert and noted speaker, suggests still another way that speakers can use the Web. He recommends posting your slides on the Web even if you are giving a face-to-face presentation. Attendees appreciate these *electronic handouts* because they don't have to carry them home.[12]

**FIGURE 15.7  Making Speaker's Notes for an Electronic Presentation**

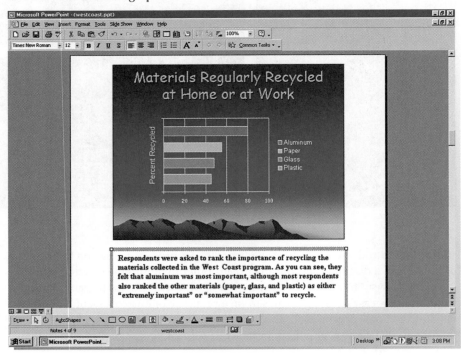

Speaker's notes enable you to print discussion items beneath each slide, thus providing handy review material for practice.

## Avoiding Being Upstaged by Your Slides

Although electronic presentations supply terrific sizzle, they cannot replace the steak. In developing a presentation, don't expect your slides to carry the show. They merely summarize important points. As the speaker, you must explain the analyses leading up to the major points. You must explain what the major points mean. Slides provide you with talking points. For each slide you should have one or more paragraphs of narration to present to your audience. The speed of the presentation is crucial. Attention will lag if there is not enough time for the audience to absorb the materials. Since PowerPoint has the words and diagrams prepared, creation time, which may have been used in the more traditional blackboard era, is now gone. Therefore, watch the trap of "speed presenting" and try to go slower rather than faster.[13] Make use of the speaker's notes feature to capture your supporting ideas while you make the slides. And don't let a PowerPoint presentation "steal your thunder." You must maintain control of the presentation rather than allowing the electronics to take over. In addition to your narration, you can maintain control by using a laser pen or pointer to connect you with the screen. Keep in mind that your slides and transparencies merely supply a framework for your presentation. Your audience came to see and hear *you*.

## POLISHING YOUR DELIVERY AND FOLLOWING UP

Once you've organized your presentation and prepared visuals, you're ready to practise delivering it. Here are suggestions for selecting a delivery method, along with specific techniques to use before, during, and after your presentation.

*5*

## Delivery Method

Inexperienced speakers often feel that they must memorize an entire presentation to be effective. Unless you're an experienced performer, however, you will sound wooden and unnatural. Moreover, forgetting your place can be disastrous! Therefore, memorizing an entire oral presentation is not recommended. However, memorizing significant parts—the introduction, the conclusion, and perhaps a meaningful quotation—can be dramatic and impressive.

If memorizing won't work, is reading your presentation the best plan? Definitely not! Reading to an audience is boring and ineffective. Because reading suggests that you don't know your topic very well, the audience loses confidence in your expertise. Reading also prevents you from maintaining eye contact. You can't see audience reactions; consequently, you can't benefit from feedback.

Neither the memorizing nor the reading method creates very convincing presentations. The best plan, by far, is a "notes" method. Plan your presentation carefully and talk from note cards or an outline containing key sentences and major ideas. By preparing and then practising with your notes, you can talk to your audience in a conversational manner. Your notes should be neither entire paragraphs nor single words. Instead, they should contain a complete sentence or two to introduce each major idea. Under the topic sentence(s), outline subpoints and illustrations. Note cards will keep you on track and prompt your memory, but only if you have rehearsed the presentation thoroughly.

Novice speakers often speed up their delivery, perhaps out of nervousness or eagerness to sit down. Preparation and practice are keys to improving presentation skills.

# Delivery Techniques

**Stage fright is both natural and controllable.**

Nearly everyone experiences some degree of stage fright when speaking before a group. "If you hear someone say he or she isn't nervous before a speech, you're talking either to a liar or a very boring speaker," says corporate speech consultant Dianna Booher.[14] Being afraid is quite natural and results from actual physiological changes occurring in your body. Faced with a frightening situation, your body responds with the fight-or-flight response, discussed more fully in the accompanying Career Coach box. You can learn to control and reduce stage fright, as well as to incorporate techniques for effective speaking, by using the following strategies and techniques before, during, and after your presentation.

## Before Your Presentation

**Thorough preparation, extensive rehearsal, and stress-reduction techniques can lessen stage fright.**

- **Prepare thoroughly.** One of the most effective strategies for reducing stage fright is knowing your subject thoroughly. Research your topic diligently and prepare a careful sentence outline. Those who try to "wing it" usually suffer the worst butterflies—and make the worst presentations.

- **Rehearse repeatedly.** When you rehearse, practise your entire presentation, not just the first half. Place your outline sentences on separate cards. You may also wish to include transitional sentences to help you move to the next topic. Use these cards as you practise, and include your visual aids in your rehearsal. Rehearse alone or before friends and family. Also try rehearsing on audio- or videotape so that you can evaluate your effectiveness.

- **Time yourself.** Most audiences tend to get restless during longer talks. Thus, try to complete your presentation in no more than 20 minutes. Set a timer during your rehearsal to measure your speaking time.

- **Request a lectern.** Every beginning speaker needs the security of a high desk or lectern from which to deliver a presentation. It serves as a note holder and a convenient place to rest wandering hands and arms.

- **Check the room.** Before you talk, make sure that a lectern has been provided. If you are using sound equipment or a projector, be certain they are operational. Check electrical outlets and the position of the viewing screen. Ensure that the seating arrangement is appropriate to your needs.

- **Greet members of the audience.** Try to make contact with a few members of the audience when you enter the room, while you are waiting to be introduced, or when you walk to the podium. Your body language should convey friendliness, confidence, and enjoyment.

- **Practise stress reduction.** If you feel tension and fear while you are waiting your turn to speak, use stress-reduction techniques, such as deep breathing. Additional techniques to help you conquer stage fright are presented in the accompanying Career Coach box.

## During Your Presentation

**Eye contact, a moderate tone of voice, and natural movements enhance a presentation.**

- **Begin with a pause.** When you first approach the audience, take a moment to adjust your notes and make yourself comfortable. Establish your control of the situation.

- **Present your first sentence from memory.** By memorizing your opening, you can immediately establish rapport with the audience through eye contact. You'll also sound confident and knowledgeable.

## How to Avoid Stage Fright

Ever get nervous before giving a speech? Everyone does! And it's not all in your head, either. When you face something threatening or challenging, your body reacts in what psychologists call the *fight-or-flight* response. This response provides your body with increased energy to deal with threatening situations. It also creates those sensations—dry mouth, sweaty hands, increased heartbeat, and stomach butterflies—that we associate with stage fright. The fight-or-flight response arouses your body for action—in this case, giving a speech.

Since everyone feels some form of apprehension before speaking, it's impossible to eliminate the physiological symptoms altogether. But you can help reduce their effects with the following techniques:

- **Breathe deeply.** Use deep breathing to ease your fight-or-flight symptoms. Inhale to a count of ten, hold this breath to a count of ten, and exhale to a count of ten. Concentrate on your counting and your breathing; both activities reduce your stress.

- **Convert your fear.** Don't view your sweaty palms and dry mouth as evidence of fear. Interpret them as symptoms of exuberance, excitement, and enthusiasm to share your ideas.

- **Know your topic.** Feel confident about your topic. Select a topic that you know well and that is relevant to your audience.

- **Use positive self-talk.** Remind yourself that you know your topic and are prepared. Tell yourself that the audience is on your side—because it is!

- **Shift the spotlight to your visuals.** At least some of the time the audience will be focusing on your slides, transparencies, handouts, or whatever you have prepared—and not on you.

- **Ignore any stumbles.** Don't apologize or confess your nervousness. If you keep going, the audience will forget any mistakes quickly.

- **Feel proud when you finish.** You'll be surprised at how good you feel when you finish. Take pride in what you've accomplished, and your audience will reward you with applause and congratulations. And, of course, your body will call off the fight-or-flight response and return to normal!

### Career Application

Interview someone in your field or in another business setting who must make oral presentations. How did he or she develop speaking skills? What advice can this person suggest to reduce stage fright? When you next make a class presentation, try some or all of the techniques described above and note which are most effective for you.

- **Maintain eye contact.** If the size of the audience overwhelms you, pick out two individuals on the right and two on the left. Talk directly to these people.

- **Control your voice and vocabulary.** This means speaking in moderated tones but loudly enough to be heard. Eliminate verbal static, such as *ah, er, you know,* and *um.* Silence is preferable to meaningless fillers when you are thinking of your next idea.

- **Put the brakes on.** Many novice speakers talk too rapidly, displaying their nervousness and making it very difficult for audience members to understand their ideas. Slow down and listen to what you are saying.

- **Move naturally.** You can use the lectern to hold your notes so that you are free to move about casually and naturally. Avoid fidgeting with your notes, your clothing, or items in your pockets. Learn to use your body to express a point.

- **Use visual aids effectively.** You should discuss and interpret each visual aid for the audience. Move aside as you describe it so that it can be seen fully. Use a pointer if necessary.

- **Avoid digressions.** Stick to your outline and notes. Don't suddenly include clever little anecdotes or digressions that occur to you on the spot. If it's not part of your rehearsed material, leave it out so that you can finish on time. Remember, too, that your audience may not be as enthralled with your topic as you are.

- **Summarize your main points.** Conclude your presentation by reiterating your main points or by emphasizing what you want the audience to think or do. Once you have announced your conclusion, proceed to it directly.

## After Your Presentation

The time to answer questions, distribute handouts, and reiterate main points is after a presentation.

- **Distribute handouts.** If you prepared handouts with data the audience will need, pass them out when you finish.

- **Encourage questions.** If the situation permits a question-and-answer period, announce it at the beginning of your presentation. Then, when you finish, ask for questions. Set a time limit for questions and answers.

- **Repeat questions.** Although the speaker may hear the question, audience members often do not. Begin each answer with a repetition of the question. This also gives you thinking time. Then, direct your answer to the entire audience.

- **Reinforce your main points.** You can use your answers to restate your primary ideas ("I'm glad you brought that up because it gives me a chance to elaborate on . . ."). In answering questions, avoid becoming defensive or debating the questioner.

- **Keep control.** Don't allow one individual to take over. Keep the entire audience involved.

- **Avoid *Yes, but* answers.** The word *but* immediately cancels any preceding message. Try replacing it with *and*. For example, *Yes, X has been tried. And Y works even better because* . . . .

- **End with a summary and appreciation.** To signal the end of the session before you take the last question, say something like *We have time for just one more question*. As you answer the last question, try to work it into a summary of your main points. Then, express appreciation to the audience for the opportunity to talk with them.

Preparing and organizing an oral presentation, as summarized in the checklist that begins on page 510, requires attention to content and strategy. Along with the care you devote to developing your talk, consider also its ethics, so that you won't be guilty of committing the "worst deadly sin" spotlighted in the accompanying Ethical Insights box.

## ADAPTING TO INTERNATIONAL AND CROSS-CULTURAL AUDIENCES

Every good speaker adapts to the audience, and cross-cultural presentations call for special adjustments and sensitivity. When working with an interpreter or speaking before individuals whose English is limited, you'll need to be very careful about your language.

## The "Worst Deadly Sin" in a Presentation

Audiences appreciate speakers with polished delivery techniques, but they are usually relatively forgiving when mistakes occur. One thing they don't suffer gladly, though, is unethical behaviour. Executives in a comprehensive research survey agreed that the "worst deadly sin" a speaker can commit in a presentation is demonstrating a lack of integrity.[15]

What kinds of unethical behaviour do audiences reject? They distrust speakers who misrepresent, exaggerate, and lie. They also dislike cover-ups and evasiveness. Everyone expects a speaker who is trying to "sell" a product or idea to emphasize its strong points. Promotion, however, becomes unethical when the speaker intentionally seeks to obscure facts or slant issues to deceive the audience. The following situations clearly signal trouble for speakers because of the unethical actions involved:

- A sales rep, instead of promoting his company's products, suggests that his competitor's business is mismanaged, is losing customers, or offers seriously flawed products.

- A manager distorts a new employee insurance plan, underemphasizing its deficiencies and overemphasizing its strengths.

- An accountant for a charity recommends that management authorize lax bookkeeping practices in order to mislead the public regarding the use of donors' money.

- A sales rep fabricates an answer to a tough question instead of admitting ignorance.

- A financial planner tries to prove her point by highlighting an irrelevant statistic.

- A real estate broker compares dissimilar properties and locations to inflate the value of some property.

- A speaker deliberately uses excessively technical language to make an idea or proposal seem more important and complex than it is.

- A project manager claims personal credit for a proposal developed largely by consultants.

How can you make certain that your own presentations are ethical? The best strategy, of course, is to present your information honestly, fairly, and without deception. Be aware of your own biases and prejudices so that you don't unconsciously distort data. Remember that the goals of an ethical communicator, discussed in Chapter 1, include telling the truth, labelling opinions so that they can be distinguished from facts, being objective, writing clearly, and giving credit when you use others' ideas or words.

### Career Application

Watch TV or read news stories about parliamentary debates. Note how proponents on each side of an issue (usually the government and the opposition) present their views in a positive light and cast their opponents' views in a negative light. Make notes of any unethical presentation techniques.

---

Beyond these basic language adaptations, however, more fundamental sensitivity is often necessary. In organizing a presentation for a cross-cultural audience, think twice about delivering your main idea up front. Many people (notably those in Japanese, Latin American, and Arabic cultures) consider such directness to be brash and inappropriate. Remember that others may not share our cultural emphasis on straightforwardness.[16]

Also consider breaking your presentation into short, discrete segments. In the Middle East, for example, Arab speakers "mix circuitous, irrelevant (by North American standards) conversations with short dashes of information that go directly to the point." Presenters who are patient, tolerant, and "mature" (in the eyes of the audience) will make the sale or win the contract.[17]

**Addressing cross-cultural audiences requires a speaker to consider audience expectations and cultural conventions.**

## *Esteem Team Revisited*

Champion Canadian snowboarder Mike Kwiatkowski reflects on his public speaking experience with the Esteem Team and its impact. "Never would I have imagined that what I do, who I am, and what I say could positively affect so many young people across British Columbia," he writes on the Esteem Team Web site. As he recounts his public-speaking experiences in grade school, Mike writes, "Gone are the days of cue cards and sweaty palms. Still with me, though, is the occasional butterfly (but sometimes one butterfly and all his friends) as I walk into the gymnasium filled with eager students, awaiting the spoken word from some National Team snowboarder named 'Mike.' For me, the anxiety lies in the enormous amount of responsibility I possess for exactly 60 minutes. Imagine having the full attention of 200–300 students who are all at that magical 'impressionable' age."

Key to developing and delivering valuable presentations is gathering feedback, and the feedback from the presentations of Esteem Team says the program is working. Almost 90 percent of students rank the Esteem Team presentations as good or excellent, and educators report that the students enjoy the variety of techniques that the athletes use in their presentations. Comments about presenters such as "captivating speaker with the right mix of humour and a fabulous message" and "wonderful job of speaking to the level of the students. Often speakers speak down to children, but he was very engaging" reflect the importance of effective audience analysis.

### CRITICAL THINKING

- What questions should the Esteem Team athletes ask themselves about their anticipated audiences?
- Why are simplicity and flexibility important in an oral presentation and why is it particularly important for school children?
- Why are visual aids critical for all types of audiences?

**www.esteemteam.com**

---

Match your presentation to the expectations of your audience. In Germany, for instance, successful presentations tend to be dense with facts and precise statistics. Canadians might say "around 30 percent" while a German presenter might say "30.4271958 percent."

Remember, too, that some cultures prefer greater formality than Westerners exercise. Writing on a flipchart or transparency seems natural and spontaneous in this country. Abroad, though, such informal techniques may suggest that the speaker does not value the audience enough to prepare proper visual aids in advance.[18]

This caution aside, you'll still want to use visual aids to communicate your message. These visuals should be written in both languages, so that you and your audience understand them. Never use numbers without writing them out for all to see. If possible, say numbers in both languages. Distribute translated handouts, summarizing your important information, when you finish. Finally, be careful of your body language. Looking people in the eye suggests intimacy and self-confidence in this country, but in other cultures such eye contact may be considered disrespectful.

## CHECKLIST FOR PREPARING AND ORGANIZING ORAL PRESENTATIONS

### Getting Ready to Speak

✓ **Identify your purpose.** Decide what you want your audience to believe, remember, or do when you finish. Aim all parts of your talk toward this purpose.

✓ **Analyze the audience.** Consider how to adapt your message (its organization, appeals, and examples) to your audience's knowledge and needs.

## Organizing the Introduction

✓ **Get the audience involved.** Capture the audience's attention by opening with a promise, story, startling fact, question, quote, relevant problem, or self-effacing joke.

✓ **Establish yourself.** Demonstrate your credibility by identifying your position, expertise, knowledge, or qualifications.

✓ **Preview your main points.** Introduce your topic and summarize its principal parts.

## Organizing the Body

✓ **Develop two to four main points.** Streamline your topic so that you can concentrate on its major issues.

✓ **Arrange the points logically.** Sequence your points chronologically, from most important to least important, by comparison and contrast, or by some other strategy.

✓ **Prepare transitions.** Between each major point write "bridge" statements that connect the previous item to the next one. Use transitional expressions as verbal signposts (*first, second, then, however, consequently, on the contrary,* and so forth).

✓ **Have extra material ready.** Be prepared with more information and visuals in case you have additional time to fill.

## Organizing the Conclusion

✓ **Review your main points.** Emphasize your main ideas in your closing so that your audience will remember them.

✓ **Provide a final focus.** Tell how your listeners can use this information, why you have spoken, or what you want them to do.

## Designing Visual Aids

✓ **Select your medium carefully.** Consider the size of your audience, degree of formality desired, cost and ease of preparation, and potential effectiveness.

✓ **Highlight main ideas.** Use visual aids to illustrate major concepts only. Keep them brief and simple.

✓ **Use aids skillfully.** Talk to the audience, not to the visuals. Paraphrase their contents.

## Developing Electronic Presentations

✓ **Learn to use your software program.** Study template and slide layout designs to see how you can adapt them to your purposes.

✓ **Select a pleasing colour palette.** Work with five or fewer colours for your entire presentation.

✓ **Use bulleted points for major ideas.** Make sure your points are all parallel and observe the Rule of Seven.

✓ **Make speaker's notes.** Jot down the narrative supporting each slide and use these notes to practise your presentation.

✓ **Maintain control.** Don't let your slides upstage you. Use a laser pointer to connect you to the slides and your audience.

## IMPROVING TELEPHONE AND VOICE MAIL SKILLS

*7*

**Telephone calls and voice mail should promote goodwill and increase productivity.**

The telephone is the most universal—and, some would say, the most important—piece of equipment in offices today.[19] And with the addition of today's wireless technology, it doesn't matter whether you are in or out of the office. You can be reached by phone. In the Career Coach box on page 19 of Chapter 1, you learned some specific techniques for being courteous in using cell phones. In this chapter we'll focus on traditional telephone techniques as well as voice mail efficiency. As a business communicator, you can be most effective by following these suggestions for making and receiving telephone calls and for using voice mail.

## Making Productive Telephone Calls

**Making productive telephone calls means planning an agenda, identifying the purpose, being courteous and cheerful, and avoiding rambling.**

Before making a telephone call, decide whether the intended call is really necessary. Could you find the information yourself? If you wait a while, would the problem resolve itself? Perhaps your message could be delivered more efficiently by some other means. One West Coast company found that telephone interruptions consumed about 18 percent of staff members' workdays. Another study found that two thirds of all calls were less important than the work they interrupted.[20] Alternatives to telephone calls include e-mail, memos, or calls to voice mail systems. If a telephone call must be made, consider using the following suggestions to make it fully productive.

- **Plan a mini-agenda.** Have you ever been embarrassed when you had to make a second telephone call because you forgot an important item the first time? Before placing a call, jot down notes regarding all the topics you need to discuss. Following an agenda guarantees not only a complete call but also a quick one. You'll be less likely to wander from the business at hand while rummaging through your mind trying to remember everything.

- **Use a three-point introduction.** When placing a call, immediately (1) name the person you are calling, (2) identify yourself and your affiliation, and (3) give a brief explanation of your reason for calling. For example: "May I speak to Larry Lopez? This is Hillary Dahl of Sebastian Enterprises, and I'm seeking information about a software program called Power Presentations." This kind of introduction enables the receiving individual to respond immediately without asking further questions.

- **Be brisk if you are rushed.** For business calls when your time is limited, avoid questions such as "How are you?" Instead, say, "Lisa, I knew you'd be the only one who could answer these two questions for me." Another efficient strategy is to set a "contract" with the caller: "Look, Lisa, I have only ten minutes, but I really wanted to get back to you."

- **Be cheerful and accurate.** Let your voice show the same kind of animation that you radiate when you greet people in person. In your mind try to envision the individual answering the telephone. A smile can certainly affect the tone of your voice, so smile at that person. Moreover, be accurate about what you say. "Hang on a second; I'll be right back" rarely is true. Better to say, "It may take me two or three minutes to get that information. Would you prefer to hold or have me call you back?"

- **Bring it to a close.** The responsibility for ending a call lies with the caller. This is sometimes difficult to do if the other person rambles on. You may need to use suggestive closing language, such as "I've certainly enjoyed talking with you," "I've learned what I needed to know, and now I can proceed with my work," "Thanks for your help," or "I must go now, but may I call you again in the future if I need . . .?"

- **Avoid telephone tag.** If you call someone who's not in, ask when it would be best for you to call again. State that you will call at a specific time—and do it. If you ask a person to call you, give a time when you can be reached—and then be sure you are in at that time.

- **Leave complete voice mail messages.** Remember that there's no rush when you leave a voice mail message. Always enunciate clearly. And be sure to provide a complete message, including your name, telephone number, and the time and date of your call. Explain your purpose so that the receiver can be ready with the required information when returning your call.

## Receiving Productive Telephone Calls

With a little forethought you can make your telephone a productive, efficient work tool. Developing good telephone manners also reflects well on you and on your organization.

- **Identify yourself immediately.** In answering your telephone or someone else's, provide your name, title or affiliation, and, possibly, a greeting. For example, "Larry Lopez, Proteus Software. How may I help you?" Force yourself to speak clearly and slowly. Remember that the caller may be unfamiliar with what you are saying and fail to recognize slurred syllables.

- **Be responsive and helpful.** If you are in a support role, be sympathetic to callers' needs. Instead of "I don't know," try "That's a good question; let me investigate." Instead of "We can't do that," try "That's a tough one; let's see what we can do." Avoid "No" at the beginning of a sentence. It sounds especially abrasive and displeasing because it suggests total rejection.

- **Be cautious when answering calls for others.** Be courteous and helpful, but don't give out confidential information. Better to say, "She's away from her desk" or "He's out of the office" than to report a colleague's exact whereabouts.

- **Take messages carefully.** Few things are as frustrating as receiving a potentially important phone message that is illegible. Repeat the spelling of names and verify telephone numbers. Write messages legibly and record their time and date. Promise to give the messages to intended recipients, but don't guarantee return calls.

- **Explain what you're doing when transferring calls.** Give a reason for transferring, and identify the extension to which you are directing the call in case the caller is disconnected.

Receiving productive telephone calls means identifying oneself, acting responsive, being helpful, and taking accurate messages.

## Making the Best Use of Voice Mail

Voice mail links a telephone system to a computer that digitizes and stores incoming messages. Some systems also provide functions such as automated attendant menus, allowing callers to reach any associated extension by pushing specific buttons on a touch-tone telephone. Interactive systems allow callers to receive verbal information from a computer database. For example, a ski resort in Banff uses voice mail to answer routine questions that once were routed through an operator: *Welcome to Snow Paradise. For information on accommodations, touch 1; for snow conditions, touch 2; for ski equipment rental, touch 3,* and so forth.

Voice mail serves many functions, but the most important is message storage. Because as many as half of all business calls require no discussion or feedback, the messaging capabilities of voice mail can mean huge savings for businesses. Incoming information is delivered without interrupting potential receivers and without all the niceties that most two-way conversations require. Stripped of superfluous chitchat, voice mail messages allow communicators to focus on essentials. Voice mail also eliminates telephone tag, inaccurate message-taking, and time-zone barriers. Critics complain, nevertheless, that automated systems seem cold and impersonal and are sometimes confusing and irritating. In any event, here are some ways that you can make voice mail work more effectively for you.

- **Announce your voice mail.** If you rely principally on a voice mail message system, identify it on your business stationery and cards. Then, when people call, they will be ready to leave a message.

- **Prepare a warm and informative greeting.** Make your mechanical greeting sound warm and inviting, both in tone and content. Identify yourself and your organization so that callers know they have reached the right number. Thank the caller and briefly explain that you are unavailable. Invite the caller to leave a message or, if appropriate, call back. Here's a typical voice mail greeting: "Hi! This is Larry Lopez of Proteus Software, and I appreciate your call. You've reached my voice mailbox because I'm either working with customers or talking on another line at the moment. Please leave your name, number, and reason for calling so that I can be prepared when I return your call." Give callers an idea of when you will be available, such as "I'll be back at 2:30" or "I'll be out of my office until Wednesday, May 20." If you screen your calls as a time-management technique, try this message: "I'm not near my phone right now, but I should be able to return calls after 3:30."

- **Test your message.** Call your number and assess your message. Does it sound inviting? Sincere? Understandable? Are you pleased with your tone? If not, says one consultant, have someone else, perhaps a professional, record a message for you.

## SUMMARY OF LEARNING OBJECTIVES

*1* **Discuss two important first steps in preparing effective oral presentations.** First, identify what your purpose is and what you want the audience to believe or do so that you can aim the entire presentation toward your goal. Second, know your audience so that you can adjust your message and style to its knowledge and needs.

## Applying Your Skills at Esteem Team

Esteem Team's goal is to increase the number of presentations throughout the country, and it is continually seeking new program components, including developing resources for educators and leaders, encouraging the achievement of goals, and advocating for an increase in physical activity and sport participation by youth. As the program grows, new ideas for topics and content continue to be added. New programs are designed in consultation with key stakeholders.

Athletes who sign on with the Esteem Team are trained in effective presentation techniques. Program coordinators and trainers deliver public-speaking workshops to the athletes and provide in-school presentation coaching and feedback. They determine the best delivery method to ensure that the impact of the presentations is felt.

Members of the Esteem Team are trained and provided with the resources to deliver their presentations. A variety of resources is used during the presentations, including video, interaction, display, and, if feasible, demonstration of the athlete's sport. However, different delivery methods and flexibility are important. Since some presenters may not be familiar with electronic presentation software, Chris Wilson wonders whether Esteem Team presentations would be more effective if speakers used a program such as PowerPoint.

### Your Task

Chris Wilson knows that you and other students have been learning about PowerPoint in your postsecondary classes. He asks your group to collaborate in preparing a presentation that demonstrates how PowerPoint works. Before your group makes the full presentation to selected Esteem Team athletes, Chris wants to see an outline. If it looks good, you'll make the complete demonstration. Prepare an outline based on what you learned about PowerPoint in this chapter. Apply the suggestions for making presentations.

**www.esteemteam.com**

2 **Explain the major elements in organizing the content of a presentation, including the introduction, body, and conclusion.** The introduction of a good presentation should capture the listener's attention, identify the speaker, establish credibility, and preview the main points. The body should discuss two to four main points, with appropriate explanations, details, and verbal signposts to guide listeners. The conclusion should review the main points, provide a final focus, and allow the speaker to leave the podium gracefully.

3 **Identify techniques for gaining audience rapport, including using effective imagery, providing verbal signposts, and sending appropriate nonverbal messages.** You can improve audience rapport by using effective imagery including analogies, metaphors, similes, personal anecdotes, statistics, and worst/best-case scenarios. Rapport is also gained by including verbal signposts that tell the audience when you are previewing, summarizing, and switching directions. Nonverbal messages have a powerful effect on the way your message is received. You should look terrific, animate your body, punctuate your words, get out from behind the podium, and vary your facial expressions.

4 **Discuss designing and using effective visual aids, handouts, and electronic presentation materials.** Use simple, easily understood visual aids to emphasize and clarify main points. Choose transparencies, flipcharts, slides, or other visuals depending on audience size, degree of formality desired, and budget.

Generally, it's best to distribute handouts after a presentation. Speakers employing a program such as PowerPoint use templates, layout designs, and bullet points to produce effective slides. A presentation may be enhanced with slide transitions, sound, animation, and video elements. Speakers' notes and handouts may be generated from slides. Web-based presentations allow speakers to narrate and show slides without leaving their home bases. Increasing numbers of speakers are using the Web to provide copies of their slides as electronic handouts.

**5** **Specify delivery techniques for use before, during, and after a presentation.** Before your talk prepare a sentence outline on note cards or speaker's notes and rehearse repeatedly. Check the room, lectern, and equipment. During the presentation consider beginning with a pause and presenting your first sentence from memory. Make eye contact, control your voice, speak and move naturally, and avoid digressions. After your talk distribute handouts and answer questions. End gracefully and express appreciation.

**6** **Explain effective techniques for adapting oral presentations to cross-cultural audiences.** In presentations before groups whose English is limited, speak slowly, use simple English, avoid jargon and clichés, and use short sentences. Consider building up to your main idea rather than announcing it immediately. Also consider breaking the presentation into short segments to allow participants to ask questions and digest small parts separately. Beware of appearing too spontaneous and informal. Use visual aids to help communicate your message, but also distribute translated handouts summarizing the most important information.

**7** **List techniques for improving telephone and voice mail effectiveness.** You can improve your telephone calls by planning a mini-agenda and using a three-point introduction (name, affiliation, and purpose). Be cheerful and responsive, and use closing language to end a conversation. Avoid telephone tag by leaving complete messages. In answering calls, identify yourself immediately, avoid giving out confidential information when answering for others, and take careful messages. In setting up an automated-attendant voice mail menu, limit the number of choices. For your own message prepare a warm and informative greeting. Tell when you will be available. Evaluate your message by calling it yourself.

# CHAPTER REVIEW

1. The planning of an oral presentation should begin with serious thinking about what two factors? (Obj. 1)

2. Name three goals to be achieved in the introduction of an oral presentation. (Obj. 2)

3. For a 20-minute presentation, how many main points should be developed? (Obj. 2)

4. What should the conclusion to an oral presentation include? (Obj. 2)

5. List six techniques for creating effective imagery in a presentation. Be prepared to discuss each. (Obj. 3)

6. Name three ways for a speaker to use verbal signposts in a presentation. Illustrate each. (Obj. 3)

7. Why are visual aids particularly useful to inexperienced speakers? (Obj. 4)

8. Why are transparencies a favourite visual aid? (Obj. 4)

9. Name specific advantages and disadvantages of electronic presentation software. (Obj. 4)

10. How is the Rule of Seven applied in preparing bulleted points? (Obj. 4)

11. What delivery method is most effective for speakers? (Obj. 5)

12. Why should speakers deliver the first sentence from memory? (Obj. 5)

13. How might presentations before international or cross-cultural audiences be altered to be most effective? (Obj. 6)

14. What is a three-point introduction for a telephone call? (Obj. 7)

15. What is voice mail? (Obj. 7)

# CRITICAL THINKING

1. Why is it necessary to repeat key points in an oral presentation? (Objs. 2 and 5)

2. How can a speaker make the most effective use of visual aids? (Obj. 4)

3. How can speakers prevent electronic presentation software from stealing their thunder? (Obj. 4)

4. Discuss effective techniques for reducing stage fright. (Obj. 5)

5. **Ethical Issue:** How can business communicators ensure that their oral presentations are ethical?

# ACTIVITIES

## 15.1 Critiquing a Speech (Objs. 1–4)

**Your Task.** Visit your library and select a speech from *Canadian Speeches: Issues of the Day*. Write a memo report to your instructor critiquing the speech in terms of the following:

a. Effectiveness of the introduction, body, and conclusion
b. Evidence of effective overall organization
c. Use of verbal signposts to create coherence
d. Emphasis of two to four main points
e. Effectiveness of supporting facts (use of examples, statistics, quotations, and so forth)

## 15.2 Preparing an Oral Presentation From an Article (Objs. 1–5)

**Your Task.** Select a newspaper or magazine article and prepare an oral report based on it. Submit your outline, introduction, and conclusion to your instructor, or present the report to your class.

## 15.3 Overcoming Stage Fright (Obj. 5)

What makes you most nervous when making a presentation before class? Being tongue-tied? Fearing all eyes on you? Messing up? Forgetting your ideas and looking silly?
**Your Task.** Discuss the previous questions as a class. Then, in groups of three or four talk about ways to overcome these fears. Your instructor may ask you to write a memo (individual or collective) summarizing your suggestions, or you may break out of your small groups and report your best ideas to the entire class.

## 15.4 Investigating Oral Communication in Your Field (Objs. 1 and 5)

**Your Task.** Interview one or two individuals in your professional field. How is oral communication important in this profession? Does the need for oral skills change as one advances? What suggestions can these people make to newcomers to the field for developing proficient oral communication skills? Discuss your findings with your class.

## 15.5 Outlining an Oral Presentation (Objs. 1 and 2)

One of the hardest parts of preparing an oral presentation is developing the outline.

**Your Task.** Select an oral presentation topic from the list in Activity 15.8 or suggest an original topic. Prepare an outline for your presentation using the following format.

**Title**

**Purpose**

|   |   |
|---|---|
|   | I. INTRODUCTION |
| **Gain attention of audience** | A. |
| **Involve audience** | B. |
| **Establish credibility** | C. |
| **Preview main points** | D. |
| **Transition** |   |
|   | II. BODY |
| **Main point** | A. |
| **Illustrate, clarify, contrast** | 1. |
|   | 2. |
|   | 3. |
| **Transition** |   |
| **Main point** | B. |
| **Illustrate, clarify, contrast** | 1. |
|   | 2. |
|   | 3. |
| **Transition** |   |
| **Main point** | C. |
| **Illustrate, clarify, contrast** | 1. |
|   | 2. |
|   | 3. |
| **Transition** |   |
|   | III. CONCLUSION |
| **Summarize main points** | A. |
| **Provide final focus** | B. |
| **Encourage questions** | C. |

## 15.6 Discovering New Presentation Tips (Objs. 2–5)

**INFOTRAC**

**Your Task.** Using InfoTrac, perform a subject guide search for *business presentations*. Read at least three articles that provide suggestions for giving business presentations. If possible, print the most relevant findings. Select at least eight good tips or techniques that you did *not* learn from this chapter. Your instructor may ask you to bring them to class for discussion or submit a short memo report outlining your tips.

## 15.7 Researching Job-Application Information (Objs. 1–5)

**INFOTRAC**

**Your Task.** Using InfoTrac, perform a subject search for one of the following topics. Find as many articles as you can. Then organize and present a five- to ten-minute informative talk to your class.

a. Do recruiters prefer one- or two-page résumés?
b. How do applicant tracking systems work?
c. How are inflated résumés detected and what are the consequences?
d. What's new in writing cover letters in job applications?
e. What is online résumé fraud?
f. What are some new rules for résumés?

## 15.8 Choosing a Topic for an Oral Presentation (Objs. 1–5)

**Your Task.** Select a topic from the list below or from the report topics on this book's Web site: "Student Resources," "Web Links by Chapter," "Chapter 12." Prepare a five- to ten-minute oral presentation. Consider yourself an expert who has been called in to explain some aspect of the topic before a group of interested people. Since your time is limited, prepare a concise yet forceful presentation with effective visual aids.

a. What is the career outlook in a field of your choice?
b. How has the Internet changed job searching?
c. How can attendance be improved in a minor sports field (your choice) at your school?
d. How do employees use online services?
e. What is telecommuting, and for what kind of workers is it an appropriate work alternative?
f. How much choice should parents have in selecting schools for their young children (parochial, private, and public)?

**g.** What travel location would you recommend for college students in December (or another school break)?

**h.** What is the economic outlook for a given product (such as domestic cars, laptop computers, digital cameras, fitness equipment, or a product of your choice)?

**i.** How can your organization or institution improve its image?

**j.** Why should people invest in a company or scheme of your choice?

**k.** What brand and model of computer and printer represent the best buy for postsecondary students today?

**l.** What franchise would offer the best investment opportunity for an entrepreneur in your area?

**m.** How should a job candidate dress for an interview?

**n.** What should a guide to proper cell phone use include?

**o.** Are internships worth the effort?

**p.** How is an administrative assistant different from a secretary?

**q.** Where should your organization hold its next convention?

**r.** What is your opinion of the statement "Advertising steals our time, defaces the landscape, and degrades the dignity of public institutions"?[21]

**s.** How can businesspeople reduce the amount of e-mail spam they receive?

**t.** What is the outlook for real estate (commercial or residential) investment in your area?

**u.** What are the pros and cons of videoconferencing for [name an organization]?

**v.** What do the personal assistants for celebrities do, and how does one become a personal assistant? (Investigate the Association of Celebrity Personal Assistants.)

**w.** What kinds of gifts are appropriate for businesses to give clients and customers during the holiday season?

**x.** Search the Web site of Industry Canada's Competition Bureau <**http://cb-bc.gc.ca**> under Consumer Information for various types of scams that have been identified by the Bureau. What scams are listed, and how can consumers avoid falling for them?

**y.** How are businesses and conservationists working together to protect the world's dwindling tropical forests?

**z.** Should employees be able to use computers in a work environment for anything other than work-related business?

## 15.9 Improving Telephone Skills by Role-Playing (Obj. 7)

**Your Task.** Your instructor will divide the class into pairs. For each scenario take a moment to read and rehearse your role silently. Then play the role with your partner. If time permits, repeat the scenarios, changing roles.

**Partner 1**

**A.** You are the personnel manager of Datatronics, Inc. Call Elizabeth Franklin, office manager at Computers Plus. Inquire about a job applicant, Chelsea Chavez, who listed Ms. Franklin as a reference.

**B.** Call Ms. Franklin again the following day to inquire about the same job applicant, Chelsea Chavez. Ms. Franklin answers today, but she talks on and on, describing the applicant in great detail. Tactfully close the conversation.

**C.** You are now the receptionist for Tom Wing, of Wing Imports. Answer a call for Mr. Wing, who is working in another office, at ext. 134, where he will accept calls.

**D.** You are now Tom Wing, owner of Wing Imports. Call your lawyer, Michael Murphy, about a legal problem. Leave a brief, incomplete message.

**E.** Call Mr. Murphy again. Leave a message that will prevent telephone tag.

**Partner 2**

You are the receptionist for Computers Plus. The caller asks for Elizabeth Franklin, who is home sick today. You don't know when she will be able to return. Answer the call appropriately.

You are now Ms. Franklin, office manager. Describe Chelsea Chavez, an imaginary employee. Think of someone with whom you've worked. Include many details, such as her ability to work with others, her appearance, her skills at computing, her schooling, her ambition, and so forth.

You are now an administrative assistant for lawyer Michael Murphy. Call Tom Wing to verify a meeting date Mr. Murphy has with Mr. Wing. Use your own name in identifying yourself.

You are now the receptionist for lawyer Michael Murphy. Mr. Murphy is skiing at Whistler and will return in two days, but he doesn't want his clients to know where he is. Take a message.

Take a message again.

# C.L.U.E. REVIEW 15

On a separate sheet edit the following sentences to correct faults in grammar, punctuation, spelling, and word use.

1.  The CEOs assistant asked my colleague and I to explain why our proposed method was better then the one previously used.

2.  My friend and me were definitly inexperienced in making presentations, therefore him and I decided to learn more about public speaking.

3.  We learned that the introduction to a presentation should accomplish 3 goals (a) capture attention, (b) establish credibility and (c) preview main points.

4.  In the body of a short presentation which is usually 20 or less minutes we should focus on 2 to 4 principle points.

5.  One of the most important ways to end a presentation are focusing on what you want the audience to do think or remember.

6.  Speakers must remember that listeners unlike readers' can not controll the rate of presentation, or flip back thorough pages to review main points.

7.  In working with electronic presentation softwear experts suggest chosing 1 transition effect, and using it consistantly.

8.  The range of effects are staggering but presenters using electronic slides must control there urge to pile on to many dazzling features.

9.  Every good speaker adapt to his audience and cross cultural presentations call for special adjustments and sensitivity.

10. One study found that $2/3$ of telephone calls were less important then the work it interupted.

520

# Chapter 16
## Employment Communication

### LEARNING OBJECTIVES

*1* Prepare for employment by identifying your interests, evaluating your assets, recognizing the changing nature of jobs, choosing a career path, and studying traditional and electronic job search techniques.

*2* Compare and contrast chronological, functional, and combination résumés.

*3* Organize, format, and produce a persuasive résumé.

*4* Identify techniques that prepare a résumé for computer scanning, posting at a Web site, faxing, and e-mailing.

*5* Write a persuasive letter of application to accompany your résumé.

*6* Write effective employment follow-up letters and other messages.

*7* Evaluate successful job interview strategies.

# Maritime Life

"Our policy has always been to stay away from their business. This is a Canadian corporation, and I can't believe we would score any points by having Americans tell their Canadian colleagues how to run their company." So said E. James Morton, a president of the fifth-largest insurance company in the United States, the John Hancock Mutual Life Insurance of Boston, in speaking of the Halifax-based Maritime Life Assurance Company.[1] While Maritime Life has been a wholly owned subsidiary of Hancock since 1968, it has maintained its Canadian identity.*

Three decades ago Maritime Life ranked 58th out of 60 Canadian life insurance companies; today it's among the top five. In 2003 the company was named among *The Globe and Mail*'s *ROB Magazine*'s Top 50 best companies to work for in Canada for the fourth consecutive year. Maritime Life has also been listed among Canada's Top 100 Employers by Mediacorp Canada Inc.

What sets Maritime Life apart from its competition? First is its location. While most major insurance companies are headquartered in Toronto, Maritime stays close to its roots in Halifax. In 2003 the 24-storey Maritime Life Tower opened at the corner of Queen and Yonge in Toronto—as a branch office. The company's more than 2 200 employees are spread throughout Canada and serve more than 2 million policyholders. Ninety percent of the company's business is conducted west of the Maritimes. Second is its growth rate. Between 1995 and 2003, Maritime Life acquired operations of Confederation Life Assurance Company, Aetna Life Insurance Company of Canada, Royal & Sun Alliance Life Insurance Company of Canada, and Liberty Health. Third is the company's focus on customer and employee satisfaction. Despite the challenges created by these acquisitions, employee-satisfaction ratings remain high.

Believing that the key to the organization's success is its philosophy that satisfied employees lead to satisfied customers, Maritime Life president and CEO Bill Black attributes much of the company's success to its employees. "We owe a lot of gratitude to our employees," he says. "Their continued interest and commitment to our vision and values greatly contribute to our success."

In speaking of the company's U.S. owners, Black goes on to say, "I told Steve [Stephen Brown, president of Maritime] the reason we're so successful is that Hancock lets us run it, and he said the reason they let us run it is that it's so successful."[2]

## CRITICAL THINKING

- What factors must Maritime Life consider in balancing employee satisfaction, customer satisfaction, and growth?
- How can a U.S.-owned company maintain its distinctive Canadian identity? What relationship must exist between the parent company and its subsidiary?
- Should job-seekers be concerned about a company's ultimate ownership? Why or why not?

www.maritimelife.ca

* In 2003, Manulife Insurance of Toronto purchased John Hancock Mutual Life Insurance of Boston. You may wish to research these three companies to determine the impact of this acquisition.

## PREPARING FOR EMPLOYMENT

*1*

One day you may be sending your résumé to a recruiting specialist who reads thousands of such résumés annually. What can you do to make your résumé and cover letter stand out? This chapter provides many tips for writing dynamite résumés and cover letters, as well as suggestions for successful interviewing. But the job search process actually begins long before you are ready to write a résumé. Whether you are looking for an internship, applying for a full-time position, searching for a part-time job, competing for a promotion, or changing careers, you must invest time and effort preparing yourself. You can't hope to find the position of your dreams without first (1) knowing yourself, (2) knowing the job market, and (3) knowing the employment process.

One of the first things you should do is obtain career information and choose a specific job objective. At the same time, you should be studying the job market and becoming aware of substantial changes in the nature of work. You'll want to understand how to use the latest Internet resources in your job search. Finally, you'll need to design a persuasive résumé and letter of application appropriate for small businesses as well as for larger organizations that may be using résumé-scanning programs. Following these steps, summarized in Figure 16.1 and described in this chapter, gives you a master plan for landing a job you really want.

**Finding a satisfying career means learning about oneself, the job market, and the employment process.**

## Identifying Your Interests

The employment process begins with introspection. This means looking inside yourself to analyze what you like and dislike so that you can make good employment choices. Career counsellors charge large sums for helping individuals learn about themselves. You can do the same kind of self-examination—without spending a dime. For guidance in choosing a field that eventually proves to be satisfying, answer the following questions. If you have already chosen a field, think carefully about how your answers relate to that choice.

**Answer specific questions to help yourself choose a career.**

- *Do I enjoy working with people, data, or things?*
- *How important is it to be my own boss?*
- *How important are salary, benefits, technology support, and job stability?*
- *How important are working environment, colleagues, and job stimulation?*
- *Would I rather work for a large or small company?*
- *Must I work in a specific city, geographical area, or climate?*
- *Am I looking for security, travel opportunities, money, power, or prestige?*
- *How would I describe the perfect job, boss, and coworkers?*

**FIGURE 16.1  The Employment Search**

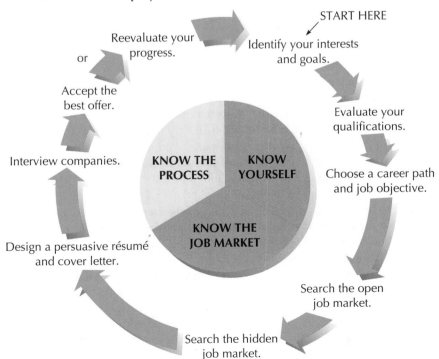

## Evaluating Your Qualifications

In addition to your interests, assess your qualifications. Employers today want to know what assets you have to offer them. Your responses to the following questions will target your thinking as well as prepare a foundation for your résumé. Remember, though, that employers seek more than empty assurances; they will want proof of your qualifications.

- *What computer skills can I offer?* Employers are often interested in specific software programs.

- *What other skills have I acquired in school, on the job, or through activities?* How can I demonstrate these skills?

- *Do I work well with people?* What proof can I offer? Consider extracurricular activities, clubs, and jobs.

- *Am I a leader, self-starter, or manager?* What evidence can I offer?

- *Do I speak, write, or understand another language?*

- *Do I learn quickly? Am I creative?* How can I demonstrate these characteristics?

- *Do I communicate well in speech and in writing?* How can I verify these talents?

## Recognizing the Changing Nature of Jobs

**People feel less job security after downsizing and movement to flatter organizations.**

As you learned in Chapter 1, the nature of the workplace is changing. One of the most significant changes involves the concept of the "job." Following the downsizing in recent years and the movement toward flattened organizations, fewer people are employed in permanent positions. Many employees are feeling less job security, although they are doing more work.

In his best-selling book *JobShift*, William Bridges describes the disappearance of the traditional job. The notion of a full-time permanent job with a specific job description, he claims, is giving way to more flexible work arrangements. Work is completed by teams assigned to projects, or work is outsourced to a group that's not even part of an organization.[3] He sees the migration of work away from fixed "boxes" that we've always called jobs.

At the same time that work is becoming more flexible; big companies are no longer the main employers. In fact, over 78 percent of businesses in Canada have fewer than five employees,[4] and self-employment is growing rapidly. According to a Statistics Canada manager, almost one in five workers is self-employed.[5] Over 80 percent of new jobs in Canada fall into the category of self-employment, while large businesses (those that hire 20 or more employees) account for less than 20 percent of employment created in Canada.[6] People seem to be working for smaller companies, or they are becoming consultants or specialists who work on tasks or projects under arrangements too fluid to be called "jobs." And because new technologies can spring up overnight, making today's skills obsolete, employers are less willing to hire people into jobs with narrow descriptions.

**"Jobs" are becoming more flexible and less permanent.**

What do these changes mean for you? For one thing, you should probably no longer think in terms of a lifelong career with a single company. In fact, you can't even expect reasonably permanent employment for work well done. This social contract between employer and employee is no longer a given. And predictable career paths within companies have largely disappeared. The result is that career advancement is in your own hands.[7] In the new workplace you can expect to work for multiple employers on flexible job assignments associated with teams and projects. You'll strive for career durability rather than job security.[8] For maximum durability, you should be prepared for constant retraining to update your skills. People who learn quickly and adapt to change are "high-value-added" individuals who will always be in demand even in a climate of surging change.

## Choosing a Career Path

There's no escaping the fact that the employment picture today is much different from that of a decade or two ago. By the time you are 30, you can expect to have had five to seven jobs. The average employee will have worked at 12 to 15 jobs over the course of a career, staying an average of 3.6 years at each job.[9] Some of you probably have not yet settled on your first career choice; others are returning to college to retrain for a new career. Although you may be changing jobs in the future, you still need to train for a specific career area now. In choosing an area, you'll make the best decisions when you can match your interests and qualifications with the requirements and rewards in specific careers. But where can you find career data? Here are some suggestions:

- **Visit your campus career centre.** Most have literature, inventories, software programs, and Internet connections that allow you to investigate such fields as accounting, finance, office technology, information systems, hotel management, and so forth. Additionally, they may provide assistance in résumé preparation and interview skills development.

- **Search the Web.** Many job search sites on the Web offer career-planning information and resources. For example, at the Canadian Association of Career Educators and Employers site <**www.cacee.com**>, you can link to career/life planning sites for college and university students and graduates. Updated descriptions of and links to the best career counselling and job search Web sites can be found at this book's Student Resources Web site <**www.businesscommunication-4th. nelson.com**>. Click on "Careers and Job Search."

- **Use your library.** Many print and online resources are especially helpful. Consult the latest edition of the *Blue Book of Canadian Business, Canadian Key Business Directory*, and *The Financial Post 100 Best Companies to Work for in Canada*. Look at the appropriate Scott's Directory for the geographical area (city, town) of your search.

- **Take a summer job, internship, or part-time position in your field.** Nothing is better than trying out a career by actually working in it or an allied area. Many companies offer internships and temporary jobs to begin training college students and to develop relationships with them. These relationships sometimes blossom into permanent positions. Consult Career Edge <**www.careeredge.ca**>, a privately financed program that has placed over 4 000 interns in Canadian companies. It offers internships of 6, 9, or 12 months in 450 companies and non-profit organizations. Companies such as GE Canada, Sears Canada, and the Royal Bank have participated and been pleased with the results. In fact, about 85 percent of Career Edge interns find work in their chosen field.[10]

- **Interview someone in your chosen field.** People are usually flattered when asked to describe their careers. Inquire about needed skills, required courses, financial and other rewards, benefits, working conditions, future trends, and entry requirements.

- **Monitor the classified ads.** Early in your postsecondary career, begin monitoring want ads and Web sites of companies in your career area. Check job availability, qualifications sought, duties, and salary range. Don't wait until you're about to graduate to see how the job market looks.

Career information can be obtained at campus career centres and libraries, from the Internet, in classified ads, and from professional organizations.

Summer and part-time jobs and internships are good opportunities to learn about different careers.

Preparing for a career begins long before you search the Web or want ads and write your résumé. Some of the best ways to learn about career paths involve talking with a campus counsellor, taking a summer or part-time job, or signing up for an internship. Most often internships and part-time jobs in your field don't just fall into your lap. They require determination and effort.

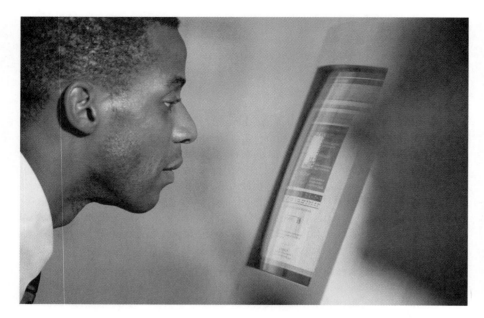

- **Join professional organizations in your field.** Frequently, they offer student membership status and reduced rates. You'll get inside information on issues, career news, and possibly jobs.

## Using Traditional Job Search Techniques

**A traditional job search campaign might include checking classified ads and announcements in professional publications, contacting companies, and developing a network of contacts.**

Finding the perfect job requires an early start and a determined effort. Whether you use traditional or online job search techniques, you should be prepared to launch an aggressive campaign. And you can't start too early. Some Canadian colleges and universities offer job search strategies as part of their curriculum, while others have separate career and employment centres for student use. Students are told early on that a college diploma or university degree alone doesn't guarantee a job. They are cautioned that grade-point averages make a difference to employers. And they are advised of the importance of experience. Here are some traditional steps that job candidates take:

- **Check classified ads in local and national newspapers.** Be aware, though, that classified ads are only one small source of jobs, as discussed in the accompanying Career Coach box.

- **Check announcements in publications of professional organizations.** If you do not have a student membership, ask your professors to share current copies of professional journals, newsletters, and so on. Your school library is another good source.

- **Contact companies in which you're interested, even if you know of no current opening.** Write an unsolicited letter and include your résumé. Follow up with a telephone call. Check the company's Web site for employment possibilities and procedures.

- **Sign up for campus interviews with visiting company representatives.** Campus recruiters may open your eyes to exciting jobs and locations.

- **Ask for advice from your professors.** They often have contacts and ideas for expanding your job search.

## How to Use Traditional and Online Networking to Explore the Hidden Job Market

Not all jobs are advertised in classified ads or listed in job databases. The "hidden" job market, according to some estimates, accounts for as much as two thirds of all positions available. Companies don't always announce openings publicly because it's time-consuming to interview all the applicants, many of whom are not qualified. But the real reason that companies resist announcing a job is that they dislike hiring "strangers." One recruiter says that when she needs to hire, she first looks around among her friends and acquaintances. If she can't find anyone suitable, she then turns to advertising.[11] It's clear that many employers are more comfortable hiring a person they know.

The key to finding a good job, then, is converting yourself from a "stranger" into a known quantity. One way to become a known quantity is by networking. You can use either traditional methods or online resources.

### Traditional Networking

**Step 1: Develop a List.** Make a list of anyone who would be willing to talk with you about finding a job. List your friends, relatives, former employers, former coworkers, classmates from grade school and high school, college friends, members of your church, people in social and athletic clubs, present and former teachers, neighbours, and friends of your parents.

**Step 2: Make Contacts.** Call the people on your list or, even better, try to meet with them in person. To set up a meeting, say "I'm looking for a job and I wonder if you could help me out. When could I come over to talk about it?" During your visit be friendly, well organized, polite, and interested in what your contact has to say. Provide a copy of your résumé, and try to keep the conversation centred on your job search area. Your goal is to get two or more referrals. In pinpointing your request, ask two questions. "Do you know of anyone who might have an opening for a person with my skills?" If not, "Do you know of anyone else who might know of someone who would?"

**Step 3: Follow Up on Your Referrals.** Call the people whose names are on your referral list. You might say something like, "Hello. I'm Carl Ramos, a friend of Connie Cole. She suggested that I call and ask you for help. I'm looking for a position as a marketing trainee, and she thought you might be willing to see me and give me a few ideas." Don't ask for a job. During your referral interview ask how the individual got started in this line of work, what he or she likes best (or least) about the work, what career paths exist in the field, and what problems must be overcome by a new-comer. Most important, ask how a person with your background and skills might get started in the field. Send an informal thank-you note to anyone who helps you in your job search, and stay in touch with the most promising contacts. Ask whether you may call every three weeks or so during your job search.

### Online Networking

As with traditional networking, the goal is to make connections with people who are advanced in their fields. Ask for their advice about finding a job. Most people like talking about themselves, and asking them about their experiences is an excellent way to begin an online correspondence that might lead to "electronic mentoring" or a letter of recommendation from an expert in the field. "Hanging out" at an online forum, discussion group, or newsgroup where industry professionals can be found is also a great way to keep tabs on the latest business trends and potential job leads.

- **Web-Based Discussion Groups, Forums, and Boards.** Forum One <**www.forumone.com**> is a Web site with a topical index that allows you to search thousands of discussion groups, forums, and boards on the Web. An especially good discussion group resource for beginners is Yahoo! Groups <**http://ca.groups.yahoo.com**>.

- **Mailing Lists and Newsgroups.** The most relevant Internet discussions can be found on mailing lists. You can subscribe to an e-mail newsletter or discussion group at Topica <**www.topica.com**>. To post and read newsgroup (Usenet) messages, try the Google Web site <**www.google.ca**> and click "Groups."

### Career Application

Begin developing your network. Conduct at least one referral interview or join one professional mailing list or newsgroup. Ask your instructor to recommend an appropriate mailing list or newsgroup for your field. Take notes, and report your reactions and findings to your class.

527

- **Develop your own network of contacts.** Networking still accounts for most of the jobs found by candidates. Therefore, plan to spend a considerable portion of your job search time developing a personal network. The previous Career Coach box gives you step-by-step instructions for traditional networking as well as some ideas for online networking.

## Using Electronic Job Search Techniques

An electronic job search campaign includes searching career and company Web sites for job listings.

Just as the Internet has changed the way the world works, it's also changing the nature of the job search. One software maker observed, "Employers are more proactive now, and there's less 'pounding the pavement' for job seekers."[12] Increasing numbers of employers are listing their job openings at special Web sites that are similar to newspaper classified ads. Companies are also listing job openings at their own Web sites providing a more direct connection to employment opportunities. Although we will describe five of the best Internet job sites here, you can find a more extensive and continuously updated list with clickable hot links at this book's Student Resources Web site.

- **Canada WorkInfoNet** <www.canworknet.ca> is sponsored by Human Resources Development Canada and provides over 2 000 Canadian Web sites. It describes itself as "the primary source of career, education, and labour market information for Canadians." This collaborative venture, developed by the public, private, and not-for-profit sectors, is a great place to start. There are valuable links to provincial and territorial partner sites.

- **Globecareers.com**, combined with Workopolis, calls itself "Canada's biggest job site." This Canada-only database provides more than 7 000 available jobs and has a Career Alert feature that will e-mail listings to you that match your profile.

- **Human Resources Development Canada** <www.hrdc-drhc.gc.ca> provides a variety of resources such as career counselling information and a national job bank. Its most unique feature is the Electronic Labour Exchange. A database of available jobs is compared to the candidate's skill profile. With a match, the profile is forwarded to the potential employer.

- **CACEE WorkWeb** <www.cacee.com> is dedicated to helping students and recent graduates find "meaningful" employment. Its WorkWeb (created by the Canadian Association of Career Educators and Employers) provides job search advice, links to employers, and access to government and professional home pages. It even includes information about the rights of the job-seeker.

- **monster.ca** (see Figure 16.2) offers access to information on jobs across Canada, while <http://workabroad.monster.com> lists jobs available in the United States and many other countries. Monster will find job listings that match your profile and e-mail them to you once a week. Although most of its jobs are aimed at experienced candidates, it also has plenty of entry-level positions.

Perhaps even better are the job openings listed at company Web sites. Check out a promising company to see what positions are open. What's the fastest way to find a company's Web address? We recommend Hoover's <www.hoovers.com> for quick company information and Web site links. If that fails, use your favourite search engine to learn whether a company has its own Web site. Some companies even provide online résumé forms that encourage job candidates to submit their qualifications immediately.

Hundreds of job sites now flood the Internet, and increasing numbers of companies offer online recruiting. In fact, a recent COMPAS Inc. survey revealed that 47 percent of Canadian companies are now using online recruiting methods, such as company Web sites or Internet-based search firms, to fill positions. Monster's

**FIGURE 16.2** Using the Web to Search for a Job

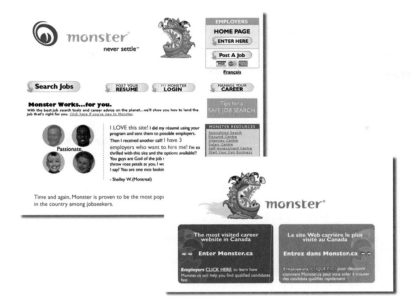

Canadian site posts over 25 000 jobs and 1.3 million résumés and gets 1.5 million visits each month. Companies like AGM Management Ltd. and Hewlett-Packard go directly to online job boards to find new hires, as well as posting positions on their own Web sites.[13] An additional survey by Ipsos-Reid shows that more than 7 million Canadians (31 percent) have used an online job listing service to search for a job in the last three years.[14] However, the harsh reality is that landing a job still depends largely on personal contacts. One employment expert said, "Online recruiting is a little like computer dating. People may find dates that way, but they don't get married that way."[15] Another professional placement expert said, "If you think just [posting] your résumé will get you a job, you're crazy. [Electronic services are] just a supplement to a core strategy of networking your buns off."[16]

> Many jobs are posted on the Internet, but most hiring is still done through personal contact.

## THE PERSUASIVE RÉSUMÉ

After using both traditional and online resources to learn about the employment market and to develop job leads, you'll focus on writing a persuasive résumé. Such a résumé does more than merely list your qualifications. It packages your assets into a convincing advertisement that sells you for a specific job. The goal of a persuasive résumé is winning an interview. Even if you are not in the job market at this moment, preparing a résumé now has advantages. Having a current résumé makes you look well organized and professional should an unexpected employment opportunity arise. Moreover, preparing a résumé early helps you recognize weak qualifications and gives you two or three years in which to bolster them.

### Choosing a Résumé Style

Your qualifications and career goal will help you choose from among three résumé styles: chronological, functional, and combination.

**FIGURE 16.3** Chronological Résumé

## Prewriting 1

**Analyze:** The purpose is to respond to a job advertisement and win an interview.

**Anticipate:** The reader probably sees many résumés and will skim this one quickly. He or she will be indifferent and must be persuaded to read on.

**Adapt:** Emphasize the specific skills that the targeted advertisement mentions.

## Writing 2

**Research:** Investigate the targeted company and its needs. Find the name of the person who will be receiving this résumé.

**Organize:** Make lists of all accomplishments and skills. Select those items most appropriate for the targeted job.

**Compose:** Experiment with formats to achieve readability, emphasis, and attractiveness.

## Revising 3

**Revise:** Use present-tense verbs to describe current experience. Bullet experience items. Check for parallel phrasing. Adjust spacing for best effect.

**Proofread:** Run spell checker. Read for meaning. Have a friend proofread and critique.

**Evaluate:** Will this résumé impress a recruiter in 30 seconds?

---

MICHELLE E. MARTIN
49 South Edgware Road
St. Thomas, ON N5P 2H5
(519) 814-9322

Includes detailed objective in response to advertisement

**OBJECTIVE**  Position with financial services organization installing accounting software and providing user support, where computer experience and proven communication and interpersonal skills can be used to improve operations.

**EXPERIENCE**  **Accounting software consultant,** Financial Specialists, London, Ontario
June 2003 to present
• Design and install accounting systems for businesses like 21st Century Real Estate, Illini Insurance, Aurora Lumber Company, and others
• Provide ongoing technical support and consultation for regular clients
• Help write proposals, such as recent one that won $250 000 contract

Uses present-tense verbs for current job

**Office manager** (part-time), Post Premiums, London, Ontario
June 2002 to May 2003
• Conceived and implemented improved order processing and filing system
• Managed computerized accounting system; trained new employees to use it
• Helped install local area network

Shows job titles in bold for readability

Chronological format arranges jobs and education by dates

**Bookkeeper** (part-time), Sunset Avionics, St. Thomas, Ontario
August 1998 to May 2002
• Kept books for small airplane rental and repair service
• Performed all bookkeeping functions including quarterly internal audit

**EDUCATION**  **University of Western Ontario**, London, Ontario
Business Administration, June 2003
Graduated with A– average

**Computer Associates** training seminars, summer and fall 2003
Certificates of completion
Seminars in consulting ethics, marketing, and ACCPAC accounting software

White space around headings creates open look

**SPECIAL SKILLS**  • Proficient in Word ME, PageMaker, PowerPoint, and Excel
• Skilled in ACCPAC Plus, MAS90, and Solomon IV accounting software
• Trained in technical writing, including proposals and documentation
• Experienced in office administration and management
• Competent at speaking and writing French

Highlights technical, management, and communication skills

**HONOURS AND ACTIVITIES**  Dean's list, three semesters
Member, Academic Affairs Advisory Committee, U.W.O., 2001–03

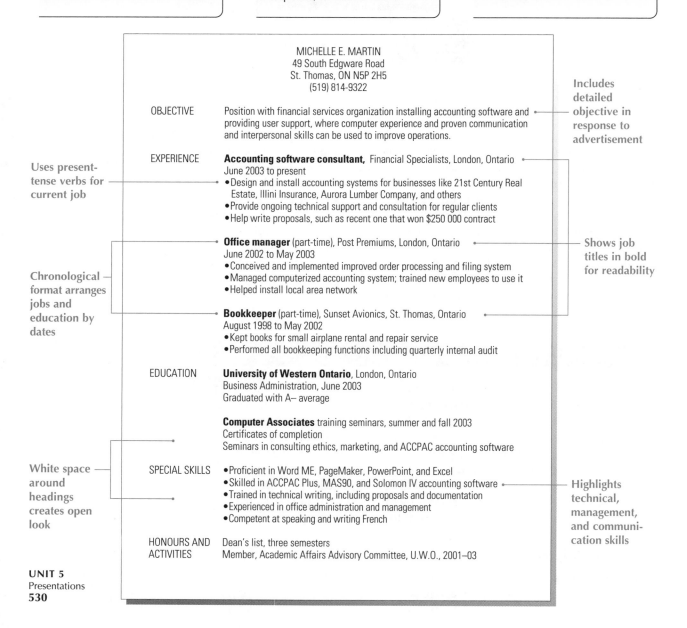

*Chronological.* Most popular with recruiters is the chronological résumé, shown in Figure 16.3. It lists work history job by job, starting with the most recent position. Many recruiters favour the chronological style because such résumés quickly reveal a candidate's education and experience record. One corporate recruiter said, "I'm looking for applicable experience; chronological résumés are the easiest to assess."[17] The chronological style works well for candidates who have experience in their field of employment and for those who show steady career growth. But for many college and university students and others who lack extensive experience, the functional résumé format may be preferable.

*Functional.* The functional résumé, shown in Figure 16.4, focuses attention on a candidate's skills rather than on past employment. Like a chronological résumé, the functional résumé begins with the candidate's name, address, telephone number, job objective, and education. Instead of listing jobs, though, the functional résumé groups skills and accomplishments in special categories, such as *Supervisory and Management Skills* or *Retailing and Marketing Experience.* This résumé style highlights accomplishments and can de-emphasize a negative employment history. People who have changed jobs frequently or who have gaps in their employment records may prefer the functional résumé. Recent graduates with little employment experience often find the functional résumé useful.

The functional format is especially good for students because it allows skills attained from experiences other than paid employment to be listed within the skills clusters. For example, one student chose leadership as a skills category, and she listed supporting experiences such as the presidency of a campus organization and other leadership positions. Your goal is to demostrate transferable skills attained through experience in traditional and nontraditional venues, including domestic management, volunteer work, and academic activities.

Functional résumés are also called *skill* résumés. Although the functional résumé of Donald Vinton shown in Figure 16.4 concentrates on skills, it does include a short employment section because recruiters expect it. Notice that Donald breaks his skills into three categories. An alternative—and easier—method is to make one large list, perhaps with a title such as *Areas of Accomplishment, Summary of Qualifications,* or *Areas of Expertise and Ability.*

*Combination.* The combination résumé style, shown in Figure 16.5, draws on the best features of the chronological and functional résumés. It emphasizes a candidate's capabilities while also including a complete job history. For recent graduates the combination résumé is a good choice because it enables them to profile what they can do for a prospective employer. If the writer has a specific job in mind, the items should be targeted to that job description.

## Deciding on Its Length

Experts simply do not agree on how long a résumé should be. Conventional wisdom has always held that recruiters prefer one-page résumés. However, a recent carefully controlled study of 570 recruiters revealed that they *claimed* they preferred one-page résumés. However, the recruiters actually *chose* to interview the applicants with two-page résumés.[18] Apparently, recruiters who are serious about candidates often prefer a full picture with the kind of details that can be provided in a two-page résumé.

The entire question may become moot as recruiters increasingly encourage online résumés, which are not restricted by page lengths. Perhaps the best advice is to make your résumé as long as needed to sell your skills.

## FIGURE 16.4 Functional Résumé

Donald, a recent graduate, chose this functional format to de-emphasize his meagre work experience and emphasize his potential in sales and marketing. He included an employment section to satisfy recruiters.

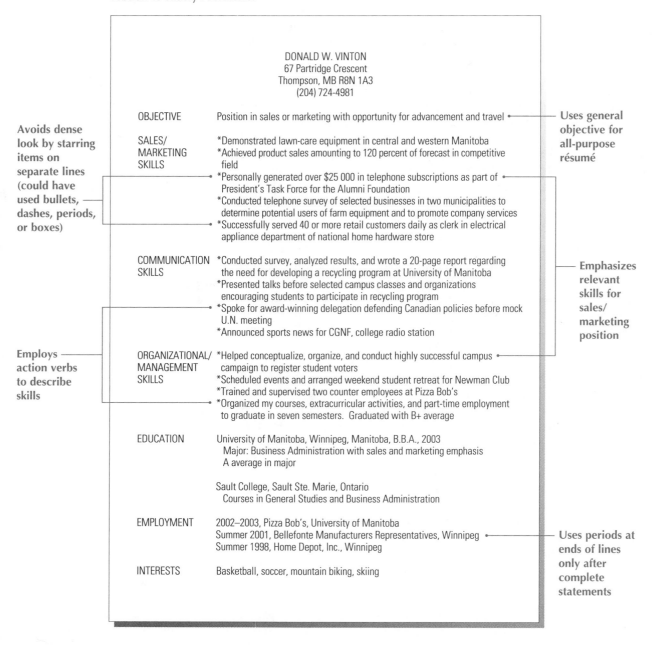

Avoids dense look by starring items on separate lines (could have used bullets, dashes, periods, or boxes)

Employs action verbs to describe skills

Uses general objective for all-purpose résumé

Emphasizes relevant skills for sales/ marketing position

Uses periods at ends of lines only after complete statements

DONALD W. VINTON
67 Partridge Crescent
Thompson, MB R8N 1A3
(204) 724-4981

**OBJECTIVE** — Position in sales or marketing with opportunity for advancement and travel

**SALES/ MARKETING SKILLS**
*Demonstrated lawn-care equipment in central and western Manitoba
*Achieved product sales amounting to 120 percent of forecast in competitive field
*Personally generated over $25 000 in telephone subscriptions as part of President's Task Force for the Alumni Foundation
*Conducted telephone survey of selected businesses in two municipalities to determine potential users of farm equipment and to promote company services
*Successfully served 40 or more retail customers daily as clerk in electrical appliance department of national home hardware store

**COMMUNICATION SKILLS**
*Conducted survey, analyzed results, and wrote a 20-page report regarding the need for developing a recycling program at University of Manitoba
*Presented talks before selected campus classes and organizations encouraging students to participate in recycling program
*Spoke for award-winning delegation defending Canadian policies before mock U.N. meeting
*Announced sports news for CGNF, college radio station

**ORGANIZATIONAL/ MANAGEMENT SKILLS**
*Helped conceptualize, organize, and conduct highly successful campus campaign to register student voters
*Scheduled events and arranged weekend student retreat for Newman Club
*Trained and supervised two counter employees at Pizza Bob's
*Organized my courses, extracurricular activities, and part-time employment to graduate in seven semesters. Graduated with B+ average

**EDUCATION**
University of Manitoba, Winnipeg, Manitoba, B.B.A., 2003
  Major: Business Administration with sales and marketing emphasis
  A average in major

Sault College, Sault Ste. Marie, Ontario
  Courses in General Studies and Business Administration

**EMPLOYMENT**
2002–2003, Pizza Bob's, University of Manitoba
Summer 2001, Bellefonte Manufacturers Representatives, Winnipeg
Summer 1998, Home Depot, Inc., Winnipeg

**INTERESTS** Basketball, soccer, mountain biking, skiing

## Arranging the Parts

3 Although résumés have standard parts, their arrangement and content should be strategically planned. The most persuasive résumés emphasize skills and achievements aimed at a particular job or company. They show a candidate's most important qualifications first, and they de-emphasize any weaknesses. In arranging the parts, try to create as few headings as possible; more than six generally looks cluttered. No two

## FIGURE 16.5  Combination Résumé

Because Susan wanted to highlight her skills and capabilities along with her experience, she combined the best features of functional and traditional résumés.  This résumé style is becoming increasingly popular.

Note: For more résumé models, see Figures 16.10–16.12, starting on page 541.

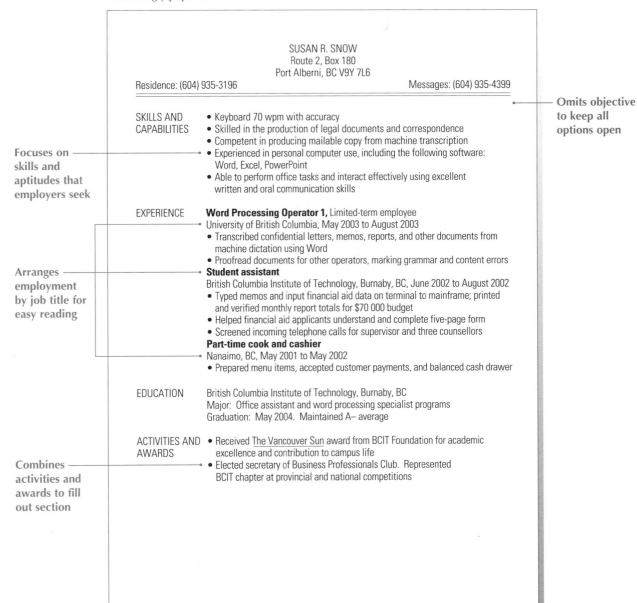

**SUSAN R. SNOW**
Route 2, Box 180
Port Alberni, BC V9Y 7L6

Residence: (604) 935-3196                          Messages: (604) 935-4399

Omits objective to keep all options open

Focuses on skills and aptitudes that employers seek

**SKILLS AND CAPABILITIES**
- Keyboard 70 wpm with accuracy
- Skilled in the production of legal documents and correspondence
- Competent in producing mailable copy from machine transcription
- Experienced in personal computer use, including the following software: Word, Excel, PowerPoint
- Able to perform office tasks and interact effectively using excellent written and oral communication skills

Arranges employment by job title for easy reading

**EXPERIENCE**
**Word Processing Operator 1,** Limited-term employee
University of British Columbia, May 2003 to August 2003
- Transcribed confidential letters, memos, reports, and other documents from machine dictation using Word
- Proofread documents for other operators, marking grammar and content errors
**Student assistant**
British Columbia Institute of Technology, Burnaby, BC, June 2002 to August 2002
- Typed memos and input financial aid data on terminal to mainframe; printed and verified monthly report totals for $70 000 budget
- Helped financial aid applicants understand and complete five-page form
- Screened incoming telephone calls for supervisor and three counsellors
**Part-time cook and cashier**
Nanaimo, BC, May 2001 to May 2002
- Prepared menu items, accepted customer payments, and balanced cash drawer

**EDUCATION**
British Columbia Institute of Technology, Burnaby, BC
Major:  Office assistant and word processing specialist programs
Graduation:  May 2004.  Maintained A– average

Combines activities and awards to fill out section

**ACTIVITIES AND AWARDS**
- Received The Vancouver Sun award from BCIT Foundation for academic excellence and contribution to campus life
- Elected secretary of Business Professionals Club.  Represented BCIT chapter at provincial and national competitions

---

résumés are ever exactly alike, but most writers consider including all or some of these items: main heading, career objective, education, experience, capabilities and skills, awards and activities, personal information, and references.

**The parts of résumés should be arranged with the most important qualifications first.**

*Main Heading.* Your résumé should always begin with your name, address, and telephone number. If possible, include a number where messages may be left for you.

Prospective employers tend to call the next applicant when no one answers. Avoid showing both permanent and temporary addresses; some specialists say that dual addresses immediately identify about-to-graduate college students. Keep the main heading as uncluttered and simple as possible. And don't include the word *résumé*; it's like putting the word *letter* above correspondence.

**Career objectives are most appropriate for specific, targeted openings, but they may limit a broader job search.**

*Career Objective.* Opinion is divided about the effect of including a career objective on a résumé. Recruiters think such statements indicate that a candidate has made a commitment to a career. Moreover, career objectives make the recruiter's life easier by quickly classifying the résumé. But such declarations can also disqualify a candidate if the stated objective doesn't match a company's job description.[19] One expert warned that putting a job objective on a résumé has "killed more opportunities for candidates . . . than typos."[20] What should you do?

You have four choices regarding career objectives. One option is to include a career objective when applying for a specific, targeted position. For example, the following responds to an advertised position: *Objective: To work in the health care industry as a human resources trainee with exposure to recruiting, training, and benefit administration.* A second choice—one that makes sense if you are preparing an all-purpose résumé—is to omit the career objective. A third possibility involves using a general statement, such as *Objective: Challenging position in urban planning* or *Job Goal: Position in sales/marketing.* A fourth possibility is omitting an objective on the résumé but including it in the cover letter, where it can be tailored to a specific position.[21]

Some consultants warn against using the words *entry-level* in your objective, as these words emphasize lack of experience. Because companies generally prefer individuals with experience, it's smart to get all the experience you can while in school. It's also wise to prepare individual résumés that are targeted for each company or position sought. Thanks to word processing, the task is easy.

*Education.* The next component is your education—if it is more noteworthy than your work experience. In this section you should include the name and location of schools, dates of attendance, major fields of study and diplomas or degrees received. Your grade-point average and/or class ranking are important to prospective employers. One way to enhance your GPA is to calculate it in your major courses only (for example, 3.6 in major, A = 4.0). By the way, it is not unethical to showcase your GPA in your major—as long as you clearly indicate what you are doing.

Some applicants want to list all their courses, but such a list makes for very dull reading. It's better to refer to courses only if you can relate them to the position sought. When relevant, include certificates earned, seminars attended, and workshops completed. Because employers are interested in your degree of self-sufficiency, you might wish to indicate the percentage of your education for which you paid. If your education is incomplete, include such statements as *B.S.C. degree expected 6/05* or *80 units completed in 120-unit program.* Entitle this section *Education, Academic Preparation,* or *Professional Training.*

*Work Experience or Employment History.* If your work experience is significant and relevant to the position sought, this information should appear before education. List your most recent employment first and work backward, including only those jobs that you think will help you win the targeted position. A job application form may demand a full employment history, but your résumé may be selective. (Be aware, though, that time gaps in your employment history will probably be questioned in the interview.) For each position show the following:

- Employer's name, city, and province

- Dates of employment
- Most important job title
- Significant duties, activities, accomplishments, and promotions

Describe your employment achievements concisely but concretely. Avoid generalities like *Worked with customers*. Be more specific, with statements such as *Served 40 or more retail customers a day, Successfully resolved problems about custom stationery orders*, or *Acted as intermediary among customers, printers, and suppliers*. If possible, quantify your accomplishments, such as *Conducted study of equipment needs of 100 small businesses in Halifax, Personally generated orders for sales of $90 000 annually, Keyboarded all the production models for a 250-page employee procedures manual*, or *Assisted editor in layout, design, and news writing for 12 issues of division newsletter*. One professional recruiter said, "I spend a half hour every day screening 50 résumés or more, and if I don't spot some [quantifiable] results in the first 10 seconds, the résumé is history."[22]

The work experience section of a résumé should list specifics and quantify achievements.

In addition to technical skills, employers seek individuals with communication, management, and interpersonal capabilities. This means you'll want to select work experiences and achievements that illustrate your initiative, dependability, responsibility, resourcefulness, and leadership. Employers also want people who can work together in teams. Thus, include statements like *Collaborated with interdepartmental task force in developing ten-page handbook for temporary workers* and *Headed student government team that conducted most successful voter registration in campus history*.

Statements describing your work experience can be made forceful and persuasive by using action verbs, such as those listed in Figure 16.6 and demonstrated in Figure 16.7. You'll also want to include plenty of solid nouns, which we'll present shortly.

*Capabilities and Skills.* Recruiters want to know specifically what you can do for their companies. Therefore, list your special skills, such as *Proficient in preparing correspondence and reports using Word ME*. Include your ability to use computer programs, office equipment, foreign languages, or sign language. Describe proficiencies you have acquired through training and experience, such as *Trained in computer accounting, including general ledger, accounts receivable, accounts payable, and payroll*. Use expressions like *competent in, skilled in, proficient with, experienced in,* and *ability to;* for example, *Competent in keyboarding, editing, and/or proofreading reports, tables, letters, memos, manuscripts, and business forms*.

Emphasize the skills and aptitudes that recommend you for a specific position.

You'll also want to highlight exceptional aptitudes, such as working well under stress and learning computer programs quickly. If possible, provide details and evidence that back up your assertions; for example, *Mastered PhotoShop in 25 hours with little instruction*. Search for examples of your writing, speaking, management, organizational, and interpersonal skills—particularly those talents that are relevant to your targeted job.

For recent graduates, this section can be used to give recruiters evidence of your potential. Instead of *Capabilities*, the section might be called *Skills and Abilities*.

*Awards, Honours, and Activities.* If you have three or more awards or honours, highlight them by listing them under a separate heading. If not, put them with activities. Include awards, scholarships (financial and other), fellowships, honours, recognition, commendations, and certificates. Be sure to identify items clearly. Your reader may be unfamiliar with scholarships and awards; tell what they mean. Instead of saying *Recipient of Star award*, give more details: *Recipient of Star award given by Mount Allison University to outstanding graduates who combine academic excellence and extracurricular activities*.

Awards, honours, and activities are appropriate for résumés; most personal data are not.

CHAPTER 16
Employment Communication
535

**FIGURE 16.6  Action Verbs for Persuasive Résumés***

| MANAGEMENT SKILLS | COMMUNICATION SKILLS | RESEARCH SKILLS | TECHNICAL SKILLS | TEACHING SKILLS |
|---|---|---|---|---|
| administered | addressed | clarified | assembled | adapted |
| analyzed | arbitrated | collected | built | advised |
| consolidated | arranged | critiqued | calculated | clarified |
| coordinated | collaborated | diagnosed | computed | coached |
| delegated | convinced | evaluated | designed | communicated |
| developed | developed | examined | devised | coordinated |
| directed | drafted | extracted | engineered | developed |
| evaluated | edited | identified | executed | enabled |
| improved | explained | inspected | fabricated | encouraged |
| increased | interpreted | interpreted | maintained | evaluated |
| organized | negotiated | interviewed | operated | explained |
| planned | persuaded | investigated | overhauled | guided |
| prioritized | promoted | organized | programmed | instructed |
| recommended | recruited | summarized | repaired | persuaded |
| strengthened | translated | surveyed | solved | set goals |
| supervised | wrote | systematized | upgraded | trained |

*The underlined words are especially good for pointing out accomplishments.

**FIGURE 16.7  Using Action Verbs to Strengthen Your Résumé**

**Identified** weaknesses in internships and **researched** five alternative programs

**Reduced** delivery delays by an average of three days per order

**Streamlined** filing system, thus reducing 400-item backlog to 0

**Organized** holiday awards program for 1200 attendees and 140 awardees

**Created** a 12-point checklist for use when requesting temporary workers

**Designed** five posters announcing new employee suggestion program

**Calculated** shipping charges for overseas deliveries and **recommended** most economical rates

**Managed** 24-station computer network linking data in three departments

**Distributed** and **explained** voter registration forms to over 500 prospective student voters

**Praised** by top management for enthusiastic teamwork and achievement

**Secured** national recognition from Communities in Bloom Foundation for tree project

**FIGURE 16.6  Continued**

| FINANCIAL SKILLS | CREATIVE SKILLS | HELPING SKILLS | CLERICAL OR DETAIL SKILLS | MORE VERBS FOR ACCOMPLISHMENTS |
|---|---|---|---|---|
| administered | conceptualized | assessed | approved | achieved |
| allocated | created | assisted | catalogued | directed |
| analyzed | customized | clarified | classified | expanded |
| appraised | designed | coached | collected | facilitated |
| audited | developed | counselled | compiled | formulated |
| balanced | established | demonstrated | generated | improved |
| budgeted | founded | diagnosed | monitored | oversaw |
| calculated | illustrated | educated | operated | pioneered |
| computed | initiated | expedited | organized | reduced (losses) |
| developed | instituted | facilitated | prepared | resolved (problems) |
| forecasted | introduced | familiarized | processed | spearheaded |
| managed | invented | guided | recorded | transformed |
| marketed | originated | motivated | screened | |
| planned | planned | referred | specified | |
| projected | revitalized | represented | systematized | |
| researched | | | tabulated | |

It's also appropriate to include postsecondary, community, and professional activities. (High school activities and accomplishments are not generally included.) Employers are interested in evidence that you are a well-rounded person. This section provides an opportunity to demonstrate leadership and interpersonal skills. Strive to use action statements. For example, instead of saying *Treasurer of business club*, explain more fully: *Collected dues, kept financial records, and paid bills while serving as treasurer of 35-member business management club.*

*Personal Data.* Today's résumés omit personal data, such as birth date, marital status, height, weight, and religious affiliation. Such information doesn't relate to genuine occupational qualifications, and recruiters are legally barred from asking for such information. Some job-seekers do, however, include hobbies or interests (such as skiing or photography) that might grab the recruiter's attention or serve as conversation starters. Naturally, you wouldn't mention dangerous pastimes (such as bungee jumping or sports car racing) or time-consuming interests. But you should indicate your willingness to travel or to relocate, since many companies will be interested.

**Omit personal data not related to job qualifications.**

*References.* Listing references on a résumé is favoured by some recruiters and opposed by others.[23] Such a list takes up valuable space. Moreover, references are not normally instrumental in securing an interview—few companies check them before the interview. Instead, recruiters prefer that a candidate bring to the interview a list of individuals willing to discuss her or his qualifications. If you do list them, use

**References are unnecessary for the résumé, but they should be available for the interview.**

parallel form. For example, if you show a title for one person (*Professor, Dr., Mrs.*), show titles for all. Include addresses and telephone numbers.

Whether or not you include references on your résumé, you should have their names available when you begin your job search. Ask three to five instructors or previous employers whether they will be willing to answer inquiries regarding your qualifications for employment. Be sure, however, to provide them with an opportunity to refuse. No reference is better than a negative one. Do not include personal or character references, such as friends, family, or neighbours, because recruiters rarely consult them. Companies are more interested in the opinions of objective individuals.

One final note: personnel officers see little reason for including the statement *References furnished upon request.* "It's like saying the sun comes up every morning," remarked one human resources professional.[24]

## PREPARING FOR COMPUTER SCANNING

Thus far we've aimed our résumé advice at human readers. However, the first reader of your résumé may well be a computer. An increasing number of companies are now using electronic applicant-tracking (also called *résumé management*) systems to reduce hiring costs, make résumé information more accessible, and rank candidates.[25] These systems scan incoming résumés, as shown in Figure 16.8.

### Making Your Résumé Computer-Friendly

Before you send your résumé, you should learn whether the recipient uses scanning software. One simple way to find out is to call any company where you plan to apply and ask if it scans résumés electronically. If you can't get a clear answer and you have even the slightest suspicion that your résumé might be read electronically, you'll be smart to prepare a plain, scannable version.

A scannable résumé must sacrifice many of the graphics possibilities that wise writers employ. Computers aren't impressed by graphics; they prefer plain "vanilla" résumés—free of graphics and fancy fonts. To make a computer-friendly "vanilla" résumé, you'll want to apply the following suggestions about its physical appearance.

- **Avoid unusual typefaces, underlining, and italics.** Moreover, don't use boxing, shading, or other graphics to highlight text. These features don't scan well. Most applicant-tracking programs, however, can accurately read bold print, solid bullets, and asterisks.

- **Use 10- to 14-point type.** Because touching letters or unusual fonts are likely to be misread, it's safest to use a large, well-known font, such as 12-point Times Roman or Helvetica. This may mean that your résumé will require two pages. After printing, inspect your résumé to see whether any letters touch—especially in your name.

- **Use smooth white paper, black ink, and quality printing.** Avoid coloured and textured papers as well as dot-matrix printing.

- **Be sure that your name is the first line on the page.** Don't use fancy layouts that may confuse a scanner.

- **Provide white space.** To ensure separation of words and categories, leave plenty of white space. For example, instead of using parentheses to enclose a telephone area code, insert blank spaces, such as 514 799-2415. Leave blank lines around headings.

- **Avoid double columns.** When listing job duties, skills, computer programs, and so forth, don't tabulate items into two- or three-column lists. Scanners read across and may convert tables into gobbledygook.

**Computer-friendly résumés are free of graphics and fancy fonts.**

## FIGURE 16.8  What a Résumé-Scanning Program Does

Reads résumé with scanner

Identifies job categories and ranks applicants

1  2  3

Generates letters of rejection or interview offers

OFFER

Stores information or actual résumé image for future searches

Applicant-tracking programs scan incoming résumés and store the information for future hiring.

- **Don't fold or staple your résumé.** Send it in a large envelope so that you can avoid folds. Words that appear on folds may not be scanned correctly. Avoid staples because the indentions left after they are removed may cause pages to stick.
- **Use abbreviations carefully.** Minimize unfamiliar abbreviations, but maximize easily recognized abbreviations—especially those within your field, such as CAD, COBRA, or JIT. When in doubt, though, spell it out! Computers are less addled by whole words.
- **Include all your addresses and telephone numbers.** Be sure your résumé contains your e-mail address, as well as your land address, telephone numbers, and fax number, if available.
- **Be prepared to send your résumé in ASCII.** Pronounced "AS kee," this format offers text only and is immediately readable by all computer programs. It eliminates italics, bold, underlining, and unusual keyboard characters.

## Emphasizing Keywords

In addition to paying attention to the physical appearance of your résumé, you must also be concerned with keywords. These are usually nouns that describe what an employer wants. Suppose a supervisor at Nike wants to hire an administrative assistant with special proficiencies. That supervisor might submit the following keywords to the Nike applicant-tracking system: *Administrative Assistant, Computer Skills, Microsoft Word, Self-Starter, Report Writing, Proofreading, Communication Skills.* The system would then search through all the résumés on file to see which ones best match the requirements.

Joyce Lain Kennedy, nationally syndicated career columnist and co-author of *Electronic Résumé Revolution,*[26] suggests using a keyword summary. This list of keyword descriptors immediately follows your name and address on your résumé. A keyword summary, as illustrated in Figure 16.9, should contain your targeted job title and alternative labels, as well as previous job titles, skills, software programs, and selected jargon known in your field. It concentrates on nouns rather than on verbs or adjectives.

To construct your summary, go through your core résumé and mark all relevant nouns. Also try to imagine what eight to ten words an employer might use to describe the job you want. Then select the 25 best words for your summary. Because interpersonal traits are often requested by employers, consult Figure 16.9. It shows

Keywords are usually nouns that describe specific candidate traits or job requirements.

**FIGURE 16.9  Interpersonal Keywords Most Requested by Employers Using Résumé-Scanning Software***

| | | | |
|---|---|---|---|
| Ability to delegate | Creative | Leadership | Self-accountable |
| Ability to implement | Customer-oriented | Multitasking | Self-managing |
| Ability to plan | Detail-minded | Open communication | Setting priorities |
| Ability to train | Ethical | Open-minded | Supportive |
| Accurate | Flexible | Oral communication | Takes initiative |
| Adaptable | Follow instructions | Organizational skills | Team building |
| Aggressive worker | Follow through | Persuasive | Team player |
| Analytical ability | Follow up | Problem solving | Tenacious |
| Assertive | High energy | Public speaking | Willing to travel |
| Communication skills | Industrious | Results-oriented | |
| Competitive | Innovative | Safety conscious | |

*Reported by Resumix, a leading producer of résumé-scanning software.

the most frequently requested interpersonal traits, as reported by Resumix, one of the leaders in résumé-scanning software.

You may entitle your list *Keyword Summary, Keyword Profile,* or *Keyword Index.* Here's an example of a possible keyword summary for a junior accountant:

**A computer-friendly résumé may contain a keyword summary filled with words (usually nouns) that describe the job or candidate.**

**Keyword Summary**
Accountant: Public. Junior. Staff. Dipl. Durham College—Business Administration. BA, York University—Accounting. Payables. Receivables. Payroll Experience. Quarterly Reports. Unemployment Reports. Communication Skills. Computer Skills. Excel. Microsoft Word. PCs. Mainframes. Internet. Web. Networks. J. D. Edwards Software. Ability to learn software. Accurate. Dean's List. Award of Merit. Team player. Willing to travel. Relocate.

After an introductory keyword summary, your résumé should contain the standard parts discussed in this chapter. Remember that the keyword section merely helps ensure that your résumé will be selected for inspection. Then human eyes take over. Therefore, you'll want to observe the other writing tips you've learned to make your résumé attractive and persuasive. Figures 16.10 through 16.12 show additional examples of chronological and combination résumés. Notice that the scannable résumé in Figure 16.13 is not drastically different from the others. It does, however, include a keyword summary.

## Preparing an Online, Hypertext Résumé

**An online résumé contains hypertext links to work samples or a portfolio of additional information.**

To give your résumé life and make it stand out from others, you might wish to prepare an online résumé. This is actually an HTML (Hypertext Markup Language) document located at a Web site. Posting an online résumé has some distinct advantages—and a few disadvantages.

On the plus side, merely preparing an online résumé suggests that you have exceptional technical ability. (You would, of course, give credit for any borrowed graphics or code.) An online résumé can be viewed whenever it is convenient for an

## FIGURE 16.10 Enhanced Résumé

Although Jeffrey had little paid work experience off campus, his résumé looks impressive because of his relevant summer, campus, and extern experiences. He describes specific achievements related to finance, his career goal. This version of his résumé is enhanced with desktop publishing features because he knows it will not be scanned.

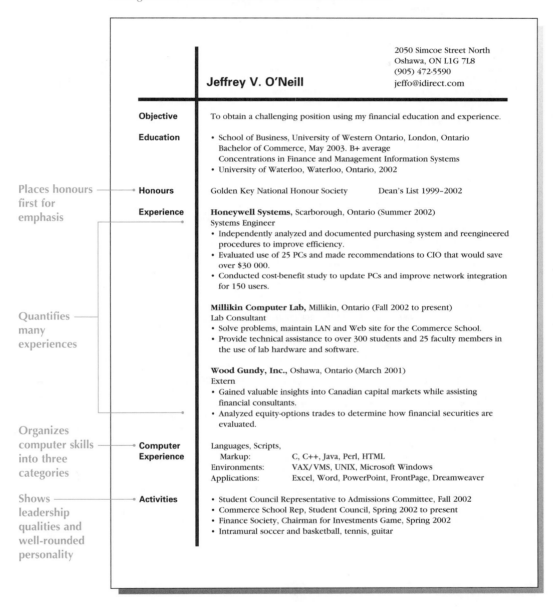

**Jeffrey V. O'Neill**

2050 Simcoe Street North
Oshawa, ON L1G 7L8
(905) 472-5590
jeffo@idirect.com

**Objective**    To obtain a challenging position using my financial education and experience.

**Education**
- School of Business, University of Western Ontario, London, Ontario
  Bachelor of Commerce, May 2003. B+ average
  Concentrations in Finance and Management Information Systems
- University of Waterloo, Waterloo, Ontario, 2002

*Places honours first for emphasis →*

**Honours**    Golden Key National Honour Society      Dean's List 1999–2002

**Experience**

**Honeywell Systems,** Scarborough, Ontario (Summer 2002)
Systems Engineer
- Independently analyzed and documented purchasing system and reengineered procedures to improve efficiency.
- Evaluated use of 25 PCs and made recommendations to CIO that would save over $30 000.
- Conducted cost-benefit study to update PCs and improve network integration for 150 users.

**Millikin Computer Lab,** Millikin, Ontario (Fall 2002 to present)
Lab Consultant
- Solve problems, maintain LAN and Web site for the Commerce School.
- Provide technical assistance to over 300 students and 25 faculty members in the use of lab hardware and software.

**Wood Gundy, Inc.,** Oshawa, Ontario (March 2001)
Extern
- Gained valuable insights into Canadian capital markets while assisting financial consultants.
- Analyzed equity-options trades to determine how financial securities are evaluated.

*Quantifies many experiences →*

*Organizes computer skills into three categories →*

**Computer Experience**

Languages, Scripts,
   Markup:      C, C++, Java, Perl, HTML
Environments:      VAX/VMS, UNIX, Microsoft Windows
Applications:      Excel, Word, PowerPoint, FrontPage, Dreamweaver

*Shows leadership qualities and well-rounded personality →*

**Activities**
- Student Council Representative to Admissions Committee, Fall 2002
- Commerce School Rep, Student Council, Spring 2002 to present
- Finance Society, Chairman for Investments Game, Spring 2002
- Intramural soccer and basketball, tennis, guitar

---

employer, and it can be seen by many individuals in an organization without circulating a paper copy. But the real reason for preparing an online résumé is that it can become an electronic portfolio with links to examples of your work.

You could include clickable links to reports you have written, summaries of projects completed, a complete list of your course work, letters of recommendation (with permissions from your recommenders), and extra information about your work experience. An advanced portfolio might include links to electronic copies of your artwork, film projects, blueprints, and photographs of classwork that might

**CHAPTER 16**
Employment Communication
**541**

## FIGURE 16.11 Combination Résumé

Rick's résumé responds to an advertisement specifying skills for a staff accountant. He uses the combination format to allow him to highlight the skills his education and limited experience have provided. To make the résumé look professional, he uses the italics, bold, and scalable font features of his word processing program.

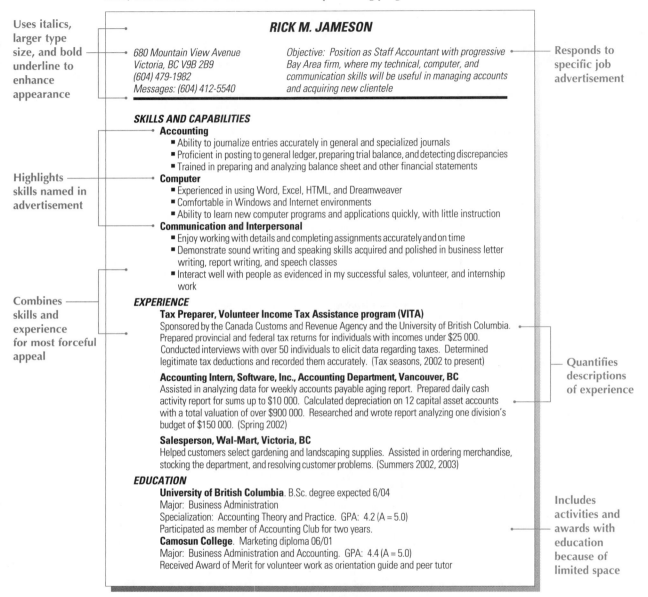

Uses italics, larger type size, and bold underline to enhance appearance

Highlights skills named in advertisement

Combines skills and experience for most forceful appeal

Responds to specific job advertisement

Quantifies descriptions of experience

Includes activities and awards with education because of limited space

### RICK M. JAMESON

680 Mountain View Avenue
Victoria, BC V9B 2B9
(604) 479-1982
Messages: (604) 412-5540

Objective: Position as Staff Accountant with progressive Bay Area firm, where my technical, computer, and communication skills will be useful in managing accounts and acquiring new clientele

#### SKILLS AND CAPABILITIES

**Accounting**
- Ability to journalize entries accurately in general and specialized journals
- Proficient in posting to general ledger, preparing trial balance, and detecting discrepancies
- Trained in preparing and analyzing balance sheet and other financial statements

**Computer**
- Experienced in using Word, Excel, HTML, and Dreamweaver
- Comfortable in Windows and Internet environments
- Ability to learn new computer programs and applications quickly, with little instruction

**Communication and Interpersonal**
- Enjoy working with details and completing assignments accurately and on time
- Demonstrate sound writing and speaking skills acquired and polished in business letter writing, report writing, and speech classes
- Interact well with people as evidenced in my successful sales, volunteer, and internship work

#### EXPERIENCE

**Tax Preparer, Volunteer Income Tax Assistance program (VITA)**
Sponsored by the Canada Customs and Revenue Agency and the University of British Columbia. Prepared provincial and federal tax returns for individuals with incomes under $25 000. Conducted interviews with over 50 individuals to elicit data regarding taxes. Determined legitimate tax deductions and recorded them accurately. (Tax seasons, 2002 to present)

**Accounting Intern, Software, Inc., Accounting Department, Vancouver, BC**
Assisted in analyzing data for weekly accounts payable aging report. Prepared daily cash activity report for sums up to $10 000. Calculated depreciation on 12 capital asset accounts with a total valuation of over $900 000. Researched and wrote report analyzing one division's budget of $150 000. (Spring 2002)

**Salesperson, Wal-Mart, Victoria, BC**
Helped customers select gardening and landscaping supplies. Assisted in ordering merchandise, stocking the department, and resolving customer problems. (Summers 2002, 2003)

#### EDUCATION

**University of British Columbia**. B.Sc. degree expected 6/04
Major: Business Administration
Specialization: Accounting Theory and Practice. GPA: 4.2 (A = 5.0)
Participated as member of Accounting Club for two years.
**Camosun College**. Marketing diploma 06/01
Major: Business Administration and Accounting. GPA: 4.4 (A = 5.0)
Received Award of Merit for volunteer work as orientation guide and peer tutor

otherwise be difficult to share with potential employers. Moreover, you can include razzle-dazzle effects such as colour, animation, sound, and graphics. An online résumé provides ample opportunity to show off your creative talents, but only if the position calls for creativity.

On the minus side, online résumés must be more generic than print résumés. They cannot be altered easily if you apply for different positions. Moreover, they present a security problem unless password protected. You may want to include only an e-mail address instead of offering your address and telephone number. Perhaps

## FIGURE 16.12  Chronological Résumé

Because Rachel has many years of experience and seeks high-level employment, she focuses on her experience. Notice how she includes specific achievements and quantifies them whenever possible.

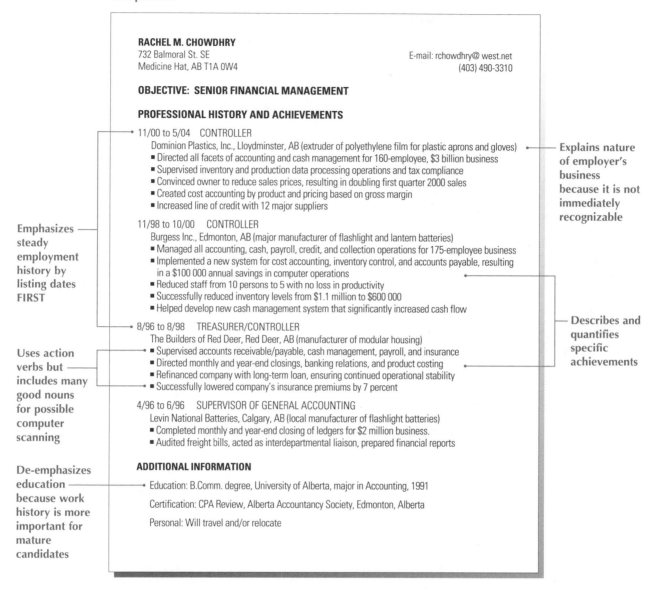

Emphasizes steady employment history by listing dates FIRST

Uses action verbs but includes many good nouns for possible computer scanning

De-emphasizes education because work history is more important for mature candidates

Explains nature of employer's business because it is not immediately recognizable

Describes and quantifies specific achievements

**RACHEL M. CHOWDHRY**
732 Balmoral St. SE
Medicine Hat, AB T1A 0W4

E-mail: rchowdhry@ west.net
(403) 490-3310

**OBJECTIVE:  SENIOR FINANCIAL MANAGEMENT**

**PROFESSIONAL HISTORY AND ACHIEVEMENTS**

11/00 to 5/04   CONTROLLER
Dominion Plastics, Inc., Lloydminster, AB (extruder of polyethylene film for plastic aprons and gloves)
- Directed all facets of accounting and cash management for 160-employee, $3 billion business
- Supervised inventory and production data processing operations and tax compliance
- Convinced owner to reduce sales prices, resulting in doubling first quarter 2000 sales
- Created cost accounting by product and pricing based on gross margin
- Increased line of credit with 12 major suppliers

11/98 to 10/00   CONTROLLER
Burgess Inc., Edmonton, AB (major manufacturer of flashlight and lantern batteries)
- Managed all accounting, cash, payroll, credit, and collection operations for 175-employee business
- Implemented a new system for cost accounting, inventory control, and accounts payable, resulting in a $100 000 annual savings in computer operations
- Reduced staff from 10 persons to 5 with no loss in productivity
- Successfully reduced inventory levels from $1.1 million to $600 000
- Helped develop new cash management system that significantly increased cash flow

8/96 to 8/98   TREASURER/CONTROLLER
The Builders of Red Deer, Red Deer, AB (manufacturer of modular housing)
- Supervised accounts receivable/payable, cash management, payroll, and insurance
- Directed monthly and year-end closings, banking relations, and product costing
- Refinanced company with long-term loan, ensuring continued operational stability
- Successfully lowered company's insurance premiums by 7 percent

4/96 to 6/96   SUPERVISOR OF GENERAL ACCOUNTING
Levin National Batteries, Calgary, AB (local manufacturer of flashlight batteries)
- Completed monthly and year-end closing of ledgers for $2 million business.
- Audited freight bills, acted as interdepartmental liaison, prepared financial reports

**ADDITIONAL INFORMATION**

Education: B.Comm. degree, University of Alberta, major in Accounting, 1991

Certification: CPA Review, Alberta Accountancy Society, Edmonton, Alberta

Personal: Will travel and/or relocate

the best approach is to submit a traditional résumé and letter of application and treat your online résumé only as a portfolio of your work.

## Applying the Final Touches

Because your résumé is probably the most important message you will ever write, you'll revise it many times. With so much information in concentrated form and with so much riding on its outcome, your résumé demands careful polishing, proofreading, and critiquing.

# FIGURE 16.13 Computer-Friendly Résumé

Casandra prepared this "vanilla" resume (free of graphics and fancy formatting) so that it would scan well if read by a computer. Notice that she begins with a keyword summary that contains job titles, skills, traits, and other descriptive words. She hopes that some of these keywords will match those submitted by an employer. To improve accurate scanning, she avoids italics, vertical and horizontal lines, and double columns.

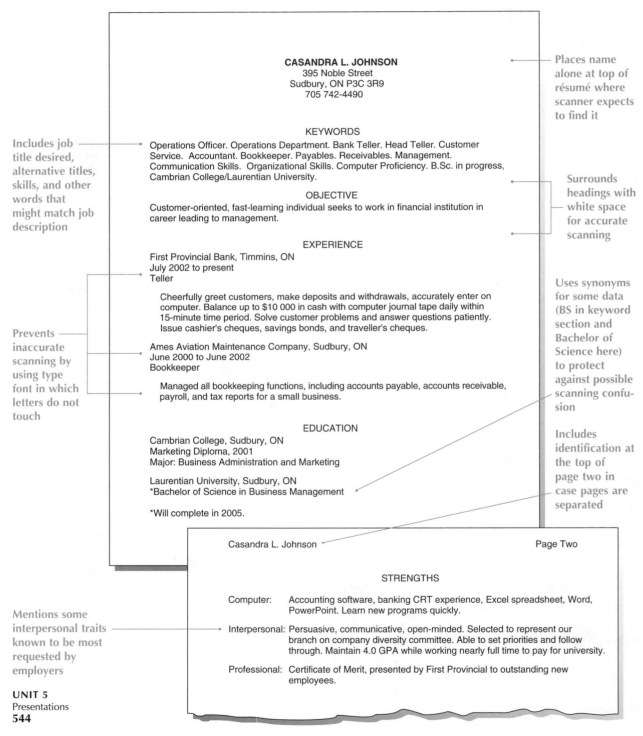

Places name alone at top of résumé where scanner expects to find it

Includes job title desired, alternative titles, skills, and other words that might match job description

Surrounds headings with white space for accurate scanning

Uses synonyms for some data (BS in keyword section and Bachelor of Science here) to protect against possible scanning confusion

Prevents inaccurate scanning by using type font in which letters do not touch

Includes identification at the top of page two in case pages are separated

Mentions some interpersonal traits known to be most requested by employers

**CASANDRA L. JOHNSON**
395 Noble Street
Sudbury, ON P3C 3R9
705 742-4490

KEYWORDS
Operations Officer. Operations Department. Bank Teller. Head Teller. Customer Service. Accountant. Bookkeeper. Payables. Receivables. Management. Communication Skills. Organizational Skills. Computer Proficiency. B.Sc. in progress, Cambrian College/Laurentian University.

OBJECTIVE
Customer-oriented, fast-learning individual seeks to work in financial institution in career leading to management.

EXPERIENCE
First Provincial Bank, Timmins, ON
July 2002 to present
Teller

Cheerfully greet customers, make deposits and withdrawals, accurately enter on computer. Balance up to $10 000 in cash with computer journal tape daily within 15-minute time period. Solve customer problems and answer questions patiently. Issue cashier's cheques, savings bonds, and traveller's cheques.

Ames Aviation Maintenance Company, Sudbury, ON
June 2000 to June 2002
Bookkeeper

Managed all bookkeeping functions, including accounts payable, accounts receivable, payroll, and tax reports for a small business.

EDUCATION
Cambrian College, Sudbury, ON
Marketing Diploma, 2001
Major: Business Administration and Marketing

Laurentian University, Sudbury, ON
*Bachelor of Science in Business Management

*Will complete in 2005.

Casandra L. Johnson                                    Page Two

STRENGTHS

Computer:       Accounting software, banking CRT experience, Excel spreadsheet, Word, PowerPoint. Learn new programs quickly.

Interpersonal: Persuasive, communicative, open-minded. Selected to represent our branch on company diversity committee. Able to set priorities and follow through. Maintain 4.0 GPA while working nearly full time to pay for university.

Professional:  Certificate of Merit, presented by First Provincial to outstanding new employees.

As you revise, be certain to verify all the facts, particularly those involving your previous employment and education. Don't be caught in a mistake, or worse, distortion of previous jobs and dates of employment. These items likely will be checked. And the consequences of puffing up a résumé with deception or flat-out lies are simply not worth the risk. Other ethical traps you'll want to avoid are described in the accompanying Ethical Insights box.

In addition to being well written, a résumé must be carefully formatted and meticulously proofread.

As you continue revising, look for other ways to improve your résumé. For example, consider consolidating headings. By condensing your information into as few headings as possible, you'll produce a clean, professional-looking document. Study other résumés for valuable formatting ideas. Ask yourself what graphics highlighting techniques you can use to improve readability: capitalization, underlining, indenting, and bulleting. Experiment with headings and styles to achieve a pleasing, easy-to-read message. Moreover, look for ways to eliminate wordiness. For example, instead of *Supervised two employees who worked at the counter*, try *Supervised two counter employees.* Review Chapter 7 for more tips.

Above all, make your résumé look professional. Avoid anything humorous or "cute," such as a help-wanted poster with your name or picture inside. Eliminate the personal pronoun *I*. The abbreviated, objective style of a résumé precludes the use of personal pronouns. Use white, off-white, or buff-coloured heavy bond paper (24-pound) and a first-rate printer.

After revising, proofread, proofread, and proofread again: for spelling and mechanics, for content, and for format. Then, have a knowledgeable friend or relative proofread it again. This is one document that must be perfect.

Because résumés must be perfect, they should be proofread many times.

By now you may be thinking that you'd like to hire someone to write your résumé. Don't. First, you know yourself better than anyone else could know you. Second, you'll end up with either a generic or a one-time résumé. A generic résumé in today's highly competitive job market will lose out to a targeted résumé nine times out of ten. Equally useless is a one-time résumé aimed at a single job. What if you don't get that job? Because you will need to revise your résumé many times as you seek a variety of jobs, be prepared to write (and rewrite) it yourself.

A final word about résumé-writing services. Some tend to produce eye-catching, elaborate documents with lofty language, fancy borders, and fuzzy thinking. Here's an example of empty writing: "Seeking a position which will utilize academic achievements and hands-on experience while providing for career-development opportunities."[27] Save your money and buy a good interview suit instead.

## FAXING OR E-MAILING YOUR RÉSUMÉ

In this hurry-up world, employers increasingly want information immediately. If you are asked to fax or e-mail your résumé, take a second look at it. The key to success is SPACE. Without it, letters and characters blur. Underlines blend with the words above, and bold print may look like an ink blot.[28] How can you improve your chances of making a good impression when you must fax or e-mail your résumé?

Résumés to be faxed should have ample space between letters, be printed in 12-point or larger font, and avoid underlines.

If you are faxing your printed résumé, select a font with adequate space between each character. Thinner fonts—such as Times, Palatino, New Century Schoolbook, Courier, and Bookman—are clearer than thicker ones. Use a 12-point or larger font, and avoid underlines, which may look broken or choppy when faxed. To be safe, get a transmission report to ensure that all pages were transmitted satisfactorily. Finally, follow up with your polished, printed résumé.

If you are e-mailing your résumé, you may wish to prepare an ASCII version (text only). It will eliminate bold, italics, underlining, tabulated indentions, and unusual characters. To prevent lines from wrapping at awkward spots, keep your line length to

## Are Inflated Résumés Worth the Risk?

A résumé is expected to showcase a candidate's strengths and minimize weaknesses. For this reason, recruiters expect a certain degree of self-promotion. But some résumé writers step over the line that separates honest self-marketing from deceptive half-truths and flat-out lies. Distorting facts on a résumé is unethical; lying is illegal. And either practice can destroy a career.

Given the competitive job market, it might be tempting to puff up your résumé. And you wouldn't be alone in telling fibs or outright whoppers. One study found that one in seven job applicants makes false claims about education.[29] Although recruiters can't check everything, most will verify previous employment and education before hiring candidates. Over half will require official transcripts.

After hiring, the checking process may continue. At one of the nation's top accounting firms, the human resources director described the posthiring routine: "If we find a discrepancy in GPA or prior experience due to an honest mistake, we meet with the new hire to hear an explanation. But if it wasn't a mistake, we terminate the person immediately. Unfortunately, we've had to do that too often."[30]

No job-seeker wants to be in the unhappy position of explaining résumé errors or defending misrep-resentation. Avoiding the following common problems can keep you off the hot seat:

- **Inflated education, grades, or honours.** Some job candidates claim diplomas or degrees from colleges or universities when in fact they merely attended classes. Others increase their grade-point averages or claim fictitious honours. Any such dishonest reporting is grounds for dismissal when discovered.

- **Enhanced job titles.** Wishing to elevate their status, some applicants misrepresent their titles. For example, one technician called himself a "programmer" when he had actually programmed only one project for his boss. A mail clerk who assumed added responsibilities conferred upon herself the title of "supervisor." Even when the description seems accurate, it's unethical to list any title not officially granted.

- **Puffed-up accomplishments.** Some job-seekers inflate their employment experience or achievements. One clerk, eager to make her photocopying duties sound more important, said that she assisted the *vice president in communicating and distributing employee directives*. One graduate who spent the better part of six months

---

**Résumés that are sent by e-mail transmit best as ASCII (text-only) files without tabs, underlines, italics, bold, or unusual characters.**

65 characters or less. You can, of course, transmit a fully formatted, attractive résumé if you send it as an attachment and your receiver is using a compatible e-mail program.

Nearly everyone writes a résumé by adapting a model, such as those in Figures 16.3 through 16.5 and 16.10 through 16.13. The chronological résumé for Rachel shown in Figure 16.12 is typical of candidates with considerable working experience. Although she describes four positions that span a 14-year period, she manages to fit her résumé on one page. However, two-page résumés are justified for people with long work histories.

As you prepare to write your current résumé, consult the following checklist to review the job search process and important résumé-writing techniques.

## CHECKLIST FOR WRITING A PERSUASIVE RÉSUMÉ

### Preparation

 **Research the job market.** Learn about available jobs, common qualifications, and potential employers. The best résumés are targeted for specific jobs with specific companies.

watching rented videos on his VCR described the activity as *Independent Film Study*. The latter statement may have helped win an interview, but it lost him the job.[31] In addition to avoiding puffery, guard against taking sole credit for achievements that required many people. When recruiters suspect dubious claims on résumés, they nail applicants with specific—and often embarrassing—questions during their interviews.[32]

- **Altered employment dates.** Some candidates extend the dates of employment to hide unimpressive jobs or to cover up periods of unemployment and illness. Let's say that several years ago Cindy was unemployed for 14 months between working for Company A and being hired by Company B. To make her employment history look better, she adds seven months to her tenure with Company A and seven months to Company B. Now her employment history has no gaps, but her résumé is dishonest and represents a potential landmine for her.

The employment process can easily lure you into ethical traps, such as those described in Chapter 1. Beware of these specific temptations:

- **The relative-filth trap:** "A little fudging on my GPA is nothing compared with the degrees that some people buy in degree mills."

- **The rationalization trap:** "I deserve to call myself 'manager' because that's what I really did."

- **The self-deception trap:** "Giving myself a certificate from the institute is OK because I really intended to finish the program, but I got sick."

Falling into these ethical traps risks your entire employment future. If your honest qualifications aren't good enough to get you the job you want, start working now to improve them.

**Career Application**

As a class, discuss the ethics of writing résumés. What's the difference between honest self-marketing and deception? What are some examples from your experience? Where could college students go wrong in preparing their résumés? Is a new employee "home free" if an inflated résumé is not detected in the hiring process? Are job candidates obligated to describe every previous job on a résumé? How can candidates improve an unimpressive résumé without resorting to "puffing it up"?

✓ **Analyze your strengths.** Determine what aspects of your education, experience, and personal characteristics will be assets to prospective employers.

✓ **Study models.** Look at other résumés for formatting and element placement ideas. Experiment with headings and styles to achieve an artistic, readable product.

## Heading and Objective

✓ **Identify yourself.** List your name, address, and telephone number. Skip the word *résumé*.

✓ **Include a career objective for a targeted job.** If this résumé is intended for a specific job, include a statement tailored to it (*Objective: Cost accounting position in the petroleum industry*).

## Education

✓ **Name your diploma or degree, date of graduation, and institution.** Emphasize your education if your experience is limited.

✓ **List your major and GPA.** Give information about your studies, but don't inventory all your courses.

# Maritime Life Revisited

According to Maritime Life president and CEO Bill Black, "We strive to be an excellent employer and this achievement—along with high satisfaction results on our recent employment survey—confirms that our company is an attractive workplace where talented people want to work."

Maritime Life has been conducting employee-satisfaction surveys for more than 25 years and offers flexible benefit programs, attractive offices with day-care and workout facilities, on-site masseuses, well-appointed corporate dining rooms with a stunning view of the sailboats on Halifax's Northwest Arm, and a reputation for innovation. With its career-investment account, the company provides an amount equivalent to a percentage of an employee's salary—2.5 percent for managers and 4 percent for administrative staff—for career training, even if not related directly to the employee's current job.[33]

Ranked among the Top 50 best companies to work for in Canada for an impressive fourth consecutive year in 2003, Maritime Life is the only company on the list that is headquartered in Halifax. Although the Top 50 companies prove to provide higher pay and other impressive benefits, overall employee morale continues

to be the number one factor that makes these companies truly exceptional among their competitors and peers.

In addition to being in the Top 50, Maritime Life is also among Canada's Top 100 Employers according to Mediacorp Canada Inc. The list showcases companies with the country's best practices in managing people. To be considered for this list, companies must be expanding and hiring new people. Mediacorp also looks at how organizations communicate with their employees in terms of personal and corporate progress, whether or not the employment benefits are exceptional or the physical work environment is stimulating, and how involved the organization is with its community.[34]

## CRITICAL THINKING

- How important should employee-satisfaction ratings be to job-seekers? How can job-seekers find this information?
- In your own job search, would you consider such things as the physical work environment and professional development opportunities in making your decisions? Why or why not?

**www.maritimelife.ca**

## Work Experience

✓ **Itemize your jobs.** Start with your most recent job. Give the employer's name and city, dates of employment (month, year), and most significant job title.

✓ **Describe your experience.** Use action verbs to summarize achievements and skills relevant to your targeted job.

✓ **Promote your "soft" skills.** Give evidence of communication, management, and interpersonal talents. Employers want more than empty assurances; try to quantify your skills and accomplishments (*Collaborated with six-member task force in producing 20-page mission statement*).

## Special Skills, Achievements, and Awards

✓ **Highlight computer skills.** Remember that nearly all employers seek employees who are proficient in using the Internet, e-mail, word processing, databases, and spreadsheets.

✓ **Show that you are a well-rounded individual.** List awards, experiences, and extracurricular activities—particularly if they demonstrate leadership, teamwork, reliability, loyalty, industry, initiative, efficiency, and self-sufficiency.

## Final Tips

✓ **Consider omitting references.** Have a list of references available for the interview, but don't include them or refer to them unless you have a specific reason to do so.

✓ **Look for ways to condense your data.** Omit all street addresses except your own. Consolidate your headings. Study models and experiment with formats to find the most readable and efficient groupings.

✓ **Double-check for parallel phrasing.** Be sure that all entries have balanced construction, such as similar verb forms (*Organized files, trained assistants, scheduled events*).

✓ **Make your résumé scannable.** If there's a chance it will be read by a computer, use a common font, remove graphics, and consider adding a keyword summary.

✓ **Project professionalism and quality.** Avoid personal pronouns and humour. Use 24-pound bond paper and a high-quality printer.

✓ **Proofread, proofread, proofread.** Make this document perfect by proofreading at least three times.

## THE PERSUASIVE LETTER OF APPLICATION

To accompany your résumé, you'll need a persuasive letter of application (also called a *cover letter*). The letter of application has three purposes: (1) introducing the résumé, (2) highlighting your strengths in terms of benefits to the reader, and (3) gaining an interview. In many ways your letter of application is a sales letter; it sells your talents and tries to beat the competition. It will, accordingly, include many of the techniques you learned for sales messages (Chapter 10).

5

Letters of application introduce résumés, relate writer strengths to reader benefits, and seek an interview.

Personnel professionals disagree on how long to make the letter of application. Many prefer short letters with no more than four paragraphs; instead of concentrating on the letter, these readers focus on the résumé. Others desire longer letters that supply more information, thus giving them a better opportunity to evaluate a candidate's qualifications. The latter personnel professionals argue that hiring and training new employees is expensive and time-consuming; therefore, they welcome extra data to guide them in making the best choice the first time. Follow your judgment in writing a brief or a longer letter of application. If you feel, for example, that you need space to explain in more detail what you can do for a prospective employer, do so.

Regardless of its length, a letter of application should have three primary parts: (1) an opening that gains attention, (2) a body that builds interest and reduces resistance, and (3) a closing that motivates action.

## Gaining Attention in the Opening

The first step in gaining the interest of your reader is addressing that individual by name. Rather than sending your letter to the "Personnel Manager" or "Human Resources Department," try to identify the name of the appropriate individual. Make it a rule to call the organization for the correct spelling and the complete address. This personal touch distinguishes your letter and demonstrates your serious interest.

How you open your letter of application depends largely on whether the application is solicited or unsolicited. If an employment position has been announced and

The opener in a letter of application gains attention by addressing the receiver by name.

applicants are being solicited, you can use a direct approach. If you do not know whether a position is open and you are prospecting for a job, use an indirect approach. Whether direct or indirect, the opening should attract the attention of the reader. Strive for openings that are more imaginative than *Please consider this letter an application for the position of . . .* or *I would like to apply for . . . .*

*Openings for Solicited Jobs.* Here are some of the best techniques to open a letter of application for a job that has been announced:

- **Refer to the name of an employee in the company.** Remember that employers always hope to hire known quantities rather than complete strangers:

  Mitchell Sims, a member of your Customer Service Department, told me that IntriPlex is seeking an experienced customer service representative. The attached summary of my qualifications demonstrates my preparation for this position.

  At the suggestion of Ms. Jennifer Larson of your Human Resources Department, I submit my qualifications for the position of staffing coordinator.

**Openers for solicited jobs refer to the source of the information, the job title, and qualifications for the position.**

- **Refer to the source of your information precisely.** If you are answering an advertisement, include the exact position advertised and the name and date of the publication. For large organizations it's also wise to mention the section of the newspaper where the ad appeared:

  Your advertisement in Section C-3 of the June 1 *Daily News* for an accounting administrator greatly appeals to me. With my accounting training and computer experience, I believe I could serve Quad Graphics well.

  The September 10 issue of *The Globe and Mail* reports that you are seeking a mature, organized, and reliable administrative assistant with excellent communication skills.

  Susan Butler, placement director at Durham College, told me that DataTech has an opening for a technical writer with knowledge of Web design and graphics.

- **Refer to the job title and describe how your qualifications fit the requirements.** Personnel directors are looking for a match between an applicant's credentials and the job needs:

  Will an honours graduate with a degree in recreation and two years of part-time experience organizing social activities for a convalescent hospital qualify for your position of activity director?

  Because of my specialized training in computerized accounting at the University of Regina, I feel confident that I have the qualifications you described in your advertisement for a cost accountant trainee.

**Openers for unsolicited jobs show interest in and knowledge of the company, as well as spotlighting reader benefits.**

*Openings for Unsolicited Jobs.* If you are unsure whether a position actually exists, you may wish to use a more persuasive opening. Since your goal is to convince this person to read on, try one of the following techniques:

- **Demonstrate interest in and knowledge of the reader's business.** Show the personnel director that you have done your research and that this organization is more than a mere name to you:

  Since Signa HealthNet, Inc., is organizing a new information management team for its recently established group insurance division, could you use the services of a well-trained information systems graduate who seeks to become a professional systems analyst?

- **Show how your special talents and background will benefit the company.**
  Personnel directors need to be convinced that you can do something for them:

  > Could your rapidly expanding publications division use the services of an editorial assistant who offers exceptional language skills, an honours degree from the University of Prince Edward Island, and two years' experience in producing a campus literary publication?

In applying for an advertised job, Nancy Sullivan James wrote the solicited letter of application shown in Figure 16.14. Notice that her opening identifies the position and the newspaper completely so that the reader knows exactly what advertisement Nancy means. More challenging are unsolicited letters of application, such as Donald Vinton's shown in Figure 16.15. Because he hopes to discover or create a job, his opening must grab the reader's attention immediately. To do that, he capitalizes on

**FIGURE 16.14** Solicited Letter of Application

Creates own stationery

**Nancy Sullivan James**

8011 Davies Road NW, Edmonton, AB T6E 4Z6

May 23, 2005

Addresses proper person by name and title

Ms. Kesha M. Scott
Manager, Human Resources
Premier Enterprises
57 Bedford Drive NE
Calgary, AB T3K 1L2

Dear Ms. Scott:

Your advertisement for an assistant product manager, appearing May 22 in Section C of the *Calgary Herald,* immediately caught my attention because my education and training closely parallel your needs.

*Identifies specific ad and job title*

Relates writer's experiences to job requirements

According to your advertisement, the job includes "assisting in the coordination of a wide range of marketing programs as well as analyzing sales results and tracking marketing budgets." A recent internship at Ventana Corporation introduced me to similar tasks. I assisted the marketing manager in analyzing the promotion, budget, and overall sales success of two products Ventana was evaluating. My ten-page report examined the nature of the current market, the products' life cycles, and the company's sales/profit return. In addition to this research, I helped formulate a product merchandising plan and answered consumers' questions at a local trade show. This brief but challenging introduction to product management convinced me that I could be successful and happy in a marketing career.

*Discusses experience*

Intensive course work in marketing and management, as well as proficiency in computer spreadsheets and databases, has given me the kind of marketing and computing training that Premier demands in a product manager. Moreover, I have had some retail sales experience and have been active in campus organizations. I'm confident that my academic preparation, my marketing experience, and my ability to work well with others qualify me for this position.

*Discusses schooling*

Refers reader to résumé

After you have examined the enclosed résumé for details of my qualifications, I would be happy to answer questions. Please call me to arrange an interview at your convenience so that we may discuss how my marketing, computing, and interpersonal skills could contribute to Premier Enterprises.

*Asks for interview and repeats main qualifications*

Sincerely,

*Nancy Sullivan James*

Nancy Sullivan James

Enclosure

551

**FIGURE 16.15** Unsolicited Letter of Application

2250 Tupper Street
Thunder Bay, ON P7A 4A5

May 29, 2005

Mr. Richard M. Jannis
Vice President, Operations
Sports World, Inc.
245 Maitland Street
London, ON N6B 2Y2

Dear Mr. Jannis:

Today's London Free Press reports that your organization plans to expand its
operations to include national distribution of sporting goods, and it occurs to me
that you will be needing highly motivated, self-starting sales representatives
and marketing managers. I have these significant qualifications to offer:

- Four years of formal training in business administration, including
  specialized courses in sales management, retailing, marketing promotion,
  and consumer behaviour.

- Practical experience in demonstrating and selling consumer products, as
  well as successful experience in telemarketing.

- A strong interest in most areas of sports and good communication skills
  (which helped me become a sportscaster at U.W.O.'s radio station CGNF).

I would like to talk with you about how I can put these qualifications, and
others summarized in the enclosed résumé, to work for Sports World as it
develops its national sales force. I'll call during the week of June 5 to discuss
your company's expansion plans and the opportunity for an interview.

Sincerely yours,

Donald W. Vinton

Enclosure

*Keeps letter brief to retain reader's attention*

*Refers to résumé*

*Shows knowledge of company and resourcefulness*

*Focuses on three most important qualities*

*Takes initiative for follow-up*

company information appearing in the newspaper. Notice, too, that Donald purposely kept his cover letter short and to the point because he anticipated that a busy executive would be unwilling to read a long, detailed letter.

Donald's unsolicited letter "prospects" for a job. Some job candidates feel that such letters may be even more productive than efforts to secure advertised jobs, since "prospecting" candidates face less competition.

## Building Interest in the Body

**The body of a letter of application should build interest, reduce resistance, and discuss relevant personal traits.**

Once you have captured the attention of the reader, you can use the body of the letter to build interest and reduce resistance. Keep in mind that your résumé emphasizes what you have *done*; your application letter stresses what you *can do* for the employer.

Your first goal is to relate your remarks to a specific position. If you are responding to an advertisement, you'll want to explain how your preparation and experience fill the stated requirements. If you are prospecting for a job, you may not know the exact requirements. Your employment research and knowledge of your field, however, should give you a reasonably good idea of what is expected for this position.

It's also important to emphasize reader benefits. In other words, you should describe your strong points in relation to the needs of the employer. In one employment survey many personnel professionals expressed the same view: "I want you to tell me what you can do for my organization. This is much more important to me than telling me what courses you took in college or what 'duties' you performed on your previous jobs."[35] Instead of *I have completed courses in business communication, report writing, and technical writing*, try this:

> Courses in business communication, report writing, and technical writing have helped me develop the research and writing skills required of your technical writers.

Choose your strongest qualifications and show how they fit the targeted job. And remember, students with little experience are better off spotlighting their education and its practical applications, as these candidates did:

> Because you seek an architect's apprentice with proven ability, I submit a drawing of mine that won second place in the Sinclair College drafting contest last year.

> Successfully transcribing over 100 letters and memos in my college transcription class gave me experience in converting the spoken word into the written word, an exacting communication skill demanded of your administrative assistants.

In the body of your letter, you'll also want to discuss relevant personal traits. Employers are looking for candidates who, among other things, are team players, take responsibility, show initiative, and learn easily. Notice how the following paragraph uses action verbs to paint a picture of a promising candidate:

**Employers seek employees who are team players, take responsibility, show initiative, and learn easily.**

> In addition to developing technical and academic skills at Dalhousie University, I have gained interpersonal, leadership, and organizational skills. As vice president of the business students' organization, I helped organize and supervise two successful fundraising events. These activities involved conceptualizing the tasks, motivating others to help, scheduling work sessions, and coordinating the efforts of 35 diverse students in reaching our goal. I enjoyed my success with these activities and look forward to applying such experience in your management trainee program.

Finally, in this section or the next, you should refer the reader to your résumé. Do so directly or as part of another statement, as shown here:

> Please refer to the attached résumé for additional information regarding my education, experience, and references.

> As you will notice from my résumé, I will graduate in June with a bachelor's degree in business administration.

## Motivating Action in the Closing

After presenting your case, you should conclude with a spur to action. This is where you ask for an interview. If you live in a distant city, you may request an employment application or an opportunity to be interviewed by the organization's nearest representative. However, never ask for the job. To do so would be presumptuous and naive. In requesting an interview, suggest reader benefits or review your strongest points. Sound sincere and appreciative. Remember to make it easy for the reader to

**The closing of a letter of application should motivate action and include a request for an interview.**

agree by supplying your telephone number and the best times to call you. And keep in mind that some personnel directors prefer that you take the initiative to call them. Here are possible endings:

> I hope this brief description of my qualifications and the additional information in my résumé indicate to you my genuine desire to put my skills in accounting to work for you. Please call me at (604) 655-4455 before 10 a.m. or after 3 p.m. to arrange an interview.

> To add to your staff an industrious, well-trained administrative assistant with proven word processing and communication skills, call me at (705) 555-5555 to arrange an interview. I can meet with you at any time convenient to your schedule.

> Next week, after you have examined the attached résumé, I will call you to discuss the possibility of arranging an interview.

## Final Tips

**Look for ways to reduce the overuse of "I."**

As you revise your letter of application, notice how many sentences begin with *I*. Although it's impossible to talk about yourself without using *I*, you can reduce "I" domination with this writing technique. Make activities and outcomes, and not yourself, the subjects of sentences. For example, rather than *I took classes in business communication and computer applications*, say *Classes in business communication and computer applications prepared me to . . . .* Instead of *I enjoyed helping customers*, say *Helping customers was a real pleasure*.

**A letter of application should look professional and suggest quality.**

Like the résumé, your letter of application must look professional and suggest quality. This means using a traditional letter style, such as block or modified block. Also, be sure to print it on the same bond paper as your résumé. And, as with your résumé, proofread it several times yourself; then, have a friend read it for content and mechanics. The following checklist provides a quick summary of suggestions to review when you compose and proofread your cover letter.

## CHECKLIST FOR WRITING A PERSUASIVE LETTER OF APPLICATION

### Opening

✓ **Use the receiver's name.** Whenever possible, address the proper individual by name.

✓ **Identify your information source, if appropriate.** In responding to an advertisement, specify the position advertised as well as the date and publication name. If someone referred you, name that person.

✓ **Gain the reader's attention.** Use one of these techniques: (1) tell how your qualifications fit the job specifications, (2) show knowledge of the reader's business, (3) describe how your special talents will be assets to the company, or (4) use an original and relevant expression.

### Body

✓ **Describe what you can do for the reader.** Demonstrate how your background and training fill the job requirements.

- ✓ **Highlight your strengths.** Summarize your principal assets from education, experience, and special skills. Avoid repeating specific data from your résumé.

- ✓ **Refer to your résumé.** In this section or the closing, direct the reader to the attached or enclosed résumé. Do so directly or incidentally as part of another statement.

## Closing

- ✓ **Ask for an interview.** Also consider reviewing your strongest points or suggesting how your assets will benefit the company.

- ✓ **Make it easy to respond.** Tell when you can be reached during office hours or announce when you will call the reader. Note that some recruiters prefer that you call them.

## FOLLOW-UP LETTERS AND OTHER EMPLOYMENT DOCUMENTS

Although the résumé and letter of application are your major tasks, other important letters and documents are often required during the employment process. You may need to make requests, write follow-up letters, or fill out employment applications. Because each of these tasks reveals something about you and your communication skills, you'll want to put your best foot forward. These documents often subtly influence company officials to arrange an interview or offer a job.

## Reference Request

Most employers expect job candidates at some point to submit names of individuals who are willing to discuss the candidates' qualifications. Before you list anyone as a reference, however, be sure to ask permission. Try to do this in person. Ask an instructor, for example, if he or she would be willing and has the time to act as your recommender. If you detect any sign of reluctance, don't force the issue. Your goal is to find willing individuals who think well of you.

> **To get good letters of recommendation, find willing people and provide ample data about yourself.**

What your recommenders need most is information about you. What should they stress to prospective employers? Let's say you're applying for a specific job that requires a letter of recommendation. Professor Orenstein has already agreed to be a reference for you. To get the best letter of recommendation from Professor Orenstein, help her out. Write a letter telling her about the position, its requirements, and the recommendation deadline. Include a copy of your résumé. You might remind her of a positive experience with you (*You said my report was well organized*) that she could use in the recommendation. Remember that recommenders need evidence to support generalizations. Give them appropriate ammunition, as the student has done in the following request:

Dear Professor Orenstein:

Recently I applied for the position of administrative assistant in the Human Resources Department of Host International. Because you kindly agreed to help me, I am now asking you to write a letter of recommendation to Host.

> Identify the target position and company. Tell immediately why you are writing.

The position calls for good organizational, interpersonal, and writing skills, as well as computer experience. To help you review my skills and training, I

*(continued)*

Specify the job requirements so that the recommender knows what to stress in the letter. Also, supply data to jog the memory of the writer.

enclose my résumé. As you may recall, I earned an *A* in your business communication class, and you commended my long report for its clarity and organization.

Please send your letter before July 1 in the enclosed stamped, addressed envelope. I'm grateful for your support, and I promise to let you know the results of my job search.

Provide a stamped, addressed envelope.

## Application Request Letter

Some organizations consider candidates only when they submit a completed application form. To secure a form, write a routine letter of request. But provide enough information about yourself, as shown in the following example, to assure the reader that you are a serious applicant:

Dear Mr. Franklin:

Because you expect a positive response, announce your request immediately.

Please send me an application form for work in your Human Resources Department. In June I will be completing my studies in psychology and communications at Sir Wilfrid Laurier University in Waterloo, Ontario. My program included courses in public relations, psychology, and communications.

Supply an end date, if it seems appropriate. End on a forward-looking note.

I would appreciate receiving this application by May 15 so that I may complete it before making a visit to your city in June. I'm looking forward to beginning a career in personnel management.

## Application or Résumé Follow-Up Letter

If your letter or application generates no response within a reasonable time, you may decide to send a short follow-up letter like the one shown here. Doing so (1) jogs the memory of the personnel officer, (2) demonstrates your serious interest, and (3) allows you to emphasize your qualifications or to add new information.

Dear Ms. Farmer:

Open by reminding the reader of your interest.

Please know I am still interested in becoming an administrative support specialist with Quad, Inc.

Substitute *letter* or *résumé* if appropriate. Use this opportunity to review your strengths or to add new qualifications.

Since I submitted an application in May, I have completed my schooling and have been employed as a summer replacement for office workers in several downtown offices. This experience has honed my word processing and communication skills. It has also introduced me to a wide range of office procedures.

Close by looking forward positively; avoid accusations that make the reader defensive.

Please keep my application in your active file and let me know when I may put my formal training, technical skills, and practical experience to work for you.

## Interview Follow-Up Letter

After a job interview you should always send a brief letter of thanks. This courtesy sets you apart from other applicants (most of whom will not bother). Your letter also reminds the interviewer of your visit as well as suggesting your good manners and genuine enthusiasm for the job. Follow-up letters are most effective if sent immediately after the interview. In your letter refer to the date of the interview, the exact job title for which you were interviewed, and specific topics discussed. Avoid worn-out phrases, such as *Thank you for taking the time to interview me.* Be careful, too, about overusing *I*, especially to begin sentences. Most important, show that you really want the job and that you are qualified for it. Notice how the following letter conveys enthusiasm and confidence:

Dear Ms. Ouchi:

Talking with you Thursday, May 23, about the graphic designer position was both informative and interesting. — Mention the interview date and specific position.

Thanks for describing the position in such detail and for introducing me to Ms. Thomas, the senior designer. Her current project designing the annual report in four colours on a Macintosh sounds fascinating as well as quite challenging. — Show appreciation, good manners, and perseverance—traits that recruiters value.

Now that I've learned in greater detail the specific tasks of your graphic designers, I'm more than ever convinced that my computer and creative skills can make a genuine contribution to your graphic productions. My training in Macintosh design and layout ensures that I could be immediately productive on your staff. — Personalize your letter by mentioning topics discussed in the interview. Highlight a specific skill you have for the job.

You will find me an enthusiastic and hard-working member of any team effort. I'm eager to join the graphics staff at your Kitchener headquarters, and I look forward to hearing from you soon. — Remind the reader of your interpersonal skills as well as your enthusiasm and eagerness for this job.

## Job Acceptance Letter

When you accept a job offer, it is a good policy to put your acceptance in writing. This letter, which should clarify and confirm details of the employment offer, will become part of your human resources file. Your acceptance letter follows the direct format. Verify details such as starting time, place, and conditions, and, if applicable, mention that the forms the employer has requested you to fill out have been completed and are enclosed. Finally, extend appreciation and confirm your decision to accept the job.

Dear Mr. Frappier:

Thanks very much for offering me the position of accounting clerk for the JCET Group. I am pleased to accept your offer. — Begin by thanking the reader for the job offer and identifying the position.

As we discussed, I will begin work on July 12, reporting to Norman McKie at 9:00 a.m. in the main foyer. Enclosed is the health form you requested I complete. — Reiterate key details.

My goal is to meet and exceed the expectations you have of me. I appreciate your support and look forward to joining your company in July. — Close with a forward-looking comment about your future with the company.

## Job Declination Letter

When you are offered a job you do not want, good manners demand that you put your declination in writing. Although you may not want the position, you still want to retain goodwill. In the future, you may want to work for that company, or you may have to work with that company. Therefore, it is important to keep the door open. After you decline the job offer, write a letter to offer some form of explanation. Your declination letter follows the indirect format. It should acknowledge the offer, provide reasons that reflect careful consideration of it, and end with a forward-looking statement.

Dear Ms. Howson:

Begin by acknowledging the offer and making a positive comment about the organization.

The Sigma Group is an excellent consulting organization that is well respected in this area. For that reason, I was honoured to be chosen for the position of marketing coordinator.

Thank the reader for her or his interest. Close positively, thus leaving the door open for future correspondence.

Since our meeting, I have been thinking carefully about my future career aspirations. Although marketing appeals to me, the area of computer programming is also an interest of mine. Because I am returning to school for another year to develop my computer expertise, your offer must be declined at this time.

## Rejection Follow-Up Letter

If you didn't get the job and you think it was perfect for you, don't give up. Employment consultant Patricia Windelspecht advises, "You should always respond to a rejection letter . . . . I've had four clients get jobs that way." In a rejection follow-up letter, it's OK to admit you're disappointed. Be sure to add, however, that you're still interested and will contact them again in a month in case a job opens up. Then follow through for a couple of months—but don't overdo it. "There's a fine line between being professional and persistent and being a pest," adds consultant Windelspecht.[36] Here's an example of an effective rejection follow-up letter:

Dear Mr. O'Neal:

Subordinate your disappointment to your appreciation at being notified promptly and courteously.

Although I'm disappointed that someone else was selected for your accounting position, I appreciate your promptness and courtesy in notifying me.

Emphasize your continuing interest. Express confidence in meeting the job requirements.

Because I firmly believe that I have the technical and interpersonal skills needed to work in your fast-paced environment, I hope you will keep my résumé in your active file. My desire to become a productive member of your Trillium staff remains strong.

Refer to specifics of your interview. If possible, tell how you are improving your skills.

I enjoyed our interview, and I especially appreciate the time you and Mr. Samson spent describing your company's expansion into international markets. To enhance my qualifications, I've enrolled in a course in International Accounting at NBU.

Take the initiative; tell when you will call for an update.

Should you have an opening for which I am qualified, you may reach me at (506) 719-3901. In the meantime, I will call you in a month to discuss employment possibilities.

## Application Form

Some organizations require job candidates to fill out job application forms instead of submitting résumés. This practice permits them to gather and store standardized data about each applicant. Here are some tips for filling out such forms:

- Carry a card summarizing those vital statistics not included on your résumé. If you are asked to fill out an application form in an employer's office, you will need a handy reference to the following data: social insurance number; graduation dates; beginning and ending dates of all employment; salary history; full names, titles, and present work addresses of former supervisors; and full names, occupational titles, occupational addresses, and telephone numbers of persons who have agreed to serve as references.

- Look over all the questions before starting. Fill out the form neatly, printing if your handwriting is poor.

- Answer all questions. Write *Not applicable* (*N.A.*) if appropriate.

- Be prepared for a salary question. Unless you know what comparable employees are earning in the company, the best strategy is to suggest a salary range or to write in *Negotiable* or *Open*.

- Ask if you may submit your résumé in addition to the application form.

## INTERVIEWING FOR EMPLOYMENT

Job interviews, for most of us, are intimidating; no one enjoys being judged and, possibly, rejected. You can overcome your fear of the interview process by knowing how it works and how to prepare for it.

Trained recruiters generally structure the interview in three separate activities: (1) establishing a cordial relationship, (2) eliciting information about the candidate, and (3) giving information about the job and company. During the interview its participants have opposing goals. The interviewer tries to uncover any negative information that would eliminate a candidate. The candidate, of course, tries to minimize faults and emphasize strengths to avoid being eliminated. You can become a more skillful player in the interview game if you know what to do before, during, and after the interview.

### Before the Interview

- **Research the organization.** Never enter an interview cold. Visit the library or use your computer to search for information about the target company or its field, service, or product. Visit the company's Web site and read everything. Call the company to request annual reports, catalogues, or brochures. Ask about the organization and possibly the interviewer. Learn something about the company's size, number of employees, competitors, reputation, and strengths and weaknesses.

- **Learn about the position.** Obtain as much specific information as possible. What are the functions of an individual in this position? What is the typical salary range? What career paths are generally open to this individual? What did the last person in this position do right or wrong?

- **Plan to sell yourself.** Identify three to five of your major selling points regarding skills, training, personal characteristics, and specialized experience. Memorize them; then in the interview be certain to find a place to insert them.

- **Prepare answers to possible questions.** Imagine the kinds of questions you may be asked and work out sample answers. Although you can't anticipate precise questions, you can expect to be asked about your education, skills, experience, and availability. The accompanying Career Coach box shows ten of the most common questions and suggests responses.

- **Prepare success stories.** Rehearse two or three incidents that you can relate about your accomplishments. These may focus on problems you have solved, promotions you have earned, or recognition or praise you have received.

- **Arrive early.** Get to the interview five or ten minutes early. If you are unfamiliar with the area where the interview is to be held, you might visit it before the scheduled day. Locate the building, parking facilities, and office. Time yourself.

A job interview gives you a chance to explain your résumé and sell your technical expertise as well as your communication and interpersonal skills. But the interview also allows the recruiter to promote the company and explain the duties of the position. Be prepared to ask meaningful questions.

# Answering Ten Frequently Asked Interview Questions

Interviewers want to learn about your job experiences and education so that they can evaluate who you are and predict how you might perform on the job. Study each of the following frequently asked interview questions and the strategies for answering them successfully.

- **Why do you want to work for us?** Questions like this illustrate the need for you to research an organization thoroughly before the interview. Go to the company's Web site, read its annual report, conduct library research, ask friends, and read the company's advertisements and other printed materials to gather data. Describe your desire to work for them not only from your perspective but also from their point of view. What have you to offer them?

- **Why should we hire you?** Here is an opportunity for you to sell your strong points in relation to this specific position. Describe your skills, academic preparation, and relevant experience. If you have little experience, don't apologize—the interviewer has read your résumé. Emphasize strengths as demonstrated in your education, such as initiative and persistence in completing assignments, ability to learn quickly, self-sufficiency, and excellent attendance.

- **What can you tell me about yourself?** Use this chance to promote yourself. Stick to professional or business-related strengths; avoid personal or humorous references. Be ready with at least three success stories illustrating characteristics important to this job. Demonstrate responsibility you have been given; describe how you contributed as a team player.

- **What are your strongest (or weakest) personal qualities?** Stress your strengths, such as "I believe I am conscientious, reliable, tolerant, patient, and thorough." Add examples that illustrate these qualities: "My supervisor said that my research was exceptionally thorough." If pressed for a weakness, give a strength disguised as a weakness: "Perhaps my greatest fault is being too painstaking with details." Or, "I am impatient when tasks are not completed on time." Don't admit weaknesses, not even to sound human. You'll be hired for your strengths, not your weaknesses.

- **What do you expect to be doing ten years from now?** Formulate a realistic plan with respect to your present age and situation. The important thing is to be prepared for this question.

- **Do you prefer working with others or by yourself?** This question can be tricky. Provide a middle-of-the-road answer that not only suggests your interpersonal qualities but also reflects an ability to make independent decisions and work without supervision.

- **Have you ever changed your major during your education? Why?** Another tricky question. Don't admit weaknesses or failures. In explaining changes, suggest career potential and new aspirations awakened by your expanding education, experience, or maturity.

- **What have been your most rewarding or disappointing work (or school) experiences?** If possible, concentrate on positive experiences such as technical and interpersonal skills you acquired. Avoid dwelling on negative or unhappy topics. Never criticize former employers. If you worked for an ungrateful, penny-pinching slave driver in a dead-end position, say that you learned all you could from that job. Move the conversation to the prospective position and what attracts you to it.

- **Have you established any new goals lately?** Watch out here. If you reveal new goals, you may inadvertently admit deficiencies. Instead of "I've resolved to finally learn something about graphics design," try "Although I'm familiar with simple graphics programs, I decided to get serious about graphics design by mastering the tools of Adobe PhotoShop and Illustrator."

- **What are your long- and short-term goals?** Suggest realistic goals that you have consciously worked out before the interview. Know what you want to do with your future. To admit to an interviewer that you're not sure what you want to do is a sign of immaturity, weakness, and indecision.

## Career Application

In teams of two to four, role-play an employment interview. Take turns playing interviewer and interviewee. Each student should answer four to five questions. Imagine a company where you'd like to work and answer accordingly.

- **Dress appropriately.** Heed the advice of one expert: "Dress and groom like the interviewer is likely to dress—but cleaner."[37] Don't overdo perfume, jewellery, or after-shave lotion. Avoid loud colours; strive for a coordinated, natural appearance. Favourite "power" colours for interviews are grey and dark blue. It's not a bad idea to check your appearance in a restroom before entering the office.

## During the Interview

- **Establish the relationship.** Shake hands firmly. Don't be afraid to offer your hand first. Address the interviewer formally ("Hello, Mrs. Jones"). Allow the interviewer to put you at ease with small talk.

- **Act confident but natural.** Establish and maintain eye contact, but don't get into a staring contest. Sit up straight, facing the interviewer. Don't cross your arms and legs at the same time (review body language cues in Chapter 3). Don't manipulate objects, like a pencil or keys, during the interview. Try to remain natural and at ease.

*During an interview, applicants should act confident, focus on their strengths, and sell themselves.*

- **Don't criticize.** Avoid making negative comments about previous employers, instructors, or others. Such criticism may be taken to indicate a negative personality. Employers are not eager to hire complainers. Moreover, such criticism may suggest that you would do the same to this organization.

- **Stay focused on your strengths.** Be prepared to answer questions such as those shown in the previous Career Coach box. If the interviewer asks a question that does not help you promote your strongest qualifications, answer briefly. Alternatively, try to turn your response into a positive selling point, such as this: "I have not had extensive paid training in that area, but I have completed a 50-hour training program that provided hands-on experience using the latest technology and methods. My recent training taught me to be open to new ideas and showed me how I can continue learning on my own. I was commended for being a quick learner."

- **Find out about the job early.** Because your time will be short, try to learn all you can about the target job early in the interview. Ask about its responsibilities and the kinds of people who have done well in the position before. Inquiring about the company's culture will help you decide if your personality fits with this organization.

*Asking questions about the job helps applicants learn whether this position is right for them.*

- **Prepare for salary questions.** Remember that nearly all salaries are negotiable, depending on your qualifications. Knowing the typical salary range for the target position helps. The recruiter can tell you the salary ranges—but you will have to ask. If you've had little experience, you will probably be offered a salary somewhere between the low point and the midpoint in the range. With more experience you can negotiate for a higher figure. A word of caution, though. One personnel manager warns that candidates who emphasize money are suspect because they may leave if offered a few thousand dollars more elsewhere.

- **Be ready for inappropriate questions.** If you are asked a question that you think is illegal, politely ask the interviewer how that question is related to this job. Ask the purpose of the question. Perhaps valid reasons exist that are not obvious.

- **Ask your own questions.** Often, the interviewer concludes an interview with "Do you have any questions about the position?" Inquire about career paths, orientation or training for new employees, or the company's promotion policies. Have a list of relevant questions prepared. If the interview has gone well, ask the recruiter about his or her career in the company.

# Applying Your Skills at Maritime Life

When Maritime Life acquired Liberty Health in 2003, David McFarlane, senior vice president, Consumer and Small Business Markets, Liberty Health, stated, "The fit between our companies, both culturally and strategically, makes sense. We share a number of values, including a strong focus on both employee and customer satisfaction, and we also share a commitment to continuing growth and innovation in the Canadian marketplace in the years ahead."

This cultural fit is critical to the ongoing success of Maritime Life as it continues its rapid growth and keeps employee satisfaction at the forefront. But equally important to the corporate culture is customer satisfaction. Offering customers coast to coast a variety of personal insurance, disability and critical illness insurance, investment products, pension and retirement solutions, and group life and health products and services, the company strives to consistently provide excellent customer service by focusing on relationships and service.

Another part of the culture is a commitment to giving back to the community. Maritime Life is an Imagine* company and supports its communities through its community investment programs. In addition, Maritime Life employees across Canada participate in their national Annual Giving Campaign to raise funds in support of the United Way, favourite charities, and community organizations. Maritime Life matches the employee contributions dollar for dollar.[38]

## Your Task

As a member of the company's human resources consulting team, you have been asked to prepare a brochure to be distributed at college and university career fairs. The brochure should highlight Maritime Life's values-centred approach to business and discuss the organization's reputation as a good company with great benefits. Remember that customer satisfaction, self-motivation, pride in one's work, support, and contribution to the community are just a few of the values that Maritime Life shares with its employees. Also remember the company's recent rankings by *The Globe and Mail*'s *ROB Magazine* and Mediacorp.

Use point-form style to prepare a one-page outline of the various points you want to address in the brochure. The document must clearly address Maritime Life's strengths as an employer, while also containing information that will appeal to recent college and university graduates.

**www.maritimelife.ca**

*Imagine is Canada's national program to promote public and corporate giving, volunteering, and support for the community <www.imagine.ca>.

- **Conclude positively.** Summarize your strongest qualifications, show your enthusiasm for obtaining this position, and thank the interviewer for a constructive interview. Be sure you understand the next step in the employment process.

## After the Interview

**Keeping notes of the meeting helps candidates remember what happened.**

- **Make notes on the interview.** While the events are fresh in your mind, jot down the key points—good and bad.

- **Write a thank-you letter.** Immediately write a letter thanking the interviewer for a pleasant and enlightening discussion. Be sure to spell her or his name correctly.

## SUMMARY OF LEARNING OBJECTIVES

*1* **Prepare for employment by identifying your interests, evaluating your assets, recognizing the changing nature of jobs, choosing a career path, and studying traditional and electronic job search techniques.** The employment process begins with an analysis of your likes and your qualifications. Because the nature of jobs is changing, your future work may include flexible work assignments, multiple employers, and constant retraining. You can learn more about career opportunities through your campus career centre, the Web, your library, internships, part-time jobs, interviews, classified ads, and professional organizations. Traditional job search techniques range from newspaper ads to developing your own network of friends and relatives. Electronic job search techniques include visiting Internet job sites and company Web sites.

*2* **Compare and contrast chronological, functional, and combination résumés.** Chronological résumés, listing work and education by dates, rank highest with recruiters. Functional résumés, highlighting skills instead of jobs, appeal to people changing careers or those having negative employment histories. Combination résumés, including a complete job history along with skill areas, are increasingly popular.

*3* **Organize, format, and produce a persuasive résumé.** Target your résumé for a specific job. Study models to arrange most effectively your main heading, career objective (optional), education, work experience, capabilities, awards and activities, personal data, and references (optional). Use action verbs to show how your assets will help the target organization.

*4* **Identify techniques that prepare a résumé for computer scanning, posting at a Web site, faxing, and e-mailing.** Computer-friendly résumés avoid unusual typefaces, underlining, and italics. They use 10- to 14-point type, smooth white paper, and quality printing. The applicant's name appears on the first line. The résumé includes ample white space, avoids double columns, and is not folded or stapled. It emphasizes keywords, which are nouns that an employer might use to describe the position and skills desired. Résumés posted at Web sites must be prepared in HTML (Hypertext Markup Language). They may include links to résumé extras such as work samples and letters of recommendation. Faxed résumés must avoid small fonts and underlining. E-mailed résumés should probably be sent in ASCII (text-only format). Follow up faxed and e-mail résumés with polished copies.

*5* **Write a persuasive letter of application to accompany your résumé.** Gain attention in the opening by mentioning the job or a person who referred you. Build interest in the body by stressing what you can do for the targeted company. Refer to your résumé, request an interview, and motivate action in the closing.

*6* **Write effective employment follow-up letters and other messages.** Follow up all your employment activities with appropriate messages. After submitting your résumé, after an interview—even after being rejected—follow up with letters that express your appreciation and continuing interest.

**7** **Evaluate successful job interview strategies.** Learn about the job and the organization. Prepare answers to possible questions and be ready with success stories. Act confident and natural. Be prepared to ask or answer salary questions. Have a list of your own questions, summarize your key strengths, and stay focused on your strong points. Afterward, send a thank-you letter.

# CHAPTER REVIEW

1. Name at least five questions that you should ask yourself to identify your employment interests. (Obj. 1)

2. List five sources of career information. (Obj. 1)

3. How are most jobs likely to be found? Through classified ads? The Internet? Employment agencies? Networking? (Obj. 1)

4. What is the goal of your résumé? (Obj. 2)

5. Describe a chronological résumé and discuss its advantages. (Obj. 2)

6. Describe a functional résumé and discuss its advantages. (Obj. 2)

7. What are the disadvantages of a functional résumé? (Obj. 2)

8. When does it make sense to include a career objective on your résumé? (Obj. 3)

9. On a chronological résumé what information should you include for the jobs you list? (Objs. 2 and 3)

10. In addition to technical skills, what traits and characteristics do employers seek? (Objs. 2 and 3)

11. What changes must be made in a typical résumé to make it effective for computer scanning? (Obj. 4)

12. What are the three purposes of a letter of application? (Obj. 5)

13. How can you make it easy for a recruiter to reach you? (Obj. 5)

14. Other than a letter of application, name five kinds of letters you might need to write in the employment process. (Obj. 6)

15. What information should a candidate gather in preparing for a job interview? (Obj. 7)

# CRITICAL THINKING

1. How has the concept of the "job" changed, and how will it affect your employment search? (Obj. 1)

2. How is a résumé different from a company employment application? (Objs. 1 and 2)

3. Some job candidates think that applying for unsolicited jobs can be more fruitful than applying for advertised openings. Discuss the advantages and disadvantages of letters that "prospect" for jobs. (Obj. 5)

4. How do the interviewer and interviewee play opposing roles during job interviews? What strategies should the interviewee prepare in advance? (Obj. 7)

5. **Ethical Issue:** Job candidate Karen accepts a position with Company A. One week later she receives a better offer from Company B. She wants very much to accept it. What should she do?

# ACTIVITIES

## 16.1 Identifying Your Employment Interests (Obj. 1)

**Your Task.** In an e-mail or a memo addressed to your instructor, answer the questions in the section "Identifying Your Interests" at the beginning of the chapter. Draw a conclusion from your answers. What kind of career, company, position, and location seem to fit your self-analysis?

## 16.2 Evaluating Your Qualifications (Objs. 1, 2, and 3)

**Your Task.** Prepare four worksheets that inventory your qualifications in these areas: employment, education, capabilities and skills, and honours and activities. Use active verbs when appropriate.

a. **Employment.** Begin with your most recent job or internship. For each position list the following information: employer; job title; dates of employment; and three to five duties, activities, or accomplishments. Emphasize activities related to your job goal. Strive to quantify your achievements.

b. **Education.** List degrees, diplomas, certificates, and training accomplishments. Include courses, seminars,

564

or skills that are relevant to your job goal. Calculate your grade-point average in your major.

**c. Capabilities and skills.** List all capabilities and skills that recommend you for the job you seek. Use words like *skilled, competent, trained, experienced,* and *ability to.* Also list five or more qualities or interpersonal skills necessary for a successful individual in your chosen field. Write action statements demonstrating that you possess some of these qualities. Empty assurances aren't good enough; try to show evidence (*Developed teamwork skills by working with a committee of eight to produce a . . .*).

**d. Awards, honours, and activities.** Explain any awards so that the reader will understand them. List campus, community, and professional activities that suggest you are a well-rounded individual or possess traits relevant to your target job.

## *16.3 Choosing a Career Path* (Obj. 1)

**WEB**

Many people know amazingly little about the work done in various occupations and the training requirements. **Your Task.** Visit your institution's library, local library, or campus career centre. Consult the National Occupational Classification (NOC) binder and guide, published by Human Resources Development Canada, or the latest release of Job Futures <**www.jobfutures.ca**>. From either of the two sources, print or photocopy the pages that describe the employment area in which you are interested. If your instructor directs, attach these copies to the letter of application you will write in Activity 16.9.

## *16.4 Searching the Job Market* (Obj. 1)

**Your Task.** Clip a job advertisement from the classified section of a newspaper or print one from a career site on the Web. Select an ad describing the kind of employment you are seeking now or plan to seek when you graduate. Save this advertisement to attach to the résumé you will write in Activity 16.8.

## *16.5 Posting a Résumé on the Web* (Obj. 4)

**WEB**

**Your Task.** Prepare a list of at least three Web sites where you could post your résumé. Describe the procedure involved and the advantages for each site.

## *16.6 Draft Document: Résumé* (Objs. 2 and 3)

**Your Task.** Analyze the following résumé. Discuss its strengths and weaknesses. Your instructor may ask you to revise sections of this résumé before showing you an improved version.

**Wendy Lee Cox**
**9 Franklin Terrace**
**Timmins, Ontario**
Phone: (d) (705) 834-4583 (n) (705) 594-2985
E-mail: wendycox22@aol.com

Seeking to be hired at Mead Products as an intern in Accounting

SKILLS: Accounting, Internet, Windows 98, Excel, PowerPoint, Freelance Graphics

EDUCATION
Now working on diploma in Business Administration. Major, Management and Accounting; GPA is 3.5. Expect to graduate in June 2005.

EXPERIENCE
Assistant Accountant, 2000 to present. March and McLennan, Inc., Bookkeeping/Tax Service, Timmins. I keep accounting records for several small businesses accurately. I prepare 150 to 200 individual income tax returns each year. At the same time for Hill and Hill Truck Line I maintain accurate and up-to-date A/R records. And I prepare payroll records for 16 employees at three other firms.

Peterson Controls Inc., Timmins. Data Processing Internship, 2004 to present. I design and maintain spreadsheets and also process weekly and monthly information for production uptime and downtime. I prepare graphs to illustrate uptime and downtime data.

Timmins Country Club. Accounts Payable Internship, 2003 to 2003. Took care of accounts payable including filing system for the club. Responsible for processing monthly adjusting entries for general ledger. Worked closely with treasurer to give the Board budget/disbursement figures regularly.

Northern College, Timmins. I marketed the VITA program to Northern students and organized volunteers and supplies. Official title: Coordinator of Volunteer Income Tax Assistance Project. I did this for three years.

COMMUNITY SERVICE: Canadian Cancer Society, Central Park High School; All Souls Unitarian Church, assistant director of Children's Choir

## 16.7 Draft Document: Letter of Application (Obj. 5)

**Your Task.** Analyze each section of the following letter of application written by an accounting major about to graduate.

Dear Human Resources Director:

Please consider this letter as an application for the position of staff accountant that I saw advertised in the *Whig-Standard*. Although I have had no paid work experience in this field, accounting has been my major in college and I'm sure I could be an asset to your company.

For four years I have studied accounting, and I am fully trained for full-charge bookkeeping as well as electronic accounting. I have taken 36 units of college accounting and courses in business law, economics, statistics, finance, management, and marketing.

In addition to my course work, during the tax season I have been a student volunteer for VITA. This is a project to help individuals in the community prepare their income tax returns, and I learned a lot from this experience. I have also received some experience in office work and working with figures when I was employed as an office assistant for Copy Quick, Inc.

I am a competent and responsible person who gets along pretty well with others. I have been a member of some college and social organizations and have even held elective office.

I feel that I have a strong foundation in accounting as a result of my course work and my experience. Along with my personal qualities and my desire to succeed, I hope that you will agree that I qualify for the position of staff accountant with your company.

Sincerely,

## 16.8 Résumé (Objs. 2 and 3)

**Your Task.** Using the data you developed in Activity 16.2, write your résumé. Aim it at a full-time job, part-time position, or internship. Attach a job listing for a specific position (from Activity 16.4). Use a computer. Revise your résumé until it is perfect.

## 16.9 Letter of Application (Obj. 5)

**Your Task.** Write a cover letter introducing your résumé. Again, use a computer. Revise your cover letter until it is perfect.

## 16.10 Interview Follow-Up Letter (Obj. 6)

**Your Task.** Assume you were interviewed for the position you seek. Write a follow-up thank-you letter.

## 16.11 Reference Request (Obj. 6)

**Your Task.** Your favourite professor has agreed to recommend you. Write to the professor and request that he or she send a letter of recommendation to a company where you are applying for a job. Provide data about the job description and about yourself so that the professor can target its content.

## 16.12 Résumé Follow-Up Letter (Obj. 6)

**Your Task.** A month has passed since you sent your résumé and letter of application in response to a job advertisement. Write a follow-up letter that doesn't offend the reader or damage your chances of employment.

## 16.13 Application Request (Obj. 6)

**Your Task.** Select a company for which you'd like to work. Write a letter requesting an employment application, which the company requires for all job-seekers.

## 16.14 Interview Cheat Sheet (Obj. 7)

Even the best-rehearsed applicants sometimes forget to ask the questions they prepared, or they fail to stress their major accomplishments in job interviews. Sometimes applicants are so rattled they even forget the interviewer's name. To help you keep your wits during an interview, make a "cheat sheet." It summarizes key facts, answers, and questions. Use it before the interview and also review it as the interview is ending to be sure you have covered everything that is critical.
**Your Task.** Prepare a cheat sheet with the following information:

Day and time of interview:

Meeting with: (Name of interviewer, title, company, city, province, postal code, telephone, fax, pager, e-mail)

Major accomplishments: (four to six)

Management or work style: (four to six)

Things you need to know about me: (three to four items)

Reason I left my last job:

Answers to difficult questions: (four to five answers)

Questions to ask interviewer:

Things I can do for you:

### 16.15 Rejection Follow-Up Letter (Obj. 6)

**Your Task.** Assume you didn't get the job. Although someone else was selected, you hope that other jobs may become available. Write a follow-up letter that keeps the door open.

### 16.16 Special Tips for Today's Résumé Writers (Obj. 4)

**INFOTRAC**

**Your Task.** Using InfoTrac, research the topic of employment résumés. Read at least three recent articles. In a memo to your instructor list eight or more good tips that are not covered in this chapter. Pay special attention to advice concerning the preparation of online résumés. The subject line of your memo should be "Special Tips for Today's Résumé Writers."

### 16.17 Résumé Swapping (Obj. 2)

A terrific way to get ideas for improving your résumé is seeing how other students have developed their résumés.
**Your Task.** Bring your completed résumé to class. Attach a plain sheet with your name at the top. In small groups exchange your résumés. Each reviewer should provide at least two supportive comments and one suggestion for improvement on the cover sheet. Reviewers should sign their names with their comments.

# C.L.U.E. REVIEW 16

On a separate sheet edit the following sentences to correct faults in grammar, punctuation, numbers, spelling, proofreading, and word use.

1. You cant hope to find the job of your dreams' without first: (1) Knowing yourself; (2) knowing the job market and (3) know the employment process.

2. Only about 1/3 of the people currently employed works for companys with more then five hundred employees.

3. If your looking for a job you should check classified ads, as well as online job banks.

4. Preparing a résumé while you are still in school, help you recognize week qualifications, and give you 2 or 3 years in which to bolster it.

5. Recruiters like to see career objectives on résumés, however it may restrict a candidates chances.

6. Todays résumés omit personel data such as birth date, martial status, hite, weigt, and religious affiliation.

7. When listing job duties, skills, computer skills, and so forth; don't tabulate them into 2 or 3 colume tables.

8. Did you see the article entitled Which is better—A functional or a chronologial résumé? in the latest issue of Canadian Business.

9. Although its impossable to talk about your self without using *I* you should try to reduce *I* domination in your cover letter.

10. Before going to a job interview learn something about the: companies size, number of employees, competitors, reputation, and strengths, and weakness.

# Appendix A

## Competent Language Usage Essentials (C.L.U.E.)

### A BUSINESS COMMUNICATOR'S GUIDE

In the business world, people are often judged by the way they speak and write. Using the language competently can mean the difference between individual success and failure. Often a speaker sounds accomplished; but when that same individual puts ideas in print, errors in language usage destroy his or her credibility. One student observed, "When I talk, I get by on my personality; but when I write, the flaws in my communication show through. That's why I'm in this class."

### What C.L.U.E. Is

This appendix provides a condensed guide to competency in language usage essentials (C.L.U.E.). Fifty-four guidelines review sentence structure, grammar, usage, punctuation, capitalization, number style, and abbreviations. These guidelines focus on the most frequently used—and abused—language elements. Presented from a business communicator's perspective, the guidelines also include realistic tips for application. And frequent checkpoint exercises enable you to try out your skills immediately. In addition to the 54 language guides in this appendix, you'll find a list of 165 frequently misspelled words plus a quick review of selected confusing words.

The concentrated materials in this guide will help novice business communicators focus on the major areas of language use. The guide is not meant to teach or review *all* the principles of English grammar and punctuation. It focuses on a limited number of language guidelines and troublesome words. Your objective should be mastery of these language principles and words, which represent a majority of the problems typically encountered by business writers.

### How to Use C.L.U.E.

Your instructor may give you a language diagnostic test to help you assess your competency. After taking this test, read and work your way through the 54 guidelines. Concentrate on areas where you are weak. Memorize the spelling list and definitions for the confusing words located at the end of this appendix.

Two kinds of exercises are available for your practice. (1) *Checkpoints*, located in this appendix, focus on a small group of language guidelines. Use them to test your comprehension as you complete each section. (2) *C.L.U.E. Review exercises*, located in the text chapters, cover all guidelines, spelling words, and confusing words. Use the review exercises to reinforce your language skills at the same time you are learning about the processes and products of business communication. As you complete the review exercises, you may wish to use the standard proofreading marks shown on the inside front cover.

Many students want all the help they can get in improving their language skills. For additional assistance with grammar and language fundamentals, try these resources:

- **CD-ROM Interactive Skill Builders.** On the enclosed CD-ROM, you will find sentence competency drills that are similar to the C.L.U.E. exercises, as well as spelling and vocabulary exercises. In addition, a Grammar Review is provided on this book's Web site at <**www.businesscommunication-4th.nelson.com**>

- **Reference Books.** More comprehensive treatment of grammar and punctuation guidelines can be found in Clark and Clark's *A Handbook for Office Workers*; Jack Finnbogason and Al Valleau's *A Canadian Writer's Pocket Guide*, ISBN 0-17-616973-3; Joanne Buckley's *Checkmate: A Writing Reference for Canadians*, ISBN 0-17-622440-8; and *The Harbrace Handbook for Canadians* by John Hodges and Andrew Stuffs, ISBN 0-17-622509-9.

- **Study Guide C.L.U.E. Exercises.** The Student Study Guide accompanying this textbook provides many additional C.L.U.E. review exercises, and the answers are available for immediate checking.

## Guidelines: Competent Language Usage Essentials

### Sentence Structure

GUIDE 1: **Express ideas in complete sentences.** You can recognize a complete sentence because it (a) includes a subject (a noun or pronoun that interacts with a verb), (b) includes a verb (a word expressing action or describing a condition), and (c) makes sense (comes to a closure). A complete sentence is an independent clause. One of the most serious errors a writer can make is punctuating a fragment as if it were a complete sentence. A fragment is a broken-off part of a sentence.

| **Fragment** | **Improved** |
|---|---|
| Because 90 percent of all business transactions involve written messages. Good writing skills are critical. | Because 90 percent of all business transactions involve written messages, good writing skills are critical. |
| The recruiter requested a writing sample. Even though the candidate seemed to communicate well. | The recruiter requested a writing sample, even though the candidate seemed to communicate well. |

**Tip.** Fragments often can be identified by the words that introduce them—words like *although, as, because, even, except, for example, if, instead of, since, so, such as, that, which,* and *when*. These words introduce dependent clauses. Make sure such clauses are always connected to independent clauses.

DEPENDENT CLAUSE      INDEPENDENT CLAUSE

Since she became supervisor, she had to write more memos and reports.

**GUIDE 2: Avoid run-on (fused) sentences.** A sentence with two independent clauses must be joined by a coordinating conjunction (*and, or, nor, but*) or by a semicolon (;). Without a conjunction or a semicolon, a run-on sentence results.

| **Run-on** | **Improved** |
|---|---|
| Robin visited resorts of the rich and the famous he also dropped in on luxury spas. | Robin visited resorts of the rich and famous, and he also dropped in on luxury spas. |
| | Robin visited resorts of the rich and famous; he also dropped in on luxury spas. |

**GUIDE 3: Avoid comma-splice sentences.** A comma splice results when a writer joins (splices together) two independent clauses—without using a coordinating conjunction (*and, or, nor, but*).

| **Comma Splice** | **Improved** |
|---|---|
| Disney World operates in Orlando, EuroDisney serves Paris. | Disney World operates in Orlando; EuroDisney serves Paris. |
| | Disney World operates in Orlando, and EuroDisney serves Paris. |
| Visitors wanted a resort vacation, however they were disappointed. | Visitors wanted a resort vacation; however, they were disappointed. |

**Tip.** In joining independent clauses, beware of using a comma and words like *consequently, furthermore, however, therefore, then, thus,* and so on. These conjunctive adverbs require semicolons.

## ✓ Checkpoint

Revise the following to rectify sentence fragments, comma splices, and run-ons.

1. When McDonald's tested pizza, Pizza Hut fought back. With aggressive ads ridiculing McPizza.

2. Aggressive ads can backfire, consequently, marketing directors consider them carefully.

3. Corporations study the legality of attack advertisements they also retaliate with counterattacks.

4. Although Pizza Hut is the country's number one pizza chain. Domino's Pizza leads in deliveries.

5. About half of the 6 600 outlets make deliveries, the others concentrate on walk-in customers.

For all the Checkpoint sentences, compare your responses with the answers at the end of Appendix A (page A-23).

# Grammar

## Verb Tense

GUIDE 4: Use present tense, past tense, and past participle verb forms correctly.

| Present Tense (Today I _____ ) | Past Tense (Yesterday I _____ ) | Past Participle (I have _____ ) |
|---|---|---|
| am | was | been |
| begin | began | begun |
| break | broke | broken |
| bring | brought | brought |
| choose | chose | chosen |
| come | came | come |
| do | did | done |
| give | gave | given |
| go | went | gone |
| know | knew | known |
| pay | paid | paid |
| see | saw | seen |
| steal | stole | stolen |
| take | took | taken |
| write | wrote | written |

The package *came* yesterday, and Kevin *knew* what it contained.

If I *had seen* the shipper's bill, I *would have paid* it immediately.

I *know* the answer now; I wish I *had known* it yesterday.

**Tip.** Probably the most frequent mistake in tenses results from substituting the past participle form for the past tense. Notice that the past participle tense requires auxiliary verbs such as *has, had, have, would have,* and *could have.*

| **Faulty** | **Correct** |
|---|---|
| When he *come* over last night, he *brung* pizza. | When he *came* over last night, he *brought* pizza. |
| If he *had came* earlier, we *could have saw* the video. | If he *had come* earlier, we *could have seen* the video. |

## Verb Mood

GUIDE 5: Use the subjunctive mood to express hypothetical (untrue) ideas. The most frequent misuse of the subjunctive mood involves using *was* instead of *were* in clauses introduced by *if* and *as though* or containing *wish.*

If I *were* (not *was*) you, I would take a business writing course.

Sometimes I wish I *were* (not *was*) the manager of this department.

He acts as though he *were* (not *was*) in charge of this department.

**Tip.** If the statement could possibly be true, use *was.*

If I *was* to blame, I accept the consequences.

## ✓ Checkpoint

Correct faults in verb tenses and mood.

**6.** If I was in your position, I would have wrote the manager a letter.

**7.** You could have wrote a better résumé if you have read the chapter first.

**8.** When Trevor seen the want ad, he immediately contacted the company.

**9.** I wish I was able to operate a computer so that I could have went to work there.

**10.** Because she had took many computer courses, Maria was able to chose a good job.

## Verb Voice

For a discussion of active- and passive-voice verbs, see page 170 in Chapter 6.

## Verb Agreement

GUIDE 6: **Make subjects agree with verbs despite intervening phrases and clauses.** Become a detective in locating *true* subjects. Don't be deceived by prepositional phrases and parenthetic words that often disguise the true subject.

> Our study of annual budgets, five-year plans, and sales proposals *is* (not *are*) progressing on schedule. (The true subject is *study*.)
>
> The budgeted item, despite additions proposed yesterday, *remains* (not *remain*) as submitted. (The true subject is *item*.)
>
> A salesperson's evaluation of the prospects for a sale, together with plans for follow-up action, *is* (not *are*) what we need. (The true subject is *evaluation*.)

**Tip.** Subjects are nouns or pronouns that control verbs. To find subjects, cross out prepositional phrases beginning with words like *about, at, by, for, from, of,* and *to*. Subjects of verbs are not found in prepositional phrases. Also, don't be tricked by expressions introduced by *together with, in addition to,* and *along with*.

GUIDE 7: **Subjects joined by *and* require plural verbs.** Watch for true subjects joined by the conjunction *and*. They require plural verbs.

> The CEO and one of his assistants *have* (not *has*) ordered a limo.
>
> Considerable time and money *were* (not *was*) spent on remodelling.
>
> Exercising in the gym and jogging every day *are* (not *is*) how he keeps fit.

GUIDE 8: **Subjects joined by *or* or *nor* may require singular or plural verbs.** The verb should agree with the closest subject.

> Either the software or the printer *is* (not *are*) causing the glitch. (The verb is controlled by closer subject, *printer*.)
>
> Neither Montreal nor Calgary *has* (not *have*) a chance of winning. (The verb is controlled by *Calgary*.)

**Tip.** In joining singular and plural subjects with *or* or *nor*, place the plural subject closer to the verb. Then, the plural verb sounds natural. For example, *Either the manufacturer or the distributors are responsible*.

GUIDE 9:  Use singular verbs for most indefinite pronouns.  For example: *anyone, anybody, anything, each, either, every, everyone, everybody, everything, neither, nobody, nothing, someone, somebody,* and *something* all take singular verbs.

> Everyone in both offices *was* (not *were*) given a bonus.

> Each of the employees *is* (not *are*) being interviewed.

GUIDE 10:  Use singular or plural verbs for collective nouns, depending on whether the members of the group are operating as a unit or individually.  Words like *faculty, administration, class, crowd,* and *committee* are considered *collective* nouns. If the members of the collective are acting as a unit, treat them as singular subjects. If they are acting individually, it's usually better to add the word *members* and use a plural verb.

**Correct**
The Finance Committee *is* working harmoniously. (*Committee* is singular because its action is unified.)

The Planning Committee *are* having difficulty agreeing. (*Committee* is plural because its members are acting individually.)

**Improved**
The Planning Committee members *are* having difficulty agreeing. (Add the word *members* if a plural meaning is intended.)

**Tip.**  In North America collective nouns are generally considered singular. In Britain these collective nouns are generally considered plural.

##  Checkpoint

Correct the errors in subject–verb agreement.

**11.** A manager's time and energy has to be focused on important issues.

**12.** Promotion of women, despite managerial training programs and networking efforts, are disappointingly small.

**13.** We're not sure whether Mr. Murphy or Ms. Wagner are in charge of the program.

**14.** Each of the Fortune 500 companies are being sent a survey regarding women in management.

**15.** Our CEO, like other good executives, know how to be totally informed without being totally involved.

## Pronoun Case

GUIDE 11:  Learn the three cases of pronouns and how each is used.  Pronouns are substitutes for nouns. Every business writer must know the following pronoun cases.

| Nominative or Subjective Case | Objective Case | Possessive Case |
|---|---|---|
| Used for subjects of verbs and subject complements | Used for objects of prepositions and objects of verbs | Used to show possession |
| I | me | my, mine |
| we | us | our, ours |

| Nominative or Subjective Case | Objective Case | Possessive Case |
|---|---|---|
| you | you | you, yours |
| he | him | his |
| she | her | her, hers |
| it | it | its |
| they | them | their, theirs |
| who, whoever | whom, whomever | whose |

**GUIDE 12: Use nominative case pronouns as subjects of verbs and as complements.** Complements are words that follow linking verbs (such as *am, is, are, was, were, be, being,* and *been*) and rename the words to which they refer.

*She* and *I* (not *her* and *me*) prefer easy-riding mountain bikes. (Use nominative case pronouns as the subjects of the verb *prefer.*)

We think that *she* and *he* (not *her* and *him*) will win the race. (Use nominative case pronouns as the subjects of the verb *will win.*)

It must have been *she* (not *her*) who called last night. (Use a nominative case pronoun as a subject complement.)

**Tip.** If you feel awkward using nominative pronouns after linking verbs, rephrase the sentence to avoid the dilemma. Instead of *It is she who is the boss,* say *She is the boss.*

**GUIDE 13: Use objective case pronouns as objects of prepositions and verbs.**

Send the e-mail to *her* and *me* (not *she* and *I*). (The pronouns *her* and *me* are objects of the preposition *to.*)

The CEO appointed *him* (not *he*) to the position. (The pronoun *him* is the object of the verb *appointed.*)

**Tip.** When a pronoun appears in combination with a noun or another pronoun, ignore the extra noun or pronoun and its conjunction. Then, the case of the pronoun becomes more obvious.

Jason asked Jennifer and *me* (not *I*) to lunch. (Ignore *Jennifer and.*)

The waiter didn't know whether to give the bill to Jason or *her* (not *she*). (Ignore *Jason or.*)

**Tip.** Be especially alert to the following prepositions: *except, between, but,* and *like.* Be sure to use objective pronouns as their objects.

Just between you and *me* (not *I*), that mineral water comes from the tap.

Computer grammar checkers work well for writers like Lee and *him* (not *he*).

**GUIDE 14: Use possessive case pronouns to show ownership.** Possessive pronouns (such as *hers, yours, whose, ours, theirs,* and *its*) require no apostrophes.

All reports except *yours* (not *your's*) have to be rewritten.

The printer and *its* (not *it's*) fonts produce exceptional copy.

A-7

Tip. Don't confuse possessive pronouns and contractions. Contractions are shortened forms of subject–verb phrases (such as *it's* for *it is, there's* for *there is, who's* for *who is*, and *they're* for *they are*).

## ✓ Checkpoint

Correct errors in pronoun case.

**16.** Although my friend and myself are interested in this computer, it's price seems high.

**17.** Letters addressed to he and I were delivered to you and Ann in error.

**18.** Just between you and I, the mailroom and its procedures need improvement.

**19.** Several applications were lost; your's and her's were the only ones delivered.

**20.** It could have been her who sent the program update to you and I.

GUIDE 15: Use *self*-ending pronouns only when they refer to previously mentioned nouns or pronouns.

> The president *himself* ate all the M & Ms.
>
> Send the package to Marcus or *me* (not *myself*).

Tip. Trying to sound less egocentric, some radio and TV announcers incorrectly substitute *myself* when they should use *I*. For example, "Jerry and *myself* (should be *I*) are cohosting the telethon."

GUIDE 16: Use *who* or *whoever* for nominative case constructions and *whom* or *whomever* for objective case constructions. In determining the correct choice, it's helpful to substitute *he* for *who* or *whoever* and *him* for *whom* or *whomever*.

> For *whom* was this software ordered? (The software was ordered for *him*.)
>
> *Who* did you say called? (You did say *he* called?)
>
> Give the supplies to *whoever* asked for them. (In this sentence the clause *whoever asked for them* functions as the object of the preposition *to*. Within the clause *whoever* is the subject of the verb *asked*. Again, try substituting *he: he asked for them*.)

## ✓ Checkpoint

Correct any errors in the use of *self*-ending pronouns and *who/whom*.

**21.** The boss herself is willing to call whoever we nominate for the position.

**22.** Who would you like to see nominated?

**23.** These supplies are for whomever ordered them.

**24.** The meeting is set for Tuesday; however, Jeff and myself cannot attend.

**25.** Incident reports are to be written by whomever experiences a sales problem.

## Pronoun Reference

GUIDE 17: Make pronouns agree in number and gender with the words to which they refer (their antecedents). When the gender of the antecedent is obvious, pronoun references are simple.

One of the boys lost *his* (not *their*) new tennis shoes. (The singular pronoun *his* refers to the singular *One*.)

Each of the female nurses was escorted to *her car* (not *their cars*). (The singular pronoun *her* and singular noun *car* are necessary because they refer to the singular subject *Each*.)

Somebody on the girls' team left *her* (not *their*) headlights on.

When the gender of the antecedent could be male or female, sensitive writers today have a number of options.

| **Faulty** | **Improved** |
|---|---|
| Every employee should receive *their* cheque Friday. (The plural pronoun *their* does not agree with its singular antecedent *employee*.) | All employees should receive *their* cheques Friday. (Make the subject plural so that the plural pronoun *their* is acceptable. This option is preferred by many writers today.) |
| | All employees should receive cheques Friday. (Omit the possessive pronoun entirely.) |
| | Every employee should receive *a* cheque Friday. (Substitute *a* for a pronoun.) |
| | Every employee should receive *his* or *her* cheque Friday. (Use the combination *his* or *her*. However, this option is wordy and should be avoided.) |

**GUIDE 18: Be sure that pronouns such as *it, which, this,* and *that* refer to clear antecedents.** Vague pronouns confuse the reader because they have no clear single antecedent. The most troublesome are *it, which, this,* and *that*. Replace vague pronouns with concrete nouns, or provide these pronouns with clear antecedents.

| **Faulty** | **Improved** |
|---|---|
| Our office recycles as much paper as possible because *it* helps the environment. (Does *it* refer to *paper, recycling,* or *office*?) | Our office recycles as much paper as possible because *such efforts* help the environment. (Replace *it* with *such efforts*.) |
| The disadvantages of local area networks can offset their advantages. That merits further evaluation. (What merits evaluation: advantages, disadvantages, or offsetting of one by the other?) | The disadvantages of local area networks can offset their advantages. That fact merits further evaluation. (*Fact* supplies a concrete noun for the vague pronoun *that*.) |
| Negotiators announced an expanded health care plan, reductions in dental coverage, and a proposal of on-site child-care facilities. *This* caused employee protests. (What exactly caused employee protests?) | Negotiators announced an expanded health care plan, reductions in dental coverage, and a proposal of on-site child-care facilities. *This* reduction in dental coverage caused employee protests. (The pronoun *This* now has a clear reference.) |

A-9

**Tip.** Whenever you use the words *this, that, these,* and *those* by themselves, a red flag should pop up. These words are dangerous when they stand alone. Inexperienced writers often use them to refer to an entire previous idea, rather than to a specific antecedent, as shown in the preceding example. You can often solve the problem by adding another idea to the pronoun (such as *this announcement*).

##  Checkpoint

Correct the faulty and vague pronoun references in the following sentences. Numerous remedies exist.

**26.** Every employee is entitled to have their tuition reimbursed.

**27.** Flexible working hours may mean slower career advancement, but it appeals to me anyway.

**28.** Any subscriber may cancel their subscription at any time.

**29.** Every voter must have their name and address verified at the polling place.

**30.** Obtaining agreement on job standards, listening to coworkers, and encouraging employee suggestions all helped to open lines of communication. This is particularly important in team projects.

## Adjectives and Adverbs

**GUIDE 19: Use adverbs, not adjectives, to describe or limit the action of verbs.**

Andrew said he did *well* (not *good*) on the exam.

After its tune-up, the engine is running *smoothly* (not *smooth*).

Don't take the manager's criticism *personally* (not *personal*).

She finished her prescription *more quickly* (not *quicker*) than expected.

**GUIDE 20: Hyphenate two or more adjectives that are joined to create a compound modifier before a noun.**

Follow the *step-by-step* instructions to construct the *low-cost* bookshelves.

A *well-designed* keyboard is part of their *state-of-the-art* equipment.

**Tip.** Don't confuse adverbs ending in *-ly* with compound adjectives: *newly enacted* law and *highly regarded* CEO would not be hyphenated.

## ✔ Checkpoint

Correct any problems in the use of pronouns, adjectives, and adverbs.

**31.** My manager and myself prepared a point by point analysis of the proposal.

**32.** Because we completed the work so quick, we were able to visit the recently-opened snack bar.

**33.** If I do good on the placement exam, I qualify for many part time jobs and a few full time positions.

**34.** The vice president told him and I not to take the announcement personal.

**35.** In the not too distant future, we may enjoy interactive television.

# Punctuation

**GUIDE 21:  Use commas to separate three or more items (words, phrases, or short clauses) in a series.**

> Downward communication delivers job instructions, procedures, and appraisals.

> In preparing your résumé, try to keep it brief, make it easy to read, and include only job-related information.

> The new ice cream flavours include cookie dough, chocolate raspberry truffle, cappuccino, and almond amaretto.

**Tip.**  Some professional writers omit the comma before *and*. However, most business writers prefer to retain that comma because it prevents misreading the last two items as one item. Notice in the third example how the final two ice cream flavours could have been misread if the comma had been omitted.

**GUIDE 22:  Use commas to separate introductory clauses and certain phrases from independent clauses.**  This guideline describes the comma most often omitted by business writers. Sentences that open with dependent clauses (often introduced by words such as *since, when, if, as, although,* and *because*) require commas to separate them from the main idea. The comma helps readers recognize where the introduction ends and the big idea begins. Introductory phrases of more than five words or phrases containing verbal elements also require commas.

> If you recognize introductory clauses, you will have no trouble placing the comma. (Comma separates introductory dependent clause from main clause.)

> When you have mastered this rule, half the battle with commas will be won.

> As expected, additional explanations are necessary. (Use a comma even if the introductory clause omits the understood subject: *As we expected.*)

> In the spring of last year, we opened our franchise. (Use a comma after a phrase containing five or more words.)

> Having considered several alternatives, we decided to invest. (Use a comma after an introductory verbal phrase.)

> To invest, we needed $100 000. (Use a comma after an introductory verbal phrase, regardless of its length.)

**Tip.**  Short introductory prepositional phrases (four or fewer words) require no commas. Don't clutter your writing with unnecessary commas after introductory phrases such as *by 2005, in the fall,* or *at this time.*

**GUIDE 23:  Use a comma before the coordinating conjunction in a compound sentence.**  The most common coordinating conjunctions are *and, or, nor,* and *but.* Occasionally, *for* and *so* may also function as coordinating conjunctions. When coordinating conjunctions join two independent clauses, commas are needed.

> The investment sounded too good to be true, *and* many investors were dubious. (Use a comma before the coordinating conjunction *and* in a compound sentence.)

> Niagara Falls is the honeymoon capital of the world, *but* some newlyweds prefer to go to more exotic desinations.

**Tip.** Before inserting a comma, test the two clauses. Can each of them stand alone as a complete sentence? If either is incomplete, skip the comma.

> Promoters said the investment offer was for a limited time and couldn't be extended even one day. (Omit a comma before *and* because the second part of the sentence is not a complete independent clause.)

> Home is a place you grow up wanting to leave but grow old wanting to return to. (Omit a comma before *but* because the second half of the sentence is not a complete clause.)

## ✓ Checkpoint

Add appropriate commas.

**36.** Before he entered this class Jeff used to sprinkle his writing with commas semi-colons and dashes.

**37.** After studying punctuation he learned to use commas more carefully and to reduce his reliance on dashes.

**38.** At this time Jeff is engaged in a strenuous body-building program but he also finds time to enlighten his mind.

**39.** Next spring Jeff may enroll in accounting and business law or he may work for a semester to earn money.

**40.** When he completes his degree he plans to apply for employment in Montreal, Ottawa or Toronto.

**GUIDE 24: Use commas appropriately in dates, addresses, geographical names, degrees, and long numbers.**

> September 30, 1963, is her birthday. (For dates use commas before and after the year.)

> Send the application to James Kirby, 3405 120th Ave. N. W. Edmonton, AB T5W 1M3, as soon as possible. (For addresses use commas to separate all units except the two-letter province abbreviation and the postal code.)

> She expects to move from Salmon Arm, British Columbia, to Mississauga, Ontario, next fall. (For geographical areas use commas to enclose the second element.)

> Karen Munson, CPA, and Richard B. Larsen, Ph.D., were the speakers. (For professional designations and academic degrees following names, use commas to enclose each item.)

> The latest census figures show the city's population to be 342 000. (In figures use commas to separate every three digits, counting from the right. The metric system, as used in this book, uses a space instead of a comma.)

**GUIDE 25: Use commas to set off internal sentence interrupters.** Sentence interrupters may be verbal phrases, dependent clauses, contrasting elements, or parenthetical expressions (also called transitional phrases). These interrupters often provide information that is not grammatically essential.

> Medical researchers, working steadily for 18 months, developed a new cancer therapy. (Use commas to set off an interrupting verbal phrase.)

> The new therapy, which applies a genetically engineered virus, raises hope among cancer specialists. (Use commas to set off nonessential dependent *clauses*.)

Dr. James C. Morrison, who is one of the researchers, made the announcement. (Use commas to set off nonessential dependent clauses.)

It was Dr. Morrison, not Dr. Arturo, who led the team effort. (Use commas to set off a contrasting element.)

This new therapy, by the way, was developed from a herpes virus. (Use commas to set off a parenthetical expression.)

**Tip.** Parenthetical (transitional) expressions are helpful words that guide the reader from one thought to the next. Here are representative parenthetical expressions that require commas:

| | | |
|---|---|---|
| as a matter of fact | in addition | of course |
| as a result | in the meantime | on the other hand |
| consequently | nevertheless | therefore |
| for example | | |

**Tip.** Always use *two* commas to set off an interrupter, unless it begins or ends a sentence.

##  Checkpoint

Insert necessary commas.

**41.** Sue listed 222 George Henry Blvd. Toronto ON M2J 1E6 as her forwarding address.

**42.** The personnel director felt nevertheless that the applicant should be given an interview.

**43.** Employment of paralegals which is expected to increase 32 percent next year is growing rapidly because of the expanding legal services industry.

**44.** The contract was signed April 1 1999 and remained in effect until January 1 2003.

**45.** As a matter of fact the average North American drinks enough coffee to require 12 pounds of coffee beans annually.

**GUIDE 26: Avoid unnecessary commas.** Do not use commas between sentence elements that belong together. Don't automatically insert commas before every *and* or at points where your voice might drop if you were saying the sentence out loud.

**Faulty**
Growth will be spurred by the increasing complexity of business operations, and by large employment gains in trade and services. (A comma unnecessarily precedes *and*.)

All students with high grades, are eligible for the honour society. (A comma unnecessarily separates the subject and verb.)

One of the reasons for the success of the business honour society is, that it is very active. (A comma unnecessarily separates the verb and its complement.)

Our honour society has, at this time, over 50 members. (Commas unnecessarily separate a prepositional phrase from the sentence.)

A-13

## ✓ Checkpoint

Remove unnecessary commas. Add necessary ones.

**46.** Businesspeople from all over the world, gathered in Windsor for the meeting.

**47.** When shopping for computer equipment consider buying products that have been on the market for at least a year.

**48.** The trouble with talking fast is, that you sometimes say something before you've thought of it.

**49.** We think on the other hand, that we must develop management talent pools with the aim of promoting women minorities and people with disabilities.

**50.** A powerful reason for online purchasing is, that customers save time.

## Semicolons, Colons

**GUIDE 27: Use a semicolon to join closely related independent clauses.** Mature writers use semicolons to show readers that two thoughts are closely associated. If the ideas are not related, they should be expressed as separate sentences. Often, but not always, the second independent clause contains a conjunctive adverb (such as *however*, *consequently*, *therefore*, or *furthermore*) to show the relationship between the two clauses.

> Learning history is easy; learning its lessons is almost impossible.
>
> He was determined to complete his degree; consequently, he studied diligently.
>
> Most people want to be delivered from temptation; they would like, however, to keep in touch.

**Tip.** Don't use a semicolon unless each clause is truly independent. Try the sentence test. Omit the semicolon if each clause could not stand alone as a complete sentence.

| **Faulty** | **Improved** |
| --- | --- |
| There's no point in speaking; unless you can improve on silence. (The second half of the sentence is a dependent clause. It could not stand alone as a sentence.) | There's no point in speaking unless you can improve on silence. |
| Although I cannot change the direction of the wind; I can adjust my sails to reach my destination. (The first clause could not stand alone.) | Although I cannot change the direction of the wind, I can adjust my sails to reach my destination. |

**GUIDE 28: Use a semicolon to separate items in a series when one or more of the items contains internal commas.**

> Representatives from as far away as Longueil, Quebec; Vancouver, British Columbia; and Whitehorse, Yukon Territory, attended the conference.
>
> Stories circulated about Henry Ford, founder, Ford Motor Company; Lee Iacocca, former CEO, Chrysler Motor Company; and Dr. Shoichiro Toyoda, honorary chairman, Toyota Motor Corporation.

GUIDE 29: Use a colon after a complete thought that introduces a list of items. Words such as *these*, *the following*, and *as follows* may introduce the list or they may be implied.

> The following cities are on the tour: Toronto, Ottawa, and Winnipeg.
>
> An alternative tour includes several western cities: Calgary, Saskatoon, and Edmonton.

**Tip.** Be sure that the statement before a colon is grammatically complete. An introductory statement that ends with a preposition (such as *by*, *for*, *at*, and *to*) or a verb (such as *is*, *are*, or *were*) is incomplete. The list following a preposition or a verb actually functions as an object or as a complement to finish the sentence.

| **Faulty** | **Improved** |
|---|---|
| Three Big Macs were ordered by: Pam, Jim, and Lee. (Do not use a colon after an incomplete statement.) | Three Big Macs were ordered by Pam, Jim, and Lee. |
| Other items that they ordered were: fries, Cokes, and salads. (Do not use a colon after an incomplete statement.) | Other items that they ordered were fries, Cokes, and salads. |

GUIDE 30: Use a colon after business letter salutations and to introduce long quotations.

> Dear Mr. Duran:          Dear Lisa:
>
> The Asian consultant bluntly said: "North Americans tend to be too blabby, too impatient, and too informal for Asian tastes. To succeed in trade with Pacific Rim countries, North Americans must become more willing to adapt to native cultures."

**Tip.** Use a comma to introduce short quotations. Use a colon to introduce long one-sentence quotations and quotations of two or more sentences.

##  Checkpoint

Add appropriate semicolons and colons.

**51.** My short-term goal is an entry-level job my long-term goal however is a management position.

**52.** Reebok interviewed the following candidates Joni Sims Simon Fraser University James Jones University of Saskatchewan and Madonna Farr Ryerson University.

**53.** The recruiter was looking for three qualities initiative versatility and enthusiasm.

**54.** Reebok seeks experienced individuals however it will hire recent graduates who have excellent records.

**55.** Mississauga is an expanding area therefore many business opportunities are available.

## Apostrophe

**GUIDE 31:** **Add an apostrophe plus *s* to an ownership word that does not end in an *s* sound.**

> We hope to show a profit in one year's time. (Add *'s* because the ownership word *year* does not end in an *s*.)
>
> The company's assets rose in value. (Add *'s* because the ownership word *company* does not end in *s*.)
>
> All the women's votes were counted. (Add *'s* because the ownership word *women* does not end in *s*.)

**GUIDE 32:** **Add only an apostrophe to an ownership word that ends in an *s* sound—unless an extra syllable can be pronounced easily.**

> Some workers' benefits will cost more. (Add only an apostrophe because the ownership word *workers* ends in an *s*.)
>
> Several months' rent are now due. (Add only an apostrophe because the ownership word *months* ends in an *s*.)
>
> The boss's son got the job. (Add *'s* because an extra syllable can be pronounced easily.)

**Tip.** To determine whether an ownership word ends in an *s*, use it in an *of* phrase. For example, *one month's salary* becomes *the salary of one month*. By isolating the ownership word without its apostrophe, you can decide whether it ends in an *s*.

**GUIDE 33:** **Use *'s* to make a noun possessive when it precedes a gerund, a verb form used as a noun.**

> We all protested *Laura's* (not *Laura*) smoking.
>
> *His* (not *Him*) talking interfered with the movie.
>
> I appreciate *your* (not *you*) answering the telephone while I was gone.

##  Checkpoint

Correct erroneous possessives.

**56.** Both companies presidents received huge salaries, even when profits were falling.

**57.** Within one months time we were able to verify all members names and addresses.

**58.** Bryans supporters worry that there's little chance of him being elected.

**59.** The position requires five years experience in waste management.

**60.** Ms. Jackson car is serviced every six months.

**GUIDE 34:** **Use one period to end a statement, command, indirect question, or polite request. Never use two periods.**

> Matt worked at BioTech, Inc. (Statement. Use only one period.)
>
> Deliver it before 5 p.m. (Command. Use only one period.)
>
> Stacy asked whether she could use the car next weekend. (Indirect question)
>
> Will you please send me an employment application. (Polite request)

Tip. Polite requests often sound like questions. To determine the punctuation, apply the action test. If the request prompts an action, use a period. If it prompts a verbal response, use a question mark.

**Faulty**
Could you please correct the balance on my next statement? (This polite request prompts an action rather than a verbal response.)

**Improved**
Could you please correct the balance on my next statement.

GUIDE 35: Use a question mark after a direct question and after statements with questions appended.

Are they hiring at BioTech, Inc.?

Most of their training is in-house, isn't it?

GUIDE 36: Use a dash to (a) set off parenthetical elements containing internal commas, (b) emphasize a sentence interruption, or (c) separate an introductory list from a summarizing statement. The dash has legitimate uses. However, some writers use it whenever they know that punctuation is necessary, but they're not sure exactly what. The dash can be very effective, if not misused.

Three top students—Gene Engle, Donna Hersh, and Mika Sato—won awards. (Use dashes to set off elements with internal commas.)

Executives at IBM—despite rampant rumours in the stock market—remained quiet regarding dividend earnings. (Use dashes to emphasize a sentence interruption.)

Dell, Hewlett-Packard, and Apple—these were the three leading computer manufacturers. (Use a dash to separate an introductory list from a summarizing statement.)

GUIDE 37: Use parentheses to set off nonessential sentence elements, such as explanations, directions, questions, or references.

Researchers find that the office grapevine (see Chapter 1 for more discussion) carries surprisingly accurate information.

Only two dates (February 15 and March 1) are suitable for the meeting.

Tip. Careful writers use parentheses to de-emphasize and the dash to emphasize parenthetical information. One expert said, "Dashes shout the news; parentheses whisper it."

GUIDE 38: Use quotation marks to (a) enclose the exact words of a speaker or writer; (b) distinguish words used in a special sense, such as slang; or (c) enclose titles of articles, chapters, or other short works.

"If you make your job important," said the consultant, "it's quite likely to return the favour."

The recruiter said that she was looking for candidates with good communication skills. (Omit quotation marks because the exact words of the speaker are not quoted.)

This office discourages "rad" hair styles and clothing. (Use quotes for slang.)

A-17

In *Business Week* I saw an article entitled "Communication for Global Markets."
(Use quotation marks around the title of an article; use all caps, underlines, or
italics for the name of the publication.)

**Tip.** Never use quotation marks arbitrarily, as in *Our "spring" sale starts April 1.*

##  Checkpoint

Add appropriate punctuation.

**61.** Will you please send me your latest catalogue as soon as possible

**62.** (Direct quote) The only thing you get in a hurry said the professor is trouble

**63.** (De-emphasize) Two kinds of batteries see page 16 of the instruction booklet
may be used in this camera.

**64.** (Emphasize) The first three colours that we tested red, yellow, and orange were
selected.

**65.** All letters with erroneous addresses were reprinted weren't they

## Capitalization

GUIDE 39: **Capitalize proper nouns and proper adjectives.** Capitalize the *specific*
names of persons, places, institutions, buildings, religions, holidays, months, organizations, laws, races, languages, and so forth. Don't capitalize common nouns that
make *general* references.

| **Proper Nouns** | **Common Nouns** |
|---|---|
| Michelle DeLuca | the manufacturer's rep |
| Algonquin Provincial Park | the wilderness park |
| College of the Rockies | the community college |
| CN Tower | the downtown building |
| Environmental Assessment Agency | the federal agency |
| Persian, Armenian, Hindi | modern foreign languages |

| **Proper Adjectives** | |
|---|---|
| French markets | Italian dressing |
| Xerox copy | Japanese executives |
| Swiss chocolates | Red River economics |

GUIDE 40: **Capitalize only specific academic courses and degrees.**

Professor Jane Mangrum, Ph.D., will teach Accounting 121 next spring.

James Barker, who holds bachelor's and master's degrees, teaches marketing.

Jessica enrolled in classes in management, English, and business law.

GUIDE 41: **Capitalize courtesy, professional, religious, government, family, and
business titles when they precede names.**

Mr. Jameson, Mrs. Alvarez, and Ms. Robinson (Courtesy titles)
Professor Andrews, Dr. Lee (Professional titles)
Rabbi Cohen, Pastor Williams, Pope John (Religious titles)
Prime Minister Martin, Mayor Tremblay (Government titles)
Uncle Edward, Aunt Louise, Cousin Vinney (Family titles)
Vice President Morris, Budget Director Lopez (Business titles)

Do not capitalize a title when it is followed by an appositive (that is, when the title is followed by a noun that renames or explains it).

Only one professor, Jonathan Marcus, favoured a tuition hike.

Local candidates counted on their premier, Ralph Klein, to raise funds.

Do not capitalize titles following names unless they are part of an address:

Mark Yoder, president of Yoder Enterprises, hired all employees.

Paula Beech, director of Human Resources, interviewed all candidates.

Send the package to Amanda Harr, Advertising Manager, Cambridge Publishers, 20 Park Plaza, Saint John, NB E2L 1G2.

Generally, do not capitalize a title that replaces a person's name.

Only the president, his chief of staff, and one senator made the trip.

The director of marketing and the sales manager will meet at 1 p.m.

Do not capitalize family titles used with possessive pronouns.

my mother, his father, your cousin

**GUIDE 42: Capitalize the principal words in the titles of books, magazines, newspapers, articles, movies, plays, songs, poems, and reports.** Do *not* capitalize articles (*a, an, the*) and prepositions of fewer than four letters (*in, to, by, for*) unless they begin or end the title. The *to* in infinitives (*to run, to say, to write*) is also not capitalized unless it appears as the first word of a title or subtitle.

I enjoyed the book *A Customer Is More Than a Name.*

Did you read the article entitled "Companies in Europe Seeking Executives With Multinational Skills"?

We liked the article entitled "Advice From a Pro: How to Say It With Pictures."

(Note that the titles of books are underlined or italicized while the titles of articles are enclosed in quotation marks.)

**GUIDE 43: Capitalize *north, south, east, west,* and their derivatives only when they represent specific geographical regions.**

from the Pacific Northwest      heading northwest on the highway
living in the East      east of the city
moving to the West Coast      western Quebec, southern Ontario

**GUIDE 44: Capitalize the names of departments, divisions, or committees within your own organization.** Outside your organization capitalize only *specific* department, division, or committee names.

Lawyers in our Legal Assistance Department met at 2 p.m.

Samsung offers TVs in its Consumer Electronics Division.

We volunteered for the Employee Social Responsibility Committee.

You might send an application to that company's personnel department.

**GUIDE 45: Capitalize product names only when they refer to trademarked items. Don't capitalize the common names following manufacturers' names.**

| | | |
|---|---|---|
| Sony portable television | Skippy peanut butter | NordicTrack treadmill |
| Eveready Energizer | Gillette razor | Kodak colour copier |
| Coca-Cola | Apple computer | Big Mac sandwich |

**GUIDE 46: Capitalize most nouns followed by numbers or letters (except in page, paragraph, line, and verse references).**

| | | |
|---|---|---|
| Room 14 | Exhibit A | Flight 12, Gate 43 |
| Figure 2.1 | Plan No. 1 | Model Z2010 |

## ✓ Checkpoint

Capitalize all appropriate words.

**66.** vice president ellis bought a toshiba computer for use on her trips to europe.

**67.** our director of research brought plan no. 1 with him to the meeting in our engineering research department.

**68.** proceed west on highway 10 until you reach the mt. vernon exit.

**69.** you are booked on american airlines flight 164 leaving from gate 5 at mirabel international airport.

**70.** to improve their english, many new canadians purchased the book entitled *the power of language is yours*.

## Number Usage

**GUIDE 47: Use word form to express (a) numbers *ten* and under and (b) numbers beginning sentences.** General references to numbers *ten* and under should be expressed in word form. Also use word form for numbers that begin sentences. If the resulting number involves more than two words, however, the sentence should be recast so that the number does not fall at the beginning.

We answered *six* telephone calls for the *four* sales reps.

*Fifteen* customers responded to the *three* advertisements today.

A total of 155 cameras were awarded as prizes. (Avoid beginning the sentence with a long number such as *one hundred fifty-five*.)

**GUIDE 48: Use words to express general references to small fractions. Use words or figures to refer to periods of time or to ages.**

When she reached *twenty-one* (or *21*), she received *one half* of the estate.

James owns a *one-third* interest in the electronics business. (Note that fractions are hyphenated only when they function as adjectives.)

That business was founded *thirty-five* (or *35*) years ago.

**Tip.** Exact ages and specific business terms should be expressed in figures.

> Both Meredith Jones, 55, and Jack Jones, 57, appeared in the article.
>
> The note is payable in 60 days.

**GUIDE 49:** Use figures to express most references to numbers *11* and over.

> Over *150* people from *53* companies attended the two-day workshop.
>
> A 114-mL serving of Haagen-Dazs toffee crunch ice cream contains *300* calories and *19* grams of fat.

**GUIDE 50:** Use figures to express money, dates, clock time, decimals, and percents. Use a combination of words and figures to express sums of 1 million and over.

> One item cost only *$1.95*; most, however, were priced between *$10* and *$35*. (Omit the decimals and zeros in even sums of money.)
>
> A total of *3 700* employees approved the contract *May 12* at *3 p.m.*
>
> When sales dropped *4.7* percent, net income fell *9.8* percent. (Use the word *percent* instead of the symbol %.)
>
> Orion lost *$62.9 million* in the latest fiscal year on revenues of *$584 million*. (Use a combination of words and figures for sums of 1 million and over.)

**Tip.** To ease your memory load, concentrate on the numbers normally expressed in words: numbers *ten* and under, numbers at the beginning of a sentence, and small fractions. Nearly everything else in business is generally written with figures.

##  Checkpoint

Correct any inappropriate expression of numbers.

**71.** McDonald's former McLean Deluxe, priced at one dollar and fifty-nine cents, had only three hundred ten calories and nine percent fat.

**72.** 175 employees will attend the meeting January tenth at one p.m.

**73.** The Nordstrom family, which owns forty percent of the company's stock, recently added four co-presidents.

**74.** Our three branch offices, with a total of ninety-six workers, needs to add six computers and nine printers.

**75.** On March eighth we paid thirty-two dollars per share to acquire one third of the shares.

## Abbreviations

Abbreviations should be used only when they are clear and appropriate. Be aware that every field (such as technology and engineering) has its own specialized abbreviations. Therefore, be certain before you use such abbreviations that the receiver of your information is familiar with them.

A-21

GUIDE 51: Use abbreviations for titles before and after proper names.

*Mr.* Peter Mansbridge          Joshua Paul, *Jr.*
*Rev.* Simon Brownsley          Samford Amhas, *M.D.*
*Hon.* Judy Sgro                Ronny Muntroy, *Ph.D.*

GUIDE 52: Learn when to use periods with abbreviations.
Use a period with conventional abbreviations.

Mrs.    Ms.    Mr.    Dr.    Hon.    Prof.

Acronyms (shortened forms), which are pronounced as a word, do not have periods.

AIDS    scuba    laser    VIP    UNICEF    NAFTA

Latin abbreviations have periods.

e.g.    i.e.    etc.    vs.

GUIDE 53: Use abbreviations for familiar institutions, organizations, associations, corporations, and people.

**Institutions**
UBC    UWO    WLU    CNIB

**Organizations and Associations**
NDP    CIA    YMCA    CAW    CAPIC    CMA
OPEC    G7    OSSTF    NHLPA    CHRP    CSIS

**Corporations**
IBM    CTW    CBC

**People**
PET    FDR    LBJ    JFK

GUIDE 54: Remember your audience when using abbreviations.    If the short form or abbreviation is not well known, spell it out it before using it throughout the discussion.

The CBE (Council of Biology Editors) documentation style is used primarily in the sciences. Consult a reference text for information about how to use CBE documentation.

✓ Checkpoint

Correct any inappropriate use of abbreviations.

**76.** My dr., Samnik Shanban, m.d., has wonderful credentials.

**77.** To save both money and time, the specialist recommended l.a.s.e.r. surgery.

**78.** The question was addressed to Prof Antle.

**79.** You should remember to use a large-sized font when preparing overheads, eg, 24-point or greater.

**80.** Mrs. Cathrick was n.a. for comment.

## Key to C.L.U.E. Checkpoint Exercises in Appendix A

This key shows all corrections. If you marked anything else, double-check the appropriate guideline.

1. Pizza Hut fought back with
2. backfire; consequently,
3. advertisements; they
4. chain, Domino's
5. deliveries; the
6. If I *were* . . . I would have *written*
7. could have *written* . . . if you *had* read
8. When Trevor *saw*
9. I wish I *were* . . . could have *gone*
10. she had *taken* . . . able to *choose*
11. energy *have*
12. efforts, *is* disappointingly
13. Ms. Wagner *is* in charge
14. companies *is* being
15. *knows* how
16. my friend and *I* . . . *its* price
17. to *him* and *me*
18. between you and *me*
19. *yours* and *hers*
20. could have been *she* . . . to you and *me*
21. *whomever* we nominate
22. *Whom* would you
23. *whoever* ordered
24. Jeff and *I*
25. by *whoever* experiences
26. to have *his or her* tuition; to have *the* tuition; *all employees are entitled to have their tuition reimbursed*
27. but *this advancement plan* appeals (*Revise to avoid vague pronoun* it.)
28. may cancel *his or her* subscription; may cancel *the* subscription; *subscribers* may cancel *their* subscriptions
29. *his or her* name and address; *all voters must have their names and addresses*
30. *These activities are* particularly important (*Revise to avoid the vague pronoun* this.)
31. my manager and *I* . . . point-by-point
32. completed the work *so quickly* . . . recently opened (*Omit hyphen.*)
33. If I do *well* . . . part-time . . . full-time
34. told him and *me* . . . *personally*

A-23

35. *not-too-distant* future

36. class, Jeff . . . commas, semicolons, and

37. punctuation, (*No comma before* and!)

38. program, but

39. business law, or

40. degree, he . . . Montreal, Ottawa, or

41. 222 George Henry Blvd., Toronto, ON M2J 1E6, as her

42. felt, nevertheless,

43. paralegals, which . . . year,

44. April 1, 1999, . . . January 1, 2003.

45. As a matter of fact,

46. (*Remove comma.*)

47. equipment,

48. (*Remove comma.*)

49. think, on the other hand, . . . women, minorities, and

50. (*Remove comma.*)

51. entry-level job; my . . . goal, however,

52. candidates: Joni Sims, Simon Fraser University; James Jones, University of Saskatchewan; and Madonna Farr, Ryerson University.

53. qualities: initiative, versatility, and

54. individuals; however,

55. area; therefore,

56. companies'

57. one month's time . . . members'

58. Bryan's . . . *his* being elected

59. years' experience

60. Jackson's car

61. possible.

62. "The only thing you get in a hurry," said the professor, "is trouble."

63. batteries (see page 16 of the instruction booklet) may be

64. tested—red, yellow, and orange—were selected.

65. reprinted, weren't they?

66. Vice President Ellis . . . Toshiba computer . . . Europe

67. Our . . . Plan No. 1 . . . Engineering Research Department

68. Proceed . . . Highway 10 . . . Mt. Vernon exit.

69. You . . . American Airlines Flight 164 . . . Gate 5 at Mirabel International Airport.

70. To improve their English, many new Canadians . . . *The Power of Language Is Yours.*

71. priced at $1.59, had only 310 calories and 9 percent fat.

72. A total of 175 employees . . . January 10 at 1 p.m.

73. 40 percent

74. 96 workers

75. March 8 . . . $32

76. doctor ... M.D.,

77. laser

78. Professor

79. e.g.

80. not available

## Confusing Words

| | | | |
|---|---|---|---|
| accede: | to agree or consent | council: | governing body |
| exceed: | over a limit | counsel: | (v) to give advice; |
| accept: | to receive | | (n) advice |
| except: | to exclude; (prep) but | credible: | believable |
| adverse: | opposing; antagonistic | creditable: | good enough for praise |
| averse: | unwilling; reluctant | | or esteem; reliable |
| advice: | suggestion, opinion | desert: | arid land; to abandon |
| advise: | to counsel or recom- | dessert: | sweet food |
| | mend | device: | invention or mechanism |
| affect: | to influence | devise: | to design or arrange |
| effect: | (n) outcome, result; (v) | disburse: | to pay out |
| | to bring about, to create | disperse: | to scatter widely |
| all ready: | prepared | elicit: | to draw out |
| already: | by this time | illicit: | unlawful |
| all right: | satisfactory | envelop: | (v) to wrap, surround, or |
| alright: | unacceptable variant | | conceal |
| | spelling | envelope: | (n) a container for a |
| altar: | structure for worship | | written message |
| alter: | to change | every day: | each single day |
| appraise: | to estimate | everyday: | ordinary |
| apprise: | to inform | farther: | a greater distance |
| ascent: | (n) rising or going up | further: | additional |
| assent: | (v) to agree or consent | formally: | in a formal manner |
| assure: | to promise | formerly: | in the past |
| ensure: | to make certain | grate: | (v) to reduce to small |
| insure: | to protect from loss | | particles; to cause irrita- |
| capital: | (n) city that is seat of | | tion; (n) a frame of |
| | government; wealth of | | crossed bars blocking a |
| | an individual; (adj) chief | | passage |
| capitol: | building that houses | great: | (adj) large in size; |
| | state or national | | numerous; eminent or |
| | lawmakers | | distinguished |
| cereal: | breakfast food | hole: | an opening |
| serial: | arranged in sequence | whole: | complete |
| cite: | to quote; to summon | imply: | to suggest indirectly |
| site: | location | infer: | to reach a conclusion |
| sight: | a view; to see | lean: | (v) to rest against; (adj) |
| coarse: | rough texture | | not fat |
| course: | a route; part of a meal; | lien: | (n) a legal right or claim |
| | a unit of learning | | to property |
| complement: | that which completes | liable: | legally responsible |
| compliment: | to praise or flatter | libel: | damaging written |
| conscience: | regard for fairness | | statement |
| conscious: | aware | loose: | not fastened |

| | | | |
|---|---|---|---|
| *lose:* | to misplace | *principal:* | (n) capital sum; school official; (adj) chief |
| *miner:* | person working in a mine | *principle:* | rule of action |
| *minor:* | a lesser item; person under age | *stationary:* | immovable |
| | | *stationery:* | writing material |
| *patience:* | calm perseverance | *than:* | conjunction showing comparison |
| *patients:* | people receiving medical treatment | *then:* | adverb meaning "at that time" |
| *personal:* | private, individual | *their:* | possessive form of *they* |
| *personnel:* | employees | *there:* | at that place or point |
| *plaintiff:* | (n) one who initiates a lawsuit | *they're:* | contraction of *they are* |
| *plaintive:* | (adj) expressive of suffering or woe | *to:* | a preposition; the sign of the infinitive |
| *populace:* | (n) the masses; population of a place | *too:* | an adverb meaning "also" or "to an excessive extent" |
| *populous:* | (adj) densely populated | | |
| *precede:* | to go before | *two:* | a number |
| *proceed:* | to continue | *waiver:* | abandonment of a claim |
| *precedence:* | priority | *waver:* | to shake or fluctuate |
| *precedents:* | events used as an example | | |

# 165 Frequently Misspelled Words

| | | | |
|---|---|---|---|
| absence | convenient | familiar | license (v) |
| accommodate | correspondence | fascinate | maintenance |
| achieve | courteous | feasible | manageable |
| acknowledgment | criticize | February | manufacturer |
| across | decision | fibre | mileage |
| adequate | deductible | fiscal | miscellaneous |
| advisable | defendant | foreign | mortgage |
| analyze | definitely | forty | necessary |
| annually | dependant | fourth | nevertheless |
| appointment | dependent | friend | ninety |
| argument | describe | genuine | ninth |
| automatically | desirable | government | noticeable |
| bankruptcy | destroy | grammar | occasionally |
| becoming | development | grateful | occurred |
| beneficial | disappoint | guarantee | offered |
| budget | dissatisfied | harass | omission |
| business | division | height | omitted |
| calendar | efficient | hoping | opportunity |
| cancelled | embarrass | immediate | opposite |
| catalogue | emphasis | incidentally | ordinarily |
| centre | emphasize | incredible | paid |
| changeable | employee | independent | pamphlet |
| column | envelope | indispensable | permanent |
| committee | equipped | interrupt | permitted |
| congratulate | especially | irrelevant | pleasant |
| conscience | evidently | itinerary | practical |
| conscious | exaggerate | judgment | prevalent |
| consecutive | excellent | knowledge | privilege |
| consensus | exempt | legitimate | probably |
| consistent | existence | library | procedure |
| control | extraordinary | licence (n) | profited |

prominent
qualify
quantity
questionnaire
receipt
receive
recognize
recommendation
referred
regarding
remittance

representative
restaurant
schedule
secretary
separate
similar
sincerely
software
succeed
sufficient
supervisor

surprise
tenant
therefore
thorough
though
through
truly
undoubtedly
unnecessarily
usable
usage

using
usually
valuable
vigorous
   (*but* vigour)
volume
weekday
writing
yield

# Appendix B

## Guide to Document Formats

Business documents carry two kinds of messages. Verbal messages are conveyed by the words chosen to express the writer's ideas. Nonverbal messages are conveyed largely by the appearance of a document. If you compare an assortment of letters and memos from various organizations, you will notice immediately that some look more attractive and more professional than others. The nonverbal message of the professional-looking documents suggests that they were sent by people who are careful, informed, intelligent, and successful. Understandably, you're more likely to take seriously documents that use attractive stationery and professional formatting techniques.

Over the years certain practices and conventions have arisen regarding the appearance and formatting of business documents. Although these conventions offer some choices (such as letter and punctuation styles), most business letters follow standardized formats. To ensure that your documents carry favourable nonverbal messages about you and your organization, you'll want to give special attention to the stationery and formatting of your letters, envelopes, memos, e-mail messages, and fax cover sheets.

### Stationery

Most organizations use high-quality stationery for business documents. This stationery is printed on select paper that meets two qualifications: weight and cotton-fibre content.

Paper is measured by weight and may range from 9 pounds (thin onionskin paper) to 32 pounds (thick card and cover stock). Most office stationery is in the 16- to 24-pound range. Lighter 16-pound paper is generally sufficient for internal documents, including memos. Heavier 20- to 24-pound paper is used for printed letterhead stationery.

Paper is also judged by its cotton-fibre content. Cotton fibre makes paper stronger, softer in texture, and less likely to yellow. Good-quality stationery contains 25 percent or more cotton fibre.

### Letter Placement

The easiest way to place letters on the page is to use the defaults of your word processing program. These are usually set for side margins of 2.5 cm. Many companies today find these margins quite acceptable.

If you wish to adjust your margins to better balance shorter letters, use the following chart.

| Words in Body of Letter | Side Margins | Blank Lines After Date |
|---|---|---|
| Under 200 | 4 cm | 4 to 10 |
| Over 200 | 2.5 cm | 2 to 3 |

By the way, experts say that a "ragged" right margin is easier to read than a justified (even) margin. Consider turning off the justification feature of your word processing program if it automatically justifies the right margin.

## Letter Parts

Professional-looking business letters are arranged in a conventional sequence with standard parts. Following is a discussion of how to use these letter parts properly. Figure B.1 illustrates the parts in a block-style letter. (See Chapter 9 for additional discussion of letters and their parts.)

**Letterhead.** Most business organizations use $8\frac{1}{2}$- by 11-inch paper printed with a letterhead displaying their official name, land address, e-mail address, telephone number, and fax number. The letterhead may also include a logo and an advertising message.

**Dateline.** On letterhead paper you should place the date one blank line below the last line of the letterhead or 5 cm from the top edge of the paper. On plain paper place the date immediately below your return address. Start the return address about 4 to 5 cm from the top. The most common dateline format is as follows: *June 9, 2005*. Don't use *th* (or *rd*) when the date is written this way. For European or military correspondence, use the following dateline format: *9 June 2005*. Notice that no commas are used.

**Addressee and Delivery Notations.** Delivery notations such as *FAX TRANSMITTAL, FEDERAL EXPRESS, MESSENGER DELIVERY, CONFIDENTIAL,* or *CERTIFIED MAIL* are typed in all capital letters one blank line above the inside address.

**Inside Address.** Type the inside address—that is, the address of the organization or person receiving the letter—single-spaced, starting at the left margin. The number of lines between the dateline and the inside address depends on the size of the letter body, the type size (point or pitch size), and the length of the typing lines. Generally, two to seven blank lines are appropriate.

Be careful to duplicate the exact wording and spelling of the recipient's name and address on your documents. Usually, you can copy this information from the letterhead of the correspondence you are answering. If, for example, you are responding to *Jackson & Perkins Company*, don't address your letter to *Jackson and Perkins Corp.*

Always be sure to include a courtesy title such as *Mr., Ms., Mrs., Dr.,* or *Professor* before a person's name in the inside address—for both the letter and the envelope. Although many women in business today favour *Ms.,* you'll want to use whatever title the addressee prefers.

Remember that the inside address is not included for readers who already know who and where they are. It's there to help writers accurately file a copy of the message.

**FIGURE B.1** Block and Modified Block Letter Styles

**Block style**
**Mixed punctuation**

Letterhead ———————————

*island*graphics
893 Dillingham Boulevard, Vancouver, BC V5A 1B1

Dateline ———————————
September 13, 2005
↓ 5 cm from the top or 1 blank line below letterhead

↓ 2 to 7 blank lines

Inside address ———————
Mr. T. M. Wilson, President
Visual Concept Enterprises
2166 Ocean Forest Drive
Surrey, BC V3A 7K2
↓ 1 blank line

Salutation ————————
Dear Mr. Wilson:
↓ 1 blank line

Subject line ————————
SUBJECT:  BLOCK LETTER STYLE
↓ 1 blank line

This letter illustrates block letter style, about which you asked.  All typed lines begin at the left margin.  The date is usually placed two inches from the top edge of the paper or 1 blank line below the last line of the letterhead, whichever position is lower.

Body ———————————
This letter also shows mixed punctuation.  A colon follows the salutation, and a comma follows the complimentary close.

If a subject line is included, it appears 1 blank line below the salutation.  The word *SUBJECT* is optional.  Most readers will recognize a statement in this position as the subject without an identifying label.  The complimentary close appears 1 blank line below the end of the last paragraph.
↓ 1 blank line

Complimentary ——————
close
Sincerely,
↓ 3 blank lines

Signature block ———————
Mark H. Wong
Graphics Designer
↓ 1 blank line

MHW:pil

**Modified block style**
**Mixed punctuation**

In the modified block-style letter shown at the left, the date is centred or aligned with the complimentary close and signature block, which start at the centre.  Mixed punctuation includes a colon after the salutation and a comma after the complimentary close, as shown above and at the left.

In general, avoid abbreviations (such as *Ave.* or *Co.*) unless they appear in the printed letterhead of the document being answered.

**Attention Line.** An attention line allows you to send your message officially to an organization but to direct it to a specific individual, officer, or department. However, if you know an individual's complete name, it's always better to use it as the first line of the inside address and avoid an attention line. Here are two common formats for attention lines:

MultiMedia Enterprises
27 Fairlance Boulevard
Nepean, ON K2E 5H3

MultiMedia Enterprises
Attention: Marketing Director
27 Fairlance Boulevard
Nepean, ON K2E 5H3

ATTENTION MARKETING DIRECTOR

Attention lines may be typed in all caps or with upper- and lowercase letters. A colon following *Attention* is optional. Notice that an attention line may be placed one blank line below the address block or printed as the second line of the inside address. You'll want to use the latter format if you're composing on a word processor because the address block may be copied to the envelope and the attention line will not interfere with the last-line placement of the postal code. (Mail can be sorted more easily if the postal code appears in the last line of a typed address.)

Whenever possible, use a person's name as the first line of an address instead of putting that name in an attention line. Some writers use an attention line because they fear that letters addressed to individuals at companies may be considered private. They worry that if the addressee is no longer with the company, the letter may be forwarded or not opened. Actually, unless a letter is marked "Personal" or "Confidential," it will very likely be opened as business mail.

**Salutation.** For most letter styles, place the letter greeting, or salutation, one blank line below the last line of the inside address or the attention line (if used). If the letter is addressed to an individual, use that person's courtesy title and last name (Dear Mr. Lanham). Even if you are on a first-name basis (Dear Leslie), be sure to add a colon (not a comma or a semicolon) after the salutation. Do not use an individual's full name in the salutation (not Dear Mr. Leslie Lanham) unless you are unsure of gender (Dear Leslie Lanham).

For letters with attention lines or those addressed to organizations, the selection of an appropriate salutation has become more difficult. Formerly, *Gentlemen* was used generically for all organizations. With increasing numbers of women in business management today, however, *Gentlemen* is problematic. Because no universally acceptable salutation has emerged as yet, you'll probably be safest with *Ladies and Gentlemen* or *Gentlemen and Ladies.*

One way to avoid the salutation dilemma is to address a document to a specific person. Another alternative is to use the simplified letter style, which conveniently omits the salutation (and the complimentary close).

**Subject and Reference Lines.** Although experts suggest placing the subject line one blank line below the salutation, many businesses actually place it above the salutation. Use whatever style your organization prefers. Reference lines often show policy or file numbers; they generally appear 1 blank line above the salutation.

**Body.** Most business letters and memorandums are single-spaced, with double line spacing between paragraphs. Very short messages may be double-spaced with indented paragraphs.

**Complimentary Close.** Typed one blank line below the last line of the letter, the complimentary close may be formal (Very truly yours) or informal (Sincerely yours or Cordially). The simplified letter style omits a complimentary close.

**Signature Block.** In most letter styles the writer's typed name and optional identification appear three to four blank lines below the complimentary close. The combination of name, title, and organization information should be arranged to achieve a balanced look. The name and title may appear on the same line or on separate lines, depending on the length of each. Use commas to separate categories within the same line, but not to conclude a line.

Sincerely yours,                          Cordially yours,

Jeremy M. Wood, Manager          Casandra Baker-Murillo
Technical Sales and Services        Executive Vice President

Courtesy titles (*Ms., Mrs.,* or *Miss*) should be used before female names that are not readily distinguishable as male or female. They should also be used before names containing only initials and international names. The title is usually placed in parentheses, but it may appear without them.

Yours truly,                               Sincerely,

(Ms.) K. C. Tripton                      (Mr.) Leslie Hill
Project Manager                          Public Policy Department

Some organizations include their names in the signature block. In such cases the organization name appears in all caps two lines below the complimentary close, as shown here.

Cordially,

LITTON COMPUTER SERVICES

Shelina A. Simpson
Executive Assistant

**Reference Initials.** If used, the initials of the typist and writer are typed one blank line below the writer's name and title. Generally, the writer's initials are capitalized and the typist's are lowercased, but this format varies.

**Enclosure Notation.** When an enclosure or attachment accompanies a document, a notation to that effect appears one blank line below the reference initials. This notation reminds the typist to insert the enclosure in the envelope, and it reminds the recipient to look for the enclosure or attachment. The notation may be spelled out

(*Enclosure, Attachment*), or it may be abbreviated (*Enc., Att.*). It may indicate the number of enclosures or attachments, and it may also identify a specific enclosure (*Enclosure: Form 1099*).

**Copy Notation.** If you make copies of correspondence for other individuals, you may use *cc* to indicate carbon or courtesy copy, *pc* to indicate photocopy, or merely *c* for any kind of copy. A colon following the initial(s) is optional.

**Second-Page Heading.** When a letter extends beyond one page, use plain paper of the same quality and colour as the first page. Identify the second and succeeding pages with a heading consisting of the name of the addressee, the page number, and the date. Use either of the following two formats:

Ms. Rachel Ruiz                    2                    May 3, 2005

Ms. Rachel Ruiz
Page 2
May 3, 2005

Both headings appear 2.5 cm from the top of the page and are followed by two blank lines to separate them from the continuing text. Avoid using a second page if you have only one line or the complimentary close and signature block to fill that page.

**Plain-Paper Return Address.** If you prepare a personal or business letter on plain paper, place your address immediately above the date. Do not include your name; you will type (and sign) your name at the end of your letter. Start your street address 4 to 5 cm from the top edge of the paper. Avoid abbreviations except for a two-letter province or state abbreviation.

580 Frontenac Street
Kingston, ON K7K 4M2
December 14, 2005

Ms. Ellen Siemens
Escrow Department
Kingston Trust
1075 Johnson Street
Kingston, ON K7M 2N6

Dear Ms. Siemens:

For letters prepared in the block style, type the return address at the left margin. For modified block-style letters, start the return address at the centre to align with the complimentary close.

## Letter Styles

Business letters are generally prepared in one of three formats. The most popular is the block style, but the simplified style has much to recommend it.

**Block Style.** In the block style, shown earlier in Figure B.1, all lines begin at the left margin. This style is a favourite because it is easy to format.

**Modified Block Style.** The modified block style differs from block style in that the date and closing lines appear in the centre, as shown at the bottom of Figure B.1. The date may be (1) centred, (2) begun at the centre of the page (to align with the closing lines), or (3) backspaced from the right margin. The signature block—including the complimentary close, writer's name and title, or organization identification—begins at the centre. The first line of each paragraph may begin at the left margin or may be indented five or ten spaces. All other lines begin at the left margin.

**Simplified Style.** Introduced by the Administrative Management Society a number of years ago, the simplified letter style, shown in Figure B.2, requires little formatting. Like the block style, all lines begin at the left margin. A subject line appears in all caps two blank lines below the inside address and two blank lines above the first paragraph. The salutation and complimentary close are omitted. The signer's name and identification appear in all caps four blank lines below the last paragraph. This letter style is efficient and avoids the problem of appropriate salutations and courtesy titles.

**FIGURE B.2** Simplified Letter Style

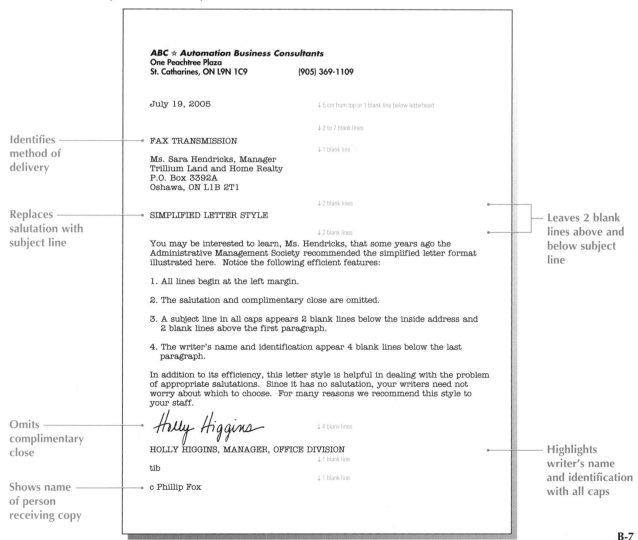

## Punctuation Styles

Two punctuation styles are appropriate for letters. *Open* punctuation contains no punctuation after the salutation or complimentary close. This style is seldom seen in business today. *Mixed* punctuation, shown with the modified block-style letter in Figure B.1, requires a colon after the salutation and a comma after the complimentary close. Many business organizations prefer mixed punctuation, even in a block-style letter.

If you choose mixed punctuation, be sure to use a colon—not a comma or semicolon—after the salutation. Even when the salutation is a first name, the colon is appropriate.

## Envelopes

An envelope should be printed on the same quality and colour of stationery as the letter it carries. Because the envelope introduces your message and makes the first impression, you need to be especially careful in addressing it. Moreover, how you fold the letter is important. For further and updated information on addressing envelopes, consult the Canada Post Corporation (CPC) home page at <**www.canadapost.ca**>. Use the Search function to locate the Canadian Postal Guide and Reference Tools section.

**Return Address.** The return address is usually printed in the upper-left corner of an envelope, as shown in Figure B.3. In large companies some form of identification (the writer's initials, name, or location) may be typed above the company name and return address. This identification helps return the letter to the sender in case of nondelivery.

**FIGURE B.3** Envelope Formats

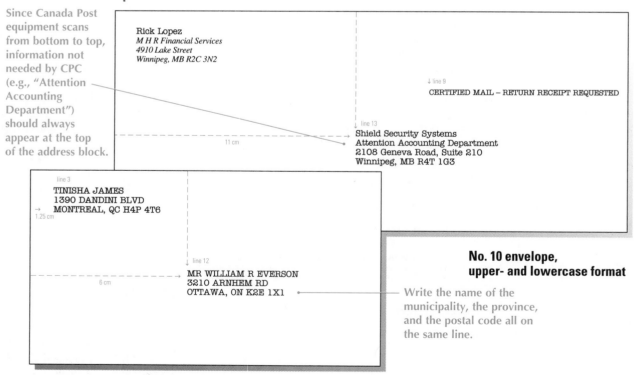

Since Canada Post equipment scans from bottom to top, information not needed by CPC (e.g., "Attention Accounting Department") should always appear at the top of the address block.

Rick Lopez
*M H R Financial Services*
*4910 Lake Street*
*Winnipeg, MB R2C 3N2*

↓ line 9
CERTIFIED MAIL – RETURN RECEIPT REQUESTED

↓ line 13
Shield Security Systems
Attention Accounting Department
2108 Geneva Road, Suite 210
Winnipeg, MB R4T 1G3

11 cm

line 3
TINISHA JAMES
1390 DANDINI BLVD
→ MONTREAL, QC H4P 4T6
1.25 cm

↓ line 12
MR WILLIAM R EVERSON
3210 ARNHEM RD
OTTAWA, ON K2E 1X1

6 cm

**No. 10 envelope,
upper- and lowercase format**

Write the name of the municipality, the province, and the postal code all on the same line.

**No. 8 envelope, uppercase format**

On an envelope without a printed return address, single-space the return address in the upper-left corner. Beginning on line 3 on the fourth space (1.25 cm) from the left edge, type the writer's name, title, company, and mailing address.

**Mailing Address.** On legal-sized No. 10 envelopes (10.4 by 24.1 cm), begin the address 5 cm from the top and about 11 cm from the left edge, as shown in Figure B.3. For No. 8 envelopes (9.2 by 16.5 cm), begin typing on line 12 about 6 cm from the left edge.

Canada Post Corporation recommends that addresses be consistent and accurate to "ensure that mail is 'delivered on time, the first time, every time.'" Writers can take advantage of word processing programs to "copy" the inside address to the envelope, thus saving keystrokes and reducing errors. Having the same format on both the inside address and the envelope also looks more professional and consistent. For these reasons you may choose to use the familiar upper- and lowercase combination format. But you will want to check with your organization to learn its preference.

In addressing your envelopes for delivery in this country or in the United States, use the two-letter province and state abbreviations shown in Figure B.4. Notice that these abbreviations are in capital letters without periods.

**Folding.** The way a letter is folded and inserted into an envelope sends additional nonverbal messages about a writer's professionalism and carefulness. Most businesspeople follow the procedures shown here, which produce the least number of creases to distract readers.

For large No. 10 envelopes, begin with the letter face up. Fold slightly less than one third of the sheet toward the top, as shown above. Then fold down the top third to within about 1 cm of the bottom fold. Insert the letter into the envelope with the last fold toward the bottom of the envelope.

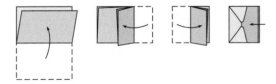

For small No. 8 envelopes, begin by folding the bottom up to within about 1 cm of the top edge. Then fold the right third over to the left. Fold the left third to within about 1 cm from the last fold. Insert the last fold into the envelope first.

## Memorandums

As discussed in Chapter 8, memorandums deliver messages within organizations. Many offices use memo forms imprinted with the organization name and, optionally, the department or division names, as shown in Figure B.5 on page B-11. Although the design and arrangement of memo forms vary, they usually include the

**FIGURE B.4  Abbreviations of Provinces, Territories, and States**

| PROVINCE OR TERRITORY | TWO-LETTER ABBREVIATION | STATE OR TERRITORY | TWO-LETTER ABBREVIATION |
|---|---|---|---|
| Alberta | AB | Kansas | KS |
| British Columbia | BC | Kentucky | KY |
| Manitoba | MB | Louisiana | LA |
| New Brunswick | NB | Maine | ME |
| Newfoundland/Labrador | NL | Maryland | MD |
| Northwest Territories | NT | Massachusetts | MA |
| Nova Scotia | NS | Michigan | MI |
| Nunavut | NU | Minnesota | MN |
| Ontario | ON | Mississippi | MS |
| Prince Edward Island | PE | Missouri | MO |
| Quebec | QC | Montana | MT |
| Saskatchewan | SK | Nebraska | NE |
| Yukon Territory | YT | New Hampshire | NH |
| | | New Jersey | NJ |
| | | New Mexico | NM |
| | | New York | NY |
| **STATE OR TERRITORY** | **TWO-LETTER ABBREVIATION** | North Carolina | NC |
| | | North Dakota | ND |
| Alabama | AL | Ohio | OH |
| Alaska | AK | Oklahoma | OK |
| Arizona | AZ | Oregon | OR |
| Arkansas | AR | Pennsylvania | PA |
| California | CA | Puerto Rico | PR |
| Canal Zone | CZ | Rhode Island | RI |
| Colorado | CO | South Carolina | SC |
| Connecticut | CT | South Dakota | SD |
| Delaware | DE | Tennessee | TN |
| District of Columbia | DC | Texas | TX |
| Florida | FL | Utah | UT |
| Georgia | GA | Vermont | VT |
| Guam | GU | Virgin Islands | VI |
| Hawaii | HI | Virginia | VA |
| Idaho | ID | Washington | WA |
| Illinois | IL | West Virginia | WV |
| Indiana | IN | Wisconsin | WI |
| Iowa | IA | Wyoming | WY |

basic elements of DATE, TO, FROM, and SUBJECT. Large organizations may include other identifying headings, such as FILE NUMBER, FLOOR, EXTENSION, LOCATION, and DISTRIBUTION.

Because of the difficulty of aligning computer printers with preprinted forms, many business writers store memo formats in their computers and call them up when preparing memos. The guide words are then printed with the message, thus eliminating alignment problems.

**FIGURE B.5  Printed Memo Forms**

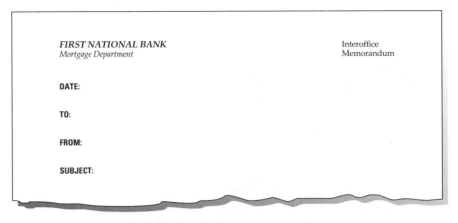

If no printed or stored computer forms are available, memos may be typed on company letterhead or on plain paper, as shown in Figure B.6 on page B-12. On a full sheet of paper, start the guide words 5 cm from the top; on a half sheet, start 2.5 cm from the top. Double-space and type in all caps the guide words: DATE:, TO:, FROM:, SUBJECT:. Align all the fill-in information 2 spaces after the longest guide word (SUBJECT:). Leave 3 lines between the last line of the heading and the first line of the memo. Like business letters, memos are single-spaced.

Memos are generally formatted with side margins of 3 cm, or they may conform to the printed memo form. (For more information about memos, see Chapter 8.)

## E-Mail Messages

Because e-mail is a developing communication medium, formatting and usage are still fluid. The following suggestions, illustrated in Figure B.7 on page B-12 and also in Figure 8.3 in Chapter 8, may guide you in setting up the parts of an e-mail message. Always check, however, with your organization so that you can follow its practices.

*To* **Line.**  Include the receiver's e-mail address after *To*. If the receiver's address is recorded in your address book, you just have to click on it. Be sure to enter all addresses very carefully since one mistyped letter prevents delivery.

**FIGURE B.6** Memo on Plain Paper

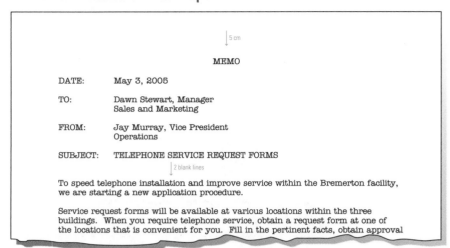

*From* **Line.** Most mail programs automatically include your name and e-mail address after *From*.

*Cc* **and** *Bcc*. Insert the e-mail address of anyone who is to receive a copy of the message. *Cc* stands for carbon copy or courtesy copy. Don't be tempted, though, to send needless copies just because it's so easy. *Bcc* stands for *blind carbon copy*. Some

**FIGURE B.7** E-Mail Message

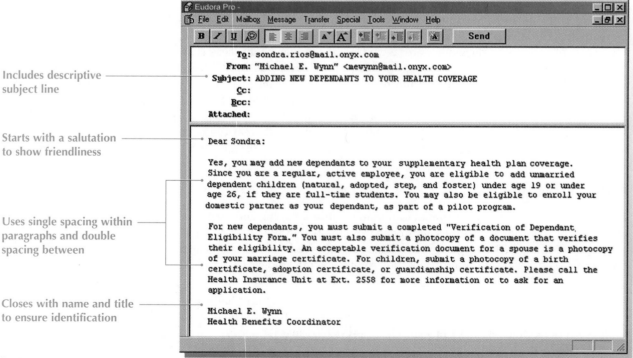

writers use this to send a copy of the message without the addressee's knowledge. Sending blind carbon copies, however, is dangerous because you just might make an address error, and the addressee could learn of the intended *bcc*. Use the *bcc* feature when sending a message to many people. It protects their privacy by concealing their e-mail addresses.

**Subject.** Identify the subject of the e-mail message with a brief but descriptive summary of the topic. Be sure to include enough information to be clear and compelling. Capitalize the initial letters of principal words, or capitalize the entire line if space permits.

**Salutation.** Include a brief greeting to show friendliness, if you like. Some writers use a salutation such as *Dear Sondra* followed by a comma or a colon. Others are more informal with *Hi, Sondra!* or *Good morning* or *Greetings*. Some writers stimulate a saluation by including the name of the receiver in an abbreviated first line. Other writers treat an e-mail message like a memo and skip the salutation entirely.

**Message.** Cover just one topic in your message, and try to keep your total message under two screens in length. Single-space and be sure to use both upper- and lower-case letters. Double-space between paragraphs.

**Closing.** Conclude an external message, if you like, with *Cheers, Best wishes,* or *Warm regards,* followed by your name and e-mail address (because some programs and routers do not transmit your address automatically). If the recipient is unlikely to know you, it's not a bad idea to include your title and organization. Some veteran e-mail users include a *signature file* with identifying information embellished with keyboard art. Use restraint, however, because signature files take up precious space. Writers of e-mail messages sent within organizations may omit a closing and even skip their names at the ends of messages because receivers recognize them from indentification in the opening lines.

**Attachment.** Use the attachment window or button to select the path and file name of any file you wish to send with your e-mail message. You can also attach a Web page to your message.

## Fax Cover Sheet

Documents transmitted by fax are usually introduced by a cover sheet, such as that shown in Figure B.8. As with memos, the format varies considerably. Important items to include are (1) the name and fax number of the receiver, (2) the name and fax number of the sender, (3) the number of pages being sent, and (4) the name and telephone number of the person to notify in case of unsatisfactory transmission.

When the document being transmitted requires little explanation, you may prefer to attach an adhesive note (such as a Post-It fax transmittal form) instead of a full cover sheet. These notes carry essentially the same information as shown in our printed fax cover sheet. They are perfectly acceptable in most business organizations and can save considerable paper and transmission costs.

**FIGURE B.8** Fax Cover Sheet

**FAX TRANSMISSION**

DATE: _____

TO: _____     FAX
      _____     NUMBER: _____
      _____

FROM: _____     FAX
        _____     NUMBER: _____
        _____

NUMBER OF PAGES TRANSMITTED INCLUDING THIS COVER SHEET: _____

MESSAGE:

If any part of this fax transmission is missing or not clearly received, please call:

NAME: _____

PHONE: _____

# Appendix C

# Documentation Formats

For many reasons business writers are careful to properly document report data. Citing sources strengthens a writer's argument, as you learned in Chapter 12. Acknowledging sources also shields writers from charges of plagiarism. Moreover, good references help readers pursue further research.

Before we discuss specific documentation formats, you must understand the difference between *source* notes and *content* notes. Source notes identify quotations, paraphrased passages, and author references. They lead readers to the sources of cited information, and they must follow a consistent format. Content notes, on the other hand, enable writers to add comments, explain information not directly related to the text, or refer readers to other sections of a report. Because content notes are generally infrequent, most writers identify them in the text with a raised asterisk (*). At the bottom of the page, the asterisk is repeated with the content note following. If two content notes appear on one page, a double asterisk identifies the second reference.

Your real concern will be with source notes. These identify quotations or paraphrased ideas in the text, and they direct readers to a complete list of references (a bibliography) at the end of your report. Researchers have struggled for years to develop the perfect documentation system, one that is efficient for the writer and crystal clear to the reader. As a result, many systems exist, each with its advantages. The important thing for you is to adopt one system and use it consistently.

Students frequently ask, "But what documentation system is most used in business?" Actually, no one method dominates. Many businesses have developed their own hybrid systems. These companies generally supply guidelines illustrating their in-house style to employees. Before starting any research project on the job, you'll want to inquire about your organization's preferred documentation style. You can also look in the files for examples of previous reports.

References are usually cited in two places: (1) a brief citation appears in the text, and (2) a complete citation appears in a bibliography at the end of the report. The two most common formats for citations and bibliographies are those of the Modern Language Association (MLA) and the American Psychological Association (APA). Each has its own style for textual references and bibliography lists. For more discussion and examples of citations for electronic formats, visit "Study Resources" at <**www.businesscommunication-4th.nelson.com**>.

## Modern Language Association Format

Writers in the humanities frequently use the MLA format, as illustrated in Figure C.1. In parentheses close to the textual reference appears the author's name and page cited.

# FIGURE C.1 Portions of MLA Text Page and Bibliography

Peanut butter was first delivered to the world by a St. Louis physician in 1890. As discussed at the Peanut Advisory Board's Web site, peanut butter was originally promoted as a protein substitute for elderly patients ("History," screen 2). However, it was the 1905 Universal Exposition in St. Louis that truly launched peanut butter. Since then, annual peanut butter consumption has zoomed to 3.3 pounds a person in the United States (Barrons 46). America's farmers produce 1.6 million tons of peanuts annually, about half of which is used for oil, nuts, and candy. Lisa Gibbons, executive secretary of the Peanut Advisory Board, says that "peanuts in some form are in the top four candies: Snickers, Reese's Peanut Butter Cups, Peanut M & Ms, and Butterfinger" (Meadows 32).

Works Cited

Barrons, Elizabeth Ruth. "A Comparison of Domestic and International Consumption of Legumes." *Journal of Economic Agriculture* 23 (1998): 45–49.

"History of Peanut Butter." Peanut Advisory Board. Retrieved 19 Jan. 2003 <http://www.peanutbutterlovers.com/History/index.html>.

Meadows, Mark Allen. "Peanut Crop Is Anything but Peanuts at Home and Overseas." *Business Monthly* 30 Sept. 2002: 31–34.

If no author is known, a shortened version of the source title is used. At the end of the report, the writer lists alphabetically all references in a bibliography called "Works Cited." To see a long report illustrating MLA documentation, turn to Figure 14.4 in Chapter 14. For more information consult Joseph Gibaldi, *MLA Handbook for Writers of Research Papers*, Sixth Edition (New York: The Modern Language Association of America, 2003).

**MLA In-Text Format.** In-text citations generally appear close to the point where the reference is mentioned or at the end of the sentence inside the closing period. Follow these guidelines:

- Include the last name of the author(s) and the page number. Omit a comma, as (Smith 310).

- If the author's name is mentioned in the text, cite only the page number in parentheses. Do not include either the word *page* or the abbreviations *p.* or *pp.*

- If no author is known, refer to the document title or a shortened version of it, as (Facts at Fingertips 102).

**MLA Bibliographic Format.** The "Works Cited" bibliography lists all references cited in a report. Some writers include all works consulted. A portion of an MLA bibliography is shown in Figure C.1. A more complete list of model references appears in Figure C.2. Following are selected guidelines summarizing important points regarding MLA bibliographic format:

- Use italics or underscores for the titles of books, magazines, newspapers, and journals. Check with your organization or instructor for guidance. Capitalize all important words.

**FIGURE C.2** MLA Bibliography Sample References

Works Cited

Air Canada. *2003 Annual Report.* Dorval, QC.     — Annual report

Berss, Marcia. "Protein Man." *Forbes* 24 Oct. 2002: 65–66.   — Magazine article

Connors, H. Lee. "Saturn's Orbit Still High with Consumers." *Marketing News Online* 31 Aug. 2002. Retrieved 1 Sept. 2002 <http://www.marketingnews.com/08-31-02.htm>.  — Magazine article, online

"Globalization Often Means That the Fast Track Leads Overseas." *National Post* 17 June 2002: A10.  — Newspaper article, no author

Lancaster, Hal. "When Taking a Tip from a Job Network, Proceed with Caution." *The Globe and Mail* 7 Feb. 2001: B1.  — Newspaper article, one author

Markoff, John. "Voluntary Rules Proposed to Help Insure Privacy for Internet Users." *The New York Times on the Web* 5 June 2002. Retrieved 9 June 2002 <http://www.nytimes.com/library/tech/02/05/biztech/articles/05privacy.html>.  — Newspaper article, online

Pinkerton Investigation Services. *The Employer's Guide to Investigation Services,* 2nd ed. Atlanta: Pinkerton Information Center, 2002.  — Brochure

Rivers, Frank. Personal interview. 16 May 2004.  — Interview

Rose, Richard C., and Echo Montgomery Garrett. *How to Make a Buck and Still Be a Decent Human Being.* New York: HarperCollins, 2001.  — Book, two authors

"Spam: How to Eliminate It from Your Workplace." *SmartPros.* 8 Aug. 1997. Retrieved 12 Sept. 2002 <http://accounting.smartpros.com/x10434.xml>.  — Internet document, no author

Statistics Canada. *A Portrait of Persons with Disabilities: Target Groups Project.* Ottawa: Ministry of Industry, Science and Technology, 1995.  — Government publication

Wetherbee, James C., Nicholas P. Vitalari, and Andrew Milner. "Key Trends in Systems Development in Europe and North America." *Journal of Global Information Management* 3.2 (2001): 5–20. ["3.2" signifies volume 3, issue 2]  — Journal article with volume and issue numbers

Wilson, Craig M. "E-Mail Bill May Fail to Curtail Spamming." *eWeek.* 9 July 2001: 49. InfoTrac College Edition. Retrieved 26 Aug. 2002 <http://infotrac.thomsonlearning.com/>.  — Article from online database

Yeller, Martin. "E-commerce Challenges and Victories." Online posting. 4 Dec 2002. Google Group biz—ecommerce. Retrieved 14 Jan. 2004 <http://groups.google.com/groups?h1-en@safe=off&group=biz.eco>.  — Message from online forum or discussion group

Note: If a printed document is viewed electronically and you have no reason to believe the electronic version is different from the print version, use the same format as for the print citation.

- Enclose the titles of magazine, newspaper, and journal articles in quotation marks. Include volume and issue numbers for journals only.
- For Internet citations, include a retrieval date. Although MLA format does not include the words "Retrieved" or "Accessed," such wording helps distinguish the retrieval date from the document date.

# American Psychological Association Format

Popular in the social and physical sciences, the American Psychological Association (APA) documentation style uses parenthetic citations. That is, each author reference is shown in parentheses when cited in the text, as shown in Figure C.3. At the end of the report, all references are listed alphabetically in a bibliography called "References." For more information about APA formats, see the *Publication Manual of the American Psychological Association*, Fifth Edition (Washington, DC: American Psychological Association, 2001).

**APA In-Text Format.** Within the text, document each specific textual source with a short description in parentheses. Following are selected guidelines summarizing important elements of APA style:

- Include the last name of the author(s), date of publication, and page number, as (Jones, 2002, p. 36). Use "n.d." if no date is available.

- If no author is known, refer to the first few words of the reference list entry and the year, as (Computer Privacy, 2003, p. 59).

- Omit page numbers for general references, but always include page numbers for direct quotations.

**APA Bibliographic Format.** List all citations alphabetically in a section called "References." A portion of an APA bibliography is shown in Figure C.3. A more complete list of model references appears in Figure C.4. APA style requires specific capitalization and sequencing guidelines, some of which are summarized here:

- Include an author's name with the last name first followed by initials, such as *Smith, M. A.* First and middle names are not used.

**FIGURE C.3** Portions of APA Text Page and Bibliography

Peanut butter was first delivered to the world by a St. Louis physician in 1890. As discussed at the Peanut Advisory Board's Web site, peanut butter was originally promoted as a protein substitute for elderly patients ("History," n.d.). However, it was the 1905 Universal Exposition in St. Louis that truly launched peanut butter. Since then, annual peanut butter consumption has zoomed to 3.3 pounds a person in the United States (Barrons, 1998, p. 46). America's farmers produce 1.6 million tons of peanuts annually, about half of which is used for oil, nuts, and candy. Lisa Gibbons, executive secretary of the Peanut Advisory Board, says that "peanuts in some form are in the top four candies: Snickers, Reese's Peanut Butter Cups, Peanut M & Ms, and Butterfinger" (Meadows, 2002, p. 32).

References

Barrons, E. (1998). A comparison of domestic and international consumption of legumes. *Journal of Economic Agriculture, 23,* 45–49.

History of peanut butter (n.d.). Peanut Advisory Board. Retrieved January 19, 2003, from http://www.peanutbutterlovers.com/History/index.html

Meadows, M. A. (2002, September 30). Peanut crop is anything but peanuts at home and overseas. *Business Monthly,* 31–34.

**FIGURE C.4** Model APA Bibliography Sample References

References

Air Canada. (2003). *2003 Annual Report.* Dorval, QC. —————— Annual report

Atamian, R. M., & Ferranto, M. (2000). *Driving market forces.* New York: HarperCollins. —————— Book, two authors

Berss, M. (2002, October 24). Protein man. *Forbes, 154,* 64–66. —————— Magazine article

Cantrell, M. R., & Watson, H. (2001). Violence in today's workplace [Electronic version]. —————— Magazine article, viewed
    *Office Review, 26*(1), 24–29.     electronically

Globalization often means that the fast track leads overseas. (2002, June 16). *National Post,* —————— Newspaper article, no author
    p. A10.

Lancaster, H. (2002, February 7). When taking a tip from a job network, proceed with caution. —————— Newspaper article, one author
    *The Globe and Mail,* p. B1.

Lang, R. T. (2001, March 2). Most people fail to identify nonverbal signs. *The New York* —————— Newspaper article, online
    *Times.* Retrieved November 15, 2001, from http://www.nytimes.com

Moon, J. (1999). Solid waste disposal. *Microsoft Encarta 2000* [CD-ROM]. Redmond, WA: —————— CD-ROM encyclopedia article
    Microsoft.

Pinkerton Investigation Services. (2001). *The employer's guide to investigation services* (3rd ed.) —————— Brochure
    [Brochure]. Atlanta: Pinkerton Information Center.

Wetherbee, J. C., Vitalari, N. P., & Milner, A. (2001). Key trends in systems development —————— Journal article with volume
    in Europe and North America. *Journal of Global Information Management, 3*(2), 5–20.     and issue numbers
    ["3(2)" signifies volume 3, series or issue 2]

Wilson, G. & Simmons, P. (2001). *Plagiarism: What it is, and how to avoid it.* Retrieved July 4, —————— World Wide Web document
    2001, from Biology Program Guide 2001/2002 at the University of British Columbia Web     with author and date
    site: http://www.zoology.ubc/ca/bpg/plagiarism.htm

*WWW user survey reveals consumer trends.* (n.d.). Retrieved August 2, 2002, from http://www —————— World Wide Web document,
    .cc.gatech.edu/gvu/user_surveys/survey-2001-10/     no author, no date

Yudkin, M. (2001, July 4). The marketing minute: Truth is always in season [Msg. ID: —————— Message to online forum or
    ruf6kt0aiu5eui6523qsrofhu70h21evoj@4ax.com]. Message posted to news://biz.ecommerce     discussion group

- Show the date of publication in parentheses immediately after the author's name, as *Smith M. A. (2002).*

- Italicize the titles of books. Use "sentence-style" capitalization. This means that only the first word of a title, proper nouns, and the first word after an internal colon is capitalized.

- Do not italicize or underscore the titles of magazine and journal articles. Use sentence-style capitalization for article titles.

- Italicize the names of magazines and journals. Capitalize the initial letters of all important words.

## Online Help

Various websites have been created to assist writers in creating the appropriate documentation. You may want to visit the following sites: <**www.easybib.com**>, <**www.noodletools.com**>, and <**www.workscited4u.com**>.

## Citing Electronic Sources

Standards for researchers using electronic sources are still emerging. When citing electronic media, you should have the same goals as for print sources. That is, you try to give credit to the authors and to allow others to easily locate the same or updated information. However, traditional formats for identifying authors, publication dates, and page numbers become confusing when applied to sources on the Internet. Strive to give correct credit for electronic sources by including the author's name (when available), document title, Web page title, Web address, and retrieval date. Formats for some electronic sources have been shown here. For more electronic citation format information, visit <**www.businesscommunication-4th.nelson.com**>, click "Study Resources" and go to "Documentation/Citation Style Guides."

# Appendix D

# Correction Abbreviations

In marking your papers, your instructor may use the following symbols or abbreviations to indicate writing weaknesses. You'll find that studying these symbols and suggestions will help you understand your instructor's remarks. Knowing this information can also help you evaluate and improve your own letters, memos, reports, and other writing. For specific writing guidelines and self-help exercises, see Appendix A, Competent Language Usage Essentials (C.L.U.E.).

## Strategy and Organization

| | |
|---|---|
| **Coh** | Develop coherence between ideas. Repeat key idea or add transitional expression. |
| **DS** | Use direct strategy. Start with main idea or good news. |
| **IS** | Use indirect strategy. Explain before introducing main idea. |
| **Org** | Improve organization. Keep similar topics together. |
| **Plan** | Apply appropriate plan for message. |
| **Trans** | Include transition to join ideas. |

## Content and Style

| | |
|---|---|
| **Acc** | Verify accuracy of names, places, amounts, and other data. |
| **ACE** | Avoid copying examples. |
| **ACP** | Avoid copying case problems. |
| **Act** | Use active voice. |
| **AE** | Use action ending that tells reader what to do. |
| **Awk** | Rephrase to avoid awkward or unidiomatic expression. |
| **Asn** | Check assignment for instructions or facts. |
| **Chop** | Use longer sentences to avoid choppiness. Vary sentence patterns. |
| **Cl** | Improve clarity of ideas or expression. |
| **Con** | Condense into shorter form. |
| **Emp** | Emphasize this idea. |
| **Eth** | Use language that projects honest, ethical business practices. |
| **Exp** | Explain more fully or clearly. |
| **Inc** | Expand an incomplete idea. |
| **Jar** | Avoid jargon or specialized language that reader may not know. |
| **Log** | Remedy faulty logic. |
| **Neg** | Revise negative expression with more positive view. |

| Obv | Avoid saying what is obvious. |
|---|---|
| Par | Use parallel (balanced) expression. |
| PV | Express idea from reader's point of view. |
| RB | Show reader benefits. What's in it for reader? |
| Rdn | Revise to eliminate redundant idea or expression. |
| Rep | Avoid unintentional repetition of word, idea, or sound. |
| Sin | Use language that sounds sincere. |
| Spec | Develop idea with specific details. |
| Sub | Subordinate this point to lessen its impact. |
| SX | Avoid sexist language. |
| Tone | Use more conversational or positive tone. |
| You | Emphasize "you" view. |
| Var | Vary sentences with different patterns. |
| Vag | Avoid vague pronoun. Don't use *they, that, this, which, it,* or other pronouns unless their references are clear. |
| Vb | Use correct verb tense. Avoid verb shift. |
| W | Condense to avoid wordiness. |
| WC | Improve word choice. Find a more precise word. |

## Grammar and Mechanics

| Abv | Avoid most abbreviations in text. Use correct abbreviation if necessary. |
|---|---|
| Agr | Make each subject and verb or pronoun and noun agree. |
| Apos | Use an apostrophe to show possession or contraction. |
| Art | Choose a correct article (*a, an,* or *the*). |
| Cap | Capitalize appropriately. |
| Cm | Use a comma. |
| CmConj | Use a comma preceding coordinating conjunction (*and, or, nor, but*) that joins independent clauses. |
| CmIntro | Use a comma following introductory dependent clause or long phrase. |
| CmSer | Use commas to separate items in a series. |
| CS | Rectify a comma splice by separating independent clauses with a period or a semicolon. |
| Div | Improve word division by hyphenating between syllables. |
| DM | Fix a dangling modifier by supplying a clear subject for modifying element. |
| Exp | Avoid expletives such as *there is, there are,* and *it is.* |
| Frag | Revise fragment to form complete sentence. |
| Gram | Use correct grammar. |
| Hyp | Hyphenate a compound adjective. |
| lc | Use lowercase instead of uppercase. |
| MM | Correct misplaced modifier by moving modifier closer to word it describes or limits. |
| Num | Express numbers in correct word or figure form. |
| Pn | Use correct punctuation. |
| Prep | Correct use of preposition. |
| RO | Fix run-on sentence with comma or semicolon to separate independent clauses. |
| Sem | Use semicolon to join related independent clauses. |
| Sp | Check spelling. |
| SS | Shorten sentences. |
| UnCm | Avoid unnecessary comma. |

# Format

**Cen**    Centre a document appropriately on the page.

**DSp**    Insert a double space, or double-space throughout.

**F**    Choose appropriate format for this item or message.

**GH**    Use graphic highlighting (bullets, lists, indentions, and headings) to improve readability.

**Mar**    Improve margins to frame a document on the page.

**SSp**    Insert a single space, or single-space throughout.

**TSp**    Insert a triple space.

# Key to C.L.U.E. Review Exercises

## Chapter 1

1. In today's average business office, employees spend approximately 60 percent of their time processing documents.

2. My friend and I were surprised to learn that more information has been produced in the last thirty (or 30) years than in the previous 5 000 years.

3. A typical manager, by the way, reads 1 million words every week, which is equal to reading one and a half full-length novels every day.

4. If you are defining *communication*, a principal element is the transmission of information and meaning.

5. When Ms. Diaz had three messages to send, she chose e-mail because it was definitely the fastest communication channel.

6. Five factors that make up your unique frame of reference are the following: experience, education, culture, expectations, and personality.

7. Just between you and me, who do you think will be recommended for the award?

8. To many workers, balancing family and work demands is more important than earning big salaries.

9. Matt felt that he did well (or had done well) on the exam, but he wants to do even better when it's given again next fall.

10. The grapevine may be an excellent source of employee information; however, it should not replace formal lines of communication.

## Chapter 2

1. Companies are forming teams for at least three good reasons: better decisions, faster response times, and increased productivity.

2. Although they do not hold face-to-face meetings, virtual teams exchange information and make decisions electronically.

3. Successful self-directed teams are autonomous; that is, they can hire, fire, and discipline their own members.

4. We already have a number of teams; however, our CEO and several vice presidents are advising us to add more.

5. At last month's staff meeting, the manager and he encouraged a warm, supportive climate with praise and helpful comments.

6. When conflict erupted at our team's February meeting, we made a conscious effort to confront the underlying issues.

7. The best method for reaching group decisions involves consensus, but this method is very time-consuming.

8. The team leader and I think, however, that all speakers have a right to a fair hearing.

9. Seventy-five people are expected to attend the training session on May 15; consequently, she and I must find a larger room.

10. Lawyers in our Legal Services Department distributed an agenda for participants attending their January 3 meeting.

## Chapter 3

1. Although listening is a principal activity of employees, experts say that many listen at only 25 percent efficiency.

2. When listening to instructions, be sure to take notes and review them immediately.

3. In a poll of over 9 000 employees, only one third felt that their companies sought their opinions and suggestions.

4. Well-trained customer service representatives ask gentle, probing questions to ensure clear understanding.

5. The appearance and mannerisms of a speaker affect a listener's evaluation of a message.

6. Remembering important points involves three factors: (1) deciding to remember, (2) forming relationships, and (3) reviewing.

7. A list of suggestions for paraphrasing a speaker's ideas is found in an article titled "Best Listening Habits," which appeared in *Fortune*.

8. Skilled speakers raise their voices to convey important ideas; however, they whisper to imply secrecy.

9. One successful manager says that he can tell from people's eyes whether they are focused, receptive, or distant.

10. On March 5 the president of the company announced a casual dress policy; consequently, I must buy a whole new wardrobe.

## Chapter 4

1. Gifts for the children of an Arab are welcome; however, gifts for an Arab's wife are not advisable.

2. In Latin America knives are not proper gifts; they signify cutting off a relationship.

3. Statistics Canada reports that one third of the foreign-born population of Canada is from Asia, the Caribbean, and the Middle East.

4. Although international business was already common among big companies, we now find many smaller companies seeking global markets.

5. On April 15 an article entitled "Practical Cross-Cultural Persuasion Strategies" appeared in *The Journal of International Business*.

6. Three executives agreed that their company's overseas project with France was taking twice as long as expected.

7. They recommend, therefore, that a committee study the cultural and language issues for a three-week period and submit a report of its findings.

8. The 300 representatives were told that the simple act of presenting a business card is something to which Canadians give little thought, but it is a serious formality in Japan.

9. Each of the 75 delegates was charged a fee of $40 to attend the cultural training session, although formerly the charge had been only $30.

10. Both the president and senior vice president agree that all staff members' suggestions should be sent to Human Relations. (Note: Capitalize the name of a specific department within your company.)

## Chapter 5

1. If I were you, I would memorize the following three parts of the writing process: prewriting, writing, and revising.

2. A writer's time is usually spent as follows: 25 percent worrying, 25 percent writing, 45 percent revising, and 5 percent proofreading.

3. At least four or five members of our team will probably attend the meeting scheduled with our company vice president at 3 p.m. on Tuesday, March 4.

4. We're not asking the team to alter its proposal; we are asking team members to check the proposal's figures.

5. Writers may use computer software to fight writer's block as well as to help them collect information electronically. ("Writer's block" is an expression generally used in reference to a single writer.)

6. Will you please fax me a list of all independent publishers' names and addresses. (Note: A polite request ends in a period.)

7. Writers have many communication channels from which to choose; therefore, they should choose carefully.

8. Over 250 years ago one of Canada's founding fathers recognized a fundamental writing principle.

9. If you are trying to persuade someone, be sure that your proposal and request are beneficial to the receiver (OR *to that person*).

10. By substituting everyday, familiar words for unfamiliar ones, you can make your audience comprehend your ideas more quickly.

## Chapter 6

1. Whether you are writing a short memo or a 30-page report, you should expect to conduct formal or informal research.

2. Our company vice president came to the president and me asking for help with two complex but separate desktop publishing problems.

3. Because neither of us is particularly creative, we decided to organize a brainstorming session.

4. To develop a better sense of design, we collected desirable samples from books, magazines, brochures, and newsletters.

5. We noticed that poorly designed projects often were filled with cluttered layouts, incompatible typefaces, and too many typefaces.

6. Our brainstorming session included the following individuals: Troy, Rhonda, Amanda, and Matt.

7. We encouraged participants to think visually, but most were reluctant to draw pictures.

8. One of our principal goals was to create 100 ideas in 30 minutes; however, we were prepared to meet up to one hour.

9. Because we know that ideas continue to incubate, we encouraged everyone to continue to submit ideas after the session ended.

10. Robyn Clarke's article titled "A Better Way to Brainstorm," which appeared in the magazine *Black Enterprise*, proved to be very helpful.

## Chapter 7

1. Business documents must be written clearly to ensure that readers comprehend the message quickly.

2. The prominent chairman of Monsanto in Europe complained that his managers' reports were too long, too frequent, and too unread.

3. The report contained so many redundancies that its main principles requesting provincial and federal funding were lost.

4. The information was cited in a recent article entitled "What's New in Grammar-Checking Software"; however, I can't locate the article now.

5. All three of our company's recruiters—Jim Lucus, Doreen Delgado, and Brad Kirby—criticized their poorly written procedures.

6. To help receivers anticipate and comprehend ideas quickly, two special writing techniques are helpful: parallelism, which involves balanced writing, and highlighting, which makes important points more visible.

7. When you must proofread an important document, always work from a printed copy.

8. Have you already ordered the following: a dictionary, a reference manual, and a stylebook?

9. As we completed the final step in the writing process, we wondered how feasible it would be to evaluate our message.

10. It's almost impossible to improve your communication skills alone; therefore, you should take advantage of this opportunity.

## Chapter 8

1. Today's organizations, however, are encouraging rank-and-file employees to share information and make decisions.

2. Because managers and employees are writing more messages than ever before, it's definitely important that they develop good communication skills.

3. Memos generally contain four necessary parts: subject line, opening, body, and action closing.

4. The Federal Trade Commission is holding hearings to elicit information about IBM's request to expand marketing in 21 cities.

5. Consumer buying and spending for the past five years are being studied by a federal team of analysts.

6. When you respond to an e-mail message, you should not automatically return the sender's message.

7. Wasn't it Dr. Ben Cohen, not Mr. Temple, who always wrote his e-mails in all capital letters?

8. A list of the names and addresses of e-mail recipients was sent using the "bcc" function.

9. Our Human Resources Department, which was formerly in Room 35, has moved its offices to Room 5.

10. The *Post Dispatch*, our local newspaper, featured as its principal article a story entitled "Smarter E-Mail Is Here."

## Chapter 9

1. Although we've seen an extraordinary increase in the use of e-mail, some business letters must still be written.

2. She acts as if she were the only person who ever received a compliment about her business writing.

3. Good business letters are distinguished by three characteristics: clear content, a goodwill tone, and correct form.

4. Cynthia Jones, who I think is our newly appointed vice president, writes many business letters for our company.

5. After the office manager and he returned from their meeting, we were able to sort the customers' letters more quickly.

6. Even the best-run and best-loved businesses occasionally receive claims or complaints from consumers.

7. On Wednesday we received two claims; on Thursday we received four more.

8. We enclosed a refund cheque for $200; however, we worried that it was not enough to regain the confidence of the customer.

9. If you could have seen the customer's letter, you would have been as upset as Rona and I.

10. To express thanks and show appreciation, most people write a short note on special notepaper or heavy card stock.

## Chapter 10

1. Successful persuasion results from two important elements: a reasonable request and a well-presented argument.

2. If we wanted to persuade a bank to lend you and me $10 000, we would probably use rational appeals.

3. Our senior marketing director and the sales manager want to send a sales letter to our current customers; therefore, they analyzed the product, purpose, and audience.

4. Four important parts of a persuasive message are (1) gaining the audience's attention, (2) convincing them that your purpose is worthy, (3) overcoming resistance, and (4) motivating action.

5. One of the biggest mistakes in persuasive requests is the failure to anticipate and offset audience resistance.

6. If the CEO and he had behaved more professionally, the chances of a practical settlement would be considerably greater.

7. An adjustment letter is a form of complaint; consequently, it's wise to use the indirect strategy.

8. Anger and emotion are not effective in persuasion, but many writers cannot control their tempers.

9. When we open our office in Montreal, we will need at least three people who are fluent in French and English.

10. A good news release looks and sounds credible; that is, it has no typos, no imaginative spelling, and no factual errors.

## Chapter 11

1. When delivering bad news, you can reduce the disappointment by (1) telling the reasons for the rejection and (2) revealing the news with sensitivity.

2. It's important that you make sure the receiver understands the bad news and accepts it.

3. The indirect pattern consists of four parts: buffer, reasons, bad news, and close.

4. Undoubtedly, the indirect pattern cannot be used in every situation; however, it is often better than blunt announcements of bad news.

5. When the bad news is not devastating, references to resale or promotion may be appropriate.

6. If the vice president of our company must announce a big increase in each employee's contribution to health benefits, should he use the indirect strategy?

7. Most of us prefer to be let down gently when we're being refused something; that's why the reasons-before-refusal pattern is effective.

8. Publisher Malcolm Forbes said, "To be agreeable while disagreeing—that's an art."

9. When a well-known tire company recalled hundreds of thousands of tires, its president issued an apology to all injured customers.

10. If I were you, I would be more concerned with long-term, not short-term, returns on the invested capital.

## Chapter 12

1. In a low-context culture such as North America, our values and attitudes prompt us to write many reports.

2. A reader's expectations and the content of a report determine its pattern of development.

3. The format of a report is governed by its length, topic, audience, and purpose.

4. If a report has ten or fewer pages, it's generally considered a short informal report.

5. Research reports from consultants to their clients tend to be formal; however, a conference report to your boss would be informal.

6. My colleague and I followed step-by-step instructions in preparing a work plan for our report.

7. If your report is authorized by someone, be sure to review its work plan with him or her (OR *with that person*) before proceeding.

8. Eric was offered $1 000 to finish Robert's report, but Eric said the offer was "too little and too late."

9. To search the Internet, you need a browser such as Netscape Navigator or Microsoft Internet Explorer.

10. To illustrate report data, you may choose from among the following visual aids: tables, charts, graphs, and pictures.

## Chapter 13

1. If you are conducting research for a report, you will probably face a jumble of data including printouts, note cards, copies of articles, interview notes, questionnaire results, and statistics.

2. Numerical information from surveys is usually summarized and simplified in tables.

3. Researchers use three statistical terms to describe data: mean, median, and mode.

4. When my boss and I use the word *average*, we are referring to the mean, which is the arithmetic average.

5. Readers of reports often turn right to the conclusions and recommendations; therefore, these sections must be written very carefully.

6. Report conclusions explain what the problem is; recommendations tell how to solve it.

7. In writing reports you will probably organize your data using one of the following five methods: time, component, importance, criteria, or convention.

8. The introduction to a report should tell its purpose and significance; it should also preview the main points.

9. You should, however, delay writing the introduction until after you complete the report.

10. To turn out professional-looking documents, be sure to design attractive pages and avoid using too many typefaces and graphics.

## Chapter 14

1. Proposals are written offers to do the following: solve problems, provide services, or sell equipment.

2. Our company president and vice president worked together in developing two RFPs to solicit competitive bids.

3. To make an introduction to a proposal interesting, a writer should provide a "hook" to capture the reader's attention.

4. A central item in most proposals is the budget, which is a list of proposed project costs.

5. Any proposal delivered to the manager or me should definitely explain the specific credentials and expertise of key personnel for the project.

6. Lisa and he wanted to start their own business; therefore, they wrote a business plan that included a detailed market analysis.

7. Nicolas Scott, who is a member of our Research and Development Department, presented a formal report based on thorough investigation and analysis.

8. The principal section of the report is the body; it discusses the research findings.

9. If a report is 100 pages long, it may require a 10-page executive summary. (Note: Related numbers are written as the larger number is expressed.)

10. Only one of the executives was present at the June 10 meeting when the report was presented.

## Chapter 15

1. The CEO's assistant asked my colleague and me to explain why our proposed method was better than the one previously used.

2. My friend and I were definitely inexperienced in making presentations; therefore, he and I decided to learn more about public speaking.

3. We learned that the introduction to a presentation should accomplish three goals: (a) capture attention, (b) establish credibility, and (c) preview main points.

4. In the body of a short presentation, which is usually 20 or fewer minutes, we should focus on two to four principal points.

5. One of the most important ways to end a presentation is focusing on what you want the audience to do, think, or remember.

6. Speakers must remember that listeners, unlike readers, cannot control the rate of presentation or flip back through pages to review main points.

7. In working with electronic presentation software, experts suggest choosing one transition effect and using it consistently.

8. The range of effects is staggering, but presenters using electronic slides must control their urge to pile on too many dazzling features.

9. Every good speaker adapts to his or her audience, and cross-cultural presentations call for special adjustments and sensitivity. (OR, *All good speakers adapt to their audiences* . . . .)

10. One study found that two thirds of telephone calls were less important than the work they interrupted.

# Chapter 16

1. You can't hope to find the job of your dreams without first (1) knowing yourself, (2) knowing the job market, and (3) knowing the employment process.

2. Only about one third of the people currently employed work for companies with more than 500 employees.

3. If you're looking for a job, you should check classified ads as well as online job banks.

4. Preparing a résumé while you are still in school helps you recognize weak qualifications and gives you two or three years in which to bolster them.

5. Recruiters like to see career objectives on résumés; however, they may restrict a candidate's chances. (Note: To avoid confusion, you might prefer to replace the pronoun *they* with *such objectives*.)

6. Today's résumés omit personal data such as birth date, marital status, height, weight, and religious affiliation.

7. When listing job duties, skills, computer skills, and so forth, don't tabulate them into two- or three-column tables.

8. Did you see the article entitled "Which Is Better—A Functional or a Chronological Résumé?" in the latest issue of *Canadian Business*?

9. Although it's impossible to talk about yourself without using *I*, you should try to reduce *I* domination in your cover letter.

10. Before going to a job interview, learn something about the company's size, number of employees, competitors, reputation, strengths, and weaknesses.

# Endnotes

## CHAPTER 1

1. Chris Powell, "On a Roll," *Marketing Magazine*, 1 July 2002.
2. Sonya Felix, "The Canadian Tire Way," *Benefits Canada*, January 2001, 24–29.
3. Andy Holloway, "Give Like Santa…," *Canadian Business*, 9 December 2002, 109.
4. Powell, "On a Roll."
5. Dana Flavelle, "Canadian Tire Aims to Woo Women," *Toronto Star*, 15 May 2003, C1–C12.
6. Paul Martin, 2000 Budget Speech, 5.
7. "Why Yahoo! Isn't Too Worried About Beijing's Chinese Wall," 6 November 2000 <www.business week.com> (Retrieved 15 November 2000).
8. Suzanne Bidlake, "Burger King's Euro Push," *Marketing*, 20 February 1992, 2.
9. Craig S. Smith, "Globalization Puts a Starbucks Into the Forbidden City in Beijing," *The New York Times*, 25 November 2000, B1.
10. Hal Lancaster, "Learning to Manage in a Global Workplace," *The Wall Street Journal*, 2 June 1998, B1.
11. Barbara Booth, "Beg to Differ," *International Business*, November 1996, 28.
12. Wesley Cragg, "Ethics and the Academy: Lessons From Business Ethics and the Private Sector," *Canadian Journal of Higher Education*, 2000, 127–156.
13. "The Challenges Facing Workers in the Future," *HR Focus*, August 1999, 6; Paula Jacobs, "Strong Writing Skills Essential for Success, Even in IT," *Infoworld*, 6 July 1998, 86.
14. Rosalind Stefanac, "Brain Drain Is for Real, ITAC's Duncan Argues," *Computing Canada*, 9 July 1999, 29, 33.
15. "Office Trends: More Teamwork, Less Personal Time," *Worklife Report*, 2001, 10.
16. Sharon Helldorfer and Michael Daly, "Reengineering Brings Together Units," *Best's Review*, October 1993, 82–85.
17. Marjo Johne, "What Do You Know? The Knowledge Worker and the Knowledge Environment Today Require Synergy and Collaboration More Than Ever Before," *CMA Management*, March 2001, 21–24.
18. Dwight Cunningham, "The Downside of Technology," *Chicago Tribune Internet Edition*, 2 January 2000; "Wired to the Desk," *Fortune*, Summer 1999, 164.
19. Holloway, "Give Like Santa …"
20. General Social Survey: Internet Use, The Daily: Statistics Canada, 26 March 2001 <www.statcan.ca/Daily/English/010326/d010326a.htm>.
21. Canadian Telework Studies *InnoVisions Canada*, available <www.ivc.ca/part12.htm> (Accessed 28 May 2003).
22. Kirk Johnson, "Limits on the Work-at-Home Life," *The New York Times*, 17 December 1997, A20.
23. Holloway, "Give Like Santa . . ."
24. Rosalind Stefanac (1999).
25. Lesley Meall, "Workers With Reservations," *Accountancy*, March 1997, 54–55; Ellen Bruce Keable and Mike Brill, "Hotelling: Beyond Space Reduction," *Facilities Design & Management*, June 2000, 26–28.
26. Hal Lancaster, "Hiring a Full Staff May Be the Next Fad in Management," *The Wall Street Journal*, 4 April 1998, B1.
27. Andrew Denka, "New Office Etiquette Dilemmas," *CPA Journal*, August 1996, 13.
28. Susan Thea Posnock, "The Pros and Cons of a Virtual Office," *Folio: The Magazine for Magazine Management*, October 2000, 112.
29. Elaine Carey, "Gender Gap in Earnings Staying Stubbornly High," *Toronto Star*, 12 March 2003, A9.
30. "Latest Census Figures Reveal Colourful Canada," *Toronto Star*, 21 January 2003, A1.
31. David Crane, "Census Figures Point to Three Economic Trends," *Toronto Star*, 12 February 2003, E2.
32. "Latest Census Figures Reveal Colourful Canada," *Toronto Star*.
33. Crane, "Census Figures Point to Three Economic Trends."
34. Patrick Carnevale, as quoted by Genevieve Capowski, "Managing Diversity," *Management Review*, June 1996, 6.
35. Bob Williams, "Toward a Sensible School-to-Work System," *Education Canada*, Summer 2000, 15–18.
36. G. A. Marken, "New Approach to Moving up the Corporate Ladder," *Public Relations Quarterly*, Winter 1996, 47.
37. Barrett J. Mandel and Judith Yellen, "Mastering the Memo," *Working Woman*, September 1989, 135.
38. "Australian Slang for Shagging at Root of Joke," *The Welland Tribune*, 15 November 1999, A2.
39. Cheryl Hamilton with Cordell Parker, *Communicating for Results* (Belmont, CA: Wadsworth, 1996), 7.
40. Jerry Sullivan, Naoki Karmeda, and Tatsuo Nobu, "Bypassing in Managerial Communication," *Business Horizons*, January/February 1991, 72.
41. Dorthee Ostle, "D/C Can't Bridge the Gap," *Automotive News*, 12 June 1999, 1, 3.
42. Peter Drucker, *Managing the Non-Profit Organization: Practices and Principles* (New York: HarperCollins, 1990), 46.
43. John C. Beck, Thomas Davenport, "Strategy and Structure of Firms in the Attention Economy," *Ivey Business Journal*, March/April 2002, 49–54.

44. Thomas Davenport, "Attention: The Next Information Frontier: In a World of Information Overload, the Message Has to Be Packaged So It Becomes Irresistible," *Financial Post, National Post*, 29 May 2001, M8.

45. Dave Miller, "You've Got (Too Much) Mail," *London Free Press*, 21 September 2001, available <http://www.canoe.ca/LondonBusinessMonday/01b1.html>.

46. "Canadians' Love Affair with Email Continues," *Ipsos-Reid Press Release*, 30 October 2001, available <www.angusreid.com/meidadsp_dip slaypr.prnt.cfm?ID_to_view=1345>.

47. Wilkinson, "Stop Reading!"

48. Tom Geddie, "Technology: It's About Time," *Communication World*, Special Issue Supplement, March 1998, 26–28.

49. Leslie Walker, as quoted in "Coping With Communication Overload," *Association Management*, October 1997, 32–33.

50. Mitch Betts and Tim Ouellette, "Taming the E-Mail Shrew," *Computerworld*, 6 November 1995, 1, 32.

51. Marken, "New Approach to Moving Up the Corporate Ladder."

52. Thomas J. Hackett, "Giving Teams a Tune-Up: Reviving Work Teams," *HR Focus*, November 1997.

53. Flavelle, "Canadian Tire Aims to Woo Women."

54. Powell, "On a Roll."

55. "Who Told You That?" *The Wall Street Journal*, 23 May 1985, 33.

56. Marjo Johne, "What Do You Know? The Knowledge Worker and the Knowledge Environment Today Require Synergy and Collaboration More Than Ever Before," *CMA Management*, March 2001, 21–24.

57. Stephanie Zimmermann, Beverly Davenport, and John W. Haas, "A Communication Metamyth in the Workplace: The Assumption That More Is Better," *Journal of Business Communication*, April 1996, 185–204.

58. Bob Nelson, "How to Energize Everyone in the Company," *Bottom Line/Business*, October 1997, 3.

59. Wesley Cragg, "Ethics and the Academy: Lessons From Business Ethics and the Private Sector," *Canadian Journal of Higher Education*, 2000, 127–156.

60. Deirdre McMurdy, "Figures Show There's Plenty of Green in Being Green," *The Calgary Herald*, 23 January 2003, D4.

61. "Return on Communication Investment; Social Responsibility Programs Valuable to Canadian Corporation, Survey Finds," Canadian NewsWire Limited <http://www.newswire.ca/releases/October2002/17/> 17 October 2002.

62. Tina Kelley, "Charting a Course to Ethical Profits," *The New York Times*, 8 February 1998, BU1.

63. Patrick Brethour, "Talisman Stake Sale in Sudan Delayed," 1 January 2003 <www.edmontoplus.workopolis.com>

64. Samuel Greengard, "50 Percent of Your Employees Are Lying, Cheating, and Stealing," *Workforce*, October 1997, 46–47.

65. Martha Groves, "Ethics at Work: Honor System," *Los Angeles Times*, 3 November 1997, Careers sec., 3, 15. See also Alison Boyd, "Employee Traps—Corruption in the Workplace," *Management Review*, September 1997, 9.

66. "The Values Added Banker Brings Ethics to Investing," *National Post*, 4 March 2000, E4.

67. Reported in Alison Bell, "What Price Ethics?" *Entrepreneurial Woman*, January/February, 1991, 68.

68. Competition Bureau, Government of Canada <http://strategis.ic.gc.ca//SSG/ct01250e.html> (Retrieved 18 June 2003).

69. Based on Bell, "What Price Ethics?"

70. Amy Harmon, "On the Office PC, Bosses Opt for All Work, and No Play," *The New York Times*, 22 September 1997, A1, C11.

71. Diane Cole, "Ethics: Companies Crack Down on Dishonesty," *The Wall Street Journal*, Spring 1991, Managing Your Career, Sec. 8.

72. "Hudson's Bay Company Fined $600 000 Under Misleading Advertising Provisions of the Competition Act," *Canadian Corporate News*, 4 May 1998, 73.

73. "Abtronic Muscle Stimulators Removed from Market by Competition Bureau," *Competition Bureau News Release*, 16 December 2002, available <http://strategis.ic.gc.ca/SSG/ct02481e.html>.

74. Jane Applegate, "Women Starting Small Businesses Twice as Fast as Men," *The Washington Post*, 2 September 1991, WB10.

75. Darryl Grigg and Jennifer Newman, "Five Ways to Foster Bonds, Win Trust in Business," *The Vancouver Sun*, 5 April 2003, D1.

76. "*The Wall Street Journal* Ethics Quiz," *The Wall Street Journal*, 21 October 1999, B1.

## CHAPTER 2

1. Michael Dojc, "Marrying the Media With the Message," *Toronto Star*, 24 September 2002, E03.

2. Dojc, "Marrying the Media With the Message."

3. Patricia Buhler, "Managing in the 90s: Creating Flexibility in Today's Workplace," *Supervision*, January 1996, 24–26.

4. Based on Cheryl Hamilton with Cordell Parker, *Communicating for Results*, 6th ed. (Belmont, CA: Wadsworth, 2000), 279; and Harvey Robbins and Michael Finley, *Why Teams Don't Work: What Went Wrong and How to Make It Right* (Princeton, NJ: Peterson's/Pacesetter Books, 1995), 11–12.

5. Jon R. Katzenbach and Douglas K. Smith, *The Wisdom of Teams*, (New York: HarperBusiness and Harvard Business School Press, 1994), 14.

6. Frank Mueller, Stephen Procter, David Buchanan, "Teamworking in Its Context(s): Antecedents, Nature and Dimensions," *Human Relations*, November 2000, 1387.

7. James R. DiSanza and Nancy J. Legge, *Business and Professional Communication* (Boston: Allyn and Bacon, 2000), 98.

8. Katzenbach and Smith, *The Wisdom of Teams*, 19.

9. Christine A. Spring, Paul R. Jackson, Sharon K. Parker, "Production Teamworking: The Importance of Interdependence and Autonomy for Employee Strain and Satisfaction," *Human Relations*, November 2000, 1519.

10. Kevin McManus, "Do You Have Teams?" *IIE Solutions*, April 2000, 21.

11. The discussion of Tuckman's model is adapted from Robbins and Finley, *Why Teams Don't Work*, Chapter 22. See also Jane Henderson-Loney, "Tuckman and Tears: Developing Teams During Profound Organiza-

tional Change," *Supervision*, May 1996, 3–5.

12. Based on Kenneth D. Benne and Paul Sheats, "Functional Roles of Group Members," *Journal of Social Issues*, No. 4, 1949, 41–49; Hamilton and Parker, *Communicating for Results*, 308–312; and J. Keyton, *Group Communication: Process and Analysis* (Mountain View, CA: Mayfield, 1999).

13. Allen C. Amason, Wayne A. Hochwarter, Kenneth R. Thompson, and Allison W. Harrison, "Conflict: An Important Dimension in Successful Management Teams," *Organizational Dynamics*, Autumn 1995, 20–35.

14. Kathleen M. Eisenhardt, Jean L. Kahwajy, and L. J. Bourgeois, III, "Conflict and Strategic Choice: How Top Management Teams Disagree," *California Management Review*, Winter, 1997, 42–62.

15. I. L. Janis, *Groupthink: Psychological Studies on Policy Decisions and Fiascoes* (Boston: Houghton Mifflin, 1982). See also Shaila M. Miranda and Carol Saunders, "Group Support Systems: An Organization Development Intervention to Combat Groupthink," *Public Administration Quarterly*, Summer 1995, 193–216.

16. Amason, Hochwater, "Conflict," 1.

17. Parnell, "Teamwork: Not a New Idea," 36–40.

18. Patricia Booth, "Embracing the Team Concept: Special Report—Teams at Work," *Canadian Business Review*, 22 September 1994, 10.

19. Katzennbach and Smith, *Wisdom of Teams*, 45.

20. Joel Makower, "Managing Diversity in the Workplace," *Business and Society Review*, Winter 1995, 48–54.

21. Katzenbach and Smith, *Wisdom of Teams*, 50.

22. Jon Hanke, "Presenting as a Team," *Presentations*, January 1998, 74–82.

23. Jay Robb, "More Gets Done in a No-Meeting Workplace," *The Hamilton Spectator*, 14 April 2003, D11.

24. "Office Trends: More Teamwork, Less Personal Time," *Worklife Report*, 2001, 10.

25. Tom McDonald, "Minimizing Meetings," *Successful Meetings*, June 1996, 24.

26. Lancaster, "Learning Some Ways," B1.

27. John C. Bruening, "There's Good News About Meetings," *Managing Office Technology*, July 1996, 24–25.

28. Kirsten Schabacker, "A Short, Snappy Guide to Meaningful Meetings," *Working Women*, June 1991, 73.

29. J. Keith Cook, "Try These Eight Guidelines for More Effective Meetings," *Communication Briefings Bonus Item*, April 1995, 8a. See also Morey Stettner, "How to Manage a Corporate Motormouth, *Investor's Business Daily*, 8 October 1998, A1.

30. Eli Mina, "Meeting Minutes: Should You Record Meeting Minutes Verbatim?" *Office Pro*, June/July 2001, 4.

31. Hamilton and Parker, *Communicating*, 311–312.

32. Marjo Johne, "What Do You Know? The Knowledge Worker and the Knowledge Environment Today Require Synergy and Collaboration More Than Ever Before," *CMA Management*, March 2001, 21–24.

## CHAPTER 3

1. "Minacs in Profile," Overview, available <www.minacs.com/en/company/about/> (Retrieved 2 July 2003).

2. "Minacs Honored by General Motors as 2002 Supplier of the Year" <www.minacs.com/pdf_uploads/2003/20030414_GM_Award_Rel_Final_Apr14.pdf?> (Retrieved 2 July 2003).

3. "Minacs in Profile," *The CRM Market*.

4. Based on information found at Minacs Web site <www.minacs.com> (Retrieved 1 July 2003).

5. "To Compete A PEO Must Be a Listening Organization," 1999 <www.devaindustries.com/articles/ListeningPEO.htm> (Retrieved 20 March 2003).

6. Harvey Robbins and Michael Finley, *Why Teams Don't Work* (Princeton, NJ: Peterson's/Pacesetter Books, 1995), 123.

7. L. E. Penley, E. R. Alexander, I. E. Jerigan, and C. I. Henwood, "Communication Abilities of Managers: The Relationship to Performance," *Journal of Management*, No. 17, 1991, 57–76; R. P. Ramsey and R. S. Sohi,

"Listening to Your Customers: The Impact of Perceived Salesperson Listening Behavior on Relationship Out-comes," *Journal of the Academy of Marketing Science*, No. 25 (2), 1997, 127–137; Lynn O. Cooper, "Listening Competency in the Workplace: A Model for Training," *Business Communication Quarterly*, December 1997, 75–84; and Valerie P. Goby and Justice H. Lewis, "The Key Role of Listening in Business: A Study of the Singapore Insurance Industry," *Business Communication Quarterly*, June 2000, 411.

8. Employability Skills 2000+. The Conference Board of Canada, available <www.conferenceboard.ca/nbec> (Accessed 20 March 2003).

9. Ko DeRuyter and Martin G. M. Wetzels, "The Impact of Perceived Listening Behavior in Voice-to-Voice Service Encounters," *Journal of Service Research*, February 2000, 276–284.

10. Tom W. Harris, "Listen Carefully," *Nation's Business*, June 1989, 78.

11. L. K. Steil, L. I. Barker, and K. W. Watson, *Effective Listening: Key to Your Success* (Reading, MA: Addison-Wesley, 1983); and J. A. Harris, "Hear What's Really Being Said," *Management-Auckland*, August 1998, 18.

12. Eric H. Nelson and Jan Gypen, "The Subordinate's Predicament," *Harvard Business Review*, September/October 1979, 133.

13. "Listening Factoids," International Listening Association <http://www.listen.org/pages/factoids.html> (Retrieved 7 January 2001).

14. Robert McGarvey, "Now Hear This: Lend Your Employees an Ear—and Boost Productivity," *Entrepreneur*, June 1996, 87.

15. "Good Ideas Go Unheard," *Management Review*, February 1998, 7.

16. "Good Ideas," 7.

17. Michael Render, "Better Listening Makes for a Better Marketing Message," *Marketing News*, 11 September 2000, 22–23.

18. Georges Azzam, as quoted in Jonathon Kay, "Inside the Charisma Economy," *National Post Business*, 1 December 2001, 72–82.

19. Stephen Golen, "A Factor Analysis of Barriers to Effective Listening," *The Journal of Business Communication*, Winter 1990, 25–37.

20. International Listening Association, "Listening Factoids" <http://www.listen.org/pages/factoids.html> (Retrieved 12 January 2001).
21. James Butcher, "Dominic O'Brien—Master Mnemonist," *The Lancet*, 2 September 2000, 836.
22. Andrew Wolvin and Carolyn Gwynn Coakley, *Listening*, 5th ed. (New York: McGraw-Hill, 1996), 136–137.
23. "Effective Communication," *Training Tomorrow*, November 1994, 32–33.
24. Kristin J. Anderson and Campbell Leaper, "Meta-Analyses of Gender Effects on Conversational Interruption: Who, What, When, Where, and How," *Sex Roles: A Journal of Research*, August 1998, 2251; M. Booth-Butterfield, "She Hears: What They Hear and Why," *Personnel Journal*, No. 44, 1984, 39.
25. L. P. Stewart and A. D. Stewart, *Communication Between the Sexes: Sex Differences and Sex Role Stereotypes* (Scottsdale, AZ: Gorsuch Scarisbrick, 1990).
26. Jayne Tear, "They Just Don't Understand Gender Dynamics," *The Wall Street Journal*, 20 November 1995, A12; Alan Wolfe, "Talking From 9 to 5: How Women's and Men's Conversational Styles Affect Who Gets Heard, Who Gets Credit and What Gets Done at Work," *New Republic*, 12 December 1994.
27. Based on information found at Minacs Web site <www.minacs.com> (Retrieved 2 July 2003).
28. J. Burgoon, D. Coker, and R. Coker, "Communication Explanations," *Human Communication Research*, 12, 1986, 463–494.
29. Dianna Booher, "Communication Tip of the Month," September 2000 <http://commotip.booher.com/index000018483.cfm> (Retrieved 5 July 2003).
30. Michael Tarsala, "Remec's Ronald Ragland: Drawing Rivals to His Team by Making Their Concerns His," *Investor's Business Daily*, 7 November 1997, A1.
31. Ray Birdwhistel, *Kinesics and Context* (Philadelphia: University of Pennsylvania Press, 1970).
32. "What's A-O.K. in the U.S.A. Is Lewd and Worthless Beyond," *The New York Times*, 18 August 1996, E-7.
33. "Body Speak: What Are You Saying?" *Successful Meetings*, October 2000, 49–51.
34. *The Body Language of Proxemics. The Significance of Body Proxemics*, available <http://members.aol.com/katydidit/bodylang.htm>.
35. Anne Sowden as quoted in Astrid Poei, "Has Casual Gone Too Far?" <http://travel.canoe.ca/Lifewise Work0208/16_casual2-sun.html> (Retrieved 6 July 2003).
36. "My Closet Is Full, But I Have Nothing to Wear!" 30 July 2002 <www.workopolis.com/servlet/Content/rprinter/20020730/dcode 20020730> (Retrieved 3 July 2003).
37. "Dress Codes," Queen's University Career Services <http://careers.queensu.ca/students/career counselling/dresscodes.asp> (Retrieved 3 July 2003).
38. Mary Lou Andre, "The Business Casual Dress Code" <http://editorial.careers.msn.com/articles/women/> (Retrieved 5 July 2003).
39. "Minacs Worldwide Selected to Provide CRM Services for Major Automotive Manufacturer" <www.minacs.com/pdf_uploads/2003/20030206_amerhonda.pdf> (Retrieved 2 July 2003).
40. "Not Listening Is an American Thing," *HighGain Inc. Newsletter* <http://www.highgain.com/newsletter/back-issues/e-news/06-00/hg-enews-06-00.html> (Retrieved 17 January 2001).
41. Mark L. Hickson and Don W. Stacks, *Nonverbal Communication* (Dubuque, IA: William Brown & Benchmark, 1993), 21.
42. "What's the Universal Hand Sign for 'I Goofed'?" *Santa Barbara News-Press*, 16 December 1996, D2.
43. Arthur H. Bell, "Using Nonverbal Cues," *Incentive*, September 1999, 162.
44. James Calvert Scott, "Business Casual Dress: Workplace Boon or Boondoggle?" Part 2, *Instructional Strategies*, Delta Pi Epsilon, December 1999, 5.

## CHAPTER 4

1. Kali Pearson, "Ten Trailblazers: The Adventurer and The Builder: Entrepreneurs Who Have Rocked Their Industries," May 2002 <www.profitguide.com/magazine/article.jsp?content=924> (Retrieved 2 July 2003).
2. Based on information found at "G.A.P: The Great Adventure People" Web site <www.gapadventures.ca> (Retrieved 2 July 2003); Kali Pearson, "Ten Trailblazers"; Paul Luke, "All I Want to Do Is Have a Positive Impact on the World: Poon Tip," *The Province*, Vancouver, BC, 27 October 2002; "G.A.P Adventures, Toronto, Ontario" <www.dfait-maeci.gc.ca/tna-nac/stories 23-en.asp> (Retrieved 2 July 2003); Laura Pratt, "Adventures with Ethics," *World Tibet Network News*, 19 August 2001 <www.tibet.ca/wtnarchive/2001/8/19_5.html> (Retrieved 2 July 2003).
3. Julian Beltrame, "Simply the Best," *Maclean's*, 24 March 2003, 19–24.
4. John Ward, "Census Shows Jump in Canadians with a Mother Tongue Other than English, French," *The Canadian Press*, 2002 <www.hispeed.rogers.com> (Retrieved 5 February 2003).
5. Alecia Swasy, "Don't Sell Thick Diapers in Tokyo," *The New York Times*, 3 October 1993, F9.
6. Raju Narisetti, "Can Rubbermaid Crack Foreign Markets?" *The Wall Street Journal*, 20 June 1996, B1.
7. E. S. Browning, "In Pursuit of the Elusive Euroconsumer," *The Wall Street Journal*, 23 April 1992, B1.
8. Gabriella Stern, "Heinz Aims to Export Taste for Ketchup," *The Wall Street Journal*, 21 November 1992, B1.
9. Shona Crabtree, "Cultural Differences," *Eagle-Tribune* <http://www.eagletribune.com/news/stories/19990530/BU-001.htm> (Retrieved 13 February 2001).
10. Mary O'Hara-Devereaux and Robert Johansen, *GlobalWork: Bridging Distance, Culture and Time* (San Francisco: Jossey-Bass, 1994), 245.
11. Sari Kalin, "Global Net Knits East to West at Liz Claiborne," *Computerworld*, 9 June 1997, G4–G6.
12. Elaine Carey, "City of New Faces," *Toronto Star*, 22 January 2003, A6.
13. "Facts in Canada," Canada *Information Office* <www.cio.bic.gc.ca/facts/multi_e.html> (Retrieved 8 April 2000).

14. David Harvey, "Going Global," *Home Office Computing*, October 2000, 87.

15. Steve Alexander, "Learn the Politics of Going Global," *Computerworld*, 1 January 2001, S8–S10.

16. Adam Lincoln, "Lost in Translation," *ECFO*, Spring 2001, 38; Sari Kalin, "The Importance of Being Multiculturally Correct," *Computerworld*, 6 October 1997, G16–G17.

17. Andrew Pollack, "Barbie's Journey in Japan," *The New York Times*, 22 December 1996, E3.

18. Lennie Copeland and Lewis Griggs, *Going International* (New York: Plume Books, 1985), 14.

19. James Baxter, "Canadian Identity 'Stronger Than Ever,'" *Ottawa Citizen* (online), 22 May 2000 <www.ottawacitizen.com> (Retrieved 21 June 2000).

20. Guo-Ming Chen and William J. Starosta, *Foundations of Intercultural Communication* (Boston: Allyn and Bacon, 1998), 40.

21. Iris Varner and Linda Beamer, *Intercultural Communication in the Global Workplace* (Boston: Irwin McGraw-Hill, 1995), 15.

22. Guy Rocher, "Culture," *1998 Canadian Encyclopaedia*, Electric Library Canada, 6 September 1997.

23. Edward T. Hall and Mildred Reed Hall, *Understanding Cultural Differences* (Yarmouth, ME: Intercultural Press, 1987), 183–184.

24. Kathleen K. Reardon, *Where Minds Meet* (Belmont, CA: Wadsworth, 1987), 199.

25. Vivienne Luk, Mumtaz Patel, and Kathryn White, "Personal Attributes of American and Chinese Business Associates," *The Bulletin of the Association for Business Communication*, December 1990, 67.

26. Cynthia Gallois and Victor Callan, *Communication and Culture* (New York: John Wiley Sons, 1997), 24.

27. "Canada Business, Business Culture," *Canada Business*, Electric Library Canada, 30 June 1997.

28. "Canada Business, Business Culture."

29. T. Morrison, Wayne Conaway, and George Borden. *Kiss, Bow, or Shake Hands: How to Do Business in Sixty Countries* (Holbrook, MA: Bob Adams Inc., 1994), 44.

30. Susan S. Jarvis, "Preparing Employees to Work South of the Border," *Personnel*, June 1990, 763.

31. Gallois and Callan, *Communication and Culture*, 29.

32. Copeland and Griggs, *Going International*, 94.

33. Copeland and Griggs, *Going International*, 108.

34. Copeland and Griggs, *Going International*, 12.

35. Jeff Copeland, "Stare Less, Listen More," *American Way*, American Airlines, 15 December 1990.

36. Nicholas Keung, "Learning the Signs of Communication," *Toronto Star*, 22 May 1999, L1–L2.

37. Keung, "Learning the Signs of Communication."

38. E. S. Browning, "Computer Chip Project Brings Rivals Together, But the Cultures Clash," *The Wall Street Journal*, 3 May 1994, A1, A11.

39. S. Ishii and T. Bruneau, "Silence and Silences in Cross-Cultural Perspective: Japan and the United States." *In Intercultural Communication: A Reader* (Belmont, CA: Wadsworth, 1994), 266.

40. Laura Pratt, "Adventures with Ethics," *World Tibet Network News*, 19 August 2001, <www.tibet.ca/wtnarchive/2001/8/19_5.html> (Retrieved 2 July 2003).

41. Based on information found at "G.A.P: The Great Adventure People" Web site <www.gapadventures.ca> (Retrieved 2 July 2003); Kali Pearson, "Ten Trailblazers"; Paul Luke, "All I Want to Do Is Have a Positive Impact on the World: Poon Tip," *The Province*, Vancouver, BC, 27 October 2002; "G.A.P Adventures, Toronto, Ontario" <www.dfait maeci.gc.ca/tna-nac/stories23-en.asp> (Retrieved 2 July 2003); Laura Pratt, "Adventures with Ethics," *World Tibet Network News*, 19 August 2001 <www.tibet.ca/wtnarchive/2001/8/19_5.html> (Retrieved 2 July 2003).

42. Copeland and Griggs, *Going International*, 111.

43. M. R. Hammer, "Intercultural Communication Competence," in Chen and Starosta, *Foundations of Intercultural Communication*, 247.

44. Lillian H. Chaney and Jeanette S. Martin, *Intercultural Business Communication* (Englewood Cliffs, NJ: Prentice Hall Career and Technology, 1995), 67.

45. *Do's and Taboos Around the World*, 2nd ed. (New York: Wiley, 1990), 7l.

46. Robert McGarvey, "Foreign Exchange," *USAir Magazine*, June 1992, 64.

47. Andrew W. Singer, "Ethics: Are Standards Lower Overseas?" *Across the Board*, September 1991, 31–34.

48. "Transparency International Canada Urges Quick Passage of Anti-Corruption Legislation," *Canada NewsWire*, 3 December 1998 <www.newswire.ca/releases> (Retrieved 24 March 2000).

49. Transparency International, "OECD Convention on Combating Bribery of Foreign Public Officials in International Business Transactions" <http://www.state.gov/www.issues/economic/fs_000301_oecd_conv.html> (Retrieved 13 February 2001).

50. Kent Hodgson, "Adapting Ethical Decisions to a Global Marketplace," *Management Review*, May 1992, 56.

51. Charlene Marmer Solomon, "Put Your Ethics to a Global Test," *Personnel Journal*, January 1996, 66–74. See also Larry R. Smeltzer and Marianne M. Jennings, "Why an International Code of Business Ethics Would Be Good for Business," *Journal of Business Ethics*, January 1998, 57–66.

52. Based on Kent Hodgson, "Adapting Ethical Decisions," 54.

53. "Latest Employment News from Statistics Canada Released: March 10, 2000," *Canada NewsWire Career Monitor*, 10 March 2000 <www.newswire.ca/releases/March2000/10/>.

54. Carter Hammett, "Companies Win Through Team Building," *The Toronto Sun Career Connection* <www.canoe.ca/CareerConnectionNews/030213_teambuilding.html> (Retrieved 12 February 2003).

55. Rae Andre, "Diversity Stress as Morality Stress," *Journal of Business Ethics*, June 1995, 489–496.

56. Jayne Tear, "They Just Don't Understand Gender Dynamics," *The Wall Street Journal*, 20 November 1995, A12; Anne Roiphe, "Talking Trouble," *Working Woman*, October 1994, 28–31; and Cristina Stuart, "Why Can't a Woman Be More Like a Man?" *Training Tomorrow*, February 1994, 22–24.

57. Genevieve Capowski, "Managing Diversity," *Management Review,* June 1996, 16.
58. Joel Makower, "Managing Diversity in the Workplace," *Business and Society Review,* Winter 1995, 48–54.
59. George Simons and Darlene Dunham, "Making Inclusion Happen," *Managing Diversity,* December 1995 <www.jalmc.org/mk-incl.htm> (Retrieved 9 August 1996).
60. Pearson, "Ten Trailblazers."
61. Based on information found at "G.A.P: The Great Adventure People" Web site <www.gapadventures.ca> (Retrieved 2 July 2003); Kali Pearson, "Ten Trailblazers"; Paul Luke, "All I Want to Do Is Have a Positive Impact on the World: Poon Tip," *The Province,* Vancouver, BC, 27 October 2002; "G.A.P Adventures, Toronto, Ontario" <www.dfait-maeci.gc.ca/tna-nac/stories23-en.asp> (Retrieved 2 July 2003); Laura Pratt, "Adventures with Ethics," *World Tibet Network News,* 19 August 2001, <www.tibet.ca/wtnarchive/2001/8/19_5.html> (Retrieved 2 July 2003).
62. Luke, "All I Want to Do."
63. Ken Cottrill, "The World According to Hollywood," *Traffic World,* 6 November 2000, 15.
64. "Examples of Cultural Blunders Made by U.S. Businessmen," *Eagle Tribune* <http://www.eagletribune.com/news/stories/19990530/BU_002.htm> (Retrieved 13 February 2001).
65. Michele Wucker, "Keep on Trekking," *Working Woman,* December/January 1998, 32–36.
66. Karl Schoenberger, "Motorola Bets Big on China," *Fortune,* 27 May 1996, 116–124.
67. Based on Rose Knotts and Mary S. Thibodeaux, "Verbal Skills in Cross-Culture Managerial Communication," *European Business Review,* 92, no. 2, 1992, v–vii.
68. Keith Martin and Sheila M. Walsh, "Beware the Foreign Corrupt Practices Act," October 1996, 25–27.
69. Makower, "Managing Diversity."

## CHAPTER 5

1. Mark Evans, "Man of Many Hats Navigates Rough Waters; Adventures of the Unsinkable Alex Tilley," *Financial Post,* 30 May 1992.
2. Evans, "Man of Many Hats Navigates Rough Waters; Adventures of the Unsinkable Alex Tilley."
3. Rick Eglinton, "Tilley's Tale: Design Endures," *Toronto Star,* 18 February 2002, E06.
4. Hugh Hay-Roe, "The Secret of Excess," *Executive Excellence,* January 1995, 20.
5. Charles C. Manz, Christopher P. Neek, James Mancuso, and Karen P. Manz, *For Team Members Only* (New York: AMACOM American Management Association, 1997), 3–4. See also Edward M. Marshall, *Transforming the Way We Work* (New York: AMACOM American Management Association, 1995), 5.
6. A. Lunsford and L. Ede, "Audience Addressed/Audience Invoked: The Role of Audience in Composition Theory and Pedagogy," *College Composition and Communication,* May 1984, 2; and A. Lunsford and L. Ede, "Why Write . . . Together: A Research Update," *Rhetoric Review,* Fall 1986, 1.
7. Earl N. Harbert, "Knowing Your Audience," in *The Handbook of Executive Communication,* ed. John L. DiGaetani (Homewood, IL: Dow Jones/Irwin, 1986), 3.
8. Vanessa Dean Arnold, "Benjamin Franklin on Writing Well," *Personnel Journal,* August 1986, 17.
9. Mark Bacon, quoted in "Business Writing: One-on-One Speaks Best to the Masses," *Training,* April 1988, 95. See also Elizabeth Danziger, "Communicate Up," *Journal of Accountancy,* February 1998, 67.
10. For more information see Marilyn Schwartz, *Guidelines for Bias-Free Writing* (Bloomington, IN: University Press, 1994).
11. Diane Stegmann, "Tilley Junior Redesigns Tilley Endurables," *Catalog Age,* July 2000, 22.
12. Stegmann, "Tilley Junior Redesigns Tilley Endurables."
13. Leslie Matthies, as described in Carl Heyel, "Policy and Procedure Manuals," *The Handbook of Executive Communication* (Homewood, Illinois: Dow Jones-Irwin, 1986), 212.
14. Parts of this section are based on Kristin R. Woolever's "Corporate Language and the Law: Avoiding Liability in Corporate Communi-cations," *IEE Transactions on Professional Communication,* 2 June 1990, 95–98.
15. "Effect of Product Liability Laws on Small Business: An Introduction to International Exposure through a Comparison of U.S. and Canadian Law," *Journal of Small Business Management,* 7 January 1998, 72.
16. Lewis N. Klar, "Torts," *The 1998 Canadian Encyclopedia,* Electric Library Canada, 9 June 1997.
17. Klar, "Torts."
18. Lisa Jenner, "Develop Communication and Training With Literacy in Mind," *HR Focus,* March 1994, 14.
19. 1996 Minister of Public Works and Government Services and the WWLIA "Misleading Advertisings Under the Federal Competition Act," <http://wwwlia.org/ca-compl.htm> (Retrieved 18 April 2000).
20. 1996 Minister of Public Works and Government Services and the WWLIA "Misleading Advertisings Under the Federal Competition Act," <http://wwwlia.org/ca-compl.htm> (Retrieved 18 April 2000).
21. Woolever, "Corporate Language," 96.
22. Eglinton, "Tilley's Tale: Design Endures."
23. Eglinton, "Tilley's Tale: Design Endures."
24. Jules Abend, "The enduring Alex Tilley," *Bobbin,* June 1997, 8.
25. Woolever, "Corporate Language," 95.
26. Lisa Jenner, "Employment-at-Will Liability: How Protected Are You?" *HR Focus,* March 1994, 11.
27. Judy E. Pickens, "Communication: Terms of Equality: A Guide to Bias-Free Language," *Personnel Journal,* August 1985, 5.

## CHAPTER 6

1. Andy Holloway, "Doughnuts and Drugstores Join Our List of Canada's Top 75 Companies: The Countdown Continues," *Canadian Business,* 9 June 2003.
2. Maryanna Lewyckyj, "Tim Scores in U.S.; Hortons' Chain Finally Sees a Profit Stateside," *Toronto Sun,* 1 February 2003, 43.
3. Holloway, "Doughnuts and Drugstores."
4. Hollie Shaw, "Doughnuts Outmuscle McDonald's Burgers: Tim Hortons Tops in Sales," *Financial Post,* 24 March 2003, 1.

5. Shaw, "Doughnuts Outmuscle McDonald's burgers."

6. Isabel Teotonio, "Can Tim's Stay Canadian?" *Toronto Star*, 12 February 2003, D4.

7. Adrian Furnham, "The Brainstorming Myth," *Business Strategy Review*, Winter 2000, 21–28.

8. Dean Rieck, "AH HA! Running a Productive Brainstorming Session," *Direct Marketing*, November 1999, 78.

9. Kimberly Paterson, "The Writing Process," *Rough Notes*, April 1998, 59–60.

10. Johan Rindegard, "Use Clear Writing to Show You Mean Business," *InfoWorld*, 22 November 1999, 78.

11. Alex Mlynek, "Live and Learn: Ron Joyce," *Canadian Business*, 23 June 2003.

12. Teotonio, "Can Tim's Stay Canadian?"

13. Andrew Fluegelman and Jeremy Joan Hewes, "The Word Processor and the Writing Process," in *Strategies for Business and Technical Writing*, 4th ed. Kevin J. Harty, ed. (San Diego: Harcourt Brace Jovanovich, 1989), 43. See also Lynn Quitman Troyka, *Simon & Schuster Handbook for Writers*, 4th ed. (Upper Saddle River, NJ: Prentice Hall, 1996), 49.

14. Maryann V. Piotrowski, *Effective Business Writing* (New York: HarperPerennial, 1996), 12.

15. Eric McLuhan, "The Changing Face of Literacy," *TVO*, December 2002, 12.

16. Robert W. Goddard, "Communication: Use Language Effectively," *Personnel Journal*, April 1989, 32.

17. Frederick Crews, *The Random House Handbook*, 4th ed. (New York: Random House, 1991), 152.

18. "Creating the Right Environment," *National Post* Joint Venture Supplement with the Conference Board of Canada, 27 April 1999, CB1, CB3.

19. Lewyckyj, "Tim Scores in U.S."

20. Lori Doss, "Tim Hortons Makes Plans to Roll Out Hundreds of New Branches," *Nation's Restaurant News*, 10 June 2002, 4.

21. Mlynek, "Live and Learn: Ron Joyce."

22. Doss, "Tim Hortons Makes Plans."

23. Doss, "Tim Hortons Makes Plans."

24. Doss, "Tim Hortons Makes Plans."

25. Mlynek, "Live and Learn: Ron Joyce."

## CHAPTER 7

1. Based on information found at Stiff Sentences Inc. Web site <www.stiff sentences.com.> (Retrieved 25 June 2003); "Corporate Review Including The Machinery of Language" (Ottawa: 2002, Stiff Sentences Inc.); BackDRAFT promotional material.

2. Peter Elbow, *Writing With Power: Techniques for Mastering the Writing Process* (Oxford: Oxford University Press, 1998), 30.

3. John S. Fielden, "What Do You Mean You Don't Like My Style?" *Harvard Business Review*, May/June 1982, 128.

4. Sonia Von Matt Stoddard, "Proofreading for Perfection," *Legal Assistant Today*, March/April 1997, 84–85.

5. Ralph Brown, "Add Some Informal Polish to Your Writing," *Management*, March 1998, 12.

6. *Business Week*, 6 July 1981, 107.

7. Richard E. Neff, "CEOs Want Information, Not Just Words," *Communication World*, April/May 1997, 22–25.

8. Robert Beauchemin, "How to Help Customers Look After Customers: Comprehensive Relationship Management Solution, *Computing Canada*, 13 October 1998.

9. Claire K. Cook, *Line by Line* (Boston: Houghton Mifflin, 1985), 17.

10. William Power and Michael Siconolfi, "Memo to: Mr. Ball, RE: Your Messages, Sir: They're Weird," *The Wall Street Journal*, 30 November 1990, 1; Ralph Brown, "Add Some Informal Polish to Your Writing," *Management*, March 1998, 12.

11. Carol Ann Wilson, "Be On the Cutting Edge: Learn These Seven Plain Language Principles Now!" <www.wwlia.org/plainlan.htm> (Retrieved 20 April 2000).

12. "Plain Language," *National Literacy Secretariat* <www.nald.ca/nls.nlsild/fact6.htm> (Retrieved 5 July 2003).

13. "Making it Plain: Government Releases Model Plain Language Loan Disclosure Documents,"

Ottawa, 15 March 2001 <www.fin.gc.ca/news01/01-028e.html> (Retrieved 5 July 2003).

14. Peter Calamai, "How Can Anyone See Through This Smog?" *Toronto Star*, 28 August 1999, J3.

15. Joel Shore, "Suites Still Depend on 'Feature Creep' to Grow," *Computer Reseller News*, 11 November 1996, 202.

16. Spell checker poem has appeared in many publications without attribution.

17. Louise Lague, *People* Magazine editor, interview with Mary Ellen Guffey, 5 February 1992.

18. *The Canadian Style: A Guide to Writing and Editing* (Toronto: Dundurn Press Limited, 1996).

19. Laurie Bildfell, "Standard Time: The Canadian Style? Versatile and Not Pushy," *Quill and Quire*, December 1994, 12–13.

20. *The Canadian Style: A Guide to Writing and Editing.*

## CHAPTER 8

1. Based on information found at Research in Motion Web site, <www.rim.com> (Retrieved 6 July 2003).

2. "Canadians' Love Affair with Email Continues," Ipsos-Reid, 30 October 2001 <www.angusreid.com/media/dsp_displaypr.prnt.cfm?ID_to_view=1345> (Retrieved 18 June 2003).

3. Sana Reynolds, "Composing Effective E-Mail Messages," *Communication World*, July 1997, 8–9.

4. Reynolds, "Composing Effective E-Mail," 8.

5. Paula Jacobs, "Strong Writing Skills Essentials for Success, Even in IT," *InfoWorld*, 6 July 1998, 86.

6. Rachel Ross, "E-mail Chewing Up More Paper," *Toronto Star*, 8 April 2003, E3.

7. James Brooke, "That Secure Feeling of a Printed Document," *The New York Times*, 21 April 2001, B1.

8. Rosalind Gold, "Reader-Friendly Writing," *Supervisory Management*, January 1989, 40.

9. Linda Himelstein, "Exhibit A: The Telltale Computer Tape," *Business Week*, 15 August 1994, 8; Lawrence Dietz, "E-Mail Is Wonderful But It Has Risks," *Bottom Line/Business*

(published by Boardroom, Inc.), 15 June 1995, 3–4; and Jenny C. McCune, "Get the Message," *Management Review*, January 1997.

10. Leslie Helm, "The Digital Smoking Gun," *Los Angeles Times*, 16 June 1994, El.
11. "Canadians' Love Affair with Email Continues."
12. "Innovations Case Study: Research in Motion Ltd.," Information Technology Association of Canada <www.itac.ca> (Retrieved 12 August 2003).
13. "Innovations Case Study: Research in Motion Ltd."
14. "Handy BlackBerry Can Be Addictive," *USA Today*, 2 June 2003, 13.
15. Joshua Partlow, "Busy Thumbs and Crossed Fingers; BlackBerry Users Not Likely to Be Left Empty-Handed," *The Washington Post*, 21 August 2003 <www.washington post.com> (Retrieved 26 August 2003).
16. "Handy BlackBerry Can Be Addictive."
17. John Fielden, "Clear Writing Is Not Enough," *Management Review*, April 1989, 51.
18. "Innovations Case Study: Research in Motion Ltd."
19. Robert Uhlig, "How Text Messages Cut a Sentence Down to Size," 16 February 2001 <www.telegraph .co.uk> (Retrieved 25 July 2003).
20. Laura Liebeck, "Novelty Hasn't Worn Off for Candy Manufacturers," *Discount Store News*, 13 July 1998, 8, 110.
21. Nan DeMars, "Confidentiality Maintenance," *OfficePro*, February 2001, 22–23.
22. Based on Maggie Jackson, "Casual Day a Bad Fit?" *Los Angeles Times Careers*, 19 January 1998, 27–28.
23. Based on Charles Waltner, "Web Watchers," *Informationweek*, 27 April 1998, 121–126; and Howard Millman, "Easy EDI for Everyone," *InfoWorld*, 17 August 1998, 38–39.
24. George D. Webster, "Internal Communications Issues," *Association Management*, May 1995, 150–153.
25. Joann S. Lublin, "You Should Negotiate A Severance Package—Even Before Job Starts," *The Wall Street Journal*, 13 March 2001, B1.

## CHAPTER 9

1. Based on information found at Rocky Mountaineer Web site <www.rockymountaineer.com> (Retrieved 15 July 2003).
2. Malcolm Forbes, "How to Write a Business Letter," International Paper Company, reprinted in *Strategies for Business and Technical Writing*, 4th ed., ed. Kevin Harty (Boston: Allyn and Bacon, 1999), 108.
3. Bill Knapp, "Communication Breakdown," *World Wastes*, February 1998, 16.
4. Hugh Hay-Roe, "The Secret of Excess," *Executive Excellence*, January 1995, 20.
5. Dennis Chambers, *Writing to Get Action* (Bristol, VT: Velocity Business Publishing, 1998), 12.
6. Max Messmer, "Enhancing Your Writing Skills," *Strategic Finance*, January 2001, 8–10.
7. Eugene E. Brussell, *Dictionary of Quotable Definitions* (Eaglewood Cliffs, NJ: Prentice-Hall, 1970), 550.
8. Geoffrey Brewer, "The Customer Stops Here," *Sales & Marketing Management*, March 1998, 30–36.
9. Malcolm MacKillop, "How to Handle Requests for a Reference," *Human Resource Professional*, April/May 1997, 10.
10. "A 'Catch 22' in Honesty," *The Wall Street Journal*, 2 December 1990, F25. See also Brian Gill, "Establishing Job References Policies," *American Printer*, January 1998, 66.
11. Steven N. Spertz and Glenda S. Spertz, *The Rule of Law: Canadian Business Law*, 2nd ed. (Toronto: Copp Clark Ltd., 1995), 289.
12. Gary L. Clark, Peter F. Kaminski, and David R. Rink, "Consumer Complaints: Advice on How Companies Should Respond Based on an Empirical Study," *Journal of Services Marketing*, Winter 1992, 41–50.
13. Laura Hansen and Karen Curtis, "Keep the Customer Satisfied," *Marketing Tools*, 6 January 2000, 44.
14. Robert Klara, "Press 1 to Gripe," *Restaurant Business*, 15 May 1998, 96–102.
15. Stephanie Armour, "Companies Grapple with Gripes Posted on Web," *USA Today*, 16 September 1998, O5B.

16. "Grove's Internet Apology," *Computer Reseller News*, 5 December 1994, 313.
17. Marcia Mascolini, "Another Look at Teaching the External Negative Message," *The Bulletin of the Association of Business Communication*, June 1994, 46; Robert J. Aalberts and Lorraine A. Krajewski, "Claim and Adjustment Letters," *The Bulletin of the Association for Business Communication*, September 1987, 2.
18. Elizabeth Blackburn Brockman and Kelly Belanger, "You-Attitude and Positive Emphasis: Testing Received Wisdom in Business Communication," *The Bulletin of the Association for Business Communication*, June 1993, 1–5; C. Goodwin and I. Ross, "Consumer Evaluations of Responses to Complaints: What's Fair and Why," *Journal of Consumer Marketing*, 7, 1990, 39–47; Marcia Mascolini, "Another Look at Teaching the External Negative Message," *The Bulletin of the Association for Business Communication*, June 1994, 46.
19. Based on information found at Rocky Mountaineer Web site <www.rockymountaineer.com> (Retrieved 15 July 2003).
20. Pamela Gilbert, "Two Words That Can Help a Business Thrive," *The Wall Street Journal*, 30 December 1996, A12.
21. Saburo Haneda and Hirosuke Shima, "Japanese Communication Behavior as Reflected in Letter Writing," *The Journal of Business Communication* 1, 1982, 29. See also Iris I. Varner and Linda Beamer, *Intercultural Communication* (Chicago: McGraw-Hill Irwin, 2001), 131–132.
22. Zhu Yunxia, "Building Knowledge Structures in Teaching Cross-Cultural Sales Genres," *Business Communication Quarterly*, December, 2000, 49.
23. Wolfgang Manekeller, as cited in Iris I. Varner, "Internationalizing Business Communication Courses," *The Bulletin of the Association for Business Communication*, December 1987, 10.
24. Dr. Annette Luciani-Samec, French instructor, and Dr. Pierre Samec, French businessman, interviews with Mary Ellen Guffey, May 1995.

25. Retha H. Kilpatrick, "International Business Communication Practices," *The Journal of Business Communication*, Fall 1984, 42–43.
26. Based on articles by Frank Edward Allen, "McDonald's to Reduce Waste in Plan Developed With Environmental Group," *The Wall Street Journal*, 17 April 1991, B1; and Mark Hamstra, "McD Supersizes Efforts to Cut Down on Costs," *Nation's Restaurant News*, 29 June 1998, 1, 60.

## CHAPTER 10

1. Based on information found at United Way Web site <www.unitedway.ca> (Retrieved July 2003).
2. Seth Faison, "Trying to Play by the Rules," *The New York Times*, 22 December 1991, Sec. 3, 1.
3. "How to Ask For—And Get—What You Want!" *Supervision*, February 1990, 11.
4. Rob Yogel, "Sending Your Message Electronically," *Target Marketing*, June 1998, 77–78.
5. Dean Rieck, "Great Letters and Why They Work," *Direct Marketing*, June 1998, 20–24.
6. Molly Prior, "Amazon: King of the On-Line Jungle, Master of All Domains," *Dsn Retailing Today*, 20 November 2000, 18.
7. Dennis Chambers, *The Agile Manager's Guide to Writing to Get Action* (Bristol, VT: Velocity Press, 1998), 86.
8. Kevin McLaughlin, "Words of Wisdom," *Entrepreneur*, October 1990, 101.
9. Based on Richard Gibson, "Merchants Mull the Long and the Short of Lines," *The Wall Street Journal*, 3 September 1998, B1.
10. Lin Grensing-Pophal, "Training Employees to Telecommute: A Recipe for Success," *HRMagazine*, December 1998, 76; Jeffery D. Zbar, "Training to Telework," *Home Office Computing*, March 2001, 72.
11. Laura Johannes, "Globe-Trotting Shutterbug Slaps Kodak With the Bill for a Reshoot," *The Wall Street Journal*, 24 April 1998, B1.
12. Virginia Galt, "Getting Fit on the Job," *The Globe and Mail*, 6 November 2002, C1

<www.globeandmail.com> (Retrieved 2 August 2003).
13. Based on "U.S. Company Pays Big Bucks for Used Athletic Footwear," *Sporting Goods Business*, 23 January 1998; "Your Feet Are Paved With Gold," *Canadian Business*, October 1996, 113.

## CHAPTER 11

1. Based on information found at Hyundai Auto Canada Web sites <www.Hyundaicanada.com> and <www.Hyundaiupdate.ca> (Retrieved July 2003).
2. Mohan R. Limaye, "Further Conceptualization of Explanations in Negative Messages," *Business Communication Quarterly*, June 1997, 46.
3. Carol David and Margaret Ann Baker, "Rereading Bad News: Compliance-Gaining Features in Management Memos," *The Journal of Business Communication*, 31, No. 4, 268.
4. Robert Mirguet, information security manager, Eastman Kodak Co., Rochester, New York, quoted in *Computerworld*, cited in "Telecommunicating," *Boardroom Reports*, 1 March 1995, 15; Sandy Sampson, "Wild Wild Web: Legal Exposure on the Internet," *Software Magazine*, November 1997, 75–78.
5. Elizabeth A. McCord, "The Business Writer, the Law, and Routine Business Communication: A Legal and Rhetorical Analysis," *Journal of Business and Technical Communication*, April 1991, 183.
6. Phillip M. Perry, "E-Mail Hell: The Dark Side of the Internet Age," *Folio: The Magazine for Magazine Management*, June 1998, 74–75.
7. McCord, "The Business Writer," 183, 193.
8. Marcia Mascolini, "Another Look at Teaching the External Negative Message," *The Bulletin of the Association for Business Communication*, June 1994, 47.
9. "Letters to Lands' End," *February 1991 Catalog* (Dodgeville, WI: Lands' End, 1991), 100.
10. Elizabeth M. Dorn, "Case Method Instruction in the Business Writing Classroom," *Business Communication Quarterly*, March 1999, 51–52.

11. James E. Goodwin, chairman and CEO, United Airlines, letter to Mary Ellen Guffey, 1 September 2000.
12. Malcolm Forbes, "How to Write a Business Letter," International Paper Company, reprinted in *Strategies for Business and Technical Writing*, 4th ed., ed. Kevin Harty (Boston: Allyn and Bacon, 1999), 108.
13. Based on information found at Hyundai Auto Canada Web sites, <www.Hyundaicanada.com> and <www.Hyundaiupdate.ca> (Retrieved July 2003).
14. Jeanette W. Gilsdorf, "Metacommunication Effects on International Business Negotiating in China," *Business Communication Quarterly*, June 1997, 27.
15. Based on Gene Sloan, "Under 21? Carnival Says Cruise Is Off," *USA Today*, 29 November 1996.
16. Based on Robert L. Simison, "'Forget Paris,' GM Tells Journalists; Instead They Get to Visit Detroit," *The Wall Street Journal*, 12 August 1998, B1.
17. Andrew Ross Sorkin, "J. Crew Web Goof Results in Discount," *The New York Times*, 11 November 1999, D3.
18. Based on Julia King, "SunGard Stung by Virus," *Computerworld*, 6 February 1995, 73.
19. Laura Johannes, "Globe-Trotting Shutterbug Slaps Kodak With the Bill for a Reshoot," *The Wall Street Journal*, 24 April 1998, B1.

## CHAPTER 12

1. "It Figures: StatsCan's No. 1," *Financial Post*, 12 November 1994, 16.
2. Melanie Brooks, "The World's Top Number Cruncher: Researchers Last Night Honoured StatsCan Chief Ivan Fellegi for Telling Canada's Story by the Numbers," *Ottawa Citizen*, 25 October 2002, A2.
3. Haroon Siddiqui, "Ivan Fellegi Has It All Figured Out," *Toronto Star*, 12 December 2002, A35.
4. Brooks, "The World's Top Number Cruncher."
5. "We Are Statistics Canada" <www.statcan.ca> (Accessed 16 June 2003).
6. "What We Do" <www.statcan.ca> (Accessed 16 June 2003).
7. "More Than Numbers, Census Tells a Story," *Sudbury Star*, 24 November 2002, A6.

8. "Unlocking History," *The Expositor (Brantford)*, 11 February 2003, A10.
9. Kerry Gillespie, "Forget the Sensible Shoes; Librarians Turn a New Leaf," *Toronto Star,* 14 June 2003, A23.
10. Gillespie, "Forget the Sensible Shoes."
11. Joellen Perry and Janet Rae-Dupree, "Searching the Web Gets Easier With Engines That Try To Read Your Mind," *U.S. News & World Report*, 16 April 2001, 52.
12. Rona Maynard, "Making Your Life Simpler," *Chatelaine's Essential Web Guide*, Third Annual Web Guide, September 2002, 2.
13. Tina Pittaway, "Smart Search Strategies," *Chatelaine's Essential Web Guide*, Third Annual Web Guide, September 2002, 47.
14. Kim Zetter and Harry McCracken, "How To Stop Searching and Start Finding," *PC World*, September 2000, 129.
15. H. B. Koplowitz, "The Nature of Search Engines," *Link-Up*, September/October 1998, 28.
16. Based on Konnie G. Kustron, "Searching the World Wide Web," *Records Management Quarterly*, July 1997, 8–12.
17. Susan Feldman quoted in Annette Skov, "Internet Quality," *Database*, August/September 1998.
18. M. Theodore Farries, II, Jeanne D. Maes, and Ulla K. Bunz, "References and Bibliography: Citing the Internet," *Journal of Applied Business Research*, Summer 1998, 33–36.
19. Christopher Velotta, "How To Design and Implement a Question-naire," *Technical Communication*, Fall 1991.
20. Robin Toner, "Politics of Welfare: Focusing on the Problems," *The New York Times*, 5 July 1991, 1.
21. Daphne A. Jameson, "The Ethics of Plagiarism: How Genre Affects Writers' Use of Source Materials," *The Bulletin of the Association for Business Communication*, June 1993, 18.
22. Writing Tutorial Services, Indiana University, "Plagiarism: What It Is and How to Recognize and Avoid It" <http://www.indiana.edu/~wts/wts/plagiarism.html> (Retrieved 22 August 2001).
23. Chris Sorenson, "A Web of Cheating," *Toronto Star*, 18 March 2003, D1.
24. "It Figures."
25. Brooks, "The World's Top Number Cruncher."
26. "Contacting Canadians: Improving Data Collection and Reporting," <www.statcan.ca/about/online.htm> (Accessed 16 June 2003).
27. Gerald J. Alred, Walter E. Oliu, and Charles T. Brusaw, *The Professional Writer* (New York: St. Martin's Press, 1992), 78.
28. "Gulf States Centralizes HR/Payroll Functions," *Workforce*, December 1998, 70.
29. "On Target American Retailing; America's Other Wal-Mart," *Economist (U.S.)*, 5 May 2001, 6.

## CHAPTER 13

1. Dana Flavelle, "Bay Cans 15% of Suppliers Over Conduct," *Toronto Star*, 13 June 2003, E6.
2. Bob Jeffcott, "Wal-Mart Wins Sweatshop of the Year Award," *Organic Consumers Association*, 16 January 2003.
3. David Finlayson, "The Value of Trust: Companies See Their Reputations as Concrete Assets Worth Protecting," *Edmonton Journal*, 4 August 2001, F1.
4. Hudson's Bay Company 2002 Corporate Social Responsibility Report, 1.
5. Hudson's Bay Company, 3.
6. Flavelle, "Bay Cans 15%."
7. Charlene Marmer Solomon, "Marriott's Family Matters," *Personnel Journal*, October 1991, 40–42; Jennifer Laabs, "They Want More Support—Inside and Outside of Work," *Workforce*, November 1998, 54–56.
8. Chuck Hawkins, "FedEx: Europe Nearly Killed the Messenger," *Business Week*, 25 May 1992, 124–126.
9. David Finlayson, "The Value of Trust."
10. Lesia Strangre, "Trademarks Are Not Tools for Censorship. Some Companies Seek Shield from Criticism on Web," *National Post*, 24 June 2000, D6.
11. Hudson's Bay Company 2002 Corporate Social Responsibility Report, "Community Investment," 13.
12. Katherine Raso, "Hbc Continues to Differentiate Itself with the Introduction of New Brands in 2003," *Canada Newswire Ltd.* <www.newswire.ca> 28 May 2003.
13. Timony Aeppel, "Firestone Recall Fuels Interest in 'Smart' Tires," *The Wall Street Journal*, 20 November 2000, B1.
14. Katherine Raso, "Hudson's Bay Company and Thrifty Car Rental Announce Loyalty Partnership Program," *Canada NewsWire Ltd.* <www.newswire.ca> 12 March 2003 (Accessed 12 July 2003).
15. Dana Flavelle, "Shopaholics, Start Your Engines," *Toronto Star*, 20 February 2003, C1.
16. Flavelle, "Shopaholics."
17. Katherine Raso, "Home Outfitters Continues Expansion Across Canada," *Canada NewsWire Ltd.* <www.newswire.ca> 27 March 2003 (Retrieved 12 July 2003).

## CHAPTER 14

1. Nancy Rivera Brooks and Jesus Sanchez, "U.S. Firms Map Ways to Profit From the Accord," *Los Angeles Times*, 13 August 1992, D1, D2.
2. Herman Holtz, *The Consultant's Guide to Proposal Writing* (New York: John Wiley, 1990), 188.

## CHAPTER 15

1. Based on information found at <www.esteemteam.com>.
2. Peter Urs Bender, *Secrets of Power Presentations* (Toronto: The Achievement Group, 1991).
3. Rod Plotnik, *Introduction to Psychology* (Pacific Grove, CA: Brooks/Cole, 1993). 484.
4. Lisa Wright, "Executives Learn How to Beat Stage Fight," *Toronto Star*, 19 August 1998, E1.
5. Wright, "Executives Learn."
6. Wharton Applied Research Center, "A Study of the Effects of the Use of Overhead Transparencies on Business Meetings, Final Report" cited in "Short, Snappy Guide to Meaningful Presentations," *Working Woman*, June 1991, 73.
7. Stanford communications professor Clifford Nass quoted in Tad Simons, "When Was the Last Time Power-Point Made You Sing?" *Presentations*, July 2001, 6. See also Geoffrey

E-10

NEL

Nunberg, "The Trouble With PowerPoint," *Fortune*, 20 December 1999, 330–334.

8. James Gray, "The Perils of PowerPoint Slides," *The Globe and Mail*, 6 September 2002, C1.
9. Jennifer Rotondo, "Customized PowerPoint Templates Make Life Easier," *Presentations*, July 2001, 25–26.
10. Jim Endicott, "For Better Presentations, Avoid PowerPoint Pitfalls," *Presentations*, June 1998, 36–37.
11. Victoria Hall Smith, "Gigs by the Gigabyte," *Working Woman*, May 1998, 114.
12. Smith, "Gigs," 115.
13. Michael A. Russell and Walter M. Shriner, "Creating Effective PowerPoint Presentations," available <www.gst-d21.com/TLC> (Accessed 11 March 2003).
14. Dianna Booher, *Executive's Portfolio of Model Speeches for All Occasions* (Englewood Cliffs, NJ: Prentice Hall, 1991), 259.
15. Raymond Slesinski, "Giving a Topnotch Executive Presentation," *Management*, April 1990, 16.
16. Peter Schneider, "Scenes From a Marriage: Observations on the Daimler-Chrysler Merger From a German Living in America," *The New York Times Magazine*, 12 August 2001, 47.
17. Ronald E. Dulek, John S. Fielden, and John S. Hill, "International Communication: An Executive Primer," *Business Horizons*, January/February 1991, 23. See also Susan J. Marks, "Nurturing Global Workplace Connections," *Workforce*, September 2001, 76+.
18. Dulek, Fielden, and Hill, "International Communication," 22.
19. Patricia A. LaRosa, "Voice Messaging Is Quality 'Lip Service,'" *The Office*, May 1992, 10.
20. "Did You know That . . .," *Boardroom Reports*, 15 August 1992, 15.
21. Michael Jackson, quoted in "Garbage In, Garbage Out," *Consumer Reports*, December 1992, 755.

## CHAPTER 16

1. Harry Bruce, "Some U.S. Takeovers Are Good News," *Guelph Mercury*, 7 January 2003, A6.
2. Based on information found at Maritime Life Web site <www.maritimelife.ca> (Retrieved July 2003).
3. Caitlin P. Williams, "The End of the Job As We Know It," *Training & Development*, January 1999, 52–54. See also John A. Challenger, "The Changing Workforce: Workplace Rules in the New Millennium," *Vital Speeches of the Day*, 15 September 2001, 721–728.
4. "Small Business Sentinel," *National Post*, 4 March 2000, E8.
5. "Financial Outlook," *Maclean's*, 22 March 1999, 37.
6. Brian Mairs, "Are Resume Banks Worth the Effort?" *Job Searching: Canada* <jobsearchcanada. about.com.library/weekly/99120998. htm> (Retrieved 26 October 2000).
7. George B. Weathersby, "Responding to Change," *Management Review*, October 1998, 5.
8. Anne Kates Smith, "Charting Your Own Course," *U.S. News & World Report*, 6 November 2000, 56.
9. Smith, "Charting," 57.
10. Ellen Roseman, "Internship Program Praised," *Toronto Star*, 24 May 2000, E7.
11. Judith Schroer, "Seek a Job With a Little Help From Your Friends," *USA Today*, 19 November 1990, B1.
12. Michele Pepe, "ResumeMaker Turns a Complete Circle," *Computer Reseller News*, 29 September 1997, 173.
13. Kate MacNamara, "Recruiters Turning to Internet," *National Post*, 31 December 2002, FP1.
14. "More Than 7 Million Canadians Have Used Online Job Listing Services," Ipsos-Reid <www. ipsos-reid.com/media/> (Retrieved 28 May 2003).
15. Professor Mark Granovetter, quoted in Susan J. Wells, "Many Jobs on Web," *The New York Times*, 12 March 1998, A12.
16. George Crosby of the Human Resources Network, as quoted in Hal Lancaster, "When Taking a Tip From a Job Network, Proceed With Caution," *The Wall Street Journal*, 7 February 1995, B1.
17. Dan Moreau, "Write a Résumé That Works," *Changing Times*, June 1990, 91. See also Natalie Bortoli, "Resumes in the Right: New Rules Make Writing a Winner Easy," *Manage*, August 1997, 20–21.
18. Elizabeth Blackburn-Brockman and Kelly Belanger, "One Page or Two?: A National Study of CPA Recruiters' Preferences for Résumé Length," *The Journal of Business Communication*, January 2001, 29–57.
19. Bortoli, "Resumes in the Right," 20.
20. H. B. Crandall, quoted in Jacqueline Trace, "Teaching Résumé Writing the Functional Way," *The Bulletin of the Association for Business Communication*, June 1985, 41.
21. Bortoli, "Resumes in the Right," 20.
22. Tom Washington, "Improve Your Résumé 100 Percent" <http://www .nbew.com/archive/961001-001 .html> (Retrieved 27 September 1998).
23. Robert Lorentz, James W. Carland, and Jo Ann Carland, "The Résumé: What Value Is There in References?" *Journal of Technical Writing and Communication*, Fall 1993, 371.
24. "As Graduation Approaches . . . ," *Personnel*, June 1991, 14.
25. William H. Baker, Kristen DeTeinne, and Karl L. Smart, "How Fortune 500 Companies Are Using Electronic Résumé Management Systems," *Business Communication Quarterly*, September 1998, 8–19.
26. Joyce Lain Kennedy and Thomas J. Morrow, *Electronic Résumé Revolution* (New York: John Wiley & Sons, 1994), Chapter 3.
27. Marc Silver, "Selling the Perfect You," *U.S. News & World Report*, 5 February 1990, 70–72.
28. Rhonda D. Findling, "The Résumé Fax-periment," *Résumé Pro Newsletter*, Fall 1994, 10.
29. Jude M. Werra and Associates, publisher of the semiannual Liars Index, as cited in Drew Robb, "Résumé Writing," *Network World*, 8 October 2001, 65.
30. Diane Cole, "Ethics: Companies Crack Down on Dishonesty," *The Wall Street Journal, Managing Your Career* supplement, Spring 1991, 8.
31. "Managing Your Career," *National Business Employment Weekly*, Fall 1989, 29.
32. Joan E. Rigdon, "Deceptive Resumes Can Be Door-Openers but Can Become an Employee's Undoing," *The Wall Street Journal*, 17 June 1992, B1. See also Barbara Solomon, "Too Good to Be True?" *Management Review*, April 1998, 28.

33. Canada's Top 100 Employers—
   Walking the Walk," *Maclean's*,
   28 October 2002, 115(43), 26.
34. "Canada's Top 100 Employers—
   Walking the Walk." *Maclean's*.
35. Harriett M. Augustin, "The Written
   Job Search: A Comparison of the
   Traditional and a Nontraditional
   Approach," *The Bulletin of the
   Association for Business Communi-
   cation*, September 1991, 13.
36. Julia Lawlor, "Networking Opens
   More Doors to Jobs," *USA Today*,
   19 November 1990, B7.
37. J. Michael Farr, *The Very Quick Job
   Search* (Indianapolis, IN: JIST
   Works, 1991), 158.
38. Based on information found at
   Maritime Life Web site
   <www.maritimelife.ca> (Retrieved
   July 2003).

# Acknowledgments

## CHAPTER 1

**p. 7** Figure 1.2 Canadian Tire website: <http://www2.canadiantire.ca/CTenglish/h_ourstory.html>. Used by permission of Canadian Tire.

**p. 9** Figure 1.3 "Canadian cities more diverse." Sources: StatsCan, 2001 Census; Australian Bureau of Statistics, 2001; U.S. Census Bureau, 2000; appeared with *Toronto Star* article, Jan. 22, 2003, Elaine Carey, "City of new faces." Reprinted with permission – Torstar Syndication Services.

**p. 17** Figure 1.5 Canadian Tire letter used by permission of Canadian Tire.

**p. 19** Career Coach box (cell phone use) based on Edwin Powell, "Cell Phone Etiquette," *OfficeSolutions*, March, 2001, 13; and Catherine Siskos, "Cell Phone Sanctions," *Kiplinger's Personal Finance Magazine*, November, 2000, 27.

**p. 21** Figure 1.8 Volume and source of daily messages for average worker. Source: Pitney Bowes Inc. Reprinted by permission of Pitney Bowes, Inc.

## CHAPTER 2

**p. 44** Tech Talk box based on David Armstrong, "Building Teams Across Borders," *Executive Excellence*, March 2000, 10; Deborah S. Kezsbom, "Creating Teamwork in Virtual Teams," *Cost Engineering*, October 2000, 33–36; Larry Greenemeier, "Teamwork Via the Web," *Informationweek*, 25 September 2000, 211; Steve Alexander, "Virtual Teams Going Global," *InfoWorld*, 13 November 2000, 55–56; and Cheryl Hamilton with Cordell Parker, *Communi-

cating for Results* (Belmont, CA: Wadsworth, 2000), 320.

**p. 45** Discussion of team development based on Jon R. Katzenbach and Douglas K. Smith, *The Wisdom of Teams* (New York: HarperCollins, 1994); Harvey Robbins and Michael Finley, *Why Teams Don't Work* (Peterson's/Pacesetter, 1995); Jon R. Katzenbach, *Teams at the Top* (Boston: Harvard Business School Press, 1997); and Jane Henderson-Loney, "Tuckman and Tears: Developing Teams During Profound Organizational Change," *Supervision*, May 1996, 3–5.

**p. 46** Figure 2.1 based on Jon R. Katzenbach and Jason A. Santamaria, "Firing Up the Front Line," *Harvard Business Review*, May/June 1999, 107–117; and Suzanne K. Bishop, "Cross-Functional Project Teams in Functionally Aligned Organizations," *Project Management Journal*, September 1999, 6–12.

**p. 47** Discussion of group and team roles based on K. E. Benne and Paul Sheats, "Functional Roles and Group Members," *Journal of Social Issues*, 1948, No. 4, 41–49; Cheryl Hamilton and Cordell Parker, *Communicating for Results* (Belmont, CA: Wadsworth, 2000), 309–311; Gerald M. Goldhaber, *Organizational Communication*, 6e (Madison, WI: WCB Brown & Benchmark, 1993), 247–249.

**p. 48** Figure 2.2. Portions reprinted with permission of Peterson's, a division of International Thomson Publishing, FAX 800-730-2215. Adapted from *Why Teams Don't Work* © 1995 by Harvey A. Robbins and Michael Finley.

**p. 49** Discussion of conflict and groupthink based on Stephanie Reynolds, "Managing Conflict

Through a Team Intervention and Training Strategy," *Employee Relations Today*, Winter 1998, 57–64; Odette Pollar, "Sticking Together," *Successful Meetings*, January 1997, 87–90; Kathleen M. Eisenhardt, "How Management Teams Can Have a Good Fight," *Harvard Business Review*, July/August 1997, 77–85; and Erich Brockmann, "Removing the Paradox of Conflict from Group Decisions," *Academy of Management Executive*, May 1996, 61–62.

**p. 49** Discussion about reaching group decisions based on Harvey Robbins and Michael Finley, *Why Teams Don't Work* (Princeton, NJ: Peterson's/Pacesetter Books, 1995), 42–45; and Steven A. Beebe and John T. Masterson, *Communicating in Small Groups* (New York: Longman, 1999), 198–200.

**p. 52** Ethical Insights box based on Gerald L. Wilson, *Groups in Context* (New York: McGraw-Hill, 1996), 24–27; and Harvey Robbins and Michael Finley, *Why Teams Don't Work* (Princeton, NJ: Peterson's/Pacesetter Books, 1995), 88–89.

**p. 53** Discussion of team-based presentations based in part on Jon Hanke, "Presenting as a Team," *Presentations*, January 1998, 74–82; Frank Jossi, "Putting It All Together: Creating Presentations as a Team," *Presentations*, July 1996, 18–26; and Jon Rosen, "10 Ways to Make Your Next Team Presentation a Winner," *Presentations*, August 1997, 31.

**p. 55** Discussion on meetings based on Hal Lancaster, "Learning Some Ways to Make Meetings Slightly Less Awful," *The Wall Street Journal*, 26 May 1998, B1; Melinda Ligos, "Why Your Meetings Are a Total Bore," *Sales & Marketing Management*, May 1998, 84; Jana

M. Kemp, "The Writing's on the Wall," *Successful Meetings*, August 1996, 74; Charles R. McConnell, "The Chairperson's Guide to Effective Meetings," *Health Care Supervisor*, March 1997, 1–9; and John C. Bruening, "There's Good News About Meetings," *Managing Office Technology*, July 1996, 24–25.

**p. 62** Discussion on groupware based on James R. Borck, "As E-Collaboration Tools Mature, They Can Help You Work Out a Competitive Advantage," *InfoWorld*, 27 November 2000, 73; Marion Agnew, "Collaboration on the Desktop," *Informationweek*, 10 July 2000, 87–94; Dennis Fisher, "Taming Web Projects: Project Management Software Embraces the Web, Opens Up More Choices," *eWeek*, 20 November 2000, 48; Steve Jefferson, "Groove Takes to New Level," *InfoWorld*, 30 October 2000, 29; Todd Coopee, "Outsourced Teamware Gains Ground," *InfoWorld*, 17 April 2000, 55–56; Howard Millman, "On Track and in Touch: You Want It When?" *Computerworld*, 26 June 2000, 88; Carla Catalano, "Web-Based Groupware," *Computerworld*, 7 June 2000, 105; Bradley C. Wheeler, Alan R. Dennis, and Laurence I, "Groupware Comes to the Internet: Charting a New World," *Database for Advances in Information Systems*, Summer, 1999, 8–21; Steve Gillmor and Jeff Angus, "Teamware Comes of Age," *Informationweek*, 20 September, 1999, 69–78; and Craig R. Scott, Laura Quinn, C. Erik Timmerman, and Diana M. Garrett, "Ironic Uses of Group Communication Technology: Evidence from Meeting Transcripts and Interviews with Group Decision Support System Users," *Communication Quarterly*, Summer 1998, 353.

## CHAPTER 3

**p. 72** Tips for Workplace Listening based on Kenneth R. Johnson, "Effective Listening Skills," The itmWEB Site of Web Media Corporation <http://www.itmweb.com/essay514.htm> (Retrieved 15

January 2001); Shari Caudron, "Listen Up!" *Workforce*, August 1999, 25–27; and Hal Lancaster, "It's Time to Stop Promoting Yourself and Start Listening," *The Wall Street Journal*, 10 June 1997, B1.

**p. 73** Listening to Superiors based on Lynn O. Cooper, "Listening Competency in the Workplace: A Model for Training," *Business Communication Quarterly*, December 1997, 75–84; Valerie Priscilla Goby and Justus Helen Lewis, "The Key Role of Listening in Business: A Study of the Singapore Insurance Industry," *Business Communication Quarterly*, June 2000, 411; and Michael C. Dennis, "Effective Communication Will Make Your Job Easier, *Business Credit*, June 1995, 45.

**p. 73** Listening to Employees based on Max E. Douglas, "Creating Distress in the Workplace: A Supervisor's Role, *Supervision*, October 1996, 6–9; Robert McGarvey, "Now Hear This: Lend Your Employees an Ear—and Boost Productivity," *Entrepreneur*, June 1996, 87; Brian Tracy, "Effective Communication," *Executive Excellence*, October 1998, 13; and Stuart Silverstein, "But Do They Listen? Companies Making an Effort to Build Skill," *Los Angeles Times*, 19 July 1998, D5.

**p. 73** Listening to Customers based on Nick Langley, "Looking After the Customers," *Computer Weekly*, 2 November 2000, 100; Jeff Caplan, "Golden Age Customer Service Returns," *Direct Marketing*, July 2000, 60; Rosemary P. Ramsey and Ravipreet S. Sohi, "Listening to Your Customers: The Impact of Perceived Salesperson Listening Behavior on Relationship Outcomes," *Journal of the Academy of Marketing Science*, Spring 1997, 127–137; Daniel Pedersen, "Dissing Customers: Why the Service Is Missing from America's Service Economy," *Newsweek*, 23 June 1997, 56; Michael Render, "Better Listening Makes for a Better Marketing Message," *Marketing News*, 11 September 2000, 22–23; Lynn Thomas, "Listening: So What's in It for Me?" *Rough Notes*, December 1998, 63–64; and Susan A. Timm, Timothy W. Aurant, and

Rick E. Ridnout, "Listening Competence Within Marketing and Other Business Disciplines: Phase I —Measuring College Student Perceptions," *The Delta Pi Epsilon Journal*, Spring 2000, 78–89.

**p. 74** Figure 3.1 based on Watson Wyatt Worldwide, as reported in "Good Ideas Go Unheard," *Management Review*, February 1998, 7.

**p. 75** Figure 3.2 based on Lynn Thomas, "Listening: So What's in It for Me?" *Rough Notes*, December 1998, 63–64.

**p. 77** Figure 3.4 based on "Listening Factoids," International Listening Association <http://www.listen.org/pages/factoids.html> (Retrieved 13 January 2001).

**p. 79** Career Coach box (Listening to Nonnative Speakers) based on Tom Marshall and Jim Vincent, "Improving Listening Skills: Methods, Activities, and Resources," Instructor's Manual, *Business Communication: Process and Product*, 4e; Iris Varner and Linda Beamer, *Intercultural Communication in the Global Workplace* (Boston: Irwin McGraw-Hill, 1995), 37; and Chris Lee, "How to Deal with the Foreign Accent," *Training*, January 1993, 72, 75.

**p. 84** Figure 3.5 Olympic Games hand signals, *Atlanta Committee for the Winter Games* as presented by Sam Ward, "The Olympics Don'ts of Gestures," *USA Today* (Thursday, March 14, 1996), p 7C. USA TODAY. Copyright March 14, 1996. Reprinted with permission.

## CHAPTER 4

**p. 100** Figure 4.1 Screen capture of <sonymusic.de>. Reprinted by permission of Sony Music Entertainment Germany.

**p. 101** Tech Talk box based on Sari Kalin, "The Importance of Being Multiculturally Correct," *Computer World*, 6 October 1997, G16–17; B. G. Yovovich, "Making Sense of All the Web's Numbers," *Editor & Publisher*, Mediainfo.com Supplement, November 1998, 30–31; Laura Morelli, "Writing for a Global Audience on the Web," *Marketing News*, 17 August 1998, 16.

**p. 105** Figure 4.2 based on J. Chung's analysis appearing in Guo-Ming Chen and William J. Starosta, *Foundations of Intercultural Communication* (Boston: Allyn and Bacon, 1998), 51; and Mary O'Hara-Devereaux and Robert Johansen, *Globalwork: Bridging Distance, Culture, and Time* (San Francisco: Jossey-Bass, 1994), 55.

**p. 112** Figure 4.3 based on Sondra Ostheimer, "Internationalize Yourself," *Business Education Forum*, February 1995, 45. Reprinted with permission of Sondra Ostheimer, Southwest Wisconsin Technical College.

**p. 114** Figure 4.4 based on William Horton, "The Almost Universal Language: Graphics for International Documents," *Technical Communication*, Fourth Quarter, 1993, 690.

## CHAPTER 5

**p. 141** Figure 5.4 Tilley Endurables letter. Reprinted by permission of Tilley Endurables.

## CHAPTER 7

**p. 187** Picture caption for Wall Street photo based on J. Peder Zane, "For Investors, an Initial Public Offering of English," *The New York Times*, 25 August 1996; U. S. Securities and Exchange Commission, *A Plain English Handbook*, Washington, DC, 13 January 1997.

**p. 203** Activity 7.7 based on Paula J. Pomerenke, "Teaching Ethics with Apartment Leases," *Business Communication Quarterly*, December 1998, 119.

## CHAPTER 8

**p. 213** Discussion in Tech Talk (Paperless Workplace) box, based on James Brooke, "That Secure Feeling of a Printed Document," *New York Times*, 21 April 2001, B1; Ted Needleman, "Not Exactly a Paperless Office, But Close," *Investor's Business Daily*, 4 December 1998, A1; and William M. Bulkeley, "Advances in Networking and Software Push Firms Closer to Paperless Office," *The Wall Street Journal*, 5 August 1993, B1.

**p. 215** The discussion on pages 215 to 220 ("Smart E-Mail Practices") is based on Dale Bowen and Bryan Gold, "Policies and Education Solve E-Mail Woes," *American City & County*, May 2001, 8; Reg Pirie, "Ask an Expert: E-Mail Etiquette," *CA Magazine*, December 2000, 11; Ruth Davidhizar, Ruth Shearer, and Becky Castro, "A Dilemma of Modern Technology: Managing E-Mail Overload," *Hospital Materiel Management Quarterly*, February 2000, 42–47; Margaret Boles and Brenda Paik Sunoo, "Don't Let E-Mail Botch Your Career," *Workforce*, February 1998, 21; Brenda Paik Sunoo, "What If Your E-Mail Ends Up in Court?" *Workforce*, July 1998, 36–41; G. A. Marken, "Think Before You Click," *Office Systems*, March 1998, 44–46; Howard Millman, "Easy EDI for Everyone," *InfoWorld*, 17 August 1998, 38–39; Joe Dysart, "Establishing an Internet Policy," *Credit Union Executive*, May/June 1998, 18–22; "Do's and Don'ts for E-Mail Use," *CA Magazine*, June/July 1998, 40; and Sana Reynolds, "Composing Effective E-Mail Messages," *Communication World*, July 1997, 8–9.

## CHAPTER 9

**p. 257** Figure 9.6 Raptors letter. Reprinted by permission of the Toronto Raptors and NBA.

**p. 258** Ethical Insights (Using Caution in Writing Letters of Recommendation) based on Ellen Harshman and Denise R. Chachere, "Employee References: Between the Legal Devil and the Ethical Deep Blue Sea," *Journal of Business Ethics*, January, 2001, 29–39; Jeffrey L. Seglin, "Too Much Ado About Giving References," *The New York Times*, 21 February 1999, BU4; Lauren Picker, "Job References: To Give or Not to Give," *Working Woman*, February 1992, 21; and Amy Saltzman, "Suppose They Sue," *U.S. News & World Report*, 22 September 1997, 68–70.

**p. 259** Discussion (claim and adjustment letters) is based on Ed Foster, "Don't Blame the Vendor: Web Shoppers Are Not Always Innocent Victims," *InfoWorld*, 12 March 2001, 73; Kevin Lawrence, "How to Profit from Customer Complaints: Turning Problems into Opportunities," *Canadian Manager*, Fall 2000, 25; Jeffrey J. Roth, "When the Customer's Got a Beef," *ABA Banking Journal*, July 1998, 24–29; Geoffrey Brewer, "The Customer Stops Here," *Sales & Marketing Management*, March 1998, 30–36; Bill Knapp, "Communication Breakdown," *World Wastes*, February 1998, 16; Stephen S. Tax, Stephen W. Brown, and Murali Chandrashekaran, "Customer Evaluations of Service Complaint Experiences: Implications for Relationship Marketing," *Journal of Marketing*, April 1998, 60–76; Edmund S. Fine, "Are You Listening to Your Customers?" *Quality Progress*, January 1998, 120; Robert Klara, "Press 1 to Gripe," *Restaurant Business*, 15 May 1998, 96–102; "Foiling the Rogues: 'Anti' Web Sites Are Great for Angry Customers, But Now Companies Are Trying to Fight Back," *Newsweek*, 27 October 1997, 80; Roberta Furger, "Don't Get Mad, Get Online," *PC World*, October 1997, 37; Gary Hren, "The Sales Behind the Scowl," *American Demographics, Marketing Tools Supplement*, March/April 1996, 14–17; Gwendolyn N. Smith, Rebecca F. Nolan, and Young Dai, "Job-Refusal Letters: Readers' Affective Responses to Direct and Indirect Organizational Plans," *Business Communication Quarterly*, March 1996, 67–73; Carol David and Margaret Ann Baker, "Rereading Bad News: Compliance-Gaining Features in Management Memos," *The Journal of Business Communications*, October 1994, 267–290.

**p. 262** Internal picture (responding to claims) based on Kevin Lawrence, "How to Profit from Customer Complaints: Turning Problems into Opportunities," *Canadian Manager*, Fall 2000, 25.

## CHAPTER 10

**p. 292** Discussion (Ethical Insights—Logical Fallacies) is based on Lynn Quitman Troyka, *Simon & Schuster Handbook for Writers* (Upper Saddle River, NJ: Prentice Hall, 1996), 144–146; Frederick Crews, *The Random House Handbook* (New York: Random House, 1987), 76–78; and Stephen Downes, "Stephen's Guide to the Logical Fallacies" <www.assiniboinc.mb.ca/user/downes/fallacy/falla.htm> (Retrieved 6 December 1998).

**p. 303** Photo caption for iMac photo based on Stewart Alsop, "My Old Flame: The Macintosh," *Fortune*, 25 June 2001, 60.

**p. 308** Figure 10.8 Bell Canada Enterprises media release re: Vince Carter. Reprinted by permission of Bell.

## CHAPTER 11

**p. 328** Caption for internal picture of REI: Michael Fickes, "REI Explores New Heights," *Sporting Goods Business*, 2 January 2001, 62.

## CHAPTER 12

**p. 376** Figure 12.6 based on Kim Zetter and Harry McCracken, "How to Stop Searching and Start Finding," *PC Magazine*, September 2000, 129.

**p. 379** Figure 12.7 <www.google.ca> Webpage reprinted by permission of Google. Yahoo! Canada Webpage reproduced with permission of Yahoo! Inc. © 2001 by Yahoo! Inc. Yahoo! and the Yahoo! logo are trademarks of Yahoo! Inc.

**p. 381** Figure 12.8 based on "Search Engines and Directories: The Quest for the Best," *PC Magazine*, September 2000, 131.

**p. 384** Picture caption based on Phil Levine, Bill Ahlhauser, Dale Kulp, and Rick Hunter, "Pro and Con: Internet Interviewing," *Marketing Research*, Summer 1999, 33–36.

## CHAPTER 13

**p. 422** Career Coach box based on Dianna Booher, "E-Writing," *Executive Excellence*, April 2001, 16; Janet Bigham Bernstel and Hollis Thomases, "Writing Words for the Web," *Bank Marketing*, March 2001, 16–21; and Pat R. Graves and Jack E. Murry, "Enhancing Communication with Effective Page Design and Typography," *Delta Pi Epsilon* Instructional Strategies Series, Summer 1990.

## CHAPTER 14

**p. 458** Career Coach based on "The Business Plan—Road Map to Success," Small Business Administration <http://www.sba.gov/starting/indexbusplans.html> (Retrieved 21 September 2001) and "So You Wanna Write a Business Plan?," SoYouWanna.com <http://www.soyouwanna.com/site/sywsbizplan/bizplan2.html> (Retrieved 22 September 2001).

## CHAPTER 15

**p. 491** Figure 15.1 based on Janet G. Elsea, "Strategies for Effective Presentations," *Personnel Journal*, September 1985, 31–33 appearing in Cheryl Hamilton, *Communicating for Results* (Wadsworth/Thomson Learning, 2001), 340.

**p. 493** Career Coach box based on Bert Decker, "Successful Presentations: Simple and Practical," *HR Focus*, February 1992, 19; Lawrence Stevens, "The Proof Is in the Presentation," *Nation's Business*, July 1991, 33; Hal Lancaster, "Practice and Coaching Can Help You Improve Um, Y'Know, Speeches," *The Wall Street Journal*, 9 January 1996, B1.

**p. 496** Discussion of vivid imagery based on Jeff Olson, *Giving Great Presentations* (Bristol, VT: Velocity Business Publishing, 1997), 32–37; Kevin Daley, "Using the Right Evidence for Effective Presentations," *Communication Briefings*, April 1997, 8a; Patricia Calderon, "Anatomy of a Great Presentation," *Windows Magazine*, June 1998, 203+; and Al Borowski, "To Connect with Audiences, Learn How to Build Rapport," Presentations.com <http://www.presentations.com/deliver/speak/2000/03/31> (Retrieved 31 May 2001).

**p. 499** Discussion of electronic presentations based on Scott Heimes, "Add Some Visual Thunder to Your Presentations," *Presentations*, March 1998, 11–12; Stuart Kahan, "Capturing Clients Through High-Powered Presentations," *Practical Accountant*, February 1997, 39–42; Jim Endicott, "For Better Presentations, Avoid PowerPoint Pitfalls," "How to Make Presentations That Audiences Will Love," *Training*, March 1997, S4; Jean Mausehund and R. Neil Dortch, "Presentation Skills in the Digital Age," *Business Education Forum*, April 1999, 30–31; "Presentation Superguide," *PC Computing*, June 1999, 176+; Greg Jaffe, "What's Your Points, Lieutenant? Just Cut to the Pie Charts," *The Wall Street Journal*, 26 April 2000, A1; Julie Hill, "How to Create a QuickTime Movie for PowerPoint," *Presentations*, September 2001, 20; Ken Bluttman, "Exploring PowerPoint 2002," *Presentations*, August 2001, 42–45.

## CHAPTER 16

**p. 527** Networking Career Coach box based on Steve Morris, "Forget Jobs Vacant . . . ," *Asian Business*, August 2001, 66; J. Michael Farr, *The Very Quick Job Search* (Indianapolis: JIST Works, Inc., 1991), 50–52; Bob Rosner, "What Color Is HR's Parachute?" *Workforce*, September 1998, 50–51; and Rebecca Smith, "NetKnocking," *Computer Bits*, January 1997 <www.computerbits.com/archive,9701;netknock.hrm> (Retrieved 14 January 1999).

**p. 528** Using Electronic Job Search Resources based on Alan S. Kay, "Recruiters Embrace the Internet," *Informationweek*, 20 March 2000, 72–80; Gary M. Stern, "Applicants Use Web to Get Scoop on Firms," *Investor's Business Daily*, 13 June 2000, A2; and Michael E. Ryan and Ben Z. Gottesman, "Job Hunting and Hiring on the Web," *PC Magazine*, 25 May 1999, 159+.

**p. 529** Figure 16.2 <www.monster.ca> Webpage reprinted by permission of Monster.ca.

**p. 536** Figure 16.6 Action Verbs for Persuasive Résumés adapted from Yana Parker, *The Damn Good*

*Résumé Guide* (Berkeley, CA: Ten Speed Press, 1996). Reprinted with permission from THE DAMN GOOD RESUME GUIDE by Yana Parker. Copyright © 1996 by Yana Parker, Ten Speed Press, Berkeley, CA. Available from Ten Speed Press by calling 1-800-841-2665, or online at <www.tenspeed.com>.

**p. 540** Figure 16.9 Interpersonal Keywords Most Requested by Employers Using Résumé-Scanning Software. Source: Joyce Lain Kennedy and Thomas J. Morrow, *Electronic Résumé Revolution* (New York: John Wiley & Sons), 70. Reprinted by permission of John Wiley & Sons, Inc.

**Photo Credits:**

**p. 2** © Dick Hemingway, **p. 5** © ELIPSA/CORBIS SYGMA/ Magmaphoto.com, **p. 13** © Novastock/Index Stock Imagery, **p. 20** Rob Melnyschuk/PhotoDisc, **p. 25** PhotoDisc, Inc., **p. 28** Courtesy of Mountain Equipment Co-op, **p. 41** Courtesy of Ronald Alepian and National Public Relations, **p. 43** Superstock, **p. 46** PhotoDisc, Inc., **p. 47** Superstock, **p. 54** CP/Ottawa Citizen (Kier Gilmour), **p. 68** PhotoDisc, Inc., **p. 69** PhotoDisc, Inc., **p. 70** Courtesy of Minacs, **p. 74** R.W. Jones/CORBIS/MAGMA, **p. 80** ©Anton Vengo/SuperStock, **p. 83** Reuters NewMedia Inc./CORBIS/ MAGMA, **p. 94** PhotoDisc, Inc., **p. 96** Courtesy of G.A.P Adventures, **p. 99** Susan Van Etten, **p. 102** CP (John Ulan), **p. 106** Courtesy of Isadore Sharp, **p. 118** Michael Newman/PhotoEdit, **p. 125** PhotoDisc, Inc., **p. 127** PhotoDisc, Inc., **p. 130** Courtesy of Tilley Endurables, **p. 138** PhotoDisc, Inc., **p. 144** James A. Sugar/CORBIS, **p. 145** © Dick Hemingway, **p. 155** © Dick Hemingway, **p. 169** ©Lisette Le Bon/SuperStock, **p. 179** PhotoDisc, Inc., **p. 183** Courtesy of Stiff Sentences, **p. 187** © Rufus F. Folkks/CORBIS, **p. 195** © Dick Hemingway, **p. 204** PhotoDisc, Inc., **p. 208** © Rick Chard/CORBIS, **p. 210** PhotoDisc, Inc., **p. 219** © Didrik Johnck/CORBIS/MAGMA, **p. 226** PhotoDisc, Inc., **p. 241** Copyright Great Canadian Railtour Company Ltd., **p. 254** © Orion Press/Index Stock Imagery, **p. 262** © Eyewire, **p. 284** Courtesy of United Way, **p. 303** © David H. Wells/CORBIS/Magmaphoto.com, **p. 317** PhotoDisc, Inc., **p. 320** © Gerhard Van Roon/Hollandse Hoogte/CORBIS SYGMA/ MagmaPhoto.com, **p. 328** © David Samuel Robbins/CORBIS, **p. 338** PhotoDisc, Inc., **p. 354** PhotoDisc, Inc., **p. 358** PhotoDisc, Inc., **p. 377** CP (Geoff Howe), **p. 384** PhotoDisc, Inc., **p. 392** PhotoDisc, Inc., **p. 405** © Dick Hemingway, **p. 418** © Layne Kennedy/CORBIS, **p. 429** Mary Guffey, **p. 450** Courtesy of Matthew Myers, **p. 463** Ryan McVay/Photodisc Green/Getty Images, **p. 488** Courtesy of Esteem Team, **p. 505** © Powerstock/ SuperStock, **p. 518** PhotoDisc, Inc., **p. 521** Courtesy of Maritime Life Assurance Company, **p. 526** PhotoDisc, Inc., **p. 559** PhotoDisc, Inc.

# Index

Page numbers in italics refer to figures.

## Y

# INDEX TO SPECIAL TOPICS